FROM CHRIST TO THE WORLD

From *Christ*

Introductory Readings

to the *World*

in Christian Ethics

Edited by

Wayne G. Boulton,
Thomas D. Kennedy, and
Allen Verhey

WILLIAM B. EERDMANS PUBLISHING COMPANY
GRAND RAPIDS, MICHIGAN / CAMBRIDGE, U.K.

© 1994 Wm. B. Eerdmans Publishing Co.

Wm. B. Eerdmans Publishing Co.
255 Jefferson Ave. S.E., Grand Rapids, Michigan 49503 /
P.O. Box 163, Cambridge CB3 9PU U.K.
www.eerdmans.com

Printed in the United States of America

11 10 09 08 07 06 05   17 16 15 14 13 12 11 10

Library of Congress Cataloging-in-Publication Data

From Christ to the world: introductory readings in Christian ethics /
    edited by Wayne G. Boulton, Thomas D. Kennedy, and Allen Verhey.
        p.   cm.
    Includes bibliographical references.
    ISBN-10 0-8028-0640-6 / ISBN-13 978-0-8028-0640-6 (pbk.)
    1. Christian ethics. I. Boulton, Wayne G.
II. Kennedy, Thomas D., 1955–   . III. Verhey, Allen.
BJ1191.F76   1994
241 — dc20   94-21944
                                                   CIP

The editors and publisher gratefully acknowledge
permission granted by the publishers listed on
pages 530-533 to reprint copyrighted works.

Contents

III. ISSUES IN CHRISTIAN ETHICS

Preface

The three editors of this volume were colleagues at Hope College during the academic years 1984-1987. Although we are each trained in Christian ethics, we differ in our interests, our understandings of Christian ethics, and the ways in which we teach Christian ethics. These differences led to many happy and healthy discussions during those three years and to many rich disagreements.

In the midst of our disagreements, we discovered unanimity on at least one point. There is no anthology which does what we think needs to be done in an introductory course in Christian ethics. While there are several fine collections of readings in Christian ethics, each focuses upon only a part of what needs to be discussed in introductory courses in Christian ethics.

There are introductory readers in Christian ethics which focus on particular moral problems, but students who are introduced only to issues frequently fail to appreciate the theological issues at stake in the very strategy someone adopts to address an issue. Christian ethics is not just about deciding but about deciding how to decide. Attention to specific ethical issues belongs in an introductory course and in an introductory reader, but we believe that ethical issues are best addressed when attention is also given to the resources and strategies for Christian moral discernment and judgment.

There are also texts which direct the student's attention to readings in the history of Christian ethics. We applaud these efforts and agree that some familiarity with the Christian tradition of moral reflection — some attention to Scripture, to individuals like Clement of Alexandria, Augustine, Aquinas, Luther, and Calvin, and to movements like monasticism, the radical reformation, and the social gospel — is critical for an adequate introduction to Christian ethics. But sometimes the tradition is handled as if it were only of antiquarian interest. We believe that if the tradition is engaged at the same time contemporary issues are engaged, both the tradition and the discipline can be seen by students as valuable and exciting.

We have put together a collection of readings which will engage students in reflection upon concrete moral problems, disciplined by attention to some of the basic issues of Christian ethics and enriched by consideration of some of the finest minds in the Christian tradition. We have collected readings which will expose students to a wide diversity of voices in Christian ethics, past and present, and to the complexity of the discipline of Christian ethics. We have, in short, constructed an anthology which we believe will draw students into the exciting discipline of Christian ethics. We hope our readers will agree.

Finally, we should note and thank some of the undergraduates who have been our students and our assistants and intimately involved in the production of this volume. From Hope College, David Johnson, Timothy Verhey, Melanie Waldron, Alene Weber, and Rameen Zahed reviewed early drafts of the chapters, and made perceptive criticisms and suggestions. From Valparaiso University, Andrew Fields and Michael Kessler assisted in the preparation of biographical information.

Chapter 1

An Introduction to Christian Ethics

Understanding Ethics

Even now, almost 2,500 years after his death, the philosopher Socrates stands out as one of the most important figures in world history. Born in 427 B.C.E., he challenged not only the reigning scientists of his day, too busy to think about the meaning of their own lives, but also the political officials, the business people, and the religious leaders of Athens. He challenged them not by what he wrote, for he wrote nothing. The difference he made in Athens and for Western intellectual history was a result of what he taught and how he lived.

In a nutshell, Socrates taught that the most important question to be answered has to do with the meaning of one's life and how one lives. "What sort of life is worth living? If I want to be fulfilled and happy, what sort of person should I be?" These were the questions which Socrates thought each person needs to confront and answer. Socrates was concerned foremost with the good life.

Ironically, his understanding of the good life is perhaps best exhibited in his death. Socrates was placed on trial on several "trumped-up" political charges. He was found guilty, but he could have escaped punishment by renouncing his beliefs, by refusing to examine "the good life," or by fleeing to another country. He refused these options, for he believed that dying well is an integral part of living well. So he accepted his punishment, drank the hemlock and died, having faced his death calmly and serenely. Socrates was, his friend Phaedo told his companions, "the best, and also the wisest and the most upright" of all the people they knew.

It is no wonder, then, that Socrates' successors found his fundamental question, "What would a life worth living look like?" inescapable in their philosophical musings. Plato and Aristotle, the best-known philosophers after Socrates, spent a good part of their intellectual lives developing answers to this very question. They pondered and puzzled and finally wrote down some answers. And their followers have continued that legacy of trying to make sense of the good life to this day.

You and I, if we are the least bit reflective, ponder Socrates' question ourselves, in one form or another. The likelihood is that you are reading these words as part of a university class. But why are you taking the class? In most cases the answer is because in some way the class will lead to a degree from your university. But why is a university degree worth having? Because in some way it will contribute to your getting the sort of job you want. But why is that sort of job worth getting? Well probably, you think, it will lead to some sort of personal satisfaction or fulfillment; you probably think that a decent job is an integral part of a good life. But your pondering about vocation and the good life will not end once you have gotten the job you want, not if you are anything like most of us. Many will be the night you lie awake wondering whether your work is really making yours a good life. Many will be the morning when leaving your family to go to work does not seem to mesh with your idea of a good life.

Of course, not all of us know what we want to do with our lives. Many of us have thought a lot and still haven't sorted out exactly what our vocation is. But even if we have, the questions still remain, "What more is there to the good life? What should I do with my life? What sort of person do I want to be?"

We don't start thinking about these questions only when we reflect upon work and our future, though at this time in your lives vocation is a major concern. Our reflection upon this question

1

of a life worth living is far more extensive and arises in a far more piecemeal fashion in the daily routines of our lives. For example, you may have quarreled with your roommate when you got up this morning. Somehow you two are going to have to fix that if you are going to continue living together. But who should make the first move? Is your roommate always the one who makes the first move towards reconciliation? If so, what does that indicate about you, the kind of person you are, and the kind of life you are leading?

Many of us are trying to figure out exactly what responsibilities we have to our parents. They may be footing a large part of our educational bills, but we are adults too. Must we still obey them? When? And why? Or perhaps you are trying to decide whether to "break up" with a friend, or whether to become sexually involved, or whom to vote for. All of these questions, in one way or another, are about who we are and who we want to be. All of these questions are bits and pieces of that larger question that Socrates asked, "What sort of life is worth living?" All of these questions are, we might say, questions about *morality,* about who we are and how we ought to live, about what we ought to do and what we ought to leave undone. *Morality* has to do with our character and our behavior towards ourselves and others. A good person, we might say, cares a great deal about whether she is the sort of person it is good to be. She may not be a great philosopher, like Socrates, but she cares deeply about morality, about the things Socrates cared about.

What Socrates was most concerned about, then, was morality. The good life, as far as Socrates was concerned, consists of living morally. We, the editors of this volume, think Socrates was right. Morality is, or ought to be, a primary concern of everyone, or so we maintain. We think everyone should care about others and should care about themselves. But *caring* about what is moral and *thinking* about what is moral are not exactly the same thing. Most of us know persons whom we admire for how good they are, despite the fact that they have spent little time self-consciously thinking about the moral life.

My friend Walt is a case in point. Walt is now retired, but he remains quite active, building and repairing homes for individuals trapped in horrible conditions in the inner city. I've talked with Walt about the moral life, and I think he is confused and mistaken about a number of issues I think are important. I would not encourage students to take any course with him. But I would encourage students to watch Walt, to get to know him, to learn what he cares about. Students will learn better how to understand and *think* about morality from me. But if they want to *be* good people, if they want to *care* about what it is important to care about, Walt's life and his actions are better teachers. So, while we think that it is a good thing for individuals to reflect upon and think carefully about the moral life, thought about the moral life is, to our minds, not nearly so important as caring about persons and their world. It is better, we think, to be a moral person, like Walt, than merely to be a person who thinks carefully about morality.

Nevertheless, it is important to think carefully about morality. Everyone has a stake in answering for himself or herself, as well as for his or her community, "What sort of person should I be? "What sort of people should we be?" We have a stake in this because thinking about morality can help us become more moral people. Socrates maintained that the unexamined life is not worth living. That, we think, is to overstate the case, is to forget that there may be something morally destructive about too much reflection upon one's life. Still, Socrates is close to the truth. Usually, reflecting upon the good life is critical for living a good life. Reflecting upon morality and the moral life may help us discover inconsistencies between what we say and what we do, may help us discover answers and better answers to questions that bother us about morality and the good life.

At first glance, it might seem that questions about the good life could be answered pretty quickly and simply. History would suggest otherwise. As mentioned above, Plato and Aristotle, two of Socrates' most immediate successors, spent a good portion of their careers attempting to develop a coherent, sound answer to the question of what a good life looks like. They wanted their answers to be systematic, to hold together, to be comprehensive, addressing all of the basic questions about morality, and to be persuasive to others. This project, the examination and study of morality, is normally referred to as *ethics.*

Normative ethics is the attempt to identify

norms, or standards, of right or good behavior. Normative ethics is the attempt to answer Socrates' questions, "How should I behave? What should I do? What sort of person should I be?" In normative ethics, these questions are answered by presenting arguments and explanations, by appealing to certain norms, or standards, and explaining why the appeal to these particular norms is appropriate. "What norms are relevant in this situation? Why? What types of appeals are adequate? Which appeals are reasonable for us to make in these circumstances?" These are the concerns of normative ethics. For example, should I think primarily about what is likely to happen to me and Sally if we marry and compare this to what is likely to happen to us if we do not marry and choose the better outcome? Or are there some principles that should guide my conduct, such as "Never promise to be faithful when you do not intend to keep your promise"? Or perhaps I should ask myself whether I have the traits of character that are necessary in order for a marriage to flourish.

Questions like these, attempts to identify and illuminate standards or norms for a good life, are the concerns of the philosopher or theologian engaged in normative ethics.

Understanding Christian Ethics

So far, we have discussed what morality, ethics, and normative ethics are. But this is a collection of readings in *Christian ethics*. What, you may be wondering, is different about Christian ethics? There are, as you may know, many introductory readers in ethics. What is so special about Christian ethics that we need an entirely different set of readings? What does Christianity add to ethics? How does "Christian" qualify ethics?

We can explain it this way. All normative ethics attempts to identify the characteristics of a life worth living, and all examines and articulates standards to inform and guide us in shaping our actions and character. Christian ethics undertakes the same task with reference to Jesus of Nazareth.

All ethics is "qualified" in one way or another. Every attempt to identify the characteristics of a life worth living or the standards for conduct or character makes certain assumptions about where the standards come from and how we know them. These different assumptions lead people to undertake the task of ethics with reference to different fundamental accounts of reality. This is the reason there are disagreements about what the standards or norms of morality are, exactly to whom these standards apply, and what the point of the study of normative ethics is — what the study is supposed to do for the student.

To begin to clarify how reference to Jesus qualifies ethics we need to consider a second historical figure, Jesus of Nazareth, the one whom Christians identify as the Christ, the one who made known and made real the cause of God, and the one in terms of whom Christians undertake both the task of living lives of discipleship and the task of thinking about the sort of lives that are worthy of followers of Christ.

Jesus resembled Socrates in many ways. He was primarily a teacher, and he wrote nothing. He was profoundly concerned with the lives of his followers and whether the people he addressed were leading worthy lives. The testimony of his followers is that he, like Socrates, lived what he taught and was a morally admirable person. And like Socrates, rather than renounce his deepest commitments and beliefs, he died for what he believed. Again, there were "trumped-up" political charges, and the punishment was death.

We ought not neglect the similarities between Socrates and Jesus, but neither should we ignore their profound differences. Those who followed Jesus professed that a rather remarkable thing happened following the crucifixion of Jesus. They claimed that God raised Jesus up from the dead. They claimed that Jesus the Christ was crucified, that he died and was buried, but that having been raised up from the dead by God the Father, he continues to live and continues to be present and to reach those who would follow him.

It is this confession — that Jesus is the Christ, that in him, in his works and words, and in the suffering love of his cross, God is present to humanity in a special way, that God did not abandon Jesus to the grave but vindicated him and restored him to life — that is the starting point for Christian ethics. It is here that the most fundamental differences between Christian ethics and secular ethics arise. Socrates would think it the greatest of confusions if his followers were to make reference back to him in their attempt to identify the good life. One should not ask, "What would Socrates think about this?" for Socrates denied that he had any moral expertise at all. He maintained, perhaps a bit ingenuously, that he knew only the right questions, not the right answers. In any case, the proper moral questions make no reference to Socrates, for he, like us, is in pursuit of moral truth.

Christians, by contrast, believe that the failure to refer to Jesus Christ, the failure to somehow "think from" the perspective of the story of Jesus, is a failure of the greatest significance. Whether or not the name of Jesus is made explicit in moral enquiry, *the starting point of Christian ethics must always take account of what God has done in human history in Jesus Christ.* Christ's disciples said that he came teaching "as one with authority." Minimally, this means that somehow Jesus is authoritative for Christian ethics — that the person and work of Jesus establish a vantage point for thinking about what ethics is meant to do, and establish and explain norms for the character and behavior of Christians.

We might think of it this way. Morality always involves a person or community living in a certain way towards other persons and things as well as themselves. For example, go back to your quarrel with your roommate. This involves you and how you feel and behave towards your roommate. Because you want to be a good person, you want to know what is o.k. for you to do or feel in these circumstances. Part of the concern of ethics is to help you answer that question.

Typically, in nonreligious ethics we might think of ethics as informing you of what attitudes and actions are appropriate in these circumstances. In ethics, we consider questions about what norms are relevant in the situation, about what sort of person the moral agent is, and about who the recipient of the action/attitude is. Having pondered these questions, we propose an answer as to what is right or good to do or feel in the situation. We could illustrate it as in the illustration below.

Christian ethics reinterprets what is going on here, somehow interjecting the person of Jesus Christ into the relationship between the moral agent — the person doing or feeling something, and the moral patient — the person who is the recipient of the action or feeling. As Søren Kierkegaard might have put it, Jesus Christ is the "middle term" in Christian ethics. In Christian ethics, Jesus Christ is always in the middle. We could illustrate it as in the illustration on the facing page.

Somehow, Christian ethics insists, you need to think about the relevance of Jesus Christ, you need to refer back to the person and work of Christ in

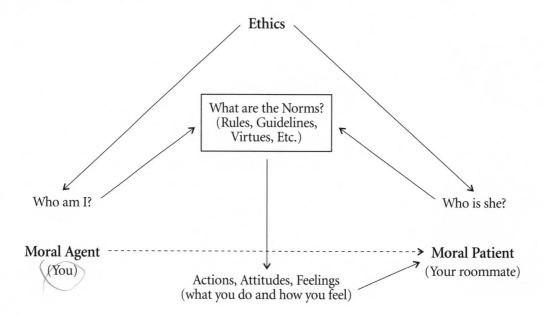

identifying moral norms, in understanding your identity as one who stands in a particular relation to God in Jesus Christ, and in understanding who the recipient of your action or attitude is, as another related to God in Jesus Christ, and in understanding what is good for him or her. In Christian ethics Jesus Christ is the middle term in the answer to the question, "What is the good or right way to feel and act towards my roommate in light of our quarrel?"

To summarize, we might put the differences between Christian ethics and secular ethics this way: Whereas secular ethics identifies the primary questions of ethics as "What is the good life? What is the life worth living?" Christian ethics identifies the primary questions of ethics as "Who am I as a follower of Jesus? What life is worthy of one who recognizes the authority of Jesus? What sort of people should those who confess Jesus as Christ be?"

The Diversity of Christian Ethics

Christian ethics, then, is the careful, systematic examination of how the life and person of Jesus Christ should impinge upon our moral lives, of who we should be and what we should do in light of what Jesus reveals to us about God and the cause of God. Christian ethics is the disciplined attempt to explain what the significance of morality is for Christians and to identify those norms which should inform and guide the Christian in his or her way of living towards the world.

Again, one might think these questions are easily answered, but a moment's reflection upon the diversity and complexity of the Christian tradition will convince you that this is not so. No one is just a Christian. As Christians we are part of some particular community and tradition of Christians. We are, for starters, Catholic Christians, Orthodox Christians, or Protestant Christians. The editors of this volume are Protestant Christians, but even that won't tell you much about our perspectives, for there are Lutheran Protestants, Reformed or Calvinist Protestants, Baptist Protestants, Anabaptist Protestants, Anglican Protestants, Pentecostal Protestants, nondenominational Protestants, etc. Two of the editors of this volume are Reformed or Calvinist Protestants, but even this will not tell you much about our perspectives, for within Reformed Protestantism there are a multitude of theological understandings. There are theological liberals, evangelicals, fundamentalists, and liberationists. Within Reformed Protestantism there are women, men, white people, people of color, Africans, Indonesians, Europeans, and Americans.

The Christian tradition today encompasses an

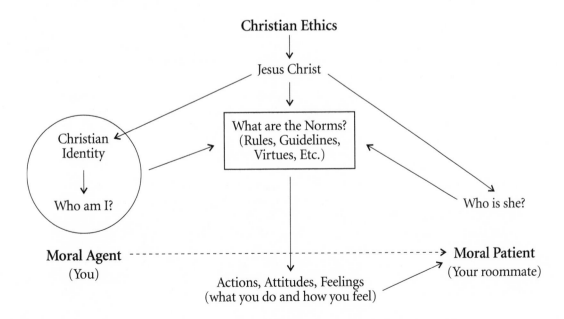

extraordinary diversity of persons throughout the world. Moreover, diversity has been characteristic of the Church since the very beginning of the Christian tradition. Whatever a person's specific identity in this diverse community, of course, each Christian is called by God to faithfulness to Christ. However, how different Christians understand that faithfulness may well vary depending upon how they understand the Bible, what their particular Christian traditions are, and upon their experiences as Christians and as human beings. This is not to say that all theological understandings are equal, that there are no better or worse understandings of God, Scripture, and tradition. It is to simply acknowledge that there is a surprising diversity of theological understandings.

In acknowledging the diversity of Christian visions and voices we should also remember that we currently stand at the end of nearly two thousand years of Christian belief and practice. Untold numbers of Christian believers before us have tried to live lives faithful to Jesus; numerous Christian thinkers have tried to think carefully about what a life in which Christ is the "middle term" looks like. It would be a mistake, we think, to suppose that any one of these previous Christian thinkers has answered all the questions there are about the moral life. But likewise, we think it would be a mistake to underestimate their wisdom. Even if we cannot learn everything from those who have gone before us, there is a lot we can learn if we are willing to listen.

Because the editors of this book want you to be aware that there is an historical Christian tradition and that there is much to be gained from the careful study of that tradition, we have made a special effort to provide access to voices from past Christian tradition in the chapters of this volume. You may find, for example, that your understanding of your responsibility to the poor is aided by hearing the words of Clement, who lived 1,700 hundred years ago, and John Calvin, who lived some 400 years ago, as well as two mighty voices from earlier in this century, Walter Rauschenbusch and Reinhold Niebuhr.

We make no pretense of introducing you to the whole of the Christian tradition in all its richness and diversity. We hope, rather, to expose you to glimpses of the treasures of that tradition and to provide you with incentives for further examination of the Christian voices of the past.

The Complexity of Christian Ethics

We have mentioned the great diversity of voices, past and present, in Christian ethics. This range of voices goes some distance in accounting for how complex Christian ethics can be. But the complexity of Christian ethics cannot be wholly accounted for by diversity. The subject matter of the moral life itself accounts for complexity, especially when one is attempting to think about morality from some type of Christian perspective.

The complexity of Christian ethics is illustrated well through the topic of *abortion*. This subject has dominated many religious press stories — and hence much of the popular religious consciousness — for some time now. Indeed for the past twenty-five years, Lutherans, Presbyterians, Methodists, Episcopalians, and others have been debating the morality of abortion with, at best, mixed results. (Roman Catholics have argued about abortion, too, but the Magisterium, or the official teaching authority, of the Roman Catholic Church has consistently opposed abortion.)

The Lutheran Church in America, for example, issued a statement on abortion in 1970 with a clarifying note in 1978. A sister church, the American Lutheran Church, issued similar statements in 1974, 1976, and 1980. After the merger of these churches into the Evangelical Lutheran Church of America a new study of abortion was presented to the denomination for approval in 1991. In its opening section the report admits "Induced abortion . . . is one of the issues about which members of the Evangelical Lutheran Church in America have serious differences. These differences are also found within society."

Why do differences on abortion remain within the churches, even after more than twenty-five years of discussion? In part, this question can be answered just in terms of the diversity of the church.

Things are not as simple as that, however. The complexity of the abortion issue itself — and abortion is not unlike a number of issues in Christian ethics — lends itself to disagreements, and these disagreements become loud when any new normative ethical study is presented to the churches for approval. Some within the ELCA recognized the ELCA report as capturing important middle ground in the debate over abortion, and thus recommended the approval of the report by the church. Others thought the report a step in the right direction, but too halting and unsteady a step. Still others found the report repressive and thought that, without warrant, it advocated a narrowed range of choices for Lutherans.

It may be tempting for us to dash in and state our own views of this report, and whether we agree with its conclusions about the morality of abortion. But more instructive for our purposes is a look at some of the objections that were raised to the report, for these objections can tell us much about the actual substance of the discipline of Christian ethics, and about the sorts of appeals usually made in the attempt to identify norms of Christian living.

The ELCA report on abortion appeals to Holy Scripture to identify basic convictions of Christian faith relevant to the abortion issue, passages which speak of the creative work of God and the image of God in human beings. Still, many objected that the report was too reserved in its appeals to Scripture, too reluctant to let Scripture have the first and last word. Others faulted the final draft of the report for leaving out what had been included in the first draft, the recognition "that specific passages [of Scripture] do not solve the dilemma." One group of objections to the report, then, had to do with the interpretation of biblical materials and how biblical materials are relevant to the moral life and whether the report adequately recognized the authority of Scripture for our moral lives.

Some who objected to the report suggested that the report was self-consciously ignoring the relevance of the Lutheran theological heritage in addressing the issue of abortion, that the task force which composed the report heard almost every theological voice except that of its own tradition. This alleged abandonment of tradition was seen as both arrogant and ignorant. The result could only be an impoverished understanding of human nature and the mysteries of God's creative activity and the loss of the church's distinctive identity in a secular culture. One Lutheran ethicist objected that inattentiveness to the Lutheran heritage

guaranteed theological and ethical mediocrity. So, while part of the debate over the document was about the interpretation of Scripture and the legitimate use of Scripture in the identification of moral norms, another part of the debate was over the role and authority of tradition.

The significance of science for the moral life was another issue. This was most evident in the analysis of the status of the fetus. According to some, the report assumed that unborn life is "human," and thus worthy of protection from the moment of conception on. But why identify conception as the point at which we are dealing with a "human"? Indeed, these individuals maintained, scientific evidence indicates that "humanlike" features emerge in the fetus only eight to ten weeks after conception; so the report, they claimed, was scientifically irresponsible in suggesting that the fetus is human from the moment of conception on.

Now just as one can dispute the best interpretation of what Scripture or the Christian tradition says, so one can dispute whether the "findings" of science really are findings, or whether they are but one possible interpretation of the data among many equally valid interpretations. And just as one can dispute what authority Scripture or Christian tradition ought to have for contemporary Christians, so one can dispute what authority contemporary science ought to have for the moral life. Even if science does tell us that at eight to ten weeks "humanlike" features emerge in the fetus, can science tell us what moral responsibility we have for the fetus? Or must our moral norms — and our interpretation of the facts of a case — have some other basis, say Scripture, or what the church has historically taught?

There is one other point of contention about what sources should be recognized as authoritative for the Christian moral life that is harder to put a finger on but is, nevertheless, very important. We started off this introduction by discussing the interest of Socrates, Plato, and Aristotle in ethics. Each of these philosophers attempted to identify moral norms and standards not by consulting a holy book, but merely by thinking hard and carefully about his own life and experience. And each was able to identify some norms or standards for the moral life. A final issue in the debate over abortion concerns the relevance and authority of philosophical thought for the morality of Christians. What if a contemporary Aristotle has presented some apparently powerful arguments for the conclusion that only full-fledged human persons can have moral rights and that although the fetus at eight to ten weeks may possess "humanlike" features, it is not a person and thus is entitled to no moral respect and protection? Should this argument be relevant for Christian believers? May it override the teachings of Holy Scripture or the Christian tradition? Some who objected to the ELCA document on abortion thought that it failed to listen attentively to voices outside of the Christian community.

The debate of Christians about whether or not abortion is ever morally permissible for Christians, and, if so, under what circumstances, involves, you see, a debate about the very character of Christian ethics. What are the sources for the moral reflection of Christians? The Bible, the Christian tradition, science, and philosophy are each recognized as sources by most Christians, and each of these is frequently appealed to, but does any one of these have greater moral authority than the others? And if so, why? In what does its greater authority lie? Does Scripture always have the first and last word? Or only the first word, the last word belonging to either tradition, philosophy, or science? These are difficult questions, but they are among the most crucial for Christian ethics.

Of course, even after we have provided, to our own satisfaction, an account of the sources of Christian moral reflection, questions remain for Christian ethics. One set of questions has to do with what we might call strategies for moral reflection. We need to decide *how* to decide. The strategy for moral reflection will be coherent with a judgment about how best to understand the moral life.

One strategy focuses directly on conduct and is primarily concerned with the articulation and application of moral norms that can help us to *decide* and *do* the right or the good moral action. This approach to Christian ethics can be described as *decisionist ethics*.

While decisionists agree about focusing directly on conduct, they disagree about the the type of norms decisions should be guided by. Some Christian thinkers maintain that we can identify specific principles for Christian morality — for example,

principles of love and justice — which establish certain duties and rights. Let's call this variant of decisionist ethics the *rights and duties* strategy. According to it, the task of the Christian is to know rules that should govern conduct and obey them. We do the right thing by engaging in only those actions which are compatible with the relevant moral principle.

Other Christian decisionists maintain that we do the good thing not by concentrating on the fit between actions and principles, but by looking at the fit between the consequences or outcomes of actions and principles. Let's call this variant or decisionist ethics the *outcome,* strategy. According to it the task is to maximize good consequences and to minimize bad consequences.

Too simplistically, we might illustrate the disagreement in the following way. Elaine, who is our first type of decisionist, believes that in ordinary circumstances we ought not to tell a lie. Lying, she believes, does not comport well with the respect for others which both love and justice require of us, so "Do not lie" is a moral principle which Christians ought to be very reluctant to violate. She has, she believes, a *duty* to tell the truth, and others have a *right* to it. So, even though it will cause her and her parents a great deal of pain if she answers truthfully their question "Have you broken up with Mark?" (whom her parents despise), she will do so. Her parents, she may think, are entitled to the truth.

Mark, by contrast, is our second type of decisionist. For him the Christian moral life consists of doing the loving thing by trying to bring about the best results or *outcomes*. When Mark's parents ask whether he and Elaine (whom they think bad for Mark) have ended their relationship, Mark considers what the consequences of telling the truth would be and what the consequences of deceiving his parents would be. If he tells the truth, a major argument will ensue, along with anger and pain. More loving, Mark concludes, to deceive them about the way things are going.

Of course, you could agree with Elaine about a rights and duties strategy for making a decision and disagree with her decision, contending, for example, that because her parents had violated her right to privacy, they had forfeited their right to be told the truth. And one could clearly agree with Mark about an outcomes strategy but disagree with his decision because he neglected certain (more distant) consequences of his deception. The strategies do not tell us what to decide, only how to decide.

There are other Christian thinkers who believe the strategies of both Mark and Elaine to be mistaken, who maintain the *decisionist* approach to be fundamentally misguided. These thinkers suggest an alternative strategy for Christian ethics. Let's call it *virtue ethics*. In virtue ethics, the emphasis is not placed directly upon what one decides or what one does, but upon one's character. Virtue ethicists maintain that our attention should be upon the character traits or virtues that a person must possess in order to live well. Of course, decisions about conduct still have to be made, but the strategy here is to do the sort of thing that a virtuous person would do. So we might imagine Allen, Mark's roommate, committed to this strategy for Christian ethics. When Mark asks Allen (who thinks that Mark is taking advantage of Elaine) whether the two should break up, Allen does not first consider the consequences of telling the truth and compare these with the consequences of not telling the truth. Nor does he consider whether he has some kind of duty to tell the truth to Mark. If he is inclined to lie to Mark, he regards this as a temptation to be resisted, for he knows that truthfulness is a virtue that is required for living well. Allen considers what sort of person he would be revealing himself to be were he to lie and, disapproving of the sort of person who tells lies of convenience, Allen speaks the truth.

Much of the discussion in Christian ethics in the last fifty years has been over which of these three strategies — decisionist ethics in its two strands and virtue ethics — is most truthful to the Christian story, which best captures a Christian way of living towards the world. That debate continues today. Some think that when we address the issue of abortion we should consider only the consequences for everyone involved. Others maintain that foremost in our minds should be rules or principles, delivered by Scripture or tradition, and the compatibility of abortion with those principles. Still others maintain that Christians must think about abortion in light of what sort of people they and the church are called to be, and what the act of abortion would reveal about themselves and their character.

Even after we have decided or reached a conclusion about which strategy or strategies to adopt, there is work to do, for we still need to identify the "stuff" of that model; we need to think about what the most significant principles, outcomes, or virtues are. Our first type of decisionist will have to identify what rules and principles are to guide our conduct. Our second type of decisionist will have to address what makes for a good outcome. The virtue ethicists will need to identify what character traits are required for living well and explain how these character traits contribute to a life well lived.

There is ready agreement that *agape*, love or neighbor-love, must play a central part in any Christian ethic. Both types of decisionists, as well as virtue ethicists, are in agreement that love is a fundamental norm of Christian ethics. However, the meaning of love can vary according to the strategy adopted. In the rights and duties model, "love" usually means regard and (minimally) respect for the neighbor. In the outcomes model, "love" means to do good for the neighbor, to achieve good consequences for the neighbor. And for virtue ethics, we learn what "love" means by looking at Christ and the cross. Upon reflection, then, it is not obvious exactly what love is or what it requires and prohibits. Could it be loving to have an abortion? There is a good deal of disagreement among those who profess to be Christians whether this could be the case, in part because there are disagreements about what "love" is and requires.

Some Christian thinkers have argued that love is not the only norm for Christians. Some of these thinkers suggest that reading the entire Christian Scriptures points to a second norm, justice. But it is almost as difficult to understand what justice requires as what love requires.

Having sorted out what justice and love require will not end our puzzles about the "stuff" of Christian ethics. Christian thinkers will also need some account of how love and justice are related. Some thinkers believe justice and love are inseparable, that anything truly just will also be truly loving. Other Christian thinkers suggest a perpetual tension between love and justice. Still others maintain that frequently love and justice will conflict, that we will be able, at best, to satisfy but one of these norms.

There are other candidates for fundamental norms of Christian living as well. The imitation of Christ, humility, wisdom, mercy, courage, moderation — the case can be made that each of these is necessary for a Christian way of living towards the world. The complexity of Christian ethics shows itself, then, not just in debates about the relative weight of various *sources* of Christian norms, or in the debates about which *strategy* for moral reflection best captures the Christian way of living, but also about *what standards* are to be gleaned from the sources and worked into one of the strategies for moral reflection.

We should muddy the waters of complexity once more before moving on to other matters. It is very easy to think of Christian ethics as though it is only about who *I* am and what *I* do. Christian ethics can be thought of as only the examination of how the individual should live towards the world. But to think of Christian ethics in this limited way would be to lose much of its richness and its complexity. All Christians understand themselves to be part of the body of Christ, the Church. And, as human beings, we recognize our lives to be surrounded by and structured by a multitude of other communities and institutions — the state, economic systems, etc. Christian ethics addresses questions about who we are and how we should think about and act in response to these institutions. Christian ethics, thus, is also concerned about the *context* of our being and doing, about who we are and what we do in relation to the church, the state, economic systems, and other institutions. If, for example, I think abortion is the killing of a human life, but the state permits abortions, should I disobey some of the state's laws in order to protect human life? Or how should I respond to an economic system that leaves many women and children hungry?

Christian ethics is not only about the individual and the individual's posture towards institutions. The Church stands apart as a distinct type of community or institution for Christians. My identity is shaped by my participation in a community of believers, and I reveal who I am by my participation in that community of believers. Christian ethics must address, then, questions about the character of the communities in which we live.

Christian ethics speaks, then, to questions about what the church should be and do, as well as what the individual Christian should be and do. Christian ethics also addresses what these other institutions are to be and do if our lives and our world are to be as God desires. Christian ethics is concerned with providing guidance not only to individuals in relations with other individuals, but also to individuals in relations with institutions, and to these institutions themselves. It is critical for Christian ethics that we be mindful of what our context is, for the moral words spoken to the church are not necessarily the words of moral guidance that should be given to the state. Perhaps, as some Christian ethicists maintain, the church is called to a higher ideal, a more radical obedience, than it is appropriate to expect of non-religious communities or the state.

Is the study of Christian ethics simple and elementary? Not if you attend to the diversity of voices that are part of the conversation of Christian ethics. Not if you recognize and examine the rich complexity of Christian ethics. The study of Christian ethics can be valuable for all Christians, but we should not think that there will be anything simple or elementary about it.

In this collection of readings we have tried to capture the diversity, the complexity, and the richness that characterize the study of Christian ethics. In every chapter of this book, we have tried to provide you with voices from the past Christian tradition, as well as modern voices that represent not only the "mainstream" views of Christian ethics, but voices too little heard in the mainstream. Contemporary Christians need to listen to the saints who led the way before them. Protestant, Catholic, and Orthodox Christians need to listen to one another. Men need to listen to women, and white people need to listen to people of color. If the most frequently heard voices in this volume are white males, we hope that that can be attributed not to any insensitivity on our part, but rather to the fact that, historically, white males have been those most engaged in the discipline of Christian ethics. We can easily and happily envision a similar anthology one hundred years from now looking much different from this one.

As you read this text, you will be exposed not only to the diversity of voices in Christian ethics, but also to some of the complexity and richness of Christian moral reflection. In chapters 2-5 you will engage the debate over the sources of Christian ethics and their relative authority for the Christian moral life. In chapters 6-8 we present discussions of the strategies for reflection about the Christian moral life, the standards for Christian ethics, and the posture of Christians towards various institutions which structure our lives. At the end of this introduction and of chapters 5 and 8-13, you will find "Try It Yourself" exercises — case studies that serve to focus your attention upon the specific issues raised in and by the discipline.

Chapters 2-8 could be said to address foundational issues in Christian ethics. At chapter 9 we turn to issues which many most readily identify with the discipline of Christian ethics. Here we see the foundations and theories developed in the first two parts of this anthology applied to issues of sex and love, to medical practice, to violence and war, to economic matters, and to the environment.

This collection of readings, with its attentiveness to the diversity and complexity of Christian ethics will, we hope, engage you and draw you into reflection upon the Christian moral life. If it succeeds at that, it will have served its purpose. The editors of this volume are not merely scholars, however, but also individuals active in Christian communities, concerned about church and the world. Better, we think, if this anthology not only draws you into the study of Christian ethics, but also draws you toward more faithful lives, if it points you toward Christ and then — with Christ as the "middle term" — toward the world.

Try It Yourself:
Holy Unions (I)

CASE STUDY 1

The case studies in this volume are intended to give you an opportunity to do a little Christian ethics on your own. We hope that the cases will require you not only to make a decision but also to consider the sources, strategies, standards, and contexts for Christian moral decisions. After responding to this case, keep alert for ways in which subsequent chapters might strengthen your answer. The second part of this case can be found on page 180.

For some time now, you have known that Steve is gay. Most of Sheldon Dormitory knows it, too.

Sheldon Dorm is a non-smoking, residential hall on Eastern University's campus. Though not your roommate, Steve lives on your second-floor hall. You are both seniors.

It is a Friday evening in early spring. Steve has gone home for the weekend. A friend asks you to come up to a third-floor room in Sheldon where a spirited discussion is going on. The topic is Steve's "lifestyle." You sit quietly, and hear the following:

"I'm as tolerant as anybody at Eastern, man. 'Live and let live' is my philosophy. But last week he talked to me about eventually marrying his lover. Having a 'holy union' or something like that, is what he called it. That's where I draw the line. I couldn't support him in that, and I sure would leave any Christian church that allowed it. Pronto. It's abnormal."

"I can see you not liking it, Bob. But where do you get off calling gay sex and homosexual marriage 'abnormal'? What makes it so? The fact that there is no procreation? I think marriage between two gay people could be beautiful."

"I'm not what you call a fundamentalist," Bob replies, "but we eventually have to talk about sin here. In the Bible, homosexuality is a sin. That is the bottom line."

"Even if I believed that," George replies, "it doesn't help us decide what church policy should be. The church is a hospital for sinners, you know, not a fortress for the righteous. Besides, I'm not a biblical literalist."

Do you agree with Bob, George, or a third position? Why, and with what justification?

PART I
SOURCES OF CHRISTIAN ETHICS

Chapter 2

Scripture and Christian Ethics

Introduction

"All Scripture is inspired by God and is useful . . . for training in righteousness." That claim by Paul (or a later Paulinist) in the second letter to Timothy (see reading 1) has echoed down the centuries in Christian churches. With virtually one voice, Christians acknowledge the authority of Scripture for the moral life.

The argument *that* Scripture has authority, however, does not by itself settle the question concerning *how* Scripture's authority should function. To say that Scripture has authority for the moral life is to say that it must bear on the formation of character or the choices of conduct *somehow*, but it does not say *how*. The one voice acknowledging the authority of Scripture suddenly becomes many voices when Scripture is *used* "for training in righteousness."

The issue is fundamental to Christian ethics, and it will come up again and again in the selections of this anthology. Of course, it has already come up in the case study, "Holy Unions" (page 13). The argument between Bob and George there was in part an argument about how Scripture bears on moral judgment. They could probably agree *that* Scripture has authority, and they could probably agree that there are a few texts of Scripture that refer to homosexual conduct (Gen. 19:5; Lev. 18:22, 20:13; Rom. 1:26-27; 1 Cor. 6:9; 1 Tim. 1:10), but they might still disagree about the relevance of Scripture — and these few texts — to moral discernment and judgment. How might Bob and George — and all of us — begin to think together and to talk together about *how* to use Scripture appropriately in moral reflection?

It might be useful for Bob and George to begin with an account of the diverse ways in which Scripture has been and might be used in moral reflection. The essay by Jim Gustafson (see reading 2) gives such a description. They — and you — might consider what difference it makes to the discussion of "Holy Unions" if you use Scripture as a source of laws, or ideals, or analogies, or a "great variety" of morally relevant materials, or as a source of knowledge of God and the cause of God. If they do, they will quickly encounter many of the issues Gustafson identifies as important issues within the options he describes.

It might also be useful to take some of the proposals for using Scripture that are found in the subsequent readings and to ask how, according to those proposals, Scripture bears on the argument between Bob and George. How, for example, would the feminist hermeneutic of Sister Margaret Farley (see reading 8), with its convictions concerning equality and mutuality and its emphasis on "nonviolent" appeals to Scripture, bear on the understanding of Scripture's relevance to "Holy Unions"? And how would Richard Mouw's account of the commands of God in Scripture (see reading 6), which are not to be reduced to "love" or simply identified with any locution that has the form of an imperative, license and restrict appeals to Scripture by Bob or George — or you? In order to answer that question, you will probably need to form a judgment about what Mouw calls the "broader pattern of divine address."

Indeed, in order to think and talk about the appropriate use of Scripture in "Holy Unions" or about any of these proposals for the use of Scripture, Bob and George — and you — may need to form judgments not only about the "broader" message or "wholeness" of Scripture with which any particular use of Scripture must cohere, but also about the nature of Scripture, about the questions appropriate to Scripture, and about the relation of Scripture to other sources of moral insight. Of course, such judgments may not be idiosyncratic; they need to be formed in the context of the whole church gathered around the whole Scripture.

According to Stanley Hauerwas (see reading 7), the church gathers around Scripture for the sake of remembrance, and she learns certain virtues not only *from* the reading of Scripture but *for* the reading of Scripture. You might consider whether Hauerwas's account of the ecclesial practice of reading Scripture is based on judgments like those identified in the previous paragraph, whether it is an alternative to such judgments, as he suggests, or whether it is a proposal for the context within which such judgments must finally be made and tested. You might also consider — in the light of Hauerwas's strong correlation of church and Scripture — what particular church is reading Scripture. Does it include Steve and other homosexuals? And would and should the church's reading of Scripture be modified if Steve's experience of the authority of Scripture were attended to as part of the church's remembering?

Suggestions for Further Reading

Birch, Bruce C., and Larry L. Rasmussen. *Bible and Ethics in the Christian Life,* rev. ed. Minneapolis: Augsburg Fortress, 1983.

Daly, Robert J., S.J. *Christian Biblical Ethics.* New York: Paulist Press, 1984.

Fowl, Stephen E., and L. Gregory Jones. *Reading in Communion: Scripture and Ethics in Christian Life.* Grand Rapids, Mich.: Wm. B. Eerdmans, 1991.

Fiorenza, Elisabeth Schüssler. *In Memory of Her: A Feminist Theological Reconstruction of Christian Origins.* New York: Crossroad, 1985.

McDonald, J. I. H. *Biblical Interpretation and Christian Ethics.* Cambridge: Cambridge University Press, 1993.

Meeks, Wayne. *Inventing Christian Morality.* New Haven: Yale University Press, 1994.

Ogletree, Thomas W. *The Use of the Bible in Christian Ethics.* Philadelphia: Fortress Press, 1983.

Verhey, Allen. *The Great Reversal: Ethics and the New Testament.* Grand Rapids, Mich.: Wm. B. Eerdmans, 1984.

1. 2 Timothy 3:16-17

All scripture is inspired by God and is useful for teaching, for reproof, for correction, and for training in righteousness, so that everyone who belongs to God may be proficient, equipped for every good work.

2. Biblical Ethics

ALLEN VERHEY

Biblical ethics is inalienably religious. Reflection on issues of moral conduct and character in Scripture is always qualified by religious convictions and commitments. To abstract biblical ethics from its religious context is to distort it.

Biblical ethics is unyieldingly diverse. The Bible contains many books and more traditions, each addressed once to a particular community in a specific cultural and social context facing concrete questions of moral conduct and character. Biblical ethics does not provide an autonomous and timeless and coherent set of rules; it provides an account of the work and will and way of the one God and evokes the creative and faithful response of those who would be God's people. The one God of Scripture assures the unity of biblical ethics, but there is no simple unitive understanding even of that one God or of that one God's will. To force biblical ethics into a timeless systematic unity is to impoverish it.

Ethics in Torah

The one God of Scripture stands behind the formation and continuation of a people as liberator and ruler. The story was told in countless recitals of faith: the God of Abraham heard our groanings when we were slaves, rescued us from Egypt, and made us a people with a covenant.

The covenant of God and the people was like

Allen Verhey (1945–) is the Blekkink Professor of Religion at Hope College.

From *The Oxford Companion to the Bible*, ed. Bruce M. Metzger and Michael D. Coogan (New York: Oxford University Press, 1993).

an ancient suzerainty treaty, acknowledging and confirming that God will be their great king and they will be God's faithful people. Like other suzerainty treaties the covenant begins by identifying the great king and reciting his works (e.g. Exod. 20:2), continues with stipulations forbidding conflicting loyalties and assuring peace in the land (e.g. Exod. 20:3-17), and ends with provisions for periodic renewal of the covenant and assurances of blessings upon faithful observance and curses upon infidelity (e.g. Exod. 25:22-33).

This story and covenant provided a framework for the gathering of stories and stipulations until the literary formation of Torah, the first five books of the Bible, and the acceptance of it as having Mosaic authority.

"Torah" is usually translated "law," and much of it is legal material. Various collections can be identified (e.g. Exod. 20:22–23:19, the Book of the Covenant; Lev. 17–16, the Holiness Code; Deut. 4:44–28:44, the Deuteronomic Book of the Law) and associated with particular social contexts of Israel's history. The later collections sometimes include older material, but it is not the case that the whole law was given once as a timeless code. Rather, the lawmakers were evidently both creative with and faithful to the legal traditions.

There are two forms of law, causistic and apodictic. The causistic regulations are similar in form and content to other Near Eastern law codes. The apodictic prohibitions, rejecting other gods and marking out the boundaries of freedom (and so securing it), seem a special contribution of Torah.

There is no nice differentiation in the law between "ceremonial" and "civil" and "moral" laws. All of life is covenanted. As "ceremonial" the Torah struggles against the temptations to covenant infidelity in foreign cults and nurtures a communal memory and commitment to covenant. As "civil" the Torah is fundamentally theocratic, and the theocratic conviction that the rulers are ruled too, that they are subject to law, not the final creators of it, has a democratizing effect. As "moral" the Torah protects the family and its economic participation in God's gift of the land, protects persons and property (but persons more than property), requires fairness in settling disputes and economic transactions, and provides for the care and special protection of the vulnerable, widows, orphans, the poor, the sojourner. This last characteristic is perhaps the most remarkable (although it is not absent from other ancient codes) — but it is hardly surprising, given the story that surrounds the stipulations.

The legal materials never escape the story and its covenant, and "Torah" is finally better rendered "teachings." The narrative and covenant preserve the responsiveness of obedience to the law; gratitude then stands behind obedience as its fundamental motive. The story, moreover, forms and informs the law and its use. The concern about the vulnerable reflects the story of one God who heard the cries of slaves (e.g. Exod. 22:21-23; Lev. 19:33-34). And the stories of Moses as the champion of the oppressed should shape the use of the law by any who honor its Mosaic authority.

The narratives of Torah, it needs finally to be said, were morally significant in their own right; artfully told, they nurtured dispositions more effectively than the stipulations themselves. The Yahwist, for example, had told the stories of the patriarchs not only to trace the blessings of David's empire to God but to evoke the readiness to use the power of empire to bless the subject nations (e.g. Gen. 12:1-2; 18-19; 26; 30:27-28; 39-41).

Ethics in the Prophets

The one God who rescued and established a people visited them in the prophets. They came always with a particular word for a particular time, but the word they brought was always related to covenant. Their "Thus saith the Lord . . ." was familiar language of diplomacy in the ancient Near East for the "announcement" of a messenger of a suzerain. The prophets were not social reformers nor skilled in the craft and compromise of politics; they were messengers of the great king and announced his word of judgment.

The sum of that judgment was always the same: The people have forsaken the covenant (1 Kings 19:10, 14; Hos. 8:1 etc.). Concretely — and the message of the prophet was always concrete — some specific idolatry or injustice was condemned as covenant infidelity. The infidelity of idolatry was never "merely" religious. The claims of Ba'al involved the fertility of wombs and land and a theory of ownership. The prophet's announce-

ment of God's greater power freed the people to farm a land stripped of divinity but acknowledged as God's gift and bound them to leave the edges unharvested for the poor. The infidelity of injustice was never "merely" moral, for covenant faithfulness does justice, and the welfare of the poor and powerless is the best index of fidelity and justice. So the prophets irritated and denounced unjust rulers, greedy merchants, corrupt judges, the complacent rich, but they saved their harshest words for those who celebrated covenant in ritual and ceremony without caring about justice, without protecting the powerless, without faithfulness (e.g. Amos 5:21-24).

On the other side of God's judgment the prophets saw and announced God's faithfulness to God's own good future. God will reign and establish both peace and justice — not only in Israel but among all the nations, and not only among the nations but in nature itself. That future is not contingent on human striving, but it already affects human vision and dispositions and actions, readying the faithful even to suffer for the sake of God's cause in the world.

Ethics in Wisdom

The way and will of the one God can be known not only in the great events of liberation and covenant, not only in the great oracles of God's messengers, but also in the regularities of nature and experience. The moral counsel of the sage was not founded on the Torah or the covenant; reflection on moral character and conduct among the wise was rather grounded and tested in experience.

Careful attention to nature and experience allowed the wise to comprehend the basic principles operative in the world, the regularities to which it was both prudent and moral to conform. The one God is the creator who established and secures the order and stability of ordinary life. So the sage could give counsel about eating and drinking and sleeping and working, the way to handle money and anger, the way to relate to friends and enemies and women and fools, when to speak and when to be still, in short, about everything that was a part of experience.

The ethics of wisdom tend to be conservative,

for the experience of a community over time provided a fund of wisdom, but the immediacy of experience keeps the tradition open to challenge and revision. The ethics of wisdom tend to be prudential, but a little experience is enough to teach that the righteous may suffer and that there is no neat fit between morality and prudence (Job). The ethics of wisdom tend to delight both in the simple things of life, like the love of a man and woman (Song of Solomon), and in the quest for wisdom itself, but experience itself teaches the hard lessons that wisdom has its limit in the inscrutable (Job 28) and that the regularities of nature and experience cannot simply be identified with the cause of a covenanted God (Ecclesiastes).

Wisdom reflects about conduct and character quite differently than the Torah and the prophets, but "the end of the matter," like "the beginning of wisdom" (Prov. 1:7), is a reminder of covenant: "Fear God, and keep his commandments" (Eccles. 12:13). That beginning and end keeps wisdom in touch with Torah; between that beginning and end wisdom struggles mightily to keep Torah in touch with experience and covenant in touch with creation.

Ethics in the New Testament

Jesus of Nazareth came announcing that the kingdom of God was at hand and already making its power felt in his words and deeds. He called the people to repent, to form their conduct and character in response to the good news of that coming future.

To welcome a future where the last will be first (Mark 10:31), a future already gestured in Jesus' humble service, is to be ready to be "servant of all" (Mark 10:35). To delight in a kingdom where the poor will be blessed is now to be carefree about riches and to give alms. To repent before a kingdom which belongs to children, which is already gestured in table-fellowship with sinners, and which is signaled in open conversation with women, is now to turn from conventional standards of value and worth to bless children, to welcome sinners, and to treat women as equals.

Because Jesus announced and already unveiled the coming reign of God, he spoke with authority, not simply on the basis of law and tradition. And

because the coming reign of God demanded a response of the whole person and not merely external observance of the law, his words made radical demands on character. So, Jesus' radical demand for truthfulness replaced (and fulfilled) the legal casuistry about oaths. The readiness to forgive and be reconciled set aside (and fulfilled) the legal limitations on revenge. The disposition to love even enemies put aside legal debates about the meaning of "neighbor." The ethic was based neither on the precepts of law nor the regularities of experience, but it did not discard them either; law and wisdom were both qualified and fulfilled in this ethic of response to the future reign of the one God of Scripture.

Jesus died on a Roman cross, but God raised him up in an act of power which was at once vindication of this Jesus and prelude to God's final triumph and reign. Moral reflection in the New Testament always looks back to the vindicated Jesus and forward to God's cosmic sovereignty.

The Gospels used the tradition of Jesus' words and deeds to tell his story creatively and faithfully and so to shape the conduct and character of the particular communities they addressed. Each has its own distinctive emphasis. Mark represents Jesus as calling for heroic discipleship ready to suffer and die and ready as well to live in ordinary relationships with heroic confidence, not in Jewish law or Roman justice, but in God. In Matthew, the law holds and Jesus is represented as upholding the law and as its best interpreter even as he demands a righteousness that "exceeds that of the scribes and Pharisees" (5:20). Luke's emphasis falls on care for the poor and women and sinners and upon the mutual respect due Jew and Gentile in the Christian community. John tells the story quite differently that his reader might "have life" (20:31) and might know that life in his name entails love for one another.

The epistles of Paul make little use of the tradition of Jesus' words and deeds. He proclaims the gospel of the cross and resurrection as "the power of God for salvation" (Rom. 1:16) to his churches, but sometimes in the indicative mood and sometimes in the imperative mood. The indicative describes the power of God in the crucified and risen Christ to provide an eschatological salvation of which Christians have the "first fruits" (Rom. 8:23) and "guarantee" (2 Cor. 5:5) in the Spirit.

The imperative acknowledges that the powers of the old age still threaten Christians; so, "if we live by the Spirit, let us also walk by the Spirit" (Gal. 5:25).

Reflection about conduct and character ought to be radically affected by God's power in the cross and resurrection (cf. Rom. 12:2). Paul provides no recipe for this new discernment, but some features are clear. (1) Their self-understanding as moral agents was determined by their incorporation into Christ (e.g. Gal. 2:20, Rom. 6:1–11). (2) Their perspective on situations was eschatological. (The Corinthian enthusiasts, who claimed to be already fully in the new age, were consistently reminded of the "not yet" character of their existence, while the Colossians, tempted to submit again to angelic powers and their taboos, were told that Christ was "already" Lord.) (3) Freedom (Gal 5:1, 2 Cor. 3:17) and love (1 Cor. 13, Phil. 1:9) were values which provided tokens of the new age. (4) The moral traditions of the church, the synagogue, and the Greek schools were not to be discarded but selected, assimilated, and qualified by the gospel. The new discernment does not create guidelines and judgments *ex nihilo,* but the existing traditions are brought under the critical and transforming power of God. Paul and his churches exercised such discernment on various moral problems: the relation of Jew and Gentile, slave and free, male and female, rich and poor, church and state. The judgments are not "timeless truths" in the style of either a philosopher or a code-maker; they are timely applications of the gospel to specific problems in particular contexts.

The unyielding diversity of biblical ethics is only confirmed by other New Testament writings. For example, the pastorals use common hellenistic moral vocabulary and urge commonplace moral judgment against the Gnostics. James provides *paraenesis,* a didactic text collecting instructions into a moral miscellany. Revelation provides a symbolic universe to make intelligible both the experience of injustice at the hands of Caesar and the conviction that Jesus is Lord, and to make plausible both patient endurance of suffering and faithful resistance to the values of the empire.

The ethical voices are "many and various," but the one God of Scripture still makes known in all the unyielding diversity — and richness — of these writings the power of God to renew life, to transform identity, to sanctify a people, to bring the whole creation into coherence with God's reign.

3. Ways of Using Scripture

JAMES M. GUSTAFSON

*Authority
in scripture?
How use it?*

The existence of a variety of materials in Scripture necessitates some general principles for clarifying a more coherent and simpler view of the message of Scripture. The use of Scripture in Christian ethics first involves the determination of the theological and ethical principles which will be used to bring coherence to the "meaning" of Scripture's witness. In a previous publication I distinguished a view of Scripture as the revelation of a morality that is authoritative for the judgments of Christians from a view of it as a revelation of theological principles that are used to interpret what "God is doing," and thus, in turn, can give clues to what man as a moral agent is to do in particular historical circumstances.[1] If Scripture is the revelation of a morality, its application to the Cambodian invasion would require that one judge that event in accordance with moral laws, precepts, and commands given in Scripture. If Scripture is the revelation of the action of God, one applies it to

1. "Christian Ethics in America," *Christian Ethics and the Community,* pp. 23-82.

James M. Gustafson (1925–) taught at Yale Divinity School and the University of Chicago before becoming the Henry R. Luce Professor of Humanities and Comparative Studies at Emory University. His work includes *Can Ethics be Christian?*, *Christ and the Moral Life*, *Protestant and Roman Catholic Ethics*, and *Ethics from a Theocentric Perspective.*

From "The Place of Scripture in Christian Ethics: A Methodological Study" in James M. Gustafson, *Theology and Christian Ethics* (Philadelphia: United Church Press, 1974).

the Cambodian invasion by interpreting that event in the light of an answer to the question, "What is God doing in our contemporary history, and particularly in Cambodia?" Here I would like to refine these types before proceeding to suggest a more constructive statement.

The most stringent use of Scripture as revealed morality can be stated in the following way. Those actions of persons and groups which violate the moral law revealed in Scripture are to be judged morally wrong. The idea of moral law becomes the principle for ethical interpretation. Two issues immediately emerge. One is the content of the moral law, and the other is the mode of its application. For Jewish religion these can be answered more simply than they can for Christians, although even in Judaism the answers are complex. The law would be the Torah, and *halachah* would provide the tradition for application. The parts of Torah that would be applicable, and the procedures for its application through Mishna, Talmud, the Codes, the Responsa, all involve judgments on the part of the learned rabbi who might come to a decision. But there would be clear biblical authority in the tradition for using biblical law, and the tradition provides a continuity of historical judgments and general procedures by which a new judgment might be made.

For Christian religion this use of Scripture is even more difficult. What is the moral law that is revealed in the Bible? Torah would be an insufficient answer. There is also the "new law," and just what that is has to be determined. If the teachings of Jesus as recorded in the Gospels are the new law, then something like the method of *halachah* might be appropriate; but on the whole the Christian theologians have not worked in this way. Further, if the new law is the "grace of the Holy Spirit written in the heart," as it has been judged to be by both the Catholic and Protestant traditions, it can no longer be limited in its references to the moral teachings of the Scriptures interpreted to be law. It is "the life-giving law of the Spirit," to quote Romans 8:2 (NEB), a text that is persistently cited in the history of Christian ethical thought.

Christians have no codifications of the moral law of Scripture and its interpretations comparable to the *Shulhan Arukh* and the Code of Maimonides; even the codifications of law in the canon law tradition of the Catholic Church appeal heavily to the natural law tradition developed in the West, rather than to Scripture. Even Fundamentalists have highly selective[2] ways of using biblical evidence. There are clearly ethical principles at work that govern their choices of texts to be applied to particular moral situations and that provide ways of explaining texts which *prima facie* would contravene the positions they would take.

Perhaps agreement on the primacy, if not the exclusiveness, of the "law of love" could be asserted about the Christian Scriptures, recognizing their continuity with Jewish Scriptures. "For the whole law can be summed up in a single commandment: 'Love your neighbor as yourself,'" writes Paul (Gal. 5:14, NEB), a claim also found in other parts of the Scripture. If this were judged to be the material content of the new moral law, the modes of its application to situations like the Cambodian venture would vary markedly. For some persons it might have a pacifist application; one does not love himself by taking his own life; surely one does not love his neighbor by taking his. For others it becomes a high-level general principle which is applied to the complexities of a war through the mediation of the structure and principles of just-war thinking.

A second use of Scripture as revealed morality could be stated as follows: Those actions of persons and groups which fall short of *the moral ideals* given in Scripture are to be judged morally wrong, or at least morally deficient. The notion of moral ideals becomes the principle of ethical interpretation. Three issues emerge here. The first is whether the language of moral ideals is itself warranted by Scripture. Is the language of ideals as intrinsic to the Scriptures as is the language of law?

2. See the arguments in support of capital punishment developed by H. J. Vellenga in "Christianity and the Death Penalty," *The Death Penalty in America,* ed. Hugo A. Bedau (Garden City: Doubleday Anchor Books, 1964), pp. 123-30. With reference to Matt. 5:21f, Vellenga writes: "It is evident that Jesus was not condemning the established law of capital punishment, but was actually saying that hate deserved capital punishment" (p. 126), "If one accepts the authority of Scripture, then the issue of capital punishment must be decided on what Scripture actually teaches and not on the popular, naturalistic ideas of sociology and penology that prevail today" (p. 129).

How these questions would be answered depends to some extent upon how one interprets "ideals." If a moral notion has to refer to some timeless entity, a metaphysical value, in order to be an ideal, it is safe to say that the language of ideals is more at home in Greek ethics than in biblical ethics. If, however, it refers to a vision of the future in which "The wolf shall live with the sheep, and the leopard lie down with the kid; the calf and the young lion shall grow up together" (Isa. 11:6, NEB), the promised fulfillment might well function as a vision of the ideal future. The New Testament idea of the kingdom of God has functioned this way in Christian ethics from time to time in Christian history, most prominently in the social gospel writers.

The theological doctrine that qualifies the use of the language of ideals is eschatology. Whether an ethician uses the vision of an ideal future is governed by his eschatological views. If he finds a warrant for the language of ideals within those views, then *how* that vision is used is also determined to a considerable degree by his eschatology. The double problem of the use of Scripture which we pointed out previously confronts us again: One part of the problem is the significance of the eschatological context within the Scriptures for understanding properly the biblical visions of ideal futures; the other is the authority that the biblical eschatological context has for the use of those visions in constructive Christian theological ethics.

The second issue that emerges in the use of the language of ideals is that of their material content. The biblical imagery in Isaiah, as well as elsewhere, suggests harmony between natural enemies, the resolution of struggles in idyllic peace — a theme often portrayed in Christian art. The social gospel writers did not hesitate to find consistent with the biblical vision of the coming kingdom of God almost all values that were judged to promote human welfare: peace, love, justice, harmony. They courageously developed these in terms of ideals and goals for the society of their own time. Clearly, there is a deep and broad gulf between the ideal of universal peace as part of the biblical vision of the fulfillment and any war, including the Cambodian venture.

The third issue is the mode of application of a moral ideal to the Cambodian or any other historical situation. If the basis for using an ideal is that reality ought to be conformed to the ideal in all human actions and states of affairs, a condemnatory verdict on the Cambodian venture is clear. If, however, the use of the ideal leads to the reckoning of *compromises* that men can live with, or *approximations* with which they can be satisfied, then a sliding scale of judgment has been introduced. The adoption of a more realistic view of the possibilities of political and moral achievement under the conditions of historical finitude and corruption leads to such applications. How much compromise with the ideal do the conditions of history, the particular circumstances, require? What degree of approximation of the vision of the ideal future ought one to strive for under the political, social, and military conditions of our time? To give warrant for a judgment against the Cambodian venture one has to indicate, in this mode of thought, that the compromises are too great, that the present approximations are insufficient to merit moral approval of the policies of the government.

A third use of Scripture as a revealed morality would be stated as follows: Those actions of persons and groups are to be judged morally wrong which are similar to actions that are judged to be wrong or against God's will under similar circumstances in Scripture, or are discordant with actions judged to be right or in accord with God's will in Scripture. Here the method is roughly one of analogy, and it has its share of difficulties. One is the problem of providing persuasive evidence that the circumstances of, for example, a political and military situation in our time are similar in any significant respects to the circumstances in biblical times. A second is the problem of determining which biblical events will be used for purposes of an analogical elucidation of the moral significance of present events. Some prior ethical commitment is likely to determine this choice. For example, one might choose the account of the "liberation" of the Hebrew people from bondage in Egypt as the biblical narrative most applicable to present history. This choice might be made on either one of two separate grounds or on a combination of them. First, it might be judged that the Vietnamese and Cambodian people are like the Hebrew people of old and that American power is like the power of Egypt. With more refined intervening steps provided, we might conclude that intervention in

Cambodia is morally wrong just as repression of the Hebrews in Egypt was morally wrong. Second, we might judge that the crucial moral issue of our time, and of biblical times, is that of liberation from oppression and repression. A general moral and biblical theme, namely, liberation, is judged on theological and ethical grounds to be central to Christian ethics. On the basis of this judgment one could turn to Scripture to find the historical events which reveal and elucidate this theme, and in turn use these events as analogies for events of the present time which seem to elucidate the same theme.

The primary question in the use of Scripture for moral analogies is that of control. If present events are in control, then one first responds to these events and then on the basis of that response seeks biblical events that are similar to the present ones. The predisposition is to seek those events which will confirm one's present judgments. Thus, the choice of the Exodus would be more congenial for a negative judgment on present repression of a small power by a great power than would some of the prophetic interpretations of the role of a great power in chastising a lesser power for its violation of God's ways for the nations. The biblical materials would be chosen on the basis of their affinity for a present moral judgment arrived at perhaps independently of biblical considerations. Biblical support could be found for the opinions one has formed on independent ethical bases.

If Scripture is in control, then one is faced with the persistent question of which events are most nearly consistent with certain central tendencies of the biblical, theological, and moral witness. One would have to decide whether the Hebrew wars of conquest of Canaan were "truer" to the central themes of biblical morality than was the liberation accomplished by the Exodus. (I have been told that the Calvinists in South Africa used the analogy of the chosen people's right to the land of Canaan to justify their expansion into the territory of the Africans in the nineteenth century.) Some theological and ethical principle would have to be judged as normative for the whole of scriptural witness; this would in turn determine which events would be used as analogies normatively proper to current events, and thus as the basis for judging the moral rightness of present actions.

A fourth use of Scripture is looser than the first three. It could be stated as follows: Scripture witnesses to a great variety of moral values, moral norms and principles through many different kinds of biblical literature: moral law, visions of the future, historical events, moral precepts, paraenetic instruction, parables, dialogues, wisdom sayings, allegories. They are not in a simple way reducible to a single theme; rather, they are directed to particular historical contexts. The Christian community judges the actions of persons and groups to be morally wrong, or at least deficient, on the basis of reflective discourse about present events *in the light of* appeals to this variety of material as well as to other principles and experiences. Scripture is one of the informing sources for moral judgments, but it is not sufficient in itself to make any particular judgment authoritative.

The obvious problem with this use is its looseness. The questions that were raised about what is in control are also pertinent here. It would be very easy to make a judgment on the basis of feelings or prevailing cultural values and then find *some support for it* in the variety of Scripture's texts. The maintenance of any objective authority for the moral witness of the Scriptures is difficult if one recognizes the variety of norms and values present there and also the historical character of the occasions in which these emerge. Thus, some efforts at generalization are necessary in order to bring some priorities of biblical morality into focus. The generalizations that are most nearly consistent with certain theological, ethical statements that appear to be more at the heart of the matter in the development of biblical religion would be used. Informed in a general way by biblical faith and morality, as well as by other relevant beliefs and moral commitments, one might judge the Cambodian venture to be wrong and proceed to cite biblical norms and values as corroborative evidence for one's judgment. We admittedly have less than absolute certitude that the judgment is biblically authorized, both because of the variety of material contents in the Scriptures and because of the looseness of the way in which it is used. The necessity for appeals to the continuing tradition of Christian morality beyond the closing of the canon is taken for granted, and the fact that biblical moral-

ity is in many ways inapplicable, and in other ways wrong, is accepted.

Each of the ways in which the morality in the Scripture is used can be given theological justification. Thus, no sharp line can be drawn between primarily moral and primarily theological uses of Scripture in Christian ethics. But attention to some of the basically theological uses of Scripture in Christian ethics, which subordinate its ethical content to its theological importance, helps us to see the range of opinion. I have argued elsewhere that the most significant alterations in Christian ethics in mid-twentieth century took place not as a result of the reassessment of the liberal and optimistic interpretation of human nature, but as a result of the introduction into ethical thinking of the idea of a "God who acts," or a "God who speaks" in particular historical circumstances. Without further elaboration of that, it should be clear that biblical theology provided a framework for the interpretation of the historical events in which men and nations were involved; and out of this interpretation came certain assessments of the moral significance of events, certain clues about how they were to be judged, and what persons ought to do in them. The primary question became not "How ought we to judge this event?" nor even "What ought we to do in this event?" but "What is God doing in this event? What is he saying to us in this event?" Three articles published by H. Richard Niebuhr during World War II have titles which illustrate this: "War as the Judgment of God," "Is God in the War?" and "War as Crucifixion."[3]

The inspiration of a biblical understanding of an active God has to be specified by asking two sorts of questions. First, who is this God who acts? What do we know about him as "subject" or "person" or about his "nature" which will give a clue to the sorts of things he might be doing and saying? Second, what sorts of things has he said and has he done? What does he wish to accomplish by his acting? What do we know about his actions?

Insofar as Scripture provides "data" for answering these questions, we are again faced with the task of formulating generalizations based upon a variety of materials.[4] Here we shall only indicate

3. The three appeared in *The Christian Century* 59 (1942): 630-33; 953-55; and 60 (1943): 513-15.

4. For a critical analysis of the work that has been

some of the themes that have been used in theological ethics. The theme of liberation currently finds wide usage with reference to the struggle both of black people in the United States and of colonial peoples of the world. "Jesus' work is essentially one of liberation," writes the articulate and influential James H. Cone, in his *Black Theology and Black Power*.[5] This becomes a warrant for both an evaluative description of the situation of black people in America and a normative direction for the activity in which Christians ought to be engaged. The themes of crucifixion and resurrection are used by another influential contemporary theologian, Richard Shaull, of Princeton. These terms provide a theologically warranted framework for interpreting the present course of events in a world of revolutions; the old orders must die in order for new life to be born, a life of hope and justice for all who are oppressed.[6] As does the liberation theme, so the crucifixion and resurrection theme provides a way of describing and evaluating the events of our times, and a normative thrust for the actions of Christians. They ought to be involved in the destruction of oppressive forms of life in order for new life to come into being. Jürgen Moltmann's highlighting of the theme of hope as central to biblical theology, Paul Lehmann's development of God's doing humanizing work, H. Richard Niebuhr's more complex view of God's creative, governing, judging, and redeeming work: each provides a theological ground upon which is constructed both an interpretation of the significance of events and a positive normative thrust with reference to what Christians ought to be doing. James Sellers, in his very suggestive *Theological Ethics*, takes the theme of promise and fulfillment to be central to the biblical witness. Traditional Lutheran theologians have used gospel and law, and orders of creation; Barth offers an interpretation of the God of grace who is yet the commander as a biblical theological foundation.

The use of biblical theological concepts to provide an evaluative description of historical events requires that further moves be made to determine how a particular event is to be judged and what ought to be done in those circumstances. These moves can be made in two ways or in a combination of them. One such move is from the built-in, normative content of the evaluative-descriptive terms to the basis both for moral judgment on the events and for prescriptions or guidelines for action in them. If, in Lehmann's ethics, one discerns what God is doing to make and keep human life human, whatever is not in accord with the human is judged to be wrong, and the prescriptions or guidelines for further action would be whatever is in accord with the human. The second move is a methodological one. In Lehmann's case, for example, the method for discerning both what is morally wrong and what one ought to do is akin in crucial respects to what philosophers designate as moral intuitionism; the judge and actor is sensitive to what God is doing, and in his theonomous conscience he perceives what is wrong and what he ought to do. In the case of others, however, the move from the evaluative-descriptive enterprise to the moral judgment and the prescription for action might involve a more elaborate and rational process of practical moral reasoning. The normative elements in the concepts used for the evaluative description are lifted out in statements of moral principles and values, and their application both to the judgment and to subsequent action is developed according to methods of rational moral argumentation.[7]

How the various biblical theologies of ethics use the morality or ethical teachings found in Scripture is contingent upon methodological choices that can be given both theological and philosophical justification. For example, within Barth's theological ethics, it is the command of God, heard by the moral agent, that determines whether something is right or wrong. But this command is not a capricious one; it is likely to be in accord with the moral teachings of the decalogue and of Jesus. These moral teachings provide "prominent lines"; they are not unexceptionable

called biblical theology see Brevard Childs, *Biblical Theology in Crisis* (Philadelphia: Westminster Press, 1970).

5. James H. Cone, *Black Theology and Black Power* (New York: Seabury Press, 1968), p. 35.

6. See, for example, Shaull's article, "Christian Theology and Social Revolution (I)," *The Perkins School of Theology Journal* 21 (1967-68): 5-12.

7. I have developed these issues in "Two Approaches to Theological Ethics," *Christian Ethics and the Community*, pp. 127-38.

rules or laws of conduct, nor are they moral ideals. They are coherent with the revelation of God in the Scriptures; and thus, if one's judgment is not in accord with these prominent lines, it is doubtful whether one is really hearing God's command.

4. Scripture and the Love of God

ST. AUGUSTINE

XXXV

The sum of all we have said since we began to speak of things thus comes to this: It is to be understood that the plenitude and the end of the Law and of all the sacred Scriptures is the love of a Being which is to be enjoyed and of a being that can share that enjoyment with us, since there is no need for a precept that anyone should love himself. That we might know this and have the means to implement it, the whole temporal dispensation was made by divine providence for our salvation. We should use it, not with an abiding but with a transitory love and delight like that in a road or in vehicles or in other instruments, or, if it may be expressed more accurately, so that we love those things by which we are carried along for the sake of that toward which we are carried.

St. Augustine (354–430), under the influence of Neo-platonic philosophy, converted to the Christian faith as a young man. Following his conversion, he pursued the knowledge of God in a monastic community prior to being drafted to be the Bishop of Hippo in North Africa. His *Confessions* and his *City of God* have had widespread influence on psychology and political philosophy as well as theology in the West.

From St. Augustine, *On Christian Doctrine*, part 1, chaps. 35-36, 40, trans. D. W. Robertson, Jr. (New York: Macmillan, 1958).

XXXVI

Whoever, therefore, thinks that he understands the divine Scriptures or any part of them so that it does not build the double love of God and of our neighbor does not understand it at all. Whoever finds a lesson there useful to the building of charity, even though he has not said what the author may be shown to have intended in that place, has not been deceived, nor is he lying in any way.

XL

Therefore, when anyone knows the end of the commandments to be charity "from a pure heart, and a good conscience, and an unfeigned faith," and has related all of his understanding of the divine Scriptures to these three, he may approach the treatment of these books with security. For when he says "charity" he adds "from a pure heart," so that nothing else would be loved except that which should be loved. And he joins with this "a good conscience" for the sake of hope, for he in whom there is the smallest taint of bad conscience despairs of attaining that which he believes in and loves. Third, he says "an unfeigned faith." If our faith involves no lie, then we do not love that which is not to be loved, and living justly, we hope for that which will in no way deceive our hope.

5. Social Ideas in the New Testament

WALTER RAUSCHENBUSCH

When the Bible gets through startling us, either it will have lost its vitality or we shall be well on in holiness. There is more light to break forth from God's Word, and, when we suddenly look into more light, it makes us blink. Let us be entirely honest with the Bible and state just what every passage means as it stands; then if we feel that it has to be modified by collateral truth or adapted to changed conditions, we can apply those modifications afterward without doing violence to our own honesty or to the meaning of the Scripture writers.

Let us take up first the teaching of Jesus in the synoptic Gospels; then the ideas prevailing in the Jewish-Christian Church; and, finally, the teachings of Paul.

The Teaching of Jesus

If we were to cut out and put together all the passages in which Jesus discussed questions of property, they would exceed, in mere bulk, his teaching on any question in ethics. They would also be conspicuous by a severity of tone not found in the treatment of other evils, except in-

---

Walter Rauschenbusch (1861–1918) was an influential leader of the social gospel movement and a professor of church history at Rochester Seminary. His works include *Christianity and the Social Crisis, A Theology for the Social Gospel,* and *The Social Principles of Jesus.*

From Walter Rauschenbusch, *The Treasury of Religious Thought* 17, no. 2 (June 1899): pp. 155-59.

sincerity and hypocrisy. Do questions of property receive the same quantity and quality of attention either in the teaching or the practice of the Christian Church as a whole? We demand as much as he in regard to chastity; namely, purity of thought as well as of action. We demand more than he in temperance. But neither in the letter nor in the spirit do we demand what he did about property.

Jesus never advised men to acquire wealth or to "rise in life," which is so often set forth as an object of ambition for young men today. He forbade his disciples to lay up treasures for the reason that their hearts would inevitably be where their treasure was; their inward light would be darkened; and the attempt to serve two masters would prove a failure (Matt. 6:19-24). The good seed cannot compete with the rank and rapid growth of the thorns; the higher life is choked by "the deceitfulness of riches" (Matt. 13:22). He told his dumbfounded disciples that it was next to impossible for a rich man to enter the kingdom (Mark 10:23, 24). He explained this by saying: "How hard it is for them that *trust* in riches to enter into the kingdom of God," and we are sometimes told that riches are no danger, as long as one does not trust in them. But, if we take this saying in connection with the passages just quoted, we see that he held such an inward devotion to wealth to be almost inseparable from the possession of it. Tell a man who is bathing: "You can tie as many pounds of lead to your feet as you please, as long as you keep your head above water"; and then tell young men: "You can be as rich as you please, but you must not let your property, either in the getting or the having or the spending, have any evil effect on your moral and spiritual life." The passage is often misunderstood, because we understand the phrase, "enter the kingdom of God," to mean, "get to heaven." If we paraphrase it: "How hard it is for a rich man to live a right life," it becomes clearer. It is a hard thing for a man to become wealthy without offending against justice and the finer shades of honesty and truthfulness, and without developing the acquisitive instinct at the expense of the nobler faculties of the soul; it is hard for a man even to possess wealth inherited from another, without drifting into luxurious habits, associating with idle people, and being alienated from his poorer fellows and ceasing to be a brother of men.

Jesus applied this principle by demanding of one man that he get rid of his wealth before he entered the discipleship. Another rich man was hailed by him gladly, but it was after he had promised to give away 50 percent of his property outright, and out of the balance to restore fourfold what he had taken wrongfully. I wonder how much Zaccheus had left when he got through his figuring, and I wonder what Mrs. Zaccheus thought of it. How did Zaccheus come to express his conversion in that fashion anyway? Why did he not announce that henceforth he intended to attend church and have family worship again? Was it so notorious a quality of this revivalist from Galilee to demand restitution and a squaring of accounts, that Zaccheus knew without having heard him that he must let daylight into his property affairs before he could hope to please Jesus?

Christ was profoundly suspicious of the desire to get wealth and to accumulate. When a man asked him to intervene with his brother so that he would get his share of the inheritance, Jesus followed up his refusal by a warning against covetousness. The attitude of the rich farmer who congratulated himself on his crops he called folly (Luke 12:13-21). We should call it legitimate business sense. There are said to be about thirty-six different interpretations of the parable of the unjust steward. There are real difficulties in it, but the reason why the most obvious meaning is set aside seems to be that it is unpalatable to us. I understand it to be addressed to men of wealth; they have only a short time of authority left to them before the coming of the Messianic kingdom sweeps away their privileges; they are advised to use that time with shrewd foresight, like the steward, to win the favor of the children of the kingdom, who may then, after the coming of the kingdom, show them kindness in turn. That the parable somehow bears down sharply on the rich is clearly indicated by Luke (Luke 16:14); the Pharisees, "who were lovers of money," understood the parable better than modern interpreters, for they scoffed at him. (The Greek word means: "They turned up their noses at him.") And Jesus replied to their attitude by telling them the story of Dives and Lazarus, which ends with a significant reference to certain five brothers of Dives, who are still in this world, living presumably as Dives did, unwilling to listen to Moses and the prophets, and on the road to the same place.

When the Messiah returns to judgment and to the inauguration of his kingdom, the decisive test of men will be the attitude they have taken to the social want and misery of men (Matt. 25:31-46). We are told to look for his coming; but to look for it does not appear to mean that we must talk about it and have clear theories about the time and manner of his return. That steward is unprepared and unmindful, who beats his fellow-servants and eats and drinks with the drunken (Matt. 24:48-51); that is, who exploits his position of power and influence to tyrannize over his subordinates and to use up his master's possessions for his own luxurious enjoyment.

Like the prophets, Jesus hated the combination of religion with indifference to social wrong, the tithing of mint, anise, and cummin, while justice, mercy, and fidelity are neglected. He quotes repeatedly the saying of Hosea: "Mercy, not sacrifice."

Some of Christ's moral precepts are practicable only in a social condition of approximate equality. For instance the command to give to him that asks and to lend to him that wishes to borrow, is possible among neighbors of fairly equal standing, who help one another out with tools or work or seed-corn or money. It becomes increasingly difficult when a rich man lives among poor people. So that the working chance of a really Christian morality depends in a measure on the general social condition.

It is almost amusing to notice with what comfort some men face this mass of radical teaching with the saying: "The poor ye have with you always." As if Jesus said: "Strive to have the poor always with you. Beware of any condition in which you might lessen their number." It is simply a statement of fact, and eighteen centuries have borne it out only too well.

In the Jewish-Christian Church

It is cause for regret that our information about the life of the Jewish-Christian churches is not more copious and at first hand. And even what there is of it has often been overshadowed by the intellectual and spiritual power of Paul's writings. There must have been a rich and interesting life in the Jewish churches, before the destruction of Jerusalem and the growth of Gentile Christianity gradually ended their separate existence. Certainly their Christian ideas were strongly tinged by social aspirations. They could not help being so, for they were the direct continuance of the best Jewish thought. "He hath put down princes from their thrones, and hath exalted them of low degree; the hungry he hath filled with good things and the rich he hath sent empty away." That revolutionary sentiment is an expression of the thought current among pious Jews before the coming of Christ; it was uttered by one who probably had more influence in shaping the thoughts of Jesus than any other human being.

John the Baptist called on them to prepare for the coming of the Messiah by straightening out the crooked paths, filling up the low places and levelling down the high. He explained this by demanding fruits meet for repentance. And when they asked him for a more definite statement of what he meant by repentance, he told them to even out social inequalities by sharing with one another, and not to misuse positions of legal or physical superiority for extorting profits from (Luke 3:3-14).

The Church at Jerusalem began its life by sharing. It is urged that this is an isolated case, and that is quite true. We have no indication that communism prevailed in any of the churches to which Paul wrote. But the anxiety to deprive this isolated instance of any binding force strikes one a little unpleasantly when coming from men who otherwise insist on prooftexts. If there were as clear an utterance of Scripture for the method of administering the ordinances, or for the form of church government, how it would be seized and insisted on! This communion originated under the fresh impulse of the Holy Spirit, and Luke at least tells of it with evident enthusiasm. The assertion that the later poverty of the church at Jerusalem was due to its early communism may be true, but there is no evidence to sustain the assertion. It is juster to say that both the early sharings inside of the same church, and the later system of sharing between entire churches by collections, were due to the same condition of poverty and devised by the same Christian spirit of love and fellowship. The collections from Antioch and the large fund brought by Paul and a committee of Gentile brethren were an application of communism on a large scale.

It is justly pointed out that the sharing at Jerusalem was voluntary. But the feeling in the Church was so strong that even covetous souls like Ananias and Sapphira felt the compulsion and tried to satisfy public sentiment and their own conscience by at least a show of compliance. That is precisely what is lacking in churches today. We have a public sentiment compelling men to abstain from swearing, drinking, and licentiousness. But we elect Ananias to our board of trustees and have Sapphira run the church fair and they never feel that anybody expects them to sell their real estate or to lay even a considerable portion of their capital at the feet of the Apostles.

The Epistle of James is usually regarded as a sample of the teaching prevailing in the Jewish church. It has the ring of the old prophets in its denunciation of the property distinctions that were creeping into the church. With him, as with the prophets, the rich are the oppressors, and the poor are the heirs of the kingdom. His woes on the rich who live delicately by defrauding the laborers of their hire are pretty bold speech. I have never heard them preached on and seldom heard them read.

The Apocalypse of John is one of the fullest and most authentic expressions of the thought prevailing in the Jewish churches early in the first century. When we look it frankly in the face, it is a revolutionary book, picturing the cataclysm that is to sweep away existing society, and the establishment of a new social order. Whether we understand the author to have spoken only of the world powers of his own day, or to have used these as representatives and symbols of the world powers of far distant times, the general bearing remains the same. The great city which is the centre of commerce and the incarnation of wealth and luxury (18:1-24), is to him a vile and evil thing, doomed to destruction. The political and intellectual powers of the Word are symbolized in the image of beasts. The book ends with the description of the ideal city on earth, four-square in the symmetry of perfectness, where the wail of the oppressed shall be heard no more.

The Social Teaching of Paul

Paul was a radical in theology, but a conservative in social matters. Yet in him too we recognize the ring of Christian democracy when he glories in the lowliness of the Christian community (1 Cor. 1:26-31), and charges the rulers of the world collectively with the death of Christ, because as a class they are without the wisdom of God (1 Cor. 2:6-9). He advises contentment and warns against the anxiety to be rich as a snare to the soul and a cause of all lusts, because the love of money is a root of all evils (1 Tim. 6:9, 10). Those who are rich are to beware of pride and the concentration of their hope on the uncertainty of riches, but are to cultivate the spirit of generous fellowship (1 Tim. 7:17-19). He emphasizes the demand concerning all the officers of the church, that they must not be lovers of money (1 Tim. 3:3, 8). He kept himself in voluntary poverty, lest he be tripped up in his Christian race (1 Cor. 9). He insists on the obligation of honest work and refuses idlers the right to eat — a principle that would have interesting results if applied today. He places the covetous man and the extortioner in the same list with the drunkard, idolater, and adulterer as unfit for the kingdom, and as proper subjects for exclusion from Christian fellowship (1 Cor. 5:11; 6:9, 10). It would be interesting to inquire whether the churches today ever exclude anyone for covetousness. I have heard of a few instances, but the burden of the accusation usually was that the excluded man failed to contribute to the support of the church, which lowers the moral level of the act of exclusion somewhat.

Paul does not demand a levelling of wealth. But neither does he look for a democratic levelling of rank, or even the abolition of slavery, both of which we regard as worthy achievements of the spirit of Christianity. He advised all Christians to remain in the social condition in which their conversion found them and to act well their part as Christians in that position (1 Cor. 7:18-24). That advice rested on the assumption that the present scheme of things was to last but a short time longer; at the return of the Lord the fashion of this present world would pass away; therefore those who had wives were to be as though they had none, and those who bought as though they possessed not (1 Cor. 7:29-31). That attitude of mind is feasible in regard to social discomforts and wrongs, if they are sure to come to an end soon. A man can bear a leaky flue with equanimity if he expects to leave the house the next day; if he has to stay there and expects his children to live there for generations, he will probably attempt to repair the flue. Those who believe the end of the world to be close at hand are entirely consistent, if they are indifferent to any efforts to change the structure of society; but they must be indifferent to their real estate titles and the security of their banks too, otherwise they may give the impression that their indifference is for others and their solicitude for themselves. If, on the other hand, a man does not share in that belief, he ought to lend a hand in social efforts even though they may take generations for their fruition.

The New Testament does not, like the Old, attempt to legislate. It is the expression of a spirit that entered humanity and fashions our actions by the free compulsion of moral ideals. Yet the statements which we have gathered from the New Testament and have tried to interpret, certainly are guideposts to show the direction in which that spirit is urging us. A survey of Church history will show that with every awakening of religious life and every attempt to realize New Testament ideals, there has also been an attempt to create a better social life, with more equality, justice, and brotherly kindness. Many of these attempts were crude and hasty and foredoomed to failure, but they were still far nobler than an indolent acceptance of present conditions as satisfactory or inevitable. For the larger sweep of the history of mankind the social spirit of Christianity has been an immense motive power. Modern democracy is a child of Christianity. The question for us today is: Are the stores of social force in the New Testament now exhausted? Have we gone as far as it wants us to go? If not, what is the further message to our times? Whither does the Spirit of Christ in us, that never hastes and never rests, point us . . . ?

6. Biblical Imperatives

RICHARD J. MOUW

My own commitment, in dealing with issues of religious authority, is to the kind of *sola scriptura* emphasis that was a prominent feature of the Protestant Reformation, and is still dear to the hearts of many conservative Protestants. But I want in no way to imply that a belief in the moral relevance of divine commands is the exclusive property of people who spell out the issues of authority in a strong bibliocentric manner. For example, some Christians — especially some Anglicans and Roman Catholics — understand "natural law" in such a way that when someone makes moral decisions with reference to natural law that person is obeying divine commands. Others hold that submission to the *magisterium* of a specific ecclesiastical body counts as obedience to divine directives. Others assume that individual Christians, even those who are not members of ecclesiastical hierarchies, can receive specific and extrabiblical commands from God, such as, "Quit smoking!" or, "Get out of New Haven!" Still others hold that the will of God can be discerned by examining our natural inclinations or by heeding the dictates of conscience.

None of these is, strictly speaking, incompatible with a *sola scriptura* emphasis. One could hold, for example, that the Bible itself commands us to conform to natural law, or to submit to the

Richard J. Mouw (1940–) is professor of Christian philosophy and ethics and president of Fuller Theological Seminary. He is the author of three works of Christian moral and political theory, *Political Evangelism, Politics and the Biblical Drama,* and *The God Who Commands.*

From Richard J. Mouw, *The God Who Commands* (Notre Dame: Notre Dame Press, 1990).

church's teachings, or to consult our consciences. Or one could simply view these alternative sources as necessary supplements to, or glosses on, biblical revelation. The view which I am attempting to elucidate here, while formulated in terms that signal my own *sola scriptura* orientation, is not meant to rule out the propriety of appeals to these other sources. Rather, I am assuming a perspective from which the Bible is viewed as a clarifier of these other modes, as the authoritative source against which deliverances from these other sources must be tested.

I should also make it clear that I will be assuming in this discussion that the Bible offers detailed moral guidance to us. On the view that I mean to be elucidating, the good life must be pursued with serious and sustained attention to the rich message of the Scriptures. This is no trivial matter to mention. There have been Christian ethicists in recent years who contend that there is only one divine commandment that is morally relevant, namely, the command to love God and neighbor. That seemed to be Joseph Fletcher's contention when he described himself, in *Situation Ethics,* as "rejecting all 'revealed' norms but the one command — to love God in the neighbor."[1]

If the command to love is the only biblical command which has normative relevance to moral decision making, then much of the substance of Christian ethics can be established without reference to the Scriptures. But if the Bible does offer other commands and considerations which bear on our decision making, then the task will be one of finding correlations between biblical revelation and moral issues at many different points.

It is interesting, though, that when Fletcher explained his grounds for his mono-imperativism, his arguments were not so much directed against the moral relevance of other divine commands as they were against their "absoluteness." To hold, however, that there is a plurality of divine commands which are morally relevant and binding is not to commit oneself to the view that each of these commands is indefeasible. It may well be that there is only one indefeasible command, the so-called "law of love" — such that in any situation

in which the course of action prescribed by the law of love is one's duty, it is one's actual duty, and that only the law of love has this property. But this does not rule out the possibility that there are other divine commandments which prescribe courses of action which are at least one's *prima facie* duties to perform in those situations in which the commands in question are morally relevant.

Not that *all* the commandments which are found in the Bible are morally relevant for us today. As Lewis Smedes puts it, they do not all "tell us what God wants us to do."[2] For example, God commanded Abraham to leave Ur of the Chaldees, and Jonah was told by the Lord to preach in Nineveh; it would be silly to suppose that it is a part of our contemporary Christian duty to obey these commands, or even to think of them as included in our functioning moral repertoire.

I do not mean to promote, then, a fascination with all of those biblical sentences that are in the imperative mood. In fact, my references to "commands" here should be taken as a kind of shorthand that I am using to refer to a somewhat broader pattern of divine address. The Bible is much more than a compendium of imperatives; the sacred writings contain historical narratives, prayers, sagas, songs, parables, letters, complaints, pleadings, visions, and so on. The moral relevance of the divine commandments found in the Scriptures can only be understood by viewing them in their interrelatedness with these other types of writings. The history, songs, predictions, and so on, of the Bible serve to sketch out the character of the biblical God; from this diversity of materials we learn what God's creating and redeeming purposes are, what sorts of persons and actions the Lord approves of, and so on. Divine commands must be evaluated and interpreted in this larger context.

Furthermore, we would actually miss some of the divine imperatives which the Bible transmits to us if we only attended to grammatical imperatives. For example, nowhere in the New Testament is there a literal command to the original followers of Jesus to stop discriminating against the Samaritans. But the New Testament record has Jesus tell-

---

1. Joseph Fletcher, *Situation Ethics: The New Morality* (Philadelphia: Westminster Press, 1966), 26.

2. Lewis B. Smedes, *Mere Morality: What God Expects from Ordinary People* (Grand Rapids, Mich.: Eerdmans, 1983), 5.

ing stories and engaging in activities which make it very clear that he is directing his disciples to change their attitudes toward Samaritans. Thus it is accurate to say that Jesus "commanded" his disciples to love the Samaritans, even though the words (or their Greek or Aramaic equivalents) "Stop discriminating against Samaritans" never appear in the Bible.

When the writer of Ecclesiastes concludes, then, that our whole duty consists in obeying God's commandments, we must not understand him to be instructing us to attend only to divine utterances which have a specific grammatical form. He is telling us, rather, that we must conform to whatever God requires of us, to all that the Creator instructs us to do — whether that guidance is transmitted through parables, accounts of divine dealings with nations and individuals, or sentences which embody commands.

7. The Moral Authority of Scripture

STANLEY HAUERWAS

A Proposal for Understanding the Moral Authority of Scripture

The canon does not contain its own self-justification but rather directs our attention to the tradition which it mediates. For to say the least which has to be said, without the tradition there is no shared memory and therefore no community. Our study of the canon has led to the conclusion that no one interpretation of the tradition can be accorded final and definitive status. The presence of prophecy as an essential part of the canon means that it will always be possible and necessary to remold the tradition as a source of life-giving power.[1]

Joseph Blenkinsopp's claim about the canon and its relation to prophecy and a community sufficient to sustain prophecy is crucial for understanding how Scripture does and/or should function ethically. We currently have difficulty in appreciating the moral role of Scripture because we have forgotten that the authority of Scripture

1. Joseph Blenkinsopp, *Prophecy and Canon* (Notre Dame: University of Notre Dame Press, 1977), p. 152.

Stanley Hauerwas (1940–) is professor of theological ethics at Duke University. He has authored numerous books in Christian ethics including *Truthfulness and Tragedy: Further Investigations in Christian Ethics, A Community of Character, The Peaceable Kingdom, Suffering Presence, Against the Nations,* and *After Christendom.*

From Stanley Hauerwas, *A Community of Character* (Notre Dame: University of Notre Dame Press, 1981).

is a political claim characteristic of a very particular kind of polity. By "political" I do not mean, as many who identify with liberation theology, that Scripture should be used as an ideology for justifying the demands of the oppressed. The authority of Scripture derives its intelligibility from the existence of a community that knows its life depends on faithful remembering of God's care of his creation through the calling of Israel and the life of Jesus.

To construe the authority of Scripture in this way, moreover, is most nearly faithful to the nature of biblical literature as well as the best insights we have learned from the historical study of the Bible. The formation of texts as well as the canon required the courage of a community to constantly remember and reinterpret its past. Such remembering and reinterpretation is a political task, for without a tradition there can be no community. That we no longer consider remembering as an ethical or political task manifests our questionable assumption that ethics primarily concerns decisions whereas politics brokers power.

When we so limit ethics and politics, the Scripture, particularly in its narrative mode, cannot but appear as a "problem." For the narrative requires a corresponding community who are capable of remembering and for whom active reinterpreting remains the key to continuing a distinctive way of life. But when one begins to look to an ethic sufficient for guiding the wider society, the narrative aspects of Scripture have to be ignored. Such an ethic, though often claimed to be biblically "inspired" or "informed," must be freed from the narratives of Scripture if it is to be the basis for judging or making common cause with those who do not share those narratives in their own history. So what is presented as the "biblical ethic" has been made over into a universal ethic that does not depend on memory for its significance but turns on "reason" or "nature."

As a result, we could easily forget that a biblical ethic requires the existence of a community capable of remembering in the present, no less than it did in the past. Where such a community does not exist the most sophisticated scholarly and hermeneutical skills cannot make Scripture morally relevant. What John Yoder describes as the free church understanding of the significance of community is necessary for any appreciation of the moral significance of Scripture. He points out that the:

> bridge between the words of Jesus or of the apostolic writings and the present is not a strictly conceptual operation, which could be carried out by a single scholar in an office, needing only an adequate dictionary and an adequate description of the available action options. The promise of the presence of Christ to actualize a definition of his will in a given future circumstance was given not to professional exegetes but to the community which would be gathered in his name (Matt. 18:19) with the specific purpose of "binding and loosing" (Matt. 18:18). Classical Protestantism tended to deny the place of this conversational process, in favor of its insistence on the perspicuity and objectivity of the words of Scripture. Catholicism before that has provoked that extreme Protestant answer by making of this hermeneutical mandate a blank check which the holders of ecclesiastical office could use with relative independence. The free church alternative to both recognizes the inadequacies of the text of Scripture standing alone uninterpreted and appropriates the promise of the guidance of the spirit throughout the ages, but locates the fulfillment of that promise in the assembly of those who gather around Scripture in the face of a given real moral challenge. Any description of the substance of ethical decision-making criteria is incomplete if this aspect of its communitarian and contemporary form is omitted.[2]

Failure to appreciate how the biblical narratives have and continue to form a polity is part of the reason that the ethical significance of Scripture currently seems so problematic. Indeed, many of the articles written on the relation of Scripture and ethics focus on ways Scripture

---

2. John Howard Yoder, "Radical Reformation Ethics in Ecumenical Perspective," *Journal of Ecumenical Studies,* Fall 1978, p. 657. I think it is no accident that the best recent book that utilizes Scripture for ethics is Yoder's *The Politics of Jesus* (Grand Rapids, Mich.: Eerdmans, 1972). Yoder was able to see the New Testament with fresh eyes because he came from a separated community with the physical and intellectual space and time to appreciate the radical demands in Scripture.

should not be used for ethical matters. Yet if my proposal is correct, that very way of putting the issue — i.e., how should Scripture be used ethically — is already a distortion. For to put it that way assumes that we must first clarify the meaning of the text in the sense that we understand its historical or sociological background — and only then can we ask its moral significance. David Kelsey has reminded us, however, that claims about the authority of Scripture are in themselves moral claims about the function of Scripture for the common life of the church. The Scripture's authority for that life consists in its being used so that it helps to nurture and reform the community's self-identity as well as the personal character of its members.[3]

To reinstate the moral and political context required for the interpretation of Scripture, moreover, demands that we challenge what Kelsey has characterized as the "standard picture" of the relation between Scripture and theology. The "standard picture," supported by a variety of theological agendas, assumes that if Scripture is to be meaningful it must he translated into a more general theological medium.[4] Such "translation" is often deemed necessary because of the texts' obscurity, cultural limits, and variety, but also because there seems to be no community in which the Scripture functions authoritatively. As a result we forget that the narratives of Scripture were not meant to describe our world — and thus in need of translation to adequately describe the "modern world" — but to change the world, including the one in which we now live. In the classic words of Erich Auerbach, Scripture is not meant:

merely to make us forget our own reality for a few hours, it seeks to overcome our reality: we are to fit our own life into its world, feel ourselves to be elements in its structure of universal history. . . . Everything else that happens in the world can only be conceived as an element in this sequence; into it everything that is known about the world . . . must be fitted as an ingredient of the divine plan.[5]

I would only add that Scripture creates more than a world; it shares a community which is the bearer of that world. Without that community, claims about the moral authority of Scripture — or rather the very idea of Scripture itself — make no sense. Furthermore, I shall argue that claims about the authority of Scripture make sense only in that the world and the community it creates are in fact true to the character of of God. In order to develop this proposal, the concepts of "moral authority" and "Scripture" must be analyzed to show how each gains its intelligibility only in relation to a particular kind of community. Before doing so, however, it should prove useful to examine how many current problems associated with the moral use of Scripture are, in part, the result of attempts to ignore or avoid the necessity of a community in which it is intelligible for Scripture to function authoritatively.

The Scripture as a Moral Problem

James Gustafson has observed that "in spite of the great interest in ethics in the past thirty years, and in spite of the extensive growth of biblical studies, there is a paucity of material that relates the two areas of study in a scholarly way. Writers in ethics necessarily make their forays into the Bible without the technical exegetical and historical acumen and skills to be secure in the way they use biblical materials. But few biblical scholars

3. David Kelsey, *The Uses of Scriptures in Recent Theology* (Philadelphia: Fortress Press, 1975), pp. 208-209.

4. Ibid., pp. 185-192. Kelsey observes, "the translation picture wrongly assumes that 'meaning' has only one meaning. By suggesting that theological proposals express the same 'meaning' as the biblical texts that authorize them, it obliges one to assume that the texts do have some sort of meaning. What the translation picture obscures, however, is that 'meaning' may be used here in two different senses. That is, it obscures the possible conceptual discontinuity between text and proposal," p. 190. See also James Barr, *The Bible in the Modern World* (New York: Harper & Row, 1973), p. 141.

5. Erich Auerbach, *Mimesis* (Princeton, N.J.: Princeton University Press, 1968), p. 48. This is, of course, the quote as well as the theme which dominates Hans Frei's *The Eclipse of Biblical Narrative* (New Haven, Conn.: Yale University Press, 1974), p. 3. That Frei's analysis is crucial for the argument of this essay is obvious. Frei, even more than Barth, has helped me see that the problem is not in our Scriptures but in ourselves.

have provided studies from which writers in ethics can draw."[6] Likewise, Brevard Childs suggests that "there is no outstanding modern work written in English that even attempts to deal adequately with Biblical material as it relates to ethics."[7]

No doubt the problem of specialization is a real one, but our current inability to use the Scriptures ethically involves more fundamental conceptual and methodological issues. For, as we shall see, appeal to Scripture is not equivalent to appeal to the text in itself and it is the latter, rightly or wrongly, which is the subject of most current scholarly effort.[8] I am not suggesting that critical analysis of the development of the biblical text is theologically questionable, but that often it is simply unclear what theological significance such work should have. However, for Christian ethics the Bible is not just a collection of texts but Scripture that makes normative claims on a community.

6. James Gustafson, "Christian Ethics" in *Religion,* ed. Paul Ramsey (Englewood Cliffs, N.J.: Prentice-Hall, 1965), p. 337. See also Gustafson, *Christian Ethics and the Community* (Philadelphia: Pilgrim Press, 1971) for an excellent overview of recent attempts to use the Scripture ethically. For Gustafson's own more constructive proposals, see his *Theology and Christian Ethics* (Philadelphia: Pilgrim Press, 1974), pp. 121-159. Bruce Birch and Larry Rasmussen provide an equally helpful account in their *Bible and Ethics in the Christian Life* (Minneapolis: Augsburg, 1976), pp. 45-78.

7. Brevard Childs, *Biblical Theology in Crisis* (Philadelphia: Westminster Press, 1970); p. 124.

8. This is, of course, the problem that Childs is struggling with in his *Introduction to the Old Testament as Scripture* (Philadelphia: Fortress, 1979). I think he is right to suggest that the crucial issue resides in how we understand the significance and function of the canon, but I think that Childs fails to adequately indicate the interdependence of canon and community. Therefore his sense of the status of the text appears too unmediated. However, he rightly suggests that "the fixing of a canon of Scripture implies that the witness to Israel's experience with God lies not in recovering such historical processes, but is testified in the effect on the biblical text itself. Scripture bears witness to God's activity in history on Israel's behalf, but history per se is not a medium of revelation which is commensurate with a canon," p. 76. For a very helpful analysis of the differences between the Bible as Scripture and as text, see Kelsey, pp. 198-201.

The confusion surrounding the relation of text to Scripture has not resulted in ethicists (and theologians) paying too little attention to current scholarly work concerning the Bible; rather their attention is far too uncritical. It has been observed that there is finally no substitute for knowing the text, and it is often unfortunately true that theologians and ethicists alike know the current theories about the development of the text better than the text itself.[9] As a result, claims about an ethic being biblically informed too frequently turn out to mean that the ethic is in accordance with some scholar's reconstruction of "biblical theology," e.g., the centrality of covenant or love in the Bible.[10] And ironically, as James Barr has shown, the very notion of "biblical theology" dis-

9. It is important not only that theologians know text, but it is equally important how and where they learn the text. It is my hunch that part of the reason for the misuse of the Scripture in matters dealing with morality is that the text was isolated from a liturgical context. There is certainly nothing intrinsically wrong with individuals reading and studying Scripture, but such reading must be guided by the use of the Scripture through the liturgies of the church. For the shape of the liturgy over a whole year prevents any one part of Scripture from being given undue emphasis in relation to the narrative line of Scripture. The liturgy, in every performance and over a whole year, rightly contextualizes individual passages when we cannot read the whole. As Aidan Kavanagh has recently observed, "the liturgy is Scripture's home rather than its stepchild, and the Hebrew and Christian Bibles were the church's first liturgical books." *The Shape of Baptism: The Rite of Christian Initiation* (New York: Pueblo Publishing Co., 1978), p. xiii.

10. Even more damaging in this respect than the subsequent ethical concentration of a limited range of "biblical concepts" is the underwriting of destructive prejudices of the Scripture scholars. For example, Joseph Blenkinsopp has documented the often implicit anti-Semitism involved in portrayals of the history of Israel, so that the second temple period was invariably interpreted as a time of "decline." See his "The Period of the Second Commonwealth in the Theology of the Old Testament," forthcoming from Paulist Press, New York. E. P. Sanders has exposed the equally distorting interpretation of Paul by Protestants who tended to read back into Paul's relation to Judaism the issues of the relation of Protestantism to Catholicism. See his *Paul and Palestinian Judaism* (Philadelphia: Fortress Press. 1977).

torts the variety of biblical material by failing to take the text seriously.[11]

The conceptual issues raised by the ethical use of Scripture involve not only how we should understand Scripture, but also how ethics should be understood. We often have a far too restricted understanding of the "ethical." For example, Childs asks, "How does the Bible aid the Christian in the making of concrete ethical decisions," without considering whether "ethics" is or should be primarily about "decisions"?[12] Consequently, attempts to explicate the "ethics" of Scripture have tended to concentrate on those aspects — Decalogue, the Sermon on the Mount, Wisdom books, the command to love — that fit our intuitive assumptions about what an "ethic" should look like. But this manner of locating the "biblical ethic" not only confuses the questions of the ethics in the Scripture with the ethical use of Scripture, but has the unfortunate effect of separating and abstracting the ethics from the religious (and narrative) contexts that make them intelligible.

Gustafson has often observed that how authors use Scripture is determined as much by how they define the task of Christian ethics as how they understand the nature and status of Scripture.[13] Birch and Rasmussen have also suggested that once the moral life is understood as not only involving decisions but also how actions mold the character of individuals and of a community, the narratives of Scripture are as important as the commandments; the Psalms afford the most ex-

plicit moral teachings.[14] But pictures die harder even than habits and many persist in thinking that a biblical ethic must be one that tells us "what to do in circumstances X or Y." When ethics is equivalent to advice, issues of interpretation or community need not arise.

In fairness it should be said that the persistence of the idea that the Bible is some sort of "revealed morality"[15] has been deeply ingrained in our culture by the church itself. Moreover it is an idea shared by conservative and liberal alike as they appeal to different parts of Scripture in support of ethical positions that they have ironically come to hold on grounds prior to looking to Scripture. Thus claims about the moral significance of Scripture are used to reinforce decisions about ethics derived from nonscriptural sources.

Though they may appear to be radically different, those who would have us obey everything in the Scripture that looks like moral advice — e.g., that women should keep quiet in church (1 Cor. 14:34-36) — and those who would have us act according to the more general admonitions — e.g., that we should be loving (1 Cor. 13) — share many common assumptions. Both look to Scripture as containing a revealed morality that must or should provide guidance. And each, often in quite different ways, has a stake in maintaining that the "biblical ethic" be distinctive or unique when compared with other ethics.[16]

---

11. See, for example, James Barr's criticism of "biblical theology" in his *The Bible in the Modern World*, pp. 135-136. Kelsey's critique of the "biblical concept" approach to scripture is equally devastating. *The Uses of Scripture in Recent Theology*, pp. 25-29.

12. Childs, *Biblical Theology in Crisis*, p. 130. For a particularly egregious example of the failure to appreciate the significance of the question of how "ethics" should be understood as well as the claim that the New Testament ethic must be judged by its adequacy for negotiating the "modern world," see Jack Sanders, *Ethics in the New Testament* (Philadelphia: Fortress Press, 1975). For a critique of Sanders, see my "A Failure in Communication: Ethics and the Early Church," *Interpretation*, 32/2 (April 1978), pp. 196-200.

13. Gustafson, *Theology and Christian Ethics*, pp. 122-123.

14. Birch and Rasmussen, p. 185. Birch and Rasmussen's book has the virtue of being the most methodologically aware of how different conceptions of ethics will determine not only what and how one identifies descriptively the "ethics in the Scripture," but also the continuing status of that ethic for use today.

15. Gustafson has drawn and analyzed the distinction between "revealed morality" and "revealed reality" in *Theology and Christian Ethics*, pp. 129-138 and in *Christian Ethics and the Community*, pp. 48-51. He notes that the Bible as revealed morality can be understood in terms of law, ideals, analogies, and as a pattern of interpretation.

16. For example, Paul Ramsey maintains that the conception of justice in the Bible is radically different from all others because it consists in the principle: "To each according to the measure of his real need, not because of anything human reason can discern inherent in the needy, but because his need alone is the measure of God's righteousness toward him." *Basic Christian*

The assumption that to be ethically significant the Bible must contain some kind of "revealed morality" not only creates a nest of unfruitful problems but finally betrays the character of the biblical literature. The very idea that the Bible is revealed (or inspired) is a claim that creates more trouble than it is worth. As Barr has pointed out, "the term *revelation* is not in the Bible a common general term for the source of man's knowledge of God, and some of the main cases found are eschatological, i.e., they look forward to a revealing of something *in the future*. Perhaps this suggests another way of thinking. The main relation of revelation to the Bible is not that of an antecedent revelation, which generates the Bible as its response, but that of a revelation which *follows upon* the existent tradition, or, once it has reached the fixed and written stage, the existent Scripture. The Scripture provides the frames of reference within which new events have meaning and make sense."[17]

The problem of revelation aside, however, the view that the Bible contains a revealed morality that can be applied directly by the individual agent, perhaps with some help from the biblical critic, flounders when considering the status of individual commands. For some moral aspects of Scripture — such as the *Haustafeln* (household codes: Col. 3:18–4:1; Eph. 5:21–6:9; 1 Pet. 2:13–3:7) — strike many today as not only morally irrelevant but morally perverse. The common strategy for dealing with such statements is to dismiss them as the product of the limitations of the early church's culture, which had not been sufficiently subjected to the searching transformation of the gospel. But that strategy suffers from being too powerful, for why should the *Haustafeln* be singled out as culturally relative and texts more appealing to modern ears such as "there is neither Jew nor Greek, there is neither slave nor free, there is neither male nor female;

for you are all one in Christ Jesus" (Gal. 3:28) be exempted?

Besides moral positions that simply strike us as wrong, Scripture also contains commands that many feel are too "idealistic" to be workable. The admonition not to resist "one who is evil" (Matt. 5:39) may work at an interpersonal level, but most Christians assume that it makes no sense as a social policy. Attempts to "explain" such statements as "ideals," or as "law that provides consciousness of sin," or as requiring eschatological interpretation result in a feeling that we really do not need to treat them with moral seriousness after all.[18]

Thus attempts to formulate a "biblical ethic" result in the somewhat embarrassing recognition that the "morality" that is said to be "biblical" is quite selective and even arbitrary. Various strategies are used to justify our selectivity, such as appealing to "central" biblical themes or images, like love. No doubt love has a central place in the Bible and the Christian life, but when it becomes the primary locus of the biblical ethic it turns into an abstraction that cannot be biblically justified. Indeed when biblical ethics is so construed one wonders why appeals need be made to Scripture at all, since one treats it as a source of general principles or images that once in hand need no longer acknowledge their origins. In fact, once we construe Christian ethics in such a way, we find it necessary to stress the "uniqueness" of the "biblical concept of love covenant," or some other equally impressive sounding notion.

Finally the attempt to capture the ethical significance of Scripture by a summary image or concept makes it difficult to be faithful to our growing awareness that the ethics in the Scripture are bound in an intimate way with the life of Christ; nor can they be dissociated from the life of the

---

Ethics (New York: Scribner's, 1950), pp. 13-14. Ramsey is a classical example of an ethicist exploiting the assumption that biblical theology is primarily a matter of locating the central "biblical" concepts. Thus Ramsey stresses the centrality of love and covenant on the assumption that by doing so his ethic is thereby "biblical."

17. Barr, *The Bible in the Modern World*, p. 122.

18. For what remains a very useful discussion of these issues, see John Knox, *The Ethics of Jesus in the Teaching of the Church* (Nashville: Abingdon Press, 1961). As noted this issue involves the still controversial question of eschatology and ethics in the New Testament. In that respect it is still worth anyone's time to read Amos Wilder, *Eschatology and Ethics in the Teaching of Jesus* (New York: Harper & Row, 1939) and Hans Windisch, *The Meaning of the Sermon on the Mount* (Philadelphia: Westminster Press, 1949).

community that arose around his life.[19] The more we try to mine Scripture for a workable ethic, the more we are drawn to separate such an ethic from the understanding of salvation that makes such an ethic intelligible in the first place.[20] Insisting that the biblical ethic is first an indicative before being an imperative[21] will hardly suffice to provide an account of the complex nature of the moral life manifest in the early Christian community, nor can that distinction inform us how we are to live and think in a manner appropriate to Christian convictions regarding God and his relation to our existence.

In an attempt to avoid separating the ethics of Scripture from the theological context that makes them intelligible, the suggestion has been made that Scripture is not so much a revealed morality as a revealed reality. Thus for H. R. Niebuhr the Bible is not morally important in that it gives us knowledge of itself, "but because it gives us knowledge of God acting on men, and of ourselves before God."[22] What the Bible makes known, then, "is not a morality, but a reality, a living presence to whom man responds."[23] The Bible does not so much provide a morality as it is the source of images and analogies that help us understand and interpret the nature of our existence.[24]

19. Victor Paul Furnish in his *Theology and Ethics in Paul* (Nashville: Abingdon, 1968) and *The Love Command in the New Testament* (Nashville: Abingdon, 1972) has emphasized both these themes with great effect.

20. See, for example, Robert Tannehill's *Dying and Rising with Christ* (Berlin: Verlag Alfred Topelmann, 1967), pp. 80-83, for substantiation of this point.

21. Furnish resorts to this means of expression simply because he has no other conceptual or moral means to articulate the way Paul's ethics is but an extension of his theology. For an effective critique of Furnish's method in this respect, see Gilbert Meilander, "Does Gift Imply Task? Some Ethical Reflections" (unpublished paper read to Ethics Section of the AAR, 1979).

22. James Gustafson, "Introduction" to H. R. Niebuhr's *The Responsible Self* (New York: Harper and Row, 1963), p. 23. For an extensive analysis of H. R. Niebuhr's use of Scripture, see Ben Jordan, "The Use of Scripture in the Ethics of H. R. Niebuhr" (diss., Emory University, 1974).

23. Gustafson, *Christian Ethics and the Community*, pp. 50-51.

24. See, for example, Gustafson's attempt to illuminate the Cambodian invasion through the use of scrip-

This suggestion that Scripture is revealed reality has the virtue of being more appropriate to the nature of Scripture than does the idea of "revealed morality." But it too lacks appreciation for the political nature of the very concepts of authority and Scripture associated with the idea of "revealed morality." As a result, Scripture is mined for concepts and images, which are claimed to be biblically warranted but have the effect of legitimating the loss of any continuing engagement of a community with the biblical narratives. Emphasis on the Bible as the revelation of God can give the impression that Scripture can be known and used apart from a community that has been formed and sustained by the reality that gives substance both to the Scripture and to that community. No image of God, no matter how rich, can substitute for the "life-giving power" which Blenkinsopp suggests arises from a community's capacity to sustain the prophetic activity of remembering and reinterpreting the traditions of Yahweh.

The Moral Authority of Scripture

Thus, the very definition of the problem of the relation of Scripture and ethics, as well as the suggestions designed to deal with that problem, often suffer from a failure to appreciate how claims for the authority of Scripture are political. Indeed, the overtly political assertion that Scripture has authority is seldom analyzed. Rather it is accepted as a statement of fact, when it is by no means clear what it means to say that Scripture or anything else has authority. Therefore it is necessary to provide an account of authority that may illumine how Scripture is or should be used in the life of church.

Although my analysis of authority will be distinct from an explicit discussion of Scripture, the very meaning of Scripture entails authoritative judgment. As David Kelsey has reminded us, to say "these texts are Christian Scripture" is but a way of saying "these texts are authoritative for the life of the Christian church." So claims about the authority of Scripture are analytic, since the scrip-

tural analogies in *Theology and Christian Ethics*, pp. 138-145.

tural texts' "authority for theology is logically grounded in and dependent on their authority for the life of the church generally. But since, concretely speaking, the life of church taken as some sort of organic whole *is* 'tradition,' that means that the texts' authority for theology is dependent on their being authority for 'tradition.'"[25] Therefore, to call certain texts "Scripture" means in part that the church relies upon them in a normatively decisive manner.

This situation is not peculiar to the Christian community, for the very meaning of authority is community dependent. Though authority is often confused with power or coercion, it draws its life from community in a quite different manner. Like power, authority is directive; unlike power, however, it takes its rationale not from the deficiencies of community but from the intrinsic demands of a common life.[26] The meaning of authority must be grounded in a community's self-understanding, which is embodied in its habits, customs, laws, and traditions; for this embodiment constitutes the community's pledge to provide the means for an individual more nearly to approach the truth.

The language of community is open to a great deal of misunderstanding, given its association with small, tightly knit groups. Yet the fact that a community requires authority indicates that it is a mistake to think of community in personal rather than institutional terms. A community is a group of persons who share a history and whose common set of interpretations about that history provide the basis for common actions. These interpretations may be quite diverse and controversial even within the community, but are sufficient to provide the individual members with the sense that they are more alike than unlike.

The diversity of accounts and interpretations of a community's experiences is exactly the basis

of authority. For authority is that power of a community that allows for reasoned interpretations of the community's past and future goals. Authority, therefore, is not contrary to reason but essential to it. Authority is the means by which the wisdom of the past is critically appropriated by being tested by current realities as well as by challenging the too often self-imposed limits of the present. A person or institution may be the way authority is exercised, but their authority derives only from their ability to justify their decision in terms of the shared traditions of the community.

Thus, there is an essential connection between authority, tradition, and change. Reasoning from tradition is the primary form and method of authority. As James Mackey has pointed out, tradition "is a dimension of life itself. It is the whole way of life of a people as it is transmitted from generation to generation. So tradition shares with life the characteristic of being something which we do (if that is the correct word) and may do very well indeed, and may do for a very long time, before we bother to provide ourselves with a general theory about what it is that we are doing."[27]

Traditions by their nature require change, since there can be no tradition without interpretation. And interpretation is the constant adjustment that is required if the current community is to stay in continuity with tradition. As Mackey suggests, "Change and continuity are two facets of the same process, the process we call tradition. So much so that continuity can only be maintained by continual development, and development or change is only such (and not simply replacement) because of continuity. Tradition means continuity and change, both together and both equally."[28]

25. Kelsey, p. 97.

26. Those familiar with the work of Yves Simon will recognize how dependent this account of authority is on his work. In particular, see his *Philosophy of Democratic Government* (Chicago: University of Chicago Press, 1951), pp. 1-71, 144-194. See also Clarke Cochran's very helpful "Authority and Community: The Contributions of Carl Friedrich, Yves Simon, and Michael Polanyi," *American Political Science Review*, 71/2 (June 1977), pp. 546-558.

27. J. P. Mackey, *Tradition and Change in the Church* (Dayton, Ohio: Pflaum Press, 1968), p. x. Ironically Catholic theologians at Tübingen were among the first to realize the importance of this for understanding the significance of Scripture. It is a tragedy that they were silenced before they were appreciated. See James Burtchaell's *Catholic Theories of Biblical Inspiration Since 1810* (Cambridge: Cambridge University Press, 1969).

28. Mackey, pp. 42-43. Those familiar with Kuhn's analysis of the development and change in science will see that many of the issues discussed and debated about his account are relevant here. Indeed I suspect a very interesting comparison could be drawn between the

This is even more true when the tradition of a community is based on witnessing to non-repeatable events. For such events must be fitted within a narrative that is an interpretation. But that interpretation must remain open to a new narrative display not only in relation to the future, but also whenever we come to a new understanding of our past. That is why, as Barr reminds us, it is so often the case that interpretation of the Scripture does not mean the discovery of new meaning (as if there was no previous meaning there), but the reappropriation of the tradition with a greater depth of understanding.[29] Interpretation does not mean or require departure from the tradition, though justified discontinuity is not illegitimate, but rather that the Scripture is capable of unanticipated relevancy through reinterpretation.[30]

---

breakdown and reinterpretation of traditions in the Bible and those in science. That Kuhn's work might be relevant to such an analysis should not be surprising, for I suspect that Kuhn's interpretation of science gains its inspiration from politics. For an attempt to develop this suggestion, see Richard Vernon, "Politics as Metaphor: Cardinal Newman and Professor Kuhn," *The Review of Politics*, 41/4 (October 1979), pp. 513-535.

29. James Barr, *Old and New Interpretation* (New York: Harper and Row, 1966), p. 190. However Barr goes on to remind us that "this positive evaluation of the 'tradition,' i.e., of the body of previous decisions and interpretations, of customs and accepted methods, nevertheless should not conceal from us the fact that this tradition can constitute the chief agency for the damaging and distorting of the meaning of the Bible." He notes, however, that this cannot be corrected by the possession of "pure" theological presuppositions, but rather the "primary ethical problem in interpretation will very often, perhaps always, lie *within* the church," p. 191. That is why the church must always remember that the Bible belongs to the world and not the church only. "When the church addresses the world on the basis of the Bible, it invites people to look for themselves and see if these things are not so. The possibility that people may do this looking for themselves carries with it a consequence on the more scholarly level: non-Christian interpretation of the Bible is a possibility, indeed it is more, it is a reality," p. 191.

30. "What is needed is more awareness of how religious texts live by reinterpretation. The very mechanics of creative interpretation in the religious realm requires that we understand the Bible, not as a philosophical text

It is particularly useful to note how fundamentally political is this understanding of the relation of tradition and authority. Although revolutions may occur without tradition,[31] politics depends on tradition, for politics is nothing else but a community's internal conversation with itself concerning the various possibilities of understanding and extending its life. In fact, the very discussion necessary to maintain the tradition can be considered an end in itself, since it provides the means for the community to discover the goods it holds in common. Without the authority of the tradition to guide such a discussion there would be no possibility of the community drawing nearer to the truth about itself or the world.

Yves Simon illustrates this feature by his refusal to justify authority from what he called a deficiency theory of community. The deficiency theory holds that authority is necessary to secure the unified action of a community because not everything is normal, because wills are weak or perverse and intellects ignorant or blinded.[32] In contrast Simon argued that authority is required, not because we are deficient, but because as the number of deficiencies in a society or individuals decreases, the number of available choices increases. Therefore, according to Simon, "The function of authority with which we are concerned, i.e., that of procuring united action when the means to the common good are several, does not disappear but grows as deficiencies are made up; it originates not in the defects of men and

---

expressing certain ideas, but as Scripture, inspired and authoritative and consequently capable of assuming new meanings. This understanding leads to the puzzling insight that in the living religious traditions continuity is affirmed and achieved by discontinuity. Authority is affirmed and relevance asserted by reinterpretation." Krister Stendahl, "Biblical Studies in the University," in *The Study of Religion in Colleges and Universities*, ed. P. Ramsey and J. Wilson (Princeton, N.J.: Princeton University Press, 1970), pp. 30-31.

31. See, for example, Jon Gunnemann's extremely interesting interpretation of revolutions in terms of Kuhn's understanding of a paradigm shift in his *The Moral Meaning of Revolution* (New Haven, Conn.: Yale University Press, 1979).

32. Simon, pp. 29-30.

societies but in the nature of society. It is an essential function."[33]

Authority is required, not because there is any one perception of the common good that controls all the others, but because there are many ways of seeking such a good. The necessity of authority grows from the fact that morality unavoidably involves judgments that by their nature are particular and contingent — that is, they could be otherwise. Tradition is but the history of a community's sharing of such judgments as they have been tested through generations. Authority is not, therefore, an external force that commands against our will; rather it proceeds from a common life made possible by tradition. Authority is

not only compatible with freedom, but requires it, since the continued existence and excellence of the community is possible only by forming and perfecting new members. Yet freedom is not an end in itself, but the necessary condition for a community to come to a more truthful understanding of itself and the world.

Particularly important in this respect is Simon's contention that true authority must always call a community to what it has not yet become. He does not deny that authority must be grounded in community, or that whatever is identified as the common good must be built on what the community is, but he sees that authority must always continue to act as a witness to the truth if it is to be legitimate. Authority, therefore, functions at those points where the tradition of a community engages in the discussion necessary to subject its politics to the search of and judgment by the truth.

The fact that truth is known only by the conversation initiated by the tradition and carried out through political means signals something essential about the character of truth. For if truth could be known without struggle, there would be no need for the kind of politics I am suggesting is integral to its discovery. Truth in this sense is like a "knowing how" — a skill that can only be passed from master to apprentice. Tradition and authority are crucial to such a process, as they must guide us to what others have found to be true, even though in the process we may well find that in order to be faithful to the tradition we must criticize our current guides. The place of tradition and authority in this sense is no less required for the development of intellectual disciplines, including science, than the more practical aspects of our existence.

In summary I have suggested that authority requires community, but it is equally true that community must have authority. For authority is that reflection initiated by a community's traditions through which a common goal can be pursued.[34] Authority is, therefore, the means

---

33. Ibid., p. 33. In his *A General Theory of Authority* (Notre Dame: University of Notre Dame Press, rpt. 1980), Simon points out that the "need for authority and the problem of the need for a distinct governing personnel have often been confused: it is already clear that they are distinct and that the argumentation which establishes the need for authority, even in a society made of ideally enlightened and well-intentioned persons, leaves open the question of whether some communities may be provided with all the authority they need without there being among them any distinct group of governing persons," p. 49. So to claim Scripture as authority does not preclude the necessity of distinct officers and others in the church exercising authority. But again as Simon reminds us, "when an issue is one of action, not of truth, the person in authority has the character of a leader; but when the issue is one of truth, not of action, the person in authority has the character of a witness. Indeed, a witness may also be a leader and, in the capacity of leader, exercise command. But in the mere witness, and universally in the witness as such, authority does not involve, in any sense or degree, the power to give orders and to demand obedience. We would say that an event, for some time considered doubtful, finally has been established by the authority of sound and numerous witnesses. We would go so far as to say that yielding to their testimony is a duty and a matter of honesty. The authority of the mere witness is nothing else than truthfulness as expressed by signs which make it recognizable in varying degrees of assurance," p. 84. In this respect the authority of scripture is surely that of a witness which, however, tests the authority of any who would lead in the church. For the development of this idea of authority in relation to the papacy, see my and Robert Wilken's "Protestants and the Pope," *Commonweal*, 107/3 (February 15, 1980), pp. 80-85.

34. Cochran observes that the modern attack "on tradition as such, however, is fundamentally an attack on history. It is at bottom an attempt to escape history and the necessarily historical (and therefore limited) existence of man. Tradition is what makes historical existence bearable by giving some meaning and perspec-

through which a community is able to journey from where it is to where it ought to be. It is set on its way by the language and practices of the tradition, but while on its way it must often subtly reform those practices and language in accordance with its new perception of truth.

By regarding Scripture as an authority Christians mean to indicate that they find there the traditions through which their community most nearly comes to knowing and being faithful to the truth. Scripture is not meant to be a problem-solver. It rather describes the process whereby the community we call the church is initiated by certain texts into what Barr has called the "vivid and lively pattern of argument and controversy" characteristic of biblical traditions.[35]

The Scripture is not an authority because it sets a standard of orthodoxy — indeed the very categories of orthodoxy and heresy are anachronistic when applied to Scripture — but because the traditions of Scripture provide the means for our community to find new life.[36] Blenkinsopp reminds us:

That those responsible for the editing of the biblical material did not on the whole expunge views in conflict with their own, but rather allowed them to exist side by side in a state of unresolved

tension or unstable equilibrium, is clearly a fact of significance for the understanding of Judaism — and, *mutatis mutandis*, of Christianity also. It suggests that one may appeal to a fixed tradition with absolute seriousness and still affirm its "infinite interpretability" (Scholem). Given the formative influence of different interpretations of the tradition on the shape and self-understanding of the community at different times, it also suggests that the community must be prepared to accept creative tension as a permanent feature of its life.[37]

Therefore when Christians claim Scripture as authority for their community they are not claiming that the Bible is without error; or that the genres of the Bible are unique; or that the Bible contains a unique understanding of man, history, or even God as opposed to Greek or some other culture; or that the Bible manifests a unique *Weltanschauung* or contains an implicit metaphysics that still remains largely misunderstood; or that the Bible contains images without which we cannot achieve an adequate self-understanding; and so on. Rather to claim the Bible as authority is the testimony of the church that this book provides the resources necessary for the church to be a community sufficiently truthful so that our conversation with one another and God can continue across generations.

---

tive to the distance between the given and the demanded. Political theorists can do little, perhaps, directly to respond to the practical crisis of authority. Yet ideas have consequences, and the practical crisis of authority has roots in the undernourished soil of our theoretical understanding of authority, tradition, knowledge, and community," p. 557. The church, however, not only has the opportunity to enrich "ideas" but to provide the positive experience of tradition and community.

35. Barr, *The Bible in the Modern World*, p. 147.

36. Of course it is true, as Barr observes, that tradition comes before Scripture, as well as following after it. *Bible in The Modern World*, p. 127. However as Kelsey has observed the concepts of "tradition" and "Scripture" are not on a logical par. " 'Tradition' is used to name, not something the church uses, but something the church *is*, insofar as her reality lies in a set of events and practices that can be construed as a single activity. 'Scripture' is used to name, not something the church is, but something she must *use*, according to some concepts of 'church,' to preserve her self-identity," p. 96.

37. Blenkinsopp, *Prophecy and Canon*, p. 94. For a fascinating study of the problem of authority in Paul, see John Schutz, *Paul and the Anatomy of Apostolic Authority* (Cambridge: Cambridge University Press, 1975). Schutz's primary thesis is that "Jesus' death brings life to the Christian, but not without Jesus' life. So Paul's death is also Paul's life, his weakness, his power; and this weakness or suffering alone can stand for the union of the two, just as the cross stands for Christ's death and new life. The work of Christ is the work of God and cannot be taken from God's hand. But the appropriation puts Paul into the life of the communities alongside of the gospel, itself power and weakness. This is how the authority of the apostle is to be understood. In Paul's whole apostolic life one sees the manifestations of God's same act which one sees in the gospel itself," p. 246.

Scripture as Moral Authority

This analysis of the authority of Scripture lacks concreteness, however, since it leaves what Scripture means quite unanalyzed. One can agree formally that Scripture has or should have such authority for Christians, but still ask what it is about Scripture that compels such authority. Even before that, however, one must ask what is meant by *Scripture,* for I have already noted that Scripture cannot simply be identified with the collection of texts we find in the Bible.

David Kelsey's analysis of the way theologians use Scripture demonstrates that theologians "do not appeal to some objective text-in-itself but rather to a text construed *as* a certain kind of whole having a certain kind of logical force. To call each different way of construing the text 'Scripture' is to use 'Scripture' in importantly different ways. In short, the suggestion that Scripture might serve as a final court of appeals for theological disputes is misleading because there is no one, normative concept of 'Scripture.' Instead, there seems to be a family of related but importantly different concepts of 'Scripture.' "[38]

As a means for exploring the different concepts of Scripture Kelsey suggests that in each case we must ask what aspect of Scripture is taken to be authoritative. His book consists in an analysis of three ways that theologians have located the au-

thoritative aspect of biblical writing, namely: (1) the Bible as containing doctrinal or conceptual content; (2) the Bible as the source of mythic, symbolic, or imagistic expression of a saving event; (3) the Bible as the recital of a narrative. One of the interesting results of Kelsey's analysis is that those who look at the Bible as a source of doctrine and those who criticize this approach as failing to appreciate the Bible as a record of God's action in history equally fail to appreciate the narrative mode of much of the material in Scripture. Ironically, as Kelsey shows, the emphasis on "God acting in history" is structurally similar to the construal of Scripture in terms of concepts such as covenant, promise, and so on.[39]

There is no need for me to repeat here the work that Kelsey has already done so well. But one aspect of his analysis is critical for the development of my proposal. Kelsey notes the difference between Scripture's uses in the common life of the church and its uses in theology.[40] A theologian's "working canon" and the "Christian canon" are not identical, for the theologian is obliged to decide what it is *in* Scripture that is authoritative. And such a decision often results in an appeal to certain patterns characteristically exhibited by whatever aspect of Scripture the theologian takes to be authoritative.[41]

So a theologian's claim that the Scriptures have authority for the church will involve ascribing some sort of wholeness to the text or set of texts.[42] But because various kinds of wholeness can be ascribed to the texts, there can be no one concept of Scripture. The theologian's attempt to propose how Scripture should be understood and used in the church derives from an act of imagination that Kelsey, borrowing from Robert Johnson, calls a *discrimen* — that is, "a configuration of criteria that are in some way organically related to one another as reciprocal coefficients."[43]

---

38. Kelsey, pp. 14-15. Elsewhere Kelsey suggests "To call a text or set of texts 'Scripture' is not only to say that their use in certain ways in the church's life is essential to the preservation of her identity, and therefore to say that they are 'authoritative' over that life, it is also to ascribe some sort of wholeness to the text or set of texts. However, there is an irreducible variety of kinds of wholeness that may be ascribed to the texts. Thus 'Scripture' turns out to be, not one concept, but a set of different concepts that bear one another some family resemblances. All uses of 'Scripture' are dialectically related to uses of the concept of 'church' and entail ascribing authoritativeness and wholeness to the texts called 'Scripture'; this much all uses of 'Scripture' share. But in the actual practice of appealing to Scripture in the course of doing theology, there turns out to be an irreducible logical diversity of ways the texts are concretely construed as 'whole,' " pp. 100-101. Later I will suggest that the kind of "wholeness" that is most appropriate to the Scripture is that of a story.

39. Kelsey, pp. 37ff.

40. Ibid., p. 94.

41. Ibid., p. 101.

42. It is important to note that ascriptions of "wholeness" to the canon are not identical with claims about the "unity" of the canon. Kelsey, p. 106. See also Barr's very useful discussion of the problem of the "unity" of Scripture, *The Bible in the Modern World,* pp. 98ff.

43. Kelsey, p. 160.

Therefore, according to Kelsey, the relationship between the church, Scripture, and theology turns out to be formally similar to the notorious "hermeneutical circle." For "the concrete ways in which biblical texts are used as Scripture in the church's common life help shape a theologian's imaginative construal of the way that use is conjoined with God's presence among the faithful. The determinate patterns in Scripture suggest a range of images from which he may select or construct a root metaphor for that *discrimen*. The particularities of the concrete use of Scripture unique to the common life of the church as he experiences it will shape which image strikes him as most apt. Then, secondly, it is that imaginative characterization of the central reality of Christianity, 'what it is finally all about,' that is decisive for the way the theologian actually construes and uses biblical texts as Scripture in the course of doing theology."[44]

Kelsey's analysis is particularly illuminating for exposing the influence the church has on how we construe Scripture. Theologians, to be sure, make suggestions about how Scripture can or should be understood, but such suggestions must be fueled by the common life of the church in both its liturgical and moral forms. So a theologian may construe and use Scripture in ways determined by a "logically prior imaginative judgment," but that is not all that needs to be said. For such judgment, as Kelsey suggests, must be schooled by a community whose life has been shaped by the narratives of the Scripture. How we use Scripture is finally an affair of the imagination, but it is nonetheless a political activity, since our imagination depends on our ability to remember and interpret our traditions as they are mediated through the moral reality of our community.

For all its perspicacity, however, Kelsey's analysis fails to do justice to the ways in which Scripture morally shapes a community. The idea of a *discrimen* suggests a far too singular and unifying image, whereas the actual use of Scripture in the church, in liturgy, preaching, and in morality, is not so easily characterized. In fact I would maintain that many of the difficulties attendant upon locating the authoritative aspect of Scripture in doctrine, concepts, or saving event(s) revolve around the attempt to provide a far too coherent account of Scripture. Put differently, one reason the church has had to be content with the notion of a canon rather than some more intellectually satisfying summary of the content of Scripture is that only through the means of a canon can the church adequately manifest the kind of tension with which it must live. The canon marks off as Scripture those texts that are necessary for the life of the church without trying to resolve their obvious diversity and/or even disagreements.

Still, it may be asked, why these texts? My answer is simply: these texts have been accepted as Scripture because they and they alone satisfy what Reynolds Price has called our craving for a perfect story which we feel to be true. Put briefly, that story is: "History is the will of a just God who knows us."[45] Therefore the status of the Bible as Scripture "separated both from other written works and from the continuous accretion of oral tradition, represents a fundamental decision to assign a special status to the material it contains and to recognize it as the classic model for the understanding of God."[46] We continue to honor that decision made by the ancient church, however, because it is a decision that makes sense "in relation to the basic nature of Christian faith. Faith is Christian because it relates itself to classically expressed models. This is much the same as what people mean when they say, rather vaguely and ambiguously, that 'Christianity is a historical religion.' Christian faith is not whatever a modern Christian may happen to believe, on any grounds at all, but faith related to Jesus and to the God of Israel. The centrality of the Bible is the recognition of the classic sources for the expression of Jesus and of God."[47]

---

44. Ibid., p. 205.

45. Reynolds Price, *A Palpable God: Thirty Stories Translated from the Bible: With an Essay on the Origins and Life of Narrative* (New York: Atheneum, 1978), p. 14. Of course as Price himself would emphasize such a story is indeed complex — so complex it requires the many narrative lines of Scripture for us to understand what the existence of such a God entails.

46. Barr, *The Bible in the Modern World*, pp. 117-118.

47. Ibid., p. 118. For an extremely interesting account of the concept of a "classic" and its importance for Christian theology, see David Tracy, "Theological Classics in Contemporary Theology," *Theology Digest*, 25/4 (winter 1977), pp. 347-355.

The Scripture functions as an authority for Christians precisely because by trying to live, think, and feel faithful to its witness they find they are more nearly able to live faithful to the truth. For the Scripture forms a society and sets an agenda for its life that requires nothing less than trusting its existence to the God found through the stories of Israel and Jesus. The moral use of Scripture, therefore, lies precisely in its power to help us remember the stories of God for the continual guidance of our community and individual lives. To be a community which lives by remembering is a genuine achievement, as too often we assume that we can insure our existence only by freeing ourselves from the past.

The Morality of Remembering: The Scripture as Narrative

Obviously I am convinced that the most appropriate image — or as Kelsey insists, *discrimen* — for characterizing Scripture, for the use of the church as well as morally, is that of a narrative or a story. James Barr rightly points out that the dealings of God with man in the Bible are indeed describable as a cumulative process, "in which later elements do build upon what was said and done at an earlier time. As I have argued, the literature is meant to be read as a story with a beginning and a progression. All 'acts of God' and incidents of the story make sense because a framework of meaning has already been created by previous acts, remembered in the tradition; they are 'further acts of one already known, of one with whom the fathers have already been in contact and have passed on the tradition of this contact.' "[48]

It is certainly true, as Barr recognizes, that Scripture contains much material that is not narrative in character. But such material, insofar as it is Scripture, gains its intelligibility by being a product of and contribution to a community that lives through remembering. The narrative of Scripture not only "renders a character"[49] but renders a community capable of ordering its existence appropriate to such stories. Jews and Christians believe this narrative does nothing less than render the character of God and in so doing renders us to be the kind of people appropriate to that character. To say that character is bound up with our ability to remember witnesses to the fact that our understanding of God is not inferred from the stories but is the stories.[50]

One of the virtues of calling attention to the narrative nature of Scripture is the way it releases us from making unsupportable claims about the unity of Scripture or the centrality of the "biblical view of X or Y." Rather, the Scripture must be seen as one long, "loosely structured non-fiction novel" that has subplots that at some points appear minor but later turn out to be central.[51] What is crucial, however, is that the Scripture does not try to suppress those subplots or characters that may challenge, or at least qualify, the main story line, for without them the story itself would be less than truthful.[52]

---

48. Barr, *The Bible in the Modern World*, p. 147. See also, Barr, *Old and New in Interpretation*, pp. 21ff and his "Story and History in Biblical Theology," *Journal of Religion*, 56/1 (January 1976), pp. 1-17. In the latter Barr suggests that the narrative form of the Old Testament better merits the title of story rather than history, though much of it illumines as well as recounts history. I cannot here try to deal with what Frei calls the "history-like" quality of the biblical narrative and the questions thereby raised about the "accuracy" of Scripture. However I think Frei is exactly right to challenge the assumption that the "real" meaning of the text resides

in how accurately or inaccurately the writers report occurrences. For an extremely fruitful discussion of these issues, see Julian Hartt's chapter "Story as the Art of Historical Truth," in his *Theological Method and Imagination* (New York: Seabury Press, 1977), and James Coughenour, "Karl Barth and the Gospel Story: A Lesson in Reading the Biblical Narrative," *Andover Newton Quarterly*, 20 (1979), pp. 97-110.

49. Kelsey interprets Barth in this manner, pp. 39ff.

50. Kelsey, p. 45.

51. Ibid., p. 48.

52. From this perspective the most important question about how to tell the story in the Scripture still involves how to understand the connections between the two testaments. And it is important to note that this is not just a matter of studying the text but, as I have argued, continues to be a political issue of the nature of the Christian community as well as Judaism. As Blenkinsopp has suggested, "In view of the break between Christianity and Judaism towards the end of the Second Commonwealth — profoundly tragic in its consequences as it has been — the two faiths must neces-

Through Scripture we see that at crucial periods in the life of Israel and the church, questions about how to remember the stories were not just questions about "fact" or accuracy, but about what kind of community we must be to be faithful to Yahweh and his purposes for us. So the question of the status of the Davidic kingship for Israel now in Exile could not be avoided as Israel sought to survive as a community without being a "nation."[53] The issue is not just one of interpretation but of what kind of people can remember the past and yet know how to go on in a changed world.

Moreover one does not need to be a New Testament scholar to recognize that questions in the early church about how to tell the life of Jesus were also issues about the kind of community needed to live in keeping with the significance of that life. How the story should be told was basically a moral issue, since it was also a question about what kind of people we ought to be. The unity of the Gospels is not dependent, therefore, on whether they can be made to agree on the details of Jesus' life or even whether various theologies are compatible; rather, the unity of the Gospels is based on the unquestioned assumption that the unity of these people required the telling of the story of this man who claimed to be nothing less than the Messiah of Israel.[54]

The fact that we now have a canon and recognize its authority in the church does not mean that we can be any less concerned about what kind of community we must be to remember rightly through the biblical narrative. Our selectivity and arbitrariness in using Scripture ultimately result from our attempt to be something less than a people capable of carrying God's story in the world. For who "wants to hear about brave deeds when he is ashamed of his own, and who likes an open, honest tale from someone he's deceiving?"[55] The canon is not an accomplishment but a task, since it challenges us to be the kind of people capable of recalling the stories of our fathers and mothers, on which our existence continues to depend.

The temptation, now that we have the canon, is either to objectify Scripture in a manner that kills its life, or to be willing in principle to accept the validity of any interpretation by way of acknowledging the Scripture's variety. Both responses fail to meet the moral challenge of being a people who derive their identity from a book. The continued existence of Israel is alone enough to make us recognize that the question of what kind of community we must be to be faithful to God is not an issue settled by the mere fact we possess a canon. I have tried to show how the very nature of the biblical literature requires us to be as able to remember as those who produced the literature.

The question of the moral significance of Scripture, therefore, turns out to be a question

---

sarily address a critique to each other, and such a critique will necessarily inform any attempt to give a theological account of the classical texts to which both bodies appeal. Is it inconceivable that such mutual testing be carried out in dialogue and cooperation? And, from the Christian side, what would an Old Testament theology look like which at least envisioned such a situation by taking Judaism with absolute theological seriousness?" "The Period of the Second Commonwealth in the Theology of the Old Testament," p. 29. In his *Discerning the Way* (New York: Seabury, 1980), Paul Van Buren rightly argues that the relationship between the Hebrew Scriptures and the apostolic writings is "unavoidably a question of the relationship between the Jewish people and the Gentile church," p. 139. I am in deep sympathy with Van Buren's attempt to take seriously the fact that the God Christians worship is Israel's God.

53. Blenkinsopp, *Prophecy and Canon,* pp. 78-79.

54. Charles Talbert has suggested that though the early Christians agreed that God was present in Jesus for our salvation, they differed about how that presence was manifest in Jesus. As a result the gospel was

preached and written down in different ways — some concentrated on the miracles, some morality, some knowledge of the future. But what is important is that the "canonical Gospels appear to be attempts to avoid the reductionism of seeing the presence of God in Jesus in only one way and attempts to set forth a comprehensive and balanced understanding of both the divine presence and the discipleship it evokes." "The Gospel and the Gospels," *Interpretation,* 33/4 (October 1979), pp. 351-362. As Talbert has shown elsewhere, what was crucial about the Gospels is not their genre, but the kind of discipleship they assumed appropriate to the character of Jesus. See his *What is a Gospel: The Genre of the Canonical Gospels* (Philadelphia: Fortress Press, 1977).

55. This is a statement by Fiver from Richard Adams' *Watership Down* (New York: Avon Books, 1972), p. 124.

about what kind of community the church must be to be able to make the narratives of Scripture central for its life. I have already argued that such a community must be capable of sustaining the authority of Scripture through use in its liturgy and governance. But first and foremost the community must know that it has a history and tradition which separate it from the world. Such separation is required by the very fact that the world knows not the God we find in the Scripture.[56]

The virtues of patience, courage, hope, and charity must reign if the community is to sustain its existence. For without patience the church may be tempted to apocalyptic fantasy; without courage the church would fail to hold fast to the traditions from which it draws its life; without hope the church risks losing sight of its tasks; and without charity the church would not manifest the kind of life made possible by God. Each of these virtues, and there are others equally important, draws its meaning and form from the biblical narrative, and each is necessary if we are to continue to remember and to live faithful to that narrative.

As I have suggested, Christians continue to honor the decision of their ancestors to fashion a canon because they believe the Scripture reflects the very nature of God and his will for their lives. Put more concretely, Scripture has authority for Christians because they have learned as a forgiven people they must also be able to forgive.[57] But to

be a people capable of accepting forgiveness separates them from the world: The world, under the illusion that power and violence rule history, assumes that it has no need to be forgiven. Part of the meaning of the "world," therefore, is it is that which assumes it needs no Scripture, since it lives not by memory made possible by forgiveness, but by power.

Being a community of the forgiven is directly connected with being a community sustained by the narratives we find in Scripture, as those narratives do nothing less than manifest the God whose very nature is to forgive. To be capable of remembering we must be able to forgive, for without forgiveness we can only forget or repress those histories that prove to be destructive or at least unfruitful. But Christians and Jews are commanded not to forget, since the very character of their community depends on their accepting God's forgiveness and thus learning how to remember, even if what they must remember is their sin and unrighteousness.[58] By attending closely to

---

56. Blenkinsopp suggests that "the prophetic canon found a place alongside Torah as a compromise or way of maintaining a balance between law and prophecy, institution and charisma, the claims of the past and those of the future. Such an inclusive canon, which contained within itself both the seeds of tension and the means of overcoming it, corresponds to something important in the makeup of Judaism and Christianity. Both faiths can test the truth of the proposition that a theocratic institution which excludes prophecy and the millenarian hope leaves itself open to assimilation, while prophecy left to itself tends of its nature toward disunity and sectarianism. It is the fate of prophecy to be always necessary and never sufficient." *Prophecy and Canon,* p. 116. However, as I have tried to suggest, without a prophetic community there is no chance that the moral force of the Scripture story can be intelligible.

57. On the political presuppositions of forgiveness, see Hadden Willmer, "The Politics of Forgiveness," *The Furrow,* April 1979, and my "Forgiveness and Political

Community," *Worldview,* 23/1-2 (January-February 1980), pp. 15-16.

58. In his otherwise admirable *The First Followers of Jesus* (London: SCM Press, 1977), Gerd Theissen suggests "in the New Testament for the first time the revolutionary — and healthy — insight that to take any human ethical requirement seriously will demonstrate its inadequacy, that ethics without forgiveness is a perversion, and that there is more to morality than morality, if it is to remain human. This recognition certainly points far beyond the particular historical context in which it came into being. But at one time it was a contribution towards overcoming a deep-rooted crisis in Judaism. The identity of Judaism could not be achieved by rival intensifications of the demands of the Torah, each of which sought to outbid the others; the only answer was the recognition of divine grace. In the last resort, solidarity between men could not be achieved by an intensification of norms; this could only heighten latent and open aggressiveness. What was needed was a new relationship to all norms: putting trust and freedom from anxiety before demands of any kind," p. 107. Not only does this accept a far too restricted sense of "morality," but more damaging is the assumption that forgiveness was absent prior to the coming of Jesus and the church. I have tried to suggest that the ability of Israel to reinterpret her traditions presumed a profound experience and understanding of forgiveness. Theissen's argument in this respect still

the example of those who have given us our Scripture, we learn how to be a people morally capable of forgiveness and thus worthy of continuing to carry the story of God we find authorized by Scripture.

The Moral Use of "Biblical Morality"

Some may well wonder whether this account of the moral authority of Scripture has really helped us advance beyond the problems concerning the use of "biblical morality" described in section two. It may be objected that all I have done is redescribe as "moral" aspects of Scripture and the process of its development which we already knew.[59] I may be right that remembering is a moral activity that requires a particular kind of community, especially if the stories we find in the Scripture are to be remembered, but that still does not help us to know what to do with the more straightforwardly "moral" aspects of Scripture — i.e., the Decalogue or the Sermon on the Mount. Nor does it help us understand what we are to do with those aspects of Scripture that now seem irrelevant or, even worse, morally perverse.

For example, the complexity of the analysis offered here tends to obscure the straightforward command "Thou shalt not commit adultery" (Exod. 20:14) or the equally significant, "Do not resist one who is evil" (Matt. 5:39). In spite of all that one must say about the need to understand such passages in context, I am impressed by those who live as if such commands should directly govern their affairs. None of us should lose the

suspicion that our sophistication concerning the cultural and theological qualifications about "biblical morality" often hides a profound unwillingness to have our lives guided by it.

Yet I contend that the position developed here does help us better comprehend the more straightforwardly moral portions of Scripture. It keeps us from turning commands found there into isolated rules or principles that are assumed to have special status because they are in the Bible. Rather it proposes that Christians (and we hope others) take them to heart (and mind) because they have been found to be crucial to a people formed by the story of God. Such commands stand as reminders of the kind of people we must be if we are to be capable of remembering for ourselves and the world the story of God's dealing with us.

To take the prohibition of adultery, it does not claim to be intelligible in itself, but draws its force from the meaning and significance of marriage in the Jewish and Christian communities. Marriage in those communities derives from profound hope in and commitment to the future, witnessed by the willingness and duty to bring new life into the world. Moreover for those traditions family and marriage have special significance as they are also an expression of the relation these people have with their God. The prohibition against adultery does not therefore derive from a set of premises concerned directly with the legitimacy of sexual expression, though without doubt it has often been so interpreted, but from the profoundest commitment of the community concerning the form of sexual life necessary to sustain their understanding of marriage and family.

Nor does the prohibition against resisting evil derive from an assumption about violence as inherently evil, but rather from the community's understanding of how God rules his creation. For how can a people who believe God is Lord of their existence show forth that conviction if they act as if the meaning of their existence, and perhaps even history itself, must be insured by the use of force? The nonviolence of the church derives from the character of the story of God that makes us what we are — namely a community capable of witnessing to others the kind of life made possible when trust rather than fear rules our relation with one another.

I do not assume that all the moral advice and

---

betrays the Protestant reading of Paul that has recently been challenged by E. P. Sanders in his *Paul and Palestinian Judaism*. Sanders rather decisively shows that for Paul the problem with Judaism was not the law, but that it is not Christianity — that is, a new community based on the work and person of Jesus, p. 552.

59. If this is the case, it is but another indication that ethics at best is only bad poetry — that is, it seeks to help us see what we see every day but fail to see rightly. Put differently, ethics is an attempt to help us feel the oddness of the everyday. If ethicists had talent, they might be poets, but in the absence of talent, they try to make their clanking conceptual and discursive chains do the work of art.

admonitions found in Scripture have the same significance or should positively be appropriated. Each must be evaluated separately and critically. Of course, before we decide that certain aspects of Scripture are no longer relevant — e.g., the *Haustafeln* — we must make sure we understand them through an exegesis as accurate as we can muster. And we must remember that a set of historical-critical skills will not guarantee an accurate reading. Our analysis will also depend on the questions we learn to put to the text from participating in a community which acknowledges their formative role.

The command for wives to be subject to their husbands, for example, comes only after the admonition that everyone in the church must be subject to the other out of "reverence for Christ" (Eph. 5:21). It does not say that wives should be subject to husbands as an end in itself, but rather as "to the Lord." So the manner of being "subject" cannot be read off the face of the text nor can it be made clear by exegesis alone. In fact, exegesis itself points us to recall the ways in which we as members of the church have learned to be subject to one another as faithful disciples of Christ. That direction should effectively restrain a contemporary reader from trying to understand "subordinate" from a perspective that assumes all moral relations which are not "autonomous" are morally suspect.

There is no doubt that the *Haustafeln* are in danger of great distortion and harm if they are lifted out of their theological and community context and turned into general admonitions meant to apply to any community. But that is just what their existence in Scripture should prohibit. One need not agree with Yoder's argument that the *Haustafeln* were necessary because the freedom established by this new community created the possibility of insubordination in order to appreciate how the *Haustafeln* are but reminders of the radical nature of the new community that has been called into existence — namely, one where service to the other is freed from concern with status and envy.[60]

Finally, there can be no ethical use of Scripture unless we are a community capable of following the admonition to put "away falsehood, let every one speak the truth with his neighbor, for we are members of one another. Be angry but do not sin; do not let the sun go down on your anger, and give no opportunity to the devil. Let the thief no longer steal, but rather let him labor, doing honest work with his hands, so that he may be able to give to those in need. Let no evil talk come out of your mouths, but such as is good for edifying, as fits the occasion, that it may impart grace to those that hear. And do not grieve the Holy Spirit of God, in whom you were sealed for the day of redemption. Let all bitterness and wrath and anger and clamor and slander be put away from you, with all malice, and be kind to one another, tenderhearted, forgiving one another, as God in Christ forgave you" (Eph. 4:25-32).

60. Yoder, *The Politics of Jesus*, p. 178.

8. Feminist Consciousness and the Interpretation of Scripture

MARGARET A. FARLEY

"When the women returned from the tomb they told all this to the Eleven and to all the others. The women were Mary of Magdala, Joanna, and Mary the mother of James. The other women with them also told the apostles, but this story of theirs seemed pure nonsense, and [the apostles] did not believe them" (Luke 24:9-11, JB). At least one motivation for developing a feminist interpretation of the Christian Scriptures is the need that many of us feel to address the question: Is the testimony of these women to be believed; and, if it is, what does it really mean?

What is at stake in developing a feminist hermeneutic — a feminist theory of interpretation — in relation to the Bible is, of course, the interpretation of the biblical witness as a whole. Is it a witness that is life-giving for women and for men, a witness that opens access to some truth that is freeing for all? Is it a witness that enables us to make choices that are authentic and good, that are faithful to the deepest needs of the human community and consonant with its noblest aspira-

Margaret A. Farley (1935–) is the Gilbert L. Stark Professor of Christian Ethics at Yale University Divinity School. She has authored numerous essays in Christian feminist ethics. Her books include *Personal Commitments: Beginning, Keeping, Changing* (1986).

From *Feminist Interpretation of the Bible,* ed. Letty M. Russell (Louisville, Ky.: Westminster/John Knox Press, 1985).

tions? Are the women returning from the tomb beguiled by an illusion, used by traditions of which they are a part, adding one more turn to the plot of a story that is only fiction or perhaps even deception or, worse, a story that will serve forever to injure the women who either tell it or hear it?

My aim here is to probe the consequences of feminist consciousness for the interpretation of Scripture. I will not attempt to identify the whole of what can be called "feminist consciousness" or begin the task of actual interpretation of Scripture. What I will do is try to identify some important elements in feminist consciousness, show how these yield interpretive principles in relation to Scripture, and reflect on the function of these for our understanding and use of Scripture. In order to set the stage for this, however, I want to consider how feminist consciousness, like any other "consciousness" that includes deeply held convictions about the way things are and ought to be, inevitably and profoundly influences our interpretation of and our belief in the biblical witness.

Authority and Content: The Test of "Recognition"

Is the testimony of the women returning from the tomb to be believed? And, if it is, what does it really mean? To put the questions in this way suggests that it is possible to separate them, to separate the question of authenticity, or authority, from the question of content, or meaning. This, however, cannot be done. Herein lies a stumbling block for many who would otherwise like to take seriously a feminist hermeneutic for the Bible. If the question of the authority of the witness is made contingent in any way upon our recognition of the "truth" of its message or the "justice" of its aims, this seems to make of the Bible a secondary source for our knowledge, one that is subject to the test of insights generated from some other more fundamental source. Is this not tantamount to bringing to Scripture a test of one's own, a criterion of truth, rather than approaching Scripture as a revelatory word, a test of all other claims to truth?

This problem is not easily dismissed, whether a negative or positive resolution is chosen. For many persons, a *recognition* of truth as well as truthfulness is necessary if the Bible is to be a source of life. The authority question is indeed inseparable from the question of content. The reason for this need not be a sophisticated skepticism, certainly not a stiff-necked self-righteousness. It can be, rather, an intuitive or reflective awareness that no communication has real and living power unless it can elicit in us a responding recognition. Call it grace, or previous insight, or a receptivity for truth — unless there is some way in which a new revelation can be recognized by us as true, it cannot free us further from ignorance of falsehood and it cannot awaken us to love.

Massive difficulties are entailed by such an assertion, of course. Qualifications of all kinds may be necessary. I think, however, its plausibility can be shown fairly simply if I treat it for now as a "negative limit." Let me try to explain what I mean by this.

Theologians and ethicists always make some judgments about what sources they will use and how they will use them. For example, they determine that secular disciplines (like philosophy) should be included or excluded as sources for theology; they decide which of their sources takes priority (as when Scripture is given priority over the teaching of church leaders); they raise up certain biblical texts and relativize the value of others. Implicit or explicit in these judgments are beliefs about the nature of human understanding, human experience, divine revelation, the authenticity of particular religious traditions, logical consistency, the nature of reality itself. At the heart of such judgments there can be convictions so basic that to contradict them would be to experience violence done to the integrity of the self. The making of such judgments is not unique to theologians and ethicists. It is part of any approach — that of individual believers or whole churches — to the sources of faith and understanding, to discernment of what we can believe and how we are to live what we believe.

My concern here is precisely for the kind of conviction so basic to a person's understanding that a contradictory witness cannot be believed without doing violence to one's self. One can, of course, come to see that the contradictory witness is more true than one's own previous belief. But in this case, it is not violence to the understanding that is experienced. If in such an instance a kind

of letting-go of internal barriers to fuller vision is necessary (barriers such as fear of the new or unwillingness to change behavior in accordance with new insights), this does not do violence to our deepest selves, but liberates them. As long as what is presented actually *contradicts* what remain our most fundamental convictions, however, we cannot surrender our minds to it without experiencing violence done to our own integrity.

The biblical witness, on the contrary, claims to present a truth that will heal us, make us whole; it will free us, not enslave us to what violates our very sense of truth and justice. Its appeal to us might be described, in the words of philosopher Paul Ricoeur, as a "nonviolent appeal."[1] As a revelation of truth, it asks for something less like a submission of will and more like an opening of the imagination — and thence the whole mind and heart. In its own terms, then, it cannot be believed unless it rings true to our deepest capacity for truth and goodness. If it contradicts this, it is not to be believed. If it falsifies this, it cannot be accepted.

Does this characterization of the biblical witness (that is, that its authority can be acknowledged only if its meaning is perceived as true) risk reducing it to "cheap grace"? Is the Bible really required to answer the demands of reason and the cries of the human heart? It depends, of course, on what one means by the demands of reason and the desires of the human heart. But surely there is a sense in which every religious tradition has power only insofar as it offers just this — insofar as it helps to make sense of the whole of human life, to give meaning to human tragedy and horizons to human hopes. "Hard sayings" can be liberating truths; reason need not be opposed to mystery, nor desire to great-hearted love.

The minimal claim I want to make, however, is that included in feminist consciousness are some fundamental convictions so basic and so important that contradictory assertions cannot be accepted by feminists without violence being done to their very understandings and valuations. These convictions serve as a kind of negative test for any revelation in knowledge. They can serve, too, as a positive key to the fullness of revelation regarding the reality and

1. See Paul Ricoeur, *Essays on Biblical Interpretation,* ed. by Lewis S. Mudge (Philadelphia: Fortress Press, 1980), p. 95.

destiny of human persons. These convictions must, then, function in a feminist interpretation of Scripture — discerning the meaning of the biblical witness as a whole and in its parts and thus (though not only thus) whether it is to be believed. Moreover, they serve as principles for selective and interpretive judgments in relation to *all* potential sources for feminist theology and ethics — not only Scripture but the history of theology, the comparative study of religions, philosophy, and the sciences, historical events, contemporary social arrangements, and every woman's own experience. If we can identify some of these convictions, it will be possible both to illustrate better their function in a feminist hermeneutic and at the same time to clarify just what a *feminist* hermeneutic may be.

Principles for a Feminist Hermeneutic

Feminist consciousness includes many elements, not all of which are agreed upon by every feminist. There is pluralism within feminism as in any other rich and comprehensive interpretation of humanity and the world. Yet some central convictions are shared at least by large groups of feminists. Most fundamental, perhaps, is the conviction that women are fully human and are to be valued as such. The content of this conviction, however, is different from some similar affirmations that are nonfeminist. Thus, for example, it is not to be mistaken for the view that women are human, though derivatively and partially so. Hence, a feminist belief about the humanness of women is specified by the inclusion of principles of mutuality. Further, feminist consciousness recognizes the importance of women's own experience as a way to understanding; it takes seriously the essential embodiment of human persons; it opens to an ecological view of the value of all of nature and the context of the whole of the universe; it affirms a mode of collaboration as the primary mode for human interaction.

But let me focus somewhat narrowly on the conviction that women are fully human and are to be valued as such. This conviction could well be formulated as the underlying principle for a feminist hermeneutic. In order not to risk trivializing the central insight of feminism, however, it must (as I have already suggested) be understood to include within it at least two closely related principles: (1) the principle of equality (women and men are equally fully human and are to be treated as such) and (2) the principle of mutuality (based on a view of human persons as embodied subjects, essentially relational as well as autonomous and free). In at least one major version of feminism, these are truth claims, founded on a new understanding of the reality of women (and therefore also of men). So profound is their persuasive appeal that they give rise to an experience of a moral imperative. They function, then, as interpretive principles but also as normative ethical principles in a feminist theory of justice. They function, moreover, to ground a strategy of commitment to the well-being of women, to counter whatever biases perpetuate gender inequalities and structural barriers to human mutuality.

Feminists, quite obviously, are not the only persons who have come to convictions about the principles of equality and mutuality. Yet for feminists the content of these principles is not simply equatable with every other articulation of them. It is not the case, for example, that when feminists argue for equality among women and men, they simply extend to women the insights of modern liberal philosophy; or that when feminists raise up the importance of mutuality, they simply repeat the conclusions of theorists of sociality such as George Herbert Mead, Martin Buber, and John Macmurray. Feminists have, of course, learned from all these sources. But they also know that no other tradition or movement has adequately addressed the situation of women. This is not just a failure of extension. Rather, it represents a fundamental need for deeper analysis of the contexts of human life, concepts of the human self, categories of human relation. It makes clear the urgency for taking account of the experience of all groups of human persons. From the interpretive vantage point of the experience of women — of our oppression and our achievements, our needs and our contributions, our freedom and our responsibilities — feminism assumes groundbreaking work on questions of human dignity and models of human relationships. It also assumes transformative experiences of new and growing insight on the part of individuals, deeply formed convictions about the capabilities and possibilities of each human being.

Equality

Contemporary feminist consciousness, developed through a careful listening to women's own experience (largely prompted by new modes of sharing this experience), incorporates certain conclusions. First, all efforts to justify the inferiority of women to men falsify women's experience. Traditional warrants for gender inequality have been demystified and rejected; women have recognized the contradiction between received interpretations of our identity and function on the one hand and our own experience of ourselves and our lives on the other.

Women have also unmasked deceptive theories that assert a principle of equality but still assume basic inequalities among persons determined by gender, or race, or any property of individuals and groups not essential to their humanity as such. Thus, the long-standing formal principle of equal treatment for equals has been recognized by women in its radical powerlessness by itself to discern who are the "equals." Further, where "equal protection under the law" was said to apply to all persons, women learned only too well that this did not necessarily include them, just as it did not apply to slaves. And strong theories of "complementarity" have been exposed that cover for patterns of inequality — for relationships in which the role of one partner is always inferior to, dependent upon, instrumental to the role of the other.

Feminist consciousness opens, then, to acknowledge for women those essential features of personhood that modern liberal philosophy identified for human persons as such: individual autonomy and a capacity for free choice. Once these features are appropriated for women as well as men, the conclusion follows that women, too, must be respected as "ends," not as mere "means." And their interests and aims must be respected no less than men's.

Equitable Sharing

But women have learned more from their experience than the lessons of liberal philosophy. Their own experience of disadvantage, and their perception of the disadvantaged histories of others who are similarly fully human, have impelled a feminist universalization of the principle of equality that includes a claim by all to an equitable share in the goods and services necessary to human life and basic happiness. The accumulated experience of life situations in which inequality is not limited to political powerlessness or personal lack of esteem but is a matter of hunger and homelessness, sickness and injury, has pushed feminist consciousness to a positive form of the principle of equality — one based not only on the self-protective right of each to freedom but on the positive, self-yielding as well as self-enhancing, participation of all in human solidarity.

Mutuality

Finally, then, women have found in their experience clear indications of the inadequacy of a view of human persons that respects them by isolating them one from another. When autonomy is the sole basis of human dignity and the single principle for social arrangements, individuals are atomized. Their primary mode of relating becomes one of opposition and competition between the self and the other. Women claim that gross forms of individualism not only undermine the common good but fail to take account of another essential feature of personhood — the feature of relationality, that feature which ultimately requires mutuality as the primary goal of relationships between persons.

Only with a principle of mutuality can human persons truly be affirmed as embodied subjects; as beings whose value lies not only in their freedom but also in their capacity to know and be known, to love and be loved; as beings whose destiny is communion.

Deep in women's experience lies the long-standing awareness of the reality that theorists of sociality have come to see. Feminist consciousness stands as a corrective to a liberal philosophy that fails to understand human solidarity and the importance and need for mutuality. But it also stands as a corrective to theories of sociality that fail to incorporate a requirement for basic human equality; that fail to affirm the feature of autonomy along with the feature of relationality. Feminists thus reject romantic returns to organic models of society where woman's relation is determined, each in her own place, without regard for free agency or for personal identity and worth that transcend roles. Yet feminists are convinced that persons, women and men, are centers of life, capable (without contradiction) of being centered more and more in themselves as they are centered more and more beyond themselves in one another. They are convinced, too, that in this mystery of autonomy and relationality, equality and mutuality, lie the clues we need for the relation of persons to the whole universe in which we live. But what can these convictions, and the principles that express them, mean for the interpretation and use of the biblical witness?

Feminist Interpretation of Scripture

The need for interpretation of Scripture is clear. Without interpretation, we are not able to believe the witness that is presented. This is not only because there is reason to be suspicious of Scripture, but because without interpretation we are not able to "hear" what was spoken in another time, to understand its meaning for us. In this, contemporary feminists are not unique. The necessity for interpretation exists for all those who struggle to know what was written in another context, who ask whether a tradition is living in which they can stand. This does not mean that no one can experience a present direct address through the mediation of Scripture, but even the immediacy of such experience is not free of the need for interpretation — interpretation of the experience and what is encountered in it. Interpretation of sacred Scriptures from *within* the tradition for which they are Scriptures, and sacred, is precisely the bringing together of the horizons of a far-reaching tradition and present life situations. For Christians the task of interpretation has been under way from the beginning — as, for example, when a New Testament hermeneutic was addressed to the Old Testament, and when Paul interpreted the story of Jesus in relation to the lives of the early churches, and when in each century there was acknowledged the need to hear and hear again.[2]

For those who are reluctant to bring to Scripture what seems to be a measure for its meaning and authority, one solution suggests itself in the face of a seeming dilemma. That is, it might be argued that Scripture itself provides the basis for

2. Ibid., pp. 49-72.

feminist consciousness. True discernment of the biblical witness yields feminist insights, which in turn become principles of interpretation for the rest of Scripture. In other words, convictions regarding the full humanity of women emerge precisely from the bringing of women's experience to the address of Scripture.

The difficulty with attributing solely to Scripture the genesis of feminist consciousness is that it seems clearly contrary to fact. Not all feminists have come to their beliefs about the reality of women, about equality and mutuality, simply by reading the Bible. Some, at least, have come to these convictions influenced by the intellectual history of our civilization, by the cultural milieu which this intellectual history has helped to form, by the changes in women's own lives, by the sharing of women's recognition of contradictions between received traditions and their own experience. Insight into women's reality may be prompted for some by encounter with biblical texts, confirmed and expanded for others, left untouched for still others, contradicted for others still. Within the potential religious experience of women, the fundamental question is not whether original vision is generated by Scripture but how, given this vision, Scripture is to be approached.

Some fairly standard ways in which Christian ethicists think about Scripture as a source can be helpful to us here. For example, most Christian ethicists would not claim that the Bible (or Christian theology, for that matter) provides exclusive access to moral insight.[3] Scripture is indeed a source for Christian ethics in a variety of ways. It can reveal moral principles, ideals, guidelines, values. It can aid moral discernment by illuminating the human condition, possibilities of human agency, obstacles to moral goodness. It can motivate moral action by making present a divine promise and call, a history of people formed in

3. See, for example, Beverly Wildung Harrison, *Our Right to Choose: Toward a New Ethic of Abortion* (Boston: Beacon Press, 1983), chapter 3; James M. Gustafson, *The Contributions of Theology to Medical Ethics* (Milwaukee: Marquette University Press, 1975), pp. 84-90; Richard A. McCormick, *How Brave a New World: Dilemmas in Bioethics* (New York: Doubleday, 1981), p. 9; Thomas W. Ogletree, *The Use of the Bible in Christian Ethics* (Philadelphia: Fortress Press, 1983).

faith, a glimpse of what is to be hoped for. It can empower persons religiously and morally by mediating a fundamental meaning for their lives, stretching them always beyond themselves, challenging self-deception, enabling self-acceptance. But in all of this, the Bible may not yield very specific moral rules or action guides, and the general principles it offers may have no ready application to contemporary life. Without other sources of moral wisdom, the power of Scripture cannot be mediated into the contemporary context.

On this basis can we ask, then, what it might mean to acknowledge the authority of Scripture as a source for Christian and feminist faith, theology, ethics? First, it is helpful to be clear about what it does *not* mean (or at least need not mean, within a traditionally recognized pluralism of approaches by Christians to Scripture). It does not mean that some important insights — regarding life, morality, even hope — cannot come both from the Bible and from other sources, or only from other sources. It does not mean, moreover, that Scripture is sufficient in itself for the development of a wholly adequate Christian feminist theology or ethic.

Positvely, what it *can* mean for feminists to acknowledge the authority of Scripture as a source for understanding human persons and human life is that (1) at least Scripture contains something more than a patriarchal view of human life, a support for sexism, and (2) the "more" that Scripture embodies rings at least in harmony with the truth of women's reality as it is understood in feminist consciousness — touches it, perhaps unfolds it, makes it resonate with other truths, perhaps can help to test fidelity to it. For those for whom Scripture has this authority, the interpretive task becomes imperative.

We must ask more specifically, however, in what way feminist consciousness can function in the interpretation of Scripture. I have already said that principles of a feminist hermeneutic will serve first as a negative limit. It may be clearer now what it means to say that deep convictions, when they are brought to the interpretation of Scripture or any other source for faith, for theology, for ethics, serve precisely as a negative limit. Whatever contradicts those convictions cannot be accepted as having the authority of an authentic revelation

of truth. It is simply a matter of there being no turning back. We can be dispossessed of our best insights, proven wrong in our judgments. But as long as those insights continue to make sense to us, and as long as our basic judgments seem to us incontrovertible, there can be no turning back. So it is with feminist consciousness and the interpretation of Scripture.

Feminists quite readily acknowledge the historical nature of human knowledge and the social nature of the interpretation of human experience. Yet feminist consciousness is experienced as an immeasurable advance over the false consciousness it replaces or the implicit consciousness it renders explicit. Scales have fallen from persons' eyes, and they cannot be put back. The fact that present insights are still partial, that present formulations of principles may change, that the meaning of principles can vary significantly from context to context — none of this changes the requirement that new understandings must be tested for truth (for accuracy and adequacy) against the reality of women's lives as revealed in women's experience. It is no fancy, no illusion, that feminists believe they bring to the interpretation of Scripture.

If, within the negative limit, the biblical witness as a whole is experienced as authentic — if, in other words, some religious authority is given to Scripture — then the interpretive task remains in relation to all the parts of the whole. That is, insofar as Scripture is judged by feminists to be a source for faith, for theology, ethics, and life, then the negative limit also functions in discerning the meaning of specific texts, specific aspects of the biblical story. On the basis of feminist convictions, then, some interpretations are ruled out (just as an overall acceptance of the love commandment as central to Christian life and to the teaching of Scripture rules out final interpretations that contradict it). Thus, for example a divine imperative which universalizes a requirement that women fill inferior roles is ruled out as the final word of the biblical witness. Different feminist interpreters will rule out such interpretations different ways, of course. Within a pluralism of approaches, some will deny the validity of texts that hold such content; some will relativize the importance of such texts; some will interpret the texts under a feminist paradigm that makes them negative symbols of what the overall witness is portraying.

But, as I have said, feminist principles of interpretation serve more than as a negative limit in discerning the meaning of Scripture. Insofar as Scripture is believed to shed light on human experience, feminist interpretive principles must function to probe its stories and its teachings, its poetry and its oracles, searching for positive clues for the ongoing task of finding meaning and making decisions in our concrete lives (just as the love commandment sets questions for discernment, searching for analogies between the tradition and the lives of those who approach the tradition). New questions are themselves principles of movement in understanding. It is possible that a feminist hermeneutic can allow more scales to drop from our eyes, so that the biblical witness is freed for our seeing in a way that must otherwise remain forever obscured.

Two final observations may be in order. When an interpretive principle rises out of experience that is importantly characterized by oppression and suffering, it carries with it a moral imperative for use. Feminists must approach Scripture, and every other source of religious faith and practice, with hermeneutical principles that not only render the sources accessible to feminist consciousness but more and more inaccessible for the harmful aims of sexism. Whatever problems its writers had in attaining anything like a feminist consciousness, they knew well the tragic fact that persons "hear and hear, but do not understand; see and see, but do not perceive" (Isa. 6:9). Thus was their own task set. Thus, too, is set the task of feminist interpretation for a long time to come.

Last of all, it may not be nonsense to suggest that feminists have powerful reasons to hope that the women returning from the tomb bear a witness that is life-giving and that can help to deepen and widen every understanding of life and destiny. Human persons need, after all, an ongoing word to meet the word in our hearts. We need religious symbols whose power is a power of access to reality; a promise that can allow us to risk basic trust in life and the world; a call that can help us to be faithful to the truth we hold. We need, also, to acknowledge an essential human openness to any sacred truth and any sacred presence. If the story of the women is to be believed, it will do more than pass a critical test. It will do more than reveal new meaning. Feminists can know the risks — but also the inestimable hope — of giving these women a hearing.

9. Biblical Revelation and Social Existence

JAMES CONE

Black Theology's answer to the question of hermeneutics can be stated briefly: *The hermeneutical principle for an exegesis of the Scriptures is the revelation of God in Christ as the liberator of the oppressed from social oppression and to political struggle, wherein the poor recognize that their fight against poverty and injustice is not only consistent with the gospel but is the gospel of Jesus Christ.* Jesus Christ the liberator, the helper and the healer of the wounded, is the point of departure for valid exegesis of the Scriptures from a Christian perspective. Any starting point that ignores God in Christ as the liberator of the oppressed or that makes salvation as liberation secondary is *ipso facto* invalid and thus heretical. The test of the validity of this starting point, although dialectically related to Black cultural experience, is not found in the particularity of the oppressed culture alone. It is found in the One who freely grants us freedom when we were doomed to slavery. In God's revelation in Scripture we come to the recognition that the divine liberation of the oppressed is not determined by our perceptions but by the God of the Exodus, the prophets, and Jesus Christ who calls the oppressed into a liber-

ated existence. Divine revelation *alone* is the test of the validity of this starting point. And if it can be shown that God as witnessed in the Scriptures is not the liberator of the oppressed, then Black Theology would have to either drop the "Christian" designation or choose another starting point.

James Cone (1938–) is the Charles A. Briggs Distinguished Professor of Systematic Theology at Union Theological Seminary in New York. The leading figure in African-American theology, his works include *Black Theology and Black Power; A Black Theology of Liberation; Speaking the Truth: Ecumenism, Liberation, and Black Theology;* and *Martin and Malcolm.*

From *Interpretation* 28 (October 1974): pp. 422-40.

Chapter 3

Tradition and Christian Ethics

Introduction

The biblical readings which stand at the head of this chapter display different attitudes toward tradition — and so have Christian moral theologians. Some have been suspicious of what has been handed down as moral wisdom within the religious community and are ready to challenge the authority of tradition in order to keep "the command of God," whether that "command" is found in Scripture or in the present moment or in some vision of a future which breaks the hold of both the past and the present. Others have honored tradition, have held fast to it, and have been suspicious of change.

Every living tradition, however, as more than one of the readings will remind us (see readings 13, 14, and 16; also 7), involves both continuity and change. If that is so, then the critical question will be the fidelity of both continuity and change. However, to ask that question is to ask others as well. How will fidelity be tested? Who will test it? To what must traditions — in continuity and change — be faithful?

Before we can consider those questions, however, it will be important to identify the "tradition" we are talking about. There is more than one tradition, after all. We might be talking about the broad Christian tradition, the wisdom handed down by saints and sinners and received by contemporary Christians. Moreover, we might be talking of that tradition in such a way as to include Scripture as a part, even the normative part, of it, or as to exclude Scripture in an effort to identify a second source for Christian ethics in addition to Scripture. Or we might be talking about a particular tradition within the history of Christian moral reflection, the tradition of the veneration of saints, for example (see reading 13, but also reading 16,

where this tradition is accused of infidelity, of becoming "a new paganism"). Or, the particular tradition might be the prohibition of contraception, or the tradition of "just war" (see reading 16), or the tradition of the exclusion of homosexual persons like Steve from "Holy Unions."

Moreover, we all receive, by virtue of our life in the world, traditions for our life and for our common life that do not have their source in the Christian community. There is, for example, an enlightenment tradition that contrasts tradition with "reason" (see reading 11). We are, in fact, surrounded by traditions. By selective retrieval from any of them we create for ourselves a life and a common life. But, again, what are the principles of selection? How can we test continuity and change for fidelity? and fidelity to what or to whom?

Douglas Ottati (reading 14) warns against occasionalism, individualism, utopianism, and traditionalism. John Howard Yoder (reading 16) urges us always to be "looping back," to remember Scripture and especially the stories of Jesus, as the test for traditions and reformation. Rosemary Radford Ruether (reading 15) requires suspicion of any chauvisim. And James Tunstead Burtchaell (reading 13) suggests testing traditions against the experience of faithful members of the Christian community, whose membership also includes some gifted and charged to "groom" ancient wisdom. You might consider how these different proposals for testing tradition would bear on the tradition or traditions at stake in "Holy Unions."

Burtchaell's recommendation may remind us of another question you may want to raise with respect to "Holy Unions." It is the question of who will — and who should — test the traditions. Who's in control? The magisterium, the teaching office of the church? Or the community as a whole, with the diversity of gifts that belong to a congregation? Is testing the tradition a right of personal and private judgment? Do men control and test the tradition (see reading 15); should they? Do straight men control and test the tradition? How would answers to these questions shape the conversation between Bob and George? How do they shape your own views of moral discernment and judgment, so that you might be able to live faithfully and creatively with your traditions?

Suggestions for Further Reading

Congar, Yves. *Tradition and Traditions.* New York: Macmillan, 1967.

Farley, Edward. *Ecclesial Reflection: An Anatomy of Theological Method.* Philadelphia: Fortress Press, 1982.

Florovski, George V. *Bible, Church, Tradition: An Eastern Orthodox View.* Nordland Pub., 1972.

MacIntyre, Alasdar. *Three Rival Versions of Moral Enquiry: Encyclopedia, Geneology, and Tradition.* Notre Dame: University of Notre Dame Press, 1990.

Stout, Jeffrey. *Ethics after Babel: The Languages of Morals and Their Discontents.* Boston: Beacon Press, 1988.

Troeltsch, Ernst. *The Social Teachings of the Christian Churches.* 2 vols. (German original published in 1911; trans. Olive Wyon), New York: Harper & Row, 1960.

10. Mark 7:1-13;
2 Thessalonians 2:15

Mark 7:1-13

Now when the Pharisees and some of the scribes who had come from Jerusalem gathered around him, they noticed that some of his disciples were eating with defiled hands, that is, without washing them. (For the Pharisees, and all the Jews do not eat unless they thoroughly wash their hands, thus observing the tradition of the elders; and they do not eat anything from the market unless they wash it; and there are also many other traditions that they observe, the washing of cups, pots, and bronze kettles.) So the Pharisees and the scribes asked him, "Why do your disciples not live according to the tradition of the elders, but eat with defiled hands?" He said to them, "Isaiah prophesied rightly about you hypocrites, as it is written,

'This people honors me with their lips,
  but their hearts are far from me;
in vain do they worship me,
  teaching human precepts as doctrines.'

You abandon the commandment of God and hold to human tradition."

Then he said to them, "You have a fine way of rejecting the commandment of God in order to keep your tradition! For Moses said, 'Honor your father and your mother'; and, 'Whoever speaks evil of father or mother must surely die.' But you say that if anyone tells father or mother, 'Whatever support you might have had from me is Corban' (that is, an offering to God) — then you no longer permit doing anything for a father or mother, thus making void the word of God through your tradition that you have handed on. And you do many things like this."

2 Thessalonians 2:15

So then, brothers and sisters, stand firm and hold fast to the traditions that you were taught by us, either by word of mouth or by our letter.

11. Tradition in Ethics

JEFFREY STOUT

The term "tradition" can refer either to something handed down from generation to generation *(traditum)* or to the mode of transmission itself *(traditio)*. No one doubts that there are ethical traditions in both senses, but there is no consensus among students of morality concerning the nature and significance of tradition in ethics. Several major movements in modern ethical thought portray tradition as inessential to ethics or even as morally dangerous, though each has met with serious opposition.

Some Protestants have argued that Scripture, interpreted by human reason in light of the Holy Spirit, should serve as the sole rule of faith and morals. Their point has been to deny tradition the essential role ascribed to it in Catholicism, where the living magisterium functions not only as the definitive interpreter of scriptural revelation but also as the official organ of nonscriptural divine traditions. Against the doctrine of *sola scriptura*, Catholics have maintained that Scripture cannot operate independently as a rule of faith and morals, for Scripture is silent on some important matters, requires interpretation disciplined by tradition, and does not provide a criterion for determining which writings are genuinely scriptural. Without denying the authority of Scripture, Catholics have therefore insisted upon the necessity of acknowledging tradition as a source of au-

Jeffrey Stout (1950–) is director of graduate studies at the Princeton University department of religion. His work includes *The Flight From Authority* and *After Babel*.

From *Westminster Dictionary of Christian Ethics*, ed. James F. Childress and John Macquarrie (Louisville, Ky.: Westminster/John Knox Press, 1986).

thority as well. On the other hand, Protestants have often seen tradition as too inconsistent and corruptible to be a genuine source of moral authority. Not all Protestants, however, have taken such a dim view of tradition, and Protestant theologians like James Gustafson and Stanley Hauerwas are among those now assigning tradition a central role in ethics.

Many modern moral philosophers have viewed tradition as, at best, an ultimately dispensable aid to fallible human reason and, at worst, a repository of superstition and a threat to autonomy. They have therefore attempted to ground moral knowledge and action in something not essentially dependent upon tradition. For intuitionists, moral knowledge is derived from a foundation of certitudes accessible in principle to all rational persons. For followers of Immanuel Kant (1724-1804), morality is a set of rules required by pure reason, rules we legislate for ourselves out of respect for free rational agency. Even the received moral teachings of Christ, according to Kant, must be subjected to scrutiny by autonomous reason before being accepted as authoritative.

Intuitionists and Kantians face a common difficulty — that of how to square moral variety or disagreement with the idea that moral knowledge derives from foundational certitudes or from the requirements of pure reason. Why, if moral knowledge is what intuitionists and Kantians have said it is, do some ethical traditions differ significantly from others? One answer, Kant's own, is that some traditions are simply more fully rational than others. They are further along the road to moral perfection. Kant, who took a more favorable view of tradition than many of his followers have, interpreted religious traditions as "vehicles" of perfect moral rationality, vehicles that help fallible human beings make progress toward pure rational faith. Religious traditions, while dispensable in the long run, are suited to the failings of sensuous humanity, but some represent relatively little progress toward perfection, others more. Kant thus explains moral variety by judging some traditions less rational than others and then endeavoring to show how nonrational factors enter in. His successors, however, have been reluctant to declare alien tradition irrational without closer examination. Some have tried to show that much of the putative evidence of moral diversity is merely apparent.

Others, agreeing that Kant's ascriptions of irrationality cannot be supported but remaining unpersuaded that moral diversity can simply be explained away, have suggested that practical reason makes use of tradition-bound presuppositions and that variation in such presuppositions explain variation in moral conclusions.

This last option in effect grants what the proponents of tradition have insisted upon all along — that tradition is essential to moral reasoning, that the rational acceptability of a moral conclusion can be determined only relative to a context of inherited assumptions and that "pure reason" does not suffice to generate a uniquely rational moral system. Once this much has been granted, however, it becomes hard to avoid the further conclusion that pure reason is an empty abstraction lacking any explanatory power whatsoever. This was the conclusion G. W. F. Hegel (1770-1831) drew in his critique of Kant, and recent defenses of tradition as an essential dimension of the moral life continue to show Hegel's influence. Those most deeply influenced by Hegel — philosophers like Hans-Georg Gadamer and Alasdair MacIntyre, theologians like David Tracy — have taken pains to dissociate themselves from a picture of tradition as basically continuous and conservative. For such thinkers, traditions are ongoing conversations or arguments subject to dramatic reversal and, at times, revolutionary innovation. Tradition, for them, far from being opposed to critical reason, is its necessary embodiment.

12. The Transmission of Divine Revelation

VATICAN II

In his gracious goodness, God has seen to it that what he had revealed for the salvation of all nations would abide perpetually in its full integrity and be handed on to all generations. Therefore Christ the Lord, in whom the full revelation of the supreme God is brought to completion (cf. 2 Cor. 1:20; 3:16; 4:6), commissioned the apostles to preach to all men that gospel which is the source of all saving truth and moral teaching, and thus to impart to them divine gifts. This gospel had been promised in former times through the prophets, and Christ himself fulfilled it and promulgated it with his own lips. This commission was faithfully fulfilled by the apostles who, by their oral preaching, by example, and by ordinances, handed on what they had received from the lips of Christ, from living with Him, and from what he did, or what they had learned through the prompting of the Holy Spirit. The commission was fulfilled, too, by those apostles and apostolic men who under the inspiration of the same Holy Spirit committed the message of salvation to writing.

But in order to keep the gospel forever whole and alive within the church, the apostles left bishops

---

The Second Vatican Council was called by Pope John XXIII in 1959. It met in four sessions from 1962 to 1965 and ended with the solemn promulgation of sixteen conciliar documents by the new pope, Paul VI, and the bishops in council. It was the twenty-first ecumenical council recognized by Roman Catholics and the first since Vatican I in 1869-70.

From "The Dogmatic Constitution on Divine Revelation" in Walter M. Abbot, S.J., *The Documents of Vatican II* (New York: America Press, 1966).

as their successors, "handing over their own teaching role" to them. This sacred tradition, therefore, and sacred Scripture of both the Old and the New Testament are like a mirror in which the pilgrim church on earth looks at God, from whom she has received everything, until she is brought finally to see him as he is, face to face (cf. 1 John 3:2).

And so the apostolic preaching, which is expressed in a special way in the inspired books, was to be preserved by a continuous succession of preachers until the end of time. Therefore the apostles, handing on what they themselves had received, warn the faithful to hold fast to the traditions which they have learned (cf. 2 Thess. 2:15), and to fight in defense of the faith handed on once and for all (cf. Jude 3). Now what was handed on by the apostles includes everything which contributes to the holiness of life, and the increase in faith of the people of God; and so the church, in her teaching, life, and worship, perpetuates and hands on to all generations all that she herself is, all that she believes.

This tradition which comes from the apostles develops in the church with the help of the Holy Spirit. For there is a growth in the understanding of the realities and the words which have been handed down. This happens through the contemplation and study made by believers, who treasure these things in their hearts (cf. Luke 2:19, 51), through the intimate understanding of spiritual things they experience, and through the preaching of those who have received through episcopal succession the sure gift of truth. For, as the centuries succeed one another, the church constantly moves, forward toward the fullness of divine truth until the words of God reach their complete fulfillment in her.

The words of the holy Fathers witness to the living presence of this tradition, whose wealth is poured into the practice and life of the believing and praying church. Through the same tradition the full canon of the sacred books becomes known to the church, and the sacred writings themselves are more profoundly understood and unceasingly made active in her; and thus God, who spoke of old, uninterruptedly converses with the bride of his beloved Son; and the Holy Spirit, through whom the living voice of the gospel resounds in the church, and through her, in the world, leads unto all truth those who believe and makes the word of Christ dwell abundantly in them.

Hence there exists a close connection and communication between sacred tradition and sacred Scripture. For both of them, flowing from the same divine wellspring, in a certain way merge into a unity and tend toward the same end. For sacred Scripture is the word of God inasmuch as it is consigned to writing under the inspiration of the divine Spirit. To the successors of the apostles, sacred tradition hands on in its full purity God's word, which was entrusted to the apostles by Christ the Lord and the Holy Spirit. Thus, led by the light of the Spirit of truth, these successors can in their preaching preserve this word of God faithfully, explain it, and make it more widely known. Consequently, it is not from sacred Scripture alone that the church draws her certainty about everything which has been revealed. Therefore both sacred tradition and sacred Scripture are to be accepted and venerated with the same sense of devotion and reverence.

Sacred tradition and sacred Scripture form one sacred deposit of the word of God, which is committed to the church. Holding fast to this deposit, the entire holy people united with their shepherds remain always steadfast in the teaching of the apostles, in the common life, in the breaking of the bread, and in prayers (cf. Acts 2:42, Greek text), so that in holding to, practicing, and professing the heritage of the faith, there results on the part of the bishops and faithful a remarkable common effort.

The task of authentically interpreting the word of God, whether written or handed on, has been entrusted exclusively to the living teaching office of the church, whose authority is exercised in the name of Jesus Christ. This teaching office is not above the word of God, but serves it, teaching only what has been handed on, listening to it devoutly, guarding it scrupulously, and explaining it faithfully by divine commission and with the help of the Holy Spirit; it draws from this one deposit of faith everything which it presents for belief as divinely revealed.

It is clear, therefore, that sacred tradition, sacred Scripture, and the teaching authority of the church, in accord with God's most wise design, are so linked and joined together that one cannot stand without the others, and that all together and each in its own way under the action of the one Holy Spirit contribute effectively to the salvation of souls.

13. Community Experience as a Source of Christian Ethics

JAMES TUNSTEAD BURTCHAELL

A primary wellspring of Christian ethical wisdom is the believing community's reflection on human experience and on the personal aftermath of that experience. That is the proposition I want to expound.

Moral Wisdom, Not Moral Law

I speak of wisdom, not law, because of the impediments Christians have tended to find when using "law" as their analogy for moral norms. Law requires obedience to another's stated will, under pain of estrangement and punishment. I say obedience, not just conformity, for law implies a conscious relation between lawgiver and subject: a known command, announced sanctions for disobedience, and intentional submission to the command. Now Christians have no awkwardness in understanding God as a sovereign. Both as creator and as re-creator, God is presented in the

James Tunstead Burtchaell (1934–) was professor of theology at the University of Notre Dame. His works include *Bread and Salt; Rachel Weeping; For Better, For Worse;* and *There is No More Just War: The Teaching and Trial of Don Lorenzo Milani.*

From James Tunstead Burtchaell, *The Giving and Taking of Life: Essays Ethical* (Notre Dame: University of Notre Dame Press, 1989).

Scriptures as establishing a long-hoped-for reign beyond all hopes: over the disciples of Jesus, over all humankind, and indeed over all creation. Nor is it confusing for Christians to suppose that immoral behavior incurs inexorable penalties. Jesus' teaching gains its urgency from his warning that if we do not repent and extricate ourselves from sin we shall be dead even before our obituaries appear. Right behavior is a matter of life and death.

The risky element in the analogy of law is its implication that our good or evil behavior will determine God's attitude towards us. Quite naturally (and quite contrary to the gospel) when we construe our moral performance as obedience to God's law or as violation of divine law, we infer that God will cherish and bless those who submit, and that God will take offense at those who take the law into their own hands. But Jesus who dies for those that kill him reveals a love that defies defiance, that is persistent to the point of wrathlessness, that is determined to cherish us quite beyond our ability to alienate him. He consummates our understanding of the character of his Father, the God of Abraham and Sarah, Isaac and Rebecca, and Jacob and Leah and Rachel. That God, we finally can see, has no wrath, no curse, no doom. It is not we who control God's stance towards us, for that is fixed and fast in love beyond all telling.

How, then, if there be no wrath in the God that Christians know, is the course of human behavior a matter of life and death? In our passage through this time-life, while change is possible, we must grow from selfishness into love. Our failure to do that will not bring reaction from the Lord but will leave us unredeemably incapacitated to clasp that love, to take it in, to be God's (or anyone else's) intimate. The tragedy of being fixed in selfishness is not that God will cease to love us but that we shall have stifled our capacity to enter the eternal embrace.

It is more illuminating, then, to speak of moral wisdom, which does not require obedience to another's will to avoid that person's wrath, but allows one to benefit from another's mind. This conforms to the Christian notion of Good News as revelation rather than statute; urgent invitation rather than command. When your physician pleads with you that three packs of cigarettes a day will tend to give you emphysema until you con-

tract lung cancer, no matter how peremptory her mood and voice are, she is giving you wisdom, not orders. You ignore her at your risk, but it is not she who will penalize you. Doctors tell patients about their bodies and about what favors their bodies and thus their selves. If they are right and we ignore them, what ensues is not of their doing, only of their telling.

The church is a community of moral wisdom accumulated, passed on, challenged, and revised. The primary font of that savvy is our own experience and observation. Experience, of course, does not consist in merely being there. Inspector Clouseau is always in the right spot at the right time, yet he never gets the point. He hath eyes yet seeth not. Experience consists in figuring out what is going on.

A young graduate, formerly my student, returned to campus to tell me of his work. As a precinct worker from high school days he easily found patronage work in the city assessor's office while he was earning money to go to law school. His task was to explain to the walk-in public the mysteries of property evaluation and taxation. It was with special warmth that he recounted how helpful he had been to an elderly Italian couple that week, taking more than an hour to explain to them the whys and wherefores of the recent upward assessment of their home. "They were so grateful," he beamed, "that when they were leaving the old man slipped a ten-dollar bill into my hand!" It was at this point in our visit that the sun refused to give its light and the moon turned to blood. I stormed at him for having just made his entry into the sleaze and graft of the Chicago underworld, for taking bribes and extorting the savings of the poor. How did he imagine big-time dishonesty started? I was not warning him of criminal indictments or threatening him with my anger. I was telling him what becomes of the souls of public servants on the take. Ours was a transaction of ethical wisdom.

It put me in mind of an incident when I was five years old and told my mother a lie. I distinctly recall a savage right uppercut that sent me cannonading across the room into the far wall. Our explanatory conversation is less clear in my memory, but somehow I understood that it was not her fist but my weakness I had to fear. Moral wisdom was being conveyed.

How does the community evaluate any kind of act as good or evil? By seeing what that action does to us. The gospel, for instance, cues us about wealth: wealth carries a high risk. Taking the tip, the community takes a long look at the affluent and develops an even more trenchant and shareable conviction that few of us are strong enough to survive wealth. The same with marijuana, dictatorship, red-lining, slavery, embezzlement, and child abuse. If we share or if we dispute the received ethical assessments of such activities, it is primarily because of our own moral appraisal of what they do to people: most of all, to those who engage in them. And the evidence most influential for us comes from those who have made a life out of these kinds of behavior and then looked back on it with dismay.

We begin by being told, by listening to the tradition, whether it comes to us from the gospel, the clergy, wise Uncle Harry, Miss Manners, or the *Tribune*'s resident anthropologist. They tell us what's what. But just listening is passive. As we leave childhood behind it is our need to look about us (and within us) as closely as did those whose wisdom has been passed on to us like a sourdough starter, so to speak, and to make the tradition our own. As that happens, we no longer have moral guidance by hearsay. We come to the point where we can vouch for it ourselves. That is an act of judgment, not one of mere memory and acceptance. It is moral maturity.

In our anxiety to persuade others how to live rightly we sometimes offer them motives why they should not do thus or so. Stealing violates property rights and persons' integrity; bribery violates the law; pollution violates the environment. Promiscuity will get you VD. Drunkenness will lose you your job. Or: hard study will get you into Cal Tech. Fair wages will hire you a steady workforce. Meditation will lower your pulse and skin tension. Now all of that may be true, but it is secondary. In fact, it may eclipse what is primary.

Our primary moral concern must be: How do certain courses of behavior tend to make us thrive or induce us to wither . . . personally, spiritually, in our character, our self?

The ultimate outcome of your life is your self, and it is the course and pattern of what you have done and what you have withheld that will be most of the making of you: acts coalescing into traits combining to develop your self.

Christians have a chronic handicap in understanding a graced ethical wisdom, for Christians believe they benefit from a revealed faith, a faith that includes our moral doctrine. And Christians often have crude ideas about revelation. They imagine that their faith emerges from some specially inspired persons or gatherings, say, from Moses and Paul and their like; or from Augustine and Kierkegaard and Barth and their like; or from the bishop of Rome who has no like; or from their charismatic prayer meeting which may be like nothing else you ever saw. What may underlie (and compromise) their appeals to revelation is the supposition that certain privileged persons were visited by direct inner disclosures entrusted to them to be shared with us.

Revelation better understood is neither so passive nor so exotic. Revelation, in Israel and in the church, comes as an insight into experience on the strength of the God who capacitates someone. Consider the paragons of revealing inspiration, the classical prophets of Israel and Judah. Their rivals, the prophets on the royal payroll, delivered oracles to order in some sort of induced ecstasy, oracles that were respected as divine because the prophets' normal mode of thinking and speaking had been deactivated. The classical prophets, by contrast, were not professional seers and they had no truck with all the dance and trance of prophecy-for-hire. They were persons so acutely aware of Israel's calling and of the inevitable outcome of national life as it unfolded before their muck-raking eyes, that they blurted out what was at stake: loudly, articulately, antagonizingly. It was only by hindsight that the community — the sadder but wiser girl was she — came to treasure those oracles as coming from Yahweh's true visionaries: men and women who had eyes to see. Their divine disclosures came when their powers of thinking and speaking and authorship were at full alert, not when they were shut down. It was not their process of learning but their message of prophetic insight that convinced Israel of its divine origin.[1]

1. James Tunstead Burtchaell, C.S.C., *Catholic Theories of Biblical Inspiration Since 1810: A Review and Critique* (Cambridge: Cambridge University Press, 1969), 289-294.

Revelation is graced insight into experience. Moses came by it the same way we do, only more abundantly. What we inherit under the byline of Moses is a code of law. It was not delivered, it was derived — from some especially graced leaders of the clans of Israel who had great wisdom: that knack of settling disputes and setting rules that enabled touchy families and competitive tribes to dwell beside one another in peace. What we have from Paul is not so much what came to him during his solitary meditation in the Syrian desert as it is the convictions he acquired when he was shouting in those toe-to-toe arguments with Peter over who should eat at whose house. It is the same with any great person in the church: divinely given insight emerges from graced yet energetic scrutiny of what is really going on and what is really worth, in the prospect of death and the perspective of eternity.[2]

Grooms of the Tradition

Revealed moral wisdom is uncommon insight into common events. It is cumulative, in that we are always starting from what our predecessors saw and said. It is also current, for we have never appropriated the wisdom tradition until we have tried it out ourselves to the point where we can pass it on, not as hearsay or in quotes, but as a complex of insights we vouch for in our own name. John Cassian, the Gaul who visited late fourth-century Egypt to see for himself the communities of ascetic monks in the desert there, reported that they gathered in large caves during long stretches of the night to praise God with the Psalms, led by one singer who read by a single lampflame. So often had they chanted those 150 Psalms, he observed, that they sang as if composing them extemporaneously as they went along. That is a fit image for a community of faith, which makes the wisdom it receives its very own. No matter how many scores of hundreds of forebears had a hand in shaping its contours and picking out its highlights, we learn it well and then put it to the test in our own time. Then we can utter it

2. This point is most effectively expounded in George Lindbeck, "Scripture, Consensus, and Community," *This World* 23 (fall 1988): 5-24.

as if it were our own fresh discovery. Which, by that time, it is.

It is inevitable that some elements of the wisdom handed down would give us pause, and that a few might even stick in our throats. It is inevitable, and it is good. For as grooms of a vital tradition we must reconstrue and improve on those few matters on which our particular generation may have been given further light. The tradition is not inert. But our reconsideration of it is a nervous task, for it is as likely to be astigmatism or blindness which puts us in stress with our elders in the faith as it is their backwardness and our enhanced vision. Still, we must take our misgivings out to the plaza of human experience for newly inquisitive study. If it goes well we shall either disagree more articulately with the tradition because we know better why we must revise it, or we shall appreciate the older wisdom more than ever because we did take a second look.

The authentic and sound Christian tradition would insist that ethical truth must be discerned, not decided. And that discernment, I am claiming here, is primarily an act of the believing community which remembers what happens to us in the aftermath of certain ways of living.

Pastors and Scholars

By now it must be obvious that this exposition has gone out of its way to omit any reference to a privileged role in this moral endeavor for two kinds of person who have been prominent in Christian norm-making: the officers of the church and its experts: the hierarchy (or clergy) and the scholars. They do have special services to offer, but those services have not always been carefully understood.

The task of the cleric (within any tradition), and its corresponding charism, is to preside. Whether any individual officeholder in the church actually possesses the requisite charism or empowerment, the duty of office is to preside, to convene the community, to call it to listen to the gospel, to provoke it to respond, to orchestrate its care and service, to cultivate its peace. To preside is not always to lead. Actually, few of those ordained to preside seem to have been chosen for their manifest graces of leadership. They are rarely learned in the faith, rarely the ones whose imagination is strongest in keeping the community on the *qui vive,* or the ones whose courage and candor help others to see through the legerdemain of current fashion. But if those and the other essential gifts are at the community's disposition in other members, the one who presides can call on them for the common benefit.

In this matter of moral discernment most church officers will not be so possessed of the prophetic spirit that their insights will revitalize the tradition. But those who preside will commonly have to review or summarize or recite the tradition. That is an important task, and there are more articulate ways and less articulate ways of doing it. When it goes wrong it is often because the presiding official fancies himself, not to be enunciating what the community and its predecessors have worked to elaborate, but to be in the position of giving orders which others should obey. This, of course, is the authority of the scribes. It is exactly the same as when a pastor of a church treats the congregational bank account as his own money.

As one who presides, the cleric enjoys no *ex officio* insight save possibly a presidential concern lest any sector of the community not find its voice or be squelched. But since, in the Christian tradition, the officers who preside are also charged with pastoral care, this other role can and should advantage the cleric with a privileged exposure to the consciences and experiences of the community. It is especially providential that by ancient tradition the presbyter who is deputed to preside at the eucharist and expound the gospel is also entrusted with the initiatives of forgiveness. The one who calls the community into the fire of the Lord's summons is the same one who must look each one lovingly in the eye when he fails that call. Thus the gospel is more realistically preached and forgiveness less sentimentally transacted for their both having the same minister. A cleric who is energetically and effectively active in pastoral ministry has an extraordinary opportunity to elicit and study and witness to prophetic insight in the church. But one who presides without that experience is quite disadvantaged, and must have it all on hearsay. In fact, pastoral involvement is so essential to effective presidency in the church that one who holds office without it may do much mischief without being aware.

This interpretation is allied to that expounded by Newman's essay, "On Consulting the Faithful in Matters of Doctrine." Though he construes faith as tenacity in holding what has descended from the apostles more than as inquiry into what those ancient insights might mean further and later, Newman argues that in a season of most urgent crisis, that of the Arian controversy, it was not the bishops but the laity who by instinct and stubbornness held fast to the orthodox faith.[3]

The other special role in moral inquiry belongs to the scholar. A tradition that is historical, scrutiny of human behavior that is systematic, and constructive reflection that is principled are all activities that scholars should be able to assist with skill and method. In Christian moral inquiry scholars are essential. They could, I suppose, be considered the sheep dogs of the flock, running from side to side and barking and biting. Yet everything the theological scholar does is derivative, for the communal inquiry cannot be monopolized out of the hands of the church. In the end it will probably be the scholar that writes it all up. But it is always "as told to" him or her. The scholar is the ghost writer of faith, not its hero.

The moral inquiry of the church is crucially assisted by these two ministries, so that it can move from learning to expounding, from description to prescription, from what they see happens to people who behave in certain ways to conclusions about how we must all live in order to live well.

Recognizing Saints

Now I would like to illustrate this by some examples. The first is the largest, for it entails the most tested ethical wisdom in the long centuries of Christian experience. It begins in the apostolic age itself and is still incomplete: it is the designation and veneration of saints.[4]

3. John Henry Newman, *On Consulting the Faithful in Matters of Doctrine*, ed. John Coulson (London: Collins, 1961 [first published 1859]), 75-76.

4. For what follows, see Peter Brown, *The Cult of the Saints: Its Rise and Function in Latin Christianity* (Chicago: University of Chicago Press, 1981); Hippolyte Delehaye [S.J.], *Sanctus: Essai sur le culte des saints dans l'antiquité* (Brussels: Société des Bollandistes, 1927);

There is an inveterate question that has occupied some theologians and canonists ever since the Roman See reserved to itself the prerogative of canonization: Is a solemn declaration of sainthood an infallible act, guaranteed free from error? By and large canonists have said no and theologians have said yes.[5] Those who have held for infallibility have argued that too much is at stake in the church for God to allow the pope to err in such a decree. Their concern, typically, has been that papal teaching would be worthless were it fallible. No one seems to have noted the much more significant matter at stake: that the identification of a specific person as a saint is perhaps the most fundamental moral statement that the church has occasion to make. It is the validity of the statement, more than the reputation of the one who utters it, that counts most here.

What I should like to propose is that the designation of saints is not merely a specific application of all that the Christian community knows about good and evil; it is a major source for our ethical doctrine. It is popularly believed ("popularly" means that this is a misunderstanding of the learned to which the unlearned seem more immune) that we hold and study a body of knowledge about good and evil human behavior which we then apply to individuals. It is more radically true to say that we derive any reliable general notions about ethical value from our exposure (either personally or through stories) to very virtuous and very sinful people, and to no one more significantly than to the saints. We come to know about sanctity by meeting saints.

*   *   *

Even under modern church legislation which governs both canonization and cult, it is important to realize that the driving force in the entire veneration of saints is essentially popular. It is the familiars of a deceased person who have been struck by his or her single-minded generosity, that have petitioned for a consideration of his or her life and charismatic evidences. It is the laity who, in the absence of recognized categories, press for acknowledgment of any new sort of saint. It is the reflective and assertive experience of the apprecative lay witnesses which is the driving force in the entire process.

No matter who is exercising jurisdiction — a local bishop, a synod, a regional council, a pope or his curia or a general council — the role of presidency is less to initiate than to preside: to discipline, to challenge, to look for conflicts of interest or superstition or inconsistency. It is a superficial and incomplete observation that the cult of the saints has been enlarged in its perspective at the same time it has been taken over by the clergy from the laity. It is certainly the case that procedure has evolved. As Kemp puts it, "Canonization in the age of the martyrs was a spontaneous act of the local community."[6] No one imagines that this is true today. Yet the basic ecclesiastical act of recognizing signal holiness and distinguishing it from sham and mediocrity remains within the popular grasp. Scholars and pastors may through their keen questioning induce the community to scrutinize more closely, for that is the proper relationship of scholars and pastoral officers to the community. But the prophetic insight that discerns heroic sanctity belongs the membership as much as to the officers or scholars.

*   *   *

People may mistakenly suppose that the church has an analytic checklist of the qualifications required for sanctity, against which it examines the recorded lives of the candidates: certain virtues, a rigorous consistency of character, the potency of miracles, and the like. In actuality, our process has been the reverse of that. We have beheld saints. We have seen them with our eyes and touched

---

idem, *Les origines du culte des martyrs,* 2nd ed. (Brussels: Société des Bollandistes, 1933); idem, *Les passions des martyrs et les genres littéraires,* 2nd ed. (Brussels: Société des Bollandistes, 1966); Ludwig Hertling, S.J., "Materiali per la storia del processo di Canonizzazione," *Gregorianum* 16 (1935): 170-195; Eric Waldram Kemp, *Canonization and Authority in the Western Church* (London: Oxford University Press [Geoffrey Cumberledge], 1948); André Vauchez, *La sainteté en occident aux derniers siècles du moyen age d'après les procès de canonisation et les documents hagiographiques* (Rome: École Française de Rome, 1981).

5. Kemp, 151-170.

6. Kemp, 7.

them with our hands and heard them with our ears and been awestruck at their luminous likeness to Jesus. Only after beholding them did we begin to reflect what we saw and recognized. That reflection led eventually to the criteria which later authorities could use to verify sanctity in others who come along. But if you have seen a saint, and are believer yourself, you should know her for a saint. It may take you some time and some care to portray her adequately. But your knowledge of what a saint is comes from your exposure to that person and to her intense dedication, not to theological treatises or sociological surveys. And this manifests what I have been trying to illustrate: that sanctity is in the eye of the beholder, and the primary beholder is the believing community.

Now let me offer two other illustrations of how moral wisdom is enacted and managed in the Christian tradition. The first is the controversy one century ago about the legitimacy of belonging to the Knights of Labor. The second is much more recent: the dispute over the moral acceptability of contraception.

The Knights of Labor Dispute

To assess the conflict regarding the Knights of Labor in North America one must first be knowledgeable about the odium visited upon secret societies by the Roman See.

The origins of Freemasonry are usually dated back to 1717, but that era begat numerous fraternal organizations offering alternative allegiance to aristocrats, professionals, and bourgeois who were disaffected towards the increasingly activist exercise of authority by both national sovereigns and the established churches. Those who looked for a religion more amenable to rational discourse without priestcraft and dogma found these new societies refreshing, as did those who aspired to more popular forms of government with or without monarchy. Often it was the same men whose thoughts ran to both those restive hopes and looked for comrades with whom to ventilate their ideas more freely, beyond the ears of civil or ecclesiastical orthodoxy. As sometimes happens, the fraternities were organized into more levels of rank and honor than any sovereign's court, and created a pastiche of borrowed mystical lore and costume and ritual more exotic than anything to be seen in church.

The Freemasons found soaring success in both northern and southern Europe. By 1735 they were being outlawed in Holland; two years later Louis XIV forbade them in France; and in 1738 Pope Clement XII issued the first, fierce papal condemnation.[7]

Clement itemized four reasons why Freemasonry was a threat to both church and state. First, their mixed composition put Catholics indiscrimininately into fellowship with members of many religious affiliations (all heretical). Second, the Deism which pervaded the organization refused to countenance divine revelation, church authority, or even divine intiatives towards humankind; its adherents saw no need for dogmatic belief so long as a sound morality was fostered. Third, members bound themselves by a solemn oath which created an allegiance so strong it overrode prior obligations to princes and prelates. Lastly, the aims and doings of the Masons were surrounded by a palisade of sworn secrecy. Catholics were forbidden on pain of excommunication either to join or to associate with the Freemasons, and Catholic rulers were instructed to suppress the organization with the rigor appropriate to a virulent heresy.

*   *   *

What had begun, however, as the condemnation of one specific society eventually targeted a *kind* of institution.[8] As the grievance becomes more generic, opposing first an institution and later a movement, it is typical that among the various elements or traits of the offending entity, one or two would emerge as definitory. Specific condemnations need reasons; but generic condemnations need definitions as well. This inevitably affects

7. Clement XII, Apostolic Constitution *In Eminenti*, 28 April 1738; *Bullarum Diplomatum et Privilegiorum Sanctorum Romanorum Pontificum Taurinensis Editio*, ed. A. Tomassetti 24 (Turin: Vecco, 1872): 366-367.

8. This can be seen in the document which, in a way, brought to a close this series of documents: the 1918 *Code of Canon Law*. Canon 2335 prescribes: "Those who enroll in a Masonic sect or in other associations of the same sort which conspire against the church or lawful civil authorities incur *ipso facto* an excommunication reserved simply to the Apostolic See."

both the rhetoric and the vocabulary of the moral doctrine. In this case it was the oath and the secrecy that became highlighted as essential.

This identification of telltale signs of evil is all the more needful because later popes were insisting that the subversive sects were so cunning that the average Catholic would tend to be deceived when confronted by their publicity. The two elements that adequately betray sinister character and intent became the oath (which commits a member to unquestioning obedience) and the secrecy (which insulates that obedience from supervision by any lawful authority). Thus the long and articulate condemnation becomes known as "the church's outlawing of secret societies." If they are covert, you know enough to be sure they are godless and subversive.

It is significant that in its origins the moral assessment of these fraternal organizations spread its findings on the page: the reader was asked to take note of the data which give rise to the papal judgment. But at a certain point that changed. The popes instructed the faithful that they were no longer to try to join in the assessment; they needed only to obey. For the movement had proven too cunning and deceptive for the public to be able to judge it capably. It was precisely at this point (Leo XII in 1825) that the tradition was transformed. Until then the character and purposes and drift of the brotherhoods were presented alongside the account of their tactics. Thereafter the evidence was separated from the conclusion. The faithful were no longer enjoined to observe how these indicators embodied those pursuits. It would now be enough to verify that the indicators (the oath and secrecy) were present for a Catholic to reject an organization as seditious and diabolic.

This was the traditional message of official Catholic moral doctrine in 1884, the year of Leo XIII's encyclical, *Arcanum*. It was an eventful year for fraternal societies in North America. The senior Catholic churchman in Canada [Archbishop Taschereau] was waiting for Rome to issue the judgment he had requested on the Knights of Labor. The Knights of Labor had an oath of membership and a sworn obligation to secrecy. They thus encountered a *prima facie* suspicion of being an organization forbidden to Catholics. That same year all the Catholic bishops in the United States assembled in the Third Plenary Council of Bal-

timore and decided not to condemn the Knights of Labor.[9] [Archbishop Gibbons]

* * *

Rome at first ruled (in 1884, responding to Taschereau's inquiry) that membership was forbidden and later, after [Archbishop]Gibbons' presentation of a strong majority stance by the U.S. bishops, receded to the point of decreeing that membership in the Knights could be tolerated, provided the Order amended its constitutional documents somewhat.[10]

That the Knights never did revise their documents to suit the Vatican, but for other reasons entered thereafter into a swift decline, is incidental to our interest. The episode was significant for two reasons that quite transcended the fortunes of that fraternal union. The position defended by Gibbons and his allies put the United States hierarchy aggressively on record in behalf of the right and need of workers to act collectively in their own

9. For what follows, see Henry J. Browne, *The Catholic Church and the Knights of Labor* (Washington, DC: Catholic University of America Press, 1949); John Tracy Ellis, *The Life of James Cardinal Gibbons, Archbishop of Baltimore 1834-1921*, 1 (Milwaukee: Bruce, 1952): 439-546; Marvin O'Connell, *John Ireland and the American Catholic Church* (St. Paul: Minnesota Historical Society, 1988), 229-239; Fergus Macdonald, C.P., *The Catholic Church and the Secret Societies in the United States*, ed. Thomas J. McMahon, (New York: U.S. Catholic Historical Society, 1946).

10. The ruling read, in part: "In view of the latest statement of the case, the Society of the Knights of Labor may be allowed for the time being, provided whatever in its statutes is improperly expressed or susceptible of wrong interpretation shall be corrected. Especially in the preamble of the constitutions for local assemblies words which seem to savor of socialism and communism must be emended in such a way as to make clear that the soil was granted by God to man, or rather the human race, that each might have the right to acquire some portion of it, by use however of lawful means and without violation of the right of private property." Browne, 324.

Gibbons was meticulous in restricting his advocacy to the Knights in the United States; he specifically disclaimed any desire to interfere with the Canadian church and its discipline. This was his adroit way of rebuking Taschereau for having published his ruling from Rome as one that should apply below the border as well.

interests. Although Rome gave them scant satisfaction in their specific effort, their advocacy was to be a major influence on the perspective of Leo XIII, whose previous encyclicals (somewhat like those of his predecessor) in defense of the lawful social order were to be followed by *Rerum novarum* (1891) which pleaded eloquently that no social order could be tolerable unless workers had standing and institutionalized power to secure their own rightful welfare.

The second outcome of the Knights of Labor conflict has received no mention in studies of the controversy, but it has relevance to our inquiry into the way the church elaborates its moral wisdom. The conflict was an instance of a moral judgment that had originated in community experience, then had been codified for transmission the tradition in a way that eventually severed it from its original insight, and finally encountered challenge by observant churchmen who could not square it with their moral estimate.

The two groups of bishops differed, of course, in their moral judgments, but more interesting than their respective conclusions on the merits of the case were their very different modes of proceeding.

The critics of the Knights began with the conviction that their people needed a decision from them, and must not be left without pastoral direction. Elzéar-Alexandre Taschereau, years before he was aware of a single member of the Knights of Labor in his archdiocese of Quebec, prevailed upon Rome for a ruling which he forthwith published. The record abounds in Irish pastors burdened by the obligation to decide whether to permit their parishioners to become members. Gibbons, by contrast, sought to slow down the rush to judgment by what he called a "masterly inactivity."[11] His party did not want to decide whether laypeople could or could not enroll. Also, while the critics thought such an issue ought be decided by the Holy See, the advocates preferred to have it resolved at home by those directly involved. There was this wide gulf between their estimates of how determinative their pastoral office should be.

There is further significance in the evidence on which the two parties grounded their arguments. The critics went by the book. Taschereau submitted the current constitutions of the Order

(actually they were already outdated) as his only exhibit. To assess that booklet against the various papal statements would have to be an act of documentary analysis, a legal judgment.

Gibbons' *plaidoyer* was quite different. Yes, it was a fact that Catholics were in fellowship with Protestants in the Order. The actual result, however, was not religious indifference but a helpful influence by the Catholics on the Protestant minority. Yes, it was a fact that there were rituals that smacked of Masonic hokum. In practice, though, they were not the carriers of Deism or any other religion. They were simply quaint solemnities no one would ever confuse with what he did in church. Yes, there was an oath and a commitment to secrecy. But the oath had been changed to a promise in order to allay ecclesiastical misgivings, and Knights were permitted to breach their secrecy in the privacy of the confessional. Knowledge of the people, Gibbons argued, must govern interpretation of the facts: it showed that the oath and promise were, in the case of the Knights, no evidence of impiety or sedition. The Order required solidarity and confidentiality, not to put it beyond the reach of church or state, but as a protective measure against reprisals by employers. Yes, they sometimes resorted to the strike and the closed shop and the boycott, but as countervailing measures against punitive dismissal, the lockout, and unfair wages. They were not to be condemned by a different standard than had been imposed on ownership and management. Gibbons offered a personal appraisal of the religious sincerity and practice of Powderly and other union leaders as evidence of the character of the organization itself. Yes, the Order was not a Catholic association run by the church, but Gibbons stated sternly that that was just as well:

> I sincerely admire the efforts of this sort which are made in countries where the workers are led astray by the enemies of religion; but thanks be to God, that is not our condition. We find that in our country the presence and explicit influence of the clergy would not be advisable where our citizens, without distinction of religious belief, come together in regard of their industrial interests alone.[12]

11. Ibid., 165.

12. Ibid., 370. This document, Gibbons' formal

In brief, one group of bishops was using naked documentary evidence to show that the papal excommunication devised against Freemasonry applied to the Knights of Labor. The other group appealed to its immediate, pastoral acquaintance with the workers and their leaders as the appropriate pivot of interpretation on which any moral appraisal of their organization should turn. Archbishop Riordan of San Francisco said it plainly: "The majority are honest men who apart from this association know no other means of attaining their rights."[13] The advocates of the Knights were nineteenthcentury prelates, and were surely disposed to reverence a tradition of papal teaching. They were emboldened to confront that tradition because what they knew of these people obligated them to reexamine the received wisdom of the past. The men they saw did not qualify for the odium of popes.

*   *   *

A ruling passively accepted from tradition and legally applied without making active moral appraisals in the present is bound to go wrong. In a word, Gibbons' argument provoked his contemporaries to honor the tradition of moral judgment by becoming its active trustees and by engaging in the same kind of experiential appraisal when applying a point of moral wisdom that had led its originators to formulate it in the first place. It is as strenuous and discriminating a task to apply moral wisdom from the past as it is to enact it for the future.

Clement XII and his successors perceived the church threatened by an upbeat Freemasonry with a power struggle for the primary loyalties of the more willful classes in the Old and New Worlds. James Gibbons and those pastors who supported him were stating on their own say-so — that is, they were vouching for what they had witnessed — that despite *prima facie* appearances, this was not at stake in the Knights of Labor.

The Birth Control Controversy

Our [third illustration is a story that] is not yet complete. The lessons it yields for our purposes arise from the history of a relatively small papal advisory group that met from 1963 to 1966. The issue contemplated was the morality of contraception.

The birth control commission, as it was commonly known, had the attendance and advice of John Noonan just as he was publishing his great historical study, *Contraception*.[14] The commission's own chapter in that ongoing serial which has as yet no finale is capably told by Robert Kaiser, one of the two or three most effective journalists at Vatican II. His account, *The Politics of Sex and Religion*,[15] is the other documentary source for our inquiry.

Let Noonan's masterful (one should say magisterial) reconstruction suffer here a summary. The earliest Christians had few developed convictions about sex. The esteem for fecundity inherited from Israel had been doubly moderated by the Old Testament's wariness of some features of sex (e.g., incest, adultery, homosexuality, bestiality) and the New Testament's innovative appreciation for widowhood and virginity. The rabbinical prohibitions of certain sexual practices (such as intercourse during menstruation, or withdrawal), though without counterpart in Christian moral lore of the early years, may reflect a tradition not entirely dormant in the synagogue's cousin, the church.

That community was goaded to elaborate its own sexual ethic, however, by two attitudes it found repulsive: Roman society's indifference to promiscuity and to the unborn, and Gnosticism's distaste for procreation. Gnosticism, an elusive amalgam of austerity and licentiousness, was anti-marriage, anti-fertility, and anti-law. In their reaction the Christian intellectuals of the second century drew on the slender resources of Scripture,

---

memorandum to the Holy See, is also available in *Documents of American Catholic History*, ed. John Tracy Ellis, 2 (Wilmington: Glazier, 1987): 444-457.

13. Browne, 212.

14. John T. Noonan, Jr., *Contraception: A History of Its Treatment by the Catholic Theologians and Canonists* (Cambridge, Mass.: Harvard University Press, 1965). An enlarged edition, adding an essay written in 1980, has been issued in 1986 by the same press.

15. Robert Blair Kaiser, *The Politics of Sex and Religion: A Case History in the Development of Doctrine, 1962-1984* (Kansas City, Mo.: Leaven, 1985).

but found readier help in the Stoic teaching that marriage was for procreation. The Stoics' premium on rationality had obliged them to resolve how an act as passionate as sexual intercourse could be licit. Their answer was that procreation was what made sex good. Christians came to adopt that view, and to frown therefore on intercourse disabled by infertility (during pregnancy or after menopause or through contraception). Their fierce opposition to abortion, at a time when biological competence could not distinguish accurately between it and contraception, was an added reason for them to disallow the latter. Thus it was that explicit repudiations of contraception first emerged in the Christian literature of the third century.

Two centuries later that doctrine was called up to oppose the anti-sexual teachings of the Manichees. The borrowed Stoic rule found new eloquence in the polemics of Augustine. Against an anti-procreational ethic he found both sex and procreation good — by being utterly identified with each other. And among the three benefits of marriage — offspring (proles), fidelity (fides), and indissolubility (sacramentum) — it was the first he usually designated as fundamental.

It was Augustine's awesome usage of the Stoic doctrine that the only purpose of conjugal intercourse was procreation which gave it authority for ages to follow. Noonan observes that the teaching had little occasion to draw on personal and pastoral experience, with the obvious exception of Augustine's eleven-year liaison with his mistress, an experience he never regarded as one of unselfish love on his part. Augustine's doctrine failed to incorporate major themes of the faith. Neither love nor friendship nor affection, for instance, was related to sexuality. Had Chrysostom, who taught that it was love which validated sex, become the classical authority instead, or even been remembered as a valuable supplement to an incomplete presentation, the Christian moral teaching might have developed differently.

For centuries this doctrine was handed on by the monks, who were both the pastors and the scholars of Christian Europe. They evinced little appreciation for marriage and much distrust of sex. The tradition made its way thither into the penitentials and thence into the codifications of canon law, acquiring along the way an apparatus

of penalties for every manner of sexual misbehavior intended to avoid pregnancy.

The threat of the Cathars (or Albigensians), who in the twelfth century revived the old repugnance to marriage and sex, put the traditional Catholic doctrine in bold face. Procreation was good: so good that it made sex good and even mitigated the sinfulness of the attendant enjoyment and pleasure (for which the still-Stoicized tradition could find no other apology). It seems amazing that a church so persistently in favor of sex should have been so ill at ease with its carnal joy.

A change set in. The schoolmen of the High Middle Ages began to pursue insights at odds with the Augustinian synthesis. Albert the Great put forth a little-noticed suggestion that intercourse to reinforce the bond of marriage might be licit without reference to fecundity. Something other than procreation was being proposed as validating sex. His pupil Aquinas caused a bigger stir when he defended Aristotle's dictum that delight which proceeds from any act shares the moral value of the act itself. The new sympathy to sexual pleasure found a following among other scholars like Bonaventure.

> All of this rearrangement of values into a synthesis permitting or favoring contraception was possible. . . . The doctrine on sexuality, as it stood, was a balance — not the logical projection of a single value, but a balance of a whole set of competing values. The balance was weighted at a particular point which excluded contraception. If it held where it did at the height of the Middle Ages, the influence of St. Augustine, the reaction to the Cathars, and the mating habits of the age were together responsible. It was not inevitable that the balance remain so. In what follows we shall see a gradual shift.[16]

Denis the Carthusian in the fifteenth century wrote *The Praiseworthy Life of the Married*, with positive regard for sexual enjoyment. Noonan introduces us to a remarkable contemporary, Martin Le Maistre, who bolted radically from the Augustinian doctrine. Virtue being moderation, he says, conjugal chastity must pursue a middle course between incontinence and insensi-

16. Noonan, 300.

bility. It is quite right to relish pleasure, provided it does not obliterate other considerations. The older doctrine, he grieves, had done harm. Though Martin made no disciples, his was "a sweeping legitimation of the nonprocreational purposes of marriage." Noonan sees here a shift in method:

> The key is the experience of Christian couples. When Augustine found in his acquaintance not a single couple who had intercourse only for procreation, he was not in the least deterred from stamping all nonprocreative purpose as sinful. In the different Christian community of fifteenth-century France — much more established in its traditions than that of fifth-century North Africa, and innocent of advocates of Manicheanism — a different approach is valued. On another subject of much importance to the laity, usury, Christian moralists were beginning to look to the custom and practice of good Christian merchants in determining whether a particular contract was sinful. Similarly Le Maistre . . . invoke[s] the experience of Christian married folk to determine workable rules for intercourse, and urge[s] the perils of negative reaction that an unrealistic harshness may engender.[17]

Eventually the new view became established. The old pessimism inherited from Augustine waned even more among Catholics because of the favor he enjoyed among the Reformers. The Augustinian revival among the Jansenists only fortified the new theory among the Catholics, which found an authoritative new synthesis in the work of Alphonsus Liguori, the experienced pastor who made it settled doctrine that the purposes of marriage were the purposes of marital intercourse. Writers began to relate sex to pleasure, to health, even to love.[18]

The thinkers who were freeing marital intercourse from its single-purpose destiny, however, were still continuing to hand on intact the ancient ban on contraception.

17. Ibid., 312.
18. In noticing how absent pastoral experience was from this tradition, Noonan remarks that any serious attention to the experience of married couples would have uprooted the entire Augustinian outlook, ibid., 24.

At the close of the seventeenth century the Holy See began to criticize and sometimes to condemn some of the innovations, but speculation continued. It was in that century that authors for the first time opined that economic need might justify denying the marital debt to one's spouse in order to avoid pregnancy.

The seventeenth and eighteenth centuries were notable, not for any further development of doctrine but for the increasing frequency with which confessors were advised they need not interrogate or disturb penitents whom they supposed were using contraception. This was, at the least, a policy of pastoral diffidence.

The last episode in Noonan's narrative, one as decisive as Augustine or Aquinas or Liguori, was inaugurated by the nineteenth century birth control movement, the abrupt population increase due to public health improvements, and the advances in contraceptive technology. Catholic clergy went out to meet this "godless materialism" as belligerently as they had campaigned against the Gnostics, Manichees, and Cathars. This eventually culminated in *Casti Connubii,* the encyclical letter of Pius XI in 1930. The document was faithful to the primitive sexual doctrine but not to its historical development. All the themes were there: the Hebrew favor for procreation, the anti-Gnostic teaching, Augustine's marital goods with offspring still in first place, Thomas on the biologically determined nature of intercourse, and Onan as the founder and namesake of birth control.

The rigor of *Casti Connubii* was attenuated twenty years later when Pius XII countenanced rhythm for medical, eugenic, economic, or social motives. It was the development of chemical anovulants in the 1960s that was destined to push Rome beyond its theological supply lines.

When bishops throughout the world were submitting their requests for agenda items to be considered at Vatican II, not a single one asked for the birth control ban to be reconsidered. This may have been an indicator, however, not of low interest but of low expectation. For it was during the conciliar years that bishops, theologians, pastors, and articulate laypeople displayed impatient and restive dissatisfaction with the papal teaching.

Those voices were heard in St. Peter's basilica, and the bishops there drafted an astonishingly permissive enactment. Pope Paul VI succeeded in having the document docked on the strength of his commitment to a thorough study by an expert commission. Before considering what transpired within that group let us give ear once more to John Noonan, whose narrative leaves off just at that point.

> The lay voice on marriage was never entirely lost after the fifteenth century, when it played a part in framing the new doctrine on the purposes of marital intercourse. It was not much listened to. When Bishop Bouvier [in the early nineteenth century] cited the belief of younger couples of Le Mans that contraception was not a sin, the testimony of the laity never rose to the dignity of an argument that contraception was lawful, but was used to support the plea that their good faith not be unsettled. The laity spoke, but their testimony was individual, oral, unsystematic, and not expressed in theological categories. To most theologians it failed to be persuasive or even relevant.[19]

John XXIII had quietly appointed an advisory group shortly before he died. Called eventually the Commission for the Study of Population, Family, and Birth, it was put to use by Paul VI and met for five sessions between October 1963 and June 1966. Paul added members at every gathering. The charter group of six European social scientists grew to an international crowd of seventy-one: demographers, psychologists and sociologists, physicians, moral and systematic theologians, diocesan bishops, officials of the curia, and three married couples.[20]

When the commission met first in 1963, no Catholic prelate or theologian or lay leader anywhere in the world had yet stated publicly that contraception judiciously used was morally acceptable. That was true of these people as well. Yet when they submitted their report to Paul VI less than three years later they had, by a substantial and vigorous majority, determined that contraception was not intrinsically illicit, that the position taken by *Casti Connubii* should be rescinded,

that birth control could be integrated with the most abiding Christian values of marriage and childbearing, and that the misdirection of official Catholic teaching on this subject should swiftly be corrected. How then was it that so varied and responsible a task force underwent so unforeseen and drastic a change?

First, one must note that they claimed for their deliberations a free and frank exchange. In early sessions members assumed their participation would be limited by the discreet deference due to any explicit papal policy. Soon they resolved that they must send up their own best convictions as advice and no longer calculate how the pope was going to receive it. From that day the commissioners not only spoke their minds, they found their minds. In the very liberty of debate they came to clarify and affirm convictions long held subliminally but never openly known or shared.

Second, each category of member functioned in its characteristic way. There were no mere layfolk present. Even the three married couples were each centrally involved in large marriage-related enterprises. Pat and Patty Crowley from Chicago, for instance, were founders and leading couple of the international Christian Family Movement, the first organization in the Catholic Action movement in which spouses belonged and functioned as couples. These three couples came less for witness to their own marital experience than as persons with intense and confidential exposure to many Catholic households. All the other professionals (mostly lay but some clerical) thought and spoke as persons giving access to vast human experience and opinion.

It is noteworthy that this mostly lay group was not the source of initiative in the commission. That came from the theologians. It was the theologians more than either the secular professionals or the bishops who were familiar with the history and official pronouncements of the past. It was these scholars of the tradition who questioned its inadequacies, rearticulated the question as it lurched forward, and at the end produced a position paper that could speak for the group. The theologians were, so to speak, the engineers of the commission's work.

But once prompted, the lay professionals gave the project most of its impetus. Pierre van Rossum, a Belgian physician from the original membership of six, was quick to criticize the clerical

---

19. Ibid., 489.

20. Only a select number of the full commission was convoked for the decisive final session, however, so that the final statement was actually considered by a cohort comprising less than half the membership.

bias of the magisterium. " 'You think of sex as something you must avoid in order to be faithful to your vocation. That's all right for you. But our vocation is to love one another.' They all knew what he meant by 'love.' "[21]

Albert Görres, a psychologist from Frankfurt, spoke more bitingly of a "celibate psychosis" that had rendered some moral theologians emotionally handicapped by unconscious reactions of resentment, envy, and aggression.[22] The Crowleys brought in two surveys they had conducted of their CFM membership: activist, devout, and procreative couples (average children per family: six). The evidence showed that most had tried rhythm valiantly but found it stunted their marital intimacy. About half had moved on to using the pill, which they did with no sense of wrongdoing.[23]

Washington psychiatrist John Cavanagh then displayed an extensive survey of his own in which 71 percent of the women responding (2,300 users of rhythm) asserted that their sexual desire was greatest precisely at the time of ovulation. Rhythm, he observed, is more psychologically harmful than other methods because it deprives a woman of the sexual embrace during the time of her greatest natural desire. "Abstinence as the only means of controlling conception has left Catholics immature emotionally and impoverished financially . . . . Serious psychiatric disorders have arisen as a result."[24] Demographers pointed out that abortion tended to be most used where contraception was least accessible.[25] One entire meeting was given to frank and moving testimony by women on the commission about how integral and effective sexual intercourse was as a nourishment of their marital affection.[26] The psychologists deplored what they perceived as a dualist view of sex as an animal act to be controlled by the spirit[27] Had the Manichees emerged victorious after all? The lay evidence was especially sharp in accusing the church officials of combining an irrationally rigorous public standard with a private pastoral indulgence that kept couples on an infantile level. Lay believers were not asking for a permissive or lenient norm, only a valid one.[28]

It took this dam-burst of lay testimony to persuade the theologians that the conscientious, experienced convictions of the faithful are evidence of high authority in moral inquiry, and especially on the subject of marriage.[29]

The participation of the hierarchy in the commission was also characteristic. They proved not to be cogent defenders of the official teaching; few of them knew much of the history or the theology. But once exposed to the momentum of the lay participants (which was well underway by the time the bishops were added for the final session), and put at their ease by the finding of the theologians that the papal policy was modifiable, the cardinals and bishops reverted from prelates to pastors. Shehan of Baltimore, Döpfner of Munich, Dupuy of Albi, Zoa of the Cameroun, Dearden of Detroit, Reuss of Mainz, Suenens of Malines — they testified to their experience in the confessional, their canvass of parish priests, what they had learned from couples, and how that had led them to suspect the pope had somehow got it wrong, though they had never before said it to themselves in so many words. By contrast, the few prelates who held back from the gathering consensus were either in the pontifical establishment or dismayed at the prospect of approving a practice for which they had so willingly consigned offenders to hell in the past.[30]

It was not the bishops, in fact, who had the most stressful change to undergo. It was the theologians. At their first meeting (the commission's second) there was no convergence. At the next they rejected contraception: nine to five. At the fourth session they looked over the brink and then drew back. It was only at the extensive final session that, by a decisive majority, the theologians at last saw their way clear to accepting contraception as licit and responsible.

What made their journey so toilsome was that, while the lay experience of the present commanded immediate respect and the pastoral assessment of the lay testimony rather swiftly ratified those lay

---

21. Kaiser, 45.
22. Ibid., 139.
23. Ibid., 92-95, 135-136.
24. Ibid., 136-137.
25. Ibid., 150-151.
26. Ibid., 140-142.
27. Ibid., 151.

28. Ibid., 142-143.
29. Ibid., 57, 137, 142, 158.
30. Ibid., 164-174.

insights, for the scholars those experiences and appraisals of the present were insufficient. The scholarly calling was to submit that evidence to a twofold test. They had to see whether it was both coherent and inclusive: whether it honored all the major faith-insights about marriage, fidelity, and childbearing and did so without inner contradiction. And they had to verify that this conviction in the present was in communion with those haunting and prophetic insights of the past, which had marked the road of doctrinal development.

One might have expected the hierarchy to be slowest and most reluctant to accept a reversal of doctrine, but it was not so. Once freed from fear of reprisal for free thought and free speech (Vatican II had initiated this emancipation), their pastoral orientation made them quickly and honestly ready to reconsider.[31] Cardinal Heenan said it was the seeming abruptness of the theologians' reversal that made him hesitate.[32] But Heenan misper-

ceived. The bishops who joined the new consensus did so through the course of one month at the last session; the theologians had needed three years to cover the same distance. The theologians had rightly heeded the lay testimony and that of the pastors. Those who lead valiant lives of service under the gospel are presumed to know what they are talking about, and the good shepherd must heed their voices. But the scholar must then apply critical and historical analysis. What unnerved Heenan was being present only at the finale when the scholars finally saw it all fall into place.

Together the commissioners gave their advice to the pope:

> The morality of sexual acts between married people takes its meaning first of all and specifically from the ordering of their actions in a fruitful married life: that is, one which is practised with responsible, generous, and prudent parenthood. It does not then depend upon the direct fecundity of each and every particular act. Moreover, the morality of every marital act depends upon the requirements of mutual love in all its aspects. . . .

> More and more clearly, for a conscience correctly formed, a willingness to raise a family with full acceptance of the various human and Christian responsibilities is altogether distinguished from a mentality and a way of married life which in its totality is egotistically and irrationally opposed to fruitfulness.[33]

The Community and Its Servants

These have been three quite different stories: the recognition of sanctity, the vindication of independent working people keeping their own counsel, and the struggle to reconstrue conjugal sexuality. All three illustrate in helpfully distinct ways how moral wisdom emerges from the church's primal moral experience: assessing what becomes of

---

31. This is not to say they did not need help. Kaiser records this sharp encounter, ibid., 167-168:

[Cardinal] Heenan had already mentioned the Pope's fear: that a change in the church's teaching might damage the church's credibility. How, Heenan had asked, could the church change its stand and avoid losing its moral influence. Or, if the church did not change, how could it preserve its authority over couples? Now [Thomas Burch, a population expert from Georgetown University] stood up and called Heenan's stand "hypocrisy." Almost 20 years later, Burch told . . . about his feelings at the time. "I think my very strong reaction was, 'What the heck's going on here? You guys are saying that you might have been wrong for nigh on thirty to forty years on some details about methods; you've caused millions of people untold agony and unwanted children; brought on stresses and strains and tremendous feelings of guilt. You've told people they were going to hell because they wouldn't stop using condoms, and now you're saying maybe you're wrong. But you want to say it in such a way that you can continue to tell people what to do bed?'"

32. "Although my heart tells me that at almost any cost, we must bring relief to the magnificent Christian couples who are finding the discipline of the church intolerable, my head warns me against accepting too readily the arguments of converted theologians who now argue against the accepted doctrine. . . . theologians who until a few months ago, not twenty or thirty years ago, dogmatically taught the old doctrine," ibid., 167.

33. Ibid., 252. That the pope rejected the commission's work, and commissioned some of the minority to draft an encyclical much in line with *Casti Connubii*, does not diminish the significance of what transpired within the commission. For comment upon the emergent encyclical, *Human Vitae*, see Burtchaell, *The Giving and Taking of Life*, chapter 4.

people — ourselves and others — when they act in certain ways.

Pius IX, in the last days of heated dispute before the conciliar definition of papal infallibility when some cautioned that such a doctrine lacked adequate grounding in the tradition, was reported to have said: *La tradizione son' io,* "I *am* the tradition!"[34] For a pope, the statement is perhaps extravagant. But for the people, the church, it may not be.

The community's gaze will often be whistled up by those rare individuals called prophets: foretopmen who see first and far. But the community has its own inspiration and will follow the prophets with their sight and their insight. The saints will be there first. Pastors who preside will be reminding the community of its store of tried insight from the past. But the past is cue, not script, for the present. The tradition is dangerous in the hands of any generation that can only quote it without vouching for it. As any generation puts its ancestral moral wisdom to the test there will be new insights — or so it will seem. The scholars have their service especially at these moments of stress, to construe to the community the landscape and inscape of the older wisdom, to help them be humble enough to acquiesce in the abiding truth others left to them, and humble enough to accept as well those moments when they, and no one prior to them, must utter moral insights that give the tradition new nourishment.

There are, then, these three gifts that groom the ancestral wisdom: the charisms of prophecy, pastorate, and scholarship. But the title to ownership of the tradition is communal, never private. The primary wellspring of Christian ethical wisdom is the believing community's reflection on human experience and on the personal aftermath of the experience.

34. The source is highly questionable: Johann Joseph Ignaz von Döllinger, writing from Rome under the pseudonym "Quirinus."

14. What It Means to Stand in a Living Tradition

DOUGLAS F. OTTATI

Our constant endeavor, day and night, is not just to transmit the tradition faithfully, but also to put it in the form we think will prove best.

JOHN CALVIN

Contemporary christology is in crisis. Some ask whether Christianity is possible without incarnation, others cite an "increasing discomfort with the Christ image even within the church."[1] We read varied interpretations of Christ as liberator and as revolutionary, as wise teacher and as friend, as crucified God and as risen Lord, as the one who brings eternity to earth and as the man who is for the world. Some say that Jesus means freedom, others that he means consent to our limitations. A young Uruguayan claims, "For us, Jesus Christ

1. Maurice Wiles, "Christianity without Incarnation?" in *The Myth of God Incarnate*, ed. John Hick (Philadelphia: Westminster Press, 1977), 1-10; and John B. Cobb, Jr., *Christ in a Pluralistic Age* (Philadelphia: Westminster Press, 1975), 17.

Douglas F. Ottati (1950–) is professor of theology at Union Theological Seminary in Richmond, Virginia. He has written *Meaning and Method in H. Richard Niebuhr's Theology* and *Jesus Christ and Christian Vision.*

From Douglas F. Ottati, *Jesus Christ and Christian Vision* (Minneapolis: Augsburg Fortress, 1989).

is Che Guevara."[2] One leading theologian writes, "It seems there are as many images of Christ as there are minds."[3] Another says flatly that traditional christology "has fallen apart in our time."[4]

The character of the current crisis should not be misunderstood. It is not particularly difficult to say what christology is. Christology is talk and reflection about Jesus Christ. It is not especially taxing to identify the aim of christology. The aim is to give an interpretation of the meaning and significance of Jesus Christ. Neither have we suddenly been blinded to its historic importance. Christology has been central to much Christian theology because Jesus Christ is pivotal for a Christian vision of God and humanity's place in God's world. Christology is now in crisis because the great affirmations of classical christological doctrine have become questionable. The result is that Christian theology today often appears to be a historic inquiry that has lost its coherence as well as its traditional bearings.

The Context of Christology

To address this crisis one needs to account for the sense of the classical tradition, its meanings and its dynamic patterns, in a fashion that clarifies how they may yet guide and inform contemporary talk and reflection about Jesus Christ. Before turning to that task, however, it is important to set the work of interpretation in the wider context of the ongoing life of the Christian community. Jesus Christ is the focus of a worshiping and ministering community in the present world. To develop a sustained christology, then, is to propose a contemporary statement of the Christian community's center of meaning. A narrowly traditional christology, which merely repeats the past tradition, does not automatically address the current crisis.

Partly, this is because the horizons of many

contemporary Christians have been extended, even as their world has grown small, thanks to travel, mass media, and communications. In their homes, they see and hear reports about poverty in urban ghettos, the plight of the small farmer, the nuclear arms race, anti-apartheid demonstrations, Shi'ite Muslims, moonshots, and the "greenhouse effect." They view television series and read magazines and books about different cultures and about the cosmos, its possible beginnings and endings. In their airports, they see devotees of imported Eastern religions, even as the security systems remind them of violent conflicts raging around the globe. They inhabit what Richard R. Niebuhr calls a "radial world," in which a global nervous system transmits images, messages, perspectives. ideas, and passions from people and places well beyond the bounds of any local horizon.[5] They are struck by the galaxy of human creeds, the tremendous power and risks of new technologies, recent advances in scientific knowledge, and the enormity of the universe. They are Christians who are curious about and interested in the world, and who seem unwilling and unable to leave their social and cultural premises at the doors of the sanctuary when they assemble to worship. Indeed, they value the experience of interacting with the world. They tend inevitably to evaluate their churches and theologies in light of other interpretations of life, and to evaluate the perspectives presented by their culture in light of their theologies.[6]

For these people, christology is in crisis. In an age that values empirical inquiry more than metaphysics, they are unsure what it means to say that Jesus Christ is truly human and truly divine. In a culture that is only dimly aware of any human fault, they are uncertain what it means to say that Jesus Christ is the redeemer who has won the decisive victory over the forces of sin and darkness. In a society that is often suspicious of large institutions, they are also confused over what official pronouncements have to do with the New Testament and Jesus of Nazareth. Because the

2. José Míguez Bonino, *Doing Theology in a Revolutionary Situation* (Philadelphia: Fortress Press, 1975), 2.

3. Hans Küng, *On Being a Christian,* trans. Edward Quinn (New York: Doubleday & Co., 1976), 129.

4. Edward Schillebeeckx, *Jesus: An Experiment in Christology,* trans. Hubert Hoskins (New York: Seabury Press, 1979), 29.

5. Richard R. Niebuhr, *Experiential Religion* (New York: Harper & Row, 1972), xii-xiii, 1-14.

6. James M. Gustafson, "The Vocation of the Theological Educator," *Austin Seminary Bulletin* 101, no. 7 (1986): 13-26.

great affirmations of classical christology have become questionable, many Christians are perplexed as to whether and how these affirmations may yet guide and inform Christian life and piety in the contemporary world. No mere repetition of past phrases and formulas will adequately address their perplexity.

More profoundly, perhaps, given the inherent dynamic of a living tradition, there is a sense in which a narrowly traditional christology hardly seems possible. A living tradition is a primary source for a community's distinctive identity. It is the "story" of community transmitted for reappropriation in each generation by means of varied artifacts (e.g., texts, art, music, buildings) and activities (e.g., ceremony, commentary, moral behavior). A living tradition shapes present life by furnishing a common memory or heritage that, in turn, yields a guiding orientation.

Let me illustrate. Some time ago, the legislature of the state of New Jersey required that every student in its public high schools take at least two years of courses in American history to graduate. The point of these courses was not to produce a new generation of critical historians but to contribute to the vital transmission of the story of the American nation. Exposure to interpreted documents, monuments, and historical sites sought to ensure that the common memory or heritage of the national community would continue to inform the civic behavior of another generation of Americans, people with names like Smith, Javna, Iwahashi, and Hajinlian. The classes did not exclusively concern the past; they also included attention to current events. The vitalization of a living tradition was reinforced by student government associations and Young Enterprisers' Clubs, as well as by civic rituals on Memorial Day and the Fourth of July.

As any taxpayer will recognize, this process was expensive. The cost was justified by the fact that traditions may be living or dead, and once they have died, they are not easily revived. The vitality of a community depends upon the continuing viability of its tradition. If Smith and Iwahashi do not learn the story and extend its meanings to illumine the challenges and realities of their own experiences, then the distinctive orientation of the American political community is threatened. When the tradition ceases to be reappropriated

and extended, the characteristic orientation of the community dies. Traditional artifacts are not destroyed, but they are rendered mute. The interpretative activities by means of which they spoke and were invested with the power to motivate and guide cease. What dies is the vital commitment and willingness of persons to be shaped by the heritage in question and to carry it further in their own time and place. A living tradition enters into the constitution of meaningful life because, by persistent questioning and interpretation, it continues to yield an orientation that makes sense of the continuing experiences of a society of persons. Therefore, to write a sustained christology is to take up the eminently practical task of interpreting and re-presenting the living orientation of the historical Christian community.

Yet not every portion of a heritage carries the same weight or significance.[7] Traditions have varied topographies. They contain high points and low points, peaks, valleys, and plains. So, for example, among participants in the life of the American nation, the presidency of John Tyler is generally thought to have less significance than the presidencies of Abraham Lincoln or Franklin D. Roosevelt. A living tradition contains classic expressions and less compelling ones, and it is part of the work of interpretation to discern which are which.

A classical tradition is that set of expressions that gives seminal representation to the essential characteristics of the community's distinctive orientation or stance. It is constituted by representations that emerge from community-forming figures and events, such as Thomas Jefferson and the Declaration of Independence. A classical tradition both embodies and points toward a cause or an object of devotion, for example, democracy. Its constitutive expressions become the classic origi-

7. Many of the basic concepts and contentions of this chapter are drawn from Ernst Troeltsch's "What Does 'Essence of Christianity' Mean?" in *Ernst Troeltsch: Writings on Philosophy and Religion,* ed. and trans. Robert Morgan and Michael Pye (London: Gerald Duckworth & Co., 1977), 124-79. I also have learned more than I can adequately acknowledge here from David Tracy's discussions of "the religious classic" in *The Analogical Imagination: Christian Theology and the Culture of Pluralism* (New York: Crossroad, 1981), 99-229.

nals to which subsequent interpretations must refer. Otherwise, the later interpretations make no genuine claim to furthering the distinctive orientation of the particular community in question. Subsequent interpretations do not simply repeat the originals. If genuine, they stand as creative developments that draw out and extend the fuller meanings of the originals to engage the distinctive challenges and realities of another time. Moreover, a genuinely creative development that truly engages the realities of a subsequent time and place cannot simply be read back into the field of older expressions.

If a subsequent interpretation succeeds at a critical turn in the community's history, it too becomes a benchmark for the interpretations that follow. For example, Lincoln's Emancipation Proclamation and the Nineteenth Amendment to the Constitution of the United States are regarded as compelling developments of the original cause of democracy embodied by Jefferson's Declaration and its revolutionary notion that "all men are created equal" — this despite the fact that Jefferson owned slaves and the Nineteenth Amendment gives *women* the right to vote. Lincoln's Proclamation and the Nineteenth Amendment have taken their places as compelling developments of the essential characteristics of the American political community's identity and orientation. As truly creative developments, they cannot be retroactively translated into the language of Jefferson's Declaration. Nevertheless, no contemporary interpretation of the distinctive identity of the American political community is complete without reference to the compelling meanings of these later documents.

To stand in a living tradition, then, is to participate in a dynamic process of interpretation — one that moves between received heritage and the realities and challenges of the present world in order to express a continuing and vital orientation or identity. The classics remain the criteria for subsequent developments even as their continuing vitality — and the continuing vitality of the entire tradition — depends upon the continuing success of subsequent developments. The classic originals retain a privileged position. There must be a historical chain of connection between them and all subsequent expressions. Nevertheless, subsequent interpretations do not repeat the origi-

nals. Indeed, literal repetition often loses a community's distinctive orientation because, in another time and place, the originals do not carry precisely the same meanings that they did in the foundational period. A contemporary interpretation must do no more and no less than engage the community's experiences of the distinctive realities of the present, yet stand in a meaningful measure of continuity with the originals and the subsequent expressions determined to be classical.

The interpretative task is complicated further when the original expressions are multifaceted and contain a number of polarities or tensions that subsequently have been drawn out and resolved in a variety of ways. For example, the originating expressions of the American political community appear to contain a tension between individual liberty and corporate responsibility. This polarity seems to have been resolved differently during the "New Deal" than under the administration of Calvin Coolidge. An inherently dynamic and tensive set of original expressions enables a living tradition to adapt to diverse circumstances — now emphasizing one element or dimension and now another, occasionally spawning new elements and combinations. However, this also means that the interpreter is faced with originating classics that have given rise to differing and sometimes conflicting further developments.

The originating classics of the Christian movement are multifaceted. They include a number of variations on particulars of faith and practice. For example, different titles and images are ascribed to Jesus Christ, and there are differently nuanced statements about divorce. They also contain a variety of general polarities or tensions between knowledge gained from the distinctive heritage of the believing community and from other sources, between the propensities of created nature and the regenerating effects of grace, between sin and the powers of goodness, between law and gospel, and

8. These polarities might be stated in a variety of ways and probably are not exhaustive. They appear as elements of H. Richard Niebuhr's analysis of basic stances in Christian ethics in *Christ and Culture* (New York: Harper & Row, 1975). I have discussed them in *Meaning and Method in H. Richard Niebuhr's Theology* (Washington, D.C.: University Press of America, 1982), 98-125.

between church and world.[8] Subsequent interpreters draw out these polarities and resolve them in a variety of ways. Thomas Aquinas's interpretation of the tension between nature and grace differs from Martin Luther's. Neither Aquinas nor Luther understand the relation between law and gospel in a way that accords with the more radical ethic of discipleship exposited by the Hutterite, Peter Ridemann, and so on. Then too, none of these three figures simply repeats one or another biblical understanding of law, and it would be unfair to Luther, for example, were one to assume that his interpretation of moral law either can or should be translatable without remainder into Pauline terms. Still, each of these subsequent interpretations stands in some measure of continuity with the multifaceted and tensive originals, and each has been accepted as classic by differing strands within the wider Christian movement. Moreover, even within these differing strands, significant variations occur with respect both to particulars of faith and practice and the general polarities. Within the Reformed strand, for example, Ulrich Zwingli and John Calvin maintain different understandings of the Lord's Supper; Emil Brunner resolves the tension between law and gospel differently than Calvin; and Karl Barth delivers a more negative judgment upon natural theology than any of his Reformed predecessors.

In the face of divergent developments, no single self-consistent interpretation of the distinctive orientation of the Christian movement can stand in unbroken continuity with all that has gone before. Even within specific strands of the wider Christian movement, one must be prepared to tolerate a legitimate (although not an unqualified) plurality of interpretations. This, of course, does not mean that the interpreter is released from the responsibility of showing how his or her work stands in meaningful continuity with some construction of the originals and with at least some of the subsequent expressions accepted as classical. It does mean that the most one can accomplish is a contemporary statement that engages the distinctive realities and challenges of the present age and that stands in a measure of continuity with selected themes presented in the originals and selected subsequent expressions. No self-consistent Christian theology responsibly can claim to comprehend the totality of the historical Chris-

tian movement and its varied and multifaceted traditional expressions. To stand in the living tradition of the Christian community, then, means not only to attend to what one has received in its original and subsequent expressions, and not only to attend to present challenges and resources, but also to select constructively from the totality of the historical tradition those themes and strands that seem best.

There is an unavoidably subjective element in any self-consistent theological interpretation. There can be no substitute for the interpreter's personal study of the widest possible cross section of the historical Christian movement. Neither can there be a substitute for the interpreter's personal appropriation of the distinctive orientation of the Christian movement within the living context of the Christian community. He or she therefore will prize both the cloud of witnesses from other times and places available in books and libraries, and close relationships with present Christian congregations, for these provide critical avenues toward one's own judgments about the distinctive past, vital present, and beckoning future of the Christian movement. They comprise transsubjective checks, which may help to remove the one-sided prejudices and superficialities of initial impressions.

Nevertheless, one's final interpretation of the distinctive orientation or pattern must be offered personally. It is no longer merely a disciplined judgment about the past, but also a constructive act aimed at the present and future. To stand within the living tradition of the Christian community is to take the responsibility of shaping afresh the distinctive orientation of the Christian movement — of defining it anew for a given time and place. The interpreter labors to clarify the continuity that obtains between a contemporary interpretation and the varied historical expressions of the community's distinctive orientation. At the same time, he or she also seeks to shape the living reality for the present. Thus, a contemporary statement of the community's distinctive orientation cannot simply be identified with any one of its past expressions. Neither can it be fairly translated back into the language of previous historical expressions.

Such, then, is the mélange of disciplined and constructive judgments by which one enters the interpretative process that seeks to further the distinctive orientation of the historical Christian community. A living tradition "is the occasion for thought; and precisely because it is something mobile, it requires to be transmitted, not passively or mechanically, but by a conscious, creative act."[9] Those who believe it to be the office of theology to instill absolute certainty are likely to remain dissatisfied with this, since nowhere does the process promise complete assurance as to the truth or correctness of an interpretation. Yet such an assurance seems unavailable as soon as we honestly face the multiplicity and dynamism of the historical Christian movement and the conditioned limitations of our own judgments and aims. What does seem possible, however, is a reasonable confidence that one's careful interpretation of the historical tradition falls within a plausible range of legitimate outgrowths of the originals, and that one's theology makes a credible effort to engage the distinctive challenges and realities of the community's present and foreseeable future. One's labors may contribute to the vital identity of an ongoing community precisely because one dares to risk a constructive statement of a historical orientation for present life.[10]

9. B. A. Gerrish, *Tradition and the Modern World: Reformed Theology in the Nineteenth Century* (Chicago: University of Chicago Press, 1978), 181.

10. The primary aim of Christian theology is to serve God and neighbor. Where this is attempted in full recognition of our creaturely limits and sinful tendencies, it will be apparent that theology does not secure an absolute certainty that we are correct and others are wrong. One submits one's theological work for the critical scrutiny of the wider Christian community, a community whose life continues to be informed by the originating and subsequent classics of Scripture and church history. This community may determine the range of positions that it finds legitimate, although those charged with this responsibility by one or another institution do well to remember that their task is to establish a *range* of legitimate positions rather than a single, self-consistent, and detailed theology. Within this community, one has the right to expect that measure of tolerance and humility that appropriately follows the recognition that no one occupies a place of such authority as to control the meaning of the Scriptures.

Recurrent Challenges

From time to time, the vital power of a tradition may become faint or even fall into disrepute. The past inheritance is thought to be untenable, an irksome burden to be escaped.[11] Then the creative process of interpretation that we have been discussing may be cut short by occasionalist, individualist, and utopian alternatives.[12]

Occasionalists, by concentrating on the reality of the present, overlook both the past and the future. The present consumes past and future. In its most radical forms, occasionalism regards tradition as nothing more than an archaic survival. Rather than consult a received heritage, the occasionalist tries to construct identity exclusively from a reading of present circumstances. The truth in occasionalism is that the present identities of individuals and groups are never forged on the basis of the past alone. At times, therefore, occasionalism may furnish a needed corrective to an uncritical reliance upon a received tradition. It may mount a challenge to entrenched, static, and one-sided interpretations of what we have received, which fail genuinely to risk engaging the distinctive challenges and insights of the present situation.

Nevertheless, occasionalism does not see that the past is unavoidably a part of the present. It fails to recognize that present institutions, values, and behavior are always indissolubly intertwined with a particular past, its material objects, beliefs, images of persons and events, practices, and institutions. Indeed, it fails to comprehend that our perspectives on the present environment and what is at stake in it are partly shaped by the stories of our communities. When it comes to ordering the lives of our families, for example, we cannot escape the orienting power of our responses to our parents, our ancestors, and to the historic ethos of our wider society. Again, it took more than reasoned argument about the contemporary situation of American society to alter the attitudes of many Americans toward certain racial and ethnic minorities. For

11. Edward Shils, *Tradition* (Chicago: University of Chicago Press, 1981), 1-33.

12. I use the terms "occasionalism," "individualism," and "utopianism" here, as also the term "traditionalism" later on, merely to signify general and illustrative types.

many American citizens, Martin Luther King, Jr.'s appeals to the classic expressions of the American political community were among his most effective rhetorical strategies. In part, King would say, "Look, by the oppression of black people in this society we fail to live up to the best of our own historical tradition. We fail genuinely to appropriate and develop our true historical identity." The principal value of occasionalism with respect to forming personal and communal identity is that it insists upon the significance of the contemporary situation. In conjunction with received patterns and values, a judicious and critical estimate of the present environment's distinctive features makes a needed contribution to present identity.

Isolated individualism, by concentrating on the self to the exclusion of others, overlooks the common meanings of past, present, and future. It represents the disintegration of community. In its radical form, it regards tradition as a collective mold that threatens to suffocate personal vitality. Rather than work with a received heritage, then, individualism tries to forge identity from individual choice and decision alone. Its slogans will approximate "Decide who you shall be" or "You can choose who you will be." The truth in individualism is that identity is never formed apart from personal responses to what has been given to us, to our present possibilities, and to our aspirations for the future. At times, therefore, individualism may counterbalance oppressive and authoritarian interpretations of common identity that foreclose or limit inappropriately our personally creative responses.

Nevertheless, isolated individualism fails to see that the past is not necessarily a collective threat to personality. It fails to see that the past is an inevitable companion of choosing and deciding subjects. It fails to recognize that the orientations of choosing and deciding individuals are inevitably shaped by timely encounters with other people, the longer histories of their social groups, their participation in institutions, customs, morals, and so on. When a young man rebels against his parents or his home town, for example, he rebels in response to his history with his family and the continuing ethos of his immediate surrounding community. His identity may take on the characteristics of a counter-identity, but he is still identified in part by that which he rejects. The

principal value of individualism for identity is that it seeks to protect the integrity of personal creativity. An integral individuality that operates creatively in conjunction with received patterns and values in the context of the present environment makes an indispensable contribution to present identity.

Idealistic utopianism, by concentrating on the reality of the future, overlooks both the past and the present. This is its strength and its weakness. Utopianism is a strategy of revolutionary change which, in its most radical forms, regards received tradition as a burden to be overcome. Rather than working within the given tradition, it tries to redirect present identity by constructing an imaginative vision of a changed future. The truth in utopianism is that the present identity of individuals and groups is never forged without reference to an anticipated future, and the future is never a simple extension of the past and the present. Therefore, there are times and situations when utopianism functions as a needed corrective to interpretations of common or individual identity that do not genuinely engage a vision of future possibilities.

Nevertheless, utopianism fails to see that present identity is always responsive to the past as well as to the challenges and realities of the present. Even after revolutionary political change has taken place, the identity of a community does not escape the orienting influences of its prerevolutionary past, nor does the community effectively understand itself apart from the distinctive features of the present. For example, communist China is not only shaped by its responses to the rich and varied heritage of Chinese culture but also by the present realities of international relations and by domestic challenges. Because the present orientation of a community is always formed partly by past and present circumstances, utopianism alone never successfully constitutes present identity. Still, no vital identity is possible without attention to some vision of an anticipated future in conjunction with a received heritage and an interpretation of the present environment.

Partly in response to the acids of occasionalism, individualism, and utopianism, a traditionalism may emerge that regards the distinctive challenges of the present, the creative responses of individuals, and visions of a changed future as threats to be avoided. In its extreme forms, traditionalism attempts to construct present identity entirely out of the past. The truth in this is precisely that the present identities of individuals and groups are never fabricated *de novo*. Therefore, at times when a tradition weakens or falls into disrepute, traditionalism may at least uphold the sense that present identity necessarily is connected with a common heritage.

Nevertheless, traditionalism fails to see that interpretations of present circumstances, personally creative acts, and visions of future possibilities always play a part in the constitution of present identity. It fails to recognize that historic institutions, beliefs, values, and behavior inevitably are shaped by creative responses to present realities and future aspirations. Traditionalistic attempts merely to repeat a past heritage come to grief for at least two reasons. First, the traditionalist is by no means absolved of the necessity of selecting certain themes and expressions from the longer tradition as being especially compelling or classic representations of the historic community's distinctive orientation. Such selections, however, almost always betray some reading or estimate of the distinctive challenges facing the community's present life as well as its future possibilities. Consciously or unconsciously, traditionalistic stances tend to import interpretations of contemporary circumstances and visions of the future into the larger effort to shape the community's present identity. Second, due to the shifting circumstances of history, the past expressions of a given tradition, when repeated in the present, almost never carry the same meanings they had in their original situations. To repeat is to innovate. For example, a decision to repeat Lincoln's Gettysburg Address as a particularly compelling expression of the orientation of the American national community implies the prior judgment that this document, rather than some other, is classic. The mere repetition of Lincoln's address will likely carry different meanings today, given the different challenges and aspirations that now presumably engage "government of the people, by the people, and for the people." Moreover, any effort to specify these challenges and aspirations in effect will develop the present meaning of the address, by an interpretation of present circumstances and future possibilities, in directions that Lincoln and his hearers could not have anticipated. Similar things might

be said about any mere repetition of the slogan "one man, one vote" in our present environment. Traditionalism fails genuinely to interpret and re-appropriate the heritage anew because it trades the dynamic reality of a living community for a static blueprint. It exchanges a living tradition for a dead one, and this is why it often provokes occasionalistic, individualistic, and utopian replies.

To stand in a living tradition is to participate in a community that is consciously informed by its common memory, actively engaged in the realities of the present, vitally concerned about its future direction, and genuinely responsive to personally creative acts of appropriation. It is to acknowledge that the identities of individuals and groups are formed in creative responses to past, present, and future. In short, it is to recognize that a historical tradition, although indispensable, is not an exclusive source for a community's present identity. Vital contributions are made by other resources as well.

Resources for the Identity of the Christian Community

This last statement especially applies to the Christian community because its historical tradition and christological center point toward the God who is an active power and universal presence. The distinctive orientation of this community is tied to an apprehension of the living Lord whose dominion includes all things in nature and in history, past, present, and future. Given this perception of God in relation to humanity and the world, there can be no exclusive inquiry into the distinctive orientation of the Christian community that eliminates things other than the historical Christian tradition from consideration. To inquire about God from the perspective of the Christian community's historical tradition is always to inquire about other things in our experience and the varied ways in which they may be understood. Continued engagement in the world is mandated by the Christian community's historical perception of God. What is presently known about anything in nature, history, and society is at least potentially relevant for understanding God's purposes and the orientation in human life that coheres with them.

This would not be so if the historic tradition of the Christian community had a limited reality as its cherished object of devotion — if, for example, it had in view a limited lord of the seas or the reality of the human race. Then the field of experiences that might count for or against one's understanding of the object of devotion and its purposes would be less than universal. One or another aspect of nature or history might then be left out of account because it would not count in relation to the cherished object. Yet the cherished object, in relation to which the Christian community dares to say that we live and move and have our being, is no limited reality. For Christians, no corner of nature or history is of no account in relation to God and God's purposes. To be faithful to the theological integrity of *this* particular orientation and identity, Christians must interpret it intelligibly in light of what is currently known about the world from other sources of insight.[13]

There are multiple reference points for present identity within historical Christian community.[14] Scripture, or the classic literary expressions of the initial stages of the community's life, is most distinctive because it constitutes the original and seminal expression of orientation of the Christian movement. The closing of the canon stabilizes this resource and makes it the charter document of historical Christian identity.[15] Subsequent expressions of the community whose life is informed by this charter document constitute an emerging and developing tradition, which may be grouped as a second reference point under the rubric of church history. Finally, other resources include the culture in which members of the Christian community participate (e.g., the arts, sciences, philosophy) and the common sense or experiential wisdom of day-to-day life.[16]

A continuing intellectual task of the Christian community is to bring these diverse resources and their varied perspectives into a conversation that maintains meaningful continuity with the distinctive features of its historical tradition. While there is a predisposition toward the confirmation of traditional meanings, this conversation cannot accord equal weight to all of the varied and sometimes conflicting insights of Scripture and church history. Instead, it necessarily involves a selective retrieval of certain themes and expressions regarded as classical, giving reasons for how one works with the traditional resources for the selections that are made. It also entails a critical appraisal of varied and sometimes conflicting insights proffered by the arts, sciences, philosophy, and common sense.

To interpret Jesus Christ as the focused representation of the guiding orientation for the Christian community's present identity requires that one attend to each aspect of this mutually correcting conversation. One needs to show how a contemporary interpretation stands in meaningful continuity with selected scriptural themes and subsequent classical expressions. Again, one needs to weigh the diverse insights of the arts, sciences, philosophy, and common sense to discover whether and how they may contribute to a vital contemporary christology. Here, too, one personally must offer one's contemporary statement for the critical appraisal of the wider community, knowing that it is not the only statement possible.

---

13. The relationship between Christian theology and other disciplines is complex. I have outlined my understanding of this relationship in "Christian Theology and Other Disciplines," *Journal of Religion* 64, no. 2 (1984): 173-87.

14. Lisa Sowle Cahill makes a similar proposal in *Between the Sexes: Foundations for a Christian Ethics of Sexuality* (Philadelphia: Fortress Press; Paramus, N.J.: Paulist Press, 1985), 4-7.

15. See H. Richard Niebuhr, *The Meaning of Revelation* (New York: Macmillan Co., 1960), 44-45; and idem, "Introduction to Biblical Ethics" in *Christian Ethics: Sources of the Living Tradition*, ed. Waldo Beach and H. Richard Niebuhr (New York: Ronald Press Co., 1955), 4-5, 10-11. Niebuhr here compares the "book of Christian beginnings" with the foundational documents of other communities.

16. Gerrish (*Tradition and the Modern World,* 7, 183) says that it is typical of liberal Protestantism that Scripture no longer serves as the exclusive critical norm. Theology takes on a "mediating" character because it opens the door to other points of reference besides Scripture and attempts to mediate among them. The appropriating and transforming of the past or the *development* of doctrine is what theology is all about. Its statements are to be constantly retested by the dual norm of fidelity to the tradition and intelligibility in the modern world. My own approach, in some sense, is a mediating one.

15. Feminist Interpretation: A Method of Correlation

ROSEMARY RADFORD RUETHER

It has been frequently said that feminist theology and theory of interpretation draw upon women's experience as a source of knowledge. It has not been entirely clear what this means. It is generally assumed by traditional theology that any experience, let alone "women's experience," is merely a subjective and culture-bound source of ideas and cannot be compared with the objectivity of Scripture, which discloses the "Word of God" outside of, over, and against the subjectivity and sinful impulses of human experience. As a narrow and contemporary source, experience cannot compare with the accumulated weight of theological tradition. It is sheer impertinence to suggest that "women's experience" can be used to judge Scripture and theological tradition.

Such a response, aside from its trivializing of women's persons, misunderstands the role of human experience in the formation of Scripture and theological tradition. Human experience is both the starting point and the ending point of

Rosemary Radford Ruether (1936–) is the Georgia Harkness Professor of Applied Theology at Garrett-Evangelical Theological Seminary. Her work includes *Faith and Fratricide, The Radical Kingdom: The Western Experience of Messianic Hope, Sexism and God-Talk,* and *Toward a Feminist Theology.*

From *Feminist Interpretation of the Bible,* ed. Letty M. Russell (Louisville, Ky.: Westminster/John Knox Press, 1985).

the circle of interpretation. Codified tradition both reaches back to its roots in experience and is constantly renewed through the test of experience. Experience includes experience of the divine and experience of oneself, in relationship to society and the world, in an interacting dialectic. Received symbols, formulas, and laws are either authenticated or not through their ability to illuminate and interpret existence in a way that is experienced as meaningful. Systems of authority try to reverse this relationship and make received tradition dictate both what may be experienced and how it may be interpreted. But the relationship is the opposite. If the symbol does not speak authentically to experience, it becomes dead and is discarded or altered to provide new meaning.

Religious traditions begin with breakthrough experiences that shed revelatory light on contemporary events so as to transform them into paradigms of ultimate meaning. These experiences, such as the exodus experience or the resurrection experience, are the primary data of the religious tradition. But such experiences, however new and transformative, do not interpret themselves. They are always interpreted in the context of an accumulated heritage of symbols and codes, which are already available to provide touchstones of meaning. The new revelatory experience becomes meaningful by being related to this heritage, and also it allows the contemporary community to transform, revise, and recombine the traditional touchstones of meaning in new ways, which allows the new experience to become a new insight into the ultimate nature of things.

Just as the foundational revelatory experience is available only in a transformative dialectic between experience and accumulated interpretive keys, so it, in turn, becomes an interpretive key which interacts with and continues to be meaningful through its ability to make ongoing experience of the individual in the community meaningful. This key then continues to live because it is able to continue to make contemporary experience meaningful, and it itself is constantly revised or reinterpreted through this same process. Traditions die when a new generation is no longer able to reappropriate the foundational paradigm in a meaningful way; when it is experienced as meaningless or even as demonic: that is, disclosing a meaning that points to false or inauthentic life.

Thus if the cross of Jesus would be experienced by women as pointing them only toward continued victimization and not redemption, it would be perceived as false and demonic in this way, and women could no longer identify themselves as Christians.

Women's Experience and Feminist Hermeneutics

What is new about feminist hermeneutics, then, is not the category of experience as a context of interpretation but rather the appeal to *women's experience.* It is precisely women's experience that has been shut out of hermeneutics and theological reflection in the past. This has been done by forbidding women to study and then to teach and preach the theological tradition. Women have not been able to bring their own experience into the public formulation of the tradition. Not only have women been excluded from shaping and interpreting the tradition from their own experience, but the tradition has been shaped and interpreted against them. The tradition has been shaped to justify their exclusion. The traces of their presence have been suppressed and lost from the public memory of the community. The androcentric bias of the male interpreters of the tradition, who regard maleness as normative humanity, not only erase women's presence in the past history of the community but silence even the questions about their absence. One is not even able to remark upon or notice women's absence, since women's silence and absence is the norm.

Thus the criticism of the tradition in the context of women's experience does not merely add another point of view to the prevailing one. Women's experience explodes as a critical force, exposing classical theology, including its foundational tradition in Scripture, as shaped by male experience rather than human experience. Women's experience makes the androcentric bias of the original formulations and ongoing interpretations of the tradition visible, rather than hidden behind the mystifications of divine authority. It throws the universality of the claims of the tradition into question.

What is meant by women's experience? Surely all women do not have the same experiences.

There are many variations in the consciousness of women, shaped by different cultural contexts and life experiences. How then can one generalize about women's experience? Is one suggesting that women, because of biological differences from men, possess a distinctively "feminine" psychology, and that it is this distinctive psychology they bring to biblical hermeneutics?

Biological differences are not completely irrelevant. Women, as persons who live in and through a female body, have some distinctive experiences of the world that men do not have. A woman who has experienced her bodily rhythms in menstruation, or who has borne and suckled a child, feels some things which males have never experienced. One need not reject out of hand that women may bring such experiences to the interpretive task. One finds, for example, in the writings of women mystics, the use of experiences of birthing and suckling that draw on such women's experiences as paradigms of divine-human relationships.

However, in this context we are not talking about women's experience primarily in terms of experiences created by biological differences in themselves but, rather, women's experiences created by the social and cultural appropriation of biological differences in a male-dominated society. In such a society, women experience even their biological differences in ways filtered and biased by male dominance and by their own marginalization and inferiorization. Menstruation and childbirth are interpreted to them as pollution, over against a male-controlled sacred sphere, for example, which alienates them from a positive understanding of their own bodily experiences. Insofar as they appropriate their own experiences, such as the experience of menstruation, as a positive and creative rhythm of ebb and flow, they must do so in contradiction to the male hermeneutic of their own experience imposed upon them by the dominant culture. Their positive appropriation of their experience from their own vantage point becomes a covert critical counter-culture over against the official culture.

Women in patriarchal culture are surrounded by messages that negate or trivialize their existence. Their bodily sexual presence is regarded as a dangerous threat to male purity and, at the same time, as a justification for constant verbal and physical abuse. They experience their bodies as constantly vulnerable to assault and are told, at the same time, that they deserve such assault because they "cause" it by their sexual presence. Similarly, women find their own viewpoints and judgments of events trivialized, and this trivialization is justified on the grounds that women are inherently stupid, uninformed, lacking in authority, and incapable of forming significant understandings. Thus they are alienated from their own minds, from being able to trust their own perceptions. These judgments upon the woman's body and mind are, in turn, used to justify women's exclusion from cultural opportunities and leadership. Women are asked to accept this, too, as normal, natural, divinely sanctioned.

By women's experience as a key to hermeneutics or theory of interpretation, we mean precisely that experience which arises when women become critically aware of these falsifying and alienating experiences imposed upon them as women by a male-dominated culture. Women's experience, in this sense, is itself a grace event, an infusion of liberating empowerment from beyond the patriarchal cultural context, which allows them to critique and stand out against these androcentric interpretations of who and what they are. Women begin to name these experiences of negation and trivialization as wrong and contrary to their authentic humanity. They begin to find an alternative stand in their own shared reflection on this experience from which to judge it. They affirm their own bodies and bodily experiences as good and normative for them, rather than deviant; their own feelings and thoughts as intelligent and healthy, rather than stupid. From this empowerment to self-affirmation, they are able to place under judgment — and also progressively to free themselves from — that culture which negates them.

It is this process of the critical naming of women's experience of androcentric culture that we refer to when we say that women's experience is an interpretive key for feminist theology. Women's experience, then, implies a conversion experience through which women get in touch with, name, and judge their experiences of sexism in patriarchal society. Not all cultures create exactly the same experiences of sexism, and individual women may have experienced this differently as well. So women do not come to exactly

the same criticisms of these experiences or the same conclusions about them. Feminism must leave room for such individual and cross-cultural differences. Nevertheless, patriarchy by its very nature provides enough of a common body of experiences that women, even from different cultures and religions, find commonalities. But this conversation can happen only when women become freed and empowered to criticize the experience of sexism as an unjustified assault upon their beings, rather than accepting it as the norm.

The critique of sexism implies a fundamental principle of judgment. This critical principle of feminist theology is the affirmation of and promotion of the full humanity of women. Whatever denies, diminishes, or distorts the full humanity of women is, therefore, to be appraised as not redemptive. Theologically speaking, this means that whatever diminishes or denies the full humanity of women must be presumed not to reflect the divine or authentic relation to the divine, or to reflect the authentic nature of things, or to be the message or work of an authentic redeemer or a community of redemption.

This negative principle also implies the positive principle: What does promote the full humanity of women is of the Holy, does reflect true relation to the divine, is the true nature of things, is the authentic message of redemption and the mission of redemptive community. But the meaning of this positive principle — namely, the full humanity of women — is not fully known. It has not existed in history as we have known it. What we have known is only the negative principle of the denigration and marginalization of women's humanity. But the humanity of women, although diminished, has not been destroyed. It has constantly affirmed itself, albeit at times only in limited and subversive ways. It is the touchstone by which we test and criticize all that diminishes us. In the process we experience our larger potential, which allows us to begin to imagine a world without sexism.

This principle is hardly new. In fact, the correlation of original and authentic human nature (*imago dei*/Christ) over against diminished, fallen humanity has traditionally provided the basic structure of classical Christian theology. The uniqueness of feminist theology is not the critical principle of "full humanity" but that women claim this principle for themselves. Women name themselves as subjects of authentic and full humanity.

In this light, the use of this principle in male theology is perceived to have been corrupted by sexism. By naming males as norms of authentic humanity, women have been scapegoated for sin and marginalized in both original and redeemed humanity. This distorts and turns to the opposite the theological understanding of the created and redeemed image of God. Defined as male humanity against or above women, as ruling-class humanity above servant classes, the *imago dei/* Christ paradigm becomes an instrument of sin rather than a disclosure of the divine and an instrument of grace.

But this also implies that women cannot just reverse the sin of sexism. Women cannot just blame males for historical evil in a way that makes themselves only innocent victims. Women cannot affirm themselves as created in the image of God and as subjects of full human potential in a way that diminishes male humanity. Women, as the denigrated half of the human species, must reach for a continually expanding definition of the inclusive humanity: inclusive of both genders, inclusive of all social groups and races. Any principle of religion or society that marginalizes one group of persons as less than fully human diminishes us all. In rejecting androcentrism (males as norms of humanity), women must also criticize all other forms of chauvinism: making white Westerners the norm of humanity, making Christians the norm of humanity, making privileged classes the norm of humanity. They must also criticize humanocentrism: making humans the norm and "crown" of creation in a way that diminishes other beings in the community of creation. This is not a question of "sameness" but of recognition of value which, at the same time, affirms genuine variety and particularity. It reaches for a new mode of relationship: neither a hierarchical model that diminishes the potential of the "other" nor an "equality" defined by a ruling norm drawn from the dominant group, but rather a mutuality that allows us to affirm different ways of being.

16. The Authority of Tradition

JOHN HOWARD YODER

"Why do you transgress the commandment of God for the sake of your tradition? Isaiah rightly prophesied of you: 'This people serves me with their lips, but their heart is far from me; the worship they offer me is in vain, for they teach as doctrine nothing but human regulations.'"

MATT. 15:3, 8f.

How tradition exercises authority is one of those questions which put to us the prior challenge of choosing which league we want to play in. In the classical debate between scholastic Protestantism and scholastic Roman Catholicism after Trent[1] the term "tradition" not only pointed to the general

1. Without reaching back to the origins of this high scholastic debate in Bellarmine and Canisius, we find it very adequately summarized in a recent article by Kevin McNamara of Maynooth, on the thought of Patrick Murray, also of Maynooth, 1811-1882, in a symposium honoring the ecumenist and ecclesiologist Joseph Höfer: "Patrick Murray's Teaching on Tradition," in R. Bäumer and H. Dolch, eds., *Volk Gottes* (Freiburg: Herder, 1967), pp. 455f.

John Howard Yoder (1927–) is professor of theology at the University of Notre Dame. His works include *The Original Revolution: Essays in Christian Pacifism, Karl Barth and the Problem of War, The Priestly Kingdom: Social Ethics as Gospel,* and *The Politics of Jesus: Vicit Agnus Noster.*

From John Howard Yoder, *The Priestly Kingdom: Social Ethics and the Bible* (Notre Dame: University of Notre Dame Press, 1985).

observation that the substance of faith and the framework of its interpretation are passed on from one generation to the next: "tradition" also meant the specific set of units of information which have been passed down and cherished in such a way that they can claim a kind of revelatory authority, complementary to and not completely dependent on that of the canonical Scriptures.[2]

For the Protestants in that debate, it was profoundly important to say that *all* necessary information bearing revelatory authority is contained in the Holy Scriptures as they stand, sufficiently clear and self-interpreting as to need no more hermeneutic aids than every believer has available in the Holy Spirit and his or her human reason. Thus it was important for the Catholics to say the opposite: namely, that there are specific items of information (not merely additional perspectives useful for interpretation) which have been handed down without being written (or at least without being written in sacred Scriptures) "as if from hand to hand." It lies within the authority of the teaching hierarchy to clarify and promulgate this knowledge as they may see fit, subject to the internal accountability structures of the hierarchy, but independent of what other believers may hold the Bible text itself to say.

As this debate was framed after Trent and administered from both sides until a generation ago, it by definition cannot move to a resolution. It could however be bypassed, if one could step back from the issue of locating in the papal office the authority to declare *which* units of information have the status of revelatory tradition. Thus it is no surprise that it was first in the Faith and Order movement (that division of the World Council of Churches which devotes its attention to classical issues of dogma and polity, and which for all practical purposes was long mostly a bilateral conversation between mainstream Western Protestants and the Eastern Orthodox) that the post-Tridentine formulation of the problem could be bypassed. In the documents of the Faith and Order Assembly in 1963 at Montreal, the issue was raised to a higher level of sophistication, and thereby practically laid to rest. The absence of formal

Roman Catholic representation in the WCC at that time, and the practical silence within the Faith and Order conversations of the radical free-church traditions, made this major progress easier. The Montreal formulation used "Tradition" with a capital *T* to refer globally to all that each Christian community and all the Christian communities together think and speak. It is a stream of handing-down processes which is prior to and wider than the tradition of any one denominational communion. Secondly, the "traditions" (small *t*) are the several sets of sectarian understandings. They may properly be cultivated in separate places, but by their nature do not justify dividing the church. Thirdly, "tradition" (singular with a lower case *t*) means the event or process of handing down the substance of a community's faith. Everyone affirms all three. Since it is fitting that local "traditions" (lower case, plural) should differ, we can recognize one another without demanding uniformity or centralization.

But then what has become of the problem, the classical problem of Bellarmine and Canisius? Has it been resolved? Or has it been simply declared nonexistent by definition or repressed? Is this like a military retreat from a battle line, where the trenches had been dug at the wrong point, without its being clear that we know now where we will meet an enemy? Has something been learned by backing away from that wrong battle? Albert Outler, one of the participants in the Montreal process (whose own brief book *The Christian Tradition and the Unity We Seek*[3] had contributed to that development), does think we have learned something. Of most disagreements between Christians that went to the point of schism, Outler argues that the break was not necessary. Even at the point of schism, the common beliefs remaining were more fundamental than the crucial differences. Outler holds that the wider stream of common experience and confession, binding all Christians together even though they have never met, is weightier than the issues about which we do battle with one another. Tradition and Scripture are not separate forces or substances but two different expressions of the same function of "handing on" what has been "given over" to us all in Christ.

---

2. I say "units of information" rather than "propositions" because the way in which this knowledge was transmitted is not always held to have retained one particular fixed linguistic form.

3. Albert Outler, *The Christian Tradition and the Unity We Seek* (Oxford, 1975).

That handing-on process includes organic evolution such as produced the later definitions of Nicea and Chalcedon. Simply facing that fact will, according to Outler, be a strong step forward "toward the unity we seek."

I grant that this sense of progress and learning is appropriate on the level of etiquette. Christians of all kinds have learned to be more polite and pluralistic in dealing with difference. If we had not been taught this by the gospel, we should have had to learn it from the culture of disestablishment.

The reading Outler gives is appropriate as a description of the mutual recognition for which mainstream Western Protestant churches are ready. Openness of previously separated denominational bodies to mutual recognition has been purchased partly by serious theological labor like Outler's and partly by the extent to which these Protestant denominations have brought into the pluralistic mood of the surrounding cultures.

Yet I must record doubt as to whether this more appeased mood has taken care of the root of the problem. This kind of irenic restatement was achieved in a context where the parties with the strongest convictions were absent, namely the Roman Catholics and the "free-church" Protestants. The old agenda was also left in the shadow, in favor of this more formal analysis. The specific issues that had been fought about before were not resolved but left to withdraw into a penumbra of polite pluralism. That is no reproach. Ecumenical movements do not have to discuss all the issues all the time. Some issues to which a new generation turns may well be of more immediate importance, without claiming that the older ones have been resolved.

My task here is not so much to add to the discipline of ethics[4] some new resource which might be discovered in the name of "tradition," but rather to ask with reference to ethics whether the issue of tradition, as irenically reorganized at Montreal, is rightly put and readily resolved.

I mentioned before the absence at Montreal not only of Roman Catholics, but also of radical evangelicals and conservative Protestants. The absence of conservative Protestants made it easier to reach

4. This paper was originally presented to a consultation at Notre Dame on "Remembering and Reforming: Toward a Constructive Christian Ethic."

a relatively moderate consensus. Yet their critique of inclusive pluralism is valid in one way that I must mention.

The Abiding Challenge

The critical claim of evangelical biblicism is not answered by the "you-too" of the Catholics from Bellarmine to Patrick Murray. To retort to the "biblicists" (a label I propose to use descriptively, not pejoratively), who claim to grant authority to "the Scriptures alone," "you too have a context of interpretation, you too make assumptions, you too choose arbitrarily a canon within a canon" is true but is not to meet the issue worthily. This kind of put-down speaks to the cultural naiveté of some precritical evangelicals, but it does not speak to their theological tradition, which in its original age (that of Wyclif and Hus or of Luther and Calvin) was by no means naive nor disrespectful of tradition as a hermeneutical matrix. To recognize that there is no reading of Scripture without an interpreting frame does not set aside the canonical witness as a baseline and a critical instance, or make it only one of "two sources." One's "hermeneutical matrix" is like the microscope in microbiology. You cannot see the tiny organisms without the microscope, but the microscope never becomes the microbe. The use of the microscope might impose upon the microbe certain very severe conditions before it can be seen. The microbe will need to be put on a slide. It may need to be killed or dyed, but still it remains distinct from the microscope. If the microscope is immensely more powerful we approach the frontier where the interference of the instrument with the object becomes uncontrollable: but even here the electron which the microscope uses to see with is not the molecule. It is, in other words, thoroughly possible to distinguish in principle between the object of knowledge and the way of knowing it, and to affirm the priority of the former. In a similar sense, Protestant biblicists do not deny that they use language and logic, but they need not grant that that makes their reading hopelessly subjective. They can grant that the Scripture was produced by churches out of traditions that were not "Scripture" until long after they were edited and recorded, and that contemporary interpretation is moved by contemporary priorities and challenges, without thereby conceding as desirable or even as possible that all of that process be controlled by a particular agent in the teaching church.

The old notion of tradition, as challenged by the Protestants, is inadequately represented by such concepts as unfolding, clarification, or reformulation. There can very properly be forms of change to which the "biblicist" would not object, if they have about them the organic quality of growth from seed, faithful translation, or fecundation. In fact, most of the theology of the conservative Protestant was reformulated after 1500 and much of it has evolved since 1600 (though not much since 1900). What is at stake is not whether there can be change but whether there is such a thing as unfaithfulness. Is there a difference between compatible extrapolation and incompatible deviation?

The linguistic line between treason and tradition is very fine. Both terms come from the same root. Yet in substance there is a chasm between the two, a chasm which the modern debate about tradition has not helped to survey. The semantic puzzles are enormous when we try to distinguish between faithful organic development on one hand and a sell-out on the other. Both are formed in historical continuity. Both are explainable within historicist axioms of causality and analogy. Both use the same words. Yet if the notion of fidelity is not to fade into a fog where nothing is verifiable, the notion of infidelity as a real possibility must continue to be operational.

* * *

Perpetual Reform

. . . We are not plagued merely by a hard-to-manage diversity, by a wealth of complementary variations on the same theme. We are faced with error, into which believers are seduced by evil powers seeking to corrupt the church and to disqualify her witness. To denounce those errors we must appeal to the common traditions from which those who fall into error are falling away, which they previously had confessed together with us. As the Apostle Paul was already doing in 1 Corinthians 15 and Galatians 1, we appeal to a

prior commonality against an innovation. Such an innovation, already having been handed down for more than one generation, but recognizable as not valid from the root, is what Jesus in Matthew 15:3ff. (followed by Zwingli and the Puritans) called "human traditions." The need is not that *those* traditions be integrated in a richer pluralism. They must be uprooted (v. 13). There are no grounds for claiming that they had been handed down in unwritten form "as if from hand to hand" ever since the apostles. Against these new-fangled "traditions of man" we appeal to the original traditions which enshrine the commandments of God. The clash is not tradition versus Scripture but faithful tradition versus irresponsible tradition. Only if we can with Jesus and Paul (and Francis, Savonarola, Milton, and the others) denounce *wrong* traditioning, can we validly affirm the rest. Scripture comes on the scene not as a receptacle of all possible inspired truths, but rather as witness to the historical baseline of the communities' origins and thereby as link to the historicity of their Lord's past presence.

Far from being an ongoing growth like a tree (or a family tree), the wholesome growth of a tradition is like a vine: a story of constant interruption of organic growth in favor of pruning and a new chance for the roots. This renewed appeal to origins is not primitivism, nor an effort to recapture some pristine purity. It is rather a "looping back," a glance over the shoulder to enable a midcourse correction, a rediscovery of something from the past whose pertinence was not seen before, because only a new question or challenge enables us to see it speaking to us. To stay with the vinedresser's image, the effect of pruning is not to harm the vine, but to provoke new growth out of the old wood nearer to the ground, to decrease the loss of food and time along the sap's path from roots to fruit, and to make the grapes easier to pick. *Ecclesia reformata semper reformanda* is not really a statement about the church. It is a statement about the earlier tradition's permanent accessibility, as witnessed to and normed by Scripture at its nucleus, but always including more dimensions than the Bible itself contains, functioning as an instance of appeal as we call for renewed faithfulness and denounce renewed apostasy. The most important operational meaning of the Bible for ethics is not that we do just what it says in some way that we can derive deductively. It is rather that we are able, thanks to the combined gifts of teachers and prophets, to become aware that we do not do what it says, and that the dissonance we thereby create enables our renewal.[5]

There is no reproach involved when we affirm this need for correction. *Sometimes* a need for correction is the result of culpable failure or disobedience. Sometimes it is the result of not having listened or waited. Yet often the need for continuing historical correction is blameless, intrinsic to the quality or historically rooted community. We should feel guilty not when we need to be corrected but when we claim to bypass that need, as if our link to our origins were already in our own hands.

What we then find at the heart of our tradition is not some proposition, scriptural or promulgated otherwise, which we hold to be authoritative and to be exempted from the relativity of herme-

---

5. This way of remembering in reforming is a pattern for aggressive and optimistic forward movement in the life of the church. Not only is the church *reformata* and *semper reformanda*. She is also always in the process of further reformation. When the need for further reformation is affirmed, as in this standard slogan, yet without providing an instrument for it, the slogan *semper reformanda* becomes an acquiescence in imperfection rather than an affirmation of vulnerability to change. When the concrete subservience to political establishment belies the commitment to further reformation, then the *semper reformanda* becomes a defense ("nobody's perfect") instead of a power to renew. The standard interpretation of the position which others pejoratively call "sectarian" is, on the other hand, that it affirms the recoverable purity of the pristine pentecostal community. That would mean no forward movement but only a constant and always implicitly, almost immediately defeated effort to start over from scratch. That is not the vision that has been lived by any radical free-church community in history, nor is it the one I suggest. Each time a new perception of unfaithfulness is provoked by a new recourse to the canonical testimony, thereby calling forth from the ancient heritage "treasures old and new" (Matt. 13:4), the history of the community and even of the world has been moved not back but forward. It is not the free church but the establishment model that attempts to freeze history in the claim thereby to be taking responsibility for it.

neutical debate by virtue of its inspiredness. What we find at the origin is already a process of reaching back again to the origins, to the earliest memories of the event itself, confident that that testimony, however intimately integrated with the belief of the witnesses, is not a wax nose, and will serve to illuminate and sometimes adjudicate our present path.

New Receptivity

One way the same old data yields new information is that we bring to it another set of questions, just as the natural sciences find more facts in the same plant or animal than before their present instruments were developed. A new question permits the old event to respond in ways that earlier patterns of questioning had not made self-evident or perhaps had hidden.

Within the last century, and for many of us within the generation, there has been a fundamental paradigm shift in the readiness to see the Gospel story in particular, and the biblical revelatory story in general, as social and political. Earlier generations had intentionally filtered out that part of the light, considering it as the particular conditioned dimension that should not be permitted to get in the way of the more authentically religious data. It is now possible to talk about the Eucharist as relating to world hunger, or about Jesus as a liberator. We are finding in the old sources help which was always there, but which previously was not drawn from them because we did not expect them to speak to those issues. Nor did we think that we needed much help in that area anyway. In other words, we have just lived a new episode of the "reaching back" phenomenon. Having learned that our models for understanding social structures and their moral weight in the light of the faith were not adequate, we were free for a new approach to the same old canonical texts. Some of our questions are now reformulated in such a way that the texts are ready to speak to them.

There have always been radio waves bringing messages to us from distant stars. Only the development of radio technology has empowered us to receive those signals. The Bible was always a liberation storybook: now we are ready to read it that way. Tomorrow some other question will provoke another "reaching back" for yet another level of meaning that was always there. In this study, our interest is that what the "reaching back" has brought forward recently has to do with ethics. It corrects a model of Christian social ethics that thought it did not need that specific story, because it got its guidance from "nature" or "conscience" or later history.

The commercials invite us to "reach out and touch someone." They tell us we can do it by phone. The healing communication we need for ethical reforming is also to reach and to touch someone. Here, though, the touching must be done through documents, and through our modest capacity for understanding what documents originally meant. More than when the reformation debate arose, we are aware that these documents point to events beyond themselves, namely to the utterly human, vulnerable, dubitable, rejectable presence of Jesus among us, and that the quality of historical testimony which they offer is that of believing witness. Nonetheless this process of "reaching back" once again, to participate in the process of the believing witnesses' "reaching back" at their time, must be the shape of our discipline if our claim to be his disciples is not to be evacuated of moral substance.

The radio analogy stated in lay cultural terms what a free-church alternative to the Tridentine debate would have said biblically. There is continuing revelation. Jesus promised that there would be (John 14:12-26; 16:7-15). The Lucan and Pauline pictures of prophecy assume that there will be. 1 John 4:1ff, and 1 Corinthians 12:1ff. assume that there will be and provide criteria for it. At Trent the defense against Protestant biblicism made the wrong move. Instead of granting to the Protestants that all revelation must be apostolic and then claiming to have some leftover unwritten apostolic information, Trent might have granted that later developments had gone beyond Scripture, but agreed to face the challenges of dialogue about justifying at the bar of Scripture the movement beyond Scripture. Then it would have surfaced that the real debate was not about apostolic memories but about which kind of church can have an open dialogue.

So the term "tradition" has exploded beyond the point where it could have functioned as a "second source." It now represents a river in which we all float, or swim, seeking our bearings as we move. It is not like Scripture in the high scholastic Protestant view, uniquely inspired literature, whose credibility has been undermined by the perspectives of historical criticism. The acids of historicism that have weakened it are not challenges to the precise historicity of particular Gospel accounts, or to naive traditions about authorship and redaction, but rather the broader awareness of the plurality and the conditioned quality of all meanings and institutions.

Most of the above applies intentionally to the wider questions of how tradition functions in all social groups claiming to be faithful to some formative or founding event. It may apply more specifically just now to ethics because it is a realm where the reality check is met soon. In ritual or in dogma it is not surprising or alienating for language to be a little old or other-worldly. There the past, at least the moderately recent past, has a hold on us against which we do not rebel. Social behavior has by its nature a present meaning.

Models of Unfaithfulness

It is in the realm of ethics that the strongest appeals have been made to kinds of information that do not need scriptural warrant, since they are held to be common to all mankind: the famous "natural" sources of moral insight. People would be less likely to suggest there are natural sources of ritual knowledge or of creedal information.

The realm of the social is accordingly the one where the dynamics of accommodation and the tendencies to sell out are the strongest, as the church lives at the interface with the world of unbelief, its powers and pressures. Thus if we want to know how we need to proceed in a debate about tradition going astray and being called to order by tradition, we should find such a mistake to analyze.

If I knew more, I should like to begin with the betrayal of the Jewishness of the early church, as the Christian apologetes of the second and third centuries moved into Hellenistic culture, or with the betrayal of the feminist thrust that had begun with the Gospels. I would, if I could, study when the veneration of the saints became a new pa-

ganism, or when Easter became a fertility ritual. If I were a Marxist, or a historian of the eleventh century in Milan, we could talk about wealth as apostasy.

Instead of focusing on a debatable negative case of ethical evolution that needs to be called into question, it might have been desirable first to use some positive ones, which we would all agree to be good, and others that we would all agree to be bad. As an example of good change we could have taken the acceptance by most Christians in our time of religious liberty, or of democracy. I doubt, however, that that would really have produced more clarity. The grounds on which these affirmations, ancient in some Christian communities and recent in others, have been integrated in recent Christian thought are not agreed upon. It seems to have been a part of the price of the acceptance of religious liberty, by Vatican II, as desirable from now on in the modern world that there needed to be no express disavowal of its rejection by Catholics in past centuries. There is not full agreement about whether the particular lines of argument which led to the acceptance of religious liberty in Vatican II, thanks to the leadership of John Courtney Murray, were the best way to move in that case. It would seem then that the acceptance of religious liberty is not a better test case for evaluating our differences about how tradition functions to criticize tradition.

The other approach would be to broaden our conspectus with something that we would all agree was a bad evolution, properly rejected by "all Christians everywhere always," on the grounds of an appeal to the older tradition. We might ethically agree to condemn support given to Adolf Hitler by the *Deutsche Christen,* but that case would not really count, because it was not sanctioned by a hierarchy. We could critique the Crusades, but that would involve us in a complicated conceptual debate among specialists about the sense in which the Crusades were and were not expressions of the just war logic.

We could discuss the Iberian conquest of South America and the first four and a half centuries of bad colonial manners, but that would point us to an unfinished debate still going on within in the dominant Catholic communion rather than to real agreement. Even many theologians of "liberation," while very clear in their present criticism of the colonial heritage, do not want to use ethical concepts which would reject the colonial pattern in principle, nor the pattern of Constantinian establishment from which it was derived. Some would seem to say that Constantine was all right for his time, and Charlemagne for his, and Charles V for his: then it is only in our age that we must replace the imperial vision of civil righteousness with a revolutionary one.

This would leave us with the Inquisition as one possible case where we might all agree today that that pattern, once solidly accepted by the entire hierarchy, has come to be rejected on the grounds of a fundamental appeal to what the earlier Christian tradition was about. Yet even here, we would have some more history to study before we could be sure that what undercut the Inquisition for those whose direct predecessors had believed in it, was really a renewed appeal to the New Testament, or to Christology, or to the fundamental nature of religion or of the human being as a religious person, rather than acquiescence to the power of modernity, which tore such instruments from the hands of the hierarchy on quite other grounds.[6]

The Legitimation of War

Yet the demonstration will be simpler if I stay with the classical agenda of the divergent Christian views about the morality of the violence of the state, not to be argued for its own sake but as a well-known specimen of what we are trying to isolate.

From Tertullian and Origen at the end of the second century to Bernard a millennium later, the view of Christians on the morality of violence in the public realm was reversed. The development

---

6. My assignment has otherwise dealt with a purely formal question: normative past and debatable present, treason and fidelity. The theme would have been richer, but less manageable, if the debate had been specified materially as well. Might an ethic of martyrdom be more readily betrayed than one of stewardship? Might love of enemy be harder to hold to than love of spouse or homeland? Might an ethic of vocation be more easily secularized than one of charisma? Then some elements of the Christian moral message might be more crucial, more in jeopardy of being jettisoned than others. In this respect, the just war sample is a good one.

came in phases. The first was a rather modest borrowing from the Roman legal tradition by Ambrose and Augustine, to speak to questions the New Testament did not help them with. The legitimate violence which they approved was the function of the police in domestic peacekeeping or at most the defense of the empire against the Vandals. The category of "vengeance" was present in their thought, to account for the wars in the Old Testament, but they did not see the contemporary international undertakings of the Roman Empire as being vengeance commanded by God. The Crusades were quite another phase, which went far beyond the old Roman just war categories to make the Middle East adventures a specifically religious cause.

The end product of these and other shifts is a fundamentally new political ethic, not organically evolved from the social stance of the early Christians, as that stance had been evolving up to and through Tertullian and Origen. The new stance rejects the privileged place of the enemy as the test of whether one loves one's neighbor. It rejects the norm of the cross and the life of Jesus Christ as the way of dealing with conflict. It assigns to civil government, not only to Caesar as an ecumenical savior figure but even, later, to fragmented local regimes, a role in carrying out God's will that is quite incompatible with the fruit of the progressive relativization of kingship from Samuel to Jeremiah to Jesus and Jochanan ben Zakkai.

This "just war tradition" is now dominant.[7] It

has crowded the earlier pacifist tradition to the Franciscan and Waldensian fringes of Christendom. Yet it has never been promulgated as an official teaching by a council or a pope, never studied with great intensity, never formulated in a classical outline, and never applied with much consistency. It is dominant without being clear. It has taken over without being tested.

Having a real case of change in view, there is no difficulty in observing that the Tridentine notion of a second source is ludicrously inept. There was not a "just war" undercurrent in the first centuries, waiting unused yet faithfully passed on orally until the Constantinian opportunity let it come out of the catacombs. Rather, there were new challenges to which the separatist ethic of the apocalypse or of the pacifist fathers did not seem to speak sufficiently. It would have been good at that time to have had a new prophetic voice to save the church of the third and fourth centuries from the no-win choice between separatism and sell-out. Tragically, there was no such prophet. Ambrose and Augustine did the best they could. They did not mean to sell out, but they did buy

---

7. There are at least the following distinct ways of using the language of "the just war":

a. The term was classically used to describe the holy wars of the age of Joshua and the Crusades, whose cause is transcendentally accredited by hierarch or prophet.

b. The same language is used to describe the moral autonomy of a ruler who is properly answerable to no one in his decisions about cause and means.

c. It may speak of the application of a set of rigorously logical formal criteria, whose objective clarity permits them to be applied by the citizen, the theologian, or the politician.

d. There is the transmutation of the logical and formal criteria into legal and procedural rules: conventions, tribunals, mediators.

e. There is justifiable insurrection, which claims that exceptionally the criterion of "legitimate authority" must yield to that of just cause.

f. There is "nothing like success" argument, which claims that policies of mass retaliation and assured destruction, while contrary to the traditional rules of proportionality and discrimination, nevertheless are morally justified, because they deter effectively by making their application unthinkable.

g. There is what some now call "just war pacifism"; the application to particular contemporary cases of the classical criteria, in such a way as to condemn rather than approve of a war that is otherwise seriously likely, or is going on.

h. There is the "war is hell" view. The outbreak of war suspends most moral discourse. Everything we do is sin. Yet the judgments of military necessity must still be made responsibly. Hiroshima was still an atrocity.

These views differ in many concrete ways. Type c is structurally different from types a and b, although in the Middle Ages the distinction was not made clearly. Type f contradicts c in all its details, but agrees in its basically utilitarian logic. Type d is a development from type c. Type e is a development from c and/or from d. Type g is a serious revitalization of type c, beginning with its logic yet producing unprecedented conclusions. Type h is like f in that it differs deeply from c yet nonetheless claims to discriminate responsibly. Thus this *new* "tradition" does not have in its favor that it has done away with ambiguity.

into a system whose inherent dynamism they could no longer control. The one explanation that can *not* be claimed is that they got their new ideas about the just war from a not yet recorded oral treasury of apostolic memories. They themselves would not have said that. They knew they were borrowing from Cicero. What needs to be debated is not the "two sources" notion but the criteria for the church's necessary appropriation of non-Christian moral ideas.

Our concern here is not to debate the ethics of violence as an issue for its own sake. The observation is purely formal. A change has taken place which must be described as a reversal rather than as an organic development. This case shows that when the issue is whether change has been faithful or unfaithful, *then* the reason the reformers challenge some usage or idea is not that it is not in the Scriptures, but that it is counter to the Scriptures; not that it is an ancient idea insufficiently validated by ancient texts, but that it is a later introduction invalidated by its contradicting the ancient message. So the issue — if there be a genuine issue — is not tradition versus Scripture, nor Scripture versus some one fragment of the rest of tradition, nor (as Montreal said) the scriptural fraction of tradition versus some other one of many traditions. The issue is (as Jesus said it) the traditions of men versus the commandment of God. That rough word of Jesus introduces seriousness that ecumenical politeness had hidden. Not all varieties of vision — or of ethics — can fit together within a tolerant pluralism. What we need is tools to identify and denounce error, while welcoming variety and celebrating complimentarity.

The problem with which the truce of Montreal cannot help is not that we talk different languages, or that each of us is so integrated in his own culture that our several patterns are very different. The problem is that within the same culture we take positions so fundamentally contradictory that we cannot both be faithfully serving the same Lord. To adjudicate that question, the thrust of Trent and Bellarmine is no help. However prestigious be the center which claims to rule over the universal community, it will always be in some sense provincial. Its claim to possess a side channel of revelation reaching all the way back to the apostles by an unbroken oral chain is even less credible, in the face of the perspectives of scientific histori-

cism, than are the claims for the univocal meaning of Scripture texts. Nor has it ever been seriously claimed in the field of social ethics that there exist particular data preserved within the unbroken hierarchy by oral transmission. If we treat as more or less equivalent (a) the claim that there is valid nonscriptural tradition received from the apostles and (b) the practice of Roman councils and popes of promulgating specific claims, if necessary *ex cathedra,* then it is significant that it is not in the field of social ethics that this authority has been exercised. Such a fundamental innovation as the just war attitude was never given that kind of ratification. A stronger claim in fact would have been to exploit the promises in the New Testament of further leading beyond the teachings of Jesus, and to claim continuing specific concrete guidance in line with Matthew 10:19f., yet for other reasons Trent could not have taken that path, and the just war doctrine would not have fit the context of Matthew 10.

The scholastic Protestant view has been no less undermined by the age of historical awareness. With regard to the Bible itself, we know, without being threatened by the fact, that a process of traditioning had been going on for a generation before the texts took on their present form, that those texts were always interpreted within a wider context of meanings and logic, and that the plurality of the texts testifies to an even greater variety in those early communities. In a similar way, historical relativity makes us aware that the way we read a text is also the product of our education, language, and logic.

Thus both sides of the scholastic debate have been undermined. The three definitions from Montreal, while not harmful, are of no help here. It was not the intention of the Montreal redefinition to adjudicate apostasy or heresy. Its purpose was to insist that not all divergence is heresy and that no one is without tradition. That approach is especially fitting when the divergences we talk about are matters of ritual, where the variations in the language of the doxology need not be measured in dogmatic terms, because they do not exclude the appropriateness of quite different language in other places. This same quality of pluralism will not work in the same way, and has not been advocated aggressively by any convinced theologian, in the field of social ethics.

We are not talking about "the authority of tradition" as if tradition were a settled reality and we were then to figure out how it works. We are asking how, within the maelstrom of traditioning processes, we can keep our bearings and distinguish between the way the stream should be going and side channels which eddy but lead nowhere. Can we do this by some criterion beyond ourselves? The peculiarity of the term "tradition" is that it points to that criterion beyond itself, to which it claims to be a witness. We are therefore doing no violence to the claim of tradition when we test it by its fidelity to that origin. A witness is not being dishonored when we test his fidelity as an interpreter of the events to which he testifies. That is his dignity as witness; he wants to be tested for that.

Returning to the particular sample case: how would we proceed if we desired to let reforming and renewing through memory apply to the tradition of the just war? It would not suffice to say that these new ideas came into Christian thought in the fourth century and are therefore wrong. Neither can we say that they were brought into Christian thought in the fourth century by bishops who were later sainted and that therefore they are all right. Nor can we bring justification like that of Reinhold Niebuhr, to the effect that any growing community will have to dilute its morality a little in order to take charge of a society for the good of that society.

We must therefore ask much more careful questions about the vision of history as a whole that led to this change in critics. What kind of formulation of the Christian hope was at work when this ethical change seemed to make sense? What was the quality of Christian spirituality and character that made the shift seem "natural"?

If this questioning is careful and is not simply polemic, we shall come to the awareness that the early just war thinkers, more than our contemporaries who use the same words, were still thinking in terms of a minority ethic. They were attempting to "drag their feet" as the mass of Christianity rapidly moved into a new relationship of church and world. Unwilling to admit that their ethical commitment to the sacredness of life and the dignity of the enemy was irrelevant, or to accept that their morality was only for the monastery, they transposed their Christian defense of the sacred life of the enemy into a doctrine of the right of the enemy not to be harmed except for cause, which should have made sense to the Caesars and their heirs. They were not saying that war is "just" in the sense of moral righteousness. They were saying that, to the extent to which this exceptional degree of violence, which obviously is *prima facie* opposed to the gospel, can be justified at all, it must be subject to the vigilant application of the solid criteria of just cause, right intention, legitimate authority, necessary and proportionate means, etc. They were not describing a good society or a Christian moral order but continuing to drag their feet as they saw Christians drawn into administering a bad one.

Seeing the pastoral and culture-critical intent of early just war thought provides us the criteria by which we can evaluate it after a trial run of fifteen centuries. It has very seldom functioned as an efficacious restraint, as it was supposed to. It has more often been transmuted, in the hands of people less critical than Augustine or Aquinas or Vitoria, into a simple affirmation that war is acceptable if it meets certain requirements. Augustine himself would reject that use made of his language. He was adapting the *prima facie* original Christian pacifism, which he still thought he was faithfully supporting, in his continuity with the early Christians, against abuse by people improperly claiming that their responsibilities for the civil order authorized them to be free of restraint. He said it in the language of human rights (the right of the enemy not to be jeopardized without due cause) rather than in the simple language of the Gospel, because he was willing to grant that this simple language would be written off as irrelevant. He had given up on the claim that the Jesus of the Gospel account was relevant and was accepting the apologetes' demand that ethical insight be transmuted into Hellenistic and Roman juridical forms.

A fundamental critique must then address not merely the space that was made for justifiable violence, but the prior acceptance of the irrelevance of Jesus to the political existence of his disciples, or the prior commitment to the imperative of using the world's language if we want to challenge the world's imperatives. That is the point at which the sell-out can now be seen to have occurred. The debate is not about whether the Christian prohibition of violence might have loopholes. The question is whether the pertinence of the Jesus story for our present agenda has to be filtered through some other language and its frame of reference.

I have in the past said it affirmatively: Jesus is presented by the Gospel writers as a model when he renounces the justifiable insurrection of the Zealots. Now I say it as critique. A millennium and a half of efforts to use the more "natural," and therefore supposedly more "applicable" categories of the just war tradition have not successfully translated Christian concern for the enemy's dignity into real politics. We are more able than the medievals to see that justifiable insurrection, as a form of the "just war," *is* a theme to which Jesus does speak: a perception for which neither Saint Francis or Tolstoy was yet ready. The newer urgency of the arms race and of liberation rhetoric frees a deeper stratum of the gospel. We reconstruct by critiquing and by remembering.

Chapter 4

Philosophy and Christian Ethics

Introduction

"You can't live with 'em, you can't live without 'em," sings Rowlf the dog in Jim Henson's *The Muppet Movie*. Rowlf is expressing his male view of females, but a similar sentiment is felt by many theologians when they think about philosophers. On one hand, theologians are aware that a great many philosophers look upon theology with scorn, viewing theologians as, at best, gullible, naive, and unsophisticated. On the other hand, no discipline has altered and continues to alter the course of theology and theological ethics so much as the discipline of philosophy. Theologians may find it hard to live with philosophers, but few have been willing to go it without them.

We can date the current antagonism of philosophy towards theology from roughly the middle of the 1700s. While eighteenth-century philosophy is overwhelmingly characterized by theistic belief, it is David Hume's suspicion of religious belief and his ridicule of Christian believers that is most reflected in the philosophy of the past two hundred fifty years, this hostility perhaps reaching its apex earlier in this century in the philosophical school of logical positivism. If philosophy strikes us as an unlikely source for theological ethics, we must realize that this attitude is a relatively recent one.

As our readings make clear, the relationship between philosophy and theology has not always been characterized by hostility and suspicion. Our biblical texts indicate that in Christian Scripture there is some ambivalence about philosophy. The two passages from Romans seem to suggest a natural revelation of God and God's will by means of which sensitive and alert individuals might read what is required for moral goodness, might have the building blocks for developing a philosophical theory of ethics independent of, but consistent with, that which Scripture discloses about the moral life. Systematic human thought might very well lead us to important truths about the moral life. But even if that is possible, philosophy can, nevertheless, be used for ill as well as good, can be in service to the principalities of the earth rather than God, the Pauline author of Colossians warns us.

It is not surprising that the early Christian theologians should turn to Greek philosophy as a source of moral insight. Aristotle (reading 18) is one of the Greek philosophers whose thought has been found most fertile for moral reflection. Aristotle's approach is that of common sense; observing human practices and beliefs, he concludes that our lives are purposeful, the telos, or goal, of our lives being the achievement of happiness. But happiness cannot consist of just what anyone wants it to consist of, that goal must be one which comports well with our human natures, and what is best in our natures. Moral and intellectual virtues are required not just for the achievement of happiness, in a very real sense they constitute human happiness.

If we leap forward some sixteen hundred years we find the greatest of Christian philosophers attempting to employ the insights of the newly rediscovered Aristotle in the service of Christian thought. St. Thomas Aquinas (reading 19) draws upon biblical teaching and the Christian tradition passed on to him, most notably in the thought of St. Augustine, as he examines the goal of human life. It is not so much that Aristotle is mistaken about the goal of human life as that his thought is incomplete. Aristotle has misidentified our ultimate telos and the nature of the human activity involved in the achievement of that final goal, and St. Thomas sets him right.

The second part of the readings from St. Thomas displays him wrestling with a legacy of Roman thought about natural law as well as with our biblical texts from Romans. St. Thomas's writings asserting the existence of moral laws of nature knowable by the wise, but not only the wise, are difficult, but among the most influential in Western theological ethics even to the present day.

We continue with the Catholic tradition of moral theology in the excerpt from Pope John Paul II's recent encyclical letter *Veritatis Splendor* (reading 20). In our second passage from Romans, Paul writes of the presence of conscience in all humans and the idea of an internal guide or conscience bearing witness against our wrong actions and, perhaps directing us to what is good. Some notion of conscience has been a common feature of theological reflection upon the moral life throughout the history of Christian thought. One finds a view of conscience as a moral source in the writings of Protestants such as John Calvin, the English Puritans, and Bishop Joseph Butler as well as in Catholic moral theology. In our excerpt from *Veritatis Splendor,* the Pope develops a contemporary Catholic view of the authority of conscience in the moral life.

In Richard Mouw's essay on moral justification (reading 21), we find a fine example of how the tools of contemporary philosophy can be of service to moral theology. Wrestling with the perennial problem of the relationship between morality and God's commands, he introduces distinctions which enable us to think more clearly and carefully about this relation. At the very least, Mouw argues, Christians will want to contend that God's commands *indicate* what is morally required even if God's commands by themselves do not always *make* actions right.

In significantly different ways, the two final essays in this chapter challenge too easy a reliance upon philosophy as a moral source. Christos Yannaras (reading 22) describes the work of those the church has identified as "fools for Christ." Taking to heart the "foolishness of the gospel," and rejecting the adequacy of philosophical reflection for grasping the fundamental truths of the Christian faith, these "fools" live their lives in defiance of "reason" as prophetic witnesses to the love of Christ.

This chapter concludes with Stanley Hauer-was's brilliant indictment of the love affair between much of contemporary theological ethics and philosophy (reading 23). Hauerwas carefully details the history of the discipline of Christian ethics (shrewdly introducing many of the ethicists whose works appear in this volume), and examines the contextual and theological motivations that have led Christian ethicists to minimize the theological character of their thought. Hauerwas concludes with the affirmation that theological ethicists do have something important to contribute to contemporary moral discussion but that their contributions will be significant only insofar as they roundly declare their Christian identity and attempt to think through moral questions in the light of this identity and not a universal, objective identity truer to the aims of Enlightenment philosophy.

Suggestions for Further Reading

Bonhoeffer, Dietrich. *Ethics.* New York: Macmillan, 1955.

Cronin, Kieran. *Rights and Christian Ethics.* Cambridge: Cambridge University Press, 1992.

Helm, P., ed. *Divine Commands and Morality.* New York: Oxford University Press, 1981.

John Paul II. *Veritatis Splendor.* New York: Daughters of St. Paul, 1993.

MacIntyre, Alasdair. *After Virtue,* 2nd ed. Notre Dame: University of Notre Dame Press, 1984.

———. *Three Rival Versions of Moral Enquiry* Notre Dame: University of Notre Dame Press, 1990.

Mouw, Richard J. *The God Who Commands.* Notre Dame: University of Notre Dame Press, 1990.

Outka, G., and Paul Ramsey, eds. *Norm and Context in Christian Ethics.* London: SCM Press, 1968.

Outka, G., and John P. Reeder, Jr., eds. *Religion and Morality.* Garden City: Anchor/Doubleday, 1973.

Taylor, Charles C. *Sources of the Self.* Cambridge, Mass.: Harvard University Press, 1989.

Ward, Keith. *Ethics and Christianity.* London: George Allen & Unwin, 1970.

17. Romans 1:18-25
Romans 2:14-16
Colossians 2:8-15

Romans 1:18-25

For the wrath of God is revealed from heaven against all ungodliness and wickedness of those who by their wickedness suppress the truth. For what can be known about God is plain to them, because God has shown it to them. Ever since the creation of the world his eternal power and divine nature, invisible though they are, have been understood and seen through the things he has made. So they are without excuse; for though they knew God, they did not honor him as God or give thanks to him, but they became futile in their thinking, and their senseless minds were darkened. Claiming to be wise, they became fools; and they exchanged the glory of the immortal God for images resembling a mortal human being or birds or four-footed animals or reptiles.

Therefore God gave them up in the lusts of their hearts to impurity, to the degrading of their bodies among themselves, because they exchanged the truth about God for a lie and worshiped and served the creature rather than the Creator, who is blessed forever! Amen.

Romans 2:14-16

When Gentiles, who do not possess the law, do instinctively what the law requires, these, though not having the law, are a law to themselves. They show that what the law requires is written on their hearts, to which their own conscience also bears witness; and their conflicting thoughts will accuse or perhaps excuse them on the day when, according to my gospel, God, through Jesus Christ, will judge the secret thoughts of all.

Colossians 2:8-15

See to it that no one takes you captive through philosophy and empty deceit, according to human tradition, according to the elemental spirits of the universe, and not according to Christ. For in him the whole fullness of deity dwells bodily, and you have come to fullness in him, who is the head of every ruler and authority. In him also you were circumcised with a spiritual circumcision, by putting off the body of the flesh in the circumcision of Christ; when you were buried with him in baptism, you were also raised with him through faith in the power of God, who raised him from the dead. And when you were dead in trespasses and the uncircumcision of your flesh, God made you alive together with him, when he forgave us all our trespasses, erasing the record that stood against us with its legal demands. He set this aside, nailing it to the cross. He disarmed the rulers and authorities and made a public example of them, triumphing over them in it.

18. Excerpts from the *Nicomachean Ethics*

ARISTOTLE

Every craft and every investigation, and likewise every action and decision, seems to aim at some good; hence the good has been well described as that at which everything aims.

However, there is an apparent difference among the ends aimed at. For the end is sometimes an activity, sometimes a product beyond the activity; and when there is an end beyond the action, the product is by nature better than the activity.

*   *   *

Suppose, then, that (a) there is some end of the things we pursue in our actions which we wish for because of itself, and because of which we wish for the other things; and (b) we do not choose everything because of something else, since (c) if we do, it will go on without limit, making desire empty and futile; then clearly (d) this end will be the good, i.e. the best good.

*   *   *

Let us, then, begin again. Since every sort of knowledge and decision pursues some good, what

Aristotle (384–322 B.C.E.) studied philosophy in Athens with Plato and authored numerous works in both natural science and philosophy. The range and depth of his thought is virtually unrivaled. Among his most significant works are the *Physics*, the *Metaphysics*, and the *Nicomachean Ethics*. He was called "the philosopher" by Thomas Aquinas, who synthesized his thought with Christianity.

From Aristotle, *Nicomachean Ethics*, trans. Terence Irwin (Indianapolis: Hackett Publishing Co., 1985).

is that good which we say is the aim of political science? What [in other words] is the highest of all the goods pursued in action?

As far as its name goes, most people virtually agree [about what the good is], since both the many and the cultivated call it happiness, and suppose that living well and doing well are the same as being happy. But they disagree about what happiness is, and the many do not give the same answer as the wise.

For the many think it is something obvious and evident, e.g. pleasure, wealth, or honour, some thinking one thing, others another; and indeed the same person keeps changing his mind, since in sickness he thinks it is health, in poverty wealth. And when they are conscious of their own ignorance, they admire anyone who speaks of something grand and beyond them.

[Among the wise,] however, some used to think that besides these many goods there is some other good that is something in itself, and also causes all these goods to be goods.

*   *   *

Each kind of animal seems to have its own proper pleasure, just as it has its own proper function; for the proper pleasure will be the one that corresponds to its activity.

This is apparent if we also study each kind. For a horse, a dog and a human being have different pleasures; and, as Heracleitus says, an ass would choose chaff over gold, since asses find food pleasanter than gold. Hence animals that differ in species also have pleasures that differ in species; and it would be reasonable for animals of the same species to have the same pleasures also.

In fact, however, the pleasures differ quite a lot, in human beings at any rate. For the same things delight some people, and cause pain to others; and while some find them painful and hateful, others find them pleasant and lovable. The same is true of sweet things. For the same things do not seem sweet to a feverish and to a healthy person, or hot to an enfeebled and to a vigorous person; and the same is true of other things.

But in all such cases it seems that what is really so is what appears so to the excellent person. If this is correct, as it seems to be, and virtue, i.e. the good person in so far as he is good, is the measure of each thing, then what appear pleasures to him will also *be* pleasures, and what is pleasant will be what he enjoys.

And if what he finds objectionable appears pleasant to someone, that is nothing surprising, since human beings suffer many sorts of corruption and damage. It is not pleasant, however, except to these people in these conditions.

Clearly, then, we should say that the pleasures agreed to be shameful are not pleasures at all, except to corrupted people.

But what about those pleasures that seem to be decent? Of these, which kind, or which particular pleasure, should we take to be the pleasure of a human being? Surely it will be clear from the activities, since the pleasures are consequences of these.

Hence the pleasures that complete the activities of the complete and blessedly happy man, whether he has one activity or more than one, will be called the human pleasures to the fullest extent. The other pleasures will be human in secondary and even more remote ways corresponding to the character of the activities.

*   *   *

Some activities are necessary, i.e. choiceworthy for some other end, while others are choiceworthy in themselves. Clearly, then, we should count happiness as one of those activities that are choiceworthy in themselves, not as one of those choiceworthy for some other end. For happiness lacks nothing, but is self-sufficient; and an activity is choiceworthy in itself when nothing further beyond it is sought from it.

This seems to be the character of actions expressing virtue; for doing fine and excellent actions is choiceworthy for itself.

*   *   *

If happiness, then, is activity expressing virtue, it is reasonable for it to express the supreme virtue, which will be the virtue of the best thing.

The best is understanding, or whatever else seems to be the natural ruler and leader, and to understand what is fine and divine, by being itself either divine or the most divine element in us.

Hence complete happiness will be its activity expressing its proper virtue; and we have said that this activity is the activity of study. This seems to agree with what has been said before, and also with the truth.

For this activity is supreme, since understanding is the supreme element in us, and the objects of understanding are the supreme objects of knowledge.

Besides, it is the most continuous activity, since we are more capable of continuous study than of any continuous action.

We think pleasure must be mixed into happiness; and it is agreed that the activity expressing wisdom is the pleasantest of the activities expressing virtue. At any rate, philosophy seems to have remarkably pure and firm pleasures; and it is reasonable for those who have knowledge to spend their lives more pleasantly than those who seek it.

Moreover, the self-sufficiency we spoke of will be found in study above all.

For admittedly the wise person, the just person and the other virtuous people all need the good things necessary for life. Still, when these are adequately supplied, the just person needs other people as partners and recipients of his just actions; and the same is true of the temperate person and brave person and each of the others.

But the wise person is able, and more able the wiser he is, to study even by himself; and though he presumably does it better with colleagues, even so he is more self-sufficient than any other [virtuous person].

Besides, study seems to be liked because of itself alone, since it has no result beyond having studied. But from the virtues concerned with action we try to a greater or lesser extent to gain something beyond the action itself.

Happiness seems to be found in leisure, since we accept trouble so that we can be at leisure, and fight wars so that we can be at peace. Now the virtues concerned with action have their activities in politics or war, and actions here seem to require trouble.

This seems completely true for actions in war, since no one chooses to fight a war, and no one continues it, for the sake of fighting a war; for someone would have to be a complete murderer if he made his friends his enemies so that there could be battles and killings.

But the actions of the politician require trouble also. Beyond political activities themselves these actions seek positions of power and honours; or at least they seek happiness for the politician himself and for his fellow-citizens, which is something different from political science itself, and clearly is sought on the assumption that it is different.

Hence among actions expressing the virtues those in politics and war are preeminently fine and great; but they require trouble, aim at some [further] end, and are choiceworthy for something other than themselves.

But the activity of understanding, it seems, is superior in excellence because it is the activity of study; aims at no end beyond itself; has its own proper pleasure, which increases the activity, and is self-sufficient, leisured and unwearied, as far [as these are possible] for a human being. And whatever else is ascribed to the blessedly happy person is evidently found in connection with this activity.

Hence a human being's complete happiness will be this activity, if it receives a complete span of life, since nothing incomplete is proper to happiness.

Such a life would be superior to the human level. For someone will live it not in so far as he is a human being, but in so far as he has some divine element in him. And the activity of this divine element is as much superior to the activity expressing the rest of virtue as this element is superior to the compound. Hence if understanding is something divine in comparison with a human being, so also will the life that expresses understanding be divine in comparison with human life.

We ought not to follow the proverb-writers, and 'think human, since you are human', or 'think mortal, since you are mortal.' Rather, as far as we can, we ought to be pro-immortal, and go to all lengths to live a life that expresses our supreme element; for however much this element may lack in bulk, by much more it surpasses everything in power and value.

Moreover, each person seems to be his understanding, if he is his controlling and better element; it would be absurd, then, if he were to choose not his own life, but something else's.

And what we have said previously will also apply now. For what is proper to each thing's nature is supremely best and pleasantest for it; and hence for a human being the life expressing understanding will be supremely best and pleasantest, if understanding above all is the human being. This life, then, will also be happiest.

*   *   *

In another way also it appears that complete happiness is some activity of study. For we traditionally suppose that the gods more than anyone are blessed and happy; but what sorts of actions ought we to ascribe to them? Just actions? Surely they will appear ridiculous making contracts, returning deposits and so on. Brave actions? Do they endure what [they find] frightening and endure dangers because it is fine? Generous actions? Whom will they give to? And surely it would be absurd for them to have currency or anything like that. What would their temperate actions be? Surely it is vulgar praise to say that they do not have base appetites. When we go through them all, anything that concerns actions appears trivial and unworthy of the gods.

However, we all traditionally suppose that they are alive and active, since surely they are not asleep like Endymion. Then if someone is alive, and action is excluded, and production even more, what is left but study? Hence the gods' activity that is superior in blessedness will be an activity of study. And so the human activity that is most akin to the gods' will, more than any others, have the character of happiness.

A sign of this is the fact that other animals have no share in happiness, being completely deprived of this activity of study. For the whole life of the gods is blessed, and human life is blessed to the extent that it has something resembling this sort of activity; but none of the other animals is happy, because none of them shares in study at all. Hence happiness extends just as far as study extends, and the more someone studies, the happier he is, not coincidentally but in so far as he studies, since study is valuable in itself. And so [on this argument] happiness will be some kind of study.

However, the happy person is a human being, and so will need external prosperity also; for his nature is not self-sufficient for study, but he needs a healthy body, and needs to have food and the other services provided.

Still, even though no one can be blessedly happy without external goods, we must not think that to be happy we will need many large goods. For self-sufficiency and action do not depend on excess, and we can do fine actions even if we do not rule earth and sea; for even from moderate resources we can do the actions expressing virtue. This is evident to see, since many private citizens seem to do decent actions no less than people in power do — even more, in fact. It is enough if moderate resources are provided; for the life of someone whose activity expresses virtue will be happy.

*   *   *

The person whose activity expresses understanding and who takes care of understanding would seem to be in the best condition, and most loved by the gods. For if the gods pay some attention to human beings, as they seem to, it would be reasonable for them to take pleasure in what is best and most akin to them, namely understanding; and reasonable for them to benefit in return those who most of all like and honour understanding, on the assumption that these people attend to what is beloved by the gods, and act correctly and finely.

Clearly, all this is true of the wise person more than anyone else; hence he is most loved by the gods. And it is likely that this same person will be happiest; hence the wise person will be happier than anyone else on this argument too.

19. Excerpts from *Summa Contra Gentiles,* and *Summa Theologica*

ST. THOMAS AQUINAS

Summa Contra Gentiles
Book III, Chapters 34, 37, 48, 63

That Man's Ultimate Felicity Does Not Lie in Acts of the Moral Virtues

It is clear, too, that the ultimate felicity of man does not consist in moral actions.

In fact, human felicity is incapable of being ordered to a further end, if it is ultimate. But all moral operations can be ordered to something else. This is evident from the most important instances of these actions. The operations of fortitude, which are concerned with warlike activities, are ordered to victory and to peace. Indeed, it would be foolish to make war merely for its own sake.[1] Likewise, the operations of justice are ordered to the preservation of peace among men,

---

1. Aristotle, *Nicomachean Ethics,* X, 7 (1177b 9).

St. Thomas Aquinas (1225–1274) was a professor of theology in Paris and Naples. He is widely regarded as the most important of Christian philosophers. His moral theory is developed in numerous passages in his works *Summa Theologica* and *Summa Contra Gentiles.* Note his use of Aristotle.

From Thomas Aquinas, *Summa Contra Gentiles,* trans. V. Bourke (Notre Dame: University of Notre Dame Press, 1975) and *Summa Theologica,* trans. Fathers of the English Dominican Province (Indianapolis: Hackett Publishing Co., 1988).

by means of each man having his own possessions undisturbed. And the same thing is evident for all the other virtues. Therefore, man's ultimate felicity does not lie in moral operations.

Again, the moral virtues have this purpose: through them the mean is preserved in the internal passions, and in regard to external things. Now, it is not possible for such a measuring of passions, or of external things, to be the ultimate end of human life, since these passions and exterior things are capable of being ordered to something else. Therefore, it is not possible for man's ultimate felicity to lie in acts of the moral virtues.

Besides, since man is man by virtue of his possession of reason, his proper good which is felicity should be in accord with what is appropriate to reason. Now, that is more appropriate to reason which reason has within itself than which it produces in another thing. So, since the good of moral virtue is something produced by reason in things other than itself, it could not be that which is best for man; namely, felicity. Rather would felicity seem to be a good situated in reason itself.

Moreover, it was shown above[2] that the ultimate end of all things is to become like unto God. So, that whereby man is made most like God will be his felicity. Now, this is not a function of moral acts, since such acts cannot be attributed to God, except metaphorically. Indeed, it does not befit God to have passions, or the like, with which moral acts are concerned. Therefore, man's ultimate felicity, that is, his ultimate end, does not consist in moral actions.

Furthermore, felicity is the proper good for man. So, that which is most proper among all human goods, for man in contrast to the other animals, is the good in which his ultimate felicity is to be sought. Now, an act of moral virtue is not of this sort, for some animals share somewhat, either in liberality or in fortitude, but an animal does not participate at all in intellectual action. Therefore, man's ultimate felicity does not lie in moral acts.

*   *   *

2. Summa Contra Gentiles (SCG), III, ch. 19.

That the Ultimate Felicity of Man Consists in the Contemplation of God

So, if the ultimate felicity of man does not consist in external things which are called the goods of fortune, nor in the goods of the body, nor in the goods of the soul according to its sensitive part, nor as regards the intellective part according to the activity of the moral virtues, nor according to the intellectual virtues that are concerned with action, that is, art and prudence — we are left with the conclusion that the ultimate felicity of man lies in the contemplation of truth.

Indeed, this is the only operation of man which is proper to him, and in it he shares nothing in common with the other animals.

So, too, this is ordered to nothing else as an end, for the contemplation of truth is sought for its own sake.

Also, through this operation man is united by way of likeness with beings superior to him, since this alone of human operations is found also in God and in separate substances.

Indeed, in this operation he gets in touch with these higher beings by knowing them in some way.

Also, for this operation man is rather sufficient unto himself, in the sense that for it he needs little help from external things.

In fact, all other human operations seem to be ordered to this one, as to an end. For, there is needed for the perfection of contemplation a soundness of body, to which all the products of art that are necessary for life are directed. Also required are freedom from the disturbances of the passions — this is achieved through the moral virtues and prudence — and freedom from external disorders, to which the whole program of government in civil life is directed. And so, if they are rightly considered, all human functions may be seen to subserve the contemplation of truth.

However, it is not possible for man's ultimate felicity to consist in the contemplation which depends on the understanding of principles, for that is very imperfect, being most universal, including the potential cognition of things. Also, it is the beginning, not the end, of human enquiry, coming to us from nature and not because of our search for truth. Nor, indeed, does it lie in the area of the sciences which deal with lower things, because felicity should lie in the working of the intellect in relation to the noblest objects of understanding. So, the conclusion remains that man's ultimate felicity consists in the contemplation of wisdom, based on the considering of divine matters.

From this, that is also clear by way of induction, which was proved above by rational arguments,[3] namely, that man's ultimate felicity consists only in the contemplation of God.

*   *   *

That Man's Ultimate Felicity Does Not Come in This Life

If, then, ultimate human felicity does not consist in the knowledge of God, whereby he is known in general by all, or most, men, by a sort of confused appraisal, and again, if it does not consist in the knowledge of God which is known by way of demonstration in the speculative sciences, nor in the cognition of God whereby he is known through faith, . . . and if it is not possible in this life to reach a higher knowledge of God so as to know him through his essence, or even in such a way that, when the other separate substances are known, God might be known through the knowledge of them, as if from a closer vantage point, . . . and if it is necessary to identify ultimate felicity with some sort of knowledge of God, . . . then it is not possible for man's ultimate felicity to come in this life.

Again, the ultimate end of man brings to a termination man's natural appetite, in the sense that, once the end is acquired, nothing else will be sought. For, if he is still moved onward to something else, he does not yet have the end in which he may rest. Now, this termination cannot occur in this life. For, the more a person understands, the more is the desire to understand increased in him, and this is natural to man, unless, perchance, there be someone who understands all things. But in this life this does not happen to anyone who is a mere man, nor could it happen, since we are not able to know in this life the separate substances, and they are most intelligible, . . . Therefore, it is not possible for man's ultimate felicity to be in this life.

Besides, everything that is moved toward an end naturally desires to be stationed at, and at rest in, that end; consequently, a body does not move away from the place to which it is moved naturally, unless by virtue of a violent movement which runs counter to its appetite. Now, felicity is the ultimate end which man naturally desires. So, there is a natural desire of man to be established in felicity. Therefore, unless along with felicity such an unmoving stability be attained, he is not yet happy, for his natural desire is not yet at rest. And so, when a person attains felicity he likewise attains stability and rest, and that is why this is the notion of all men concerning felicity, that it requires stability as part of its essential character. For this reason, the philosopher says, in *Ethics I,* that "we do not regard the happy man as a sort of chameleon."[4] Now, in this life there is no certain stability, for to any man, no matter how happy he is reputed to be, illnesses and misfortunes may possibly come, and by them he may be hindered in that operation, whatever it may be, with which felicity is identified. Therefore, it is not possible for man's ultimate felicity to be in this life.

*   *   *

For these and like reasons, Alexander and Averroes claimed that man's ultimate felicity does not consist in the human knowledge which comes through the speculative sciences, but through a connection with a separate substance, which they believed to be possible for man in this life. But, since Aristotle saw that there is no other knowledge for man in this life than through the speculative sciences, he maintained that man does not achieve perfect felicity, but only a limited kind.

On this point there is abundant evidence of how even the brilliant minds of these men suffered from the narrowness of their viewpoint. From which narrow attitudes we shall be freed if we grant in accord with the foregoing proofs that man can reach true felicity after this life, when man's soul is existing immortally; in which state the soul will understand in the way that separate substances understand, as we showed in Book Two of this work.[5]

And so, man's ultimate felicity will lie in the knowledge of God that the human mind has after

---

3. SCG, III, ch. 25. Ch. 26-37 contain an elaborate instance of inductive argument by exclusion.

4. Aristotle, *Nicomachean Ethics,* I, 10 (1100b 5).
5. SCG, II, ch. 81.

this life, according to the way in which separate substances know him. For which reason our Lord promises us "a reward in heaven" and says that the saints "shall be as the angels . . . who always see God in heaven," as it is said (Matt. 5:12; 22:30; 18:10).

*　　*　　*

How Man's Every Desire Is Fulfilled In That Ultimate Felicity

From the foregoing it is quite apparent that, in the felicity that comes from the divine vision,[6] every human desire is fulfilled, according to the text of the Psalm (102:5): "Who satisfieth thy desire with good things." And every human effort attains its completion in it. This, in fact, becomes clear to anyone who thinks over particular instances.

For there is in man, in so far as he is intellectual, one type of desire, concerned with the *knowledge of truth;* indeed, men seek to fulfill this desire by the effort of the contemplative life. And this will clearly be fulfilled in that vision, when, through the vision of the First Truth, all that the intellect naturally desires to know become known to it. . . .

There is also a certain desire in man, based on his possession of reason, whereby he is enabled to manage lower things; this, men seek to fulfill by the work of the active and civic life. Indeed, this desire is chiefly for this end, that the entire life of man may be arranged in accord with reason, for this is to *live in accord with virtue.* For the end of the activity of every virtuous man is the good appropriate to his virtue, just as, for the brave man, it is to act bravely. Now, this desire will then be completely fulfilled, since reason will be at its peak strength having been enlightened by the divine light, so that it cannot swerve away from what is right.

Going along, then, with the civic life are certain goods which man needs for civic activities. For instance, there is a high position of honor, which makes men proud and ambitious, if they desire it inordinately. But men are raised through this vision to the highest peak of honor, because they are in a sense united with God. . . . For this reason, just as God himself is the "King of ages" (1 Tim. 1:17), so are the blessed united with him

6. SCG, IV, ch. 54.

called *kings:* "They shall reign with Christ" (Rev. 20:6).

Another object of desire associated with civic life is *popular renown;* by an inordinate desire for this men are deemed lovers of vainglory. Now, the blessed are made men of renown by this vision, not according to the opinion of men, who can deceive and be deceived, but in accord with the truest knowledge, both of God and of all the blessed. Therefore, this blessedness is frequently termed *glory* in sacred Scripture; for instance, it is said in the Psalm (149:5): "The saints shall rejoice in glory."

There is, indeed, another object of desire in civic life; namely, *wealth.* By the inordinate desire and love of this, men become illiberal and unjust. But in this beatitude there is a plenitude of all goods, inasmuch as the blessed come to enjoy him who contains the perfection of all good things. For this reason it is said in Wisdom (7:11): "All good things came to me together with her." Hence it is also said in the Psalm (111:3): "Glory and wealth shall be in his house."

There is even a third desire of man, which is common to him and the other animals, *to enjoy pleasures.* Men chiefly seek after this in the voluptuous life, and they become intemperate and incontinent through immoderation in regard to it. However, the most perfect delight is found in this felicity: as much more perfect than the delight of the sense, which even brute animals can enjoy, as the intellect is superior to sense power; and also as that good in which we shall take delight is greater than any sensible good, and more intimate, and more continually delightful, and also as that delight is freer from all admixture of sorrow, or concern about trouble. Of this it is said in the Psalm (35:9): "They shall be inebriated with the plenty of thy house, and thou shalt make them drink of the torrent of thy pleasure."

There is, morover, a natural desire common to all things by which they desire *their own preservation,* to the extent that this is possible: men are made fearful and excessively chary of work that is hard for them by immoderation in this desire. But this desire will then be completely satisfied when the blessed attain perfect sempiternity and are safe from all harm; according to the text of Isaiah (49:10) and Revelation (7:16; 21): "They shall no more hunger or thirst, neither shall the sun fall on them, nor any heat."

And so, it is evident that through the divine

vision intellectual substances obtain true felicity, in which their desires are completely brought to rest and in which is the full sufficiency of all the goods which, according to Aristotle,[7] are required for happiness. Hence, Boethius also says that "happiness is a state of life made perfect by the accumulation of all goods."[8]

Now, there is nothing in this life so like this ultimate and perfect felicity as the life of those who contemplate truth, to the extent that it is possible in this life. And so, the philosophers who were not able to get full knowledge of this ultimate happiness identified man's ultimate happiness with the contemplation which is possible in this life.[9] On this account, too, of all other lives the contemplative is more approved in divine Scripture, when our Lord says: "Mary hath chosen the better part," namely, the contemplation of truth, "which shall not be taken from her" (Luke 10:42). In fact, the contemplation of truth begins in this life, but reaches its climax in the future; whereas the active and civic life does not go beyond the limits of this life.

Summa Theologica
Books I-II, Question 94, Articles 2-6

Does the Natural Law Contain Several Precepts or One Only?

Obj. 1. It would seem that the natural law contains, not several precepts, but one only. For law is a kind of precept, as stated above.[1] If, therefore, there were many precepts of the natural law, it would follow that there are also many natural laws.

Obj. 2. Further, the natural law is consequent to human nature. But human nature as a whole is one, though, as to its parts, it is manifold. Therefore, either there is but one precept of the law of nature, on account of the unity of nature as a whole, or there are many by reason of the number of parts of human nature. The result would be that even things relating to the inclination of the concupiscible faculty belong to the natural law.

Obj. 3. Further, law is something pertaining to reason, as stated above.[2] Now, reason is but one in man. Therefore, there is only one precept of the natural law.

On the contrary, the precepts of the natural law in man stand in relation to practical matters as the first principles to matters of demonstration. But there are several first indemonstrable principles. Therefore, there are also several precepts of the natural law.

I answer that, as stated above, the precepts of the natural law are to the practical reason what the first principles of demonstrations are to the speculative reason because both are self-evident principles.[3] Now a thing is said to be self-evident in two ways: first, in itself; secondly, in relation to us. Any proposition is said to be self-evident in itself if its predicate is contained in the notion of the subject, although, to one who knows not the definition of the subject, it happens that such a proposition is not self-evident. For instance, this proposition, "Man is a rational being," is in its very nature self-evident, since who says "man" says "a rational being," and yet to one who knows not what a man is, this proposition is not self-evident.

7. Aristotle, *Nicomachean Ethics*, X, 7 (1177a 24).

8. Boethius, *De consolatione philosophiae*, III, prose 2 (*PL*, 63, col. 724).

9. Aristotle, *Nicomachean Ethics*, X, 7 (1177a 18).

1. *Summa Theologica* (ST), I-II, Q. 92, A. 2.

2. ST, I-II, Q. 90, A. 1.

3. ST, I-II, Q. 91, A. 3.

Hence it is that, as Boethius says,[4] certain axioms or propositions are universally self-evident to all, and such are those propositions whose terms are known to all, as, "Every whole is greater than its part," and, "Things equal to one and the same are equal to one another." But some propositions are self-evident only to the wise who understand the meaning of the terms of such propositions; thus to one who understands that an angel is not a body, it is self-evident that an angel is not circumspectively in a place, but this is not evident to the unlearned, for they cannot grasp it.

Now, a certain order is to be found in those things that are apprehended universally. For that which, before aught else, falls under apprehension, is "being," the notion of which is included in all things whatsoever a man apprehends. Wherefore the first indemonstrable principle is that the same thing cannot be affirmed and denied at the same time, which based on the nature of "being" and "not-being," and on this principle all others are based, as it is stated in *Metaphysics* IV.[5] Now, as "being" is the first thing that falls under the apprehension simply, so "good" is the first thing that falls under the apprehension of the practical reason, which is directed to action, since every agent acts for an end under the aspect of good. Consequently, the first principle in the practical reason is one founded on the notion of good, viz., that good is that which all things seek after. Hence this is the first precept of law, that good is to be done and pursued, and evil is to be avoided. All other precepts of the natural law are based upon this, so that whatever the practical reason naturally apprehends as man's good (or evil) belongs to the precepts of the natural law as something to be done or avoided.

Since, however, good has the nature of an end, and evil the nature of a contrary, hence it is that all those things to which man has a natural inclination are naturally apprehended by reason as being good and, consequently, as objects of pursuit, and their contraries as evil and objects of avoidance. Wherefore the order of the precepts of the natural law is according to the order of natural inclinations. Because in man there is first of all an inclination to good in accordance with the nature which he has in common with all substances, inasmuch as every substance seeks the preservation of its own being according to its nature, and by reason of this inclination, whatever is a means of preserving human life and warding off its obstacles belongs to the natural law. Secondly, there is in man an inclination to things that pertain to him more specially according to that nature which he has in common with other animals, and in virtue of this inclination, those things are said to belong to the natural law "which nature has taught to all animals,"[6] such as sexual intercourse, education of offspring, and so forth. Thirdly, there is in man an inclination to good according to the nature of his reason, which nature is proper to him; thus man has a natural inclination to know the truth about God and to live in society, and in this respect, whatever pertains to this inclination belongs to the natural law, for instance, to shun ignorance, to avoid offending those among whom one has to live, and other such things regarding the above inclination.

Reply Obj. 1. All these precepts of the law of nature have the character of one natural law inasmuch as they flow from one first precept.

Reply Obj. 2. All the inclinations of any parts whatsoever of human nature, e.g., of the concupiscible and irascible parts: insofar as they are ruled by reason, belong to the natural law and are reduced to one first precept, as stated above, so that the precepts of the natural law are many in themselves but are based on one common foundation.

Reply Obj. 3. Although reason is one in itself, yet it directs all things regarding man, so that whatever can be ruled by reason is contained under the law of reason.

Are All Acts of Virtue Prescribed by the Natural Law?

Obj. 1. It would seem that not all acts of virtue are prescribed by the natural law because, as stated above, it is essential to a law that it be ordained to the common good.[7] But some acts of virtue are ordained to the private good of the individual, as is evident especially in regard to acts of temperance. Therefore, not all acts of virtue are the subject of natural law.

Obj. 2. Further, every sin is opposed to some

---

4. *De hebdom.* PL 64, 1311.
5. 3. 1005b29-34.

6. *Digest* I, 1, 1. K I, 29a.
7. ST, I-II, Q. 90, A. 2.

virtuous act. If, therefore, all acts of virtue are prescribed by the natural law, it seems to follow that all sins are against nature, whereas this applies to certain special sins.

Obj. 3. Further, those things which are according to nature are common to all. But acts of virtue are not common to all, since a thing is virtuous in one and vicious in another. Therefore, not all acts of virtue are prescribed by the natural law.

On the contrary, Damascene says that "virtues are natural."[8] Therefore, virtuous acts also are a subject of the natural law.

I answer that we may speak of virtuous acts in two ways: first, under the aspect of virtuous; secondly, as such and such acts considered in their proper species. If, then, we speak of acts of virtue considered as virtuous, thus all virtuous acts belong to the natural law. For it has been stated that to the natural law belongs everything to which a man is inclined according to his nature.[9] Now each thing is inclined naturally to an operation that is suitable to it according to its form; thus fire is inclined to give heat. Wherefore, since the rational soul is the proper form of man, there is in every man a natural inclination to act according to reason and this is to act according to virtue. Consequently, considered thus, all acts of virtue are prescribed by the natural law, since each one's reason naturally dictates to him to act virtuously. But if we speak of virtuous acts considered in themselves, i.e., in their proper species, thus not all virtuous acts are prescribed by the natural law; the many things are done virtuously to which nature does not incline at first, but which, through the inquiry of reason, have been found by men to be conducive to well-living.

Reply Obj. 1. Temperance is about the natural concupiscences of food, drink, and sexual matters, which are indeed ordained to the natural common good, just as other matters of law are ordained to the moral common good.

Reply Obj. 2. By human nature we may mean either that which is proper to man — and in this sense all sins, as being against reason, are also against nature, as Damascene states[10] — or we may mean that nature which is common to man and other animals, and in this sense certain special

sins are said to be against nature, thus, contrary to heterosexual intercourse, which is natural to all animals, is male homosexual union, which has received the special name of the unnatural vice.

Reply Obj. 3. This argument considers acts in themselves. For it is owing to the various conditions of men that certain acts are virtuous for some as being proportionate and becoming to them, while they are vicious for others as being out of proportion to them.

Is the Natural Law the Same in All Men?

Obj. 1. It would seem that the natural law is not the same in all. For it is stated in the *Decretum* that "the natural law is that which is contained in the Law and the Gospel."[11] But this is not common to all men because, as it is written, "all do not obey the gospel."[12] Therefore, the natural law is not the same in all men.

Obj. 2. Further, "Things which are according to the law are said to be just," as stated in *Ethics* V.[13] But it is stated in the same book that nothing is so universally just as not to be subject to change in regard to some men. Therefore, even the natural law is not the same in all men.

Obj 3. Further, as stated above, to the natural law belongs everything to which a man is inclined according to his nature.[14] Now, different men are naturally inclined to different things, some to the desire of pleasures, others to the desire of honors, and other men to other things. Therefore, there is not one natural law for all.

On the contrary, Isidore says, "The natural law is common to all nations."[15]

I answer that, as stated above, to the natural law belong those things to which a man is inclined naturally, and among these, it is proper to man to be inclined to act according to reason.[16] Now the process of reason is from the common to the proper, as stated in *Phys.* I.[17] The speculative reason, however, is differently situated in this matter

---

8. *De fide orth.* III, 14. PG 94, 1045.
9. ST, I-II, Q. 94, A. 2.
10. *De fide orth.* II, 30. PG 94, 976.

11. *Decretum* I, 1, 1. RF I, 1.
12. Rom. 10:16.
13. 3. 1129b12.
14. ST, I-II, Q. 94, AA. 2, 3.
15. *Etym.* V, 4. PL 82, 199.
16. ST, I-II, Q. 94, AA. 2, 3.
17. 1. 184a16.

from the practical reason. For, since the speculative reason is concerned chiefly with necessary things, which cannot be otherwise than they are, its proper conclusions, like the universal principles, contain the truth without fail. The practical reason, on the other hand, is concerned with contingent matters, about which human actions are concerned, and consequently, although there is necessity in the general principles, the more we descend to matters of detail, the more frequently we encounter deviations. Accordingly, then, in speculative matters, truth is the same for all men both as to principles and as to conclusions, although the truth is not known to all as regards the conclusions but only as regards the principles which are called common notions. But in matters of action, truth or tactical rectitude is not the same for all as to matters of known to all.

It is, therefore, evident that, as regards the general principles, whether of speculative or practical reason, truth or rectitude is the same for all and is equally known by all. As to the proper conclusions of the speculative reason, the truth is the same for all but is not equally known to all; thus it is true for all that the three angles of a triangle are together equal to two right angles, although it is not known to all. But as to the proper conclusions of the practical reason, neither is the truth or rectitude the same for all, nor, where it is the same, it is equally known by all. Thus it is right and true for all to act according to reason, and from this principle, it follows as a proper conclusion that goods entrusted to another should be restored to their owner. Now this is true for the majority of cases, but it may happen in a particular case that it would be injurious, and therefore unreasonable, to restore goods held in trust, for instance, if they are claimed for the purpose of fighting against one's country. And this principle will be found to fail the more according as we descend further into detail, e.g., if one were to say that goods held in trust should be restored with such and such a guarantee or in such and such a way, because the greater the number of conditions added, the greater the number of ways in which the principle may fail, so that it be not right to restore or not to restore.

Consequently, we must say that the natural law as to general principles is the same for all both as to rectitude and as to knowledge. But as to certain matters of detail, which are conclusions, as it were, of those general principles, it is the same for all in the majority of cases both as to rectitude and as to knowledge, and yet, in some few cases, it may fail both as to rectitude by reason of certain obstacles (just as natures subject to generation and corruption fail in some few cases on account of some obstacle) and as to knowledge, since, in some, the reason is perverted by passion or evil habit or an evil disposition of nature; thus, formerly, theft, although it is expressly contrary to the natural law, was not considered wrong among the Germans, as Julius Caesar relates.[18]

Reply Obj. 1. The meaning of the sentence quoted is not that whatever is contained in the Law and the Gospel belongs to the natural law, since they contain many things that are above nature, but that whatever belongs to the natural law is fully contained in them. Wherefore Gratian, after saying that "the natural law is what is contained in the Law and the Gospel," adds at once, by way of example, "by which everyone is commanded to do to others as he would be done by."

Reply Obj. 2. The saying of the philosopher is to be understood of things that are naturally just, not as general principles but as conclusions drawn from them, having rectitude in the majority of cases but failing in a few.

Reply Obj. 3. As, in man, reason rules and commands the other powers, so all the natural inclinations belonging to the other powers must needs be directed according to reason. Wherefore it is universally right for all men that all their inclinations should be directed according to reason.

Can the Natural Law Be Changed?

Obj. 1. It would seem that the natural law can be changed because, on Sir. 17:9, "He gave them instructions, and the law of life," a gloss says: "He wished the law of the letter to be written in order to correct the law of nature."[19] But that which is corrected is changed. Therefore, the natural law can be changed.

Obj. 2. Further, the slaying of the innocent, adultery, and theft are against the natural law. But we find these things changed by God, as when God

---

18. *De bello Gal.* VI, 23.
19. *Glossa ordin.* PL 109, 876.

commanded Abraham to slay his innocent son,[20] and when he ordered the Jews to borrow and purloin the vessels of the Egyptians,[21] and when he commanded Hosea to take to himself "a wife of fornications."[22] Therefore, the natural law can be changed.

Obj. 3. Further, Isidore says that "the possession of all things in common and universal freedom are matters of natural law."[23] But these things are seen to be changed by human laws. Therefore, it seems that the natural law is subject to change.

On the contrary, it is said in the *Decretum:* "The natural law dates from the creation of the rational creature. It does not vary according to time but remains unchangeable.[24]

I answer that a change in the natural law may be understood in two ways. First, by way of addition. In this sense, nothing hinders the natural law from being changed, since many things, for the benefit of human life, have been added over and above the natural law both by the divine law and by human laws.

Secondly, a change in the natural law may be understood by way of subtraction, so that what previously was according to the natural law ceases to be so. In this sense, the natural law is altogether unchangeable in its first principles, but in its secondary principles, which, as we have said, are like certain proper conclusions closely related to the first principles, the natural law is not changed so that what it prescribes be not right in most cases. But it may be changed in some particular cases of rare occurrence[25] through some special causes hindering the observance of such precepts, as stated above.[26]

Reply Obj. 1. The written law is said to be given for the correction of the natural law, either because it supplies what was wanting to the natural law or because the natural law was perverted in the hearts of some men as to certain matters, so that they esteemed those things good which are naturally evil, which perversion stood in need of correction.

20. Gen. 22:2.
21. Ex. 12:25.
22. Hos. 1:2.
23. *Etym.* V, 4. PL 82, 199.
24. *Decretum* I, 1, 5. RF I, 7.
25. ST, I-II, Q. 94, A. 4.
26. A. 4.

Reply Obj. 2. All men alike, both guilty and innocent, die the death of nature, which death of nature is inflicted by the power of God on account of original sin, according to I Kings: "The Lord kills and makes alive."[27] Consequently, by the command of God, death can be inflicted on any man, guilty or innocent, without any injustice whatever. In like manner, adultery is intercourse with another's wife, who is allotted to him by the law handed down by God. Consequently, intercourse with any woman, by the command of God, is neither adultery nor fornication. The same applies to theft, which is the taking of another's property. For whatever is taken by the command of God, to whom all things belong, is not taken against the will of its owner, whereas it is in this that theft consists. Nor is it only in human things that whatever is commanded by God is right but also in natural things — whatever is done by God is, in some way, natural, as stated in the First Part.[28]

Reply Obj. 3. A thing is said to belong to the natural law in two ways. First, because nature inclines thereto, e.g., that one should not do harm to another. Secondly, because nature did not bring in the contrary; thus we might say that for man to be naked is of the natural law because nature did not give him clothes, but art invented them. In this sense, "the possession of all things in common and universal freedom" are said to be of the natural law because, to wit, the distinction of possessions and slavery were not brought in by nature but devised by human reason for the benefit of human life. Accordingly, the law of nature was not changed in this respect except by addition.

Can the Law of Nature Be Abolished from the Heart of Man?

Obj. 1. It would seem that the natural law can be abolished from the heart of man because, on Rom. 2:14, "When the Gentiles who have not the law," etc., a gloss says that "the law of righteousness, which sin had blotted out, is graven on the heart of man when he is restored by grace.[29] But the law of righteousness is the law of nature. Therefore, the law of nature can be blotted out.

27. 2:6.
28. ST, I, Q. 105, A. 6, *ad* 1.
29. *Glossa.* PL 191, 1345.

Obj. 2. Further, the law of grace is more efficacious than the law of nature. But the law of grace is blotted out by sin. Much more, therefore, can the law of nature be blotted out.

Obj. 3. Further, that which is established by law is made just. But many things are legally established which are contrary to the law of nature. Therefore, the law of nature can be abolished from the heart of man.

On the contrary, Augustine says, "Thy law is written in the hearts of men, which iniquity itself effaces not."[30] But the law which is written in men's hearts is the natural law. Therefore, the natural law cannot be blotted out.

I answer that, as stated above, there belong to the natural law, first, certain most general precepts that are known to all; and secondly, certain secondary and more detailed precepts which are, as it were, conclusions following closely from first principles.[31] As to those general principles, the natural law, in the abstract, can nowise be blotted out from men's hearts. But it is blotted out in the case of particular action insofar as reason is hindered from applying the general principles of a particular point of practice on account of concupiscence or some other passion, as stated above.[32] But as to the other, i.e., the secondary precepts, the natural law can be blotted out from the human heart either by evil persuasions, just as in speculative matters errors occur in respect of necessary conclusions, or by vicious customs and corrupt habits, as among some men theft and even unnatural vices, as the apostle states,[33] were not esteemed sinful.

Reply Obj. 1. Sin blots out the law of nature in particular cases, not universally, except perchance in regard to the secondary precepts of the natural law, in the way stated above.

Reply Obj. 2. Although grace is more efficacious than nature, yet nature is more essential to man and therefore more enduring.

Reply Obj. 3. The argument is true of the secondary precepts of the natural law, against which some legislators have framed certain enactments which are unjust.

30. *Conf.* II, 4. PL 32, 678.
31. ST, I-II, Q. 94, AA. 4, 5.
32. ST I-II, Q. 77, A. 2.
33. Rom. 1:24.

20. Conscience and Truth

POPE JOHN PAUL II

Man's Sanctuary

The relationship between man's freedom and God's law is most deeply lived out in the "heart" of the person, in his moral conscience. As the Second Vatican Council observed: "In the depths of his conscience man detects a law which he does not impose on himself, but which holds him to obedience. Always summoning him to love good and avoid evil, the voice of conscience can when necessary speak to his heart more specifically: 'do this, shun that.' For man has in his heart a law written by God. To obey it is the very dignity of man; according to it he will be judged" (cf. Rom. 12:14-16).[1]

The way in which one conceives the relationship between freedom and law is thus intimately bound up with one's understanding of the moral conscience. Here the cultural tendencies referred to above in which freedom and law are set in opposition to each other and kept apart, and free-

1. Pastoral Constitution on the Church in the Modern World *Gaudium et Spes,* 16.

John Paul II (1920–) (born Karol Wojtyla) is the current bishop of Rome and pope of the Roman Catholic Church. Trained in moral theology, he has written *Sources of Renewal: The Implementation of the Second Vatican Council; Signs of Contradiction; The Redeemer of Man;* and *Christian Meaning of Human Suffering.*

From "Encyclical Letter *Veritatis Splendor* Addressed by the Supreme Pontiff Pope John Paul II to All the Bishops of the Catholic Church regarding Certain Fundamental Questions of the Church's Moral Teaching" (1993).

dom is exalted almost to the point of idolatry — lead to a *"creative" understanding of moral conscience,* which diverges from the teaching of the Church's tradition and her Magisterium.

According to the opinion of some theologians, the function of conscience had been reduced, at least at a certain point in the past, to a simple application of general moral norms to individual cases in the life of the person. But those norms, they continue, cannot be expected to foresee and to respect all the individual concrete acts of the person in al their uniqueness and particularity. While such norms might somehow be useful for a correct *assessment* of the situation, they cannot replace the individual personal *decision* on how to act in particular cases. The critique already mentioned of the traditional understanding of human nature and of its importance for the moral life has even led certain authors to state that these norms are not so much a binding objective criterion for judgments of conscience, but a *general perspective* which helps man tentatively to put order into his personal and social life. These authors also stress the *complexity* typical of the phenomenon of conscience, a complexity profoundly related to the whole sphere of psychology and the emotions, and to the numerous influences exerted by the individual's social and cultural environment. On the other hand, they give maximum attention to the value of conscience, which the Council itself defined as "the sanctuary of man, where he is alone with God whose voice echoes within him."[2] This voice, it is said, leads man not so much to a meticulous observance of universal norms as to a creative and responsible acceptance of the personal tasks entrusted to him by God.

In their desire to emphasize the "creative character of conscience, certain authors no longer call its actions "judgments" but "decisions": only by making these decisions "autonomously" would man be able to attain moral maturity. Some even hold that this process of maturing is inhibited by the excessively categorical position adopted by the Church's Magisterium in many moral questions; for them, the Church's interventions are the cause of unnecessary *conflicts of conscience.*

In order to justify these positions, some authors have proposed a kind of double status of moral truth. Beyond the doctrinal and abstract level, one would have to acknowledge the priority of a certain more concrete existential consideration. The latter, by taking account of circumstances and the situation, could legitimately be the basis of certain *exceptions to the general rule* and thus permit one to do in practice and in good conscience what is qualified as intrinsically evil by the moral law. A separation, or even an opposition, is thus established in some bases between the teaching of the precept, which is valid in general, and the norm of the individual conscience, which would in fact make the final decision about what is good and what is evil. On this basis, an attempt is made to legitimize so-called "pastoral" solutions contrary to the teaching of the Magisterium, and to justify a "creative" hermeneutic according to which the moral conscience is in no way obliged, in every case, by a particular negative precept.

No one can fail to realize that these approaches pose a challenge to the very identity of the moral conscience in relation to human freedom and God's law. Only the clarification made earlier with regard to the relationship, based on truth, between freedom and law makes possible a *discernment* concerning this "creative" understanding of conscience.

The Judgment of Conscience

The text of the Letter to the Romans which has helped us to grasp the essence of the natural law also indicates the *biblical understanding of conscience, especially in its specific connection with the law:* "When Gentiles who have not the law do by nature what the law requires, they are a law unto themselves, even though they do not have the law. They show that what the law requires is written on their hearts, while their conscience also bears witness and their conflicting thoughts accuse or perhaps excuse them" (Rom. 2:14-15).

According to Saint Paul, conscience in a certain sense confronts man with the law, and thus becomes a *"witness" for man:* a witness of his own faithfulness or unfaithfulness with regard to the law, of his essential moral rectitude or iniquity. Conscience is the *only* witness, since what takes place in the heart of the person is hidden from the eyes of everyone outside. Conscience makes its witness known only to the person himself. And,

2. Ibid.

in turn, only the person himself knows what his own response is to the voice of conscience.

The importance of this interior *dialogue of man with himself* can never be adequately appreciated. But it is a also a *dialogue of man with God,* the author of the law, the priomordial image and final end of man. Saint Bonaventure teaches that "conscience is like God's herald and messenger; it does not command things on its own authority, but commands them as coming from God's authority, like a herald when he proclaims the edict of the king. This is why conscience has binding force."[3] Thus it can be said that conscience bears witness to man's own rectitude or iniquity to man himself but, together with this and indeed even beforehand, conscience is the *witness of God himself,* whose voice and judgment penetrates the depths of man's soul, calling him *fortiter et suaviter* to obedience. "Moral conscience does not close man within an insurmountable and impenetrable solitude, but opens him to the call, to the voice of God. In this, and not in anything else, lies the entire mystery and the dignity of the moral conscience: in being the place, the sacred place where God speaks to man."[4]

Saint Paul does not merely acknowledge that conscience acts as a "witness"; he also reveals the way in which conscience performs that function. He speaks of "conflicting thoughts" which accuse or excuse the Gentiles with regard to their behavior (cf. Rom 2:15). The term "conflicting thoughts" clarifies the precise nature of conscience: it is a *moral judgment about man and his actions,* a judgment either of acquittal or of condemnation, according as human acts are in conformity or not with the law of God written on the heart. In the same text the apostle clearly speaks of the judgment of actions, the judgment of their author, and the moment when that judgment will be definitively rendered: "(This will take place) on that day when, according to my gospel, God judges the secrets of men by Christ Jesus" (Rom. 2:16).

The judgment of conscience is a *practical judgment,* a judgment which makes known what man must do or not do, or which assesses an act already performed by him. It is a judgment which applies to a concrete situation the rational conviction that one must love and do good and avoid evil. This first principle of practical reason is part of the natural law; indeed it constitutes the very foundatIon of the natural law, inasmuch as it expresses the primordial insight about good and evil, that reflection of God's creative wisdom which, like an imperishable spark *(scintilla animae),* shines in the heart of every man. But whereas the natural law discloses the objective and universal demand so the moral good, conscience is the application of the law to a particular cause; this application of the law thus becomes an inner dictate for the individual, a summons to do what is good in this particular situation. Conscience thus formulates *moral obligation* in the light of the natural law: it is the obligation to do what the individual, through the workings of his conscience, *knows* to be a good he is called to do *here and now.* The universality of the law and its obligation are acknowledged, not suppressed, once reason has established the law's application in concrete present circumstances. The judgment of conscience states "in an ultimate way" wherther a certain particular kind of behavior is in conformity with the law; it formulates the proximate norm of the morality of a voluntary act, "applying the objective law to a particular case."[5]

Like the natural law itself and all practical knowlege, the judgment of conscience also has an imperative character: man must act in accordance with it. If man acts against this judgment or, in a case where he lacks certainty about the rightness and goodness of a determined act, still performs that act, he stands condemned by his own conscience, *the proximate norm of personal morality.* The dignity of this rational forum and the authority of its voice and judgments derive from the truth about moral good and evil, which it is called to listen to and to express. This truth is indicated by the "divine law," *the universal and objective norm of morality.* The judgment of conscience does not establish the law; rather it bears witness to the authority of the natural law and of the practical reason with reference to the supreme

3. *In II Librum Sentent.,* dist. 39, a. 1, q. 3, conclusion: Ed. Ad Claras Aquas, II, 907b.

4. *Address* (General Audeince, 17 August 1983), 2: *Insegnamenti,* VI, 2 (1983), 256.

5. Supreme Sacred Congregation of the Holy Office, Instruction on "Situation Ethics" *Contra Doctrinam* (2 February 1956): AAS 48 (1956), 144.

good, whose attractiveness the human person perceives and whose commandments he accepts. "Conscience is not an independent and exclusive capacity to decide what is good and what is evil Rather there is profoundly imprinted upon it a principle of obedience vis-à-vis the objective norm which establishes and conditions the correspondence of its decisions with the commands and prohibitions which are at the basis of human behaviour."[6]

The truth about moral good, as that truth is declared in the law of reason, is practically and concretely recognized by the judgment of conscience, which leads one to take responsibility for the good or the evil one has done. If man does evil, the just judgment of his conscience remains within him as a witness to the universal truth of the good, as well as to the malice of his particular choice. But the verdict of conscience remains in him also as a pledge of hope and mercy: while bearing witness to the evil he has done, it also reminds him of his need, with the help of God's grace, to ask forgiveness, to do good and to cultivate virtue constantly.

Consequently, *in the practical judgment of conscience,* which imposes on the person the obligation to perform a given act, *the link between freedom and truth is made manifest.* Precisely for this reason conscience expresses itself in acts of "judgment" which reflect the truth about the good, and not in arbitrary "decisions." The maturity and responsibility of these judgments — and, when all is said and done, of the individual who is their subject — are not measured by the liberation of the conscience from objective truth, in favor of an alleged autonomy in personal decisions, but, on the contrary, by an insistent search for truth and by allowing oneself to be guided by that truth in one's actions.

Seeking What is True and Good

Conscience, as the judgment of an act, is not exempt from the possibility of error. As the Council

puts it, "not infrequently conscience can be mistaken as a result of invincible ignorance, although it does not on that account forfeit its dignity; but this cannot be said when a man shows little concern for seeking what is true and good, and conscience gradually becomes almost blind from being accustomed to sin."[7] In these brief words the Council sums up the doctrine which the Church down the centuries has developed with regard to the *erroneous conscience.*

Certainly, in order to have a "good conscience" (1 Tim. 1:5), man must seek the truth and must make judgments in accordance with that same truth. As the Apostle Paul says, the conscience must be "confirmed by the Holy Spirit" (cf. Rom. 9:1); it must be "clear" (2 Tim. 1:3); it must not "practice cunning and tamper with God's word," but "openly state the truth" (cf. 2 Cor. 4:2). On the other hand, the apostle also warns Christians: "do not be conformed to this world but be transformed by the renewal of your mind, that you may prove what is the will of God, what is good and acceptable and perfect" (Rom. 12:2).

Paul's admonition urges us to be watchful, warning us that in the judgments of our conscience the possibility of error is always present. Conscience *is not an infallible judge;* it can make mistakes. However, error of conscience can be the result of an *invincible ignorance,* an ignorance of which the subject is not aware and which he is unable to overcome by himself.

The Council reminds us that in cases where such invincible ignorance is not culpable, conscience does not lose its dignity, because even when it directs us to act in w ays not in conformity with the objective moral order, it continues to speak in the name of that truth about the good which the subject is called to seek sincerely.

In any event, it is always from the truth that the dignity of conscience derives. In the case of the correct conscience, it is a question of the *objective truth* received by man; in the case of the erroneous conscience, it is a question of what man, mistakenly, *subjectively* considers to be true. It is never acceptable to confuse a "subjective" error about moral good with the "objective" truth

6. Encyclical Letter *Dominum et Vivificantem* (18 May 1986), 43: *AAS* 78 (1986), 859; cf. Second Vatican Ecumenical Council, Pastoral Constitution on the Church in the Modern World *Gaudium et Spes,* 16; Declaration on Religious Freedom *Dignitatis Humanae,* 3.

7. Second Vatican Ecumenical Council, Pastoral Constitution on the Church in the Modern World *Gaudium et Spes,* 16.

rationally proposed to man in virtue of his end, or to make the moral value of an act performed with a true and correct conscience equivalent to the moral value of an act performed by following the judgment of an erroneous conscience.[8] It is possible that the evil done as the result of invincible ignorance or a non-culpable error of judgment may not be imputable to the agent; but even in this case it does not cease to be an evil, a disorder in relation to the truth about the good. Furthermore, a good act which is not recognized as such does not contribute to the moral growth of the person who performs it; it does not perfect him and it does not help to dispose him for the supreme good. Thus, before feeling easily justified in the name of our conscience, we should reflect on the words of the Psalm: "Who can discern his errors? Clear me from hidden faults" (Ps. 19:12). There are faults which we fail to see but which nevertheless remain faults, because we have refused to walk toward the light (cf. John 9:39-41).

Conscience, as the ultimate concrete judgment, compromises its dignity when it is *culpably* erroneous, that is to say, "'when man shows little concern for seeking what is true and good, and conscience gradually becomes almost blind from being accustomed to sin."[9] Jesus alludes to the danger of the conscience being deformed when he warns: "The eye is the lamp of the body. So if your eye is sound, your whole body will be full of light; but if your eye is not sound, your whole body will be full of darkness. If then the light in you is darkness, how great is the darkness!" (Matt. 6:22-23).

The words of Jesus just quoted also represent a call to *form our conscience*, to make it the object of a continuous conversion to what is true and to what is good. In the same vein, Saint Paul exhorts us not to be conformed to the mentality of this world, but to be transformed by the renewal of our mind (cf. Rom. 12:2). It is the "heart" converted to the Lord and to the love of what is good which is really the source of true judgments of conscience. Indeed, in order to "prove what is the will of God, what is good and acceptable and per-

fect" (Rom. 12:2), knowledge of God's law in general is certainly necessary, but it is not sufficient: what is essential is a sort of *"connaturality" between man and the true good*.[10] Such a connaturality is rooted in and develops through the virtuous attitudes of the individual himself: prudence and the other cardinal virtues, and even before these the theological virtues of faith, hope and charity. This is the meaning of Jesus' saying: "He who does what is true comes to the light" (John 3:21).

Christians have a great help for the formation of conscience in the Church and her Magisterium. As the Council affirms: "In forming their consciences the Christian faithful must give careful attention to the sacred and certain teaching of the Church. For the Catholic Church is by the will of Christ the teacher of truth. Her charge is to announce and teach authentically that truth which is Christ, and at the same time with her authority to declare and confirm the principles of the moral order which derive from human nature itself."[11] It follows that the authority of the Church, when she pronounces on moral questions, in no way undermines the freedom of conscience of Christians. This is so not only because freedom of conscience is never freedom "from" the truth but always and only freedom "in" the truth, but also because the Magisterium does not bring to the Christian conscience truths which are extraneous to it; rather it brings to light the truths which it ought already to possess, developing them from the starting point of the primordial act of faith. The Church puts herself always and only at the *service of conscience*, helping it to avoid being tossed to and fro by every wind of doctrine proposed by human deceit (cf. Eph. 4:14), and helping it not to swerve from the truth about the good of man, but rather, especially in more difficult questions, to attain the truth with certainty and to abide in it.

8. Cf. St. Thomas Aquinas, *De Veritate*, q. 17, a. 4.

9. Second Vatican Ecumenical Council, Pastoral Constitution on the Church in the Modern World *Gaudium et Spes*, 16.

10. Cf. St. Thomas Aquinas, *Summa Theologica*, II-II, q. 45, a. 2.

11. Declaration on Religious Freedom *Dignitatis Humanae*, 14.

21. Moral Justification

RICHARD J. MOUW

As a way of showing the relevance of a specific philosophical topic to the larger worldview agenda, I will briefly examine the relationship between the questions of moral justification and an emphasis on the importance of divine commands. I will not provide elaborate details about this relationship because, as I will explain, I do not possess a full-blown theory which provides those details. But it will perhaps be helpful to sketch out some important matters bearing on the relationship.

Let us say that a person has a direct moral justification for a given course of action if that person directly ascertains that the course of action in question, in the light of all relevant and available factual information, satisfies what she takes to be the correct fundamental moral criterion or criteria. Furthermore, let us understand normative theories such as consequentialism, deontology, and virtue accounts as providing different possible understandings of what constitutes the correct moral criterion or criteria. Thus, in one version of consequentialism, a person who is wondering whether to keep a specific promise will ask whether the keeping of that promise will bring about a situation in which there is a greater excess of good over bad consequences than the situation

Richard Mouw (1940–) is professor of Christian philosophy and ethics and president of Fuller Theological Seminary. He is the author of three works of Christian moral and political theory, *Political Evangelism, Politics and the Biblical Drama,* and *The God Who Commands.*

From Richard J. Mouw, *The God Who Commands* (Notre Dame: University of Notre Dame Press, 1990).

that would result if the promise is not kept. Or a deontologist would ask whether, say, telling Peter that I will give him twenty-five dollars on Wednesday conforms to a rule of practice whose obligatoriness is rationally defensible (or intuitively obvious), and whether in conforming to that rule I would not be violating another rule whose obligatoriness is weightier in that situation.

When a person has gone through the proper moral operations regarding a course of action, with direct reference to fundamental moral criteria, we can say that a person has a *direct* moral justification for what she decides. But there are situations in which persons do not have direct moral justifications — where, for example, sufficient factual information is unavailable, or where there is no time to calculate consequences or to engage in appropriate rational reflection. Nonetheless, in such situations there may be other grounds for making justified moral judgments.

Let us say that a person has an *indirect* moral justification for a course of action under conditions of this sort: the course of action possesses some property distinct from the property of being supportable by fundamental moral criteria, and the person reasonably believes that the possession of this property by a course of action makes it either logically certain or inductively probable that the action has the property of satisfying the correct moral criteria.

Perhaps an analogy will be helpful. Suppose that my car engine's being fixed consists in certain adjustments having been made to the engine. But suppose I do not possess the skills to ascertain whether those adjustments have been made. But if I believe that when my mechanic, Mary, says that the engine is fixed then it is in all likelihood fixed — so that Mary's saying that it is fixed makes it highly probable that it is fixed — then knowing that Mary says so constitutes an indirect justification for the claim that it is fixed. Mary herself, in this case, has a direct justification for that claim.

The following might be a situation in which I have an indirect moral justification for some course of action: I am a consequentialist and have not calculated the consequences of some act, but I know that Jane, whom I believe to be a skilled consequentialist calculator, wants me to perform that act. Or I am a deontologist and have not engaged in proper reflection regarding some course of action, but I know that Jimmy, whose intuitive powers I greatly respect, generally reacts with favor when the course of action is recommended in similar circumstances. In these cases, knowing that Jane or Jimmy approves of a given course of action would count as an indirect justification for my approving of that course of action.

It is important to distinguish between two questions which relate to moral decision making: What *makes* an action right? and How do I *decide* that an action is right? We can decide, of course, that an action is right by directly investigating whether it possesses what we take to be the proper right-making characteristics. But sometimes the two questions receive very different answers. Very often people decide what to do by listening to moral authorities or by looking at moral examples. This is sometimes a dangerous basis for decision making, but not always. Sometimes, as I am suggesting, the appeal to an authority or an example can constitute an indirect justification for a specific decision. In both car repair and morality, the appeal to authority or example must take into account the credentials of the person to whom reference is made.

Right-Making or Right-Indicating

I am suggesting here that Christians who believe that the good life consists in obeying divine commands have a choice regarding how to spell out the way in which that posture of obedience relates to issues of moral justification. In brief, we can view God's commanding something as either a right-*making* or a right-*indicating* characteristic.

The stronger view, of course, is the one that views God's commanding something as a right-making characteristic. This view has been receiving favorable attention again in recent years. Indeed, very attractive versions of it have been elaborated, especially by Robert Merrihew Adams[1]

— although, as James Hanink and Gary Mar have observed, many of these recent "defenses have employed sophisticated metaethical, causal, or 'paradigmatic' versions" of a divine command ethic, of a sort that a "simple believer" might fail to recognize them as supporting a straightforward account of God's will as right-making.[2]

It is significant, though, that even Adams concedes, in response to Alasdair MacIntyre's insistence that we must approach obedience to God's will with an understanding of authority grounded in justice, that "[i]t matters what God's attributes are."[3] And Hanink and Mar develop a version of divine command ethics that employs a helpful distinction between God's "legislative" and "creative" wills; we obey God's legislative demands because we believe that God, in creating us, wants us to "flourish" in the realizing of our happiness by means of "such basic goods as life, knowledge, family, community, play, work, and worship of God."[4]

These accounts do place an important emphasis on the examination of the divine credentials. We obey God because God is just. We serve the Lord because that is the way to attain the "abundant life" for which we were created by a God who wants us to be happy.

These nuances seem to suggest that the will of God is at least being viewed as a right-indicating factor. A morally justified action will certainly be one that promotes justice, or that contributes to human flourishing. And since we believe that God is just, or that God aims at human flourishing, we can at least take God's commands as very reliable indicators that what is being commanded does indeed satisfy the requirements for moral justification.

Is it possible, though, to view God's willing something as nothing more than a right-indicating characteristic? Perhaps. It may not be necessary to insist that knowing that God has commanded something constitutes a direct moral

---

1. For a good collection of Robert Merrihew Adams's essays see his *The Virtue of Faith and Other Essays in Philosophical Theology* (New York: Oxford University Press, 1987). Some of Adams's essays are included also in the useful anthology *Divine Commands and Morality*, Oxford Readings in Philosophy, ed. Paul Helm (Oxford: Oxford University Press, 1981).

2. James G. Hanink and Gary R. Mar, "What Euthyphro Couldn't Have Said," *Faith and Philosophy* 4 (July 1987): 241.

3. Robert M. Adams, "Divine Commands and the Social Nature of Obligation," *Faith and Philosophy* 4 (July 1987): 272.

4. Hanink and Mar, "Euthyphro," 249.

justification for that course of action; one could believe that even God, in commanding a course of action, satisfies certain moral criteria (which are distinct from God s having commanded it). For example, God's commanding marital fidelity may not necessarily be what *makes* marital fidelity right. By holding a loose view of the connection here the Christian believer could open-mindedly consider a number of different theoretical accounts of what constitutes a direct moral justification of a course of action. God might be a consequentialist or a deontologist or a virtue ethicist.

And ordinary Christian piety does seem to leave some conceptual room for this kind of loose view of the connection. Christian believers often say things of this sort: "I don't know why God wants me to do that, or to put up with this hardship, or to cultivate these traits; but I am confident that God knows best." This suggests that what goes into God's "knowing best" is a subject for legitimate theoretical, even metaethical, speculation. We do not have to offer decisive answers to such speculative questions before we can confidently accept God's commands as reliable moral guidelines.

But in the final analysis it does not seem quite right to treat connection between God's willing something and that something's being morally right in *too* loose a manner. God is, after all, perfect righteousness in the biblical scheme of things. It is difficult to put this matter concisely — but it does seem appropriate to think that in some mysterious sense the right-indicating and the right-making begin to merge as soon as we pause to reflect upon divine goodness.

22. A Historical Example: The Challenge of the "Fools for Christ"

CHRISTOS YANNARAS

Mockery of the World

In the life of the church, there is a historical example which represents the most extreme and extraordinary way of obeying the Gospel preaching about overturning and rejecting individual morality. This is the example of the holy "fools for Christ." In the lives and behavior of these saints, the church has seen the expression of a particular gift of the Holy Spirit, one of the most acute forms of prophetic preaching.[1]

The fools are usually monks who come down

---

1. Bibliography on fools for Christ is somewhat limited. For my very summary treatment of them here, I have used primarily a study by Ernst Benz, "Heilige Narrheit," in *Kyrios* 3 (1938), pp. 1-55, and the critical edition of the life of St. Symeon "who for Christ's sake was called the fool, written by Leontius bishop of Neapolis in the island of Cyprus," published in Uppsala in 1963, by Lennart Rydén (*Das Leben des heiligen Symeon von Leontios von Neapolis*). There is also the written account of the life of St. Andrew the Fool for Christ in PG 111, 611ff. I also note two interesting articles by Stephanus Hilpisch: "Die Torheit um Christi Willen," in *Zeitschrift für Aszese und Mystik* 6 (1931), pp. 121-131, and "Die Schmach der Sunde um Christi Willen," in the same periodical 8 (1933), pp. 289-299.

Christos Yannaras (1935–) is professor of philosophy at the Panteios Institute, Athens. His works include *Person and Love* and *The Freedom of Morality*.

From Christos Yannaras, *The Freedom of Morality* (Crestwood, N.Y.: St. Vladimir's, 1984).

into the "world," into the cities and into "Christian" society, and perform strange and senseless actions — the actions of a madman. Yet these actions always have a deeper meaning: they always aim to uncover the reality and truth hidden behind the practices of this world. The fool goes into taverns and brothels and keeps bad company. He lives on the streets like a vagabond, with disreputable people like prostitutes and street urchins. He appears to fall in with their way of life, whereas in fact he is revealing to them the truth of salvation in a way accessible to them and on their own spiritual level, through extraordinary antics, jokes, and absurdities.

He rebukes sinners, and often performs miracles to prevent them falling further. He will usually have the gift of insight, of reading men's hidden depths; and he derides their secret transgressions in public, but in such a way that only the offender can understand the reproach. The fool himself gives the appearance of being very sinful: he provocatively breaks the fasts of the church before men, while in reality he practises the strictest asceticism in his eating. He poses as a *habitué* of the brothels, but when he is there he admonishes the prostitutes and gives money to save them from vice. At night he returns to the community of the saints, to the seclusion of his prayer and the vision of the face of God; and in the morning, he dons once again the mask of foolishness, "mocking the vain and slanderous world." This is indeed a mockery of the world: it is the most extreme form of asceticism, ultimate self-denial, absolute rejection of the world's standards, and complete renunciation of the ego.

The fools come to remind us that the gospel message is "foolishness," and that salvation and sanctity cannot be reconciled with the satisfaction that comes from society's respect and objective recognition. They present themselves during periods of "secularization" among Christians, when the Christian identity seems to depend on the conventional standards and ideas of a world which measures the true life and virtue of man with the yardsticks of social decorum and deontology.

The fool is a vessel of grace, who has immediate experience of the Kingdom of God and undertakes to manifest prophetically the contrast between the "present age" and the age of the Kingdom, the basic difference in standards and criteria.

He refuses any objective recognition of virtue and piety for himself, and takes to the limit his rejection of praise and honor among men. He knows that individual virtue separates man from God because it leads to self-satisfaction; and also that it separates man from his fellow-men, because they dare not expose to him their need and their weakness.

The fool does not pursue his ascetic way in the secure spirituality of a monastery, but alone, in the world. He grapples at close quarters with the world and the devil, taking up the cross of the church, the cross of those who are tormented and sinful. This is another form of revelatory "tragedy": of his own accord, he takes on the grotesque mask of foolishness so as to reveal the truth of the person, the artificiality of the nice-looking masks of a conventional decorum which destroys personal distinctiveness and freedom. In the artificial "reality" of a world which changes good into evil and evil into good, and where "the ruler of this world" is on the watch to see that this falsity is maintained, the fool takes it upon himself to leap into the house of the strong man and seize his goods.[2] The only way the saint can make this leap is to go into the midst of the world wearing the mask of foolishness, of social irresponsibility, and uncover the true reality before people's very eyes, tearing apart the veils of conventional morality, established attitudes and deceptive value-judgments. This is not an ironic, Socratic disclosure but a personal awakening, actively forcing people to arouse themselves. Fools for Christ do not choose this foolishness as a form of asceticism, but are chosen for it by God. They do it "involuntarily." That is where their way has taken them. And this is a taste of truth and of dangerous freedom.

Taking on Another's Guilt

.... In the *Lausiac History* . . . and in St. John of the Ladder and elsewhere in ascetic writings and church history we frequently encounter isolated actions and examples corresponding to those of the fools. Thus we read of how St. Macarius of Egypt was living as a monk in a hut outside some

2. See Matt. 12:29.

village, when the parents of a girl accused him of seducing their daughter. They tied a rope round his neck and led him through all the village, crying, "Look at this 'anchorite' who raped our daughter!" They demanded that he should pay compensation and undertake the maintenance of the child which was to be born. Without defending himself, the saint accepted his disgrace and returned to his cell. He began to work twice as hard as before, weaving rush mats and baskets, and saying to himself, "Macarius, now you have a wife, and you must work harder in order to feed her." Every day he would take whatever money he had earned to the girl's house, and received blows and insults in return. This went on until the girl, in the pangs of childbirth, admitted the monk's innocence. Then, however, Macarius fled into the desert to avoid being honored as a saint.[3]

The same story is told of Eustathius of Caesarea when he was still in minor orders, a simple reader, and also of Nicon of Sinai.[4] Another monk, Andrew of Messina, later abbot of a monastery, was accused of theft and accepted the accusation without objection until his innocence was proved.[5]

For the monks, this act of taking on another's guilt, voluntarily and without protest, was not simply an opportunity to increase in humility. It was a practical manifestation of their conviction that sin is common to all, an obvious way of participating in the common cross of the church, in the fall and failure of all mankind. The monk is "apart from all" but also "joined with all," and he sees the sins of others as his own, as sins common to the human nature in which we all partake. Distinguishing the sins of individuals does not have any real meaning, any more than does distinguishing individual virtues. What condemns or saves us is our refusal or our striving to "alter" the rebellion of our common nature into a personal relationship of repentance and communion. Man must imitate the self-emptying of Christ, his renunciation of any individual claim for justification: he must voluntarily take on the failure common to all and bring it to God, embodying in his own

person the words of the Apostle Paul, "I fill up that which is lacking in the afflictions of Christ in my flesh for His body's sake, which is the Church" (Col. 1:24). Only thus do the saints who live according to the trinitarian mode of existence overcome the fragmentation of our nature caused by sin, altering sin into a humble acceptance of others, a fact of communion and love.

Characteristic is the story of Theophilus and Maria (c. 540) related by John of Ephesus. They were only children from aristocratic families in Antioch, both of exceptional beauty, betrothed to each other, "who sought to apply to their own lives the words of the Bible, 'He hath made him to be sin for us, who knew no sin'" (2 Cor. 5:21). Theophilus played the buffoon, the jester, while Maria dressed as a prostitute. They roamed the city streets acting as comics, telling jokes and talking nonsense: and people laughed at them, and sometimes even struck them. They sought the contempt of men, the utter degradation of their own ego, in order to gain that ineffable freedom and taste of life which comes as a gift when the last resistance of egocentric individuality is dead. On one occasion, a woman asked Maria, "Why do you wallow in sin, my child"; and she replied without hesitation, "Madam, pray that God will raise me up from the filth of sin."[6]

Complete Abandonment of the Ego

The most abundant and striking historical evidence is preserved in the complete biographies of St. Symeon of Emesa and St. Andrew of Constantinople. In the persons of these two saints we have a complete picture of the holy fools' spiritual gift and the prophetic message they embody.

St. Symeon was an anchorite in the wilderness beyond the Jordan when he received the call from God to live as a fool. He said to his companion in the ascetic life, "In the power of Christ, I am going to mock the world."[7] Then he went down into the city of Emesa "and performed miracles, but for God's sake he pretended to be a fool": he hid his virtue, denigrating himself and shunning any respect or honor that might come from men. For

3. *Lausiac History*, ch. 70, ed. Butler, Texts and Studies VI (Cambridge, 1904), pp. 165f.

4. PG 65, 310.

5. PL 74, 178-179.

6. *Patrologia Orientalis*, vol. 19, pp. 164-179.

7. PG 93, 1704B; Rydén, p. 142, II.25-26.

the gifts of holiness were certainly manifest in him: he had the gifts of healing, foresight, and insight, as well as "pure prayer" and tears.

Thus on one occasion, as his biographer tells us, "on a Sunday, he took some walnuts and went into the church at the beginning of the Liturgy, cracking walnuts and putting out the lamps. When they threw themselves upon him to drive him out, he went up into the pulpit and from there he pelted the women with walnuts. With a great deal of effort, they managed to drive him out; but as he went out he overturned the tables of the pastry-sellers, and they gave him wounds which nearly killed him."[8] Actions such as this testify to the effort he made to refuse at any cost recognition and fame as a saint. He preferred to be considered a half-crazy monk without even the rudiments of social decorum — that decorum which safeguards and preserves the ego.

On another occasion, Symeon was working as an apprentice in a wine shop; but his virtue had started to become known, and people were coming to the shop to see him and find in his person a confirmation of the objective type of a virtuous man. Then, in order to avoid men's honor and esteem, Abba Symeon pretended that he felt carnal desire towards the shopkeeper's wife and that he wanted to assault her to satisfy his lust. "While the man's wife was asleep on her own," says the biographer, "and he himself was pouring wine, Abba Symeon went up to her and made as if to take off his cloak. When she cried out, her husband came in and she said to him, 'Throw out this thrice-accursed fellow — he wanted to rape me.' And they struck him with their fists, and drove him out of the shop into the cold."[9] And the shopkeeper put it about all through the city that "he wanted to commit adultery with my wife, if he had had his way."

For the same reason, St. Symeon used to keep company with the city's prostitutes and dance with them in the streets, monk of the Church though he was, and would endure their lewd gestures: "He had reached such a state of purity and freedom from passions that he would often caper and dance with a chorus-girl on either side of him, and associate with them and play with them in public;

and sometimes the shameless women would put their hands into his bosom and provoke and slap him. But the old man, like pure gold, was in no way defiled by them."[10]

In men's eyes, St. Symeon sometimes appeared to transgress even the canonical order of the Church, the basic obligations of fasting: "The righteous man often ate meat, while he did not taste bread all week. As for his fasting, no one observed it; but he used to eat meat in front of all, to deceive them."[11] "In Lent, he would not taste anything until Great Thursday. But on Great Thursday he would sit from morning eating cake, so that the people who saw him were scandalized, saying that he did not fast even on Great Thursday."[12] This provocation which scandalized the faithful recalls Christ's "provocative" breaking of the Sabbath: the way he took responsibility for the paralytic "taking up his bed" (John 5:1-16), and excused the disciples who "began to pluck ears of corn and to eat" on the Sabbath day (Matt. 7:1-16). Christ does not destroy the law, but shows that the law is transcended in the Kingdom. And St. Symeon is a citizen of the Kingdom: in his person, he embodies the transcendence of the law, the "transgression," which is a scandal only to those of us who still live in need of the law, in need of obedience, because we have not yet attained or know nothing about the "end" of the law which is the freedom of the saints. In Emesa, it seems that Symeon deliberately provoked scandal. Once, he managed to enter the women's public baths — "as it were to the glory of God," notes his biographer, Bishop Leontius of Neapolis in Cyprus — "and they all rushed upon him and drove him out with blows."[13] There are moral and social restraints, like the law, for those who are subject to the passions. But there is also the reality of the "passionlessness" of the saints; and this is what Symeon reveals, liberating our spiritual vision from the shadow and the narrowness of the law.

Side by side with their essential content, these extraordinary tactics also had their social dimension, as Symeon's biographer assures us: the saint succeeded in gaining the liking and trust of sin-

8. PG 93, 1708D; Rydén, p. 145, 25-29, and p. 146, 1-3.

9. PG 93, 1712C; Rydén, p. 148, 1-5.

10. PG 93, 1724C; Rydén, p. 154, 27-29, and p. 155, 1-4.

11. PG 93, 1712D; Rydén, p. 148, 10-13.

12. PG 93, 1728AB; Rydén, p. 156, 23-28.

13. PG 93, 1713BC; Rydén, p. 149, 1-18.

ners, of the destitute and disreputable.[14] He saved women who were living in brothels; providing them with money, he liberated them from vice and brought them to lawful marriage or even to monastic life.[15] He also won over unbelievers and heretics, and helped them to return to right faith. "His whole aim was this: firstly, to save souls, whether through the attacks he unleashed on them either in jest or by guile, or again through the miracles which he performed in folly, or through exhortations addressed to them as though he were playing the fool. And secondly, to prevent his virtue from becoming known, and himself from receiving praise and honor from men."[16] He advised an archdeacon in the city, "I beseech you never to hold any soul in contempt, and particularly not a monk or a poor man, as has happened. For love knows that among the poor, and especially among the blind, there are people who shine like the sun, cleansed by their endurance and the ills they have suffered."[17]

Symeon also had a blessed end. "The Lord glorified him and translated him [in the body]. Then everyone came to their senses, as if waking from sleep, and told one another what miracles he had performed for each of them, and how it was for God that he had pretended to be a fool."[18]

An exact parallel is to be found in the story of St. Andrew the Fool for Christ. He was born a Scythian and came to Constantinople as the slave of Theognostus, *protospatharios* to Leo the Wise (886-911). Theognostus gave him a Greek education and made him steward of his house. Andrew accepted the monastic vocation, and lived as a fool for about thirty years; he died at the age of sixty-six in about 946. He had a particular spiritual bond with Nicephorus, a priest at the church of Haghia Sophia in Constantinople; it was to him that Andrew confided his strict asceticism, and Nicephorus gave the saint his support. His biographer, too, relates that he saw Andrew the Fool in his secret cell transfigured and radiant with the light of divine glory: like Christ on Tabor.

14. PG 93, 1713D; Rydén, p. 149, 16-18.
15. PG 93, 1708B; Rydén, p. 145, 9-15.
16. PG 93, 1728C; Rydén, p. 157, 12-16.
17. PG 93, 1741CD; Rydén, p. 166, 29, and .p. 167, 1-3.
18. PG 93, 1745B; Rydén, p. 168, 68-69.

Freedom without Bounds

The fools for Christ seem to reject the Apostle Paul's admonition to accept any personal deprivation and sacrifice in order to avoid scandalizing the faithful (1 Cor. 8:13). But what kind of scandal is St. Paul talking about? It is something that causes confusion in the realm of truth, and may thus deprive others of the possibility of participating in truth — the possibility of salvation. If by eating food offered to idols you give your brother's "weak conscience" grounds for supposing that there is some connection between idol worship and the truth and life of the church, then the responsibility for the confusion you cause is great indeed.

The challenge of the fools, however, does not create confusion in people's faith, nor does it obscure the truth of the church. It simply surprises those who have identified faith and truth with the secularized concept of moral uprightness and conventional decorum. Fools for Christ have the gift, and the audacity, to manifest openly the human fall and sin which is common to us all: this is the reality of our nature, and it is not cancelled out by individual cases of "improvement," nor by concealment behind social externals.

In this sense, every monk in the Orthodox East is a kind of "fool for Christ." He wears a garment of mourning, openly declaring that he accepts our common fall and sin; and he withdraws into the ascetic life, waging war on this fall and this sin on behalf of us all. This same acceptance is the calling of every member of the church. If we persist in ignoring the gospel of salvation and continue to identify the regeneration of man with the social recognition of individual virtues, with worldly success in gaining individual moral respectability, then the fault is ours alone — and it is an error which bars us from truth and life.

The prototype to which the church has always looked is not individual moral self-sufficiency, but the monks' lament of repentance. This lament is ultimately joyful — a "joyful sorrow" — and turns sin into a measure of the acceptance of Christ's love. Man is able to mourn and lament only when he knows exactly what he has lost, and experiences this loss as a personal deprivation, a personal thirst. This is why repentance, the *personal* sense of the loss of God, is also a first revelation, our first acquaintance with his person, our first discovery of the extent of his love.

In the case of the fools for Christ, certainly their shocking freedom from every law, rule, restriction, or code of obligations is not simply didactic in its purpose, reminding us of the danger of identifying virtue and holiness with conventional social decorum and egocentric moral rectitude. No one can ever really teach simply by calling into question mistaken conceptions and ways of life: one has to make the fulness of the saving truth incarnate in oneself. The shocking freedom of the fools is first and foremost a total death, a complete mortification of every individual element in their lives. This death is the freedom which can break and destroy every conventional form; it is resurrection into a life of personal distinctiveness, the life of love which knows neither bounds nor barriers.

The example of the "fools for Christ," then, is neither extreme nor inexplicable, as it may perhaps seem to many people. It is the incarnation of the gospel's fundamental message: that it is possible for someone to keep the whole of the law without managing to free himself from his biological and psychological ego, from corruption and death. And that on the other hand, it is enough if someone humbly accepts his own sin and his fall, without differentiating it from the sin and fall of the rest of mankind, trusting in the love of Christ which transfigures this acceptance into personal nearness and communion, into a life of incorruption and immortality.

23. On Keeping Theological Ethics Theological

STANLEY HAUERWAS

The Ethical Significance of Saying Something Theological

"Say something theological," is a request, as Gustafson notes, theologians frequently hear.[1] Such a request, often made in a more oblique manner, may be entirely friendly, as the inquirer — possessed by an archaeological curiosity in still-living antiquities simply wants an example of a religious relic. More likely, however, the request is really a challenge: "Say something theological in a way that convinces me that you are not talking nonsense." Such a challenge thus assumes that anyone using theological language seriously — that is, as though that language is essential for telling us about how things are or how we ought to be — bears the burden of proof.

---

1. James Gustafson, "Say Something Theological," 1981 *Nora and Edward Ryerson Lecture* (Chicago: University of Chicago, 1981), 3. Gustafson notes that he has the presence of mind to say "God."

Stanley Hauerwas (1940–) is professor of theological ethics at Duke University. He has authored numerous books in Christian ethics, including *Truthfulness and Tragedy: Further Investigations in Christian Ethics, A Community of Character, The Peaceable Kingdom, Suffering Presence, Against the Nations,* and *After Christendom.*

From *Revisions: Changing Perspectives in Moral Philosophy,* ed. Stanley Hauerwas and Alasdair MacIntyre (Notre Dame: University of Notre Dame Press, 1983).

This is particularly the case in matters having to do with ethics. For even though at a popular level many continue to assume there must be a close connection between religion and morality, this has not been compellingly evidenced on the philosophical level. Indeed the persistence of such an assumption only testifies how hard it is to kill certain habits of thought. For the assumption that there is a strong interdependence between religion and morality is but the remains of the now lost hegemony of Christianity over Western culture. That many still persist in assuming religion is essential to motivate us to do the good is an indication, however, that no satisfactory alternative has been found to replace Christianity, as world view and cult, in sustaining the *ethos* of our civilization. We, therefore, find ourselves in the odd situation where many of our society's moral attitudes and practices are based on Jewish and Christian beliefs that are thought to be irrelevant or false in themselves. This situation does not provide an argument for the continued viability of religious practices, but only an indication that as a culture we still have not fully faced the implications of generating a genuine secular morality.

Our culture's lingering failure to find an adequate substitute for Christianity has presented theologians with a temptation almost impossible to resist. Even if they cannot demonstrate the truth of theological claims, they can at least show the continued necessity of religious attitudes for the maintenance of our culture. Of course it would be unwise to continue to use the explicit beliefs derived from the particular historic claims associated with Christianity (and Judaism) as the basis of a secular morality. Such beliefs bear the marks of being historically relative and contingent. If religion is to deserve our allegiance, so the thinking goes, it must be based on the universal. Thus, theologians have sought, at least since the Enlightenment, to demonstrate that theological language can be translated into terms that are meaningful and compelling for those who do not share Christianity's more particularistic beliefs about Jesus of Nazareth. In short, theologians have tried to show that we do not need to speak theologically in order to "say something theological," as other forms of speech are really implicitly religious. After all, hasn't talk of

God always really been but a way to talk about being human?[2]

Even though this understanding of the theological task is relatively recent, there is ample precedent for this endeavor in Christian tradition. As early as the second century, Christians felt their faith contained enough in common with the nonbeliever to legitimate an apologetic strategy. Moreover, such a strategy seems required by a faith that claims a strong continuity between the God who redeems and the God who creates. Thus Christians should not be surprised to find their specific religious beliefs confirmed by the best humanistic alternatives.

Without denying some continuity between recent theological strategies and some modes of past Christian theology, it is equally important that we see the fundamental differences. The apologist of the past stood in the church and its tradition and sought relationship with those outside. Apologetic theology was a secondary endeavor because the apologist never assumed that one could let the questions of unbelief order the theological agenda. But now the theologian stands outside the tradition and seeks to show that selected aspects of that tradition can no longer pass muster from the perspective of the outsider. The theologian thus tries to locate the "essence," or at least what is essential to religion, in a manner that frees religion from its most embarrassing particularistic aspects.

Ironically, just to the extent this strategy has been successful, the more theologians have underwritten the assumption that anything said in a theological framework cannot be of much interest. For if what is said theologically is but a confirmation of what we can know on other grounds or can be said more clearly in nontheological language, then why bother saying it theologically at all? Of course there may still be reason to keep theologians around to remind us of what people used to

2. This development is as true of Roman Catholic as well as Protestant theology. See, for example, Thomas Sheehan's review of Karl Rahner's *Foundations of Christian Faith,* in which he applauds Rahner's attempt to carry out Feuerbach's program of transforming theology into anthropology. Of course, the odd thing about Sheehan's enthusiasm for this move is that Feuerbach assumed that to do so was the agenda of atheism, not theism. "The Drama of Karl Rahner," *New York Review of Books,* February 4, 1981, 13-14.

believe, or to act as a check against the inevitable perversities of those in our culture who persist in the more traditional forms of religious practices and belief, but theology as such cannot be considered a serious intellectual endeavor. Nor is this meant to deny that theologians may have important insights concerning general human and moral issues, but that situation testifies to their individual intelligence and insight rather than their particular theological convictions or training.

For example, much of the recent work in "medical ethics" has been done by theologians, but their prominence in that area has been purchased largely by demonstrating that they can do "medical ethics" just as well as anyone who is not burdened by a theological agenda. As a result it is very hard to distinguish between articles in medical ethics written by theologians and those written by nontheologians except that often the latter are better argued.[3]

The fact that it has become hard to distinguish work done by theologians in ethics from that of philosophers has only reinforced the impression that theologians have nothing interesting to say as theologians. Theologians and religious ethicists avidly read philosophers; the compliment is seldom returned. There are signs, however, that philosophers are beginning to turn their attention to matters that were discussed in the past by theologians. We may, therefore, have the odd situation where philosophers began thinking about religious issues while theologians continue to plumb issues no longer at the center of philosophical discussions.

For example, many philosophers writing about ethics are beginning to challenge the assumption that ethics is best understood on analogy with law, or at least, how many assume lawlike morality should function. For centuries Christian theologians have discussed that question and at no time more intensely than the Reformation. That discus-

sion has had rich results, for Christian thinkers have consistently maintained that the law is not sufficient to depict the Christian moral life.[4] In a related manner many challenge overly optimistic assumptions about humanity and moral rationality. Nowhere in modern literature have such assumptions been more decisively challenged than by Reinhold Niebuhr[5] And still further, some suggest that ethicists must free themselves from their fascination with quandaries and rules, and pay more attention to the virtues and character. Again religious traditions provide rich resources for such an analysis and some theologians, for example, James Gustafson, have developed well-argued accounts of ethics so understood.[6] Yet each of these significant developments in theology has largely been ignored outside the theological community. Why is that the case?

At least part of the fault can be attributed to the sheer prejudice of many secular thinkers. They are simply ignorant of the disciplined nature of theological reflection and assume any reflection informed by religious claims cannot possibly be intelligible. But I suspect that there is a further reason, not so easily addressed, that is internal to how theological reflection about ethics has been done in our time: the lack of attention to the inability of Christian theologians to find a sufficient medium to articulate their own best insights for those who do not share their convictions. In order to understand why that is the case, it will be necessary to describe the development of Christian ethics during this century. For it is only against this historical background that we can understand the failure of Christian ethics to command attention, and furthermore, why failure should not be perpetuated, since those convictions still offer a powerful resource for ethical reflection, even for those who find they are unable to envision and construe the world through them.

---

3. That is not to say that much of the work done by philosophers in medical ethics is free from difficulty. By "better argued" I mean it is more adept at working within the set paradigms of philosophical analysis. However I am by no means happy with these paradigms. For example, see my *Suffering Presence: Essays on Medical Ethics, the Mentally Handicapped, and the Church* (Notre Dame: University of Notre Dame Press, 1985).

4. See, for example, Edward Long's fine article "Soteriological Implications of Norm and Context," in *Norm and Context in Christian Ethics*, edited by Eugene Outka and Paul Ramsey (New York: Scribner's, 1968) 265-296.

5. In particular, see Reinhold Niebuhr, *The Self and the Dramas of History* (New York: Scribner's, 1955).

6. James Gustafson, *Can Ethics Be Christian?* (Chicago: University of Chicago Press, 1975).

The Difficulty of Keeping
Christian Ethics Christian

The very idea of Christian ethics as a distinct discipline is a relatively recent development.[7] Of course, Christians have always had a lot to say about moral matters, but neither in their practical discourse nor their more systematic reflection did they try to make ethics a subject separable from their beliefs and convictions. The Church fathers did not write ethics *per se;* rather their understanding of theology shaped their view of the moral life. Prior to the Enlightenment, the notion that there might be an independent realm called "morality" to which one must try to determine one's relation religiously and theologically simply did not exist.

The story of the development of "Christian ethics" as a distinct field, at least in the Protestant context, has two different strands — one philosophical and the other more pastoral. The first begins in Europe, especially in Germany, where Protestant liberalism tried to save the soul of theology by rescuing its essence — the fatherhood of God and the brotherhood of man. The great exponent of this solution, of course, was Kant who, with his characteristically admirable clarity, maintained that:

> since. the sacred narrative, which is employed solely on behalf of ecclesiastical faith, can have and, taken by itself, ought to have absolutely no influence upon the adoption of moral maxims, and since it is given to ecclesiastical faith only for the vivid presentation of its true object (virtue striving toward holiness), it follows that this narrative must at all times be taught and expounded

in the interests of morality; and yet (because the common man especially has an enduring propensity within him to sink into passive belief) it must be inculcated painstakingly and repeatedly that true religion is to consist not in the knowing or considering of what God does or has done for our salvation, but in what we must do to become worthy of it.[8]

Thus morality becomes the "essence" of religion, but ironically it is understood in a manner that makes positive religious convictions secondary.

The other part of our story does not begin with such an explicit intellectual agenda, but involves a group of Protestant pastors in the late nineteenth and early twentieth centuries and their attempt to respond to the economic crisis of their people.[9] These men challenged the widespread assumption that poverty was the fault of the poor. Taking their bearings from the prophetic traditions of the Hebrew Scripture, they preached against political and economic structures which they believed were the roots of poverty. In the process they thought they discovered an old truth that had been lost through centuries of Christian accommodation with the status quo — namely that the essential characteristic of the Christian religion is its insistence on organic unity between religion and morality, theology and ethics.[10] For Christian salvation consists in nothing less than

> an attitude of love in which we would freely coordinate our life with the life of our fellows in obedience to the loving impulses of the spirit of God, thus taking our part in a divine organism of mutual service. God is the all-embracing source and exponent of the common life and good of mankind. When we submit to God, we submit to the supremacy of the common good. Salvation is the voluntary socializing of the soul.[11]

7. I am keenly aware of the inadequacy of the brief overview of the development of Christian ethics over the last century. Not only do I leave out of the account many of the main actors, even those I treat are not analyzed with the nuance they deserve. I hope soon to write a more adequate book-length account that will do justice to this complex story. However, for present purposes I thought it worthwhile to tell the history in a somewhat contentious manner, since my interests are more systematic than historical. Moreover, I am certainly ready to defend the interpretive features of my account, even though I have not taken the time here to document them adequately.

8. Immanuel Kant, *Religion Within the Limits of Reason Alone,* translated with an introduction by Theodore Greene and Hoyt Hudson (New York: Harper, 1960), 123.

9. C. H. Hopkins, *The Rise of the Social Gospel in American Protestantism, 1865-1915* (New Haven: Yale University Press, 1940).

10. Walter Rauschenbusch, *A Theology for the Social Gospel* (Nashville: Abingdon Press, 1945), 140.

11. Ibid., 98-99.

The "social gospel," as we learned to call this movement, cared little for the development of Christian ethics as a reflective mode of discourse. Rather Christian ethics meant for them the mobilization of the energy and power of the church for social renewal. That does not mean they were unsophisticated, for they were deeply influenced by Protestant liberalism, particularly the Kantianism of Albrecht Ritschl. Thus they were adamant in their opposition to all eschatologies that might justify passive Christian response to societal injustice. The social gospel sought "to develop the vision of the Church toward the future and to cooperate with the will of God which is shaping the destinies of humanity."[12]

Yet with the social gospel, for the first time, serious courses began to be taught in American Protestant seminaries in Christian ethics — though they were often called Christian sociology. Taking their inspiration from the social gospel, these courses tended to be primarily concerned with why Christians should be committed to social justice and what economic and social strategy best accomplished that end. As a result, one of the central agendas of Christian ethics, still very much present, was a concern to make use of the social sciences for social analysis and action.[13] A Christian ethicist often became but a social scientist with a religious interest. More importantly, however, this emphasis meant that the primary conversation partners for most Christian ethicists were not philosophers but social scientists.

It was not long, however, before some of the more naive theological and social assumptions of the social gospel began to be questioned in the light of experience and historical criticism. For example, the social gospel's conviction that "the first step in the salvation of mankind was the achievement of the personality of Jesus"[14] was rendered problematic by the increasing knowledge that the Gospels do not pretend to portray Jesus "the way he really was." Thus the attempt of liberal Protestantism to free Jesus from past "schemes of redemption," to base his divine quality not in metaphysical questions but on the free and ethical acts of his personality, ironically failed to meet the challenges of a critical approach to Scripture.

Moreover the social strategy of the social gospel was soon called into question by the change of attitude occasioned by World War I and the intractability of many social problems with regard to unambiguous solutions. In spite of their trenchant criticism of American capitalism, the social gospelers were after all completely committed to American progressive ideology and policies. They never doubted the uniqueness of the American experience or entertained any critical doubt about the achievement of the American ideal, which they saw as nothing less than the realization of the Kingdom of God. The only question was how to bring the economic institutions of American life under the same spirit of cooperation that our political institutions had already achieved. The primary difference between "saved and unsaved organizations" for the social gospel is that the former are democratic and the latter are autocratic and competitive. Their attempt to turn American business into worker cooperatives was but the continuing attempt to create the secure "saved institutions."[15]

Though often more realistic and theologically profound than these aims suggest, it was clear that the movement started by the social gospel required a new theological rationale as well as social strategy.[16] "Christian ethics" became the discipline pledged to find just such a rationale and strategy. The great figure representing this project was Reinhold Niebuhr, who began his long career as a social gospel advocate, became its most powerful critic, and was quite possibly the last publicly accessible and influential theologian in America. Niebuhr seemed to be saying something theological that was

---

12. Ibid., 224.

13. For example, in his fine article on one of the early social gospelers, Francis Greenwood Peabody, David Little observes that "like many of his contemporaries, Peabody recommended wide exposure to the methods of social science as the basis for sound moral action. Since the ethical aims of true religion and manifest patterns of social development were believed to be rooted in one and the same phenomenon, inductive empirical investigation of social life could only complement and enrich the moral task. He is very clear about this: 'Ethics is finally social science and social science is ethics. *Ethics is the end of sociology.*'" "Francis Greenwood Peabody," *Harvard Library Bulletin* 15, 3 (July 1967), 287-300.

14. Rauschenbusch, 151.
15. Rauschenbusch, 112-113.

compelling to a wide range of people, including people in government, but, as we shall see, his accomplishment was fraught with ambiguity.

Niebuhr's criticism of the social gospel originally centered on his increasing dissatisfaction with its optimistic view of social institutions and change. His own experience as a pastor in Detroit during the great labor struggles taught him to distrust any idea that institutions *qua* institutions are capable of moral transformation, much less salvation.[17] Rather, under the influence of Marx, he began to appreciate the necessity of power and coercion as essential for achieving, not a saved society, but at least one that might be more relatively just.

Niebuhr's theological transformation was at least partly the result of his having to wrestle with the implications of this changed perspective on social action. Theologically, how can we come to terms with living in a world which might well require us to kill for a relative political good, and with the full knowledge that any achievement of some justice that may require violence necessarily results in some injustice. Thus Niebuhr came to conclude that "the tragedy of human history consists precisely in the fact that human life cannot be creative without being destructive, that biological urges are enhanced and sublimated by demonic spirit and that this spirit cannot express itself without committing the sin of pride."[18]

Though by education a theological liberal, Niebuhr found the liberal optimistic understanding of mankind insufficient to sustain his social vision. He turned to that line of Christian theology represented by Augustine, Luther, and Kierkegaard, who emphasized humanity's fallenness and the need for a redemption not of human

making. What we need to sustain us in the struggle for social justice is not, as the social gospel presumed, a grand idealistic vision, but a forgiveness which is necessarily a "moral achievement which is possible only when morality is transcended in religion."[19] Thus, for Niebuhr, Jesus' cross represents the ultimate sacrificial love that will always call into question every social and political order. Such a cross is necessary to sustain moral action in an inherently unjust world, for only as it stands on the edge of history do we have the basis for a hope that does not result in either despair or utopianism.[20]

Under Niebuhr's influence, the agenda of Christian ethics became, for many, the attempt to develop those theological, moral, and social insights necessary to sustain the ambiguous task of achieving more relatively just societies. Although this would seem to indicate a decisive break with his social gospel forebears, in fact Niebuhr continued their most important theological and social presuppositions. Like them he assumed that the task of Christian ethics was to formulate the means for Christians to serve their societies, particularly American society. His understanding and justification of democracy was more sophisticated, but like the social gospelers he never questioned that Christianity has a peculiar relationship to democracy. For Niebuhr and the social gospelers the subject of Christian ethics was America.[21]

16. For a particularly able defense of Rauschenbusch, see Max Stackhouse's, "The Continuing Importance of Walter Rauschenbusch," which introduces Rauschenbusch's *The Righteousness of the Kingdom* (Nashville: Abingdon Press, 1968), 13-59.

17. Niebuhr's reflections on his change of mind can be found in his *Leaves from the Notebook of a Tamed Cynic* (New York: Living Age Books, 1957). See also Niebuhr's "Intellectual Autobiography," in *Reinhold Niebuhr: His Religious, Social, and Political Thought*, ed. Charles Kegley and Robert Bretall (New York: Macmillan, 1956), 1-24.

18. Reinhold Niebuhr, *The Nature and Destiny of Man* (New York: Scribner's, 1941), 1:10-11.

19. Reinhold Niebuhr, *An Interpretation of Christian Ethics* (New York: Living Age Books, 1956), 201. It is interesting that Niebuhr's stress on forgiveness as the hallmark of Christian ethics is not carried forward in his later work. Rather his emphasis is almost entirely on self-sacrificial love. It is my hunch that Niebuhr was much closer to being right by focusing on forgiveness than love as more important for the systematic display of Christian ethics.

20. In his *Christian Realism and Liberation Theology* (Maryknoll: Orbis Books, 1981) Dennis McCann suggests that rather than providing a strategy for social action Niebuhr is best interpreted as trying to form a "spirituality" necessary to sustain political activity. That seems to me to be a particularly fruitful way to read Niebuhr, as it helps account for the lack of any conceptually clear connections between Niebuhr's theological views and his strategic judgments.

21. See, for example, Niebuhr's *The Children of Light and the Children of Darkness* (New York: Scribner's,

They differed only on how nearly just such a society could be and the theological presupposition necessary to understand and sustain social involvement.

Niebuhr, far more than was seen at the time, continued to he essentially a liberal theologian. His emphasis on the sinfulness of man in his magisterial *Nature and Destiny of Man* led many to associate him with the "neo-orthodox" movement of Bultmann, Brunner, and Barth. Yet Niebuhr never shared Barth's theological rejection of liberalism as a basic theological strategy; he, like Bultmann, continued liberal theology's presumption that theology must be grounded in anthropology. Thus, his compelling portrayal of our sinfulness, which appeared *contra* liberal optimism, only continued the liberal attempt to demonstrate the intelligibility of theological language through its power to illuminate the human condition. In spite of Niebuhr's personally profound theological convictions, many secular thinkers accepted his anthropology and social theory without accepting his theological presuppositions.[22] And it is not clear that in doing so they were making a mistake, as the relationships between Niebuhr's theological and ethical positions were never clearly demonstrated.

It was becoming increasingly apparent that Christian ethics must be written in a manner that allowed, and perhaps even encouraged, the separation of ethics from its religious roots. Perhaps this seems an odd result for a movement that began by asserting the "organic unity" between religion and ethics, but it was a development that was a necessary outgrowth of the social gospel commitments. The social gospelers were able to make direct appeals to their religious convictions to justify their social involvement, because in the late nineteenth century they could continue to presuppose that America was a "religious" or even a "Christian civilization and country." Niebuhr, more aware of our religious pluralism as well as the secular presuppositions underlying the American experience, attempted to provide a theological rationale for why Christians should not seek to make their theological commitments directly relevant for social policy and strategy. Even though he appeared extremely critical of the Lutheran law-gospel distinction, in fact, he drew on the resources of that tradition, now reinterpreted in existential categories, to justify an understanding of justice and its attainment that did not require any direct theological rationale.

Niebuhr's views prevailed for no other reason than that they were more in accord with the changing social and religious situation in America. American society was increasingly becoming a pluralist and secular society.[23] As a result Christian theologians, particularly as they dealt with social issues, felt it necessary to find ways in which their ethical conclusions could be separated from their theological framework. In the hope of securing

---

1944) and *The Irony of American History* (New York: Scribner's, 1962). This perhaps helps explain the oft made observation that Niebuhr paid almost no attention to the social significance of the church — for finally, in spite of all the trenchant criticism he directed at America, America was his church. Thus the criticism that failed to sustain his trenchant perspective in the last years of his life in some ways is misplaced, since it fails to note that Niebuhr from beginning to end was involved in a stormy love affair with America. In some ways the social gospelers were less accomodationist than Niebuhr in this respect; Rauschenbusch, in particular, assumed the necessity of the church to stand as a critic against American society.

The importance of America as the subject of Christian ethics can also be seen in the tendency of many Christian ethicists to think of ethics as a form of "American studies." H. R. Niebuhr's *The Kingdom of God in America* (New York: Harper, 1937) remains the classical text for this genre.

22. Niebuhr profoundly influenced such people as Hans Morgenthau, George Kennan; Arthur Schlesinger, Jr., and many others. It is, perhaps, a mark of the instability of Niebuhr's position that often both sides of a political issue, particularly in foreign affairs, can claim with some justice to be Niebuhrians.

23. Arthur Schlesinger documents this well in his "The Political Philosophy of Reinhold Niebuhr," in *Reinhold Niebuhr: His Religious, Social, and Political Thought*, 125-150. Schlesinger rightly notes that Niebuhr, the penetrating critic of the social gospel and of pragmatism, ended up "the powerful reinterpreter and champion of both. It was the triumph of his own remarkable analysis that it took what was valuable in each, rescued each by defining for each the limits of validity, and, in the end, gave the essential purposes of both new power and vitality. No man has had as much influence as a preacher in this generation; no preacher has had as much influence in the secular world" (149).

societal good, the task of Christian ethics thus became the attempt to develop social strategies which people of goodwill could adopt even though they differed religiously and morally.

Therefore, even though Niebuhr criticized the Catholic natural law tradition for "absolutizing the relative," he nonetheless was a natural law thinker. Only the natural law, through which justice was defined, involves "not so much fixed standards of reason as they are rational efforts to apply the moral obligation, implied in the love commandment, to the complexities of life and the fact of sin, that is, to the situation created by the inclination of men to take advantage of each other.[24] In fact, Niebuhr's understanding of the "law of love" as an unavoidable aspect of the human condition was in many ways a powerful attempt to provide a natural theology that could make the cross intelligible as a symbol of human existence.[25]

If Reinhold Niebuhr's work resulted in an ambiguous account of Christian ethics, in many ways his brother's work proved to be a more decisive challenge for that task. H. Richard Niebuhr was less concerned with the difficulties of sustaining the social imperatives of the social gospel; instead, he tended to pursue the theological difficulties that the social gospel had occasioned. Deeply influenced by Troeltsch, he was acutely aware that the social gospelers' attempt to move directly from their theological convictions to social strategies was fraught not only with social ambiguities but with theological difficulties. Moreover, he was increasingly doubtful of any position which assumed that God could be used to underwrite mankind's interests, even if those interests were most impressive.

Under H. Richard Niebuhr's influence it became the business of Christian ethics to find the most adequate conceptual means to explicate what kind of moral implications might follow from Christian convictions.[26] Thus, Christian theologians began to give more serious attention to what philosophers were doing, hoping they would supply just such conceptual tools. But the kind of philosophical ethics to which Niebuhr's students looked had exactly the opposite effect. They learned from those philosophical sources that there was an inherent problem in trying to move from theological claims to normative recommendations, for in doing so one commits the "supernaturalistic fallacy."[27] As a result, theological ethicists began to pay even less attention to positive theological claims and instead attempted to show that, formally, a theological basis for ethics was not inherently incoherent and, in particular, that theological claims could underwrite anti-relativist and objectivist concerns.[28] In the hands of some, Christian ethics became but another form of metaethics. In the process, it became just as ahistorical as its philosophical counterpart.

That was certainly not a result which would have made H. Richard Niebuhr happy. Even though in his work Christian ethics was less an aid to action than an aid to understanding, he did not want Christian ethics to lose its theological agenda. On the contrary, his attempt to focus attention on the question "What is going on?" rather than "What should we do?" was an attempt to keep theological questions primary for ethical reflection. It was H. R. Niebuhr's task to show that the former question could only be answered adequately in theological terms. Thus, in *The Re-*

---

24. Reinhold Niebuhr, *Faith and History* (New York: Scribner's, 1951), 188-189.

25. Niebuhr's stress on the sinfulness of man leads some to forget that for Niebuhr theology is still primarily anthropology. As a result Niebuhr never answered satisfactorily how the cross of Jesus is necessary for our adequately understanding why the cross is the necessary symbol of "the perfection of *agape* which transcends all particular norms of justice and mutuality in history." *(Nature and Destiny of Man)* 2:74.

26. For the best short introduction to H. R. Niebuhr's work see James Gustafson, "Introduction," in H. R. Niebuhr, *The Responsible Self: An Essay in Christian Moral Philosophy* (New York: Harper and Row, 1963), 6-41.

27. H. R. Niebuhr was not himself very taken with ethics done out of the analytical tradition, but instead was influenced more by the pragmatist tradition of Royce and Perry. However, a latter generation of students, trained by Gustafson, turned increasingly to Moore, Ross, Hare, in attempts to think through the problems they had inherited from Niebuhr.

28. Art Dyck's enthusiasm for and theological justification of the "ideal-observer" theory is a good example of this tendency. See his *On Human Care: An Introduction to Ethics* (Nashville: Abingdon, 1977).

sponsible Self, he maintained the central Christian claim is "God is acting in all actions upon you. So respond to all actions upon you as to respond to his action."[29]

For H. R. Niebuhr the problem was not how to secure justice in an unjust world, but rather how to account for moral activity amid the relativities of history. His theological project was to provide a theological interpretation of the relativity of our existence so that the knowledge of our finitude was relativized by our relation to a God who alone deserves our complete loyalty. For H. R. Niebuhr, the task of Christian ethics was a theological task, but ironically, his own theology made it difficult to keep Christian ethics Christian. For the very idea of "Christian ethics" suggested a far too narrow conception of God to do justice to the relativities of our existence.[30]

In spite of the undeniable influence of Barth on H. R. Niebuhr, the influence of Schleiermacher was stronger. He strongly reacted against the christocentrism of Barth, but just as importantly, like his brother he continued the liberal project to secure the intelligibility of theological discourse by demonstrating how it reflects as well as describes the human condition. Therefore, while differing deeply with his brother on particular theological issues, he remained essentially in the tradition of Calvinism, as opposed to Reinhold's Lutheranism, but in many ways the structure of their theologies was similar. H. Richard Niebuhr's *The Responsible Self* was an attempt to analyze the inherent relatedness of human to human, human to nature, human and nature to God who enters a covenant with his creation.[31]

The recent history of Christian ethics has largely been the story of the attempt to work out the set of problems bequeathed to us by the social gospel and the Niebuhrs. The other figure in the drama of late has been Roman Catholic moral theology. Under the impetus of Vatican II, Roman Catholic moral theologians have increasingly made contact with their Protestant counterparts in hopes they could learn from them how to put their natural law commitments in a more compelling theological framework. Protestant thinkers, struggling with the failure of their own tradition to develop discriminating forms of argument, looked to the Catholic casuistical tradition for help in thinking about such issues as marriage, abortion, and war. No thinker better represents this tendency of Protestant thinkers than Paul Ramsey. For Ramsey continues to assume that the task of Christian ethics is to address the American body politic. Yet now the issue is not the transformation of that polity but how the ethos that underwrites that polity can be sustained under the increasing onslaught of relativistic and consequential moral theories. The heir of both Niebuhrs, Ramsey found that neither the Niebuhrs nor Protestant thought in general provided the framework appropriate for disciplined ethical argument. Thus Ramsey looked to the Catholic tradition for principles to structure arguments that, at least in principle, would be publicly acceptable. Still, the influence of the Niebuhrs meant that Ramsey could not accept Roman Catholic assumptions about the relative autonomy of natural law and morality. As a result, his work clearly manifests the tension inherent in the development of Christian ethics —

---

29. H. R. Niebuhr. *The Responsible Self,* 126.

30. For H. R. Niebuhr, Jesus is normative only as he "represents the incarnation of radical faith," which is faith that "Being is God, or better, that the principle of being, the source of all things and the power by which they exist, is good, as good for them and good to them" *Radical Monotheism and Western Culture* (New York: Harper and Row, 1960), 38.

31. Thus he says, "Man responsive and responsible before nature, fitting his actions into those of nature; man responsive in political or economic or cultural society as responsible citizen; responsible businessman, responsible educator, responsible scientist, responsible parent, responsible churchman — such men we know and understand. But what ties all these responsivities

and responsibilities together and where is the responsible *self* among all these roles played by the individual being? Can it be located within the self, as though by some mighty act of self-making it brought itself into being as one 'I' among these many systems of interpretation and response? The self as one self among all the systematized reactions in which it engages seems to be the counterpart of a unity that lies beyond, yet expresses itself in, all the manifold systems of actions upon it. In religious language, the soul and God belong together; or otherwise stated, I am one within myself as I encounter the One in all that acts upon me" *The Responsible Self,* 122.

namely, a concern to provide a theological account of the moral life while at the same time underplaying the significance of theology for purposes of public discussion.[32]

Much of Ramsey's perspective on this wider set of issues was set by the situation ethics debate of the 1950s and '60s. Against Joseph Fletcher's acceptance of act-utilitarianism as the most appropriate expression of Christian love, Ramsey insisted that Christian love must be in-principled. Moreover, the principles he thought best expressed or embodied their love were very much like the traditional Roman Catholic prohibitions against unjust life-taking, lying, sexual misconduct, and so on. Thus Ramsey maintained that Christian ethics, as well as Christian responsibility to maintain the best moral insights of Western civilization, was clearly aligned with deontological normative theories and against all consequentialism.[33]

Perhaps it is hard to see how this agenda has anything in common with the social gospel, but in many interesting ways Ramsey stands in continuity with that project. Even though he does not seek to underwrite a social activism that the social

gospelers thought was required by the "organic unity between religion and ethics," Ramsey nonetheless shares their assumption that the first subject of Christian ethics is how to sustain the moral resources of American society. Moreover, like Reinhold Niebuhr, he assumes that this project requires an account sufficient to underwrite a politics of realism in which we see that we may well have to kill in the name of a lesser evil; but unlike Niebuhr, Ramsey sought to provide, through a theological reinterpretation of the just war tradition, a control on realism's tendency to consequentialism.[34]

Ramsey claims that what makes ethics Christian is that theological convictions are necessary to sustain the deontological commitments of our culture. Therefore, in Ramsey's work in such areas as medical ethics, most of the theology can be done in the "Preface" of his books. As a result, even many of those who are sympathetic with Ramsey's construal of the ethos of medicine in deontological terms see no reason why those deontological commitments require Ramsey's peculiar theological views about the significance of covenant love to sustain that ethos. Or again, many may well side with Ramsey against the act-utilitarianism of Fletcher, but see no reason why that debate involves theological questions, since it is simply a straightforward philosophical matter involving whether a coherent deontological or teleological normative theory can be defended. All the talk about love by both Fletcher and Ramsey is but a confusion of the issue.

Therefore, contemporary theologians find

32. The theological side of Ramsey's work was more apparent in his early work where he was emphatic that "natural law" must be transformed by love. See in particular his *War and the Christian Conscience* (Durham, N.C.; Duke University Press, 1961). Ramsey's shift to the motif of covenant fidelity as the central metaphor for Christian reflection also seems to have been accompanied with a greater appreciation for the continuity between the "natural" covenants we find in our lives and that which God has made with us. As a result he is able to proceed with much less direct appeal to theological warrants. See, for example, his *The Patient as Person* (New Haven: Yale University Press, 1970).

33. Thus Ramsey argues that "Protestant Christian ethics is often too profoundly personal to be ethically relevant, if in this is included even a minimum of concern for the social habits and customs of a people. Ordinarily, we do not take Christian ethics with enough seriousness to illumine the path that men, women, and *society* should follow today. This suggests that only some form of rule-agapism, and not act-agapism, can be consistent with the elaboration of a Christian's social responsibilities. No social morality ever was founded, or ever will be founded, upon a situational ethic." *Deeds and Rules in Christian Ethics* (New York: Scribner's, 1967), 20.

34. Ramsey's profound debt to Niebuhr can be most clearly seen in his *The Just War: Force and Political Responsibility* (New York: Scribner's, 1968). There Ramsey, like Niebuhr argues that the failure of all peace movements is they presume the illusion that force can be avoided in politics and as a result only increase the likelihood of war. In contrast the just war tradition influenced by the theological insights of Augustine rightly sees that war can never be fought for peace, but only for more relative just ends. Thus Ramsey argues the ethos necessary to control violence through just war principles must ultimately draw on religious presuppositions. For only if you think death is not ultimate power over life can you be willing to expose yourself to death and to kill others for the limited moral goods of political community.

themselves in a peculiar situation. Increasingly they turned to philosophical sources to help them illumine the logic of their ethical commitments, but just to the extent they did so it became harder to say what, if anything, Christian ethics had to contribute to discussions in ethics. What they failed to see was that the very philosophical sources from which they drew to clarify the nature of their normative claims made it difficult to suggest how religious convictions might challenge just those philosophical frameworks. Thus theologians assumed, along with their philosophical colleagues, that ethics must basically be about dealing with quandaries, the only question being whether Christian convictions are more basically deontological or teleological or some as yet unspecified combination of the two.

The distinctive nature of theological ethics continued to be shown not in its philosophical expression, but rather in the range of interests each theologian addressed. By continuing to draw on the inspiration of the social gospel, the theologian continued to be concerned about questions of social and economic justice, marriage and the family, the status of the nation state, that hitherto had tended to be ignored by the philosopher. Yet, with the work of Rawls and the rise of journals such as *Philosophy and Public Affairs*, the theologian could no longer even claim that mark of distinction. The only alternatives left seemed to be to retreat to working in a confessional stance or analyzing the methodological issues and alternatives for understanding how theological ethics has been or should be done.

Much of the later work has been done by James Gustafson — a student of H. R. Niebuhr — who has sought through careful analysis of historical and current options within theological ethics to keep the discourse alive.[35] Though much of Gustafson's work is descriptive, his concerns are primarily constructive. It is, therefore, not accidental that Gustafson began to direct attention to the importance for ethics of the "sort of persons we are," of character and virtue, as the appropriate context for assessing the significance of theological language for ethical behavior.[36]

Above all, Gustafson's work is centered on the question "Can ethics be Christian?" For him the Christian theologian's ethical task is done for the sake of a community which shares a set of common experiences and beliefs about God and his particular revelation in Jesus Christ.

The Christian community is not, however, the exclusive audience. Since the intention of the divine power for human well-being is universal in its scope, the historically particular medium through which that power is clarified for Christians also has universal significance. The theologian engaged in the task of "prescriptive" ethics formulates principles and values that can guide the actions of persons who do not belong to the Christian community. They will be persuasive to others, however, on the basis of supporting reasons different from those that Christians might respond to. In effect, the theologian moves from the particular Christian belief to a statement of their moral import in a more universal language. These statements will be persuasive to nonreligious persons only by the cogency of the argument that is made to show that the "historical particularity" sheds light on principles and values that other serious moral persons also perceive and also ought to adhere to. Indeed, since the Christian theologian shares in the general moral experience of secular people, and since one facet of this work that is theologically warranted is the inferring of principles and values from common experience, he or she need not in every practical circumstance make a particular theological case for what is formulated. The theologian ought, however, to be able to make a Christian theological case if challenged to do so.[37]

35. See, for example, Gustafson's *Christian Ethics and the Community* (Philadephia: Pilgrim Press, 1971) and *Theology and Christian Ethics.* (Philadelphia: Pilgrim Press, 1974), both of which are collections of his essays that attempt to bring some intellectual clarity to the activity of other Christian ethicists.

36. This emphasis, of course, is but an indication of Gustafson's indebtedness to H. R. Niebuhr's attempt to identify the central issue of Christian ethics as that of the "self." Unfortunately many of the interpreters of H. R. Niebuhr tend to stress more his account of "responsibility" and, as a result, fail to see that Niebuhr's primary concern was the "self."

37. Gustafson, *Can Ethics Be Christian?*, 163.

Gustafson's reasoning is based on his theological belief that God's purposes are for "the well-being of man and creation, and thus on most occasions the reasons that justify any moral act would justify the moral acts of Christians. The only case he can give that might be an exception to this is some Christians' commitment to nonviolent resistance to evil, since the justification of such a response clearly must rely on appeal to certain "religious" reasons that go beyond what we mean by morality.[38]

If this is all that is to be gained by speaking theologically about morality, then one may well question if it is worth the effort. As I have tried to show through this brief history of the development of the "discipline" of Christian ethics, the primary subject theologically became how to keep Christian ethics Christian. This situation is no doubt partly the result of the changing historical and sociological stance of the churches vis-a-vis American society. For as that society increasingly becomes secular, Christians, insofar as they endeavor to remain political actors, must attempt to translate their convictions into a nontheological idiom. But once such a translation is accomplished, it becomes very unclear why the theological idiom is needed at all.

The difficulty of making and keeping Christian ethics Christian, however, derives not only from social strategies, but, as we have seen, also from theological difficulties. For the recovery of the ethical significance of theological discourse was part of a theological movement within Protestantism that in large measure sought to avoid the more traditional particularistic claims of Christianity. Ironically, just to the extent that the development of Christian ethics as a field was a success, it reinforced the assumption that more positive theological convictions had little purchase on the way things are or should be. It is no wonder, therefore, that the dominant modes of philosophical ethics received little challenge from the theological community. Indeed, exactly to the contrary, theologians and religious thinkers have largely sought to

38. It is telling, I think, that in his recent constructive work *Ethics from a Theocentric Perspective* (Chicago: University of Chicago Press, 1981), Gustafson thinks John Howard Yoder's "sectarian" stance to be the most intelligible alternative to his own position.

show that the modes of argument and conclusions reached by philosophical ethicists are no different from those reached by ethicists with more explicit religions presuppositions. The task of Christian ethics, both socially and philosophically, was not revision but accommodation.

A Revision of Theological Ethics

I have tried to suggest why the development of Christian ethics during this century provided no significant alternative to the dominant modes of ethical reflection done by philosophers. To be sure there are aspects in the work of Rauschenbusch, the Niebuhrs, Ramsey, and Gustafson that stand in sharp contrast with the accepted mode of doing philosophical ethics. But it is simply the case that their work has failed to influence or even to be taken very seriously by others working in ethics in a nontheological context.

Of course part of the reason for that is more sociological than intellectual. Religion has increasingly become marginal in our culture, both politically and intellectually. Those types of religion that attempt to assert their relevancy in the social and political realm do so with a crudeness that only underwrites the general assumption that our society will do better to continue to relegate religious concerns to the private and subjective realm. This same kind of relegation has occurred in the intellectual realm, often with much less good reason. Few modern intellectuals feel the obligation to read the better work done in theology, because they prejudicially assume that theology must inherently be a form of special pleading.

As I suggested at the beginning, attempts to address this prejudice on its own terms are doomed to failure. The more theologians seek to find the means to translate theological convictions into terms acceptable to the nonbeliever, the more they substantiate the view that theology has little of importance to say in the area of ethics. It seems that the theologian is in a classical "no win" situation.

Yet I think in many ways this is not the case. It may be that theology can make a virtue of necessity. In many ways the social and intellectual marginality of the church in our culture is an intellectual resource that can provide the opportunity to recover some of the more important aspects of Christian reflection, particularly concerning morality. As I have tried to suggest, the very development of "Christian ethics" as a branch of theology was inspired by an attempt to re-awaken Christian social responsibility. But the very terms of that reawakening and its underlying theology had already accommodated itself far too much to the secular ethos. Therefore, in spite of the significant advances in Christian reflection represented by the development of Christian ethics, in many ways it failed to represent adequately the resources for ethical reflection within the Christian tradition. Thus one of the ironies is that many of the challenges made by philosophers against the reigning paradigm could have been made, and perhaps made even more forcefully, from a theological perspective. But they were not, and they were not because Christians in general and theologians in particular continued to assume that they had built a home within Western civilization that they had a stake in continuing. As a result, Christian ethicists accepted an account of the social good that fails to manifest the struggle, the transformation of the self necessary for any adequate account of the moral life.

It is odd that Christians, of all people, could have made that mistake, since who could know better than they that the moral good is not an achievement easily accomplished by the many, but a demanding task that only a few master. Christians have not been called to do just the right, to observe the law, though doing the right and observing the law are not irrelevant to being good. Rather, for Christians the moral life, at least scripturally, is seen as a journey through life sustained by fidelity to the cross of Christ, which brings a fulfillment no law can ever embody. Thus Aquinas says:

> there is a twofold element in the law of the gospel. There is the chief element, namely, the grace of the Holy Ghost bestowed inwardly. And as to this the new law justifies. Hence Augustine says: "There (that is, in the Old Testament) it is given in an inward manner, that they might be justified." The other element of the Evangelical law is secondary; namely, the teachings of faith, and those commandments which direct human affections and human actions. And as to this, the new law does not justify. Hence the apostle says: "The letter

killeth, but the spirit quickeneth" (II Cor. 3:6), and Augustine explains this by saying that the letter denotes any writing that is external to man, even that of the moral precepts such as are contained in the gospel. Therefore the letter, even of the gospel would kill, unless there were the inward presence of the healing grace of faith.[39]

From such a perspective Christian thinkers, above all, should have been among the first to criticize the attempt to model the moral life primarily on the analogy of the law. Instead, fearing moral anarchy, like our philosophical colleagues, Christian thinkers assumed that questions of "right" were more primary than questions of good, that principles were more fundamental than virtues, that for morality to be coherent required some one principle from which all others could be derived or tested, that the central task of moral reflection was to help us think straight about quandaries, and that we had to see the world as neatly divided into facts and values, rather than an existence filled with many valuational possibilities, some of which may well be in conflict. Perhaps most ironical, Christian theology attempted to deny the inherent historical and community-dependent nature of our moral convictions in the hopes that our "ethics" might be universally persuasive.

But as Schneewind reminds us, the justification of our moral principles and assertions cannot be done from the point of view of anyone, but rather requires a tradition of moral wisdom.[40] Such a tradition is not a "deposit" of unchanging moral "truth," but is made up of the lives of men and women who are constantly testing and changing

---

39. Thomas Aquinas, *Summa Theologia*, I-II.106.2 translated by Fathers of the English Dominican Province (Chicago: William Benton Publisher, 1952). Many others besides Aquinas could be quoted to substantiate this point. I purposely chose Aquinas, since many who defend a natural law approach to Christian ethics appeal to him as their primary authority. Yet as the quotation makes clear, Aquinas assumed that an adequate theological ethics could not be limited to or based on an analogy with law.

40. J. B. Schneewind, "Moral Knowledge and Moral Principles," in *Revisions: Changing Perspectives in Moral Philosophy*, edited by Stanley Hauerwas and Alasdair MacIntyre (Notre Dame: University of Notre Dame Press, 1983), 113-126.

that tradition through their own struggle to live it. The maintenance of such a tradition requires a community across time sufficient to sustain the journey from one generation to the next. The Christian word for the community is church.[41]

It is my suspicion that if theologians are going to contribute to reflection on the moral life in our particular situation, they will do so exactly to the extent they can capture the significance of the church for determining the nature and content of Christian ethical reflection. This may seem an odd suggestion, for it seems such a move would only make the theologian that much further removed from being a serious conversation partner. It is assumed, by theologian and philosopher alike, that any distinctive contribution of theological ethics must begin with beliefs about God, Jesus, sin, and the like, and the moral implications of those beliefs. And of course there is much truth to that. Yet the problem with putting the matter in that way is that such "beliefs" look like descriptions of existence, some kind of primitive metaphysics, that one must then try to analyze for their moral implications. To force Christian moral reflection into such a pattern is to make it appear but another philosophical account of the moral life.

But that is exactly what it is not. For Christian beliefs about God, Jesus, sin, the nature of human existence, and salvation are intelligible only if they are seen against the background of the church — that is, a body of people who stand apart from the "world" because of the peculiar task of worshiping a God whom the world knows not. This is a point as much forgotten by Christian theologians as by secular philosophers, since the temptation is to make Christianity another "system of belief." Yet what was original about the first Christians was not the peculiarity of their beliefs, even beliefs about Jesus, but their social inventiveness in creating a community whose like had not been seen before. To say they believed in God is true but uninteresting. What is interesting is that they thought that their belief in God as they had encountered him in Jesus required the formation of

a community distinct from the world exactly because of the kind of God he was. You cannot know what kind of God you disbelieve in, from a Christian perspective, unless you see what kind of community is necessary to worship him across time. The flabbiness of contemporary atheism is, thus, a judgment on the church's unwillingness to be a distinctive people.

Therefore, when asked to say something theological, especially when the questioner is seeking to understand the ethical significance of religious convictions, we should perhaps not say with Gustafson "God," but "Church." For the criticism of the emphasis in contemporary ethics on law, on rights, on principles, on quandaries, on facts distinguished from values, is the result of trying to write ethics for anyone, as if ethics can be abstracted from any community. It is not surprising that the law becomes the primary analogue for such an ethic as law is often seen as the minimal principles needed to secure order between people who share little in common. Ethics, like law, thus becomes the procedural means to settle disputes and resolve problems while leaving our individual "preferences" and desires to our own choice. To say more about morality requires not simply a conception of the good, but a tradition that carries the virtues necessary for training in movement toward the good.

Many philosophers and theologians are calling for a fuller account of the moral life. They rightly criticize the thinness of much of contemporary ethical theory; yet they offer no persuasive alternative. They point to the need for revision, but the social and political practices necessary for that revision to be institutionalized are missing. Moreover, any attempts to create them appear utopian or totalitarian. Of course, appeals can be made to particular individuals as paradigms of the kind of moral life desired, but moral geniuses are never sufficient to sustain our best moral convictions. For sustenance we need a community to direct attention toward, and sustain the insights of, those who have become more nearly good.

As Christians we believe we not only need a community, but a community of a particular kind to live well morally. We need a people who are capable of being faithful to a way of life, even when that way of life may be in conflict with what passes as "morality" in the larger society. Christians are

---

41. For a fuller account of this perspective see my *A Community of Character: Toward a Constructive Christian Social Ethic* (Notre Dame: University of Notre Dame Press, 1981).

a people who have learned that belief in God requires that we learn to look upon ourselves as creatures rather than as creators. This necessarily creates a division between ourselves and others who persist in the pretentious assumption that we can and should be morally autonomous. Of course Christians are as prone to such pretensions as non-Christians. What distinguishes them is their willingness to belong to a community which embodies the stories, the rituals, and others committed to worshipping God. Such a community, we believe, must challenge our prideful pretensions as well as provide the skills for the humility necessary for becoming not just good, but holy.

Theologians, therefore, have something significant to say about ethics, but they will not say it significantly if they try to disguise the fact that they think, write, and speak out of and to a distinctive community. Their first task is not, as has been assumed by many working in Christian ethics and still under the spell of Christendom, to write as though Christian commitments make no difference in the sense that they only underwrite what everyone already in principle can know, but rather to show the difference those commitments make. At least by doing that, philosophers may have some idea how the attempt to avoid presuming any tradition or community may distort their account of the moral life as well as moral rationality. Our task as theologians remains what it has always been — namely, to exploit the considerable resources embodied in particular Christian convictions which sustain our ability to be a community faithful to our belief that we are creatures of a graceful God. If we do that we may well discover that we are speaking to more than just our fellow Christians, for others as a result may well find we have something interesting to say.

Chapter 5

Science and Christian Ethics

Introduction

The impact of science on Christian ethical reflection has been immense. As a distinctive way of knowing and as a source of new techniques, modern scientific investigation continues to rock the religious world in which the activity of Christian ethics takes place. The debate about gays in the church, for example, is inconceivable apart from the concept of a "homosexual," a decidedly untraditional notion drawn from the discipline of psychology and the social sciences. (See reading 30, and then case study 2 at the end of this chapter.)

As James Gustafson indicates (reading 28), the range of empirical sciences that influence Christian ethics is wide. Data from political science, economics, sociology and psychology impinge on ethical investigation in a variety of ways. Harder data from the science of biology enrich the ethics of medical practice (see chapter 10), frame many of the issues related to care of the environment (see chapter 13), and finally, inform the knotty question of abortion (see above, pages 17ff.).

Surveying the Christian tradition as a whole, one quickly senses a certain ambivalence about science, an ambivalence clearly visible in the essays selected for this chapter. In reading 25, Pope Paul VI examines what may be the most remarkable and fateful of powers we receive from modern science — control over our own reproduction. While he appreciates the insights of science regarding conception, the pope believes that the ethical criteria that one might derive from these insights are too limited to guide Christians in the larger questions of when to limit birth and by what means. This is the task of the church. Note the way in which this reading, *Humanae Vitae,* is clearly rooted in a living tradition (see reading 14) and

displays a sacramental view of marriage and family (as in reading 57).

E. O. Wilson is both a noted scientist and an atheist. In reading 26, he shows how religious belief and scientific knowledge could be completely opposing ways of depicting the universe. In reading 27, C. S. Lewis notes that in a particular sort of science today, there is a popular (though finally misguided) attempt to stand outside of religion and values while investigating "facts." Carol Gilligan argues that by leaving out the experience of women, the psychological literature on human development has imitated the patriarchy of the Christian church and of Western society as a whole (reading 29).

Human investigation of the world has value, states the biblical writer in Job (reading 25). But one should not place too much confidence there. True wisdom is of a different order. "Mortals do not know the way to it, and it is not found in the land of the living."

Suggestions for Further Reading

Barbour, Ian G., ed. *Science and Religion: New Perspectives on the Dialogue.* New York: Harper & Row, 1968.

Birtel, Frank T., ed. *Religion, Science, and Public Policy.* New York: Crossroad, 1987.

Heyward, Carter. *Touching Our Strength: The Erotic as Power and the Love of God,* chapter 4. New York: Harper & Row, 1989.

Kass, Leon. *Toward a More Natural Science: Biology and Human Affairs.* New York: Macmillan, Free Press, 1985.

Merchant, Carolyn. *The Death of Nature: Women, Ecology, and the Scientific Revolution.* New York: Harper & Row, 1980.

Nelson, J. Robert. *On the New Frontiers of Genetics and Religion.* Grand Rapids, Mich.: Wm. B. Eerdmans, 1994.

Rolston, Homes, III. *Science and Religion: A Critical Survey.* New York: Random House, 1987.

Russell, Colin. *Cross-Currents: Interactions between Science and Faith.* Grand Rapids, Mich.: Wm. B. Eerdmans, 1985.

24. Job 28:9-14, 23-28

"They put their hand to the flinty rock,
   and overturn mountains by the roots.
They cut out channels in the rocks,
   and their eyes see every precious thing.
The sources of the rivers they probe;
   hidden things they bring to light.

"But where shall wisdom be found?
   And where is the place of understanding?
Mortals do not know the way to it,
   and it is not found in the land of the living.
The deep says, 'It is not in me,'
   and the sea says, 'It is not with me.' . . .

"God understands the way to it,
   and he knows its place.
For he looks to the ends of the earth,
   and sees everything under the heavens.
When he gave to the wind its weight,
   and apportioned out the waters by measure;
When he made a decree for the rain,
   and a way for the thunderbolt;
then he saw it and declared it;
   he established it, and searched it out.
And he said to humankind,
'Truly, the fear of the Lord, that is wisdom;
   and to depart from evil is understanding.'"

25. Excerpt from *Humanae Vitae*

POPE PAUL VI

Encyclical Letter of his Holiness on the Regulation of Birth

To the venerable Patriarchs, Archbishops and Bishops, and other local ordinaries in peace and communion with the Apostolic See, to priests, the faithful, and to all men of good will.

Venerable brothers and beloved sons:

The Transmission of Life

The most serious duty of transmitting human life, for which married persons are the free and responsible collaborators of God the Creator, has always been a source of great joys to them, even if sometimes accompanied by not a few difficulties and by distress.

At all times the fulfillment of this duty has posed grave problems to the conscience of married persons, but, with the recent evolution of society, changes have taken place that give rise to new questions which the Church could not ignore, having to do with a matter which so

---

Pope Paul VI (1897–1978) (born Giovanni Battista Montini) was bishop of Rome and pope of the Roman Catholic Church between 1963 and 1978. Among the papal documents of his bishopric are *Sacerdotalis Coelibatus* and *Humanae Vitae*.

From Paul VI, *Humanae Vitae* (Boston: St. Paul Editions, 1968).

closely touches upon the life and happiness of men. . . .

Doctrinal Principles

A Total Vision of Man

The problem of birth, like every other problem regarding human life, is to be considered, beyond partial perspectives — whether of the biological or psychological, demographic or sociological orders — in the light of an integral vision of man and of his vocation, not only his natural and earthly, but also his supernatural and eternal vocation. And since, in the attempt to justify artificial methods of birth control, many have appealed to the demands both of conjugal love and of "responsible parenthood" it is good to state very precisely the true concept of these two great realities of married life, referring principally to what was recently set forth in this regard, and in a highly authoritative form, by the Second Vatican Council in its pastoral constitution *Gaudium et Spes* (Constitution on the Church in the Modern World).

Conjugal love reveals its true nature and nobility when it is considered in its supreme origin, God, who is love[1] "the Father, from whom every family in heaven and on earth is named."[2]

Marriage is not, then, the effect of chance or the product of evolution of unconscious natural forces; it is the wise institution of the Creator to realize in mankind his design of love. By means of the reciprocal personal gift of self, proper and exclusive to them, husband and wife tend towards the communion of their beings in view of mutual personal perfection, to collaborate with God in the generation and education of new lives.

For baptized persons, moreover, marriage invests the dignity of a sacramental sign of grace, inasmuch as it represents the union of Christ and of the Church.

---

1. Cf. 1 John 4:8.
2. Cf. Eph. 3:15.

Its Characteristics

Under this light, there clearly appear the characteristic marks and demands of conjugal love, and it is of supreme importance to have an exact idea of these.

This love is first of all fully human, that is to say, of the senses and of the spirit at the same time. It is not, then, a simple transport of instinct and sentiment, but also, and principally, an act of the free will, intended to endure and to grow by means of the joys and sorrows of daily life, in such a way that husband and wife become one only heart and one only soul, and together attain their human perfection.

Then, this love is total, that is to say, it is a very special form of personal friendship, in which husband and wife generously share everything, without undue reservations or selfish calculations. Whoever truly loves his marriage partner loves not only for what he receives, but for the partner's self, rejoicing that he can enrich his partner with the gift of himself.

Again, this love is faithful and exclusive until death. Thus in fact do bride and groom conceive it to be on the day when they freely and in full awareness assume the duty of the marriage bond. A fidelity, this, which can sometimes be difficult, but is always possible, always noble and meritorious, as no one can deny. The example of so many married persons down through the centuries shows, not only that fidelity is according to the nature of marriage, but also that it is a source of profound and lasting happiness and finally, this love is fecund for it is not exhausted by the communion between husband and wife, but is destined to continue, raising up new lives. "Marriage and conjugal love are by their nature ordained toward the begetting and educating of children. Children are really the supreme gift of marriage and contribute very substantially to the welfare of their parents."[3]

Responsible Parenthood

Hence conjugal love requires in husband and wife an awareness of their mission of "responsible par-

enthood," which today is rightly much insisted upon, and which also must be exactly understood. Consequently it is to be considered under different aspects which are legitimate and connected with one another.

In relation to the biological processes, responsible parenthood means the knowledge and respect of their functions; human intellect discovers in the power of giving life biological laws which are part of the human person.[4]

In relation to the tendencies of instinct or passion, responsible parenthood means that necessary dominion which reason and will must exercise over them.

In relation to physical, economic, psychological and social conditions, responsible parenthood is exercised, either by the deliberate and generous decision to raise a numerous family, or by the decision, made for grave motives and with due respect for the moral law, to avoid for the time being, or even for an indeterminate period, a new birth.

Responsible parenthood also and above all implies a more profound relationship to the objective moral order established by God, of which a right conscience is the faithful interpreter. The responsible exercise of parenthood implies, therefore, that husband and wife recognize fully their own duties towards God, towards themselves, towards the family and towards society, in a correct hierarchy of values.

In the task of transmitting life, therefore, they are not free to proceed completely at will, as if they could determine in a wholly autonomous way the honest path to follow; but they must conform their activity to the creative intention of God, expressed in the very nature of marriage and of its acts, and manifested by the constant teaching of the Church.[5]

Respect for the Nature and Purpose of the Marriage Act

These acts, by which husband and wife are united in chaste intimacy, and by means of which human

---

3. Cf. Second Vatican Council, Pastoral constitution *Gaudium et Spes*, no. 50.

4. Cf. St. Thomas, *Summa Theologica*, I-II, q. 94, art. 2.

5. Cf. Pastoral constitution *Gaudium et Spes*, nos. 50, 51.

life is transmitted, are, as the council recalled, "noble and worthy,"[6] and they do not cease to be lawful if, for causes independent of the will of husband and wife, they are foreseen to be infecund, since they always remain ordained towards expressing and consolidating their union. In fact, as experience bears witness, not every conjugal act is followed by a new life. God has wisely disposed natural laws and rhythms of fecundity which, of themselves, cause a separation in the succession of births. Nonetheless the Church, calling men back to the observance of the norms of the natural law, as interpreted by its constant doctrine, teaches that each and every marriage act *(quilibet matrimonii usus)* must remain open to the transmission of life.[7]

Two Inseparable Aspects: Union and Procreation

That teaching, often set forth by the magisterium, is founded upon the inseparable connection, willed by God and unable to be broken by man on his own initiative, between the two meanings of the conjugal act: the unitive meaning and the procreative meaning. Indeed, by its intimate structure, the conjugal act, while most closely uniting husband and wife, capacitates them for the generation of new lives, according to laws inscribed in the very being of man and of woman. By safeguarding both these essential aspects, the unitive and the procreative, the conjugal act preserves in its fullness the sense of true mutual love and its ordination towards man's most high calling to parenthood. We believe that the men of our day are particularly capable of seizing the deeply reasonable and human character of this fundamental principle.

Faithfulness to God's Design

It is in fact justly observed that a conjugal act imposed upon one's partner without regard for his or her condition and lawful desires is not a true act of love, and therefore denies an exigency of right moral order in the relationships between husband and wife. Hence, one who reflects well must also recognize that a reciprocal act of love, which jeopardizes the responsibility to transmit life which God the Creator, according to particular laws, inserted therein, is in contradiction with the design constitutive of marriage, and with the will of the Author of life. To use this divine gift destroying, even if only partially, its meaning and its purpose is to contradict the nature both of man and of woman and of their most intimate relationship, and therefore it is to contradict also the plan of God and his will. On the other hand, to make use of the gift of conjugal love while respecting the laws of the generative process means to acknowledge oneself not to be the arbiter of the sources of human life, but rather the minister of the design established by the Creator. In fact, just as man does not have unlimited dominion over his body in general, so also, with particular reason, he has no such dominion over his generative faculties as such, because of their intrinsic ordination towards raising up life, of which God is the principle. "Human life is sacred," Pope John XXIII recalled; "from its very inception it reveals the creating hand of God."[8]

Illicit Ways of Regulating Birth

In conformity with these landmarks in the human and Christian vision of marriage, we must once again declare that the direct interruption of the generative process already begun, and, above all, directly willed and procured abortion, even if for therapeutic reasons, are to be absolutely excluded as licit means of regulating birth.[9]

Equally to be excluded, as the teaching authority of the Church has frequently declared, is direct sterilization, whether perpetual or temporary, whether of the man or of the woman.[10] Similarly

---

6. Ibid., no. 49.

7. Cf. Pius XI, encyc. *Casti Connubii,* in *Acta Apostolicae Sedis* XXII (1930), p. 560; Pius XII, in AAS XLIII (1951), p. 843.

8. Cf. John XXIII, encyc. *Mater et Magistra,* in AAS LIII (1961), p. 447.

9. Cf. *Catechismus Romanus Concilii Tridentini,* part. II, Ch. VIII; Pius XI, encyc. *Casti Connubii,* in AAS XXII (1930), pp. 562-564; Pius XII, *discorsi e Radiomessaggi,* VI (1944), pp. 191-192; AAS XLIII (1951), pp. 842-843; pp. 857-859; John XXIII, encyc. *Pacem in Terris,* Apr. 11, 1963, in AAS LV (1963), pp. 259-260; *Gaudium et Spes,* no. 51.

10. Cf. Pius XI, encyc. *Casti Connubii,* in AAS XXII

excluded is every action which, either in anticipation of the conjugal act, or in its accomplishment, or in the development of its natural consequences, proposes, whether as a end or as a means, to render procreation impossible.[11]

To justify conjugal acts made intentionally infecund, one cannot invoke as valid reasons the lesser evil, or the fact that such acts would constitute a whole together with the fecund acts already performed or to follow later, and hence would share in one and the same moral goodness. In truth, if it is sometimes licit to tolerate a lesser evil in order to avoid a greater evil or to promote a greater good,[12] it is not licit, even for the gravest reasons, to do evil so that good may follow therefrom,[13] that is, to make into the object of a positive act of the will something which is intrinsically disordered, and hence unworthy of the human person, even when the intention is to safeguard or promote individual, family or social well-being. Consequently it is an error to think that a conjugal act which is deliberately made infecund and so is intrinsically dishonest could be made honest and right by the ensemble of a fecund conjugal life.

Licitness of Therapeutic Means

The Church, on the contrary, does not at all consider illicit the use of those therapeutic means truly necessary to cure diseases of the organism, even if an impediment to procreation, which may be foreseen, should result therefrom, provided such impediment is not, for whatever motive, directly willed.[14]

Licitness of Recourse to Infecund Periods

To this teaching of the Church on conjugal morals, the objection is made today, as we have elsewhere observed, that it is the prerogative of the human intellect to dominate the energies offered by irrational nature and to orientate them towards an end conformable to the good of man. Now, some may ask: in the present case, is it not reasonable in many circumstances to have recourse to artificial birth control if, thereby, we secure the harmony and peace of the family, and better conditions for the education of the children already born? To this question it is necessary to reply with clarity: the Church is the first to praise and recommend the intervention of intelligence in a function which so closely associates the rational creature with his Creator; but she affirms that this must be done with respect for the order established by God.

If, then, there are serious motives to space out births, which derive from the physical or psychological conditions of husband and wife, or from external conditions, the Church teaches that it is then licit to take into account the natural rhythms immanent in the generative functions, for the use of marriage in the infecund periods only, and in this way to regulate birth without offending the moral principles which have been recalled earlier.[15]

The Church is coherent with herself when she considers recourse to the infecund periods to be licit, while at the same time condemning, as being always illicit, the use of means directly contrary to fecundation, even if such use is inspired by reasons which may appear honest and serious. In reality, there are essential differences between the two cases; in the former, the married couple make legitimate use of a natural disposition; in the latter, they impede the development of natural processes. It is true that, in the one and the other case, the married couple are concordant in the positive will of avoiding children for plausible reasons, seeking the certainty that offspring will not arrive; but it is also true that only in the former case are they able to renounce the use of marriage in the fecund periods when, for just motives, procreation is not desirable, while making use of it

---

(1930), p. 565; decree on the Holy Office, Feb. 22, 1940, in AAS L (1958), pp. 734-735.

11. Cf. *Catechismus Romanus Concilii Tridentini*, part II, Ch. VIII; Pius XI, encyc. *Casti Connubii*, in AAS XXII (1930), pp. 559-561; Pius XII, AAS XLIII (1951), p. 843; AAS L (1958), pp. 734-735; John XXIII, encyc. *Mater et Magistra*, in AAS LIII (1961), p. 447.

12. Cf. Pius XII, alloc. to the National Congress of the Union of Catholic Jurists, Dec. 6, 1953, in AAS XLV (1953), pp. 798-799.

13. Cf. Rom. 3:8.

14. Cf. Pius XII, alloc. to Congress of the Italian Association of Urology, Oct. 8, 1953, in AAS XLV (1953), pp. 674-675; AAS L (1958), pp. 734-735.

15. Cf. Pius XII, AAS XLIII (1951), p. 846.

during infecund periods to manifest their affection and to safeguard their mutual fidelity. By so doing, they give proof of a truly and integrally honest love.

Grave Consequences of Methods of Artificial Birth Control

Upright men can even better convince themselves of the solid grounds on which the teaching of the Church in this field is based, if they care to reflect upon the consequences of methods of artificial birth control. Let them consider, first of all, how wide and easy a road would thus be opened up towards conjugal infidelity and the general lowering of morality. Not much experience is needed in order to know human weakness, and to understand that men — especially the young, who are so vulnerable on this point — have need of encouragement to be faithful to the moral law, so that they must not be offered some easy means of eluding its observance. It is also to be feared that the man, growing used to the employment of anticonceptive practices, may finally lose respect for the woman and, no longer caring for her physical and psychological equilibrium, may come to the point of considering her as a mere instrument of selfish enjoyment, and no longer as his respected and beloved companion.

Let it be considered also that a dangerous weapon would thus be placed in the hands of those public authorities who take no heed of moral exigencies. Who could blame a government for applying to the solution of the problems of the community those means acknowledged to be licit for married couples in the solution of a family problem? Who will stop rulers from favoring, from even imposing upon their peoples, if they were to consider it necessary, the method of contraception which they judge to be most efficacious? In such a way men, wishing to avoid individual, family, or social difficulties encountered in the observance of the divine law, would reach the point of placing at the mercy of the intervention of public authorities the most personal and most reserved sector of conjugal intimacy.

Consequently, if the mission of generating life is not to be exposed to the arbitrary will of men, one must necessarily recognize insurmountable limits to the possibility of man's domination over his own body and its functions; limits which no man, whether a private individual or one invested with authority, may licitly surpass. And such limits cannot be determined otherwise than by the respect due to the integrity of the human organism and its functions, according to the principles recalled earlier, and also according to the correct understanding of the "principle of totality" illustrated by our predecessor Pope Pius XII.[16]

The Church, Guarantor of True Human Values

It can be foreseen that this teaching will perhaps not be easily received by all: Too numerous are those voices — amplified by the modern means of propaganda — which are contrary to the voice of the Church. To tell the truth, the Church is not surprised to be made, like her divine founder, a "sign of contradiction,"[17] yet she does not because of this cease to proclaim with humble firmness the entire moral law, both natural and evangelical. Of such laws the Church was not the author, nor consequently can she be their arbiter; she is only their depositary and their interpreter, without ever being able to declare to be licit that which is not so by reason of its intimate and unchangeable opposition to the true good of man.

In defending conjugal morals in their integral wholeness, the Church knows that she contributes towards the establishment of a truly human civilization; she engages man not to abdicate from his own responsibility in order to rely on technical means; by that very fact she defends the dignity of man and wife. Faithful to both the teaching and the example of the Savior, she shows herself to be the sincere and disinterested friend of men, whom she wishes to help, even during their earthly sojourn, "to share as sons in the life of the living God, the Father of all men."[18]

16. Cf. AAS XLV (1953), pp. 674-675; AAS XLVIII (1956), pp. 461-462.

17. Cf. Luke 2:34.

18. Cf. Paul VI, encyc. *Populorum progressio*, March 26, 1967, no. 21.

26. Scientific Humanism and Religion

EDWARD O. WILSON

At the Cologne Cathedral, in 1980, Pope John Paul II said that science has added "wings to the spirit of modern awareness." Yet science does not threaten the core of religious belief:

> We have no fear, indeed we regard it as excluded, that a branch of science or branch of knowledge, based on reason and proceeding methodically and securely, can arrive at knowledge that comes into conflict with the truth of faith. This can be the case only where the differentiation between the orders of knowledge is overlooked or denied.

That last sentence, reaffirming Augustine's two books on God, takes us to the heart of the real dialogue between religion and science. Although many theologians and lay philosophers like to deny it, I believe that traditional religious belief and scientific knowledge depict the universe in radically different ways. At bedrock they are incompatible and mutually exclusive. The materialist (or "humanist" or "naturalist") position can be put in a phrase: There is only one book, and it was written in a manner too strange and subtle to be foretold by the prophets and church fathers.

But, there is another side to the story, one that

makes the contrast in world views still more interesting. The materialist position presupposes no final answers. It is an undeniable fact that faith is in our bones, that religious belief is a part of human nature and seemingly vital to social existence. Take away one faith, and another rushes in to fill the void. Take away that, and some secular equivalent such as Marxism intrudes, replete with sacred texts and icons. Take away all these faiths and rely wholly on skepticism and personal inquiry — if you can — and the fabric of society would likely start to unravel. This phenomenon, so strange and subtle as to daunt materialist explanation, is in my opinion the most promising focus for a dialogue between theologians and scientists.

From early Greek philosophy, there has always been a great divide in thought. Humanity is faced with a choice between two metaphysics, two differing views of how the world works from the top down and, hence, of the ultimate means for the selection of moral codes. The first view holds that morality is transcendental in origin and exists both within and apart from the human species. This doctrine has been refined within the church by the conception of natural law, which is the reading of the eternal law in God's mind: People reason out God's intent through a reflection of human nature, obedient to the principle that, as Aquinas expressed it, "man has a natural inclination to know the truth about God and to live in society." The opposing view is that morality is entirely a human phenomenon. In the modern, evolutionary version of this materialist philosophy, its precepts represent the upwelling of deep impulses that are encoded in our genes and find expression within the setting of particular cultures. They have nothing directly to do with divine guidance, at least not in the manner conceived by traditional religions.

I may be wrong (and, in any case, do not speak for all scientists), but I believe that the correct metaphysic is the materialist one. It works in the following way. Our profound impulses are rooted in a genetic heritage common to the entire species. They arose by evolution through natural selection over a period of tens or hundreds of thousands of years. These propensities provide survival for individuals and for the social groups on which personal survival depends. They are transmuted

Edward O. Wilson (1929–) is the Frank B. Baird, Jr. Professor of Science and Mellon Professor of the Sciences at Harvard University and the leading articulator of sociobiology. Among his publications are *The Insect Societies, On Human Nature,* and *Genes, Mind, and Culture.*

From *Free Inquiry,* spring 1991, pp. 20-23, 56.

through rational processes and the formation of culture into specific moral codes that are integrated into religion and the sacralized memories of revolutions, conquests, and other historical events by which cultures secured their survival. Although variations in the final codes are inevitable, different societies share a great deal in their perception of right and wrong. By making the search for these similarities part of the scientific enterprise, and by taking religious behavior very seriously as a key part of genetically evolved human nature, a tighter consensus on ethical behavior might be reached.

Let me interpose, at this point, a very brief account of evolution by natural selection. Genetic variation among individuals in a population of the same species, say a population of human beings, arises by mutations, which are random changes in the chemical composition and relative positions of genes. Of the thousands of mutations that typically occur throughout a population in each generation, all but a minute fraction are either neutral in effect or deleterious to some degree. They include, for example, the altered genes that cause hemophilia and Tay-Sachs disease and the abnormally duplicated chomosomes responsible for Down's syndrome. When a new mutant (or novel combination of rare preexisting genes) happens to be superior to the ordinary "normal" genes, it tends to spread through the population over a period of many generations and, hence, become by definition the new genetic norm. If human beings were to move into a new environment that somehow gave hemophiliacs a survival and reproductive advantage over non-hemophiliacs, then, in time, hemophilia would predominate in the population and be regarded as the norm.

Two features of evolution by natural selection conspire to give it extraordinary creative potential. The first is the driving power of mutations. All populations are subject to a continuous rain of new genetic types that test the old. The second feature is the ability of natural selection to create immensely complicated new structures and physiological processes, including new patterns of behavior, with no blueprint and no force behind them other than the selection process itself. This is a key point missed by creationists and other critics of evolutionary theory, who often argue

that the probability of assembling an eye or a hand (or life itself) by genetic mutations is infinitesimally small — in effect, impossible. But, the following thought experiment shows that the opposite is true. Suppose that a new trait emerges if two new gene forms (mutations), which I will call A and B, occur simultaneously. The chance of A occurring is one in a million, the chance of B occurring is also one in a million. Then, chance of both A and B occurring simultaneously as mutants is one in a trillion, a near impossibility — as the critics intuited. However, natural selection subverts this process. If A has even a slight advantage by itself alone, it will become the dominant gene at its position. Now, the chance of AB appearing is one in a million. In even moderately sized species of plants and animals (which often contain more than a million individuals), the change-over to AB is a virtual certainty.

This very simple picture of evolution at the level of the gene has altered our conception of both the nature of life and humanity's place in nature. Before Darwin, it was customary to use the great complexity of living organisms per se as proof of the existence of God. The most famous expositor of this "argument from design" was the Reverend William Paley, who in 1802 introduced the watchmaker analogy. The existence of a watch implies the existence of a watchmaker. In other words, great effects imply great causes. Common sense would seem to dictate the truth of this deduction, but common sense, as Einstein once noted, is only our accumulated experience up to the age of eighteen. Common sense tells us that one-ton satellites cannot hang suspended two hundred miles above a point on the earth's surface, but they do.

We have arrived at the conception of the one book of creation to which I alluded earlier. Given the combination of mutation and natural selection, the biological equivalent of watches can be created without a watchmaker. But, did blind natural selection also lead to the human mind, including moral behavior and spirituality? That is the grandmother of questions in both biology and the humanities. Common sense would seem, at first, to dictate the answer to be "No." But, I and many other scientists believe that the answer may be "Yes." Furthermore, it is possible by this means to explain the very meaning of human life.

The key proposition based on evolutionary biology is the following: Everything human, including the mind and culture, has a material basis and originated during the evolution of the human genetic constitution and its interaction with the environment. To say this much is not to deny the great creative power of culture or to minimize the fact that most causes of human thought and behavior are still poorly understood. The important point is that modern biology already can account for many of the unique properties of our species. Research on that subject is accelerating quickly enough to lend plausibility to the proposition that more complex forms of social behavior, including religious belief and moral reasoning, will eventually be understood to their foundations.

A case in point, useful for its simplicity and tractability, is the avoidance of brother-sister incest. In order to avoid misunderstanding, let me define *incest* as strong sexual bonding among close biological relatives that includes intercourse of the kind generally associated with cohabitation and procreation and excludes transient forms of adolescent experimentation. Incest taboos are very nearly universal and a cultural norm. The avoidance of brother-sister incest originates in what psychologists have called "prepared learning." This means that people are innately prone to learn one alternative as opposed to another. They pick it up more readily, they enjoy it more, or both. The avoidance of sibling incest comes from the "potty rule" in mental development: Individuals reared in close domestic proximity during the first six years of life (they share the same potty) are automatically inhibited from strong sexual attraction and bonding when they reach sexual maturity. The rule works even when the children reared together are biologically unrelated and later encouraged to marry and have children, as in the Israeli kibbutzim and traditional minor marriages of prerevolutionary China. Those affected are usually quite unable to offer a rational explanation of why they have no attraction. Some unconscious process ticked over in the brain and the urge, they explain, never came.

The inhibitory rule is an example not only of prepared learning but also of "proximate causation" as it is understood by evolutionary biologists. This means that the learning channels a response of importance to the survival or reproduction of the organism. Proximate causes are put into place by the assembly of genes through the process of natural selection. The ultimate causation — in other words, the particular selection regime that enabled certain genes to predominate in the first place — is the well-documented effect of inbreeding depression. When mating occurs between brother and sister, father and daughter, or mother and son, the probability of matching debilitating genes in both homologous chromosomes of the offspring is greatly increased. The end result is a rise in abortion, physical defects, and genetic disease. Hence, genes prescribing a biological propensity to avoid incest will be favored over those that do not. Most animal and plant species display proximate devices of one kind or another, and it does indeed protect them from inbreeding depression. In some, the response is rigidly determined. In others, especially the brighter mammals, it is based on prepared learning. Interestingly enough, the human proximate form is nearly identical to that of the chimpanzee, the species to which we are most closely related genetically.

It is exquisitely human to semanticize innate tendencies. In many societies, incest avoidance is underwritten by symbolically transmitted taboos, myths, and laws. These, not the emotions and programs of prepared learning, are the values we perceive by direct, casual observation. They are easily transmitted from one person to the next, and they are the behaviors most readily studied by scholars. But, the phenomenon of greatest interest is the etiology of the moral behavior: The chain of events leading from ultimate cause in natural selection to proximate cause in prepared learning to reification and legitimation in culture. If the terminal cultural form were somehow to be stripped away by a collective loss of memory, people would still avoid sibling incest. Given enough time, they would most likely invent religious and ethical rationalizations to justify their feelings about the wrongness of incest.

Crude genetic determinism has no part in this process. The existence of the three-step etiology in mental development, genes to learning rules to culture, in no way contradicts free will. Individual choice persists, even when learning is strongly prepared by heredity. If some future society decides to encourage brother-sister incest, for whatever bizarre and unlikely reason, it now has the knowledge to do so efficiently. The possibility, however, is vanishingly remote, because the same knowledge tells us that incest avoidance is programmed as a powerful rule and protects families from genetic damage. We are likely to agree still more firmly than before that the avoidance is a part of human nature to be fostered. In short, incest avoidance is and will continue to be one of our common values.

It will immediately occur to you that incest avoidance might be no more than a special case in the evolution of social behavior. A vast difference separates this relatively simple phenomenon from economic cycles, religious rites, and presidential elections. Might such particularities fall within a wholly different domain of explanation and require a different metaethic? Perhaps, but I don't think so.

The evidence favoring the evolutionary approach to moral reasoning is as follows. By mid-1985, no fewer than 3,577 human genes had been identified, of which about six hundred had been placed on one or another of the twenty-three pairs of chromosomes. This is a respectable fraction of the entire human complement. New techniques for separation and identification make it possible to map most of the genes and specify all of the DNA sequences — perhaps, by early in the next century. Hundreds of the genes already known alter behavior in one way or another. In most cases, the effect is crude or indirect. But a few change behavior in a precise manner as for example those modulating expression, reading ability, and performance on spatial tests. Twin and adoption studies have implicated other genes — as yet unmapped and probably working in complex multiples — in schizophrenia, toward homosexuality, performance on tests measuring empathy, and a wide range of personality traits from introversion-extroversion to athleticism and proneness to alcoholism. Moreover, prepared learning and biases in perception have been discovered in virtually every category of behavior thus far studied. In their seminal book *The Biology of Religion,* Vernon Reynolds and Ralph Tanner showed that survival and genetic reproduction can be favored by the traditional practices of religion, including evangelism, marriage rites, and even celibacy and asceticism, the latter

through their positive effects on group cohesion and welfare.

But, to come quickly to the point that most troubles critics of evolutionary ethics, it does not follow that the genetic programs of cognition and prepared learning are automatically beneficial, even in a crude Darwinian sense. Behaviors such as xenophobia and territorial expansion may have been very adaptive in the earlier, formative stages of human evolutionary history, but they are destructive now, even for those who practice them. Although the cultural *ought* is more tightly linked to the genetic *is* than philosophers have traditionally conceded, the two do not automatically translate one into the other. A workable moral code can be obtained not just by understanding the foundations of human nature but by the wise choice of those constraints needed to keep us alive and free in a rapidly changing cultural environment that renders some of our propensities maladaptive.

Let me illustrate this approach to moral reasoning by taking an example that has proved troublesome to the Church. In *Humanae Vitae,* Pope Paul VI used the best interpretation concerning human nature available to him to proscribe artificial birth control and to protect the family. He said, in effect, that you should not prevent conception when having sex because that is what sex is for and, as such, reflects the will of God: "To use this divine gift destroying, even if only partially, its meaning and its purpose is to contradict the nature both of man and of woman and of their most intimate relationship, and, therefore, it is to contradict also the plan of God and his will."

I believe that there is a way out of the impasse that this strict argument from natural law has created. All that we have learned of biology in recent years suggests that the perception of human nature expressed by Pope Paul VI was only half true. A second major function of sexual intercourse, one evolved over vast periods of time, is the bonding of couples in a manner that enhances the long-term care of children. Only a minute fraction of sexual acts can result in conception, but virtually all can tighten the conjugal bonds. Many circumstances can be imagined, and in fact exist, in which family planning by artificial birth control leads to an improvement of the bonding function while promoting the rearing of healthy, secure children.

If this more recent and better substantiated view of human sexuality is accepted, a revision of *Humanae Vitae* could easily be written that accomplishes the main purpose of Pope Paul VI and the modern [Roman Catholic] Church, permits artificial birth control, and, in fact, serves as a model of the utilization of scientific findings by religious thinkers.

I am now going to close with a truly radical suggestion: The choice among the foundations of moral reasoning is not likely to remain arbitrary. Metaethics can be tested empirically. One system of ethics and, hence, one kind of religion is not as good as another. Not only are some less workable, they are, in the most profound sense, less human. The corollary is that people can be educated readily only to a narrow range of ethical precepts. This leaves a choice between evolutionary ethics and transcendentalism. The idea of a genetic origin of moral codes can be further tested by a continuance of biological studies of complex human behavior, including religious thought itself. To the extent that the sensory and nervous systems appear to have evolved by natural selection or some other purely natural process, the evolutionary interpretation will be supported. To the extent that they do not appear to have evolved in this manner, or to the extent that complex human behavior cannot be linked to a physical basis in the sensory and nervous systems, the evolutionary explanation will have to be abandoned and a transcendental explanation sought.

Which position — scientific materialism or religious transcendentalism — proves correct will eventually make a very great difference in how humanity views itself and plans its future. But, for the years immediately ahead, this distinction makes little difference if the following overriding fact is realized: Human nature is, at the very least, far more a product of self-contained evolution than ordinarily conceded by philosophers and theologians. On the other hand, religious thought is far richer and more subtle than present-day science can explain — and too important to abandon. Meanwhile, the areas of common concern are vast, and the two enterprises can converge in most of the areas of practical moral reasoning at the same time that their practitioners disagree about the ultimate causes of human nature.

What, then, is the best relation between religion and science toward which we might aim? I would say an uneasy but fruitful alliance. The role of religion is to codify and put into enduring poetic form the highest moral values of a society consistent with empirical knowledge and to lead in moral reasoning. The role of science is to test remorselessly every conclusion about human nature and to search for the bedrock of ethics — by which I mean the material basis of natural law. Science faces in religion its most interesting challenge, while religion will find in science the necessary means to meet the modern age.

Epilogue

That concludes my talk to the Catholic bishops. Now an additional thought: If I'm right about the deep biological origins of religion, no amount of debunking and confrontation will significantly alter the colossi of organized religion. They won't collapse like the Soviet empire, with the leaders declaring that they have seen the light; for billions of religionists and their leaders there will be no reverse epiphany; the sacred texts won't crumble like the Berlin Wall. But the great organized religions *can* be humanized. They can evolve, through friendly truth and reason as opposed to hostile truth and reason, laid forth in a conciliatory style. Superstition will rarely or never be repudiated, it will simply be abandoned during the gradual humanization of organized religion. It's been said that the great problems of history are never solved, they are merely forgotten. And so it will be during the Darwinian sifting of ideas, hastened by open communication, total honesty, and warmth of spirit, in the best tradition of humanism. For both sides, let the chips fall where they may.

27. The Abolition of Man

C. S. LEWIS

"Man's conquest of nature" is an expression often used to describe the progress of applied science. "Man has nature whacked" said someone to a friend of mine not long ago. In their context the words had a certain tragic beauty, for the speaker was dying of tuberculosis. "No matter," he said, "I know I'm one of the casualties. Of course there are casualties on the winning as well as on the losing side. But that doesn't alter the fact that it is winning." I have chosen this story as my point of departure in order to make it clear that I do not wish to disparage all that is really beneficial in the process described as "man's conquest," much less all the real devotion and self-sacrifice that has gone to make it possible. But having done so I must proceed to analyse this conception a little more closely. In what sense is man the possessor of increasing power over nature?

Let us consider three typical examples: the aeroplane, the wireless, and the contraceptive. In a civilized community, in peace-time, anyone who can pay for them may use these things. But it cannot strictly be said that when he does so he is exercising his own proper or individual power over nature. If I pay you to carry me, I am not therefore myself a strong man. Any or all of the three things I have mentioned can be withheld from some men by other men — by those who

sell, or those who allow the sale, or those who own the sources of production, or those who make the goods. What we call man's power is in reality, a power possessed by some men which they may, or may not, allow other men to profit by. Again, as regards the powers manifested in the aeroplane or the wireless, man is as much the patient or subject as the possessor, since he is the target both for bombs and for propaganda. And as regards contraceptives, there is a paradoxical, negative sense in which all possible future generations are the patients or subjects of a power wielded by those already alive. By contraception simply, they are denied existence; by contraception used as a means of selective breeding, they are, without their concurring voice, made to be what one generation, for its own reasons, may choose to prefer. From this point of view, what we call man's power over nature turns out to be a power exercised by some men over other men with nature as its instrument.

It is, of course, a commonplace to complain that men have hitherto used badly, and against their fellows, the powers that science has given them. But that is not the point I am trying to make. I am not speaking of particular corruptions and abuses which an increase of moral virtue would cure: I am considering what the thing called "man's power over nature" must always and essentially be. No doubt, the picture could be modified by public ownership of raw materials and factories and public control of scientific research. But unless we have a world state this will still mean the power of one nation over others. And even within the world state or the nation it will mean (in principle) the power of majorities over minorities, and (in the concrete) of a government over the people. And all long-term exercises of power, especially in breeding, must mean the power of earlier generations over later ones.

The latter point is not always sufficiently emphasized, because those who write on social matters have not yet learned to imitate the physicists by always including time among the dimensions. In order to understand fully what man's power over nature, and therefore the power of some men over other men, really means, we must picture the race extended in time from the date of its emergence to that of its extinction. Each generation exercises power over its successors; and each in so far as it modifies the environment bequeathed to

C. S. Lewis (1898–1963), a professor of medieval and Renaissance literature at Oxford and later Cambridge University, is best known for his fiction and his popular works in Christian apologetics. His works include *The Chronicles of Narnia, The Screwtape Letters, Mere Christianity,* and *Surprised by Joy.*

From C. S. Lewis, *The Abolition of Man* (New York: Macmillan, 1978).

it and, rebels against tradition, resists and limits the power of its predecessors. This modifies the picture which is sometimes painted of a progressive emancipation from tradition and a progressive control of natural processes resulting in a continual increase of human power. In reality, of course, if any one age really attains, by eugenics and scientific education, the power to make its descendants what it pleases, all men who live after it are the patients of that power. They are weaker, not stronger: for though we may have put wonderful machines in their hands we have pre-ordained how they are to use them. And if, as is almost certain, the age which had thus attained maximum power over posterity were also the age most emancipated from tradition, it would be engaged in reducing the power of its predecessors almost as drastically as that of its successors. And we must also remember that, quite apart from this, the later a generation comes — the nearer it lives to that date at which the species becomes extinct — the less power it will have in the forward direction, because its subjects will be so few. There is therefore no question of a power vested in the race as a whole steadily growing as long as the race survives. The last men, far from being the heirs of power, will be of all men most subject to the dead hand of the great planners and conditioners and will themselves exercise least power upon the future. The real picture is that of one dominant age — let us suppose the hundredth century A.D. — which resists all previous ages most successfully and dominates all subsequent ages most irresistibly, and thus is the real master of the human species. But even within this master generation (itself an infinitesimal minority of the species) the power will be exercised by a minority smaller still. man's conquest of nature, if the dreams of some scientific planners are realized, means the rule of a few hundreds of men over billions upon billions of men. There neither is nor can be any simple increase of power in man's side. Each new power won *by* man is a power *over* man as well. Each advance leaves him weaker as well as stronger. In every victory, besides being the general who triumphs, he is also the prisoner who follows the triumphal car.

I am not yet considering whether the total result of such ambivalent victories is a good thing or a bad. I am only making clear what man's con-

quest of nature really means and especially that final stage in the conquest, which, perhaps, is not far off. The final stage is come when man by eugenics, by prenatal conditioning, and by an education and propaganda based on a perfect applied psychology, has obtained full control over himself. *Human* nature will be the last part of nature to surrender to man. The battle will then be won. We shall have 'taken the thread of life out of the hand of Clotho' and be henceforth free to make our species whatever we wish it to be. The battle will indeed be won. But who, precisely, will have won it?

For the power of man to make himself what he pleases means, as we have seen, the power of some men to make other men what *they* please. In all ages, no doubt, nurture and instruction have, in some sense, attempted to exercise this power. But the situation to which we must look forward will be novel in two respects. In the first place, the power will be enormously increased. Hitherto the plans of educationalists have achieved very little of what they attempted and indeed, when we read them — how Plato would have every infant 'a bastard nursed in a bureau,' and Elyot would have the boy see no men before the age of seven and, after that, no women,[1] and how Locke wants children to have leaky shoes and no turn for poetry[2] — we may well thank the beneficent obstinacy of real mothers, real nurses, and (above all) real children for preserving the human race in such sanity as it still possesses. But the man-molders of the new age will be armed with the powers of an omnicompetent state and an irresistible scientific technique: we shall get at last a race of conditioners who really can cut out all posterity in what

1. *The Boke Named the Governour*, I.iv: "Al men except physitions only shulde be excluded and kepte out of the norisery." I.vi: "After that a childe is come to seuen yeres of age . . . the most sure counsaile is to withdrawe him from all company of women."

2. *Some Thoughts concerning Education*, §7: "I will also advise his *Feet to be wash'd* every Day in cold Water, and to have his Shoes so thin that they might leak and *let in Water*, whenever he comes near it." §174: "If he have a poetick vein, 'tis to me the strangest thing in the World that the Father should desire or suffer it to be cherished or improved. Methinks the Parents should labour to have it stifled and suppressed as much as may be." Yet Locke is one of our most sensible writers on education.

shape they please. The second difference is even more important. In the older systems both the kind of man the teachers wished to produce and their motives for producing him were prescribed by the *Tao* — a norm to which the teachers themselves were subject and from which they claimed no liberty to depart. They did not cut men to some pattern they had chosen. They handed on what they had received: they initiated the young neophyte into the mystery of humanity which over-arched him and them alike. It was but old birds teaching young birds to fly. This will be changed. Values are now mere natural phenomena. Judgements of value are to be produced in the pupil as part of the conditioning. Whatever *Tao* there is will be the product, not the motive, of education. The conditioners have been emancipated from all that. It is one more part of nature which they have conquered. The ultimate springs of human action are no longer, for them, something given. They have surrendered — like electricity: it is the function of the conditioners to control, not to obey them. They know how to *produce* conscience and decide what kind of conscience they will produce. They themselves are outside, above. For we are assuming the last stage of man's struggle with nature. The final victory has been won. Human nature has been conquered — and, of course, has conquered, in whatever sense those words may now bear.

The conditioners, then, are to choose what kind of artificial *Tao* they will, for their own good reasons, produce in the human race. They are the motivators, the creators of motives. But how are they going to be motivated themselves? For a time, perhaps, by survivals, within their own minds, of the old "natural" *Tao*. Thus at first they may look upon themselves as servants and guardians of humanity and conceive that they have a "duty" to do it "good." But it is only by confusion that they can remain in this state. They recognize the concept of duty as the result of certain processes which they can now control. Their victory has consisted precisely in emerging from the state in which they were acted upon by those processes to the state in which they use them as tools. One of the things they now have to decide is whether they will, or will not, so condition the rest of us that we can go on having the old idea of duty and the old reactions to it. How can duty help them to

decide that? Duty itself is up for trial: it cannot also be the judge. And "good" fares no better. They know quite well how to produce a dozen different conceptions of good in us. The question is which, if any, they should produce. No conception of good can help them to decide. It is absurd to fix on one of the things they are comparing and make it the standard of comparison.

To some it will appear that I am inventing a factitious difficulty for my conditioners. Other, more simple-minded, critics may ask "Why should you suppose they will be such bad men?" But I am not supposing them to be bad men. They are, rather, not men (in the old sense) at all. They are, if you like, men who have sacrificed their own share in traditional humanity in order to devote themselves to the task of deciding what "humanity" shall henceforth mean. "Good" and "bad," applied to them, are words without content: for it is from them that the content of these words is henceforward to be derived. Nor is their difficulty factitious. We might suppose that it was possible to say, "After all, most of us want more or less the same things — food and drink and sexual intercourse, amusement, art, science, and the longest possible life for individuals and for the species. Let them simply say, 'This is what we happen to like,' and go on to condition men in the way most likely to produce it. Where's the trouble?" But this will not answer. In the first place, it is false that we all really like the same things. But even if we did, what motive is to impel the conditioners to scorn delights and live laborious days in order that we, and posterity, may have what we like? Their duty? But that is only the *Tao*, which they may decide to impose on us, but which cannot be valid for them. If they accept it, then they are no longer the makers of conscience but still its subjects, and their final conquest over nature has not really happened. The preservation of the species? But why should the species be preserved? One of the questions before them is whether this feeling for posterity (they know well how it is produced) shall be continued or not. However far they go back, or down, they can find no ground to stand on. Every motive they try to act on becomes at once a *petitio*. It is not that they are bad men. They are not men at all. Stepping outside the *Tao*, they have stepped into the void. Nor are their subjects necessarily unhappy men. They are not men at all: they are artefacts. Man's final conquest has proved to be the abolition of man.

Yet the conditioners will act. When I said just now that all motives fail them, I should have said all motives except one. All motives that claim any validity other than that of their felt emotional weight at a given moment have failed them. Everything except the *sic volo, sic jubeo* has been explained away. But what never claimed objectivity cannot be destroyed by subjectivism. The impulse to scratch when I itch or to pull to pieces when I am inquisitive is immune from the solvent which is fatal to my justice, or honour, or care for posterity. When all that says, "It is good" has been debunked, what says, "I want" remains. It cannot be exploded or "seen through" because it never had any pretensions. The conditioners, therefore, must come to be motivated simply by their own pleasure. I am not here speaking of the corrupting influence of power nor expressing the fear that under it our conditioners will degenerate. The very words *corrupt* and *degenerate* imply a doctrine of value and are therefore meaningless in this context. My point is that those who stand outside all judgements of value cannot have any ground for preferring one of their own impulses to another except the emotional strength of that impulse. We may legitimately hope that among the impulses which arise in minds thus emptied of all "rational" or "spiritual" motives, some will be benevolent. I am very doubtful myself whether the benevolent impulses, stripped of that preference and encouragement which the *Tao* teaches us to give them and left to their merely natural strength and frequency as psychological events, will have much influence. I am very doubtful whether history shows us one example of a man who, having stepped outside traditional morality and attained power, has used that power benevolently. I am inclined to think that the conditioners will hate the conditioned. Though regarding as an illusion the artificial conscience which they produce in us their subjects, they will yet perceive that it creates in us an illusion of meaning for our lives which compares favourably with the futility of their own: and they will envy us as eunuchs envy men. But I do not insist on this, for it is mere conjecture. What is not conjecture is that our hope even of a "conditioned" happiness rests on what is ordinarily called "chance" — the chance that benevolent impulses may on the whole predominate in our conditioners. For without the judgement "Benevolence is good" — that is, without re-entering the *Tao* — they can have no ground for promoting or stabilizing their benevolent impulses rather than any others. By the logic of their position they must just take their impulses as they come, from chance. And chance here means nature. It is from heredity, digestion, the weather, and the association of ideas, that the motives of the conditioners will spring. Their extreme rationalism, by "seeing through" all "rational" motives, leaves them creatures of wholly irrational behaviour. If you will not obey the *Tao*, or else commit suicide, obedience to impulse (and therefore, in the long run, to mere "nature") is the only course left open.

At the moment, then, of man's victory over nature, we find the whole human race subjected to some individual men, and those individuals subjected to that in themselves which is purely "natural" — to their irrational impulses. Nature, untrammelled by values, rules the conditioners and, through them, all humanity. Man's conquest of nature turns out, in the moment of its consummation, to be nature's conquest of man. Every victory we seemed to win has led us, step by step, to this conclusion. All nature's apparent reverses have been but tactical withdrawals. We thought we were beating her back when she was luring us on. What looked to us like hands held up in surrender was really the opening of arms to enfold us for ever. If the fully planned and conditioned world (with its *Tao* a mere product of the planning) comes into existence, nature will be troubled no more by the restive species that rose in revolt against her so many millions of years ago, will be vexed no longer by its chatter of truth and mercy and beauty and happiness. *Ferum victorem cepit*: and if the eugenics are efficient enough there will be no second revolt, but all snug beneath the conditioners, and the conditioners beneath her, till the moon falls or the sun grows cold.

My point may be clearer to some if it is put in a different form. Nature is a word of varying meanings, which can best be understood if we consider its various opposites. The natural is the opposite of the artificial, the civil, the human, the spiritual, and the supernatural. The artificial does not now concern us. If we take the rest of the list of opposites, however, I think we can get a rough idea of what men have meant by nature and what it is they oppose to her. Nature seems to be the spatial and temporal, as distinct from what is less fully so or not so at all. She seems to be the world of quantity, as against the world of quality: of objects as against consciousness: of the bound, as against the wholly or partially autonomous: of that which knows no values as against that which both has and perceives value: of efficient causes (or, in some modern systems, of no causality at all) as against final causes. Now I take it that when we understand a thing analytically and then dominate and use it for our own convenience we reduce it to the level of "nature" in the sense that we suspend our judgments of value about it, ignore its final cause (if any), and treat it in terms of quantity. This repression of elements in what would otherwise be our total reaction to it is sometimes very noticeable and even painful: something has to be overcome before we can cut up a dead man or a live animal in a dissecting room. These objects *resist* the movement of the mind whereby we thrust them into the world of mere nature. But in other instances too, a similar price is exacted for our analytical knowledge and manipulative power, even if we have ceased to count it. We do not look at trees either as Dryads or as beautiful objects while we cut them into beams: the first man who did so may have felt the price keenly, and the bleeding trees in Virgil and Spenser may be far-off echoes of that primeval sense of impiety. The stars lost their divinity as astronomy developed, and the dying god has no place in chemical agriculture. To many, no doubt, this process is simply the gradual discovery that the real world is different from what we expected, and the old opposition to Galileo or to "body-snatchers" is simply obscurantism. But that is not the whole story. It is not the greatest of modern scientists who feel most sure that the object, stripped of its qualitative properties and reduced to mere quantity, is wholly real. Little scientists, and little unscientific followers of science, may think so. The great minds know very well that the object, so treated, is an artificial abstraction, that something of its reality has been lost.

From this point of view the conquest of nature appears in a new light. We reduce things to mere nature *in order that* we may "conquer" them. We are always conquering nature, because "nature" is the name for what we have, to some extent, conquered. The price of conquest is to treat a thing as mere nature. Every conquest over nature increases her domain. The stars do not become nature till we can weigh and measure them: the soul does not become nature till we can psychoanalyze her. The wresting of powers *from* nature is also the surrendering of things *to* nature. As long as this process stops short of the final stage we may well hold that the gain outweighs the loss. But as soon as we take the final step of reducing our own species to the level of mere nature, the whole process is stultified, for this time the being who stood to gain and the being who has been sacrificed are one and the same. This is one of the many instances where to carry a principle to what seems its logical conclusion produces absurdity. It is like the famous Irishman who found that a certain kind of stove reduced his fuel bill by half and thence concluded that two stoves of the same kind would enable him to warm his house with no fuel at all. It is the magician's bargain: give up our soul, get power in return. But once our souls, that is, our selves, have been given up, the power thus conferred will not belong to us. We shall in fact be the slaves and puppets of that to which we have given our souls. It is in man's power to treat himself as a mere "natural object" and his own judgements of value as raw material for scientific manipulation to alter at will. The objection to his doing so does not lie in the fact that his point of view (like one's first day in a dissecting room) is painful and shocking till we grow used to it. The pain and the shock are at most a warning and a symptom. The real objection is that if man chooses to treat himself as raw material, raw material he will be: not raw material to be manipulated, as he fondly imagined, by himself, but by mere appetite, that is, mere nature, in the person of his dehumanized conditioners.

We have been trying, like Lear, to have it both ways: to lay down our human prerogative and yet at the same time to retain it. It is impossible. Either we are rational spirit obliged for ever to obey the absolute values of the *Tao*, or else we are mere nature to be kneaded and cut into new shapes for the pleasures of masters who must, by hypothesis, have no motive but their own "natural" impulses. Only the *Tao* provides a common human law of action which can overarch rulers and ruled alike. A dogmatic belief in objective value is necessary to the very idea of a rule which is not tyranny or an obedience which is not slavery.

I am not here thinking solely, perhaps not even chiefly, of those who are our public enemies at the moment. The process which, if not checked, will abolish man, goes on apace among Communists and Democrats no less than among Fascists. The methods may (at first) differ in brutality. But many a mild-eyed scientist in pince-nez, many a popular dramatist, many an amateur philosopher in our midst, means in the long run just the same as the Nazi rulers of Germany. Traditional values are to be "debunked" and mankind to be cut out into some fresh shape at the will (which must, by hypothesis, be an arbitrary will) of some few lucky people in one lucky generation which has learned how to do it. The belief that we can invent "ideologies" at pleasure, and the consequent treatment of mankind as mere ὑλη, specimens, preparations, begins to affect our very language. Once we killed bad men: now we liquidate unsocial elements. Virtue has become *integration* and diligence *dynamism,* and boys likely to be worthy of a commission are "potential officer material." Most wonderful of all, the virtues of thrift and temperance, and even of ordinary intelligence, are *sales-resistance.*

The true significance of what is going on has been concealed by the use of the abstraction man. Not that the word *man* is necessarily a pure abstraction. In the *Tao* itself, as long as we remain within it, we find the concrete reality in which to participate is to be truly human: the real common will and common reason of humanity, alive, and growing like a tree, and branching out, as the situation varies, into ever new beauties and dignities of application. While we speak from within the *Tao* we can speak of man having power over himself in a sense truly analogous to an individual's self-control. But the moment we step outside and regard the *Tao* as a mere subjective product, this possibility has disappeared. What is now common to all men is a mere abstract universal, an H.C.F., and man's conquest of himself means simply the rule of the conditioners over the conditioned human material, the world of post-humanity which, some knowingly and some unknowingly, nearly all men in all nations are at present laboring to produce.

Nothing I can say will prevent some people from describing this lecture as an attack on science. I deny the charge, of course: and real nat-ural philosophers (there are some now alive) will perceive that in defending value I defend *inter alia* the value of knowledge, which must die like every other when its roots in the *Tao* are cut. But I can go further than that. I even suggest that from Science herself the cure might come. I have described as a "magician's bargain" that process whereby man surrenders object after object, and finally himself, to nature in return for power. And I meant what I said. The fact that the scientist has succeeded where the magician failed has put such a wide contrast between them in popular thought that the real story of the birth of science is misunderstood. You will even find people who write about the sixteenth century as if magic were a medieval survival and science the new thing that came to sweep it away. Those who have studied the period know better. There was very little magic in the Middle Ages: the sixteenth and seventeenth centuries are the high noon of magic. The serious magical endeavour and the serious scientific endeavour are twins: one was sickly and died, the other strong and throve. But they were twins. They were born of the same impulse. I allow that some (certainly not all) of the early scientists were actuated by a pure love of knowledge. But if we consider the temper of that age as a whole we can discern the impulse of which I speak. There is something which unites magic and applied science while separating both from the "wisdom" of earlier ages. For the wise men of old the cardinal problem had been how to conform the soul to reality, and the solution had been knowledge, self-discipline, and virtue. For magic and applied science alike the problem is how to subdue reality to the wishes of men: the solution is a technique; and both, in the practice of this technique, are ready to do things hitherto regarded as disgusting and impious — such as digging up and mutilating the dead. If we compare the chief trumpeter of the new era (Bacon) with Marlowe's Faustus, the similarity is striking. You will read in some critics that Faustus has a thirst for knowledge. In reality, he hardly mentions it. It is not truth he wants from his devils, but gold and guns and girls. "All things that move between quiet poles shall be at his command" and "a sound magician is a mighty god."[3]

3. *Dr. Faustus,* 77-90.

In the same spirit Bacon condemns those who value knowledge as an end in itself: this, for him, is to use as a mistress for pleasure what ought to be a spouse for fruit.[4] The true object is to extend man's power to the performance of all things possible. He rejects magic because it does not work,[5] but his goal is that of the magician. In Paracelsus the characters of magician and scientist are combined. No doubt those who really founded modern science were usually those whose love of truth exceeded their love of power; in every mixed movement the efficacy comes from the good elements, not from the bad. But the presence of the bad elements is not irrelevant to the direction the efficacy takes. It might be going too far to say that the modern scientific movement was tainted from its birth: but I think it would be true to say that it was born in an unhealthy neighbourhood and at an inauspicious hour. Its triumphs may have been too rapid and purchased at too high a price: reconsideration, and something like repentance, may be required.

Is it, then, possible to imagine a new natural philosophy, continually conscious that the "natural object" produced by analysis and abstraction is not reality but only a view, and always correcting the abstraction? I hardly know what I am asking for. I hear rumours that Goethe's approach to nature deserves fuller consideration — that even Dr. Steiner may have seen something that orthodox researchers have missed. The regenerate science which I have in mind would not do even to minerals and vegetables what modern science threatens to do to man himself. When it explained it would not explain away. When it spoke of the parts it would remember the whole. While studying the *It* it would not lose what Martin Buber calls the *Thou*-situation. The analogy between the *Tao* of Man and the instincts of an animal species would mean for it new light cast on the unknown thing, instinct, by the inly known reality of conscience and not a reduction of conscience to the category of instinct. Its followers would not be free with the words *only* and *merely*. In a word, it would conquer nature without being at the same time

conquered by her and buy knowledge at a lower cost than that of life.

Perhaps I am asking impossibilities. Perhaps, in the nature of things, analytical understanding must always be a basilisk which kills what it sees and only sees by killing. But if the scientists themselves cannot arrest this process before it reaches the common reason and kills that too, then someone else must arrest it. What I most fear is the reply that I am "only one more" obscurantist, that this barrier, like all previous barriers set up against the advance of science, can be safely passed. Such a reply springs from the fatal serialism of the modern imagination — the image of infinite unilinear progression which so haunts our minds. Because we have to use numbers so much we tend to think of every process as if it must be like the numeral series, where every step, to all eternity, is the same kind of step as the one before. I implore you to remember the Irishman and his two stoves. There are progressions in which the last step is *sui generis* — incommensurable with the others — and in which to go the whole way is to undo all the labor of your previous journey. To reduce the *Tao* to a mere natural product is a step of that kind. Up to that point, the kind of explanation which explains things away may give us something, though at a heavy cost. But you cannot go on "explaining away" for ever: you will find that you have explained explanation itself away. You cannot go on "seeing through" things for ever. The whole point of seeing through something is to see something through it. It is good that the window should be transparent, because the street or garden beyond it is opaque. How if you saw through the garden too? It is no use trying to "see through" first principles. If you see through everything, then everything is transparent. But a wholly transparent world is an invisible world. To "see through" all things is the same as not to see.

---

4. *Advancement of Learning*, Bk. I (p. 60 in Ellis and Spedding, 1905; p. 35 in Everyman Edn.).

5. *Filum Labyrinthi*, i.

28. The Relationship of Empirical Science to Moral Thought

JAMES M. GUSTAFSON

The extensive development of empirical sciences in the United States and abroad has had several consequences for moral thought, particularly for practical moral theology and ethics. The range of empirical sciences that impinge upon moral thought is almost as extensive as the range of actual problems that are discussed. Moral theologians have become intrigued with the rapid development of the social and/or behavioral sciences. It is no longer possible to discuss economic ethics, for example, at the level of generalization used in the great social encyclicals. Now one must have technical knowledge of the gross national product, the economics of development, the function of monetary and fiscal policies, etc. Nor is it possible to discuss political ethics without awareness of the structure and the functions of various political systems, the ways in which they operate in relation to law and constitutions, and even the behavior of voters. Sociology provides a basis for the critiques of moral thought itself, as one finds in Karl Mannheim's essays on sociology of knowledge, and particularly, for example, in his essays, "Conservative

Thought."[1] Sociology also provides concepts and data about social behavior, institutions, and class structures. Psychology is used to understand the nature of moral agents, and also increasingly to assist in the definition of moral norms of fulfillment, happiness, and well-being.

The harder data of the biological and physical sciences impinge on other areas of concern to moral theologians. The science of fetology bears in many ways upon the ethical arguments about abortion. The technology developing from the science of genetics has attracted the attentions not only of moral theologians such as Paul Ramsey, but also of the dogmatic theologian Karl Rahner.[2]

Further suggestions about the general impingements of the empirical sciences on moral thought are not necessary. In this chapter I shall address several foci of the relationship. The assigned task is a large one, and thus the essay is more an exercise in clarification and exploration than a thorough study. The relevant literature is relatively sparse.[3] Philosophical issues whose development require more intensive development than is possible in this chapter will be alluded to.

The order of discussion in this essay is as follows: (A) The areas of moral thought in which one finds significant use of empirical sciences. These are (1) the understanding of the nature of persons as moral agents, (2) the understanding of the circumstances in which decisions and actions occur, (3) the prediction of potential consequences of various courses of action, and (4) the development of moral norms. (B) Major problems involved in the use of empirical sciences in moral thought.

James M. Gustafson (1925–) taught at Yale Divinity School and the University of Chicago before becoming the Henry R. Luce Professor of Humanities and Comparative Studies at Emory University. His work includes *Can Ethics be Christian?*, *Christ and the Moral Life*, *Protestant and Roman Catholic Ethics*, and *Ethics from a Theocentric Perspective*.

From *Proceedings of the Catholic Theological Society of America* 26 (1971): pp. 122-137.

1. Karl Mannheim, "Conservative Thought," *Essays in Sociology and Social Psychology* (London: Routledge & Kegan Paul, 1953), pp. 74-164.

2. Paul Ramsey, *Fabricated Man* (New Haven: Yale University Press, 1970); Karl Rahner, "Experiment Mensch" *Schriften zur Theologie*, VIII (Einsiedeln: Benziger Verlag, 1967), pp. 260-85; "Zum Problem der Genetischen Manipulation," Ibid., pp. 286-321. The first Rahner article is digested in "Experiment: Man," *Theology Digest*, Sesquicentennial Issue (1968), pp. 57-69.

3. See Gibson Winter, *Elements for a Social Ethic* (New York: Macmillan, 1966), pp. 3-82; Max Stackhouse, "Technical Data and Ethical Norms," *Journal for the Scientific Study of Religion*, 5, pp. 191-203; and Wilhelm Koyff, "Empirical Social Study and Ethics," *Concilium*, 5 (no. 4), pp. 5-13.

These all affect the selection of empirical materials: (1) the judgment about what data and concepts are relevant to the moral issue involved; (2) this first raises the issues of the principles of interpretation in the empirical studies, of what are involved in the selection and significance of the data used; and (3) it secondly raises the issue of the normative biases built into the empirical studies.

Use of Empirical Sciences in Moral Thought

1. Psychological, sociological, and anthropological studies have had a very significant impact in recent decades on the *understanding of persons*. The question to which these sciences have offered tentative answers is this: How can the behavior of persons be explained? Included in human behavior is moral action. Explanations are offered not only to account for particular acts, but also for the kind of person an individual has become, which in turn conditions, if not determines what one does. The central concern that erupts in these accounts is the degree of answerability that agents have for their conduct. It is not as if the question of free will and determinism is raised for the first time with the development of social and behavioral sciences in recent decades. The question has been answered by philosophers and theologians in different ways throughout the history of Western thought. But the discussion of answers has shifted from the realm of metaphysics to the realm of descriptive and analytical accounts of human persons and their behavior. Indeed, one might begin such an account at the presocial level of the genotypes of individuals, which have some determinative significance on their capacities to become and to act.

Another concern that emerges from these accounts is the extent to which individual differences between persons have to be taken into account in moral judgments. One can ask whether on the basis of empirical accounts of individual differences, one does not have to make moral judgments about actions with reference to the specific persons who have acted, rather than to a class of actions. For example, would we morally excuse one person for committing adultery, while morally blaming another?

In general, it is clear that the persuasive power

of scientific accounts of the development of persons and explanations of their actions have deeply affected moral thought with regard to these two concerns. There has been a major trend toward the willingness to excuse persons from moral accountability for their actions in the light of knowledge we have about their relationships with their parents, about the moral values of the communities in which they grew up, and the social circumstances in which they have been nurtured. In the arena of legal accountability one sees that psychiatric data are used to warrant an excusing condition. Data and concepts from psychiatry (or other fields) are used to make a case for the limitations of answerability. Men are not as prone to believe that an agent has "free will" in the strong sense that they once believed, and thus in some circles there is an erosion of the notion of moral responsibility itself. Although the concept of causality employed in the social scientific account of behavior has been subject to rigorous philosophical criticism in recent decades, partially in the interest of retaining a meaningful concept of moral responsibility, "blame" is often laid for moral faults not so much on the agent, as on the conditions over which he presumably has no control.

The accounts given of the formation of persons and of their actions also, quite consistently, have led to a trend to make judgments of moral actions increasingly specific with reference to the individuals who engaged in them. While this trend is ambiguous, it is nonetheless present: there are moralists who would suggest, for example, that adultery is morally indifferent, if not approvable, for two individuals who have particular needs under particular circumstances, while it is morally wrong for other individuals with other needs in other circumstances.

Thus far we have assumed that there is a vague and general agreement among the empirical sciences about the determination of human persons and behavior. It would appear at this point that one could speak of "the contemporary scientific understanding of man."[4] That such a generaliza-

---

4. John Giles Milhaven, *Toward a New Catholic Morality* (Garden City, N.Y.: Doubleday, 1970), p. 118. In general I am writing a critical but sympathetic response to Milhaven's chapter "The Behavioral Sciences," and to essays of Robert Springer, S.J.

tion is not warranted is apparent to the critical reader of psychology, sociology, and other fields. Thus, our later discussion of critical problems in the employment of empirical sciences can be anticipated here by indicating that any moral theologian chooses from a number of renderings of the explanation of persons and behavior. Let us hypothetically suggest that he has read Freud, B. F. Skinner, and Rollo May, and has thought about the implications of the writings of each of these three persons for understanding the moral agent. The critical questions are which one should he choose, and why choose the one he does. It is likely that the moralist will choose the one whose interpretation is most in accord with his philosophical, moral, or theological predilections. If this is the case, one can ask whether he can claim "scientific" authority for the view of the agent that he adopts. If he chooses to claim such authority, he obviously has to make his case on scientific grounds, which implies that he will have to adjudicate between the scientific claims made by each of his three authors. The moral theologian could, however, make a weaker claim for one or more of the authors, namely, that the authors are sources of "insight" into the nature of persons and into human behavior. If such a claim is made, he bears his own authority for the way in which he combines or uses the insights he gleans from one or more of the authors. He might take recourse to the justification that his own combination of insights "makes sense" to him, and hopefully to others — a justification which has its own implicit empirical references, but which does not rely upon the sorts of scientific evidences offered by Freud, Skinner, and May.

The choice actually is more difficult than we have thus far suggested, for it involves not only some selection of empirical data, but also the selection of certain concepts and principles of explanation. In each of the authors the data, concepts, and principles of explanation have been systematized to the degree that there is coherence in the overall position. Thus, as we shall note more extensively, the concepts and principles of explanation are already involved in the isolation of certain data about persons and behavior as being significant and the ruling out of other data.

Enough has been said to rule out the simple use of a simple notion, namely "the contemporary scientific understanding of man" in developing a view of the moral agent. Here we only note the complexity of the issues involved in the use of empirical sciences in this area of moral thought.

2. The social and other sciences are often used to get a more precise and complete *understanding of the circumstances* in which a moral problem occurs, and thus in defining both the causes and options for action. This has been clear for a long time in the arena of medical ethics. For example, Catholic moralists have long been schooled in the biological processes of conception and birth, and have argued their moral cases using the best available scientific data that pertain to the related moral issues. In areas of social morality some Protestants and Catholics have been operating in a similar way.

Let us take the interest in developing a social ethics for urban problems as a general instance in which empirical sciences would pertain. All ethicians would readily admit that a study of the history of cities would not provide sufficiently accurate and insightful information for understanding contemporary urban existence, though Lewis Mumford's *The City in History* might provide insight and perspective.[5] All would also admit that cities are much too complex for any one person to have a full range of experience of their life; each person is likely to have a partial experience of urban existence, as a participant in its productive economy, a resident of a particular neighborhood, a driver on its expressways, etc. Thus, some supplemental information, some concepts for ordering it, and some principles for interpreting its significance are necessary beyond reliance on the knowledge of history and personal experience.

Among other things, one needs to know something of the structure and dynamics of the social order, the political order, and the economic order, to name but three factors. On the face of it, to turn to the social sciences makes sense. When one does, however, he is faced with choices comparable in principle to those above between Freud, Skinner, and Rollo May. Let us confine ourselves simply to the question of how best to understand the dis-

5. Lewis Mumford. *The City in History* (New York: Harcourt, Brace and World, 1961). See also Max Weber's classic study, *The City* (Glencoe, Ill.: The Free Press, 1958).

tribution of power in the city. A few years ago, for example, the social ethician had choices to make between the model of *The Power Elite*, described by C. Wright Mills with reference to the nation as a whole, which had structural similarities to Floyd Hunter's *Community Power Structure*, a study of Atlanta, on the one hand, and on the other hand, Robert A. Dahl's widely acclaimed study of New Haven, *Who Governs?*[6] Hunter and Mills found evidence for the existence of interlocking elites who by virtue of social and familial connections, responsibilities in industrial, political, military, and other institutions, seemed to be in control of what was going on in American urban life. Dahl explicitly challenged this interpretation with evidences he gathered for the existence of much greater diversity of centers of power in a city. (The issue of locus and distribution of power is complicated even more by the shifts that are rapidly taking place; all the books I refer to were written before the emergence of black power, chicano power, and other ethnic developments in American cities.)

How would the moralist decide between the option of Hunter and Dahl? First, he might review the evidences of each author, and seek to determine what evidences were omitted. He might assess the methods of research that were used, and judge which has the greater degree of sufficiency for the study of urban power structures. If he finds one to be a superior scientific study, he might use its authority for his work precisely on those grounds. But second, he might probe behind the scientific work to inquire into the concepts, the principles of interpretation, and indeed, the basic assumptions about the political and social process that inform each of the studies. Are there reasons why Hunter is predisposed to a power elite model of analysis? Is there a view of man involved in his choice? One which, in a sense, sees men as power-seeking (in a quiet conspiratorial sort of way) in their efforts to retain control of urban institutions for their own class interests? Are there reasons why Dahl is predisposed to an analysis which finds

power more widely dispersed? Does Dahl's empirical work rest on confidence in the liberal democratic process, and does this confidence affect his analysis in crucial ways? Does it shade his awareness of power elites? Does it heighten his awareness of pluralism? If the moralist finds answers to these questions, he makes not simply a choice of the best scientific study, but a choice of a point of view that involves philosophical commitments, and that leads to certain predispositions in the area of morality. The choice of model will have a significant influence on the kinds of social ethical policies he develops and supports; if these policies inform institutions and programs, they will in turn affect actions and their consequences.

3. Max Weber, in his sophisticated studies of the methodology of the social sciences, long ago indicated that one of the functions of such research for moral and policy choices is to assist one in *predicting the consequences of certain choices.*[7] His argument is part of a larger concern, namely, one that attempts to limit the value biases in social sciences. Whatever one thinks of the total effort in this regard, one would have to admit that social and other empirical research can make the prediction of consequences more accurate. The point is this: if on moral grounds you choose course of action a under the known circumstances, then consequences l, m, and n are likely to occur; but if you choose course of action b, consequences o, p, and q are likely to occur.

The arena in which the moral choices are made is significant for the degree of accuracy in prediction. In the situation of a dying patient, predictions can have a high degree of accuracy. If a physician decides that patient x no longer has any right to use artificial life support systems, there is no question that by "pulling the plug" one creates the circumstances in which he will die. In the arena of social problems, however, the accuracy of predictions is not as precise. (I once read an article

6. C. Wright Mills, *The Power Elite* (New York: Oxford University Press, 1956); Floyd Hunter, *Community Power Structure* (Chapel Hill, N.C.: University of North Carolina Press, 1953); Robert A. Dahl, *Who Governs?* (New Haven: Yale University Press, 1961).

7. Max Weber, *The Methodology of the Social Sciences* (Glencoe, Ill.: The Free Press, 1949). The essays in this volume were first published between 1903 and 1917 during the "method controversies" going on in German scholarship and the natural and "human" sciences. They, together with other literature of that struggle, are still worth serious study today.

which indicated that the Ford Motor Company developed the Edsel on the basis of potential markets that were indicated by social research. As I recall, the research suggested that persons who moved from lower- to higher-priced cars tended to stay in the same automobile "family." Thus, it was predicted that by building a car in the Ford family that was more elaborate than the Ford, the company could increase its share of the total auto market. The illustration is trivial, but it makes the point.)

The moralist can make certain maximalist or minimalist claims for the authority of empirical research in the prediction of consequences for moral action. Hypothetically, he might establish a set of ends to be "good," and on the basis of social research define the policies and actions that would guarantee the achievement of those ends. (Max Millikan, in his essay on the uses of research in policy, in Daniel Lerner's *The Human Meaning of the Social Sciences* indicates that researchers are often frustrated because persons who formulate policy and engage in the exercise of power rarely simply follow recommendations of the research. Millikan argues that policy-makers have other matters to bring to bear than those in the purview of the researcher, and that the contribution of research is "to deepen, broaden, and extend the policy-maker's capacity for judgment — not to provide him with answers.")[8] The moralist, however, is not likely to have so mechanistic a view of social developments that research would permit him to function as a social technocrat or engineer who can control events to guarantee their outcome.

A more modest claim is likely. In the light of empirical research the moralist is likely to gain insight into the potential consequences of various courses of morally determined action. Insofar as the consequences of action have moral weight, that is, insofar as they can be judged to be morally good or better, evil or less evil, calculation of consequences is of major importance. In this regard social research can fulfill an important role in more precise calculation. This is possible without

accepting a view of absolute determinism; what one accepts is at least the degree of determinism that is assumed in all views of human action, namely, that to initiate an act is to intend certain consequences and to exercise such powers as one has to make those consequences most likely to occur.

4. The more problematic use of the empirical sciences is in the *development of moral norms*. It is problematic because it raises the philosophical questions of the relations of fact to value, of the *is* to the *ought*. Our concern is not to rehearse that question in terms of the logical problems involved, or to review the hundreds of pages of discussion about it in the past seventy years. Rather, we shall indicate some of the problems involved in the relation of empirical sciences to moral norms. Since the range of such sciences is so wide and the applicability so multiple, our investigation takes on even more of an outline form at this point.

First, let us examine the possibility that the moral norms for economic justice might arise out of economic science, out of economic data. In the introduction I indicated that one no longer finds the level of generality of the great social encyclicals to be satisfactory for social ethics. Thus, it is clear that I am positive about the contribution of economic science to economic ethics. But one immediately is pressed to ask: what are the principles used to judge a "good" economic system from the standpoint of economics? Not being well versed in economics, I can only indicate some hunches in this area; but it does not take much reading to find out that there are differences of opinion about what constitutes a good economics system. Clearly, the science seeks *to minimize radical instability* in the economic system when economic knowledge is applied to policy. However, there are differences of opinion about how much instability is tolerable, and at what costs to whom in the society. Certainly *growth* has been a factor in recent decades in judging a "good" economic system. Growth clearly affects stability, and depending on where the growth is, it affects some persons adversely and other persons advantageously.

The more clearly ethical questions emerge when a word like *distribution* is introduced into the discourse, for it immediately evokes tones of justice. But it also calls attention to differences of opinion within the science itself. For example, I

8. Max F. Millikan, "Inquiry and Policy: The Relation of Knowledge to Action," *The Human Meaning of the Social Sciences*, ed. Daniel Lerner (New York: Meridian Books, 1959), p. 167.

believe there was a strong opinion a few years ago that the way in which the economy might best grow would be for some persons to have sufficient resources beyond their needs in order to plow the surplus back into the economy in the form of capital investments. There was alongside of that the opinion that the pump should be primed at the other end, that is, by increasing the consumer power of the masses sufficiently to create increased demands which in turn would call forth increased capital investment. (I do not mean to suggest that these two opinions were not reconcilable at some levels.) My point is to suggest that the question of how wealth should be distributed is a factor within the development of the system, and does not necessarily, from the standpoint of the economist, immediately raise the questions of justice. But the question of distributive justice with all its ramifications does enter rather quickly into a critical discussion. If one takes either of two famous formulas, "To each his due," and "Equals shall be treated equally," one quickly sees that economic science alone cannot determine what is due to each person, or who are the equals who ought to be treated equally, except on the assumption that the free market system takes care of the question of justice — that is, in a free market system persons would receive what was due them, and if they did not receive much they were not due much.

I hope it does not enlarge issues too swiftly or too much to suggest that when economists address policy questions (and the purpose of their science is in large part to contribute to policy and the direction of society), the themes of liberty, justice, and power are always latent. Indeed, one difference between state-controlled economies, such as that of the Soviet Union, and freer economies, such as that of the United States, is the difference between the allocations of liberty, justice, and power. One might argue, I suppose, that from an economic standpoint one reaches decisions about these distributions; that is, one might develop norms for the distribution of liberty, justice, and power out of assessments about what it takes to make the economy function with a minimum basis of instability and a necessary rate of growth. Yet what might be judged to be best for the economic system to function as a system does not from various moral points of view satisfy, for example, the concern for distributive justice. What

determines the norms of justice are noneconomic judgments about whether persons are to be rewarded according to need, or according to productive contribution or other criteria of merit, or according to ascribed status due to inherited social class. Clearly, if need were the criterion, it would have significant consequences on the allocations of power and liberty in the society. These would be different from the consequences that occur if one or several criteria of merit were used, or if there were a mixture of need and merit. The moral norm of distributive justice does not arise from economic science, but is independent of it.

When one is addressing questions of economic *policy,* one is in an arena in which ethical considerations and economic science interact with each other. At this level a case might be made that policy norms, used to determine the exercise of economic power, take on a character that is both empirically and ethically informed. (In a sense, the encyclicals have not been policy statements, but guides for policy; the policies illumined or directed by them had to be worked out under particular economic, not to mention political and other social conditions.) Yet even at the level of economic policy it is not possible to say that good economics is good ethics, since the reference of the word good in each case is different. Good economics usually refers to the successful functioning of an economic system as this is interpreted from a particular point of view in that science, and not to concepts such as distributive justice. Policy norms are informed by economic science, and refer to a given set of conditions in which the ends of human and moral values are sought, but policy norms are not in a restrictive sense purely moral norms.

In an essay, "What Is the Normatively Human?" I have addressed the question of the relation of empirical sciences to the answer to that question in more detail. One example from that essay might be instructive at this point. In the area of obligations to keep life alive, at certain points the statistically human functions to establish the moral norm. These points pertain to birth defects. Birth anomalies of the grossest order are often called "monstrosities," and no moralist questions whether an obstetrician has the right not to sustain such living matter. Such monstrosities deviate so significantly from the statistical norm of the physically human that they are not judged morally to be human. At the other end of the spectrum are the "normal" infants, who are within the statistical range of the descriptively human, and here there is no argument about the obligations of obstetricians to sustain the life of such infants. Increasingly, questions are being raised about genetically defective fetuses, and about the relation of the statistical norm to the moral norm, or put in the form of a question, how defective (statistically deviant from the norm) does a fetus have to be before it is judged not to be normatively human from a moral point of view? Is the mongoloid fetus to be so judged? Is the fetus that has the dreaded Tay-Sachs disease? It is clear that the statistical norm refers not only to individual humans in such cases, but also to a normative conception of the human gene pool. A judgment about the benefits or cost to the future of the human race is based upon statistical extrapolations.

Clearly, in the cases purported to be ambiguous the moral norm of the right to life is determined not merely by empirical evidence, but also by what the human community values as normatively human. There are appeals to moral values which are not embedded in the empirically (physically) normative in all the instances in which the moralist would insist upon the right to life of fetuses or infants who deviate. Yet it should be clear that by permitting a judgment in cases of gross deformities that is based on empirical evidence alone, the moralist has opened the door to the use of such evidence in other cases as well. There might be several responses to this dilemma. One, it could be argued that even in the cases of gross deformities there are appeals to moral values which enter into the judgment, and these support the contention that there is no obligation to sustain the living matter. Another might be an elaboration of the first, namely, that there is a dialectic between the empirical and the ethical, and that this must be worked out with references to particular instances or to classes of instances. If this is granted, however, one must accept a degree of necessary uncertitude of moral judgment, for one would be appealing both to "facts" and to "values" which do not cohere perfectly.[9]

9. The choice of both the previous example from

Major Problems Involved in the Use of Empirical Sciences

The purpose of this part of the essay is to specify some of the issues previously suggested. This can be done by formulating three major questions.

1. What data and concepts are relevant to the moral issue under discussion?

The answers to this question involve a number of difficult considerations. First, responses to "moral" problems are made in terms of the delineations of what empirically is the issue; such delineations are made in terms of experiential or empirical data. Thus, what is included and excluded is crucial to what the actual moral issue is. One simple example will make the point clear. What is the situation of a dying patient? One has a different definition of the moral issues if the financial circumstance of his family is included in the situation than if it is excluded. If the use of artificial life support systems is draining the family resources, is this a relevant consideration in the determination? From some moral points of view it is not, from others it is. To include such information reflects a moral point of view; at the same time the exclusion of the information would state the moral issues in a different way.

Second, in many instances the empirical studies used in moral theology and social ethics were not designed to help the moralist answer his questions; the studies were not done to resolve the moral questions. Thus, the studies are in a profound sense "translated" from their own arena of purpose to another. Certain information which is crucial for the moralist might not have been crucial for another purpose. Great care must be taken in acknowledging the limitations and difficulties of this translation process, for it might not only distort the data used, but also require a reformulation of the moral questions in such a way that crucial aspects from an ethician's point of view are ignored.

---

economics and this one from medicine is intended to respond to John Giles Milhaven's statements in his "Exit for Ethicists," *Commonweal*, 91 (Oct. 31, 1969), p. 139. "Thus the ethical question can be purely a question of economics and an economics course appropriately replace the encyclicals." "Good medicine was good morality, and vice versa."

Third, it is possible that a predetermination of which data and concepts are relevant to the moral issue might foreclose awareness of other studies, points of view, and information that are in the end of equal, if not greater relevance. For example, as one proceeds with a question of economic ethics, he might foreclose it if he is not aware that political and social issues studied by other sciences are at least as significant, if not more so, in coming to a resolution. The ethician clearly needs to be open to a wide range of studies that might possibly pertain to the issues he is specifically attending to. The peril of openness should also be noted: since most human problems defy the boundaries within which research is conducted, it is possible to develop a degree of complexity of information and concepts that makes thinking unmanageable and resolution impossible.

2. What interpretation of a field should be accepted? And on what grounds?

This question has been addressed at several points previously, and the considerations need only to be summarized here. If the moralist accepts an interpretation on its "scientific" adequacy, he has the burden of making his case for his choice on scientific grounds. Clearly, most moralists are in no position to do that. Yet a counsel of despair is out of order. There are ways available to the moralist for determining which scholars are more reliable, and which interpretations are at least most questionable. The moralist clearly needs to be in communication with scholars in the areas from which he borrows in order to avoid horrendous mistakes of judgment, but he has to accept responsibility for making choices within the best of his knowledge.

If he chooses those studies that have an affinity with his own philosophical or theological point of view, he must be prepared to defend such decisions. In such an instance he would argue for the researcher's philosophical point of view as being more adequate, accurate, or at least plausible with reference to the understanding of man and society. For example, if he has a preference for social research that maximally takes into account man's capacity to choose, decide, and act (in short, a high measure of free will), he is in a sense not only under obligation to defend that philosophically, but also to argue that studies done from such a position are more likely to be empirically adequate.

The moralist's third possibility is more eclectic, namely, to use empirical research for sources of "insight" into the nature of man and society. Here he takes full responsibility to be his own thinker, and not to borrow authority from the research. To defend such use he will probably make claims for interpretations and data on the basis of the "sense" that they make to him and to his purposes. His uses are subject to critical judgment and to revision when the insights appear to be inadequate or the data invalid.

3. How does the moralist deal with the value biases of the studies that he uses?

If it is conceded that value preferences are involved in many dimensions of empirical research, this question can be difficult to answer. The researcher's choice of an area of study at least refers to his interests, if not to what he values as being significant for the human good. Thus, there is a reference to value in the choice of what to study. In addition, his preference for certain values is likely to have a considerable measure of effect on how he defines his research problem, what he is looking for, and what he consequently sees. This has become clear in the conflicts within some of the social sciences between those who have revolutionary tendencies and those who are "liberal reformers."

Again, a counsel of despair is out of order, for while the postempirical and even postethical (in the sense of decisions about values or ways of life that can never be fully defended on rational grounds alone) are at work, there are canons of evaluation about good research which mitigate some of the potential idiosyncratic consequences of these assumptions. As empirical sciences become more sophisticated about these matters, there is greater articulation of them by the researchers, and this facilitates the moralists' discourse.

The moralist has to accept responsibility for his own way of answering all three of these questions. He is, after all, finite. He can, after all, only do what he has the capacities to do. Within awareness of these questions, he is more likely to be a better moralist by being widely and deeply informed from the side of empirical research. But empirical research will never replace ethical arguments in the resolution of moral issues.

29. A Different Voice in Moral Decisions

CAROL GILLIGAN

I have in my own work sought to represent the voices of contemporary American girls and women as they talked about moral conflict and choice, and to amplify and validate these voices by associating them with voices in the western literary tradition. When I entitled my book *In a Different Voice,* I meant simply that there is a voice different from the voices represented in the Western intellectual tradition, different from the voices that have defined morality, the human condition, and women. My central point in trying to identify that voice is that we must become curious about its origins and meaning, notice it, listen to it carefully, hear its presence not only in women, but also in men.

I want to stress the importance of not assimilating this voice too quickly to schemes of interpretation that repeatedly have both observed its difference, and then systematically left it out. In a sense the most honest statement we can make at this point is that we have *not* listened to the voices of girls and women, and therefore we probably do not understand these voices, because all of our categories of understanding and interpretation in the West have been based on the investigation,

Carol Gilligan (1936–) is professor of education at the Graduate School of Education at Harvard University. She is author of *In a Different Voice: Psychological Theory and Women's Development,* and the editor of *Making Connections: The Relational Worlds of Adolescent Girls at Emma Willaerd School.*

From *Speaking of Faith,* ed. Diana Eck and Devaki Jain (Philadelphia: New Society Publishers, 1987).

consideration and analysis of the experience of men.

Once one notices the omission of women, it becomes a long and complicated task to explore what the inclusion of women's voices might mean. To recognize women's voices as human voices means to recognize that women's experience might inform, even transform, our understanding of the human condition. To discover that over half the population essentially has not been studied is, in one sense, an enormous opportunity. It opens the possibility that there may be in that group, in our group, ways of thinking and knowing that have not been explored. There may be new ways of thinking about questions on which we seem to have arrived at something of a dead end.

I am a researcher and I confess I did not set out to study women. In a way, I was part of the very problem I want to present. I set out in my research with two questions. One was the question of the relationship between moral judgement and action. I was interested in how people think about real, as opposed to hypothetical, moral problems. The second question was the relationship of experience to moral development. How does one's actual experience of moral conflict and choice affect one's thinking about morality and one's view of oneself as a moral actor or agent?

In pursuing these questions I made a change in the traditional instruments of measurement, which was absolutely crucial to the subsequent findings of my research, especially to my findings about women. This I offer here as the single most important point of my presentation. The point of the change was to free the instruments of research or investigation, i.e. the questions that are asked, from presuppositions about what morality is, what a moral problem is, what moral conflicts are, what the nature of moral choice is, what identity is, and what the categories are by which we define ourselves. In the prevailing research instruments that are used in Western psychology, the scales of moral development, the questions which lead to the responses that are assessed, and the scales of identity contain two central value presuppositions: first, that morality is basically justice, and second, that identity is basically autonomy.

The first value presupposition goes back to Socrates: Virtue is one and its name is justice. Jean Piaget, studying the moral development of the child, said all morality consists of systems of rules, and the question to be studied is, "How does the mind come to respect rules?" From this, he traced the development of the ideas of justice. Lawrence Kohlberg, setting out to study moral development in adolescents, sought to measure reasoning about justice in a sample of male adolescents. But the very questions that were posed in the investigation were premised on this particular, presupposed definition of the moral domain.

In my research, however, I did not begin by posing a moral problem and then asking, "How would you resolve it?" Rather, I asked people how they would define what a moral problem is. What experiences in their lives had they construed as moral conflicts? Thus, the research questions were: Have you ever been in a situation where you faced a moral conflict? Have you ever had to make a decision where you were not sure what the right thing to do was? What was the situation? What was the conflict *for you* in that situation? It is clear that here we were shifting our starting point to allow the participant in the research to define the moral domain. What was conflict *for you*? What did you consider in thinking about how to resolve the problem? What did you do? Do you think it was the right thing to do?

With regard to the question of identity, we, the research team, began with the simple question, "How would you describe yourself to yourself?" Then we would ask such questions as, "Is the way you see yourself now different from how you saw yourself in the past? What led to the change?"

This shift in the questions asked made it possible to identify a different construction of the moral problem, that is, different from that presupposed in the psychological literature. Against the prevailing definition of morality as a problem of justice, and identity as the achievement of separation, morality emerges as a problem of care and responsibility, and identity the achievement of relationship.

It is important to remember that I began with the question of the relationship between moral judgement and action. I was looking for a real moral choice to study, and I selected a sample of pregnant women who were considering abortion. Obviously, choosing the abortion decision, I ended up with a sample of women, and I began to hear where it was that these women attached

moral language to their consideration of the abortion problem. The first question of the interview was, "How did you get pregnant, and how have you been thinking about it so far?" The goal was to map the decision-making process in the woman's own terms, and to see if those terms were moral terms. The responses of the women studied contrasted dramatically with the public discussion of abortion in America. The public discussion casts the conflict as one between the right to life and the right to choice. These women, however, articulated a different way of framing the issue. Whenever they used moral language — words like "should," "better," "ought," "right," "wrong" — I would ask, "When you say this would be the better choice, or the right choice, what do you mean?" The women identified repeatedly the moral problem as a problem of *responsibility*. If one is to be responsible for having a child, one has to ask, "Is it possible to care for this child?"

The whole view of choice, of the relationship between other and self, was fundamentally different. Choice, rather than being seen as an isolated moment, was a moment in an ongoing narrative of events, which in the abortion decision were specifically the events of relationship. There were the events that led to the pregnancy, and the events that would occur if the pregnancy were continued. Choice was not abstracted from the context, the story, the narrative of lives. Self and other, rather than being seen as separate and opposed, were seen as interdependent. This means that, for the woman, hurting herself was harmful to the developing child and hurting the developing child was harmful to herself. There was no way to separate self and other into a distinct opposition. So in this as well as in a variety of other conflict situations, women searched for an inclusive solution, for a way to avoid harm both to others *and* to themselves. Failing to find such a solution, the women in the abortion-decision study tended to ask which alternative would do the least harm. They did not ask what was the ideal solution, even the "right" solution, but the least harmful solution for everyone involved. This different voice, then, revealed a different way of thinking about the self and the other, about the causes of conflict, and about the strategies for arriving at a "better" solution.

It was in identifying this voice that I began to

notice its absence from Western psychological literature on development. Here I simply want to add a note of caution to all those who have occasion to use Western psychology. In making use of its conceptions of morality, its conceptions of identity, and its scales of measurement, one is borrowing a tradition that has been sustained by systematically leaving out women, by silencing women, and by eclipsing their experience in the definition of the human condition. But the omission of women also tells you that this is a tradition that has been blind to the facts of human relationship.

Let me cite Freud as an example. To say, as Freud did, that we have a theory of sexuality, a psychology of love, and that we know nothing about women is to reveal a psychology of love and sexuality that has very little to do with relationships. In 1926, Freud observed that "the sexual life of adult women is a dark continent for psychology." To put it in this metaphorical language, to say that women's sexuality — a subject so central for Freud — is a "dark continent," is to imply that women's experience occurs on some continent *apart* from the rest of human experience, a continent that can be illuminated, somehow, without changing the rest of the map. This way of thinking is especially interesting to us here, for it obviously parallels the leaving out of so many cultures in our theoretical formulations about human society and human nature.

The question is, "What has been missed by leaving out women, and how might the inclusion of women *change* the mapping of human growth?" How might it challenge, revise, expand, or correct our current assumptions about morality, truth, conflict and choice, as well as our assumptions about women and men? The absence of women's voices in Western moral and religious traditions, and relegation of women to ancillary roles in the central stories that have been told in these traditions, make it possible that women and women's thinking might inform these traditions in new ways.

There have been two strands to the Western moral tradition. One focuses on contract, on enlightened self-interest, and on the extension to the other of the rights and claims that are one's own. This might be called a self-interested form of morality, and it is tied to the notion of social contract in its modern formulation. The second tradition is that of self-sacrifice, which is tied to the notion of altruism. For centuries, these two lines of morality have wandered through the Western tradition, appearing in the contrast between reason and compassion, fairness and forgiveness, justice and mercy, and emerging repeatedly, although by no means exclusively, in the contrast between men and women. These distinctions implied an underlying division between thought and feeling, a separation between the process of discerning what is just and the capacity for response. But the division between reason and compassion focuses a problem in this formulation, since the implication that women are thoughtless and men without feeling clearly cannot be sustained. Instead, there appear to be two modes of thinking, carrying differing implications of feeling and signifying different ways of perceiving others and of knowing oneself. However, to observe that this contrast has been framed within a tradition that has not itself included women's voices is also to raise the question of how the inclusion of women's voices might change the very framing of the problem.

Listening to women talk about moral conflict and choice, and about themselves in relation to others, I have observed that women tend to translate the abstract language of moral discourse into the vernacular of human relationships. This is usually grounds for criticizing women's moral thinking, i.e. for saying that women confuse moral problems with problems of interpersonal relationships. But the very "confusion" is revealing. The two moral languages, of self-interest and self-sacrifice, came to be labelled as "selfish" and "selfless" by women. These were the recurrent words that I heard, interviewing American women, the word "selfish" always meaning bad, the word "selfless" always good. And the criticism of these two words, indeed a criticism of the very polarity of self-interest and self-sacrifice, is that they both exclude relationship. Selfish means excluding the other, and selfless implies excluding the self, which creates a special problem with moral choice, since there is then no self, actor, or agent in the situation of choice. In any case, both selfishness and selflessness imply an exclusion which destroys relationships. There is no relationship if others are not present in their own terms, or if the self is silenced.

Listening to women's voices as they spoke about moral conflict and choice raised the question as to whether women were calling attention to the extent to which both of the central lines of the Western moral tradition are ways of thinking that diminish relationships, and thus limit the possibilities for care, love and response.

In identifying two different moral voices, I wondered whether these voices could be identified systematically in responses to moral questions. The answer was yes. Different observers reading the same interview could agree about the distinction between these voices, and which considerations in thinking about moral problems belonged to which of the two domains. Systematically encoding this distinction then made it possible to investigate it in a series of studies across samples mainly composed of advantaged, Western-educated men and women — a sample chosen deliberately to refute the "gender difference" hypothesis. In other words, the sample was chosen so that the women, whether black or white, would be highly educated and have professional opportunities, since the absence of opportunities is generally cited as the explanation for differences observed in women's moral thinking.

Within the sample studied, most people, in thinking about moral problems, used both voices — that is, introduced considerations of both justice and care. This is very important, for it means that both ways of thinking are understood by both women and men. But in both men and women one voice tended to be more salient. That is, in deciding what are moral problems, in resolving moral problems, and in evaluating moral choices, people tended to focus their thinking either on issues of justice, equality, reciprocity and rights or on issues of care, connection, responsibility and response. One voice tended to be salient, suggesting that the two voices articulated two different organizing perspectives. As major and minor modes appear in music, major and minor modes appeared in most people's thinking about moral decision.

There was a strong correlation in the population studied between the major mode of moral thinking and gender. Although neither mode of moral thinking was gender specific, and most people used both modes, the salience of these modes was gender related. Men in these studies tended to use "justice" as their predominant mode of moral reasoning and to define themselves as separate in relation to others. Women in these studies tended to use "care" as their predominant mode of moral reasoning and to define themselves as connected with others.

Psychologically, how can one explain the presence of these two different ways of moral thinking? By looking, I believe, at two different dimensions of human relationships, not by thinking of one mode of moral thinking as connected to relationships and the other as isolated from relationships. *Both* of these moral visions — of justice and of care — come out of experiences of relationship which are universal in human life. The first is the experience of inequality: as long as adults are larger than children, every person has experienced being in an unequal situation. This situation of inequality grounds a vision of justice, fairness, equality, rights. The second is the experience of attachment: since human survival depends on adults attaching to children, every person has experienced attachment and the consequent vulnerability to separation and loss. Attachment creates interdependence, and therefore it creates a vision of morality as caretaking — as perceiving, attending, and responding to need.

In a study of high school girls, I asked the question, What does "dependence" mean to you? All of us might think how we would respond to this question, and to the question, What is the opposite of dependence? Most Americans will say that the opposite of "dependence" is "independence," because that opposition is so firmly rooted in the American tradition. But adolescent girls often opposed dependence to isolation. For them, dependence meant: "Someone would be there when you need them," "Someone would listen to you, would try to understand." By opposing dependence to isolation, the girls conveyed the assumption that dependence is positive, that the human condition *is* a condition of dependence, and that people need to rely on one another for understanding, comfort and support. Therefore, dependence was *not* simply the condition of the unequal, the one controlled by someone else, the one who lacks independence. Dependence, rather, was created by choices to be there for others, to take care of them, to listen, to try to understand, and to help. In this way, a whole range of activities which have been traditionally associated with women and linked with passivity and inequality become represented as active moral choices that create and sustain relationships of attachment. This vision extends from interpersonal to intercultural relations.

It is human experience — the experience of inequality, and of attachment — that gives rise to two moral visions. One, the social-contract vision of justice, has been dominant in Western thinking thus far. But these two ways of moral thinking reveal different perspectives on the relationship between self and others — as unequal or equal, attached or detached. As we listen more carefully to the moral voice that speaks about interdependence and the problems of detachment, a voice articulated more frequently by women, different ways of thinking about power emerge as well as different ways of understanding violence to others and to self.

The crucial questions this work leaves me with are these: First, in whose terms do we speak? Who is to define the terms of the discussion? Who is going to set the terms of the dialogue? Noticing that the terms have been set in the past by men, we must ask how women's experience might change the very terms of the discussion. In the field of psychology, the discussion of attachment is always subsumed to the focus on inequality, and the "justice/autonomy" view of morality and self defines the mainline of human development. It becomes very crucial to reframe the questions.

How does one empower women to speak in situations where women have been silent? One way is simply to represent and to validate women's experience and vision, to articulate the order of women's experience, and to validate it as human experience. In my research, my focus is now on adolescent girls because of the observation that it is at this time in the life cycle that girls tend to become silent. At the time when thinking becomes interpretive, and one is taught to think through interpretive schemes that have not represented women's experience, or even noted its omission, it becomes very hard for girls and for women to render that experience coherent.

Finally, I would like to close with the suggestion that, in our age of nuclear weapons, international interdependence has become a reality of life. Autonomy, which has been taken as a premise for our sense of "identity," conversely becomes an illusion. And the images of winning and losing, in games and in making moral decisions, begin to appear as very dangerous images of relationship. For this reason, looking to our own experiences as women, and realizing that these experiences have not been systematically explored, we must look for different images of relationships, different ways of thinking about values and about development, and different ways of affirming our human interdependence.

30. Using Empirical Information

LISA SOWLE CAHILL

The special helpfulness of descriptive, especially empirical, research lies in its ability to illumine the reality of situations that the ethicist evaluates. This does not necessarily make empirical studies a uniformly more important ethical source than tradition and philosophy, but in the present historical, socio-cultural context, they offer some of the most provocative evidence and further the critique of other sources upon which Christian ethics has relied more frequently in the past. While these studies bear out the pervasiveness of the institutionalization of sex in marriage and family, they also clarify the circumstances of variance. Certainly not all societies accommodate sex, marriage, and procreation in the same ways, nor do individuals engage in nonprocreative or nonmarital sexual activity for the same reasons, with the same motives, or with the same social and personal consequences.

The contribution that empirical evidence has made to the Christian evaluation of homosexuality is a case in point. The biblical tradition has been associated by and large with negative prohibitions of homosexuality. Recently the empirical sciences have been associated with challenges to

biblically supported condemnations of homosexual acts as "unnatural," "ungodly," and "wrong." Since Christians not only come from a faith tradition but are also human beings living in human societies in history, it is necessary to take these challenges seriously. The sciences of anthropology, sociology, psychology, and biology have turned a good deal of attention to and have a good deal to say about the phenomenon of human being as sexual being, including homosexual being. The homosexual orientation and relationship are today understood to differ from what biblical and traditional authors interpreted simply as willful perversion.[1]

Alfred Kinsey was among the first to establish some reliable instruments for documenting the incidence and variety of homosexual behavior.[2] According to his studies, only 4 percent of males and 2 to 3 percent of females are "exclusively homosexual throughout their lives," but 37 percent of males and 13 percent of females have had a least one significant homosexual experience after adolescence.[3] It has been estimated that the population of the United States includes two million homosexuals.[4] In 1973, the American Psychiatric Association removed homosexuality from its diagnostic manual of psychiatric disorders.[5] In 1982 the Kinsey Institute also suggested that homosexuality may have a biological basis, and that 10 percent of children appear to lack from a very early age a strong gender conformity and an attraction to the toys and games traditionally

---

Lisa Sowle Cahill (1948–) is professor of Christian ethics at Boston College. She is author of *Between the Sexes: Foundations for a Christian Ethics of Sexually,* and co-author with Thomas Shannon of *Religion and Artificial Reproduction: An Inquiry into the Vatican "Instruction on Respect for Human Life in its Origin and on the Dignity of Human Reproduction."*

From Lisa Sowle Cahill, *Between the Sexes* (Philadelphia: Fortress Press, 1985).

1. Robin Scroggs is particularly helpful in elucidating the socio-cultural contexts of biblical prohibitions of homosexuality (*The New Testament and Homosexuality* (Philadelphia: Fortress Press, 1983).

2. Alfred Kinsey et al., *Sexual Behavior in the Human Male* (Philadelphia: Saunders, 1948); and Alfred Kinsey et al., *Sexual Behavior in the Human Female* (Philadelphia: Saunders, 1953).

3. Kinsey, *Human Male*, 651.

4. Jack Thomas, "Television: A Courageous Look at Growing up Gay," *The Boston Globe* (5 January, 1983): 57.

5. Charles N. Socarides, M.D., "Homosexuality Is Not Just an Alternative Life Style," in *Male and Female: Christian Approaches to Sexuality,* ed. Ruth Tiffany Barnhouse and Urban T. Holmes III (New York: Seabury Press, 1976), 149.

6. Thomas, "Growing Up Gay," 57.

favored by their gender.[6] Some researchers have offered evidence that homosexuality may originate in the genetic makeup the human zygote, and may be related to chromosomal and hormonal anomalies.[7] Whatever its origins, and, in fact, these may very well be diverse, the homosexual orientation and its accompanying lifestyles can take many forms.[8] These forms occur cross-culturally, although perhaps not universally. And it has been demonstrated by anthropologists[9] and historians[10] that different cultures vary in acceptance, rejection, and even institutionalization of homosexuality. Although most psychiatrists in Western culture do not advocate therapy aimed at changing the sexual orientation of persons who are exclusively homosexual by the Kinsey scale, they do appreciate the importance of assisting the homosexual person to improve self-image, interpersonal relationships, and social adjustment. The evaluative norm for these "improvements" appears to be ability to sustain stable, affective, sexual relationships, particularly with one other person.[11]

What does the increasingly plentiful data about the frequency and etiology of a human sexual phenomenon like homosexuality "prove" about its moral character? Despite the fact that homosexuality remains incompletely understood, we find what appears to be a consensus that most persons discover their sexual orientation as a "given," if an ambiguous and confusing given, rather than choosing it. Furthermore, homosexuality is a variation in human sexual orientation that occurs consistently even though with less frequency than heterosexuality. Although neither consistency nor frequency in and of themselves establish whether a phenomenon of human constitution or behavior is biologically or psychologically healthy or pathological,[12] much less whether it is morally right or wrong, they do have implications for moral judgment. If certain biological or psychological conditions constantly recur in human societies, then the members of those societies have the obligation to enhance human life as far as possible in the midst of those conditions, whether the conditions themselves are desirable or undesirable.

Empirical studies are able to tell us something about the cooperation of male and female physiology in reproduction; about the relative frequency of conception in humans; about the nature and causes of sexual pleasure; about the psychic components of human sexual interaction. They also are able to discriminate between male and female sexual response, both physiological

7. James A. Monteleone, M.D., "The Physiological Aspects of Sex," in *Human Sexuality and Personhood: Proceedings of the Workshop for the Hierarchies of the United States and Canada Sponsored by the Pope John Center through a Grant from the Knights of Columbus* (St. Louis: Pope John Center, 1981), 71-85.

8. Alan P. Bell and Martin S. Weinberg, *Homosexualities: A Study of Diversity among Men and Women* (New York: Simon and Schuster, 1978).

9. Margaret Farley, "Sexual Ethics," in *Encyclopedia of Bioethics,* ed. Warren T. Reich (New York: Free Press, 1978), 1583; Clellan S. Ford and Frank A. Beach, *Patterns of Sexual Behavior* (New York: Harper & Brothers, 1951), 130 (cited by Farley); Harriet Whitehead, "The Bow and the Burden Strap: A New Look at Institutionalized Homosexuality in Native North America," Sexual Meanings (New York: Cambridge Univ. Press, 1981), 80-115.

10. John Boswell, *Christianity, Social Tolerance, and Homosexuality: Gay People in Western Europe from the Beginning of the Christian Era to the Fourteenth Century* (Chicago: Univ. of Chicago Press, 1980).

11. Bell and Weinberg, *Homosexualities,* 220.

12. The content of the norm "health" is not as self-evident as it might at first appear. One frequently proposed and reasonable definition of biological and psychological health is "the successful functioning of an organism in its environment." This definition lends credence to the proposal that the active homosexual who is personally and socially well-adjusted is also sexually "healthy." However, at second sight, we discover that there is in this definition a certain circularity. The health of a sexual orientation is contingent upon "successful function"; but "success" and even "function" are evaluative concepts that return us to the unavoidable question of what we consider to be adequate or normative human sexual functioning, and whether or not the directing of one's genital sexuality to members of the same sex fulfills that definition, even if one's sexual orientation does not impinge detrimentally upon one's ability to perform other social roles. An *evaluative* component, then, is unavoidable, even in ostensibly "empirical" notions of health and sickness. It is no less problematic when the agenda behind the definition of "health" is the justification of homosexuality, than when it is its denigration by inclusion in a list of psychiatric disorders.

and psychological, and tell us something about the roles that sexual interactions and commitments play in society, culture, and history. But they are not able, by dint of empirically based description alone, to tell us conclusively what place such factors *ought* to have. Beyond the level of the de facto occurrence of certain behaviors or social arrangements, there lie the levels of biological and psychological evaluation, and, finally, of moral evaluation. It is necessary to introduce moral categories in order to move beyond statistical norms, and even beyond norms of "health," which depend to some extent upon *evaluation* of what is observed to occur in "nature." No simple definitions of what is morally "normative," or even what is "healthy," in human sexuality will be available from sheer empirical investigations, even though the latter augment ethical reflection immensely. It must be remembered that even empirical "data" are organized and interpreted with the help of categories that are themselves not wholly "value free." The decisive question for Christian ethics is which "naturally" occurring and even functionally "healthy" facts, states, and relations also represent moral ideals. Empirical evidence can be appropriated meaningfully in Christian ethics only if interpreted in the light of other, complementary sources: Scripture, tradition, and normative, as distinct from descriptive, accounts of the human.

Try It Yourself:
Holy Unions (II)

CASE STUDY 2

We have now reviewed the key sources in Christian ethics — Scripture, tradition, philosophy, and science. The following case illustrates the way in which ethical "source questions" often appear in ordinary conversation and argument. The first part of this case can be found on page 13, and the last part on page 315.

Saturday morning, George bursts into your room with an excited look on his face. "You thought that argument last night was fun? Wait until this afternoon! Professor Smarts from our anthropology department is lecturing on 'Gays and Straights' at 2:00 p.m., and he's having an informal and open discussion with students on the same subject later this morning in the cafeteria. Let's go over."

As you arrive, Smarts is responding to a student whose face is still a little red from the passion of his remarks. "I understand where you are coming from, Tim. The book that Christians hold to be sacred does not say a thing positive about homosexuals. I wish it did, but it doesn't."

"The book *is* sacred," Tim said, his color rising again. "And you have conveniently left out the fact that everything the Bible does say about homosexuality is negative. There is simply no way a Christian can accept your views and remain Christian."

"But remember, Tim," the anthropology professor continued, "the notion of a 'homosexual' — a person with settled erotic preferences for the same sex — is completely modern. It appears first about a hundred years ago as a product of social scientific investigation. No biblical writer, including Paul, had it in view. Strictly speaking, the word does not belong in the Bible. The only reason you find it there is that some recent translators have decided to import it."

A burly, articulate sophomore named Sam then jumped in. "What you failed to mention, Tim, is that what the Bible does say about gays hardly adds up to three complete sentences. Jesus says nothing at all about it. Keep a sense of proportion here. Most of all, you ought to meet some real gays before you spout off more about 'what the Bible says.' Let me tell you: the ones I have met I would never want to condemn. They are fine, upright people. You should consult your *experience* a little more, Tim, before rushing to judgment."

"I think Tim has a point." The speaker was Nancy Miles, vice president of the Student Council. The entire group turned to watch her speak. "After all, it's not a case of the Bible being against homosexuality and everyone else being for it. The gay rights movement, only twenty-five years old, may be confusing us a little. Even today, the clear and obvious weight of the Christian tradition is against placing homosexuals and heterosexuals on the same level. So we are not talking about just the Bible. Rather, we are talking about millions of people over thousands of years who have reached the same conclusion. I think I am correct that other world religions tilt in precisely the same way. Shouldn't Chesterton's 'democracy of the dead' have some role to play in this conversation?"

"Well now, Nancy," Smarts replied, "haven't we seen over and over again that this 'Christian tradition' has the capacity to be mistaken? Wasn't it mistaken when it permitted Christians to live comfortably with slavery? Both slaves and women were oppressed minorities. Aren't gays and lesbians in a similar position today? It seems to me that the revolutionary insights of science are helping to reduce our fears and to see more clearly in this area."

Tim began to leave the cafeteria, but put in one last comment. "The insights of science will never match the Bible. Tolstoi got it right a hundred years ago: forget about science. It can't help on the big questions. Stick to anthropology, Dr. Smarts." He waved, and left the room.

Who gets the better of this argument, and why? Which sources do you think are relevant? How would you use them to enter this argument?

PART II

FEATURES OF CHRISTIAN ETHICS

Chapter 6

The Forms of Christian Ethics

Introduction

When we begin to examine the moral teachings of the Christian Scriptures, we find a vast array of material. We discover Moses who issues laws not only forbidding murder but demanding that we honor our parents. We encounter Jesus who advocates a purity of heart, a humility of spirit, and an expansiveness of love few of us can begin to imagine. We hear the apostle Paul who calls our attention away from the works of the law and the radical obedience required by Jesus to focus instead upon the life and death of Jesus. And these are but a small selection of the voices of Scripture. Christian thinkers throughout the ages have pondered over the nature of a moral theory which could accommodate these diverse types of scriptural teaching. How can these pieces be ordered coherently?

Some thinkers, like Martin Luther (reading 32), have taken their inspiration first and foremost from Pauline literature. In their view, a very real danger is attached to too close a consideration of the law of God. God's law stands over us, to be sure, and judges us. But inevitably our tendency will be to attempt to justify ourselves by our own efforts rather than to humbly rely upon God's gift in Jesus the Christ. Better that we focus upon faith in Christ, by whom we are forgiven and justified before God. Better that we, like Paul, learn the hard, the humbling, but the extraordinarily liberating message that Christ has done it all. Luther, thus, resists a systematic inquiry into the moral teaching of the Scriptures, for the systematization might itself lead to a hubris that prevents us from hearing the law's judgment of us and the free offer of forgiveness from Christ. Instead, Luther would have the gospel preached and heard by God's faithful children who, upon rightly hearing the gospel proclaimed, will freely do God's work in the world.

H. Richard Niebuhr's essay, "The Meaning of Responsibility" (reading 33), may well be the richest single essay in Christian ethics of this century. Niebuhr carefully lays out the three most common symbols, metaphors, or theoretical forms employed in reflection upon the moral life. Some thinkers have thought of humans primarily as *makers*. So it was that Aristotle and Aquinas (readings 18 and 19) viewed human life as shot through with purpose. With our purpose, or goal, determined by our human natures, our task is to mold the material of our lives in order to achieve that *telos*. We give shape to our lives and to the world around us in order to realize and accomplish our final good. Other theologians — John Calvin comes readily to mind — have tended to think the metaphor of humans as *citizens, as law-makers and law-abiders,* most illuminating. God is understood as the mighty and benevolent ruler of the universe who issues laws which direct us to our true good and enable us better to live together. Niebuhr himself recommends a third metaphor to guide our thoughts — humans as *answerers, as responders to action*. Often we find ourselves in circumstances which seem incompatible with our purposes as humans and outside of our control, but if we think of ourselves as responsible agents, choosing that which fits into the pattern of our past actions and what we anticipate in our future, we find that we are able to achieve a wholeness absent of the more fragmentary metaphors of maker and citizen.

Joseph Fletcher (reading 34) also identifies three models or forms of moral theory, but rather than what we might call the teleological (human as maker), deontological (human as law-maker, law-abider), and aretaic (human as responder) models identified by Niebuhr, Fletcher identifies the models as *legalistic, antinomian,* and *situ-*

ational. Fletcher opts for the situational approach, a type of teleological approach virtually indistinguishable from a philosophical theory known as *act utilitarianism.* Fletcher believes each person has a duty in each situation to try to do that which is the most loving action in those circumstances. The place of moral laws or rules is relatively insignificant; they merely provide us with helpful insight into what has seemed to work in the past in somewhat similar situations. But all situations are different, so the Christian's final guide is love.

If Joseph Fletcher is the best example of a Christian ethicist embracing a *consequentialist* moral theory — the consequences of an action alone determine that action's goodness or badness — then Paul Ramsey is perhaps the best contemporary example of a Christian ethicist whose outlook is decidedly *deontological* and, hence, anti-consequentialist. Ramsey (reading 35), like Fletcher, recognized love, or *agape,* as the fundamental principle of Christian ethics. But, unlike Fletcher, Ramsey believed it was the nature or character of the action, and not its consequences, which determined whether or not an action was loving. To be guided only by a consequentialist interpretation of love is to open oneself to the performance of many actions which wrong human beings, violating the most basic principles of respect for persons without which no act can be genuinely loving.

James Gaffney (reading 36) and James McClendon (reading 37) turn our attention back from teleological and deontological moral theories to the type of theory advocated by H. Richard Niebuhr. Gaffney surveys recent developments in Catholic moral theology describing what he sees as the strengths and weaknesses of these developments. He finds most helpful the type of moral theory McClendon articulates, one that focuses not so much upon discrete, isolated decisions made by a moral agent as upon the formation of moral character. What is most important morally is the type of persons we are, who we become as we live through the vicissitudes of our lives. What is most important is the story we can tell of ourselves. Here *vision,* or how we see God acting in our world, and *community,* or the communal context for an appropriate Christian viewing of the world, overshadows *decisions* as the building-blocks of a moral life.

Our readings in this chapter conclude with Carol Robb's attempt to articulate the parameters of a feminist ethical theory (reading 38). While suggesting that feminist ethical theories will tend to be teleological in character, her essay clearly shows that this is but one minor aspect of feminist moral theory. More important, by far, is the feminist attention to and analysis of the concrete experiences of women and the loyalty of women to women.

In this chapter, then, we find a number of attempts to establish what form a Christian moral theory should take — one that attends foremost to the goals of human nature or the consequences of our actions, or one that examines the character of individual actions and their compatibility with rules or principles, or one that sees the hand of God in the world and shapes one's character so as to tell a story that fits God's action, or one that inductively moves from the concrete experiences of a particular group to a program of liberation from oppression. Undoubtedly more variations on these themes and new themes as well might have been included, but these selections indicate not only the diversity and complexity of Christian moral theories, but also those types of theories which are today most prevalent among Christian ethicists.

Suggestions for Further Reading

Fletcher, Joseph. *Situation Ethics.* Philadelphia: Westminster Press, 1966.

Harrison, Beverly Wildung. *Making the Connections.* Boston: Beacon Press, 1985.

Hauerwas, Stanley. *Vision and Virtue.* Notre Dame: Fides, 1974.

Holmes, Arthur F. *Ethics.* Downers Grove: Inter-Varsity Press, 1984.

Mahoney, John P. *The Making of Moral Theology.* Oxford: Oxford University Press, 1987.

Meilaender, Gilbert. *The Theory and Practice of Virtue.* Notre Dame: University of Notre Dame Press, 1984.

Niebuhr, H. Richard. *The Responsible Self.* New York: Harper & Row, 1963.

O'Donovan, Oliver. *Resurrection and Moral Order.* 2nd ed., Grand Rapids, Mich.: Wm. B. Eerdmans, 1994.

Ramsey, Paul. *Basic Christian Ethics.* Louisville, Ky.: Westminster/John Knox Press, 1993.

Thielicke, Helmut. *Theological Ethics.* Grand Rapids, Mich.: Wm. B. Eerdmans, 1979.

Welch, Sharon. *A Feminist Ethic of Risk.* Minneapolis: Fortress Press, 1990.

31. Exodus 20:1-17; Matthew 5:1-11, 17-48; Galatians 2:15-21

Exodus 20:1-17

Then God spoke all these words:

I am the LORD your God, who brought you out of the land of Egypt, out of the house of slavery: you shall have no other gods before me.

You shall not make for yourself an idol, whether in the form of anything that is in heaven above, or that is on the earth beneath, or that is in the water under the earth. You shall not bow down to them or worship them: for I the LORD your God am a jealous God, punishing children for the iniquity of parents, to the third and the fourth generation of those who reject me, but showing steadfast love to the thousandth generation of those who love me and keep my commandments.

You shall not make wrongful use of the name of the LORD your God, for the LORD will not acquit anyone who misuses his name.

Remember the sabbath day, and keep it holy. Six days you shall labor and do all your work. But the seventh day is a sabbath to the LORD your God; you shall not do any work — you, your son or your daughter, your male or female slave, your livestock, or the alien resident in your towns. For in six days the LORD made heaven and earth, the sea, and all that is in them, but rested the seventh day; therefore the LORD blessed the sabbath day and consecrated it.

Honor your father and your mother, so that your days may be long in the land that the LORD your God is giving you.

You shall not murder.

You shall not commit adultery.

You shall not steal.

You shall not bear false witness against your neighbor.

You shall not covet your neighbor's house; you shall not covet your neighbor's wife, or male or female slave, or ox, or donkey, or anything that belongs to your neighbor.

Matthew 5:1-11, 17-48

When Jesus saw the crowds, he went up the mountain; and after he sat down, his disciples came to him. Then he began to speak, and taught them, saying:

"Blessed are the poor in spirit, for theirs is the kingdom of heaven.

"Blessed are those who mourn, for they will be comforted.

"Blessed are the meek, for they will inherit the earth.

"Blessed are those who hunger and thirst for righteousness, for they will be filled.

"Blessed are the merciful, for they will receive mercy.

"Blessed are the pure in heart, for they will see God.

"Blessed are the peacemakers, for they will be called children of God.

"Blessed are those who are persecuted for righteousness' sake, for theirs is the kingdom of heaven.

"Blessed are you when people revile you and persecute you and utter all kinds of evil against you falsely on my account. Rejoice and be glad, for your reward is great in heaven, for in the same way they persecuted the prophets who were before you. . . .

"Do not think that I have come to abolish the law or the prophets: I have come not to abolish but to fulfill. For truly I tell you, until heaven and earth pass away, not one letter, not one stroke of a letter, will pass from the law until all is accomplished. Therefore, whoever breaks one of the least of these commandments, and teaches others to do the same, will be called least in the kingdom of heaven; but whoever does them and teaches them will be called great in the kingdom of heaven. For I tell you, unless your righteousness exceeds that of the scribes and Pharisees, you will never enter the Kingdom of Heaven.

"You have heard that it was said to those of ancient times, 'You shall not murder'; and 'whoever murders shall be liable to judgment.' But I say to you that if you are angry with a brother or sister, you will be liable to judgment; and if you insult a brother or sister, you will be liable to the council; and if you say, 'You fool,' you will be liable to the hell of fire. So when you are offering your gift at the altar, if you remember that your brother or sister has something against you, leave your gift there before the altar and go; first be reconciled to your brother or sister, and then come and offer your gift. Come to terms quickly with your accuser while you are on the way to court with him, or your accuser may hand you over to the judge, and the judge to the guard, and you will be thrown into prison. Truly I tell you, you will never get out until you have paid the last penny.

"You have heard that it was said, 'You shall not commit adultery.' But I say to you that everyone who looks at a woman with lust has already committed adultery with her in his heart. If your right eye causes you to sin, tear it out and throw it away; it is better for you to lose one of your members than for your whole body to be thrown into hell. And if your right hand causes you to sin, cut it off and throw it away; it is better for you to lose one of your members than for your whole body to go into hell.

"It was also said, 'Whoever divorces his wife, let him give her a certificate of divorce.' But I say to you that anyone who divorces his wife, except on the ground of unchastity, causes her to commit adultery; and whoever marries a divorced woman commits adultery.

"Again, you have heard that it was said to those of ancient times, 'You shall not swear falsely, but carry out the vows you have made to the Lord.' But I say to you, do not swear at all, either by heaven, for it is the throne of God, or by the earth, for it is his footstool, or by Jerusalem, for it is the city of the great King. And do not swear by your head, for you cannot make one hair white or black. Let your word be 'Yes, Yes' or 'No, No'; anything more than this comes from the evil one.

"You have heard that it was said, 'An eye for an eye and a tooth for a tooth.' But I say to you, do not resist an evildoer. But if anyone strikes you on the right cheek, turn the other also; and if anyone wants to sue you and take your coat, give your cloak as well; and if anyone forces you to go one mile, go also the second mile. Give to everyone who begs from you, and do not refuse anyone who wants to borrow from you.

"You have heard that it was said, 'You shall love your neighbor and hate your enemy.' But I say to you, love your enemies and pray for those who persecute you, so that you may be children of your Father in heaven: for he makes his sun rise on the evil and on the good, and sends rain on the righteous and on the unrighteous. For if you love those who love you, what reward do you have? Do not even the tax collectors do the same? And if you greet only your brothers and sisters, what more are you doing than others? Do not even the Gentiles do the same? Be perfect, therefore, as your heavenly Father is perfect.

Galatians 2:15-21

We ourselves are Jews by birth and not Gentile sinners; yet we know that a person is justified not by the works of the law but through faith in Jesus Christ. And we have come to believe in Christ Jesus, so that we might be justified by faith in Christ, and not by doing the works of the law, because no one will be justified by the works of the law. But if, in our effort to be justified in Christ, we ourselves have been found to be sinners, is Christ then a servant of sin? Certainly not! But if I build up again the very things that I once tore down, then I demonstrate that I am a transgressor. For through the law I died to the law, so that I might live to God. I have been crucified with Christ; and it is no longer I who live, but it is Christ who lives in me. And the life I now live in the flesh I live by faith in the Son of God, who loved me and gave himself for me. I do not nullify the grace of God; for if justification comes through the law, then Christ died for nothing.

32. Treatise on Christian Liberty

MARTIN LUTHER

Many people have considered Christian faith an easy thing and not a few have given it a place among the virtues. They do this because they have not experienced it and have never tasted the great strength there is in faith. It is impossible to write well about it or to understand what has been written about it unless one has at one time or another experienced the courage which faith gives a man when trials oppress him. But he who has had even a faint taste of it can never write, speak, meditate, or hear enough concerning it. It is a living "spring of water welling up to eternal life," as Christ calls it in John 4[:14].

*   *   *

To make the way smoother for the unlearned — for only them do I serve — I shall set down the following two propositions concerning the freedom and the bondage of the spirit:

A Christian is a perfectly free lord of all, subject to none.

A Christian is a perfectly dutiful servant of all, subject to all.

These two theses seem to contradict each other. If, however, they should be found to fit together

Martin Luther (1483–1546) was a professor of theology at Wittenberg University and a reforming activist in Germany. His work includes *An Appeal to the Nobility of the German Nation, On the Babylonian Captivity of the Church, Liberty of the Christian Man;* and numerous studies of Christian Scriptures.

From Martin Luther, *Three Treatises,* in *The American Edition of Luther's Works* (Philadelphia: Muhlenberg Press, 1943).

they would serve our purpose beautifully. Both are Paul's own statements, who says in 1 Cor. 9[:19], "For though I am free from all men, I have made myself a slave to all," and in Rom. 13[:8], "Owe no one anything, except to love one another." Love by its very nature is ready to serve and be subject to him who is loved. So Christ, although he was Lord of all, was "born of woman, born under the law" [Gal. 4:4], and therefore was at the same time a free man and a servant, "in the form of God" and "of a servant" [Phil. 2:6-7].

Let us start, however, with something more remote from our subject, but more obvious. Man has a twofold nature, a spiritual and a bodily one. According to the spiritual nature, which men refer to as the soul, he is called a spiritual, inner, or new man. According to the bodily nature, which men refer to as flesh, he is called a carnal, outward, or old man, of whom the apostle writes in 2 Cor. 4[:16], "Though our outer nature is wasting away, our inner nature is being renewed every day." Because of this diversity of nature the Scriptures assert contradictory things concerning the same man, since these two men in the same man contradict each other, "for the desires of the flesh are against the Spirit, and the desires of the Spirit are against the flesh," according to Gal. 5[:17].

First, let us consider the inner man to see how a righteous, free, and pious Christian, that is, a spiritual, new, and inner man, becomes what he is. It is evident that no external thing has any influence in producing Christian righteousness or freedom, or in producing unrighteousness or servitude. A simple argument will furnish the proof of this statement. What can it profit the soul if the body is well, free, and active, and eats, drinks, and does as it pleases? For in these respects even the most godless slaves of vice may prosper. On the other hand, how will poor health or imprisonment or hunger or thirst or any other external misfortune harm the soul? Even the most godly men, and those who are free because of clear consciences, are afflicted with these things. None of these things touch either the freedom or the servitude of the soul. It does not help the soul if the body is adorned with the sacred robes of priests or dwells in sacred places or is occupied with sacred duties or prays, fasts, abstains from certain kinds of food, or does any work that can be done by the body and in the body. The righteousness

and the freedom of the soul require something far different, since the things which have been mentioned could be done by any wicked person. Such works produce nothing but hypocrites. On the other hand, it will not harm the soul if the body is clothed in secular dress, dwells in unconsecrated places, eats and drinks as others do, does not pray aloud, and neglects to do all the above-mentioned things which hypocrites can do.

Furthermore, to put aside all kinds of works, even contemplation, meditation, and all that the soul can do, does not help. One thing, and only one thing, is necessary for Christian life, righteousness, and freedom. That one thing is the most holy word of God, the gospel of Christ, as says, John 11[:25], "I am the resurrection and the life; he who believes in me, though he die, yet shall he live"; and John 8[:36], "So if the Son makes you free, you will be free indeed"; and Matt. 4[:4], "Man shall not live by bread alone, but by every word that proceeds from the mouth of God." Let us then consider it certain and firmly established that the soul can do without anything except the word of God and that where the word of God is missing there is no help at all for the soul. If it has the word of God it is rich and lacks nothing, since it is the word of life, truth, light, peace, righteousness, salvation, joy, liberty, wisdom, power, grace, glory, and of every incalculable blessing. This is why the prophet in the entire Psalm [119] and in many other places yearns and sighs for the word of God and uses so many names to describe it.

On the other hand, there is no more terrible disaster with which the wrath of God can afflict men than a famine of the hearing of his word, as he says in Amos [8:11]. Likewise there is no greater mercy than when he sends forth his word, as we read in Psalm 107[:20]: "He sent forth his word, and healed them, and delivered them from destruction." Nor was Christ sent into the world for any other ministry except that of the word. Moreover, the entire spiritual estate — all the apostles, bishops, and priests — has been called and instituted only for the ministry of the word.

You may ask, "What then is the Word of God, and how shall it be used, since there are so many words of God?" I answer: The apostle explains this in Romans 1. The word is the gospel of God concerning his Son, who was made flesh, suffered, rose from the dead, and was glorified through the

Spirit who sanctifies. To preach Christ means to feed the soul, mark it righteous, set it free, and save it, provided it believes the preaching. Faith alone is the saving and efficacious use of the word of God, according to Rom. 10[:9]: "If you confess with your lips that Jesus is Lord and believe in your heart that God raised him from the dead, you will be saved." Furthermore, "Christ is the end of the law, that every one who has faith may be justified" [Rom. 10:4]. Again, in Rom. 1[:17], "He who through faith is righteous shall live." The word of God cannot be received and cherished by any works whatever but only by faith. Therefore it is clear that, as the soul needs only the word of God for its life and righteousness, so it is justified by faith alone and not any works; for if it could be justified by anything else, it would not need the word, and consequently it would not need faith.

This faith cannot exist in connection with works — that is to say, if you at the same time claim to be justified by works, whatever their character — for that would be the same as "limping with two different opinions" [1 Kings 18:21], as worshiping Baal and kissing one's own hand [Job 31:27-28], which, as Job says, is a very great iniquity. Therefore the moment you begin to have faith you learn that all things in you are altogether blameworthy, sinful, and damnable, as the apostle says in Rom. 3[:23], "Since all have sinned and fall short of the glory of God," and, "None is righteous, no, not one; . . . all have turned aside, together they have gone wrong" (Rom. 3:10-12). When you have learned this you will know that you need Christ, who suffered and rose again for you so that, if you believe in him, you may through this faith become a new man in so far as your sins are forgiven and you are justified by the merits of another, namely, of Christ alone.

Since, therefore, this faith can rule only in the inner man, as Rom. 10[:10] says, "For man believes with his heart and so is justified," and since faith alone justifies, it is clear that the inner man cannot be justified, freed, or saved by any outer work or action at all, and that these works, whatever their character, have nothing to do with this inner man. On the other hand, only ungodliness and unbelief of heart, and no outer work, make him guilty and a damnable servant of sin. Wherefore it ought to be the first concern of every Christian to lay aside all confidence in works and

increasingly to strengthen faith alone and through faith to grow in the knowledge, not of works, but of Christ Jesus, who suffered and rose for him, as Peter teaches in the last chapter of his first Epistle (1 Pet. 5:10). No other work makes a Christian. Thus when the Jews asked Christ, as related in John 6[:28], what they must do "to be doing the work of God," he brushed aside the multitude of works which he saw they did in great profusion and suggested one work, saying, "This is the work of God, that you believe in him whom he has sent" [John 6:29]; "for on him has God the Father set his seal" [John 6:27].

Therefore true faith in Christ is a treasure beyond comparison which brings with it complete salvation and saves man from every evil, as Christ says in the last chapter of Mark [16:16]: "He who believes and is baptized will be saved; but he who does not believe will be condemned." Isaiah contemplated this treasure and foretold it in chapter 10: "The Lord will make a small and consuming word upon the land, and it will overflow with righteousness" [Cf. Isa. 10:22]. This is as though he said, "Faith, which is a small and perfect fulfillment of the law, will fill believers with so great a righteousness that they will need nothing more to become righteous." So Paul says, Rom. 10[:10], "For man believes with his heart and so is justified."

Should you ask how it happens that faith alone justifies and offers us such a treasure of great benefits without works in view of the fact that so many works, ceremonies, and laws are prescribed in the Scriptures, I answer: First of all, remember what has been said, namely, that faith alone, without works, justifies, frees, and saves; we shall make this clearer later on. Here we must point out that the entire Scripture of God is divided into two parts: commandments and promises. Although the commandments teach things that are good, the things taught are not done as soon as they are taught, for the commandments show us what we ought to do but do not give us the power to do it. They are intended to teach man to know himself, that through them he may recognize his inability to do good and may despair of his own ability. That is why they are called the Old Testament and constitute the Old Testament. For example, the commandment, "You shall not covet" [Exod. 20:17], is a command which proves us all to be sinners, for no one can avoid coveting no matter how much he may struggle against it. Therefore, in order not to covet and to fulfill the commandment, a man is compelled to despair of himself, to seek the help which he does not find in himself elsewhere and from someone else, as stated in Hosea [13:9]: "Destruction is your own, O Israel: your help is only in me." As we fare with respect to one commandment, so we fare with all, for it is equally impossible for us to keep any one of them.

Now when a man has learned through the commandments to recognize his helplessness and is distressed about how he might satisfy the law — since the law must be fulfilled so that not a jot or tittle shall be lost, otherwise man will be condemned without hope — then, being truly humbled and reduced to nothing in his own eyes, he finds in himself nothing whereby he may be justified and saved. Here the second part of Scripture comes to our aid, namely, the promises of God which declare the glory of God, saying, "If you wish to fulfill the law and not covet, as the law demands, come, believe in Christ in whom grace, righteousness, peace, liberty, and all things are promised you. If you believe, you shall have all things; if you do not believe, you shall lack all things." That which is impossible for you to accomplish by trying to fulfill all the works of the law — many and useless as they all are — you will accomplish quickly and easily through faith. God our Father has made all things depend on faith so that whoever has faith will have everything, and whoever does not have faith will have nothing. "For God has consigned all men to disobedience, that he may have mercy upon all," as it is stated in Rom. 11[:32]. Thus the promises of God give what the commandments of God demand and fulfill what the law prescribes so that all things may be God's alone, both the commandments and the fulfilling of the commandments. He alone commands, he alone fulfills. Therefore the promises belong to the New Testament. Indeed, they are the New Testament.

*   *   *

From what has been said it is easy to see from what source faith derives such great power and why a good work or all good works together cannot equal it. No good work can rely upon the word of God or live in the soul, faith alone and the word of God rule in the soul. Just as the heated iron glows like fire because of the union of fire with it, so the word imparts its qualities to the soul.

It is clear, then, that a Christian has all that he needs in faith and needs no work to justify him; and if he has no need of works, he has no need of the law; and if he has no need of the law, surely he is free from the law. It is true that "the law is not laid down for the just" [1 Tim. 1:9]. This is that Christian liberty, our faith, which does not induce us to live in idleness or wickedness but makes the law and works unnecessary for any man's righteousness and salvation.

*   *   *

From this you once more see that much is ascribed to faith, namely, that it alone can fulfill the law and justify without works. You see that the first commandment, which says, "You shall worship one God," is fulfilled by faith alone. Though you were nothing but good works from the soles of your feet to the crown of your head, you would still not be righteous or worship God or fulfill the first commandment, since God cannot be worshiped unless you ascribe to him the glory of truthfulness and all goodness which is due him. This cannot be done by works but only by the faith of the heart. Not by the doing of works but by believing do we glorify God and acknowledge that he is truthful. Therefore faith alone is the righteousness of a Christian and the fulfilling of all the commandments, for he who fulfills the first commandment has no difficulty in fulfilling all the rest.

But works, being inanimate things, cannot glorify God, although they can, if faith is present, be done to the glory of God. Here, however, we are not inquiring what works and what kind of works are done, but who it is that does them, who glorifies God and brings forth the works. This is done by faith which dwells in the heart, and is the source and substance of all our righteousness. Therefore it is a blind and dangerous doctrine which teaches that the commandments must be fulfilled by works. The commandments must be fulfilled before any works can be done, and the works proceed from the fulfillment of the commandments [Rom 13:10], as we shall hear.

*   *   *

From this anyone can clearly see how a Christian is free from all things and over all things so that he needs no works to make him righteous and save him, since faith alone abundantly confers all these things. Should he grow so foolish, however, as to presume to become righteous, free, saved, and a Christian by means of some good work, he would instantly lose faith and all its benefits, a foolishness aptly illustrated in the fable of the dog who runs along a stream with a piece of meat in his mouth and, deceived by the reflection of the meat in the water, opens his mouth to snap at it and so loses both the meat and the reflection.

*　*　*

To return to our purpose, I believe that it has now become clear that it is not enough or in any sense Christian to preach the works, life, and words of Christ as historical facts, as if the knowledge of these would suffice for the conduct of life; yet this is the fashion among those who must be regarded as our best preachers. Far less is it sufficient or Christian to say nothing at all about Christ and to teach instead the laws of men and the decrees of the fathers. Now there are not a few who preach Christ and read about him that they may move men's affections to sympathy with Christ, to anger against the Jews, and such childish and effeminate nonsense. Rather ought Christ to be preached to the end that faith in him may be established that he may not only be Christ, but be Christ for you and me, and that what is said of him and is denoted in his name may be effectual in us. Such faith is produced and preserved in us by preaching why Christ came, what he brought and bestowed, what benefit it is to us to accept him. This is done when that Christian liberty which he bestows is rightly taught and we are told in what way we Christians are all kings and priests and therefore lords of all and may firmly believe that whatever we have done is pleasing and acceptable in the sight of God, as I have already said.

*　*　*

Now let us turn to the second part, the outer man. Here we shall answer all those who, offended by the word "faith" and by all that has been said, now ask, "If faith does all things and is alone sufficient unto righteousness, why then are good works commanded? We will take our ease and do no works and be content with faith." I answer: Not so, you wicked men, not so. That would indeed be proper if we were wholly inner and perfectly spiritual men. But such we shall be only at the last day, the day of the resurrection of the dead. As long as we live in the flesh we only begin to make some progress in that which shall be perfected in the future life. For this reason the apostle in Rom. 8[:23] calls all that we attain in this life "the first fruits of the Spirit" because we shall indeed receive the greater portion, even the fullness of the Spirit, in the future. This is the place to assert that which was said above, namely, that a Christian is the servant of all and made subject to all. Insofar as he is free he does no works, but insofar as he is a servant he does all kinds of works. How this is possible we shall see.

Although, as I have said, a man is abundantly and sufficiently justified by faith inwardly, in his spirit, and so has all that he needs, except insofar as this faith and these riches must grow from day to day even to the future life; yet he remains in this mortal life on earth. In this life he must control his own body and have dealings with men. Here the works begin; here a man cannot enjoy leisure; here he must indeed take care to discipline his body by fastings, watchings, labors, and other reasonable discipline and to subject it to the Spirit so that it will obey and conform to the inner man and faith and not revolt against faith and hinder the inner man, as it is the nature of the body to do if it is not held in check. The inner man, who by faith is created in the image of God, is both joyful and happy because of Christ in whom so many benefits are conferred upon him; and therefore it is his one occupation to serve God joyfully and without thought of gain, in love that is not constrained.

While he is doing this, behold, he meets a contrary will in his own flesh which strives to serve the world and seeks its own advantage. This the spirit of faith cannot tolerate, but with joyful zeal it attempts to put the body under control and hold it in check, as Paul says in Rom. 7[:22-23], "For I delight in the law of God, in my inmost self, but I see in my members another law at war with the law of my mind and making me captive to the law of sin," and in another place, "But I pommel my body and subdue it, lest after preaching to others I myself should be disqualified" [1 Cor. 9:27], and in Galatians [5:24], "And those who belong to Christ Jesus have crucified the flesh with its passions and desires."

In doing these works, however, we must not think that a man is justified before God by them, for faith, which alone is righteousness before God, cannot endure that erroneous opinion. We must, however, realize that these works reduce the body to subjection and purify it of its evil lusts, and our whole purpose is to be directed only toward the driving out of lusts. Since by faith the soul is cleansed and made to love God, it desires that all things, and especially its own body, shall be purified so that all things may join with it in loving and praising God. Hence a man cannot be idle, for the need of his body drives him and he is compelled to do many good works to reduce it to subjection. Nevertheless the works themselves do not justify him before God, but he does the works out of spontaneous love in obedience to God and considers nothing except the approval of God, whom he would most scrupulously obey in all things.

*   *   *

The following statements are therefore true: "Good works do not make a good man, but a good man does good works; evil works do not make a wicked man, but a wicked man does evil works." Consequently it is always necessary that the substance or person himself be good before there can be any good works, and that good works follow and proceed from the good person as Christ also says, "A good tree cannot bear evil fruit, nor can a bad tree bear good fruit" [Matt. 7:18]. It is clear that the fruits do not bear the tree and that the tree does not grow on the fruits, also that, on the contrary, the trees bear the fruits and the fruits grow on the trees. As it is necessary, therefore, that the trees exist before their fruits and the fruits do not make trees either good or bad, but rather as the trees are, so are the fruits they bear; so a man must first be good or wicked before he does a good or wicked work, and his works do not make him good or wicked, but he himself makes his works either good or wicked.

Illustrations of the same truth can be seen in all trades. A good or a bad house does not make a good or a bad builder; but a good or a bad builder makes a good or a bad house. And in general, the work never makes the workman like itself, but the workman makes the work like himself. So it is with the works of man. As the man is,

whether believer or unbeliever, so also is his work — good if it was done in faith, wicked if it was done in unbelief. But the converse is not true, that the work makes the man either a believer or unbeliever. As works do not make a man a believer, so also they do not make him righteous. But as faith makes a man a believer and righteous, so faith does good works. Since, then, works justify no one, and a man must be righteous before he does a good work, it is very evident that it is faith alone which, because of the pure mercy of God through Christ and in his word, worthily and sufficiently justifies and saves the person. A Christian has no need of any work or law in order to be saved since through faith he is free from every law and does everything out of pure liberty and freely. He seeks neither benefit nor salvation since he already abounds in all things and is saved through the grace of God because in his faith he now seeks only to please God.

Furthermore, no good work helps justify or save an unbeliever. On the other hand, no evil work makes him wicked or damns him; but the unbelief which makes the person and the tree evil does the evil and damnable works. Hence when a man is good or evil, this is effected not by the works, but by faith or unbelief, as the wise man says, "This is the beginning of sin, that a man falls away from God" [Cf. Sirach 10:14-15], which happens when he does not believe. And Paul says in Heb. 11[:6], "For whoever would draw near to God must believe. . . ." And Christ says the same: "Either make the tree good, and its fruit good; or make the tree bad, and its fruit bad" [Matt. 12:33], as if he would say, "Let him who wishes to have good fruit begin by planting a good tree." So let him who wishes to do good works begin not with the doing of works, but with believing, which makes the person good, for nothing makes a man good except faith, or evil except unbelief.

*   *   *

From this it is easy to know how far good works are to be rejected or not, and by what standard all the teaching of men concerning works are to be interpreted. If works are sought after as a means to righteousness, are burdened with this perverse leviathan, and are done under the false impression that through them one is justified, they are made necessary and freedom and faith are destroyed;

and this addition to them makes them no longer good but truly damnable works. They are not free, and they blaspheme the grace of God, since to justify and to save by faith belongs to the grace of God alone. What the works have no power to do they nevertheless — by a godless presumption through this folly of ours — pretend to do and thus violently force themselves into the office and glory of grace. We do not, therefore, reject good works; on the contrary, we cherish and teach them as much as possible. We do not condemn them for their own sake but on account of this godless addition to them and the perverse idea that righteousness is to be sought through them; for that makes them appear good outwardly, when in truth they are not good. They deceive men and lead them to deceive one another like ravening wolves in sheep's clothing [Matt. 7:15].

*   *   *

Let this suffice concerning works in general and at the same time concerning the works which a Christian does for himself. Lastly, we shall also speak of the things which he does toward his neighbor. A man does not live for himself alone in this mortal body to work for it alone, but he lives also for all men on earth; rather, he lives only for others and not for himself. To this end he brings his body into subjection that he may the more sincerely and freely serve others, as Paul says in Rom. 14[:7-8], "None of us lives to himself, and none of us dies to himself. If we live, we live to the Lord, and if we die, we die to the Lord." He cannot ever in this life be idle and without works toward his neighbors, for he will necessarily speak, deal with, and exchange views with men, as Christ also, being made in the likeness of men [Phil. 2:7], was found in the form as a man and conversed with men, as Baruch 3[:37] says.

Man, however, needs none of these things for his righteousness and salvation. Therefore he should be guided in his works by this thought and contemplate this one thing alone, that he may serve and benefit others in all that he does, considering nothing except the need and the advantage of his neighbor. Accordingly the apostle commands us to work with our hands so that we may give to the needy, although he might have said that we should work to support ourselves. He says, however, "that he may be able to give to those in

need" [Eph. 4:28]. This is what makes caring for the body a Christian work, that through its health and comfort we may be able to work, to acquire, and lay by funds with which to aid those who are in need, that in this way the strong member may serve the weaker, and we may be sons of God, each caring for and working for the other, bearing one another's burdens and so fulfilling the law of Christ [Gal. 6:2]. This is a truly Christian life. Here faith is truly active through love [Gal. 5:6], that is, finds expression in works of the freest service, cheerfully and lovingly done, with which a man willingly serves another without hope of reward; and for himself he is satisfied with the fullness and wealth of his faith.

Accordingly Paul, after teaching the Philippians how rich they were made through faith in Christ, in which they obtained all things, thereafter teaches them, saying, "So if there is any encouragement in Christ, any incentive of love, any participation in the Spirit, any affection and sympathy, complete my joy by being of the same mind, having the same love, being in full accord and of one mind. Do nothing from selfishness or conceit, but in humility count others better than yourselves. Let each of you look not only to his own interests, but also to the interests of others" [Phil. 2:1-4]. Here we see clearly that the apostle has prescribed a rule for the life of Christians, namely, that we should devote all our works to the welfare of others, since each has such abundant riches in his faith that all his other works and his whole life are a surplus with which he can by voluntary benevolence serve and do good to his neighbor.

*   *   *

So a Christian, like Christ his head, is filled and made rich by faith and should be content with this form of God which he has obtained by faith; only, as I have said, he should increase this faith until it is made perfect. For this faith is his life, his righteousness, and his salvation: it saves him and makes him acceptable, and bestows upon him all things that are Christ's, as has been said above, and as Paul asserts in Gal. 2[:20] when he says, "And the life I now live in the flesh I live by faith in the Son of God." Although the Christian is thus free from all works, he ought in this liberty to empty himself, take upon himself the form of a servant, be made in the likeness of men, be found in human form, and to serve, help, and in every way deal with his neighbor as he sees that God through Christ has dealt and still deals with him. This he should do freely, having regard for nothing but divine approval.

He ought to think: "Although I am an unworthy and condemned man, my God has given me in Christ all the riches of righteousness and salvation without any merit on my part, out of pure, free mercy, so that from now on I need nothing except faith which believes that this is true. Why should I not therefore freely, joyfully, with all my heart and with an eager will do all things which I know are pleasing and acceptable to such a Father who has overwhelmed me with his inestimable riches? I will therefore give myself as a Christ to my neighbor, just as Christ offered himself to me; I will do nothing in this life except what I see is necessary, profitable, and salutary to my neighbor, since through faith I have an abundance of all good things in Christ."

Behold, from faith thus flow forth love and joy in the Lord, and from love a joyful, willing, and free mind that serves one's neighbor willingly and takes no account of gratitude or ingratitude, of praise or blame, of gain or loss. For a man does not serve that he may put men under obligations. He does not distinguish between friends and enemies or anticipate their thankfulness or unthankfulness, but he most freely and most willingly spends himself and all that he has, whether he wastes all on the thankless or whether he gains a reward. As his Father does, distributing all things to all men richly and freely, making "his sun rise on the evil and on the good" [Matt. 5:45], so also the son does all things and suffers all things with that freely bestowing joy which is his delight when through Christ he sees it in God, the dispenser of such great benefits.

Therefore, if we recognize the great and precious things which are given us, as Paul says [Rom. 5:5], our hearts will be filled by the Holy Spirit with the love which makes us free, joyful, almighty workers and conquerors over all tribulations, servants of our neighbors, and yet lords of all. For those who do not recognize the gifts bestowed upon them through Christ, however, Christ has been born in vain; they go their way with their works and shall never come to taste or feel those things. Just as our neighbor is in need and and lacks that in which we abound, so we were in need before God and lacked his mercy. Hence, as our heavenly Father has in Christ freely come to our aid, we also ought freely to help our neighbor through our body and its works, and each one should become as it were a Christ to the other that we may be Christs to one another and Christ may be the same in all, that is, that we may be truly Christians.

33. The Meaning of Responsibility

H. RICHARD NIEBUHR

The word *responsibility* and cognate terms are widely used in our time when men speak about that phase of human existence to which they customarily referred in the past with the aid of such signs as *moral* and *good*. The *responsible citizen,* the *responsible society,* the *responsibilities of our office,* and similar phrases are often on our lips. This meaning of *responsibility* is of relatively recent origin. There was a time when *responsible* meant *correspondent* as in the statement "The mouth large but not responsible to so large a body." But its use in sentences such as "The great God has treated us as responsible beings," seems to have become common only in the nineteenth and twentieth centuries.[1] It is a relatively late-born child, therefore, in the family of words in which duty, law, virtue, goodness, and morality are its much older siblings. This history may mean nothing more, of course, than that men have found a new sign for a well-known phenomenon and an old idea; many writers, indeed, so use it, as their definitions plainly show. But it is also possible that the word gives us a new symbol with which to grasp and understand not a really well-known phenomenon or an old idea but the actuality of

1. *Oxford English Dictionary.*

H. Richard Niebuhr (1894–1962) was professor of Christian ethics at Yale University Divinity School. Among his works are *Christ and Culture, The Meaning of Revelation, The Kingdom of God in America,* and *The Responsible Self.*

From H. Richard Niebuhr, *The Responsible Self* (New York: Harper & Row, 1963).

that human existence of which other aspects came into view when we employed the older symbols of *the mores,* or of *the ethos,* or of *what is due,* or of *being virtuous,* that is, being manly. I believe that this is the case; the symbol of responsibility contains, as it were, hidden references, allusions, and similes which are in the depths of our mind as we grope for understanding of ourselves and toward definition of ourselves in action. But we are not concerned with the word nor with our subjective intentions as we use it. Our task rather is to try with the aid of this symbol to further the double purpose of ethics: to obey the ancient and perennial commandment, *"Gnothi seauton,"* "Know thyself"; and to seek guidance for our activity as we decide, choose, commit ourselves, and otherwise bear the burden of our necessary human freedom.

In the history of man's long quest after knowledge of himself as agent — that is, as a being in charge of his conduct — he has used fruitfully several other symbols and concepts in apprehending the form of his practical life and in giving shape to it in action. The most common symbol has been that of the maker, the fashioner. What is man like in all his actions? The suggestion readily comes to him that he is like an artificer who constructs things according to an idea and for the sake of an end. Can we not apply to the active life as a whole the image we take from our technical working in which we construct wheels and arrows, clothes and houses and ships and books and societies? So not only common-sense thinking about ideals, and ends and means, but much sophisticated philosophy has construed human existence. Thus Aristotle begins his *Ethics* — the most influential book in the West in this field — with the statement: "Every art and every inquiry and similarly every action and pursuit, is thought to aim at some good."[2] Beyond all the arts of bridle-making and horse-riding and military strategy there must be then, he says, an art of arts, a master art, whose end is the actualization of the good man and the good society, whose material is human life itself. For the Greek philosopher and many who knowingly or unknowingly follow him, man is the

2. *The Works of Aristotle,* ed. W. D. Ross (Oxford: Clarendon Press, 1925), Vol. IX, *Ethica Nicomachea,* Bk. I, 1.

being who makes himself — though he does not do so by himself — for the sake of a desired end. Two things in particular we say about ourselves: we act toward an end or are purposive; and, we act upon ourselves, we fashion ourselves, we give ourselves a form. Aristotle's great Christian disciple saw eye to eye with him. "Of the actions done by man," wrote Thomas Aquinas, "those alone are called properly *human,* which are proper to man as man. Now man differs from the irrational creatures in this, that he is master of his own acts. . . . But man is master of his own acts by reason and will: hence free will is said to be *a function of will and reason.* Those actions, therefore, are properly called *human,* which proceed from a deliberate will. . . . Now it is clear that all the actions that proceed from any power are caused by that power acting in reference to its object. But the object of the will is some end in the shape of good. Therefore all human actions must be for an end."[3]

The image of man-the-maker who, acting for an end, gives shape to things is, of course, refined and criticized in the course of its long use, by idealists and utilitarians, hedonists and self-realizationists. But it remains a dominant image. And it has a wide range of applicability in life. Purposiveness and humanity do seem to go together. Everyone, even a determinist undertaking to demonstrate the truth of determinism, knows what it is to act with a purpose or a desired future state of affairs in mind, and knows also how important it is to inquire into the fitness of the steps taken moment by moment in his movement toward the desired goal. In most affairs of life we employ this practical ends-and-means reasoning and ask about our purposes. Education has its goals and so has religion; science is purposive though it defines its purpose only as knowledge of fact or as truth. Justice uses the idea when it asks about the culpability of the accused by raising the further question concerning his intentions and his ability to foresee consequences. Legislation thinks teleologically, that is, with respect to the telos — the goal — when it inquires into the desires of individual citizens and the various social groups, taking for granted that they all pursue some ends,

3. *Summa Theologica,* Prima Secundae, Q.I., Resp. Translation above by J. Rickaby, S.J., *Aquinas Ethicus* (London: Burns and Oates, Ltd., 1896), vol. I.

whether these be power or prosperity or peace or pleasure; and when it raises the further question how manifold individual purposes can be organized into one common social purpose. Moral theories and moral exhortations to a large extent presuppose the future-directed, purposive character of human action and differ for the most part only — though seriously enough — in the ends they recommend or accept as given with human nature itself. The will to pleasure, the will to live, the will to power, the will to self-fulfillment, the will to love and be loved, the will to death and many another hormetic drive may be posited as most natural to man, whether as most compulsive or as setting before him the most attractive future state of affairs. When we are dealing with this human nature of ours, in ourselves and in others, as administrators of our private realms of body and mind or as directors of social enterprises — from families seeking happiness to international societies seeking peace — we cannot fail to ask: "At what long- or short-range state of affairs are we aiming, and what are the immediate steps that must be taken toward the attainment of the possible goal?" So the teleologist, in that double process of self-definition we call morals, interprets human life and seeks to direct it. The symbol of man-the-maker of many things and of himself also throws light not only on many enterprises but also on this strange affair of personal existence itself. The freedom of man appears in this context as the necessity of self-determination by final causes; his practical reason appears as his ability to distinguish between inclusive and exclusive, immediate and ultimate ends and to relate means to ends.

The men who have employed this image of man-the-maker in understanding and in shaping their conduct have, of course, by no means been unanimous in their choice of the ideals to be realized nor in their estimate of the potentialities of the material that is to be given the desired or desirable form. Whether the human end is to be achieved for the sake of delight or for further use toward another end, whether it is to be designed for the delight or the use of the self, or of the immediate society or of a universal community — these remain questions endlessly debated and endlessly submitted to individuals for personal decision. But the debates and decisions are carried on against the background of a common understanding of the nature of our personal existence. We are in all our working on selves — our own selves or our companions — technicians, artisans, craftsmen, artists.

Among many men and at many times another grand image of the general character of our life as agents prevails. It is the image of man-the-citizen, living under law. Those who conceive themselves and human beings in general with the aid of this great symbol point out the inadequacies and defects, as they see them, of that view of personal life which interprets it as *technē* or as art. In craftsmanship, they say, both the end and the means are relatively under our control. But neither is at our disposal when we deal with ourselves as persons or as communities.

Man-the-maker can reject material which does not fit his purposes. It is not so when the material is ourselves in our individual and in our social nature. Our body, our sensations, our impulses — these have been given us; whether to have them or not have them is not under our control. We are with respect to these things not as the artist is to his material but as the ruler of a city is to its citizens. He must take them for better or for worse. And so it is also with respect to the future. The favors or disfavors of fortune, as well as the "niggardly provisions of a step-motherly nature," put us at the mercy of alien powers so far as the completion of our lives as works of art is concerned. What use would it have been, had Socrates designed for himself that happy life which Aristotle described? This life we live amidst our fellow men and in the presence of nature's forces cannot be built over many generations like a cathedral. Who can plan his end? Who can by taking thought guarantee that his being, his character, his work, will endure even in the memory of those that come after? Neither the material then with which we work nor the future building is under our control when the work is directed toward ourselves. This life of ours is like politics more than it is like art, and politics is the art of the possible. What is possible to us in the situation in which we find ourselves? That we should rule ourselves as being ruled, and not much more.

Many moral philosophers and theologians, otherwise disagreeing with each other, agree at least in this, that they understand the reality of our personal existence with the aid of the political image. It is indeed, as in the case of the technical symbol, more than an image for it is derived from our actual living. As a symbol it represents the use of a *special* experience for the interpretation of *all* experience, of a part for the whole. We come to self-awareness if not to self-existence in the midst of *mores,* of commandments and rules, *Thou shalts* and *Thou shalt nots,* of directions and permissions. Whether we begin with primitive man with his sense of *themis,* the law of the community projected outward into the total environment, or with the modern child with father and mother images, with repressions and permissions, this life of ours, we say, must take account of morality, of the rule of the mores, of the ethos, of the laws and the law, of heteronomy and autonomy, of self-directedness and other-directedness, of approvals and disapprovals, of social, legal, and religious sanctions. This is what our total life is like, and hence arise the questions we must answer: "To what law shall I consent, against what law rebel? By what law or system of laws shall I govern myself and others? How shall I administer the domain of which I am the ruler or in which I participate in rule?"

As in the case of the symbol of the maker, the symbol of the citizen has a wide range of applicability in common life and has been found useful by many a special theorist. In intellectual action, for instance, man not only directs his thoughts and investigations toward the realization of a system of true knowledge that will be useful to other ends or give delight in itself, but carries on his work of observation, conceptualization, comparison, and relation under laws of logic or of scientific method. It is important for him, if he is a person and not only a reasoning animal, that he govern his inquiries by adherence to such rules or laws. Again, what man does in the political realm is not only or perhaps even primarily to seek the ends of order, peace, prosperity, and welfare but to do all that he does under the rule of justice. If we are to associate the two symbols with each other, as indeed we often do, we must say that justice itself is an end, though when we do this peculiar difficulties arise. The image has applicability to all our existence in society. We come into being under the rules of family, neighborhood, and nation, subject to the regulation of our action by others. Against these rules we can and do rebel, yet find it necessary — morally necessary, that is — to consent to some laws and to give ourselves rules, or to administer our lives in accordance with some discipline.

Again, as in the case of the maker image, those who employ the citizen symbol for the understanding and regulation of self-conduct, have various domains in view. For some the republic that is to be governed is mostly that of the multifarious self, a being which is a multiplicity seeking unity or a unity diversifying itself into many roles. It is a congeries of many hungers and urges, of fears and angers and loves that is contained somehow within one body and one mind, which are two, yet united. The multiplicity of the body is matched by an at least equal variety of mental content. How to achieve that unity of the self, that organization of manifoldness we call personality, is a challenging question for the administrative self. It is not done in fact without external rule and regulation, but also not without internal consent and self-legislation. How this self-government is in fact achieved is one of the problems of much psychology and the concern of moralists. Or the republic in view is a human community of selves in which the manifoldness is that of many persons with many desires and subject to many regulations issuing from each other. The communal life then is considered as both consenting to law and as law-giving. Or again, the community we have in mind may be universal society, and the quest may be after those laws of nature or that will of the universal God which the person is asked to accept not only with consent but actively, as legislating citizen in a universal domain.

The effort so to conceive the self in its agency as legislative, obedient, and administrative has had a long history. Its use has raised many theoretical and practical problems, but it has also been very fruitful. The symbol of man the law-maker and law-abider may be a primordial or only a cultural symbol; but in any case it has been helpful in enabling us to understand large areas of our existence and to find guidance in the making of complex decisions.

In the history of theoretical ethics, but also in practical decisions, the use of these two great symbols for the understanding of our personal existence as self-acting beings has led to many disputes as well as to many efforts at compromise and adjustment. Those who consistently think of man-as-maker subordinate the giving of laws to the work of construction. For them the right is to be defined by reference to the good; rules are utilitarian in character; they are means to ends. All laws must justify themselves by the contribution they make to the attainment of a desired or desirable end. Those, however, who think of man's existence primarily with the aid of the citizen image seek equally to subordinate the good to the right; only right life is good and right life is no future ideal but always a present demand. Federalist schools, as they have been called by C. D. Broad, tend to say that we cannot apprehend our existence with the aid of one image but must employ both. They leave us as a rule with a double theory, of which the two parts remain essentially unharmonized. The conflict of theories is but an extension of the practical one which takes place in the personal and social life as we try to answer the questions: "What shall *I* do?" or "What shall *we* do?" We find ourselves moving there from the debate about the various ideals according to which we might shape our personal and social existence to the debate about what is required or demanded and by whom it is required. Or the movement may be from debate about the law to be obeyed to the question: "What laws can be justified in view of the ideal before us?" Practical debate on the achievement of desegregation, for example, moves between the insistence that the law of the country must be obeyed and the young Negroes' demand that the ideal state of affairs be realized.

What these debates suggest to us is that, helpful as the fundamental images are which we employ in understanding and directing ourselves, they remain images and hypotheses, not truthful copies of reality, and that something of the real lies beyond the borders of the image; something more and something different needs to be thought and done in our quest for the truth about ourselves and in our quest for true existence.

In this situation the rise of the new symbolism of responsibility is important. It represents an alternative or an additional way of conceiving and defining this existence of ours that is the material of our own actions. What is implicit in the idea of responsibility is the image of man-the-answerer, man engaged in dialogue, man acting in response to action upon him. As in the case of maker and of citizen, man-the-answerer offers us a synecdochic analogy. In trying to understand ourselves in our wholeness we use the image of a part of our activity; only now we think of all our actions as having the pattern of what we do when we answer another who addresses us. To be engaged in dialogue, to answer questions addressed to us, to defend ourselves against attacks, to reply to injunctions, to meet challenges — this is common experience. And now we try to think of all our actions as having this character of being responses, answers, to actions upon us. The faculty psychology of the past which saw in the self three or more facient powers, and the associationist psychology which understood the mind to operate under laws of association, have been replaced by a psychology of interaction which has made familiar to us the idea that we act in reaction to stimuli. Biology and sociology as well as psychology have taught us to regard ourselves as beings in the midst of a field of natural and social forces, acted upon and reacting, attracted and repelling. We try also to understand history less by asking about the ideals toward which societies and their leaders directed their efforts or about the laws they were obeying and more by inquiring into the challenges in their natural and social environment to which the societies were responding. It will not do to say that the older images of the maker and the citizen have lost their meaning in these biological, psychological, sociological, and historical analyses, but when we compare a modern psychology, a modern study of society, a modern history, with older examples of similar studies the difference thrusts itself upon one. The pattern of thought now is interactional, however much other great images must continue to be used to describe how we perceive and conceive, form associations, and carry on political, economic, educational, religious, and other enterprises.

The use of this image in the field of ethics is not yet considerable. When the word responsibility is used of the self as agent, as doer, it is usually translated with the aid of the older images as meaning direction toward goals or as ability to be moved by respect for law.[4] Yet the

understanding of ourselves as responsive beings, who in all our actions answer to action upon us in accordance with our interpretation of such action, is a fruitful conception, which brings into view aspects of our self-defining conduct that are obscured when the older images are exclusively employed.

The understanding of ourselves with the aid of this image has been prefigured, as it were, by certain observations made by moralists of an older time. Aristotle may have had something of the sort in mind (something of the idea of what we would call a fitting response) when he described what he meant by the *mean* which constitutes virtue. He said that to feel fear, confidence, appetite, anger, and pity "at the right times, with reference to the right objects, towards the right people, with the right motive and in the right way, is what is intermediate and best. . . ."[5] Stoic ethics is usually interpreted as either primarily teleological or as primarily concerned with law; but it receives much of its peculiar character from the way in which it deals with the ethics of suffering, that is, with the responses which are to be made to the actions upon them that men must endure. The Stoic's main question is: "How may one react to events not with passion — that is, as one who is passive or who is subject to raw emotions called forth by events — but with reason?" And this reason for him is not first of all the law-giving power which rules the emotions, nor yet the purposive movement of the mind seeking to realize ideals. It is rather the interpretative power which understands the rationale in the action to which the self is subject and so enables it to respond rationally and freely rather than under the sway of passion. In Spinoza this idea of response guided by rational interpretation of the events and beings to which the self reacts plays a major role. To be sure, he is an idealist after a fashion, who asks how he may "discover and acquire the faculty of enjoying throughout eternity continual supreme happi-

---

4. Cf. W. Fales, *Wisdom and Responsibility* (Princeton: Princeton University Press, 1946). "There is much evidence that man is . . . determined by final ends which

are not an object of his contemplation although they account for his personality and constitute his will. The pressure which the final ends exert upon man is felt as responsibility" (pp. 4f.). Fales tries to account for the *feeling* of responsibility but never analyzes that feeling itself. Cf. pp. 56-58, 67, 71, 144.

5. Op. cit., Bk. II, 6.

ness."[6] But he quickly notes that this end is not attainable except through that correction of the understanding which will permit men to substitute for the unclear and self-centered, emotion-arousing interpretations of what happens to them, a clear, distinct interpretation of all events as intelligible, rational events in the determined whole. The freedom of man from his passions, and from the tyranny of events over him exercised via the passions, is freedom gained through correct interpretation with the consequent changing of responses by the self to the events that go on within it and happen to it. Other intimations of the idea of response are to be found in naturalistic ethics and Marxism.

Outside the realm of philosophic theory practical life has made this approach to the solution of the problem of our action almost inevitable in two particular situations, in social emergencies and in personal suffering. It has often been remarked that the great decisions which give a society its specific character are functions of emergency situations in which a community has had to meet a challenge. Doubtless ideals, hopes and drives toward a desirable future play their part in such decisions; inherited laws are also important in them. Yet the decision on which the future depends and whence the new law issues is a decision made in response to action upon the society, and this action is guided by interpretation of what is going on. The emergence of modern America out of the Civil War when measures were adopted in response to challenges that the founding fathers had not foreseen; the welfare-state decisions of the New Deal era in reaction to depression and the entrance of the nation into the sphere of international politics in reaction to foreign wars despite all desire for isolation — such events give evidence in the social sphere of the extent to which active, practical self-definition issues from response to challenge rather than from the pursuit of an ideal or from adherence to some ultimate laws. In the case of individuals we are no less aware of the way in which opportunity on the one hand, limiting events on the other, form the matrix in which the self defines itself by the nature of its responses.

6. *Tractatus de intellectus emendatione*, I, 1

Perhaps this becomes especially evident in the case of suffering, a subject to which academic ethical theory, even theological ethics, usually pays little attention. Yet everyone with any experience of life is aware of the extent to which the characters of people he has known have been given their particular forms by the sufferings through which they have passed. But it is not simply what has happened to them that has defined them; their responses to what has happened to them have been of even greater importance, and these responses have been shaped by their interpretations of what they suffered. It may be possible to deal with the ethics of suffering by means of the general hypothesis of life's purposiveness; however when we do so there is much that we must leave out of consideration. For it is part of the meaning of suffering that it is that which cuts athwart our purposive movements. It represents the denial from beyond ourselves of our movement toward pleasure; or it is the frustration of our movement toward self-realization or toward the actualization of our potentialities. Because suffering is the exhibition of the presence in our existence of that which is not under our control, or of the intrusion into our self-legislating existence of an activity operating under another law than ours, it cannot be brought adequately within the spheres of teleological and deontological ethics, the ethics of man-the-maker, or man-the-citizen. Yet it is in the response to suffering that many and perhaps all men, individually and in their groups, define themselves, take on character, develop their ethos. And their responses are functions of their interpretation of what is happening to them as well as of the action upon them. It is unnecessary to multiply illustrations from history and experience of the actuality and relevance of the approach to man's self-conduct that begins with neither purposes nor laws but with responses; that begins with the question, not about the self as it is in itself, but as it is in its response-relations to what is given with it and to it. This question is already implied, for example, in the primordial action of parental guidance: "What is the fitting thing? What is going on in the life of the child?"

In summary of the foregoing argument we may say that purposiveness seeks to answer the question: "What shall I do?" by raising as prior the question: "What is my goal, ideal, or telos?" Deon-

200

THE FORMS OF CHRISTIAN ETHICS

tology tries to answer the moral query by asking, first of all: "What is the law and what is the first law of my life?" Responsibility, however, proceeds in every moment of decision and choice to inquire: "What is going on?" If we use value terms then the differences among the three approaches may be indicated by the terms, the *good*, the *right*, and the *fitting;* for teleology is concerned always with the highest good to which it subordinates the right; consistent deontology is concerned with the right, no matter what may happen to our goods; but for the ethics of responsibility the *fitting* action, the one that fits into a total interaction as response and as anticipation of further response, is alone conducive to the good and alone is right.

The idea of responsibility, if it is to be made useful for the understanding of our self-action, needs to be brought into mind more clearly than has been done by these preliminary references to its uses in past theory and in common experience. Our definition should not only be as clear as we can make it; it should, if possible, be framed without the use of symbols referring to the other great ideas with which men have tried to understand their acts and agency. Only so will it be possible for us to develop a relatively precise instrument for self-understanding and also come to an understanding of the instrument's possibilities and limitations.

The first element in the theory of responsibility is the idea of *response.* All action, we now say, including what we rather indeterminately call moral action, is response to action upon us. We do not, however, call it the action of a self or moral action unless it is response to *interpreted* action upon us. All actions that go on within the sphere of our bodies, from heartbeats to knee jerks, are doubtless also reactions, but they do not fall within the domain of self-actions if they are not accompanied and infused, as it were, with interpretation. Whatever else we may need to say about ourselves in defining ourselves, we shall need, apparently, always to say that we are characterized by awareness and that this awareness is more or less that of an intelligence which identifies, compares, analyzes, and relates events so that they come to us not as brute actions, but as understood and as having meaning. Hence though our eyelids may react to the light with pure reflex, the self responds to it as *light,* as something interpreted,

understood, related. But, more complexly, we interpret the things that force themselves upon us as parts of wholes, as related and as symbolic of larger meanings. And these large patterns of interpretation we employ seem to determine — though in no mechanical way — our responses to action upon us. We cannot understand international events, nor can we act upon each other as nations, without constantly interpreting the meaning of each other's actions. Russia and the United States confront each other not as those who are reflexively reacting to the manufacture of bombs and missiles, the granting of loans, and the making of speeches; but rather as two communities that are interpreting each other's actions and doing so with the aid of ideas about what is in the other's mind. So Americans try to understand Russia's immediate actions as expressions of the Communist or the Russian mind, which is the hidden part of the overt action, and we make our responses to the alien action in accordance with our interpretation of it as symbolic of a larger, an historic whole. The process of interpretation and response can be followed in all the public encounters of groups with each other. When we think of the relations of managers and employees we do not simply ask about the ends each group is consciously pursuing nor about the self-legislated laws they are obeying but about the way they are responding to each other's actions in accordance with their interpretations. Thus actions of labor unions may be understood better when we inquire less about what ends they are seeking and more about what ends they believe the managers to be seeking in all managerial actions. One must not deny the element of purposiveness in labor and in management, yet in their reactions to each other it is the interpretation each side has of the other's goals that may be more important than its definition of its own ends. Similarly in all the interactions of large groups with each other, law and duty seem to have a larger place in the interpretation of the other's conduct to which response is being made than they have in the immediate guidance of the agent's response. We use the idea of law less as a guide to our own conduct than as a way of predicting what the one will do to whom we are reacting or who will react to us. When lawyers try to discover under what law the judge will make his decisions, they are doing something akin to what we do in all our group relations; as Catholics or Protestants, also, we act less with an eye to our own law than to the other's action under his law, as we understand that law.

The point so illustrated by reference to groups applies to us as individuals. We respond as we interpret the meaning of actions upon us. The child's character may be formed less, the psychologists lead us to believe, by the injunctions and commandments of parents than by the child's interpretation of the attitudes such commandments are taken to express. The inferiority and superiority feelings, the aggressions, guilt feelings, and fears with which men encounter each other, and which do not easily yield to the commandment of neighbor-love, are dependent on their interpretations of each other's attitudes and valuations. We live as responsive beings not only in the social but also in the natural world where we interpret the natural events that affect us — heat and cold, storm and fair weather, earthquake and tidal wave, health and sickness, animal and plant — as living-giving and death-dealing. We respond to these events in accordance with our interpretation. Such interpretation, it need scarcely be added, is not simply an affair of our conscious, and rational, mind but also of the deep memories that are buried within us, of feelings and intuitions that are only partly under our immediate control.

This, then, is the second element in responsibility, that it is not only responsive action but responsive in accordance with our *interpretation* of the question to which answer is being given. In our responsibility we attempt to answer the question: "What shall I do?" by raising as the prior question: "What is going on?" or "What is being done to me?" rather than "What is my end?" or "What is my ultimate law?" A third element is *accountability* — a word that is frequently defined by recourse to legal thinking but that has a more definite meaning, when we understand it as referring to part of the response pattern of our self-conduct. Our actions are responsible not only insofar as they are reactions to interpreted actions upon us but also insofar as they are made in anticipation of answers to our answers. An agent's action is like a statement in a dialogue. Such a statement not only seeks to meet, as it were, or to fit into, the previous statement to which it is an answer, but is made in anticipation of reply. It

looks forward as well as backward; it anticipates objections, confirmations, and corrections. It is made as part of a total conversation that leads forward and is to have meaning as a whole. Thus a political action, in this sense, is responsible not only when it is responsive to a prior deed but when it is so made that the agent anticipates the reactions to his action. So considered, no action taken as an atomic unit is responsible. Responsibility lies in the agent who stays with his action, who accepts the consequences in the form of reactions and looks forward in a present deed to the continued interaction. From this point of view we may try to illuminate the question much debated in modern times of the extent to which a person is to be held socially accountable for his acts. In terms of responsibility the question is simply this: "To whom and in what way ought a society through its courts and other agencies respond?" If a homicide has taken place, is the only one to whom there is to be reaction the killer himself, or is there to be response also to the society in which he acted as a reactor? Further, is the reaction to the individual criminal agent to be reaction guided by purely legal thinking, which interprets him solely as an unobedient and perhaps a self-legislating being, or is it to be informed by a larger interpretation of his conduct — one which takes into account other dimensions of his existence as a self? Is the criminal to be dealt with as a self who can anticipate reactions to his actions and so be acted upon as a potentially responsive person, or is the social reaction to him to be confined to his antisocial physical body only and he be regarded as a being that cannot learn to respond with interpretation and anticipation? Is education, psychiatry, or only incarceration the fitting response?

This third element in responsibility — the anticipation of reaction to our action — has brought us within view of what at least for the present seems to be its fourth and final significant component, namely *social solidarity*. Our action is responsible, it appears, when it is response to action upon us in a continuing discourse or interaction among beings forming a continuing society. A series of responses to disconnected actions guided by disconnected interpretations would scarcely be the action of a self but only of a series of states of mind somehow connected with the same body — though the sameness of the body would be apparent only to an external point of view. Personal responsibility implies the continuity of a self with a relatively consistent scheme of interpretations of what it is reacting to. By the same token it implies continuity in the community of agents to which response is being made. There could be no responsible self in an interaction in which the reaction to one's response comes from a source wholly different from that whence the original action issued. This theme we shall need to develop more fully in the second lecture.

The idea or pattern of responsibility, then, may summarily and abstractly be defined as the idea of an agent's action as response to an action upon him in accordance with his interpretation of the latter action and with his expectation of response to his response; and all of this is in a continuing community of agents.

The idea of the moral life as the responsible life in this sense not only has affinities with much modern thinking but it also offers us, I believe, a key — not *the* key — to the understanding of that biblical ethos which represents the historic norm of the Christian life. In the past many efforts have been made to understand the ethos of the Old and New Testaments with the aid of the teleological theory and its image of man-the-maker. Thus the thinking of the lawgivers and prophets, of Jesus Christ and the apostles, has been set before us in the terms of a great idealism. Sometimes the ideal has been described as that of the vision of God, sometimes as perfection, sometimes as eternal happiness, sometimes as a harmony of all beings: or at least of all men, in a kingdom of God. Each of these interpretations has been buttressed by collections of proof texts, and doubtless much that is valid about the Bible and about the Christian life which continues the scriptural ethos has been said within the limits of this interpretation. But much that is in Scriptures has been omitted by the interpreters who followed this method, and much material of another sort — the eschatological, for instance — has had to be rather violently wrenched out of its context or laid aside as irrelevant in order to make the Scriptures speak in this fashion about the self. At all times, moreover, but particularly among the German interpreters in whom the Kantian symbolism holds sway, the deontological interpretation of man the obedient legislator has been used not only as the key to

biblical interpretation but for the definition of the true Christian life. For Barth and Bultmann alike in our times, not to speak of most interpreters of the Old Testament, the ethics of the Bible, and Christian ethics too, is the ethics of obedience. How to interpret Christian freedom and what to make of eschatology within this framework has taxed the ingenuity of the interpreters severely. Bultmann has transformed eschatology into existentialism in order to maintain an ethics of radical obedience; Barth has had to transform the law into a form of the gospel and the commandment into permission in order to reconcile the peculiarity of gospel ethos with deontological thinking. There is doubtless much about law, commandment, and obedience in the Scriptures. But the use of this pattern of interpretation does violence to what we find there.

If now we approach the Scriptures with the idea of responsibility we shall find, I think, that the particular character of this ethics can be more fully if not wholly adequately interpreted. At the critical junctures in the history of Israel and of the early Christian community the decisive question men raised was not "What is the goal?" nor yet "What is the law?" but "What is happening?" and then "What is the fitting response to what is happening?" When an Isaiah counsels his people, he does not remind them of the law they are required to obey nor yet of the goal toward which they are directed but calls to their attention the intentions of God present in hiddenness in the actions of Israel's enemies. The question he and his peers raise in every critical moment is about the interpretation of what is going on, whether what is happening be, immediately considered, a drought or the invasion of a foreign army, or the fall of a great empire. Israel is the people that is to see and understand the action of God in everything that happens and to make a fitting reply. So it is in the New Testament also. The God to whom Jesus points is not the commander who gives laws but the doer of small and of mighty deeds, the creator of sparrows and clother of lilies, the ultimate giver of blindness and of sight, the ruler whose rule is hidden in the manifold activities of plural agencies but is yet in a way visible to those who know how to interpret the signs of the times.

It will not do to say that the analysis of all our moral life in general and of biblical ethics in particular by means of the idea of responsibility offers us an absolutely new way of understanding man's ethical life or of constructing a system of Christian ethics. Actuality always extends beyond the patterns of ideas into which we want to force it. But the approach to our moral existence as selves, and to our existence as Christians in particular, with the aid of this idea makes some aspects of our life as agents intelligible in a way that the teleology and deontology of traditional thought cannot do.

Some special aspects of life in responsibility are to occupy us in the succeeding lectures. In none of them shall I take the deontological stance, saying, "We *ought* to be responsible"; nor yet the ideal, saying, "The *goal* is responsibility"; but I shall simply ask that we consider our life of response to action upon us with the question in mind, "To whom or what am I responsible and in what community of interaction am I myself?"

34. Three Approaches

JOSEPH FLETCHER

There are at bottom only three alternative routes or approaches to follow in making moral decisions. They are: (1) the legalistic; (2) the antinomian, the opposite extreme — i.e., a lawless or unprincipled approach; and (3) the situational. All three have played their part in the history of Western morals, legalism being by far the most common and persistent. Just as legalism triumphed among the Jews after the exile, so, in spite of Jesus' and Paul's revolt against it, it has managed to dominate Christianity constantly from very early days. As we shall be seeing, in many real-life situations legalism demonstrates what Henry Miller, in a shrewd phrase, calls "the immorality of morality."[1]

There is an old joke which serves our purposes. A rich man asked a lovely young woman if she would sleep the night with him. She said, "No." He then asked if she would do it for $100,000? She said, "Yes!" He then asked, "$10,000?" She replied, "Well, yes, I would." His next question was, "How about $500?" Her indignant "What do you think I am?" was met by the answer, "We have already

1. *Stand Still Like the Hummingbird* (New Directions, 1962), pp. 92-96.

Joseph Fletcher (1905–1993) was professor of pastoral theology and Christian ethics at the Episcopal Theological Seminary at Cambridge, Massachusetts, and later a visiting professor of medical ethics at the University of Virginia Medical College. His works include *Morals and Medicine, Situation Ethics: The New Morality,* and *Moral Responsibility: Situation Ethics at Work.*

From Joseph Fletcher, *Situation Ethics* (Philadelphia: Westminster Press, 1966).

established *that*. Now we are haggling over the price." Does any girl who has "relations" (what a funny way to use the word) outside marriage automatically become a prostitute? Is it always, regardless of what she accomplishes for herself or others — is it *always* wrong? Is extramarital sex inherently evil, or can it be a good thing in some situations? Does everybody have his price, and if so, does that mean we are immoral and ethically weak? Let's see if we can find some help in answering these questions.

Approaches to Decision-Making

Legalism

With this approach one enters into every decision-making situation encumbered with a whole apparatus of prefabricated rules and regulations. Not just the spirit but the letter of the law reigns. Its principles, codified in rules, are not merely guidelines or maxims to illuminate the situation; they are *directives* to be followed. Solutions are preset, and you can "look them up" in a book — a Bible or a confessor's manual.

Judaism, Catholicism, Protestantism — all major Western religious traditions have been legalistic. In morals as in doctrine they have kept to a spelled-out, "systematic" orthodoxy. The ancient Jews, especially under the post-exilic Maccabean and Pharisaic leadership, lived by the law or Torah, and its oral tradition (halakah).[2] It was a code of 613 (or 621) precepts, amplified by an increasingly complicated mass of Mishnaic interpretations and applications.

Statutory and code law inevitably piles up, ruling upon ruling, because the complications of life and the claims of mercy and compassion combine — even with code legalists — to accumulate an elaborate system of exceptions and compromise, in the form of rules for breaking the rules! It leads to that tricky and tortuous now-you-see-it, now-you-don't business of interpretation that the rabbis called pilpul — a hairsplitting and logic-chopping study of the letter of the law, pyramiding from codes (e.g., the Covenant and

Holiness) to Pentateuch to Midrash and Mishna to Talmud. It was a tragic death to the prophets' "pathos" (sharing God's loving concern) and "ethos" (living by love as *norm,* not program). With the prophets it had been a question of sensitively seeking "an understanding of *the situation*."[3]

Any web thus woven sooner or later chokes its weavers. Reformed and even Conservative Jews have been driven to disentangle themselves from it. Only Orthodoxy is still in its coils. Something of the same pilpul and formalistic complication may be seen in Christian history. With Catholics it has taken the form of a fairly ingenious moral theology that, as its twists and involutions have increased, resorts more and more to a casuistry that appears (as, to its credit, it does) to evade the very "laws" of right and wrong laid down in its textbooks and manuals. Love, even with the most stiff-necked of system builders, continues to plead mercy's cause and to win at least partial release from law's cold abstractions. Casuistry is the homage paid by legalism to the love of persons, and to realism about life's relativities.

Protestantism has rarely constructed such intricate codes and systems of law, but what it has gained by its simplicity it has lost through its rigidity, its puritanical insistence on moral rules.[4] In fact, the very lack of a casuistry and its complexity, once people are committed to *even the bare principle* of legalistic morality or law ethics, is itself evidence of their blindness to the factors of doubt and perplexity. They have lost touch with the headaches and heartbreaks of life.

What can be worse, no casuistry at all may reveal a punishing and sadistic use of law to hurt people instead of helping them. How else explain burning at the stake in the Middle Ages for homosexuals (death, in the Old Testament)? Even today imprisonment up to sixty years is the penalty in one state for those who were actually consenting adults, without seduction or public disorder! This is really unavoidable whenever law instead of love is put first. The "puritan" type is a

---

2. The prophetic J tradition gave way to the E-D tradition, with its precepts and laws.

3. Abraham J. Heschel, *The Prophets* (Harper & Row, 1962), pp. 225, 307-315.

4. There are, however, atypical works such as Richard Baxter, *Christian Directory* (1673), and William Ames (Amesius), *De conscientia, eius jure et Casibus* (1632).

well-known example of it. But even if the legalist is truly sorry that the law requires unloving or disastrous decisions, he still cries, *"Fiat justitia, ruat caelum!"* (Do the "right" even if the sky falls down). He is the man Mark Twain called "a good man in the worst sense of the word."

The Christian situation ethicist agrees with Bertrand Russell and his implied judgment, "To this day Christians think an adulterer more wicked than a politician who takes bribes, although the latter probably does a thousand times as much harm."[5] And he thoroughly rejects Cardinal Newman's view: "The Church holds that it were better for sun and moon to drop from heaven, for the earth to fail, and for all the many millions who are upon it to die of starvation in extremest agony . . . than that one soul, I will not say should be lost, but should commit one single venial sin."[6]

A Mrs. X was convicted (later cleared in appellate court) of impairing the morals of her minor daughter. She had tried to teach the child chastity but at thirteen the girl bore the first of three unwanted, neglected babies. Her mother then had said, "If you persist in acting this way, at least be sure the boy wears something!" On this evidence she was convicted and sentenced. The combined forces of "secular" law and legalistic puritanism had tried to prevent loving help to the girl, her bastard victims, and the social agencies trying to help her. Situation ethics would have praised that woman; it would not have pilloried her.

* * *

Legalism in the Christian tradition has taken two forms. In the Catholic line it has been a matter of legalistic *reason,* based on nature or natural law. These moralists have tended to adumbrate their ethical rules by applying human reason to the facts of nature, both human and subhuman, and to the lessons of historical experience. By this procedure they claim to have adduced universally agreed and therefore valid "natural" moral laws. Protestant moralists have followed the same adductive and deductive tactics. They have taken Scripture and

done with it what the Catholics do with nature. Their scriptural moral law is, they argue, based on the words and sayings of the law and the prophets, the evangelists and the apostles of the Bible. It is a matter of legalistic *revelation.* One is rationalistic, the other biblicistic; one natural, the other scriptural. But both are legalistic.

Even though Catholic moralists deal also with "revealed law" (e.g., "the divine positive law of the Ten Commandments") and Protestants have tried to use reason in interpreting the sayings of the Bible (hermeneutics), still both by and large have been committed to the doctrines of law ethics.

Antinomianism

Over against legalism, as a sort of polar opposite, we can put antinomianism. This is the approach with which one enters into the decision-making situation armed with no principles or maxims whatsoever, to say nothing of *rules.* In every "existential moment" or "unique" situation, it declares, one must rely upon the situation of itself, *there and then,* to provide its ethical solution.

The term "antinomianism" (literally, "against law") was used first by Luther to describe Johannes Agricola's views. The ethical concept has cropped up here and there, as among some Anabaptists, some sects of English Puritanism, and some of Wesley's followers. The concept is certainly at issue in 1 Corinthians (e.g., ch. 6:12-20). Paul had to struggle with two primitive forms of it among the Hellenistic Jew-Christians whom he visited. They took his attacks on law morality too naively and too literally.

One form was libertinism — the belief that by grace, by the new life in Christ and salvation by faith, law or rules no longer applied to Christians. Their ultimate happy fate was now assured, and it mattered no more *what* they did. (Whoring, incest, drunkenness, and the like are what they did, therefore! This explains the warning in 1 Peter 2:16, "Live as free men, yet without using your freedom as a pretext for evil, but live as servants of God." This license led by inevitable reaction to an increase of legalism, especially in sex ethics, under which Christians still suffer today.) The other form, less pretentious and more enduring, was a Gnostic claim to special knowledge, so that neither principles nor rules were needed any

5. *Why I Am Not a Christian* (Simon and Schuster, Inc., 1957), p. 33.

6. J. H. Newman, *Certain Difficulties Felt by Anglicans in Catholic Teaching* (Longmans, Green & Co., Inc., 1918), p. 190.

longer even as guidelines and direction pointers. They would just *know* what was right when they needed to know. They had, they claimed, a super-conscience. It is this second "gnostic" form of the approach which is under examination here.

While legalists are preoccupied with law and its stipulations, the Gnostics are so flatly opposed to law — even in principle — that their moral decisions are random, unpredictable, erratic, quite anomalous. Making moral decisions is a matter of spontaneity; it is literally unprincipled, purely *ad hoc* and casual. They follow no forecastable course from one situation to another. They are, exactly, anarchic — i.e., without a rule. They are not only "unbound by the chains of law" but actually sheer extemporizers, impromptu and intellectually irresponsible. They not only cast the old Torah aside; they even cease to think seriously and *carefully* about the demands of love as it has been shown in Christ, the love norm itself. The baby goes out with the bath water!

This was the issue Paul fought over with the antinomians at Corinth and Ephesus. They were repudiating all law, as such, and all principles, relying in all moral action choices solely upon guidance in the situation. Some were what he called *pneumatikoi*, spirit-possessed. They claimed that *their* guidance came from outside themselves, by the Holy Spirit. Of what use are principles and laws when you can depend on the Holy Spirit? It was a kind of special-providence idea; a version of the inspiration theory of conscience.[7] Other antinomians claimed, and still do, that their guidance comes from within themselves, as a sort of built-in radarlike "faculty," a translegal or clairvoyant conscience as promised in Jer. 31:31-34, written "upon their hearts." This second and more common form of Gnostic antinomianism, found among both Christians and non-Christians, is close to the intuition theory or faculty theory of conscience.[8]

* * *

Another version of antinomianism . . . is the ethics of existentialism. Sartre speaks of "nausea,"

which is our anxious experience of the *incoherence* of reality. For him any belief in coherence (such as the Christian doctrine of the unity of God's creation and his lordship over history) is "bad faith." In every moment of moral choice or decision "we have no excuses behind us and no justification before us." Sartre refuses to admit to any *generally* valid principles at all, nothing even ordinarily valid, to say nothing of universal *laws*.[9] Simone de Beauvoir in *The Ethics of Ambiguity* cannot quite bring herself to accept either "the contingent absurdity of the discontinuous" or "the rationalistic necessity of the continuous," proving herself to be less sturdily existentialist than Sartre, but she admits that the real world is after all "bare and incoherent."[10] She shrinks from a candid antinomianism. But the plain fact is that her ontology — her idea of basic reality — is, like Sartre's, one of radical discontinuity, so that there can be no connective tissue between one situation or moment of experience and another. There is no fabric or web of life, hence no basis for generalizing moral principles *or* laws. Every situation has only its particularity!

On this view, of course, the existentialists rightly reject even all principles, all "generally valid" ethical norms or axioms, as well as all rules or laws or precepts that legalistically absolutize (idolize) such general principles. Radical discontinuity in one's theory of being forces the "absolute particularity" of *tout comprendre, tout pardonner*. Sartre is at least honest and tough-minded. In the absence of any faith in love as the norm and in any God as the norm-giver, he says resolutely: "Ontology itself cannot formulate ethical precepts. It is concerned solely with what is, and we cannot possibly derive imperatives from ontology's indicatives."[11] He is, on this score at least, entirely correct!

Situationism

A third approach, in between legalism and antinomian unprincipledness, is situation ethics. (To

---

7. See warnings in Eph. 6:12; 1 Tim. 4:1.

8. Thomas tied conscience to a faculty, synteresis; for a critique, see Eric D'Arcy, *Conscience and the Right to Freedom* (London: Sheed & Ward, Ltd., 1961).

9. Jean-Paul Sartre, *Existentialism*, tr. by B. Frechtman (Philosophical Library, Inc., 1947), p. 27.

10. (Philosophical Library, Inc., 1948), pp. 44, 122.

11. *Being and Nothingness*, tr. by Hazel Barnes (Philosophical Library, Inc., 1956), p. 625.

jump from one polarity to the other would be only to go from the frying pan to the fire.) The situationist enters into every decision-making situation fully armed with the ethical maxims of his community and its heritage, and he treats them with respect as illuminators of his problems. Just the same he is prepared in any situation to compromise them or set them aside *in the situation* if love seems better served by doing so.

Situation ethics goes part of the way with natural law, by accepting reason as the instrument of moral judgment, while rejecting the notion that the good is "given" in the nature of things, objectively. It goes part of the way with scriptural law by accepting revelation as the source of the norm while rejecting all "revealed" norms or laws but the one command — to love God in the neighbor. The situationist follows a moral law or violates it according to love's need. For example, "Almsgiving is a good thing *if* . . ." The situationist never says, "Almsgiving is a good thing. Period!" His decisions are hypothetical, not categorical. Only the commandment to love is categorically good. "Owe no one anything, except to love one another" (Rom. 13:8). If help to an indigent only pauperizes and degrades him, the situationist refuses a handout and finds some other way. He makes no law out of Jesus' "Give to every one who begs from you." It is only one step from that kind of biblicist literalism to the kind that causes women in certain sects to refuse blood transfusions even if death results — even if they are carrying a quickened fetus that will be lost too. The legalist says that even if he tells a man escaped from an asylum where his intended victim is, if he finds and murders him, at least only one sin has been committed (murder), not two (lying as well)!

As Brunner puts it, "The basis of the divine command is always the same, but its content varies with varying circumstances." Therefore, the "error of casuistry does not lie in the fact that it indicates the infinite variety of forms which the command of love may assume; its error consists in deducing particular laws from a universal law . . . as though all could be arranged beforehand. . . . Love, however, is free from all this predefinition."[12] We might say, from the situationist's perspective, that

it is possible to derive general "principles" from whatever is the one and only universal law (*agape* for Christians, something else for others), but not laws or rules. We cannot milk universals from a universal!

William Temple put it this way: "Universal obligation attaches not to particular judgments of conscience but to conscientiousness. What acts are right may depend on circumstances . . . but there is an absolute obligation to will whatever may on each occasion be right."[13] Our obligation is relative *to* the situation, but obligation *in* the situation is absolute. We are only "obliged" to tell the truth, for example, if the situation calls for it; if a murderer asks us his victim's whereabouts, our duty might be to lie. There is in situation ethics an absolute element and an element of calculation, as Alexander Miller once pointed out.[14] But it would be better to say it has an absolute *norm* and a calculating method. There is weight in the old saying that what is needed is "faith, hope, and clarity." We have to find out what is "fitting" to be truly ethical, to use H. R. Niebuhr's word for it in his *The Responsible Self.*[15] Situation ethics aims at a contextual appropriateness — not the "good" or the "right" but the *fitting.*

A cartoon in a fundamentalist magazine once showed Moses scowling, holding his stone tablet with its graven laws, all ten, and an eager stonecutter saying to him, "Aaron said perhaps you'd let us reduce them to 'Act responsibly in love.'" This was meant as a dig at the situationists and the new morality, but the legalist humor in it merely states exactly what situation ethics calls for! With Dietrich Bonhoeffer we say, "Principles are only tools in God's hands, soon to be thrown away as unserviceable."[16]

One competent situationist, speaking to students, explained the position this way. Rules are "like 'Punt on fourth down,' or 'Take a pitch when the count is three balls.' These rules are part of the wise player's know-how, and distinguish him from

---

12. *The Divine Imperative,* tr. by Olive Wyon (Westminster Press, 1947), pp. 132ff.

13. *Nature, Man and God* (Macmillan, 1934), p. 405.

14. *The Renewal of Man* (Doubleday, 1955), p. 44.

15. (Harper & Row, 1963), pp. 60-61. Precedents are Samuel Clarke, *Unchangeable Obligations of Natural Religion* (London, 1706), and A. C. Ewing, *The Definition of the Good* (Macmillan, 1947).

16. *Ethics,* tr. by N. H. Smith (Macmillan, 1955), p. 8.

the novice. But they are not unbreakable. The best players are those who know when to ignore them. In the game of bridge, for example, there is a useful rule which says 'Second hand low.' But have you ever played with anyone who followed the rule slavishly? You say to him (in exasperation), 'Partner, why didn't you play your ace? We could have set the hand.' And he replies, unperturbed, 'Second hand low!' What is wrong? The same thing that was wrong when Kant gave information to the murderer. He forgot the purpose of the game. . . . He no longer thought of winning the hand, but of being able to justify himself by invoking the rule."[17]

This practical temper of the activist or *verb*-minded decision maker, versus contemplative *noun*-mindedness, is a major biblical rather than Hellenistic trait. In Abraham Heschel's view, "The insistence upon generalization at the price of a total disregard of the particular and concrete is something which would be alien to prophetic thinking. Prophetic words are never detached from the concrete, historic situation. Theirs is not a timeless, abstract message; it always refers to an actual situation. The general is given in the particular and the verification of the abstract is in the concrete."[18] A "leap of faith" is an action decision rather than a leap of thought, for a man's faith is a hypothesis that he takes seriously enough to act on and live by.

There are various names for this approach: situationism, contextualism, occasionalism, circumstantialism, even actualism. These labels indicate, of course, that the core of the ethic they describe is a healthy and primary awareness that "circumstances alter cases" — i.e., that in actual problems of conscience the situational variables are to be weighed as heavily as the normative or "general" constants.

The situational factors are so primary that we may even say "circumstances alter rules and principles." It is said that when Gertrude Stein lay dying she declared, "It is better to ask questions than to give answers, even good answers." This is the temper of situation ethics. It is empirical, fact-minded, data conscious, inquiring. It is antimoralistic as well as antilegalistic, for it is sensitive to variety and complexity. It is neither simplistic nor perfectionistic. It is "casuistry" (case-based) in a constructive and nonpejoritive sense of the word. We should perhaps call it "neocasuistry." Like classical casuistry, it is case-focused and concrete, concerned to bring Christian imperatives into practical operation. But unlike classical casuistry, this neocasuistry repudiates any attempt to anticipate or prescribe real-life decisions in their existential particularity. It works with two guidelines from Paul: "The written code kills, but the Spirit gives life" (II Cor. 3:6), and "For the whole law is fulfilled in one word, 'You shall love your neighbor as yourself' " (Gal. 5:14).

*   *   *

As we shall see, *Christian* situation ethics has only one norm or principle or law (call it what you will) that is binding and unexceptionable, always good and right regardless of the circumstances. That is "love" — the *agape* of the summary commandment to love God and the neighbor.[19] Everything else without exception, all laws and rules and principles and ideals and norms, are only *contingent*, only valid *if they happen* to serve love in any situation. Christian situation ethics is not a system or program of living according to a code, but an effort to relate love to a world of relativities through a casuistry obedient to love. It is the strategy of love. This strategy denies that there are, as Sophocles thought, any unwritten immutable laws of heaven, agreeing with Bultmann that all such notions are idolatrous and a demonic pretension.[20]

In non-Christian situation ethics some other highest good or *summum bonum* will, of course, take love's place as the one and only standard — such as self-realization in the ethics of Aristotle. But the *Christian* is neighbor-centered first and last. Love is for people, not for principles; i.e., it is personal — and therefore when the impersonal universal conflicts with the personal particular, the

17. E. La B. Cherbonnier, unpublished address, Trinity College, December 14, 1964.

18. *God in Search of Man: A Philosophy of Judaism* (Farrar, Strauss & Cudahy, Inc., 1956), p. 204.

19. Matt. 5:43-8 and ch. 22:34-40; Luke 6:27-28; 10:25-28 and vs. 29-37; Mark 12:28-34; Gal. 5:14; Rom. 13:8-10; etc.

20. Rudolf Bultmann, *Essays Philosophical and Theological* (Macmillan, 1955), pp. 22, 154.

latter prevails in situation ethics. Because of its mediating position, prepared to act on moral laws or in spite of them, the antinomians will call situationists soft legalists, and legalists will call them cryptoantinomians.

Principles, Yes, but Not Rules

It is necessary to insist that situation ethics is willing to make full and respectful use of principles, to be treated as maxims but not as laws or precepts. We might call it "principled relativism." To repeat the term used above, principles or maxims or general rules are *illuminators*. But they are not *directors*. The classic rule of moral theology has been to follow laws but do it *as much as possible* according to love and according to reason (*secundum caritatem et secundum rationem*). Situation ethics, on the other hand, calls upon us to keep law in a subservient place, so that *only* love and reason really count when the chips are down!

Situationists have no invariable obligation to what are sometimes called "middle axioms," logically derived as normative propositions based on love. An example of what is meant is the proposition that love of the neighbor in practice *usually* means putting human rights before property rights. The term "middle axiom," first used by J. H. Oldham and William Temple, and notably by John C. Bennett in America, is well meant but unfortunate, since an axiom is a self-validating, nonderivative proposition and it cannot stand in the "middle" between something logically prior to it and a subsequent derivative. Middle-axiom theorists must beware lest they, too, slip into the error of deriving universals from universals.

There are usually two rules of reason used in moral inquiry. One is "internal consistency," and nobody has any quarrel with it — a proposition ought not to contradict itself. The other is "external consistence" (analogy), the principle that what applies in one case should apply in all similar cases. It is around this second canon that the differences arise. Antinomians reject analogy altogether, with their doctrine of radical particularity. Situationists ask, very seriously, if there ever are enough cases enough alike to validate a law or to support anything more than a cautious generalization. In Edmond Cahn's puckish phrase, "Every case is like every other case, and no two cases are alike."[21]

There is no real quarrel here between situationism and an ethic of principles, unless the principles are hardened into laws.[22] Bishop Robinson says: "Such an ethic [situationism] cannot but rely, in deep humility, upon guiding rules, upon the cumulative experience of one's own and other people's obedience. It is this bank of experience which gives us our working rules of 'right' and 'wrong,' and without them we could not but flounder."[23] Nevertheless, in situation ethics even the most revered principles may be thrown aside if they conflict in any concrete case with love. Even Karl Barth, who writes vehemently of "absolutely wrong" actions, allows for what he calls the *ultima ratio* the outside chance that love in a particular situation might override the absolute. The instance he gives is abortion.[24]

Using terms made popular by Tillich and others, we may say that Christian situationism is a method that proceeds, so to speak, from (1) its one and only law, *agape* (love), to (2) the *sophia* (wisdom) of the church and culture, containing many "general rules" of more or less reliability, to (3) the *kairos* (moment of decision, the fullness of time) in which *the responsible self in the situation* decides whether the *sophia* can serve love there, or not. This is the situational strategy in capsule form. To legalists it will seem to treat the *sophia* without enough reverence and obedience; to antinomians it will appear befuddled and "inhibited" by the *sophia*.

Legalists make an idol of the *sophia*, antinomians repudiate it, situationists *use* it. They cannot give to any principle less than love more than tentative consideration, for they know, with Dietrich Bonhoeffer, "The question of the good is

---

21. "The Lawyer as Scientist and Scoundrel," *New York University Law Review*, vol. 36 (1961), p. 10.

22. J. M. Gustafson sees this clearly in "Context Versus Principle: A Misplaced Debate in Christian Ethics," *Harvard Theological Review* 58 (1965): pp. 171-202; less clearly in "Christian Ethics," in *Religion*, ed. Paul Ramsey (Prentice-Hall, Inc., 1965), pp. 285-354.

23. *Honest to God* (Philadelphia: Westminster Press, 1963), pp. 119-120.

24. *Church Dogmatics* (Edinburgh: T. & T. Clark, 1961), vol. 3, bk. 4, pp. 420-421.

posed and is decided in the midst of each definite, yet unconcluded, unique and transient situation of our lives, in the midst of our living relationships with men, things, institutions and powers, in other words in the midst of our historical existence."[25] And Bonhoeffer, of course, is a modern Christian ethicist who was himself executed for trying to kill, even *murder*, Adolf Hitler — so far did he go as a situationist.

* * *

The basic legalism of classical Christian ethics will resist the situational love ethic by any and every tactic. Nevertheless, the growing jeopardy of law-ethics is clear. We need only to recall how the dean of Anglican moral theologians, Bishop Kenneth Kirk, ended his effort to be a casuist, a *practical moralist*. Pointing out that at most the number of unalterable principles must be "very small," Kirk admitted that "if we followed out this line of thought to the end (as has rarely been done in Christian ethics), there could strictly speaking be only one such principle. For if any principle has an inalienable right to be observed, *every* other principle would have to be waived if the two came into conflict in a given case."[26] *Exactly!* Christian ethics has indeed failed to follow up that line of thought! But situation ethics picks it up. It holds flatly that there is only one principle, love, without any prefabricated recipes for what it means in practice, and that *all other* so-called principles or maxims are relative to particular, concrete situations! If it has any rules, they are only rules of thumb.

Kirk mourned, further, that "it seems that we have reached a point at which the whole ambitious structure of moral theology is revealed as a complete futility. Every man must decide for himself according to his own estimate of conditions and consequences; and no one can decide for him or impugn the decision to which he comes. Perhaps this is the end of the matter after all."[27] *This is precisely what this book is intended to show.*

25. *Ethics,* p. 185.

26. *Conscience and Its Problems* (London: Longmans, Green & Co., Ltd., 1927), p. 331.

27. Ibid., pp. 375-376.

Abortion: A Situation

In 1962 a patient in a state mental hospital raped a fellow patient, an unmarried girl ill with a radical schizophrenic psychosis. The victim's father, learning what had happened, charged the hospital with culpable negligence and requested that an abortion to end the unwanted pregnancy be performed at once, in an early stage of the embryo. The staff and administrators of the hospital refused to do so, on the ground that the criminal law forbids abortion except "therapeutic" ones when the mother's life is at stake — because the *moral* law, it is supposed, holds that any interference with an embryo after fertilization is murder, i.e., the taking of an innocent human being's life.

Let's relate the three ethical approaches to this situation. The rape has occurred and the decisional question is: May we rightly (licitly) terminate this pregnancy, begun in an act of force and violence by a mentally unbalanced rapist upon a frightened, mentally sick girl? Mother and embryo are apparently healthy on all the usual counts.

The legalists would say *NO.* Their position is that killing is absolutely wrong, inherently evil. It is permissible only as self-defense and in military service, which is held to be presumptive self-defense or justifiable homicide. If the mother's life is threatened, abortion is therefore justified, but for no other reasons. (Many doctors take an elastic view of "life" and thereby justify abortions to save a patient's *mental* life as well as physical.) Even in cases where they justify it, it is only *excused* — it is still held to be inherently evil. Many Protestants hold this view, and some humanists.

Catholic moral theology goes far beyond even the rigid legalism of the criminal law, absolutizing their prohibition of abortion *absolutely,* by denying all exceptions and calling even therapeutic abortion wrong. (They allow killing in self-defense against malicious, i.e., deliberate, aggressors but not in self-defense against innocent, i.e., unintentional aggressors.) Thus if it is a tragic choice of the mother's life or the baby's, as can happen in rare cases, neither can be saved.

To this ethical nightmare legalism replies: "It is here that the Church appears merciless, but she is not. It is her logic which is merciless; and she promises that if the logic is followed the woman will receive a reward far greater than a number of years of life."[28] Inexplicably, shockingly, Dietrich Bonhoeffer says the same thing: "The life of the mother is in the hand of God, but the life of the child is arbitrarily extinguished. The question whether the life of the mother or the life of the child is of greater value can hardly be a matter for a human decision."[29]

The antinomians — -but who can predict what *they would say? Their ethic is by its nature and definition outside the reach of even generalities. We can only guess, not unreasonably, that if the antinomian lives by a love norm, he will be apt to favor abortion in this case.*

The situationists, if their norm is the Christian commandment to love the neighbor, would almost certainly, *in this case,* favor abortion and support the girl's father's request. (Many purely humanistic decision makers are of the same mind about abortion following rape, and after incest too.) They would in all likelihood favor abortion for the sake of the patient's physical and mental health, not only if it were needed to save her life. It is even likely they would favor abortion for the sake of the victim's self-respect or reputation or happiness or simply on the ground that *no unwanted and unintended* baby should ever be born.

They would, one hopes, reason that it is *not* killing because there is no person or human life in an embryo at an early stage of pregnancy (Aristotle and St. Thomas held that opinion), or even if it *were* killing, it would not be murder because it is self-defense against, in this case, not one but two aggressors. First there is the rapist, who being insane was morally and legally innocent, and then there is the "innocent" embryo which is continuing the ravisher's original aggression! Even self-defense legalism would have allowed the girl to kill her attacker, no matter that he was innocent in the forum of conscience because of his madness. The embryo is no more innocent, no less an aggressor or unwelcome invader! Is not the most loving thing possible (the right thing) in this case a responsible decision to terminate the pregnancy?

What think ye?

---

28. Alan Keenan, O.F.M., and John Ryan, M.D., *Marriage: A Medical and Sacramental Study* (Sheed & Ward, Inc., 1955), p. 53.

29. *Ethics,* p. 131n.

35. The Problem of Protestant Ethics Today

PAUL RAMSEY

Protestant ethics today comes from a long line of prudent people. The pacifism which between the world wars spread widely in the non-peace churches, the non-pacifism which gradually overcame this as World War II approached and which continues today, the increasing pragmatism of the Niebuhrians, the current increase of "no greater evil" nuclear pacifism, and in general the rejection of natural law and "middle axioms" in favor of contextualism and the study of "decision making" — all this has been largely a matter of determining the "lesser evil" or perchance the "greater good" among the supposed *consequences* of actions. By calculating the facts and speculating about the expected results, we have sought to find the path along which action should be directed in order to defend or secure some sort of values at the end of the road toward which action reaches, yet never reaches. We have had an ethics derived from some future good (or evil), not in any significant degree an ethics of *right,* right action or proper conduct. We have understood morality to be a matter of prudential calculation. This is the case even if

---

Paul Ramsey (1913–1988) was professor of religion at Princeton University and a founding scholar of the Center for Theological Inquiry at Princeton. His work includes *Basic Christian Ethics; The Ethics of Fetal Research; The Just War: Force and Political Responsibility;* and *War and the Christian Conscience.*

From Paul Ramsey, *War and the Christian Conscience* (Durham, N.C.: Duke University Press, 1961).

Christian *agape* directs the estimate made of the utility of an action to be done. Such an ethic is well calculated to reduce every present reality — people and principles no less than facts — to what may be done to bring in the future.

Against this, it should be affirmed, first of all, that "prudence" has rightly to be understood to be in the service of some prior principle, whether in application of natural-law principles or (if, as I believe, these alone are inadequate) in application of divine charity. Against this, secondly, it should be affirmed that *agape* does not first and always face toward the future alone. Rather does *agape* face in the present also toward a man's existing neighbors and companions in God, seeking to determine what love permits and requires to be now done or not done toward them. Thus, love posits or takes form in principles of right conduct which express the difference it discerns between permitted and prohibited action, and these are not wholly derived from reflection upon the consequences.

In what way, then, should moral decision be based on anticipation of greater good or lesser evil among the consequences of action? Not every action that is licit is therefore to be done; what love permits, it does not without more ado require. For sound judgment to be made that a certain conduct is commanded, the Christian must, of course, also consult the consequences to see as best he can that the good outweighs the evil, or that evil is minimized by his proposed action. Yet, in order to make a decision about what should *be done,* a Christian would attempt to trammel up the consequences only among alternative courses of action which do not directly violate the love-commandment, or fall outside of the work of love in depositing, in-forming or taking the form of certain principles of right conduct. The good or the best or the lesser evil among the goals of action is to be chosen, yet by action that is not intrinsically and from the beginning wrong in itself.

We must affirm that a wholly teleological ethic — even a *wholly future-facing agape*-ethic — amounts to the suspension of a great part of morality. If no more can be said about the morality of *action* than can be derived backward from the future goal (thus unrolling toward the present the path that we shall have to tread by deeds determined by calculating their utility) ethics has already more than half-way vanished, i.e., it has become mere calculation of the means to projected ends. Of course, the ends and values toward which ethico-political calculation or prudence is directed may in themselves be of great importance; and we cannot deny that it makes a great deal of difference what the objectives a society seeks are, especially when, so far as Christian action is concerned, *agape* is in any measure the director of action toward the greater good or lesser evil (which, of course, means the same as the greatest possible good). Still, to say only this about morality is to say that there is nothing that should not be done which a future-facing calculation seems to require; and no action which can be prudently calculated to produce the described result which should not *therefore* be defined as a right action. Such a view has to be rejected as the suspension of a great part of ethics, without in any sense minimizing the significance of calculation, in its proper place, both for morality and for political decision.

* * *

In the past an ethics that attempted to determine right action and the proper conduct of affairs may have been too rigid, too certain in its statements about legitimate means; and "moralism" may often have prevented good people from being sufficiently wise or free or flexible in their deeds or in the choice of political programs. However, this should not blind us to the fact that rigid moralism has long since been overcorrected; and that today Protestant ethics points every which way in search of the useful and prudent thing to do. We call by the name of "social ethics" our wanderings over the wasteland of utility since the day we completely surrendered to technical political reason the choice of the way to the goals we seek.

Morality, including political morality, has to do with the definition of right *conduct,* and this not simply by way of the ends of action. *How* we do *what* we do is as important as our goals. An "idealist" in politics is one who goes on his way and finds his way under the lure of such goals as the greatest happiness of the greatest number, etc. A "realist" is one who knows that there are many ways that may reasonably be supposed to lead there, ranging all the way from the noblest to the most wicked political decisions and actions; and he reminds the calculative idealist that in politics he had better know more than this about right and wrong conduct. No properly ethical statement has yet been made so long as our moral imperatives are tied to unlimitedly variable ends. Nor has a properly ethical statement yet been made so long as the means are unlimitedly variable that are supposed to lead to fixed, universal ends, even the ends determined by *agape*.

* * *

A wholly future-facing love-ethic necessarily produces some version of the opinion that the end justifies the means, and a reading of the means-end situation only from the end backward. Nevertheless, an emphasis upon the significance of means, and upon principles of justice and right conduct, need not neglect concern with the good and evil consequences. For while the end may never justify the means, one effect often justifies another effect that is linked with it. Thus, moral theology has long taught that an unavoidable evil effect may be produced if that is the only way, by an action not wrong in itself, to secure some very good result. Now only at this point do we come to the proper work of calculation, in the comparison of the mixed effects of right or neutral actions, weighing their gravity, estimating the sufficiency of the reasons for them, and balancing greater against lesser goods or lesser evils.

* * *

Finally, we must conclude that today Protestant theories of politics have a very odd shape indeed. Those theologians who most stress the fact that Christian ethics is wholly predicated upon redemption or upon the divine indicative, and who say that decisive action is made possible by virtue of *justification* in Christ and by God's *forgiveness*, are often precisely the thinkers who strip politics of norms and principles distinguishing between right and wrong action. For them policy decisions are always wholly relative or "contextual," pragmatically relating available means to ends. On their view, a policy may be inept or erroneous, but it is difficult to see how decision could be *wrong*. This makes it difficult to see what there is in need of forgiveness, except inner motives. Even the politics of deferred repentance is made quite im-possible, where there is nothing in violation of fundamental principle to repent of, and to negotiate out of the realm of possibility. It would seem that an ethics grounded in justification in Christ has no such urgent need to avoid making judgments of right and wrong in politics. The statesman who lives out of faith and love is under no necessity of theorizing contextually to the effect that there is no right he did not do and no wrong he was under continuing complicity in doing. This is not to say that sin must abound in order that faith may the more abound. But where there is faith there is surely no need for the removal of the principles of civil righteousness by which wrong gains some meaning; and where there is justification it is sinners and wrong-doers who may be sustained in office, and not merely prudent politicians. It is only an *agape*-ethic facing exclusively toward the future consequences that today allows outstanding theologians to reduce the morality of means to prudential calculation of results. Certainly, the moral problem of war will never be correctly analyzed unless there is a return to a morality of means as well as ends in warfare that can at all be justified for the Christian. This requires also an *agape*-ethic precipitating some principled judgment about means that are permitted or prohibited. Such an understanding of Christian morality may be described as "faith effective through in-principled love." The task of Christian ethical analysis is to articulate what this should mean in political action, and for the vocation of citizen or statesman.

214

36. Values, Victims, and Visions

JAMES GAFFNEY

A little more than a century ago, as a tribute to his recently deceased wife, a great English poet wrote an extraordinary poem. It is admirable in a number of respects, not least its telling of a truly fascinating story. But what continues to interest me is that, from start to finish, it is a poem about moral thinking.

The masterpiece called *The Ring and the Book,* which Robert dedicated to Elizabeth Barrett Browning, is about the once very famous murder of an adolescent Italian girl and her elderly parents by her middle-aged husband, allegedly to avenge the girl's infidelity with a young local priest. Because the defendant himself had received minor orders, he succeeded in having the case transferred from civil to ecclesiastical jurisdiction. The case was eventually decided in a criminal tribunal of the Vatican.

The connection of all this with moral thinking is the remarkable way Browning constructed his dramatic monologue. He causes the entire story to be retold, time after time, by very different people, each with contrasting social positions, backgrounds, interests, assumptions, ambitions, and degrees of personal involvement. We are compelled to view the same crude facts from a variety of personal and social moral viewpoints. We discover that what one account presents as momen-

tous appears trivial in another. We find motives not even suspected in one taken for granted in another. We see heroes transform into villains and villains into nonentities. Virtues turn into vices, bystanders into participants, and neutral circumstances into compelling influences. Each account is a peculiar mosaic of lights and shadows, and the pattern of vividness and obscurity constantly changes. Hence, for the reader, even though a definite fabric of facts remains substantially unaltered, the moral picture is repeatedly transformed. What causes the transformations are different human viewpoints from which it is perceived. G. K. Chesterton characterized *The Ring and the Book* as a "spiritual detective story." When the mystery is concluded in the final scene what assures us of the verdict is neither knowledge of facts nor knowledge of law, but the spiritual discernment of an aged saint, dedicated to justice, trustful of God, close to death, and unconcerned about anything this world could bestow or withhold.

To me, it has come to seem fairly clear that changes in the way modern Catholics think about morality are explicable, to a considerable extent, in much the same way as those transformations of moral perception that are the most original feature of Browning's poem. Moral cases, including typical ones look different, and therefore are analyzed and judged differently, depending on the perspective in which they are viewed. And that perspective depends on who the viewers are, and how they are enabled and accustomed to do their seeing. In this respect, moral judgment is similar to legal judgment, and the practical significance of differing perspectives for legal judgment is something of which we all become acutely aware whenever we watch trial lawyers in a selection of jurors.

For a very long time, nearly since the Protestant Reformation, and until quite recently, Catholic moral judgments exhibited a remarkable degree of uniformity. A major reason for that was the control exerted on such judgments by a body of doctrine called moral theology, censored and authorized by the church, and developed for the most part to assist priests in administering the sacrament of Penance. The main assistance it offered was twofold: first, to identify the kinds of sins being confessed; and second, to ascertain the guilt of the person who confessed them.

Many things, both favorable and unfavorable,

James Gaffney (1931–) is professor and chairperson of the department of religious studies at Loyola University in New Orleans. His work includes *Focus on Doctrine; Newness of Life;* and *Sin Reconsidered.*

From *Commonweal* 113 (15 August 1986): pp. 426-429.

can be said about that confessional system and the moral theology that derived its character from it. But it also had a confining effect on moral perspective, and therefore on moral thinking.

That confinement depended on both the setting and the characters. Because the setting was juridical, it had to rely on a definite set of statutes, in effect criminal and penal laws official specifications of punishable offenses. Penitents had the task of translating their recent moral histories into terms of infraction of these laws. The confessor was there to help them do so, and moral theology was his equipment for that function. From the nature of the case, the laws had to be stable and uniform, and so did the procedures for interpreting them. Under such circumstances moral theology had every reason to be conservative and dogmatic. It had no reason to be original or philosophical.

The confessional orientation confined moral thinking for other reasons as well. Among them must be included the fact that the whole procedure was directed not only by a quite rigid set of norms, but also by a highly specialized set of persons. All of them were men; none women. All of them were celibate; none spouses, and none parents. Nearly all had received a very similar, and quite peculiar education. All were full-time functionaries of a vast, hierarchical institution. None of these characteristics is objectionable in itself. But even with maximum allowance for individuality, and maximum resistance to clerical stereotyping, it remains obvious that no random assortment of Roman Catholic priests could be seriously regarded as a cross-section of humanity at large. Yet no one else was ever allowed to have much to do with formulating or administering moral theology, until very recently.

In still other ways, the penitent's role contributed to a confinement of moral thought. Penitents, of course, included all sorts of people. Yet each penitent appeared alone, as the doer of certain morally objectionable deeds. Hence, the only moral picture readily obtainable in the confessional was a picture taken of — or from the viewpoint of — an individual moral agent. Most of the sins confessed were, of course, actions that offended and injured other people, sometimes great numbers of other people and in extremely complicated ways. Yet, because none of those

people was heard from, their moral perspectives could scarcely be introduced. Not surprisingly, then, Catholic moral thinking habitually understood sin in relation to sinners more than in relation to the victims of sinners. There were no plaintiffs and, apart from the defendant, who confessed and pleaded guilty, there were no witnesses. Even with maximum sincerity, such an arrangement is hardly calculated to generate a comprehensive picture of moral realities.

Penitents, it should also be recalled, came always, until very recently, as isolated individuals, to confess the particular individual deeds for which they sought forgiveness. Under such circumstances moral vision is seriously incapacitated for perceiving either morality or immorality as socially organized, institutionally entailed, ideologically sustained, or culturally perpetuated. To adopt familiar jargon, moral theology, as shaped by the exigencies of the confessional system, tended greatly to emphasize what may be called micro-morality, and to overlook macro-morality. Social sin, as it has come to be called, tended to slip through the meshes of the confessional system, and consequently to slip the minds of moral theologians and of Catholics who took their moral cues from them.

One last consideration along the same lines: what penitents were expected to report, and what confessors were expected to interpret, were not traits or tendencies of moral character, but particular misdeeds. One confessed what one was doing, not what one was becoming. Moral theology focused on rules rather than on virtues, and on the intermittent breaking of rules rather than on the progressive deterioration of character. By the same token, moral theology typically gave far more attention to doing things one should not do, than to not doing the things one should. The only sins of omission commonly attended to were those involving very precise, usually ritual, obligations.

The functional relationship between moral theology and the confessional system had far-reaching effects, both in assuring the relative invariance of Catholic moral thinking, and in skewing that thinking in a number of important ways. To recapitulate, among the changes in moral thinking that have recently been most conspicuous among Catholics, we can plainly see a number of reversals of, or compensations for the following five broadly-stated tendencies, separately or in combination:

- First, moral norms were regarded as a definite and permanent set of fixed statutes.
- Second, moral issues were interpreted with both insights and oversights typical of celibate, male clergy.
- Third, moral perspective was dominated by the viewpoint of agents of wrongdoing rather than that of sufferers from it.
- Fourth, sins were identified with individual misdeeds, with little attention to their involvement in social practices, policies, and structures.
- And fifth, immorality was thought of rather as a quality of actions than as a disposition of character.

It should be noted that the recent wave of change and diversification in Catholic moral thinking has been simultaneous with rapid decline of moral theology, at least as traditionally understood, and with widespread neglect of sacramental confession, despite some interesting experiments changing its procedures.

1. For quite some time now, there has been a widespread reluctance to attribute absolute validity to any but the the most comprehensive moral norms. The most extreme reaction has been to discredit moral generalizations altogether, and then replace then all by a sweeping injunction to love. Very often, the obvious practical inadequacy of such an approach leads to interpreting love as that which contributes to happiness, thereby turning Christian morality into a pure consequentialism indistinguishable from secular utilitarianism. In more moderate circles, the tendency is to pay much more attention than formerly to proportional consequences, while honoring certain other norms as well.

2. For a somewhat shorter time, doubt has been cast on a number of familiar moral assumptions by a growing suspicion that they embody prejudices rooted in ignorance of typical female and conjugal experience, intensified by institutionally encouraged attitudes of authoritarian paternalism. Here the most extreme reactions have taken the form of ideological feminism and anti-clericalism. More balanced reactions have explored the effects of sexism on distributive justice, and cultivated a sexual and conjugal morality more sensitive to the realities of family life.

3. A subtler, more profound reassessment of moral priorities has been broached by deliberately adopting outlooks and evaluations proper to those who may be described as morally victimized, those, that is, whose sufferings are intensified and whose decent aspirations are frustrated by the moral indifference and social irresponsibility of others, more fortunately situated.

4. Catholics are steadily becoming aware of the extent to which moral wrongdoing is rooted in corporate action or inaction, facilitated by social systems, and supported by underlying ideologies, mainly political and economic. Indeed, such wrongdoing may even be so effectively disguised by these same factors as to be commonly overlooked by the moral criticism of conscientious people. Altering those factors has come to be seen as a primary demand of social justice.

5. Several lines of thought, psychological and theological as well as ethical, have conspired in recent years to recommend the centering of moral assessment not on rules but on virtue. The basic idea is that moral goodness is primarily a quality of human lives, constituted not by a record of unbroken regulations, but by the cultivation and integration of certain basic habits, attitudes, and outlooks, of which conformity to rules is only one indication. Such goodness is adequately demonstrated only by the story of a life, in which not only overt action, but vision and expectation shape the evolution of a character within the unfolding of a plot.

What answer can be given to the very basic, practical question of whether Catholic moral thinking in recent years has been getting better or worse? I can only answer: both. All five of the trends I have described are, in my opinion, progressive. But at the same time, because they are a response to a given historical moment, they can be too readily exaggerated, and allowed to supersede rather than supplement elements of moral wisdom from the past.

In my own view, the most celebrated of modern trends in Catholic moral thinking, often called situation ethics, is the most superficial and least innovative. After all, throughout the entire history of Christianity, circumstantial limits to most moral rules have been readily admitted. Even the most venerable Christian moralists, for example, made lots of exceptions to "Thou shalt not kill," and at least a few to "Thou shalt not steal." The same cannot be said of "Thou shalt not commit adultery," and it is notorious that when situation ethicists get down to cases, it is very largely in the realm of sexual morality that they draw controversy and condemnation. We are thus reminded of that peculiar inflexibility which overtakes the traditional Roman Catholic moral theological mind whenever moral rules are rules affecting sexual behavior. Here, I suppose, is the most deplorable effect of a centuries-old hegemony of male celibates in moral theology.

Looking again at the kinds of exceptions to moral norms that have long been taken for granted, one notices that most of them have obviously been based on some kind of consequentialism and proportionalism, that is, on comparing, in particular circumstances, the values of what would happen if the norm were conformed with. That, for example, is clearly the basis on which moral approval has been given to thefts by the very poor from the very rich, and to lethal violence by defenders against aggressors. There is nothing new in principle about consequentialism and proportionalism, but only about certain of their applications. And it cannot be overlooked that here too, at least in official Catholic circles, it is about sex that nearly all the fuss is made.

Up to a point, consequentialism and proportionalism express sound common-sense morality. Obviously the foreseeable results of our actions should be major factors in judging their moral rightness or wrongness. It is elementary morality to try to do more good than harm. But it is not the whole of even elementary morality. The serious problems about consequentialism are not in the realm of sex, but in the realm of justice. For no one can realistically doubt that occasions can arise when doing something plainly unjust really is likely to accomplish more good than any alternative just behavior. That is not only how tyrants defend their disregard of human rights, but how terrorists opposing those tyrants defend their massacres of the innocent. It is also how governments defend mining foreign harbors, how tax-evaders defend cheating the public, how disciplinarians defend indiscriminate punishment, and

how ideologues defend suppressing the truth. Within limits, consequentialism is indispensable to reasonable morality. Beyond those limits, it annihilates the sense of justice.

Subtler and more innovative than these trends is the tendency in modern Catholic moral thinking to adopt the perspective not only of those who perform moral or immoral actions, but also of those who are chiefly affected by them. Phrases like "option for the poor" and "solidarity with victims" are significant expressions of this perspective in recent Catholic social ethics. There is a growing awareness that, from the receiving end of morality and immorality, one gets a different view, and in some respects a clearer and truer one. Demands on our generosity or responsibility take on a completely different moral quality as we shift our focus from concentrating on our own limited resources to entering into the predicaments of those who ask us to share them. The closer one gets to the sufferer, the harder it becomes to refuse help. And the farther one stays from the sufferer, the farther one remains from the central moral reality of the situation. Thus we chase the beggars off our streets, keep the slums off our itineraries, and usher the helpless off our premises because their near presence mocks the complacency of our consciences.

Yet, even this wholesome trend of thought has, perhaps, a dark side in moral thinking. For, given our congenital egocentrism, it is an easy step from paying moral attention to the victimization of others, to thinking about our own moral situations more in passive than in active terms, that is, thinking of ourselves as the objects of other people's moral or immoral behavior.

I think there is reason to fear something of this kind of recurring. The main indication I would point to is a change in the prevailing language of ordinary moral discourse. I have in mind the rapidly increasing frequency of references to rights, and a corresponding diminution of references to duties and obligations. This is a transferral of properly legal language to the realm of ethics. One thing to be said for the confessional system was that it required Catholics regularly to interrupt preoccupation with their rights and pay serious attention to their obligations. We may need to recall that. In a world where all moral thoughts were concerned with rights, and none with obligations, moral life would inevitably cease. The converse is not true.

Perhaps no recent trend has had greater impact on Catholic moral thinking than that which emphasizes the collective and socially structured nature of so much ethical behavior. The practical corollary is that our own responsibility concerning such actions depends on what we can do about the collectivities and social structures involved, and about our personal relations with them. Social justice, as a moral virtue, has come to be understood as a disposition, on the one hand, to try to make societies more just and, on the other, to detach oneself from societies bent on injustice. The velocity of progress in this regard is well demonstrated by attitudes towards conscientious objection, such a short time ago reprobated by the entire fraternity of Catholic moral theologians, and now enjoying praises and blessings from bishops, popes, and an ecumenical council. At the present time, the moral reinterpretation of political, economic, and professional life seems to be well under way.

The least developed, and in some ways the most interesting of the trends I have listed is the last one, with its reinterpretation of moral goodness as the development — over a course of time, experience, and choice — of a certain kind of human being. The interesting thing is that this point of view is not in the least *new* to Catholic thought, even though it is rather new to Catholic theorizing about morality and ethics. The fact is, if one wants to find Catholic thought of the kind here recommended, one can easily find it in any well-stocked Catholic library. To get to it, though, you must make a wide berth of the sections labeled "moral theology" and settle down among the volumes marked spirituality and hagiography. A long, long time ago, spirituality and moral theology went separate ways, eventually separating even more widely. Bringing them together again would be a natural result of addressing questions about what we ought to do with questions about what we are supposed to become. That, it seems to me, is the only possible way a distinctively Christian morality might come into being.

37. From Decision to Story

JAMES W. McCLENDON, JR.

Decisionism

What's wrong with decisions as the substance of morality? Certainly in other realms decision-making is given high billing. Doctors decide, and lawyers, and merchant chiefs. Why not the moral self? Is not "the hour of decision" all-important? What can morality consist in, if *not* in decisions? That we find these questions natural, even unanswerable, may say more about our times, our *Zeitgeist,* than about Christian ethics. The dawn of our era in the North European Renaissance brought a strong new emphasis upon the *will* in human nature. This emphasis was, to be sure, as old as the Hebrew prophets, but for the men and women of the Renaissance the will arose with a strange fascination, like a malevolent beast from the abyss. Marlowe's Doctor Faustus is a character in whom not knowledge but the lust for it is revealed as ruinous. Shakespeare, in *Julius Caesar,* paints portraits of men in whom the will to power or its fatal converse shapes destiny. For the Elizabethans, "ambition" was a vice, for beneath it lay a power they could little understand but knew to dread — the unruly human will. And it is at least worth noting that *Lady* Macbeth is perhaps

James W. McClendon, Jr. (1924–) is professor of theology at Church Divinity School of the Pacific and the Graduate Theological Union in Berkeley, California. His work includes *Biography as Theology, Ethics: Systematic Theology;* and, with others, *Understanding Religious Convictions,* and *Is God God?*

From James W. McClendon, Jr., *Ethics: Systematic Theology,* vol. 1 (Nashville: Abingdon Press, 1986).

Shakespeare's purest incarnation of this chaotic force.

Little wonder, then, that when the eighteenth century sought to impose order on the world it had inherited from the Renaissance, the moral government of the human will would be seen as the chief task of the Enlightened intellect. Thus Immanuel Kant (1724-1804), master philosopher of the Enlightenment, found the locus of morality to be the direction of the transcendent human will in accordance with the categorical imperative, and held that in a world of radical evil the only truly good thing was a good will. And to shorten a complex story, when William James (1842-1910) sought the vital nerve by which he himself might be roused from impotence to vibrant action, the ganglion of selfhood that he seized was precisely the self-direction of the will by an act of will. Dangerous will, purely good will, impotent will — the history of moral philosophy for five centuries parallels the changing concept of the human will.

All that remained for recent ethicists was to localize those primal acts of will in *decisions,* and to say that *morality consists in decision-making.* The perfect expression of this last stage may be found in Jean-Paul Sartre (1905-1980), the French existentialist, for whom true morality consisted not in deciding this or that, but purely and merely in deciding. Decide, and you have acted morally, while not to decide is — bad faith.

The two chief sorts of decisionism, however, come from the eighteenth century. One is *utilitarianism,* whose distinctive creator was an English student of law, Jeremy Bentham (1748-1832). He presented two fundamental doctrines. One is the principle of utility or welfare or pleasure: We act in order to attain the perceived good, and that good, according to Bentham, is our own *happiness* (hedonism), though this may be conceived in more than one way by utilitarians. The other is the hedonic *calculus:* Human pleasure in any given set of circumstances may be quantified and calculated by summing up the pleasure to be realized by each in any proposed action. Suppose that I am deliberating whether to take my little niece, Erica, to the circus. I apply the calculus: To her very great pleasure, assign +5 units. To my own mild inconvenience, -2. To the relief her mother will feel in getting the little brat off her hands for the after-noon, +3. To expense of tickets and refreshments, estimated at $38, assign -4. To benefit to the circus of two extra patrons, +1. Slight risk of harm to self or to niece, -1. The net value is +2, so a utilitarian (happily, we presume) takes his niece to the circus. And the utilitarian claim is that such a decisionist calculus will be the guide to life.

At the other end of the spectrum of decisionism stands the moral philosophy of Immanuel Kant. Here the question will be not, What *good* may I achieve, but, What is *right* in itself? To will is to walk the path of moral duty. For example, I must not lie. Confronted with temptation to do so, I sense the categorical imperative as the claim upon my will. I ought to tell the truth for truth's sake. With that pure motive, without self-interest, I decide to tell the truth; morality has prevailed. These two schemes, the consequentialist and the deontological, seem to differ at almost every point; what interests us now, though, is what they have in common: morality as deciding.

To see how this decisionist emphasis captured Christian ethics, still another development must be recognized. The same centuries that saw the growth of the emphasis upon the will in human nature brought also an intense interiorization of the Christian life. Puritanism, pietism, revivalism — all emphasized the inner struggles of the soul. Krister Stendahl, a Lutheran scholar, has shown in an important essay, "The Apostle Paul and the Introspective Conscience of the West" (1976), how little this interiorization is biblical and how much it is due to Augustine and Luther. We misread Romans 7, Stendahl argues, if we fail to see that Paul was a Christian (and Jew) of robust conscience, whose concern in that famous chapter was with the place of the law since Messiah has come — and *not* with the (Lutheran) role of conscience in leading sinners to the gospel. It was through Augustine, not Paul, that the introspective interpretation of justification by faith was first sounded, and it was through Luther, an Augustinian monk deeply enmeshed in the practice of penance, that this introspective conscience became the standard hermeneutic by which, says Stendahl, *we* read the whole New Testament — and misread Paul. He goes on to claim that the introspective approach, once it has entered the stream of history, is inescapable. We cannot like Paul be men and women of robust conscience; our questions must be Augustine's and Luther's, for we live in the modern West.

However that may be, see how the emphases upon will and inwardness converge in the concept of deciding. Originally "decide" and its Latin original meant "to cut off" — to end a battle by a "decisive" victory, or to settle a lawsuit with an award to one of the contestants. Hence the word implied (1) a struggle, and (2) its termination. Then the same word was applied to an interior "battle" in which the mind wavers until one "side" of the mind overcomes the other — as in the uncertainty of a lover torn between two loves. So "decision" comes to mean the end of an *inner* contest. Unquestionably, such inner struggle is a recurrent feature of human life. But in modern Christianity, the new exaltation of the will, together with the interiorization of the Christian life, made it seem that such struggles are not part but the whole of morality — as if being continually divided against itself were the soul's main business, as if a self divided were the normal moral status of the Christian life. My point is not to deny that such "sick souls" (William James) exist but to ask whether their perpetual sickness is the moral norm of the Christian life.

Some recent ethicists, at any rate, have entered a strong dissent. Dietrich Bonhoeffer, with perhaps typical German abruptness, argued that the very idea of ethics as *our* knowing good and evil is the sign and consequence of the fall away from our primal unity with God. This fall is represented in the Eden story as the eating of forbidden fruit. Its effect is that we usurp the place of God ("you will be like God, knowing good and evil" Gen. 3:5 RSV); we take to ourselves the divine role of choosing and become the source of moral decisions rather than the objects of God's choice for us. To know good and evil, to be *ethicists,* to choose — these are the marks of our *fallen* creaturehood (Bonhoeffer). And on the other hand, in Christ's redemption, the single-minded one (James 1:8) is freed from that spurious "knowledge." "Not fettered by principles, but bound by love for God, he has been set free from the conflicts of ethical decisions." Perhaps this seems one-sided, but it does point to a Christian morality other than decisionism.

For the present argument is not that no Christian ever need decide: there are perplexities, there is surely temptation; our minds are sometimes divided. It is only to claim that decisionism with its entailed voluntarism and interiorization cannot be an adequate or full account of the moral life. As clearly as anywhere, this can be seen in the great sheep and goats judgment parable of Matthew 25. There, when the righteous are summoned to inherit the kingdom, they are startled by the recital of their deeds of love and mercy. So far from having been deliberate and calculated acts of moral decision, their conduct, insofar as it reflected their destiny, seems to have been constituted by deeds that unconsciously registered their character and their faith: "Lord, when saw we thee hungry, and fed thee? or athirst, and gave thee drink?" (25:37 ASV). The King's judgment is based, not on their deliberate decisions if any, but on their unreckoned generosity, their uncalculating love, their "aimless" faithfulness.

The Bunyan Narrative

But the Christian alternative to decisionism may better be represented by a life story than by a parable. Consider a writer who stands in a truly borderline position between the medieval world and our own, John Bunyan (1628-1688), the Bedford tinker, roisterer, convert, baptist preacher, and prisoner for the sake of conscience. In Bunyan we find a theologian (Greaves, 1969) who embodies the psychology of Western introspection, but who has retained or recovered an outlook sufficiently biblical to save him from subjective decisionism.

Bunyan's two best-known works (among fifty or more) are his autobiography, *Grace Abounding* (1666), and his allegorical novel, *The Pilgrim's Progress,* completed in 1684. These should be read together, not only because together they establish his reputation as the earliest master of English narrative prose, but because they show the inside and the outside of Bunyan's storied conception of the Christian life.

There is indeed an inner side to the Christian story. *Grace Abounding* is the account of a conversion almost purely Augustinian and Lutheran in its onset of guilt, its struggles, its accession of grace, and its continuing dynamic of struggle and relapse and renewed grace. At its outset, Bunyan acknowledges the inevitable judgment of the world: This will be called the tale of an unsound mind. Indeed, what keeps it from being just that is the outcome — the richly redemptive life that issues from the struggle. The symbolic outer sins that are the counters in this fierce spiritual battle — swearing, dancing, bell-ringing — are, like Augustine's stolen pears, the tokens of titanic inner struggles.

After he relates being driven to agonies of conscience over whether he should, at an inner urging he later recognized as Satanic, drop his food while he sat at table and rush away to pray, Bunyan goes on to tell of a morning when,

> . . . as I did lie in my bed, I was, as at other times, most fiercely assaulted with this temptation to sell and part with Christ; the wicked suggestion still running in my mind, Sell him, sell him, sell him, sell him, as fast as a man could speak; against which also, in my mind, as at other times, I answered, No, no, not for thousands, thousands, at least twenty times together. But at last, after much striving, even until I was almost out of breath, I felt this thought pass through my heart, Let him go, if he will! And I thought also, that I felt my heart freely consent thereto. Oh, the diligence of Satan! Oh, the desperateness of man's heart!

What saves these agonies from bathos, gives them an almost biblical flavor, distinguishing them from Kantian writhings after pure conscience and Benthamite calculation of the pains and pleasures of taking Little Erica to the circus, is I believe twofold: On the one hand, Bunyan's interiority is made vivid by being linked to a whole life story which we learn as we read *Grace Abounding;* on the other, the struggles are directly linked to the central issue, to the question of his life-changing conversion and union with Christ.

This double linkage becomes explicit in *Pilgrim's Progress.* In its two parts, the Christian life is unfolded in a journey of pilgrims from the City of Destruction to the Celestial City. The allegory is at once (1) realistic, earthy narrative of an imaginary journey, (2) the symbolic representation of the life journey of any Christian pilgrim, and (3) a recall of the link between that life journey and the Scripture story. In the weaving together of these three, the symbols (characters with names like Pliable and Mr. Worldlywiseman, a county fair called

Vanity, companions named Faithful and Mr. Greatheart, a wicket gate, a burden, a cross) together form links between interiority and realism and biblical story, making of these one vision.

But again Bunyan's own dialogue may better convey the flavor. Bunyan tells how as Christian advances toward the heavenly city he is met along the way by two men who have turned back in terror. They describe the scene that lies ahead.

CHR. But what have you seen? said Christian.
MEN. Seen! Why the valley itself, which is as dark as pitch; we also saw there the hobgoblins, satyrs, and dragons of the pit; we heard also in that valley a continual howling and yelling, as of a people under unutterable misery, who there sat about in affliction and irons; and over that valley hangs the discouraging clouds of confusion; death also doth always spread his wings over it. In a word it is every whit dreadful, being utterly without order.
CHR. Then said Christian, I perceive not yet, by what you have said, but that this is my way to the desired haven.
MEN. Be it thy way; we will not choose it for ours. So they parted, and Christian went on his way, but still with his sword drawn in his hand, for fear lest he should be assaulted.

And the journey goes on. Bunyan's own life story, here so fleetingly indicated, seems to me to represent well the true place of decisions in the moral life. They are not everything there. Some decisions are spurious — the devil's word, Bunyan said. And others are evanescent, as O'Connell has also recognized, being no part of a Christian's fundamental stance. But what of that one great decision, when the pilgrim stands at the foot of the cross, and the burden of sin rolls away to disappear into the empty tomb? That decision, Bunyan would be the first to say, is in no straightforward way one's own, for the "I" that might have decided is the "I" that ever refused the way, the truth, the life, whereas the "I" that is created in that decisive moment is, as Bonhoeffer also saw, God's election, not our own. So Bunyan's narratives point us away from moral decisionism, but toward a Christian life where vision and community and hope converge in the disciples' way. As Valiant, one of Christian's companions, sings in *Pilgrim's Progress:*

Hobgoblin nor foul fiend
Can daunt his spirit;
He knows he at the end
Shall life inherit.
Then fancies fly away,
He'll fear not what men say,
He'll labour night and day
To be a pilgrim.

38. A Framework for Feminist Ethics

CAROL S. ROBB

Introduction

The diversity among feminist perspectives is reflected in the diversity of feminist ethical theories. A major indicator of this diversity is the way feminists answer the question, "Who is accountable to feminist ethics?" The seat of accountability rests in some of the following areas: to women solely, according to radical feminists; to families and schools, for sex-role theorists; to the working class, according to Marxist-Leninist feminists; to all women and the working class, for socialist-feminists. Considering these responses, this paper takes the position that feminists are making claims on social structures and aggregates of people — government, child-care systems, families, schools, churches, and the corporate sphere. In this light, feminist ethics are social ethics, and can guide our reflection with the tools and questions which pertain to the discipline of social ethics.

On the other side, social ethics is a discipline still in the forge, in process, with some of its outlines yet to be shaped. Developments in feminist ethical theory provide the basis for a contribution to the formation of social ethics: a vision of the breadth of scope that the discipline must encompass. Without a scope broad enough to include, among other things, the task of analyzing the roots

Carol S. Robb (1945–) is professor of Christian social ethics at San Francisco Theological Seminary. She has edited *Making the Connections: Essays in Feminist Social Ethics.*

From *The Journal of Religious Ethics* 9, no. 1 (spring 1981): pp. 48-68.

of women's oppression, our ethical reflection is subject to a major difficulty, to fail to account for the systemic quality of the grounds for women's complaints and claims. Secondarily, without recognizing the importance of that analysis to feminist ethics, we will miss understanding a major reason why feminists take such diverse and even conflicting normative stances, ranging from separatism to institutional reformism to commitment to socialist revolution.

Yet the analysis of women's oppression is only one aspect of feminist ethics, as the analysis of the root of any situation is only one aspect of social ethics in general. Several factors constitute ethical theories, and ethicists, including feminist ethicists, may differ along any or all of these factors, thus expressing different normative stances. In this paper I propose a schema which can make explicit how ethical theories differ from each other and share points of commonality. This schema can be shared by feminist ethics and social ethics.

This schema contains many factors which appear in contemporary and traditional ethical theory, though this particular configuration is one which I propose to encourage viewing the ethical enterprise in a broad way. Ethicists in general, including feminist ethicists, tend to focus their attention on one or a few of these factors, as the notes will indicate, making contributions to the total enterprise in the context of others' contributions in different ways.

Elements of Ethical Theories

Proposing this schema necessitates attentiveness to a dialogue between the traditions of the discipline of ethics and new voices which are both appropriating and challenging the traditions. One of the outcomes of this dialogue is an awareness of the impact on ethical reflection of the analysis of the roots of oppression. We have seen attention to analysis before in the ethics of Latin American liberation theology. My concern is to make this aspect of ethical reflection explicit, since to do so confronts us with the importance of making explicit the social theories at the base of our various social ethics.

Specifically in relation to feminist ethics, analyses among feminists differ, as I shall take some care to show. Thus, while all feminist ethics begins

with or assumes a criticism of the historical, including contemporary, roles of women in society, or a complaint about those roles, the attempt to understand the grounds for the criticism and the requirements for liberation requires analysis. Because the analyses of the roots of women's oppression yield such divergent normative stances, I will make the case that this particular factor is heavily weighted in relation to all the other factors.

Starting Point for Ethical Reflection

The starting point is the first of nine analytically distinct aspects of ethical reflection. In the tradition of ethics we have learned the significance of how people define problems appropriate for ethical reflection, or pose issues, and in this sense *start* the ethical enterprise.

On the one hand, one can proceed by reflecting on very concrete historical experiences, and attempt to arrive at more general understandings of the ethical situation by that "reflection on praxis," to borrow liberation theology terminology. On the other hand, one can begin with a definition of the good life, the virtuous person, the "nature" of anything in an idealist sense, and deduce the definition of an ethical situation from that basis.[1]

To date there has been a nearly consistent tendency for feminist ethicists to take as their starting points reflection upon very concrete situations. This procedure is one way, and a main way, in which dominant ideology is unmasked. In this procedure, there is commonality or at least a basis for commonality with those who articulate ethical reflections from other oppressed groups. For until the dominant ideology of a social structure can be exposed as manufactured instead of natural, the terms of an ethical problem will tend to reflect assumptions which support a dominant ideology. For this reason, the act of defining a problem is a political act; it is an exercise of power to have accepted one's terms of a "problem."[2]

1. For an illustration of this particular distinction in terms of the abortion question, see English (1977) and Cohen (1977).
2. Gilligan (1977) claims that the proclivity of women to reconstruct hypothetical dilemmas in terms of the real, to request or supply the information missing about the nature of people and the places where they

Data about the Historical Situation

Ethical decisions must take into account all of the relevant data. Social ethicists are accountable for basing their definition of the ethical situation on inclusive data. Those formulating feminist ethical theory are inclined to challenge social ethicists in two ways, as to the *sufficiency* of the data to be considered, whether it adequately reflects what is happening to women and what it is that women are doing, and as to the *weight given* to the data which reflects or impacts women's lives.[3]

Analysis of the Roots of Oppression

Dependent upon but not collapsible to the data about the historical situation, the location of the roots of oppression informs all aspects of ethical reflection. The purpose of this factor is to locate causal dynamics.[4]

---

live, shifts their judgment away from the hierarchical ordering of principles and the formal procedures of decision-making that are critical for scoring at Kohlberg's highest level.

3. Card (1978) claims we cannot presuppose a requisite publicity of the data for our inquiries, thus the need for autobiographies. Lebacqz (1979) says that if only logical analysis of "facts" is considered appropriate data, one takes the decision away from those most intimately involved, and obfuscates the value-laden nature of data. Mary Pellauer teaches a course, "Violence and Violation," at Union Theological Seminary which organizes often-ignored data about various forms of violence against women.

4. For an illustration of the significance of analysis on a common data fund, compare Ehrenreich and Ehrenreich (1977) with Daly (1978) on the treatment of the development of gynecology in the medical profession. The Ehrenreichs argue that that development was part of the de-skilling of the working class. Midwifery, which played an important role in the culture of European immigrant groups and rural black and white Americans, was outlawed or discredited in the early 1900s and replaced by professionally-dominated care. De-skilling the working class was involved in the rise of the professional managerial class, whose function is to reproduce capitalist class relations. Daly views the rise of the professional field of gynecology as a reactionary response of men to the first wave of feminism. "For of course the purpose and intent of gynecology was/is not healing in a deep sense but violent enforcement of the sexual caste system."

Feminist ethical theory reflects at least four different analyses of the roots of oppression which I will examine later. They share one perspective, however: that the causative factors in women's situation, whether prehistorical, historical, or currently operative, are not collapsible to, even if they are related to, causes of other social inequalities. Women's oppression cannot be "liquidated" by abolishing the class structure alone, racism alone, or the need for democratic reforms alone.

Loyalties

On whose behalf ought we to make ethical judgments? Some ethicists have treated this factor as a pre-ethical factor, one about which persons have made some judgment when they enter into ethical reflection. However, the approach I suggest is that one may intentionally and after reflection take a position of partiality, or loyalty to a particular group, and consequently it is appropriate to treat "loyalties" as an ethical factor.

Feminist ethical theory confronts all proponents of justice in the social-ethical tradition as to whether loyalty to women *as women* is operative. It is not sufficient to espouse justice for women solely or even primarily as a means to achieve justice for the underdeveloped, a racial or ethnic group, or a nationality. On the other hand, there is among feminist ethicists a continuing search for the relationship between loyalty to women and loyalty to other oppressed groups. With some exceptions, feminist ethicists are loyal to women in a way which is consistent to a loyalty to all of humanity.

Theory of Value

Value theories contain rank orders of values according to priority. Rank orderings are based on an assumption that many if not all ethical decisions are made in situations in which some values must be chosen at the expense of some others. Thus theories of value may posit how to choose between life and freedom, unity and justice, affiliation and autonomy, to name some examples of choices often posed. Theories of value are often implied in anthropologies, theologies, and visions of future social orders as they are expressed in utopic science fiction, for example.

An ongoing discussion among those developing theories of feminist values concerns whether feminists have claim to any values independent of either a theory that biology is determinative, or a commitment to social justice shared with others with commitments to racial or economic justice. The substance of feminist value theory remains an open discussion.[5]

Mode of Making Ethical Decisions

The discipline of social ethics generally recognizes three primary models for decision-making, and there is some discussion about whether there are in fact only two. That is, in reflecting upon the teleological, deontological, and situation-response modes, one can detect within the third mode aspects are essentially teleological or deontological, depending on the ethicist in question.

Feminist ethics is in large part done in the teleological mode when the understanding of teleology allows for inclusion of the relational mode. Feminist ethics is oriented toward the liberation of women and weighs the value of acts or policy in those terms, but it is important to distinguish teleology from utilitarianism.[6] For while utilitar-

ian theories are teleological, not all teleological theories are subject to the difficulties of utilitarianism. That is, when utilitarianism calculates the greater good, it can be done in such a way as to make minority groups, including women, pay the cost for social policy. There are trends of feminist ethics which view the liberation of women as inclusive of or consistent with the liberation of other oppressed groups, and also of white men.[7]

Source or Justification of Ethical Claims

Some typical sources of ethical claims have traditionally included reference to the revelation of God, tradition, rational reflection, history, or lived experience. When lived experience is the source of ethical claims, further questions must be asked to clarify *whose* experience and under what interpretation. A further issue involves how persons are able to claim objectivity for their ethical sources when cultural, personal, and political perspectives on those claims are significant.

In relation to the various modes of making ethical decisions, it appears unlikely that those using a teleological mode would claim revelation as the source or justification of ethical claims, whereas those using a deontological or relational mode might do so. There is no rigid relation between the various sources and modes. For instance, one might claim natural law as the source for ethical claims and use either a teleological or

---

5. Haney (1980) has articulated a notion of feminist ethics as a vision for a values revolution, and proposes the paradigm nourishment-friendship as the central values. It is the task of feminists, she claims, to redefine moral excellence, virtue, and the good person, and to hold suspect definitions from the past of justice, love, and mercy.

6. Just as H. Richard Niebuhr is credited by Gustafson (1978) as having claimed that ethics is reflection upon ethos, when that means that his task is to analyze "ethos," to lay bare the roots and fundamental character of a community's moral life, so too might the metaethics of Daly (1978) be understood: "I would say that radical feminist metaethics is of a *deeper intuitive* type than 'ethics.' The latter, generally written from one of several (but basically the same) patriarchal perspectives, works out of hidden agendas concealed in the texture of language, buried in mythic reversals which control 'logic' most powerfully because unacknowledged. Thus for theologians and philosophers, Eastern and Western, and particularly for ethicists, woman-identified women do not exist. The metaethics of radical feminism seeks to uncover the background. . . . It is able to do this because our primary concern is *not* male ethics and/or ethicists, but our own Journeying." Further considering the mode

of decision-making, Gilligan (1979) characterizes women's patterns of moral reasoning in terms of an ethic of responsibility: "Sensitivity to the needs of others and the assumption of responsibility for taking care, lead women to attend to voices other than their own and to include in their judgment other points of view. Women's moral weakness, manifest in an apparent diffusion and confusion of judgment, is thus inseparable from women's moral strength, an overriding concern with relationships and responsibilities. The reluctance to judge itself can be indicative of the same care and concern for others that infuses the psychology of women's development. . . ."

7. I am indebted to a March, 1980 discussion within the Consultation on Social Ethics in Feminist Perspective, at Andover Newton Theological School, Newton Centre, Massachusetts, in which Lisa Cahill made the point that the inclusiveness of ends may distinguish teleological ethics from utililarian ethics.

a deontological mode of making ethical decisions, or justifying them.

Those developing feminist ethical theory are overwhelmingly inclined to refer to lived experience as the source for ethical claims, granting the complexities of this method.[8]

Presupposition of Ethical Action, Autonomy

The theory with regard to autonomy must necessarily be complex if it is to take seriously both the meaning of ethical propositions as well as behavioral research uncovering the very powerful forces which limit autonomy. While a measure of autonomy is necessary before moral choice can be exercised — and in this sense is an important goal — the notion of the moral agent as dispassionate and disengaged is distinct from the former notion of autonomy, and has come under criticism for its failure to recognize the social foundation of self.

Feminist ethical theory, in general terms, presupposes a criticism of the forces which limit women's autonomy in the ethical realm. In this sense, the economic dependency of women in the family, the inequality of pay and promotion in the labor force tied to women's role as child-bearer and child-rearer, the possibility of sexual harassment or physical abuse from a stranger or an intimate, and further, in psychological terms, the tendency toward lack of ego differentiation in women's personality formation, are all factors impinging upon women's sense of self which can be autonomous confronting or defining ethical situations.[9]

Motivation

How do we view the way ethical action begins and what keeps it going, recognizing that knowledge of what is the right thing to do does not necessarily result in the will to do the right? This is a classical question in the ethical tradition. Developing feminist perspectives bring to light the energy unleashed when women become engaged in collective efforts of self-definition, an energy which overcomes or at least mitigates against the alienation between the will and the right.[10]

To include all these factors in the ethical reasoning process is significant in itself, as there is not general agreement that the scope of social ethics should be so broadly conceived. While ethicists have proposed schemas including some of these factors, or more factors than these, it has been only recently, in relation to Latin American theologians of liberation, that the analysis of the roots of oppression has been suggested as necessary. In the field of social ethics we have had no trouble viewing "data" as a significant factor in ethical theory. However, *analysis* is the process of organizing data according to a theory which attempts to locate the historical causes of the situation. Some of the most important work impacting ethical reflection on women's experience is explicitly in this area.

* * *

In sum, to do feminist ethics we need a view of ethics in this broad scope. And in particular, we need to recognize analysis of the roots of oppression as an ethical factor.

* * *

Conclusion

In the preceding discussion, my purpose was to indicate why the term "feminist ethics" does not by itself indicate the content of feminist ethical theory. Indeed, there are at least four different social-political theories and programs which

---

8. Lived-world experience, feminist consciousness, "our bodies ourselves," women's efforts to achieve full recognition as persons — all serve as sources for norms in the work of Beverly Harrison (1975; 1978).

9. In response to this and related issues, Ruth Smith, doctoral candidate at Boston University, is developing a notion of the social self as moral agent, and Kate Cannon, doctoral student at Union Theological Seminary, is judging the applicability of the autonomous self to survival ethics of black women.

10. Ehrenreich (1978:3) says that Marxism and feminism are both outlooks which "lead to conclusions which are jarring and disturbing at the same time that they are liberating. There is no way to have a Marxist or feminist outlook and remain a spectator. To understand the reality laid bare by these analyses is to move into action to change it."

could provide a foundation for feminist ethics. However, the analysis of the roots of oppression is a key factor in feminist ethics. It has a direct bearing on the way we pose problems, gather data, commit our loyalties, rank values, engage in moral reasoning, justify claims, structure autonomy, and heighten motivation. Some examples might point to the validity of the exercise.

I made the point earlier that feminist ethicists generally agree that the appropriate starting point for ethical reflection is to attend to the very concrete situations, the fabric of women's lives. But just as few ethicists use the inductive mode at the expense of the deductive mode, feminists take into their reflection some assumptions which affect how they define the problem. Consequently, one can compare a radical feminist way of posing the problem, "In what ways are problematic situations the results of patriarchal control?" to a sex-rolist approach, "Is this a problem for both women and men, or do the conditions which resolve it apply equally for women and men?" A socialist feminist approach might look for concrete ways in which race and sexual dynamics benefit the owners of capital in the situation, and Marxist-Leninist feminists would probably share this starting point. Thus, at a fundamental level, the analysis of women's oppression affects the way the problem is posed.

Again, earlier I made the point that feminist ethicists have a loyalty to women *as women,* but that there is not across-the-board agreement as to how this loyalty relates to loyalties to other oppressed groups. Hence, the loyalties of radical feminists are to women, and perhaps even to radical feminist women, whereas the loyalties of sex-rolists are to all people, in the vision of situation-specific behaviors rather than sex-defined behaviors. Marxist-Leninist feminists have loyalties to women and men in the working class, and to all groups exploited by capital, as well as to those women and men who swing in their class allegiance toward the working class, thereby committing class suicide. Socialist feminists, because of a class analysis which views many professionals and white collar workers as working class, would view their loyalties in similar but broader terms than Marxist-Leninist feminists.

Values take on new meaning when they are defined in terms of the different political theories.

"Control over our own bodies" can evoke images of the petit bourgeoisie, a class of individualists, in light of a Marxist-Leninist feminist position on reproductive rights. On the other hand, reproductive rights as democratic rights needed by working class women to participate in the revolutionary struggle can sound like a mask of male hegemony in the context of a socialist feminist or a radical feminist perspective.

Yet there is no necessary disagreement among feminists about a value theory. Self-determination for women, autonomy, and an inviolable sense of embodiedness figure prominently in all feminists' visions of a new social order. There might be disagreement, however, on the understanding about why to articulate a feminist value theory, which would determine the weight it is given. Ethicists who have integrated an historical materialist world view are likely to articulate a value theory as one task to be accomplished in addition to other, more social-structural tasks. It could be that ethicists who do not operate with an historical materialist world view project the reordering of values as primary among the tasks involved in creating new structures for special relations. This thesis explains in some measure the emphasis given to value theory among radical feminists and sex-role theorists. However, some sex-role theorists actually place more emphasis on restructuring the institutions of family and school than socialist or Marxist-Leninist feminists. Since the sex-role theorists do not face the task of restructuring the economy and political relations, they can attend to and focus on a limited range of institutions.

In the radical feminist perspective, motivation to ethical activity is a function of coming to awareness of being female in a woman-hating culture. In sex-rolism, motivation is the result of having insight as to all the levels of experience which have been defined as socially inappropriate by virtue of an irrational factor, gender. Socialist feminism and Marxist-Leninist feminism acknowledge a motivation of commitment to justice for all victims of private property, even if one has race, class, or sex privilege.

And so on. These paragraphs should be suggestive of further possibilities in connecting the analysis of the roots of oppression to other factors in ethical theory. The emphasis on the role of this factor in feminist ethics reflects two things: first, that social-political theory contains a broad range of ethical factors, and, second, that ethicists, in the narrow sense of this term, do have social-political analyses, often unacknowledged.

By implication, ethicists are accountable to make clear their analyses of the roots of oppression, so that they can be held accountable for adequacy to the full range of data. In so doing we are broadening the range of accountability for attending to such analyses in two directions: to all ethicists, insofar as their work is in any way related to the social sphere; and to claims for adequacy to women regardless of race and class. In the context of such claims we can sense that the discipline of social ethics is full of possibilities for people seeking to take control of their lives in the midst of community formation.

Chapter 7

The Norms of Christian Ethics

Introduction

Most of the readers of this anthology will have heard of the Beatles and their 1967 recording *Sergeant Pepper's Lonely Hearts Club Band,* even if they have not heard the entire album. Most will be familiar with the song that seemed to capture not only an era of popular culture but a popular strand of Christian moral thought. "All you need is love," is an apt summary of the heart of Joseph Fletcher's situation ethics (see chapter 6). But as we saw in the last chapter, agreement that love is the ultimate principle of Christian ethics does not guarantee agreement about what form the matter of love must take. In this chapter, our readings indicate the conviction of Christian ethicists that love is not the only moral principle. Few Christian ethicists join in the chorus with Fletcher and the Beatles, "Love is all you need, love is all you need."

The passage from the prophet Micah declares straightforwardly that God delights when we do justice, love kindness, and walk humbly with God. The passage from Luke tells us of Jesus' demand that we follow him in a radical, self-sacrificial love of neighbor, and Paul sings in the sweetest voice of the beauty and goodness of love. But agreement with respect to the biblical demands of love and justice and mercy does not guarantee agreement about exactly what love, justice, and mercy require. One of the central tasks for Christian ethicists, then, is not only to identify the relevant norms for Christian ethics, but to elaborate what these norms actually require and how they should be employed in reflection upon the moral lives of Christians.

In our first reading, St. Augustine links love with peace of the soul and the proper order of human society. The starting point of neighbor love, he suggests, is the prohibition of harm to others. Following this, we have a duty to assist others. But Augustine, like the Greek philosophers who so influenced him, thinks that the moral life is not merely a matter of obeying the divine law, but also a matter of having an appropriate character, of possessing the excellences or virtues appropriate to rational creatures. Genuine virtue is not possible without God, and in the second part of the reading, Augustine presents a picture of what the four cardinal virtues — to Augustine's mind four forms of love — look like when transformed by the grace of God.

Kenneth Kirk (reading 41), the most significant Anglican moral theologian of the twentieth century, takes up where Augustine leaves off, translating the cardinal virtues into a modern context. The task of the church today is to explain and amplify the principles of Christian ethics handed to the church by the Scriptures and the tradition. Kirk thus discusses the four cardinal virtues and identifies many additional virtues related to these.

Reinhold Niebuhr (reading 42) sets before us the radical demand of sacrificial love exemplified in the life and death of Jesus. In the face of this demand, we are inclined either to entirely deny its relevance to our lives or to affirm its relevance by transforming the demand for self-sacrifice into common-sense moral wisdom. Niebuhr will have none of this. The law of love is not exhausted by common sense moral principles such as equality or justice, nor is it irrelevant to the Christian moral life. Rather, the law of love stands over and above all moral principles, judging them when they fall short of its demands, and remaining an ideal to which we aspire — ever aware of the impossibility of satisfying its demands.

Paul Tillich, like Reinhold Niebuhr, is one of the giants of twentieth-century American theology. Tillich's thought is teleological, the goal being the actualization or self-realization of all as "persons." In reading 43 Tillich identifies three ethical norms which are relevant to every moral decision, co-operatively enabling the self and others to realize "centeredness" and fullfillment. Tillich identifies these three principles as justice, love, and wisdom though, interestingly, he is reluctant to speak of love because of its contemporary trivialization.

Nicholas Wolterstorff (reading 44) turns our attention to the cause of God as disclosed in the biblical vision of *shalom*. Shalom is the peace, enjoyment, and fulfillment of God, humans, and the creation alike. Shalom requires justice, a commitment to the rights of all persons, but it requires right relationships with God and the creation as well. Hand-in-hand go the twin requirements, then, of the struggle for justice and mastery of the world in order to enrich human life.

Karen Lebacqz, too (reading 45), affirms the importance of justice and invites us to a deeper understanding of the requirements of justice. She argues that justice is primarily corrective of the concrete injustices that confront us here and now. Listening to the stories of those who suffer injustice we discern what means will liberate the oppressed and establish a new beginning apart from injustice. Lebacqz concludes with a brief critique of six contemporary theories of justice. (Readers may find it illuminating to review Carol Robb's discussion of feminist ethics in chapter 6 prior to reading Lebacqz's exploration of justice.)

Gordon Graham is among the many Christian thinkers who identify love and justice as two primary moral principles. In his essay (reading 46) he examines a common assumption in liberation theology that love and justice are identical. Graham rejects this conflation, distinguishing between two distinct ideas of justice and charity, or beneficence towards those who suffer. He argues that, in fact, much of the suffering that occurs in the world is not the result of some violation of human rights, so talk of justice in these circumstances is less accurate than talk of charity, despite the greater rhetorical impact of the former.

The last two essays in this chapter turn from the relation of love and justice to the relation of love to other values and virtues. Gilbert Meilaender ponders the goodness of the preferential love of friendship in light of Christian love (reading 47). *Agape* must be offered to all without preference or partiality, *agape* expects nothing in return, and *agape* remains steadfast and faithful to the other, come what may. Meilaender here explores the compatibility of friendship, always open to change, with the radical fidelity of Christian love.

Sidney Callahan's concern (reading 48) is with the virtue of patience and its relation to both love and justice. She argues for a resurrection of the virtue of patience, and carefully identifies just what it might mean to "bear wrongs patiently." Patience is revealed to be not only a great moral strength but also of practical benefit. Callahan concludes her discussion with advice on how to develop the excellence of patience.

Laws of God, moral principles, virtues — as the readings in this chapter and the last make clear, the norms or standards of the Christian life may come packaged in many different forms. And what is packaged — *agape*, *shalom*, justice, courage, fidelity, patience — may differ as well. Here we observe a few, but only a few, of the many norms and standards Christians have identified as relevant to the moral life.

Suggestions for Further Reading

Farley, Margaret. *Personal Commitments*. San Francisco: Harper & Row, 1986.

Lebacqz, Karen. *Six Theories of Justice*. Minneapolis: Augsburg Press, 1986.

————. *Justice in an Unjust World*. Minneapolis: Augsburg Press, 1986.

Lewis, C.S. *The Four Loves*. New York: Harcourt Brace Jovanovich, 1960.

Meilaender, Gilbert. *Friendship*. Notre Dame: University of Notre Dame Press, 1981.

Outka, Gene. *Agape: An Ethical Analysis*. New Haven: Yale University Press, 1972.

Perkins, Pheme. *Love Commands in the New Testament*. New York: Paulist Press, 1982.

Pieper, Josef. *About Love*. Chicago: Franciscan Herald Press, 1974.

39. Micah 6:6-8;
Luke 10:25-37;
1 Corinthians 13

Micah 6:6-8

"With what shall I come before the Lord,
  and bow myself before God on high?
Shall I come before him with burnt offerings,
  with calves a year old?
Will the Lord be pleased with thousands
    of rams?
  with ten thousands of rivers of oil?
Shall I give my firstborn for my transgression,
  the fruit of my body for the sin of my soul?"
He has told you, O mortal, what is good;
  and what does the Lord require of you
but to do justice, and to love kindness,
  and to walk humbly with your God?

Luke 10:25-37

Just then a lawyer stood up to test Jesus. "Teacher," he said, "what must I do to inherit eternal life?" He said to him, "What is written in the law? What do you read there?" He answered, "You shall love the Lord your God with all your heart, and with all your soul, and with all your strength, and with all your mind; and your neighbor as yourself." And he said to him, "You have given the right answer; do this, and you will live."

But wanting to justify himself, he asked Jesus, "And who is my neighbor?" Jesus replied, "A man was going down from Jerusalem to Jericho, and fell into the hands of robbers, who stripped him, beat him, and went away, leaving him half dead. Now by chance a priest was going down that road; and when he saw him, he passed by on the other side. So likewise a Levite, when he came to the place and saw him, passed by on the other side. But a Samaritan while traveling came near him; and when he saw him, he was moved with pity. He went to him and bandaged his wounds, having poured oil and wine on them. Then he put him on his own animal, brought him to an inn, and took care of him. The next day he took out two denarii, gave them to the innkeeper, and said, 'Take care of him; and when I come back, I will repay you whatever more you spend.' Which of these three, do you think, was a neighbor to the man who fell into the hands of the robbers?" He said, "The one who showed him mercy." Jesus said to him, "Go and do likewise."

1 Corinthians 13

If I speak in the tongues of mortals and of angels, but do not have love, I am a noisy gong or a clanging cymbal. And if I have prophetic powers, and understand all mysteries and all knowledge, and if I have all faith, so as to remove mountains, but do not have love, I am nothing. If I give away all my possessions, and if I hand over my body so that I may boast, but do not have love, I gain nothing.

Love is patient; love is kind; love is not envious or boastful or arrogant or rude. It does not insist on its own way; it is not irritable or resentful; it does not rejoice in wrongdoing, but rejoices in the truth. It bears all things, believes all things, hopes all things, endures all things.

Love never ends. But as for prophecies, they will come to an end; as for tongues, they will cease; as for knowledge, it will come to an end. For we know only in part, and we prophesy only in part; but when the complete comes, the partial will come to an end. When I was a child, I spoke like a child, I thought like a child, I reasoned like a child; when I became an adult, I put an end to childish ways. For now we see in a mirror, dimly, but then we will see face to face. Now I know only in part; then I will know fully, even as I have been fully known. And now faith, hope, and love abide, these three; and the greatest of these is love.

40. Excerpts from *The City of God* and *The Morals of the Catholic Church*

ST. AUGUSTINE

The City of God

The Order and Law, Earthly or Heavenly, by which Government Serves the Interests of Human Society

We see, then, that all man's use of temporal things is related to the enjoyment of earthly peace in the earthly city; whereas in the heavenly city it is related to the enjoyment of eternal peace. Thus, if we were irrational animals, our only aim would be the adjustment of the parts of the body in due proportion, and the quieting of the appetites — only, that is, the repose of the flesh, and an adequate supply of pleasures, so that bodily peace might promote the peace of the soul. For if bodily peace is lacking, the peace of the irrational soul is also hindered, because it cannot achieve the quieting of its appetites. But the two together promote that peace which is a mutual concord between soul and body, the peace of an ordered life and of health. For living creatures show their love of bodily peace by their avoidance of pain, and by their pursuit of pleasure to satisfy the demands of their appetites they demonstrate their love of peace of soul. In just the same way, by shunning death they indicate quite clearly how great is their love of the peace in which soul and body are harmoniously united.

But because there is in man a rational soul, he subordinates to the peace of the rational soul all that part of his nature which he shares with the beasts, so that he may engage in deliberate thought and act in accordance with this thought, so that he may thus exhibit that ordered agreement of cognition and action which we called the peace of the rational soul. For with this end in view he ought to wish to be spared the distress of pain and grief, the disturbances of desire, the dissolution of death, so that he may come to some profitable knowledge and may order his life and his moral standards in accordance with this knowledge. But he needs divine direction, which he may obey with resolution, and divine assistance that he may obey it freely, to prevent him from falling, in his enthusiasm for knowledge, a victim to some fatal effort through the weakness of the human mind. And so long as he is in this mortal body, he is a pilgrim in a foreign land, away from God; therefore he walks by faith, not by sight.[1] That is why he views all peace, of body or of soul, or of both, in relation to that peace which exists between mortal man and immortal God, so that he may exhibit an ordered obedience in faith in subjection to the everlasting law.

Now God, our master, teaches two chief precepts, love of God and love of neighbour; and in them man finds three objects for his love: God, himself, and his neighbour; and a man who loves God is not wrong in loving himself. It follows, therefore, that he will be concerned also that his neighbour should love God, since he is told to love his neighbour as himself; and the same is true of his concern for his wife, his children, for the members of his household, and for all other men, so far as is possible. And, for the same end, he will wish his neighbour to be concerned for him, if he happens to need that concern. For this reason he

---

St. Augustine (354–430), under the influence of Neoplatonic philosophy, converted to the Christian faith as a young man. Following his conversion he pursued the knowledge of God in a monastic community prior to being drafted to be the Bishop of Hippo in North Africa. His *Confessions* and his *City of God* have had widespread influence on psychology and political philosophy as well as theology in the West.

From St. Augustine, *The City of God,* trans. Henry Bettenson (London: Penguin Classics, 1984) and *The Basic Writings of St. Augustine,* ed. Whitney Oates (New York: Random House, 1948).

1. Cf. 2 Cor. 5:6f.

will be at peace, as far as lies in him, with all men, in that peace among men, that ordered harmony; and the basis of this order is the observance of two rules: first, to do no harm to anyone, and, secondly, to help everyone whenever possible. To begin with, therefore, a man has a responsibility for his own household — obviously, both in the order of nature and in the framework of human society, he has easier and more immediate contact with them; he can exercise his concern for them. That is why the apostle says, "Anyone who does not take care of his own people, especially those in his own household, is worse than an unbeliever — he is a renegade."[2] This is where domestic peace starts, the ordered harmony about giving and obeying orders among those who live in the same house. For the orders are given by those who are concerned for the interests of others; thus the husband gives orders to the wife, parents to children, masters to servants. While those who are the objects of this concern obey orders; for example, wives obey husbands, the children obey their parents, the servants their masters. But in the household of the just man who "lives on the basis of faith" and who is still on pilgrimage, far from that heavenly city, even those who give orders are the servants of those whom they appear to command. For they do not give orders because of a lust for domination but from a dutiful concern for the interests of others, not with pride in taking precedence over others, but with compassion in taking care of others.

*　　*　　*

True Virtues Impossible without True Religion

The fact is that the soul may appear to rule the body and the reason to govern the vicious elements in the most praiseworthy fashion; and yet if the soul and reason do not serve God as God himself has commanded that he should be served, then they do not in any way exercise the right kind of rule over the body and the vicious propensities. For what kind of a mistress over the body and the vices can a mind be that is ignorant of the true God and is not subjected to his rule, but instead is prostituted

2. 1 Tim. 5:8.

to the corrupting influence of vicious demons? Thus the virtues which the mind imagines it possesses, by means of which it rules the body and the vicious elements, are themselves vices rather than virtues if the mind does not bring them into relation with God in order to achieve anything whatsoever and to maintain that achievement. For although the virtues are reckoned by some people to be genuine and honourable when they are related only to themselves and are sought for no other end, even then they are puffed up and proud, and so are to be accounted vices rather than virtues. For just as it not something derived from the physical body itself that gives life to that body, but something above it, so it is not something that comes from man, but something above man, that makes his life blessed; and this is true not only of man but of every heavenly dominion and power whatsoever.

The Morals of the Catholic Church

The Christian Definition of the Four Virtues

As to virtue leading us to a happy life, I hold virtue to be nothing else than perfect love of God. For the fourfold division of virtue I regard as taken from four forms of love. For these four virtues (would that all felt their influence in their minds as they have their names in their mouths!), I should have no hesitation in defining them: that temperance is love giving itself entirely to that which is loved; fortitude is love readily bearing all things for the sake of the loved object; justice is love serving only the loved object, and therefore ruling rightly; prudence is love distinguishing with sagacity between what hinders it and what helps it. The object of this love is not anything, but only God, the chief good, the highest wisdom, the perfect harmony. So we may express the definition thus: that temperance is love keeping itself entire and incorrupt for God; fortitude is love bearing everything readily for the sake of God; justice is love serving God only, and therefore ruling well all else, as subject to man; prudence is love making a right distinction between what helps it towards God and what might hinder it.

*　　*　　*

235

Description of the Duties of Temperance, according to the Sacred Scriptures

It is now time to return to the four virtues, and to draw out and prescribe a way of life in conformity with them, taking each separately. First, then, let us consider temperance, which promises us a kind of integrity and incorruption in the love by which we are united to God. The office of temperance is in restraining and quieting the passions which make us pant for those things which turn us away from the laws of God and from the enjoyment of his goodness, that is, in a word, from the happy life. For there is the abode of truth; and in enjoying its contemplation, and in cleaving closely to it, we are assuredly happy; but departing from this, men become entangled in great errors and sorrows. For, as the apostle says, "The root of all evils is covetousness; which some having followed, have made shipwreck of the faith, and have pierced themselves through with many sorrows."[1] And this sin of the soul is quite plainly, to those rightly understanding, set forth in the Old Testament in the transgression of Adam in Paradise. Thus, as the apostle says, "In Adam we all die and in Christ we shall all rise again."[2] Oh, the depth of these mysteries! But I refrain; for I am now engaged not in teaching you the truth, but in making you unlearn your errors, if I can, that is, if God aid my purpose regarding you.

Paul then says that covetousness is the root of all evils: and by covetousness the old law also intimates that the first man fell. Paul tells us to put off the old man and put on the new.[3] By the old man he means Adam who sinned, and by the new man him whom the Son of God took to himself in consecration for our redemption. For he says in another place, "The first man is of the earth, earthy; the second man is from heaven, heavenly. As is the earthy, such are they also that are earthy; and as is the heavenly, such are they also that are heavenly. And as we have borne the image of the earthy, let us also bear the image of the heavenly"[4] — that is, put off the old man, and put on the new. The whole duty of temperance, then, is to put off the old man, and to be renewed in God — that is, to scorn all bodily delights, and the popular applause, and to turn the whole love to things divine and unseen. Hence that following passage which is so admirable: "Though our outward man perish, our inward man is renewed day by day."[5] Hear, too, the prophet singing, "Create in me a clean heart, O God, and renew a right spirit within me."[6] What can be said against such harmony except by blind barkers?

We Are Required to Despise All Sensible Things and to Love God Alone

Bodily delights have their source in all those things with which the bodily sense comes in contact, and which are by some called the objects of sense; and among these the noblest is light, in the common meaning of the word, because among our senses also, which the mind uses in acting through the body, there is nothing more valuable than the eyes, and so in the Holy Scriptures all the objects of sense are spoken of as visible things. Thus in the New Testament we are warned against the love of these things in the following words: "While we look not at the things which are seen, but at the things which are not seen; for the things which are seen are temporal, but the things which are not seen are eternal."[7] This shows how far from being Christians those are who hold that the sun and moon are to be not only loved but worshipped. For what is seen if the sun and moon are not? But we are forbidden to regard things which are seen. The man, therefore, who wishes to offer that incorrupt love to God must not love these things too. This subject I will inquire into more particularly elsewhere. Here my plan is to write not of faith, but of the life by which we become worthy of knowing what we believe. God then alone is to be loved; and all this world, that is, all sensible things, are to be despised — while, however, they are to be used as this life requires.

* * *

1. 1 Tim. 6:10.
2. Col. 3:9, 10.
3. 1 Cor. 15:22.
4. 1 Cor. 15:47-49.
5. 2 Cor. 4:16.
6. Ps. 51:10.
7. 2 Cor. 4:18.

Fortitude Comes from the Love of God

On fortitude we must be brief. The love, then, of which we speak, which ought with all sanctity to burn in desire for God, is called temperance, in not seeking for earthly things, and fortitude, in bearing the loss of them. But among all things which are possessed in this life, the body is, by God's most righteous laws, for the sin of old, man's heaviest bond, which is well known as a fact, but most incomprehensible in its mystery. Lest this bond should be shaken and disturbed, the soul is shaken with the fear of toil and pain; lest it should be lost and destroyed, the soul is shaken with the fear of death. For the soul loves it from the force of habit, not knowing that by using it well and wisely its resurrection and reformation will, by the divine help and decree, be without any trouble made subject to its authority. But when the soul turns to God wholly in this love, it knows these things, and so will not only disregard death, but will even desire it.

Then there is the great struggle with pain. But there is nothing, though of iron hardness, which the fire of love cannot subdue. And when the mind is carried up to God in this love, it will soar above all torture free and glorious with wings beauteous and unhurt, on which chaste love rises to the embrace of God. Otherwise God must allow the lovers of gold, the lovers of praise, the lovers of women, to have more fortitude than the lovers of Himself, though love in those cases is rather to be called passion or lust. And yet even here we may see with what force the mind presses on with unflagging energy, in spite of all alarms, towards that it loves; and we learn that we should bear all things rather than forsake God, since those men bear so much in order to forsake him.

*   *   *

Of Justice and Prudence

What of justice that pertains to God? As the Lord says, "Ye cannot serve two masters,"[8] and the apostle denounces those who serve the creature rather than the Creator,[9] was it not said before in the Old Testament "Thou shalt worship the Lord thy God, and him only shalt thou serve?"[10] I need say no more on this, for these books are full of such passages. The lover, then, whom we are describing, will get from justice this rule of life, that he must with perfect readiness serve the God whom he loves, the highest good, the highest wisdom, the highest peace; and as regards all other things, must either rule them as subject to himself, or treat them with a view to their subjection. This rule of life, is, as we have shown, confirmed by the authority of both Testaments.

With equal brevity we must treat of prudence, to which it belongs to discern between what is to be desired and what is to be shunned. Without this, nothing can be done of what we have already spoken of. It is the part of prudence to keep watch with most anxious vigilance, lest any evil influence should stealthily creep in upon us. Thus the Lord often exclaims, "Watch";[11] and he says, "Walk while ye have the light, lest darkness come upon you."[12] And then it is said, "Know ye not that a little leaven leaveneth the whole lump?"[13] And no passage can be quoted from the Old Testament more expressly condemning this mental somnolence, which makes us insensible to destruction advancing on us step by step, than those words of the prophet, "He who despiseth small things shall fall by degrees."[14] On this topic I might discourse at length did our haste allow of it. And did our present task demand it, we might perhaps prove the depth of these mysteries, by making a mock of which profane men in their perfect ignorance fall, not certainly by degrees, but with a headlong overthrow.

---

8. Matt. 6:24.
9. Rom. 1:25.
10. Deut. 6:13.
11. Matt. 24:42.
12. John 12:35.
13. 1 Cor. 5:6.
14. Ecclus. 19:1.

41. The Cardinal Virtues

KENNETH E. KIRK

The Christian ideal of character, we have seen, is the person of Christ, as manifested in his earthly life. Nothing short of that suffices as a guide. And the simplest summary of this pattern of Christian goodness is to say that it exemplifies in the highest form the love and the service of God and our fellow men.[1] To love God and to serve him; to love men and to serve them; this is the essence and the whole of Christian duty — the purpose of man's life.

But this pattern requires to be articulated and examined, and its leading *motifs* set out in plain form, in order that its demands may be brought into relation with the circumstances of a more elaborate civilisation than that of Galilee and Judea.

It is, of course, open to the Christian to separate himself from the world and its business and live a life of evangelical simplicity in poverty, celibacy, and even seclusion. There are those, no doubt, for whom such a course is the only one by which they can attain to single-hearted union with God. If de Cressy's estimate of John Inglesant was the right one, the latter was one of these: "You are like the young man who came to Jesus," the Benedictine said, "and whom Jesus loved, for you have great possessions. You have been taught all that men

1. *Summa,* II, 2, Q.25, A.1.

Kenneth E. Kirk (1886–1954) was the Anglican bishop of Oxford. His work includes *Vision of God, Some Principles of Moral Theology; The Threshold of Ethics; The Ministry of Absolution;* and *The Coherence of Christian Doctrine.*

From Kenneth E. Kirk, *Some Principles of Moral Theology* (London: Longman, Green, & Co., 1920).

desire to know, and are accomplished in all that makes life delightful. You have the knowledge of the past and know the reality of men's power and wisdom and beauty, which they possess of themselves, and did possess in the old classic times. . . . You wish this life's wisdom, and to walk with Christ as well; and you are your own witness that it cannot be. The two cannot walk together as you have found. To you especially this is the great test and trial that Christ expects of you to the very full. We of this religious order have given ourselves to learning, as you know; nay, in former years to that pagan learning which is so attractive to you. . . . But even this you must keep yourself from. *To most men this study is no temptation: to you it is fatal.* I put before you your life with no false colouring, no tampering with the truth. Come with me to Douay; you shall enter our house according to the strictest rule; you shall engage in no study that is any delight or effort to the intellect; but you shall teach the smallest children in the schools, and visit the poorest people, and perform the duties of the household — and all for Christ. I promise you on the faith of a gentleman and a priest — I promise you for I have no shade of doubt — that in this path you shall find the satisfaction of the heavenly walk; you shall walk with Jesus day by day growing ever more and more like to him; and your path, without the least fall or deviation, shall lead more and more into the light, until you come unto the perfect day; and on your deathbed — the deathbed of a saint — the vision of the smile of God shall sustain you, and Jesus himself shall meet you at the gate of eternal life."[2]

Characters such as the one here described — men and women with sensibilities abnormally alive to the absorbing interest of truth and beauty, but without the stability of purpose which will enable them to keep such sensibilities under control — can perhaps only develop their spiritual life after a violent and irrevocable act of self-detachment from the world. The world is too strong for them. "Get thee to a nunnery" was advice not so much due to any desire on Hamlet's part for Ophelia's happiness; it was the outcome of some such sense that only complete alienation from a world which fascinated and terrified him

2. J. H. Shorthouse, *John Inglesant,* chap. 19. The italics are not in the original.

at once could save *his own* reason and soul. It expressed a longing for seclusion for himself rather than for her.

Other circumstances, too, and other temperamental conditions may make what is technically called the "religious life" the best way in which any given Christian can grow into conformity with his master's pattern. Christianity recognises to the full the fact of *vocation*.[3] There is only one ideal of the Christian life; but it will express itself in many different forms according as a man is called, by circumstance or endowment, to the cloister, the library, the workshop or the office. And the cloister, we may say, is the vocation of comparatively few. The majority of Christian men and women have to live in the world, though not of it; occupied with its problems and beset with its temptations. For their guidance we need a translation, into terms of business and home life, of the spirit and example of him who had neither business entanglements nor home itself. He himself laid down the principles upon which this expansion of the essential elements in the Christian life through all the accidents of its varying circumstances must be conducted; more than that he left to the church to provide. The apostles, who from the first attempted to regulate home and social intercourse on Christian principles, laid the foundations of Christian ethics; its amplification has gone on in the church ever since.

The first business of Christian ethics, then, is to enumerate the main duties of a Christian in normal circumstances. The sketch must not be too vague: for that would leave it out of relation with the situations in which the duties have to be performed. On the other hand, it must not be too detailed, for, as we have seen, the Christian dispensation has always tried to avoid the rigidities of the Jewish law. We need not, however, treat of this branch of our subject at any length; for the ground has been continually traversed, and any of the recognised textbooks on Christian ethics give all that is required. We may, however, notice one or two features about the treatment of the subject which are of importance.

First of all, our attention is drawn by the wealth of material from which selection can be made. From the Bible alone we can choose any one of innumerable different passages or pictures as a groundwork. Greatest of all of them is the person of our Lord as revealed in the Gospels. That pattern can be, and has often been, studied until its main features stand out clearly as a model for all time. So too with his teaching as with his life; it has been formulated time after time with a view to giving a clear but comprehensive survey of the Christian virtues. In particular, the Beatitudes have been used for this purpose. Their half-dozen clauses enshrine the greatest virtues of the Christian character.

From the apostolic writings can be chosen the hymn of love (1 Cor. 13), or the fruits of the Spirit (Gal. 5:22), or the "soberness, righteousness, and godliness"[4] of Titus 2:12, or St. James's brief summary (James 1:27) — "to visit the fatherless and widows in their affliction and to keep himself unspotted from the world."

The Old Testament too, interpreted in the light of the New, is no less illuminating. The decalogue, read in the spirit of the Sermon on the Mount, with its negative enactments emphasised on the positive side, has been used in this way throughout the church's history.[5] The gifts of the Spirit (Isa. 11:2, 3) have passed into Christian usage in the Confirmation service; the various pictures of the righteous man (Ps. 1, 15, 24, etc.) or the wise man (Prov. 3, etc.) can all be used as true outlines of an ideal to which the New Testament supplies color and detail. There is no set form or scheme with which theologians have approached their task; every student of Christian ethics is at liberty to travel by the path which suits him best.

Yet it is to be noticed — and this is the second point to which we should give attention — that Western theology, at all events, under the successive guidance of Ambrose, Augustine, Gregory, and Aquinas, has on the whole chosen to base its picture of the Christian ideal not upon any one of these scriptural foundations, but upon a pagan

---

3. E.g. Matt. 14:11; Mark 3:13-15; Acts 9:15, 16; 1 Cor. 7:7, 17-24, 27, 12:6-21; Gal. 1:16, 2:7; Eph. 4:7, 11, 6:5-9.

4. This is the basis of Jeremy Taylor's scheme in *Holy Living*, where "soberness" is taken as covering our duty to ourselves; "righteousness," our duty to our neighbour; "godliness," our duty to God.

5. But see C. Gore, *Dominant Ideas*, etc., chap. 6, and *Supra*, p. 10.

classification of virtue. Through the medium of Cicero's "De Officiis" St. Ambrose first of all, and then his successors, drew from Plato and Aristotle that Greek classification which has always gone by the name of the cardinal virtues[6] — prudence, justice, temperance, and fortitude. But Christian theology did not adopt them in any slavish spirit of imitation. It reinterpreted them and filled them with a Christian content, so much so that in the end it reversed those parts of their meaning which had a pagan, as distinct from a Christian, outlook.

"The virtues are recognisable indeed," says Dr. Strong, in summarising the end of this process of adaptation as it appears in the *Summa Theologica,* "There can be no question but that they are the true lineal descendants of those of Aristotle. Fortitude is still the cool steady behaviour of a man in the presence of danger, the tenacious preservation of that which is dearer to him than his life. But its range is widened by the inclusion of dangers to soul as well as body; it is the bravery of one who dwells in a spiritual world. Temperance is still the control of the bodily passions; but it is also more positively than negatively the right placing of our affections. Justice is still the negative of all self-seeking, of all angry conflict with the interests of others; but the source of it all and the ground of its possibility lies in giving God the love and adoration which are his due. Prudence is still the practical moral sense which chooses the right course of concrete action; but it is the prudence of men who are pilgrims towards a country where the object of their love is to be found. The four are recognisable, then, as I have said, but they have suffered serious change."[7]

We need scarcely remind ourselves that these virtues are called "cardinal" because all other Christian duties "hinge" on, or may be referred to, one or other of them. Two-thirds of the second division of Part II of the *Summa Theologica* is devoted to a discussion of the virtues dependent upon the four,[8] and their meaning is further developed by discussion of the vices contrary to each. More modern examples of the same method are to be found in Dr. Ottley's essay in *Lux Mundi* or in his *Christian Ideas and Ideals,* and in Professor Sorley's *The Moral Life.* Putting together these various accounts we may therefore summarise the Christian duties something after the following fashion:

Prudence: the habit of referring all questions, whether of ideals or of courses of action, to the criterion of God's will for us. From it derive such virtues as docility, conscientiousness, impartiality, and tact.

Justice: the giving to everyone (including to God and to oneself) his due. Under this head are comprised truthfulness, benevolence, forgiveness, compassion, and the duties of religion[9] — reverence, devotion, obedience, and gratitude to God.

Temperance: self-control "for the highest possible development of our nature both for personal and for social ends";[10] including purity, humility, patience, meekness, and even thrift.

Fortitude: the spirit which not only resists and endures, but even triumphs over, the trials and temptations of life; "glorifying in its afflictions." To it we may refer not only such high virtues as moral courage and righteous indignation, but the more everyday yet equally Christian duties of industry and thoroughness.

That such a catalogue is at best of a highly artificial and almost unreal kind can hardly be denied. Yet it has a value of its own for the guardian of souls. It gives him a scheme on which he can build much of his exhortation and his preaching, as well as a rude criterion by which to test the spiritual welfare of his flock. We should all agree, surely, that the clergy would benefit both themselves and their people by greater study of the

---

6. Also called the *natural* or *moral* virtues: *natural,* as distinct from *theological; moral,* as distinct from *intellectual.* This last distinction dates from the confusion of the Greek word ἀρετὴ, meaning at once *virtue* in the ordinary sense, and *excellence* or *perfection.* See T. B. Strong, *Christian Ethics,* Lect. 3, note 1. The cardinal virtues are mentioned together in the Wisdom literature — e.g. *Wisd.* 8:7.

7. T. B. Strong, *Christian Ethics,* p. 141. Cp. *Summa,* II, 2, Q. 47-170, and Augustine *De Moribus Eccl. Cath.* 15, 25, where all four are defined in terms of loving God.

8. For the exact relation which St. Thomas thought to exist between the cardinal virtues and the minor moral virtues, see W. H. V. Reade, *Moral System of Dante's Inferno,* pp. 148-152.

9. Thus St. Thomas makes penance a "part" of justice, as being the acknowledgment of a debt incurred to God by sin. *Summa,* III, Q.85, A.3.

10. W. R. Sorley, *The Moral Life,* p. 36.

principal Christian virtues and their demands. English morality, as has already been argued, suffers today not from over-rigidity but from vagueness — from an inability to decide what is right and what is wrong;[11] one cause at least of this lies in the fact that we have ceased to give clear thought and expression to the leading principles of Christian action. The cardinal virtues and their dependent virtues cannot be regarded as anything more than such leading principles; but so much at least they are, and the priest who is armed with a knowledge of them and their parts goes to his work with a surer touch than one who has no more than a vague idea of "goodness."

42. The Relevance of an Impossible Ethical Ideal

REINHOLD NIEBUHR

Prophetic Christianity faces the difficulty that its penetration into the total and ultimate human situation complicates the problem of dealing with the immediate moral and social situations which all men must face. The common currency of the moral life is constituted of the "nicely calculated less and more" of the relatively good and the relatively evil. Human happiness in ordinary intercourse is determined by the difference between a little more and a little less justice, a little more and little less freedom, between varying degrees of imaginative insight with which the self enters the life and understands the interests of the neighbour. Prophetic Christianity, on the other hand, demands the impossible; and by that very demand emphasizes the impotence and corruption of human nature, wresting from man the cry of distress and contrition, "The good that I would, do I do not: but the evil that I would not, that I do. . . . Woe is me . . . who will deliver me from the body of this death?" Measuring the distance between mountain peaks and valleys and arriving at the conclusion that every high mountain has a "tim-

Reinhold Niebuhr (1892–1971) was professor of theology at Union Theological Seminary and, arguably, the most important figure in theological ethics in this century. Among his many works are *Moral Man and Immoral Society; Children of Light, Children of Darkness;* and *The Nature and Destiny of Man.*

From Reinhold Niebuhr, *An Interpretation of Christian Ethics* (New York: Harper & Row, 1935).

11. Stevenson, *Lay Morals.*

ber line" above which life cannot maintain itself, it is always tempted to indifference toward the task of building roads up the mountainside, and of coercing its wilderness into a sufficient order to sustain human life. The latter task must consequently be assumed by those who are partly blind to the total dimension of life and, being untouched by its majesties and tragedies, can give themselves to the immediate tasks before them.

Thus prophetic religion tends to disintegrate into two contrasting types of religion. The one inclines to deny the relevance of the ideal of love to the ordinary problems of existence, certain that the tragedy of human life must be resolved by something more than moral achievement. The other tries to prove the relevance of the religious ideal to the problems of everyday existence by reducing it to conformity with the prudential rules of conduct which the common sense of many generations and the experience of the ages have elaborated. Broadly speaking, the conflict between these two world-views is the conflict between orthodox Christianity and modern secularism. In so far as liberal Christianity is a compound of prophetic religion and secularism it is drawn into the debate in a somewhat equivocal position but, on the whole on the side of the secularists and naturalists.

Against orthodox Christianity, the prophetic tradition in Christianity must insist on the relevance of the ideal of love to the moral experience of mankind on every conceivable level. It is not an ideal magically superimposed upon life by a revelation which has no relation to total human experience. The whole conception of life revealed in the Cross of Christian faith is not a pure negation of, or irrelevance toward, the moral ideals of "natural man." While the final heights of the love ideal condemn as well as fulfil the moral canons of common sense, the ideal is involved in every moral aspiration and achievement. It is the genius and the task of prophetic religion to insist on the organic relation between historic human existence and that which is both the ground and the fulfilment of this existence, the transcendent.

Moral life is possible at all only in a meaningful existence. Obligation can be felt only to some system of coherence and some ordering will. Thus moral obligation is always an obligation to promote harmony and to overcome chaos. But every

conceivable order in the historical world contains an element of anarchy. Its world rests upon contingency and caprice. The obligation to support and enhance it can therefore only arise and maintain itself upon the basis of a faith that it is the partial fruit of a deeper unity and the promise of a more perfect harmony than is revealed in any immediate situation. If a lesser faith than this prompts moral action, it results in precisely those types of moral fanaticism which impart unqualified worth to qualified values and thereby destroy even their qualified worth. The prophetic faith in a God who is both the ground and the ultimate fulfilment of existence, who is both the creator and the judge of the world, is thus involved in every moral situation. Without it the world is seen either as being meaningless or as revealing unqualifiedly good and simple meanings. In either case the nerve of moral action is ultimately destroyed. The dominant attitudes of prophetic faith are gratitude and contrition; gratitude for creation and contrition before judgment; or, in other words, confidence that life is good in spite of its evil and that it is evil in spite of its good. In such a faith both sentimentality and despair are avoided. The meaningfulness of life does not tempt to premature complacency, and the chaos which always threatens the world of meaning does not destroy the tension of faith and hope in which all moral action is grounded.

The prophetic faith, that the meaningfulness of life and existence implies a source and end beyond itself, produces a morality which implies that every moral value and standard is grounded in and points toward an ultimate perfection of unity and harmony, not realizable in any historic situation. An analysis of the social history of mankind validates this interpretation.

In spite of the relativity of morals every conceivable moral code and every philosophy of morals enjoins concern for the life and welfare of the other and seeks to restrain the unqualified assertion of the interests of the self against the other. There is thus a fairly universal agreement in all moral systems that it is wrong to take the life or the property of the neighbour, though it must be admitted that the specific applications of these general principles vary greatly according to time and place. This minimal standard of moral conduct is grounded in the law of love and points toward it as ultimate fulfilment. The obligation to affirm and protect the life of others can arise at all only if it is assumed that life is related to life in some unity and harmony of existence. In any given instance motives of the most calculating prudence rather than a high sense of obligation may enforce the standard. Men may defend the life of the neighbour merely to preserve those processes of mutuality by which their own life is protected. But that only means that they have discovered the interrelatedness of life through concern for themselves rather than by an analysis of the total situation. This purely prudential approach will not prompt the most consistent social conduct, but it will nevertheless implicitly affirm what it ostensibly denies — that the law of life is love.

Perhaps the clearest proof that the law of love is involved as a basis of even the most minimal social standards, is found in the fact that every elaboration of minimal standards into higher standards makes the implicit relation more explicit. Prohibitions of murder and theft are negative. They seek to prevent one life from destroying or taking advantage of another. No society is content with these merely negative prohibitions. Its legal codes do not go much beyond negatives because only minimal standards can be legally enforced. But the moral codes and ideals of every advanced society demand more than mere prohibition of theft and murder. Higher conceptions of justice are developed. It is recognized that the right to live implies the right to secure the goods which sustain life. This right immediately involves more than mere prohibition of theft. Some obligation is felt, however dimly, to organize the common life so that the neighbour will have fair opportunities to maintain his life. The various schemes of justice and equity which grow out of this obligation, consciously or unconsciously imply an ideal of equality beyond themselves. Equality is always the regulative principle of justice; and in the ideal of equality there is an echo of the law of love, "Thou shalt love thy neighbour *as thyself*." If the question is raised to what degree the neighbour has a right to support his life through the privileges and opportunities of the common life, no satisfactory, rational answer can be given to it, short of one implying equalitarian principles: He has just as much right as you yourself.

This does not mean that any society will ever achieve perfect equality. Equality, being a rational, political version of the law of love, shares with it the quality of transcendence. It ought to be, but it never will be fully realized. Social prudence will qualify it. The most equalitarian society will probably not be able to dispense with special rewards as inducements to diligence. Some differentials in privilege will be necessary to make the performance of certain social functions possible. While a rigorous equalitarian society can prevent such privileges from being perpetuated from one generation to another without regard to social function, it cannot eliminate privileges completely. Nor is there any political technique which would be a perfect guarantee against abuses of socially sanctioned privileges. Significant social functions are endowed by their very nature with a certain degree of social power. Those who possess power, however socially restrained, always have the opportunity of deciding that the function which they perform is entitled to more privilege than any ideal scheme of justice would allow. The ideal of equality is thus qualified in any possible society by the necessities of social cohesion and corrupted by the sinfulness of men. It remains, nevertheless, a principle of criticism under which every scheme of justice stands and a symbol of the principle of love involved in all moral judgments.

But the principle of equality does not exhaust the possibilities of the moral ideal involved in even the most minimal standards of justice. Imaginative justice leads beyond equality to a consideration of the special needs of the life of the other. A sensitive parent will not make capricious distinctions in the care given to different children. But the kind of imagination which governs the most ideal family relationships soon transcends this principle of equality and justifies special care for a handicapped child and, possibly, special advantages for a particularly gifted one. The "right" to have others consider one's unique needs and potentialities is recognized legally only in the most minimal terms and is morally recognized only in very highly developed communities. Yet the modern public school, which began with the purpose of providing equal educational opportunities for all children, has extended its services so that both handicapped and highly gifted children receive special privileges from it. Every one of these achievements in the realm of justice is logically related, on the one hand, to the most minimal standards of justice, and on the other to the ideal of perfect love — i.e., to the obligation of affirming the life and interests of the neighbour as much as those of the self. The basic rights to life and property in the early community, the legal minima of rights and obligations of more advanced communities beyond those which are legally enforced, the further refinement of standards in the family beyond those recognized in the general community — all these stand in an ascending scale of moral possibilities in which each succeeding step is a closer approximation of the law of love.

The history of corrective justice reveals the same ascending scale of possibilities as that of distributive justice. Society begins by regulating vengeance and soon advances to the stage of substituting public justice for private vengeance. Public justice recognizes the right of an accused person to a more disinterested judgment than that of the injured accuser. Thus the element of vengeance is reduced, but not eliminated, in modern standards of punitive justice. The same logic which forced its reduction presses on toward its elimination. The criminal is recognized to have rights as a human being, even when he has violated his obligations to society. Therefore modern criminology, using psychiatric techniques, seeks to discover the cause of antisocial conduct in order that it may be corrected. The reformatory purpose attempts to displace the purely punitive intent. This development follows a logic which must culminate in the command, "Love your enemies." The more imaginative ideals of the best criminologists are, of course, in the realm of unrealized hopes. They will never be fully realized. An element of vindictive passion will probably corrupt the corrective justice of even the best society. The collective behaviour is not imaginative enough to assure more than minimal approximations of the ideal. Genuine forgiveness of the enemy requires a contrite recognition of the sinfulness of the self and of the mutual responsibility for the sin of the accused. Such spiritual penetration is beyond the capacities of collective man. It is the achievement of only rare individuals. Yet the right to such understanding is involved in the most basic of human rights and follows logically if the basic right to life is rationally elaborated. Thus all standards of corrective justice are organically related

to primitive vengeance on the one hand, and the ideal of forgiving love on the other. No absolute limit can be placed upon the degree to which human society may yet approximate the ideal. But it is certain that every achievement will remain in the realm of approximation. The ideal in its perfect form lies beyond the capacities of human nature.

Moral and social ideals are always a part of a series of infinite possibilities not only in terms of their purity, but in terms of their breadth of application. The most tender and imaginative human attitudes are achieved only where consanguinity and contiguity support the unity of life with life, and nature aids spirit in creating harmony. Both law and morality recognize rights and obligations within the family which are not recognized in the community, and within the community which are not accepted beyond the community. Parents are held legally responsible for the neglect of their children but not for the neglect of other people's children. Modern nations assume qualified responsibilities for the support of their unemployed, but not for the unemployed of other nations. Such a sense of responsibility may be too weak to function adequately without the support of political motives, as, for instance, the fear that hungry men may disturb the social peace. But weak as it is, it is yet strong enough to suggest responsibilities beyond itself. No modern people is completely indifferent toward the responsibility for all human life. In terms of such breadth the obligation is too weak to become the basis for action, except on rare occasions. The need of men in other nations must be vividly portrayed and dramatized by some great catastrophe before generosity across national boundaries expresses itself. But it can express itself, even in those rare moments, only because all human life is informed with an inchoate sense of responsibility toward the ultimate law of life — the law of love. The community of mankind has no organs of social cohesion and no instruments for enforcing social standards (and it may never have more than embryonic ones); yet that community exists in a vague sense of responsibility toward all men which underlies all moral responsibilities in limited communities.

As has been observed in analyzing the ethic of Jesus, the universalism of prophetic ethics goes beyond the demands of rational universalism. In rational universalism obligation is felt to all life because human life is conceived as the basic value of ethics. Since so much of human life represents only potential value, rational universalism tends to qualify its position. Thus in Aristotelian ethics the slave does not have the same rights as the freeman because his life is regarded as of potentially less value. Even in Stoicism, which begins by asserting the common divinity of all men by reason of their common rationality, the obvious differences in the intelligence of man prompts Stoic doctrine to a certain aristocratic condescension toward the "fools." In prophetic religion the obligation is toward the loving will of God; in other words, toward a more transcendent source of unity than any discoverable in the natural world, where men are always divided by various forces of nature and history. Christian universalism, therefore, represents a more impossible possibility than the universalism of Stoicism. Yet it is able to prompt higher actualities of love, being less dependent upon obvious symbols of human unity and brotherhood. In prophetic ethics the transcendent unity of life is an article of faith. Moral obligation is to this divine unity; and therefore it is more able to defy the anarchies of the world. But this difference between prophetic and rational universalism must not obscure a genuine affinity. In both cases the moral experience on any level of life points toward an unrealizable breadth of obligation of life to life.

If further proof were needed of the relevance of the love commandment to the problems of ordinary morality it could be found by a negative argument: Natural human egoism, which is sin only from the perspective of the law of love, actually results in social consequences which prove this religious perspective to be right. This point must be raised not against Christian orthodoxy which has never denied this negative relevance of the law of love to all human situations, but against a naturalism which regards the law of love as an expression of a morbid perfectionism, and declares "we will not aim so high or fall so low." According to the thesis of modern naturalism, only excessive egoism can be called wrong. The natural self-regarding impulses of human nature are accepted as the data of ethics; and the effort is made to construct them into forces of social harmony and cohesion. Prophetic Christianity, unlike modern liberalism, knows that the force of egoism cannot be broken by moral suasion and that on certain levels qualified harmonies must be achieved by building conflicting egoisms into a balance of power. But, unlike modern naturalism, it is unable to adopt a complacent attitude toward the force of egoism. It knows that it is sin, however natural and inevitable it may be, and its sinfulness is proved by the social consequences. It is natural enough to love one's own family more than other families and no amount of education will ever eliminate the inverse ratio between the potency of love and the breadth and extension in which it is applied. But the inevitability of narrow loyalties and circumscribed sympathy does not destroy the moral and social peril which they create. A narrow family loyalty is a more potent source of injustice than pure individual egoism, which, incidentally, probably never exists. The special loyalty which men give their limited community is natural enough; but it is also the root of international anarchy. Moral idealism in terms of the presuppositions of a particular class is also natural and inevitable; but it is the basis of tyranny and hypocrisy. Nothing is more natural and, in a sense, virtuous, than the desire of parents to protect the future of their children by bequeathing the fruits of their own toil and fortune to them. Yet this desire results in laws of testation by which social privilege is divorced from social function. The social injustice and conflicts of human history spring neither from a pure egoism nor from the type of egoism which could be neatly measured as excessive or extravagant by some rule of reason. They spring from those virtuous attitudes of natural man in which natural sympathy is inevitably compounded with natural egoism. Not only excessive jealousy, but the ordinary jealousy, from which no soul is free, destroys the harmony of life with life. Not only excessive vengeance, but the subtle vindictiveness which insinuates itself into the life of even the most imaginative souls, destroys justice. Wars are the consequence of the moral attitudes not only of unrighteous but of righteous nations (righteous in the sense that they defend their interests no more than is permitted by all the moral codes of history). The judgment that "whosoever seeketh to gain his life will lose it" remains true and relevant to every moral situation even if it is apparent that no human being exists who does not in some sense lose his life by seeking to gain it.

A naturalistic ethics, incapable of comprehending the true dialectic of the spiritual life, either regards the love commandment as possible of fulfilment and thus slips into utopianism, or it is forced to relegate it to the category of an either harmless or harmful irrelevance. A certain type of Christian liberalism interprets the absolutism of the ethics of the Sermon on the Mount as Oriental hyperbole, as a harmless extravagance, possessing a certain value in terms of pedagogical emphasis. A purely secular naturalism, on the other hand, considers the absolutism as a harmful extravagance. Thus Sigmund Freud writes: "The cultural superego . . . does not trouble enough about the mental constitution of human beings; it enjoins a command and never asks whether it is possible for them to obey it. It presumes, on the contrary, that a man's ego is psychologically capable of anything that is required of it, that it has unlimited power over the id. This is an error; even in normal people the power of controlling the id cannot be increased beyond certain limits. If one asks more of them one produces revolt or neurosis in individuals and makes them unhappy. The command to love the neighbour as ourselves is the strongest defence there is against human aggressiveness and it is a superlative example of the unpsychological attitude of the cultural superego. The command is impossible to fulfil; such an enormous inflation of the ego can only lower its value and not remedy its evil."[1] This is a perfectly valid protest against a too moralistic and optimistic love perfectionism. But it fails to meet the insights of a religion which knows that the law of love is an impossible possibility and knows how to confess, "There is a law in my members which wars against the law that is in my mind." Freud's admission that the love commandment is "the strongest defence against human aggressiveness" is, incidentally, the revelation of a certain equivocation in his thought. The impossible command is admitted to be a necessity, even though a dangerous one. It would be regarded as less dangerous by Freud if he knew enough about the true genius of prophetic religion to realize that it has resources for relaxing moral tension as well as for creating it.

If the relevance of the love commandment must be asserted against both Christian orthodoxy and against certain types of naturalism, the impossibility of the ideal must be insisted upon against all those forms of naturalism, liberalism, and radicalism which generate utopian illusions and regard the love commandment as ultimately realizable because history knows no limits of its progressive approximations. While modern culture since the eighteenth century has been particularly fruitful of these illusions, the logic which underlies them was stated as early as the fourth century of the Christian faith by Pelagius in his controversy with Augustine: He said:

> We contradict the Lord to his face when we say: It is hard, it is difficult; we cannot, we are men; we are encompassed with fragile flesh. O blind madness! O unholy audacity! We charge the God of all knowledge with a twofold ignorance, that he does not seem to know what he has made nor what he has commanded, as though forgetting the human weakness of which he is himself the author, he imposed laws upon man which he cannot endure.[2]

There is a certain plausibility in the logic of these words, but unfortunately, the facts of human history and the experience of every soul contradict them. The faith which regards the love commandment as a simple possibility rather than an impossible possibility is rooted in a faulty analysis of human nature which fails to understand that though man always stands under infinite possibilities and is potentially related to the totality of existence, he is, nevertheless, and will remain, a creature of finiteness. No matter how much his rationality is refined, he will always see the total situation in which he is involved only from a limited perspective; he will never be able to divorce his reason from its organic relation with the natural impulse of survival with which nature has endowed him; and he will never be able to escape the sin of accentuating his natural will-to-live into an imperial will-to-power by the very protest which his yearning for the eternal tempts him to make against his finiteness.

There is thus a mystery of evil in human life to

---

1. Freud, *Civilization and its Discontents*, pp. 139-140.

2. Quoted by N. P. Williams, op. cit., p. 342.

which modern culture has been completely oblivious. Liberal Christianity, particularly in America, having borrowed heavily from the optimistic credo of modern thought, sought to read this optimism back into the Gospels. It was aided in doing this by the fortuitous circumstance that the impossibility of an impossible possibility was implicit rather than explicit in the thought of Jesus. It became explicit only in the theology of Paul. Modern Christianity could thus make the "rediscovery of Jesus" the symbol and basis of its new optimism. The transcendent character of the love ideal was covert rather than overt in the words of Jesus because of the eschatological mould in which it was cast. Jesus thus made demands upon the human spirit, which no finite man can fulfil, without explicitly admitting this situation. This enabled modern liberalism to interpret the words of Jesus in terms of pure optimism.[3] The interpretation of Jesus' own life and character was also brought into conformity with this optimism. For liberal Christianity Christ is the ideal man, whom all men can emulate, once the persuasive charm of his life has captivated their souls. In Christian theology, at its best, the revelation of Christ, the God-man, is a revelation of the paradoxical relation of the eternal to history, which it is the genius of mythical-prophetic religion to emphasize. Christ is thus the revelation of the very impossible possibility which the Sermon on the Mount elaborates in ethical terms. If Christian orthodoxy sometimes tends to resolve this paradox by the picture of a Christ who has been stripped of all qualities which relate him to man and history, Christian liberalism resolves it by reducing Christ to a figure of heroic love who reveals the full possibilities of human nature to us. In either case the total human situation which the mythos of the Christ and the Cross illumines, is obscured. Modern liberalism significantly substitutes the name of "Jesus" for that of "Christ" in most of the sentimental and moralistic exhortations by which it encourages men to "follow in his steps." The relation of the Christ of Christian faith to the Jesus of history cannot be discussed within the confines of

this treatise in terms adequate enough to escape misunderstanding. Perhaps it is sufficient to say that the Jesus of history actually created the Christ of faith in the life of the early church, and that his historic life is related to the transcendent Christ as a final and ultimate symbol of a relation which prophetic religion sees between all life and history and the transcendent. In genuine prophetic Christianity the moral qualities of the Christ are not only our hope, but our despair. Out of that despair arises a new hope centred in the revelation of God in Christ. In such faith Christ and the Cross reveal not only the possibilities but the limits of human finitude in order that a more ultimate hope may arise from the contrite recognition of those limits. Christian faith is, in other words, a type of optimism which places its ultimate confidence in the love of God and not the love of man, in the ultimate and transcendent unity of reality and not in tentative and superficial harmonies of existence which human ingenuity may contrive. It insists, quite logically, that this ultimate hope becomes possible only to those who no longer place their confidence in purely human possibilities. Repentance is thus the gateway into the Kingdom of God.

---

3. Typical statements of this liberal interpretation of gospel ethics may be found, *inter alia,* in Shailer Matthews' *The Gospel and the Modern Man,* and in Francis Peabody's *Jesus Christ and the Social Question.*

43. Ethical Principles of Moral Action

PAUL J. TILLICH

Now I come to the next, and what is perhaps to most of you the most urgent question: "What are the principles of moral action which we find in man's natural structure, which might be called the natural law of morals?" There are three ethical norms which work together in every ethical decision if it is what it should be, namely: (1) the principle of *justice*, (2) the principle of *love* (translated from the Greek word *agape*), and (3) the principle of *wisdom*. All three must operate in the affirmation of self as a centered self.

Now, first, in what sense is justice an ethical principle of moral action? We ask again, "How can we become persons?" How is it possible to establish oneself as a centered person? How do we experience the unconditional imperative? There is only one way to do this, namely, in the encounter with the other persons. In the person-to-person encounter, both persons are created as persons. There is no other way for the creation of the person as person than the "person-to-person" encounter. This is not true in our encounter with nature outside of the realm of persons, nor in our encounter with natural phenomena. We can analyze and control nature, and we can do it today in an unprecedented measure. We can pull it to pieces by analysis and then rebuild it technically.

Paul J. Tillich (1886–1965) was professor of theology at the University of Chicago, Harvard University, and Union Theological Seminary. His works include *The Courage to Be; Systematic Theology*, 3 vols.; *Theology of Culture;* and *Dynamics of Faith*.

From *Being and Doing*, ed. John J. Carey (Macon, Ga.: Mercer University Press, 1987).

We can analyze the question of nature and the adaptation of it to us in all directions. Where the boundaries lie of man's finitude nobody knows. In the last ten years we are aware that they are much much broader than humanity has ever imagined except in myths and fables. We have no limits in our dealings with whatever is not potentially a person. We can deal with nature in this manner, but another human being — he or she who is potentially a person — creates an absolute limit for us. If we want to use another person like a piece of nature we fail. It is a persistent human weakness which causes us to make a potential person into an object; this keeps us from saying "Thou" to the other. There is an unconditional command to accept the other one as another one, namely, as a potential person.

This command is valid regardless of the socio-economic status of people and regardless of their legal status. For instance, in the ancient world slaves, children, and the women were not accepted as equals in terms of being person. They were considered to be "things," protected to certain extent by the paterfamilia, but were not accorded equal rights, social status, or human dignity. We can now recognize that the master who followed this legal scheme — who carried it radically through and treated the slave as a thing; or the man who treated the woman as a thing; and the parent who treated the child as a thing — all destroyed in the process not only them but also something of their own humanity. This is the foundation of justice. *All justice is derived from this fundamental principle of the person-to-person encounter.* In the moment in which we meet a potential person and don't acknowledge him as such, not only in our thinking but also in our acting, we are ourselves prevented from realizing, or actualizing, ourselves as persons.

This, however, puts a limit on the description of justice that I have just given. It is a true description, but a description which has a formalistic character. I can acknowledge the other one as a person, but as long as this acknowledgment remains outside of him, it is merely a formal, legal, or an "external" acknowledgment, not an acknowledgment of the full reality of the other person. A realistic acknowledgment of another person is always connected with some kind of participation, and the name of this participation is love. Therefore, the principle of justice by itself is partial and not independent as an ethical principle. It must be united with the principle of love so that it becomes a structural element within love.

And now we ask, "What is love?" I will make a confession: For years I have been reluctant to use this word in any of my articles, speeches, or sermons, or anywhere else I speak publicly, even to small groups of people. This word has become so flat, has lost so much of its power, that one cannot use it simply. Anytime I have not been extremely cautious about the use of this word — and it is hard not to use it since the solution of this or that problem is love — I have experienced blank eyes looking at me, and I felt no reaction, perhaps rightly so. I was responsible for that because this word has suffered, as have many other words, but perhaps more than most other words, which speak of matters of the spirit. In any case, let me give a preliminary definition which I often have given which may help to overcome this flatness. *Love is the urge for the reunion of the separated.* I previously described justice as an element in love. It is the element which accepts the other one as a person. Recall, however, that I said this element is not sufficient alone, for there remains a barrier and a coldness in all abstract justice. "Abstract" here means isolated from the reunion with another person. On the other hand, "love without justice" is mere sentimentality. This is the basic sickness which has distorted the concept of love like cancer, and almost ruined the possibility of its use. If we speak in terms of love, we must first remove the sentimentalization of the concept of love, which is the identification of love with mere emotions. Unless this is done, love can in no way be the ultimate principle of moral action, and the attacks against this principle are justified.

Let me give you one or two examples of attacks on love as sentimentality. One comes from Friedrich Nietzsche, who said that "Christian love is merely sentimental piety, and is an expression of the weak ones and not of the strong ones, of those who deny life instead of those who affirm life." If Christian love were this sentimentalized love, Nietzsche's attack on Christianity would be absolutely justified. It is justified in many respects against much of what the Church is preaching, singing in hymns, and even praying. The other attack which I hear again and again comes from my Jewish friends. The Jews have suffered from injustice probably more than any other human group during thousands of years, and especially during the two thousand years of Christian history. For this reason, the Jews are extremely sensitive about the problems of justice. If any one speaks with a Jew about love as the ultimate principle of moral action, the Jew asks, "But what about justice?" Often he says with passion and bitterness, "I don't want love — I want justice!" And it is not only the Jews who say this. If love means something which doesn't include the principle of justice as its backbone, its iron structure, then both attacks are justified.

If you look at love in the light of these two attacks, we can recognize the misuse of the term *love* and can perhaps answer better what love means. I already defined love as the reunion of the separated, or as the urge toward the reunion of the separated, and this refers to all dimensions of love: of *eros,* the love toward the good, the true, and the beautiful; to *philia,* the love of friendship, which expresses intimacy and trust between persons; and the *libido,* the most important part of which is the sexual love. Love contains all these facets. I would like to speak much more about this, but the only thing I can say in this moment is that in all these nuances, *Love is one.* It is always this one thing — the urge towards the reunion of the separated. Perhaps you have noticed the little syllable "re" in reunion, because that means that essentially all creatures belong together. In order to become persons they first must be separated. They must be able to stand upon themselves and their centered self. They are lonely in their centeredness and they must be so. The person who is not able to be in solitude never can become a person. Now beyond this, the power of love is the continuous desire to break through this necessary isolation, which is connected with the centeredness of every person.

We have this principle of love — we call it in an ultimate sense *agape.* This is the quality within love which prevents the other forms of love from becoming distorted into selfishness. We look at it and say, "But this is not enough for a principle of moral action, because how shall we act? Even if the power of love is one, and is determined by *agape,* how shall we act?" The urgent question arises again. Now let me give you the following answer. Love is the only reality which has two sides which seem to be contradictory. When completely united on the one hand, it is unconditional and it is always love. And on the other hand, it is more flexible than any other spiritual reality. It is the one power in us which is able to adapt itself to every concrete situation. And so my answer concerning moral action is rooted in the power of love. Listen to the situation, the concrete situation, the here and now which changes every moment. This situation has another voice also, a silent voice, but with this silent voice it cries out to us. It says, "This is the situation. Listen to me in the power of love which is in you, because only love can listen to the concrete situation." For instance, in the relationship with the other one, the friend, the husband, the child, the parent — listen to what the other one in this moment really wants and may not be able to say. Listen what he or she is lacking without knowing it.

At this point, I would like to draw from another religious and ethical point of view, often called the "psychology of depth." It refers to our insights into the dynamics of the human soul, and the dynamic tensions between the conscious and the unconscious. If we use a little bit of these insights in our relationships with others, listening to them with the help of our insight into these movements — then our acts of love may be much more adequate, and much more able of expressing what the other one really is and means and wants. We can better grasp what he wants with his essential being, not with his contingent willfulness. This is the listening power of love as related to the ever changing concrete situation. This insight in the concrete situation, this power to listen to it, liberates us from conventions and traditions which never fit any one concrete situation completely. No moral law fits any concrete situation totally. Only one principle can do this: that principle of moral action which by its very essence, while remaining always the same, changes toward the concrete situation in each moment. That principle is love.

Let me speak for one moment of the different qualities of love which I mentioned. We need the principle of *agape* with its concrete listening to its situations. For instance, the abstract rules of the libido quality of love — the abstract rules, how to relate to the other sex, how to eat, how to drink, or

how not to eat or drink — such rules are not valid at all from the point of view of the principle of love. There is the only demand to listen to what *agape* — love in this concrete situation — demands, so that a self-realization of the person through reunion with the other person is possible. This is the only criterion, and this liberates us from what I called at the beginning of this lecture, a "distorted type of moralism" of which we still hear so much in Protestant preaching. We also hear it in judgments which are based on secularized Puritan principles, and which identify the Christian message with the prohibition of eating this or that, of drinking this or that; or of acting in sexual relations in this or that way. Instead of that, *agape* binds us responsibly to the other person, to ourselves, and to the world as a whole. The same criterion must be applied to the relationship of friends, which easily become ego-centered and selfish. Many other moral maxims, judgments, values, and folkways must be put under the principle of love.

Now I conclude with the third consideration, *wisdom*. I would like for you to see it as a diagram of the following structure. We have love immovable in itself, yet changing in every moment, as the ultimate principle of moral action. We have then, deep down, the concrete situation; the situation here and now in this moment — not yesterday, not tomorrow, but now in this moment, when somebody talks to you or encounters you. But now, you have this ultimate principle about the concrete situation which we call love but still you feel something must be added. All right, we have the ultimate principle of love. We have the concrete situation which cries out with a voice so that we can listen if we are driven by the power of love. But there is something between love and the situation, and these are the laws of religions, the laws of nations, and the laws of society. They are embodied in the traditional laws which we read and learn. How can we judge them?

My answer is that we must draw on the inspiration of wisdom. Wisdom was once upon a time a great concept. He who knows the Old Testament knows that wisdom has a position beside God, helping him in his creation and then coming down into the hearts of the man on the street. It is often later identified with the Christ or with his spirit. It was a medium of the creation of the world. This wisdom is present in us, and out of this wisdom the tables of laws came once upon a time. The Ten Commandments are the results of the revelatory power of wisdom in the history of mankind. In this way all the commands of religion and cultures are derived, but these commands — although they are principles of wisdom — are not abstract laws which can be applied like a technical tool to the appropriate material. This would be against the principle of love, and on the other side, irrelevant to the needs of the concrete situation. Laws are between the principle of love and the concrete situation, and they are guides given us to help us make decisions. But nobody should feel compelled — religiously or morally — to follow them unconditionally.

The principles of wisdom certainly are largely valid. They are so valid that opposition against them is a great risk; they guide our moral conscience, but they are not ultimately valid except as modified by the principle of love. Even the Ten Commandments are not expressions of man's essential nature alone; they are also expressions of the wisdom of a feudal culture with all its limitations. This means there is also a risk if one slavishly follows the Commandments. There is a risk in both cases, and that means a decision for any ethical act has in itself the character of risk. *Nobody can be a person who doesn't risk in his or her ethical decisions.* Those who did it — who broke through — were the most lonely people, and if you, any of you, want to break through the values of this wisdom of mankind, you might be right. You risk much and you will be lonely, but perhaps if you do so you will have become a person, and if you do not so, you may have missed your own fulfillment as a person. This is the dimension in which our ethical situation stands.

Most people are not able to stand this loneliness and they follow conventional morals. Conventional morals are not only evil — they are wisdom, but they are wisdom in the state of compromise, in the state of weakness, of subjection to a foreign law. I conclude by saying, *a moral action is an action in which we actualize ourselves as persons within person-to-person encounters. Its principles are the love whose backbone is justice; the love which, though unconditional itself, listens to the concrete situation and its changes, and is guided by the wisdom of the past.*

44. For Justice in Shalom

NICHOLAS WOLTERSTORFF

To guide our thoughts, we need some vision . . . Of course there is no substitute for careful, informed, and specific reflection; but is there some comprehensive vision that can serve to orient those reflections and thereby keep us from losing our way? When architects design buildings, they begin with an image of forms and lights and shadows to which they gradually give increasing articulation. Is there any such image for us here?

I think there is. It is the vision of *shalom — peace —* first articulated in the Old Testament poetic and prophetic literature but then coming to expression in the New Testament as well. We shall see that shalom is intertwined with justice. In shalom, each person enjoys justice, enjoys his or her rights. There is no shalom without justice. But shalom goes beyond justice.

Shalom is the human being dwelling at peace in all his or her relationships: with God, with self, with fellows, with nature. It is shalom when:

> The wolf shall dwell with the lamb,
>   and the leopard shall lie down with the kid,
> and the calf and the lion and the
>   fatling together,
>   and a little child shall lead them.
> The cow and the bear shall feed;
>   their young shall lie down together;

Nicholas Wolterstorff (1932–) is professor of philosophical theology at the Divinity School of Yale University. His works include *Lament for a Son; Reason within the Bounds of Religion; Until Justice and Peace Embrace;* and *Educating for Responsible Action.*

From Nicholas Wolterstorff, *Until Justice and Peace Embrace* (Grand Rapids, Mich.: Wm. B. Eerdmans, 1983).

and the lion shall eat straw like the ox.
The sucking child shall play over the hole
    of the asp,
  and the weaned child shall put his hand
    on the adder's den.

                  (Isa. 11:6-8)

But the peace which is shalom is not merely the absence of hostility, not merely being in right relationship. Shalom at its highest is *enjoyment* in one's relationships. A nation may be at peace with all its neighbors and yet be miserable in its poverty. To dwell in shalom is to *enjoy* living before God, to *enjoy* living in one's physical surroundings, to *enjoy* living with one's fellows, to *enjoy* life with oneself.

Shalom in the first place incorporates right, harmonious relationships to *God* and delight in his service. When the prophets speak of shalom, they speak of a day when human beings will no longer flee God down the corridors of time, a day when they will no longer turn in those corridors to defy their divine pursuer. Shalom is perfected when humanity acknowledges that in its service of God is true delight. "The mountain of the house of the Lord," says the prophet,

shall be established as the highest
    of the mountains,
  and shall be raised above the hills;
and all the nations shall flow to it,
  and many peoples shall come, and say:
"Come, let us go up to the mountain
    of the Lord,
  to the house of the God of Jacob;
that he may teach us his ways
  and that we may walk in his paths."

                  (Isa. 2:2-3)

Secondly, shalom incorporates right harmonious relationships to other *human beings* and delight in human community. Shalom is absent when a society is a collection of individuals all out to make their own way in the world. And of course there can be delight in community only when justice reigns, only when human beings no longer oppress one another. When "justice shall make its home in the wilderness, / and righteousness dwell in the grassland" — only then will it be true that "righteousness shall yield shalom, / and its fruit be

quietness and confidence for ever" (Isa. 32:16-17). In shalom,

Love and Fidelity now meet,
  Justice and Peace now embrace;
Fidelity reaches up from earth
  and Justice leans down from heaven.

              (Psalm 85:10-11)

Thirdly, shalom incorporates right, harmonious relationships to *nature* and delight in our physical surroundings. Shalom comes when we, bodily creatures and not disembodied souls, shape the world with our labor and find fulfillment in so doing and delight in its results. In speaking of shalom the prophet spoke of a day when the Lord would prepare:

a banquet of rich fare for all the people,
a banquet of wines well matured
    and richest fare,
well matured wines strained clear.

                  (Isa. 25:6)

He spoke of a day when the people "shall live in a tranquil country, / dwelling in shalom, in houses full of ease" (Isa. 32:18).

I said that justice, the enjoyment of one's rights, is indispensable to shalom. That is because shalom is an *ethical* community. If individuals are not granted what is due them, if their claim on others is not acknowledged by those others, if others do not carry out their obligations to them, then shalom is wounded. That is so even if there are no *feelings* of hostility between them and the others. Shalom cannot be secured in an unjust situation by managing to get all concerned to feel content with their lot in life. Shalom would not have been present *even if* all the blacks in the United States had been content in their state of slavery; it would not be present in South Africa *even if* all the blacks there felt happy. It is because shalom is an ethical community that it is wounded when justice is absent.

But the right relationships that lie at the basis of shalom involve more than right relationships to other human beings. They involve right relationships to God, to nature, and to oneself as well. Hence, shalom is more than an ethical community. Shalom is the *responsible* community in which

God's laws for the multifaceted existence of his creatures are obeyed.

Shalom goes beyond even the responsible community. We may all have acted responsibly and yet shalom may be wounded, for delight may be missing. Always there are sorrows in our human existence that we are at a loss to heal. It is in this context that we must ultimately see the significance of technology. Technology does make possible advance toward shalom; progress in mastery of the world can bring shalom nearer. But the limits of technology must also be acknowledged: technology is entirely incapable of bringing about shalom between ourselves and God, and it is only scarcely capable of bringing about the love of self and neighbor.

I have already cited that best known of all shalom passages, the one in which Isaiah describes the anticipated shalom with a flourish of images of harmony — harmony among the animals, harmony between man and animal: "Then the wolf shall live with the sheep. . . ." That passage, though, is introduced with these words:

> Then a shoot shall grow from the stock of Jesse,
> and a branch shall spring from his roots.
> The spirit of the Lord shall rest upon him,
> a spirit of wisdom and understanding,
> a spirit of counsel and power,
> a spirit of knowledge and the fear of the Lord.
> (Isa. 11:1-2)

That shoot of which Isaiah spoke is he of whom the angels sang in celebration of his birth: "Glory to God in highest heaven, and on earth his *peace* for men on whom his favor rests" (Luke 2:24). He is the one of whom the priest Zechariah said that he "will guide our feet into the way of *peace*" (Luke 1:79). He is the one of whom Simeon said, "This day, Master, thou givest thy servant his discharge in *peace;* now thy promise is fulfilled" (Luke 2:29). He is the one of whom Peter said that it was by him that God preached "good news of *peace*" to Israel (Acts 10:36). He is the one of whom Paul, speaking as a Jew to the Gentiles, said that "he came and preached *peace* to you who were far off and *peace* to those who were near" (Eph. 2:17). He is in fact Jesus Christ, whom Isaiah called the "prince of peace" (Isa. 9:6).

It was this same Jesus who said to the apostles in his farewell discourse, "The words that I say to you I do not speak on my own authority; but the Father who dwells in me does his works. Believe me that I am in the Father and the Father in me; or else believe me for the sake of the works themselves" (John 14:10-11). And then he added, "I say to you, he who believes in me will also do the works that I do; and greater works than these will he do" (John 14:12).

Can the conclusion be avoided that not only is shalom God's cause in the world but that all who believe in Jesus will, along with him, engage in the works of shalom? Shalom is both God's cause in the world and our human calling. Even though the full incursion of shalom into our history will be divine gift and not merely human achievement, even though its episodic incursion into our lives now also has a dimension of divine gift, nonetheless it is shalom that we are to work and struggle for. We are not to stand around, hands folded, waiting for shalom to arrive. We are workers in God's cause, his peace-workers. The *missio Dei* is *our* mission.

An implication of this is that our work will always have the two dimensions of a struggle for justice and the pursuit of increased mastery of the world so as to enrich human life. Both together are necessary if shalom is to be brought nearer. Development and liberation must go hand in hand. Ours is both a cultural mandate and a liberation mandate — the mandate to master the world for the benefit of mankind, but also the mandate:

> to loose the chains of injustice
> and untie the cords of the yoke,
> to set the oppressed free
> and break every yoke . . .
> to share your food with the hungry
> and to provide the poor wanderer
> with shelter —
> when you see the naked, to clothe him,
> and not to turn away from your own
> flesh and blood.
> (Isa. 58:6-7)

45. Implications for a Theory of Justice

KAREN LEBACQZ

Roots: Foundations for a Theory of Justice

Philosophy has long held that the formal principle of justice is "give to each what is due." The task of a substantive theory of justice, then, is determining what is "due." Many contenders seek the throne: need, effort, merit, contribution, equality, market demands, and so on.

The approach taken here suggests a different beginning point, and with it a different understanding of justice. I begin with the realities of injustice. The formal principle of justice is therefore not to give to each what is due but to correct injustices. This simple shift in starting point has profound implications for a theory of justice.

If justice begins with the correction of injustices, then the most important tools for understanding justice will be the stories of injustice as experienced by the oppressed and the tools of social and historical analysis that help to illumine the process by which those historical injustices arose and the meaning of them in the lives of the victims. A theory of justice will therefore not be primarily dependent upon philosophical reasoning. Philosophical reasoning plays a role in locating the nature of injustices, but does not provide

a full picture of them. Rather, we must make use of tools from the social sciences to analyze what is happening and to locate the present injustices. I have not provided a catalog of useful tools from the social sciences here. A number can be found enumerated in Bonino's approach to ethics for Latin America.[1]

Injustice takes different primary forms in different parts of the world: sexism here, racism there, economic oppression in one place, political repression in another, and so on. The forms of injustice . . . will each reign at different times and in different places. The task of justice and a theory of justice will be different depending on which forms of injustice are primary.

For this reason it is inadequate to begin any theory of justice with discussions of whether justice requires distribution on the basis of "need" versus "merit," "effort" versus "contribution," and so on. Such concerns are not alien to a full theory of justice. But they are not an adequate beginning point. If racism is a reality in our world, then justice cannot consist simply in giving to each according to "need." If sexism is a reality in our world, then justice cannot consist simply in giving to each according to "merit." Racism and sexism bring claims in justice that go beyond determinations of need or merit.

A theory of justice therefore cannot begin with philosophical arguments for one or another "criterion" for what is "due." What is "due" is not due in the abstract but in the concrete. And that concrete is determined by history — by exchanges made, by contracts forced, by covenants broken, by disrespect, by exploitation, by all the myriad ways in which human beings violate the fundamental covenant of life with life.[2] Violations of the covenant of mutual responsibility result in the need for correctives. Relationships in history create demands in justice. A theory of justice must be historical.

Perhaps most important, current patterns of distribution can be taken as *prima facie* evidence

Karen Lebacqz (1945–) is professor of Christian ethics at the Pacific School of Religion. She is author of a two-volume study of justice, *Six Theories of Justice: Perspectives from Philosophical and Theological Ethics* and *Justice in an Unjust World* as well as works addressing sexual ethics.

From Karen Lebacqz, *Justice in an Unjust World* (Minneapolis: Augsburg Press, 1987).

1. José Miguez Bonino, *Toward a Christian Political Ethics* (Philadelphia: Fortress, 1983).
2. Note that the covenant symbolized by the rainbow includes not just human life but all life forms. This suggests that a theory of justice might encompass non-human life as well as human life.

of past injustices. A theory of justice cannot provide a formula for distribution — e.g., to each according to the choices made by others[3] — in abstraction from the concrete realities of history. As the early church fathers argued, and as contemporary peasants concur, the fact of inequalities of wealth is itself a likely indicator of gross injustices. Johanna Masilela's circumstances are not simply "unfortunate"; they are "unfair." The circumstances themselves suggest the injustices perpetrated on this black, crippled, disenfranchised, poor woman.

. . . the forms of injustice are interlocking: one feeds another, and they result in a web of injustice. Being poor and being female go together. Being disenfranchised and being poor go together. Injustices are not random events. They form patterns. The meaning of any injustice, and therefore the justice necessary to correct it will be dependent on its place in the pattern.

This means that justice begins with stories of injustice. Justice takes a narrative form. Narratives are what give meaning to disparate events and relate them into patterns. Justice therefore is not so much a concept as a story. It is an invitation, not a program. Injustice is like a parable: a story that invites the question, "What's wrong with this picture?" Justice is the answer to the question.

But whose stories are to be told? And from whose perspective are they to be told? We all know that the same story told by two different people will sound very different. This is the stuff on which marital disputes thrive! It is important, then, not only to tell stories of injustice, but to make choices about whose stories are told and from whose perspective.

The perspective on justice offered here holds that justice requires an "option for the poor" or an "epistemological privilege of the oppressed." It is the stories of injustice as experienced by the victims that count. It is the perspective of the fish who swim in an ocean of usury rather than the perspective of the birds who fly through airy breezes that must be taken seriously. This makes for a profound shift from traditional approaches in the field of ethics, where logical discourse and dialog have

been largely confined to the well-educated birds. Because justice emerges in protest against injustice, the task of justice is different for the oppressed than it is for the oppressor. The victim of injustice must resist, rage, and attempt to bring the injustice to the fore and expose it for the injustice that it is. The perpetrator of injustice must make reparations or redress — attempting to correct the injustice and set things right again. Distinguishing the task of oppressed and oppressor is supported in Scripture. God's word to each is different, and the appropriate response of each is different.

Yet this is not a common approach in contemporary theory. Theories of justice look for rules or principles that are applicable to all people at all times. While I would argue that principles of resistance and redress are generalizable, I would not argue that the specific forms of justice must be the same everywhere and always. Since justice emerges in response to injustice, it will partake of the particular corrective qualities required by the circumstances. Thus I would concur with Major Jones that the answer to the question, "What ought I to do?" will vary according to whether one is oppressed or oppressor.[4]

But this suggests that a search for absolute rules of justice is not appropriate. Justice is not "to each according to need." Nor is it "benefit the least advantaged." Nor is it "the greatest good for the greatest number." Because justice emerges out of protest against injustice, justice is not so much a state of being as a struggle and a constant process. It is the process of correcting what is unjust. It is the process of providing new beginnings, not an ideal state of distribution.

Justice must be both preeminently historical and radically free from history. It must be preeminently historical because it originates in the protest against injustice. In order to understand the injustice, and to know where justice would lie in correcting it, attention must be paid to history. Justice is not simply treating people in accord with "need," because it makes a difference why the need arose. Where someone has been wronged by another, there are special obligations of justice in addition to any obligations created by the mere existence of need.

3. I have characterized Nozick's theory this way in *Six Theories of Justice* (Minneapolis: Augsburg, 1986), p. 118.

4. Major J. Jones, *Christian Ethics for Black Theology* (Nashville: Abingdon, 1974), p. 17.

At the same time, justice must be radically free from history, for the future to be posited is not dependent on the possibilities inherent in the past. If the future depends on the past, then patterns of injustice will be perpetuated into that future. Once a button is buttoned up wrong, it takes the entire row of buttons with it. What is needed is a new start: unbuttoning the button and starting again free of the limitations of the original buttoning. This is what the image of the jubilee provides.

But it should not be expected that the jubilee is perfect justice, or that no new injustices will arise. The jubilee is not a program for perfect justice. Some who have worked hard to increase their holdings will lose those holdings in the jubilee. There is a kind of injustice built into the corrections of other injustices. The jubilee is a vision of new beginnings, but it is a cyclical vision implying the need for a new jubilee. The story goes on. And as the human community writes its story, new injustices will happen. Justice is a constant process of correction, not a once-and-for-all program. Justice is restorative, and restoration is a constant necessity. What is restored is new sociopolitical beginnings (jubilee), new attitudes of community (jubilation), and new life (the logic is that the people may live).

Nonetheless, underlying restorative justice there is a vision. It is a vision incorporating the exodus image of liberation, the rainbow image of covenant, the jubilee image of new beginnings, and the Christological image of identification with the poor and oppressed. In one sense, then, there is a single standard of justice that applies to both oppressed and oppressor. Injustice originates with violations of the responsibilities of covenant. Injustice is "wrong relationship." We know that it is wrong because we have some glimpse of the rainbow of right relationship.

Justice is not "relative," therefore. Justice in the world will consist primarily in liberation from oppression and in jubilee restructurings. But these will be contextual, depending on the historical circumstances for their exact expression. To say that the corrections of justice will be contextual, however, is not to say that they will be relative. They are demanded by circumstances, in accord with a vision.

At the root of my approach to justice, therefore, there is a concept of justice perceived, however dimly. To know that something is "unjust" and requires correction means that we must have some idea of what justice requires. But we cannot approach justice directly, because we already live in the midst of injustice. The "rupture" of justice in the world, and the "rue" of the Christian who knows that her history is part of that rupture, cannot be ignored.

Finally, the Bible must be for Christians a *sine qua non*. No theory of justice can claim to be Christian unless it takes seriously the common record considered canon by the Christian community. But here the pitfalls are particularly great, for the temptation is to look to Scripture for rules of justice: "give away half," "leave the edges of the fields for gleaning by the poor," and even "do unto others as you would have them do unto you."

The approach to justice proposed here does not permit such a use of Scripture. The Bible is not a rule book. It is the living memory of a people. It is a collection of stories and poems and laws and sayings that give expression to a people's understanding of God's response to injustice and the people's response to God. The Bible must be used accordingly. It provides stories that illumine justice. Part of the power of biblical stories is that they have stood the test of time. They have relevance today. It is not wrong, therefore, to look for contemporary situations that appear to provide parallels to biblical stories.

At the same time, even those stories are subject to the distortions of the human community. The history of rue suggests that the Bible itself, as the record of a human community, will be limited by that community. Thus, biblical stories are illustrative for a theory of justice, but they do not provide that theory. They offer windows through which we might glimpse injustice and justice, but they do not offer a plan for the perfectly just world.

Rudiments: Beginnings of a Theory of Justice

It has not been my intention here to offer a theory of justice, but only to offer foundations for a Christian approach to justice. We see now what some of those foundations are: a historical perspective on injustice, the use of narrative, biblical stories as illustrative, and a willingness to be contextual. All of these "roots" for a theory of justice emerge from taking injustice seriously as the reality of our world. But they are not yet a theory of justice.

Such a theory is beyond the scope of this work. But I can suggest now some rudiments of the theory of justice that might emerge from such an approach.

First, "justice" will be conceived very broadly. It will participate in the richness of the biblical concept of justice in which justice is nothing less than "right relationship" or righteousness. Emil Brunner once noted that the Christian concept of justice is far broader than the philosophical "give to each what is due."[5] It is precisely that broader notion that must be recaptured. Justice will move toward *sedaqah,* righteousness, as its plumb line.

Second, justice will reside in responsibilities and duties, not in rights. The covenant of mutual responsibility of which the rainbow is a sign gives clues to a theory of justice. The covenant implies care of one for another. The covenant suggests that the welfare of each depends on the other. Thus, justice will be located in responsibilities and mutuality, not in "rights" that are asserted against one another.

Third, the primary injustice is therefore exploitation. Domination and oppression are injustices because they are violations of a covenant of mutual responsibility. They violate the relationship and they violate the personhood of *both* parties. The victim is clearly violated. But just as surely, the perpetrator of injustice fails to live according to God's covenant and therefore violates her or his own personhood. When an injustice is done, the entire human community experiences a breach of covenant.

Fourth, since injustice is rooted in exploitation and oppression, justice as the process of correction of injustice takes shape primarily in rescue/resistance and in rebuke/reparations. God's justice for the oppressed consists in liberation from oppression. The struggle for justice by the oppressed therefore consists in resistance to forms of oppression and in actions consonant with liberation as the goal. God's justice for the oppressor consists in rebuke and requisition. Those responsible for

injustice have the duty of redress — of making amends, setting things right. This includes not only ending the exploitation or oppression, but making reparations for the harms caused by past injustices. Both together participate in the restoration of the proper order of relationships in which exploitation and domination would not exist.

Fifth, any such justice will be understood to be incomplete and partial. No theory of justice is adequate that does not provide for an assessment of the incomplete and partial nature of the historical jubilees that are created. The Rainbow Workers Cooperative was a jubilee occurrence that enacted justice; but because it was also a response to previous injustice, the cooperative itself was not able to overcome all injustices. Self-analysis and self-correction will therefore be a crucial part of a theory of justice.

This approach to justice is strikingly different from some approaches currently dominating American thought. In *Six Theories of Justice: Perspectives from Philosophical and Theological Ethics,* I reviewed six such approaches. A brief word about each will indicate what is distinctive about my own approach here, as well as lifting up common grounds from which we might move toward a more full theory of justice.

In the utilitarian approach, *justice* is the term used for those categories of acts which are not only right, but which have such utility that they become defended as claims. Claims of justice, however, may always be overridden by the "greater good" in the circumstance.[6] The strength of the utilitarian approach to justice lies in its acknowledgment of an arena larger than that of individual claims.[7] The utilitarian sees a concept of the common good in which justice is not antithetical to the greater good overall.

The notion that justice is broader than individual claims fits well with the approach taken here. Justice is truncated if it is limited to individual claims brought on the basis of need or merit or contribution or market laws of supply and demand.

---

5. Emil Brunner, *Justice and the Social Order* (London: Lutterworth, 1945), p. 19.

6. See John Stuart Mill, *Utilitarianism* (New York: Bobbs-Merrill, 1957).

7. For a discussion of this approach, see Lebacqz, *Six Theories of Justice,* chap. 1.

At the same time, the approach taken here would say a resounding no to utilitarianism, for reasons similar to those adopted by Rawls and other critics: the utilitarian approach to justice provides no special protections for the poor and oppressed. In no way does it root justice precisely in corrections of injustice or in liberation from oppression.

My approach therefore shares some affinities with Rawls' theory, which provides that justice is done when the least advantaged are benefited.[8]

However, though there are affinities, the two approaches differ. Rawls' approach to justice appears to leave open the possibility that "justice" consists in anything that leaves the poor or disadvantaged better off than they were before. This is contrary to the liberation/rescue motif. "We don't want our chains made more comfortable; we want them removed."[9] Justice requires liberation, not simply improvements within an oppressive structure. Rawls' theory protects the least advantaged but does not appear to require any new beginnings. My approach suggests that justice consists primarily in liberation from oppression and in "new beginnings" that undo oppressive structures.

Perhaps most important here are some methodological differences. Rawls approaches justice as an issue in rational deliberation. His contract model is tempting. But it is not adequate to a world in which injustice is already rampant. It is not adequate to a world in which rationality itself is distorted by human sin.

Moreover, injustice is multifaceted. Rawls' approach assumes that one can separate political from economic justice, holding equal political rights in the face of economic inequalities. I assume that injustices feed each other, and that "jubilee" requires both political emancipation and economic restructuring. Political rights are not genuine without economic liberation.

Because liberation is a primary theme in my approach to justice, it might seem that Nozick's stress on freedom would be compatible with the theory of justice sketched here.[10] For Nozick, justice consists primarily in honoring human freedom — particularly freedom of exchange. Whatever distribution of goods results from exchange will be fair so long as the original acquisition and the subsequent exchanges of goods were fair. Where Rawls would protect the least advantaged, no such protections are included for Nozick. Rather, what is protected is freedom of choice.

I have indicated above that there is some strength in this theory. Peasants who think the current distribution is not fair often link that unfairness to a presumption that exchanges were not free and hence that the resulting distribution is really the result of coercion. They appear to support Nozick's stress on freedom in choosing.

What is missing in Nozick's theory, however, is a historical perspective that would assess the "freedom" of the choices actually made. That is, he offers no room for the possibility that current distributions are *prima facie* evidence of unfairness.

Second, his approach offers no room for the jubilee vision. Nozick suggests that corrective principles are necessary, but does not provide them. In the approach suggested here, corrective principles are central to a theory of justice. There is always a need for new beginnings, and for a jubilee. Where Nozick would assume that the market system is generally free of the need for correction, I would assume precisely the opposite, based on the concrete realities of injustice.

Moreover, where Nozick's approach takes seriously the freedom and the separateness of individuals, it does not take seriously the interrelationship of individuals. It does not begin with the fact of relationship. It begins with "rights," not with covenantal responsibilities. The biblical remembrance used here provides instead a covenant image of mutual responsibility. It is this that permits "jubilation" at the restructuring that deprives the oppressor.

Where Nozick fails to see the interconnections between humans, this vision looms large in Catholic theology. The National Conference of Catholic Bishops affirms that "biblical justice . . . is not

---

8. John Rawls' *A Theory of Justice* (Cambridge, Mass.: Harvard University Press, 1971) is the subject of chap. 2 of *Six Theories of Justice*.

9. Mrs. Motlana, quoted by Desmond Tutu, *Hope and Suffering* (Grand Rapids: Eerdmans, 1983), p. 128.

10. For a discussion of Robert Nozick's *Anarchy, State and Utopia* (New York: Basic Books, 1974), see *Six Theories of Justice,* chap. 3.

concerned with a strict definition of rights and duties, but with the rightness of the human condition before God and within society."[11] This vision of interrelatedness yields a "preferential option for the poor."[12]

Justice for the bishops, then, cannot be limited to fairness in exchange alone. Such "commutative justice," is complemented by requirements of "distributive justice," which emphasizes the needs of the poor, and by "social justice," which requires productive participation in society.[13] The common good demands justice in this full sense. Personal rights provide minimum conditions for justice.[14]

Resting as it does on a biblical vision, it is to be expected that this view would share many affinities with my Christian approach. And to a certain extent it does. I also would affirm the preferential option for the poor. And I urge a justice that goes beyond mere commutative exchange.

However, there are some important differences. First, the bishops stress creation and covenant as primary biblical themes. I stress covenant, but only within the context of liberation. The liberating acts of God are more central to my view. Because I begin with injustice, I cannot assume the coherence of the interests of all parties, as the bishops seem to do. I find not one word on justice, but two: different words spoken to the oppressed and to the oppressor.

Second, I find the jubilee theme missing in the bishops' view. Although they stress the priority of meeting the needs of the poor, the theme of new beginnings, and with it the willingness to envision a radical break from the past, does not loom large in their approach.

Reinhold Niebuhr's approach to justice shares affinity with the view presented here in that it recognizes the partial and imperfect nature of all earthly justice.[15] For Niebuhr, only the fullness of

love constituted perfect justice — the mutual affirmation of life with life. This is at root a covenant view similar to the one adopted here. Moreover, Niebuhr recognized the realities of injustice and the need for struggle and force to correct injustice.

However, when Niebuhr turned to find principles of "justice," he separated the "self-sacrificial" love of Jesus so completely from the social world that he was then forced to turn to philosophy for his principles. Both equality and liberty loomed large for Niebuhr, and I would not disagree with the importance of these principles.

But *liberation* never became a theme of justice for Niebuhr. Nor did he draw on biblical remembrance to illumine the meaning of other principles, such as redress. Above all, he separated love and justice in ways that I have suggested tend to render justice a "second class citizen"; such separation is not consonant with the biblical view.

Miranda then provides an important corrective in affirming a biblical view that unites love and justice.[16] His impressive study of *mishpat* yields a liberation view that has many affinities with mine. Of particular importance is his stress on the way of knowing that is central to the Bible. God is known, argues Miranda, only in the doing of justice. He thus gives an "epistemological privilege" to the oppressed and to those engaged in concrete praxis of struggle for justice.

I concur in this privilege, and in the need for a justice that is known in and emerges out of the struggles of the oppressed. Indeed, I consider my own approach to be an instance of "liberation" theology and ethics.

Nonetheless, there are differences between Miranda's approach and mine. First, although he clearly perceives the struggle between oppressed and oppressor, he offers no specific words of justice addressed to the oppressor. Second, he does not incorporate a recognition of the limited nature of every earthly achievement of justice and therefore of the necessity for constant "jubilee" occurrences that break the injustices brought about by previous jubilees. Third, and perhaps most important, he uses a word study of *mishpat*

---

11. *Economic Justice for All: Pastoral Letter on Catholic Social Teaching and the U.S. Economy* (Washington, D.C.; U.S. Catholic Conference, 1986), §39. The second draft of this letter is the subject of chap. 4 of *Six Theories of Justice.*

12. Ibid., §52.

13. Ibid., §§69-71.

14. Ibid., §79.

15. A discussion of Niebuhr's view of justice is the subject of chap. 5 of *Six Theories of Justice.*

16. Jose Porfirio Miranda's *Marx and the Bible: A Critique of the Philosophy of Oppression* (Maryknoll, N.Y.: Orbis, 1974) is discussed in chap. 6 of *Six Theories of Justice.*

to approach a biblical perspective on justice, whereas I use a narrative approach that draws on stories from Scripture rather than on the use of words translated by the English term *justice*.

These six approachs to justice have set an agenda that challenges all other approaches: the need to recognize the greater good, the stress on the least advantaged, respect for freedom of choice, the priority of the poor, the imperfections of injustice, and the epistemological privilege of the oppressed.

I have taken this agenda seriously in these pages. And yet, doing so has yielded a different approach to justice. Precisely because I take most seriously the epistemological privilege of the oppressed, I have begun with the reality of oppression and injustice as it is experienced in the world. Once one begins there, a different understanding of justice emerges.

What I have offered here is not a full theory of justice. It is but a beginning. It is a searching for roots from which a tree of justice might grow. It is a clearing of ground in preparation for laying of foundations. It is not a finished edifice, nor yet a grown tree. Above all, I hope that it is a calling into account — a "vocation" — for all Christians, oppressed and oppressor alike, so that Johanna Masilela might make history and in the making of that history might expose the realities of injustice and move us one step closer to the jubilee.

46. Justice and Christian Charity

GORDON GRAHAM

. . . Christians are sometimes thought to have a duty to secure a socially just society, but the political justification of such a society (and of any political program adopted with such a society in view) is not that it is in accordance with the Christian gospel, but that it is a just one. It is in this way, it is said, that Christians may form alliances with secular political ideologies, for though they seek the Kingdom of God and their allies do not, certain aspects of the Kingdom of God are also things that those ideologies seek.

Such alliances are familiar throughout history. In the early years of this century they were formed more frequently with fascist than with socialist parties in the belief that Christians should join battle against the atheistical forces of Marxism alongside those to whom, for different reasons, the defeat of communism was also important. Some of these alliances still persist, but since the 1960s it is alliances with socialism of one sort or another that have come to the fore, especially in Central and South America where the theology of liberation has arisen to give them additional theoretical sanction. These alliances spring from the convic-

Gordon Graham (1949–) is a reader in moral philosophy at the University of St. Andrews, Scotland. He has written *Politics in Its Place, Contemporary Social Philosophy, Living the Good Life: An Introduction to Moral Philosophy,* and *The Idea of Christian Charity: A Critique of Some Contemporary Conceptions.*

From Gordon Graham, *The Idea of Christian Charity* (Notre Dame: University of Notre Dame Press, 1989).

tion that the evangelist of Christian love should join forces with the protagonists of social justice. Thus, Juan Luis Segundo, for instance, equates "the Gospel commandment to love all men" with the demand "to seek first justice, before all else, and universal brotherhood,"[1] and Gustavo Gutierrez sees "liberation" as a correlate of "salvation."[2]

*　　*　　*

The belief is widespread in contemporary Christendom, then, that the aspiration to social justice and a commitment to *caritas* — caring for others — share a common end.[3] As the foregoing quotations demonstrate, just how closely the two are related is a subject on which opinions differ, but several theologians appear to think them identical, and that this identity is biblical. Thus, J. P. Miranda in *Marx and the Bible* says:

> Since at least the sixth century A.D. a bald fact has been systematically excluded from theological and moral consideration: "To give alms" in the Bible is called "to do justice."[4]

Miranda goes on to cite a few of the passages "which have resisted all misrepresentation." In point of fact the passages cited are not nearly as unequivocal as he suggests, but more damaging to his argument is his lack of clarity about what *modern* conception of justice he wishes to identify the ancient Hebrew and Greek conceptions with. A similar failing is to be found in the use another moral theologian — Robert McAfee Brown — wishes to make of some of the sayings of Jeremiah. To understand Jeremiah properly we have to be

1. Juan Luis Segundo, "Social Justice and Revolution," *America* (April 1968). A general view of Segundo's extensive writings will be found in Alfred T. Hennelly, *Theologies in Conflict* (1979).

2. Gutierrez, *A Theology of Liberation.*

3. The list of books and other publications with this as their theme is almost endless. Representative are *Cry Justice* (London, 1984) by John de Gruchy, Professor of Christian Studies in the University of Capetown; *Bias to the Poor* (London, 1983) by David Sheppard, Anglican Bishop of Liverpool; *Faith and Freedom* (Belfast, 1979) by Schubert M. Ogden; and *Justice on the Agenda* (Basingstoke, 1985) by Roger Sainsbury.

4. Extracted in Gill, *A Textbook of Christian Ethics,* p. 278.

clear not only about the Hebrew "sedakah," but about the English "justice."

My purpose . . . is to prize apart the ideals of charity and justice and to show, contrary to this great current of thought, that the traditional Christian duty cannot be construed as a version of this more secular demand. To do so, however, it is obviously necessary to avoid Miranda's mistake and make clear just what conception of justice it is in which we are interested.

In the history of moral and social thought there are at least two conceptions which are translated by the English word "justice." One, that which is to be found in Plato's *Republic,* for instance, is concerned with the whole range of human conduct, private as well as public. We might, in order to distinguish it, call it "righteousness" (as, *pace* Miranda, it is usually translated in the Bible). The second is a much later development in legal and moral theory. It came to prominence first in the social contract theories of the seventeenth and eighteenth centuries and as a result of the gradual evolution of European civil and criminal law. In contrast to the first conception, this conception of justice applies only to a certain aspect of human conduct, in general that which has a public character and involves the conflict of interests, and it is closely connected with the concept of rights.

I do not mean to suggest, of course, that there is no connection between the two. The first is plainly ancestor to the second, but the second is a much more highly refined notion and is that which is dominant in contemporary moral and social thought. Its various features will emerge as the discussion proceeds, but we should begin by noting a distinction within justice, familiar to political philosophers and legal theorists, namely that between retributive and distributive justice. The former concerns the actions of individuals and, more usually, legal systems with respect to wrongdoers. Anyone who commits a criminal wrong acts unjustly and retributive justice requires that he be punished accordingly. Equally, of course, retributive justice requires that those who have not committed any wrong must be protected. The principle "the innocent must not be punished" is as fundamental an element of retributive justice as the principle that "the guilty ought to be punished," and possibly more so.

But there are occasions when questions of justice seem to arise which do not involve any redress for wrongdoing. The most obvious of these are distributions. If I am cutting up the birthday cake at my daughter's party and give the girls much larger slices than the boys, then, though no question of guilt or innocence, conviction or punishment arises, it looks as though some question of injustice does, for I have flouted another fundamental principle of justice, namely that "like cases be treated alike." Since, for the purposes of distributing birthday cake, there is no relevant difference between girls and boys, the distribution is unjust.

The idea of *social* justice is really the concept of distributive justice applied to society as a whole and to the comparative positions and possessions of its members. Now it is a matter of considerable dispute among philosophers as to what the principles of social justice are, and indeed whether there is such a thing as social justice at all,[5] but despite this uncertainty it is plain that politicians and moralists, including Christian moralists, increasingly prefer talk of justice and rights to talk of misfortune and charity. This is true even in cases that plainly are misfortunes, like earthquakes, and which do call for charity. The reason is, I think, that "justice," unlike "charity," has a high rhetorical value, in part derived from one of its logical features and in part derived from the "liberal" *mores* of the present time.

This rhetorical value is worth looking at. It is to be observed first of all that claims of justice (and consequent claims of "rights," which share this rhetorical value) justify the involvement of third parties in the way that charity and the duties of benevolence (more properly, "beneficence") do not. For instance, if a wealthy man passes a drunk who, entirely as a result of his own indolence and folly, is desperate for a few cents to get himself a little more of the only sort of satisfaction he can now appreciate, charity or beneficence may be thought to dictate that the wealthy man should give him something. But, if so, the man's charitable duty does not generate a right on the drunkard's part. From the fact, if it is one, that the man ought

to give him something it does not follow that he has a right to what he ought to be given. Should the rich man pass by on the other side, the fact that he has not done what he ought to do does not imply that he has violated the drunkard's right. Consequently, we as third parties might think him heartless or simply very mean, but the truth of our judgment upon him does not give us the right to interfere. We would not be entitled to seize his wallet forcibly, for instance, and extract something from it for the drunkard. He has done wrong, we might say, but he has not done anyone *a* wrong.

This is a feature of beneficence in general and charity as one form of it. It may be wrong for me to repay generosity with parsimony or give my close friends very poor birthday presents. But for all this, the generous host has no *right* to a return invitation and my friends have no *right* to better birthday presents. These cases, namely those in which I am or am not beneficent, are to be contrasted with those in which I act unjustly. Suppose the rich man does give the drunkard a couple of dollars and someone else, on the true but inadequate ground that the money will go on more drink, takes it away again. He believes that the rich man did wrong to give it, no doubt, but even if he is correct in this belief, he does not have the right to take it away. The money, for good or ill, has been given to the drunkard and is his. It is his *now,* by right. Consequently, a policeman or any third party, who would have had no right to transfer the money from the rich man to the beggar in the first place, does have a right to transfer it back to the beggar. The point is: though it was not his by right before he was given it (even though he ought to have been given it), having been given it, it is his by right. Third parties, when they insist upon the rights of others, act justly. But they do not act justly when they try to bring about the same material result (two dollars in the pocket of the drunkard) without that right.

It should be plain enough in the light of these remarks why there is moral and rhetorical value in construing distribution as a matter of justice. Many people across the world live in abject poverty. They do not, by and large, rise up and seize the goods of the rich, and the rich, by and large, pass by on the other side. If those who want to end this abject poverty also have the power to

5. See John Rawls, *A Theory of Justice* (Boston and Oxford, 1972); Robert Nozick, *Anarchy, State, and Utopia* (Oxford, 1974); and Anthony Flew, *The Politics of Procrustes* (London 1981).

seize the goods of the rich (or a reasonable portion of them) they can rightfully do so if the condition of the poor is one of injustice, not if it is not. If the poor have a *right* to a larger share of the world's goods than they actually enjoy, anyone who seizes it on their behalf is not engaged in stealing but in restitution and thus promoting, not subverting, justice. But if the poor do not have a right, only a *need* for assistance, their appeal must be to the the benevolence of the rich, and if this appeal goes unheard for the most part, third parties must content themselves with deploring the heartlessness of the rich.

The second source of rhetorical value in talk of justice lies in one contemporary legacy of liberalism. Why is it, one might wonder, that many good causes prefer to talk in terms of rights rather than needs? The answer is that it is thought (erroneously, I shall argue in the next chapter) that to be dependent upon the benevolence of others for what one needs is an affront to human dignity. In our common moral consciousness justice and rights form the basis of most appeals by self-respecting adult individuals, needs and wants the basis of appeals in childhood. To acknowledge a need or desire for charity is to confess an inadequacy, a lack of that self-reliance which is an important part of the ideal of autonomy at the heart of liberal individualism. It is this that has given "charity" a bad name and persuaded well-meaning people to speak (confusedly) of rights and justice instead. But unlike the implication for third parties, this feature of justice is, in my view, not a necessary but a purely contingent one and, as I shall try to show later on, there is, for the Christian at any rate, a deep sense of equal worth with which the demands and practice of charity not only do not conflict but which, in a sense, they express. (It may be worth remarking in passing on the irony that it is socialist writers who rely heavily on the rhetorical value of "social justice," while at the same time denying the ideal of the self-reliant autonomous individual upon which it rests in favor of some communitarian ideal.)

Construing the world's ills in terms of rights and social justice, then, has rhetorical value and this being so it is easy to see (a) why people concerned with poverty and deprivation talk in this way and (b) that the fact that they do so does not in itself show the foundations of their moral view

to be sound. That is to say, there are good reasons for talking about justice and rights in preference to needs and charity — it is more effective in contemporary debate — and for this reason many people speak in this way. But it does not follow that they are right to do so.

*   *   *

I have argued that the three assumptions commonly made about suffering in the third world are largely without foundation, but that, even if they were true they would not imply any injustice on the part of the rich. I should stress, however, that such a conclusion does not carry a license to turn one's back on poverty and suffering. On the contrary. It is only those whose moral thinking is blinkered by the concepts of rights and justice who will imagine that such a conclusion follows; and indeed it is part of my objection to the contemporary obsession with justice that it has this blinkering effect. In fact my main point turns on the belief that Christians *ought* to be concerned with these facts. They *should* view as a moral demand the material as well as the spiritual needs of the destitute. But if their concern is to bring about justice, they need have *no* concern with these facts. *Ergo*, justice cannot be the basis of the Christian's concern.

This simple argument, it seems to me, puts an end to a lot of well-intentioned but woolly-minded talk about social justice. Because it *assumes* a legitimate concern with material suffering its conclusion that justice has next to nothing to do with the matter cannot be accused of leading to indifference. And precisely because it disposes of justice as a basis for Christian concern, it opens the door once again to some other foundation. Moreover, if such a basis can be found, then since any strictures on a Christian use of "social justice" in this connection apply equally well to secular uses of it, Christian morality will to this extent be on firmer ground than those secular ideologies (like socialism) which, I think, Christians have often imagined to have greater intellectual robustness.

The way is open, then, and the need revealed to find some better basis than justice for a concern with world hunger and the like.

47. Friendship and Fidelity

GILBERT MEILAENDER

Does the dance cease because one dancer has gone away? In a certain sense. But if the other still remains standing in the posture which expresses a turning towards the one who is not seen, and if you know nothing about the past, then you will say, "Now the dance will begin just as soon as the other comes, the one who is expected."

KIERKEGAARD, *Works of Love*

Christian love, though not entirely incompatible with friendship, is in itself neither preferential nor reciprocal.

Friendship is not love in general; rather, it is a deep attachment to and preference for another person because of the sort of person he or she is. Yet, because this is the case, it seems necessary to say that if one of the persons changes, the relationship must change and friendship may die. If friendship is preferential love, it must cease when the characteristics which gave rise to such preference are no longer present. And if the affection of friendship fails and fades in either party, then one can only admit that the reciprocal and mutually

---

Gilbert Meilaender (1946–) is a professor in the religion department at Oberlin College. He has written *The Taste for the Other: The Social and Ethical Thought of C. S. Lewis, Friendship: A Study in Theological Ethics, The Theory and Practice of Virtue,* and *Faith and Faithfulness: Basic Themes in Christian Ethics.*

From Gilbert Meilaender, *Friendship* (Notre Dame: University of Notre Dame Press, 1981).

shared good will which friendship involves is gone. Friendship, in order to be friendship — that is, in order to be a preferential and reciprocal love — must be subject to change.

Not so with Christian love. It is determined not by the characteristics of the loved one nor by any anticipated return but solely by its own self-giving character. "How can I give you up, O Ephraim!" Yahweh cries out through his prophet (Hosea 11:9). And the evangelist depicts the standard for *agape* when he writes of Jesus that "having loved his own who were in the world, he loved them to the end" (John 13:1). The God who in nature has faithfully made his sun to rise on evil and good and sent his rain on just and unjust (Matthew 5:45) is thereby claimed to have proven himself just as faithful within history. It is not surprising that such love should make neither preference nor reciprocity central. *Agape*, in order to be *agape* — that is, in order to be a faithful love — must, it seems, be nonpreferential and unconcerned with reciprocity.

Perhaps, therefore, we ought simply to face the harsh truth to which this brief analysis gives rise: friendship and fidelity are incompatible. We can purchase permanence in love only by sacrificing the delights of preference and reciprocity, and we can enjoy friendship only by sacrificing the assurance of permanence. And yet, it is not clear that either of these is precisely what we desire. "A friend loves at all times" (Proverbs 17:17). That is what we want: faithful friendship. The hard question is whether we can have it.

I

It should be no surprise that certain friendships cease. Those ties, for example, which were based solely on the usefulness of the friends to each other are not likely to survive a change in circumstances which makes obsolete the mutually advantageous relationship which existed. Plutarch put the point well:

In the house of rich men and rulers, the people see a noisy throng of visitors offering their greetings and shaking hands and playing the part of armed retainers, and they think that those who have so many friends must be happy. Yet they can see a far greater number of flies in those persons' kitchens. But the flies do not stay on after the good food is gone, nor the retainers after their patron's usefulness is gone.[1]

And even in the case of character-friendships, if these are formed before young people reach some degree of maturity, we are neither surprised nor even particularly dismayed to discover that those who were once close friends have grown apart and fallen out of touch. Where character is not yet relatively formed, character-friendship must necessarily be unstable.

Far more tragic, yet also understandable, are friendships which falter when the friends find themselves in unalterable disagreement on some good greater even than friendship itself. If, as I argued when discussing the preferential character of friendship, the exclusiveness of friendship is meant to lead on to a more all-embracing form of community, we have to reckon with the possibility that a more universal good may, at any time, demand our loyalty in an overriding way. Thus Aristotle, referring to his friendship for the author of the *Theory of Ideas*, which he is criticizing, says that truth must be valued more highly even than friendship — a sentiment which would surely have been understood by the author of that theory who himself had written that "we must not honor a man above truth."[2]

Indeed, in Christian terms one must always presume at least one such qualification to be written into friendship: namely, that loyalty to the friend could not override faithfulness to God, if these should seem to conflict. Thus, Aelred of Rievaulx, in perhaps the most important treatise on friendship to emerge from medieval monastic life, could write:

> It is clear, then, . . . what the fixed and true limit of spiritual friendship is: namely, that nothing ought to be denied to a friend, nothing ought to be refused for a friend, which is less than the very precious life of the body, which divine authority

has taught should be laid down for a friend. Hence, since the life of the soul is of far greater excellence than that of the body, any action, we believe, should be altogether denied a friend which brings about the death of the soul, that is, sin, which separated God from the soul and the soul from life.[3]

In a rather different literary vein, Dorothy Sayers explores such a conflict in *Unnatural Death*, one of her Lord Peter Wimsey stories. Mary Whittaker, a murderess, is using Vera Findlater to provide her with an alibi. Vera is an extremely devoted and loyal friend (who mistakenly believes that the same is true of Mary) and has permitted ties of personal loyalty to lead her to lie on Mary's behalf. In a conversation with Miss Climpson, who seems an innocuous spinster but is really investigating for Lord Peter, the theological issue is raised:

> "But a great friendship does make demands," cried Miss Findlater eagerly. "It's got to be just everything to one. It's wonderful the way it seems to color all one's thoughts. Instead of being centred in oneself, one's centred in the other person. That's what Christian love means — one's ready to die for the other person."
>
> "Well, I don't know," said Miss Climpson. "I once heard a sermon about that from a most *splendid* priest — and he said that that kind of love might become *idolatry* if one wasn't very careful. He said that Milton's remark about Eve — you know, 'he for God only, she for God in him' — was not congruous with Catholic doctrine. One must get the *proportions* right, and it was *out of proportion* to see everything through the eyes of another fellow-creature."[4]

To prefer the friend above God, who gives the friend, would be an inordinate love — one in which, as Miss Climpson's splendid priest put it, the proportions were not right. And, however tragic the choice might be on certain occasions,

1. Plutarch, "On Having Many Friends," *Moralia*, II, trans. F. C. Babbott (London: William Heinemann, 1928), 94B, p. 53.

2. Cf. Aristotle, *Nicomachean Ethics*, I, vi, 1096a; and Plato, *Republic*, 595c.

3. Aelred of Rievaulx, *Spiritual Friendship*, trans. Mary Eugenia Laker, S.S.N.D., Cistercian Fathers Series Number Five (Washington, D.C.: Consortium Press, 1974), II:69.

4. Dorothy L. Sayers, *Unnatural Death* (New York: Avon Books, 1968), p. 158.

one must be willing to say to the friend what the Cavalier poet said to a different kind of beloved in conflict with a lesser god "I could not love thee, dear, so much, loved I not honor more."

Conflicts such as these are not the chief obstacle to faithful friendship. That barrier is something far less heroic-sounding, far more mundane. "The most fatal disease of friendship," Dr. Johnson wrote, "is gradual decay."[5] Perhaps time heals all wounds, but only by teaching forgetfulness of the wounds which time itself inflicts. We are temporal beings, constantly changing. And a love like friendship, which depends so greatly on shared interests and enjoyments, is easily weakened or destroyed by altered circumstances. Any change in our circumstances, our vocation, our education, our wealth will slowly have its effect on our friendships. New enjoyments and interests crowd out old ones — crowding out also thereby the friendships built on those old enjoyments and interests. The measured sentences of Dr. Johnson come to terms with the humble realities of finite existence.

> Many have talked, in very exalted language, of the perpetuity of friendship, of invincible constancy, and unalienable kindness; and some examples have been seen of men who have continued faithful to their earliest choice; and whose affection has predominated over changes of fortune, and contrariety of opinion.
>
> But these instances are memorable, because they are rare. The friendship which is to be practised or expected by common mortals, must take its rise from mutual pleasure, and must end when the power ceases of delighting each other.

Hence, Dr. Johnson suggests, "there is no human possession of which the duration is less certain." Insofar as our experience suggests this to be accurate, it merely confirms what sober analysis of the requirements of friendship and the requirements of fidelity suggests: that faithful friendship is likely to be very rare in human experience. Friendship involves the delights and enjoyments which preference and reciprocity make possible. Fidelity requires a steadfastness of purpose which perseveres even when none of those enjoyments is present.

*　　*　　*

II

If friendship's duration is so uncertain, one may well ask whether there is any way to protect friendship against dissolution. And there is one answer, often given by those who have written on friendship, which deserves to be taken seriously if only because it has been given so frequently: test the prospective friend in advance of proffering friendship. Emerson — whose essay on friendship is considerably overrated and whose "the only way to have a friend is to be one" sounds quite different when read in context — states the typical view concisely and eloquently: "Let us buy our entrance to this guild by a long probation."[6]

Cicero, living in an age when friendships were of political and not merely private importance, develops the theme of testing at great length. It is wise, he suggests, to "exercise such care in forming friendships that we should never begin to love anyone whom we might sometime hate" (XVI, 60). A qualification, one is constrained to reply, which may severely limit the circle of one's potential friends! The more detail Cicero gives us about what he has in mind, the more uncomfortable, we may become:

> It is the part of wisdom to check the headlong rush of goodwill as we would that of a chariot, and thereby so manage friendship that we may in some degree put the dispositions of friends, as we do those of horses, to a preliminary test. Some men often give proof in a petty money transaction how unstable they are; while others, who could not have been influenced by a trivial sum, are discovered in one that is large. (XVII, 63)

One feels instinctively that there is something unsatisfactory — perhaps even repugnant — about such a notion; yet most of us do so test

5. Samuel Johnson, *Essays from the 'Rambler', 'Adventurer', and 'Idler'*, ed. W. J. Bate (New Haven: Yale University Press, 1968), p. 283 (Idler #23). The citations in this paragraph are all taken from this same essay.

6. Ralph Waldo Emerson, "Friendship," *Essays and Journals,* selected by Lewis Mumford (Garden City, N.Y.: Doubleday, 1968), p. 169.

those with whom we are in danger of becoming "too close."[7]

We can, however, move beyond an initial, undeveloped reaction to Cicero's view of the necessity of testing; for there is a fundamental flaw in his suggestion, a flaw to which his own discussion points. He suggests a problem but does not pursue it:

> We ought, therefore, to choose men who are firm, steadfast and constant, a class of which there is a great dearth; and at the same time it is very hard to come to a decision without a trial, while such trial can only be made in actual friendship: thus friendship outruns the judgment and takes away the opportunity of a trial. (XVII, 62)

Friendships, if there are to be any at all, must be formed before we can have any certain knowledge that the other person is truly lovable, one suited for our friendship. This means that we may commit ourselves to persons for whom our regard may fade. Yet, in thus committing ourselves to another person, we create in that friend a set of expectations, needs, and loyalties which cannot simply be set aside without pain and grief. Again we see that the bond of friendship seems to call for a permanence which it cannot itself provide. Try to avoid making mistakes in friendship and we will have no friends at all. Acquire the necessary experience which only friendship and some "mistaken judgments" can provide and in so doing we make commitments and establish expectations which call for fidelity. Can the tension between friendship and fidelity be overcome?

When discussing reciprocity in friendship I suggested that the self-giving of *agape* may be a necessary component of friendship from the very outset, that without such self-giving no mutual love could spring up or be sustained. That provided a convenient way to suggest that *agape* and *philia* do not only stand in tension; rather, it is

equally true to suggest that the natural love of friendship stands in need of *agape,* that it is supported and sustained by a love which is not natural to the creature. It would be nice if in discussing the tension between friendship and fidelity we could do the same, but we cannot.

Aelred of Rievaulx, for example, wants to hold that true friendship can never cease. He has as authorities, after all, the scriptural passage that "a friend loves at all times" as well as a statement of Jerome's which he cites: "friendship which can end, was never true friendship." But in attempting to explain how this can be possible, Aelred is driven to a viewpoint which seems implausible. He distinguishes four elements in a bond of friendship — love (by which he means benevolence and good will), affection, security (i.e., trust), and happiness. He grants that a friendship burdened with various difficulties may come to lose affection, security, and happiness. Hence, he concludes, "that familiarity, in which such things find their place, must be denied to a former friend, but love should not be withdrawn. . . ."[8] What we have left, of course, is a bond that is neither preferential nor reciprocal — mere good will. That can last, to be sure, but it is hard to see why we should call it friendship.

We can probe the tension between friendship and fidelity more deeply if we consider what may be the most striking passage in a very striking book — Kierkegaard's *Works of Love.* St. Paul writes that "love abides," and in the light of that Kierkegaard considers the possibility of a rupture in love:

> And so the breaking-point between the two is reached. It was a misunderstanding; yet one of them broke the relationship. But the lover says, "I abide" — therefore there still is no break. Imagine a compound word which lacks the last word; there is only the first word and the hyphen (for the one who breaks the relationship still cannot take the hyphen with him; the lover naturally keeps the hyphen on his side); imagine, then, the first word and the hyphen of a compound word and now imagine that you know absolutely nothing more about how it hangs together — what will you say? You will say that the word is not complete, that it

7. The same emphasis on the importance of a probationary period appears in Aelred of Rievaulx's *Spiritual Friendship,* the high-water mark of monastic thought about friendship and a treatise heavily dependent on Cicero's *De Amicitia.* In the monastic context, of course, it is not difficult to see this emphasis take institutional shape in the concept of a novitiate.

8. *Spiritual Friendship,* III:52.

lacks something. It is the same with the lover. That the relationship has reached the breaking-point cannot be seen directly; it can be known only from the angle of the past. But the lover wills not to know the past, for he abides; and to abide is in the direction of the future. Consequently the lover expresses that the relationship which another considers broken is a relationship which has not yet been completed. . . . What a difference there is between a fragment and an unfinished sentence! In order to call something a fragment, one must know that nothing more is to come. If one does not know this, he says that the sentence is not yet completed. . . . But suppose now that it is three years since that they last spoke together. See, here it comes again. That it was three years ago one can know only in the sense of the past; but the lover, who daily renews himself by the eternal and abides, over him the past has no power at all. If you saw two persons sitting silent together and you knew nothing more, would you thereby conclude that it was three years since they spoke together? Can any one determine how long a silence must have been in order to say now, there is no more conversation; and if one can determine this, in a particular instance one can nevertheless know only from the angle of the past whether this is so, for the time must indeed be past. But the lover, who abides, continually emancipates himself from his knowledge of the past; he knows no past; he waits only for the future.[9]

The lover keeps the hyphen. Perhaps no one has ever pictured so magnificently the meaning of steadfastness in love. But clearly, it must be *agape*, not *philia*, which Kierkegaard here describes. Imagine a friendship in which neither friend has spoken for three years. To call such a bond a friendship would be contrary to what almost everyone who has written on friendship has thought it necessary to say: that friends long to spend time together; that friends want to share their interests and enjoyments with one another.

There may be deep commitment to the well-being of the neighbor in the love Kierkegaard describes, but we should not call it friendship. And,

9. Søren Kierkegaard, *Works of Love*, trans. Howard and Edna Hong (New York: Harper Torchbooks, 1964), pp. 184f.

of course, Kierkegaard himself understands this quite well. He contrasts what it means to love "the neighbor" with what it means to love a friend or a beloved.

> The beloved can treat you in such a way that he is lost to you, and you can lose a friend, but whatever a neighbour does to you, you can never lose him. To be sure, you can also continue to love your beloved and your friend no matter how they treat you, but you cannot truthfully continue to call them beloved and friend when they, sorry to say, have really changed. No change, however, can take your neighbour from you, for it is not your neighbour who holds you fast — it is your love which holds your neighbour fast. (p. 76)

Here, as is very often the case with Kierkegaard, the very strength of his insight is also its greatest danger. It becomes too easy to suggest, as Kierkegaard himself does, that if the lover holds on to love even when the beloved ruptures their relationship, then "the break has no power over him" (p. 283). And that is quite different from saying that the lover keeps the hyphen. To say that the break has no power over the lover can too easily come to mean that the relationship was of little consequence, as if only the relation with the Eternal and not our fragile, earthly bonds were important. To say that the lover keeps the hyphen on his side, that he wills not to be determined by the past but, instead, to live for the future, is to admit the relationship is of enormous significance — for what love believes when it abides is that the relationship "has not yet been completed."

We have reached a point at which the difference between *agape* and *philia* must be plain. If friendship ceases, the steadfastness of love may still be directed toward that neighbor who once was friend, but *agape* cannot simply be substituted for friendship without loss. To say, "though I can no longer love him as a friend, I can continue in a self-giving spirit to be devoted to his good," may be very important indeed. But such a simple substitution of *agape* for *philia* must be understood to be just that — a substitution of one love for another, and a substitution in which something of great importance is lost.

We achieve permanence in love by ceasing to let our love be concerned with or determined by the particular character of the loved one. Friendship never loves that way. Friendship loves and prefers a particular person because of what that person is. That is why, when the person changes, friendship changes or fades. And though it may be good to know that we are loved with a love which never fades, it is doubtful whether anyone wishes to be loved in only that way — in spite of what we are, rather than because of what we are. No doubt that is better than not to be loved at all. But being loved in that way does not offer all that we need or want. To be loved with *agape* alone is, however important, not sufficient; for it is too impersonal. It is not surprising that the words "I love you despite your failings" should as often be a subtle weapon as a genuine affirmation of the other person.

The tension between *philia* and *agape* must be permitted to stand. Friendship, in order to be preferential and reciprocal, must be subject to change. Yet, a friendship which lacks permanence seems less than perfect. *Agape,* in order to be faithful, must be nonpreferential and unconcerned with reciprocity. Yet, a love which lacks these marks of *philia* — its deep intimacy, mutuality, and preference — seems too impersonal and cold to satisfy the needs of our nature.

III

Either our desire for faithful friendship is sheer self-delusion or else it is permissible to hope for a day and a community in which such friendship might become possible, to hope that temporality and change might lose their relentless power over our commitments. *Agape,* with its steadfastness, should enter into friendship to perfect it. Friendship, with its warmth and mutuality, should be the internal fruition of *agape.* It was sound theological instinct, not mere wish-fulfillment, which led medieval thinkers to conceive of heaven as a "vast friendship." Nothing less than this, a community in which friendship and charity are coextensive, will satisfy the needs of our nature. Nothing less than this will correspond to the mutuality of the triune life of God into which he wills to draw us.

Such a hope is expressed better by Augustine's vision of life as pilgrimage toward the enjoyment of God than Kierkegaard's sterner vision of love

as duty brought about through transformation by the Eternal, a vision which tries too quickly to resolve the argument between *philia* and *agape.* To think of love solely as a duty does, to be sure, recognize that any love which is attached to the friend because of his character will be subject to change if that character changes. However, love as duty purchases permanence at the cost of mutuality. The eternal steadfastness of Christian love should not simply replace the mutuality of *philia.* If friendship ends, a willingness to serve and help must never be withdrawn, but one must also hope for something more.

That something more is expressed in the vision of human life as pilgrimage toward the community God is fashioning. This more patient image permits us to take time and its terrors seriously without being overcome by them. It permits us to express better the complexities of relating *philia* and *agape.* Attachment to friends is a school in which we are trained for that greater community. Steadfast faithfulness in love is necessary even when friendship ceases. But faithful friendship is the goal — a goal which can be realized only when the friend is loved in God. To love the friend in God is not to love what is godlike in the friend — precisely at that point Christian thought parts company with the classical conception of friendship. Not the friend's goodness but the Goodness which possesses the friend and is refracted by the friend is what the eye is to discern. Only thus is the friend seen as God's creature and loved appropriately.

We cannot resolve the tension between friendship and fidelity; we can only state some of the truths to which reflection upon this tension gives rise. Life is a journey, a pilgrimage toward that community in which friends love one another in God and time no longer inflicts its wounds on friendship. Along the way, friendship is a school, training us in the meaning and enactment of love. Friendship is also a foretaste of the internal reciprocities of love which have yet to be fully realized. And, it is important to add, friendship is a good which may have to be sacrificed here and now in order to be fully realized in the sharing of the divine life.

But to speak of faithful friendship is to conjoin in hope what cannot be fully united within human history. Time is not that easily or quickly tamed by eternity, and one must learn to be patient. Such patience is possible, however, for those who believe that the changeable character of our friendships — the work of time — need not stand in irreconcilable tension with the steadfastness of love transformed by the Eternal. Cicero could do no more than point toward such a possibility.

> How grievous and hard to most persons does association in another's misfortunes appear! Nor is it easy to find men who will go down to calamity's depths for a friend. . . . Whoever, therefore, in either of these contingencies, has shown himself staunch, immovable, and firm in friendship ought to be considered to belong to that class of men which is exceedingly rare — aye, almost divine. (XVII, 64)

Christian ethics affirms that such a love has entered history in Jesus of Nazareth and that this love is, to paraphrase Niebuhr, a tangent toward eternity in time.[10] The presence within history of such love justifies the Christian hope for faithful friendship. It is the reason for believing that, even if one partner in the dance turns away for a time, it is appropriate to remain standing in that posture which "expresses a turning towards the one who is not seen" and thereby says, "Now the dance will begin just as soon as the other comes, the one who is expected."

48. To Bear Wrongs Patiently

SIDNEY CORNELIA CALLAHAN

If you put up with suffering for doing what is right, this is acceptable in God's eyes. It was for this you were called, since Christ suffered for you in just this way and left you an example, to have you follow in his footsteps. He did no wrong; no deceit was found in his mouth. When he was insulted he returned no insult. When he was made to suffer, he did not counter with threats. Instead, he delivered himself up to the One who judges justly.

1 PETER 2:20-25

To bear wrongs patiently. In an age of liberation movements, revolution, and assertiveness training this work of mercy makes us wince at its apparent endorsement of fatalism and masochism. Have not generations of the poor and oppressed been kept down and made submissive by the idea that they should bear wrongs patiently? Today, we do not see patience as a virtue; it is impossible to imagine parents naming their daughter Patience in admiration of the attitude. Patience now is equated more often with passivity and long-suffering, an undesirable condition to be overcome.

Sidney Cornelia Callahan (1933–) teaches psychology at Mercy College in Dobbs Ferry, New York. Among her publications are *The Illusion of Eve, With All Our Heart and Mind,* and *In Good Conscience: Reason and Emotion in Moral Decision-Making.*

10. See Reinhold Niebuhr, *The Nature and Destiny of Man,* Vol. II: *Human Destiny* (New York: Charles Scribner's Sons, 1964), p. 69.

From Sidney Cornelia Callahan, *With All Our Heart and Mind: The Spiritual Works of Mercy in a Psychological Age* (New York: Crossroad, 1988).

Part of our problem with patience may stem from our American spirit. America has always been the land of ideal supermen who run faster than a speeding bullet. We are the people who wish to hurry up everything and provide instant relief, in medication, in fast food, in the fast-track career. At the same time we are programmed *not* to stand for wrongs, or as one state motto warns, "Don't Tread on Me." If you do, you will be instantly sorry. We won't tolerate delay, obstacles, or oppression — "Give me liberty or give me death," right this second. We believe that the impossible can only take a little longer; individual liberty and rights to self-defense (enabled by the possession of guns) are our paramount values. This American cultural conditioning makes it difficult for us to relate to spiritual counsels commending patience.

Feminists, blacks, American Indians, and other oppressed groups have also balked at traditional spiritual interpretations of the need for patience. Accepting suffering and injustice in the name of love has been labeled the "Uncle Tom response" that holds back liberation movements. Induced female masochism has been seen as a chief obstacle to women's progress. Indeed, masochism is much on our mind these days and has long since escaped its narrower meaning connected with sexuality. Masochism in its general cultural form applies to persons who are apathetic, resigned to suffering, and expect poor treatment from others. Their self-defeating behavior correlates with a low sense of self-worth, an inadequate sense of personal rights, and a lack of hope that things can change for the better. Who am I to deserve more or make waves? I am doomed to suffer, and besides, as a suffering victim, I may be able to garner some psychological advantages for myself, or at least avoid danger.

Self-defeating behavior can become a way of life. The martyred, long-suffering mother, the put-upon wife, the overburdened worker or middle manager — even male versions are available. Psychoanalysts have described lives in which a person manifests a persistent need for failure or the idealization of unhappiness. One can observe regularly the puzzling cases of the competent persons who, despite their innate capacity, can never quite make it and who repeatedly self-destruct, snatching defeat after defeat from the jaws of victory. An unconscious or preconscious program or script appears to have been established in early life such that unhappiness and defeat appear psychologically necessary for safety and security. Success, happiness, or victory may have become identified as dangerous for unconscious reasons — fears of provoking retaliatory jealousies or losing love, and guilt over outshining one's parental figures. Only personal defeat, suffering, and inhibition feel safe.

In self-deprecating long-suffering, a person defensively adopts the habit of abnegation. Is this psychological condition the same as bearing wrongs patiently? No; neither masochism nor fatal resignation are meant when Christians speak of bearing wrongs patiently. Christians believe that fatalism can be fatal, indeed a form of despair. When one gives up hope, self-respect, and a sense of internal agency, one gives up the struggle to change. We cannot make the Kingdom come when we have become resigned to suffering and think that nothing we can do will make any difference. We need to reconsider patience, and rethink what it means to bear wrongs patiently. How is this activity related to love? What is patience? What are wrongs?

Wrongs

What are wrongs? How does a wrong differ from injuries or from sins, the other negative things that we must cope with in the traditional list of the spiritual works of mercy? As compared to injury or sin, a wrong seems more general, less specific, less intentional, less often directed with premeditated malice toward a particular individual. The time framework is also different, in that wrongs often are long-term chronic conditions as compared to acute attacks or brief episodes. A wrong is more socially institutionalized and impersonal. Wrongs are definitely immoral and unethical in the sense that the innocent suffer, but they lack the characteristic of specific injury or specific intentional rejections of God through consciously evil action. Things should be otherwise, should be just — some things are unfair, unjust, terrible — but wrongs seem less personal than either sin or injuries.

Examples of wrongs to bear might include prejudice against one's race, sex, religion, age, class, or condition. To be subject to dislike as a member of a stigmatized group would be an example of a wrong or violation of justice. This wrong would not be directed at oneself specifically but would be a form of structural social oppression. We can think of many wrongs that exist even in our relatively free American society. To be old and denigrated is certainly one wrong that many in the society can look forward to. To be poor, homeless, or deprived of health care or other basic needs and rights is also a wrong. Other wrongs one might have to cope with include being imprisoned wrongfully, being dismissed from a job unjustly, and being wronged in some other transaction with the world or social system. Wrongs and injustice also arise from human errors, flaws, and failings.

Wrongs do not include acts of nature such as earthquakes, floods, or disease. One could not say that one has been wronged by an earthquake or pneumonia. Of course if one has intentionally been given a disease, such as AIDS, by someone who through deception spread the infection, then one could consider the suffering incurred as a wrong. Wrongs are essentially social betrayals and failings toward an individual, infringements upon justice, equality, and human dignity. In countries where one can be arrested, imprisoned, or tortured without recourse to the law there are, of course, many more wrongs to be borne. We are indeed fortunate to live in a society that does not require most of us to bear as much injustice as most people have had to bear.

But, say the skeptics, America is a land in which justice more or less prevails because Americans have never accepted the counsel that we should accept wrongs patiently. Have we not always taken arms against a sea of troubles, with the firm conviction that we could overcome difficulty and injustice through effort? The idea that God helps those who help themselves and that human beings can solve their own problems, has been at the root of our satisfactory condition of life. We have always been willing to fight for our rights. Not for us the sentimental glorification of suffering, or the excusing of failure and retreat! We are the can-do people who will try ever harder when an obstacle or wrong is in our way.

Bearing Wrongs

But does *bearing a wrong* mean passively accepting the wrong? Not when we pay attention to the meaning of *to bear*. To bear means "to support and move, to carry, to sustain, to hold up, conduct oneself in a given manner," and, of course, it also means "to produce a child." These are all intensely active human functions. Bearing is not passive after all; weak delicate persons given to apathy or masochism cannot bear up, cannot bear down, cannot bear much of anything. Other active meanings of bear are "to exercise as a power" and "to assume something." All of these activities take strength and depths of human resources. The power to sustain something, assume something, or bring something forth, requires strength and courage. This has nothing to do with fatalism or passive submission.

Once we see that bearing is an active exercise of power, we can begin to understand what we are called to do in this spiritual work of mercy. To bear wrongs patiently is an active enabling form of love and power. It is having the firmness to hold ourselves and others up, through strain, stress, and evil times, without causing more suffering and evil. One can best see this spiritual work of mercy as a call for toughness, strength of will, and strength of purpose. It is a display of firmness and fortitude rather than weakness. Is one strong enough to bear trials, to bear up when things are not working out, when things are not going one's way, when one is being oppressed or having to suffer unmerited wrongs? Passive, weak persons faced with difficulties either collapse or are driven to violent outbursts in which the wrong done them is taken out on others. Self-pity and tantrums, including the tantrums of sullen silence, are often the reaction of the childishly immature. They pass on their distress to others, often with violent abuse, and thereby multiply injustice, escalate misfortune, and magnify the amount of suffering and evil in the world.

How well one bears the wrongs one encounters in life is a true test of strength of character. Some wrong will have to be faced by almost everyone, since injustice is inherent in the disorder of the present world. If we cannot bear wrongs with fortitude, we fail in our responsibility toward those with whom we live. Everyone knows those who cannot bear stress, who cannot cope when obstacles or problems arise. Often they are people who have never had to struggle before, or people who, despite superficial indulgences, seem not to have gotten enough love or discipline.

A person needs past experience in coping in order to be able to cope when injustice or wrongs are encountered later. This aptitude seems to have less to do with physical health or strength than with psychological attitude. A certain humility, gratitude, and sense of reality is needed. When one is still a childish, self-engrossed, narcissistic person, one demands that the world conform to one's whims and wishes. Everything one encounters should be fair, just, comfortable, and instantly solvable. When reality does not oblige, the immature person disintegrates. Or alternatively, a person who has struggled to succeed, can become gradually corrupted by power, comfort, and flattery so that he or she falls into narcissistic expectation of omnipotence. A person with power can begin to ignore reality and the needs of others, slowly regressing to infancy over the course of four or five decades. Psychological strength is revealed by how well a person is able to cope over the long haul.

It is instructive to look at extreme cases in which people have had to bear wrongs, cases all too prevalent in our modern era of concentration camps, preventive detention, disappearances, and torture. Victor Frankl, the noted psychologist who was incarcerated in the Nazi concentration camps during the Second World War, was one of the first to draw pertinent psychological and spiritual conclusions from his observation of individuals in extreme situations. He saw that persons react to stress and persecution partly in common patterns determined by the horrible situation; but, more crucially, their behavior was also partly determined by their individual character. Some people were not able to cope, or bear up under the pressure. They broke down morally, spiritually, and physically. Others mustered the strength to keep their humanity alive in the grim situation, while still others were truly heroic. As Frankl reflects, "It becomes clear that the sort of person the prisoner became was the result of an inner decision, and not the result of camp influences alone." There were always decisions to be made:

Every hour offered the opportunity to make a decision, a decision which determined whether you would or would not submit to those powers which threatened to rob you of your very self, your inner freedom: which determined whether or not you would become the plaything of circumstance, renouncing freedom and dignity to become molded into the form of a typical inmate.[1]

Personal attitude makes the difference in situations of stress. Wrongs that we encounter will offer this test, this challenge of whether we will be conformed to the world or will be able to overcome through our inner resistance. We bear up and sustain and carry wrongs because we believe with Frankl that "man can preserve a vestige of spiritual freedom, of independence of mind even in such terrible conditions of psychic and physical stress." The people who have experienced the worst demonstrate that "everything can be taken from a man but one thing: the last of the human freedoms — to choose one's attitude in any given set of circumstances, to choose one's own way." When people give up choosing, give up hope, they can no longer cope psychologically, nor long survive physically.

Despair is born in many ways. One of the most insidious ways is through acquiescence in one's mind to the claims and world view of those who inflict the wrongs. To be persuaded by and accept the viewpoint of one's oppressors or torturers, to give up one's inner moral and spiritual resistance to evil, breaks the human spirit. As one young woman poet writes of her struggle to resist the guards in her Siberian prison, "Well, we'll live as the soul directs, not asking for other bread." If one begins to inwardly accede to evil, if one becomes callous to the wrongs inflicted upon oneself and others, then the oppressor has won a convert to their system of injustice and immorality. In the Gulag prisons, as the young poet proclaims, it is "the best in all the world, the most tender, who don't break." Their virtue, tenderness, and alertness to the unjust wrongs being inflicted upon the innocent, help them withstand torture and bear wrongs without succumbing. Those who harden

1. *Man's Search for Meaning* (New York: Simon & Schuster, 1963), p. 104.

break because they no longer care enough to nurture and support themselves or other sufferers.

It is important to remember that Christians, knowing that they are made in God's image and redeemed at great cost, are instructed to admonish sinners and to struggle as in childbirth so that God's love and justice can be born in the creation. However it is obvious that success can never be achieved instantly. Before the final victory one must be able to bear the wrongs that still exist in the midst of the struggle. This is true in the political communities and the larger social groups in which we live, and it is also true as we struggle and work out our salvation together in family and personal life. It is essential to get the right balance.

One must bear wrongs patiently while at the same time admonishing, resisting, and working to right the wrongs. Bearing wrongs patiently is not an instance of religion serving as the opiate of the people, or pie in the sky when you die. It has nothing to do with a pietism that retreats from the world in order to avoid conflict. In fact the spiritual resistance to injustice may precipitate or increase conflict: struggles to overcome evil with good are not compatible with certain gnostic approaches to life in which evil is thought not to exist and wrongs suffered are only an illusion. In the tradition of the Old Testament prophets, we must accept the presence of evil and recognize injustice before we can bear it or initiate change.

A belief that the status quo represents a just world has been seen by psychologists as the royal road to blaming victims and abdicating social responsibility. Since there is something in us that wants the world to be just, the temptation is always there to believe that the world is just. If the world were just, the victors would deserve their spoils and the losers would deserve what they get. When persons believe this it meets all sorts of psychological needs. If victims have somehow brought suffering on themselves, our responsibility to help them is lessened. The rest of us in a just world can also more easily deny that we, too, could be victimized. This belief serves as a protection against accepting the irrationality and injustice that exist in life. How upsetting it is to realize the truth that good people have terrible things happen to them that they certainly never deserved.

To face the disorder of the world produces deep anxiety. We try to deny it. But the counsel to bear wrongs patiently helps break through our denial by reiterating and reminding us that wrongs do exist and that the innocent and righteous suffer. We belong to the human community who endure unmerited wrongs. We cannot avoid it, nor separate ourselves from the unlucky persons who suffer.

Patience

Patience is an active exercise of power. Patience is to be expectant, to act strongly without complaint, to act with equanimity. It is the ability to continue efforts undisturbed by obstacles, delays, or the temptation to quit. Perseverance and patience are related. To expect that victory and success will come in the long run is the basis of patience and perseverance. And perseverance, as Saint Paul points out, brings hope. The activity of *keeping on* keeping on produces the change in viewpoint. One's own activity reveals to oneself and others that activity is possible. Each step that one takes changes one's position in the world.

One is patient because one believes in the future and in the ultimate victory of good. As Christ was sure of God, the One who judges justly, he could return good for evil. The ultimate triumph of justice means that one can be patient as one makes interim efforts. As Saint Teresa of Avila said, "Patience obtains all . . . all things pass, God alone suffices." When we look at the patience of the saints imitating the patience displayed by Jesus, who bore his wrongs with calmness, equanimity, and courage, we see that they were all able to act in this way because of their utter confidence in the ultimate outcome and victory. God's will *will* be done, justice *will* come. In the end all wrongs will be righted by God's power. This belief that the Kingdom will triumph and that in the end a new Jerusalem will be created gives the assurance and power to bear wrongs in the present with patience.

Victor Frankl also observed that only those people who sustain hope were able to bear wrongs patiently. To see meaning in their suffering meant that they could bear it without despair. Christians are not the only ones who have had the ability to be patient and bear wrongs; other believers have also been certain of meaning in life. Marxists and communists, for instance, have seen themselves contributing to the inevitable forces of history — and they, too, held up well in concentration camps. All believers in transcendent meaning are given strength in the present by their belief in ultimate spiritual vindication. The American Indians who could sing their victory songs while being tortured were as great a witness to the psychology of conviction as were the Jesuit martyrs whom the Indians tortured. Both groups believed that their courage was not wasted.

The conviction that suffering is not wasted helps us to act bravely and bear wrongs patiently. The ultimate despair in the modern world arises from the fact that nothing seems to have meaning when "the best have lost all conviction." Then the wrongs that we suffer are simply random occurrences in a chaotic world that has no purpose and no connection with ultimate values. This lack of meaning leads to the collapse of young persons and adolescents who so often commit suicide in the midst of material abundance. They have no sense of meaning, no sense that the wrongs they must bear might have a connection to the rest of the universe. Without a hope that God can use their suffering in some way or that they can transcend this suffering or that ultimately the forces of right will triumph, they despair and end their lives. It's also important to note that few children today are ever instructed in the virtue of patience. In a world in which immediate satisfaction is touted (go for it, and so on), where would one find a model of patience that would be admirable to a young person?

With patience we can work to right wrongs, but we know that it cannot happen immediately. Even Christians confident of final victory still have to get through the intermediate time between now and then. While we are patient in hope and trust that eventually justice will triumph, what should be our attitude toward those who are working with us, or toward those who are the oppressors, and who are creating the wrongs which we have to bear? If we take seriously both the commandment to love and the need to forgive the sins of those who oppress us, there is only one answer to this question. We must be patient and full of graciousness, kindliness, and positive joyful strength. The other alternatives are sullen apathy or varying degrees of rage.

When one gives in to wrath, anger, and — even worse — bitter resentment, it means that the enemy or the oppressor has conquered one inside as well as outside. When one hates an oppressor, the outer coercion that one cannot prevent has overcome one's inner freedom as well. Patience differs from masochism: masochists who suffer entrap themselves in the suffering insofar as they feel that they should be suffering, should be unhappy, and are unworthy to be happy. But those who bear a wrong patiently know that it is unjust, know that it is wrong for this wrong to be existing, and yet refuse to let this wrong make them miserable or enraged. When one is patient one can be joyful in the midst of the oppression. A heart that is filled with love and kindness toward one's self, toward one's fellow victims, and toward one's oppressors cannot be counted as crushed. This magnanimity and kindliness and graciousness produce the spirit of a person who is a victor and no longer a victim. It is the ultimate triumph of the inner spirit over the wrongs being inflicted. But, of course, such a victory is not easy to achieve.

Here, again, an extreme case history can be instructive to us in meeting the challenges of more ordinary experience. A woman who had been tortured in a Russian prison reported on her struggle to find an effective way to respond. As she was being subjected to systematic torture by an expert at breaking down every defense she searched for ways to find meaning in her absurd and horrible situation. When she tried to shrink into a negative posture the torturer came on stronger as bullies usually do when they sense weakness. However, if she tried to fight back in anger she also whetted his sadistic appetite. In the midst of this she prayed and tried to permeate the situation with spiritual consciousness. With this she felt that she began to understand the other person's self in a new way. But if she became in the least sentimental or overly indulgent toward her torturer, he would brutalize her all the more. Also if she became self-pitying or overindulgent of herself, again displaying weakness, the same thing happened. Slowly she found a balance between indulgence on either side, a way of serenity that she felt was founded on the "divine rock." In the presence of God within her, the core of her personality and foundation, she was able to find the strength to resist and transcend each new act of brutality. She was so grounded in God that she grew perfectly quiet despite the pain. Realizing that he could not disrupt her serenity the torturer lost interest — the sadist was freed from his obsession and she was freed by her centeredness in God.

Now most persons will never be tortured in prison, but many people have had to bear unavoidable psychological persecution in some form, often from a family member. A person under the influence of alcohol, a person being cruel in defense of his or her anxiety or guilt, or a person trying to avoid emptiness and depression can actively persecute a friend or family member.

Just as in physical torture, there can be malice and efforts to confuse and to cause pain through lies and verbal abuse. The effort can also be made to destroy a person's sense of self and confidence in their perception of reality. Objective reality threatens the psychological torturer's power, so it must be distorted by every means at hand. When this horrible kind of suffering and wrong is visited upon an individual the only defense is to seek the serenity and spiritual centeredness that can give one the power to patiently bear the wrongful persecution. In ordinary circumstances one has to seek the same balance as a person under physical torture: one can neither be indulgent and superficially forgiving of what the other person is doing nor self-pitying and self-defeating, wallowing in sweet sorrow. It is necessary to seek confidence in oneself as God's child, and confidence in one's view of the world and reality. Centeredness on God gives the patience and love needed for detachment and the transcendence of anger and bitterness.

Many of the self-help books and self-help movements that have helped so many sufferers teach the same spiritual lessons of unsentimental love and balanced detachment. A well-known example of this is the famous serenity prayer of Alcoholics Anonymous which beseeches God to grant me the serenity to accept that which I cannot change, the courage to change that which I can, and the wisdom to know the difference. This serenity is a form of patience for those who cannot avoid suffering a wrong; it helps them to center themselves and not be consumed by bitterness and the fruitless effort to change and control the uncontrollable.

Other self-help books take a similar spiritual approach. They emphasize praying for the persons who are provoking so much sorrow and trouble, thereby letting them go in order to center upon oneself and one's own spiritual affirmations and belief. This "letting go" through the cultivation of patience includes love, detachment, hope, and confidence in one's own view of reality. Bearing wrongs patiently gives peace and an ability to survive and bear the unbearable one day at a time. If one fights back and becomes angry and wrathfully obsessed with the other's wrongdoing, one allows the persecutor and oppressor to be victorious. Once again, they have made you play their game, and you lose. By fighting back one also sustains the distracting game in which wrongdoers can take refuge and justify themselves. Instead of facing their own behavior, they have in their victim's counterattacks and reactive anger a continuing excuse for their own aggression. All oppressors and wrongdoers love to provoke violence so that their own suppressions and original violence will seem justified to themselves and to others.

If one keeps one's serenity and lives up to Christ's example of patience and love, then no matter what happens one's inner spirit has not been violated by aggressive hate. It is what actively comes out of a person that defiles and disintegrates personality, not what is done to a person without consent.

It is also the case that bearing wrongs patiently may be the most prudent and shrewd course of action to accomplish one's goal. When Christ says that the meek will inherit the earth, he may be making a descriptive statement as well as giving spiritual counsel. A Christian does not bear wrongs patiently *in order* to be more successful in the world, but it often turns out to be an effective life strategy. Even those who do not share the Christian motivation have championed the advantages of nonviolent strategies to achieve certain goals. If they are not innocent as doves, they are at least wily as the serpent.

Why the Meek May Inherit the Earth

Bearing wrongs patiently may work better than anything else one can do in a struggle or conflict. It works because in order to plan and think effectively, one must be calm and able to take time to assess all the factors in any situation. Wrath and anger and the gusts of near madness one might feel when being mistreated can keep one from being able to think clearly or see the oppressor or aggressor as they really exist, that is, from their own stance and point of view as well as from one's own viewpoint. Bearing wrongs patiently has sometimes been interpreted as meaning to bear with wrongdoers patiently, and this larger understanding is important.

While trying to support and love an oppressor one will cultivate empathy and take account of his role as he sees it. This alternate point of view keeps one from subjectively overestimating or underestimating the other's power or position, as hate and fear induce one to do. What is important to this other person or to this other group's world view? What in his system is being threatened in our particular conflict or struggle? Loving my enemy I must pay sustained attention to his point of view; through careful attention I will inevitably and easily penetrate psychologically to his goals, fears, strengths, and weaknesses. As the mother knows her child, and the lover knows the beloved, so I can know my oppressor through sustained empathetic efforts to love him.

Once I know through patience what I could never know through violent hate, I can better devise a means to solve our problems. Love is creative in its free play of the mind, while hate narrows thinking into the obsessive circuits around revenge. If I would seek the best for my enemy along with the best for me and mine, I must be free, confident, and loving in my strategic actions. I can enter a dialogue willingly, for I, too, am concerned with what will serve my oppressor's best interests, including, of course, his moral well-being as well as psychological and material welfare. If he is ensnared in wrongdoing and injustice, I want to help liberate him. How can we together use what Gandhi called soul-force and truth-force to lead us to a new creative solution that will do justice to us both? When my opponent sees that I am concerned about him as well as steely in my concern for justice for myself and my people, new options become possible.

Gandhi said that means are ends in the making, and this is certainly true when one is bearing wrongs and struggling to right them. If you foment acts of aggressive violence, or collapse in self-pity back into fatalism and masochism, there is little hope for a new peaceful future. Violence begets more violence, masochism invites sadism, apathy begets inertia. If I do what my enemy does in retaliation, I become my enemy. Violent revolutionaries who come to power repress in their turn.

We are just beginning to plumb the resources of nonviolent social action in the world today. The civil rights movement, Solidarity in Poland, the Philippine revolution, and other grassroots campaigns for peace and justice are pointing to new realities of the way power is exercised. Power always depends to some extent on the cooperation of others. Waging peace instead of war is slowly becoming a real option in the world. But training and mobilizing for nonviolent action may take more discipline and sustained effort than old-fashioned warfare. What remains to be seen is whether such strategies can work without prolonged efforts to achieve high levels of collective spiritual discipline. What works for individuals and small communities should be adaptable to larger numbers but it will be a challenge to devise strategies for a whole society.

Learning to Bear Wrongs Patiently — Cultivating Patience

For a Christian, progress in bearing wrongs patiently can only mean growing in wisdom and truth. Becoming more Christlike in our own lives is the only Way to go. Once one has tried to do good to enemies and had the bitter experience of failure, one is forced to admit that it is impossible without God's help. God wins, because we learn that one cannot learn to bear wrongs patiently without being sustained and transformed by God. Only through the empowerment of Christ and the Holy Spirit helping us from within the depths of our personality can we cultivate the centeredness to become patient. We need a great deal of meditation and quiet prayer. At the same time we must have worship in community, participating in the sacrament to strengthen the bonds and beliefs which give us faith that justice will come. Only love begets love. If we do not patiently grow in love among our own that we see daily, we surely will not be able to love wrongdoers who oppress us.

277

We must also cultivate loving patience toward ourselves. We have to be patient with ourselves before we can be serene and patient with others. As with all our spiritual transactions, the way we treat others is intimately tied to the way we treat ourselves, which depends in turn on our relationship to God, the ground of reality. Bearing our own faults, and limiting our own self-destructiveness and suffering are prerequisites for bearing the faults of others and supporting them so their wrongdoing is limited. We can overcome evil only by good, through the real and deep understanding that God loves us and accepts us just as we are. With all our faults and failings we are not able to bring about instant justice and right all wrongs immediately. It takes time for the leaven of patience to work, for the seed to grow. Once we understand that God lovingly accepts our efforts and will bring about final victory, we can accept ourselves more completely. We know we're not perfect and that we fail often, just like those whose wrongdoing we must patiently bear. Perhaps one of the best ways to think about ourselves and our oppressors as we bear wrongs patiently is that we are all developing and growing — hard as that is.

All creation is groaning to be born and trying to come to the fruition that God desires. We now know that the universe is hurtling through space and that expansive change is the only constant surrounding us. However, certain things, such as our bodies and many of the material things around us are changing at such a slow rate that they seem hardly to change at all. So, too, the wrongs that we are trying to right can seem unchangeable, but if we think about the history of our world and the fact that so much change has already taken place over the centuries we gain hope and patience. Seemingly permanent structures are really only temporary crystallizations, slower in their transformations than other aspects of the universe. Our bones seem solid compared to the food that we eat but this is only because our bones change more slowly. So, too, with the mountains and the inner core of the molten earth, as well as with the explosions of the stars — everything we know from science points to a universe of perpetual movement. I make all things new, says the Lord. Surely the human spirit and our social consciousness and social worlds are also in motion.

But nothing in our human sphere happens without human effort. Only after working can we rest in God, and after rest and restoration we return to work out our salvation. We must prepare the ground of our personality so that God can act through us. This preparation and pruning require discipline. Discipline and the tools of discipline that many have spoken of are ways of training and painfully pruning, so that we are able to live in fuller happiness and joy in the long run. We cannot become patient without a certain amount of discipline and asceticism; it is the training that is necessary to run in the race. We have to learn delayed gratification. We have to learn to give up illusions and fantasy for the sake of truth and reality, and we have to learn to admit our responsibility for those things that we do and cause. We also have to become flexible and no longer rigidly fixed on perfection and the desire for absolute control. We would like to be gods — we constantly thirst after perfect and absolute order according to our will. Training ourselves in patience and serenity is much like training the body for sports. It is slow. It requires constant individual effort combined with constant reliance upon creative forces beyond us to bring about a new birth.

It is instructive to remember that in actual childbirth a form of patience is also the best of all strategies. Similar principles seem to operate in pain management. To fight the pain or to fight the body's birth contractions, to flail about in fear and loathing, to writhe and grimace and struggle, makes the pain more horrible and intense. The way to conquer is through acceptance of the body and through efforts to transform what is happening. One must concentrate mentally and simultaneously exert controlled efforts to relax in order to float through the process as a swimmer rides a wave. The body seems to follow certain laws that operate in the psyche as well. According to the "law of least effort," it is better not to struggle and focus upon a goal, but to focus upon something else and imperceptibly float toward one's goal bit by bit. In trying *not* to do things one should not focus upon the thing one does not want to do, since that only brings it to mind more acutely and makes it more difficult to resist.

The best way to bear pain and to bear wrongs is to jog along patiently, in a sense of moment-to-moment calmness and acceptance, attending to the good, and confident of eventual victory. Struggling to control a chaotic situation can only result in pain, frustration, and stress. Some unfortunate personalities (those with so-called type-A behavior) spend their lives struggling against the constraints of time, the frustrations and obstacles of matter, and the inability of the world to function perfectly. Their driven quality produces intense stress, making these persons irritable and more subject to heart disease and other stress-related diseases.

So many persons in our society suffer physically and psychologically because they have never learned even the first lessons of patience. It is such an un-American virtue. We are all too familiar with the experience of burnout, in which people struggling to help others and to fight wrongs simply have to give up and quit. They have not been able to persevere in patience and hope because of the continuing frustration of their desire to see wrongs righted; they become angry, irritable, and emotionally drained; finally a condition of emotional numbing is induced. Such numbing can happen to idealistic teachers, nurses, social workers, health workers, and others who must struggle against injustice and the wrongs of the world.

When techniques for "stress reduction" are offered to overstressed modern persons, they turn out to be secularized versions of spiritual techniques and spiritual disciplines. One changes behavior by changing thoughts and feelings, and one changes thoughts and feelings by changing behavior — all at the same time. Imagery, behavioral rehearsals, and physical strategies involving breathing exercises and health habits are used to help persons relax and to restore their sense of well-being. How hard it is for Americans to cultivate serenity, when it is so alien to our culture and to our most admired heroes!

It takes a long time to discipline the mind and the heart and the body. While techniques such as role-playing or behavioral rehearsal sound like mere jargon, they are simply old and tested means of using the human imagination to help become the way one wishes to be. By playing out new scripts and scenarios, either actually or in one's mind, one can prepare for future challenges. Watching films of the best tennis moves improves one's next game. Liturgical re-creations of the gospel inspire one's next moves in a larger game. The spirituality of Saint Ignatius, in concert with many other schools of spirituality, have known all about the power of imagination.

But alas, one cannot simply perform one's way to inner spiritual strength. We really cannot do this alone. For the Christian, the path to such strength must include prayer and worship and actual practice of certain kinds of virtues. Only through practice and the deeds that produce new habits of the heart can God act to transform us into the selves we wish to be. Christians change themselves by asking God to transform them: Give us a new heart, one that is no longer apathetic and hardened. Indeed, make us desire to be given a new heart capable of love. When we have grown in God's love, we will be able to bear wrongs patiently.

Chapter 8

The Contexts of Christian Ethics

Introduction

"The ethical," Bonhoeffer wrote, "cannot be detached from reality." Christian ethics is always "a matter of correct appreciation of real situations and of serious reflection upon them."[1] That is to say, the interpretation of the context for action is an element essential to any moral discernment and judgment.

One does not have to be a "situationist" (see reading 34) to agree with Bonhoeffer on this point. Indeed, a judgment about what principles or rules are relevant to a case — and how they are relevant — will depend on an analysis of the context.

The interpretation of the situation, however, is not simply an objective assembling of "the facts of the case." It involves evaluative description, and it is always done from a particular location, with a particular perspective on the case, a particular point of view. The importance of perspective to description is a point elegantly made by Robert Browning's *The Ring and the Book,* which tells the same story from many different perspectives. (See reading 36, where James Gaffney begins with an account of Browning's poem.)

Whenever one looks at anything, what one sees depends on where one stands. It is no different when one looks at a situation requiring a moral decison. There are two relevant senses of context here, the context (or situation) for moral decision and the context (or location) which determines our perspective on the situation.

Christian ethics stands within the Christian community and its tradition when it describes the situations in which it must struggle to live morally. So, in an important sense, the church is the context

1. Dietrich Bonhoeffer, *Ethics,* trans. N. H. Smith (New York: Macmillan, 1955), pp. 364-365.

(or location) for Christian ethics. The church itself remains "in the world" and the situations which Christians struggle to understand and to describe evaluatively are also "in the world." So, "the world" and its institutions are also the context (or situation) for Christian ethics, as it attempts to understand the context of moral conduct.

Within the church there have been different perspectives on the world, ranging from a deep suspicion of the world to indifference to affirmation. The different perspectives on the world are formed in part by different theological emphases, and the different perspectives surely form different evaluative descriptions of the particular situations in which Christians must act and different accounts of the action Christians should take.

The famous ideal types of Christian community identified by Ernst Troeltsch, the "church" and the "sect," can be described along these lines: the church accepts the necessity of compromise with its ideals for the sake of life in the world and in order to exercise its influence on the cultural ethos and institutions of the world, while the sect, deeply suspicious of the world, resists compromise and accepts distance (and marginalization) from the ethos and institutions of the world.

The typology of Troeltsch was developed by H. Richard Niebuhr into a typology of relations of Christ to culture: Christ against culture, Christ of culture, Christ above culture, Christ and culture in paradox, and Christ transforming culture. The first corresponds to Troeltsch's "sect"; the church is separated from the world and set against the world, which is regarded as ruled by sin and death. The second describes Troeltsch's "church" type when it is so thoroughly compromised with the cultural ethos and institutions of the world that no distinction between them seems either possible or necessary; the church is indistinguishable from the world, which is regarded as itself the work of God. The mediating positions describe different strategies for preserving Christian integrity without sacrificing responsibility in and for the world (and without accepting marginalization from the ethos and institutions of the world). The strategy of "Christ above culture" regards the world as in need of something additional, something it has lost in the Fall and does not possess among its own resources, in order truly to flourish. The strategy of "Christ and culture in paradox'" regards the world and its culture as the work of God as creator and preserver, while God is at work in the church as redeemer; there are, then, two orders to our moral lives as Christians, and we may have a vocation to act as executioner in the world while we have a vocation to forgive in the church. The strategy of "Christ transforming culture" regards the world as the creation of God deeply distorted by sin and in need of transformation; that transformation is finally the work of God, but the church, always in need of transformation itself, can contribute to that work of God by modifying and qualifying the ethos and the institutions of the world.

The typologies of Troeltsch and Niebuhr disclose the fact that Christian ethics can hardly be separated from the sociological status of the church which provides its location. The "strategy" adopted is hardly unrelated to the social position of the community. The typologies, moreover, have great heuristic value. They have been challenged, however, as dismissive of the "sect" and of the more radical challenges to "the world" that have emerged within those communities. And when pluralism and secularism assign the church to the margins of public life, some are asking whether a "sectarian" construction of an alternative social reality is the strategy most apt for not only for the preservation of Christian integrity but also for making a difference in the world.

The readings in this chapter are chosen to help you think about the contexts for Christian ethics. The readings from 1 John clearly set the church against "the world." There are sovereignties in conflict — the rule of God, of life, and of love in conflict with the rule of desire and pride and death. Discernment depends on loyalty to the God made known in Christ and victorious over the world in Christ. That theme of conflict with the world, with its pride and desire, is continued

in the ascetic fathers whom Tito Colliander introduced in reading 50. It continues in the radical reformation — for example, in *The Schleitheim Confession of Faith* (reading 51) and its acceptance of separation from the world and its institutions of power and greed, forsaking the sword and lawsuits and the taking of an oath for the sake of an alternative community formed by peace and truthfulness.

The reading from Romans 13, however, suggests that God is at work not only in the church but in the world, too. A more positive view of the world and of its institutions seems to many, therefore, not only possible but required by faithfulness to God. Wayne Boulton, for example, commenting on Romans 13, rejects withdrawal from political power and political responsibility (reading 52). John Courtney Murray, the eminent Roman Catholic theologian, provides an account of "pluralism," an important feature of our context, but — in spite of the fact that "religious pluralism is against the will of God" — he does not simply reject it; he urges a revisioning of it (reading 53). And Max Stackhouse considers the corporation, which to many seems the very embodiment of the desire, greed, power, and pride of "the world," and finds in it both effects of Western Christianity and possibilities to bring theological convictions to bear on public life (reading 54).

Finally, in reading 55 Larry Rasmussen returns to the church as the location for Christian ethics and as "a little piece of the world where Christ is taking community form." It invites reconsideration of the typologies of Troeltsch and Niebuhr, a reconsideration of the "sectarian" context for Christian ethics, a reconsideration of our public responsibilities in the light of the calling to be the church. To such considerations this collection of readings also invites you.

Suggestions for Further Reading

Barth, Karl. *Community, State and Church*. New York: Doubleday, 1960.

Cochrane, Charles N. *Christianity and Classical Culture*. New York: Oxford University Press, 1957.

Ellul, Jacques. *False Presence of the Kingdom*. New York: Seabury Press, 1972.

Hauerwas, Stanley, and William Willimon. *Resident Aliens*. Nashville: Abingdon Press, 1989.

Niebuhr, H. Richard. *Christ and Culture*. Harper & Row, 1951.

Troeltsch, Ernst. *The Social Teaching of the Christian Churches*. George Allen and Unwin Ltd., 1931.

Yoder, John Howard, *The Priestly Kingdom*. Notre Dame: University of Notre Dame Press, 1984.

49. 1 John 2:15-17; 1 John 4:1-7; Romans 13:1-7

1 John 2:15-17

Do not love the world or the things in the world. The love of the Father is not in those who love the world; for all that is in the world — the desire of the flesh, the desire of the eyes, the pride in riches — comes not from the Father but from the world. And the world and its desire are passing away, but those who do the will of God live forever.

1 John 4:1-7

Beloved, do not believe every spirit, but test the spirits to see whether they are from God; for many false prophets have gone out into the world. By this you know the Spirit of God: every spirit that confesses that Jesus Christ has come in the flesh is from God, and every spirit that does not confess Jesus is not from God. And this is the spirit of the antichrist, of which you have heard that it is coming; and now it is already in the world. Little children, you are from God, and have conquered them; for the one who is in you is greater than the one who is in the world. They are from the world; therefore what they say is from the world, and the world listens to them. We are from God. Whoever knows God listens to us, and whoever is not from God does not listen to us. From this we know the spirit of truth and the spirit of error.

Beloved, let us love one another, because love is from God; everyone who loves is born of God and knows God.

Romans 13:1-7

Let every person be subject to the governing authorities; for there is no authority except from God, and those authorities that exist have been instituted by God. Therefore whoever resists authority resists what God has appointed, and those who resist will incur judgment. For rulers are not a terror to good conduct, but to bad. Do you wish to have no fear of the authority? Then do what is good, and you will receive its approval; for it is God's servant for your good. But if you do what is wrong, you should be afraid, for the authority does not bear the sword in vain! It is the servant of God to execute wrath on the wrongdoer. Therefore one must be subject, not only because of wrath but also because of conscience. For the same reason you also pay taxes, for the authorities are God's servants, busy with this very thing. Pay to all what is due them — taxes to whom taxes are due, revenue to whom revenue is due, respect to whom respect is due, honor to whom honor is due.

50. On the Insufficiency of Human Strength

TITO COLLIANDER

The holy fathers say with one voice: The first thing to keep in mind is never in any respect to rely on yourself. The warfare that now lies before you is extraordinarily hard, and your own human powers are altogether insufficient to carry it on. If you rely on them you will immediately be felled to the ground and have no desire to continue the battle. Only God can give you the victory you wish.

This decision not to rely on self is for most people a severe obstacle at the very outset. It must be overcome, otherwise we have no prospect of going further. For how can a human being receive advice, instruction and help if he believes that he knows and can do everything and needs no directions? Through such a wall of self-satisfaction no gleam of light can penetrate. "Woe unto them that are wise in their own eyes, and prudent in their own sight," cries the prophet Isaiah (5:21), and the apostle St. Paul utters the warning: "Be not wise in your own conceits" (Romans 12:16). The kingdom of heaven has been "revealed unto babes," but remains hidden from "the wise and prudent" (Matthew 11:25).

We must empty ourselves, therefore, of the im-

Tito Colliander (1904–) was born in St. Petersburg, Russia, but lived most of his life in Helsinki, Finland. An artist and novelist and an Eastern Orthodox layperson, he first published *Way of the Ascetics* in Swedish in 1952.

From Tito Colliander, *Way of the Ascetics: The Ancient Tradition of Discipline and Inner Growth,* trans. Katharine Ferre (Crestwood, N.Y.: St. Vladimir's Press, 1985).

moderately high faith we have in ourselves. Often it is so deeply rooted in us that we do not see how it rules over our heart. It is precisely our egoism, our self-centredness and self-love that cause all our difficulties, our lack of freedom in suffering, our disappointments and our anguish of soul and body.

Take a look at yourself, therefore, and see how bound you are by your desire to humour yourself and only yourself. Your freedom is curbed by the restraining bonds of self-love, and thus you wander, a captive corpse, from morning till eve. "Now I will drink," "now I will get up," "now I will read the paper." Thus you are led from moment to moment in your halter of preoccupation with self, and kindled instantly to displeasure, impatience or anger if an obstacle intervenes.

If you look into the depths of your consciousness you meet the same sight. You recognize it readily by the unpleasant feeling you have when someone contradicts you. Thus we live in thraldom. But "where the Spirit of the Lord is, there is liberty" (2 Corinthians 3:17).

How can any good come out of such an orbiting around the ego? Has not our Lord bidden us to love our neighbour as ourselves, and to love God above all? But do we? Are not our thoughts instead always occupied with our own welfare?

No, be convinced that nothing good can come from yourself. And should, by chance, an unselfish thought arise in you, you may be sure that it does not come from you, but is scooped up from the wellspring of goodness and bestowed upon you: it is a gift from the Giver of life. Similarly the power to put the good thought into practice is not your own, but is given you by the Holy Trinity.

51. Excerpts from *The Schleitheim Confession of Faith*

THE SWISS BRETHREN

We are agreed [as follows] on separation: A separation shall be made from the evil and from the wickedness which the devil planted in the world; in this manner, simply that we shall not have fellowship with them [the wicked] and not run with them in the multitude of their abominations. This is the way it is: Since all who do not walk in the obedience of faith, and have not united themselves with God so that they wish to do his will, are a great abomination before God, it is not possible for anything to grow or issue from them except abominable things. For truly all creatures are in but two classes, good and bad, believing and unbelieving, darkness and light, the world and those who [have come] out of the world, God's temple and idols, Christ and Belial; and none can have part with the other.

To us then the command of the Lord is clear when he calls upon us to be separate from the evil and thus he will be our God and we shall be his sons and daughters.

He further admonishes us to withdraw from Babylon and the earthly Egypt that we may not be partakers of the pain and suffering which the Lord will bring upon them.

The Swiss Brethren (also called Taufer, and Anabaptists), prior to the Mennonite movement, organized a dissenting congregation in Zurich, Switzerland in 1525. The group disagreed with the practice of infant baptism and with the union of church and state endorsed by Ulrich Zwingli.

From *The Mennonite Quarterly Review* 19, no. 4 (October 1945), trans. John C. Wenger.

From all this we should learn that everything which is not united with our God and Christ cannot be other than an abomination which we should shun and flee from. By this is meant all popish and antipopish works and church services, meetings and church attendance, drinking houses, civic affairs, the commitments [made in] unbelief and other things of that kind, which are highly regarded by the world and yet are carried on in flat contradiction to the command of God, in accordance with all the unrighteousness which is in the world. From all these things we shall be separated and have no part with them for they are nothing but an abomination, and they are the cause of our being hated before our Christ Jesus, who has set us free from the slavery of the flesh and fitted us for the service of God through the Spirit whom he has given us.

Therefore there will also unquestionably fall from us the unchristian, devilish weapons of force — such as sword, armor and the like, and all their use [either] for friends or against one's enemies — by virtue of the word of Christ, "Resist not [him that is] evil."

* * *

We are agreed as follows concerning the sword: The sword is ordained of God outside the perfection of Christ. It punishes and puts to death the wicked, and guards and protects the good. In the law the sword was ordained for the punishment of the wicked and for their death, and the same [sword] is [now] ordained to be used by the worldly magistrates.

In the perfection of Christ, however, only the ban is used for a warning and for the excommunication of the one who has sinned, without putting the flesh to death — simply the warning and the command to sin no more.

Now it will be asked by many who do not recognize [this as] the will of Christ for us, whether a Christian may or should employ the sword against the wicked for the defense and protection of the good, or for the sake of love.

Our reply is unanimously as follows: Christ teaches and commands us to learn of him, for he is meek and lowly in heart and so shall we find rest to our souls. Also Christ says to the heathenish woman who was taken in adultery, not that one should stone her according to the law of his Father (and yet he says, "As the Father has commanded me, thus I do"), but in mercy and forgiveness and warning, to sin no more. Such an attitude we also ought to take completely according to the rule of the ban.

Secondly, it will be asked concerning the sword, whether a Christian shall pass sentence in worldly dispute and strife such as unbelievers have with one another. This is our united answer: Christ did not wish to decide or pass judgment between brother and brother in the case of the inheritance, but refused to do so. Therefore we should do likewise.

Thirdly, it will be asked concerning the sword, Shall one be a magistrate if one should be chosen as such? The answer is as follows: They wished to make Christ king, but he fled and did not view it as the arrangement of his Father. Thus shall we do as he did, and follow him, and so shall we not walk in darkness. For he himself says, "He who wishes to come after me, let him deny himself and take up his cross and follow me." Also, he himself forbids the [employment of] the force of the sword saying, "The worldly princes lord it over them, etc., but not so shall it be with you." Further, Paul says, "Whom God did foreknow he also did predestinate to be conformed to the image of his Son," etc. Also Peter says, "Christ has suffered (not ruled) and left us an example, that ye should follow his steps."

Finally it will be observed that it is not appropriate for a Christian to serve as a magistrate because of these points: The government magistracy is according to the flesh, but the Christians' is according to the Spirit; their houses and dwelling remain in this world, but the Christians' are in heaven; their citizenship is in this world, but the Christians' citizenship is in heaven; the weapons of their conflict and war are carnal and against the flesh only, but the Christians' weapons are spiritual, against the fortification of the devil. The worldlings are armed with steel and iron, but the Christians are armed with the armor of God, with truth, righteousness, peace, faith, salvation and the word of God. In brief, as is the mind of Christ toward us, so the mind of the members of the body of Christ be through him in all things, that there may be no schism in the body through which it would be destroyed. For every kingdom divided against itself will be destroyed. Now since Christ is as it is written of him, his members must also be the same, that his body may remain complete and united to its own advancement and upbuilding.

We are agreed as follows concerning the oath: The oath is a confirmation among those who are quarreling or making promises. In the law it is commanded to be performed in God's name, but only in truth, not falsely. Christ, who teaches the perfection of the law, prohibits all swearing to his [followers], whether true or false — neither by heaven, nor by the earth, nor by Jerusalem, nor by our head, — and that for the reason which he shortly thereafter gives, For you are not able to make one hair white or black. So you see it is for this reason that all swearing is forbidden: we cannot fulfill that which we promise when we swear, for we cannot change [even] the very least thing on us.

Now there are some who do not give credence to the simple command of God, but object with this question: Well now, did not God swear to Abraham by himself (since he was God) when he promised him that he would be with him and that he would be his God if he would keep his commandments — why then should I not also swear when I promise someone? Answer: Hear what the Scripture says: God, since he wished more abundantly to show unto the heirs the immutability of his counsel, inserted an oath, that by two immutable things (in which it is impossible for God to lie) we might have a strong consolation. Observe the meaning of this Scripture: What God forbids you to do, he has power to do, for everything is possible for him. God swore an oath to Abraham, says the Scripture, so that he might show that his counsel is immutable. That is, no one can withstand nor thwart his will; therefore he can keep his oath. But we can do nothing, as is said above by Christ, to keep or perform [our oaths]: therefore we shall not swear at all.

Then others further say as follows: It is not forbidden of God to swear in the New Testament, when it is actually commanded in the Old, but it is forbidden only to swear by heaven, earth, Jerusalem, and our head. Answer: Hear the Scripture, He who swears by heaven swears by God's throne and by him who sitteth thereon. Observe: It is forbidden to swear by heaven, which is only the throne of God: How much more is it forbidden [to swear] by God himself! Ye fools and blind, which is greater, the throne or him that sitteth thereon?

Further some say, Because evil is now [in the world, and] because man needs God for [the establishment of] the truth, so did the apostles Peter and Paul also swear. Answer: Peter and Paul only testify of that which God promised to Abraham with the oath. They themselves promise nothing, as the example indicates clearly. Testifying and swearing are two different things. For when a person swears he is in the first place promising future things, as Christ was promised to Abraham whom we a long time afterwards received. But when a person bears testimony he is testifying about the present, whether it is good or evil, as Simeon spoke to Mary about Christ and testified, "Behold this (child) is set for the fall and rising of many in Israel, and for a sign which shall be spoken against."

Christ also taught us along the same line when he said, "Let your communication be yea, yea; nay, nay; for whatsoever is more than these cometh of evil." He says, "Your speech or word shall be yea and nay." (However) when one does not wish to understand, he remains closed to the meaning. Christ is simply Yea and Nay, and all those who seek him simply will understand his word. Amen.

52. The Riddle of Romans 13

WAYNE G. BOULTON

In the Christian tradition, biblical thought on government continues to perform two functions. Its critical function is to challenge certain popular and dangerous conceptions of the state as a self-contained entity, existing more or less independently of biblical revelation. Its constructive function is to generate Christian theories of the state which are at once grounded in Scripture and attentive to the wide range of political theory on the subject. Its summary legal (limiting) content is quoted at the head of this chapter — those provocative verses from the thirteenth chapter of Paul's letter to the church at Rome.

As Bonhoeffer has noted, there are two reigning and important views of the state in modern political science: a "positive" theory, locating the state's origins in human nature; and a "negative" theory, basing it not in man's created nature but in the Fall or sin.[1] The first is rooted in the ancient Greek concept of the state, particularly in Aristotle's thought, and attributes great dignity to the political vocation. The state is seen as the highest consummation of the rational character of man, and to serve it is the supreme purpose of human life. The negative view, stemming from Augustine and Reformation thought, is a self-conscious attack on

1. Dietrich Bonhoeffer, *Ethics,* pp. 332-39.

Wayne G. Boulton (1941–), former professor of religion at Hope College, is currently president of the Presbyterian School of Christian Education in Richmond, Virginia. He is a co-editor of this volume.

From Wayne G. Boulton, *Is Legalism a Heresy?* (Ramsey, N.J.: Paulist Press, 1982).

the perfectibilism inherent in the Greek concept. It is man's sin, the Reformers argued, not his greatness that leads to the institution of government, which is not established by man at all but by God.

Both of these views, however — that the state is an institution of creation or an institution of preservation — suggest that government now exists by itself with no continuing relation to the revelation of God — and particularly to this revelation as contained in the New Testament. So we are led at once to a careful reading of Romans 13 in the context of the interpretation of this passage in the Christian community over the centuries. The tradition teaches that Romans 13 has an essential framework, what might be called the "beyond politics" position of the Christian movement.

The position has two parts. First, authentic Christianity has always understood itself to be called beyond politics; there is an eschatological, apolitical thrust in the Christian community which was most evident in the anti-institutional, pacifist posture of the early church. Second, Christians do have a role to play in political life, and that is neither to withdraw from politics nor to transform it into something completely new. The first point is made indirectly throughout the New Testament. The second was not elaborated fully until Augustine set forth his "two kingdoms" thesis in the *City of God;* in Scripture it is the peculiar burden of Paul's argument in the first part of Romans 13.

The political implications of Christianity have certainly not been ignored in contemporary scholarship. Charles N. Cochrane's *Christianity and Classical Culture* (1940), Oscar Cullmann's *The State in the New Testament* (1956), John C. Murray's *We Hold These Truths* (1960), S. G. F. Brandon's *Jesus and the Zealots* (1967), John Passmore's *The Perfectibility of Man* (1970), John H. Yoder's *The Politics of Jesus* (1972) and Richard Mouw's *Politics and the Biblical Drama* (1976) are among the more significant recent publications on the subject. But some definition must be given to the word "political."

Politics is a special kind of activity which has existed since the time of the first human communities. Its essence is always plurality, conflict, difference of opinion. To be sure, some sort of agreement is the goal of many political processes. But the reconciliation is by definition temporary.

For the political realm is peopled by individuals with hopes, fears and ambitions often at odds with the plans of other individuals. British journalist Henrie Fairlie has written that political decisions involve "interests which conflict, and are hard to reconcile; wills which cannot be commandeered but at best only persuaded; resources which are limited but on which the claims are many; support which must be weighed and reweighed, and may at any time slip away."

When we define politics this way, is there a distinctively Christian assessment of political life? When this question is put to the New Testament, we find the answer moving in two different directions. On the one hand, all of Scripture is firm in its resistance to polytheism, which in this case would mean marking off the public realm as a particularly demonic (or salvific) sphere. One of the most frequent claims in the Bible is that "the Lord your God is one," sovereign in and over all spheres of life, including politics, and demanding obedience there as well as elsewhere.

At the same time there are strong anti-political themes in the New Testament, most clearly in the Johannine and apocalyptic literature. The situation could hardly be otherwise, since the complicity of the Roman and Jewish political establishments in the crucifixion of Jesus was a decisive experience in the memory of early Christians. "The light shines in the darkness. . . . He was in the world, and the world was made through him, yet the world knew him not" (John 1:5, 10). There are even suggestions that the state is demonic (Revelation 13), that politics is "of the world" and to be hated (1 John), and that politicians will never understand Christianity because it is otherworldly (John 18:33-38).

Some Christians have remained sensitive to these themes. The "separationist" doctrine of American Southern Baptists, for instance, is a dramatic elaboration of the antithesis between Christianity and politics, insisting that the best political order is one in which a "wall" exists between church and state. But those who have most fully grasped the *ethical* significance of the New Testament case against politics are Christian pacifists. Their argument is simple and profound. In the synoptic Gospels and especially in the Sermon on the Mount, the way of Jesus is revealed to be the way of peace. "But I say unto you, Do not resist

one who is evil. But if anyone strikes you on the right cheek, turn to him the other also" (Matthew 5:39). The fate of Jesus reveals the true nature of political powers and principalities: they are demonic, violent and out of control; they are unmasked and disarmed only in the mysterious triumph of Christ's crucifixion and resurrection (Colossians 2:8-15). As Tolstoi insisted, Christians are to be deceived neither by Paul's fuzzy thinking in Romans nor by bourgeois apologists for "progressive" government. Christians and the state are *never* allies; following Christ means nonviolent resistance to existing political power. It is "sectarian" groups such as the Quakers and the Mennonites that have seen most clearly the contradiction between Christian morality and the values of a secular society. particularly on the issues of war, national defense, and the promotion of peace.

Once the permanent validity of this suspicion of public power and political institutions is recognized, the significance of Romans 13 becomes clearer. For the antipolitical thrust in the New Testament creates two familiar temptations in the Christian movement: "sleep" and "drunkenness" (1 Thessalonians 5). Marxists are quite correct to use their leader's phrase in naming *these aberrations* an "opiate of the people."[2] "Sleep" is spiritualizing concrete evil, pretending that political injustice and tyranny are of little consequence next to one's own purity of soul and peace of mind. "Drunkenness" is some form of the belief that Christ has already returned, and therefore the end of the world (particularly the overcoming of evil) is at hand. The temptation is either to withdraw from politics altogether, or — on fire with eschatological hope — to attempt to transform politics into a completely new order. Romans 13:1-7 is an attack on eschatological shortcuts.

Part of a section devoted to ethics (Romans 12–15) in Paul's weightiest and most influential letter, the passage contains more than specific advice about the not-altogether-friendly political in-

2. The irony is that Marxism today has become a greater opiate — in precisely Marx's sense — than Christianity ever was. Though his book bears some marks of a fanatic against his own past, Bernard-Henri Lèvy's insights on this point are stunning: *Barbarism with a Human Face,* Holoch, tr. (New York, 1979), esp. ch. 18.

stitutions of Rome. It is nascent political theory concerning the nature and office of government and of civic obligation. Paul's three points, quite carefully phrased, all have to do with *presumption*.

1. The authority of government, from a human point of view, is ideal and permanent. It comes from God, not from human judgments about governments or about this or that public act. This authority may be removed only by God, and he has not yet done so (vv. 1-2). This view of authority checks the anarchistic bent of early Christianity, which Tolstoi correctly saw reflected in the New Testament. Followers of Christ must never revolt against government on principle.

2. The office of government is to order society morally, to punish evil and reward good (vv. 3-7). Notice that when assigning the office of punishment to government, Paul makes no distinction between Christians and non-Christians. Growing persecutions of Christians made this a delicate issue, but his implication is clear: Christians are to presume that the official exercise of government's retributive arm is legitimate, even when used against Christians.

3. As Calvin was one of the first to note, however, civil disobedience can be justified in particular circumstances in which government is violating its office. Paul does not elaborate *how* such a violation might be determined. He simply states what the office of government is, and that Christians must presume existing governments to be legitimate — a position which leaves the burden of proof on resisters.

According to Romans 13, then, the sacred element in public life can be identified with some precision. It is neither power *per se*, nor kings, nor the state, but only and exclusively the *authority to rule*. In d'Entrèves' formula, the doctrine of Romans 13:1-7 is one of "the sacred character of authority, certainly not one of the divinity of power."[3] The deification of political power in general and of monarchs in particular is a pagan doctrine, institutionalized in Hellenistic monarchies and later in the Roman Empire. Christianity has consistently fought both this ancient idea and its modern version — encouraged by Hegel — that the state is divine. The heroic resistance of the

Confessing Church movement and of certain Catholic and Free churches to Hitler's Third Reich is but one recent example of this fight.[4]

The exegesis offered here combines two quite different views of Romans 13 that have had wide currency in Christian social thought, though it stresses one more than the other. The first is an "absolutist" reading characteristic of early Christianity. In this interpretation, the emphasis is almost exclusively on the providential character of power. Good or bad, tyrannical or just, all power is of God, and therefore even evil power must be endured. Christian political ethics in such an ethos commends passive obedience or subordination in some form. The position is rooted in a deeply pessimistic attitude toward political life and political institutions, and has contributed mightily to what we have called the negative theory of the state.

This "absolutist" view of power is alive and well in contemporary Christian ethics, and often does not lead where one would expect, i.e., to quietism or withdrawal from politics. It leads rather to a consistent refusal to accept the validity of classical political distinctions in Christian ethics. Jacques Ellul, for example, concludes that every state is founded on and maintained by violence, and that

---

3. A. P. d'Entrèves, *The Notion of the State* (Oxford, 1967), p. 184.

4. National Socialism could conceivably develop anywhere, of course, but the use of the Confessing Church as a model of Christian political obedience can be misleading. The capitulation of German religious institutions, labor unions, and political parties to the Third Reich, as well as the isolated and exemplary resistance here noted, reflects a number of factors peculiar to Germany and should be viewed in historical perspective. Since the Reformation, the ties between German churches and the various states in Germany had been unusually close and the seizure of church lands in the eighteenth century tightened the financial ties even further, turning Protestant as well as Catholic churches into veritable servants of the state. One irony in the immediate situation was the way growing ecumenical sympathies among German Protestant churches in the 1930's, and their interest in a more unified Christian community played right into Hitler's hands. To Pharisaic Christian eyes, the most striking biblical characteristic of official Nazi Christianity was not so much its reading of Romans 13 as its effort to revile and do away with the Old Testament. See Ernst C. Helmreich's historical survey, *The German Churches Under Hitler* (Detroit, 1979).

the ancient distinction between violence and force is an invention of lawyers and "totally un-justified."[5] John Yoder suggests that Christians put aside the idea of rebelling only against bad governments. "They should rather rebel against all and and subordinate to all. . . . It is the way we share in God's patience with a system we basically reject."[6]

A second reading of Romans 13, the one stressed here, originates with representative political theorists in the Middle Ages.[7] Its point of departure is verse 4, where Paul instructs Christians that any ruler is "God's servant for your good." Only that power which is directed toward what is good, argues this theory, comes from God. The key assumption is that since the *use* to which political power is put reflects its true character, a distinction can and must always be made between what God ordains and merely human governance. Action reflects being. When a ruler's use of power is founded on justice, it has sacred authority, and the ruler is — even when he doesn't know it — God's minister. What this interpretation does is give legitimacy to a certain form of power, force exercised according to law; it thus might be called a "legalist" view of power.

Such a view dovetails naturally with Aristotle's conception of the relation between law and the state; over against the position of Plato who preferred "government by men" to "government by laws." Though he conceded late in life that there was practical value in the rule of law, Plato's ideal remained teleological, i.e., of a government founded not upon law but upon a rational knowledge of the good. It is finally the pursuit of the good that is the reason for the state's existence. This is clearest in the *Republic* — which remains striking as a *political* treatise because it lacks a

discussion of law — where the best state is governed by wise men who "know" the good, and who therefore must not be restricted in their commands and decisions. It is these philosopher-kings themselves, together with an educated citizenry, that for Plato held the state together, not the impersonal bonds of law.

In open disagreement with Plato, Aristotle argues emphatically that a "government by laws" was superior to "government by men." Plato's preference for personal rule perhaps reflected a confusion of power in this world with power in the next. On earth, Aristotle wrote, power is never free of appetite and passion; even high spirits can pervert the judgment of office-holders, no matter how good they are. To be sure, laws must be wisely *implemented* by the government of men in all cases where the law, because of its general character, cannot lay down precise rules. But in an arresting sentence, Aristotle writes that to make law supreme in political life is to be regarded "as commanding that God and reason should rule; he who commands that a man should rule adds the character of the beast."[8]

In sum, it appears that both the "absolutist" and "legalist" theories contain truth about the nature of political power.[9] Both theories can be attributed to Paul without doing violence to his position in Romans 13. Both can be supported with other biblical texts. Advocates of either theory can turn to the history of biblical interpretation and discover entire periods when their theory was the preferred one. But neither theory follows necessarily from Romans 13. As important as they are for applying this text and generally for guiding

5. Jacques Ellul, *Violence: Reflections from a Christian Perspective,* Kings tr. (New York, 1969), p. 84, *passim.*

6. John Howard Yoder, *The Politics of Jesus,* p. 202, fn. 10.

7. It is here, and not in Greek and Roman antiquity, that the real foundations of modern constitutionalism can be found. Augustine as well must be excluded from this list, because his negative conception of the state is Platonic politics in religious garb, reflecting his spiritual insight into the complete transcendence of true justice and into the providential character of all power in this world. See Carl Friedrich's analysis in *Transcendent Justice,* ch. 1.

8. Quoted in d'Entrèves, op. cit., p. 71. We here scratch the surface of a complex conflict of ideas which recurs continually in the development of Western political theory. My position is deeply indebted to this splendid book by Alexander d'Entrèves.

9. Cf. the recent discussions between Anabaptist and Reformed communities on political questions, as reported by Richard Mouw in *Politics and the Biblical Drama,* pp. 98-116. I agree completely with his conclusion (p. 116): "If Reformed Christians, and their political fellow-travelers among the faithful, are going to emphasize the legitimacy of political involvement in political structures, it must be with an Anabaptist-type conviction that the Christian disciple must walk in a new and better way."

Christians in politics, they do not come from Paul. As a Pharisaic Christian might put it, they are part of the "traditions of the fathers," i.e., of the oral law rather than the written law.

But why is Romans 13 so controversial in the modern period? There are at least two reasons. First, the text suggests, though it never explicitly states, an anti-democratic theory of power. In the familiar circular logic of democratic thought, we obey government ultimately because government obeys us. When it doesn't, we recognize a right to resist and change it. This conception of government might be called the populist or *ascending* theory, because power is understood to ascend from the broad base of a pyramid (the people) to its apex (the premier, sovereign, president).

Directly opposed to this is the hierocratic or *descending* theory of political authority and power. Here original power is located in a Supreme Being who, when the theory is influenced by Christianity, becomes identified with the God of Abraham, Isaac, and Jacob. Thus in the fifth century St. Augustine wrote that God distributed the laws to humankind through the medium of kings. Again the metaphorical pyramid appears, but now all original power is located at its apex rather than its base. The people "below" have no power at all except what is delegated to them "from above." All officers are appointed "from above," not elected by popular assembly. The supreme officer is responsible only to God.

The descending thesis was dominant in Europe in the Middle Ages; but since the recovery of Aristotle by Thomas Aquinas, and particularly since the Renaissance and the rise of liberal democracies, it has receded into the background. In the West, few remnants remain, though the economist Heilbroner foresees its return in post-industrial societies.[10] One reason why Romans 13 is controversial today is that it reflects this theory perfectly. In fact, the passage was an essential plank in all Christian versions of the thesis in the Middle Ages. Now that the theory is practically extinct, many Christians wish the *text* were also! A deep modern objection to Romans 13, in a word, is not religious at all, but cultural. It is a political embarrassment with the stature of Holy Writ.

Also, the text remains controversial because it continues to be challenged by the same forces that led Paul to write it in the first place. If my thesis here is correct — that the New Testament harbors an abiding and perhaps justified suspicion of political life — we should not be surprised that it continually generates efforts to depoliticize its own most political text. Contemporary Christian exegesis of Romans is peppered with such attempts.

For example, in his otherwise helpful article "A New Theological Approach to Social Ethics,"[11] Hans-Werner Bartsch argues that Romans 13:1-7 should be "bracketed" in order to be correctly understood. First, its meaning must be qualified by the "eschatological bracket" of the waking and sleeping passage at the end of the chapter. Once "bracketed," the text loses its apparently establishmentarian force, and the deeper meaning of the first seven verses may be summarized thus:

1. "Governing authorities" in the text are revealed to be forces that still exist but whose power "in reality" is broken.
2. The passage does not attribute a peculiar "position" or "commission" to the state.
3. Even in the hands of a pagan civil power, Christians are not beyond the reach of the goodness of God.

Bartsch is correct in asserting that the thirteenth chapter of Romans is all of a piece, but his "eschatological bracket" illuminates exactly nothing. If the risen Christ is now Lord over all principalities so that their power, while still existing, is in principle broken, what are the implications for personal behavior, civic obligation, and the social use of power? Paul was deeply concerned with precisely these questions, and the beginning of an answer to them is to be found right in the text. No "brackets" are necessary. On personal behavior, "let us conduct ourselves becomingly . . . not in quarreling and jealousy" (v. 13); on civic obligation, "Let every person be subject to the governing authorities . . ." (v. 1). As we have seen, the passage does indeed attribute a peculiar dignity and commission to government. The fact that existing governments were pagan at the time Paul was

10. Robert Heilbroner, *An Inquiry into the Human Prospect,* chs. 4-5.

11. John C. Bennett, ed., *Christian Social Ethics in a Changing World* (New York, 1966), pp. 59-77.

writing is irrelevant if the text is political theory (about government *qua* government). Dozens of other passages in both Testaments (Romans 8 is among the most forceful) assure believers that they are never beyond God's reach; surely Christians don't need Romans 13 to learn *that*.

Bartsch's anti-institutional agenda is even clearer when he "brackets" Romans 13:1-7 with the love commandment in 12:1ff. and 13:8. This is a technique often applied in pacifist exegesis. Paul's use of the ultimate commandment to love one's neighbor, Bartsch writes, qualifies and restricts the demand to "be subject." So we must now ask: Do the regulations of government serve one's neighbor? Do I, through my obedience, rightly attest the love of God? Bartsch is asking important ethical questions here, to be sure, but again it is difficult to see their immediate bearing on Romans 13:1-7. If he means that the function of government is oral and that its highest virtue is justice for all, this point is in the text and no brackets are needed. If means that Christ's command to love is a more fundamental, comprehensive demand than to seek justice, he is right — though again the point is made more clearly elsewhere (for example, in Matthew 5–7). If he means that the love command places Christians beyond the authority of civil law and governments in principle, this interpretation contradicts the text and a hundred brackets will be insufficient.

Barsch's concern that the text will be used out of context (as German Christians did in the 1930's) is a valid one, but in his work we witness a time-honored method for dealing with biblical embarrassments: christen them "obscure," and then interpret them through passages which are "clearer." Scripture interprets Scripture. The problem with the method in this case is that the embarrassing passage itself proves to be every bit as self-evident as the others used to explain it. It is not wise to make too little of Romans 13.

Neither is it wise to make too much of it. The mistake made by pacifists who abhor the controversial verses is often imitated by conservative Christians who celebrate them. The classic error of Christian pacifists does not lie in their politics. Their insights into the demonic side of political life are often stunning (as Yoder's *The Politics of Jesus* amply confirms), and their "absolutist" view of power and iconoclastic exposure of the temptations and hypocrisy in politics have great value.

On the contrary, the typical weakness in Christian pacifism is its biblicism: the assumption that the New Testament contains a philosophy adequate to the task of "following Jesus" into politics. The Old Testament (not a favorite of pacifists) is much more concerned with politics than the New, but even there a faithful reader with political interests needs ethical and philosophical considerations to complement exegesis. Prompting faith in God is the real agenda of biblical texts, and it is probably wrong to assume that the meaning of *any* of them is directly political.

This is true even of Romans 13. It contributes controlling ideas to Christian political theory, to be sure, but the passage's center is not so much civic obligation and political power as faith and divine providence. It is Paul's theological assessment of his experience of Roman citizenship: namely, that the God who raised Jesus is the God of Abraham, Isaac, and Jacob, continuing to rule history not only above and in spite of governments, but also — mysteriously — through them.

53. The Civilization of the Pluralist Society

JOHN COURTNEY MURRAY

The "free society" seems to be a phrase of American coinage. At least it has no comparable currency in any other language, ancient or modern. The same is true of the phrase "free government." This fact of itself suggests the assumption that American society and its form of government are a unique historical realization. The assumption is generally regarded among us as unquestionable.

However, we have tended of late to pronounce the phrase, "the free society," with a rising interrogatory inflection. The phrase itself, it seems, now formulates a problem. This is an interesting new development. It was once assumed that the American proposition, both social and political, was self-evident; that it authenticated itself on simple inspection; that it was, in consequence, intuitively grasped and generally understood by the American people. This assumption now stands under severe question.

What is the free society, in its "idea"? Is this "idea" being successfully realized in the institutions that presently determine the pattern of American life, social and personal? The web of American institutions has altered, rapidly and profoundly, even radically, over the past few generations. Has the "idea" of the free society perhaps been strangled by the tightening intricacies

---

John Courtney Murray (1904–1967) was professor of theology at Woodstock College and the author of numerous essays in Catholic social theory. His works include *We Hold These Truths: Catholic Reflections on the American Proposition.*

From John Courtney Murray, *We Hold These Truths* (New York: Sheed & Ward, 1960).

of the newly formed institutional network? Has some new and alien "idea" subtly and unsuspectedly assumed the role of an organizing force in American society? Do we understand not only the superficial facts of change in American life but also the underlying factors of change — those "variable constants" that forever provide the dynamisms of change in all human life?

The very fact that these questions are being asked makes it sharply urgent that they be answered. What is at stake is America's understanding of itself. Self-understanding is the necessary condition of a sense of self-identity and self-confidence, whether in the case of an individual or in the case of a people. If the American people can no longer base this sense on naive assumptions of self-evidence, it is imperative that they find other more reasoned grounds for their essential affirmation that they are uniquely a people, uniquely a free society. Otherwise the peril is great. The complete loss of one's identity is, with all propriety of theological definition, hell. In diminished forms it is insanity. And it would not be well for the American giant to go lumbering about the world today, lost and mad.

The Civil Multitude

At this juncture I suggest that the immediate question is not whether the free society is really free. This question may be unanswerable; it may even be meaningless as a question, if only for the reason that the norms of freedom seem to have got lost in a welter of confused controversy. Therefore I suggest that the immediate question is whether American society is properly civil. This question is intelligible and answerable, because the basic standard of civility is not in doubt: "Civilization is formed by men locked together in argument. From this dialogue the community becomes a political community." This statement, made by Thomas Gilby, O.P., in *Between Community and Society*,[1] exactly expresses the mind of St. Thomas Aquinas, who was himself giving refined expression to the tradition of classic antiquity, which in its prior turn had given first elaboration to the concept of the "civil multitude," the multitude that

---

1. New York: Longmans, Green & Co., 1953.

is not a mass or a herd or a huddle, because it is characterized by civility.

The specifying note of political association is its rational deliberative quality, its dependence for its permanent cohesiveness on argument among men. In this it differs from all other forms of association found on earth. The animal kingdom is held together simply by the material homogeneity of the species; all its unities and antagonisms are of the organic and biological order. Wolves do not argue the merits of running in packs. The primal human community, the family, has its own distinctive bonds of union. Husband and wife are not drawn into the marital association simply by the forces of reason but by the forces of life itself, importantly including the mysterious dynamisms of sex. Their association is indeed founded on a contract, which must be a rational and free act. But the substance and finality of the contract is both infra- and supra-rational; it is an engagement to become "two in one flesh." The marital relationship may at times be quarrelsome, but it is not argumentative. Similarly, the union of parents and children is not based on reason, justice, or power; it is based on kinship, love, and *pietas*.

It is otherwise with the political community. I am not, of course, maintaining that civil society is a purely rational form of association. We no longer believe, with Locke or Hobbes, that man escapes from a mythical "state of nature" by an act of will, by a social contract. Civil society is a need of human nature before it becomes the object of human choice. Moreover, every particular society is a creature of the soil; it springs from the physical soil of earth and from the more formative soil of history. Its existence is sustained by loyalties that are not logical; its ideals are expressed in legends that go beyond the facts and are for that reason vehicles of truth; its cohesiveness depends in no small part on the materialism of property and interest. Though all this is true, nevertheless the distinctive bond of the civil multitude is reason, or more exactly, that exercise of reason which is argument.

Hence the climate of the city is likewise distinctive. It is not feral or familial but forensic. It is not hot and humid, like the climate of the animal kingdom. It lacks the cordial warmth of love and unreasoning loyalty that pervades the family. It is cool and dry, with the coolness and dryness that characterize good argument among informed and responsible men. Civic amity gives to this climate its vital quality. This form of friendship is a special kind of moral virtue, a thing of reason and intelligence, laboriously cultivated by the discipline of passion, prejudice, and narrow self-interest. It is the sentiment proper to the city. It has nothing to do with the cleavage of a David to a Jonathan, or with the kinship of the clan, or with the charity . . . that makes the solidarity of the church. It is in direct contrast with the passionate fanaticism of the Jacobin: "Be my brother or I'll kill you!" Ideally, I suppose, there should be only one passion in the city — the passion for justice. But the will to justice, though it engages the heart, finds its measure as it finds its origin in intelligence, in a clear understanding of what is due to the equal citizen from the city and to the city from the citizenry according to the mode of their equality. This commonly shared will to justice is the ground of civic amity as it is also the ground of that unity which is called peace. This unity, qualified by amity, is the highest good of the civil multitude and the perfection of its civility.

The Public Argument

If then society is civil when it is formed by men locked together in argument, the question rises, what is the argument about? There are three major themes.

First, the argument is about public affairs, . . . matters which are for the advantage of the public (in the phrase as old as Plato) and which call for public decision and action by government. These affairs have their origin in matters of fact; but their rational discussion calls for the Socratic dialogue, the close and easy use of the habit of cross-examination, that transforms brute facts into arguable issues.

Second, the public argument concerns the affairs of the commonwealth. This is a wider concept. It denotes the affairs that fall, at least in decisive part, beyond the limited scope of government. These affairs are not to be settled by law, though law may be in some degree relevant to their settlement. They go beyond the necessities of the public order as such; they bear upon the quality of the common life. The great "affair" of the commonwealth is, of course, education. It includes three general areas of common interest: the school system, its mode of organization, its curricular content, and the level of learning among its teachers; the later education of the citizen in the liberal art of citizenship; and the more general enterprise of the advancement of knowledge by research.

The third theme of public argument is the most important and the most difficult. It concerns the constitutional consensus whereby the people acquires its identity as a people and the society is endowed with its vital form, its entelechy, its sense of purpose as a collectivity organized for action in history. The idea of consensus has been classic since the Stoics and Cicero; through St. Augustine it found its way into the liberal tradition of the West. . . .

The state of civility supposes a consensus that is constitutional, to wit, its focus is the idea of law, as surrounded by the whole constellation of ideas that are related to the *ratio iuris* as its premises, its constituent elements, and its consequences. This consensus is come to by the people; they become a people by coming to it. They do not come to it accidentally, without quite knowing how, but deliberatively, by the methods of reason reflecting on experience. The consensus is not a structure of secondary rationalizations erected on psychological data (as the behaviorist would have it) or on economic data (as the Marxist would have it). It is not the residual minimum left after rigid application of the Cartesian axiom, "*de omnibus dubitandum*" [doubt everything]. It is not simply a set of working hypotheses whose value is pragmatic. It is an ensemble of substantive truths, a structure of basic knowledge, an order of elementary affirmations that reflect realities inherent in the order of existence. It occupies an established position in society and excludes opinions alien or contrary to itself. This consensus is the intuitional *a priori* of all the rationalities and technicalities of constitutional and statutory law. It furnishes the premises of the people's action in history and defines the larger aims which that action seeks in internal affairs and in external relations.

The whole premise of the public argument, if it is to be civilized and civilizing, is that the consensus is real, that among the people everything is not in doubt, but that there is a core of agreement, accord, concurrence, acquiescence. We hold certain truths; therefore we can argue about them. It seems to have been one of the corruptions of intelligence by positivism to assume that argument ends when agreement is reached. In a basic sense the reverse is true. There can be no argument except on the premise, and within a context, of agreement. *Mutatis mutandis,* this is true of scientific, philosophical, and theological argument. It is no less true of political argument.

On its most imperative level the public argument within the city and about the city's affairs begins with the agreement that there is a reality called, in the phrase of Leo XIII, *patrimonium generis humani,* a heritage of an essential truth, a tradition of rational belief, that sustains the structure of the city and furnishes the substance of civil life. It was to this patrimony that the Declaration of Independence referred: "These are the truths we hold." This is the first utterance of a people. By it a people establishes its identity, and under decent respect to the opinions of mankind declares its purposes within the community of nations.

. . . An effort will be made to state the contents of the public consensus in America. Briefly, its principles and doctrines are those of Western constitutionalism, classic and Christian. This is our essential patrimony, laboriously wrought out by centuries of thought, further refined and developed in our own land to fit the needs of the new American experiment in government. In addition, as will later appear, the consensus has a growing end, as American society itself has a growing end. My point at the moment, however, is that there are two reasons why the consensus furnishes the basic theme of the public argument whereby American society hopes to achieve and maintain the mark of civility.

Initially, we hold these truths because they are a patrimony. They are a heritage from history, through whose dark and bloody pages there runs like a silver thread the tradition of civility. This is the first reason why the consensus continually calls for public argument. The consensus is an intellectual heritage; it may be lost to mind or deformed in the mind. Its final depository is the public mind. This is indeed a perilous place to deposit what ought to be kept safe; for the public mind is exposed to the corrosive rust of skepticism, to the predatory moths of deceitful *doxai* (or, "opinion," in Plato's sense), and to the incessant thieveries of forgetfulness. Therefore the consensus can only be preserved in the public mind by argument. High argument alone will keep it alive, in the vital state of being "held."

Second, we hold these truths because they are true. They have been found in the structure of reality by that dialectic of observation and reflection which is called philosophy. But as the achievement of reason and experience the consensus again presents itself for argument. Its vitality depends on a constant scrutiny of political experience, as this experience widens with the developing — or possibly the decaying — life of man in society. Only at the price of this continued contact with experience will a constitutional tradition continue to be "held," as real knowledge and not simply as a structure of prejudice. However, the tradition, or the consensus, is not a mere record of experience. It is experience illumined by principle, given a construction by a process of philosophical reflection. In the public argument there must consequently be a continued recurrence to first principles. Otherwise the consensus may come to seem simply a projection of ephemeral experience, a passing shadow on the vanishing backdrop of some given historical scene, without the permanence proper to truths that are "held."

On both of these titles, as a heritage and as a public philosophy, the American consensus needs to be constantly argued. If the public argument dies from disinterest, or subsides into the angry mutterings of polemic, or rises to the shrillness of hysteria, or trails off into positivistic triviality, or gets lost in a morass of semantics, you may be sure that the barbarian is at the gates of the city.

The barbarian need not appear in bearskins with a club in hand. He may wear a Brooks Brothers suit and carry a ball-point pen with which to write his advertising copy. In fact, even beneath the academic gown there may lurk a child of the wilderness, untutored in the high tradition of civility, who goes busily and happily about his work, a domesticated and law-abiding man, engaged in the construction of a philosophy to put an end to all philosophy, and thus put an end to the possibility of a vital consensus and to civility itself. This is perennially the work of the barbarian, to undermine rational standards of judgment, to corrupt the inherited intuitive wisdom by

which the people have always lived, and to do this not by spreading new beliefs but by creating a climate of doubt and bewilderment in which clarity about the larger aims of life is dimmed and the self-confidence of the people is destroyed, so that finally what you have is the impotent nihilism of the "generation of the third eye," now presently appearing on our university campuses. (One is, I take it, on the brink of impotence and nihilism when one begins to be aware of one's own awareness of what one is doing, saying, thinking. This is the paralysis of all serious thought; it is likewise the destruction of all the spontaneities of love.)

The barbarian may be the eighteenth-century philosopher, who neither anticipated nor desired the brutalities of the Revolution with its Committee on the Public Safety, but who prepared the ways for the Revolution by creating a vacuum which he was not able to fill. Today the barbarian is the man who makes open and explicit rejection of the traditional role of reason and logic in human affairs. He is the man who reduces all spiritual and moral questions to the test of practical results or to an analysis of language or to decision in terms of individual subjective feeling.

It is a Christian theological intuition, confirmed by all of historical experience, that man lives both his personal and his social life always more or less close to the brink of barbarism, threatened not only by the disintegrations of physical illness and by the disorganizations o[mental imbalance, but also by the decadence of moral corruption and the political chaos of formlessness or the moral chaos of tyranny. Society is rescued from chaos only by a few men, not by the many. . . . It is only the few who understand the disciplines of civility and are able to sustain them in being and thus hold in check the forces of barbarism that are always threatening to force the gates of the city. To say this is not, of course, to endorse the concept of the fascist élite — barbarous concept, if ever there was one. It is only to recall a lesson of history to which our own era of mass civilization may well attend. We have not been behind our forebears in devising both gross and subtle ways of massacring ancient civilities.

The Concept of Conversation

Barbarism is not, I repeat, the forest primeval with all its relatively simple savageries. Barbarism has long had its definition, resumed by St. Thomas after Aristotle. It is the lack of reasonable conversation according to reasonable laws. Here the word "conversation" has its twofold Latin sense. It means living together and talking together.

Barbarism threatens when men cease to live together according to reason, embodied in law and custom, and incorporated in a web of institutions that sufficiently reveal rational influences, even though they are not, and cannot be, wholly rational. Society becomes barbarian when men are huddled together under the rule of force and fear; when economic interests assume the primacy over higher values; when material standards of mass and quantity crush out the values of quality and excellence; when technology assumes an autonomous existence and embarks on a course of unlimited self-exploitation without purposeful guidance from the higher disciplines of politics and morals (one thinks of Cape Canaveral); when the state reaches the paradoxical point of being everywhere intrusive and also impotent, possessed of immense power and powerless to achieve rational ends; when the ways of men come under the sway of the instinctual, the impulsive, the compulsive. When things like this happen, barbarism is abroad, whatever the surface impressions of urbanity. Men have ceased to live together according to reasonable laws.

Barbarism likewise threatens when men cease to talk together according to reasonable laws. There are laws of argument, the observance of which is imperative if discourse is to be civilized. Argument ceases to be civil when it is dominated by passion and prejudice; when its vocabulary becomes solipsist, premised on the theory that my insight is mine alone and cannot be shared; when dialogue gives way to a series of monologues; when the parties to the conversation cease to listen to one another, or hear only what they want to hear, or see the other's argument only through the screen of their own categories; when defiance is flung to the basic ontological principle of all ordered discourse, which asserts that reality is an analogical structure, within which there are variant modes of reality, to each of which there corresponds a distinctive method of thought that imposes on argument its own special rules. When things like this happen, men cannot be locked together in argument. Conversation becomes merely quarrelsome or querulous. Civility dies with the death of the dialogue.

All this has been said in order to give some meaning to the immediate question before us, [to wit], whether American society, which calls itself free, is genuinely civil. In any circumstances it has always been difficult to achieve civility in the sense explained. A group of men locked together in argument is a rare spectacle. But within the great sprawling city that is the United States the achievement of a civil society encounters a special difficulty — what is called religious pluralism.

The Experience of Religious Pluralism

The political order must borrow both from above itself and from below itself. The political looks upward to metaphysics, ethics, theology; it looks downward to history, legal science, sociology, psychology. The order of politics must reckon with all that is true and factual about man. The problem was complicated enough for Aristotle, for whom man in the end was only citizen, whose final destiny was to be achieved within the city, however much he might long to play the immortal. For us today man is still citizen; but at least for most of us his life is not absorbed in the city, in society and the state. In the citizen who is also a Christian there resides the consciousness formulated immortally in the second-century *Letter to Diognetes*: "Every foreign land is a fatherland and every fatherland is a foreign land." This consciousness makes a difference, in ways upon which we need not dwell here. What makes the more important difference is the fact of religious divisions. Civil discourse would be hard enough if among us there prevailed conditions of religious unity; even in such conditions civic unity would be a complicated and laborious achievement. As it is, efforts at civil discourse plunge us into the twofold experience of the religiously pluralist society.

The first experience is intellectual. As we discourse on public affairs, on the affairs of the commonwealth, and particularly on the problem of consensus, we inevitably have to move upward, as it were, into realms of some theoretical generality — into metaphysics, ethics, theology. This movement does not carry us into disagreement; for disagreement is not an easy thing to reach. Rather, we move into confusion. Among us there is a plurality of universes of discourse. These universes are incommensurable. And when they clash, the issue of agreement or disagreement tends to become irrelevant. The immediate situation is simply one of confusion. One does not know what the other is talking about. One may distrust what the other is driving at. For this too is part of the problem — the disposition amid the confusion to disregard the immediate argument, as made, and to suspect its tendency, to wonder what the man who makes it is really driving at.

This is the pluralist society as it is encountered on the level of intellectual experience. We have no common universe of discourse. In particular, diverse mental equivalents attach to all the words in which the constitutional consensus must finally be discussed — truth, freedom, justice, prudence, order, law, authority, power, knowledge, certainty, unity, peace, virtue, morality, religion, God, and perhaps even man. Our intellectual experience is one of sheer confusion, in which soliloquy succeeds to argument.

The second experience is even more profound. The themes touched upon in any discussion of religion and the free society have all had a long history. And in the course of discussing them we are again made aware that only in a limited sense have we severally had the same history. We more or less share the short segment of history known as America. But all of us have had longer histories, spiritual and intellectual.

These histories may indeed touch at certain points. But I, for stance, am conscious that I do not share the histories that lie behind many of my fellow citizens. The Jew does not share the Christian history, nor even the Christian idea of history. Catholic and Protestant history may be parallel in a limited sense but they are not coincident or coeval. And the secularist is a latecomer. He may locate his ancestry in the eighteenth or nineteenth centuries, or, if his historic sense is strong, he may go back to the fourteenth century, to the rise of what Lagarde has called *l'esprit läique* (the spirit of the laity). In any case, he cannot go back to Athens, Rome, or Alexandria; for his laicism is

historically conditioned. It must situate itself with regard to the Christian tradition. It must include denials and disassociations that the secularism of antiquity did not have to make; and it also includes the affirmation of certain Christian values that antiquity could not have affirmed.

The fact of our discrepant histories creates the second experience of the pluralist society. We are aware that we not only hold different views but have become different kinds of men as we have lived our several histories. Our styles of thought and of interior life are as discrepant as our histories. The more deeply they are experienced and the more fully they are measured, the more do the differences among us appear to be almost unbridgeable. Man is not only a creature of thought but also a vibrant subject of sympathies; and in the realm of philosophy and religion today the communal experiences are so divergent that they create not sympathies but alienations as between groups.

Take, for instance, the question of natural law, of which there will be much discourse in the pages that follow. For the Catholic it is simply a problem in metaphysical, ethical, political, and juridical argument. He moves into the argument naturally and feels relatively at ease amid its complexities. For the Protestant, on the contrary, the whole doctrine of natural law is a challenge, if not an affront, to his entire style of moral thought and even to his religiosity. The doctrine is alien to him, unassimilable by him. He not only misunderstands it; he also distrusts it. "Thus," says Robert McAfee Brown in *American Catholics: a Protestant-Jewish View*,[2] "Catholic appeals to natural law remain a source of friction rather than a basis of deeper understanding" as between Protestant and Catholic.

Another example might be the argument that has been made by Catholics in this country for more than a century with regard to the distribution of tax funds for the support of the school system. The structure of the argument is not complex. Its principle is that the canons of distributive justice ought to control the action of government in allocating funds that it coercively collects from all people in pursuance of its legitimate interest in universal compulsory schooling. The fact is that

2. New York: Sheed & Ward, 1959.

these canons are presently not being observed. The "solution" to the school question reached in the nineteenth century reveals injustice, and the legal statutes that establish the injustice are an abuse of power. So, in drastic brevity, runs the argument. I shall return to it in a later chapter. For my part, I have never heard a satisfactory answer to it.

This is a fairly serious situation. When a large section of the community asserts that injustice is being done, and makes a reasonable argument to substantiate the assertion, either the argument ought to be convincingly refuted and the claim of injustice thus disposed of, or the validity of the argument ought to be admitted and the injustice remedied. As a matter of fact, however, the argument customarily meets a blank stare, or else it is "answered" by varieties of the fallacy known as *ignoratio elenchi*. At the extreme, from the side of the more careerest type of anti-Catholic, the rejoinder takes this form, roughly speaking (sometimes the rejoinder is roughly spoken): "We might be willing to listen to this argument about the rights of Catholic schools if we believed that Catholic schools had any rights at all. But we do not grant that they have any rights, except to tolerance. Their existence is not for the advantage of the public; they offend against the integrity of the democratic community, whose warrant is fidelity to Protestant principle (or secularist principle, as the case may be)." This "answer" takes various forms, more or less uncomplimentary to the Catholic Church, according to the temper of the speaker. But this is the gist of it. The statement brings me to my next point.

A Structure of War

The fact is that among us civility — or civic unity or civic amity, as you will — is a thing of the surface. It is quite easy to break through it. And when you do, you catch a glimpse of the factual reality of the pluralist society. I agree with Professor Eric Voegelin's thesis that our pluralist society has received its structure through wars and that the wars are still going on beneath a fragile surface of more or less forced urbanity. What Voegelin calls the "genteel picture" will not stand the test of confrontation with fact.

We are not really a group of men singly en-gaged in the search for truth, relying solely on the means of persuasion, entering into dignified communication with each other, content politely to correct opinions with which we do not agree. As a matter of fact, the variant ideas and allegiances among us are entrenched as social powers; they occupy ground; they have developed interests; and they possess the means to fight for them. The real issues of truth that arise are complicated by secondary issues of power and prestige, which not seldom become primary.

There are numerous well-known examples. What they illustrate is that the entrenched segments of American pluralism claim influence on the course of events, on the content of the legal order, and on the quality of American society. To each group, of course, its influence seems salvific; to other groups it may seem merely imperialist. In any case, the forces at work are not simply intellectual; they are also passionate. There is not simply an exchange of arguments but of verbal blows. You do not have to probe deeply beneath the surface of civic amity to uncover the structure of passion and war.

There is the ancient resentment of the Jew, who has for centuries been dependent for his existence on the good will, often not forthcoming, of a Christian community. Now in America, where he has acquired social power, his distrust of the Christian community leads him to align himself with the secularizing forces whose dominance, he thinks, will afford him a security he has never known. Again, there is the profound distrust between Catholic and Protestant. Their respective conceptions of Christianity are only analogous; that is, they are partly the same and totally different. The result is *odium theologicum*, a sentiment that not only enhances religious differences in the realm of truth but also creates personal estrangements in the order of charity.

More than that, Catholic and Protestant distrust each other's political intentions. There is the memory of historic clashes in the temporal order; the Irishman does not forget Cromwell any more readily than the Calvinist forgets Louis XIV. Neither Protestant nor Catholic is yet satisfied that the two of them can exist freely and peacefully in the same kind of city. The Catholic regards Protestantism not only as a heresy in the order of religion but also as a corrosive solvent in the order of civilization, whose intentions lead to chaos. The Protestant regards Catholicism not only as idolatry in the order of religion but as an instrument of tyranny in the order of civilization, whose intentions lead to clericalism. . . .

This problem is particularly acute in the United States, where the Protestant was the native and the Catholic the immigrant, in contrast to Europe where the Catholic first held the ground and was only later challenged. If one is to believe certain socio-religious critics (Eduard Heimann, for instance), Protestantism in America has forged an identification of itself, both historical and ideological, with American culture, particularly with an indigenous secularist unclarified mystique of individual freedom as somehow the source of everything, including justice, order, and unity. The result has been Nativism in all its manifold forms, ugly and refined, popular and academic, fanatic and liberal. The neo-Nativist as well as the paleo-Nativist addresses to the Catholic substantially the same charge: "You are among us but you are not of us." (The neo-Nativist differs only in that he uses footnotes, apparently in the belief that reference to documents is a substitute for an understanding of them.) To this charge the Catholic, if he happens to set store . . . on meriting the blessed adjective "sophisticated," will politely reply that this is Jacobinism, *nouveau style* (new style), and that Jacobinism, any style, is out of style in this day and age. In contrast, the sturdy Catholic war veteran is more likely to say rudely, "Them's fighten' words." And with this exchange of civilities, if they are such, the "argument" is usually over.

There is, finally, the secularist (I here use the term only in a descriptive sense). He too is at war. If he knows his own history, he must be. Historically his first chosen enemy was the Catholic Church, and it must still be the enemy of his choice . . . First, it asserts that there is an authority superior to the authority of individual reason and of the political projection of individual reason, the state. But this assertion is the first object of the secularist's anathema. Second, it asserts that by divine ordinance this world is to be ruled by a dyarchy of authorities, within which the temporal is subordinate to the spiritual, not instrumentally but in dignity. This assertion is doubly anathema. It clashes with the socio-juridical monism that is always basic to the secularist position when it is consistently argued. In secularist theory there can be only one society, one law, one power, and one faith, a civic faith that is the "unifying" bond of the community, whereby it withstands the assaults of assorted pluralisms.

The secularist has always fought his battles under a banner on which is emblazoned his special device, "The Integrity of the Political Order." In the name of this thundering principle he would banish from the political order (and from education as an affair of the city) all the "divisive forces" of religion. At least in America he has traditionally had no quarrel with religion as a "purely private matter," as a sort of essence or idea or ambient aura that may help to warm the hidden heart of solitary man. He may even concede a place to religion-in-general, whatever that is. What alarms him is religion as a Thing, visible, corporate, organized, a community of thought that presumes to sit superior to, and in judgment on, the "community of democratic thought," and that is furnished somehow with an armature of power to make its thought and judgment publicly prevail. Under this threat he marshals his military vocabulary and speaks in terms of aggression, encroachment, maneuvers, strategy, tactics. He rallies to the defense of the City; he sets about the strengthening of the wall that separates the city from its Enemy. He too is at war.

The Conspiracies and Their Conspiracy

What it comes to then is that the pluralist society, honestly viewed under abdication of all false gentility, is a pattern of interacting conspiracies. There are chiefly four — Protestant, Catholic, Jewish, secularist, though in each camp, to continue the military metaphor, there are forces not fully broken to the authority of the high command.

I would like to relieve the word "conspiracy" of its invidious connotations. It is devoid of these in its original Latin sense, both literal and tropical. Literally it means unison, concord, unanimity in opinion and feeling, a "breathing together." Then it acquires inevitably the connotation of united action for a common end about which there is agreement; those who think alike inevitably join together in some manner of action to make their common thought or purpose prevail. The word was part of the Stoic political vocabulary; it was adopted by Cicero; and it has passed into my own philosophical tradition, the Scholastic tradition, that has been formative of the liberal tradition of the West. Civil society is formed, said Cicero, "*conspiratione hominum atque consensu*," that is by action in concert on the basis of consensus with regard to the purposes of the action. Civil society is by definition a conspiracy, "*conspiratio plurium in unum.*" Only by conspiring together do the many become one. *E pluribus unum.*

The trouble is that there are a number of conspiracies within American society. I shall not object to your calling Catholicism a conspiracy, provided you admit that it is only one of several. (Incidentally, I never have seen the validity of Professor Sidney Hook's distinction: "Heresy, yes; conspiracy, no." The heresy that was not a conspiracy has not yet appeared on land or sea. One would say with greater propriety of word and concept: "Conspiracy, yes; heresy, no." Heresy, not conspiracy, is the bad word for the evil thing. No one would be bothered with the Communist conspiracy if its dynamism were not a civilizational heresy, or more exactly, an apostasy from civilization.)

Perhaps then our problem today is somehow to make the four great conspiracies among us conspire into one conspiracy that will be American society — civil, just, free, peaceful, one.

Can this problem be solved? My own expectations are modest and minimal. It seems to be the lesson of history that men are usually governed with little wisdom. The highest political good, the unity which is called peace, is far more an ideal than a realization. And the search for religious unity, the highest spiritual good, always encounters the "messianic necessity," so called: "Do you think that I have come to bring peace on earth? No, but rather dissension" (Luke 12:51). In the same text the dissension was predicted with terrible explicitness of the family. It has also been the constant lot of the family of nations and of the nations themselves. Religious pluralism is against the will of God. But it is the human condition; it is written into the script of history. It will not somehow marvelously cease to trouble the city.

Advisedly therefore one will cherish only modest expectations with regard to the solution of the problem of religious pluralism and civic unity. Utopianism is a Christian heresy (the ancient pagan looked backward, not forward, to the Golden Age); but it is a heresy nonetheless. We cannot hope to make American society the perfect conspiracy based on a unanimous consensus. But we could at least do two things. We could limit the warfare, and we could enlarge the dialogue. We could lay down our arms (at least the more barbarous kind of arms!), and we could take up argument.

Even to do this would not be easy. It would be necessary that we cease to project into the future of the Republic the nightmares, real or fancied, of the past. In Victorian England John Henry Newman noted that the Protestant bore "a stain upon the imagination," left there by the vivid images of Reformation polemic against the Church of Rome. Perhaps we all bear some stain or other upon our imaginations. It might be possible to cleanse them by a work of reason. The free society, I said at the outset, is a unique realization; it has inaugurated a new history. Therefore it might be possible within this new history to lay the ghosts of the past — to forgot the ghettos and the autos-da-fé; the Star Chamber and the Committee on the Public Safety; Topcliffe with his "Bloody Question" and Torquemada with his rack; the dragonnades and the Black and Tans; Samuel F. B. Morse, the convents in Charleston and Philadelphia, the Know-Nothings and the Ku Klux Klan and what happened to Al Smith (whatever it was that did happen to him).

All this might be possible. It certainly would be useful. I venture to say that today it is necessary. This period in American history is critical, not organic (to use Professor Toynbee's distinction). We face a crisis that is new in history. We would do well to face it with a new cleanliness of imagination, in the realization that internecine strife, beyond some inevitable human measure, is a luxury we can no longer afford. Serious issues confront us on all the three levels of public argument. Perhaps the time has come when we should endeavor to dissolve the structure of war that underlies the pluralistic society, and erect the more civilized structure of the dialogue. It would be no less sharply pluralistic, but rather more so, since the real pluralisms would be clarified out of their present confusion. And amid the pluralism a unity would be discernible — the unity of an orderly conversation. The pattern would not be that of ignorant armies clashing by night but of informed men locked together in argument in the full fight of a new dialectical day. Thus we might present to a "candid world" the spectacle of a civil society.

54. Spirituality and the Corporation

MAX L. STACKHOUSE

As long as we can forecast the realistic probabilities of the future of modern societies, the economies connected to them will be mixed. Decision-making about, capitalization for, and management of production and distribution will be centered in the corporation, although governmental regulations, tax policies, expenditures, and contracting will shape and modulate corporate policies. It is not clear what precise mix of private and public control of the economy we will have, but "corporate capitalism" is likely to be the predominant social form of economic life in the foreseeable future. Both a fully planned economy managed by the state and an economy of individual entrepreneurs are highly unlikely. Indeed, where these exist around the world, economic stagnation tends to result. The modern corporation has out-employed, out-researched, out-produced, and out-distributed every other known social form of economic organization. It develops most extensively in pluralistic societies, and considerable evidence suggests that it is structurally necessary to a viable democracy.[1]

1. *The Judeo-Christian Vision and the Modern Busi-*

Max L. Stackhouse (1935–) is the Herbert Gezork Professor of Christian Social Ethics at Andover Newton Theological Seminary. His work includes *Creeds, Society, and Human Rights: A Study in Three Cultures; Ethics and the Urban Ethos: An Essay in Social Theory and Theological Reconstruction;* and *Public Theology and Political Economy: Christian Stewardship in Modern Society.*

From Max L. Stackhouse, *Public Theology and Political Economy* (Grand Rapids, Mich.: Wm. B. Eerdmans, 1987).

These facts are troubling to many theologically and ethically concerned leaders. For many, the corporation is the embodiment of profit-oriented greed, a soulless artifact that pollutes the environment, uproots people from their farms, closes plants, dislocates workers, promotes growing discrepancies between the rich and the poor, and, in its transnational form, invades other cultures and corrupts indigenous societies. It is, to some, the enemy of spiritual life and social responsibility.

Those who celebrate corporate capitalism for its rather marvelous material achievements and those who pillory it for its manifest horrors become the chief ideological advocates of capitalism or socialism. But the one frequently misunderstands the social fabric of modern economic reality by focusing too much on the individual, and the other by holding a political theory of all social life, a view that makes politics sovereign over all economic functions. Each may be correct in thinking that the other oversimplifies economic life. But it is not clear that either has accurately diagnosed the social character of this distinctive feature of modern political economies.

*　　*　　*

Where . . . shall we turn and what questions shall we pose if we want to understand production and the social forms that govern it? I think that we will have to inquire more deeply into the social and religious history behind the modern business corporation. It is the product, empirically, of a minority tradition in the history of religion and society. This minority tradition induced a particular kind of spirituality and a particular social orientation to the world that have roots in the history of the church and that have produced a "non-natural" form of organization with its own internal logic that is today both triumphant and suspect.

The first thing to say about the business corporation is that it is a *persona ficta,* an artifact with its own internal "spirit" or "character" and with legal standing as an agent, an actor, in human affairs. Owners, managers, and workers come and go in the corporation, but the corporation lives on. It can sue and be sued, issue contracts, hold, buy, or sell property, migrate from country to country, "get married" in mergers, produce offspring in the form of subsidiaries, be granted citizenship in other lands, grow and expand, or shrink and be executed by being dissolved. The corporation may be owned by individuals, families, other corporations, governments, labor unions, or church pension funds. It may be managed by males or females, blacks or whites, old or young, Hindus or Muslims, Jews or atheists. Workers may spend forty years in its employ, or there may be an employee turnover every five years. All this will make no essential difference regarding what it does or does not do. The corporation, for all its massive influence, is founded on a very narrow base. It is a community of persons designed for efficient production that must base every decision on the question of whether or not it can continue to produce. This is determined by whether or not it is likely to reap a legal profit that will perpetuate its existence. If it does not make a profit, or if it does so by illegal means, its managers will be fired, its owners will sell their interest in it, and it can be taken into receivership for either revitalization or dissolution. If it does make a profit, it is in principle immortal.

How did such a thing come about? The story is too complex to recount in full here, but clues can be found in the work of nineteenth-century legal historians,[2] by leading social theorists early in this century,[3] and in several newer works.[4] The roots of the phenomenon are decidedly religious,

---

ness Corporation, ed. Oliver Williams and John Houck (Notre Dame: University of Notre Dame Press, 1982). See also *Corporations and the Common Good,* ed. Robert Dickie and Leroy Rouner (Notre Dame: University of Notre Dame Press, 1986); and *Christianity and Capitalism,* ed. Bruce Grelle and David Krueger (Chicago: CSSR Press, 1986).

2. See H. S. Maine, *Ancient Law* (Oxford: Oxford University Press, 1888); and Otto Gierke, *Natural Law and the Theory of Society* (Boston: Beacon Press, 1957).

3. See G. P. Davis, *The Corporation* (New York: Harper, 1908); and Max Weber, *Economy and Society: An Outline of Interpretive Sociology,* 3 vols., ed. Guenther Roth and Claus Wittich, trans. E. Fischoff et al. (Totowa, N.J,: Bedminster Press, 1968).

4. See Harold Berman, *Law and Revolution: The Formation of the Western Legal Tradition* (Cambridge: Harvard University Press, 1983); and Brian Tierney, *The Crisis of Church and State, 1050-1300* (New York: The Free Press, 1964).

in spite of the fact that much of traditional religion resisted — and still resists — the corporation.

The Religious Roots of the Corporation

The early church established the household of faith, an *oikoumene,* a spiritual network of persons who were one in Christ who also formed a social-institutional center independent of both the traditional *oikos* and the regime. In doing so, the church established in practice, and later in law, the notion that it was possible to form collective identities that were "non-natural" in origin and that were dedicated to the transformation of every aspect of life. At first, as we see in the book of Acts, the church established a community only of consumption, not of production. Yet this set the precedent for disciplined use of economic resources by an organized group independent of familial or imperial control.

Throughout its early period, Christianity seems to have been most appealing precisely to those marginal groups that were not engaged in landholding, in agricultural production, or in the service of the rulers. It seems to have been quite attractive to urban workers — not only urban slaves but artisans, traders, tent-makers, and the like. In brief, Christianity has been linked from its inception to urbanized peoples involved in producing and trading. Those tied to the land and its duties of *oikos* were called pagans; those who gave primary loyalty to regime were called idolaters. Against these, the church developed its own corporate structures and disciplines that were to be the prototypes of later corporate structures of many kinds.

Much later, as the medieval cities developed, stimulated in part by the new methods of production introduced into northern Europe by the monastic missionaries, a series of legal provisions established the city itself as a corporation. Like the church, it was also independent of *oikos* and regime. In addition, hospitals, schools, and other charitable corporations were formed on the analogy of the church and its orders.

At the hands of Protestant lawyers, during the period when protodemocratic political institutions were also being formed, this long tradition was extended by the formation of the limited-lia-bility corporation, developed specifically for commercial purposes. This made it possible for people to invest in companies without risking personal, familial, or political capital distinct from that which was invested. Imbued with the Protestant work ethic, a dedication to "covenantal relationships," an inclination to bring all aspects of life under disciplined rational control, a drive toward the democratization of piety, politics, and social relationships of all kinds, and a radicalization of the sense of vocation, the limited-liability corporation developed the concept of "trustee" and invented a new social form for stewardship. The patterns consequently developed contributed to and grew with the Industrial Revolution as it introduced modern technologies of production and new occupational possibilities on a massive scale. The ethos of the corporation, which still bears the marks of this history in its deepest fabric, continues to imbue all those working in the corporation with values rooted in this history: common economic action demands a work ethic, a set of values separate from familial and political control, a discipline guided by rational control, at least a sense of "profession," and a stewardship of wealth that is not one's own. Workers and managers in modern corporations continue to be drawn into an ethos wherein these moral and spiritual presuppositions are seen as "natural," although the overt theological foundations have largely been replaced by utilitarian and contractual understandings of human relationships, and mammon has become, for many, the reigning deity.

Today, in the United States, where these developments are, if anything, more prevalent than anywhere else in the world, approximately thirteen percent of the population (and of the gross national product) is related to political and military matters, about seventeen percent of the work force is employed in nonprofit organizations, and only about three percent of the population is engaged in agriculture and family farming. All other production is in the hands of the corporations, and the profits derived make possible churches, schools, hospitals, the arts, welfare services, and various research institutes. Corporations have created more wealth than most of humankind can imagine, and they seem likely to do so in the foreseeable future. What was once rooted in *oikos* and transformed by *oikoumene* has become a corporate economy — now significantly independent not only of *oikos* and *polis* but of *oikoumene* as well.

In this context it is important to ask what "profit" is. In one sense that is what drives the corporation, and it is dedication to profit that occasions the most frequent critique of the idea that there is some viable spirituality in corporate life. Profit has a very technical and precise meaning, and organizing for it is not to be equated too quickly or too simply with either the motivation of greed or the impulse to acquisition. Max Weber already pointed that out in 1918, although theologians more than anyone else seem to have missed the point. Greed and the impulse to acquisition — indeed, the "pursuit of gain, of money, of the greatest possible amount of money" — in themselves have nothing to do with what is distinctive to the modern corporation's "profit."

> This impulse existed and has existed among waiters, physicians . . . , artists, prostitutes, dishonest officials, soldiers, nobles, crusaders, gamblers, and beggars. One may say that it has been common to all sorts and conditions of men at all times and in all countries of the earth. . . . It should be taught in the kindergarten of cultural history that this naive idea of . . . capitalism must be given up once and for all.[5]

This is so because profit involves a difference between assets and liabilities as indicated by a balance sheet figure, itself derived from the formally calculated pluses over minuses after an analytical assessment has been made on standardized principles. Profit is the estimated claim on wealth that can be used as capital for new efforts to create wealth. It is most frequently associated with the *constraint* of greed, of the impulse to acquire by chance, adventure, or expropriation and to consume. Further, profit can be understood only in the context of ongoing institutions such as corporations and exchange marts. Individuals, families, schools, hospitals, pirates, a tribe that discovers oil on its property, or a church that is the beneficiary of a will may have gains of which they want more or expenses of which they want fewer, but they do not have profits unless they are organized as corporations that produce goods and services and have rationally calculated costs and claims on income. And it is precisely such calculations that break the power of non-economic values over economic decision-making. In accounting procedures, profits serve to indicate whether previous calculations have been correct, whether economic activity has been conducted with relative efficiency and disciplined control, and whether the gain has been acquired irrespective of any special political, familial, or cultural influence that might interfere with economic calculation. This understanding of profit applies to socialist as well as capitalist economies, although in socialist economies the state calculates, collects, and deploys profits. State capitalism turns the entire nation-state into a single corporation with government as the manager of both production and markets.

Today there is another form of corporate capitalism that reigns in some regions. In the East and many developing lands, old familial networks have been incorporated into a kind of "shogunate" corporatism that is highly paternalistic, patriarchal, hierarchical, and wedded by family connections to those who control government. In India, subcastes have become corporations. And in Latin America, Indonesia, and the Philippines, military elites closely tied to the government are awarded control over corporations to form a kind of "crony capitalism." In these settings, the utilitarian, contract-based corporations exported from the West have little historic connection with the theological-ethical traditions that I outlined earlier. They have no history of breaking with the power of traditional familial and political institutions; instead, they reinforce them. Further, there seldom exists a legacy of law, a societal ethos, or genuine competition to control their behavior. Corporations thus are very different in the Third World than they are in the corporate capitalist West, or under state capitalism, and they are intensely resisted for good reasons.

At present there are no institutions at the international level that can control these institutions except other corporations that do a better job of producing at a lower price. And we must acknowledge that the drive to capture markets has led all

5. Weber, *The Protestant Ethic and the Spirit of Capitalism,* in *From Max Weber,* ed. Gerth and Mills (Oxford: Oxford University Press, 1947), p. 17.

forms of modern corporate production to engage political forces in imperialistic ways. In fact, in developing countries, most of the Western-based, transnational corporations betray the very foundations of what I have been attempting to set forth. More often than not, such corporations do not maintain the relative independence from either the leading households or the political regime that they attempt to maintain at home. They form alliances (or subsidiaries) with elite households and with military-political authorities to gain monopolistic controls, and they function as cartels to preserve the economic control of landed aristocracy over peasantry, which has been the pattern for centuries. They incline toward the fascist form of state capitalism, and they are properly opposed by both democratic capitalism and all democratic socialism as well as by every serious public theology. The obvious difficulties in which Third World countries currently find themselves are in part due to the failure of Western-based corporations to export their own fundamental assumptions and to equip the peoples to undertake corporate development, and the making of profits, on their own.

Such failures inhibit the capacity of concerned Western Christians to enhance things beyond productivity in these lands — namely, human rights and the prospects for democracy. Even in the rising economies of Asia, transnational corporate involvements have not brought about demonstrable respect for human rights or viable democracy, although they have brought about technological transformations and increased professionalization, the consequences of which are not yet clear. It could be that human rights, democracy, technology, professional development, and corporate productivity are among the things (besides Christianity) that the West has to offer the world, and that development of these things in modernizing cultures is being inhibited by contemporary corporate policies that ally corporations too closely with political authority and indigenous feudal elites, and that do not attend to the deeper principles on which corporate activities are grounded.

Reforming the Spirituality of the Corporation

If the discussion of these matters thus far can serve as a rough outline of social and spiritual factors that we must deal with in a responsible stewardship of modern political economies, and if we are fundamentally committed to a public theology that hopes to make the Word enfleshed in this kind of world, what shall the *oikoumene* now offer to corporate life?

We will have to make some very fundamental and fateful decisions before we proceed very far. One involves answering a basic question: Which form of corporative organization do we want to champion? There are only three major choices institutionally. Shall we call for state-engineered corporative life, which is the socialist route? Shall we foster an *oikos*-based corporative model, which dominates the Third World? Or shall we endorse the model of the independent corporation, an endorsement implicit in the direction the West has taken in the past? The question could be put another way: Who do we want to have calculating and making the profits and thus controlling capitalization — governments, elite families, or stockholders? I do not think it will do for ecumenical leadership to continue to duck this issue by continuing to ignore the questions of production and concentrating only on distribution, however important it is to maintain ethical witness on that front.

I think that we had better choose the model of the independent corporation (although in some situations the state-socialist model may have to be employed temporarily to remove elite families from their present positions of economic exploitation). We should do so because, in the long run, it is the system most inclined to support and sustain the prospects for human rights, democratic participation in political life, and the reduction of feudal, patriarchal, and caste structure in family life. Of course, we must beware here, because making such a choice can easily be seen as simply a sanctification of Yankee corporate capitalism and a conscious or preconscious attempt to wrap the American way of life in the Christian flag and drape it around the world. These I do not intend, and hence any move in the direction I suggest must be coupled with simultaneous prophetic judgment against and pastoral reformation of many current corporate policies.

Unlike many arguments today, the argument in these pages is not based on a dialectical reading of history. But if it were, part of what is suggested here could be understood in different terms than those used here. It could be said that *oikos*-based feudalism has produced and still tends to produce its antithesis, capitalistic individualism; and that the synthesis, "robber barons," produces its antithesis of state capitalism. That has brought us the socialisms and fascisms of the twentieth century, against which the reactionary forces of individualistic and state capitalism are presently arrayed. We do not yet have a viable antithesis to this present state of affairs except the ideal of social democracy borne by the ecumenical church, which must, without extensive political, economic, or technological power, develop a new spirituality, based on a public theology, to transform the materialist and reductionist preoccupation of all present economic forms and ideologies. This is possible because already within the modern corporation are residual ecclesiological elements wherein spiritual matters are intrinsically related to social ones, and therefore are potentially related to new patterns of material and organizational embodiment.

In order to carry out prophetic judgment against and reformation of corporations, we will have to make a second decision. Do we think that corporations have any real or potential spiritual foundations? If they do not, we can have no transformative communication base with them. We would have to see them only as mechanisms, as humanly populated machines that could be constructed or deconstructed, that break down and can be repaired, but that could not in principle be reformed by any spiritual or moral transformation.

This question is not new, although it is neglected. A generation ago, F. W. Maitland and Ernest Barker, among others, researched the question of whether institutions have souls.[6] On the whole, they argued, it cannot be held that institu-

tions will, like people, stand before the gates of heaven. Institutions can neither go to heaven nor suffer in hell. Yet that does not mean that corporations cannot have a character, even a certain esprit de corps that can be assessed on moral and spiritual grounds. It is quite possible that these *personae fictae*, which are more *ficta* than *persona*, have an inner quality that can be reformed and renewed.

After all, it is not so farfetched to hold that corporations have some kind of spirit or character. They are not, in fundamental ways, different from universities, orchestras, or athletic clubs, which do seem to have distinctive spirits and characters. Who does not know of someone who, when job-hunting, compares the characters of the firms involved, speaking easily about the moral "tone," the humane fabric of human relationships, the sense of purpose and professional excellence, the responsible attitudes toward employees? And is it not odd that clergy who rage against corporations and the profit motive rejoice when young women and men in their congregations join a "quality" company? In a special issue of *Word and World* (Spring 1984), a number of authors speak about the kinds of moral and spiritual engagement, stimulation, stretching beyond oneself, loyalty, and intensity that come from corporate participation, especially on the part of the baby-boom generation and the blacks and the women who have subsequently been most critical of male-dominated corporate capitalism. How do we account for the fact that they seem to find liberation in the disciplined work ethic and the quest for profits when they work in first-rate corporations? And do we not find among the most sensitive of the lay leaders in our churches those who can neither tolerate nor reform the inner quality of life in a particular corporation when its inner character is distorted or absent, and who change positions or simply quit, even when it involves a considerable reduction in income? Is it not so that workers and managers in "quality" unions and corporations sometimes have the same kinds of characterological and spiritual-communal experiences that pastors have in working with the best churches?

The problem still remains. What theological resources will we bring to bear on these facts of public life today, and what forms of spirituality

---

6. See Maitland's introduction to Otto Gierke's *Political Theories of the Middle Ages* (Boston: Beacon Press, 1959), and Barker's introduction to Gierke's *Natural Law and the Theory of Society*.

ought we to attempt to cultivate for corporate life? To be sure, many argue that corporate life is inevitably spiritually vacuous, that corporations today are alienating and dehumanizing, and that a commercial enterprise surely cannot have any soul, any spirituality, for it is based, as it must be, on the making of a profit, the impersonality of the market, the mechanism of engineered needs, and finally the worship of mammon. And yet that judgment does not seem to be faithful either to the deeper history of the modern corporation (as it derived from ecclesiological, free-city, and charity-organization precedents) or to the human experience that people in our churches have in corporations.

Let us not be smug about this. Let us not uncritically celebrate the corporation today when in fact many features of corporate life produce items of little lasting value, distribute them inequitably, consume inordinate quantities of the world's non-renewable resources, and cooperate with the most exploitative forces present in other lands. And let us not forget the horror stories of discrimination, pettiness, meanness, and the rat race told by executives and laborers alike. Our purpose is simply to overcome a blind spot in modern theology and ethics, one that can prevent us from even grappling with the nature and character of the corporation as a potentially moral and spiritual reality. I simply want to stress that there may be a core in the midst of corporate life that has become vacuous or can become demonic but that may also be filled and transformed by a theologically vertebrate spirituality.

If this is so, what resources from our theological tradition shall we bring to bear on the reformation of the spirituality of production as it appears in the modern corporation? Let me close this chapter by listing five motifs from the governing themes of a public theology . . . that might become the counterpoints of preaching and teaching, pastoral care, and the development of a stewardly leadership able to carry their commitments and ministries into the world of the productive corporation:

1. Vocation. From the calling of Abraham and Moses to the calling of the prophets and disciples, through the various refinements in the history of the tradition, the notion that each person was put in the world by God to serve some particular purpose and is called to serve the whole of humanity in the economy of God is a profound and penetrating insight. A vocation is not simply a job or an occupation. It comes from God and may require sacrificial suffering, discipleship, and *kenosis*. The concept has its most important application in regard to personal life, but it has social dimensions as well. Further, every institution has *its* particular vocation. Schools are to seek the truth and understanding; hospitals are devoted to healing and the care of the sick; symphonies are meant for making music. Is it possible that corporations as cooperative endeavors, as well as the people in them, have a vocation from God to do what they do? Surely this means that they must contribute to the material well-being of the human community with the particular skills and products they offer — plumbing supply, meat-packing, energy resources, or whatever — and that they must do so in a way that makes a profit.

If this is possible, common corporate vocations must be carried out under the watchful eye of the living God with no less diligence than our personal quests for vocational fulfillment. A vocation under God is proactive — not merely reactive. Not only does it minister to those harmed by bad economic policy or corporate decisions; it steels the soul for economic initiative and engenders a willingness to take moral risks. Were the sense of vocation to be reborn in modern corporations among stockholders, management, and labor, the shape of corporate economies might change.

To accent such matters is the responsibility of clergy and theologians. Who in government, in labor unions, in business schools or economic departments speaks of these matters? It is *our* task. . . .

2. Moral Law. In some circles today it seems quaint to speak of moral law, and many are so afraid of sounding self-righteous (as those who talk about it a great deal often do) that they avoid speaking of it. And yet the reluctance to speak clearly about fundamental principles of right and wrong allows people in corporate life to be satisfied on the one hand with mere legality, and on the other hand with whatever is strategic or efficient. This has allowed many to lose sight of the basic principles of human rights that must be met as a condition of any viable structure of economic life. Corporations, especially those in

such places as South Africa and developing countries, must see to it that their activities enhance human rights. And if this is not the case, they must not be surprised if churches, workers' groups, opposition parties, and oppressed minorities form coalitions to convert them.

3. Liberation. In the West, millions of middle-class people have found their economic liberation — against the expectations of many — in the disciplined, cooperative sharing of vocations in corporations. Yet many on the underside of Western economies have not had this experience, and many more around the world are oppressed by corporations. If there is to be a remedy for this problem, it will mean that the long-range planning that every corporation now does and the intervening steps taken to carry out those plans must speak to this question: Does this project somehow contribute to the liberation of those not free in a way that draws them also into communities of economic responsibility?

4. Sin. There is something tragic in all of economic life. Every act of production involves the destruction of some resource that has been given to humanity in creation, and every pattern of distribution entails disproportionate gain for some at the expense of others, and every act of consumption involves waste. Further, every organized center of economic activity thus far developed involves the domination of some over others. Let us never think that we humans can find our salvation in economic activity and its rewards, or in the building of one specific kind of economic order, including that centered in the corporation. Many corporations engender a kind of loyalty that borders on the totemic at best, on the idolatrous at worst. The tendencies to worship mammon are with us all, and can easily demand that the corporation become mammon's temple. Especially because the corporation can provide a kind of immortality, it can require human sacrifice on its altar. These perils are already suggested in the commandment that tells us that six days shall we labor, but that we must remember the Sabbath, to keep it holy. Our necessary efforts at production are disciplined and restrained by the constant and regular repair to the One who creates what we can never produce, distributes what no human system can apportion, and receives out of our willingness to consume less than we obviously could.

5. Covenant. In the face of our modern political economies, we must work out a covenantal structure for the corporation in ways framed by these other doctrines and in ways echoing the ecclesiological roots of the corporation. And we must attempt to structure economic influence by patterns that reflect what we have learned about political distributions of power. The future of corporate polity will surely demand the democratization of decision-making, the sharing of power, and the participation of labor in setting guidelines for corporate policy around the world.[7] And this means the pluralization of economic authority and a political, social, and ethical openness to corporate formation in underdeveloped regions of the world, which state capitalisms of the left and the right do not presently encourage.

To this list one might easily add creation. The modern corporation is — besides those things already discussed — the seat of modern technology that alters the structures of nature. It therefore has many implications for how we relate to the biophysical universe as a creation of God. . . .

7. See especially William J. Everett, "*Oikos:* Convergence in Business Ethics," *Journal of Business Ethics* 5 (1986): 313-25. See also Arthur Rich, *Mitbestimmung in der Industrie* (Zurich: Flamberg Verlag, 1973); S. T. Bruyn, *The Social Economy: People Transforming Modern Business* (New York: John Wiley & Sons, 1977); and Terry Deal and Allan Kennedy, *Corporate Cultures: The Rites and Rituals of Corporate Life* (Reading, Mass.: Addison-Wesley, 1982).

55. The Meaning of the Cross for Social Ethics in the World Today

LARRY RASMUSSEN

Largely missing in North American Protestant church life and culture are a distinct ecclesiology and a clear ethic as part of the understanding of "church." The social significance of the church as a piece of the world with an integrity peculiar to itself, and the meaning of that for the moral life, has been given too little consideration.

Stanley Hauerwas's polemics force the issue.

It is not the task of the church to try to develop social theories or strategies to make America work; rather the task of the church in this country is to become a polity that has the character necessary to survive as a truthful society.[1]

The first task of Christian social ethics . . . is not to make the "world" better or more just, but to help Christian people form their community consistent with their conviction that the

story of Christ is a truthful account of our existence.[2]

To many ears this will ring too sectarian. Nonetheless, it has striking familiarity with Bonhoeffer's words:

What is of importance is now no longer that I should become good, or that the condition of the world should be made better by my action, but that the reality of God should show itself everywhere to be the ultimate reality.[3]

For Bonhoeffer, as for Hauerwas, this happens for the world by letting the church be the church; that is, a piece of world where Christ is taking community form. And so the social formation of the Christian community itself becomes a prime focal point for Christian ethics. The focal point is not initially, and not only, the social formation of the wider world.

Of course, church and world are indissoluble, since the church is a piece of world. But the attention of Christian social ethics, which is often focused primarily and sometimes only on the world beyond the church, has neglected, and sometimes distorted, the relationship of ecclesiology and ethics.

It is almost startling to read Ernst Troeltsch in this connection. In *The Social Teaching of the Christian Churches* he writes:

It is a great mistake to treat the ideas which underlie the preaching of Jesus as though they were primarily connected with the "social" problem. The message of Jesus is obviously purely religious; it issues directly from a very definite idea of God, and of the divine will in relation to man. To Jesus the whole meaning of life is religious; his life and his teaching are wholly determined by his thought of God.[4]

No Jew (like Jesus) would understand this. To have one's "life and . . . teaching . . . wholly deter-

---

1. Stanley Hauerwas, *A Community of Character: Toward a Constructive Christian Social Ethic* (Notre Dame, Ind.: University of Notre Dame Press, 1981), 3.

Larry Rasmussen (1939–) is the Reinhold Niebuhr Professor of Social Ethics at Union Theological Seminary. He is co-author of *Bible and Ethics in the Christian Life* and author of *Dietrich Bonhoeffer: Reality and Resistance* and *Dietrich Bonhoeffer: His Significance for North Americans.*

From Larry Rasmussen, *Dietrich Bonhoeffer — His Significance for North Americans* (Minneapolis: Augsburg Fortress, 1990).

2. Ibid., p. 10.
3. *Ethics*, trans. by Smith (New York: Macmillan, 1965), p. 188.
4. From Troeltsch's *The Social Teaching of the Christian Churches*, p. 50 of the Macmillan edition, cited by Hauerwas, *A Community of Character*, p. 38.

mined by [one's] thought of God" but not connect that intimately to social reality and every aspect of life was unthinkable to the observant Jew.

Of the early community Troeltsch writes:

> It is worthy of special note that early Christian apologetic contains no arguments dealing either with hopes of improving the existing social situation, or with any attempt to heal social ills. Jesus began his public ministry, it is true, by proclaiming the Kingdom of God as the great hope of redemption; this "Kingdom," however, . . . was primarily the vision of an ideal ethical and religious situation, of a world entirely controlled by God, in which all the values of pure spirituality would be recognized and appreciated at their true worth.[5]

When the "Kingdom" is "the vision of an ideal ethical and religious situation," the social ethic of Jesus and the early community is of little help, except as a judging, transhistorical norm. It functions as a statement of an ideal or ideals that provide a critique and standard. In Reinhold Niebuhr's work, for example, there is indeed a central place for the cross. It is the revelation of the ultimate ethical norm, namely, *agape* (sacrificial love), and it is the revelation of the divine mercy in the form of the forgiveness of sins. The latter serves as the core of a powerful spirituality for political engagement which succumbs neither to illusion nor to cynicism. This is certainly helpful in its own deeply Lutheran way, but it is not yet a social ethic of the cross.

Reinhold Niebuhr, the most influential North American social ethicist, here reflects the Troeltschian formulation of liberal Christianity. What is crucial for our attention is the assumption that social ethics, in order to be valid, has to be relevant to society as a whole and to its governance. Its attention is not to the formation of the church community as such. (That would be the introversion of sectarianism.) As Hauerwas correctly points out, Troeltsch specifically exempts from social ethics and lists as "purely religious" such matters as the "right kind of congregational organization, the application of Christian ideals to daily life, self-discipline in the interest of personal holiness, and appropriation of spiritual inheritance."[6] These

items do not intersect the problem Christians have when they participate in running society, and *thus* are not matters of social ethics. Differently said, when the Jesus story does not help in the managing of "empire" (Hauerwas's term), it is not an adequate story for a Christian social ethic. Why? Because after Constantine and the legacy of Christendom, it is precisely the partnership of throne and altar, of a nation or a people and the church, that sets the very terms of "social ethics." Thinking from inside a post-Constantinian paradigm shifts ethics away from the New Testament focus on the shape of the believing community as a community of the new aeon and as a "public" in its own right. It simultaneously shortcuts the possibilities that await an ethic of the cross as a community ethic of the *imitatio Christi*. Until the so-called sectarian vocation is permitted, there will be no communitarian social ethic of the cross, except on the terms of a Niebuhr or a Troeltsch.

Social ethics must include the concrete organization of the imitation of Christ in the world as Christian community. That is the contention here, and it is also Bonhoeffer's. Polity is politics, sharing and table-fellowship are economics, fellowship and joining with others in their suffering and joy are healing, and lifting up the Jesus story is worship. Social ethics is *Gemeinsames Leben,* to cite the title of Bonhoeffer's book on Christian community *(Life Together).* "Christ existing as community," the theme of his earlier work, *Sanctorum Communio,* is what the church is both to be and to do in the world.

To talk about the ecclesial vocation in ethics in these terms requires further discussion of the church's relationship to culture, especially in North America. For here we live both with a strong sense that our "calling" is to conquest and control and with a religious history in which many of the strains of Christianity have seen the social ethical task as that of making the North American world "better."

Both liberal Protestant Christianity and American evangelicalism have suffered from the neglect of a clear, distinctive sense of the church as a collective moral agent. The "church" in much of American Protestantism, with the notable excep-

---

5. Ibid., pp. 39-40, from Hauerwas, *A Community of Character,* p. 38.

6. Cited by Hauerwas, *A Community of Character,* p. 38.

tion of the African American churches, has been largely the individual and the nation, with denominations supplying ecclesiastical structure. Both the stance of the Moral Majority in the 1980s and the opposition of liberal Protestants to it betray an acculturated Christianity markedly lacking a sense of a community (the church) whose normative shape is positioned over against its own wider world.

In this setting we should emphasize Christian social ethics as ecclesial in character, and the church as the *ecclesia crucis* (the community of the cross). The direction taken will, as hinted, lean as much toward the radical Reformation as toward Luther. The shift to the left wing of the Reformation is best seen in the meaning given the cross itself. We can do no better than include a passage from Mennonite theologian John Yoder:

> The believer's cross is no longer any and every kind of suffering, sickness, or tension, the bearing of which is demanded. The believer's cross must be, like his Lord's, the price of his social nonconformity. It is not, like sickness or catastrophe, an inexplicable suffering; it is the end of a path freely chosen after counting the cost. It is not, like Luther's or Thomas Muntzer's or Zinzendorf's or Kierkegaard's cross of *Anfechtung,* an inward wrestling of the sensitive soul with self and sin; *it is the social reality of representing in an unwilling world the Order to come.*[7]

There is a strikingly similar passage in *The Cost of Discipleship:*

> To endure the cross is not a tragedy; it is the suffering which is the fruit of an exclusive allegiance to Jesus Christ. When it comes, it is not an accident, but a necessity. It is not the sort of suffering which is inseparable from this mortal life, but the suffering which is an essential part of the specifically Christian life. It is not suffering *per se* but suffering-and-rejection, and not rejection for any cause or conviction of our own, but rejection for the sake of Christ.[8]

To represent, in an unwilling world, the order to come is to "realize [true] reality," to call to mind Bonhoeffer's language. It happens when the church participates in the being of Jesus by traversing the often costly way of Jesus. "The cross means sharing the suffering of Christ to the last and to the fullest."[9]

The development of the church's social ethic has been truncated by certain assumptions and arrangements described here as Constantinian. I list a few, drawing heavily from John Yoder.

1. When H. Richard Niebuhr defines "culture" in his classic volume, *Christ and Culture,* he does so in a way that assumes "culture" is something whole. We must be "of" it or "against" it, or "above" it, "transforming" it, or holding it "in paradox." We are inconsistent, maybe we even cheat, if we as Christians do not take responsibility for the whole. Culture is a package deal and there is only one fare. Thus Niebuhr criticized Tertullian for using and applauding the Latin language as a great and good gift of the Roman Empire, and then turning around and categorically rejecting Roman imperial violence.[10] Culture is a seamless web, a single garment.

2. "The civil order [meaning government] is the quintessence of the cultural mandate."[11] It takes little reflection to note there are many dimensions of culture — family, education, the arts, the economy, religious life, and so on. Yet mainline social ethics has it that the one critical for all the rest is civil governance. Without sovereignty of government all would be lost. Such sovereignty is ordained by God or imbedded in the very order of nature, according to most of Western social ethics.

3. "The sword is the quintessence of the civil order."[12] While coercion, including lethal coercion may be the means of last resort *(ultima ratio)* for governing, it is so central to the state that the civil order cannot be understood apart from it. It is necessary if society and culture are not to dissolve

7. John Howard Yoder, *The Politics of Jesus* (Grand Rapids, Mich.: Wm. B. Eerdmans, 1972), p. 97 (emphasis added).

8. *The Cost of Discipleship,* p. 98

9. Ibid.

10. John Howard Yoder, "The Apriori Difficulty of 'Reformed-Anabaptist Conversation,'" (unpublished paper, January 27, 1977), p. 7. The discussion of the four assumptions relies on Yoder's paper, though done here in highly simplified fashion.

11. Ibid.

12. Ibid.

in anarchy. The sword is God's instrument for order. It belongs to the very essence of the state that the state wields it.

As Yoder notes, this identification between the sword and the civil order is, theologically, a fusing of creation and the Fall. That there must be order is not in doubt, nor that order is a created mandate. Genesis 1 and 2 are about such patterning of creation. But that the sword belongs to creation is not part of that ordering. Such arguments — more frequently, simply assumptions — have overlaid life under the Fall onto creation and its ordering. It has made sin not only normal, but normative.

4. God's will is univocal. We have nurtured a notion that God's will is the same for all peoples, perhaps because all share a common created nature, or a common destiny in God, or hold common potential. So we strive for a common ethic. Indeed, in ethics, "universalizability" is test of the moral integrity of any contemplated behavior.

There is probably very little that supports this biblically. Again, Yoder:

> There is no self-evident reason that the will of God has the same meaning for a Jew as for a Gentile in the age of Moses, when tabernacle worship and circumcision are not expected of the nations. There is no self-evident reason to assume that the obligations of Christians and non-Christians are the same in the New Testament when one decides and acts within the reestablished covenant of grace and the other does not. There is no reason to have to assume that the moral performance of which God expects of the regenerate [God] equally expects of the unregenerate. Of course, on some much more elevated level of abstraction, our minds demand that we project a unique and univocal ultimate or ideal will of God. But it is precisely the nature of [God's] patience with fallen humanity that God condescends to deal with us on other levels.[13]

What must be emphasized is that the above Constantinian assumptions betray the perspective of those who formulate their ethic, its nature and purpose, "from above." These are the assumptions of people more accustomed to making history than "taking" it. Ethics here are for "running

society," forging and enforcing public policy for both the clean and the great unwashed. "The view from above" (Bonhoeffer's phrase) sees culture as a totality, or demands that it be such and aspires to make it so. "From above," that is, from the point of view of the privileged, the nod is given the governing function as the one where final sovereignty must rest. "From above" the heart of governance is holding and wielding of power in the form of coercion and its threat. "From above" the constant inclination is to fuse the realities of the fallen world with requirements supposedly rooted in creation itself. "From above" universalism is a test of the validity of an ethic which corresponds to God's singular will.

Of course, such assumptions can be argued on grounds other than the interests of the privileged and the requirements of rule. Order is a social necessity, and coercion as well. But it would be naive and foolish not to suspect the pervasive play of social interests here and the remnants of a Christendom marriage of the church to power.

In any case, if we do speak of some universal reach for an ethic of the cross, it should not be that of the "Christendom" ethic, either in its more theocratic forms or in its more liberal dress (the acculturated Christianity of democratic societies). The liberal version, says Yoder:

> affirms the adequacy of the religious expression of almost everyone or at least of people in almost every condition, sometimes in other religions or perhaps even in no religion, because of some inherent human qualities for which one considers the label "Christ" to be a symbol.[14]

In Bonhoeffer this way of proceeding comes clearest when, on christological grounds, he wonders whether the ethic of agnostic world-come-of-age people might not be something like "unconscious Christianity." One way or another, with faith or without, the world will be shaped "in keeping with Christian principles!" This is the Constantinian hangover in Bonhoeffer's own thought.

13. Ibid., pp. 11-12.

14. John Howard Yoder, "The Basis of Barth's Social Ethics," (unpublished paper presented to the Midwestern Section of the Karl Barth Society, Elmhurst, Illinois, 29-30 September 1978), p. 11.

The universalism of the cross, which is even stronger in Bonhoeffer, is markedly different. It is in accord with Yoder's own description, where the way of the cross is:

> that of the confessing minority whose commitment to her Lord, despite its being against the stream, is so convinced of the majesty of his Lordship that she risks trusting that his power and goodness can reach beyond the number of those who know him by his right name.[15]

Yoder adds: "The former universalism [Constantinian] is a high view of the human; the latter a high view of Jesus."[16]

We must draw our conclusions. The ethics of the community of the cross need not share *any* of the above Constantinian assumptions in order to be a theologically and morally valid, and "reasonable," social ethic. Indeed, to carry these Constantinian assumptions subverts the ethic of the cross and the character of its community. By such prevailing assumptions about the relationship of church, Christ, and culture, the theology of the cross is forced to be something it is not, namely, a perspective for society at large. The *theologia crucis* is certainly about faithful engagement in and for the world. But it is not about controlling culture and exercising dominance. The social ethic of the cross is a communitarian ethic of "life together" in Christian community, an ethic that may or may not be appropriated by the wider world. But that it is not so appropriated is not an invalidation of the ethic. The rigors of the ethic ought not be compromised just so that it will be accepted in all quarters.

Differently said, the moral vocation of the church is to "be for others." But it does so as a community of the cross. Its social ethics are thereby formulated from the nature of the new order under the lordship of Jesus, and not from the requirements of culture and its maintenance by whomever happens to possess access to power in the moment. The confidence that the good and right will triumph does not arise from the church's ability to line up might behind right so that the levers of power favor the good guys over the bad.

Its confidence arises from the strange power of Jesus and his way, the power of cross and resurrection. This is life by a very different logic from that of the enhanced strength of the good guys, or the gradual institutionalization of virtue over vice under our wise tutelage.

For people accustomed to being in charge, this way of thinking is literally almost inconceivable. It does not "make sense," given their assumptions. Thus it is labeled hopelessly sectarian, irrelevant, self-righteous, and perhaps even world-hating. Without denying that these are risks for any close community with a distinctive identity, we must also say that for the community of the cross to be such a community in an unwilling world is not to be "against culture" per se (H. Richard Niebuhr's phrase). It is to be against those continual propensities in culture which invariably shift Christian ethics from living in and with the old aeon on the terms of the new, to living in and with the new aeon on the terms of the old! It is to be against the propensity always present to fuse even new creation with the Fall! This has been rampant in our acculturated Christianity. Its most frequent form has been the marriage of throne and altar, nation and church, sword and cross, ethnic community and religion. Or, if not marriages, then, as in the case of the United States, long-term arrangements of "living together."

---

15. Yoder, "Barth's Social Ethics," p. 11.
16. Ibid.

Try It Yourself: Holy Unions (III)

CASE STUDY 3[1]

The first two parts of this case study are found on pages 13 and 180.

After hearing Professor Smarts lecture Saturday afternoon, a surprise awaits you in All Saints Episcopal Church the following morning. Father Complex, who has an earned doctorate in religious ethics, is visiting your church and will give the homily. All you know about this priest is that he has disagreed with Smarts publicly on a number of occasions.

Complex has chosen to preach on gays in the church. The sanctuary is packed. "Homosexuals," he states, "should not be judged for their condition any more than a retarded child should be judged for being retarded. One's sexual orientation is discovered, not made. A gay person should not, therefore, accept any burden of guilt for his condition. He is responsible only for what he does with his homosexual drives."

What then should gays do? Fr. Complex offers three options. First, a gay person ought to try to change his or her sexual orientation. He asserts that, though not chosen, the homosexual orientation is not what God intended when he created humanity male and female and instituted marriage. Both divine healing and psychiatric counseling should be pursued. The statistics on homosexual conversion are not promising, he concedes, but no gay person can be absolutely sure of what is possible for him or her before he or she tries.

But what if change doesn't come, even after lengthy therapy and prayer? What if a gay's orientation proves to be "constitutional"? The second option is celibacy. Celibacy is at least the affirmation that human fulfillment does not depend on sexual fulfillment, and can sometimes be a gift, a calling that signals and relies on the power of God. And what if celibacy proves finally to be impossible? Then Complex proposes a third option of fidelity and permanence with one other member of the same sex. In such a situation, some form of a Christian "holy union" ceremony would be in order.

This third option is not the best sexual morality, the priest concludes. But within these difficult and tragic circumstances, it is both permissible and the best *possible* morality.

Do you agree?

---

1. Some content in this case is drawn from Lewis B. Smedes, *Sex for Christians* (Grand Rapids, Mich.: Wm. B. Eerdmans, 1976), pp. 62-75.

PART III
ISSUES IN CHRISTIAN ETHICS

Chapter 9
Christian Sexual Ethics

Introduction

Perhaps the central premise of Christian (and Jewish) sexual ethics is that sexual contact should be linked with love, marriage and children. James Burtchaell writes:

> Jesus surprised his followers by inviting them to a new kind of marital commitment: for better or for worse, until death. It was a frighteningly bold promise of fidelity, free of all conditions or escape clauses, and so it asked for a more demanding love and a more secure trust . . . This sort of commitment is terribly difficult to live up to, which is why more seasoned believers urge younger ones to approach it with caution . . . Sex is meant to embody a surrender of privacy which comes from belonging to one another . . . It is not simply an expression of love; rather, it embodies belonging — belonging in a way that only marriage quite achieves. The love of marriage should welcome sharers, particulary children. The planning of birth is a reasonable thing, but there should be in the hearts of husbands and wives . . . hunger and reverence for children . . .[1]

Based on this premise, traditional Christian moral teaching on marriage can be summarized along the lines of the following mandates: (1) one should refrain from sexual activity until marriage (i.e., the wedding); (2) an essential and normal purpose of marriage is to produce children; (3) one should refrain from sexual activity with anyone but one's spouse; (4) one should choose a spouse from the opposite sex; and (5) the marital

estate is intended to be a permanent love relationship.

Today, debates rage around each of these mandates, particularly in Western and other societies that have experienced rapid industrialization. The resulting discussion has been rich, and some of its finest examples are collected in this chapter.

A number of our selections are in some measure of revolt against the received Christian tradition, and intend to substantially revise that tradition. According to Beverly Harrison (reading 58), an adequate Christian sexual ethic has yet to be developed. The official Christian position is marked by anti-body dualism, fear of homosexuality (homophobia), and the oppression of women (cf. readings 15 and 38). James Nelson (reading 61) calls for a "paradigmatic shift" in traditional Christian sexual ethics which has been too legalistic. He finds this to be most often — though not exclusively — true in the Roman Catholic Christian tradition.

Our other selections defend the received tradition in a variety of ways. Vigen Guroian (reading 57) believes marriage to be finally a church-like or "ecclesial" entity, and finds significant resources for understanding and strengthening it in the liturgy of the Orthodox Church. Margaret Farley reflects on the peculiarly modern assumption that the one necessary condition for sexual intercourse and for marriage as well is "falling in love" (reading 59).

In reading 60, Lewis Smedes provides us with an exposition of the commandment, "Thou shalt not commit adultery." Following his chief mentor, the sixteenth-century lawyer-turned-theologian John Calvin, Smedes argues that the range of the commandment is a good deal wider than is usually supposed, and is not simply negative. And finally, Philip Turner finds at least one sort of revision in

---

1. James T. Burtchaell, *For Better, For Worse: Sober Thoughts on Passionate Promises* (New York; Mahwah: Paulist Press, 1985), pp. 3-4.

the traditional Christian teaching about sex and marriage to be moral retrogression (reading 62).

Suggestions for Further Reading

Augustine. *Augustine: Confessions and Enchiridion.* The Library of Christian Classics, vol. 7. Philadelphia: Westminster Press, 1955.

Berry, Wendell. "The Body and the Earth." In *The Unsettling of America,* pp. 97-140. San Francisco: Sierra Club, 1977.

Didion, Joan. "On Self-Respect." In *Slouching Toward Bethlehem,* pp. 145-151. New York: Washington Square Press, 1981.

Gustafson, James M. "The Religious and Moral Wisdom of the Marriage Service." In *Ethics from a Theocentric Perspective, Vol. II: Ethics and Theology,* pp. 177-184. Chicago: University of Chicago Press, 1984.

Kierkegaard, Søren. *Works of Love.* Trans. Howard and Edna Hong. New York: Harper & Row, 1962.

McClendon, Jr., James William. "Sarah and Jonathan Edwards." In *Systematic Theology: Ethics,* pp. 110-131. Nashville: Abingdon Press, 1986.

Thielieke, Helmut. *Theological Ethics, Vol. 3: Sex.* Grand Rapids, Mich.: Eerdmans, 1964.

56. 1 Corinthians 6:9–7:16
1 Corinthians 7:25-38
Ephesians 5:21-33

1 Corinthians 6:9–7:16

Do you not know that wrongdoers will not inherit the kingdom of God? Do not be deceived! Fornicators, idolaters, adulterers, male prostitutes, sodomites, thieves, the greedy, drunkards, revilers, robbers — none of these will inherit the kingdom of God. And this is what some of you used to be. But you were washed, you were sanctified, you were justified in the name of the Lord Jesus Christ and in the Spirit of our God.

"All things are lawful for me," but not all things are beneficial. "All things are lawful for me," but I will not be dominated by anything. "Food is meant for the stomach and the stomach for food," and God will destroy both one and the other. The body is meant not for fornication but for the Lord, and the Lord for the body. And God raised the Lord and will also raise us by his power. Do you not know that your bodies are members of Christ? Should I therefore take the members of of Christ and make them members of a prostitute? Never! Do you not know that whoever is united to a prostitute becomes one body with her? For it is said "The two shall be one flesh." But anyone united to the Lord becomes one spirit with him. Shun fornication! Every sin that a person commits is outside the body; but the fornicator sins against the body itself. Or do you not know that your body is a temple of the Holy Spirit within you, which you have from God, and that you are not your own? For you were bought with a price; therefore glorify God in your body.

Now concerning the matters about which you wrote: "It is well for a man not to touch a woman."

But because of cases of sexual immorality, each man should have his own wife and each woman her own husband. The husband should give to his wife her conjugal rights, and likewise the wife to her husband. For the wife does not have authority over her own body, but the husband does; likewise the husband does not have authority over his own body, but the wife does. Do not deprive one another except perhaps by agreement for a set time, to devote yourselves to prayer, and then come together again, so that Satan may not tempt you because of your lack of self-control. This I say by way of concession, not of command. I wish that all were as I myself am. But each has a particular gift from God, one having one kind and another a different kind.

To the unmarried and the widows I say that it is well for them to remain unmarried as I am. But if they are not practicing self-control, they should marry. For it is better to marry than to be aflame with passion.

To the married I give this command — not I but the Lord — that the wife should not separate from her husband (but if she does separate, let her remain unmarried or else be reconciled to her husband), and that the husband should not divorce his wife.

To the rest I say — I and not the Lord — that if any believer has a wife who is an unbeliever, and she consents to live with him, he should not divorce her. And if any woman has a husband who is an unbeliever, and he consents to live with her, she should not divorce him. For the unbelieving husband is made holy through his wife, and the unbelieving wife is made holy through her husband. Otherwise, your children would be unclean, but as it is, they are holy. But if the unbelieving partner separates, let it be so; in such a case the brother or sister is not bound. It is to peace that God has called you. Wife, for all you know, you might save your husband. Husband, for all you know, you might save your wife.

1 Corinthians 7:25-38

Now concerning virgins, I have no command of the Lord, but I give my opinion as one who by the Lord's mercy is trustworthy. I think that, in view of the impending crisis, it is well for you to remain as you are. Are you bound to a wife? Do not seek to be free. Are you free from a wife? Do not seek a wife. But if you marry, you do not sin, and if a virgin marries, she does not sin. Yet those who marry will experience distress in this life, and I would spare you that. I mean, brothers and sisters, the appointed time has grown short; from now on, let even those who have wives be as though they had none, and those who mourn as though they were not mourning, and those who rejoice as though they were not rejoicing, and those who buy as though they had no possessions, and those who deal with the world as though they had no dealings with it. For the present form of this world is passing away.

I want you to be free from anxieties. The unmarried man is anxious about the affairs of the Lord, how to please the Lord; but the married man is anxious about the affairs of the world, how to please his wife, and his interests are divided. And the unmarried woman and the virgin are anxious about the affairs of the Lord, so that they may be holy in body and spirit; but the married woman is anxious about the affairs of the world, how to please her husband. I say this for your own benefit, not to put any restraint upon you, but to promote good order and unhindered devotion to the Lord.

If anyone thinks that he is not behaving properly toward his fiancée, if his passions are strong, and so it has to be, let him marry as he wishes; it is no sin. Let them marry. But if someone stands firm in his resolve, being under no necessity but having his own desire under control, and has determined in his own mind to keep her as his fiancée, he will do well. So then, he who marries his fiancée does well; and he who refrains from marriage will do better.

Ephesians 5:21-33

Be subject to one another out reverence for the Christ.

Wives, be subject to your husbands as you are to the Lord. For the husband is the head of the wife just as Christ is the head of the church, the body of which he is the Savior. Just as the church is subject to Christ, so also wives ought to be, in everything, to their husbands.

Husbands, love your wives, just as Christ loved

the church and gave himself up for her, in order to make her holy by cleansing her with the washing of water by the word, so as to present the church to himself in splendor, without a spot or wrinkle or anything of the kind — yes, so that she may be holy and without blemish. In the same way, husbands should love their wives as they do their own bodies. He who loves his wife loves himself. For no one ever hates his own body, but he nourishes and tenderly cares for it, just as Christ does for the church, because we are members of his body. "For this reason a man will leave his father and mother and be joined to his wife, and the two will become one flesh." This is a great mystery, and I am applying it to Christ and the church. Each of you, however, should love his wife as himself, and a wife should respect her husband.

57. An Ethic of Marriage and Family

VIGEN GUROIAN

Christian theologians and churchpersons need to be much clearer than they have been about why the state of marriage and family, particularly among those who identify themselves as Christians, is of matter to the church. This goal will not be served by immediately raising the cry that Christians need to have good marriages, raise children properly, and not divorce, because if they fail to do so the foundations of society will crumble. Christians who worry about the triumph of secularism or cultural relativism in American society would do well to direct their attention first to ecclesiology. There is nothing new in the observation that this world is fallen, however one puts it. The crucial issue for the church always has been to maintain the well-being and good functioning of its own polity. This is an obligation owed to Christ who, for the world's sake, is married to the church. Marriage, St. Paul tells us, is bound up with a profound mystery, that of "Christ and the church" (Eph. 5:32 RSV).[1] If marriage has become

---

1. Perhaps I ought to explain exactly why this biblical passage is invoked here. First, I am not intending to use it as some kind of proof text that marriage is really sacramental. The matter obviously is not quite that simple. My warrant for invoking Ephesians 5:32 is that it appears centrally in the Orthodox rites of mat-

---

Vigen Guroian (1948–) is professor of Christian ethics at Loyola College in Baltimore. He is the author of *Incarnate Love: Essays in Orthodox Ethics*.

From Vigen Guroian, *Incarnate Love: Essays in Orthodox Ethics* (Notre Dame; University of Notre Dame Press, 1987).

a problem for the church — if, from within the very life of the Church, marriage looks as if it is "out of joint" with the church's norms — then it is incumbent upon Christians to deal with this problem as a vital ecclesiological matter. The church, which is the gathering of Christ's faithful, is itself "made up of kinds of conduct that congeal into relationships and then sub-societies of the inclusive society." As Theodore Mackin goes on to observe:

> Marriage is the most substantial of these sub-societies. If the church does not understand marriage in its nature she does not understand her own. For the church's nature is to be a society in which the belief, the trust and the caring love absolutely necessary for happiness are learned and carried on. But these are learned and carried on in families first and more than in any other relationship.[2]

When Christian marriages and families lose their sense of belonging and purpose within the community of faith, the church is weakened; and lessened is its ability to witness to Christ and his Kingdom. This is a great loss to a world in need of redemption.

---

rimony as determined by tradition. Here it takes its place within a narrative setting, the "story" of marriage being told multivocally through a typological hermeneutic. In the Byzantine rite, for example, Ephesians 5:32 is read during the royal procession when the bride and groom are crowned and declared king and queen of a new creation, a new "kingdom," a type of the church. Thus marriage participates in a divine mystery, the fullness of which is revealed in Christ and the church. The reading of the story of the marriage at Cana (John 2) follows almost immediately thereafter to reinforce this. For according to the Johannine theology the miracle of the wine is the first sign of the in-breaking Kingdom of God. It seems almost obvious from what one finds in the rite that a theological interpretation going on in the rite itself endows these passages with sacramental meaning even beyond any such meaning they might obtain in the Gospel or Pauline contexts.

2. Theodore Mackin, S.J., *What Is Marriage* (Ramsey, N.J.: Paulist Press, 1982). p. 328.

The Nature of Marriage

John L. Boojamra has observed that "even monasticism makes sense only in the context of family as a mutualistic paradigm and is justified only in the context of a fallen world, a world misshapen by sin and separation. In a world whose purpose was clear and undirectional . . . the family would be the norm as the Genesis account (Gen 2:18) makes clear."[3] This basic theological affirmation about human sociality provides the source for an Orthodox ethic of marriage and family. The second chapter of Genesis illumines marriage (and the family) as a natural institution of human life rooted in the creative activity of God. Through marriage and family God enables human beings to participate in his creative activity and redemptive purpose. There belongs a "natural" sacramentality to marriage even in its fallen condition. This sacramentality, like the image of God in humankind, was not lost entirely with the primal act of disobedience and deviance from the normativity of being human. Marriage need not be reinvented by Christians. Its character and intentionality, however, must change from selfishness, carnality, and possessiveness to being married "in the Lord." Marriage must be reconnected with the divine purpose through its full integration into the sacramental life of the church, centered, as that life is, in the renewing and nurturing actions of baptism and eucharistic assembly.

Marriage, it is true, is grounded in the natural sociality of the human species. This sociality is unthinkable without rationality and the freedom of the will peculiar only to human beings. But marriage derives also from natural and biological necessity (e.g., sexual attraction, the lengthy dependency of human offspring). As Basil wrote in his *Long Rules,* we need one another because no one of us "is self-sufficient as regards corporeal necessities, . . . God, the Creator, decreed that we should require the help of one another, . . . so that we might associate with one another."[4] However, marital community, unlike the monasticism

3. Boojamra, "Theological and Pedagogical," p. 7.

4. Basil, *The Long Rules,* in *St. Basil: The Ascetical Works,* trans. M. Monica Wagner, *The Fathers of the Church,* vol. 9 (New York: Fathers of the Church, 1950), p. 248.

which Basil sought to found, is fixed in human sexuality. Human sexuality is no simple instinct for perpetuation of the species either. It is itself compounded of human freedom and *eros*. Sexual exchange is integral to marital love and the union which marriage signifies. In human life "love penetrates to the very root of instinct and 'changes even the substance of things'" (1 Tim. 2:15).[5] The Orthodox Church describes sexual intercourse as *synousia,* a term which means consubstantiality. Husband and wife are joined together as *one* in holy matrimony. They are an ecclesial entity, one flesh, one body incorporate of two persons who in freedom and sexual love and through their relationship to Christ image the triune life of the Godhead and express the great mystery of salvation in Christ's relationship to the church.

Thus, according to Orthodox teaching, marriage is founded in a sexual love which, when not deviant, aspires toward perfect union with the other. This union is the primary good of marriage. "Indeed from the beginning," wrote John Chrysostom in his homily on Ephesians 5:22-23, "God appears to have made a special provision for this union; and discoursing of the twain as one."[6] This means that marriage is no mere agreement or contract between two individuals. As Basil exhorts in the *Hexaemeron,* "May the bond of nature, may the yoke imposed by the blessing make as one those who were divided."[7] This union may be understood as an ethical imperative of marriage even as, paradoxically, it is also a divine gift, a blessed bond. Those who are married have an obligation to live a life together consistent with this norm of union. And this is not an obligation that the spouses owe only to themselves. It is an obligation owed to the church which marries them. Marriage is not, as some contemporary views have it — e.g.

the new "contractual marriages" — an utterly private, mutually agreed-upon relationship regulated by certain claims of one spouse upon the other and rights to certain goods or benefits which derive from living together. Such views deny the norms of unitive and communicative love as well as expansive community in marriage and replace them with a norm of separateness together for the sake of personal psychic satisfaction, self-fulfillment, and autonomous activity. An Orthodox ethic of marriage denies all claims of normative so-called natural egoism, self-interest, or autonomy. The first chapter of Genesis introduces the very first man and woman as one conjugal being, complementaries of one complete humanity.[8] This is declared to be good. Only with the intrusion of the demonic is this conjugal community of being, this "Adam-Eve," divided into two who are alienated from one another and their relationship disrupted by sexual shame and antagonism. Nevertheless, conjugal union and communion become fundamental analogues and metaphors in the Old Testament prophets for the alliance between God and his people and the restoration of humanity's original relationship to God. In the New Testament, marriage is a symbol for the personal, pleromic communion of God's Kingdom (Rev. 19).

---

8. John Chrysostom sums all this up in the following: "They come to be made into one body. See the mystery of love! If the two do not become one, they cannot increase; they can increase only by decreasing! How great is the strength of unity! God's ingenuity in the beginning divided one flesh into two; but he wanted to show that it remained one even after its division, so he made it impossible for either half to procreate without the other. Now do you see how great a mystery marriage is? From one man, Adam, he made Eve; then He reunited these two into one, so that their children would be produced from a single source. Likewise, husband and wife are not two, but one; if he is the head and she is the body, how can they be two? She was made from his side; so they are two halves of one organism." (John Chrysostom, *St. John Chrysostom on Marriage and Family Life,* trans. Catherine P. Roth and David Anderson [Crestwood, N.Y.: St. Vladimir's Seminary Press, 1986], p. 75 [homily 12 on Colossians 4:18]. Also available as "Homilies on Colossians," in *A Select Library of Nicene and Post-Nicene Fathers of the Christian Church,* First Series, Vol. 12 [Grand Rapids, Mich.: Wm. B. Eerdmans Publishing Co., 1956], p. 318 [homily 20].

---

5. Paul Evdokimov, "The Theology of Marriage," in *Marriage and Christian Tradition,* trans. St. Agnes Cunningham, S.S.C.M. (Techny. Ill.: Divine Word Publications, 1968), p. 89. See also Evdokimov's more exhaustive study. *The Sacrament of Love,* (Crestwood. N.Y.: St. Vladimir's Seminary Press, 1985).

6. John Chrysostom, "Homilies on Ephesians," p. 143 (homily 20).

7. Basil, *On the Hexaemeron,* in *Saint Basil: Exegetic Homilies,* trans. Sr. Agnes Way, C.D.P., *The Fathers of the Church,* vol. 46 (Washington, D.C.: Catholic University Press of America, 1963), p. 114 (homily 7).

Such an ethic of marriage is not limited to natural law. For that nature known through empirical science, however much it might yet reveal about its origins and inner workings, is fallen and deranged. As Christos Yannaras has said, "[Christian] marriage draws its identity not [only] from the natural relationship, but from the relationship in the realm of the Kingdom."[9] It is important to the Orthodox understanding of marriage as sacrament that the Gospel of John — a reading from John 2 is included in all Eastern rites of matrimony — begins with the wedding at Cana where Christ transforms the water into wine, foreshadowing the Last Supper where wine becomes the blood of Christ.[10] In Orthodox theology natural marriage founded in *eros* is translated into an image of the Kingdom of God, a way of witnessing to the Cross and participating in the communion of saints. "If the monk converts *eros* by sublimation, conjugal love effects its transformation by opening onto divine love,"[11] writes Paul Evdokimov. Conjugal union, the primary good and norm of marriage, is achieved as natural *eros* transcends itself in a movement of reciprocal self-gift of one spouse to the other. *Eros* enters into the dynamic of *agape* which, as Basil described it, "'seeketh not her own'... [and is not] concerned only with ... private interests," but is in service "to many that they might be saved."[12] Conjugal union makes agapic love possible. Marriage (as well as Basilian cenobitic monasticism) is a way in which human beings are enabled through the grace of God to overcome their *unnatural* separateness and to perfect that mutual love for which humanity was created.

In the Armenian Rite of Holy Matrimony two prayers are said immediately following the crowning of the bride and groom and just before their enthronement. In these prayers the norms of conjugal union and communion are evoked and their relation to the other goods of marriage is established. The clear meaning in word, symbol, and action is that the union of two who were once separate serves a social — even public — end, has its being in an ecclesiological setting, and prepares persons for the eschatological advent of God's Kingdom. The first prayer reads in part:

> We beseech thee, O Lord, bless this marriage, as thou didst bless the marriage of the holy patriarchs, and keep them spotless in spiritual love and in one accord during their lives.
>
> Bless, O Lord, and make their marriage fruitful with offspring, if it be thy will, so that they may inherit a life of virtuous behavior for the glory of thy all-holy name.... And make them worthy to attain the undispoilable joys of the heavenly nuptials, together with all thy saints.[13]

In this prayer spiritual love and a mutual accord are singled out as the highest goods of marriage. But conjugal union and communion are not ends in themselves. They are described as the basis for a virtuous life whose context is community with others. Children are a gift and blessing which will deepen and extend this agapic community. The family is a school for that personal and virtuous life which prepares persons of a character willing to do service to others and fit for the Kingdom of God. Through the gift of children God forges husband and wife into persons they never imagined they could be. Children teach their parents humility, tolerance, patience, and how to deal with their own limitations. But a child's presence is also the opportunity which God provides parents for discovering within themselves the capacity to love without measure, to forgive and redeem the lives of others.

The second prayer of the Armenian rite begins with a recollection of the marriages of "Abraham and Sarah, of Isaac and Rebecca, of Jacob and Rachel, of Joachim and Anna, of Zacharia and Elizabeth." These marriages the Lord blessed and by them God kept his covenant and promise. These righteous were forerunners of the Kingdom by whose example those being married not only are instructed in the virtues of the Kingdom but are assured of God's steadfast love and intention

---

9. Christos Yannaras, *The Freedom of Morality,* trans. Elizabeth Briere (Crestwood, N.Y.: St. Vladimir's Seminary Press, 1984), p. 162.

10. Evdokimov, "Theology of Marriage," pp. 71-72.

11. Ibid., p. 74.

12. Basil, *Long Rules,* p. 248.

13. *The Blessing of Marriage or The Canon of the Rite of Holy Matrimony according to the Usage of the Armenian Apostolic Orthodox Church* (New York: Armenian Church Publications, 1953), p. 54.

to make them also heirs of the Kingdom of God. "We pray thee [bless] the crowning of these thy servants into marriage, as thou didst bless the crowns of thy righteous. For thou hast made these thy servants to arrive at thy sweet blessing and hast placed upon their heads a crown of precious gems." The wedding at Cana is then mentioned as proof that Christ brought marriage into the orbit of his priestly service to the Kingdom.[14] And this is followed by the invocation of those virtues appropriate to marriage. But rather than citing the Armenian rite it would do well to quote a portion of the Coptic prayer of crowning. It is a powerful example of the intimate link between ethics and eschatology within Eastern Christianity's vision of marriage.

> Holy Lord, who crowned your holy ones with untainted crowns and joined things heavenly with things earthly in unity, . . . bless these crowns, which we have prepared, in order to place them on your servants; may they be for them the crown of glory and honour. Amen. The crown of blessing and health. Amen. The crown of rejoicing and good fortune. Amen. The crown of jubilation and gladness. Amen. The crown of virtue and justice. Amen. The crown of wisdom and understanding. Amen. Grant lavishly on your servants who wear them the angel of peace and the bond of love, deliver them from every wicked thought, and evil assaults of the devil; may your mercy be over them, hear the cry of their prayer; set fear of you in their hearts, rule their lives, so that they may live to a long old age, may they rejoice in gazing upon sons and daughters, and whoever they may bring to birth may they be useful in your one and only holy Catholic and Apostolic Church, confirmed through Orthodox faith.[15]

This prayer expresses a powerful sense of the presence of God in Christian marriage and of marriage being "in the Lord." The first blessings which God is asked to bestow upon the married couple are dispositions of joyfulness, gladness, and well-being. These blessings invoke the image of the great banquet of God's Kingdom and the wedding of the Lamb. Marital blessedness is a foretaste of that eschatological event mentioned in Revelation: "'Alleluia! The Lord our God, sovereign over all, has entered on his reign! Exult and shout for joy and do him homage, for the wedding-day of the Lamb has come.' . . . 'Happy are those who are invited to the wedding supper of the Lamb!'" (Rev. 19:7-9 NEB). Marital union is the very image of that last day when, as the author of Revelation states, "I saw a new heaven and a new earth, for the first heaven and the first earth had vanished, and there was no longer any sea. I saw the holy city, new Jerusalem, coming down out of heaven from God, made ready like a bride adorned for her husband. I heard a loud voice proclaiming from the throne: 'Now at last God has his dwelling among men! He will dwell among them and they will be his people, and God himself will be with them'" (Rev. 21:1-3 NEB).

There is no question in the Coptic prayer that the blessed bond of marriage is a matter of both personal and corporate destiny. "Is marriage an end in itself — or is it part of a nurture fitting us more ably for larger purposes?"[16] asks Donna Schaper. Her answer is the same as that given in the Coptic prayer and in similar prayers of the Eastern rites of matrimony. Marriage *is* a preparation for larger purposes. Were marriage an end in itself, the suffering and tragedy, the boredom and anxiety, the spitefulness and psychological laceration of self and others which it also often includes would be intolerable, a sure sign of the futility, meanness, and meaninglessness of life. However, "the church," as Schaper observes, "historically has understood marriage as a sacrament, an adventure into impossible commitment which has divine sanction, encouragement, and blessing."[17] Perhaps "impossible" is too strong a word. But certainly marriage is from the standpoint of Orthodox theology an eschatological commitment and venture in faith.

Orthodoxy understands sacramental marriage to be a gift bestowed upon the couple by God through the church. The sacrament of marriage is

---

14. *Rite of Holy Matrimony (Armenian)*, p. 55.

15. Quoted by Kenneth Stevenson, *Nuptial Blessing* (New York: Oxford University Press, 1983), pp. 111-12.

16. Donna Schaper, "Marriage: The Impossible Commitment," in *Moral Issues and Christian Response*, ed. Paul T. Jersild and Dale A. Johnson (New York: Holt, Rinehart & Winston, 1983), p. 103.

17. Ibid.

a passage from natural and fallen marriage into the new order of Christ's Kingdom. Marriage which is of this order would be impossible indeed, were it dependent solely upon human will. But Christian marriage is itself a medicine which heals the ruptured relationship of men and women by uniting them through grace within the eschatological community of the church. One great failure of the Western, particularly Roman Catholic, theology of marriage, is that it lost sight of this eschatological promise in marriage and the Christian vocation bestowed upon the couple by the church. Roman Catholic moral theology went far toward reducing marriage to a legal contract, a guarantee of certain rights and privileges between the contracting individuals, which terminates in death. The language of the Coptic prayer insists upon the extralegal spiritual reality of marriage as communion with God and service to his Kingdom. God bestows upon the married couple the dispositions and virtues necessary for building up his Kingdom. And in all the Eastern rites children are counted as spiritual blessings which strengthen the little church of the family, increasing its service to God and extending it from one generation to the next until Christ's second coming. Lest there be any confusion about it, the force of this logic is not utilitarian; it is eschatological.

Again in contrast to earlier Roman Catholic moral theology, the Eastern theology could never define procreation as the primary purpose of marriage. Procreation obtains a fully human value only when it occurs within a relationship which is characterized by *unselfish and unitive love*. One of the oldest prayers of the Byzantine rite orders the goods of marriage with special clarity. "Unite them in one mind: wed them in one flesh, granting unto them of the fruit of the body and the procreation of fair children."[18] And in typical Eastern fashion the Coptic prayer refers the blessing of children to the greater service to God to which all those married and "familied" "in the Lord" are called. "May they rejoice in gazing upon sons and daughters, and whoever they bring to birth may

they be *useful in your one and only holy Catholic and Apostolic Church* [my emphasis], confirmed in Orthodox faith."[19]

In the Armenian rite these ecclesiological and eschatological themes are phrased in the imagery of the Psalms. The prayer following the crowning beseeches God to "plant them [the couple] as a fruitful tree, in the house of God, . . . living in righteousness, in purity, and godliness." Such marriage is the context in which children ought to be raised and a family nurtured whose activity becomes a service to the Church. The Armenian prayer speaks of children as a fruit or blessing of marriage and asks that the spouses "live to an age that they may see the children of their children and [that] they may be a people unto thee and glorify thy holy name, and bless the all-holy Trinity."[20] Thus the special insight of the Armenian prayer is not only that children are gifts of God but that covenanted marriage "in the Lord" is the son of relationship most fit for the nurture of children who will become heirs to God's promise of salvation which he made to the patriarchs and revealed fully in Jesus Christ. Children are a gift and blessing, a human reflection within the union of husband and wife of the power and plenitude of the divine nature. And children who become "a people unto God" are an even greater gift and reward of marriage well lived. Christian marriage is the beginning of a "small church, the smallest and most important social unit of Christ's body in the world. Marriage envisioned as sacrament. lived out in marital fidelity, gives hope for steadfast love and enduring communion even beyond the brokenness of all human relationships, including marriage itself. Christian family is a promise, enfleshed in the form of children, of a future filled with joy.

*   *   *

The Ascetical Meaning of Marriage

Unlike the Roman Catholic Church, the Orthodox Church has not established formally a hierarchy of Christian life in which celibacy is designated a

18. Isabel Florence Hapgood, ed. and trans., *Service Book of the Holy Orthodox-Catholic Apostolic Church* (Englewood, N.J.: Antiochian Orthodox Christian Archdiocese, 1975), p. 297.

19. Stevenson, *Nuptial*, p. 112.
20. *Rite of Holy Matrimony (Armenian)*, p. 56.

higher state of Christian living than marriage. In fact, married life and the raising of a family has been described at times within the Orthodox tradition as a more difficult and courageous vocation than that of celibacy.[21] The Russian dissident priest Dmitri Dudko has stated in one of his famous dialogues with the faithful, translated in the West under the title *Our Hope*, "So build your domestic church — the family — together. This is the great ascetic feat of Christianity."[22] The tradition supports this affirmation of the high ethical value of Christian marriage. Clement of Alexandria wrote in Book 7 of the *Stromateis*:

> And true manhood is shown not in the choice of a celibate life; on the contrary the prize in the contest of men is won by him who has trained himself by the discharge of the duties of husband and father and by the supervision of a household, regardless of pleasure and pain — by him, I say, who in the midst of his solicitude for his family shows himself inseparable from the love of God and rises superior to every temptation which assails him through children and wife and servants and possessions. On the other hand he who has no family is in most respects untried. In any case, as he takes thought only for himself, he is inferior to one who falls short of him as regards his own salvation, but who has the advantage in the conduct of life, in as much as he actually preserves a faint image of the true providence.[23]

As Clement emphasized the ascetical struggle which is a component of the married state and the divine similitude which a husband obtains

---

21. I do not want to leave the impression that the tradition is settled on this matter. In contrast to the Roman Catholic Church, within Orthodoxy a certain ambivalence pertaining to it was allowed to stand. This ambivalence is present even within the writings of singular authors such as Clement of Alexandria, who is cited in the text which follows. Here I quote at length Paul Evdokimov's way of describing the issue. My own interpretation as developed in the following pages is strongly sympathetic with that of Evdokimov. See *Sacrament of Love*, pp. 65-66:

> There is no reason, except a pedagogic one . . . , to call one path or the other the preeminent Christianity, since what is valid for all of Christendom is thereby valid for each of the two states. The East has never made the distinction between the "precepts" and the "evangelical counsels." The gospel in its totality is addressed to each person; everyone in his own situation is called to the *absolute* of the gospel. Trying to prove the superiority of one state over the other is therefore useless: it is an abstract, because impersonal, process. The renunciation at work in both cases is as good as the positive content that the human being brings to it: the intensity of the love of God.
>
> St. Paul's pastoral sense seeks the fulfillment of an undivided service. The nuptial community, which is the "domestic church," and the monastic community shed light upon each other and help one another in this same service. Church doctrine has never lost sight of this balance. Councils and synods have defended it against the assaults of Manichaeism and extreme spirituality.

Evdokimov mentions some interesting examples of how in practice within the *ordo* and tradition marriage and celibacy actually do "shed light upon each other and help one another in . . . [the] same service." (Ibid., p. 66.)

> In marriage the nature of man is changed sacramentally, as it is, though in another mode, in the one who becomes a monk. The deepest inner relationship unites the two. The promises exchanged by the betrothed introduce them in a certain manner into a special monasticism, because here too there is a dying to the past and a rebirth into a new life. Moreover, the rite of entrance into the monastic order makes use of nuptial symbolism (the terms

"betrothed" and "spouse"), while the ancient marriage rite included the monastic tonsure, signifying the common surrender of the two wills to God. Thus marriage includes within itself the monastic state, and that is why the latter is not a sacrament. The two converge as complementary aspects of the same virginal reality of the human spirit. The ancient Russian tradition viewed the time of engagement as a monastic novitiate. After the marriage ceremony, a retreat in a monastery was prescribed for the newly married to prepare for entrance into their "nuptial priesthood" (Ibid., p. 68).

22. Dmitri Dudko, *Our Hope* (Crestwood, N.Y.: St. Vladimir's Seminary Press, 1975), p. 57.

23. Clement of Alexandria, "On Spiritual Perfection" (*Stromateis* 7), trans. John Ernest Leonard Oulton and Henry Chadwick, in *Alexandrian Christianity, The Library of Christian Classics*, vol. 3 (London: SCM Press, 1954), p. 138.

through selfless giving to wife and children, so John Chrysostom made it clear in his homily 7 on Hebrews that the highest Christian virtues are not the exclusive reserve of monks. People who are married are called by Christ to a life no less virtuous than that of those who have chosen a monastic life. Addressing married persons who would make excuses for their behavior by invoking their married state, Chrysostom said: "And if these beatitudes were spoken to solitaries only, and the secular person cannot fulfill them, yet he [Christ] permitted marriage, then he has destroyed all men. For if it be not possible, with marriage, to perform the duties of solitaries, all things have perished and are destroyed, and the functions of virtues are shut up in a strait." Chrysostom's argument is not just about the morality of Christians, married or celibate, either. It is an argument which dismisses all notions that the institution of marriage is inferior in God's plan of salvation or fails in its nature to serve his purpose. "And if persons have been hindered by marriage state, let them know that marriage is not the hindrance, but their purpose which made an ill use of marriage. Since it is not wine which makes drunkenness, but the evil purpose, and the using it beyond due measure. Use marriage with moderation, and thou shalt be first in the Kingdom."[24]

Nowhere in Orthodox tradition or practice is the high ascetical value and significance of marriage more strongly affirmed than in the central action of the rite of matrimony, the Service of Crowning. The crowns (or garlands) placed on the heads of the bride and groom have been understood in the Pauline sense as a proleptic sign of the victory of life over death, as Christians are compared to athletes who run a race under a strict discipline (I Cor. 9:24-25). The Eastern rites of matrimony identify the highest virtue of this discipline as chastity. God is asked in an opening prayer of the Service of Crowning in the Byzantine rite to "bless this marriage, as he blessed that in Cana of Galilee: That he will grant unto them [the bride and groom] chastity, and of the fruit of the womb as is expedient [of good benefit] for

them: That he will make them glad with the sight of sons and daughters."[25] Marital chastity obviously does not exclude sexual love. This is evident from the link between chastity and the blessing of children in the Byzantine prayer. Chastity purifies and transforms human love into the abundance, richness, pleromic communion, and joy of the Kingdom, just as Christ transformed the water into wine for the wedding banquet. True marriage requires giving up the sinful desire to possess, to control, and to use others for self-gratification or self-glorification. But conjugal chastity is not so limited or negative as continence. It is not primarily a remedy for sin or concupiscence as continence is in much of medieval Western moral theology. Conjugal chastity is understood in the Orthodox theology of marriage as an *askesis* of the spirit which elevates our nature and transforms the life together of husband and wife into a true communion. In the Armenian rite the prayer of crowning asks God to unite the couple "in the spirit of meekness, loving one another with modest behaviour, pure spirit, without giving cause for shame, without impudence always ready for good works."[26] Conjugal chastity is compared in the Byzantine rite to the virginal purity of Mary in her perfect obedience to God and to the holiness of the church as the bride of Christ.

In the Byzantine rite of matrimony, after the couple has drunk from the common cup and as they are led three times around the lectern in symbolic dance and celebration of their union and journey together for eternity in God's presence, the choir sings several hymns. They express in terse biblical language and by allusion to the whole story of salvation the Orthodox vision of marriage.

> Rejoice, O Isaiah! A virgin is with child, and shall bear a Son, Emmanuel, both God and man; and Orient is his name; whom magnifying we call the virgin blessed.
>
> O Holy martyrs, who fought the good fight and have received your crowns: Entreat ye the Lord that he will have mercy on your souls.
>
> Glory to thee, O Christ-God, the apostles'

---

24. John Chrysostom, "Homilies on the Hebrews," in *A Select Library of the Nicene and Post-Nicene Fathers of the Christian Church* (New York: Christian Literature Co., 1890), p. 402 (homily 7).

25. Hapgood, *Service Book*, p. 294.
26. *Rite of Holy Matrimony (Armenian)*, p. 56.

boast, the martyrs' joy, whose preaching was the consubstantial Trinity.[27]

Through the invocation of the Virgin and her son, Emmanuel, the first stanza (or hymn) recalls the whole theme of the New Creation — celebrated with such magnificent beauty on the Orthodox Feast of Epiphany. Conjugal love is like the virginal purity of Mary, who in her perfect obedience to God gave birth to the "first-born of all creation, . . . the first-born from the dead" (Col. 1:15-18 RSV). The second stanza mentions the holy martyrs, who, by their unselfish witness to the promise of salvation in Jesus Christ, confirmed that their own deaths were a birth into the new life of the Kingdom. The last stanza praises Christ, in whom the faith of all believers rests and by whom also the joy of communion in God is insured.

When natural marriage is elevated to a sacrament of the Church, it becomes a witness to the new creation in Christ. In a sinful world, such a witness inevitably requires *self*-sacrifice, that *self* understood as the ego which in spite of its pretensions to autonomy is captive to sin and death. Marriage is a form of martyrdom. The possessive self-serving ego is put to death and a new self is born, free and in mutual accord and in service to others. Marriage is an image and a proleptic experience of the New Creation in which *eros*, purified by chastity and freed from lust, is sublimated into a selfless desire and active concern for the well-being of the other (i.e., compassion). Likewise, self-sacrifice is translated into a free communion unconstrained by sin or natural necessity: Marriage is made an entrance into the Kingdom by crucifixion *(askesis)*. Indicative of this, ancient Christian wedding rings were cast "with two profiles united by a cross."[28] With like significance, in the Byzantine rite of matrimony, before the bride and groom drink from the common cup and dance the dance of Isaiah, they must wear the crowns of martyrdom. Finally a Christian marriage testifies to the fact that the "newness of life" (Rom. 6:4 RSV) is not an individualistic pursuit of salvation. There is an ancient usage no longer followed in the Armenian and Syrian rites

for the couple to exchange baptismal crosses.[29] This is a powerful symbol of the fact that the bride and groom surrender their destinies to one another and both together to Christ and the church. Christian marriage is marriage "in the Lord" because the two who are wed *already* have been united with Christ through baptism. Through baptism they have become imitators and followers of Christ. This priestly vocation is one which baptized Christians bring to marriage. Marriage does not confer it upon them. However, marriage does expand the scope of that priestly service. Marriage commences a relationship and provides an institutional framework in which the individual witness of the two can become a mutual service and take on a social and public dimension prefiguring the Kingdom. Thus, the full Christian meaning of marriage is comprehensible only when a marriage is lived within the context of the whole life of the church. Like monastic community, marriage is an *institution* with a purpose which transcends the personal goals or purposes of those who enter into it. It is an upbuilding of the church in service to the Kingdom. Marriage is not only something which happens to the individuals who are wed and the children which they bear by the grace of God. Marriage is something which happens in and to the whole church.

---

27. Hapgood, *Service Book,* p. 300.
28. Evdokimov, "Theology of Marriage," p. 101.

29. Ibid., p. 98.

58. Misogyny and Homophobia: The Unexplored Connections[1]

BEVERLY W. HARRISON

The Dualisms that Shape the Problem

Some years ago, philosopher Dorothea Krook observed that ecclesiastical statements regarding sexuality exemplify an antisensual ambivalence. Citing the Anglican bishops' *Lambeth Report on Sexuality*[2] as evidence of her thesis, she pointed out that the bishops begin well enough by criticizing any "false dualism" that makes it impossible to affirm physical love unequivocally. Then, however, their affirmation of sexuality is hedged, and finally they vigorously disapprove of any sexual expression outside of marital sexual relations. Krook concludes,

> In spite of their statements to the contrary, sexual love for the bishops is, it seems, physical, unspir-

1. This essay is a revision of one that was published in *Integrity Forum* 7:2 (1981), pp. 7-13, and excerpted and republished in *Church and Society* (November/December 1982).
2. Dorothea Krook, *Three Traditions of Moral Thought* (Cambridge: Cambridge University Press, 1959), pp. 333-347.

Beverly W. Harrison (1932–) is the Carolyn Williams Beaird Professor of Christian Ethics at Union Theological Seminary. Her work includes *Making the Connections: Essays in Feminist Social Ethics* and *Our Right to Choose: Toward a New Ethic of Abortion.*

From Beverly W. Harrison, *Making the Connections* (Boston: Beacon Press, 1985).

itual, "carnal," or "sensual" in a way that parental and pastoral love are not.[3]

The body, we may note, simply is not understood as mediating spirituality directly. The bishops' statement clearly reflects two differing and contradictory attitudes toward sexuality.

To grasp the connections between misogyny and homophobia, we need to examine this problematic tendency of Christian theological tradition to neglect, ignore, or denigrate the body. This tendency is not characteristic only of the dominant traditions of Christianity; it is expressed in the spiritualities and official ideologies of dominant groups in every society, and more especially those of males who rule over and represent the masculinist norms of those societies. Such spiritualities sacralize mental activity or consciousness as "higher" than the rest of physical existence. Thus we are conditioned by religious and philosophical orthodoxy, or the official doctrines of the elites, to view the body and bodily needs as "lower," "animal" modalities of existence that have to be tamed or in some way overcome and transcended by a higher and loftier power that is "really" rational and spiritual. This assumption of a tension between what is most deeply "spiritual" and our physical embodiment and physical needs runs so deep in Christian culture that accepting the priority of mind over body, as if mind is not a function of body experienced in a certain way, or the "transcendence" of spirit over nature, is often held to be the essence of religious conviction. "To believe" comes to mean believing such nonsense. To be religious then involves living and acting as though a split between lower "nature" and consciousness were part of fundamental reality. The connections between homophobia and misogyny are sustained by the depth of this anti-body, antisensual bias of dominant Christianity. While these anti-body attitudes do not fully explain our society's revulsion from homosexuality or any sexual "deviance," they are an important part of the story. The fear of the power of, and revulsion from sexuality itself is an important element in homophobia. Homosexuality, in our social and cultural context, represents a break with the strongest and

3. Krook, *Three Traditions of Moral Thought*, p. 342.

most familiar control on sexuality — compulsory heterosexuality — and thus is a break with that strong social patterning which, because it is familiar, makes sexuality seem safe and conventionally channeled. Homosexuality then becomes a strong metaphor for active, freely expressed sexuality. Many imagine that we have moved beyond the Christian legacy of affirming sexuality only within marriage, for the purpose of procreation, but these ancient constraints on our behavior live on in a generalized uneasiness about "loose" or unchanneled sexuality as dangerous. Any demand that homoeroticism be accepted as "healthy" therefore calls us to recognize that sexuality itself is good not merely when channeled in "reputable" and well-patterned ways but good per se.

One of the many reasons to celebrate James Nelson's fine book *Embodiment: An Approach to Sexuality and Christian Theology*[4] is that it is among the first theological treatments of sexuality to grapple deeply and frankly with this anti-body dualism in the Christian tradition. Even more important, however, is Nelson's recognition of another and related dualism that has shaped and distorted Christian history vis-à-vis sexuality. Nelson rightly connects this other dualism — male/female dualism, predicated on the view that male and female are fundamentally different, even "opposites," and that maleness is superior — with the rejection of the body.

The value accorded female "being" varies somewhat from society to society, but all existing societies are in some degree male supremacist, so male nature is held to be expressive of full humanity while female nature is held to be different from and of less value than male human nature. Male "nature" also is perceived as more complex and subtle because it is characteristic of genuine, full humanity. Whatever the value of femaleness in a given dualistic culture, women were believed to lack some ingredient necessary for the full range of ideal human functioning. In contemporary Western culture, most often, women are perceived

as lacking the full range of what we mean by rationality. As a result, many "feel" safer when men are "in charge."

An interesting variant of this ideology aimed at assuring male control was developed in the nineteenth century to prolong male dominance in the wake of the first organized women's movement and early feminism. It came to be believed then that women have a different sort of rational capacity than men have. We were said to be more "genteel" and to possess deeper "feeling," to be more sensitive morally. Such pedestalism was nothing more than a last-ditch effort to keep women in "our place" for this presumed distinctive "femininity" (a notion invented only in the nineteenth century) was never presumed to be important at the centers of power or decision making in society. Where commerce or the arts of statecraft were practiced, such qualities were dismissed as "sentimental" and "weak," much as they were being praised wherever women gathered. Unfortunately for Christianity, this sentimentalized pedestalism was adopted and eventually even "proclaimed" by Christian churches as a second-rate substitute for feminist justice. The result was a sentimentalized church, not transformation of women's lives.

We will never get the morality of male/female relations straightened out within Christianity until this pattern of male supremacy comes to be recognized for what it is — misogyny, or the hatred of women. Like all historical oppression, the practice of male supremacy over time breeds real hostility to women, hostility that runs deeper in this society than most people — especially Christians — wish to acknowledge. Since men and women live in such proximity, hostility toward women often takes on masked, mystified, or covert forms. Often it presents itself as patronizing superiority toward women's "foibles" or is expressed in slightly contemptuous humor. It will take the form of contemptuous downplaying of "women's concerns" or the effort to trivialize. A major unrecognized index of hostility against women is the degree of indirect manipulation of women's actions, use of flirtation or seductive patterns of control aimed at making sure that women respond "sweetly." The hostility toward women as a group, implicit in the pedestalism or the romanticization of the "good" (read "unassertive") woman, is rarely perceived but is powerful none-

4. James B. Nelson, *Embodiment: An Approach to Sexuality and Christian Theology* (Minneapolis: Augsburg Press, 1979). See also his *Between Two Gardens: Reflections on Sexuality and Religious Experience* (New York: Pilgrim Press, 1983).

theless. The real face of misogyny is exposed clearly only when a woman, or groups of women, behave in strong, together, assertive ways. In fact, we can identify the true measure of misogyny only by noting how strong and independent women are received. Strong women are invariably perceived and described as "aggressive" and "hostile." Where a woman, or a group of women, are competent and self-reliant, not easily controlled, others will be threatened and they in turn will project *their* hostility onto that woman or group. Rage toward women is pervasive, and invariably it is the women who point this out who become its most conspicuous victims.

It is an error to imagine that in a misogynist society antiwoman feelings are learned only by men. All of us, male and female, learn antiwoman feelings and attitudes, just as all of us, whatever our erotic practice, learn antihomosexual feelings and attitudes. Women express such antiwoman feelings by acts and attitudes of self-abnegation and by refusing to value ourselves and/or other women as much as we value men. But it is also true that women cooperate with misogyny to avoid the rage that noncompliance looses. As long as women cooperate in our subjugation, as long as we are gently unassertive or relatively undemanding, male hostility toward us expresses itself only in gentler forms. But as the massive, sustained, and universal patterns of violence toward women in this and other societies makes clear, rage toward women lies just beneath the surface of all of our social relations and our institutional life. Women's "weakness" is, often, women's unnamed terror of this reality.

Only a genuine feminist analysis, one that advocates women's well-being, can clarify why antibody, antinature dualism has had such a powerful hold on our traditions. These dualisms are irreducibly related core theses in the ideology of control developed by the ruling male elites of a patriarchal social system to keep their power in place and women in theirs. In fact, the anti-body dualism of Christian culture is so tenacious precisely because it sustains the other dualism — the male/female dualism — which in turn grounds male superiority and privilege. Patriarchal ideology idealizes disembodied rationality and the disinterested and detached modes of experience characteristic of the way of life of dominant male

groups. A feminist moral theology, by contrast, affirms the bodily grounded experience and struggle of women and nonruling groups of males and seeks to demystify and expose "spiritualistic" theories of human nature generated to perpetuate male dominance. Only when we begin to recognize that the feminist analysis is correct, that *social control of women as a group has totally shaped our deepest and most basic attitudes toward sexuality,* do we comprehend the full social functionality of enforcing compulsory heterosexuality on both women and men. The only "respectable" alternative to compulsory heterosexuality in our culture is, of course, asexuality or celibacy.

Toward an Understanding of the Historical-Cultural Connections between Homophobia and Misogyny

We need a clearer historical appreciation for the ways in which the long-standing and deeply rooted antipathy toward women in Western, Christian tradition interacted with and became entwined with anti-body, antisensual attitudes if we are also to understand why we have reached the place where the stigma of homosexuality incorporates and encompasses all of the power dynamics of misogyny. Until we develop such an analysis, we will not even begin to appreciate why homophobia is such an intense madness among us or why homophobic frenzy thrives so in the churches. Feminists and a few others have begun to pursue the concrete historical connections between the antisexual phobia that came to characterize large sectors of Christendom and the antifemale bias so strong, continuous, and as yet untranscended in Christian history.[5] Such speculation is, as yet, very provisional. Much further investigation is needed to give precision to these matters. A feminist critique must reopen fully a

5. Rosemary Radford Ruether, *New Woman: New Earth* (New York: Seabury Press, 1975); Linda Gordon, *Woman's Body, Woman's Right: A Social History of Birth Control in America* (New York: Penguin, 1974); also "Women: Sex and Sexuality," *Signs* 5, no. 4 (Summer 1980), reprinted as Catherine R. Stimpson and Ethel Specter Person, eds., *Women: Sex and Sexuality* (Chicago: University of Chicago Press, 1980).

Pandora's box of issues. Not only must we reconsider sex role definitions, that is, what is held to be the proper province of male and female activity, but we must also examine the entire range of assumptions and definitions that mapped socialization into what was accepted as "normal" gender identity in all of its aspects, including notions of what has constituted "normal eroticism"[6] in various cultures and epochs. Historians such as John Boswell have begun to identify some evidence to describe the diversity and pluralism of attitudes toward sexuality and male homosexuality in Christian history,[7] but a full picture will require examining the development of compulsory heterosexuality as a social institution and its social and political enforcement.

Neither of those ancient cultural traditions usually considered to have nurtured Christianity — the early Israelite, or Hebraic, and the classic Greek — reflected an antisexual bias that came to characterize Christian history. Ancient Israelite culture was a physically oriented culture, one in which sexuality, at least in its heterosexual expressions, was not only affirmed but celebrated. John Boswell, among other exegetes,[8] has also provided evidence for an appropriate skepticism about the once widely accepted view that Israelite culture was antihomosexual and homophobic. Hellenic culture was neither antisexual nor antiho-moerotic. It celebrated eroticism and basically affirmed sensuality. Some have claimed that classical Greek culture was strongly antifemale and predominantly homoerotic. Certainly some of the great philosophers of the Greek tradition were antifemale, and the status of male-female relations in that culture is a much-disputed question. In any case, though, what is astonishing is how readily Christian tradition became antisexual and, simultaneously, misogynist and homophobic, given a twofold cultural heritage that was neither antisexual nor sharply homophobic.

Most current evidence suggests that misogyny is a far more consistent trend in Christian history than homophobia. Even in periods when homophobia was not intense,[9] there was still a strong pattern of disvaluing things associated with females. Given some of the reigning "scientific" assumptions, thoroughly imbued with patriarchal prejudice, males usually were viewed as sexually active "by nature" and females were held "by nature" to be passive or receptive. It appears that some male homosexual activity came to be despised because one male was understood to play the passive role, that is, was penetrated. One stigma of homosexuality, then, was that it "reduced" some men to the role of females[10] Similarly, the intensity of much contemporary homophobia confirms this continuing element in the revulsion against male homosexuality. Ho-

6. The theme of enforced heterosexuality as a social institution has been widely discussed by feminist theorists. However, heterosexism has been subtly internalized in feminist theory also. Now it is being recognized that heterosexism, historically, was a necessary extension of the system of sexist control aimed at assuring women's compliance to heterosexuality as "natural," because women's emotional bonding is otherwise likely to be with other women, as men's usually is with other men. See the excellent elaboration of this thesis in Adrienne Rich, "Compulsory Heterosexuality and Lesbian Existence," *Signs* 5, No. 4 (Summer 1980), pp. 631ff. See also Ann Ferguson, Jaquelyn N. Zita, and Kathryn Pyne Addelson, "On 'Compulsory Heterosexuality and Lesbian Existence': Defining the Issues," *Signs* 7, No. 1 (Autumn 1981), pp. 158-199. See also Lillian Faderman, *Surpassing the Love of Men: Romantic Friendship and Love Between Women from the Renaissance to the Present* (New York: Morrow, 1981).

7. John Boswell, *Christianity, Social Tolerance, and Homosexuality: Gay People in Western Europe from the Beginning of the Christian Era the the Fourteenth Century* (Chicago: University of Chicago Press, 1980). Boswell notes that etymologically *homophobia* means "fear of sameness," not "fear of homosexuality." He therefore declines to use the term, though he admits the force of the phenomenon to which it refers. While I am an admirer of Boswell's work, I find this to be a linguistic affectation. It is a mistake to assume that meaning can be discovered in etymology apart from usage.

8. See John J. McNeill, *The Church and the Homosexual* (Kansas City, Mo.: Sheed, Andrews, and McMeel, 1976), and Letha Scanzoni and Virginia Mollenkott, *Is the Homosexual My Neighbor? Another Christian View* (San Francisco: Harper and Row, 1978). Useful cross-cultural data on homosexuality may be found in Clellan S. Ford and Frank A. Beach, *Patterns of Sexual Behavior* (New York: Harpers, 1951).

9. Boswell, *Christianity, Social Tolerance, and Homosexuality*, pp. 50ff.

10. Boswell, *Christianity, Social Tolerance, and Homosexuality*. pp. 50ff.

moerotic men are perceived as failed men, no better than females. The widespread but empirically mistaken equation of male homosexuality with effeminacy is further evidence that the stigma of male homosexuality involves association with females and the "feminine." Though any connection between homoeroticism and "effeminate" personality characteristics has been totally discredited through social scientific research, the stereotype persists tenaciously in the nongay community.

The truth is that all nonwhite males, or males of cultural groups not endorsed by the dominant culture, are also seen in some degree as "effeminate." Sometimes this involves the accusation that one is controlled by feeling or is less "rational" than males of dominant racial and cultural groups, or more animalistic, rhythmic, or childlike. The depth of the hatred toward women is clearly reflected in this projection of female stigma onto any males who need to be distanced from dominant norms of "real manhood" for purposes of social control. Not surprisingly, the consequence is that men in oppressed groups who internalize this oppression often "answer back" to ruling-class men by acting out super-macho patterns of relationships to women in order to "disprove" any deficiency in their manhood. Some homosexual men also appear to attempt "expiation" of this female stigma by adopting super-macho patterns of sexual relationship. Male homosexual culture bears obvious marks of such compensation and the fear that male homosexuality may really be some sort of failure in "real" manhood.

The force of homophobia in the church and in some sectors of society is such that even the long-standing symbolic superiority of "maleness" does not appear adequate to explain it. Clearly, we are dealing with something even more highly charged than a simple male chauvinism and its convoluted consequences. Feminist historical scholarship leads us to suspect that the force of homophobia rests in yet a deeper social contradiction. To understand this contradiction we must connect two historical developments. First, we need to recognize that the hierarchicalization and centralization of the Catholic tradition of Christianity, including the solidification of power in priestly orders and in a centralized hierarchy, was the result of an active attack on the growing role of women in early Christianity.[11] We feminist theologians now believe that the development of "orthodoxy" in theology and church order was the result of an active effort to disempower women in early Christianity. Those groups within early Christianity that we viewed as deviant, heterodox, or "sectarian" turn out to have been those parts of the Christian community in which women played an extensive and strong role. The centralization of power within, and the creation of, a Catholic Christian tradition controlled by a male hierarchical elite rapidly engendered the rise within Christian theology of myths of feminine evil and images of woman either as temptress or perpetual Eve, as virgin or harlot. What this means is that a concrete power struggle over the definition of and the control of Christianity took place in the church and that the "male dominance" party won. As a result, a dominant Catholic hierarchy of Christianity, over time, became a male homophile organization, one of the most successful such organizations in human history. Whatever the historical details, the fact is that the priesthood and hierarchy of Catholic Christianity evolved as institutions predicated on and sustained by a powerful impulse of male bonding. Unless this is understood, the traumatic and sometimes bizarre reactions to the ordination of women and of gay men in the dominant churches will make no sense.

My own experience and that of other self-aware women attest that we literally can "feel" the visceral power of male/male bonding and the powerful energy sustaining such bonds when we enter a room full of men wearing clerical collars or ecclesiastical garb. Furthermore, when we listen to the rhetoric of bishops referring to their obliga-

11. Elaine Pagels, *The Gnostic Gospels* (New York: Random House, 1979). Elisabeth Schüssler Fiorenza, "Word, Spirit and Power: Women in Early Christian Communities," in *Women of Spirit: Female Leadership in Jewish and Christian Traditions*, ed. Rosemary Ruether and Eleanor McLaughlin (New York: Simon and Schuster, 1979); also see Fiorenza's *In Memory of Her: A Feminist Theological Reconstruction of Christian Origins* (New York: Crossroads, 1983). On the relationship of hierarchy and sex negativity, see Samuel Lauechli, *Power and Sexuality: The Emergence of Canon Law at the Synod of Elvira* (Philadelphia: Temple University Press, 1972).

tions to keep solidarity with "brother" bishops (by, for example, not supporting women's ordination) or hear them attest the "spiritual unity" of the church embodied in the community of bishops and priests, the power and depth of this male bonding are obvious. It is not too much to say that the feelings conveyed are deeply erotic.

This historical dynamic is, however, conjoined with another that conspires to forge the depth of the historical contradiction in which Christianity is trapped and, therefore, to generate the full force of its hysterical response to homosexuality. Not only is Christianity an institution characterized by deep male erotic bonds, but it is also the dominant institutional legitimizer of society's gender system of compulsory heterosexuality. The pressure to provide the ideology for maintaining compulsory heterosexuality and to sustain male homophile bonding creates chasms in consciousness. In such an institution, where actual relational patterns of male/male contact and regard run so contrary to the publicly endorsed, and therefore publicly permissible, patterns of eroticism, strictures *against* homosexual eroticism become almost violent and compulsive. Homosexuality *and* females both, simultaneously, threaten the uneasy balance of psychic forces and ideological functions that create the "security" of the institutional elite.

The fact is that in Christianity, considerable numbers of celibate male clergy and bishops are closeted homosexuals. This is surely one reason for the powerful resistance to sacrificing the exclusivity of male bonding through the inclusion of women in priestly orders. Often, closeted homosexual priests, those who embrace "celibacy" to cover their own sexual orientation and/or practice, lead the attack against the ordination of women. These same priests often join the attack not on homosexuality but on *gayness* — that is, on the act of being a *self*-affirming and *self*-respecting person who insists that homoeroticism is good and who wants to live a life of integrity, demanding respect that any person has a moral right to expect. In the Christian churches today the sexual sin is to wish to have your "public" and "private" lives integrated. The deepest rage is aimed not against the fact that there are homosexuals in the church but against the presence of gay men and open lesbians. Homosexuality is

tolerated if homosexual persons observe secrecy and practice hypocrisy!

The viciousness of what is going on in the churches around homosexuality is that many clergy are choosing to live lives of active duplicity with the church's public encouragement while large numbers of closeted homosexual clergy, to seek acceptance in the church, actively attack women and gay men. All of this threatens the spiritual integrity and lifeblood of Christianity. Closeted priests are not per se the problem. In a homophobic church and culture, no homosexual or lesbian should be expected to "come out of the closet" unless that person's personal or professional integrity or survival requires it. No one ever should be pressured to come out. What I am talking about is the *active* misrepresentation of the truth about human sexuality and the character assassination and moral blackmail that closeted homosexual male clergy are wreaking on women, especially lesbians, and on self-affirming gay male clergy. This situation is a scandal, and it is eroding the soul of Christianity.

Where human beings do not deal honestly and directly with their own sexuality, sexual anxiety rises and begins to mystify and obscure the basic power dynamics of the community. People live in fear of being exposed, and as a result they capitulate to corrupt power, giving away their own power of intellectual and moral judgment to a presumed higher "authority," without regard to the moral value of that "higher power." In addition, when basic issues of sexuality are too threatening to face, repression occurs and the source of all our energy is suppressed. As a result, the spirituality of a community becomes a vacuous, empty formalism, filled with effete and eccentric religiosity and ritual. The power of embodiment — of flesh and blood energy to live and grow — is lost.

It is time for male clergy and bishops to own how deeply male bonding runs, how contemptuous clerical males are of women and how fearful of all but dependent and "obedient" women. Whether male clergy or bishops' own erotic preferences are homosexual or heterosexual is irrelevant here. What is relevant is how all clerical males, and powerful lay men, relate to women, most especially to strong, self-respecting women. The test is whether they can relate to women fully as peers whose basic worth and way of being in the world are recognized as fully valuable as men's. It is also time for men to acknowledge, appreciate, and respect the fact that many women are living or choose to live homosexual lives, actively preferring the support and intimacy of female/female relations, including erotic relations. For many women, lesbianism is less fate than choice, and many women choose lesbian relations because more and more women have moved beyond male dependency and will not accept intimate relations that lack mutuality.

Male clergy and bishops must also face how deeply angry they are with gay men, men who are open about their erotic bonding to other men and who demand self-respect for who they are. It is precisely these men who are often able to hear a feminist analysis of sexuality and who join us in making the connections between homophobia and misogyny. What generates rage against gay men is that, by coming out, they signal that they will no longer cooperate in refusing to rock the ecclesiastical boat: They join women in expecting the church, finally, to come of age regarding human sexuality.

Implications for Ministry and for Reformulating an Ethic of Sexuality

Since I am a moralist by profession, I cannot resist spelling out some of the implications of this analysis for a theological ethic of sexuality and for Christian ministry. Nothing is more critical at the present moment than for the dominant traditions of Christianity to recognize and begin making the connections between the dehumanizing and ancient patriarchal attitudes toward women and our present ideological entrapment in relationship to human sexuality. Contrary to popular assumptions, it happens to be the case that an adequate response to the present global political and economic crisis actually turns on a more honest and adult confrontation with these issues. Our society's fears regarding human sexuality and the widespread, confused, and phobic anxieties about same-sex eroticism, together with the disordered relations between men and women generated by deep inequalities of power and respect, are a major source of our inability to tolerate diversity and

difference in this world. Because we are uncertain and vulnerable to terror in terms of our fear of sexuality, these issues provide a perfect foil for the new political right, which uses them to silence people. Homophobia functions to mask real, deep, and growing social and economic inequity. Gay men, lesbians, and women who insist on their procreative rights or who press for full standing as citizens are joining the poor, and nonwhite women and men, as groups that became society's chief scapegoats. We are accused, preposterously, of "destroying traditional values," whereas the erosion not only of "traditional values" but of all moral concern is rooted concretely in a political-economic system that makes every human consideration except the maximization of profit irrelevant. Late advanced monopoly capitalism not only erodes traditional values but is eroding the functional capacity of all of our liberal institutions. While traditional "family values" were never adequate morally to women's situation, the political forces attacking women and gay men seeking justice have no real concern for any sort of intrinsic moral value. Right-wing groups demand women's acquiescence to traditional "family values" only because they are astute supporters of the existing economic system that cannot accommodate genuine claims to economic equity. Since women as a group are the largest systematically disadvantaged group, the new right understands perfectly well that any efforts to realize full human equality for women must be discredited along with all other claims to social justice, especially claims for racial equality. The pressure now is great to revert to some presumed conventional wisdom, to take a more traditional stance, but not because the right wing really values "tradition." Socioeconomic pressures on families will continue to escalate whatever happens; should the rate of divorce drop, it will be only because economic pressures force people to remain in unfulfilling marriages. The economic crisis of late advanced capitalism is so deep that any group's claims that require reallocation of social power and resources must be silenced. People must be pressured to accept a social system that can no longer buy off discontent by "trickling down" modest benefits to those in the middle and at the bottom of the system.

If the formerly liberal churches now fall into

line with the expectations of the new right regarding "traditional" values of sexuality, the result hardly will be a sudden increase in moral sensibility or lessening of dissolution of family life. The massive violence now characteristic of the American family will increase as long as social justice is denied. As economic pressures increase, we may count on it that violence, including spouse and child abuse will continue to escalate. If churches buy in on the antifeminist, homophobic line of the new right, the few precarious and as yet not well established strides toward justice for women and the more mature attitude toward sexuality made by whole generations of liberals, including liberal Christianity, will be wiped out. What has happened recently in the churches is that former liberals, frightened of change largely because they could not simultaneously become critical of Christianity's role in gender oppression and also become more self-aware and self-accepting of their own sexuality, have collaborated with neo-conservatives to stop constructive change.

A Christian community in the grips of homophobia is unable to grapple with the subtle challenges of ministry in the present. To have a role in the real healing of people today, to contribute to the genuine empowerment of people, to express radical love in a social context of right relationship (justice), the church must continue to walk the long road of transforming its mores of sexuality. Once and for all, the Christian community must overcome its sex-phobic fear of eroticism as a foreign and evil power that wars with positive spiritual energy. We Christians must come to recognize that our sexuality is a foundational aspect of our total, integrated bodily well-being. It is the root of our personal integrity and it must be integrated holistically into our lifestyles and value commitments if we are to possess a deep capacity for intimacy, for powerful communication and rich interaction with others.

All of this means that the churches are going to have to acknowledge that, contrary to popular opinion and customary wisdom, *Christianity has not yet developed an adequate ethic of sexuality.* The ponderous rhetoric of the Lambeth statement on sexuality and other ecclesiastical utterances notwithstanding, a new mood of modesty about the wisdom of Christian tradition is urgently required. What most historians of Christian ethics

have missed completely is that the present confusions and disagreements around the issues of human sexuality in the church parallel earlier debates on political or economic ethics when a "taken-for-granted" church monopoly on moral wisdom held sway. Precisely at the point when the church could no longer simply dictate political policy, a new moral debate had to occur. When the church could no longer dictate the meaning of science, a similar conflict ensued. When traditional Christianity is no longer viewed as possessing a monopoly on or able simply to dictate the moral meaning of an aspect of life, conflict escalates. So today we are in conflict because consensus has been lost about the meaning of sexuality. Our past sexual mores are inadequate to integrate the new insights we need.

Traditional Christianity has persistently confused sexual mores with genuine morals, assuming that earlier patterns of practice continue to have value for their own sake, quite apart from our need as rational beings continuously to justify past norms and practices in light of new conditions. In a world where women will no longer accept inferiority, where overpopulation threatens, and where new and nonexploitive patterns of communication and intimacy that sustain genuine human dignity are needed, we must, perhaps for the first time, articulate, in a self-aware and responsible way, criteria for expressing our sexuality that are not based on institutionalized relations of male hegemony, control, and possession or on social myths about our sexual "natures" that do not correlate with the experiences that actually empower our lives. Values operative in earlier social orders may have made some sense when mere physical survival of the species was a major issue,[12] but those patterns of human practice sacralized unjust power relations and are no longer justifiable. Our sexuality, like everything human, is a historical reality and as such undergoes genuine change. Patterns of human sexual expression have always varied from culture to culture, and they have altered over time. Since sexual mores, like all mores, change, there is the possi-

---

12. Marie August Neal, "Sociology and Sexuality: A Feminist Perspective," *Christianity and Crisis* 39, no. 8 (14 May 1979), pp. 118-122.

bility that the moral quality of our social-sexual relations can also deepen over time.

In the past, the Christian ethic kept women "in our place" by confining us to procreation, but it also included the simultaneous demand that males limit erotic contact only to such less-valued creatures as women. Christian cultures have had to fetishize heterosexuality to enforce contact with women on men whom it was also teaching to disvalue women. Enforced heterosexism, in the form of the assumption that heterosexuality is "natural" sex, is the ideology of a culture that simultaneously encourages and disguises its hatred for women, seeks to extend its male supremacy, and must force males to "do their duty" by "inferior" women.

If our sexual behavior were really determined "by nature," we would, of course, need no ethic of sexuality. Human beings do not need morality to deal with what is determinate or, in an older worldview, "natural." Ethics begins where necessity, or predetermination in creation, leaves off. From an adequate theological viewpoint, we need to say bluntly that traditional Christian sexual standards are too rigid to be healthy or conducive to human well-being. The newer efforts to "take thought," to "do ethics" in relation to the meaning of sexuality, are a sign of genuine faith and hope in the church. Happily, those whose lives are twisted and thwarted by society's strongly patterned "compulsory heterosexuality" are finally speaking up, no longer willing to accept social stigma for sexual expression and personal relationships that have intrinsic value. The communal process of shaping criteria for an adequate morality of sexual-social relations must be informed by the wisdom of those who have learned to affirm their sexuality in the face of society's oppressive negations.

We need also to remember that we live in a world where persons come to puberty earlier and earlier but where the young come to adulthood later and later. Our sexual ethic must come to terms with these dynamics. The prolonged period of young adulthood means that condemnation of sex outside marriage increases pressures for early and premature marriages. Today, people have double the life expectancy and nearly double the years of reproductive fertility as did persons only a few centuries ago. In a society like ours, lifelong

monogamous sexual relations mean something quite different from what they once did, and the traditional Christian ethic, continuously reiterated, has some quite unprecedented negative effects.

To disavow, once and for all, that sexuality per se is dirty or wrong will enable us to "put sex in its place" as an important, though neither all-powerful nor traumatic, dimension of our lives. It is clear that many of our society's sexual fixations and preoccupations are connected to and interrelated with our sexual repressions. Only a society so sex-preoccupied could be so sex-phobic. Because sexuality is experienced chiefly as a means of controlling others rather than as a means of deepened communication, it is often joyless, boring, and fixated! And not surprisingly, we seem to be a culture as bored by sex as we are obsessed with it!

A Christian moral reevaluation of sexuality must be posited on the sober fact that our sexual relations, broadly considered, are a problem, but it is *not* the problem envisaged in the traditional Christian sexual ethic — that is, too much or too "loose" sex. Rather, we must acknowledge that it is through our socialization to sexuality that we begin to learn "fear of equality" and either to feel "strong" by lording it over others or to feel "safe" by being controlled by them. By conforming rigidly to "masculine" or "feminine"[13] roles, we learn, at a foundational level, to tolerate inequality. Through our earliest experience of family power relations we learn whether superiority or inferiority makes us feel safe.[14] We may be sure that there

13. I place these terms in quotes because I do not believe that they designate objective psychological qualities. Psychological perspectives that presume the meaningfulness of these terms invariably result in a subtle perpetuation of sexism. An adequate theory of psychosexual identity can deal with the differences and similarities in men's and women's psychological/historical experience without resort to either term. Studies that document the dubiousness of both notions in psychological research are James Harrison, *A Critical Evaluation of the Psychological Concepts of Masculinity and Femininity* (Unpublished doctoral diss., New York University, February 1975), and Joseph Pleck, *The Myth of Masculinity* (Cambridge: MIT Press, 1981).

14. This thesis that we learn equality or lack of it through early sex role socialization is only now being

is a direct connection between this preferred form of psychic security and what "turns us on" erotically. The awful truth is that most heterosexuals, and a lot of homosexuals too, get turned on only by those who either are more powerful than they or by those dependent on them — the sort of person for whom they otherwise can easily feel contempt! The tragedy of our so-called sexual morality is that mutual respect and eroticism are utterly separated in the lives of most people. Ours is a culture where sadomasochistic relations are the most typical forms of sexual relations and the Christian traditionalist ethic is a major source of legitimation of sadomasochism.

Many seem to confuse erotic feeling with feelings of control, finding violence "more exciting" than mutual erotic expression. Ironically, violence apparently makes many feel safer and stronger than does passionate mutual sexual exchange. Violence *is* as American as apple pie, and it is the displacement of mutuality and spontaneous consent by coercion. Evidently, people prefer control to the more vulnerable and spontaneous experience of eroticism. A people who lack a genuine power of eroticism will indeed assuage their emptiness by controlling others.

When we accept that our sexual problem is fear of genuine intimacy and mutuality and security born of having others under our control or at bay, we will also accept our responsibility for teaching an ethic that supports such norms. That loveless control of another can be viewed as morally acceptable sexual expression by current Christian standards simply because it falls within the province of "normal" heterosexual marriage is a scandal. The search for an adequate Christian ethics of sexuality can begin in earnest when we face this level of truth.

A feminist moral theology requires that we ground our new ethics of sexuality in a "spirituality of sensuality."[15] Our energy — literally, the

gift of life — is body-mediated energy. Our sexuality does not detract from, but deepens and shapes, our power of personal being. Our bodies, through our senses, mediate our real, physical connectedness to all things. Our sexuality represents our most intense interaction with the world. Because this is so, it is also a key to the quality and integrity of our overall spirituality. Our body-space is literally the ground of our personhood and our means of communicating the power of our presence to and with others. How we deal with our own body-space and how we relate to others' provides a paradigm for all our moral relations to the world. Furthermore, touch is the most powerful and effectual means of human interaction; we resort to it when words and gestures are not powerful enough or do not suffice to convey what we need to communicate. We use touch either to control others or to convey bonds and feeling. Hence, sexuality is indispensable to our spirituality because it is a power of communication, most especially a power to give and receive powerful meaning — love and respect or contempt and disdain.

Because traditional Christian ethics held that communication through genital touch should be limited only to those relationships where nonphysical intimacy and an exclusivity of personal commitment prevailed, the primary, direct power of body communication has been largely denied. Genital contact and touch was viewed as less valuable in itself, morally inferior to other modes of communication. To the contrary, the intensity of touch, which warrants its tender use, is the source of its spiritual power. The idea that genital sexual expression, except within the confines of a lifelong, committed, monogamous relationship, is dirty or wrong does not stand scrutiny for many who have long since learned that sexual touch often opens the way to other dimensions of human intimacy. Orgasm, as an expression of vulnerability and receptivity to the world, is a powerful metaphor for spiritual blessing and healing.

---

recognized. See Jean Baker Miller, *Toward A New Psychology of Women* (Boston: Beacon Press, 1976), and Roland Sampson, *The Psychology of Power* (New York: Vintage, 1968). These discussions and numerous others in the feminist literature only begin to open up this crucial issue of how we learn, or fail to learn, equality.

15. On this theme of spirituality and sensuality, see the writings of Matthew Fox, *On Becoming a Musical*

Mystical Bear (New York: Paulist Press, 1979) and *A Spirituality Named Compassion* (Minneapolis: Winston Press, 1977). Also see Tom F. Driver, *Patterns of Grace: Human Experience as Word of God* (New York: Harper & Row, 1977).

A holistic approach to sexuality, free of the body/mind dualism that sustains patriarchy, will yield a rather simple ethic, one foundationally grounded in mutual respect. The giving and receiving of touch, the sharing of erotic pleasure, is a powerful bonding with another. Sexual communication, at its best, mutually enhances self-respect and valuation of the other. The moral norm for sexual communication in a feminist ethic is radical mutuality — the simultaneous acknowledgment of vulnerability to and need of another, the recognition of one's own power to give and receive pleasure and to call forth another's power of relation and to express one's own. The sexual ethic of patriarchy — our present operative ethic — has ownership as its formative value. We are to possess total right of access to and control of another's body-space and the fruits of the other's body, if the other is female. A norm of control prevails, which is why so-called marital fidelity really means only sexual exclusivity for the female spouse.

Many fear that giving up the ethics of patriarchy will result in the emergence of a sexually normless, "promiscuous" world, a world in which any and all sexual activity is all right if it "feels good and if nobody gets hurt." It is difficult to respond to the fears people have about presumed "promiscuity," since these fears are often based on the projections or unfulfilled sexual fantasies of those who are not at all at home with their own sexuality and who therefore worry that if sexuality is more fully expressed it may "explode" or get out of hand. A feminist Christian sexual ethic, by contrast, rejects as inappropriate all sexual relations or any dynamics of human relationships characterized by inequities of power and lack of mutuality. "Nobody gets hurt" is a negative standard. A more adequate ethic insists that in sexual communication our sense of self-worth should be enhanced. Power and the quality of caring are the key issues in assessing when the criterion of mutual respect obtains. Incest is wrong, for example, because it involves sexual activity between needy, vulnerable, and psychologically dependent children and parents lacking the appropriate power or capacity for adult self-control. Power inequity and the adult's inability not to exploit dependency, not its character as a genital act, make the sexual exchange wrong. A feminist moral norm in sexual relations also would rule out hard-core (that is, not playful) seduction

of one person by another or any sexual relationships or acts based on manipulation and ego aggrandizement of one person at the expense of another. But such an ethic never condemns, *a priori,* a sexual act or a sexual relationship where equality and respect prevail.

Human intimacy relations are complex, and those that include genital sexual relations are often the most complex of all. Because many of us are at our moral worst in our closest relationships, we frequently use sexual exchange, or its withholding, as a weapon to wound, punish, or reward. We need to ask honestly why this is the case. Why do we, in fact, usually "hurt the ones we love"? Why are we most uncaring and insensitive to those with whom our life relations run deepest? A feminist moral theology has a clear answer to this question that a traditional sexual ethics does not even ask, much less answer: We are most loveless in our closest personal relations because we have studied in the patriarchal school of life, learning security in intimate patterns of inequity. It is hard to repent of lessons so early and subtly learned. Few of us ever experience the healing power of eroticism rooted in mutual dependency. How we feel about ourselves most deeply, and therefore how we feel about those whom we claim to care for most, begins at our birth and is learned before we know enough to reject the lesson. If our sexuality is in trouble, we need to be perfectly clear that what has gone wrong is already embedded in the traditional patterns of family life, in our socially enforced sex role socialization, and in gender relations. These inadequacies are embedded in our traditional ethic itself. The sexual disorder of the present is itself glaring evidence that our traditional sexual mores do not deserve acceptance as an adequate morality of sexual relations. The search for a moral-theological ethic of sexuality that encourages genuine, radical love has had to await the challenging of the ancient oppression of misogyny. A world in which gender relations are deeply unjust is not a world whose traditional sexual norms should be commended. To do so is to defend the historical oppression of women and the pervasive ideology that has sustained that oppression, "natural" or compulsory heterosexuality. Homophobia will give way only when misogyny is recognized as a pathological source of human sexual disorder.

59. Excerpts from *Personal Commitments*

MARGARET A. FARLEY

When I love you, I want you to be. I am affirming your very existence, your life, your well-being. I want you to be firm and full in being. I say yes to you according to my understanding of your truest reality. My affirmation of you is "affective." My own self affirms you in a way that goes beyond any mere intellectual or verbal affirmation. A sign that loving you is different from, more self-involving than, just knowing you is that I am willing to do the deeds of love insofar as they are called for and possible. (If they are not called for, or not possible, then a lack of deeds does not negate my love.) If I behold you in need or in danger, I move to help you — if I can. If I love you with what Toner calls a "radical" love — that is, a love for you yourself, a love that is the root of my care for you, my joy in you, my desires for your well-being — I affirm you as I affirm myself.[1]

1. Jules J. Toner, *The Experience of Love* (Washington: Corpus Books, 1968), 142. My identification of the essential elements in the experience of love as affirmation, union, and response is based on the overall analysis that Toner gives.

Margaret A. Farley (1935–) is the Gilbert L. Stark Professor of Christian Ethics at Yale University Divinity School. She has authored numerous essays in Christian feminist ethics. Her books include *Personal Commitments: Beginning, Keeping, Changing.*

From Margaret Farley, *Personal Commitments: Making, Keeping, Breaking* (San Francisco: Harper Religious Books, 1987).

Affective Union

When I love you, I am in a special sense also in union with you. My loving affirmation unites me with you. Sometimes we miss seeing this aspect of love because we think of love as a *desire for* union. And it is true that love often gives rise to an intense longing to be with the one we love — to be closer in time and space, to share more fully and know more intimately. But we do not long for such intimacy with, nor are we "lonely" for, anyone we do not already love. The love itself is a union, which is not belied by its causing in us a desire for fuller union.

Affective Response

As affirming and as unifying, love is active. It is something I do. It would seem, then, to be something I can easily choose. Like every other action, I can select a given love by my power of free choice. But there is another aspect to my loving which makes it, in its beginning, not a matter of "simply choosing." That is, my love for you is "first of all" a response — a response to your lovableness, your value and beauty. This is the passive dimension of love. I must "receive" your revelation of yourself as lovable. Your self, or some aspect of it, must touch my mind and heart, awaken it, so that I respond in love. Not that you necessarily decide to reveal yourself to me, or even that you are aware that I behold you. It is enough for you to exist, and for me to encounter you.

Ah, but many will say: Love cannot be essentially a response to what is lovable — for it is the height of human love (and the ideal of Christian love) to "love the unlovable." It is only a selfish love that has to "receive" something, even a revelation of beauty, in order to love. There is truth in this objection, actually, but only a partial truth. To "love the unlovable" makes sense only if it means that we can or ought to love persons whose beauty is not immediately evident to us, whose lovableness is hidden by some terrible evil or some superficial distortion that occasions our inability to see. In such instances, we are not enjoined to love what is literally unable-to-be-loved, but to *believe* what we cannot readily see — to believe that there is worth and beauty, dignity and lovableness, in a person as a person and as this unique person who claims our love. It can be enough for us to receive the lovableness of the other through the eyes of faith, human or divine. Such faith, of course, would move us to a love the deeds of which would surely include trying to see what first we are unable to see. Hatred of another person, as Graham Greene suggests, may be "just a failure of imagination."[2]

My loving affirmation of you is, then, a *responding* as well as a *uniting affirmation*. It begins not with sheer force of "willing" to love, but in an "indeliberate, unfree, response,"[3] a spontaneous reply to the reception of your lovableness. Love, therefore, is simultaneously passion and action, receiving and giving; there are two sides to the one coin, the one reality, of loving. What, then, is the power of freedom to influence love?

Freedom and Love

Ray and Sarah have been together for five years. Their love has "settled" in that time into something less lyrical but more peaceful and sure. Is it their choices that have brought this to pass? Stephen and Ann, after twenty years of marriage and four children, say their love is "dead." The only emotions they share are anger and resentment; otherwise there is nothing any more between them. Could they have altered this course of their love by making different free choices? Susan has spent ten years living and working with a group that provides shelter for homeless poor. During those years she several times wept in rage and despair, and she almost left the group and the work for something less demanding and more likely to bring lasting results. Is this a story where freedom of choice has sustained compassion zeal? Helen has fallen painfully in love with a man who teaches in the same school as she, and with whom she shares a love of literature and the arts in a way she has never been able to share with her husband. This new love is, she feels, a "great love, a classic love" — though it may destroy her marriage and both of their careers. Does she have any real freedom in relation to her old love or her new? Only Ray and Sarah, and

Stephen and Ann, and Susan, and Helen know the answers to these questions; and even they may not be completely sure. What we can try to know, however, is whether *it is possible* that choices, made by at least some persons in some situations, can make a difference to love.

In its first awakening, love is not a matter of free choice. It is a spontaneous response to what is perceived as lovable. That we have seen. Nonetheless, I can influence love even in its beginning by choosing to attend to certain realities or not, putting myself in a position to discover lovableness if it is there, choosing to believe in the value of persons, etc. Insofar as love is like a judgment of value, I can, as Solomon says, open myself "to argument, persuasion, evidence."[4]

Even more important, once a love exists, it can offer itself (so to speak) to freedom. That is, my love can give rise to a desire in me to accept and affirm itself, to affirm the one I love, by my free choice. I, at the center of myself where I am free, can identify with my love — with this love or that, this way of loving or that, this action to express love or that. I can take responsibility for my love — not just be carried away by it or victimized by it.

My choice of my love can also shape the love. I can choose to believe in my love, even when my feelings vacillate. I can choose to pay attention to the one I love, looking again and again for the revelation that nurtures my love. I can choose to try to modify my emotions and feelings whenever they conflict with my chosen love, or to ignore them, or to give them "free" play in my mind and heart. I can use my imagination, or perform activities, in a way that will help to "de-fuse" contradictory emotions which get in the way of my loving. I can choose to interpret the words and actions of my beloved, my own feelings, our situation together in a way that undermines my love or that helps to sustain it. I can choose to do the deeds of love, and order my life, in a way that is conducive to my love's continuance and growth.

Love is not, therefore, something that merely "occurs" in me, wholly beyond my power of freedom. I do experience being able to "work at" loving relationships, being able to gather my own spirit and nudge it this way and that, gaining wisdom and power for myself and my love. I make decisions

2. Graham Greene, *The Power and the Glory* (New York: Penguin Books, 1984), 131.

3. Toner, 96.

4. Solomon, "Emotions and Choice," 270.

about ways of expressing my love (for example, with regard to my sexuality) that will, in turn, affect the form of the love. And other choices that I make, not directly regarding my love, but for the sake of it — choices about my work or my many relationships — have also consequences for my love.

Yet I do not have anything like total power in respect to my love. I experience myself as fragmented and conflicted, conditioned as well as self-determining, "swept away" as well as "self-possessed." No, there is no such thing as despotic control over any of my emotions by my faulty model of the human self, a popularized brand of Stoicism which would make reason the conqueror of emotion, rationality the mark of freedom — or the opposite, a runaway romanticism which would collapse freedom into my spontaneous emotions. It surely is blind to my complex experience — where I know that I can choose my love, but not always. I can shape my love, but oh, so slowly. I can cultivate my love, but only through long and patient attention. I can discipline my love and liberate it; but sometimes it still slips through my heart or disrupts my ordered life.

Insofar as freedom can influence love, however, it can affect its future. It seems that we can, then, make commitments to love. We need to explore more directly what that means.

Commitment and Love

Like any other commitment, a commitment to love is not a prediction, not just a resolution. It is the yielding of a claim, the giving of my word, to the one I love — promising what? It can only be promising that I will do all that is possible to keep alive my love and to act faithfully in accordance with it. Like any other commitment, its purpose is to assure the one I love of my ongoing love and to strengthen me in actually loving. Given the challenges we have seen to the wisdom, if not the possibility, of commitments to love, this purpose bears fuller examination.

Purposes of Commitments to Love

Why should I want commitment if love rises spontaneously, and if I can identify with it by my free-

dom at every moment? Why should I promise to love if there are risks to the love itself in making it a matter of obligation? Only something at the heart of our experience of loving can explain this.

There are some loves whose very power in us moves us to commitment. "Love's reasons" for commitment are at least threefold, and they go something like this. First, like all commitments, a commitment to love seeks to *safeguard* us against our own inconsistencies, what we perceive to be our possibilities of failure. If we are not naively confident that our love can never die, we sense the dangers of our forgetfulness, the contradictions of intervening desires, the brokenness and fragmentation in even our greatest loves. We sense, too, the powerful forces in our milieu — the social and economic pressures that militate against as well as support our love. We need and want a way to be held to the word of our deepest self, a way to prevent ourselves from destroying everything in the inevitable moments when we are less than this. To give to the one we love our word, to yield to her or him a claim over our love, offers a way.

Love seeks more than this, however. We know that freedom cannot once and for all determine its future affirmation of love. No free choice can settle all future free choices for the continuation of love. Yet sometimes we love in a way that makes us yearn to gather up our *whole future* and place it in affirmation of the one we love. Though we know it is impossible because our lives are stretched out in time, we long to seal our love now and forever. By commitment to unconditional love we attempt to make love irrevocable and to communicate it so. This is the one thing we can do: initiate in the present a new form of relationship that will endure in the form of fidelity or betrayal. We do this by giving a new law to our love. Kierkegaard points to this when he says, "When we talk most solemnly we do not say of two friends: 'They love one another'; we say 'They pledged fidelity' or 'They pledged friendship to one another.'"[5] Commitment is love's way of being whole while it still grows into wholeness.

Finally, love sometimes desires commitment because love wants to express itself as clearly as it

5. Søren Kierkegaard, *Works of Love*, trans. Howard and Edna Hong (New York: Harper Torchbooks, 1962), 45.

can. Commitment is destructive if it aims to provide the only remedy for distrust in a loving relationship. But it can be a ground for *trust* if its aim is honesty about intention, communication of how great are the stakes if intention fails. The decision to give my word about my future love can be part of converting my heart, part of going out of myself truly to meet the one I love (not part of hardening my heart because of excessive fear of sanctions if I break the law that I give to my love). My promise, then, not only verbally assures the one I love of my desire for constancy, but it helps to effect what it assures.

*   *   *

When we first "fall in love," the one we love is beautiful in our eyes. It does not matter that he (or she, or they, or it — in the case of a group, or a movement, or an institution) has quite ordinary features, even obvious deficiencies or impairments. These do not take away from (and may even add to) the beauty we see. "Romantic" love . . . is love that rises from our whole self in response to an "original vision" of the beloved as beautiful, as wholly lovable. Such love may come all of a sudden (there *is* love at first sight, first meeting, first coming to know), or it may dawn slowly, as the one we love is gradually revealed to us in the beauty we perceive.

We are well aware, generally, that what we behold in this original vision is not all that we shall come to see in time. We are in danger, though, both of underestimating and overestimating its importance. To avoid overestimation, we warn ourselves and others who are in love: " 'Romantic vision' is not what is important, nor is the kind of love that depends on it." "Wait until you lose your rose-colored glasses." Some, however, like the theologian and writer Charles Williams, have worried more about the danger of underestimating the importance of the vision.[6] He feared that in our cynicism or caution we would fail to understand the significance of an original "revelation" and "vision," something on which the whole relationship might ultimately depend.

We tend, according to Williams, to make three fundamental errors regarding our original vision. They are errors of overestimation, but if we do not understand them, they will lead to errors of underestimation. We think that (a) the original vision will last, just as it is, forever; (b) that it brings with it an experience of love that is sufficient in itself; and (c) that the vision and the love are given only for the two of us (or however many directly receive it and share it).[7] Alas, all three assumptions are mistaken.

Regarding the first, the original vision does, indeed, not last. There is an inevitability about its fading. When it is gone, however, the question of fidelity arises, perhaps for the first time; and the question is: Shall I remain faithful to the vision I once saw but see no more? Shall I, in darkness, now *believe* in a light I no longer see? Everything depends on how we interpret the loss of vision. Usually we believe that we now see more clearly than we did before. "Now I see what he is *really* like." Now I see what this church, or this segment of the peace movement, or this profession are "*really* like." And, in fact, we probably do know more about the ones we love than we did in the beginning — more facts, more limitations, more oddities; and we see that as persons they may be less profound than we thought, less motivated by singleness of purpose, less possessed of genuine charm, etc.

There is also the possibility, however, that we actually see *less well* than we did originally; that what we have come to know is less centrally characteristic of this person or group than what we saw at first. One small habit of Ann's that irritates Stephen, for example, may loom larger in his perception of her now than anything else, so that the beauty that is still there is blocked from his sight. When sharpness of intellect or loveliness of face appear less brilliant or less striking, we may forget that these were only *conditions* for our original seeing, and what we saw was more than any of these. Or we may simply have grown "weary of wonders," as Chesterton said, or "tired of behold-

<hr>

6. Charles Williams's primary work on a theology of romantic love appears in his *The Figure of Beatrice in Dante* (New York: Noonday Press, 1961). A very helpful study of this theme in all of his works is provided by Mary McDermott Shideler's *The Theology of Romantic Love: A Study in the Writings of Charles Williams* (Grand Rapids: Eerdmans, 1962).

7. See Shideler, 115.

345

ing beauty," in Williams's words. "Beauty ceases, in one's own sight, to be beauty, and the revelation to be revelation."[8] Yet what we once saw was real, and remains real. The problem is with our seeing, not with the beauty of the beloved.

How shall we know which is the truth, which is the more authentic way of interpreting our now not-seeing? Do we see better now, or less well? After all we *could* have made a serious mistake in first loving someone. But we could also make a serious mistake in now ceasing to love. There is no way of determining, with absolute certitude, the answer to these questions. Both authentic and inauthentic original visions, both reality and illusion, fade. We need *some* grounds of credibility, some indication of the "reasonableness" of our belief or disbelief in the ongoing beauty of the one we love. Yet the *wager* of fidelity is in our choice to believe in the original vision new when we no longer see it. If we are right, the vision will in some form be possible again. If we are wrong, we may "prove to be, of all persons, the most foolish" (1 Corinthians 15:19).

Vision and disillusionment, learning and seeming unlearning apply, too, to our knowledge of ourselves. In the original vision we can think that we, too, are filled with glory in a way that will last; that we who before have been weak will now be strong; that we who before have been self-preoccupied are now completely freed; that we will be forever faithful, forever understanding, forever filled with love. This part of the vision fades as well. Yet it, too, may hold a truth and beauty to be believed in, a positive revelation about ourselves in which we can dare to trust.

The second assumption we make regarding the original vision, thinking that our original experience of love in response to it is sufficient in itself, proves likewise to be inevitably false. Despite its importance for awakening love and for revealing something essential about the beloved and about ourselves, the event of the original vision and spontaneous love is not sufficient in itself. Even if it could last forever, it is not enough. The reason is that the vision (when it is authentic) is not so much of what *is*, but of what we can *become* together. It is meant to call us into a process of love and fidelity, not to let us settle into a present that

is closed. The original "falling in love" needs ratification by our freedom along a carefully discerned way of fidelity. For it to come to be in all of its promise, we must learn a kind of "discipline of nonfulfillment," freedom's way of not destroying the future by mistaking it for something less or demanding it before its time.[9]

The third error, thinking that the original vision is "just for the two of us," is like the second in that it tempts us to close in on ourselves and on a fleeting bliss. Love, after all, is a gift — awakened in us first by the revelation of another (and when it is mutual, the revelation of one another). No gift, no "grace," of this magnitude is ever given just for one, or just for two, or even just for our group. It is somehow given for all. The practical implications of this vary from situation to situation, from love to love. We learn, however, from our all too sobering experiences, that love tends to wither or be distorted when it is grasped too tightly, kept only for ourselves. Its growth in depth between us must be at once also growth into an open circle beyond us.

The original vision of our love and beloved comes early in a committed relationship. But its interpretation, and the choices we make in its wake, go far along the "way of fidelity." Choices in faith for remembered vision, in the present for the kind of present that has a future, in a relation that opens to wider and wider community are choices that entail conversion of our hearts. In this lies part of the secret of truthful knowing and faithfulness in love.

8. Williams, *The Figure of Beatrice in Dante*, 35.

9. This term is Ursula Niebuhr's. I was introduced to it first by a reference to it in Christopher F. Mooney's *Man Without Tears: Soundings for a Christian Anthropology* (New York: Harper & Row, 1975), 75.

60. Respect for Covenant

LEWIS SMEDES

What Does the Seventh Commandment Tell Us to Do?

The people who heard this commandment intoned at Israel's annual festivals understood it, in its narrowest sense, as a warning to Israel's males to keep away from their neighbors' wives. A concern of this commandment, just as with all the others, is our neighbor's rights — in this case a husband's right to the integrity of his marriage and certitude about his descendants. A man, married or not, committed adultery against a woman's husband when he slept with her. But a married man did not commit adultery against his own wife by having intercourse with another woman. A male broke the covenant of another man; he did not break his own covenant with his own wife.

A husband could sleep with a prostitute, and nobody much cared. No judge's finger was pointed at Samson for his sallies into the boudoirs of liberated Philistines (Judg. 16); nobody observed that Judah was a married man when he slept with his daughter-in-law Tamar under the impression that she was a prostitute (Gen. 38:12ff.). When Nathan condemned David for his disastrous affair with Bathsheba, the prophet did not say a word on

Lewis Smedes (1921–) is professor of integrative studies in the Graduate School of Psychology at Fuller Theological Seminary, where he had previously served as professor of theology and ethics. He is author of *Love within Limits: A Realist's View of 1 Corinthians 13; Mere Morality; Choices, Caring and Commitment;* and *A Pretty Good Person.*

From Lewis B. Smedes, *Mere Morality: What God Expects from Ordinary People* (Grand Rapids, Mich.: Wm. B. Eerdmans, 1983).

behalf of David's own wives (2 Sam. 11, 12). In short, adultery was almost always an injustice only to the cuckolded husband, whose human right to descendants unquestionably his own was being abridged by his wife's dalliance with a stranger.[1]

Adultery was not a private peccadillo, therefore, but a social crime that called for retribution. In early Hebrew society those who lost their heads to sexual passion and committed adultery could also literally lose their heads to the executioner (Deut. 22:22; Lev. 20:10). The straying wife was especially vulnerable; at first she was to be stoned, but later, following the Talmud, she was to be divorced without the privilege of marrying her lover. The innocent wife of a straying husband might also suffer, if Job is to be taken literally. Boasting of his own sexual innocence, he hints how he would allow vengeance against his own wife if he had violated another man's:

> If my heart has been enticed to a woman,
> and I have lain in wait at my neighbor's door;
> then let my wife grind for another
> and let others bow down upon her.
> For that would be a heinous crime . . . ,
> an iniquity to be punished by the judges.
>
> Job 31:9-12

It was only fair, as David learned, that if you slept with your neighbor's wife, he or somebody else would sleep with yours — an eye for an eye, a wife for a wife (2 Sam. 11, 12).[2]

1. Cf. Stamm, Johann J., and Maurice E. Andrew, *Ten Commandments in Recent Research* (Allenson, 1967), p. 110; G. von Rad, *Deuteronomy* (Philadelphia: Westminster, 1963), p. 59; R. Gordis, *Love and Sex: A Modern Jewish Perspective* (New York: Farrar, Straus, and Giroux, 1978), p. 179; J. L. Koole, *De Tien Geboden* (Baarn: Bosch & Keuning, 1964), p. 107.

2. Contrary to common opinion, the abused husband did not merely suffer property damage when his wife committed adultery. Abuse of a man's property rights may have been part of the picture, as G. von Rad notes in *Genesis* (Philadelphia: Westminster, 1949), p. 360; but if adultery involved only theft it could be compensated for by financial remuneration. What was probably more deeply involved was a husband's honor as lord of the family, and the wound he suffered was more like personal shame than property loss. As time went on, however, and mercy grew, a prophet named

Adultery takes on a radically new look in the New Testament. The wife comes into her own as a full partner in the covenant; it is she who is sinned against when her husband violates his commitment to her. Jesus, for example, speaks of divorce as adultery, as a breakage of the covenant. But, he says, when a man or a woman divorces a spouse (and remarries), he violates his own wife or she her own husband. For Jesus, two whole and equal persons made a marriage; those two are the primary persons hurt in a violation of the marriage partnership. Paul supported the New Testament's "equal rights amendment" to the Old Testament regulations when he insisted that a man owed sexual allegiance to his wife as much as his wife owed it to him (1 Cor. 7:4).

Violation of marriage is basically what the Seventh Commandment forbids. Adultery, as illicit sex, is prohibited as a most likely and most threatening assault on the partnership. But is this commandment also perhaps a kind of catch-all putdown of pleasure?

The Reformed tradition has tended to spread the net of this commandment over nearly every improper sexual impulse — against "any filthy or lustful intemperance of the flesh."[3] To the question, "Does God in this commandment forbid nothing more than adultery and such like gross sins?", the Heidelberg Catechism replies: "He forbids all unchaste actions, gestures, words, thoughts, desires, and whatever may entice one thereto" (Lord's Day 41). Old-time Reformed sermons on the commandment zeroed in on "whatever may entice": short skirts, bobbed hair, the cinema, ballroom dancing, and lipstick — all came in for attack. A husband might have "lustful intemperance" if he wanted intercourse more often than his wife did. Sexual fantasies were as serious as adultery itself. No one escaped the finger of the Seventh Commandment, for everyone

had reason to cringe at some "lustful intemperance" in his own life.

It is a mistake, I think, to use the Seventh Commandment as a club against sexual passions. What happens when we do is that eros seems totally defiled and passion an ugly product of sin. The real issue is obscured. We do the commandment more justice if we focus its clear light on one's duty to his or her marriage.

Covenant-Keeping[4]

The question of adultery is a question of what sort of people we want to be. Not that only bad people commit adultery, but our attitude toward adultery as a way of life depends much on the kind of person we are. In this arena, there are two kinds of characters — and both of them live within each of us. The two characters are covenant-keepers and self-maximizers. Culture tells us to be self-maximizers; the commandment tells us to be covenant-keepers.

A covenant-keeper is loyal, trustworthy, committed, dependable, even heroic — qualities that hardly throb with sexuality. The covenant-keeper in us is not what excites people with our erotic energy. But he is a person who keeps faith with people who trust him, a person who holds relationships together and in the process keeps life humane and decent.

A self-maximizer is open, self-asserting, expanding, and erotic. A self-maximizer evaluates relationships with others in terms of how they contribute to his own growth. He thinks of marriage romantically — a deep personal relationship with rich potential for mutual fulfilment. He marries in order to enrich his life, and in analyzing his marriage, he is likely to ask: Is my marriage giving me all I need to stimulate my growth? Probably the time will come in a self-maximizer's marriage when a sexual affair promises more than he is getting in the marriage — and he may grab the promise.

The self-maximizer turns life into an exciting quest for maximal happiness. Extramarital affairs can offer a lot to anyone who earnestly joins the

---

Hosea reached out in tender love to a wife who betrayed and shamed him. Flying in the face of his tradition, Hosea acted in "steadfast love" toward his errant wife, and stuck with her in reconciling devotion. As we learn, he was acting out an object lesson of Yahweh's own committed love for his adulterous people: "I will betroth thee unto me in faithfulness, and thou shalt know the Lord (Hos. 2:20).

3. Calvin, *Institutes,* II.viii.41.

4. The material in this section is borrowed heavily from my book, *Sex for Christians* (Grand Rapids: Eerdmans, 1975), Chapter 8.

hunt. They offer new love to a person whose spouse has forgotten how to love, intense passion to a person whose marriage has gone flat, beauty to people whose marriage has turned plain or ugly, new growth to a person stifled by a spouse. Few experiences seem more justifiable than a love affair to a person who feels robbed of all the glittering promises of a romantic marriage. This is why we said that the issue is basically one of what sort of person we want to be. We need a profound reason to justify staying home nights when home is next to hell. Why stick with what you are stuck with when the bright, beautiful people of our Camelot culture are living endorsements of the prevailing hunch that self-maximizing is a lot more fun than covenant-keeping?

Yet, the commandment asks us to become covenant-keepers, people who subordinate the right to maximize their potential for sexual happiness to their responsibility for a covenanted partnership with another human being. In short, the natural, human erotic urge to stretch ourselves and reach for the maximum experience must take second place to our commitment to care for the partnership which, as it were, we are stuck with. The commandment calls us to make a deep decision, not simply about sex, but about the meaning and purpose of human life.

Vow-Keeping

Covenant-making is a uniquely human way to begin an alliance. Perhaps the greatest mystery of our humanness is the power to make and keep a vow. For in a vow you freely give yourself over to a permanent identity in the face of an unpredictable future. You will change, the person to whom you make the vow will change, your circumstances will change. Moreover, the person you vow to live with is in some ways the wrong person for you — no one ever marries the right person. But, if you are a vow-keeper, you are likely to do in the changing future what you promised in the unchangeable past. No other creature manages this. A dog can be born and become attached to a human master; only a human being can promise to create a permanent identity for himself or herself as a partner to another person.

The commandment calls us to be vow-keepers in defiance of our culture. Our culture urges us

not to define our life in terms of past commitments but in terms of present needs and future possibilities. The command calls us to subordinate our needs and accommodate our possibilities to the special history we began when we vowed to be a partner in marriage.

Keeping Each Other

Within the unique relationship of marriage two people care for each other's total welfare. Each, in a total sense, becomes the spouse's keeper. Each is dedicated to the growth, healing, pleasure, and freedom of the other.

There is a reserve clause in person-keeping that prevents it from suffocating the other person in our care. A person-keeper cares for the freedom of the other person. A husband seeks his wife's freedom to be what she is capable of being, and she nurtures his freedom in turn. Care for one another's growth brings a risk into person-keeping, for the person we care for may, in growing into a fuller person, grow away from us. And growing away within a marriage increases the chances of growing toward someone outside the marriage. But the commandment asks us to take that risk.

"Freedom in Christ" is the biblical model of freedom in marriage. The Lord is married to the church; it is "subject" to him (Eph. 5:23) and he is bent on its freedom (Gal. 5:1). We are not truly experiencing subjection to Christ unless we are being set free by it. Christ's goal is always the freedom of the church. In the same way, each partner in a marriage is faithful when working at the other's happiness, healing, wholeness, and freedom. Paul was probably asking married people to be "person-keepers" when he told them to be "in subjection" to one another (Eph. 5:21).

Keeping Our Relationships

The inner essence of a marriage is a human relationship, rooted in sexual difference and human oneness. It is the one relationship that joins two people on every human level: emotion, intellect, spirit, and body. So, too, this relationship can break down at any of its levels, not just through sexual unfaithfulness. Fidelity to a marriage is therefore a steady *commitment* to the fragile network of communication between two partners.

The vow is the moral foundation; the relationship is the personal essence. And fidelity is the mortar that holds the relationship together on the grounds of the vow. Hence, fidelity is an all-embracing moral call to devote our energies to the growth, enrichment, and repair of the tender relationship of two people within the personal union of marriage.

The commandment forbidding adultery, then, comes within a compelling call to fidelity. Fidelity is a dynamic, positive posture that needs renewing and recreating constantly. It is not achieved simply by staying out of other people's beds. The question is whether it can be achieved in spite of a little "playing around." Can a husband or wife be truly faithful, in his or her way, even though making room in married life for extramarital sex? The question may seem flippant, but we cannot answer it without facing up to the further question of why human beings, alone among sexual creatures, are morally bound to confine sexual intercourse to a marriage covenant.

Why Is Adultery Forbidden?

The Bible does not explain the reason for the Seventh Commandment in so many words. Some people may believe that adultery is wrong just because God forbids it. Others might propose that this commandment is just an ancient male trick to keep women in tow and bloodlines pure, so that it has no more validity for a modern marriage than the Hebrew legislation forbidding intercourse with a menstruating woman (Lev. 20:18). A third option is to say that, if a reasonable God forbids married people to have sexual intercourse outside their partnership, there must be a good and a profound reason for it, which we will find if our minds are clear and our hearts pure. This third option encourages us to go ahead and look for reasons even if they are not explicit in the text.

Why, in the light of the commandment, is adultery to be considered a human failure, not just an infraction of a rigorous religious rule intended mainly to keep eros in check? We are not inquiring whether a single foray into illicit love is a *particularly* bad wrong as wrongs go — though it probably goes deeper than forgetting an anniversary. What we want is a signal of how fidelity is woven,

like an invisible fiber, into the design for humane living.

Borderline Reasons

People have believed adultery to be wrong for reasons that touch only the borderline of marriage and sex. Immanuel Kant, for example, thought that adultery reduced a man to his animal nature. A married man carrying on an affair of passion was losing his head.[5] Kant was wrong; hot passion is as human as cold intellect. Besides, people commit adultery for many reasons other than lust. Sometimes extramarital sex is an adventure of true personal devotion outside a marriage torn by hostility. Kant saw all evil as a fall from rationality; we who see it as a fall from love must take our cue elsewhere.

Thomas Aquinas believed adultery was wrong because when people have sex outside of marriage they wish not to conceive a child.[6] A natural sex act lets the procreative process have its own way. But adulterers always interrupt it if they can. If they do gamble with nature, they are doing wrong for another reason: they would force a child born of their illicit union to come into life at a disadvantage. The main thing wrong with adultery, however, is that it blocks nature by interfering with its urge to procreate through sex. Most of us today probably resist this strict and limited view of the purpose of sex. We want sex to be the source and symbol of personal union, the expression of fulfilled love. So "blockage of nature" is too impersonal a reason to convince us that adultery is a serious moral lapse.

A more personal approach to adultery holds that it is wrong because it hurts people.[7] It hurts adulterers, especially if they care for each other; the deeper their secret, fragmented, and finally aborted love, the worse their pain. The spouse who finds out is hurt by a sense of being unlovely,

5. Immanuel Kant, *The Doctrine of Virtue*, Part 1, Art. 2: "The ground of proof, of course, is that man surrenders his personality (throwing it away) by using himself merely as a means to satisfy his animal instincts."

6. Aquinas, *Summa Theologica*, II, 154, art. 11, ad 3.

7. If I understand him well, Joseph Fletcher's view of adultery is that it is usually wrong because, as much as we can tell, it tends to hurt people; but if it does not hurt anyone, it is not wrong. Cf. Fletcher, *Moral Responsibility* (Philadelphia: Westminster, 1967), pp. 125ff.

unwanted, and unrespected. And adultery may hurt many others besides — the friends who know and care, and the community whose frame is shaken a little by every stricken marriage.

If adultery hurts people needlessly, it is no doubt a bad thing. But suppose everyone's feelings were to change, so that we all accepted a measure of "healthy extramarital sex." And suppose, then, accepted extramarital sex brought only a pain that was quite tolerable compared to its pleasures and its opportunities for self-maximizing. If pain is the reason adultery is forbidden, we may be able to render the commandment obsolete by making adultery painless as we make it popular.

Adultery Is Wrong Because Sexual Intercourse Fits with Marriage

The reason sex outside of marriage is wrong, in the biblical way of looking at it, lies in a notion of what a marriage is. But what does sex have to do with marriage? Why is sex so tied into marriage that the Lord God should command the human race not to enjoy sexual embrace outside of marriage? To answer this, we must ask what a marriage is for and how sex fits into the purpose of the partnership. We want a biblically informed view of the connection; but to make good sense, a biblical view will have to be consistent with our own experiences and supported by what we experience and see around us.

Marriage as a sexual covenant

A marriage is a covenanted partnership between two people who give themselves to one another in committed love. We call it a covenant for two reasons. First, it is created by the free wills of the people who make it and lasts as long as those wills determine. In this sense, a covenant is different from an "estate of matrimony," indestructibly set within reality by sacramental power. Second, marriage is meant to be a personal life-sharing union; what marks it is the unreserved sharing of two human lives. The life-sharing of a covenant makes it different from a contract; a contract calls for an exchange of goods and services, and can be cancelled as soon as the arrangement is completed. The essence of covenant is different; it is a wholeness of life-sharing, not merely an exchange of goods and services to meet the needs and desires of the partners.

Sexual activity, with all its joy and sorrow and tedium, fits within the wholeness of the covenanted partnership. This is the meaning of the biblical metaphor of "one flesh."[8] I am not saying that voluptuous or joyful sex is the secret to a good marriage; but sexual intercourse *as such* is close to the core of any marriage. Happy sex does not necessarily make a happy marriage. Two people, with healthy erotic drives and a little artistry, may create sexual symphonies in the bedroom yet make life miserable with the discord of their quarrels in every other room of the house. All that I am saying here is that without any sex at all you have no marriage at all.

The intimate bond between sex and marriage is ultimately a statement of faith, for which we need some support besides our own hunch. Paul's tough words to those Corinthian Christians who apparently sought their Saturday nights' recreation at a local brothel gives us a signal. He did not say it was degrading to buy sex, nor that it was wrong to have sex with prostitutes because they are not nice people. What he did say was that in having sex you become "one flesh" with the person you are having sex with (1 Cor. 6:16). Sexual intercourse — whether with a prostitute or the man next door — somehow bonds two people in a deep personal union. Coitus is a unitive act, not because it is fun, but because its intimacy has a meaning that only someone cued into the Creator's design can fully appreciate. Sexual intercourse has a mystique beyond what can be registered on electrodes. Its mystique is that it signifies and somehow seals a personal life covenant. This is why it is of the essence of marriage. A life-unitive act fits into a life-uniting covenant.

We cannot prove that sex and marriage belong together: the intimate bond is something to be believed. But I think it gets support, not only from Paul's teachings but also from our own experience. There may be hints in our own feelings that Paul was right, hints that what most of us (believers or not) feel with regard to marriage and sex fits with Christian belief about it.

A hint from the experience of sex. Not every experience of sex reveals its deeper meaning. Sex

---

8. For a good discussion of the covenantal view of marriage, see James Olthuis, *I Pledge You My Troth,* pp. 19ff.

can be flippant or frustrating or fragmented, so that some people's experience of it tells them it has no meaning at all beyond pleasure and pain. Even at its joyful best, sexual intimacy has enough variation to keep it from being stereotyped. Still, we can capture a few signals that flow from experience. The physical intimacy — two uncovered bodies entangled in closeness, one entering the very body of the other — hints that sex belongs only where the two *persons* are very close and committed. The orgasm — two people out of their senses in ecstatic abandon — hints for most people at the need for trust, for confidence that such self-giving ought to be matched by a self-giving of the persons. And the memory — two people who have slept with each other never again see each other through the same eyes — hints that nothing which happens between two people can compare in depth with sexual intercourse.[9]

A hint from the experience of adultery. Consider the *jealousy* a man feels when he even suspects that his wife is sexually involved with someone else. He feels as if something of his own self is being ripped off, as if he is being crowded out of his own place. It is the feelings of pain at losing a person who gave herself to him. Consider the *secrecy* of adultery. Most people still keep their affairs hidden from their own friends, and very few tell their spouses, except in sorrow or revenge. Then there is the *pain* — for everyone affected, most of the time. We have already mentioned this; here we ask only why it should hurt so much — unless it is because sexual intercourse for married people just does not fit well outside their own covenanted relationship. Again, these are only hints; every reader must sense for himself or herself whether the experience of adultery signals something deeper about sex than what meets the eye.

Marriage as a link to the kingdom of God

We need a large vision of what marriage is for as well as a notion of what sex is for. Only a fool would claim to know *all* that marriage is for. But perhaps

our culture has made fools of us all by getting us to believe that marriage is only for making people happy and that successful sex is its dream come true. I suggest that we need a sense that marriage is not for making people happy, but for giving people a future; a sense that sex is God's gift for making a good future possible; and a sense that even a barely tolerable marriage can achieve its purpose.

The ancient Hebrews at least recognized one element of reality when they identified adultery as a threat to their future in the ongoing community. They recognized sex as a force for the future of God's family and their place in it. To play around with sex was to play games with the future of God's people. The kernel of truth in the Hebrew notion is that in the birth of a child God is signaling his ongoing commitment to the future of his family and kingdom. Our culture would ignore this kernel of truth, which we need — for it points to the one large vision that makes it reasonable to subordinate our needs for maximizing our sex lives to the heroic demands of fidelity in a marriage.

The line of reasoning goes this way: Families are for the Kingdom of God. Marriage is for families. And therefore, since sex is for marriage, sex is for the Kingdom of God. Maybe only a logic like this can counterbalance the seductive "nowness" of our romantic culture. This view of fidelity manages, I believe, to set sexual fidelity in a picture larger than the profile of your own and my own marriage covenant. It sees sex and adultery within the setting of the history of one's own future family and of God's future family. The questions it poses to an ordinary married person are these: Are you willing to be the sort of person who lives with an eye on the Kingdom of God? Are you willing to be the sort of person who subordinates your understandable erotic needs to what you see ahead in God's future?

To say this is obviously to link sex closely with conception.[10] But I do not mean that sex is only

---

9. Dwight Small is right, I think: "Two human beings who have shared the sex act can no longer act toward one another as if they had not done so"; *Christians Celebrate Your Sexuality* (Old Tappan, N.J.: Revell, 1974), p. 175.

10. Paul Ramsey rightly refuses to cut the tie between sex and children: "To put radically asunder what God joined together in making love procreative . . . or to attempt to establish a relation of sexual love beyond the sphere of marriage means a refusal of the image of God's creation in our own"; "A Christian Approach to the Question of Sexual Relations Outside of Marriage," *The Journal of Religion*, XV:2 (Apr. 1965). Cf. *Sex for Christians*, pp. 219f.

for having children or that adultery is wrong because people who commit it try to avoid conception. It is not always wrong to have sex without wanting a baby — or for that matter to have a baby without sex. I am saying that sex and conception are the means God normally uses to continue his family through history until the Kingdom comes on earth in the form of a new society where justice dwells. And for this great cause, fidelity to a marriage is reasonable. Fidelity is a way of opting for the ongoing pilgrimage of a people toward the renewed family of man, a way of enduring the pain and boredom of a sexually unsatisfactory marriage for the sake of a great purpose that transcends even our rightful longing for sexual fulfilment.[11] In the big picture, sexual escapades are a blur on the scene and a distortion of the view that fidelity is meant to keep clear.

If we believe the evidence from the Bible and if we share the signals hinted at by experience, we are likely to see the *why* of the commandment against adultery. The reason is the singular appropriateness of sexual intercourse to the sort of thing marriage is. We move, as it were, from this sense that sexual intercourse is very appropriate to marriage to the conviction that it is inappropriate outside of marriage. A crucifix has such intense symbolic meaning within the Christian church that it would be inappropriate hanging in a mosque. The hammer and sickle would be inappropriate in the offices of the Chamber of Commerce. And sexual intercourse is inappropriate outside the covenant of marriage because sex fits in a sexual covenant and nowhere else. And this explains why there is a primal duty to honor marriage by avoiding adultery.[12]

---

11. Stanley Hauerwas talks provocatively about the "political significance" of sex and marriage. Sex is (among other things) meant to play a role in the ongoing history of the church as the people of God. Thus, he says, "the issue is . . . whether we have lived in a manner that allows us to bring a history with us that contributes to the common history we may be called upon to develop with one another" (*Community of Character,* p. 195). Hauerwas wants us to see our sexual lives within the setting of God's purpose for his family, the church, and for us as participants in this history.

12. There is no doubt that contemporary attitudes toward marriage are changing. Much of the mood today contradicts the covenantal view of marriage. But the crucial issue for us is whether these changing attitudes require a changed norm, whether feelings about marriage change the fundamental design for marriage. As titillating books like Gay Talese's *Thy Neighhor's Wife* (New York: Doubleday, 1980) tell us in endless detail, some people want to have marriages with open doors to many people's bedrooms. But the fact that contemporary culture can digest open marriages is no proof that marriages are meant to be sexually open. There is strong cultural evidence, in fact, that most people in all cultures still think of marriage — whether monogamous or polygamous — as stable and firm in this single point: there is a covenant between the partners to keep sex within the bonds of the partnership. Cf. Clellan S. Ford and Frank A. Beach, *Patterns of Sexual Behavior* (New York: Harper, 1951), p. 123. For a view that marriage has no ideal form and can become anything we want it to be, see Jessie Bernard, *The Future Of Marriage* (New York: Bantam, 1973), pp. 301ff.

61. The Liberal Approach to Sexual Ethics

JAMES NELSON

The following diagram suggests what I believe to be a slowly emerging paradigmatic shift in at least some Protestant (and other religious) thinking about sexuality.

From the Old Paradigm
1. Theologies about human sexuality
2. Sexuality as either incidental to or detrimental to the divine-human relationship
3. Sin as essentially wrong sexual acts, violations of sexual norms
4. Salvation as antithetical to sexuality
5. Sexuality as incidental to the life of the church

To a New Paradigm
1. Sexual theologies
2. Sexuality as intrinsic to the divine-human relationship
3. Sin as alienation from our divinely intended sexuality
4. Salvation as including the recovery of sexual wholeness
5. Sexuality as fundamental to and pervasive in the life of the church

---

James Nelson (1930–) is professor of Christian ethics at United Theological Seminary of the Twin Cities in New Brighton, Minnesota. His works include *Moral Nexus: Ethics of Christian Identity and Community; Embodiment: An Approach to Sexuality and Christian Theology;* and *Between Two Gardens.*

From James Nelson, *Between Two Gardens* (New York: Pilgrim Press, 1983).

Some comment on each item is in order.

Sexual theology. The vast majority of religious statements on sexuality in the past have assumed essentially a one-way question: what does Christian theology (or the Bible, or the church's tradition) say about human sexuality? It is important now that we recognize another question as well. The clue comes from those Christians writing liberation theologies from feminist, black, and third-world perspectives. They are insisting that their own experience (in those instances, the experience of oppression) affords extraordinarily important insights into the meanings of Christian faith itself. Thus, for sexuality as well, the concern becomes two-directional, dialogical and not monological. In addition to the still-important question of what our religious tradition says about human sexuality is another question: What does our experience as sexual human beings say about the ways in which we experience God, interpret our religious tradition, and attempt to live the life of faith?

Sexuality and the divine-human relationship. How does God make the divine presence and meaning known and real to human life? Christian faith makes the bold claim that the most decisive experience of God occurs not fundamentally or primarily in doctrine, creed, ideas, or in mystical, otherworldly experience. Rather, it happens in flesh. "And the Word became flesh and dwelt among us, full of grace and truth" (John 1:14). Christian faith is one of incarnation. And while Christians confess that they have seen God with greatest clarity and focus in and through one human being — Jesus, whom we call Christ — it is an error to limit God's incarnation to that one figure, as decisive and central as he is for the faith community. By limiting God's incarnation to him alone we both deny his genuine humanity and treat him as an anomalous exception to the general human condition. Further, we close ourselves off from the richness of the incarnationalist faith itself: the realization that God continues to be experienced fundamentally in the embodied touching of human life with human life. Our sexuality, in its full sense, is both the physiological and the psychological grounding of our capacity to love. It expresses God's intention that we find our authentic humanness not in isolation but in communion, an intention that applies equally to the genitally active and to the celibate, to the aged and to the youthful, to the able-bodied and to the disabled.

Sexual sin. It has been commonplace in Christian understanding to think of sexual sin in terms of certain acts: sexual acts done with the wrong person, against divine or natural law, or harmful to others and the self. While there is, indeed, truth in the assumption that sin will be *expressed* in acts, it is a mistake to equate the two. In its better moments theology has long known that sin basically is the experience and condition of alienation. And alienation is inevitably experienced simultaneously in three dimensions: alienation from God, from the neighbor, and from the self.

This is true of sexual sin. More basic than any particular acts, sexual sin is alienation from our divinely intended sexuality. It is experienced as alienation within and from the sexual self. The sexual body becomes object, either that which is to be constrained out of fear or that which is a pleasure machine but essentially other than the self. This is spiritualistic dualism. But it is also sexist dualism, for it is alienation from the neglected half of one's intended humanness, with males fearful of tenderness, emotion, and vulnerability, and females fearful of (or kept from) claiming their strength, assertiveness, and intellect.

Sexual sin is also sexual alienation from the neighbor. Emotions and bodies are distanced, and relationships are truncated. Sexual distortions contribute to dehumanizing uses of power and manipulation, to social violence, to persisting expressions of racism, and to ecological abuse. Sexual sin, most basically, is alienation from God. Thus in Christian history both spiritualistic and sexist dualisms helped mightily to shape the notion of a hierarchical, ladder type of spirituality. As one "progressed upward" in spirituality, one loved God quite apart from any creaturely love, and both neighbor and self became incidental to, if not inimical to, the love of God. The soul was envisioned as a solitary, uncontaminated virgin contemplating a similarly solitary and uncontaminated deity. But such spirituality cannot in the end nurture and express the intimate relationship of God, neighbor, and self, for it is inherently an invitation to division and distance.

Sexual salvation. Unfortunately, throughout the greater part of Christian history, spiritualistic dualism has so marked Christian thought and ex-

perience that salvation has been associated with disembodiment and release from the realm of the flesh into the "higher" life of the spirit. Yet, more authentic to the heart of both Christian and Jewish faiths is the claim that the experience of salvation in this life, incomplete though it may be, involves a greater realization of our sexual wholeness. If sin is basically alienation, salvation is reconciliation. If sexual sin is fundamentally alienation from divinely intended sexuality, sexual salvation involves reconciliation and reintegration of the sexual self. It is "resurrection of the body."

Two classic words from the Christian tradition deserve reinterpretation in this light. The process of salvation traditionally (and quite rightly) has been understood to involve the polar experiences of justification by grace and sanctification by grace. Justification refers to God's activity directed toward the self from "outside." It is the Cosmic Lover's radical, unconditional, unearned acceptance of the person. When one experiences this, radical acceptance as directed toward the total body-self (and not toward some discarnate spirit), one begins to reclaim the lost sexual dimensions of the self. One's body feelings, one's fantasies, one's masculinity and femininity, one's heterosexuality and homosexuality, one's sexual irresponsibility as well as one's yearning for sexual integrity — all are graciously accepted by the divine Love. In the moment of that realization, everything is transformed. If the old fears, dualisms, and alienations return — as they will — still the self is not the same as before.

Sanctification, the second dynamic of salvation, refers to God's activity *within* the self. Traditionally, it has frequently been understood as growth toward a spiritualized, anti-body, antisexual "holiness." More adequately, sanctification might be seen as God's gracious empowerment within, which both includes and enables the self's increasing sexual wholeness and fulfillment.

This might mean several things. It might mean growth in self-acceptance and positive self-love, the kind that "personalizes" the body, making me more vitally aware that I can celebrate the body which I am and thus affirm the ways in which my body-self relates to the world. Sanctification can mean growth in the capacity for sensuousness, wherein the body becomes a means of grace and the graceful expression of the body a vehicle for love. It can mean renewal of the capacity for play. It can involve the diffusion of the erotic throughout the entire body rather than the narrow focus of sexual feeling in the genitals only. With such resexualization of the body might come an eroticization of the world, wherein our experienced environment reclaims the sensuous qualities that we had forgotten or failed to recognize. Sexual sanctification can mean growth in the possibility of androgyny, wherein each individual finds freedom to lay claim to his or her own unique personality configuration and expression and is not coerced into rigid sex-role stereotypes that make us half-human. Supremely, sexual sanctification means the awakening of the self to its destiny as an embodiment of love, the reintegration of our sexual dimensions around love's meanings.

If human experience of salvation is partial, incomplete, and fragmentary (as it is), surely this is true of the salvation that involves our sexuality. But its partiality does not negate its reality. The Word is made flesh, and our flesh is confirmed.

The church as a sexual community. Throughout most of Protestant history sexuality has been seen as incidental to the life of the church or even inimical to the church's purpose. It is time that this community of faith, worship, and service be understood also as a sexual community, not only because its members are sexual beings, but also because sexual meanings and feelings pervade all dimensions of the community's life, both for good and for ill. This has always been the case, and its conscious recognition can assist the church to reform the distorted sexual aspects of its life.

The church is a sexual community in its theological expressions, as the feminist movement forcefully reminds us. Stereotypically masculine language and images have pervaded Christian understandings of God and hence have given rise to a masculinized spirituality. A more androgynous theology and language can nuture a more androgynous spirituality, and both will be truer to the best in the tradition.

Reclaiming positive dimensions of sexuality in liturgy and sacramental life can enhance the connections of those experiences with the lives of the worshipers. Mainline Protestant worship has been marked, on the whole, by a masculinized emphasis on the spoken word and a suspicion of body feelings — touch, movement, color, play, and imagi-

nation. To the extent that worship patterns reflect the alienating sexual dualisms, they reinforce those dualisms in the lives of the worshipers. Further, recapturing an awareness of the rich sexual imagery in the two Protestant sacraments — baptism (the womb of new birth) and the Lord's Supper ("This is my body, given for you") — might assist the participants' understanding of the ways in which the total human sexual experience itself has sacramental potentialities. Sexual love, at its best, does have the capacity to break the self open not only to deep communion with the partner but also to the life-giving communion with God.

In education and social witness, consciousness of the church as sexual community can also expand our Christian awareness. Beyond the neglected but important role of the church in positive and effective sexuality education for its members of all ages, there can arise sensitivity to the sexual dimensions of a vast variety of social justice issues that the church is called to address. Some justice issues are quite obviously sexual: justice for women, gays, and lesbians; abortion; sexual abuse of women and children; prostitution; pornography; family planning and population control, to mention just a few. Beyond these are even larger social issues that do not appear to be sexuality-related, but in fact are. Patterns of distorted sexuality contribute enormously to social violence and militarism, to stubbornly persisting white racism, to the ecological dilemma and abuse of the natural environment. When the church can more fully realize the ways in which it is also a sexual community, when it can affirm more celebratively the potential sacramentality of human sexuality, then it may also more fully grasp the vision of an erotic sensibility toward the whole human community in a sacramental world.

Foundations for a Protestant Sexual Ethic

While there are different nuances and emphases within Roman Catholic sexual ethics, that presence of a strong natural-law tradition within that communion together with a clearly defined teaching authority, the *magesterium,* has resulted in a more coherent body of teachings than is true for Protestants. Protestantism has largely attempted to formulate sexual ethics from biblical grounds.

The resultant ethics show a considerably greater variety, coming as they do from a diversity of faith communities with looser patterns of authority in doctrine and morals.

Historically, Catholic ethics have their strengths, particularly in universality of application, objectivity of norms, and in the attempt to be specific in application. But those strengths have been matched by certain weaknesses: a rigid insistence upon absolute moral judgments about specific acts and a strong tendency to evaluate sexual acts in terms of their physical contours.

Protestant sexual ethics have been strong in their attempt to be faithful to scriptural sources, in their openness to change, uniqueness, and particularity, and in their attempt to take motives and dispositions as seriously as the physical acts themselves. But Protestant ethics perennially have had difficulty in finding a firm grounding for sexual values and norms, and in finding ways of adjudicating conflicting norms. Protestants, moreover, have been less clear methodologically. Attempting to affirm the Bible as primary authority within a plurality of other sources, mainstream Protestants have discovered that the relativity of biblical texts and themes has made it difficult to specify particular rules of sexual conduct and to demonstrate the primacy of the Bible's authority.[1]

Protestant ethics have thus struggled to find a course between legalism on one side and normlessness on the other. Legalism is the attempt to apply precise laws and rules to actions regardless of the unique features of the context of those actions. It assumes that objective standards can be applied in the same way to whole classes of actions without regard to the particular meanings those actions have to particular persons. And it might be noted that the tendency toward legalism seems stronger in sexual morality than in virtually any other arena of human behavior.

The antidote to legalism is an ethics that finds its center and direction in *love* rather than in a series of specific, absolute injunctions. Such an ethics takes the Bible seriously, but understands the need for critical awareness of how its sexual

teachings and practices not only reflect the biblical community's perception of God's intentions but also reflect sexual mores common to those historical circumstances. A love-centered ethics understands human nature as grounded in the will to communion. We are thoroughly social beings, nurtured into our humanness in community and destined for ultimate communion. This means that the positive ethical claim upon us is to become what we essentially *are*. We are to realize through our actions a responsiveness to the divine loving. Negatively, sin is not fundamentally breaking moral codes or disobeying moral laws (though it may involve that). More basically, sin is the failure to become who we are, the failure of our responsiveness to the Cosmic Lover. Sin is the estrangement and alienation that distort fulfillment and destroy communion.

Our sexuality is a dramatic sign of our destiny to communion, for its dynamism presses us toward intimacy and community. Even its distortions witness negatively to the power of sexuality by oppressing and destroying persons and their fulfillment.

If love is the central (albeit not the only) norm for Christian ethics, it is the central meaning of human sexuality and the measuring standard and justification for any particular sex act. Nevertheless, the word is dangerously slippery, and countless dehumanizing acts have been done in the name of love.

Love's source is God, the Creator, Redeemer, and Sustainer. Love takes its content from the Christian community's historic perceptions, both in scripture and tradition, of God's ways with humankind. Sexual acts that respond to the loving of God will be marked by qualities which mirror and reflect God's own creativity, reconciling activity, and sustaining, fulfilling purposes.

Love is multidimensional. Christian ethics long has utilized the four classic distinctions in speaking of love: *epithymia* or libido (the desire for sexual fulfillment); *eros* (desire and aspiration for the beloved); *philia* (mutuality and friendship); and *agape* (freely offered self-giving). These are different dimensions of love's unity, not different or opposing kinds of love. Each needs the other. Thus sexual desire *(epithymia)*, without the desire for communion with and fulfillment in the other *(eros)*, without a strong element of mutuality and

---

1. For a good overview of tendencies in recent Christian sexual ethics see Lisa Sowle Cahill, "Sexual Issues in Christian Theological Ethics," *Religious Studies Review* 4 (January 1978).

friendship *(philia)*, and without the transformative quality of self-giving abandonment *(agape)*, becomes distorted.

Love is also indivisible and nonquantifiable in regard to other-love and self-love. Self-love has been a perennial problem in Protestant ethics, and the confusion here has spawned enormous sexual confusions. Self-love has been mistakenly confused with egocentrism and selfishness, hence condemned. Thus Protestantism has had a difficult time dealing positively with sexual pleasure in general and with certain issues such as masturbation in particular. Without positive self-love, however, authentic intimacy is impossible, for the possibility of intimacy rests in considerable measure upon each individual's own sense of worth as a person. Without such self-affirmation, we elevate the other person into the center of our lives, hoping that the partner will assure us of our own reality. But that is too large an order for the other; it idolizes the partner. Self-love and other-love are not antagonists, but are mutually complementary.

Furthermore, love expresses itself in a variety of values. These can become criteria by which specific sexual acts might be measured in a nonlegalistic manner. . . .[2] Love is self-liberating. In a sexual act, it expresses one's own authentic self-affirmation and also the desire for further growth. Love is also other-enriching, displaying a genuine concern for the well-being and growth of the partner. Sexual love is honest, expressing as truthfully as possible the meaning of the relationship that actually exists between the partners. Love is faithful, expressing an ongoing commitment to this relationship, yet without crippling possessiveness. Sexual love is socially responsible, concerned that sexual acts reflect values which enhance the larger community. Love is life-serving; the power of renewed life is shared by the partners when sexual expression has been appropriate. Authentic sexual love is joyous, exuberant in its appreciation of love's mystery, life's gift, and sex's playfulness.

Does such a perception of love involve any principles and rules for sexual ethics? Yes, it can give structure to ethics without the rigidities of legalistic absolutes. It can provide general prin-

ciples. For example, love presses us toward a single and not a double standard for sexual morality. The same considerations apply equally to male and female, aged and young, able-bodied and disabled, homosexual and heterosexual. Another of love's principles is that the physical expression of one's sexuality with another person ought to be appropriate to the level of shared commitment. Such principles as these do not give exact prescriptions about specific acts, but rather provide a direction for making such decisions.

An ethics centered in love can also have specific sexual rules. It will probably understand the authority of the rules, however, in a certain way. Such rules are not likely to be understood as exceptionless absolutes (a new invitation to legalism). Nor will they be understood simply as guidelines that can be dismissed lightly if they do not seem to fit. Rather, love's sexual rules will have weight without absolutism. They will express the wisdom of the moral community and serve as a check on human finitude and sin, our limitations in both knowledge and virtue. People will take such *prima facie* rules seriously and presume in their favor. But given the rich complexity of human situations and God's freedom to intend the new expression of love, these moral rules will not be exceptionless. Yet, the community having presumed in favor of the rules, the burden of proof is upon the one who would depart from them. Now the question is: given a particular situation, will an exception to the rule actually express greater loyalty to the divine loving experienced in the neighbor, in the self, and in the wider community?

An ethics centered in this kind of love will be neither legalistic nor antinomian. It will not guarantee freedom from mistakes in the sexual life. It will place considerable responsibility upon the individual. It will be sensitive to relationships, motivations, and concrete situations, and it will be more oriented toward persons than toward abstract concepts. It will be more concerned about the authentic fulfillment of persons than the stringencies of unyielding laws or the neat cataloguing of types of sexual acts. It can serve our human becoming and our maturation as lovers in the image of the Cosmic Lover by whom and in whom we are continually being created.

2. See Anthony M. Kosnick et al., *Human Sexuality: New Directions in American Catholic Thought* (Paramus, NJ: Paulist/Newman Press, 1977), pp. 92ff.

62. Excerpts from *Limited Engagements*

PHILIP W. TURNER III

The basic argument for revision of the traditional teaching, though it may take many forms, is this. There is a distinct good in sexual desire and its fruition in freely entered and non-injurious sexual acts, just as there are distinct goods in the more wide-ranging relations of erotic love and/or marriage. Why not treat these goods as discrete, even if related, and allow their pursuit in isolation one from another? What harm is done? Is not real good prevented and real harm done by such a morally ambitious linkage? Is the traditional teaching not an ethic for "over-achievers"? Why foist such scrupulosity on others?

The answer in each case is that to make, *in principle,* a moral separation between sexual desire, erotic love, and marriage places in jeopardy the full promise of each at the same time that it exposes each to distortion and moral abuse. Suppose, for example, we were once again to say that marriage ought to be separated in principle from sexual desire and erotic love? Such a moral state is certainly the most common we have known through the course of history and we ought not to forget that it took a long time, even within the Christian tradition, to get desire, love and

Philip W. Turner III (1935–) is professor of Christian ethics and associate dean of Yale University Divinity School and president and dean of Berkeley Divinity School. His works include *Money, Sex, and Power* and *Men and Women: Sexual Ethics in Turbulent Times.*

From *Men and Women: Sexual Ethics in Turbulent Times,* ed. Philip W. Turner III (Cambridge, Mass.: Cowley Publications, 1989).

marriage linked in a moral way. What would it be like to return to those "exciting days of yesteryear" when marriage did not have a necessary moral relation to desire and love?

Would we think of such a return as a moral advance? We would, I think, on the contrary, hold it to be a moral retrogression. In the first place, marriage would be stripped of two of its most attractive goods; in the second, the man and the woman would become increasingly useful to one another for social purposes (like wealth, prestige, offspring, or security) that lie beyond their common good.

It is not, however, the proposal to separate marriage from desire and love that has the greatest attraction within our society, but the separation of desire from love and desire and love from marriage. Both these proposals illustrate the same point I have just made: both place in jeopardy the promise of the relations in question and make it more than likely that either the man or the woman will be abused in some way.

What is going on when, in a state of desire, we seek to call another person to an immediate presence in the flesh? What does it mean if we claim that the call we issue need not be motivated by love nor have love in any way in view? Does not such a moral stance skew the very direction in which desire leads? And what can be the motive for issuing such a call once its moral connection with love has been severed? Is not the motive likely to be either a vain curiosity on the one hand or a very personal and highly self-referential need on the other?

The ethic that is enjoying increasing popularity in church circles is one which makes a moral separation between sexual desire and erotic love on the one hand, and marriage on the other. The most common version of this proposal holds that if people truly desire each other and are "in love" and if there is "commitment" in their relationship, then sexual relations are morally permissible apart from the vows that convert erotic love into a permanent and exclusive union. The essence of this proposal, which is the strongest of the revisionist arguments now current, is that sexual relations ought to be loving and faithful but they need not be permanent.

There are two points at which this view requires careful assessment, and the first concerns the nature of the relation that is supposed to link the lovers involved. Looked at from one angle, it appears to rest upon the premise that the relation in question is a test and only a test. No matter how passionate, the relation is an uncertain one; within it, sex becomes a part of the way in which both love and the loved one are examined. In either case, sexual relations are part of an experiment.

Looked at from another point of view, the relation may appear as part of an exchange where each person is after something, but is unwilling to make a permanent or exclusive commitment to get it. The agreement is "for the time being" and for limited purposes — for pleasure and sexual release, or for warmth and emotional satisfaction, or simply the company of a helpful companion. From each point of vantage a different set of meanings may appear, but from all points of view the lovers in question are involved in a limited engagement: a calculation of benefits and burdens, a test of feelings, and, most of all, a deliberate assessment of the possibility or advisability of love's demise.

So not only must we assess the nature of the relationship, but also the character of the lovers. They are to be "committed," but what is the meaning of this description of their intentions and motives? Commitment is at root a power of soul — I take this virtue to be a modern substitute for chastity. A revision of this magnitude of the traditional account of sexual virtue deserves careful scrutiny. Careful scrutiny, however, is just what the word "commitment" has not received from its advocates. If one reads the literature carefully and asks exactly what the moral requirements of "commitment" are, it is in the end very difficult to say.

A recent article in a denominational newspaper spoke of "committed sexual relationships" as ones in which two people undertake for periods of "varying duration" to share their lives in "a mutually responsive, loving way."[1] James Nelson in his widely read book *Embodiment* says that the church ought to provide "guidelines" for people "who do not see marriage or remarriage as an expression of their vocation, and yet do not intend a life of complete celibacy."[2] The first of the guidelines he provides is "commitment." Nelson goes on to say of a committed relationship that it should manifest "a profound respect for the other as a person, a deep caring for the partner's well-being . . . marked by honesty and the concern for social

responsibility. In a word, it should embody openness to life."[3] Elsewhere Nelson insists that committed sexual relations embody love, care, trust, openness, and fidelity.

These are all recognizable words and they can also be found in association with the word chastity. If we ask more precisely what they involve in their new setting, however, it becomes clear that within "committed relationships" love and care are limited in both extent and duration, and that fidelity, at least in Nelson's account, does not absolutely preclude other sexual partners. Trust and openness are both guarded and subject to frequent reevaluation.

Commitment seems to refer basically to emotional sincerity and to a morally serious dedication to testing the quality of an erotic relationship. It is a virtue, in short, well suited to a limited engagement and as such is a power of soul appropriate for people whom Dante called "trimmers." Commitment, as opposed to chastity, is the expression of a soul that at its deepest level blows neither hot nor cold. It is a virtue for the tentative, one that calls to mind the image of someone testing the water of a bath by sticking their toe in. It is an questionable virtue that makes one wonder if W. H. Auden was not right when he said in his "Christmas Oratorio," "Love's not what she used to be."[4]

Auden's comment appears to be quite accurate. These limited engagements in which desire, love, and marriage are separated in principle one from another place in jeopardy the relationship which is the most fully human and the one which we most highly prize, namely, erotic love itself. The danger is twofold. In the first place, love's promise is severely endangered and the sort of relationship love requires is opened to abuse and distortion. In the second place, the power of soul necessary if sexual desire, erotic love, and marriage are to yield their promised blessing is "trimmed," or "abridged." The results of this abridgment both of the extensiveness of love's relation and of the power of soul necessary for the support of that relation, indeed mean that "love's not what she used to be."

The subject matter of all human ethics concerns not only the forms of human relationship, but also the powers of soul necessary for successful engagement in those relationships. In both ways, the proposals for revision of the churches' traditional teaching are not only inadequate but on the whole injurious to the very relation they are supposed to further. The subject matter of Christian ethics concerns the way in which God in Christ can be imaged in the various forms of human relationship and in the powers of soul which sustain and generate them. In this respect also the suggestions for revision seem inadequate, presupposing a kind of qualified fidelity and permanence that does not image Christ.

What attitude ought Christians to take toward these increasingly frequent, though limited, sexual engagements? One thing the proponents of revision rightly fear is the sort of judgmental and punitive attitude so characteristic of church life in America and so well depicted in Hawthorne's *The Scarlet Letter*. Descendants of Hester Prynne still fill the land. Critics of the traditional teaching of the church fear not only the self-righteousness that punished her, but also the damage this self-righteousness continues to inflict upon both individuals and the church as a whole.

But need the proponents of the traditional view be self-righteous and punitive? Its defenders can be neither if they understand the teaching rightly; if they do, they will know that before God none of them is chaste. The story of the crowd gathered around the woman taken in adultery is the story of what all Christians are supposed to know about themselves. There is no one who is fully chaste and there is no one who loves as God wills. None can cast the first stone because none is without guilt.

Central to Christian belief is the view that the greatest sin of all is to focus on the faults of others while ignoring one's own. The traditional teaching about sexual relations can be understood properly only within the context of the Christian doctrine of the justification of the sinner by grace through faith. Self-righteousness is thus not a necessary companion of the traditional teaching, but rather a sure sign that it has not been properly understood.

There is another concern revisionists have, however, that is far more serious. They fear that the traditional view does not take into account the very genuine good that is often involved in the "committed relationships" they support. This point recently was made with great force by the mother of a young man, who said to me, "I thank God every day for the woman my son lived with

during college. She healed a wound in him." Unspoken was the mother's conviction that the wound lay beyond her own care.

The question is therefore bound to arise: If such good can come, why not give moral license to the relationship that brings it? It is this question that exposes a place at which the traditional teaching requires a more thorough exposition than it has yet received. Can a place be found within it for the obvious good that is part of many of the limited sexual engagements we have been discussing?

Looked at in one way, no place can be found. If we take the traditional teaching *only* as a *command* given by Christ to his disciples, then we must simply say that limited sexual engagements, what we now call "committed relationships," represent a form of disobedience. If the committed relations of which the revisionists speak are viewed *only* in terms of command and obedience, they will inevitably be judged *only* in a negative light.

There is good reason to say that some disobedience is involved in these relationships. Nevertheless, there is another aspect of the traditional teaching that displays these relations in a different and more positive way than the image of command and obedience allows, and it also must be taken into account if a fully adequate moral assessment is to be made. This aspect of the tradition speaks of *good* rather than of command and obedience. It depicts in some detail and with great appreciation the goods of the various aspects of sexual relations, those associated with sexual desire and its fulfillment as well as with the wider and more encompassing relation of erotic love. These goods are, to be sure, abridged and placed in jeopardy when sexual desire, erotic love, and marriage are not held morally together. Nevertheless, the goods themselves do not disappear.

It is precisely because the goods of sex and erotic attraction need not be totally eclipsed, even in the most tentative and limited of relationships, that defenders of the churches' traditional teaching demonstrate that they have not understood their own position if they speak only of disobedience. For the traditional teaching, properly understood, implies that we may in fact find some trace of good in the most unlikely of sexual relations. Furthermore, when coupled with an adequate account of Christian believing, the traditional teaching allows us to rejoice whenever and wherever we see good, no matter how minimal or fragile it appears or how tentative and limited the relation in which it is found. Thus one may rejoice in good even when it is seen within a relation that may, for one reason or another, not be right.

To take pleasure in the good another enjoys, however, does not mean that one must close one's eyes to what is deficient, wrong, or even evil, or give up the belief that there is a better way. A person with what we may call a "traditional conscience" can, with a good heart, recognize whatever good is to be found in "committed sexual relations" and give thanks for its presence. And yet, they can and indeed ought to insist that the relation in question, no matter what good it may involve, is nonetheless wrong; it is part of the broad rather than the narrow way in which Christ calls his disciples to follow.

Furthermore, they can make these claims even if choosing the narrow path involves refusal of a "committed relation" and, with that refusal, the loss of a much-desired and much-needed good — perhaps even healing or comfort. They can make this wrenching claim because of another belief, one which displays the very foundation upon which traditional conscience rests. It is the belief that God does not call us in a way that does us final harm, nor ask of us more than we are able to bear. The way of the Cross is in fact a way of blessing, despite all indications to the contrary. Indeed, Christianity is defined by the belief that in and through the Cross of Christ God displays his power to heal and comfort us even in the most extreme of life's circumstances, and even if the cure and comfort he offers involve the infliction of more wounds.

The mother's comment which began this discussion raises in a very immediate way the abiding question of the relation between good, right, and happiness. The question is one that cannot be avoided by either theological or philosophical ethics. Looked at in one way, the history of both may be understood as the history of this debate.

No matter what the conclusions of moral philosophy may be, however, Christian theology cannot remain consistent with itself if ever it claims that the Christian life involves no sacrifice of a deficient good or temporary happiness. Many goods and much happiness must be passed by if the way to the source of all human good and all human happiness is to be followed. What Chris-

tian theology must insist upon, however, is that, in following this way, the loss of good does not mean the loss of blessing or fullness of life. Even in the loss that occurs, joys are present which exceed it. This is the meaning of one of the most enigmatic and difficult of Christ's sayings, namely, "All these things will be added unto you."

The mother's comment with which I began this discussion leaves us with another question, however, and the remarks I have made to this point do not address it adequately. Even if the traditional teaching allows us both to recognize the good in "committed sexual relation" and to continue at the same time to recommend the traditional teaching, what are we to say to the young man who may have quite deliberately chosen not to follow it? Despite justifiable fears of appearing overly harsh, it may well be appropriate both to say that the traditional teaching marks a better way and to attempt to convince him that what one says is indeed the case. It may also be appropriate to warn him of the moral and religious dangers involved in such a relationship.

There is, however, one more thing that may also be appropriate. It is to tell him that even in choosing the goods he has, these goods will, in the end, yield their full benefit only if he does not lose sight of the full description of sexual good the traditional teaching traces. In respect to his life as a sexual being, this teaching displays his good, while the fulfillment of his and everyone else's sexual good depends upon it. Thus, if the traditional teaching is kept in mind as the way in which we, as sexual beings, are meant to follow, then the abridged and fragile goods he now enjoys will not later be lost. Rather, they may well take on a fuller meaning and provide the basis for future blessing long after the relation in question is over.

Thus defenders of the traditional teaching need not deny or disparage the genuine goods that come from the various forms of limited sexual engagement our society now allows. In fact they are in a better position than the revisionists to make some lasting sense out of them, since the former are able to show that the goods enjoyed depend upon the traditional teaching for the full extent of their meaning and the full extent of the happiness they can bring. They can also look more realistically at the character of these relations and see both their deficiencies and their dangers.

Try It Yourself:
A Case of
Premarital Sex

CASE STUDY 4

In preparation for a class debate next week, your ethics professor has taken an unusual step. Your fiancé is in the class, and will be opposing you in the debate. Your professor calls both of you into his office.

"I am aware that you two have been engaged for six months now, and plan to be married a year from now. You have known each other a full three years. Since our resolution will be 'A Christian may have sexual intercourse with his or her fiancé before their wedding ceremony,' there will be more than usual interest among your classmates in what both of you say. I'm going to allow one of you to pick their side. Who will it be?"

After much discussion, your fiancé defers to you. Choose the side (pro or con) you believe in or the side towards which you lean. Defend your choice.

You may want to return to the series of case studies on "holy unions" after reading this chapter.

363

Chapter 10

Christian Medical Ethics

Introduction

In the biblical readings which stand first in this chapter the chronicler chides King Asa for consulting physicians about his (probably gangrenous) feet. Few contemporary Christians are quite so suspicious of medicine; most would follow the sage advice of Jesus ben Sirach and honor the physician — and the skill and medicine of the physician — as a gift of God, from whom all "healing comes." (*The Wisdom of Jesus ben Sirach*, or *Ecclesiasticus*, incidentally, is part of the Roman Catholic canon but not part of the Protestant canon.) Indeed, many Christians have considered the vocation of the physician and nurse "holy callings," forms of discipleship of Jesus, and tokens of the good future Jesus made known in his own healings.

However enthusiastic Christians may be about medicine in general, most Christians want to live and die — and give birth and suffer and care for the suffering — with Christian integrity, and not just with medical proficiency. They want to use the powers of medicine in ways that are faithful to their identity as Christians. Thinking about those extraordinary powers — and the limits to them — and about the ways of faith and faithfulness in the ordinary human events of giving birth, suffering, and dying are among the tasks of a Christian medical ethics.

Daniel Callahan provides "a short history of bioethics" in reading 64. He notes "the secularization of bioethics," and he finds reasons to regret it, reasons he identifies as the "discontents of secularization." The article is particulary poignant because Callahan acknowledges that his own religious belief "had all but disappeared." Many others, of course, continue in faith, and — as faith seeks understanding — they seek to relate all things (including life and death and health and suffering and medicine) to God and to relate to all things (including medicine) in ways appropriate to the relations of all things to God.

Subsequent readings take up general questions such as the relation of theology to the public debate about issues in medical ethics (see reading 65), the relation of medicine and religion (see reading 66). Then, without leaving the general questions aside, the focus shifts to particular issues like surrogacy (67), abortion (68), and the distinction between killing and allowing to die (69). We have encountered some other issues of medical ethics already in this anthology. There was, for example, an account of the Catholic tradition and position concerning contraception in readings 13 and 25, and abortion was introduced in reading 34. The essay on technology and values by C. S. Lewis (reading 27) is surely relevant. But your struggles earlier with questions about sources and strategy and contexts are also relevant, and you can here try and test your tentative conclusions there.

The case study at the end of this chapter asks you to consider "physician-assisted suicide." The article by Gilbert Meilaender (reading 69) is obviously relevant, but so are the judgments you have formed about *how* Scripture and tradition and philosophy and science contribute to Christian moral reflection; so is your judgment about whether the best strategy for moral reflection is to focus on duties and rights, on outcomes, or on character; so is your reflection about love and justice; and so, finally, is your consideration of the contexts for Christian ethics. Many of the readings deal with context in one way or another, and the case study exercise is designed to keep you from ignoring it.

Suggestions for Further Reading

Bouma, Hessel III, Douglas Diekema, Edward Langerak, Theodore Rottman, Allen Verhey. *Christian Faith, Health, and Medical Practice.* Grand Rapids, Mich.: Wm. B. Eerdmans, 1989.

Hauerwas, Stanley. *Suffering Presence: Theological Reflections on Medicine, the Mentally Handicapped, and the Church.* Notre Dame: Univeristy of Notre Dame Press, 1986.

Holifield, E. Brooks. *Health and Medicine in the Methodist Tradition: Journey toward Wholeness.* New York: Crossroad, 1986.

Lammers, Stephen E., and Allen Verhey, eds. *On Moral Medicine: Theological Reflections on Medical Ethics.* Grand Rapids, Mich.: Wm. B. Eerdmans, 1987.

Marty, Martin E. *Health and Medicine in the Lutheran Tradition: Being Well.* New York: Crossroad, 1983.

McCormick, Richard A. *Health and Medicine in the Roman Catholic Tradition: Tradition in Transition.* New York: Crossroad, 1985.

Smith, David H. *Health and Medicine in the Anglican Tradition: Conscience, Community and Compromise.* New York: Crossroad, 1986.

Vaux, Kenneth. *Health and Medicine in the Reformed Tradition; Promise, Providence, and Care.* New York: Crossroad, 1984.

Verhey, Allen, and Stephen E. Lammers, eds., *Theological Voices in Medical Ethics.* Grand Rapids, Mich.: Wm. B. Eerdmans, 1993.

63. 2 Chronicles 16:12; Wisdom of Jesus ben Sirach 38:1-15; Luke 7:19-23

2 Chronicles 16:12

In the thirty-ninth year of his reign Asa was diseased in his feet, and his disease become severe; yet even in his disease he did not seek the LORD, but sought help from physicians.

Wisdom of Jesus ben Sirach 38:1-15

Honor the physician with the honor due him,
    according to your need of him,
  for the Lord created him;
for healing comes from the Most High,
    and he will receive a gift from the king.
The skill of the physician lifts up his head,
    and in the presence of great men he is admired.
The Lord created medicines from the earth,
    and a sensible man will not despise them.
Was not water made sweet with a tree
    in order that his a power might he known?
And he gave skill to men
    that he might be glorified in his
      marvelous works.
By them he heals and takes away pain;
    the pharmacist makes of them a compound.
His works will never be finished;
    and from him health is upon the face
      of the earth.

My son, when you are sick do not be negligent,
    but pray to the Lord, and he will heal you.
Give up your faults and direct your
      hands aright,

and cleanse your heart from all sin.
Offer a sweet-smelling sacrifice, and a
    memorial portion of fine flour,
    and pour oil on your offering, as much
        as you can afford.
And give the physician his place,
    for the Lord created him;
    let him not leave you, for there is need of him.
There is a time when success lies
    in the hands of physicians,
    for they too will pray to the Lord
that he should grant them success in diagnosis
    and in healing, for the sake of preserving life.
He who sins before his Maker,
    may he fall into the care of a physician.

Luke 7:19-23

And John, calling to him two of his disciples, sent them to the Lord, saying, "Are you he who is to come, or shall we look for another?" And when the men had come to him, they said, "John the Baptist has sent us to you, saying, 'Are you he who is to come, or shall we look for another?'" In that hour he cured many of diseases and plagues and evil spirits, and on many that were blind he bestowed sight. And he answered them, "Go and tell John what you have seen and heard: the blind receive their sight, the lame walk, lepers are cleansed, and the deaf hear, the dead are raised up, the poor have good news preached to them. And blessed is he who takes no offense at me."

64. Religion and the Secularization of Bioethics

DANIEL CALLAHAN

The occasion of this special supplement on religion and bioethics serves to remind me, once again, that the field of bioethics as we now know it is a creature of its time and history. It grew up during the 1960s and 1970s in an era of affluence and social utopianism, in a culture that was experimenting with an expansive array of newly found rights and unprecedented opportunities for personal freedom, and in the context of a national history that has long struggled to find the right place for religion in its public life. For medicine it was a time that combined magnificent theoretical and clinical achievements with uncommonly difficult moral problems, many of them bearing on the self-identity and goals of medicine. The story of contemporary bioethics turns on the way in which those problems intersected with, and whose understanding was shaped by, that larger temporal and social context.

The most striking change over the past two decades or so has been the secularization of bioethics. The field has moved from one dominated by religious and medical traditions to one now increasingly shaped by philosophical and legal

Daniel Callahan (1930–) is the founding director of the Institute for Social Ethics and the Life Sciences at the Hastings Center in New York. He has written and lectured widely. His works include *Science, Ethics, and Medicine* and *Setting Limits: Medical Goals in an Aging Society.*

From *The Hastings Center Report,* July/August 1990, pp. 2-4.

concepts. The consequence has been a mode of public discourse that emphasizes secular themes: universal rights, individual self-direction, procedural justice, and a systematic denial of either a common good or a transcendent individual good.

Let me, if I may, use myself as an illustration of this trend, as well as an example of some considerable uneasiness left in its wake. When I first became interested in bioethics in the mid-1960s, the only resources were theological or those drawn from within the traditions of medicine, themselves heavily shaped by religion. In one way, that situation was congenial enough. I was through much of the 1960s a religious person and had no trouble bringing that perspective to bear on the newly emergent issues of bioethics. But that was not to be finally adequate for me. Two personal items were crucial. My religious belief was by then beginning to decline, and by the end of the decade had all but disappeared. My academic training, moreover, was that of analytic philosophy, and I wanted to bring that work to bear on bioethics. Was it not obvious, I thought, that moral philosophy, with its historical dedication to finding a rational foundation for ethics, was well suited to biomedical ethics, particularly in a pluralistic society? Just as I had found I did not need religion for my personal life, why should biomedicine need it for its collective moral life?

The answer to that last question has been less obvious than I originally thought. If my life has been, in a way, relieved by the absence of religion as a guiding force, I cannot say that it has been enriched or that I am a better person for that. Nor can it be said, I think, that biomedical ethics is demonstrably more robust and satisfying as a result of its abandonment of religion. To say that of course is not to make a case for the validity of religion, which must be made on its own merits, not on its potential contribution to bioethics. Some nineteenth-century thinkers, we might recall, came to think that, although religion was false as a way of understanding the world, it was socially useful to sustain as a source of discipline and political stability. There was always something slightly cynical in that view, and doubly so because it was meant to strengthen the hand of those in authority. Nonetheless, it is not necessary to entertain such a position to recognize that whatever the ultimate truth status of religious perspectives,

they have provided a way of looking at the world and understanding one's own life that has a fecundity and uniqueness not matched by philosophy, law, or political theory. Those of us who have lost our religious faith may be glad that we have discovered what we take to be the reality of things, but we can still recognize that we have also lost something of great value as well: the faith, vision, insights, and experience of whole peoples and traditions who, no less than we unbelievers, struggled to make sense of things. That those goods are part of a garment we no longer want to wear does not make their loss anything other than still a loss; and it is not a negligible one.

But need that be the end of the story? Can those of us who share my lack of belief still make use of at least some of the insights and perspectives of religion, even as we reject its roots? Or are they meaningless without their connection to those roots? Are there some questions about our lives and destiny that philosophy, science, or other secular disciplines can't help us get hold of with any telling force, and that only religion has been able to accommodate? Is it wrong, or a form of illogical sentimentality, to continue feeding off of religious traditions and ways of life that one has, in fact, rejected at their core? Does intellectual honesty demand that we have the courage of our convictions (or lack thereof) and construct our view of the world out of the whole cloth of unbelief, not borrowing to suit our own purposes those valuable bits, pieces, and parts of a garment we have thrown off? And of course there is another question that might be entertained: if we agree that religion, even if wrongheaded, provides ways of understanding not otherwise attainable, should we then never allow ourselves to close the door on the possibility of a renewed belief? Even if we have not the faintest idea (as I do not) about where that renewal might come from?

Those are some questions I have put to myself over the years. I will not try to answer them directly here, and do not in any event think I have good answers. I will instead say something about the unfolding of contemporary bioethics, inviting others to see whether that history provides some answers to the questions I have raised.

A Short History of Bioethics

Joseph Fletcher's book *Medicine and Morals* (1954) has often, and correctly, been cited as the first truly fresh manifestation of a growing interest in medical ethics in the post–World War II era. That Fletcher was at the time an Episcopalian theologian might easily lead one to think of the book as a "theological" contribution. Its contents, however, suggest a very different interpretation. By his emphasis upon "choice" as the heart of morality, his rejection of moral theories (particularly Roman Catholic) that would look to nature for ethical guidance, and his celebration of the power of medicine to open new opportunities for moral freedom, Fletcher was in fact opening a direct assault upon some long-standing religious constraints on medicine. That Fletcher's moral theory was based on what he called "situation ethics" — emphasizing the uniqueness of each moral choice and therefore the irrelevance of binding moral rules and principles — signalled all the more the depth of his attack on some characteristic religious values. The possibility also of detecting, just below the surface, an additional powerful strain of utilitarianism in Fletcher's book underscored the depth of the break he was working to engender.

Medicine and Morals did not, in the 1950s, have a great impact in the medical world, even if Fletcher's situation ethics had a telling appeal among many physicians whose clinical experience resisted general moral rules. But that was not an era when the writings of outsiders, religious or not, were likely to be taken seriously. It was not until the middle of the 1960s, in the controversies that developed over human subject experimentation, that those outside voices began to make themselves heard. The quick appearance thereafter of increasingly public struggles over the definition of death and the care of the terminally ill, genetic counseling and prenatal diagnosis, and organ transplantation, brought the field of bioethics into being. The Protestant theologian Paul Ramsey, first with *The Patient as Person* (1970) and then with other books in the 1970s, carried out one of the first comprehensive bioethical examinations of the newly emergent issues. James M. Gustafson added still another powerful theological impetus (even if, in what his writings actually said, the

specific contribution of theology was rendered systematically ambiguous). All the while, Jewish and Roman Catholic theologians were carrying on the long-standing work of responding to medical advances and quandaries in light of their own traditions, though now with a new intensity. The writings of Seymour Siegel or David Feldman, from the Jewish side, or Richard McCormick and Charles Curran, from the Roman Catholic, provided evidence of that intensity.

Yet in many respects this early theological role in the emergence of the field was soon to decline. Part of the reason may be that the theological seminaries and departments of religion were in the 1970s drawn more to issues of urban poverty and race, and to questions of world peace in a nuclear age, than to bioethics. After a short burst of interest, the number of younger scholars drawn to the field seemed to decline as the decade came to an end (and many of those who were attracted seemed more comfortable speaking the language of philosophy than religion). No less importantly perhaps, once the field became of public interest, commanding the attention of courts, legislatures, the media, and professional societies, there was great pressure (even if more latent than manifest) to frame the issues, and to speak, in a common secular mode.

Here the philosophers and the lawyers came to take the lead. Samuel Gorovitz organized a 1974 conference on bioethics for philosophers at Haverford College, drawing a number of newcomers to the field, many of whom went on to considerable prominence. The Karen Ann Quinlan case in 1975 had a similarly potent effect on the law, making evident that bioethics would provide a steady stream of legal cases and a considerable body of unique issues for legal scholars. As the field of medicine became itself more engaged in the issues, it sought a way of framing and discussing them that would bypass religious struggles. Lawyers and philosophers were by no means seen as congenial allies of doctors, but they were preferable to theologians (especially those who spoke out of sectarian traditions). For all the steady interest of some physicians in religion and medicine, the discipline of medicine itself is now as resolutely secular as any that can be found in our society. It is a true child of the Enlightenment.

All of these trends were nicely epitomized in

the two federal commissions established during the 1970s, the National Commission for the Protection of Human Subjects in 1974, and the President's Commission in 1979. Both the professional staffs of the two groups and those called upon to give testimony before them were drawn mainly from medicine, philosophy, the health policy sciences, and the law. The approaches and concepts commonly employed in their reports, moreover, showed not the least visible trace of religious influence. An ethic of universal principles — especially autonomy, beneficence, and justice — was given a place of prestige in the 1978 *Belmont Report* issued by the National Commission.

I do not want to imply that there was any outright hostility toward religion (even though I could detect that now and then in some philosophers I knew). On the contrary, it was for the most part bypassed altogether. Whatever place it might have in the private lives of individuals, it simply did not count as one of the available common resources for setting public policy. There was (and still is) a lurking fear of religion, often seen as a source of deep and unresolvable moral conflict as well as single-minded political pressure when aroused. For that matter, ours is a society extraordinarily wary of provoking fundamental debates about basic worldviews and ethical premises. Such debates are seen as more likely to produce destructive battles than illuminating social insights, more anger and intransigence than peace and compromise. Religious differences have commonly been seen as the most likely source of such struggles, and thus to be kept at arm's length — or, even better, off the political playing field altogether.

The Discontents of Secularization

Some important consequences of this general attitude seem apparent. It encourages a form of moral philosophy for use in the marketplace that aspires simultaneously to a kind of detached neutrality (what Thomas Nagel has called the "view from nowhere"), and a culture-free rationalistic universalism (which is suspicious of the emotions and the particularities of actual human communities). It is hardly surprising that the only theoretical debate taken to be of any great moral interest is that between deontologists (who can help the

right trump the good), and utilitarians (who can allow a calculus of pleasures, pains, or preferences to trump both the right and the good). No less banished are more speculative forms of philosophy, especially those that might look to nature or organism for moral direction. Its worst failing may be its enormous reluctance to question the conventional ends and goals of medicine, thereby running a constant risk of simply legitimating, by way of ethical tinkering and casuistical fussiness, the way things are.

Another consequence is that it has either intimidated religion from speaking in its own voice, or has driven many to think that voice can be expressed with integrity only within the confines of particular religious communities. Time and again I have been told by religious believers at a conference or symposium that they feared revealing their deepest convictions. They felt the price of acceptance was to talk the common language, and they were probably right. Religious convictions are thought "personal" in two senses: they bespeak a particular cultural and ethnic background, and they reveal someone's inner life. Those of us who spend our time in the leading scientific and intellectual salons, and who have come to know the rules of the game, take great pains to conceal those features of our lives. I am no more enthused about letting my Irish-Catholic, parochial school background show (even if now put behind me) than I am to have a spot of gravy on my Brooks Brothers striped tie. (In fact the latter is preferable to the former; we all dribble from time to time, but not everyone has had a parochial school education — a tie can be cleaned in a way a psyche cannot be).

The net result of this narrowing of philosophy and the disappearance or denaturing of religion in public discourse is a triple threat. It leaves us, first of all, too heavily dependent upon the law as the working source of morality. The language of the courts and legislatures becomes our only shared means of discourse. That leaves a great number fearful of the law (as seems the case with many physicians) or dependent upon the law to determine the rightness of actions, which it can rarely do since it tells us better what is forbidden or acceptable than what is commendable or right.

It leaves us, secondly, bereft of the accumulated wisdom and knowledge that are the fruit of long-established religious traditions. I do not have to be a Jew to find it profitable and illuminating to see how the great rabbinical teachers have tried to understand moral problems over the centuries. Nor will Jews find it utterly useless to explore what the popes, or the leading Protestant divines, have had to say about ethics. This seems an obvious kind of point to make; but few actually make it.

It leaves us, thirdly, forced to pretend that we are not creatures both of particular moral communities and the more sprawling, inchoate general community that we celebrate as an expression of our pluralism. Yet that pluralism becomes a form of oppression if, in its very name, we are told to shut up in public about our private lives and beliefs and talk a form of what Jeffrey Stout has called moral Esperanto. The rules of that language are that it deny the concreteness and irregularities of real communities, that it eschew vision and speculation about goals and meaning, and that it enshrine the discourse of wary strangers (especially that of rights) as the preferred mode of daily relations.

With so many riches at our disposal, why have we ended in the name of social peace with a salt that has lost its savor?

65. Can Theology Have a Role in "Public" Bioethical Discourse?

LISA SOWLE CAHILL

Religious groups indubitably have been active in pressing their bioethical concerns in the public arena in the United States. One thinks preeminently of the efforts of the Roman Catholic Church and its representatives, or of religiously motivated "pro-life" activists, who quite visibly aim to influence public perceptions and policies on reproductive issues such as abortion and infertility therapies, and on dilemmas of life-prolongation, such as withdrawal of artificial nutrition and direct euthanasia. Have these church-based efforts any legitimacy in public policy formulation and if so, on what grounds? Or are they attempts to foist particularistic religious convictions on a pluralistic and otherwise free society, in violation of our prized tradition of separation of church and state?

At the same time that religious involvement in policy formation may seem unduly aggressive to some, from the perspectives of bioethics literature and medical practice or research, it often appears that theology brings little to bioethics which is even

Lisa Sowle Cahill (1948–) is professor of Christian ethics at Boston College. She is author of *Between the Sexes: Foundations for a Christian Ethics of Sexuality;* and co-author with Thomas Shannon of *Religion and Artificial Reproduction: An Inquiry into the Vatican "Instruction on Respect for Human Life in its Origin and on the Dignity of Human Reproduction."*

From "Theology, Religious Traditions, and Bioethics," ed. Daniel Callahan and Courtney S. Campbell, Special Supplement, *Hastings Center Report* 20, no. 4 (1990): pp. 10-14.

identifiably religious. When one inspects the work of individual theologians rather than ecclesial bodies — and especially when one advances beyond the well-trod ground staked out around abortion to tangle with issues such as genetic research or national health insurance — it may seem that religious faith and theological reflection fail to offer any guidance that could not have been arrived at by other means. Although "theologians" and "Christian ethicists" frequently address bioethics issues both in clinical settings and in print, even major figures such as Paul Ramsey and Richard McCormick often limit or avoid directly religious appeals in the interest of expanding their audience and hence influence. One might thus ask whether the result has any specifically theological stamp to it.

If by "theological" is meant a specific and unique line of religious argument entailing conclusions that also manifest a religious imprint, then theology is scarce in bioethics. Even clearly theological foundations, premises, and commitments do not necessarily lead to substantive moral principles, to arguments, or much less to concrete conclusions of a directly religious character, even though they may be endorsed strongly by religious groups. At the same time, the presence in bioethics of persons with theological training or with religious affiliations continues to give theology influence, even though this may not manifest itself in the explicit justification of moral conclusions. But it is more appropriate to construe theological contributions as overlapping and coinciding with philosophical ones, than to see secular, philosophical bioethics and religious, theological bioethics as two distinct or even competing entities.

As I see it, public bioethical discourse (or public policy discourse) is actually a meeting ground of the diverse moral traditions that make up our society. Some of these moral traditions have religious inspiration, but that does not necessarily disqualify them as contributors to the broader discussion. Their contributions will be appropriate and effective to the extent that they can be articulated in terms with a broad if not universal appeal. In other words, faith language that offers a particular tradition's beliefs about God as the sole warrant for moral conclusions will convince only members of that tradition. But faith commitments can legitimately motivate participants in public discussion to seek a moral consensus consistent

with their faith while at the same time be congenial to members of other moral traditions, the persuasion of whom may be the object of religious groups and theologians who argue and act for social change.

A Commitment to Dialogue and Openness

As James Gustafson has indicated, theology rarely yields precise and concrete directives for bioethical decisionmaking, or commends insights and actions inaccessible to nonreligious persons. But theology does have a critical function in "public" discourse, if the edge of religious commitment can be sharpened so as to cut through cultural assumptions.[1] Theologians and religious groups can introduce the civil community to insights borne by their own traditions, *on the assumption that and provided that* these traditions are not sheerly insular nor the civil community a wholly foreign country in which values with originally religious sponsorship are entirely unintelligible.

One should not, moreover, approach the issue of the contribution of theology to bioethics on the assumption that there exists some independent realm of secular or philosophical discourse, privileged as more reasonable, neutral, or objective, and less tradition-bound, than religious discourse. If such a realm is posited, then theology is seen potentially as entering it to be talkative, or remaining outside it in silence. To speak of distinctly secular language and arguments also implies that to be intelligible, religious or theological language must undergo some sort of "translation" into the lingua franca — into some different vocabulary universally understood. But this is a distorted understanding both of religious traditions and their theologies, and of what happens in "public" discourse about bioethics.

Bioethical discussions (and other "public" or intertraditional discussions of ethics) begin in situations of common *practical* interest; a dilemma about the nature of a *practical* moral obligation gives a common starting point. A real or envisioned situation of moral agency presents questions and

1. James M. Gustafson, *The Contributions of Theology to Medical Ethics* (Milwaukee, Wis.: Marquette University Theology Department, 1975).

stimulates participants to think theoretically. Discussion partners come to be so on the basis of such situations, and they enter them as persons from quite different, yet sometimes shared, or overlapping, moral and religious communities. Attempts to fashion a life together, a life that necessarily involves moral obligations and decisions, force us to arrive at some mutual understanding of what that would mean — especially in its practical results. Yet we do not participate in this process via an objective, traditionless, secular version of philosophical reasoning. The preeminent and supposedly neutral vocabulary of public policy debates in the U.S. today (liberty, autonomy, rights, privacy, due process) itself comes out of a rather complex but distinct set of political, legal, philosophical, moral, and even religious *traditions*. Though these are far from universal to humankind, they have over a three-hundred-year period come to be constitutive of a certain shared North American perspective. As Jeffrey Stout puts it, there is no privileged vantage point "above the fray."[2]

To follow Stout's evocative terminology,[3] there is also no universal and neutral language, no "Esperanto," into which theological language can be translated. Moreover, it is mistaken to expect theologians to adopt some sort of "pidgin," implying that, even if not philosophically fluent, theologians ought to try to master some dominant language, a language rising above all special commitments and points of view, the language in which those no longer hampered by an immigrant, ghetto mentality are already conversing. What ethicists do manage, as they speak beyond but always out of their native traditions, is what Stout (reinterpreting the term from Claude Levi-Strauss) calls "bricolage," a borrowing of what is not only handy but appropriate and communicative in jostling, negotiating, and persuading toward a common moral sense.

It is also useful to keep in mind that ethical discourse occurs on different levels and in different contexts, and that differentiated methods and goals may be appropriate to each. In a reminder to this effect, James Gustafson distinguishes four

complementary modes of ethics: analytical ethics, public policy ethics, narrative ethics, and prophetic ethics.[4] The first, which Gustafson calls "ethical discourse," is aimed at finding moral justifications for specific actions and decisions, while the interrelated modes of narrative and prophetic discourse present larger questions about worldview, community identity, and basic values. Public policy discourse can be "ethical discourse" when it is more disciplined and distanced from the actual political process. But policy discourse can also be carried out by persons with institutional roles, who ask practical questions. In such a case, bioethics is not "purely" ethical because it deals with the "enabling and limiting conditions" of practical social options, rather than with a more philosophical delineation of the ideally good society, institution, or policy.[5]

Using Gustafson's categories, one will note that policy discussions occur precisely in the arena in which some common courses of action must be agreed upon, despite less agreement at the "metaethical" level. To construct a language of "principles" that will serve this purpose is a necessary achievement, however limited. We will also discover that even analyses at the highest theoretical levels take place within some "narrative" traditions, that is, within communities shaped by, to use Gustafson's language, "formative narratives.[6] Both ethical and institutional varieties of policy discussion also occur within narratives, or at least on the basis of narratives that may be partially transcended as common ground is sought. Consensus-shaping policy efforts search for and build on the existing ground shared by traditions; they seek to illumine the aspects of a narrative that can encompass more particular stories.

Like narrative ethics, prophetic ethics advances special agendas over against common views or practices, and does so both by "indictment," and by "utopian" visions that can raise human aspirations.[7] Prophetic ethics has as its agenda the introduction of particular values into the main-

---

2. Jeffrey Stout, *Ethics After Babel: The Languages of Morals and Their Discontents* (Boston: Beacon Press, 1988), 282.

3. Stout, *Ethics After Babel*, 294.

4. James M. Gustafson, "Moral Discourse About Medicine: A Variety of Forms," *The Journal of Medicine and Philosophy* 15:2 (1990), 125-42.

5. Gustafson, "Moral Discourse," 140-41.

6. Gustafson, "Moral Discourse," 137.

7. Gustafson, "Moral Discourse," 130-31.

stream, to shift the geography of the ground occupied in common, that is to say, to reconfigure the governing narrative.

It follows that it is best to construe "public discourse" not as a separate *realm* into which we can and ought to enter tradition-free, but as embodying a *commitment* to civil exchanges among traditions, many of which have an overlapping membership, and which meet on the basis of common concerns. The language of "secular" and "publicly accessible" serves exactly to exhort persons from traditions to adopt a stance of dialogue and openness, of mutual critique, of commitment to consensus and to hammering out institutions and policies that will affect the common life for "the better," as defined on the broadest consensus we can achieve. It is a commitment to the dialogic and consensual mode of discourse, or perspective, or attitude, or stance, that is indicated by the expectation that religious and other traditions will make public rather than particularistic appeals in addressing civil society or the body politic.

Community with Others

In struggling toward a conclusion within the "public" realm of discourse, Christians, Jews, or other religious persons will of course be influenced by their religiously based values. They will look for ways to live in community with others — that is, in the many communities in which they participate — that are consistent with their religious way of being (say, as a covenant people, or as disciples), as well as with their theoretical or theological reflection on that way of life. Biblical, especially New Testament, models exist for this sort of approach. St. Paul, for instance, borrows freely from the surrounding culture (as in the "vice lists" of 1 Corinthians 5:11, and 6:9-10) in his writings about morality. Paul seems to feel no necessity to carve out something that is uniquely Christian in morality, for its own sake. His primary concern is to discern what sort of activity is appropriate for persons with a special religious identity. Then, on concrete moral issues he accepts or rejects cultural practices in view of their relation to the communal vocation of discipleship. Although Christianity poses profound questions about "wordly" power, authority, and values, it does not necessarily

demand that all moral expectations which are not specifically Christian be set aside or judged irrelevant to the Christian portrayal of the moral life. As Wayne Meeks has observed, the New Testament literature expresses a process of "resocialization" in the early church, in which new social relationships and identities were forged, even though Christians might simultaneously continue to live as members of other communities with their own values, sometimes overlapping with Christian values, and sometimes challenged by them.[8]

Meeks has also suggested that the importance of religious commitment for ethics lies in its function to form communities that then interact with the broader culture in provocative ways. Just as the biblical narratives were generated by a social environment in which the new religious identity of Christianity served a critical function, so Christian communities today mediate their religious commitment into society through a "hermeneutics of social embodiment" of the biblical witness.[9] The relevance of religion to bioethics does not lie primarily in any distinct or specific contribution to the process of moral argumentation, nor in lifting up "religious" behaviors defensible only on faith, revelation, or church authority. Rather it depends on the formation of socially radical communities that challenge dominant values and patterns of social relationship, not by withdrawing from the larger society, or by speaking to it from outside, but by participating in it in challenging and even subversive ways.

A Countercultural Edge

It is important that, in thinking bioethically, theologians hone the critical edge of religious or theological interest. To be more specific, a person from a Jewish or Christian religious tradition might have sensibilities and interests that would make her or him more attuned to certain biblically based themes, such as the well-being of creation, God's providence, human responsibility, and

8. Wayne Meeks, *The Moral World of the First Christians* (Philadelphia: Westminster Press, 1955), 126.

9. Wayne Meeks, "A Hermeneutics of Social Embodiment," *Harvard Theological Review* 79:1-3 (1986), 176-86.

human finitude and sinfulness.[10] Other themes include love of neighbor and a "preferential option for the poor" and vulnerable, mercy to others as God is merciful to us, forgiveness of others as we expect to be forgiven by God, and repentance for our sins. In nonreligious terms these themes cash out as service, not only autonomy; solidarity and integration within community; the dignity of all human beings, and special advocacy for the most vulnerable; sensitivity to our own finitude and the limits that we confront in all the projects we undertake. Recognizing and retaining the countercultural edge of such commitments is the first task of the theologian, even as he or she acknowledges that it will have few direct payoffs in particular bioethical decisions and analyses.

For instance, invoking the narrative, prophetic mode, Protestant theologians Stanley Hauerwas and Allen Verhey criticize decisions to let severely abnormal newborns die. They draw on Christian themes without claiming either that these themes *require* particular decisions, or that *only* these themes would enjoin decisions to sustain life. Hauerwas claims, "The Cross provides a pattern of interpretation which allows one to locate the pointlessness of suffering within a cosmic framework,"[11] while Verhey maintains that "the eschatological vision of Christianity — and the entire Jesus story — enlists us on the side of life and health in a world where death and evil still apparently reign." This vision also "calls us to identify with and to serve especially the sick and the poor, the powerless and the despised, and all those who do not measure up to conventional standards."[12] Although many Christians would no doubt see acceptance of death as an appropriate choice for some infants, they would agree nonetheless that the tradition would make such choices a rare exception within an ethos of nurturance and sacrifice.

Hauerwas and Verhey represent a somewhat

more biblical and confessional strand within Christian theology; their audience is characteristically the Christian community itself. Hence they emphasize the specifically Christian "narrative" and themes, while "prophetically" exhorting the community to create patterns of moral action that correspond to its religious commitments. A contrasting approach is represented by Roman Catholicism. Catholic moral theology historically has manifested a greater interest in explicitly "public" discourse and has in its service developed a "natural law" moral language claiming to analyze with some precision shared human (not religious) values. While doctrines such as creation, humanity's status as "image of God," and the supernatural destiny of human beings lie in the background of the natural law approach, it still assumes that there are basic human characteristics and values which obtain cross-culturally, and which ought to provide a basis for moral thinking and social order. The nature and extent of these "basics," as well as their practical implications, provide the often controversial subject matter of ethics. As articulated by Joseph Fuchs, S.J., Catholic ethics is based in faith in the sense of a deep personal "giving and entrusting" to God, but "no concrete ethics" can be developed out of faith so understood. Thus, Catholic ethics "has generally presented itself as a philosophical ethics: its reflections, its principles, and its reasonings differ hardly at all, in a formal sense, from those of a philosopher."[13]

Yet even contemporary natural law thinkers are increasingly ready to recognize the "postmodern" emphasis on contextualism, particularity, and tradition, and hence also to recognize that Catholic natural law thinking, while aiming at the "universal," is worked out within a historically particular religious tradition: Christianity as Catholicism. Nonetheless, the tradition continues to represent a commitment to cross-traditional communication, aiming at the broadest community possible. In the modern papal encyclicals from John XXIII forward, the community addressed has even been global, for example, in regard to the "universal common good," on issues such as arms control and

---

10. Gustafson, *Contributions of Theology,* 18-25.

11. Stanley Hauerwas, "Reflections on Suffering, Death, and Medicine," in *Suffering Presence: Theological Reflections on Medicine, the Mentally Handicapped, and the Church* (Notre Dame, Ind.: University of Notre Dame Press, 1986), 31.

12. Allen Verhey, "The Death of Infant Doe: Jesus and the Neonates," in *On Moral Medicine: Theological Perspectives in Medical Ethics,* Stephen E. Lammers and Allen Verhey, eds. (Grand Rapids, Mich.: Eerdmans, 1987), 492.

13. Joseph Fuchs, " 'Catholic' Medical Moral Theology?," in *Catholic Perspectives on Medical Morals,* Edmund D. Pellegrino *et al.,* eds. (Dordrecht: Kluwer, 1989), 85, 83.

international development. In narrower political communities, such as the nation, local prelates may work to raise moral consciousness about issues whose practical importance they consider not to be limited to their own church. Their effectiveness in achieving this goal — and even their legitimacy in attempting to achieve it — depends on their success in framing the moral issues in terms that can in fact strike a responsive chord in a constituency formed from a plurality of communities within the larger political order.

If religiously motivated speakers from particular traditions are to contribute to the sort of public consensus that can support policy initiatives, they will need to do so on the basis of moral quandaries, moral sensibilities, moral images, and moral vocabulary shared among other religious and moral traditions (as an ethics without tradition does not exist). Such morally formative factors are not sheerly "universal," nor need they be. Consensus in and about the public order is contingent not on genuine universality, but on intelligibility and persuasiveness within a community of communities broad enough to encompass the society to be ordered. (This is not to deny that at least at a very fundamental level, the whole human race might be considered a "community," sharing certain minimal moral insights in common. But even if so, such insights would *practically* demand to be worked into consistent moral expectations and social institutions within derivative communities shaped historically in more differentiated ways.)

In the United States, a Roman Catholic example of the explicitly intertraditional appeal is the writings and addresses of Joseph Cardinal Bernardin. During the 1984 presidential election, Bernardin shaped a moral vision ("the consistent ethic of life") based on the interconnection of "life issues," including but not limited to abortion, capital punishment, and nuclear war. Although obviously a religious leader wielding both religious and moral authority, Bernardin does not advance his position on specifically religious grounds. In a recent address focused on abortion (Georgetown University, March 20, 1990), Bernardin tried to persuade his audience that the moral issue of who decides should not overwhelm the issue of what it is that is decided. Specifically, how does a community grant or refuse the recognition of "humanity" in debatable cases? Appealing for a consensus that

"at the very heart of public order is the protection of human life and basic human rights," Bernardin asks, "What happens to our moral imagination and social vision if the right to life is not protected for those who do not look fully human at the beginning or end of life?" Recognizing that a large percentage of Americans do not identify themselves either with pro-choice or pro-life positions, the Cardinal "invites" this constituency to agreement that the human fetus is a value to be protected, and thus to "join us in setting significant limits on abortion."[14] His intended audience may or may not come to concur that although early fetuses do not "look" human, they deserve the full protection due children and adults; nor may it be persuaded that the limits on abortion ought to be "significant." The point here is rather that Bernardin's identity as a religious leader does not disqualify his participation in the public debate, and his success in this forum will depend precisely on his ability to join issues in a way that can elicit or instigate broad agreement. No politician, philosopher, or "humanist" marches into the contest armed only with the sharp sword of reason, stripped naked of the costume of any moral culture — however invisible he or she might wish that clothing to be. Each will succeed on demonstrated ability to find and enlarge the common ground on which originally disparate forces can be joined around a mutual cause.

Jeffrey Stout's notion of a "creole" language is illuminating here: a language that begins as a simplified "bridge dialect" to enable communication among unconnected communities, but "eventually gets rich enough for use as a language of moral reflection (e.g., the language of human rights)."[15] Bernardin puts his case in the vocabulary of public order, human life, and basic human rights, hoping to be persuasive on grounds that are not narrowly "Catholic" or "religious." Where Bernardin and other Roman Catholic representatives might differ with historically more biblical communities and theologians such as Stanley Hauerwas and Allen Verhey is in the former's confidence that essential and recognizable human

14. As quoted by Thomas H. Stahel, "Cardinal Bernardin on the 'Forgotten Factor' and Other Gaps in the Abortion Debate," *America* 162:13 (1990), 354-56.

15. Stout, *Ethics After Babel*, 294.

values (e.g., human life) ground any cultural specification; in their stronger belief that religion supports these human values; and in their optimism about the ability of discussion partners in good faith to come to agreement not only on what the basic values are, but on how they should be implemented practically. Hauerwas and Verhey would emphasize the critical or "witnessing" function of religion (its narrative and prophecy), while Fuchs and Bernardin would stress the motivation it gives to join in moral analysis and public efforts toward consensus on better social institutionalization of "human" values (the contributions it makes to ethical discourse and to policy). As Gustafson has argued, these contributions are not mutually exclusive but complementary.

Roles of Theology in Bioethics

The role of theology in bioethics is, first of all, to clarify for the religious community itself what the shape of its life should be in the relevant areas. Even within the community, however, theology will yield fewer specific norms than it will more fundamental affirmations of the values and commitments that should undergird the identity and challenge the decision-making of religious persons. Indeed, articulating moral norms will usually require the interaction of religious values and theological reflection with other sources, such as philosophy, the natural and social sciences, and careful analysis of implications and consequences. The second role of theology is to move the religious community toward active participation in the broader or overlapping communities with which its members are in some way affiliated, and in which specific norms and policies for those communities are hammered out. Beginning especially from questions of common practice, theology can influence policy through a prophetic function that challenges the civil community to consider more seriously values and alternatives which other traditions and established forms of life may have neglected. Theology also contributes at a more precise analytic level, in which a common language of moral analysis is forged by traditions that are on speaking terms, and which, more importantly, share a commitment to mutual criticism and to progress toward consensus.

66. Salvation and Health: Why Medicine Needs the Church

STANLEY HAUERWAS

A Text and a Story

While it is not unheard of for a theologian to begin an essay with a text from the Scripture, it is relatively rare for those who are addressing issues of medicine to do so. However I begin with a text, as almost everything I have to say is but a commentary on this passage from Job 2:11-13:

> Now when Job's friends heard of all this evil that had come upon him, then came each from his own place, Eliphaz the Temanite, Bildad the Shuhite, and Zophar the Na'amathite. They made an appointment together to come console with him and comfort him. And when they saw him from afar, they did not recognize him; and they raised their voices and wept: and they rent their robes and sprinkled dust upon their heads toward heaven. And they sat with him on the ground seven days and seven nights, and no one spoke a word to him, for they saw that his suffering was very great.

Stanley Hauerwas (1940–) is professor of theological ethics at Duke University. He has authored numerous books in Christian ethics, including *Truthfulness and Tragedy: Further Investigations in Christian Ethics; A Community of Character; The Peaceable Kingdom; Suffering Presence; Against the Nations;* and *After Christendom.*

From Stanley Hauerwas, *Suffering Presence: Theological Reflections on Medicine, the Mentally Handicapped, and the Church* (Notre Dame: University of Notre Dame Press, 1986).

I do not want to comment immediately on the text. Instead, I think it best to begin by telling you a story. The story is about one of my earliest friendships. When I was in my early teens I had a friend, let's call him Bob, who meant everything to me. We made our first hesitant steps toward growing up through sharing the things young boys do — i.e., double dating, athletic activities, and endless discussions on every topic. For two years we were inseparable. I was extremely appreciative of Bob's friendship, as he was not only brighter and more talented than I, but also came from a family that was economically considerably better off than my own. Through Bob I was introduced to a world that otherwise I would hardly know existed. For example, we spent hours in his home playing pool in a room that was built for no other purpose; and we swam in the lake that his house was specifically built to overlook.

Then very early one Sunday morning I received a phone call from Bob requesting that I come to see him immediately. He was sobbing intensely but through his crying he was able to tell me that they had just found his mother dead. She had committed suicide by placing a shotgun in her mouth. I knew immediately I did not want to go to see him and/or confront a reality like that. I had not yet learned the desperation hidden under our everyday routines and I did not want to learn of it. Moreover I did not want to go because I knew there was nothing I could do or say to make things even appear better than they were. Finally I did not want to go because I did not want to be close to anyone who had been touched by such a tragedy.

But I went. I felt awkward, but I went. And as I came into Bob's room we embraced, a gesture that was almost unheard of between young men raised in the Southwest, and we cried together. After that first period of shared sorrow we some-how calmed down and took a walk. For the rest of that day and that night we stayed together. I do not remember what we said, but I do remember that it was inconsequential. We never talked about his mother or what had happened. We never speculated about why she might do such a thing, even though I could not believe someone who seemed to have such a good life would want to die. We did what we always did. We talked girls, football, cars, movies, and anything else that was

inconsequential enough to distract our attention from this horrible event.

As I look on that time I now realize that it was obviously one of the most important events in my life. That it was so is at least partly indicated by how often I have thought about it and tried to understand its significance in the years from then to now. As often as I have reflected on what happened in that short space of time I have also remembered how inept I was in helping Bob. I did not know what should or could be said. I did not know how to help him start sorting out such a horrible event so that he could go on. All I could do was be present.

But time has helped me realize that this is all he wanted — namely, my presence. For as inept as I was, my willingness to be present was a sign that this was not an event so horrible that it drew us away from all other human contact. Life could go on, and in the days to follow we would again swim together, double date, and generally waste time. I now think that at the time God granted me the marvelous privilege of being a presence in the face of profound pain and suffering even when I did not appreciate the significance of being present.

Yet the story cannot end here. For while it is true that Bob and I did go on being friends, nothing was the same. For a few months we continued to see one another often, but somehow the innocent joy of loving one another was gone. We slowly found that our lives were going in different directions and we developed new friends. No doubt the difference between our social and cultural opportunities helps explain to some extent our drifting apart. Bob finally went to Princeton and I went to Southwestern University in Georgetown, Texas.

But that kind of explanation for our growing apart is not sufficient. What was standing between us was that day and night we spent together under the burden of a profound sadness that neither of us had known could exist until that time. We had shared a pain so intense that for a short period we had become closer than we knew, but now the very pain that created that sharing stood in the way of the development of our friendship. Neither of us wished to recapture that time, nor did we know how to make that night and day part of our on-going story together. So we went our separate ways. I have no idea what became of Bob, though every once in a while I remember to ask my mother if she has heard about him.

Does medicine need the church? How could this text and this story possibly help us understand that question, much less suggest how it might be answered? Yet I am going to claim in this essay that it does. Put briefly, what I will try to show is that if medicine can be rightly understood as an activity that trains some to know how to be present to those in pain, then something very much like a church is needed to sustain that presence day in and day out. Before I try to develop that thesis, however, I need to do some conceptual ground-breaking to make clear exactly what kind of claim I am trying to make about the relationship of salvation and health, medicine and the church.

Religion and Medicine: Is There or Should There Be a Relation?

It is a well-known fact that for most of human history there has been a close affinity between religion and medicine. Indeed that very way of putting it is misleading, since to claim a relation suggests that they were distinguished, and often that has not been the case. From earliest times, disease and illness were not seen as matters having no religious import but rather as resulting from the disfavor of God. As Darrel Amundsen and Gary Ferngren have recently reminded us, the Hebrew Scriptures often depict God promising:

> health and prosperity for the covenant people if they are faithful to him, and disease and other suffering if they spurn his love. This promise runs through the Old Testament. "If you will diligently hearken to the voice of the Lord your God, and do that which is right in his eyes, and give heed to his commandments and keep all his statutes, I will put none of the diseases upon you which I put upon the Egyptians; for I am the Lord, your healer" (Exod. 15:26).[1]

This view of illness was not associated only with the community as a whole, but with individuals. Thus in Psalm 38 the lament is:

> There is no soundness in my flesh because of thy indignation; there is no health in my bones because of my sin. . . . My wounds grow foul and fester because of foolishness. . . . I am utterly spent and crushed; I groan because of the tumult of my heart. . . . Do not forsake me, O Lord! O my God, be not far from me! Make haste to help me, O Lord, my salvation! (vv. 3, 5, 8, 21-22)

Amundsen and Ferngren point out this view of illness as accompanied by the assumption that acknowledgment of and repentance for our sin was essential for our healing. Thus in Psalm 32:

> When I declared not my sin, my body wasted away through my groaning all day long. For day and night thy hand was heavy upon me; my strength was dried up. . . . I acknowledged my sin to thee, and I did not hide my iniquity; I said, "I will confess my transgressions to the Lord"; then thou didst forgive the guilt of my sin. (vv. 3-5)

Since illness and sin were closely connected it is not surprising that healing was also closely associated with religious practices — or, put more accurately, healing was a religious discipline. Indeed Amundsen and Ferngren make the interesting point that since the most important issue was a person's relationship with God the chief means of healing was naturally prayer. That clearly precluded magic and thus the Mosaic code excluded soothsayers, augurs, sorcerers, charmers, wizards, and other such figures who offered a means to control or avoid the primary issue of their relation to Yahweh.[2] They also suggest that this may have been why no sacerdotal medical practice developed in Israel particularly associated with the priesthood. Rather, the pattern of the Exodus tended to prevail, with illness and healing more closely associated with prophetic activity.

The early Christian community seems to have done little to change these basic presuppositions. If anything it simply intensified them by adding

---

1. Armandsen, D., and Ferngren, G. 1982. "Medicine and Religion: Early Christianity Through the Middle Ages." In M. Marty and K. Vaux, eds., *Health/Medicine and the Faith Traditions*, 93-132.

2. Armandsen and Ferngren, p. 94.

what Amundsen and Ferngren call the "central paradox" in the New Testament:

> Strength comes only through weakness. This strength is Christ's strength that comes only through dependence upon him. In the Gospel of John, Christ says: "I have said to you, that in me you may have peace. In the world you have tribulation; but be of good cheer, I have overcome the world" (16:33). "In the world you have tribulation." It is simply to be expected and accepted. But for the New Testament Christian no suffering is meaningless. The ultimate purpose and meaning behind Christian suffering in the New Testament is spiritual maturity. And the ultimate goal in spiritual maturity is a close dependence upon Christ based upon a childlike trust.[3]

Thus illness is seen as an opportunity for growth in faith and trust in God.

Because of this way of viewing both the positive and negative effect of illness, Amundsen and Ferngren note that there has always been a degree of tension in the way Christians understand the relation between theology and secular medicine, between the medicine of the soul and the medicine of the body.

> According to one view, if God sends disease either to punish or to test a person, it is to God that one must turn for care and healing. If God is both the source and healer of a person's ills, the use of human medicine would circumvent the spiritual framework by resorting to worldly wisdom. On another view, if God is the source of disease, or if God permits disease and is the ultimate healer, God's will can be fulfilled through human agents, who with divine help have acquired the ability to aid in the curative process. Most Christians have asserted that the human agent of care, the physician, is an instrument of God, used by God in bringing succor to humankind. But in every age some have maintained that any use of human medicine is a manifestation of a lack of faith. This ambivalence in the Christian attitude, among both theologians and laity, has always been present to some degree.[4]

Nor is it possible to separate or distinguish religion and medicine on the basis of a distinction between soul and body. For as Paul Ramsey has reminded us, Christians affirm that God has created and holds us sacred as embodied souls.[5] Religion does not deal with the soul and medicine with the body. Practitioners of both are too well aware of the inseparability of soul and body — or perhaps better, they know the abstractness of both categories. Moreover when religion too easily legitimates the independence of medical care by limiting medicine to mechanical understanding and care of the body, it has the result of making religious convictions ethereal in character. It may be that just to the extent Christianity is always tempted in Gnostic and Manichean directions it accepts too willingly a technological understanding of medicine. Christians, if they are to be faithful to their convictions, may not ever be able to avoid at least potential conflict between their own assumptions about illness and health and how the ill should be cared for and the assumptions of medicine. One hopes for cooperation, of course, but structurally the possibility of conflict between church and medicine cannot be excluded, since both entail convictions and practices concerned with that same subject.

Put differently, given Judaism and Christianity's understanding of humankind's relation with God — that is: how we understand salvation — health can never be thought of as an autonomous sphere. Moreover, insofar as medicine is a specialized activity distinguished from religious convictions, you cannot exclude the possibility that there may well be conflict between religion and medicine. For in many ways the latter is constantly tempted to offer a form of salvation that religiously may come close to idolatry. The ability of modern medicine to cure is at once a benefit and potential pitfall. Too often it is tempted to increase its power by offering more than care, by offering in fact alleviation from the human condition — e.g., the development of artificial hearts. That is not the fault of medical practitioners, though often they encourage such idolatry; rather the fault lies with those of us who pretentiously place undue expectations on medicine in the hope

---

3. Armandsen and Ferngren, p. 96.
4. Armandsen and Ferngren, p. 96.

5. Paul Ramsey, *The Patient as Person* (New Haven: Yale University Press, 1970), p. xiii.

of finding an earthly remedy to our death. But we can never forget that the relation between medicine and health, and especially the health of a population, is as ambiguous as the relation between the church and salvation.

In the hope of securing peace between medicine and religion, two quite different and equally unsatisfactory proposals have been suggested. The first advocates a strong division of labor between medicine and religion by limiting the scope of medicine to the mechanism of our body. While it is certainly true that medicine in a unique way entails the passing on of the wisdom of the body from one generation to another, there is no way that medical care can be limited to the body and be good medicine.[6] As Ramsey has reminded us again and again, the moral commitment of the physician is not to treat diseases, or populations, or the human race, but the immediate patient before him or her.[7] Religiously, therefore, the care offered by physicians cannot be abstracted from the moral commitment to care based on our view that every aspect of our existence is dependent upon God.

By the same token the clergy, no less than physicians, are concerned about the patient's physical well-being. No assumptions about technical skills and knowledge can legitimate the clergy retreating into the realm of the spiritual in order to claim some continued usefulness and status. Such a retreat is as unfaithful as abandoning the natural world to the physicist on the grounds that God is a God of history and not of nature. For the church and its officeholders to abandon claims over the body in the name of a lack of expertise is equivalent to reducing God to the gaps in scientific theory. Such a strategy is not only bad faith but it results in making religious convictions appear at best irrelevant and at worse foolish.

The second alternative to accepting the autonomy of medicine from our religious convictions seeks to maintain a close relationship by resacralizing medical care. Medicine requires a "holistic vision of man,"[8] because the care it brings is but one aspect of salvation. Thus the church and its theology serves medical care by promoting a holistic view of man, one that can provide a:

> comprehensive understanding of human health [that] includes the greatest possible harmony of all of man's forces and energies, the greatest possible spiritualization of man's bodily aspect and the finest embodiment of the spiritual. True health is revealed in the self-actualization of the person who has attained that freedom which marshals all available energies for the fulfillment of his total human vocation.[9]

Such a view of health, however, cannot help but pervert the kind of care that physicians can provide. Physicians rightly maintain that their skill primarily has to do with the body, as medicine promises us health, not happiness. When such a general understanding of health is made the goal of medicine, it only results in making medical care promise more than it can deliver. As a result, we are tyrannized by the agents of medicine because we have voluntarily vested them with too much power. It is already a difficult task in our society to control the expectations people have about modern medicine; we only compound that problem by providing religious legitimacy to this overblown understanding of health. Certainly we believe that any account of salvation includes questions of our health, but that does not mean that medicine can or ever should become the agency of salvation. It may be a fundamental judgment on the church's failure to help us locate wherein our salvation lies that so many today seek a salvation through medicine.

Can Medical Ethics Be Christian?

The already complex question of the relation between religion and medicine only becomes more confusing when we turn our attention to more

6. Stanley Hauerwas, "Authority and the Profession of Medicine," in *Responsibility in Health Care,* ed. G. Agich (Dordrecht, Holland: Reidel, 1982), pp. 83-104.

7. Paul Ramsey, *The Patient as Person,* pp. 36, 59.

8. Stanley Hauerwas, "On Keeping Theological Ethics Theological," in *Revisions: Changing Perspectives in Moral Philosophy,* ed. A. MacIntyre and S. Hauerwas (Notre Dame, Ind.: University of Notre Dame Press, 1983), pp. 16-42.

9. B. Haring, *Medical Ethics* (South Bend, Ind.: Fides Publishers, 1973), p. 154.

recent developments in medical ethics. For even though religious thinkers have been at the forefront of much of the work done in the expanding field of "medical ethics," it is not clear that they have been there as religious thinkers. Joseph Fletcher, Paul Ramsey, James Gustafson, Charles Curran, Jim Childress, to name just a few, have done extensive work in medical ethics, but often it is hard to tell how their religious convictions have made a difference for the methodology they employ or for their response to specific quandaries. Indeed it is interesting to note how seldom they raise issues of the meaning or relation of salvation and health, as they seem to prefer dealing with questions of death and dying, truth-telling, etc.

By calling attention to this fact by no means do I wish to disparage the kind of reflection that has been done concerning these issues. We have all benefited from their careful analysis and distinctions concerning such problems. Yet one must wonder if, by letting the agenda be set in such a manner, we have already lost the theological ball game. For the very concentration on "issues" and "quandaries" as central for medical ethics tends to underwrite the practice of medicine as we know it, rather than challenging some of the basic presuppositions of medical practice and care. Because of this failure to raise more fundamental questions, concerns that might provide more access for our theological claims are simply never considered.

There are at least two reasons for this that I think are worth mentioning. The first has to do with the character of theological ethics itself. We tend to forget that the development of "Christian ethics" is a relatively new development.[10] It has only been in the last hundred years that some have styled themselves as "ethicists" rather than simply theologians. It is by no means clear that we know how to indicate what difference it makes conceptually and methodologically to claim our ethics as Christian in distinction from other kinds of ethical reflection. In the hopes of securing greater clarity about their own work many who have identified their work as Christian have nonetheless assumed that the meaning and

10. Hauerwas, "On Keeping Theological Ethics Theological."

method of "ethics" was determined fundamentally by non-Christian sources. In a sense the very concentration on "medical ethics" was a godsend for many "religious ethicists," as it seemed to provide a coherent activity without having to deal with the fundamental issue of what makes Christian ethics Christian.

This can be illustrated by attending to the debate among Christian ethicists concerning whether Christian moral reasoning is primarily deontological or consequential. This debate has been particularly important for medical ethics, as obviously how you think about non-therapeutic experimentation, truth-telling, transplants, and a host of other issues seems to turn on this issue. For instance, Joseph Fletcher, who wrote one of the first books by a Protestant in medical ethics, has always argued in favor of a consequential stance, thus qualifying the physician's commitment to an individual patient in the name of a greater good.[11] In contrast, Paul Ramsey has emphasized that the "covenant" of the physician with the patient is such that no amount of good to be done should override that commitment.[12]

It is interesting to note how each makes theological appeals to support his own position. Fletcher appeals to love as his basic norm, interpreting it in terms of the greatest good for the greatest number, but it remains unclear how his sense of love is theologically warranted or controlled. Ramsey provides a stronger theological case for his emphasis on "covenant" as a central theological motif, but it is not clear how the many "covenants of life with life into which we are born" require the covenant of God with a particular people we find in Scripture. Ramsey's use of covenant language thus underwrites a natural law ethic whose status is unclear both from a theological and/or philosophical perspective.[13]

11. Joseph Fletcher, *Morals and Medicine* (Boston: Beacon Press, 1954).
12. Paul Ramsey, *The Patient as Person*.
13. Ramsey's position is complex and I certainly cannot do it justice here. His emphasis on "love transforming natural law" would tend to qualify the point made above. Yet it is also true that Ramsey's increasing use of covenant language has gone hand in hand with his readiness to identify certain "covenants" that need no "transformation." Of course he could object that the covenant

What is interesting about the debate between Fletcher and Ramsey is that it could have been carried on completely separate from the theological premises that each side claimed were involved. For the terms of the debate — *consequential* and *deontological* — are basically borrowed from philosophical contexts and are dependent on the presuppositions of certain philosophical traditions. Of course that in itself does not mean that such issues and concepts are irrelevant to our work as theologians, but what is missing is any sense of how the issue as presented grows, is dependent on, or informed by our distinctive commitments as theologians.

The question of the nature of theological ethics and its relation to the development of ethical reflection in and about medicine is further complicated by our current cultural situation. As Ramsey has pointed out, we are currently trying to do the impossible — namely, "build a civilization without an agreed civil tradition and [in] the absence of a moral consensus."[14] This makes the practice of medicine even more morally challenging, since it is by no means clear how one can sustain a non-arbitrary medicine in a genuinely morally pluralistic society. For example, much of the debate about when someone is "really" dead is not simply the result of our increased technological power to keep blood flowing through our bodies, but witnesses to our culture's lack of consensus as to what constitutes a well-lived life and the correlative sense of a good death. In the absence of such a consensus our only recourse is to resort to claims and counterclaims about "right to life" and "right to die," with the result of the further impoverishment of our moral language and vision. Moreover, the only way to create a "safe" medicine under such conditions is to expect physicians to treat us as if death is the ultimate enemy to be put off by every means. Then we blame physicians for keeping us alive beyond all reason, but fail to note that if they did not we would not know how to distinguish them from murderers.

Alasdair MacIntyre has raised this sort of issue directly in his "Can Medicine Dispense with a Theological Perspective on Human Nature?" Rather than calling attention to what has become problematic for physicians and surgeons — issues such as when it is appropriate to let someone die — he says he wants to direct our attention to what is still taken for granted, "namely, the unconditional and absolute character of certain of the doctor's obligations to his patients."[15] The difficulty is that modern philosophy, according to MacIntyre, has been unable to offer a persuasive account of such an obligation.

> *Either* they distort and misrepresent it *or* they render it unintelligible. Teleological moralists characteristically end up by distorting and misrepresenting. For they begin with a notion of moral rules as specifying how we are to behave if we are to achieve certain ends, perhaps *the* end for man, the *summum bonum*. If I break such rules I shall fail to achieve some human good and will thereby be frustrated and impoverished.[16]

But MacIntyre notes that this treats moral failure as if it is an educational failure and lacks the profound guilt that should accompany moral failure. More importantly, such an account fails entirely to account for the positive evil we know certain people clearly pursue.

Moral philosophers who tend to preserve the unconditional and absolute character of the central requirements of morality, however, inevitably make those "oughts" appear as if they are arbitrary. What they cannot do is show how those oughts are rationally entailed by an account of man's true end. Kant was only able to do so because he continued the presupposition (which he failed to justify within his own philosophical position) that "the life of the individual and also of that of the human race is a journey toward a goal."[17] Once that presupposition is lost, however, and MacIntyre believes that it has been lost

---

between doctor and patient is the result of Christian love operating in history.

14. Paul Ramsey, "The Nature of Medical Ethics," in *The Teaching of Medical Ethics,* ed. R. Neatch, M. Gaylin, and C. Morgan (Hastings-on-Hudson, N.Y.: Hastings Center), p. 15.

15. Alasdair MacIntyre, "Can Medicine Dispense with a Theological Perspective on Human Nature?" in *The Roots of Ethics,* ed. D. Callahan and H. Engelhardt (New York: Plenum Press, 1981), pp. 119-138.

16. MacIntyre, p. 122.

17. MacIntyre, p. 127.

in our culture, then we lack the resources to maintain exactly those moral presuppositions that seem essential to securing the moral integrity of medicine.

Such a situation seems ripe for a theological response, since it might at least be suggested that it thus becomes our task as theologians to serve our culture in general and medicine in particular by supplying the needed rationale. Yet, MacIntyre argues, such a strategy is doomed, since the very intelligibility of theological claims has been rendered problematic by the ethos of modernity. Therefore, just to the extent theologians try to make their claims in terms offered by modernity, they only underwrite the assumption that theological language cannot be meaningful.

This kind of dilemma is particularly acute when it comes to medicine. For if the theologian attempts to underwrite the medical ethos drawing on the particular convictions of Christians, just to the extent those convictions are particular they will serve only to emphasize society's lack of a common morality. Thus theologians, in the interest of cultural consensus, often try to downplay the distinctiveness of their theological convictions in the interest of societal harmony. But in the process we only reinforce the assumption on the part of many that theological claims make little difference for how medicine itself is understood or how various issues are approached. At best theology or religion is left with justifying a concern with the "whole patient," but it is not even clear how that concern depends on or derives from any substantive theological conviction that is distinguishable from humanism.

Almost as if we have sensed that there is no way to resolve this dilemma, theologians and religious professionals involved in medicine have tended to associate with the patients' rights movement. At least one of the ways of resolving our cultural dilemma is to protect the patient from medicine by restoring the patient's autonomy over against the physician. While I certainly do not want to underestimate the importance of patients recovering a sense of medicine as an activity in which we play as important a role as the physician, the emphasis on the patient's rights over against the physician cannot resolve our difficulty. It is but an attempt to substitute procedural safeguards for what only substantive convictions can supply. As a result our attention is distracted from the genuine challenge we confront for the forming of an ethos sufficient to sustain a practice of medicine that is morally worthy.

Pain, Loneliness, and Being Present: The Church and the Care of the Ill

I can offer no "solution" to the issues raised in the previous section, as I think they admit to no solution, given our social and political situation. Moreover, I think we will make little headway on such matters as long as we try to address the questions in terms of the dichotomies of religion and medicine or the relation between medical ethics and theology. Rather, what is needed is a restatement of the issue. In this section I will try to do that by returning to my original text and story to suggest how they may help remind us that more fundamental than questions of religion and morality is the question of the kind of community necessary to sustain the long-term care of the ill.

Indeed, part of the problem with discussing the question of "relation" in such general terms as "medicine" and "religion" is that each of those terms in its own way distorts the character of what it is meant to describe. For example, when we talk in general about "religion" rather than a specific set of beliefs, behaviors, and habits embodied by a distinct group of people, our account always tends to be reductionistic. It makes it appear that underlying what people actually believe and do is a deeper reality called "religion." It is as if we can talk about God abstracted from how a people have learned to pray to that God. In like manner we often tend to oversimplify the nature of medicine by trying to capture the many activities covered by that term in a definition or ideological system. What doctors do is often quite different from what they say they do.

Moreover, the question of the relation of theology to medical ethics is far too abstract. For when the issue is posed in that manner it makes it appear that religion is primarily a set of beliefs, a world view, that may or may not have implications for how we understand and respond to certain kinds of ethical dilemmas. While it is certainly true that Christianity involves beliefs, the character of those beliefs cannot be understood apart from its place in the formation of a community with cultic practices. By focusing on this fact I hope to throw a different perspective on how those who are called to care for the sick can draw upon and count on the particular kind of community we call the church.

I do not intend, for example, to argue that medicine must be reclaimed as in some decisive way dependent on theology. Nor do I want to argue that the development of "medical ethics" will ultimately require the acknowledgment of, or recourse to, theological presuppositions. Rather all I want to try to show is why, given the particular demands put on those who care for the ill, something very much like a church is necessary to sustain that care.

To develop this point I want to call attention to an obvious but often overlooked aspect of illness — namely that when we are sick we hurt and are in pain. I realize that often we are sick and yet not in pain — e.g., hardening of the arteries — but that does not ultimately defeat my general point, since we know that such an illness will lead to physical and mental pain. Nor am I particularly bothered by the observation that many pains are "psychological," having no real physiological basis. Physicians are right to insist that people who say they have pain, even if no organic basis can be found for such pain, are in fact, in pain, though they may be mistaken about what kind of pain it is.

Moreover I am well aware that there are many different kinds of pain, as well as intensity of pains. What is only a minor hurt for me may be a major trauma for someone else. Pain comes in many shapes and sizes and it is never possible to separate the psychological aspects of pain from the organic. For example, suffering, which is not the same as pain since we can suffer without being in pain, is nonetheless akin to pain inasmuch as it is a felt deficiency that can make us as miserable as pain itself.[18]

Yet given these qualifications it remains true that there is a strong connection between pain and illness, an area of our lives in which it is appropriate to call upon the skills of a physician. When

we are in pain we want to be helped. But it is exactly at this point that one of the strangest aspects of our being in pain occurs — namely, it is impossible for us to experience one another's pain. That does not mean we cannot communicate to one another our pain. That we can do, but what cannot be done is for you to understand and/or experience my pain as mine.

This puts us under a double burden because we have enough of a problem learning to know one another in the normal aspects of our lives, but when we are in pain our alienation from one another only increases. For no matter how sympathetic we may be to the other in pain, that very pain creates a history and experience that makes the other just that much more foreign to me. Our pains isolate us from one another as they create worlds that cut us off from one another. Consider, for example, the immense gulf between the world of the sick and the healthy. No matter how much we may experience the former, when we are healthy or not in pain we have trouble imagining and understanding the world of the ill.

Indeed the terms we are using are still far too crude. For we do not suffer illness in and of itself, but we suffer this particular kind of illness and have this particular kind of pain. Thus even within the world of illness there are subworlds that are not easily crossed. Think, for example, of how important it is for those suffering from the same illness to share their stories with one another. They do not believe others can understand their particular kind of pain. People with heart disease may find little basis of communion with those suffering from cancer. Pain itself does not create a shared experience; only pain of a particular kind and sort. Moreover the very commonality thus created separates the ill from the healthy in a decisive way.

Pain not only isolates us from one another, but even from ourselves. Think how quickly people with a terribly diseased limb or organ are anxious for surgery in the hope that if it is just cut off or cut out they will not be burdened by the pain that makes them not know themselves. This gangrenous leg is not mine. I would prefer to lose the leg rather than face the reality of its connection to me.

The difficulties pain creates in terms of our relation with ourselves is compounded by the

18. For a fuller account of the complex relation between pain and suffering see Stanley Hauerwas, "Reflections on Suffering, Death, and Medicine," *Ethics in Science and Medicine* 6:229-237. Reprinted in *Suffering Presence*.

peculiar difficulties it creates for those close to us who do not share our pain. For no matter how sympathetic they may be, no matter how much they may try to be with and comfort us, we know they do not want to experience our pain. I not only cannot, but I do not want to, know the pain you are feeling. No matter how good willed we may be, we cannot take another's pain as our pain. Our pains divide us and there is little we can do to restore our unity.

I suspect this is one of the reasons that chronic illness is such a burden. For often we are willing to be present and sympathetic with someone with an intense but temporary pain — that is, we are willing to be present as long as they work at being "good" sick people who try to get well quickly and do not make too much of their discomfort. We may initially be quite sympathetic with someone with a chronic disease, but it seems to be asking too much of us to be compassionate year in and year out. Thus the universal testimony of people with chronic illness that their illness often results in the alienation of their former friends. This is a problem not only for the person who is ill but also for those closely connected with that person. The family of a person who is chronically ill often discover that the very skills and habits they must learn to be present to the one in pain creates a gulf between themselves and their friends. Perhaps no case illustrates this more poignantly than a family that has a retarded child. Often they discover it is not long before they have a whole new set of friends who also happen to have retarded children.[19]

Exactly because pain is so alienating, we are hesitant to admit that we are in pain. To be in pain means we need help, that we are vulnerable to the interests of others, that we are not in control of our destiny. Thus we seek to deny our pain in the hope that we will be able to handle it within ourselves. But the attempt to deal with our pain by ourselves or to deny its existence has the odd effect of only increasing our loneliness. For exactly to the extent I am successful, I create a story about myself that I cannot easily share.

No doubt more can be and needs to be said that would nuance this account of pain and the way it tends to isolate us from one another. Yet I think I have said enough that our attention has been called to this quite common but all the more extraordinary aspect of our existence. Moreover, in the light of this analysis I hope we can now appreciate the remarkable behavior of Job's friends. For in spite of the bad press Job's comforters usually receive (and in many ways it is deserved!), they at least sat on the ground with him for seven days. Moreover they did not speak to him, "for they saw that his suffering was very great." That they did so is truly an act of magnanimity, for most of us are willing to be with sufferers, especially those in such pain that we can hardly recognize them, only if we can "do something" to relieve their suffering or at least distract their attention. Not so with Job's comforters. They sat on the ground with Job doing nothing more than being willing to be present in the face of his suffering.

Now if any of this is close to being right, it puts the task of physicians and others who are pledged to be with the ill in an interesting perspective. For I take it that their activity as physicians is characterized by the fundamental commitment to be, like Job's comforters, in the presence of those who are in pain.[20] At this moment I am not concerned to explore the moral reason for that commitment, but only to note that in fact physicians, nurses, chaplains, and many others are present to the ill as none of the rest of us are. They are the bridge between the world of the ill and the healthy.

Certainly physicians are there because they have been trained with skills that enable them to alleviate the pain of the ill. They have learned from some sick people how to help other sick people. Yet every physician soon learns of the terrible limit of his/her craft, for the sheer particularity of the patient's illness often defies the best knowledge and skill. Even more dramatically, physicians learn that using the best knowledge and skill they have on some patients sometimes has terrible results.

19. Stanley Hauerwas, "The Retarded, Society and the Family: The Dilemma of Care," in *Responsibility for Devalued Persons,* ed. Stanley Hauerwas (Springfield, Ill.: Charles C. Thomas, 1982). Reprinted in *Suffering Presence.*

20. I am indebted to a conversation with Dr. Earl Shelp for helping me understand better the significance of this point.

Yet the fact that medicine through the agency of physicians does not and cannot always "cure" in no way qualifies the commitment of the physician. At least it does not do so if we remember that the physician's basic pledge is not to cure, but to care through being present to the one in pain. Yet it is not easy to carry out that commitment on a day-to-day, year-to-year basis. For none of us have the resources to see too much pain without that pain hardening us. Without such a hardening, something we sometimes call by the name of professional distance, we fear we will lose the ability to feel at all.

Yet the physician cannot help but be touched and, thus, tainted by the world of the sick. Through their willingness to be present to us in our most vulnerable moments they are forever scarred with our pain — a pain that we the healthy want to deny or at least keep at arm's length. They have seen a world we do not want to see until it is forced on us, and we will accept them into polite community only to the extent they keep that world hidden from us. But when we are driven into that world we want to be able to count on their skill and their presence, even though we have been unwilling to face that reality while we were healthy.

But what do these somewhat random and controversial observations have to do with helping us better understand the relation between medicine and the church and/or the story of my boyhood friendship with Bob? To begin with the latter, I think in some ways the mechanism that was working during that trying time with Bob is quite similar to the mechanism that works on a day-to-day basis in medicine. For the physician, and others concerned with our illness, are called to be present during times of great pain and tragedy. Indeed physicians, because of their moral commitments, have the privilege and the burden to be with us when we are most vulnerable. The physician learns our deepest fears and our profoundest hopes. As patients, that is also why so often we fear the physician, because she/he may know us better than we know ourselves. Surely that is one of the reasons that confidentially is so crucial to the patient-physician relation, since it is a situation of such intimacy.

But just to the extent that the physician has been granted the privilege of being with us while we are in pain, that very experience creates the seeds of distrust and fear. We are afraid of one another's use of the knowledge gained, but even more deeply we fear remembering the pain as part of our history. Thus every crisis that joins us in a common fight for health also has the potential for separating us more profoundly after the crisis. Yet the physician is pledged to come to our aid again and again, no matter how we may try to protect ourselves from his/her presence.

The physician, on the other hand, has yet another problem, for how can anyone be present to the ill day in and day out without learning to dislike, if not positively detest, our smallness in the face of pain. People in pain are omnivorous in their appetite for help, and they will use us up if we let them. Fortunately the physician has other patients who can give him distance from any patient who requires too much. But the problem still remains how morally those who are pledged to be with the ill never lose their ability to see the humanity that our very suffering often comes close to obliterating. For the physician cannot, as Bob and I did, drift apart and away from those whom he or she is pledged to serve. At least they cannot if I am right that medicine is first of all pledged to be nothing more than a human presence in the face of suffering.

But how can we account for such a commitment — the commitment to be present to those in pain? No doubt basic human sympathy is not to be discounted, but it does not seem to be sufficient to account for a group of people dedicated to being present to the ill as their vocation in life. Nor does it seem sufficient to account for the acquiring of the skills necessary to sustain that presence in a manner that is not alienating and the source of distrust in a community.

To learn how to be present in that way we need examples — that is, a people who have so learned to embody such a presence in their lives that it has become the marrow of their habits. The church at least claims to be such a community, as it is a group of people called out by a God who, we believe, is always present to us, both in our sin and our faithfulness. Because of God's faithfulness we are supposed to be a people who have learned how to be faithful to one another by our willingness to be present, with all our vulnerabilities, to one another. For what does our God require of us other than our unfailing presence in the midst of the world's sin and pain? Thus our willingness to be ill and to ask for help, as well as our willingness to be present with the ill is no special or extraordinary activity, but a form of the Christian obligation to be present to one another in and out of pain.

Moreover, it is such a people who should have learned how to be present with those in pain without that pain driving them further apart. For the very bond that pain forms between us becomes the basis for alienation, as we have no means to know how to make it part of our common history. Just as it is painful to remember our sins, so we seek not to remember our pain, since we desire to live as if our world and existence were a pain-free one. Only a people trained in remembering, and remembering as a communal act, their sins and pains can offer a paradigm for sustaining across time a painful memory so that it acts to heal rather than to divide.

Thus medicine needs the church not to supply a foundation for its moral commitments, but rather as a resource of the habits and practices necessary to sustain the care of those in pain over the long haul. For it is no easy matter to be with the ill, especially when we cannot do much for them other than simply be present. Our very helplessness too often turns to hate, both toward the one in pain and ourselves, as we despise them for reminding us of our helplessness. Only when we remember that our presence is our doing, when sitting on the ground seven days saying nothing is what we can do, can we be saved from our fevered and hopeless attempt to control others' and our own existence. Of course to believe that such presence is what we can and should do entails a belief in a presence in and beyond this world. And it is certainly true that many today no longer believe in or experience such a presence. If that is the case, then I do wonder if medicine as an activity of presence is possible in a world without God.

Another way of raising this issue is to ask the relation between prayer and medical care. Nothing I have said about the basic pledge of physicians to be present to the ill entails that they should not try to develop the skills necessary to help those in pain and illness. Certainly they should, as theirs is an art that is one of our most valuable resources

for the care of one another. But no matter how powerful that craft becomes, it cannot in principle rule out the necessity of prayer. For prayer is not a supplement to the insufficiency of our medical knowledge and practice; nor is it some divine insurance policy that our medical skill will work; rather, our prayer is the means that we have to make God present whether our medical skill is successful or not. So understood, the issue is not whether medical care and prayer are antithetical, but how medical care can ever be sustained without the necessity of continued prayer.

Finally, those involved in medicine need the church as otherwise they cannot help but be alienated from the rest of us. For unless there is a body of people who have learned the skills of presence, the world of the ill cannot help but become a separate world both for the ill and/or those who care for them. Only a community that is pledged not to fear the stranger — and illness always makes us a stranger to ourselves and others — can welcome the continued presence of the ill in our midst. The hospital is, after all, first and foremost a house of hospitality along the way of our journey with finitude. It is our sign that we will not abandon those who have become ill simply because they currently are suffering the sign of that finitude. If the hospital, as too often is the case today, becomes but a means of isolating the ill from the rest of us, then we have betrayed its central purpose and distorted our community and ourselves.

If the church can be the kind of people who show clearly that they have learned to be with the sick and the dying, it may just be that through that process we will better understand the relation of salvation to health, religion to medicine. Or perhaps even more, we will better understand what kind of medicine we ought to practice, since too often we try to substitute doing for presence. It is surely the case, as Paul Ramsey reminds us, "that not since Socrates posed the question have we learned how to teach virtue. The quandaries of medical ethics are not unlike that question. Still, we can no longer rely upon the ethical assumptions in our culture to be powerful enough or clear enough to instruct the profession in virtue; therefore the medical profession should no longer believe that the personal integrity of physicians alone is enough; neither can anyone count on values being transmitted without thought."[21] All I have tried to do is remind us that neither can we count on such values being transmitted without a group of people who believe in and live trusting in God's unfailing presence.

67. Surrogate Motherhood

JANET DICKEY MCDOWELL

Now Sarai, Abram's wife, bore him no children. She had an Egyptian maid whose name was Hagar; and Sarai said to Abram, "Behold now, the Lord has prevented me from bearing children; go in to my maid; it may be that I shall obtain children by her." And Abram hearkened to the voice of Sarai. So, after Abram had dwelt ten years in the land of Canaan, Sarai, Abram's wife, took Hagar the Egyptian, her maid, and gave her to Abram her husband as a wife. And he went in to Hagar, and she conceived. (Gen. 16:1-4)

Thus begins the most ancient account of surrogate motherhood within the Judeo-Christian tradition. To those who have followed legal and medical developments in the United States over the last decade, the story of Abram, Sarai, and the surrogate Hagar has a familiar ring: years of marriage with no progeny, despair over the absence of heirs and family life, the fortuitous presence of a woman who might conceive and provide the much-desired child. Contemporary arrangements are, of course, substantially more complicated and differ in many respect from Sarai's simple offering of her slave, but consideration of the increasingly popular practice of surrogate maternity must not neglect the fact that deliberate extramarital conception has had a long history as a means of dealing with female infertility.

Janet Dickey McDowell (1954–) is Education and Training Coordinator for Planned Parenthood of the Blue Ridge and an ethics consultant for Carilion Health Systems in Roanoke, Virginia.

From *Questions about the Beginning of Life*, ed. Edward D. Schneider (Minneapolis: Augsburg Fortress, 1985).

21. Paul Ramsey, *The Patient as Person*, p. xviii.

The advantages and disadvantages of such a practice and especially its standing within a Christian ethical framework must be assessed just as any other proposed solution to involuntary childlessness is assessed, but surrogate motherhood's relative lack of novelty and its lack of dependence on sophisticated medical support (in contrast to *in vitro* fertilization or embryo transfer, for example) set it apart from most other emerging modes of reproduction. Greater attention must be focused on the potential moral hazards or benefits of surrogate motherhood and less on the medical risks (since they are few). At least four parties must be considered: the potential biological father, his wife (if he is married), the potential biological mother or surrogate, and the proposed child to result from the arrangement. The perspective of each of these individuals will be examined after a description of the contemporary practice of surrogate motherhood and a brief overview of biblical and other theological insights into a Christian view of infertility, procreation, and parenthood.

The Current Practice of Surrogate Motherhood

Most surrogate motherhood arrangements are similar in their basic structure. A woman, designated the surrogate, agrees to conceive a child via artificial insemination and to surrender the child at birth to the man who provided the semen (and to his wife, if he is married). It should be emphasized that the surrogate usually is severing all ties with the child, who is hers genetically. She allows the child's biological father to assume responsibility for the child's upbringing and permits the biological father's wife to adopt her husband's child. All of this is agreed in advance, prior to conception, and may be formalized in a written contract. Ordinarily the surrogate will be compensated for at least her medical expenses.

Beyond this basic framework, surrogate motherhood is a practice almost as diverse as the people who enter into the agreement. Surrogate motherhood is often discussed as though it were one phenomenon when, in reality, there are a great many variations in the way people come to participate in the arrangement, in their motives and reasons for participating, and in their expectations about the future interrelationships among the child, the surrogate, and those who raise the child. Some of these differences in the structure of surrogate motherhood may be morally significant; others may simply be matters of preference or convenience. The most common permutations in the arrangement will be outlined immediately below.[1]

The first variation in the contemporary practice of surrogate motherhood in the United States has to do with the nature of the problem that prevents the man desiring to be a father from conceiving a child in the ordinary way. In the vast majority of reported surrogate arrangements the man is married to a woman who is infertile as a result of any one of several medical conditions.[2] Usually the couple has considered, then rejected, adoption as a means of dealing with their infertility. They may have become discouraged by the scarcity of healthy (especially Caucasian) infants available for adoption, or they may have concluded that they would prefer to raise a child to whom one of them has a genetic connection. They may have difficulty meeting age or other requirements of adoption agencies. Unlike adoption, surrogate motherhood presents the possibility that the husband can make a genetic contribution to the child and that he and his wife can care for the child from a very early point in its life; some couples, with the surrogate's permission, even participate in the birth, and most obtain custody of the child in its first few days of life. Most of the people who seek surrogates fit this pattern and do so because as a couple they are physically incapable of having a child.

However, in a small number of surrogate arrangements there is no medically demonstrated problem preventing normal conception and pregnancy. Instead, the reason for desiring a surrogate is

---

1. For a firsthand description of surrogate motherhood as it has come to be practiced in the United States, see Noel P. Keane with Dennis L. Breo, *The Surrogate Mother* (New York: Everest House, 1981). Keane is the lawyer who came to prominence for arranging surrogate agreements.

2. These may include inovulation, severe endometriosis, scarred or absent fallopian tubes, or a general medical condition, such as diabetes, that makes pregnancy dangerous or impossible.

the absence of a wife. Some single men have entered into agreements with surrogates because they want to be fathers but do not want to be husbands. The surrogates can assure them of children of their own without entanglements. Because this reason for entering into the surrogate arrangement is comparatively rare, the majority of this essay will continue to make reference to the man's wife as a party to the agreement. Nevertheless, it should be remembered that not all surrogate structures include an infertile woman; some are created because the man does not wish to have or cannot find a suitable partner for marriage and procreation.

A second striking variation observable in surrogate motherhood arrangements concerns the relationship between the surrogate and the prospective parents: Will the surrogate be a woman already well known by the couple, or will she be a stranger selected from an application form? If she is not already acquainted with the couple, will the three meet prior to and/or during the pregnancy, or will they always remain anonymous, dealing with one another through an intermediary?

Some of the earliest reported cases of surrogate motherhood involved friends or relatives who had volunteered to be surrogates. Each of these women was apparently motivated by a personal concern for the childless couple known to her, and one would expect that her relationship with the couple and the child continued in some form after the birth.[3]

Other women responded to newspaper advertisements seeking surrogates and agreed to bear a child for people previously unknown to them. Sometimes they met and became close to the couple; in other situations anonymity was preserved. Because artificial insemination is always the means of conception, it is possible to avoid any contact between the surrogate and the couple, but it is not clear whether that is preferable.[4]

Related to the anonymity issue is the heated controversy over payment to surrogates. Surrogates who are related to or close friends with the couple desiring a child rarely if ever seek payment for the service or carrying the child, acting on altruistic or humanitarian grounds, not for any financial gain. Some of the first surrogates responding to advertisements also agreed to the arrangement without compensation beyond medical expenses, citing reasons such as compassion, curiosity, or the desire to experience pregnancy without responsibility for the results. The absence of payment was, in fact, an explicit stipulation in the contracts drawn up for some surrogate arrangements, because to offer or accept any fee beyond medical expenses would have run afoul of laws in many states that prohibit monetary exchanges for the privilege of adoption — laws to prevent a so-called "black market" in babies.[5] However, as the notion of surrogate motherhood was publicized and greater numbers of infertile couples expressed an interest in finding surrogates, it became clear to some involved with the practice that the supply of women who were medically and psychologically suitable to be surrogates and also willing to do so without compensation was quite small; certainly the numbers were not sufficient to meet the perceived demand.

Thus efforts began to legitimate a commercial version of the practice of surrogate motherhood, with fees ranging from $5000 to $20,000 or more. The strategy adopted was to attempt to alter state statutes prohibiting "baby selling" or to establish through the courts that surrogate motherhood did not fall within the proscribed practice (since the child was being surrendered to its natural father, not merely given up for adoption). Some of the earliest attempts failed, but Noel Keane, the lawyer best known for his advocacy of surrogate motherhood, continues to be optimistic that the practice of compensating surrogates will be vindicated and that commercial surrogate motherhood will be found to be compatible with public policy concerns for children's welfare.[6] Some will debate the wisdom of regulating the amount of compensa-

---

3. See the story of Debbie, George, and their surrogate, Sue, who was Debbie's friend, in Keane, Chap. 3. Sue moved in with the couple after the birth of the baby, but did not remain.

4. The artificial insemination need not be performed by a physician. When cooperative physicians could not be located by Keane's clients, the surrogate or the wife of the potential father inseminated the surrogate (Keane, passim). This reemphasizes the point that surrogate motherhood is not a complicated medical process.

5. Walter Wadlington. "Artificial Conception: The Challenge to Family Law," *Virginia Law Review* 69, no. 3 (April 1983): 479-482.

6. Keane, pp. 234-240, 273, 289, 305.

tion beyond medical expenses, while others, repulsed by the very notion of any financial remuneration for having a child, continue to argue that no payment should ever be permitted. The legal status of paid surrogates and the couples who provide payments is cloudy at best.

Also related to the anonymity issue is the question of the future relationship among the surrogate, the child, and the infertile couple. Several options are imaginable. The surrogate couple could establish and maintain a fairly close relationship with the couple and with her child, in which case the child might or might not be informed about the surrogate's biological relationship to him or her. At the other end of the spectrum, the anonymous surrogate might agree to the arrangement through a third party, surrender the child to the couple without coming to know them, and the child might never be told of the unusual circumstances of his conception and birth. Certainly, concealing information about origins was not an uncommon practice until quite recently (when adoptees became more vocal about their rights to access to such material); some may believe it would be in the best interests of both the surrogate and child to sever all relationship between them immediately after birth and perhaps even to withhold the fact that the child is not the natural offspring of both social parents. A middle ground would be making information about the child and his development available to the surrogate at her request and informing the child about the surrogate at some point judged appropriate by the natural father and his wife. Less direct contact would be encouraged than in the first option, especially during the child's early years, but the surrogate birth would not be concealed or denied.

A final difference emerging in the practice of surrogate motherhood has to do with the qualifications of the surrogate. Descriptions of the current situation suggest that surrogates are screened, with varying degrees of rigor, to rule out women with serious existing health problems or a family history of genetically transmitted disease or defects. But there is no agreement on whether the surrogate should be single or married, whether she should have carried one or more healthy children through a full term pregnancy without complications, or whether there should be age restrictions on applicants. Advertisements have been placed in

mass-circulation newspapers, but also in some college newspapers, where they are directed, one assumes, to women 18 to 22 years old. The emotional stability of candidates for surrogate motherhood and their understanding of the physical and emotional consequences of pregnancy may or may not be carefully assessed, depending entirely on the procedure adopted by persons making the agreement.[7] Individuals who are greatly concerned with the health of the potential child and the welfare of the surrogate may set high standards before embarking on the arrangement: those whose focus is on obtaining a child by whatever means are available may be less scrupulous.

In summary, the designation "surrogate motherhood" does not capture the complexity of the many arrangements that carry that label. Careless use of the term may cover up important differences, since it could be referring to a single man hiring an anonymous divorcee to bear his child for $30,000, to an infertile couple arranging with a sister-in-law to carry a child for them, or to college sophomores volunteering to be matched with couples in order to try out pregnancy and pay their tuition. As a first step, an infertile couple contemplating the option of surrogate motherhood would have to clarify the exact sort of arrangement available to them. Only then could they consider the moral implications of the agreement.

A Christian Interpretation of Procreation and Parenthood

Though in the story of Abram, Sarai, and Hagar the Bible provides an ancient account of what might be called surrogate motherhood, the Bible does not deal in any systematic way with this or any other contemporary response to human infertility. The sophisticated scientific understanding of the biological process of reproduction was absent in biblical times, and intervention to relieve childlessness was unheard-of except in the most basic of ways, such as the offering of a substitute

---

7. Keane seems to be very careful to inform surrogates of potential hazards. See the "Agreement of Understanding," the "Surrogate Mother Application," and the "Release and Hold Harmless Agreement," reprinted in *The Surrogate Mother*, pp. 275-305.

for one partner. Nevertheless, the Bible contains substantial guidance regarding the relative importance of procreation and parenthood for those within God's covenant community and indicates a remarkable sensitivity to the psychological and social stresses faced by those who desire children and cannot have them.

Procreation has an honored place in the biblical witness. In the creation narratives of Genesis human beings are created male and female with the potential to "be fruitful and multiply," but only together. From the beginning, both were needed in order to fulfill their promise; human parthenogenesis never seems to have been possible or desirable from God's perspective. Through the companionship and sexual communion of two people committed to one another was to come new life. William Graham Cole argues that "the Hebrews saw marriage as a cleaving together which created one flesh, perfectly symbolized in the children which were to be expected. They are indeed the blending of two into one in an absolutely indissoluble way.[8] Thus from a biblical standpoint procreation is a joint venture of marriage partners.

Polygamy appears to have been acceptable as a traditional form of social organization and procreation sometimes took place within that context. But procreation was never clearly endorsed in the absence of a stable relationship between the man and the woman, a relationship that was recognized by the community and acknowledged openly by both partners. The difficulties that arose from one of the few apparent exceptions, the aforementioned union of Abram and Sarai's maid, Hagar, were formidable and might stand as a warning of the complications of procreation unsupported by a genuine marital relationship.

Barrenness, particularly as presented in the Old Testament, was a tragedy. Always attributed to the woman (because of the notion of reproduction that prevailed), the failure to have a child foreclosed the most important role available to women in Hebraic society, that of mother, and denied her a substantial component of a woman's worth. Children, especially many children, were indicative of God's blessing and, while the Old Testament did not always explicitly describe barrenness as a sign of God's displeasure, one can imagine that the affected woman would interpret it to be so. The relief of infertility, as with Sarah's conception of Isaac, was the fulfillment of God's promise, a wonderful gift, for then one could fill the earth with descendants, carrying on the family name and preserving its memory.[9]

The importance of parenthood and family to the Old Testament covenant community was further reinforced by practices such as polygamy and the levirate obligation. Lineage was traced through one's father; polygamy permitted a man to produce many children who, though having different mothers, shared a common kinship and loyalty. The levirate obligation was the duty a man owed to a brother who died without offspring. By impregnating the brother's widow, a man could assure that the brother's name would not die with him, since by law the child was considered that of the deceased. Onan, who refused to fulfill this obligation, was punished with death (Gen. 38:1-11). Children were one's primary link to the future, in a sense one's immortality, and so these and other social structures were arranged to ensure such a continuation.

Nevertheless, even with the clear importance attached to the institution of the family and to procreation, at least some elements of the Old Testament temper the focus on children, elements that are picked up and extended in the New Testament. The account of Abraham's near sacrifice of his long-awaited son by Sarah, Isaac, speaks powerfully, (if somewhat brutally) of the priority one's commitments should have: obedience to God's command is to take precedence over natural family loyalties and duties, even to the extent that one would be willing to have one's child die.

This theme of ordering one's commitments is echoed and amplified in Jesus' calling of his followers, who must be prepared to leave everything:

> For I have come to set a man against his father, and a daughter against her mother, and a daughter-in-law against her mother-in-law; and a man's foes will be those of his own household. He who loves father or mother more than me is not

---

8. William Graham Cole, *Sex and Love in the Bible* (New York: Association Press, 1959), p. 275.

9. Karen Lebacqz, ed., *Genetics, Ethics and Parenthood* (New York: Pilgrim Press, 1983), pp. 16-23.

worthy of me: and he who does not take his cross and follow me is not worthy of me (Matt. 10:35-38).

The demands of the Kingdom of God may require the setting aside of traditional bonds in favor of ties created by common dedication to the faith. In one of the most striking challenges to the tightly knit, family-oriented social structure of his day, Jesus is described as responding to a request for a private word with his mother and brothers by exclaiming, "Who is my mother, and who are my brothers?" and indicating that those who serve God have rightful claim to those titles (Matt. 12:46-50). In this and other incidents Jesus appears to be deprecating the traditional Hebrew emphasis on the genetically based family as the crucible for the forging of covenant relationship with God, urging instead an individual commitment the depth of which may strain or even break family solidarity.

Though Jesus urged that the family and one's responsibilities to it be kept in perspective, subordinate — like all lesser loyalties — to one's love of God, he did not advocate its dissolution nor propose any alternative, such as "free love" or communal child care, to a biologically based unit for the procreation and rearing of children. His clear prohibition of divorce and his presence at the wedding at Cana have been seen as buttressing and blessing the monogamous union of a man and a woman as the core of family life — although it is to be a family that turns not inward on itself for ultimate meaning and fulfillment, but outward to find its significance in service to God and God's people. If one's worth and value are not found merely by one's membership in a particular tribe or family linked by blood, neither ought they be bound up with the biological creation of those who will carry on the line.

What conclusions can be drawn from this brief sketch of biblical material? At least two generalizations seem justified, and though they stand in some tension, they do not contradict one another. The first lesson is the great esteem in which the family is to be held, with God's blessing and at his command: parents are to be honored, newborn children to be celebrated as gifts from God, the capacity to procreate through loving intercourse to be cherished, and grief acknowledged when natural procreation is not possible. But the second lesson, equally significant, is that the family is not the only or even the most important dimension of human life; covenant faith with God is. If family demands or concerns jeopardize the relationship with God through Christ and threaten to eclipse the only truly ultimate source of meaning, then the family may have become a substitute for God. Jesus opposed all forms of idolatry, whether idolatries of law, economic status, or family; nothing must take God's place, not even institutions that God has sustained and that the Bible endorses.

How have contemporary moral theologians contributed to the Christian understanding of parenthood and procreation, especially as related to surrogate motherhood? Curiously, much of the current discussion can be divided into two basic camps: a "physicalist" approach that focuses on the importance of the biological family's integrity, and a "spiritualist" approach that emphasizes non-biological sources of family ties. Both perspectives claim biblical warrant, and both illuminate vital aspects of family life. It is worthwhile exploring these two fundamental understandings of parenthood and examining in some detail their implications for the surrogate-motherhood arrangement.

The following pairs of attitudes demonstrate roughly the physicalist/spiritualist poles with regard to parenthood:

Physicalist	Spiritualist
Parenthood as given	Parenthood as voluntary
Particular children as given	Children as products of series of conscious choices
Families as exclusively biological	Families as solely moral or legal constructions

The items on the left exemplify an admittedly extreme version of the physicalist approach to family life. Whether one is or is not a parent is God's choice (or nature's choice); it is "given" in that sense, not elected, and the absence of children is interpreted as indicative of the divine will. Similarly, whether one's child is male or female, affected by genetic disease or free of it, is not for the parents to choose or control.[10] An external rather

10. They may choose never to procreate as a way of avoiding genetically transmitted illness, but they may not use amniocentesis and abortion as ways of "controlling" genetic ills.

than an internal locus of control is perceived by the couple when they contemplate their procreative activity.[11] Taken to its logical conclusion, the physicalist approach to family life would cast doubt on the complete legitimacy of family units that are created without biological connections, even including adoptive arrangements, for such constructions lack the natural genetic foundation of the family. This may sound bizarre, but surely such an idea underlies the desire some couples continue to harbor to have a genetically related child even after they have adopted, or the commonly articulated reason for seeking surrogate motherhood: so that the child will be "partially ours" or "mine" (when the impetus for the arrangement comes from the fertile potential father).

Despite the partial genetic connection forged by surrogate motherhood, physicalists would unanimously oppose surrogate motherhood. The opposition stems from the importance attached to the physical integrity of the marriage and the implied commitment to procreate with (and only with) the marital partner. To conceive a child by a third party (through artificial insemination by donor, surrogate motherhood, or the newest technology, ovum transfer) is to violate marital fidelity in a fundamental way. Such a practice menaces the biological foundation of the marriage and the family and, as Richard McCormick has argued, "To weaken the biological link is to untie the family at its root and therefore to undermine it."[12]

In contrast, the elements occupying the right half of the spectrum are those engendered by a spiritualist viewpoint. Parenthood is perceived as entirely voluntary (whether through procreation or by legal or social means). It is in essence a moral commitment, not the inevitable result of a physical contribution. When biological reproduction is undertaken, means for controlling the timing of pregnancy and even the sort of child that results (including maneuvers to determine the gender and genetic health of the child) are not merely

permissible, but virtually obligatory. To do otherwise would be to surrender human responsibility. Because it discounts or denies the role of biology in creating families, this perspective tends to see the family exclusively as a moral or legal community created by human choice and purpose. Thus the presence or absence of genetic ties among family members is a matter of indifference. Joseph Fletcher asserts:

> The bonds which tie people together are moral, mental, emotional — not biological. Parents, siblings, and kinsfolk are no "closer" to us than our spouses, friends, neighbors, and fellow men in general. What constitutes a genuine relationship is shared caring and concern, not "blood" or genes or genital origin.[13]

There is no reason, according to this view, to prefer that children know and/or be reared by their genetic parents.

The essentially spiritualist position can lead to quite opposite opinions regarding surrogate motherhood. One can see that this perspective could endorse the practice, because the child's absence of a genetic link to its social mother would be inconsequential and the almost purely physical connection between the child and the surrogate would be greatly discounted. There would be little concern over the participation of a third party in procreation, for the focus of moral attention would be on the joint *decision* by the prospective parents to procreate in this way, not on the means needed to achieve their goal. The suggestion that procreation with a woman not his wife compromises the man's marriage vows of fidelity would be rejected as ludicrous, because fidelity is understood also in terms of commitment, not in terms of who receives his sperm.[14]

On the other hand, an individual embracing the spiritualist perspective might oppose surrogate motherhood on the grounds that it was a surrender to a biologically based understanding wrongly encouraging the infertile couple's misperception that a child resulting from surrogate motherhood would be "closer" to them than an adopted child.

---

11. See Sidney Callahan's provocative article, "An Ethical Analysis of Responsible Parenthood," *Birth Defects: Original Article Series* 15, no. 2 (1979), pp. 224-229.

12. Richard A. McCormick, "Genetic Medicine: Notes on the Moral Literature," *Theological Studies* 33, no. 3 (September 1972): 551.

13. Joseph Fletcher, *The Ethics of Genetic Control* (Garden City, N.Y.: Doubleday, 1974), p. 144.

14. The lack of sexual intercourse is also significant.

Surrogate motherhood, and many other means of circumventing infertility, are simply unnecessary; as long as there are some children in the world in need of loving homes, the appropriate response to involuntary childlessness is adoption.[15]

The consensus of moral theologians representing both poles of the debate seems to recommend hesitation about, if not opposition to, surrogate motherhood (although there are exceptions, such as Joseph Fletcher). The reasons cited are disparate and sometimes contradictory, but they provide insights that can be applied to each of the parties involved in the surrogate motherhood agreement. Much of the focus of the discussion of the practice of surrogate motherhood has been on the infertile couple; they are crucial, but the potential for difficulties with the arrangement seems stronger when the surrogate and the potential child are also considered.

Surrogate Motherhood:
The Infertile Couple

Would the arguments made by either the physicalists or the spiritualists persuade an infertile couple that surrogate motherhood ought not to be undertaken? Probably not, and not merely because they may be more concerned with solutions to their shared problem than with the niceties of ethic debate. If one looks critically at either perspective, there are sufficient objections to make a middle-ground position appealing. And, *judged solely from the infertile couple's viewpoint*, and from within a more moderate position than either the physicalist or the spiritualist, surrogate motherhood may be morally justifiable — if not commendable.

What is the content of an interpretation of parenthood that stands between the poles of physicalism and spiritualism? It would deny the physicalist's claim that being a parent must be grounded in biology, acknowledging the human capacity to transcend biology and be "mother" or "father" in the most important ways without contributing ova or sperm. But it would also recognize, as the spiritualist's approach does not, the abiding links forged by biology. Thus it would be sympathetic to the man's desire to procreate, to engender a child genetically connected to him without disparaging that man's wife's capability to nurture and love a child with whom she has no such connection. "Unequal" relationships to children are not uncommon; stepparents have needed to cope with such an imbalance and have done so, one imagines, with varying degrees of success. As long as both potential legal and social parents are willing to make an unqualified commitment to the child, it does not seem that the child's origins in a surrogate arrangement would necessarily jeopardize their relationship to the child.

More serious objections stem from the effects of the surrogate situation on the relationship between the man and his infertile wife and the distortion of the full meaning of procreation that the surrogate arrangement entails. Both biblical material and the commentary of some contemporary moral theologians argue that the begetting of a child ought to be the result of loving communion between its parents.[16] The conjunction of the joys of sexuality and the potential reproductive functions is not held to be incidental. Deep communication and rich pleasure are conjoined with the giving of new life. There are, of course, many instances in which children are conceived without love between sexual partners, without permanent commitment, without an intention to be responsible for the child, but these are tragic, often sinful situations — not normative ones. Surrogate motherhood requires that the husband procreate (however anonymously) with a woman with whom he has no relationship even vaguely approximating a marital one.[17] It is true that his

15. Stanley Hauerwas is well known for his position regarding other reproductive technologies such as *in vitro* fertilization. See his testimony, "Theological Reflections on IVF" in the Ethics Advisory Board document, *Appendix: HEW Support of Research Involving Human In Vitro Fertilization and Embryo Transfer*, May 4, 1979.

16. Joseph Fletcher and others who might fall under the "spiritualist" label would deny that physical loving communion is necessarily linked to procreation, emphasizing instead the joint *decision* to procreate — by means that may involve others in the physical transmission of life.

17. If the relationship were substantially similar to a marital one, the surrogate arrangement would likely collapse, as would the marriage.

behavior can be called "adulterous" only by a very strict interpretation of that term and that couples involved in the surrogate arrangement have not themselves perceived it as any betrayal of marital fidelity: nevertheless, it is surely procreation outside the marriage, and as such it falls short of the Christian norm for procreation. The end — a child specifically conceived for the couple and sharing the man's genetic constitution in part — does not ordinarily seem sufficiently serious to warrant such a major distortion of procreation. However, one can imagine circumstances in which this breach of the procreational norm might be justified — cases where there are very few or no adoptable children available or where the couple fails to meet some arbitrary criterion to qualify for adoption — and so, seen from the infertile couple's perspective, surrogate motherhood might sometimes be considered.[18]

Surrogate Motherhood: The Surrogate

From the viewpoint of the surrogate, it is hard to imagine how one could justify the surrogate-motherhood arrangement. This may seem surprising, since it has been the willingness of women to volunteer to serve as surrogates that has popularized the practice in recent years. But in light of Christian norms and values, there seem to be few if any factors that would support a woman's decision to become a surrogate, and there are many that should discourage her. This appears to be the case whether the surrogate knows the infertile couple or not, is married or single, is compensated handsomely or carries the child without remuneration. Some of these variations may be more problematic, but in any of the possible permutations, human procreation is reduced to the status of a service for hire (or for donation), and the surrogate is encouraged to engender an attitude of distance and alienation from her own child and her body. Neither of these outcomes is compatible with a Christian notion of giving life.

Surrogates have been quoted as saying that they

agreed to conceive a child and subsequently give it up for a number of reasons: curiosity; to assuage guilt over an earlier abortion; because pregnancy and birth had been or were expected to be personally rewarding experiences; or, most frequently, out of compassion for childless couples. Whether these reasons are interpreted as selfish or altruistic, both biblical and contemporary resources indicate that by themselves they are not appropriate reasons for undertaking procreation. There is no context of loving commitment to the child's father, a basic prerequisite; and unlike the husband within the infertile marriage, the surrogate has no intention to care for the child she deliberately conceives. The absence of these crucial elements reduces human procreation to the mere biological production of babies; whether the surrogate is paid or not, she has misunderstood the essential character of procreation and so degraded it.

Of the cited reasons, compassion would seem to be the least objectionable, the reason a Christian woman might be moved to become a surrogate. Compassion is commended biblically, and there can be great sorrow associated with an infertile couple's plight, sorrow that may be alleviated only by a child. However, it must be recognized that there are limits even on behavior stemming from sympathy. If an individual offered to shoot himself in the head to provide a heart or other vital organ to someone in need, the individual's action would be discouraged, no matter how sincere the desire to help.[19] A person who robbed a bank to help the poor or, in a less dramatic vein, drained her child's education fund in order to support a worthy charity would also be vulnerable to criticism, especially because the person could be seen as sacrificing someone else's interests in order to demonstrate compassion. Surrogate motherhood may be somewhat analogous to the latter example, particularly if one concedes that the child may have some interest in knowing and being reared by its genetic mother. Therefore it is not unreasonable to argue that surrogate motherhood is compassion gone awry, sympathy that steps beyond the bounds of appropriate behavior. The deliberate

---

18. The need to develop regulations regarding various kinds of artificial conception, regulations that might be similar to those currently applicable in adoption, is acknowledged in Wadlington, pp. 501-512.

19. Some vocations entail a willingness to sacrifice oneself for another, but these are special cases created by special duties.

conception of a child outside of wedlock is not a matter of indifference, and being motivated by concern for unhappy people cannot compensate for the moral deficits inherent in the action.

In defending their decisions to become surrogates, some women describe themselves as "providing the gift of life" — an action which on its surface also appears commendable. But a Christian understanding of procreation does not view children as entities to be created in order to be bestowed on others, as though they were handmade sweaters or cookies. Participation in their creation necessarily entails a responsibility for their welfare, a commitment to try to meet their physical, emotional, and spiritual needs; the surrogate has absolutely no intention of carrying out that responsibility. There are certainly other contexts in which one or both of the biological parents may be unwilling or unable to behave responsibly, in which case others may fulfill the parental role, but, again, these are not normative situations. Moreover, the premeditated character of the surrogate's decision to forfeit the parental relationship makes her choice especially repugnant.

In conclusion, it seems difficult to imagine circumstances that would warrant a Christian woman's choice to be a surrogate. Though her motives may be praiseworthy and her concern for childless couples genuine, she fails to appreciate the full value and responsibility of procreation. Surrogates who conceive primarily for financial reasons have strayed even farther from the norm, and so perhaps are more subject to censure, but all surrogates seem confused about the appropriate use of the reproductive capacity.

Surrogate Motherhood: The Potential Child

Implied in much of the foregoing discussion is a concern for the child who might be conceived as a result of a surrogate agreement. Describing the best interests of a potential child is a difficult task, since any flaws in the situation into which he is born must be balanced against the "problem" of never being conceived at all. This is frequently pointed out by advocates of surrogate motherhood — that without the cooperation of the infertile couple and the surrogate the particular child would never exist. But no one has ever argued that all potential children ought to exist, and Christians regularly try to consider a potential child's interests when making judgments about family size or the prudence of conception when the probability of genetic disease is high. Assuming that there is some value in being conceived and born, are there reasons that one might not wish to encourage conceiving and bearing children in a surrogate arrangement — for the child's sake? There may be.

The primary pitfall from the child's perspective is a confused or nonexistent relationship with his mother. If the individual contracting with the surrogate is single, the child would most likely be raised without a mother, since the supposed purpose of the surrogate arrangement for a single male is the potential of raising a biologically related child without making commitments to the child's mother. Single persons have been permitted to adopt children in many states and often seem capable of providing loving, stable homes. But the surrogate situation differs by being premeditated: there was never an intention that the child have a substantial relationship with two parents. This seems less than fair to a child and may show a lack of concern for the child's best interests, a concern that perhaps ought to overrule a single person's desire for a biological child.

The more common surrogate arrangement, in which the infertile wife adopts the child, provides the child with two parents, but the question of the child's connection to its biological mother still needs to be resolved. It is possible that the couple might not inform the child of his or her unusual origins, allowing the child to believe the social mother had given him or her birth. In addition to being a violation of the Christian commitment to truth, such deception could be very difficult to maintain. Should the child learn the truth from others, the child's trust in those who have done the rearing could be greatly undermined.

If the infertile couple chose instead to be candid with the child, the issues of trust and truthfulness might not arise, but other problems almost certainly would. If the couple acknowledged the child's surrogate birth but severed all ties with the surrogate, the child would be cut off from an important source of medical information, not to mention the less tangible contributions to personal identity that come from knowing biological kin. Whether the child met and came to know the surrogate or not, the child might feel divided loyalties between mothers, or a sense or rejection, since the biological mother never wanted the child herself but always planned to give the child away. Payment to the surrogate could complicate the child's response: what would it mean to know your mother had been paid to conceive and carry you to birth? These may not be insurmountable difficulties, but anyone considering surrogate motherhood surely ought to be aware that the child will be faced with many of the same kinds of questions and doubts that adoptees voice — and the surrogate child would have the additional burden of knowing that the separation from his or her natural mother was the result of choices freely made by the adults around the child, not the result of circumstances they could not control.

Surrogate Motherhood: The Whole Picture

Taken as a whole, does surrogate motherhood appear to be an arrangement Christians would condemn, condone, or applaud? The picture is a mixed one, but the majority of the evidence leans against surrogate motherhood. Wholesale condemnation may not be appropriate, but Christian perceptions of the significance of procreation and its place within the marital relationship are not compatible with the basic premise of surrogate motherhood: that one could deliberately conceive and bear a child with no commitment either to the child or to its father. From the perspective of the infertile couple, surrogate motherhood may appear to be a tempting solution to a heart-wrenching problem, and the child that would result would experience the awesome gift of life. But do these benefits really outweigh or justify the distortion of procreation that makes them possible? Ultimately this is a judgment that might best be left to individual conscience, but it should be a conscience informed by the Christian community and the Bible. Parenthood is affirmed as good, but only when it is kept in perspective. There is a grave danger faced by all parents but heightened by the desperation felt by infertile couples — the danger that a child may replace God, as revealed through Jesus Christ, as their center of value and meaning. Children are

wonderful gifts entrusted by God, but they are not gifts to be sought at any price. For most people the costs of creating a child through surrogate motherhood — costs to the integrity of the marriage, to the surrogate's self-understanding, and perhaps to the child — are simply too high.

68. Praying with Dirty Hands

ALLEN VERHEY

It was about the third week of class. It was time, I said, "to get our hands dirty." The case study, as I recall, had to do with whether to cooperate with a friend seeking an abortion. (The friend was eight weeks pregnant and, by her account, a victim of "date rape.") I gave the case and asked, "What should you do?" I was hoping to elicit comment about principles like "autonomy" and "the sanctity of life," some reflection about the situation, like the status of the fetus and the circumstances of conception, even perhaps some consideration of the differences between doing an act, cooperating with an act, and merely tolerating an act. It would set up a number of issues I wanted to turn to next in class.

The class did not seem quite so eager as I was to dirty our hands. I called on a young woman in the front row. "What would you do?" I asked, and her reply was, "Well, I guess I'd pray." Someone laughed, and I smiled and said, "That's nice, but then what would you do?" The class rescued her from the silence by offering what they would do and why, and the discussion started to develop in ways I wanted and in ways for which I was prepared. Prayer was not mentioned again. I thought the session went quite well.

Now I am not so sure. Indeed, it seems to me that there was in that class period a little crisis of theological integrity and that I was not altogether faithful to my identity as a Christian theologian. My agenda as a bioethicist had no room for the

---

Allen Verhey (1945–) is the Blekkink Professor of Religion at Hope College.

From *The Reformed Journal,* July 1989, pp. 11-14.

contribution of a central practice of piety. If secularism is "a negation of worship" (Alexander Schmemann, *For the Life of the World,* p. 149), then my ignoring "Well, I guess I would pray" had contributed to it. I supposed that prayer was irrelevant to discernment or at least to the class's public discussion of cases. Worse yet, I condescendingly interpreted the young woman's disposition to pray as a refusal to get her hands dirty, as either a slothful refusal to engage in the intellectual work necessary to discover what she should do or a proud claim that she had a sort of magical access to right answers.

She might legitimately have expected a theologian to treat her remark more hospitably than "That's nice, but then what would you do?" — especially when that theologian had already made claims about the relevance of Christian faith to medical ethics and indeed to public discourse about medical ethics.

I wish now I had done things differently. I wish I had *taken her seriously* — and helped the class to take her seriously. I might have said, for example, "Oh, I guess you are familiar with the last work of the great twentieth-century theologian, Karl Barth. He, too, describes the Christian life as a life of prayer, as 'the humble and resolute, the frightened and joyful *invocation* of the gracious God in gratitude, praise, and, above all, petition' " (*The Christian Life,* p. 43). Well, perhaps not; such a reply might not get the class to take her seriously. But I might have said, "It is striking that in the ordinary events of birth and death, of suffering and caring for the suffering, prayer is nearly as commonplace as medical technology."

I owed her and the class more, of course, than simply to take her remark seriously. I wish now I had asked what she thought prayer is and how it might help her discover what she ought to do. She might have replied in various ways, of course. She might have said, "*Prayer is a practice,* what Alasdair MacIntyre called:

a coherent and complex form of socially established cooperative human activity through which goods internal to that form of activity are realized in the course of trying to achieve those standards of excellence which are appropriate to, and partially definitive of, that form of activity, with the result that human powers to achieve excellence, and human conceptions of the ends and goods involved, are systematically extended. (*After Virtue*, p. 175)

Well, perhaps not, not this young woman anyway; and such a reply with its philosophical care might have done little to get the class to see the relevance of prayer.

She might have said, "*Prayer is to call upon God. It is to invoke God and to adore God as the one on whom we depend, as helper and healer, as creator and provider and redeemer.*" And if she did, and if I were then to ask, "And how does that help you to see what you ought to do?", she might reply, "Well, I don't know exactly; that is, it probably would not help me see *exactly* what I ought to do, but it would, I think, orient me to God and so reorient me to all other things in relation to God. Attending to God as God the creator might keep me from making either life or my friend or the element of choice an idol, since nothing God made is god; and it might keep me as well from turning against life or my friend or choice as though it were evil, since all that God made is good. Attending to God the creator might keep me from comfortably reducing the embodied selves God creates either to mere organisms or merely to their capacities for agency." And then I could return to my agenda, getting our hands dirty in this case, reflecting on principles and situations, but in a different context, against the background of another sort of intelligibility, with qualified — dare I say, transformed — sensibilities.

Or, she might have said, "*Prayer is confession;* it is to acknowledge the presence and power of evil in my own life and in my own heart. Prayer looks to God in repentance and remorse." "And how does that," I would ask, "help you to decide what you ought to do?" She might reply, "Well, I don't know exactly; that is, it probably would not help me see *exactly* what I ought to do, but confession would, I think, keep me from judging my friend too quickly or too severely, and it would, I hope, remind me of the evil we sometimes do in resisting evil. Perhaps repentance could remind me that I am neither the judge nor the savior and so enable me to be critical without condescension and helpful without conceit." And then I could return to my agenda, reflecting on principles and situations, but in a different context, against the background of another intelligibility, with transformed sensibilities.

Or, she might have said, "*Prayer is intercession;* it petitions God to establish God's own good future and to grant to us — and to our friends and to our enemies — already now some taste of it; in supplication prayer attends to God's future cosmic sovereignty and to God's presence and promise even now to those who cry out in pain for it." "And how does that," I would ask, "help you to decide what you ought to do?" She might reply, "Well, I don't know exactly; that is, it probably would not help me see *exactly* what to do, but intercession for my friend might let me see her in a new and different way, as one whose ultimate good depends on God rather than on my own efforts to achieve it; it might also free me to attend to those who might be hurt in pursuit of my friend's good. And intercession for my enemies might keep me from obliterating the littlest enemy from my vision. I might even see the little organism in a new and different way, less prepared by enmity and revenge to obliterate it as a nonperson. I don't know if it is a person — at what, eight weeks? — because of genetic uniqueness and completeness or brain waves or anything else, but I think intercession would ready me to practice hospitality to this nascent, inchoative life, not disposed to consign it to the powers of death and darkness, disposed, I guess, to welcome it as a sign of confidence in God's good future and of God's care for and presence to the needy and powerless while we wait and watch for that future." And then I could return to my agenda, reflecting on principles and situations, but in a different context, against the background of another intelligibility, with transformed sensibilities.

Of course, the young woman might also have said, "*Prayer is magic;* it puts God at my disposal. It's a way of getting what I want, whether an answer or a rescue or a fortune." Or, "*Prayer is appeasement;* it placates God's wrath and gives a little room to pursue our own interests." Or . . . The abuses of prayer are diverse; and we need only mention that all prayer reflects the vision of God a person has. It may, then, have been necessary to correct and reform this young woman's participation in the practice of prayer by reflection on the practice and on the God to whom it attends.

The theologian owed it to this pious young

woman to *take her seriously* and to help the public discourse of the class to take her seriously. But not only that: the theologian owed it to this young woman to evoke and *to nurture* her reflective participation in the practices of piety and her sense that attending to God in such a way could enlarge her vision and strengthen her virtue in medical moral dilemmas. The theologian owed her, that is, reflection on the priestly word of Psalm 50, "Call upon [God] in the day of trouble" (vs. 15). But not only that; the theologian might also owe this young woman *correction,* perhaps even the prophetic word from the same Psalm, "I will accept no bull from your house" (vs. 9a) — or at least the reminder of Isaiah's prophetic words,

> When you spread forth your hands, I will hide my eyes from you; even though you make many prayers, I will not listen; your hands are full of blood. Wash yourselves; make yourselves clean; . . . cease to do evil, learn to do good; seek justice, correct oppression; defend the fatherless and the widow.

It is presumptuous, of course, to suppose that this young woman needed correction. The teacher never got that far because he failed to take her seriously. The word of correction in this instance might better be addressed to the teacher, who failed (on that day, at least), for want of imagination or good sense, one critical test of a good teacher — learning from a student. This teacher may have been a slow learner, but he is now ready to answer the question theologians interested in bioethics must answer in a way most of them have not considered. "Whom should theologians address in doing bioethics?" is the question, and my answer is "God." Theologians, the teachers of the church, must learn from the communities of faith to invoke God, to attend to God, to orient themselves to God, in examining dilemmas. Such would not prevent them from getting their hands dirty, from invoking principles or attending to the situation or orienting themselves to the goods; it would rather permit them to do all that in ways appropriate to the relations of all that to God. When they get their hands dirty by attending to cases, they might learn from those they teach to lift them up in prayer.

That answer is instructive, I think, for the audiences theologians have considered. For, with whom do we pray? With whom do we invoke God and attend to God? With communities of faith, of course; and the theological ethicist as a member of such a community and as its teacher can and must provide priestly nurture and prophetic correction of their practices and of their vision of God as such bear on decisions. Faithful people want to orient their living and their dying, their suffering and their care for the suffering, to God. They want to attend to God in all things, including their attention to giving and receiving and allocating health care. The theologian who invokes God may and must serve them, attend to them, address them by reflective participation in the practices of the community, including prayer, by appeals to the sources and standards for both reflection and piety accepted by the community of faith, including Scripture, and by rejecting any slothful refusal to do the hard intellectual work necessary for discernment and every proud claim to have the truth, if not captive, at least cornered.

But suppose I had asked the young woman in class, "With whom would you pray?" She might well have said, "With any who will." And that number may include her friend even if her friend is not a member of a community of faith; that number may be a good deal larger than the church. In an age as noisily secular as our own, it *is* striking that prayer is as commonplace in hospitals as technology. Piety still evidently surrounds the undertaking and the practice of medicine and nursing for many. Some who enter the professions, even if they do not invoke any God by name, still enter and practice it with a lively sense of gratitude for the givenness (the gifts) of life and health, with a humble sense of dependence upon some dimly known but reliable order, with a sad sense of a tragic flaw that runs through our world and through our lives, with a hopeful sense of new possibilities on the horizon, and with a keen sense of responsibility to some inscrutable power who gives the gifts, sustains the order, judges the fault, and provides new possibilities. Moreover, there are many others who use medicine, not members of any community of faith, for whom the events of birth and suffering and death are surrounded not only by medical technology but by piety as well, by a sense of their dependence upon and their indebtedness to a transcendent power that bears down on human life and powers and sustains them as well.

This is an audience which could hear philosopher Iris Murdoch's call for "attention [to] a distant transcendent perfection, a source of uncontaminated energy, a source of new and quite undreamt virtue" (*The Sovereignty of Good*, p. 101). Such attention is a bridge to the invocation of God. This is an audience which could take attention to God seriously, which could hear of the invocation of God without laughing or condescendingly supposing it slothful or proud. To such an audience the theologian, as member of believing community and as spokesperson for it, by invoking God and by claiming to know this Other and to be able to name this Other aright in invocation, may serve to orient both their piety and their medicine. Of course, such claims take courage, and such courage is ever only a small step from the foolhardy presumption of claiming to know too much, of rendering the transcendent Other not only scrutable but serviceable to *our* projects (including our ecclesiastical projects). Nevertheless, with courage and humility the theologian may and must invoke God "with any who will."

It needs to be remembered, finally, that someone laughed when the young woman said she would pray and that the class discussion had to go on. The secularists are an audience, too, and the pluralism of a society (or a classroom) may not be ignored. The theologian has the responsibility, as member and spokesperson for the community, to attempt to get the secularist to take invocation of God seriously. It may not be easy. To invoke God in defense of invoking God may only turn a grin into a smirk. Priestly invitations and prophetic corrections may only win derision. But the sage, the wisdom teacher, might appeal to moral commonplaces, to experience, to prudence, to nature to defend (and to test) the moral vision enlarged by prayer, the conceptions of the ends and goods involved enriched by prayer, the moral reflection qualified by the invocation of God. Such "natural" moral wisdom is a bridge for conversation, too. The theologian has no responsibility for — and should have no interest in — discrediting "natural" moral wisdom or in engaging in an *argumentum ad hominem* on the scale of an *argumentum ad humanum*. On the contrary, even if the theo-

logian ought not to be satisfied until the invocation of God has radically reoriented "natural" moral wisdom, it is "natural" moral wisdom which is finally reoriented. The theologian may and must use "natural" moral wisdom to defend (and to test) discourse and deliberation and discernment where God is invoked, even among the secularists, and to advance (and to test) the enlargement of moral vision, the enriched conception of the human good, the reorientation of the way we attend to circumstances, also in a pluralistic context.

A theologian may not, of course, coerce the secularist to invoke God or to act in ways discerned by attending to God. Prayer must be *free* to be genuinely prayer. The Christian life must be a free response to God to be *genuinely* Christian. Perhaps that is why a theologian can work with integrity as a teacher not only of the church but also of a class. The young woman may have had a significant contribution to make to the class discussion that day. My failure as a theologian and as a teacher stood in the way. But suppose she had monopolized the discussion. The teacher in me might have said, "Uh, that's enough; thank you. Others have a right to speak." The theologian in me might now handle it a little differently:

"And for whom would you pray?"

"Why, for all, of course."

"For the poor?"

"Yes, that they may have a fair share."

"And for the voiceless?"

"Of course, that they may be heard."

"And how might that help you to discern what you ought to do?"

"Well, I don't know exactly; that is, . . . I might shut up and let others speak."

Good idea!

69. The Distinction between Killing and Allowing to Die

GILBERT MEILAENDER

In his "Notes on Moral Theology: April-September 1975,[1] Richard A. McCormick, S.J., takes up some recent treatments of the distinction between killing and allowing to die. I want to comment on one part of that discussion — his treatment of an article by Gerald J. Hughes, S.J.[2] I will suggest that neither Hughes's argument nor McCormick's discussion takes us much beyond where Paul Ramsey had already gotten in chapter 3 of *The Patient as Person*, and that we can get further only by taking seriously a remark which Ramsey makes almost in passing and perhaps does not himself take with sufficient seriousness.

Hughes presents an interesting argument designed to lead us to question whether there is a (morally relevant) distinction between killing and allowing to die. He considers two cases: (1) a patient presently receiving artificial life-support without which he will die; (2) a terminally ill patient who will die within a few days. In each case

one act on the part of the attending physician can have a decisive significance. In case 1 the doctor can switch off the life-support machine(s), and the patient can be "allowed to die." In case 2 the doctor can give the patient an injection as a result of which he would die as quickly as would the first patient when deprived of artificial life-support.

In neither case is there any hope of saving the patient, since both are irretrievably in their process of dying. In both cases the physician has at his disposal an action which will result in the death of the patient. Neither physician need *want* the patient dead in the sense of having any ulterior motives which would render his intent evil. How is it possible to say that, since in case 1 the patient is allowed to die and in case 2 the patient is killed, some morally relevant difference is involved? McCormick summarizes the conclusion to which Hughes's argument seems to lead: "The conclusion would seem to be either that euthanasia is morally permissible in those instances in which a decision not to maintain life is permissible, or that neither euthanasia nor refusal to prolong life is permissible" (p. 105).

Hughes, in fact, rejects these alternatives and suggests another possibility. However, I am less interested in his other suggestion than I am in noting that the alternatives seem strikingly similar to what Ramsey calls "the same objection from two opposite extremes" to his suggested ethic of caring (but only caring) for the dying.[3] Each of the two extremes which Ramsey discusses equates a morality of only caring for the dying with euthanasia — the one in order to oppose both, the other in order to advocate both. "Proponents of euthanasia agree with advocates of relentless efforts to save life in reducing an ethics of omitting life-sustaining treatments to a distinction without a difference from directly killing the dying."[4]

Ramsey also writes that "in omission no human agent causes the patient's death, directly or indirectly. He dies his own death from causes that it is no longer merciful or reasonable to fight by means of possible medical interventions."[5] Now the force of Hughes's example, and the source of

---

1. *Theological Studies* 37 (1976): 70-119; cf. especially pp. 100-107.
2. "Killing and Letting Die," *Month* 236 (1975): 42-45.

Gilbert Meilaender (1946–) is a professor in the religion department at Oberlin College. He has written *The Taste for the Other: The Social and Ethical Thought of C. S. Lewis, Friendship: A Study in Theological Ethics, The Theory and Practice of Virtue,* and *Faith and Faithfulness: Basic Themes in Christian Ethics.*

From *Theological Studies* 37 (September 1976): pp. 467-470

3. *The Patient as Person* (New Haven: Yale University Press, 1970), pp. 144ff.
4. Ibid., p. 146.
5. Ibid., p. 151.

McCormick's puzzlement, is that this no longer seems clear when placed against Hughes's two cases. Or, at least, it no longer seems morally relevant. In both cases there is one act which seems to result in the same consequence: the death of the patient. In neither act is there any evil intent; on the contrary, it would be possible in some contexts to argue that each is an attempt to conform to Ramsey's fundamental imperative: "Never abandon care."[6]

Can a case nevertheless be made for saying that the "two extremes" are wrong to equate a morality of only caring for the dying with euthanasia? McCormick writes: "I myself believe that there is moral significance in the traditional distinction, in the minimal sense that we ought to maintain the distinction in practice, though I am far from sure how we ought to analyze it" (p. 107). I suggest that we unpack the moral significance of the distinction by placing it in the religious context out of which it grew. It will not be enough merely to say that "in omission no human agent causes the patient's death, directly or indirectly." That, in the abstract, may not overcome the force of Hughes's examples; for in both of his cases we have a dying patient, one action by the doctor, no subjectively evil motive on the part of the doctor, and the same result. Why, then, should the omission/commission distinction bear moral weight? Because *in a certain context* we can question whether, objectively, the doctor's action in case 2 can be brought under the rubric of *care* — whether it can be an attempt to care for and comfort the patient in his dying.

In order to do this, however, I believe we must make explicit a part of Ramsey's case which he does not always underscore. He believes, of course, that a morality of only caring for the dying is the only truly humane ethic and that the two opposite extremes inflict indignity upon the patient because they ignore something essential in our human condition. But this is a human condition understood in a religious context. Ramsey himself says that the traditional ethic which distinguished killing and allowing to die grew up in a religious tradition. If that tradition should now find itself in disrepair, it may prove impossible to sustain the

moral viewpoint which it nourished. Ramsey suggests as much in a characteristic paragraph.

It may be that only in an age of faith when men know that the dying cannot pass beyond God's love and care will men have the courage to apply these limits to medical practice. It may be that only upon the basis of faith in God can there be a conscionable category of "ceasing to oppose death," making room for caring for the dying. It may also be that only an age of faith is productive of absolute limits upon the taking of the lives of terminal patients, because of the alignment of many a human will with God's care for them here and now, and not only in the there and then of the providence.[7]

What the Christian faith provides is a story which recounts the dealings of God with his creatures — a story of creation, fall, incarnation, redemption, resurrection. The Christian tries to understand his life — even, to put it more metaphysically, define his being — in terms of that story. Furthermore — and important for ethics — he tries to shape his action in such a way that it will accord with the pattern of God's action. That is part of what it means to permit this story to define the reality of his existence and world.[8]

Now if we try to understand ourselves and our world in terms of this story, what will we say about death? Surely that it is an ambivalent phenomenon. It is not God's will for mankind. It can even be said to be the result of the turn from God into

---

6. Insofar as our evaluation of intention is tied closely to our evaluation of action, it might be better to say that there is no evil *motive* in either case.

7. *The Patient as Person*, p. 156.

8. The concept of "story" is fast becoming a fad in theological circles. I would not even venture to say how many ways it is used, but I think I am using it in something like the way Hans Frei writes of "the biblical story" as a story "whose depiction allowed the reader at the same time to locate himself and his era in the real world rendered by the depiction" (*The Eclipse of Biblical Narrative* [New Haven, 1974], p. 50). Interestingly, according to Frei's account many of the hermeneutical problems which confront contemporary theologians became problems when this biblical story was no longer thought to depict the world in terms of which one ought to understand oneself. Instead, the biblical story was incorporated into a larger framework. Ramsey's paragraph cited above seems to me to make a similar point with reference to the discipline of ethical reflection.

sin. It is the triumph of Satan, of all that is opposed to God. Hence it is something to be feared, something to be fought against, something against which God himself resolves to do battle, the last enemy.

But it is something other than that as well. Death is also the means by which God achieves his victory in the incarnate Christ. He does it by accepting the limitations which bind every creature in a sinful world, including the limitation of death. The secret of defeating this great enemy — an enemy which under ordinary circumstances must be resisted — is knowing the point at which it is necessary to accept death and acknowledge its seeming finality. Only then can losing one's life lead to finding it. The paradox makes sense within the story.

If we are to talk about death in terms of this story, it must remain ambivalent. We must say *both* that it is to be resisted *and* that, for every human being, it must at some point be acknowledged. We can say one of these to the exclusion of the other only if we remove death from the context of the story and define it in some other way. Perhaps we will always remain puzzled about the point of the distinction between killing and allowing to die — feeling it to have some moral force but not being quite certain what that force is — unless we place death within the contours of this story and understand ourselves and the dying person as pilgrims who are defined by its contours. When, however, we think within this context, the distinction is meaningful. It is, presumably, no part of the pilgrim's task to propel himself or anyone else ahead to the end of the story. That cannot be called "care." Neither is it any part of his task to try desperately to hold onto this life when, for him or any other particular human being, the end — or what seems to be the end — of the story has come. That too cannot from this perspective be called "care."

Thus to return to Hughes's two cases: our evaluation of the doctors' actions in the two cases does not depend on their subjective motives. Nor does it depend *merely* on the distinction between killing and allowing to die. Instead it depends on placing that distinction within a particular context. The doctors are understood as agents within the world the Christian story depicts. In *that* world the action which hastens death by means of an injection cannot be called "care." Not because the physician is presumed to have any subjectively evil motive, but simply because in the world so understood this cannot be part of the meaning of commitment to the well-being of the neighbor. As an action in that world, it cannot reflect the shape of God's action.

If this is correct, it may help to explain McCormick's belief that there is in the distinction a "moral bite" which he cannot fully articulate. The distinction makes sense within a context, within a story. It cannot be removed from that context and turned into an abstract proposition without undergoing change. This may also mean, of course, that Christian moralists who wish to make use of the distinction will have to acknowledge its theological roots and accept the fact that these roots may be unappealing to some and unpersuasive to others. Surely, though, it is better to risk that than to try to make the distinction operate in a way it was not meant to operate; for in doing that we risk obscuring its importance altogether.

Try It Yourself:
The Death Machine

CASE STUDY 5

Exercise: Three Contexts
for Moral Discourse

Divide yourselves up into three committees. You may choose which committee to be on, but each committee should have at least four "volunteers."

The committees are these:

1. State Senate Committee on Health Care Policy
2. Local Hospital Ethics Committee
3. Local Council of Churches Advisory Committee on Health Care.

The issue each committee must deal with is "assisted suicide," especially physician involvement in "assisted suicide." Your committees are meeting in response to the reaction (some positive and some negative) to the use of Dr. Jack Kevorkian's "suicide machine" by Janet Adkins. Janet Adkins had been diagnosed as having Alzheimer's disease. She was still evidently well physically and mentally, but the prospect of her deterioration led her to seek the aid of Dr. Kevorkian in killing herself. With Dr. Kevorkian's machine she gave herself a lethal dose of potassium chloride.

Other cases are less sensational but no less important to your committee's deliberation. For example, Dr. Timothy Quill reported in the March 1991 issue of the *New England Journal of Medicine* that he had cared for "Diane" for over eight years, that she had developed an acute leukemia, that — in order to forego the possible side effects and suffering and in order to be with her family as much as possible — she had refused a course of aggressive chemotherapy and bone marrow transplantation that would have provided a twenty-five percent chance for extended survival, that he had arranged for hospice care, that she requested a prescription for barbiturates, that she wanted to know both the therapeutic dose for insomnia and pain relief and the lethal dose, and that he told her the lethal dose. The family called Dr. Quill two days later to report that she had died after having said her good-byes and asking to be alone for an hour. She took the lethal dose. Dr. Quill reported the case to the medical examiner as a death due to acute leukemia.

Your committee's mission — "should you decide to accept it" — is the following: The Senate committee should formulate in concept some legislation to prohibit or to enable or to limit assisted suicides, including those assisted by physicians. The hospital ethics committee should formulate in concept a policy with respect to assisted suicide in the hospital and for staff privileges. The local council of churches committee should draft in concept a statement of advice to Christian communities and their members, including physicians, about "assisted suicide."

Is there a morally important distinction between killing and allowing to die? How can that distinction be formulated and defended? Is Meilaender right to make the distinction and to argue that it can be most clearly seen from a particular religious perspective? Would it have to be argued on other grounds in the Senate committee? Or, to ask Cahill's question, can theology have a role in "public" bioethical discourse? And would the distinction have to be defended in some other way still in the hospital ethics committee? Or, is Hauerwas right to say that medicine needs the church to sustain this distinction, important to medicine since the Hippocratic Oath?

Each committee should have a scribe/reporter who will report to the class when you reconvene what decisions your committee reached and on what grounds it reached them.

Chapter 11

Christian Political Ethics

Introduction

"Put your sword back into its sheath," said Jesus to Peter on the night of his betrayal and arrest (John 18:11a). Is this command meant for all followers of the Prince of Peace?

The Christian community has been asking itself this question for two millennia. Since — as this chapter amply demonstrates — the question has yet to recieve a definitive answer from Christians, we have some evidence that it is a difficult question. In fact, it is three questions: (1) Is the use of force against evil ever justified? (2) If so, in what circumstances and with what justification? (3) If not, what must be said of the *consequences* of such nonresistance?

Our tradition teaches us to frame these questions broadly. They must include organized violence and warfare, but should not be limited to the battlefield. On the contrary, you can put your sword back into its sheath in the intimate realm of marriage and family as well. At the end of the chapter, case study 6 poses a provocative question: Do we expect nonviolence to "work" when a woman encounters a man intent on doing her bodily harm? Is it an appropriate response in any case? Why, or why not?

Some of the differences between Christians on this issue were displayed in 1932 in a noted exchange between two influential ethicists and brothers, H. Richard and Reinhold Niebuhr (readings 72, 73, and 74). The debate echoes the medieval distinction between pacifist monks and Christian soldiers. H. Richard argues for a type of inactivity based "on the well-nigh obsolete faith that there is a God — a real God." In war, he writes, there are times when nothing constructive can be done through human intervention. In "Must We Do Nothing?" Reinhold concedes that

his brother's position is closer to the gospel than his own, but finds it impossible "to construct an adequate social ethic out of a pure love ethic" of the gospel (cf. readings 42 and 55).

In reading 75, Martin Luther King, Jr. writes from an Alabama jail cell to Christian pastors critical of the civil rights movement in the American South. It is a classic statement of the rationale behind Christian nonviolence and reveals the linkage between peace-making and justice-making in biblical thought.

Editor Thomas Kennedy provides us with an analysis of the just war doctrine, the major alternative to pacifism in Christian circles (reading 76). Michael Walzer reviews the history of interpretation of the Old Testament story of the Israelite Exodus from Egypt, and in particular, the golden calf and Moses' decision to kill three thousand men (reading 71).

In Christian communities, the most powerful witnesses for peace have not been documents or manifestos or even movements. On the contrary, the best witnesses have been persons of peace. Therefore, reading 75 is a portrait of one such person: Dorothy Day.

Suggestions for Further Reading

Bainton, Roland. *Christian Attitudes Toward War and Peace*. Nashville: Abingdon Press, 1960.

Booth, Alan. *Not Only Peace*. New York: Seabury Press, 1967.

Cochrane, Arthur. *The Mystery of Peace*. Elgin, Ill.: Brethren Press, 1986.

Musto, Ronald. *The Catholic Peace Tradition*. Maryknoll, N.Y.: Orbis Books, 1986.

Ramsey, Paul. *War and the Christian Conscience*. Durham, N.C.: Duke University Press, 1961.

Shinn, Roger. *Wars and Rumors of Wars*. Nashville: Abingdon Press, 1972.

Yoder, John Howard. *The Original Revolution*. Scottdale: Herald Press, 1971.

70. Psalm 44:1-5, 9-12, 23-26; Matthew 5:38-48

Psalm 44:1-5, 9-12, 23-26

We have heard with our ears, O God,
    our ancestors have told us,
what deeds you performed in their days,
    in the days of old:
you with your own hand drove out the nations,
    but them you planted;
you afflicted the peoples,
    but them you set free;
for not by their own sword did they win the
      land,
    nor did their own arm give them victory;
but your right hand, and your arm,
    and the light of your countenance,
    for you delighted in them.

You are my King and my God;
    you command victories for Jacob.
Through you we push down our foes;
    through your name we tread down our
      assailants. . . .

Yet you have rejected us and abased us,
    and have not gone out with our armies.
You made us turn back from the foe,
    and our enemies have gotten spoil.
You have made us like sheep for slaughter,
    and have scattered us among the nations.
You have sold your people for a trifle,
    demanding no high price for them. . . .

Rouse yourself! Why do you sleep, O Lord?
    Awake, do not cast us off forever!
Why do you hide your face?

Why do you forget our affliction and
    oppression?
For we sink down to the dust;
    our bodies cling to the ground.
Rise up, come to our help.
    Redeem us for the sake of your steadfast love.

Matthew 5:38-48

"You have heard that it was said, 'An eye for an eye
and a tooth for a tooth.' But I say to you, Do not
resist an evildoer. But if anyone strikes you on the
right cheek, turn the other also; and if anyone
wants to sue you and take your coat, give your
cloak as well; and if anyone forces you to go one
mile, go also the second mile. Give to everyone
who begs from you, and do not refuse anyone who
wants to borrow from you.

"You have heard that it was said, 'You shall love
your neighbor and hate your enemy.' But I say to
you, Love your enemies and pray for those who
persecute you, so that you may be children of your
Father in heaven; for he makes his sun rise on the
evil and on the good, and sends rain on the righteous and on the unrighteous. For if you love those
who love you, what reward do you have? Do not
even the tax collectors do the same? And if you
greet only your brothers and sisters, what more
are you doing than others? Do not even the Gentiles do the same? Be perfect, therefore, as your
heavenly Father is perfect."

71. The Murmurings: Slaves in the Wilderness

MICHAEL WALZER

Readers . . . probably know more about the gold-
en calf than they think they do. But l will briefly
retell the story. Moses has been on the mountain-
top now for forty days, and the people are anxious
and frightened by his absence. Or rather, some of
them are anxious and frightened: one has to add
the qualification for the text makes it clear later
on that the people at the foot of the mountain
were not of one mind. "Distrust overwhelmed a
section of this great people," as Judah Halevi
writes in his *Kuzari,* "and they began to divide into
parties and factions. . . ."[1] One of these parties
approaches Aaron, Moses' brother, and demands
that he make them an idol, a visible god. Aaron
weakly complies, collecting their golden jewelry
and shaping the molten metal into a calf — or,
perhaps better, a young bull. The people worship
the idol, feasting and "playing" in front of it. The
Hebrew word for "to play," *litzachek,* has, accord-

1. Judah Halevi, *Kuzari,* ed. Isaak Heinemann, in
Three Jewish Philosophers (Philadelphia: Jewish Publication Society, 1960), p. 48 (1:97).

Michael Walzer (1935–) is professor of social science
at Princeton University. His works include *Exodus
and Revolution; Just and Unjust Wars: A Moral Argument with Historical Illustrations; The Revolution of
the Saints: A Study in the Origins of Radical Politics;*
and *Spheres of Justice: a Defense of Pluralism and
Equality.*

From Michael Walzer, *Exodus and Revolution* (New
York: Basic Books, 1985).

ing to Rashi, sexual connotations: the worship was orgiastic.[2] God, in a rage, tells Moses what is happening down below and proposes to destroy the people whom he has just delivered and make of Moses' line a "great nation." But Moses argues with God and wins his promise of ultimate forgiveness. Then Moses comes down the mountain carrying the tablets, enters the camp, sees the people (or some of them) worshiping the idol, and is as angry as God was when he saw the same thing. Moses smashes the tablets and mobilizes his supporters:

> Who is on the Lord's side? Let him come unto me. And all the sons of Levi gathered themselves together unto him. And he said unto them, Thus saith the Lord God of Israel, Put every man his sword by his side, and go in and out from gate to gate throughout the camp, and slay every man his brother, and every man his companion, and every man his neighbor. And the children of Levi did according to the word of Moses: and there fell of the people that day about three thousand men. (Exod. 32:26-28)

There are many things to talk about here, and a vast interpretive and critical literature to review. I shall focus on only a few central themes. First, the golden calf itself. Some contemporary scholars argue that the idol is of Canaanite origin and that the whole story is a late interpolation, a piece of propaganda aimed at the northern kingdom of Israel, where an altar of golden bulls was set up during the reign of King Jeroboam.[3] But the Egyptians also worshiped a bull god, Apis, and the story loses much of its meaning if it is lifted out of the Exodus context; at least, it loses the meaning it has had within the several traditions to which I am committed: the Jewish account of deliverance and the political theory of liberation. So I shall follow the philosopher Philo who says, in his *Life*

of Moses, that the people "fashioned a golden bull, in imitation of the animal held most sacred in [Egypt]"; and I shall follow the Puritan preacher who wrote in 1643: "out of Egyptian jewels, they made an Egyptian idol . . . they intended to return for Egypt"; and I shall follow Lincoln Steffens, in our own century: "the children of Israel were going back to their old gods, the gods of the Egyptians."[4] This is the great crisis of the Exodus.

Rabbinic interpreters stress the link between the golden calf and the years in Egypt at another point in the story: when Moses argues with God on behalf of the people. The textual account of the argument is brief and not wholly satisfying. Moses seems to score a debater's point: what will the Egyptians say, he asks, if you destroy a people whom they merely enslaved? The rabbis tried to imagine Moses defending the people in some more positive way. But what claim could he make on their behalf? Surely their crime was great. They had only just made their covenant with God and sworn obedience: "All that the Lord hath spoken will we do and obey" (Exod. 24:7). And now they have "corrupted themselves" with idol worship. What could Moses say? The question was of especial importance in the first centuries of the common era, for Christian polemicists used the story of the golden calf to argue that though the Jews had once been elected of God, they had almost immediately rejected the election, themselves had refused to be God's chosen people.[5] Here is one midrashic response:

> Rabbi Huna said: It can be compared to a wise man who opened a perfumery shop for his son in a street frequented by prostitutes. The street did its work, the business also did its share; and the boy's youth contributed its part, with the result that he fell into evil ways. When his father came and caught him with a prostitute, he began to

2. *Pentateuch with Rashi's Commentary,* at Exod. 32:6.

3. Ronald E. Clements, *The Cambridge Bible Commentary: Exodus* (Cambridge: Cambridge University Press, 1972), pp. 205-6. Compare U. Cassuto, *A Commentary on the Book of Exodus,* trans. Israel Abrahams (Jerusalem: The Magnes Press, 1967), pp. 408-9, who defends the integrity of the text.

4. *Life of Moses* in *Philo,* trans. F. H. Colson (London: Heinemann [Loeb Classical Library], 1935), 6:529; John Lightfoot, *An Handful of Gleanings out of the Book of Exodus* (London, 1643), p. 35; Steffens, *Moses in Red: The Revolt of Israel as a Typical Revolution* (Philadelphia: Dorrance, 1926), p. 103.

5. Leivy Smoler and Moshe Aberbach, "The Golden Calf Episode in Postbiblical Literature," *Hebrew Union College Annual* 39 (1968), pp. 91-116.

shout: "I'll kill you." But his friend who was there said: "You ruined this youth's character and yet you shout at him! You ignored all other professions and taught him only to be a perfumer, you foresook all other districts and opened a shop for him just in a street where prostitutes dwell!" This is that Moses said: "Lord of the Universe! You ignored the entire world and caused your children to be enslaved only in Egypt, where all worshipped [idols], from whom your children learned [to do corruptly]. It is for this reason that they have made a calf! . . . bear in mind whence you have brought them forth!"[6]

It is all God's fault — which is not to say that he (directly) caused the people to worship idols but that he should have foreseen the consequences of Egyptian bondage; he should understand — if he can't, who can? — the nature of historical determination. Oppression is an experience with necessary effects, and God, confronting those effects, should not now be impatient (or dispirited). Here again is the argument for gradualism. Physically, the escape from Egypt is sudden, glorious, complete; spiritually and politically, it is very slow, a matter of two steps forward, one step back. I want to stress that this is a lesson drawn from the Exodus experience again and again. A newly freed slave in America in 1862, writing to his fellows, provides a nice example: "There must be no looking back to Egypt. Israel passed forty years in the wilderness. . . . What if we cannot see right off the green fields of Canaan; Moses could not. . . . We must snap the chains of Satan and educate ourselves and our children."[7] The need for education is indeed the argument or one of the arguments of the biblical text, as we will see. The same point is made by a Latin American priest, writing in the 1960's and thinking of the Israelite murmurings: the wilderness period is a time of hardship and struggle, "a gradual pedagogy of successes and failures" in the course of a "long march."[8]

But "gradual pedagogy" is a euphemistic description of the lesson Moses taught the people at the foot of the mountain — a lesson written in blood. The mobilization of the Levites and the killing of the idol worshippers constitute, from the standpoint of politics, an absolutely crucial moment in the transition from house of bondage to promised land. I shall describe it, because this is the way it was described in the early modern period, as the first revolutionary purge. The word "purge" was brought into the vocabulary of revolution by the English Puritans:[9] they took it, I think, from Ezekiel 20, where the prophet recounts the Exodus story and promises the Babylonian exiles a new Exodus and a new wilderness:

> Like as I pleaded with your fathers in the wilderness . . . so will I plead with you, saith the Lord God. And I will cause you to pass under the rod, and I will bring you into the bond of the covenant: And I will purge out from among you . . . them that transgress against me: I will bring them forth out of the country where they sojourn [but] they shall not enter into the land of Israel. (Ezekiel 20:36-38)

The rabbis tended to talk of the "purgings" of the wilderness period as if they were a kind of law enforcement, but even they saw in the killing of the idol worshippers at the foot of Mount Sinai a political act of a special kind. For them, its extraordinary character was revealed by an omission in the text. "And [Moses] said unto them, thus saith the Lord God of Israel, Put every man his sword by his side. . . ." But God's command is not given; God nowhere orders the killing of the idol worshippers. Did Moses invent the command? Was he — once again my reference is deliberately anachronistic — a Machiavellian prince and liberator? This is the Moses that Machiavelli describes in his *Discourses*: "He who reads the Bible with discernment will see that, in order that Moses

6. *Midrash Rabbah: Exodus*, 43:7 (pp. 502-3); I have quoted the translation in Leibowitz, *Studies in Shemot*, pp. 570-71.
7. Quoted in Albert J. Raboteau, *Slave Religion: The "Invisible Institution" in the Antebellum South* (New York: Oxford, 1978), pp. 319-20.
8. Gustavo Gutierrez, *A Theology of Liberation: His-tory, Politics, and Salvation*, trans. Sister Caridad Inda and John Eagleson (Maryknoll, N.Y.: Orbis, 1973), pp. 156, 157.
9. See, for example, Samuel Faircloth, *The Troublers Troubled* (London, 1641), esp. pp. 22ff. and Francis Cheynell, *Sion's Momento and God's Alarum* (London, 1643), p. 19: "these are purging times. . . ."

might set about making laws and institutions, he had to kill a very great number of men. . . ."[10] And isn't it easier to do what in any case must be done if the prince can claim divine authority? Some of the rabbis took the Machiavellian view:

> Moses reasoned with himself and said in his heart: If I say to the Israelites, kill every man his brother, they will answer me: On what grounds do you slay three thousand men in one day? He therefore invoked the honor of the Most High and said: "Thus saith the Lord. . . ."[11]

Other rabbis argued that God had indeed issued the command, but it was too awful to record. Awful, because brothers and neighbors were slain; awful, because the slaughter was summary justice: the idol worshippers were killed without warning and without judgment. Thus the medieval commentator Nachmanides: "This was an emergency measure . . . since there was no proper judicial warning; for who had warned them of the consequences of their crime? . . . It was an order orally imparted to Moses . . . and not recorded."[12] An emergency measure: an act, so to speak, of state.

Whether the command originated with God or with Moses, it was a momentous command. After many of the other murmurings, the people who challenged Moses were killed, but not as the idol worshippers are killed here. In the other cases, the killing is God's own work, further displays of his absolute power and his terrible anger: "and his anger was kindled; and the fire of the Lord burnt among them . . ." (Num. 11:1). Only here are the agents of destruction human: Moses himself and a band of associates who rally round him at the critical moment — and who become later on the Levitical priesthood. Modern biblical scholars typically describe this part of the story as a late addition (assuming now that the whole story isn't a late addition) designed to justify the role of the Levites.[13] But the story as we have it makes a lot of sense, if not always happy sense. The pedagogy of the desert is not only slow, it is uneven; some people or some groups of people learn more quickly than others. Some of them commit themselves more wholeheartedly to the covenant, shape themselves to the new model of the chosen people, internalize the law at a time when for the others the law is still an external command, a threat to their Egyptian habits. Moses' call "Who is on the Lord's side?" draws these new-modeled men to *his* side, divides the community, creates a subgroup — we might call it a vanguard — whose members anticipate, at least in their own minds, the "free people" of the future. In fact, they become the magistrates of the future, the priests and bureaucrats. And meanwhile, in the present, they rule by force; they are the enemies of "graciousness" and gradualism.

Moses' call to the Levites is a political act of the first importance, and as such it has figured significantly in Western political thought. I want now to look at some examples of its citation and use; I don't propose an exercise in the history of ideas, but a further effort to grasp the meaning of the text through a critique of interpretations. Here the text poses a clear question about political violence and the agents of violence, and so it has been read over the years. Or not read: for one can always refuse to engage the question by ignoring Exodus 32. In his *Antiquities of the Jews,* Josephus retells the Exodus story in considerable detail but skips the incident of the golden calf, reporting only that "there fell a contention" among the people waiting for the return of Moses.[14] I suspect that Josephus wanted his readers to think that the Zealots of his own time were the first radical enthusiasts in Jewish history and that they had no biblical warrant. In fact, the Levites or the proto-Levites were the first, and they signaled their enthusiasm with the sword.

When can the sword rightly be used? And by

---

10. Machiavelli, *The Discourses,* trans. Leslie J. Walker, revised Brian Richardson (Harmondsworth: Penguin, 1970), p. 486 (3:30). Machiavelli continues: "The need for this was clearly recognized by Friar Girolamo Savonarola."

11. Quoted from *Tanna debei Eliyahu* in Leibowitz, *Studies in Shemot,* p. 621.

12. Ramban (Nachmanides), *Commentary on the Torah: Exodus,* trans. Charles B. Chavel (New York: Shilo, 1973), pp. 567-69 (on Exod. 32:27); I have quoted the translation in Leibowitz, *Studies in Shemot,* p. 623.

13. Clements, *Commentary on Exodus,* pp. 208-9.

14. Josephus, *Of the Antiquities of the Jews* in *The Famous and Memorable Works of Josephus,* trans. Thomas Lodge (London, 1620), p. 60 (2:5:7).

whom can it rightly be used? These are central issues in political thought, and for many years whenever they were discussed Exodus 32 figured in the discussions. When Saint Augustine, for example, finally brought himself to defend the persecution of heretical Christians by the Roman state, he justified his new position with an interpretation of the killing of the idol worshippers. The sword looked the same, he admitted, in the hands of Roman magistrates and Donatist heretics, but it served different purposes:

> When good and bad do the same actions and suffer the same afflictions, they are to be distinguished not by what they do or suffer, but by the causes of each: for example, Pharaoh oppressed the people of God by hard bondage; Moses afflicted the same people by severe correction when they were guilty of impiety [Augustine refers here to Exod. 32:27]: their actions were alike; but they were not alike in the motive of regard to the people's welfare — the one inflated by the lust of power, the other inflamed by love.[15]

"Inflamed by love" is a nice reading of the biblical text "and Moses' anger waxed hot." But what is most interesting about this passage, and other of Augustine's references to the story of the golden calf, is the entire absence of the Levites. Augustine wanted to defend the activity of magistrates; he didn't mean to invite private men to do the Lord's work, and so he had nothing to say about Moses' call for volunteers. Like Josephus, he fell silent at a crucial point. During the years of the Crusades, however, private men were loudly called and apparently the call was justified by invocations of Exodus 32. For had not Moses said: "Put *every* man his sword by his side . . ."? This at any rate was the passage that Thomas Aquinas had to deal with when he undertook to answer the Christian radicals of his own time. He answered by stressing the first part of Moses' speech: "Thus saith the Lord God of Israel. . . ." The Levites acted at God's direct command (Moses was nothing more than a messenger), and so the slaughter of the idol worshippers was "properly" his act and not their

own.[16] And God doesn't issue such commands, doesn't act in this way, anymore. Years later, Hugo Grotius repeated Aquinas' argument: he attributed the severity of the Levitical punishment to "divine counsel," and he insisted, with a fine show of agnostic trepidation, that such counsel cannot be a guide to contemporary politics: "No conclusive inference can be drawn . . . its depths we cannot sound . . . we are liable to run into error."[17]

For John Calvin and his followers, this sort of thing was mere cowardice. Exodus 32 was obviously a precedent, and it was a precedent that they were more willing than Augustine or Aquinas to set within a history. Since they thought they were reenacting the entire Exodus, they were able to read the entire text. The journey through the wilderness was in part a metaphor for their own politics, and in part a model. They too had escaped from (popish) oppression only to find themselves caught up in a long and difficult struggle with their own people: God's elect against what a Puritan preacher, citing Exodus, called "the opposing rage of a hardened multitude."[18] In Calvin's mind it was more important that the Levites had killed brethren than that they had killed idolaters: "You shall show yourselves rightly zealous of God's service," he told his Genevan audience, "in that you kill your own brethren without sparing, so as in this case the order of nature be put under foot, to show that God is above all."[19] The political point was made even more clearly by John Knox in a brief comment on the same text: "God's word draweth his elect after it, against worldly appearance, against natural affections, and against civil statutes and constitutions."[20] As that last phrase suggests, the distinction between magistrates and private men meant nothing to Knox. God himself gave employment to saints out of office.

But the work was never easy. Even "meek Moses," a Puritan preacher told the House of

---

15. *The Political Writings of St. Augustine,* ed. Henry Paolucci (Chicago: Henry Regnery, 1962), p. 195 (letter 93).

16. *Summa Theologica,* 2a, 2ae, Q.64, arts. 3 and 4.

17. Grotius, *The Law of War and Peace,* trans. Francis W. Kelsey (Indianapolis: Bobbs-Merrill, n.d.), p. 504 (2:22.39).

18. John Owen, *Works,* 8:156.

19. Calvin, *Sermons on the Fifth Book of Moses* (London, 1583), p. 1203.

20. Knox, *Works,* ed. D. Laing (Edinburgh, 1846-48), 3:311-12.

Commons in 1643, sometimes had to be a "man of blood."[21] The Puritans were not surprised to find the English people, freed from "bondage under the regal power," resisting any further deliverance. For hadn't the Israelites provoked and enraged the God who elected them, as Cromwell said, "through unbelief, murmuring, repining, and other temptations and sins?"[22] Why should the English be different? And God had responded harshly, sometimes with his own hand, sometimes through his appointed agents. It wasn't necessary to read the text with Machiavellian "discernment" to see the harshness; one had only to read it — though perhaps it helped to find oneself (or to imagine oneself) marching over the difficult terrain between bondage and promise. There was no way to reach the promised land except to overcome the opponents of the march and then drive on the reluctant marchers. So it seemed, at any rate: revolutions produce hard men and hard women. One can hear the hardness again and again in the 1640s, often with an Exodus "proof." "The divine policy and heavenly remedy to recover a commonwealth and church endangered," Samuel Faircloth told the Commoners as early as 1641, ". . . is that those that have authority under God do totally abolish and extirpate all the cursed things whereby it was disturbed."[23] The "cursed things" are doubled here: Faircloth's text makes it clear that he includes the idols and the idol worshippers. And those that have authority under God are first of all the Commoners, but soon the purged Commoners, and finally the parliament of saints.

Roughly three centuries later, Lincoln Steffens found in the Exodus story a complete vindication of Leninist politics, that is, of dictatorship and terror. He repeats Augustine's distinction between Moses' and Pharaoh's use of the sword in appropriately modern language: "Whenever a nation is setting up a new system of laws and customs, it has a red terror; whenever it is defending an old system, it has a white terror."[24] Indeed, Leninism

seems to be an old story: the slavish people, incapable of liberating themselves, incapable by themselves of imagining what liberation might be like; the revolutionary leader who comes from the outside, whose life experience is entirely different from that of the oppressed men and women he leads; the band of militants, recruited from among the people, but also separated from them to form an organized and disciplined cadre; and finally, the constant purging of the people by the militants. To locate these elements in the Exodus is not to misread the text, to impose Lenin's theory upon it. I would rather say that Lenin's theory of revolution (I shall leave aside his practice) is greatly strengthened by its "fit" with the Exodus text.

Nor are rabbinic readings entirely at variance with the Leninist reading. Martin Buber is faithful to three thousand years of Jewish interpretation when he writes in his *Moses* that the Exodus was "the kind of liberation which cannot be brought about by anyone who grew up as a slave."[25] Moses is separate from the people in his growing up, and later on he separates himself again. Immediately after the incident of the golden calf, "Moses took the tabernacle and pitched it without the camp, afar off from the camp" (Exod. 33:7). The standard rabbinic explanation — no reason is given in the text itself — is that Moses moved the tabernacle because of "the people's sin with the calf."[26] Neither God nor his deputy could dwell any longer in their midst. One might say, more sadly,

---

Croatto defends revolutionary violence not by reference to Moses' purge in Exodus 32 but by reference to God's far greater violence against the Egyptians — the plagues and the overthrow at the sea: "the liberating action is necessarily violent . . . or it is prepared by none too gentle persuasive means . . ." (Croatto, *Exodus*, pp. 29-30). Similarly, Steffens refers to the last of the plagues as "God's red terror" (p. 83). But it is the purges of the Israelites, not the killing of the Egyptian firstborn, that really interest him. The plagues are more central for Croatto, who seems the most radical of the liberation theologians. See Gutierrez's rejection of violence, *Theology of Liberation*, p. 250, n. 124.

21. William Bridge, *A Sermon Preached Before the House of Commons* (London, 1643), p. 18.

22. *Oliver Cromwell's Letters and Speeches*, ed. Thomas Carlyle (London, 1893), pt. 8, p. 34.

23. Faircloth, *The Troublers Troubled*, pp. 24-25.

24. Steffens, *Moses in Red*, p. 108. I should note that

25. Buber, *Moses: The Revelation and the Covenant* (New York: Harper Torchbooks, 1958), p. 35. Cf. Lenin, *What Is to Be Done?* in *Lenin on Politics and Revolution*, ed. James E. Connor (New York: Pegasus, 1968), p. 40.

26. Ramban (Nachmanides), *Commentary on Exodus*, p. 575 (on Exod. 33:7).

that neither God nor Moses could dwell among a people whose brothers, companions, and neighbors they (one or the other of them anyway) had ordered killed. So the idol, even after it has been destroyed, casts its shadow over the camp, and the people are led not, as one would expect a covenanted people to be led, from their midst and by one of their own, but from the outside, by an outsider.

But the story can be told differently. If there is a Leninist reading, there is also, as I have already suggested, a social-democratic reading — which stresses the indirection of the march and the role of Moses as the pedagogue of the people and their defender before God (and which de-emphasizes the story of the golden calf). Moses is capable of anger, but he is also the embodiment of kindness: a "man of blood" but also "meek Moses." "And Moses was very meek, above all the men which were upon the face of the earth" (Num. 12:3). In one of the rebellions against his authority, the tribal leaders Dathan and Abiram accuse Moses of trying to make himself "altogether a prince over us" (Num. 16:13). But Moses doesn't in fact rule like a prince; he is portrayed again and again arguing with the people, much as he argues with God; in neither case does he always get his way. He is rather more successful with God than with the people, and it is worth noting that the forty years in the wilderness are his achievement. When the Israelites reach the Negev, the desert south of Canaan, they send spies into the promised land, and the spies bring back a frightening report: the inhabitants are as large and as powerful as giants, "and we were in our own sight as grasshoppers, and so were we in their sight" (Num. 13:33). And then the people once again murmur against Moses and want to "make a captain and . . . return to Egypt" (Num. 14:4). They were as "sore afraid" in the desert as they were at the sea, Egyptian slaves still, though they had put many miles between themselves and their former masters. God is furious, as usual, and ready once again to destroy the people, but Moses intercedes and he settles for the forty years. The term is chosen for a purpose: so that all those Israelites who were twenty years old or older at the time of the "going out" from Egypt will die natural deaths in the wilderness (three score years, rather than three score and ten, is taken here as the conventional span of life,

though Moses himself is granted a double span). Lincoln Steffens takes this to be the chief political lesson of the Exodus: "The grown-ups must die." And so he interprets the text to mean that "the Lord God killed off the whole of the Egyptian generation of the Jews."[27] But in Numbers 14, as in other accounts of Israelite murmurings, only some of the people are killed. The greater number of the slaves live out their lives and raise a new generation of freeborn children.

Moses teaches this new generation the laws and rituals of Israel's new religion. He accepts Jethro's advice, leaves the daily government to others, and takes for himself another task: "And thou shalt teach them ordinances and laws, and shalt show them the way wherein they must walk and the work that they must do" (Exod. 18:20). This is how Moses is remembered in the Jewish interpretive tradition — not as a prince or a judge or even a "founder" (though in first-century Alexandria Philo describes him as "the best of all lawgivers in all countries, better in fact than any that have ever arisen among either the Greeks or the barbarians," and Machiavelli and Rousseau arrive at a roughly similar estimate).[28] For the Jews generally he is a prophet and teacher, *Moshe rabenu*, Moses our rabbi.[29] He is a successful teacher, which must mean that he finds apt pupils; and he makes his pupils teachers in their turn: "And these words which I command thee this day shall be in thine heart: And thou shalt teach them diligently unto thy children . . ." (Deut. 6:6-7). The result is that the Israelites at the Jordan are very different from the Israelites at the sea: they are ready at last to fight their own battles. In one of his last speeches, Moses is able to say:

> When thou goest out to battle against thine enemies, and seest horses, and chariots, and a people more than thou [the phrases recall Pharaoh's army at the sea], be not afraid of them: for the Lord thy God is with thee, which brought thee up out of the land of Egypt. (Deut. 20:1)

27. Steffens, *Moses in Red*, p. 133.
28. *Life of Moses* in *Philo*, 6:457; Machiavelli, *The Prince*, chap. 6; Rousseau, *Government of Poland*, p. 6.
29. See Daniel Jeremy Silver, *Images of Moses* (New York: Basic Books, 1982), chap. 6.

And he can feel some confidence that the people will not in fact be afraid. They are no longer "as grasshoppers" in their own eyes. They are a "political society," committed to one another and to the covenant that binds them together. This is the achievement of the four decades in the wilderness.

Was it the purging or the teaching that made the decisive difference? The text can be read either way; that is why it has been read so long and so often. Over the years, it has more frequently been used by those who want to imitate the Levites at Mount Sinai and coerce and kill their enemies in the revolutionary camp. Such people have greater need of religious or historical justification. And at some point, I suppose, the counterrevolution must be defeated if Egyptian bondage is ever to be left behind. It is important to stress, however, what the text makes clear, that the counterrevolution has deep roots; it cannot be defeated by force alone. Indeed, God and the Levites could easily kill all the people who yearn for the fleshpots (or the idols) of Egypt. But then the Levites would arrive in the promised land virtually alone, and that would not be a fulfillment of the promise. The promise is for the people, and the people can only move in gradual stages from bondage to freedom.

In the text as we have it, the portrayal of the people is consistently harsh. But they are not consistently described as slavish and servile; they are also described as "stiff-necked" (by God himself at the time of the golden calf episode) and stubborn. So they are not wholly dispirited. And to be stubborn, even in the face of God, is not wholly unattractive. Sometimes the people seem less like a slavish rabble than like ordinary men and women recalcitrant in the face of God's demand that they be something more than ordinary. For it is not God's purpose merely to bring them to the promised land. The promise itself is more complicated than milk and honey . . . and the resistance of the people has a certain saving quality, best illustrated by a midrashic story. When the Israelites were finally allowed to leave the holy mountain, it is said, they rose early, folded their tents, packed their belongings, and marched as fast as they could — not for one day, as they were commanded, but for three days. They didn't want any more laws.[30] It is a nice story; we recognize

ourselves in it, even though we have never lived, or think we have never lived, in Egypt. I would add just one word: when they marched away from the mountain, they marched toward the promised land, not "back for Egypt." They had their own vision of a better life, and sometimes they had the courage of their vision. That is why they were able, as Rabbi Eliezer said, to march into the wilderness in the first place; and this is why they were able to commit themselves to the Covenant at Sinai. The Hegelian and the Leninist views of the Exodus have no place for the Covenant, but it is central to the Jewish tradition and to much later revolutionary thought. And if the Israelites were too stiff-necked to live up to all of its requirements, they were also too stiff-necked ever to forget it entirely.

30. Ginzberg, *Legends of the Jews*, 3:242.

72. The Grace of Doing Nothing

H. RICHARD NIEBUHR

It may be that the greatest moral problems of the individual or of a society arise when there is nothing to be done. When we have begun a certain line of action or engaged in a conflict we cannot pause too long to decide which of various possible courses we ought to choose for the sake of the worthier result. Time rushes on and we must choose as best we can, entrusting the issue to the future. It is when we stand aside from the conflict, before we know what our relations to it really are, when we seem to be condemned to doing nothing, that our moral problems become greatest. How shall we do nothing?

The issue is brought home to us by the fighting in the East. We are chafing at the bit, we are eager to do something constructive; but there is nothing constructive, it seems, that we can do. We pass resolutions, aware that we are doing nothing; we summon up righteous indignation and still do nothing; we write letters to congressmen and secretaries, asking others to act while we do nothing. Yet is it really true that we are doing nothing? There are, after all, various ways of being inactive and some kinds of inactivity, if not all, may be highly productive. It is not really possible to stand aside, to sit by the fire in this world of moving times; even Peter was doing something in the

H. Richard Niebuhr (1894–1962) was professor of Christian ethics at Yale University Divinity School. Among his works are *Christ and Culture; The Meaning of Revelation; The Kingdom of God in America;* and *The Responsible Self.*

From *The Christian Century,* 23 March 1932, pp. 378-380.

courtyard of the high-priest's house — if it was only something he was doing to himself. When we do nothing we are also affecting the course of history. The problem we face is often that of choice between various kinds of inactivity rather than of choice between action and inaction.

Meaningful Inactivity

Our inactivity may be that of the pessimist who watches a world go to pieces. It is a meaningful inactivity for himself and for the world. His world, at all events, will go to pieces the more rapidly because of that inactivity. Or it may be the inactivity of the conservative believer in things as they are. He does nothing in the international crisis because he believes that the way of Japan is the way of all nations, that self-interest is the first and only law of life, and that out of the clash of national, as out of that of individual, self-interests the greater good will result. His inactivity is one of watchful waiting for the opportunity when, in precisely similar manner, though with less loss of life and fortune if possible, he may rush to the protection of his own interests or promote them by taking advantage of the situation created by the strife of his competitors. This way of doing nothing is not unproductive. It encourages the self-asserters and it fills them with fear of the moment when the new competition will begin. It may be that they have been driven into their present conflict by the knowledge or suspicion that the watchful waiter is looking for his opportunity, perhaps unconsciously, and that they must be prepared for him.

The inactivity of frustration and moral indignation is of another order. It is the way today of those who have renounced all violent methods of settling conflicts and have no other means at hand by which to deal with the situation. It is an angry inactivity like that of a man who is watching a neighborhood fight and is waiting for police to arrive — for police who never come. He has renounced for himself the method of forcible interference which would only increase the flow of blood and the hatred, but he knows of nothing else that he can do. He is forced to remain content on the sidelines, but with mounting anger he regards the bully who is beating the neighbor and his wrath issues in words of exasperation and condemnation. Having tied his own hands he fights with his tongue and believes that he is not fighting because he inflicts only mental wounds. The bully is for him an outlaw, a person not to be trusted, unfair, selfish, one who cannot be redeemed save by restraint. The righteous indignation mounts and mounts and must issue at last — as the police fail to arrive — either in his own forcible entry into the conflict despite his scruples, or in apoplexy.

Puzzled Pacifists

The diatribes against Japan which are appearing in the secular and religious press today have a distressing similarity to the righteously indignant utterances which preceded our conflicts with Spain and with Germany. China is Cuba and Belgium over again, it is the Negro race beaten by Simon Legree; and the pacifists who have no other program than that of abstention from the unrighteousness of war are likely to be placed in the same quandary in which their fellows were placed in 1860, 1898, and 1915, and — unless human attitudes have been regenerated in the interim — they are likely to share the same fate, which was not usually incarceration. Here is a situation which they did not foresee when they made their vow; may it not be necessary to have one more war to end all war? Righteous indignation, not allowed to issue in action, is a dangerous thing — as dangerous as any great emotion nurtured and repressed at the same time. It is the source of sudden explosions or the ground of long, bitter, and ugly hatreds.

If this way of doing nothing must be rejected the communists' way offers more hope. Theirs is inactivity of those who see that there is indeed nothing constructive to be done in the present situation, but that, rightly understood, this situation is after all preliminary to a radical change which will eliminate the conditions of which the conflict is a product. It is the inactivity of a cynicism which one expects no good from the present, evil world of capitalism, but also the inactivity of a boundless faith in the future. The communists know that war and revolution are closely akin, that war breeds discontent and misery and that out of

misery and discontent new worlds may be born. This is an opportunity, then, not for direct entrance into the conflict, nor for the watchful waiting of those who seek their self-interest, but for the slow laborious process of building up within the fighting groups those cells of communism which will be ready to inherit the new world and be able to build a classless international commonwealth on the ruins of capitalism and nationalism. Here is inactivity with a long vision, a steadfast hope and a realistic program of non-interfering action.

But there is yet another way of doing nothing. It appears to be highly impracticable because it rests on the well-nigh obsolete faith that there is a God — a real God. Those who follow this way share with communism the belief that the fact that men can do nothing constructive is no indication of the fact that nothing constructive is being done. Like the communists they are assured that the actual processes of history will inevitably and really bring a different kind of world with lasting peace. They do not rely on human aspirations after ideals to accomplish this end, but on forces which often seem very impersonal — as impersonal as those which eliminated slavery in spite of abolitionists. The forces may be as impersonal and as actual as machine production, rapid transportation, the physical mixture of races, etc., but as parts of the real world they are as much a part of the total divine process as are human thoughts and prayers.

Prelude to Judgment

From this point of view, naively affirming the meaningfulness of reality, the history of the world is the judgment of the world and also its redemption, and such a conflict as the present one is — again as in communism — only the prelude both to greater judgment and to a new era. The world being what it is, these results are brought forth when the seeds of national or individual self-interest are planted; the actual structure of things is such that our wishes for a different result do not in the least affect the outcome. As a man soweth so shall he reap. This God of things as they are is inevitable and quite merciless. His mercy lies beyond, not this side of, judgment. This inactive

Christianity shares with communism also the belief in the inevitably good outcome of the mundane process and the realistic insight that that good cannot be achieved by the slow accretion of better habits alone but more in consequence of a revolutionary change which will involve considerable destruction. While it does nothing it knows that something is being done, something which is divine both in its threat and in its promise.

This inactivity is like that of the early Christians whose millenarian mythology it replaces with the contemporary mythology of social forces. (Mythology is after all not fiction but a deep philosophy.) Like early Christianity and like communism today radical Christianity knows that nothing constructive can be done by interference but that something very constructive can be done in preparation for the future. It also can build cells of those within each nation who, divorcing themselves from the program of nationalism and of capitalism, unite in a higher loyalty which transcends national and class lines of division and prepare for the future. There is no such Christian international today because radical Christianity has not arrived as yet at a program and a philosophy of history, but such little cells are forming. The First Christian international of Rome has had its day; the Second Christian international of Stockholm is likely to go the way of the Second Socialist international. There is need of and opportunity for a Third Christian international.

Difference from Communism

While the similarities of a radically Christian program with the communist program are striking, there are also great dissimilarities. There is a new element in the inactivity of radical Christianity which is lacking in communism. The Christian reflects upon the fact that his inability to do anything constructive in the crisis is the inability of one whose own faults are so apparent and so similar to those of the offender that any action on his part is not only likely to be misinterpreted but is also likely — in the nature of the case — to be really less than disinterested. He is like a father, who, feeling a mounting righteous indignation against a misbehaving child, remembers that that misbehavior is his fault as much as the child's and

that indignation is the least helpful, the most dangerous of attitudes to take; it will solve nothing though it may repress.

So the American Christian realizes that Japan is following the example of his own country and that it has little real ground for believing America to be a disinterested nation. He may see that his country, for which he bears his own responsibility as a citizen, is really not disinterested and that its righteous indignation is not wholly righteous. An inactivity then is demanded which will be profoundly active in rigid self-analysis. Such analysis is likely to reveal that there is an approach to the situation, indirect but far more effective than direct interference, for it is able to create the conditions under which a real reconstruction of habits is possible. It is the opposite approach from that of the irate father who believes that every false reaction on the part of his child may be cured by a verbal, physical, or economic spanking.

In Place of Repentance

This way of doing nothing the old Christians called repentance, but the word has become so reminiscent of emotional debauches in the feeling of guilt that it may be better to abandon it for a while. What is suggested is that the only effective approach to the problem of China and Japan lies in the sphere of an American self-analysis which is likely to result in some surprising discoveries as to the amount of renunciation of self-interest necessary on the part of this country and of individual Christians before anything effective can be done in the East.

The inactivity of radical Christianity is not the inactivity of those who call evil good; it is the inaction of those who do not judge their neighbors because they cannot fool themselves into a sense of superior righteousness. It is not the inactivity of a resigned patience, but of a patience that is full of hope, and is based on faith. It is not the inactivity of the noncombatant, for it knows that there are no noncombatants, that everyone is involved, that China is being crucified (though the term is very inaccurate) by our sins and those of the whole world. It is not the inactivity of the merciless, for works of mercy must be performed though they are only palliatives to ease present pain while the process of healing depends on deeper, more actual and urgent forces.

But if there is no God, or if God is up in heaven and not in time itself, it is a very foolish inactivity.

73. Must We Do Nothing?

REINHOLD NIEBUHR

A Critique of H. Richard Niebuhr's article, "The Grace of Doing Nothing," in last week's *Christian Century**

There is much in my brother's article on "The Grace of Doing Nothing" with which I agree. Except for the invitation of the editors of *The Christian Century* I would have preferred to defer voicing any disagreement with some of his final conclusions to some future occasion; for a casual article on a specific problem created by the contemporary international situation hardly does justice to his general position. I believe the problem upon which he is working — the problem of dissociating a rigorous gospel ethic of disinterestedness and love from the sentimental dilutions of that ethic which are current in liberal Christianity — is a tremendously important one. I owe so much to the penetrating thought which he has been giving this subject that I may be able to do some justice to his general position even though I do not share his conviction that a pure love ethic can ever be made the basis of a civilization.

*H. Richard and Reinhold Niebuhr are brothers, both professors of Christian ethics, the former in Yale divinity school, the latter in Union theological seminary.

Reinhold Niebuhr (1892–1971) was professor of theology at Union Theological Seminary and, arguably, the most important figure in theological ethics in this century. Among his many works are *Moral Man and Immoral Society; Children of Light, Children of Darkness;* and *The Nature and Destiny of Man.*

From *The Christian Century*, 30 March 1932, pp. 415-417.

Dealing with a Sinful Nation

He could not have done better than to choose the Sino-Japanese conflict, and the reactions of the world to it, in order to prove the difficulty, if not the futility, of dealing redemptively with a sinful nation or individual if we cannot exorcise the same sin from our own hearts. It is true that pacifists are in danger of stirring up hatred against Japan in their effort to stem the tide of Japanese imperialism. It is true that the very impotence of an individual, who deals with a social situation which goes beyond his own powers, tempts him to hide his sense of futility behind a display of violent emotion. It is true that we have helped to create the Japan which expresses itself in terms of militaristic imperialism. The insult we offered her in our immigration laws was a sin of spiritual aggression. The white world has not only taught her the ways of imperialism but has preempted enough of the yellow man's side of the world to justify Japan's imperialism as a vent for pent-up national energies.

It is also true that American concern over Japanese aggression is not wholly disinterested. It is national interest which prompts us to desire stronger action against Japan than France and England are willing to take. It is true, in other words, that every social sin is, at least partially, the fruit and consequence of the sins of those who judge and condemn it, and that the effort to eliminate it involves the critics and judges in new social sin, the assertion of self-interest and the expression of moral conceit and hypocrisy. If anyone would raise the objection to such an analysis that it finds every social action falling short only because it measures the action against an impossible ideal of disinterestedness, my brother could answer that while the ideal may seem to be impossible the actual social situation proves it to be necessary. It is literally true that every recalcitrant nation, like every antisocial individual, is created by the society which condemns it, and that redemptive efforts which betray strong ulterior motives are always bound to be less than fully redemptive.

Inaction That Is Action

My brother draws the conclusion from this logic that it is better not to act at all than to act from motives which are less than pure, and with the use of methods which are less than ethical (coercion). He believes in taking literally the words of Jesus, "Let him who is without sin cast the first stone." He believes, of course, that this kind of inaction would not really be inaction; it would be, rather, the action of repentance. It would give every one involved in social sin the chance to recognize how much he is involved in it and how necessary it is to restrain his own greed, pride, hatred, and lust for power before the social sin is eliminated.

This is an important emphasis particularly for modern Christianity with its lack of appreciation of the tragic character of life and with its easy assumption that the world will be saved by a little more adequate educational technique. Hypocrisy is an inevitable by-product of moral aspiration, and it is the business of true religion to destroy man's moral conceit, a task which modern religion has not been performing in any large degree. Its sentimentalities have tended to increase rather than to diminish moral conceit. A truly religious man ought to distinguish himself from the moral man by recognizing the fact that he is not moral, that he remains a sinner to the end. The sense of sin is more central to religion than is any other attitude.

Shall We Never Act?

All this does not prove, however, that we ought to apply the words of Jesus, "Let him who is without sin cast the first stone," literally. If we do we will never be able to act. There will never be a wholly disinterested nation. Pure disinterestedness is an ideal which even individuals cannot fully achieve, and human groups are bound always to express themselves in lower ethical terms than individuals. It follows that no nation can ever be good enough to save another nation purely by the power of love. The relation of nations and of economic groups can never be brought into terms of pure love. Justice is probably the highest ideal toward which human groups can aspire. And justice, with its goal of adjustment of right to right, inevitably involves the assertion of right against right and interest against interest until some kind of harmony is achieved. If a measure of humility and of love does not enter this conflict of interest it will of course degenerate into violence. A rational society will be able to develop a measure of the kind of imagination which knows how to appreciate the virtues of an opponent's position and the weakness in one's own. But the ethical and spiritual note of love and repentance can do no more than qualify the social struggle in history. It will never abolish it.

An Illusory Hope

The hope of attaining an ethical goal for society by purely ethical means, that is, without coercion, and without the assertion of the interests of the under-privileged against the interests of the privileged, is an illusion which was spread chiefly among the comfortable classes of the past century. My brother does not make the mistake of assuming that this is possible in social terms. He is acutely aware of the fact that it is not possible to get a sufficient degree of pure disinterestedness and love among privi-leged classes and powerful nations to resolve the conflicts of history that way. He understands the stubborn inertia which the ethical ideal meets in history. At this point his realistic interpretation of the facts of history comes in full conflict with his insistence upon a pure gospel ethic, upon a reli-giously inspired moral perfectionism, and he re-solves the conflict by leaving the field of social theory entirely and resorting to eschatology. The Christian will try to achieve humility and disinter-estedness not because enough Christians will be able to do so to change the course of history, but because this kind of spiritual attitude is a prayer to God for the coming of his Kingdom.

I will not quarrel with this apocalyptic note, as such, though I suspect many *Christian Century* readers will. I believe that a proper eschatology in necessary to a vigorous ethic, and that the simple idea of progress is inimical to the highest ethic. The compound of pessimism and optimism which a vigorous ethical attitude requires can be expressed only in terms of religious eschatology. What makes my brother's particular kind of es-chatology impossible for me is that he identifies everything that is occurring in history (the drift

toward disaster, another world war, and possibly a world revolution) with the counsels of God, and then suddenly, by a leap of faith, comes to the conclusion that the same God, who uses brutalities and forces, against which man must maintain con-scientious scruples, will finally establish an ideal society in which pure love will reign.

A Society of Pure Love Is Impossible

I have more than one difficulty with such a faith. I do not see how a revolution in which the disin-herited express their anger and resentment, and assert their interests, can be an instrument of God, and yet at the same time an instrument which religious scruples forbid a man to use. I should think it would be better to come to ethical terms with the forces of nature in history, and try to use ethically directed coercion in order that violence may be avoided. The hope that a kingdom of pure love will emerge out of the catastrophes of history is even less plausible than the communist faith that an equalitarian society will inevitably emerge from them. There is some warrant in history for the latter assumption, but very little for the former.

I find it impossible to envisage a society of pure love as long as man remains man. His natural limitations of reason and imagination will prevent him even should he achieve a purely disinterested motive, from fully envisaging the needs of his fel-low-men or from determining his actions upon the basis of their interests. Inevitably these limita-tions of individuals will achieve cumulative effect in the life and actions of national, racial, and economic groups. It is possible to envisage a more ethical society than we now have. It is possible to believe that such a society will be achieved partly by evolutionary process and partly by catastrophe in which an old order, which offers a too stubborn resistance to new forces, is finally destroyed.

It is plausible also to interpret both the evolu-tionary and the catastrophic elements in history in religious terms and to see the counsels of God in them. But it is hardly plausible to expect divine intervention to introduce something into history which is irrelevant to anything we find in history now. We may envisage a society in which human cooperation is possible with a minimum amount of coercion, but we cannot imagine one in which there is no coercion at all — unless, of course, human beings become something quite different from what they now are. We may hope for a society in which self-interest is qualified by rigorous self-analysis and a stronger social impulse, but we cannot imagine a society totally without the assertion of self-interest and therefore without the conflict of opposing interests.

The Cost of Human Progress

I realize quite well that my brother's position both in its ethical perfectionism and in its apocalyptic note is closer to the gospel than mine. In confessing that, I am forced to admit that I am unable to construct an adequate social ethic out of a pure love ethic. I cannot abandon the pure love ideal because anything which falls short of it is less than the ideal. But I cannot use it fully if I want to assume a responsible attitude toward the problems of society. Religious perfectionism drives either to asceticism or apocalypticism. In the one case the problem of society is given up entirely; in the other individual perfection is regarded as the force which will release the redemptive powers of God for society. I think the second alternative is better than the first, and that both have elements which must be retained for any adequate social ethic, lest it become lost in the relativities of expediency. But as long as the world of man remains a place where nature and God, the real and the ideal, meet, human progress will depend upon the judicious use of the forces of nature in the service of the ideal.

In practical, specific and contemporary terms this means that we must try to dissuade Japan from her military venture, but must use coercion to frustrate her designs if necessary, must reduce coercion to a minimum and prevent it from issuing in violence, must engage in constant self-analysis in order to reduce the moral conceit of Japan's critics and judges to a minimum, and must try in every social situation to maximize the ethical forces and yet not sacrifice the possibility of achieving an ethical goal because we are afraid to use any but purely ethical means.

Life as Tragedy

To say all this is really to confess that the history of mankind is a perennial tragedy; for the highest ideals which the individual may project are ideals which he can never realize in social and collective terms. If there is a law in our members which wars against the law that is in our minds as individuals, this is even more true when we think of society. Individuals set the goal for society but society itself must achieve the goal and society is and will always remain subhuman. The goal which a sensitive individual sets for society must therefore always be something which is a little outside and beyond history. Love may qualify the social struggle of history but it will never abolish it, and those who make the attempt to bring society under the dominion of perfect love will die on the Cross. And those who behold the Cross are quite right in seeing it as a revelation of the divine, of what man ought to be and cannot be, at least not so long as he is enmeshed in the processes of history.

Perhaps that is why it is inevitable that religious imagination should set goals beyond history. "Man's reach is beyond his grasp, or what's a heaven for." My brother does not like these goals above and beyond history. He wants religion and social idealism to deal with history. In that case he must not state his goal in absolute terms. There can be nothing absolute in history, no matter how frequently God may intervene in it. Man cannot live without a sense of the absolute, but neither can he achieve the absolute. He may resolve the tragic character of that fact by religious faith, by the experience of grace in which the unattainable is experienced in anticipatory terms, but he can never resolve in purely ethical terms the conflict between what is and what ought to be.

74. The Only Way into the Kingdom of God

H. RICHARD NIEBUHR

Editor, *The Christian Century*:

Sir: Since you have given me leave to fire one more shot in the fraternal war between my brother and me over the question of pacifism, I shall attempt to place it as well as I can, not for the purpose of demolishing my opponent's position — which our thirty years' war has shown me to be impossible — but for the sake of pointing as accurately as I can to the exact locus of the issue between us. It does not lie in the question of activity or inactivity, to which my too journalistic approach to the problem directed attention; we are speaking after all of two kinds of activity. The fundamental question seems to me to be whether "the history of mankind is a perennial tragedy" which can derive meaning only from a goal which lies beyond history, as my brother maintains, or whether the "eschatological" faith, to which I seek to adhere, is justifiable. In that faith tragedy is only the prelude to fulfilment, and a prelude which is necessary because of human nature; the Kingdom of God comes inevitably, though whether we shall see it or not, depends on our recognition of its presence and our acceptance of the only kind of life which will enable us to enter it, the life of repentance and forgiveness.

For my brother God is outside the historical processes, so much so that he charges me with faith in a miracle-working deity which interferes occasionally, sometimes brutally, sometimes redemptively, in this history. But God, I believe, is always in history; he is the structure in things, the source of all meaning, the "I am that I am," that which is that it is. He is the rock against which we beat in vain, that which bruises and overwhelms us when we seek to impose our wishes, contrary to his, upon him. That structure of the universe, that creative will, can no more be said to interfere brutally in history than the violated laws of my organism can be said to interfere brutally with my life if they make me pay the cost of my violation. That structure of the universe, that will of God, does bring war and depression upon us when we bring it upon ourselves, for we live in the kind of world which visits our iniquities upon us and our children, no matter how much we pray and desire that it be otherwise.

Self-interest acts destructively in this world; it calls forth counter-assertion; nationalism breeds nationalism, class assertion summons up counter assertion on the part of exploited classes. The result is war, economic, military, verbal; and it is judgment. But this same structure in things which is our enemy is our redeemer; "it means intensely and means good" — not the good which we desire, but the good which we would desire if we were good and really wise. History is not a perennial tragedy but a road to fulfilment and that fulfilment requires the tragic outcome of every self-assertion, for it is a fulfilment which can only be designated as "love." It has created fellowship in atoms and organisms, at bitter cost to electrons and cells; and it is creating something better than human selfhood but at bitter cost to that selfhood. This is not a faith in progress, for evil grows as well as good and every self-assertion must be eliminated somewhere and somehow — by innocence suffering for guilt, it seems.

If, however, history is no more than tragedy, if there is no fulfilment in it, then my brother is right. Then we must rest content with the clash of self-interested individuals, personal or social. But in that case I see no reason why we should qualify the clash of competition with a homeopathic dose of Christian "love."

The only harmony which can possibly result from the clash of interests is the harmony imposed by the rule of the strong or a parallelogram of social forces, whether we think of the interclass structure or the international world. To import any pacifism into this struggle is only to weaken the weaker self-asserters (India, China, or the pro-

---

From *The Christian Century*, 6 April 1932, p. 447.

letariat) or to provide the strong with a facade of "service" behind which they can operate with a salved conscience. (Pacificism, on the other hand, as a method of self-assertion, is not pacifism at all but only a different kind of war.)

The method which my brother recommends, that of qualifying the social struggle by means of some Christian love, seems to me to be only the old method of making Christian love an ambulance driver in the wars of interested and clashing parties. If it is more than that it is weakening of the forces whose success we think necessary for a juster social order. For me the question is one of "either-or ;" either the Christian method, which is not the method of love but of repentance and forgiveness, or the method of self-assertion; either nationalism or Christianity, either capitalism-communism or Christianity. The attempt to qualify the one method by the other is hopeless compromise.

I think that to apply the terms "Christian perfectionism" or "Christian ideal" to my approach is rather misleading. I rather think that Dewey is quite right in his war on ideals; they always seem irrelevant to our situation and betray us into a dualistic morality. The society of love is an impossible human ideal, as the fellowship of the organism is an impossible ideal for the cell. It is not an ideal toward which we can strive, but an "emergent," a potentiality in our situation which remains unrealized so long as we try to impose our pattern, our wishes upon the divine creative process.

Man's task is not that of building Utopias but that of eliminating weeds and tilling the soil so that the Kingdom of God can grow. His method is not one of striving for perfection or of acting perfectly, but of clearing the road by repentance and forgiveness. That this approach is valid for societies as well as for individuals and that the opposite approach will always involve us in the same one ceaseless cycle of assertion and counter-assertion, is what I am concerned to emphasize.

The Divinity School,   H. Richard Niebuhr
Yale University

75. Letter from Birmingham Jail

MARTIN LUTHER KING, JR.

April 16, 1963

My Dear Fellow Clergymen:*

While confined here in the Birmingham city jail, I came across your recent statement calling my present activities "unwise and untimely." Seldom do I pause to answer criticism of my work and ideas. If I sought to answer all the criticisms that cross my desk, my secretaries would have little time for anything other than such correspondence in the course of the day, and I would have no time

*Author's Note: This response to a published statement by eight fellow clergymen from Alabama (Bishop C. C. J. Carpenter, Bishop Joseph A. Durick, Rabbi Hilton L. Grafman, Bishop Paul Hardin, Bishop Holan B. Harmon, the Reverend George M. Murray, the Reverend Edward V. Ramage, and the Reverend Earl Stallings) was composed under somewhat constricting circumstances. Begun on the margins of the newspaper in which the statement appeared while I was in jail, the letter was continued on scraps of writing paper supplied by a friendly Negro trusty, and concluded on a pad my attorneys were eventually permitted to leave me. Although the text remains in substance unaltered, I have indulged in the author's prerogative of polishing it for publication.

Martin Luther King, Jr. (1929–1968) was an ordained Baptist minister and a civil rights activist. His work includes *Stride Toward Freedom*, *Strength to Love*, *Why We Can't Wait*, *Where Do We Go from Here: Chaos or Community?*, and *Trumpet of Conscience*.

From Martin Luther King, Jr., *Why We Can't Wait* (New York: Harper & Row, 1964).

for constructive work. But since I feel that you are men of genuine good will and that your criticisms are sincerely set forth, I want to try to answer your statement in what I hope will be patient and reasonable terms.

I think I should indicate why I am here in Birmingham, since you have been influenced by the view which argues against "outsiders coming in." I have the honor of serving as president of the Southern Christian Leadership Conference, an organization operating in every southern state, with headquarters in Atlanta, Georgia. We have some eighty-five affiliated organizations across the South, and one of them is the Alabama Christian Movement for Human Rights. Frequently we share staff, educational, and financial resources with our affiliates. Several months ago the affiliate here in Birmingham asked us to be on call to engage in a nonviolent direct-action program if such were deemed necessary. We readily consented, and when the hour came we lived up to our promise. So I, along with several members of my staff, am here because I was invited here. I am here because I have organizational ties here.

But more basically, I am in Birmingham because injustice is here. Just as the prophets of the eighth century B.C. left their villages and carried their "thus saith the Lord" far beyond the boundaries of their home towns, and just as the apostle Paul left his village of Tarsus and carried the gospel of Jesus Christ to the far corners of the Greco-Roman world, so am I compelled to carry the gospel of freedom beyond my own home town. Like Paul, I must constantly respond to the Macedonian call for aid.

Moreover, I am cognizant of the interrelatedness of all communities and states. I cannot sit idly by in Atlanta and not be concerned about what happens in Birmingham. Injustice anywhere is a threat to justice everywhere. We are caught in an inescapable network of mutuality, tied in a single garment of destiny. Whatever affects one directly, affects all indirectly. Never again can we afford to live with the narrow, provincial "outside agitator" idea. Anyone who lives inside the United States can never be considered an outsider anywhere within its bounds.

You deplore the demonstrations taking place in Birmingham. But your statement, I am sorry to say, fails to express a similar concern for the con-

ditions that brought about the demonstrations. I am sure that none of you would want to rest content with the superficial kind of social analysis that deals merely with effects and does not grapple with underlying causes. It is unfortunate that demonstrations are taking place in Birmingham, but it is even more unfortunate that the city's white power structure left the Negro community with no alternative.

In any nonviolent campaign there are four basic steps: collection of the facts to determine whether injustices exist, negotiation, self-purification, and direct action. We have gone through all these steps in Birmingham. There can be no gainsaying the fact that racial injustice engulfs this community. Birmingham is probably the most thoroughly segregated city in the United States. Its ugly record of brutality is widely known. Negroes have experienced grossly unjust treatment in the courts. There have been more unsolved bombings of Negro homes and churches in Birmingham than in any other city in the nation. These are the hard, brutal facts of the case. On the basis of these conditions, Negro leaders sought to negotiate with the city fathers. But the latter consistently refused to engage in good-faith negotiation.

Then, last September, came the opportunity to talk with leaders of Birmingham's economic community. In the course of the negotiations, certain promises were made by the merchants — for example, to remove the stores' humiliating racial signs. On the basis of these promises, the Reverend Fred Shuttlesworth and the leaders of the Alabama Christian Movement for Human Rights agreed to a moratorium on all demonstrations. As the weeks and months went by, we realized that we were the victims of a broken promise. A few signs, briefly removed, returned; the others remained.

As in so many past experiences, our hopes had been blasted, and the shadow of deep disappointment settled upon us. We had no alternative except to prepare for direct action, whereby we would present our very bodies as a means of laying our case before the conscience of the local and the national community. Mindful of the difficulties involved, we decided to undertake a process of self-purification. We began a series of workshops on nonviolence, and we repeatedly asked ourselves: "Are you able to accept blows without retaliating?" "Are you able to endure the ordeal of jail?" We decided to schedule our direct-action program for the Easter season, realizing that except for Christmas, this is the main shopping period of the year. Knowing that a strong economic-withdrawal program would be the by-product of direct action, we felt that this would be the best time to bring pressure to bear on the merchants for the needed change.

Then it occurred to us that Birmingham's mayoralty election was coming up in March, and we speedily decided to postpone action until after election day. When we discovered that the Commissioner of Public Safety, Eugene "Bull" Connor, had piled up enough votes to be in the run-off, we decided again to postpone action until the day after the run-off so that the demonstrations could not be used to cloud the issues. Like many others, we waited to see Mr. Connor defeated, and to this end we endured postponement after postponement. Having aided in this community need, we felt that our direct-action program could be delayed no longer.

You may well ask: "Why direct action? Why sit-ins, marches, and so forth? Isn't negotiation a better path?" You are quite right in calling for negotiation. Indeed, this is the very purpose of direct action. Nonviolent direct action seeks to create such a crisis and foster such a tension that a community which has constantly refused to negotiate is forced to confront the issue. It seeks so to dramatize the issue that it can no longer be ignored. My citing the creation of tension as part of the work of the nonviolent-resister may sound rather shocking. But I must confess that I am not afraid of the word "tension." I have earnestly opposed violent tension, but there is a type of constructive, nonviolent tension which is necessary for growth. Just as Socrates felt that it was necessary to create a tension in the mind so that individuals could rise from the bondage of myths and half-truths to the unfettered realm of creative analysis and objective appraisal, so must we see the need for nonviolent gadflies to create the kind of tension in society that will help men rise from the dark depths of prejudice and racism to the majestic heights of understanding and brotherhood.

The purpose of our direct-action program is to create a situation so crisis-packed that it will inevitably open the door to negotiation. I therefore concur with you in your call for negotiation. Too long has our beloved Southland been bogged down in a tragic effort to live in monologue rather than dialogue.

One of the basic points in your statement is that the action that I and my associates have taken in Birmingham is untimely. Some have asked: "Why didn't you give the new city administration time to act?" The only answer that I can give to this query is that the new Birmingham administration must be prodded about as much as the outgoing one, before it will act. We are sadly mistaken if we feel that the election of Albert Boutwell as mayor will bring the millennium to Birmingham. While Mr. Boutwell is a much more gentle person than Mr. Connor, they are both segregationists, dedicated to maintenance of the status quo. I have hope that Mr. Boutwell will be reasonable enough to see the futility of massive resistance to desegregation. But he will not see this without pressure from devotees of civil rights. My friends, I must say to you that we have not made a single gain in civil rights without determined legal and nonviolent pressure. Lamentably, it is an historical fact that privileged groups seldom give up their privileges voluntarily. Individuals may see the moral light and voluntarily give up their unjust posture; but, as Reinhold Niebuhr has reminded us, groups tend to be more immoral than individuals.

We know through painful experience that freedom is never voluntarily given by the oppressor; it must be demanded by the oppressed. Frankly, I have yet to engage in a direct-action campaign that was "well timed" in the view of those who have not suffered unduly from the disease of segregation. For years now I have heard the word. "Wait!" It rings in the ear of every Negro with piercing familiarity. This "Wait" has almost always meant "Never." We must come to see, with one of our distinguished jurists, that "justice too long delayed is justice denied."

We have waited for more than 340 years for our constitutional and God-given rights. The nations of Asia and Africa are moving with jetlike speed toward gaining political independence, but we still creep at horse-and-buggy pace toward gaining a cup of coffee at a lunch counter. Perhaps it is easy for those who have never felt the stinging darts of segregation to say, "Wait." But when you have seen vicious mobs lynch your mothers and fathers at will and drown your sisters and brothers at whim; when you have seen hate-filled policemen curse, kick, and even kill your black brothers and sisters; when you see the vast majority of your twenty million Negro brothers smothering in an airtight cage of poverty in the midst of an affluent society; when you suddenly find your tongue twisted and your speech stammering as you seek to explain to your six-year-old daughter why she can't go to the public amusement park that has just been advertised on television, and see tears welling up in her eyes when she is told that Funtown is closed to colored children, and see ominous clouds of inferiority beginning to form in her little mental sky, and see her beginning to distort her personality by developing an unconscious bitterness toward white people; when you have to concoct an answer for a five-year-old son who is asking: "Daddy, why do white people treat colored people so mean?"; when you take a cross-country drive and find it necessary to sleep night after night in the uncomfortable corners of your automobile because no motel will accept you; when you are humiliated day in and day out by nagging signs reading "white" and "colored"; when your first name becomes "nigger," your middle name becomes "boy" (however old you are), and your last name becomes "John," and your wife and mother are never given the respected title "Mrs."; when you are harried by day and haunted by night by the fact that you are a Negro, living constantly at tiptoe stance, never quite knowing what to expect next, and are plagued with inner fears and outer resentments; when you are forever fighting a degenerating sense of "nobodiness" — then you will understand why we find it difficult to wait. There comes a time when the cup of endurance runs over, and men are no longer willing to be plunged into the abyss of despair. I hope, sirs, you can understand our legitimate and unavoidable impatience.

You express a great deal of anxiety over our willingness to break laws. This is certainly a legitimate concern. Since we so diligently urge people to obey the Supreme Court's decision of 1954 outlawing segregation in the public schools, at first glance it may seem rather paradoxical for us consciously to break laws. One may well ask: "How can you advocate breaking some laws and obeying others?" The answer lies in the fact that there are two types of laws: just and unjust. I would be the first to advocate obeying just laws. One has not only a legal but a moral responsibility to obey just laws. Conversely, one has a moral responsibility to disobey unjust laws. I would agree with St. Augustine that "an unjust law is no law at all."

Now, what is the difference between the two? How does one determine whether a law is just or unjust? A just law is a man-made code that squares with the moral law or the law of God. An unjust law is a code that is out of harmony with the moral law. To put it in the terms of St. Thomas Aquinas: An unjust law is a human law that is not rooted in eternal law and natural law. Any law that uplifts human personality is just. Any law that degrades human personality is unjust. All segregation statutes are unjust because segregation distorts the soul and damages the personality. It gives the segregator a false sense of superiority and the segregated a false sense of inferiority. Segregation, to use the terminology of the Jewish philosopher Martin Buber, substitutes an "I-it" relationship for an "I-thou" relationship and ends up relegating persons to the status of things. Hence segregation is not only politically, economically, and sociologically unsound, it is morally wrong and sinful. Paul Tillich has said that sin is separation. Is not segregation an existential expression of man's tragic separation, his awful estrangement, his terrible sinfulness? Thus it is that I can urge men to obey the 1954 decision of the Supreme Court, for it is morally right; and I can urge them to disobey segregation ordinances, for they are morally wrong.

Let us consider a more concrete example of just and unjust laws. An unjust law is a code that a numerical or power majority group compels a minority group to obey but does not make binding on itself. This is *difference* made legal. By the same token, a just law is a code that a majority compels a minority to follow and that it is willing to follow itself. This is *sameness* made legal.

Let me give another explanation. A law is unjust if it is inflicted on a minority that, as a result of being denied the right to vote, had no part in enacting or devising the law. Who can say that the legislature of Alabama which set up that state's segregation laws was democratically elected? Throughout Alabama all sorts of devious methods are used to prevent Negroes from becoming registered voters, and there are some counties in which, even though Negroes constitute a majority of the population, not a single Negro is registered. Can any law enacted under such circumstances be considered democratically structured?

Sometimes a law is just on its face and unjust in its application. For instance, I have been arrested on a charge of parading without a permit. Now, there is nothing wrong in having an ordinance which requires a permit for a parade. But such an ordinance becomes unjust when it is used to maintain segregation and to deny citizens the First-Amendment privilege of peaceful assembly and protest.

I hope you are able to see the distinction I am trying to point out. In no sense do I advocate evading or defying the law, as would the rabid segregationist. That would lead to anarchy. One who breaks an unjust law must do so openly, lovingly, and with a willingness to accept the penalty. I submit that an individual who breaks a law that conscience tells him is unjust, and who willingly accepts the penalty of imprisonment in order to arouse the conscience of the community over its injustice, is in reality expressing the highest respect for law.

Of course, there is nothing new about this kind of civil disobedience. It was evidenced sublimely in the refusal of Shadrach, Meshach, and Abednego to obey the laws of Nebuchadnezzar, on the ground that a higher moral law was at stake. It was practiced superbly by the early Christians, who were willing to face hungry lions and the excruciating pain of chopping blocks rather than submit to certain unjust laws of the Roman Empire. To a degree, academic freedom is a reality today because Socrates practiced civil disobedience. In our own nation, the Boston Tea Party represented a massive act of civil disobedience.

We should never forget that everything Adolf Hitler did in Germany was "legal" and everything the Hungarian freedom fighters did in Hungary was "illegal." It was "illegal" to aid and comfort a Jew in Hitler's Germany. Even so, I am sure that, had I lived in Germany at the time, I would have aided and comforted my Jewish brothers. If today I lived in a Communist country where certain principles dear to the Christian faith are suppressed, I would openly advocate disobeying that country's antireligious laws.

I must make two honest confessions to you, my Christian and Jewish brothers. First, I must confess that over the past few years I have been gravely disappointed with the white moderate. I have almost reached the regrettable conclusion that the Negro's great stumbling block in his stride toward freedom is not the White Citizens' Councilor or the Ku Klux Klanner, but the white moderate, who is more devoted to "order" than to justice; who prefers a negative peace which is the absence of tension to a positive peace which is the presence of justice; who constantly says: "I agree with you in the goal you seek, but I cannot agree with your methods of direct action"; who paternalistically believes he can set the timetable for another man's freedom; who lives by a mythical concept of time and who constantly advises the Negro to wait for a "more convenient season." Shallow understanding from people of good will is more frustrating than absolute misunderstanding from people of ill will. Lukewarm acceptance is much more bewildering than outright rejection.

I had hoped that the white moderate would understand that law and order exist for the purpose of establishing justice and that when they fail in this purpose they become the dangerously structured dams that block the flow of social progress. I had hoped that the white moderate would understand that the present tension in the South is a necessary phase of the transition from an obnoxious negative peace, in which the Negro passively accepted his unjust plight, to a substantive and positive peace, in which all men will respect the dignity and worth of human personality. Actually, we who engage in nonviolent direct action are not the creators of tension. We merely bring to the surface the hidden tension that is already alive. We bring it out in the open, where it can be seen and dealt with. Like a boil that can never be cured so long as it is covered up but must be opened with all its ugliness to the natural medicines of air and light, injustice must be exposed, with all the tension its exposure creates, to the light of human conscience and the air of national opinion before it can be cured.

In your statement you assert that our actions, even though peaceful, must be condemned because they precipitate violence. But is this a logical assertion? Isn't this like condemning a robbed man because his possession of money precipitated the evil act of robbery? Isn't this like condemning Socrates because his unswerving commitment to truth and his philosophical inquiries precipitated the act by the misguided populace in which they made him drink hemlock? Isn't this like condemning Jesus because his unique God-consciousness and never-ceasing devotion to God's will precipitated the evil act of crucifixion? We must come to see that, as the federal courts have consistently affirmed, it is wrong to urge an individual to cease his efforts to gain his basic constitutional rights because the quest may precipitate violence. Society must protect the robbed and punish the robber.

I had also hoped that the white moderate would reject the myth concerning time in relation to the struggle for freedom. I have just received a letter from a white brother in Texas. He writes: "All Christians know that the colored people will receive equal rights eventually, but it is possible that you are in too great a religious hurry. It has taken Christianity almost two thousand years to accomplish what it has. The teachings of Christ take time to come to earth." Such an attitude stems from a tragic misconception of time, from the strangely irrational notion that there is something in the very flow of time that will inevitably cure all ills. Actually, time itself is neutral; it can be used either destructively or constructively. More and more I feel that the people of ill will have used time much more effectively than have the people of good will. We will have to repent in this generation not merely for the hateful words and actions of the bad people but for the appalling silence of the good people. Human progress never rolls in on wheels of inevitability; it comes through the tireless efforts of men willing to be co-workers with God, and without this hard work, time itself becomes an ally of the forces of social stagnation. We must use time creatively, in the knowledge that the time is always ripe to do right. Now is the time to make real the promise of democracy and transform our pending national elegy into a creative psalm of brotherhood. Now is the time to lift our national policy from the quicksand of racial injustice to the solid rock of human dignity.

You speak of our activity in Birmingham as extreme. At first I was rather disappointed that fellow clergymen would see my nonviolent efforts as those of an extremist. I began thinking about the fact that I stand in the middle of two opposing forces in the Negro community. One is a force of complacency, made up in part of Negroes who, as a result of long years of oppression, are so drained of self-respect and a sense of "somebodiness" that they have adjusted to segregation; and in part of a few middle-class Negroes who, because of a degree of academic and economic security and because in some ways they profit by segregation, have become insensitive to the problems of the masses. The other force is one of bitterness and hatred, and it comes perilously close to advocating violence. It is expressed in the various black nationalist groups that are springing up across the nation, the largest and best-known being Elijah Muhammad's Muslim movement. Nourished by the Negro's frustration over the continued existence of racial discrimination, this movement is made up of people who have lost faith in America, who have absolutely repudiated Christianity, and who have concluded that the white man is an incorrigible "devil."

I have tried to stand between these two forces, saying that we need emulate neither the "do-nothingism" of the complacent nor the hatred and despair of the black nationalist. For there is the more excellent way of love and nonviolent protest. I am grateful to God that, through the influence of the Negro church, the way of nonviolence became an integral part of our struggle.

If this philosophy had not emerged, by now many streets of the South would, I am convinced, be flowing with blood. And I am further convinced that if our white brothers dismiss as "rabble-rousers" and "outside agitators" those of us who employ nonviolent direct action, and if they refuse to support our nonviolent efforts, millions of Negroes will, out of frustration and despair, seek solace and security in black-nationalist ideologies — a development that would inevitably lead to a frightening racial nightmare.

Oppressed people cannot remain oppressed forever. The yearning for freedom eventually manifests itself, and that is what has happened to the American Negro. Something within has reminded him of his birthright of freedom, and something without has reminded him that it can be gained. Consciously or unconsciously, he has been caught up by the *Zeitgeist,* and with his black brothers of Africa and his brown and yellow brothers of Asia, South America, and the Caribbean, the United States Negro is moving with a sense of great urgency toward the promised land of racial justice. If one recognizes this vital urge that has engulfed the Negro community, one should readily understand why public demonstrations are taking place. The Negro has many pent-up resentments and latent frustrations, and he must release them. So let him march; let him make prayer pilgrimages to the city hall; let him go on freedom rides — and try to understand why he must do so. If his repressed emotions are not released in nonviolent ways, they will seek expression through violence; this is not a threat but a fact of history. So I have not said to my people: "Get rid of your discontent." Rather, I have tried to say that this normal and healthy discontent can be channeled into the creative outlet of nonviolent direct action. And now this approach is being termed extremist.

But though I was initially disappointed at being categorized as an extremist, as I continued to think about the matter I gradually gained a measure of satisfaction from the label. Was not Jesus an extremist for love: "Love your enemies, bless them that curse you, do good to them that hate you, and pray for them which despitefully use you, and persecute you." Was not Amos an extremist for justice: "Let justice roll down like waters and righteousness like an ever-flowing stream." Was not Paul an extremist for the Christian gospel: "I bear in my body the marks of the Lord Jesus." Was not Martin Luther an extremist: "Here I stand; I cannot do otherwise, so help me God." And John Bunyan: "I will stay in jail to the end of my days before I make a butchery of my conscience." And Abraham Lincoln: "This nation cannot survive half slave and half free." And Thomas Jefferson: "We hold these truths to be self-evident, that all men are created equal . . ." So the question is not whether we will be extremists, but what kind of extremists we will be. Will we be extremists for hate or for love? Will we be extremists for the preservation of injustice or for the extension of justice? In that dramatic scene on Calvary's hill three men were crucified. We must never forget that all three were crucified for the same crime — the crime of extremism. Two were extremists for immorality, and thus fell below their environment. The other, Jesus Christ, was an extremist for love, truth and goodness, and thereby rose above his

environment. Perhaps the South, the nation, and the world are in dire need of creative extremists.

I had hoped that the white moderate would see this need. Perhaps I was too optimistic; perhaps I expected too much. I suppose I should have realized that few members of the oppressor race can understand the deep groans and passionate yearnings of the oppressed race, and still fewer have the vision to see that injustice must be rooted out by strong, persistent and determined action. I am thankful, however, that some of our white brothers in the South have grasped the meaning of this social revolution and committed themselves to it. They are still all too few in quantity, but they are big in quality. Some — such as Ralph McGill, Lillian Smith, Harry Golden, James McBride Dabbs, Ann Braden, and Sarah Patton Boyle — have written about our struggle in eloquent and prophetic terms. Others have marched with us down nameless streets of the South. They have languished in filthy, roach-infested jails, suffering the abuse and brutality of policemen who view them as "dirty nigger-lovers." Unlike so many of their moderate brothers and sisters, they have recognized the urgency of the moment and sensed the need for powerful "action" antidotes to combat the disease of segregation.

Let me take note of my other major disappointment. I have been so greatly disappointed with the white church and its leadership. Of course, there are some notable exceptions. I am not unmindful of the fact that each of you has taken some significant stands on this issue. I commend you, Reverend Stallings, for your Christian stand on this past Sunday, in welcoming Negroes to your worship service on a nonsegregated basis. I commend the Catholic leaders of this state for integrating Spring Hill College several years ago.

But despite these notable exceptions, I must honestly reiterate that I have been disappointed with the church. I do not say this as one of those negative critics who can always find something wrong with the church. I say this as a minister of the gospel, who loves the church; who was nurtured in its bosom; who has been sustained by its spiritual blessings and who will remain true to it as long as the cord of life shall lengthen.

When I was suddenly catapulted into the leadership of the bus protest in Montgomery, Alabama, a few years ago, I felt we would be supported by the white church. I felt that the white ministers, priests, and rabbis of the South would be among our strongest allies. Instead, some have been outright opponents, refusing to understand the freedom movement and misrepresenting its leaders; all too many others have been more cautious than courageous and have remained silent behind the anesthetizing security of stained-glass windows.

In spite of my shattered dreams, I came to Birmingham with the hope that the white religious leadership of this community would see the justice of our cause and, with deep moral concern, would serve as the channel through which our just grievances could reach the power structure. I had hoped that each of you would understand. But again I have been disappointed.

I have heard numerous southern religious leaders admonish their worshipers to comply with a desegregation decision because it is the law, but I have longed to hear white ministers declare: "Follow this decree because integration is morally right and because the Negro is your brother." In the midst of blatant injustices inflicted upon the Negro, I have watched white churchmen stand on the sideline and mouth pious irrelevancies and sanctimonious trivialities. In the midst of a mighty struggle to rid our nation of racial and economic injustice, I have heard many ministers say: "Those are social issues, with which the gospel has no real concern." And I have watched many churches commit themselves to a completely other-worldly religion which makes a strange, unbiblical distinction between body and soul, between the sacred and the secular.

I have traveled the length and breadth of Alabama, Mississippi and all the other southern states. On sweltering summer days and crisp autumn mornings I have looked at the South's beautiful churches with their lofty spires pointing heavenward. I have beheld the impressive outlines of her massive religious-education buildings. Over and over I have found myself asking: "What kind of people worship here? Who is their God? Where were their voices when the lips of Governor Barnett dripped with words of interposition and nullification? Where were they when Governor Wallace gave a clarion call for defiance and hatred? Where were their voices of support when bruised

and weary Negro men and women decided to rise from the dark dungeons of complacency to the bright hills of creative protest?"

Yes, these questions are still in my mind. In deep disappointment I have wept over the laxity of the church. But be assured that my tears have been tears of love. There can be no deep disappointment where there is not deep love. Yes, I love the church. How could I do otherwise? I am in the rather unique position of being the son, the grandson, and the great-grandson of preachers. Yes, I see the church as the body of Christ. But, oh! How we have blemished and scarred that body through social neglect and through fear of being nonconformists.

There was a time when the church was very powerful — in the time when the early Christians rejoiced at being deemed worthy to suffer for what they believed. In those days the church was not merely a thermometer that recorded the ideas and principles of popular opinion; it was a thermostat that transformed the mores of society. Whenever the early Christians entered a town, the people in power became disturbed and immediately sought to convict the Christians for being "disturbers of the peace" and "outside agitators." But the Christians pressed on, in the conviction that they were "a colony of heaven," called to obey God rather than man. Small in number, they were big in commitment. They were too God-intoxicated to be "astronomically intimidated." By their effort and example they brought an end to such ancient evils as infanticide and gladiatorial contests.

Things are different now. So often the contemporary church is a weak, ineffectual voice with an uncertain sound. So often it is an archdefender of the status quo. Far from being disturbed by the presence of the church, the power structure of the average community is consoled by the church's silent — and often even vocal — sanction of things as they are.

But the judgment of God is upon the church as never before. If today's church does not recapture the sacrificial spirit of the early church, it will lose its authenticity, forfeit the loyalty of millions, and be dismissed as an irrelevant social club with no meaning for the twentieth century. Every day I meet young people whose disappointment with the church has turned into outright disgust.

Perhaps I have once again been too optimistic.

Is organized religion too inextricably bound to the status quo to save our nation and the world? Perhaps I must turn my faith to the inner spiritual church, the church within the church, as the true *ekklesia* and the hope of the world. But again I am thankful to God that some noble souls from the ranks of organized religion have broken loose from the paralyzing chains of conformity and joined us as active partners in the struggle for freedom. They have left their secure congregations and walked the streets of Albany, Georgia, with us. They have gone down the highways of the South on tortuous rides for freedom. Yes, they have gone to jail with us. Some have been dismissed from their churches, have lost the support of their bishops and fellow ministers. But they have acted in the faith that, right defeated is stronger than evil triumphant. Their witness has been the spiritual salt that has preserved the true meaning of the gospel in these troubled times. They have carved a tunnel of hope through the dark mountain of disappointment.

I hope the church as a whole will meet the challenge of this decisive hour. But even if the church does not come to the aid of justice, I have no despair about the future. I have no fear about the outcome of our struggle in Birmingham, even if our motives are at present misunderstood. We will reach the goal of freedom in Birmingham and all over the nation, because the goal of America is freedom. Abused and scorned though we may be, our destiny is tied up with America's destiny. Before the pilgrims landed at Plymouth, we were here. Before the pen of Jefferson etched the majestic words of the Declaration of Independence across the pages of history, we were here. For more than two centuries our forebears labored in this country without wages; they made cotton king; they built the homes of their masters while suffering gross injustice and shameful humiliation — and yet out of a bottomless vitality they continued to thrive and develop. If the inexpressible cruelties of slavery could not stop us, the opposition we now face will surely fail. We will win our freedom because the sacred heritage of our nation and the eternal will of God are embodied in our echoing demands.

Before closing I feel impelled to mention one other point in your statement that has troubled me profoundly. You warmly commended the Birmingham police force for keeping "order" and "preventing violence." I doubt that you would have so warmly commended the police force if you had seen its dogs sinking their teeth into unarmed, nonviolent Negroes. I doubt that you would so quickly commend the policemen if you were to observe their ugly and inhumane treatment of Negroes here in the city jail; if you were to watch them push and curse old Negro women and young Negro girls; if you were to see them slap and kick old Negro men and young boys; if you were to observe them, as they did on two occasions, refuse to give us food because we wanted to sing our grace together. I cannot join you in your praise of the Birmingham police department.

It is true that the police have exercised a degree of discipline in handling the demonstrators. In this sense they have conducted themselves rather "nonviolently" in public. But for what purpose? To preserve the evil system of segregation. Over the past few years I have consistently preached that nonviolence demands that the means we use must be as pure as the ends we seek. I have tried to make clear that it is wrong to use immoral means to attain moral ends. But now I must affirm that it is just as wrong, or perhaps even more so, to use moral means to preserve immoral ends. Perhaps Mr. Connor and his policemen have been rather nonviolent in public, as was Chief Pritchett in Albany, Georgia, but they have used the moral means of nonviolence to maintain the immoral end of racial injustice. As T. S. Eliot has said: "The last temptation is the greatest treason: To do the right deed for the wrong reason."

I wish you had commended the Negro sit-inners and demonstrators of Birmingham for their sublime courage, their willingness to suffer and their amazing discipline in the midst of great provocation. One day the South will recognize its real heroes. They will be the James Merediths, with the noble sense of purpose that enables them to face jeering and hostile mobs, and with the agonizing loneliness that characterizes the life of the pioneer. They will be old, oppressed, battered Negro women, symbolized in a seventy-two-year-old woman in Montgomery, Alabama, who rose up with a sense of dignity and with her people decided not to ride segregated buses, and who responded with ungrammatical profundity to one who inquired about her weariness: "My feets is tired, but my soul is at rest." They will be the young high school and college students, the young ministers of the gospel and a host of their elders, courageously and nonviolently sitting in at lunch counters and willingly going to jail for conscience's sake. One day the South will know that when the disinherited children of God sat down at lunch counters, they were in reality standing up for what is best in the American dream and for the most sacred values in our Judaeo-Christian heritage, thereby bringing our nation back to those great wells of democracy which were dug deep by the founding fathers in their formulation of the Constitution and the Declaration of Independence.

Never before have I written so long a letter. I'm afraid it is much too long to take your precious time. I can assure you that it would have been much shorter if I had been writing from a comfortable desk, but what else can one do when he is alone in a narrow jail cell, other than write long letters, think long thoughts, and pray long prayers?

If I have said anything in this letter that overstates the truth and indicates an unreasonable impatience, I beg you to forgive me. If I have said anything that understates the truth and indicates my having a patience that allows me to settle for anything less than brotherhood, I beg God to forgive me.

I hope this letter finds you strong in the faith. I also hope that circumstances will soon make it possible for me to meet each of you, not as an integrationist or a civil rights leader but as a fellow clergyman and a Christian brother. Let us all hope that the dark clouds of racial prejudice will soon pass away and the deep fog of misunderstanding will be lifted from our fear-drenched communities, and in some not too distant tomorrow the radiant stars of love and brotherhood will shine over our great nation with all their scintillating beauty.

Yours for the cause of Peace
and Brotherhood,
Martin Luther King, Jr.

76. Can War Be Just?

THOMAS KENNEDY

Every new threat of war brings both supporters and detractors of the "just war theory" out of the woodwork. "It is not relevant to the conduct of war in the contemporary world," some charge. Others counter that it is precisely the criteria established by the just war theory that makes moral criticism, as well as moral support, of a war possible. Resolution of this debate is possible only if we first understand what a just war theory is, and that is the point of this essay.

The first thing to get clear about is that there is no such beast as the "just war theory." Instead, there is a *family* of theories, united by the belief that the resort to war is sometimes morally permissible, indeed, may sometimes be morally required, but differing slightly over the details on how and when the resort to war is permitted. Most Christian ethicists identify St. Augustine (354-430) as the founding parent of this family, the family developing in St. Thomas Aquinas and coming to maturity during the late medieval period. In the twentieth century perhaps the most articulate proponent of Christian just war theory has been the late Princeton University ethicist Paul Ramsey.

This family of just war theories attempts to steer a course between two alternative positions — pacifism and, what for lack of a better name, we shall call realism. The Christian pacifist argues that the way of Christ is the way of nonviolent, suffering love, that Christ condemned the use of violence. Wars are evil and wrong, the Christian pacifist argues; they cannot be morally justified, for they are incompatible with God's way in the

Thomas Kennedy (1955–) is professor of philosophy at Valparaiso University and co-editor of this anthology.

world. Render to Caesar that which is Caesar's, but render to God that which is God's — obedience and imitation of the suffering love of Jesus.

The Christian realist, by contrast, insists that we keep ever before us the sinful nature of humanity and human institutions. Nations and states will not be bound by principles of love and justice, although they may profess allegiance to these principles in the attempt to disguise their ruthless pursuit of self-interest. Better to let undisguised self-interest rule the day. You cannot ask a nation, and you cannot expect a nation, to pursue international policy on the basis of any principle other than rational self-interest. If nations intentionally pursue their own self-interest things will be better for everyone, for the the power of one self-interested state will be cancelled out by that of another. The result will be a balance of power in which nations can pursue genuine human goods. Nations, thus, should consider national interests paramount in times of international strife. To apply moral standards to the question of war is to make a category mistake, for national interests should reign in all decisions. Furthermore, to introduce moral talk into a context of war would only encourage a hypocrisy which is ultimately detrimental to morality. Let war be war, in all its hellishness. That is what is best for humanity.

Just war theories refuse to resign themselves to humanity's inhumanity to humanity. Human beings and human institutions *are* sinful: for this reason we expect wars and rumors of war until Christ returns in glory. But God's judgment still stands over sinful nations, and persons and nations ought to live in a manner consistent with the reign of God. Although we ought never identify the policies of a sinful nation as the policies of God, surely we can say that some national policies are more consistent with the justice of God than others. Nations are accountable to standards of justice, and not mere self-interest.

Furthermore, the Christian just war theorist argues, the fallen individual is also an exalted individual, never fully abandoned by God, able to know and to approximate the good. Although wars will ever exist, God has not left us helpless in their midst. Human beings can know if and when wars are morally justified, and sinful though we may be, it is within our power to act upon principles of justice. We can use this moral knowledge available to all to criticize and protest the many immoral wars that nations may wage, as well as to support the few moral wars we may confront. The Christian realist, the just war theorist contends, is too pessimistic about our ability to know and do the good. The Christian realist, because of his pessimism, gives a blank check to sinful nations and permits the reign of sinful egoism, and the result is greater and greater harm to humanity and to God's creation.

Christian just war theories, thus, are rightly seen to have more in common with Christian pacifism than with Christian realism. Like pacifism, just war theories maintain that the actions of individuals and nations are the appropriate objects of moral evaluation; moral standards apply to egoistic individuals and to self-interested states. And, like the Christian pacifist, the Christian just war theorist acknowledges the moral presumption against the use of violence. Violence *is* ordinarily wrong, and good moral reasons must be given for its use. But, unlike the pacifist, the Christian just war theorist believes there can be good moral reasons for the resort to violence. Just war theories are attempts to state those reasons.

The family of just war theories, then, maintains that sometimes the use of violence by nations is morally permissible, perhaps even required. Furthermore, these theories maintain that there are moral rules or criteria which must be satisfied before a war can be considered morally justified. The exact content of these criteria varies somewhat from theory to theory within the family, but there exists a good deal of agreement. It is this core of more or less agreed upon criteria that is applied and is the subject of debate in situations when war threatens.

This background is sufficient for our purposes. Rather than merely assuming that the moral criteria of just war handed down by the family are binding, I shall next present a fairly generic set of criteria and examine the moral logic of that criteria. Just war theories are not the exclusive property of Christian thinkers, but in this context my concern will be with a Christian just war theory.

The Moral Basis of Christian Just War Theory

Most basic in the moral teaching of Jesus is the advocacy of neighbor-love, of commitment to the weak, the oppressed, the preyed-upon innocent. We are to love our neighbors as ourselves, especially those neighbors against whom the principalities and powers of this world seem allied. This neighbor-love may take many forms, but fundamental to it is a disposition to stand on the side of and/or to take the place of the weak, to work so that justice is received by those least able to demand it. Fleshed out in a political context, this is the basis for Christian just war theories; sometimes love of neighbor may require a willingness to harm an aggressor, the stronger, in order to protect the weaker innocent neighbor. Sometimes justice may demand that harm be done to another in order to secure for a neighbor that which God desires for all humanity.

The basic claim is that under certain rare but not unthinkable conditions the use of deadly force can be morally justified, can be the right thing to do. The best way to think about this is in terms of a conflict of moral duties. Ordinarily one ought not to lie, but we all recognize that under certain circumstances the duty not to lie can conflict with some other duty, say the duty to protect a life, and in those cases lying may be justified, may be the morally appropriate thing to do. Although we know they lied, we do not blame the people of the Netherlands who lied to Nazi soldiers to save the lives of German Jews they were hiding. Not only do we think they bear no guilt, we praise them for the goodness of their action. When the duty to save a life conflicts with the duty not to lie, the duty to save a life must take priority. This is how neighbor-love is enfleshed in such a situation.

Likewise, ordinarily we ought not to harm other persons; we cannot doubt that Jesus heartily disapproved of the resort to violence. To read Jesus as readily sanctioning violence is not to read the Jesus of the Christian Scriptures, is to ignore the one who spoke "Do not resist an evildoer . . . if anyone strikes you on the right cheek, turn the other also" (Matt. 5:38-39). But sometimes our duty not to harm others can conflict with and can be overridden by our duty to protect the innocent. If the only way I can prevent a mugger from doing grave damage to you is by clubbing him, I should club the mugger. As a human being created by God you have a right to a life free from the attacks of others, and the mugger deserves punishment for the harm he would do to you.

Our reluctance to use violence must be great, and we must acknowledge a too-ready willingness to resort to violence to resolve our conflicts. But to be unwilling to intervene, to be unwilling even to do harm to defend and protect a weak and innocent victim, is not to love the weak and needy neighbor, is to neglect the demands of justice.

We think, then, that in ordinary affairs when a duty to protect the innocent conflicts with the duty not to harm others we may do the right thing by taking action that may harm someone. But we are not and cannot be happy leaving it just like that. Let us say that the twelve-year-old neighborhood bully picks a fight with my ten-year-old daughter. She jumps Katie, and starts kicking her in the shins. Surely it couldn't be right for me, with my hands of steel, to immediately leap in and start pummeling the twelve-year-old bully. Nor would I be justified in burning down her house to ensure that she never picks on my daughter again.

Neighbor-love and justice protect not only the weak and innocent neighbor but the guilty neighbor as well. I may do the right thing by responding violently to the person who is mugging you, but just any response is not morally permissible. The presumption against the use of violence is still relevant even when that presumption against violence is overridden by the duty to protect the innocent. It shows its relevance in the constraints it places upon the violence I do even in a morally permissible act. The presumption against violence requires, for example, that I must attempt all reasonable nonviolent means of resolving the problem at hand, I must use no more force than is appropriate to the harm being done, etc. I may not shoot someone stealing your favorite tulips; I may not kill your mugger if a shout or a quick kick in the butt will scare him away.

Just war theories are attempts to apply these insights about our moral responsibilities into a broader social and political context. They find an analogy to the domestic situation in the relations between nations. Sometimes a weak and innocent nation is attacked by a strong aggressor. In the domestic context neighbor-love and justice require the use of violence to protect the innocent, so shouldn't the same hold true in the international context? If violence may be justified domestically by the requirement of neighbor-love, won't this also be the case in international affairs?

Just war theories, thus, are better termed *justified* war theories. They do not specify the conditions for a *just* war, a war in which we as impartial spectators are able to determine that either one or neither of the warring nations is acting according to the standards of perfect justice. They are more modest than that. Rather, they establish criteria for a *justified* resort to force by nations. These theories are attempts to spell out the conditions under which a state may be justified in warring despite the presumptive wrongness of warring, and are attempts to identify the limits and extent of justifiable violence. A justified war theory develops criteria which must be satisfied before a war is morally justified and criteria which define a justified waging of war.

Justified war theories recognize the fact that resort to violence is ordinarily wrong, that the burden of proof is upon those who would resort to violence. The presumption against violence derived from Jesus' disapproval of violence weighs heavily upon us, insisting that neighbor-love will not permit just any and every violent action. Although in cases of conflict between the duty to protect the weak and the duty to do no harm justice and neighbor-love may require us to do violence, the duty not to harm restrains the violence we do in protection of the weak neighbor. This presumption against violence is fleshed out in the identification of the moral constraints of going to war, the *jus ad bellum* criteria, and the moral constraints upon the waging of war in *jus in bello* criteria.

Criteria for Justified War

Jus ad bellum criteria consist of a set of moral guidelines and considerations which are relevant to the decision of whether or not a nation may justifiably engage in a warring activity. These criteria say nothing about *how* a war is to be morally fought, only whether war can, under the circumstances, be morally justified.

The most basic moral rights a people can possess, rights without which any talk of international justice is meaningless, are the rights of political sovereignty and territorial integrity. As Michael Walzer has noted. "The survival and freedom of political communities . . . are the highest values of international society."[1] A people need a place in which to exercise and develop their way of life, and freedom is required for this exercise. An attack upon the place in which one lives or an attack upon the free exercise of a people's way of life is an attack upon the life of a people, and is analogous to an attack upon an individual. Thus, such an attack is presumptively wrong. Nations are justified in defending themselves against any who would threaten these fundamental national goods. Other nations may be justified in assisting a weaker nation whose territorial integrity or political sovereignty has been threatened. The protection or restoration of those goods which are vital to the life and well-being of a people is the first of the *jus ad bellum* criteria, *just cause*.

Corresponding to the requirement of just cause is *right intention*. Intention is often confused with motivation, but the two are distinct. Intention refers to one's aim, *what* one's actions may reasonably be believed to bring about, not *why* one acts. Justified war theory is meant for the evaluation of actions, not the agents who perform the action. So right intention does not address the question of what sort of people a nation ought to be, what should motivate a nation's engagements; it merely addresses the question of what aims are morally permissible.

Right intention is most plausibly interpreted as the requirement that the war actually attempt to accomplish only those ends which are morally justified, those ends identified in just cause. Where just cause refers to what must have taken place in the world before a war can be justified, right intention requires that war must be directed at only those actions which provide one with just cause. Hence, if a nation intends war actions in order to extend boundaries, or improve access to natural resources, that war cannot be justified. Right intention prohibits the execution of any war or threats of war that are incompatible with the protection of the innocent, a restoration of rights, a more stable and just order.

1. Michael Walzer, *Just and Unjust Wars* (New York: Basic Books, 1977), p. 254.

The justified war tradition, as I understand it, has attempted to identify criteria, in addition to just cause and right intention, which are important considerations in the moral justification of war. These additional criteria are not, I would maintain, equal in moral significance to just cause and right intention. They are, however, checks which may go some distance towards ensuring that a nation does not too cavalierly enter war and that a nation not trade off its moral integrity in the waging of war. The requirement of *legitimate authority*, if we are to understand it as a moral requirement, merely states that soldiers can have a duty to fight a war only if that war is commanded by someone to whom they owe obedience. Just war theories assume, rather than establish, which authorities are owed obedience. Whether, for example, the decision to wage war lies in the hands of the president or the Congress is not determined by just war theories and is not, to my mind, a matter of direct moral import. It is, instead, a question of Constitutional law.

Other justified war criteria include *last resort, reasonable hope of success at accomplishing your ends in fighting,* and *proportionality.* Proportionality is a moral requirement, demanding that the evils of war — in terms of the costs of human lives and a people's common life, the destruction of property, the drain upon financial resources. etc. — be outweighed by the good achieved, i.e., restoration of political sovereignty and territorial integrity, vindication of international law, a more just or stable order. This type of weighing of goods and evils is notoriously imprecise, and reasonable people will differ about whether the goods of a proposed war really do outweigh its evils, in part because there is no self-evident ranking of goods and evils. Furthermore, only a few individuals will be in a position accurately to predict the likely goods and evils involved in waging a war, to assess proportionality, so judgments of proportionality will normally be difficult for the average citizen. Proportionality, in any case, is better judged after the fact, a better principle for the allocation of blame, in light of the limits of our knowledge. Still, we want our leaders to recognize its binding character, to recognize their own finitude and the limitations finitude imposes upon the good they would do. We want our leaders to remember that sometimes the

unjust will flourish simply because of the heavy cost of bringing them to justice.

Last resort should not be interpreted as a condemnation of the first use of force. This would be to give the aggressor nation an upper hand. By analogy, this interpretation would force us to say that in coming to the assistance of someone being mugged I may not attack the mugger until he has turned his attack upon me. But this won't do. No, last resort requires that we make all reasonable good faith efforts to resolve political disputes by political and diplomatic means. Only upon the failure of these efforts is force justified.

Reasonable hope of success is a counsel of prudence. It reminds us that war is not a frivolous activity, that human life is too dear a price to pay for goals that are impossible to achieve. Reasonable hope of success is not a requirement of *military* success. There may be goods short of military victory that are worth dying for. As there can be individual martyrs so can there be martyr nations or states, putting their very existence as a people on the line, say, to resist the evils of Nazism.

Minimal satisfaction of these criteria may permit the waging of a war, but all that is morally permissible is not morally required. Are there any cases according to just war theory in which a nation would be required to wage war, would do wrong by not entering a war? I think so, and again this will be because justice or some type of neighbor-love demands it. One need only think back upon Hitler's Germany. For example, perhaps the United States was not required by the demands of justice to enter World War II upon Germany's invasion of Poland. And this may still have been the case with Germany's occupation of her weaker neighbors, Norway and Denmark. But there came a point, I am sure, when the wrongs of the Nazi regime were so well established that a nation with the abilities to deliver some retribution to the German regime and to aid in the protection of other nations was required by justice to do so, regardless of that nation's own interests. The occasions upon which some particular nation is morally required to play "police force of the world" are few and far between, but this is not to say that they are nonexistent.

Sometimes, I think, a duty to intervene is required not only by justice, but by another duty as well, a duty of beneficence. Imagine the following situation. Let's say that one day while browsing in the library you hear groans in the BJ section. Glancing over, you notice a three year old rather handily bashing me with a large book. His first blow has hit me in a strategic location and I can offer no protection of myself. The blows continue against me, his helpless victim. Now, were you to turn away, not wishing to dirty your hands, you would deserve our blame. You have a duty to intervene in this situation, a duty of beneficence.

Duties of beneficence can easily get out of hand, leaving us with more duties than we can handle, so we do well to identify their limits. James F. Childress and Tom L. Beauchamp suggest the following conditions as establishing a duty of beneficence: (1) The individual in need is at a risk of significant loss or damage, (2) Another individual's action is needed to prevent this loss, (3) The intervener's action would probably prevent or remove the loss or damage, (4) Intervention would not present significant risk to the intervener, and (5) The benefit the needy individual will probably gain outweighs any harms that the intervener is likely to suffer.[2] So if a nation can rebuff the aggressor of another nation at very little risk, and the aggression to be rebuffed is significant then it may be the case that neighbor-love's derivative, the duty of beneficence, requires a nation to undertake some minor risks for the sake of the well-being of a weaker nation. Not to do so would be a moral failing.

Now, even if all these *jus ad bellum* requirements are satisfied, even if a nation were to have good reason to think a war is morally justified, the work of a justified war theory is not done. Justified war theories have always insisted that there are unjustified *means of fighting*, that not only the decision whether to go to war is subject to moral assessment, but the waging of war itself must satisfy moral criteria. The moral criteria of *jus in bello*, the standards for what is morally permitted in fighting a war, are twofold: *discrimination*, sometimes referred to as non-combatant immunity, and *proportionality*.

The principle of discrimination declares that only combatants, only those who are in some way a part of the enemy nation's military force, are

2. *Principles of Biomedical Ethics*, 3rd ed. (New York: Oxford University Press, 1989), p. 201.

legitimate objects of attack. Military personnel must intend harm only to those who are combatants, and must run some risk in order to avoid the destruction of noncombatants. How to draw the line between combatants and noncombatants is a matter of some dispute for justified war theorists, but all agree that the line can and must be drawn. More plausible drawings of this line, I think, will address the threat that is posed by military personnel, rather than the "innocence" of noncombatants. In any case, although the deaths of some noncombatants are inevitable in war, there can be no moral justification for the targeting of civilians.

Proportionality requires that the military consider the consequences of each particular military action and ensure that the goods achieved in the battle outweigh the evils involved. In each battle the military may do no more damage than is required for the achievement of the war's objectives. If, for example, territory can be recaptured using spit-wads, then spit-wads and not conventional weapons must be used.

Employing the Justified War Criteria

These criteria, *jus ad bellum* and *jus in bello,* are to be considered in determining whether a particular war and its fighting is morally justified. The criteria have their basis in principles of love and justice; they attempt to ensure that enough, but no more than enough, is done to protect the weak and innocent peoples of the world.

Justified war criteria can be used prior to entering a war as a test for whether the resort to war is morally justified, They may be employed during the war to determine whether the war is being fought in a morally permissible way. And they can also be employed after a war in order to assess and to award praise and blame the warring parties.

It must also be said that justified war criteria can be used in either a positive or negative fashion, that is to say, either to support or to condemn a war. It is perhaps the case that these criteria are too often pressed into service of somewhat less than noble causes. But this need not be. The just war theory provides a powerful basis for the condemnation of morally unjustified wars, and is no friend of those who would wage war without reason. Like any other moral principle, the principles of just war theory can be manipulated and used for evil ends. But this is no fault with the just war theory, but rather with those who employ it. No moral principle is immune to abuse by morally vicious individuals.

Knowing and employing the criteria for justified war is necessary for those who would love their neighbor and who would do justice, according to justified war theories. But, although this knowledge is necessary for the performance of just and loving actions, it isn't sufficient. At least as important is that we be people who want love and justice for others, that we be the sorts of persons who are not likely to turn away from or to turn against a neighbor out of self-love. At least as important is that we not be people who tend to deceive themselves about whether the criteria for a justified war are satisfied. No moral theory can ensure this, but without this all moral theories are dangerous.

Those who adhere to a justified war theory may rightly be thought of as peace-makers and justice-makers. There is in justified war theory a moral abhorrence of war; the presumption against violence is foundational to the theory. Indeed, as those who know how horrible war can be, justified war theorists are rightly in the vanguard of those who work for peaceful resolution of conflicts. There is nothing inconsistent in the just war theorist's commitment to educating all of us to be more peaceful and peace-loving. Still, having said this, the just war theorist recognizes that sometimes love or justice may call us away from the normal expressions of justice and love to the alien expression of willful harm to a wrongdoer. That this is the case, the just war theorist regrets, and she waits eagerly for that day when every tear shall be dried and war shall be no more.

77. The Nonviolence of Dorothy Day

KATHLEEN DE SUTTER JORDAN

"Aren't we deceiving ourselves? . . . What are we accomplishing anyway for them (those coming in on the souplines, or in need of clothing or shelter), or for the world or for the common good? Are these people being 'rehabilitated' . . . ?" According to Dorothy Day (1897-1980), in an April 1964 appeal for funds written in *The Catholic Worker,* these were some of the questions most frequently asked by readers and visitors alike. But the majority, Dorothy continued, would always ask the same question: "How can you see Christ in people?"

If in the Gandhian sense nonviolence, or satyagraha, means literally a "holding on to truth," perhaps the nonviolence practiced by Dorothy Day can be best understood as flowing out of her experience of being "held onto" by truth. For Dorothy it was precisely the love of God and the grace to "see Christ in people" that inspired her radical Christian pacifism and life of nonviolence.

A convert to Catholicism, Dorothy Day was born in Brooklyn, New York, shortly before the turn of the century. Her father was a newspaper reporter who worked on various papers across the country. Dorothy, as well as her three brothers,

Kathleen De Sutter Jordan (1945–) was an associate editor of *The Catholic Worker* newspaper from 1969 to 1975, and a long-time friend of Dorothy Day. She is an R.N., and for the last several years of Dorothy's life, lived across the path from her house on the beach at Staten Island, New York.

From *The Universe Bends Toward Justice,* ed. Angie O'Gorman (Philadelphia: New Society Publishers, 1990).

would follow in his footsteps. Her youth was spent searching, at times with a degree of desperation, for some sense of purpose as well as for companionship. In 1919 she had an abortion in a futile attempt to salvage a love affair. Formal religion, for the most part experienced as "tepid," had little substance to offer: "I did not see anyone taking off his coat and giving it to the poor. I didn't see anyone having a banquet and calling in the lame, the halt, and the blind." It was rather the fervor and vision of the Socialists and Marxists, the heroic struggles taking place in the American labor movement, her first arrest and jail sentence with the Suffragettes in 1917, and the searing literary portraits drawn by Upton Sinclair and Dostoevski, that focused the lens through which Dorothy viewed the world in her teens and twenties. With a touch of irony, she admitted years later to having completely failed even to notice quotes from *Rerum Novarum,* the great social encyclical of Pope Leo XIII, appearing in the pages of the socialist magazine, *The Masses,* at the very time she was on its editorial staff.

From her early youth on, however, Dorothy also possessed a disposition of openness toward the holy and a capacity to take genuine delight in its manifestations, grand and subtle alike. It was only fitting, she noted later, that it would be during a period of great "natural happiness," culminating in the birth of her only child, that she finally found herself drawn to conversion. Dorothy was received into the Catholic Church in December 1927. But it would take another six years before she perceived an answer to her plea: "Where were the Catholics? . . . Where were the saints trying to change the social order, not just to minister to the slaves but to do away with slavery?"

The answer arrived, initially rather well-disguised, in the person of Peter Maurin. An itinerant French philosopher, Peter had spent years of study and reflection developing a synthesis of how traditional Catholicism ("so old it looked like new") might address the chaos and social injustices rampant in the early twentieth century. Peter proposed a three-point program: round table discussions for the clarification of thought; houses of hospitality where Christ could be met and served daily through the practice of the Works of Mercy; and farming communities to provide land and worthwhile work for the unemployed. In Dorothy Day,

Peter Maurin found not only a highly receptive audience, but practical-minded woman who was also a journalist. Together they launched the Catholic Worker Movement — to "make known the expressed and implied teachings of Christ" — with the first issue of *The Catholic Worker* distributed on May 1, 1933. It was a movement that Dorothy herself would lead for almost fifty years, and a movement that has continued to the present; there are currently more than seventy-five Catholic Worker communities throughout the country.

From its inception the Catholic Worker took an explicitly pacifist position in regard to war and the use of force — "We had been pacifist in class war, race war, in the Ethiopian war, in the Spanish Civil war, all through World War II, as we are now during the Korean war," Dorothy wrote in 1952 — a position maintained through the Vietnam war years and up through the present.

While this position of radical Christian pacifism would be espoused with a remarkable, prophetic clarity and fidelity, it was also to be "deeply, costingly realized." For example, in taking a stand critical of all warring parties during the Spanish Civil War, Dorothy wrote, "We got it from both sides." The young newspaper's monthly circulation of well over 150,000 dropped by nearly 100,000 by the war's end.

A much harsher test came with World War II when the position of *The Catholic Worker* was certainly not neutral; Catholic Workers had been protesting the rise of Nazism and anti-Semitism since 1935. Yet, after the U.S. entered the war, *The Catholic Worker* continued its pacifist stand: "What shall we say? . . . What shall we print? We will print the words of Christ who is with us always, even to the end of the world. 'Love your enemies, do good to those who hate you, and pray for those who persecute and calumniate you.'" Pledging to "try to be peacemakers," to pray daily, hourly, for an end to the war, readers were encouraged to combine prayer with action; with almsgiving and penance, as well as continuing to perform the Corporal and Spiritual Works of Mercy.

The pacifism of Dorothy Day and the Catholic Worker movement was anything but passive. "We are not talking of passive resistance," Dorothy wrote in 1938. On the contrary, it was based on Christ's revolutionary commandment (not merely a counsel, or recommendation, Dorothy pointed out) that his followers "Love one another as I have loved you." Its manifesto was the Sermon on the Mount; its weapons, the weapons of the Spirit: prayer, fasting, voluntary poverty, refusing to return evil for evil. "Love and prayer are not passive," Dorothy wrote, "but a most active glowing force."

Nor was it a type of quietism or retreat from the world that the Catholic Worker was promoting. Engagement with the joys and sorrows of the world is precisely where Christ is to be found. When Peter Maurin had emphasized the necessity of practicing the Works of Mercy, Dorothy said, he meant all of them. The Corporal Works of Mercy include: To feed the hungry, to give drink to the thirsty, to clothe the naked, to ransom the captive, to harbor the harborless, to visit the sick, to bury the dead. The Spiritual Works of Mercy are: to admonish the sinner, to instruct the ignorant, to counsel the doubtful, to comfort the sorrowful, to bear wrongs patiently, to forgive all injuries, to pray for the living and the dead.

From the first issue, *The Catholic Worker* announced a commitment to work toward "a reconstruction of the social order," based on the teachings of the Gospels and the papal social encyclicals. Peter Maurin was Dorothy's instructor in these matters. At the time of her conversion, she had anguished over the scandal of the Church in respect to the social order: "Plenty of charity but too little justice." Now there was to be launched a newspaper calling attention to the fact that "the Catholic Church has a social program." The Catholic Church, particularly in the thought of Thomas Aquinas, had traditionally emphasized that justice is the basis of a proper social order, and that genuine and lasting peace can only be established in the context of such a social order. That is why from the start *The Catholic Worker* was involved in the struggles of the labor movement, from support of the fledgling seamen and auto workers' unions in the 1930s (the workers raised Dorothy up through a window during the famous Flint strike), to support the farm workers and woodcutters unions in the later years of Dorothy's life (her final imprisonment was with Cesar Chavez's United Farm Workers union in 1973). The Catholic Worker helped found the Association of Catholic Trade Unionists in 1937 and picketed the Archdiocese of New York in 1949 in support of its striking gravediggers union.

When I think back about Dorothy now, words from her own biography of Therese of Lisieux come to mind: "What was there about her to make such an appeal? . . . What did she do? . . . What stands out in her life?"

Dorothy's own approach to reconstructing the social order and attempting to make visible the peace of Christ was both personal and direct. There was no distinction made between speaking at a peace rally, visiting a dying friend, going to jail to protest air raid drills, or saying evening prayers; not between walking a picket line with migrant farmworkers, fasting during Vatican II in support of a strong peace statement, working for integration in the South, or washing someone's feet. "We find they (the Works of Mercy) all go together," Dorothy reflected.

If she was prophetic in this regard, Dorothy noted wryly that it all just "came about" from attending to what needed to be done. It was the quality of her attention, closely akin to that described by Simone Weil as the very essence of love of God and love of neighbor alike, that enabled Dorothy to "see Christ in people," whether it be an "enemy" nation or a suffering neighbor. It is a reverence, a way of being, we are all called to, and capable of. "We each have our own vocation," Dorothy wrote, "the thing to do is to answer the call."

Besides this quality of attention, what made such an appeal about Dorothy was her own remarkable beauty, and the fact that she encouraged others to "feast on beauty," on God in all God's manifestations. Shortly after I was married I asked Dorothy, with an earnest seriousness, how people can combine voluntary poverty and family life. "The world will be saved by beauty," she reminded me; and that was the heart of the whole mystery.

Her own tastes, while refined, were quite simple. Books were staples, especially Tolstoy and Dostoevski, Dickens, and a smattering of good mysteries. She loved music, particularly opera, and would listen to her radio in utter rapture on Saturday afternoons when the Metropolitan Opera was broadcast. Unfailingly grateful for the plainest of meals, she would also comment on the beauty of the very common "golden wheat" patterned plate on which it had been served.

You always knew when Dorothy was in a room. Her presence, modest and deeply courteous, was nonetheless commanding — like the heavy shoes she wore, unassuming but substantial. Reserved with an Anglo-Saxon type of reticence, she loved giving and receiving gifts, often quoting St. Ignatius's dictum that "love is an exchange of gifts." Her humor was delightful, reflecting an inherent sense of irony and a keen eye for incongruity; it came often and unexpectedly. I sensed Dorothy coming to terms with her own aging, for example, when she commented on one occasion that, while she envied others who were going to sign up for an upcoming sit-in protesting arms development, she would probably have been unable to recall for the arresting officer why she had decided to take part in the demonstration.

What Dorothy did, in word and deed, was give us "at least a glimpse of eternity" (Lubac).[1] She reminded us over and over again that we are *all* called to be saints — to put on Christ and joyfully "complete the sufferings of Christ." When we pray in the Psalm, "O Lord, deliver us from fear of our enemies," it is not from our enemy that we are begging to be delivered, Dorothy pointed out, but from our own *fear*.

To "see Christ in other people" requires an act of faith ("an overwhelming act of faith," Dorothy put it). But "we have seen his hands and his feet in the poor around us. He has shown himself to us in them. We start by loving them for him, and we soon love them for themselves, each a most unique person, most special!" Such is the heart of Dorothy Day's nonviolence, and her invitation to us.

---

1. The full quote by Lubac, as it appears in an article by Dorothy Day, "Here and Now," in the book *The Third Hour,* published in 1949, is: "It is not the proper duty of Christianity to form leaders — that is, builders of the temporal, although a legion of Christian leaders is infinitely desirable. Christianity must generate saints — that is, witnesses to the eternal. The efficacy of the saint is not that of the leader. The saint does not have to bring about temporal achievements; he is one who succeeds in giving us at least a glimpse of eternity despite the thick opacity of time." This quote, a favorite of Dorothy's, also appears in Robert Ellsberg's *By Little and By Little* (New York: Alfred A. Knopf, 1983).

Try It Yourself: Nonviolence with a Rapist?

CASE STUDY 6

Does the following case amount to an "opiate" for Christian women and consequently bad advice, or does it display the kind of life that all Christians should follow?

Rather than destruction of enemies, the Christian ethic calls for their conversion and counts on enough love on my part to facilitate the process . . .

I was awakened late one night several years ago by a man kicking open the door to my bedroom. The house was empty. The phone was downstairs. He was somewhat verbally abusive as he walked over to my bed. I could not find his eyes in the darkness but could see the outline of his form. As I lay there, feeling a fear and vulnerability I had never before experienced, several thoughts ran through my head — all in a matter of seconds. The first was the uselessness of screaming. The second was the fallacy of thinking safety depends on having a gun hidden under your pillow. Somehow I could not imagine this man standing patiently while I reached under my pillow for my gun. The third thought, I believe, saved my life. I realized with a certain clarity that either he and I made it through this situation safely — together — or we would both be damaged. Our safety was connected. If he raped me he would be hurt as well. If he went to prison, the damage would be greater. That thought disarmed me. It freed me from my own desire to lash out and at the same time from my own paralysis. It did not free me from feelings of fear but from fear's control over my ability to respond. I found myself acting out of a concern for both our safety which caused me to react with a certain firmness but with surprisingly little hostility in my voice.

I asked him what time it was. He answered. That was a good sign. I commented that his watch and the clock on my night table had different times. His said 2:30, mine said 2:45. I had just set mine. I hoped his watch wasn't broken. When the atmosphere began to calm a little I asked him how he had gotten into the house. He'd broken through the glass in the back door. I told him that presented me with a problem as I did not have the money to buy new glass. He talked about some financial difficulties of his own. We talked until we were no longer strangers and I felt it was safe to ask him to leave. He didn't want to; said he had no place to go. Knowing I did not have the physical power to force him out I told him firmly but respectfully, as equal to equal, I would give him a clean set of sheets but he would have to make his own bed downstairs. He went downstairs and I sat up in bed, wide awake and shaking for the rest of the night. The next morning we ate breakfast together and he left.

Several things happened that night. I allowed someone who I was afraid of to become human to me and as a result I reacted in a surprisingly human way to him. That caught him off guard. Apparently his scenario had not included a social visit and it took him a few minutes to regain his sense of balance. By that time the vibes were all wrong for violence. Whatever had been motivating him was sidetracked and he changed his mind.

Through the effects of prayer, meditation, training, and the experience of lesser kinds of assault, I had been able to allow what I call a context for conversion to emerge.[1]

---

1. From Angie O'Gorman, "Defense Through Disarmament: Nonviolence and Personal Assault," *The Universe Bends Toward Justice*, ed. Angie O'Gorman, (Philadelphia, Pa.: New Society Publishers, 1990).

Chapter 12
Christian Economic Ethics

Introduction

"Cold, hungry, and homeless." These signs can be seen in almost any community in the Western world. Or it may be the pictures of the skinny African children — stomachs bloated, and flies on their eyes — that pulls hardest at your heartstrings. You have encountered the poor and the hungry. Perhaps you have wondered what the response of Christians to the poor and the hungry should be. Perhaps you have wondered about your appropriate response to the local and global injustice of some of us spending our money on luxury items while others of us starve.

"Make no mistake about it," the biblical readings seem to say, "you are guilty." Amos professes the impossibility of our worshiping God while the poor are in our midst. Jesus counsels us to go and sell everything we own and give to the poor if we want to be perfect, and he alerts us to the judgment day when those who have ministered to the sick, the hungry, and the naked, will be separated from those who have ignored the "least among us." These are hard words, indeed!

It is difficult, however, to know exactly what to do after we feel convicted by these biblical texts. Take the homeless person asking you for a handout, for example. To give him money does not ensure that the money will be used to satisfy his basic human needs; nor will it restore his lost dignity. It may seem to achieve nothing more than to assuage our own guilty consciences. Still, to walk by ignoring the request for alms seems uncharitable. So what should we do?

No gift we give to the poor will eliminate poverty and its accompanying problems. You and I must, by all means, reflect upon our personal stewardship of wealth, but this is only part of the struggle that Christians face in thinking about wealth and poverty. The other question which confronts us has to do with the institutions and systems which permit, or better, which encourage such great disparities of wealth as characterizes the contemporary world. What ought we to make of a global economy in which the haves so clearly prosper in the presence of so many have-nots?

Christian thinkers throughout the ages have wrestled with these questions and with the chapter's biblical texts. Wanting to be faithful, yet realistic about the demands of daily life, they have sometimes read these biblical texts less straightforwardly than we might have expected. For example, the early church father, Clement of Alexandria, in a sermon on our second text (reading 79), warns us that we ought not be satisfied with the outward show of giving away our riches. What God requires is the far more difficult purification of the soul of the possessive passions that dominate it. To sacrifice our possessions would be to make ourselves dependent upon the charity of others. It is better by far to sacrifice sinful desires.

The Protestant reformer John Calvin (reading 80), while ostensibly addressing the moral permissibility of charging interest for money loaned to others, is likewise concerned about the Christian responsibility to the poor. In the absence of clear scriptural teaching on usury, Calvin appeals to the principle of natural equity, deriving duties protecting the poor from this principle.

Although Clement and Calvin concern themselves primarily with the question of the individual response to poverty and riches, our twentieth-century commentators, Walter Rauschenbusch and Reinhold Niebuhr (readings 81 and 82), direct their attention to economic systems. Rauschenbusch sees capitalism as radically incompatible with Christianity. Capitalism, aiming only at the maximization of profit, ignores human needs and robs humanity of the unity intended by God. There is no means of transforming capitalism; a Christian economic order must replace the capitalist economic system. The economic conversion of Christians is central to this task.

Reinhold Niebuhr believed the approach of Rauschenbusch and other social gospel theologians to be excessively moralistic and at the same time ignorant of the nuts and bolts of economic mechanisms. Decrying any easy application of the law of love to the economic realm, Niebuhr insists upon the complex and pragmatic application of a general principle of justice.

In Pope John Paul II's encyclical, *Centesimus Annus* (reading 83), the fundamental goods of private property and work are reaffirmed. This papal document is critical of various aspects of contemporary capitalist economies but nevertheless acknowledges the efficiency of free-market economies and the moral legitimacy of the profit motive. Capitalism must be constrained by the demands of morality, but it can be so constrained.

The most influential theological movement in the late twentieth century has been liberation theology. A movement of some diversity, what unites liberation theologians is their expressed solidarity with the poor and oppressed. In the final reading of this chapter (reading 84), two long-time Latin American proponents of liberation theology, Leonardo and Clodovis Boff, illuminate the meaning of the "preferential option for the poor."

This chapter closes with a different type of case study. The collapse of the Soviet Union and the increasing openness of China to free-market trade have led many Christian ethicists to a rethinking of what was perhaps too easy an alignment of Christianity and socialism. The question that has since emerged is whether, in fact, capitalism as we know it can be transformed, restructured into a system more respectful of human dignity. You are asked to dive into this current debate, using as background the resources you have plumbed in these and earlier readings (see, for example, readings 44-46 and 54).

Suggestions for Further Reading

Benne, Robert. *The Ethic of Democratic Capitalism: A Moral Reassessment.* Philadelphia: Fortress Press, 1981.

Birch, Bruce, and Larry Rasmussen. *The Predicament of the Prosperous.* Philadelphia: Westminster Press, 1978.

Gutierrez, Gustavo. *A Theology of Liberation.* Maryknoll, N.Y.: Orbis, 1973.

Gay, Craig M. *With Liberty and Justice for Whom? The Recent Evangelical Debate over Capitalism.* Grand Rapids, Mich.: Wm. B. Eerdmans, 1991.

Lebacqz, Karen. *Justice in an Unjust World.* Minneapolis: Augsburg Press, 1987.

National Conference of Catholic Bishops. *Economic Justice for All: Catholic Social Teaching and the U.S. Economy.* Washington, D.C., 1986.

Novak, Michael. *The Spirit of Democratic Capitalism.* New York: Simon and Schuster, 1982.

West, Cornel. *Prophesy Deliverance! An Afro-American Revolutionary Christianity.* Philadelphia: Westminster Press, 1982.

Wogaman, J. Philip. *The Great Economic Debate.* Philadelphia: Westminster Press, 1977.

78. Amos 5:11-24;
Matthew 19:16-30;
25:31-46

Amos 5:11-24

Therefore because you trample on the poor
  and take from them levies of grain,
you have built houses of hewn stone,
  but you shall not live in them;
you have planted pleasant vineyards,
  but you shall not drink their wine.
For I know how many are your transgressions,
  and how great are your sins —
you who afflict the righteous, who take a bribe,
  and push aside the needy in the gate.
Therefore the prudent will keep silent
    in such a time;
  for it is an evil time.

Seek good and not evil,
  that you may live;
and so the LORD, the God of hosts,
    will be with you,
  just as you have said.
Hate evil and love good,
  and establish justice in the gate;
it may be that the LORD, the God of hosts,
  will be gracious to the remnant of Joseph.

Therefore thus says the LORD, the God
    of hosts, the Lord:
In all the squares there shall be wailing;
  and in all the streets they shall say, "Alas! alas!"
They shall call the farmers to mourning,
  and those skilled in lamentation, to wailing;
in all the vineyards there shall be wailing,
    for I will pass through the midst of you,
      says the LORD.

Alas for you who desire the day of the LORD!
  Why do you want the day of the LORD?
It is darkness, not light;
    as if someone fled from a lion,
    and was met by a bear;
or went into the house and rested a hand
      against the wall,
    and was bitten by a snake.
Is not the day of the LORD darkness, not light,
  and gloom with no brightness in it?

I hate, I despise your festivals,
  and I take no delight in your solemn
    assemblies.
Even though you offer me your burnt offerings
    and grain offerings,
  I will not accept them;
and the offerings of well-being of your
    fatted animals
  I will not look upon.
Take away from me the noise of your songs;
  I will not listen to the melody of your harps.
But let justice roll down like waters,
  and righteousness like an everflowing stream.

Matthew 19:16-30

Then someone came to him and said, "Teacher, what good deed must I do to have eternal life?" And he said to him, "Why do you ask me about what is good? There is only one who is good. If you wish to enter into life, keep the commandments." He said to him, "Which ones?" And Jesus said, "You shall not murder; You shall not commit adultery; You shall not steal; You shall not bear false witness; Honor your father and mother; also, You shall love your neighbor as yourself." The young man said to him, "I have kept all these; what do I still lack?" Jesus said to him, "If you wish to be perfect, go, sell your possessions, and give the money to the poor, and you will have treasure in heaven; then come, follow me." When the young man heard this word, he went away grieving, for he had many possessions.

Then Jesus said to his disciples, "Truly I tell you, it will be hard for a rich person to enter the Kingdom of Heaven. Again I tell you, it is easier for a camel to go through the eye of a needle than for someone who is rich to enter the Kingdom of

God." When the disciples heard this, they were greatly astounded and said, "Then who can be saved?" But Jesus looked at them and said, "For mortals it is impossible, but for God all things are possible."

Then Peter said in reply, "Look, we have left everything and followed you. What then will we have?" Jesus said to them, "Truly I tell you, at the renewal of all things, when the Son of Man is seated on the throne of his glory, you who have followed me will also sit on twelve thrones, judging the twelve tribes of Israel. And everyone who has left houses or brothers or sisters or father or mother or children or fields, for my name's sake, will receive a hundredfold, and will inherit eternal life. But many who are first will be last, and the last will be first."

Matthew 25:31-46

"When the Son of Man comes in his glory, and all the angels with him, then he will sit on the throne of his glory. All the nations will be gathered before him, and he will separate people one from another as a shepherd separates the sheep from the goats, and he will put the sheep at his right hand and the goats at the left. Then the king will say to those at his right hand, 'Come, you that are blessed by my Father, inherit the kingdom prepared for you from the foundation of the world; for I was hungry and you gave me food, I was thirsty and you gave me something to drink, I was a stranger and you welcomed me, I was naked and you gave me clothing, I was sick and you took care of me, I was in prison and you visited me.' Then the righteous will answer him. 'Lord, when was it that we saw you hungry and gave you food, or thirsty and gave you something to drink? And when was it that we saw you a stranger and welcomed you, or naked and gave you clothing? And when was it that we saw you sick or in prison and visited you?' And the king will answer them. 'Truly I tell you, just as you did it to one of the least of these who are members of my family, you did it to me.' Then he will say to those at his left hand, 'You that are accursed, depart from me into the eternal fire prepared for the devil and his angels; for I was hungry and you gave me no food, I was thirsty and you gave me nothing to drink, I was a stranger and you did not welcome me, naked and you did not give me clothing, sick and in prison and you did not visit me.' Then they also will answer, 'Lord, when was it that we saw you hungry or thirsty or a stranger or naked or sick or in prison, and did not take care of you?' Then he will answer them, 'Truly I tell you, just as you did not do it to one of the least of these, you did not do it to me.' And these will go away into eternal punishment, but the righteous into eternal life."

CHRISTIAN ECONOMIC ETHICS

79. The Rich Man's Salvation

CLEMENT OF ALEXANDRIA

. . . Yet indeed he who has fulfilled every demand of the law "from youth" and has made extravagant boasts, is unable to add to the tale this one thing singled out by the Savior, in order to obtain the eternal life which he longs for. He went away displeased, being annoyed at the precept concerning the life for which he was making supplication. For he did not truly wish for life, as he said, but aimed solely at a reputation for good intentions. He could be busy about many things, but the one thing, the work that brings life, he was neither able nor eager nor strong enough to accomplish. And just as the Savior said to Martha when she was busy about many things, distracted and troubled by serving, and chiding her sister because she had left the household work and was seated at his feet spending her time in learning: "Thou art troubled about many things, but Mary hath chosen the good part, and it shall not be taken away from her," — so also he bade this man cease from his manifold activities and cling to and sit beside one thing, the grace of him who adds eternal life.

What then was it that impelled him to flight, and made him desert his teacher, his supplication, his hope, his life, his previous labours? "Sell what belongs to thee." And what is this? It is not what

---

Clement of Alexandria (150–215) was a Greek theologian who attempted to synthesize Christian and Platonic thought. His works include *Protrepticus (Exhortation to the Greeks)*, *Paedagogus (Tutor)*, and *Stromata (Miscellanies)*.

From *Clement of Alexandria*, trans. G. W. Butterworth, Loeb Classical Library (Cambridge: Harvard University Press, 1919).

some hastily take it to be, a command to fling away the substance that belongs to him and to part with his riches, but to banish from the soul its opinions about riches, its attachment to them, its excessive desire, its morbid excitement over them, its anxious cares, the thorns of our earthly existence which choke the seed of the true life. For it is no great or enviable thing to be simply without riches, apart from the purpose of obtaining life. Why, if this were so, those men who have nothing at all, but are destitute and beg for their daily bread, who lie along the roads in abject poverty, would, though "ignorant" of God and "God's righteousness," be most blessed and beloved of God and the only possessors of eternal life, by the sole fact of their being utterly without ways and means of livelihood and in want of the smallest necessities.

*   *   *

What then is it that he enjoins as new and peculiar to God and alone life-giving, which did not save men of former days? If the "new creation," the Son of God, reveals and teaches something unique, then his command does not refer to the visible act, the very thing that others have done, but to something else greater, more divine and more perfect, which is signified through this; namely, to strip the soul itself and the will of their lurking passions and utterly to root out and cast away all alien thoughts from the mind. For this is a lesson peculiar to the believer and a doctrine worthy of the Savior. The men of former days, indeed, in their contempt for outward things, parted with and sacrificed their possessions, but as for the passions of the soul, I think they even intensified them. For they became supercilious, boastful, conceited, and disdainful of the rest of mankind, as if they themselves had wrought something superhuman. How then could the Savior have recommended to those who were to live for ever things that would be harmful and injurious for the life he promises? And there is this other point. It is possible for a man, after having unburdened himself of his property, to be none the less continually absorbed and occupied in the desire and longing for it. He has given up the use of wealth, but now being in difficulties and at the same time yearning after what he threw away, he endures a double annoyance, the absence of means of support and the presence of regret. For when a man lacks the necessities of life he cannot possibly fail to be broken in spirit and to neglect the higher things, as he strives to procure these necessities by any means and from any source.

And how much more useful is the opposite condition, when by possessing a sufficiency a man is himself in no distress about money-making and also helps those he ought? For what sharing would be left among men, if nobody had anything? And how could this doctrine be found other than plainly contradictory to and at war with many other noble doctrines of the Lord? "Make to yourselves friends from the mammon of unrighteousness, that when it shall fail they may receive you into the eternal habitations." "Acquire treasures in heaven, where neither moth nor rust doth consume, nor thieves break through." How could we feed the hungry and give drink to the thirsty, cover the naked and entertain the homeless, with regard to which deeds he threatens fire and the outer darkness to those who have not done them, if each of us were himself already in want of all these things? But further, the Lord himself is a guest with Zacchaeus and Levi and Matthew, wealthy men and tax-gatherers, and he does not bid them give up their riches. On the contrary, having enjoined the just and set aside the unjust employment of them, he proclaims, "Today is salvation come to this house." It is on this condition that he praises their use, and with this stipulation — that he commands them to be shared, to give drink to the thirsty and bread to the hungry, to receive the homeless, to clothe the naked. And if it is not possible to satisfy these needs except with riches, and he were bidding us stand aloof from riches, what else would the Lord be doing than exhorting us to give and also not to give the same things, to feed and not to feed, to receive and to shut out, to share and not to share? But this would be the height of unreason.

We must not then fling away the riches that are of benefit to our neighbours as well as ourselves. For they are called possessions because they are things possessed, and wealth because they are to be welcomed and because they have been prepared by God for the welfare of men. Indeed, they lie at hand and are put at our disposal as a sort of material and as instruments to be well used by those who know. An instrument, if you use it with artistic skill, is a thing of art; but if you are lacking in skill, it reaps the benefit of your unmusical nature, though not itself responsible. Wealth too is an instrument of the same kind. You can use it rightly; it ministers to righteousness. But if one use it wrongly, it is found to be a minister of wrong. For its nature is to minister, not to rule. We must not therefore put the responsibility on that which, having in itself neither good nor evil, is not responsible, but on that which has the power of using things either well or badly, as a result of choice; for this is responsible just for that reason. And this is the mind of man, which has in itself both free judgment and full liberty to deal with what is given to it. So let a man do away, not with his possessions, but rather with the passions of his soul, which do not consent to the better use of what he has; in order that, by becoming noble and good, he may be able to use these possessions also in a noble manner. "Saying good-bye to all we have," and "selling all we have," must therefore be understood in this way, as spoken with reference to the soul's passions.

80. On Usury

JOHN CALVIN

From John Calvin to one of his friends.

I have not personally experienced this, but I have learned from the example of others how perilous it is to respond to the question for which you seek my counsel. For if we should totally prohibit the practice of usury, we would restrain consciences more rigidly than God himself. But if we permit it, then some, under this guise, would be content to act with unbridled license, unable to abide any limits.

If I were writing to you alone, I would have no fear of such a thing, for your prudence and the moderation of your heart are well known to me. But because you seek counsel for another, I fear that if I say anything he might permit himself more than I would prefer. Nonetheless, since I have no doubt that, in light of human nature and the matter at hand, you will thoughtfully consider the most expedient thing to do, I will share what I think.

First, there is no scriptural passage that totally bans all usury. For Christ's statement, which is commonly esteemed to manifest this, but which has to do with lending (Luke 6:35), has been falsely applied to usury. Furthermore, as elsewhere, when

---

John Calvin (1509–1564) was a leader of the Protestant Reformation in Switzerland. A father of the Presbyterian and Reformed traditions of Protestantism, his systematic theology and his political thought have both influenced generations of thinkers. His works include commentaries on Christian Scripture, catechisms, and his major work, the *Institutes of the Christian Religion*.

From John Calvin, *Calvin's Ecclesiastical Advice*, trans. Mary Beaty and Benjamin Farley (Louisville, Ky.: Westminster/John Knox Press, 1991).

he rebukes the sumptuous guests and the ambitious invitations of the rich, he commands us to call instead the blind, the lame, and the other poor of the streets, who cannot repay. In so doing he corrects the world's vicious custom of lending money [only to those who can repay] and urges us, instead, to lend to those from whom no hope of repayment is possible.

Now we are accustomed to lending money where it will be safe. But we ought to help the poor, where our money will be at risk. For Christ's words far more emphasize our remembering the poor than our remembering the rich. Nonetheless, we need not conclude that all usury is forbidden.

The law of Moses (Deut. 23:19) is quite diplomatic, restraining us to act only within the bounds of equity and human reason. To be certain, it would be desirable if usurers were chased from every country, even if the practice were unknown. But since that is impossible, we ought at least to use it for the common good.

Passages in both the prophets and the Psalms display the Holy Spirit's anger against usurers. There is a reference to a vile evil (Ps. 55:12, Vulgate) that has been translated by the word *usura*. But since the Hebrew word *tok* can generally mean "defraud," it can be translated otherwise than "usury."

Even where the prophet specifically mentions usury, it is hardly a wonder that he mentions it among the other evil practices (Neh. 5:10). The reason is that the more often usury is practiced with illicit license, the more often cruelty and other fraudulent activities arise.

What am I to say, except that usury almost always travels with two inseparable companions: tyrannical cruelty and the art of deception. This is why the Holy Spirit elsewhere advises all holy men, who praise and fear God, to abstain from usury, so much so that it is rare to find a good man who also practices usury.

The prophet Ezekiel (22:12) goes still further, for in citing the horrible case in which the vengeance of God has been kindled against the Jews, he uses the two Hebrew words *neshek* and *tarbith* — a form of usury so designated in Hebrew because of the manner in which it eats away at its victims. *Tarbith* means "to increase," or "add to," or "gain," and with good reason. For anyone interested in expanding his personal profit will take, or rather snatch, that gain from someone else. But undoubtedly the prophets only condemned usury as severely as they did because it was expressly prohibited for Jews to do. Hence when they rejected the clear commandment of God, they merited a still sterner rebuke.

Today, a similar objection against usury is raised by some who argue that since the Jews were prohibited from practicing it, we too, on the basis of our fraternal union, ought not to practice it. To that I respond that a political union is different. The situation in which God brought the Jews together, combined with other circumstances, made commerce without usury apt among them. Our situation is quite different. For that reason, I am unwilling to condemn it, so long as it is practiced with equity and charity.

The pretext that both St. Ambrose and Chrysostom cite is too frivolous in my judgment, that is, that money does not engender money. Does the sea or the earth [engender it]? I receive a fee from renting a house. Is that where money grows? Houses, in turn, are products of the trades, where money is also made. Even the value of a house can be exchanged for money. And what? Is money not more productive than merchandise or any other possession one could mention? It is lawful to make money by renting a piece of ground, yet unlawful to make it from money? What? When you buy a field, is money not making money?

How do merchants increase their wealth? By being industrious, you answer. I readily admit what even children can see, that if you lock your money in a chest, it will not increase. Moreover, no one borrows money from others with the intention of hiding it or not making a profit. Consequently, the gain is not from the money but from profit.

We may therefore conclude that, although at first such subtleties appear convincing, upon closer examination they evaporate, since there is no substance to them. Hence, I conclude that we ought not to judge usury according to a few passages of Scripture, but in accordance with the principle of equity.

An example ought to clarify the matter. Take a rich man whose wealth lies in possessions and rents but who has no money on hand. A second, whose wealth is somewhat more moderate — though less than the first — soon comes into money. If an opportunity should arise, the second person can easily buy what he wants, while the first will have to ask the latter for a loan. It is in the power of the second, under the rules of bargaining, to impose a fee on the first's goods until he repays, and in this manner the first's condition will be improved, although usury has been practiced.

Now, what makes a contract just and honest or unjust and dishonest? Has not the first fared better by means of an agreement involving usury by his neighbor than if the second had compelled him to mortgage or pawn his goods? To deny this is to play with God in a childish manner, preferring words over the truth itself. As if it were in our power, by changing words, to transform virtue into vice or vice into virtue. I certainly have no quarrel here.

I have said enough; you will be able to weigh this more diligently on your own. Nonetheless, I should hope that you will always keep in mind that what we must bring under judgment are not words but deeds themselves.

Now I come to the exceptions. For, as I said at the beginning, we must proceed with caution, as almost everyone is looking for some word to justify his intention. Hence, I must reiterate that when I approve of some usury, I am not extending my approval to all its forms. Furthermore, I disapprove of anyone engaging in usury as his form of occupation. Finally, I grant nothing without listing these additional exceptions.

The first is that no one should take interest [usury] from the poor, and no one, destitute by virtue of indigence or some affliction or calamity, should be forced into it. The second exception is that whoever lends should not be so preoccupied with gain as to neglect his necessary duties, nor, wishing to protect his money, disdain his poor brothers. The third exception is that no principle be followed that is not in accord with natural equity, for everything should be examined in the light of Christ's precept: Do unto others as you would have them do unto you. This precept is applicable every time. The fourth exception is that whoever borrows should make at least as much, if not more, than the amount borrowed. In the fifth place, we ought not to determine what is lawful by basing it on the common practice or in accordance with the iniquity of the world, but should base it on a principle derived from the word of God. In the sixth place, we ought not to consider only the private advantage of those with whom we deal but should keep in mind what is best for the common good. For it is quite obvious that the interest a merchant pays is a public fee. Thus we should see that the contract will benefit all rather than hurt. In the seventh place, one ought not to exceed the rate that a country's public laws allow. Although this may not always suffice, for such laws quite often permit what they are able to correct or repress. Therefore one ought to prefer a principle of equity that can curtail abuse.

But rather than valuing my own opinion over yours, I desire only that you act in such a humane way that nothing more need be said on the matter. With that in mind, I have composed these thoughts more out of a desire to please you than out of any confidence of satisfying you. But owing to your kindness toward me, I know you will take to heart what I have offered.

[I commit you] to God, my most excellent and honored friend. May he preserve you and your family. Amen.

81. The Case of Christianity against Capitalism

WALTER RAUSCHENBUSCH

Let us sum up the case of Christianity against capitalism. We saw that the distinctive characteristic of the capitalistic system is that the industrial outfit of society is owned and controlled by a limited group, while the mass of the industrial workers is without ownership or power over the system within which they work. A small group of great wealth and power is set over against a large group of propertyless men. Given this line-up, the rest follows with the inevitableness of a process in physics or chemistry.

Wherever the capitalist class remains in unorganized and small units, they will struggle for the prizes held out by modern industry. Capitalism in its youth threw off the restraints upon competition created by the older social order, and a fierce, free fight followed. Wherever the competitive principle is still in operation, it intensifies natural emulation by the size of the stakes it offers, enables the greedy and cunning to set the pace for the rest, makes men immoral by fear, and puts the selfish impulses in control. The charge of Christianity against competitive capitalism is that it is unfraternal, the opposite of cooperation and teamwork.

Walter Rauschenbusch (1861–1918) was an influential leader of the social gospel movement and a professor of church history at Rochester Seminary. His works include *Christianity and the Social Crisis*, *A Theology for the Social Gospel*, and *The Social Principles of Jesus*.

From Walter Rauschenbusch, *Christianizing the Social Order* (New York: Macmillan, 1912.

Capitalism gives the owners and managers of industry autocratic power over the workers. The dangers always inherent in the leadership of the strong are intensified by that fact that in capitalistic industry this power is unrestrained by democratic checks and fortified by almost absolute ownership of the means of production and life. Consequently the master class in large domains of industry have exacted excessive toil, and have paid wages that were neither a just return for the work done nor sufficient to support life normally. The working class is everywhere in a state of unrest and embitterment. By great sacrifices it has tried to organize in order to strengthen its position against these odds, but the master class has hampered or suppressed the organizations of labor. This line-up of two antagonistic classes is the historical continuation of the same line-up which we see in chattel slavery and feudal serfdom. In recent years the development of corporations has added a new difficulty by depersonalizing the master. The whole situation contradicts the spirit of American institutions. It is the last entrenchment of the despotic principle. It tempts the class in power to be satisfied with a semimorality in their treatment of the working class. It is not Christian.

The capitalist class serves society in the capacity of the middleman, and modern conditions make this function more important than ever before. But under the capitalistic organization this wholesome function is not under public control, and the relations created call out the selfish motives and leave the higher motives of human nature dormant. Under competition business readily drifts into the use of tricky methods, sells harmful or adulterated goods, and breaks down the moral self-restraint of the buyer. Under monopoly the middleman is able to practice extortion on the consumer. The kindly and friendly relations that abound in actual business life between the dealer and the consumer are due to the personal character of the parties and the ineradicable social nature of man, and are not created by the nature of business itself.

In all the operations of capitalistic industry and commerce the aim that controls and directs is not the purpose to supply human needs, but to make a profit for those who direct industry. This in itself is an irrational and unChristian adjustment of the social order, for it sets money up as the prime aim, and human life as something secondary, or as a means to secure money. The supremacy of profit in capitalism stamps it as a mammonistic organization with which Christianity can never be content. "Profit" commonly contains considerable elements of just reward for able work; it may contain nothing but that; but where it is large and dissociated from hard work, it is traceable to some kind of monopoly privilege and power — either the power to withhold part of the earnings of the workers by the control of the means of production, or the ability to throw part of the expenses of business on the community, or the power to overcharge the public. Insofar as profit is derived from these sources, it is tribute collected by power from the helpless, a form of legalized graft, and a contradiction of Christian relations.

Thus our capitalistic commerce and industry lies alongside of the home, the school, the church, and the democratized state as an unregenerate part of the social order, not based on freedom, love, and mutual service, as they are, but on autocracy, antagonism of interests, and exploitation. Such a verdict does not condemn the moral character of the men in business. On the contrary, it gives a remarkable value to every virtue they exhibit in business, for every act of honesty, justice, and kindness is a triumph over hostile conditions, a refusal of Christianity and humanity to be chilled by low temperature or scorched by the flame of high-pressure temptation. Our business life has been made endurable only by the high qualities of the men and women engaged in it. These personal qualities have been created by the home, the school, and the church. The state has also made business tolerable by pulling a few of the teeth and shortening the tether of greed. Thus moral forces generated outside of capitalism have invaded its domain and supplied the moral qualities without which it would have collapsed. But capitalistic business in turn is invading the regenerate portions of the social order, paralyzing their activities, breaking down the respect for the higher values, desecrating the holy, and invading God's country.

Life is holy. Respect for life is Christian. Business, setting profit first, has recklessly used up the life of the workers, and impaired the life of the consumers whenever that increased profit. The life of great masses has been kept low by poverty, haunted by fear, and deprived of the joyous expression of life in play.

Beauty is a manifestation of God. Capitalism is ruthless of the beauty of nature if its sacrifice increases profit. When commerce appeals to the sense of beauty in its products, beauty is a device to make profit, and becomes meretricious, untrue, and sometimes corrupts the sense of beauty. Neither does the distribution of wealth under capitalism offer the best incentives to artistic ability.

Love is of God; the home is its sanctuary. Capitalism is breaking down or crippling the home wherever it prevails, and poisoning society with the decaying fragments of what was the spring house of life. The conditions created by capitalism are the conditions in which prostitution is multiplying. Some sections of capitalistic business are directly interested in vice and foster it. Because it is so immensely profitable the white slave traffic would speedily become a great industry if the state did not repress it; and where the state tries to grapple with it, commercialized vice is corrupting the officers of the state.

Devotion to the common good is one of the holy and divine forces in human society. Capitalism teaches us to set private interest before the common good. It follows profit, and not patriotism and public spirit. If war is necessary to create or protect profit, it will involve nations in war, but it plays a selfish part amid the sacrifices imposed by war. It organizes many of the ablest men into powerful interests which are at some points antagonistic to the interest of the community. It has corrupted our legislatures, our executive officers, and our courts, tampered with the organs of public opinion and instruction, spread a spirit of timidity among the citizens, and vindictively opposed the men who stood for the common good against the private interests.

When men of vigorous character and intellectual ability obey the laws of capitalism, and strive for the prizes it holds out to them, they win power and great wealth, but they are placed in an essentially false relation to their fellow men, the Christian virtues of their family stock are undermined, their natural powers of leadership are crippled, and the greater their success in amassing wealth under capitalistic methods the greater is the tragedy of their lives from a Christian point of view.

These are the points in the Christian indictment of capitalism. All these are summed up in this single challenge, that capitalism has generated a spirit of its own which is antagonistic to the spirit of Christianity; a spirit of hardness and cruelty that neutralizes the Christian spirit of love; a spirit that sets material goods above spiritual possessions. To set things above men is the really dangerous practical materialism. To set Mammon before God is the only idolatry against which Jesus warned us.

*   *   *

Religion declares the supreme value of life and personality, even the humblest; business negatives that declaration of faith by setting up profit as the supreme and engrossing object of thought and effort, and by sacrificing life to profit where necessary.

Christianity teaches the unity and solidarity of men; capitalism reduces that teaching to a harmless expression of sentiment by splitting society into two antagonistic sections, unlike in their work, their income, their pleasures, and their point of view.

True Christianity wakens men to a sense of their worth, to love of freedom, and independence of action; capitalism, based on the principle of autocracy, resents independence, suppresses the attempts of the working class to gain it, and deadens the awakening effect that goes out from Christianity.

The spirit of Christianity puts even men of unequal worth on a footing of equality by the knowledge of common sin and weakness, and by the faith in a common salvation; capitalism creates an immense inequality between families, perpetuates it by property conditions, and makes it hard for high and low to have a realizing sense of the equality which their religion teaches.

Christianity puts the obligation of love on the holiest basis and exerts its efforts to create fraternal feeling among men, and to restore it where broken; capitalism has created world-wide unrest, jealousy, resentment, and bitterness, which choke Christian love like weeds.

Jesus bids us strive first for the reign of God and the justice of God because on that spiritual basis all material wants too will be met; capitalism urges us to strive first and last for our personal enrichment, and it formerly held out the hope that the selfishness of all would create the universal good.

*   *   *

Christianity makes the love of money the root of all evil, and demands the exclusion of the covetous and extortioners from the Christian fellowship; capitalism cultivates the love of money for its own sake and gives its largest wealth to those who use monopoly for extortion.

Thus two spirits are wrestling for the mastery in modern life, the spirit of Christ and the spirit of Mammon. Each imposes its own law and sets up its own God. If the one is Christian, the other is antichristian. Many of the early Christians saw in the grasping, crushing hardness of Roman rule a spiritual force that was set against the dominion of Christ and that found a religious expression in the cult of the genius of the Emperor. The conflict between that brutal force and the heavenly power of salvation was portrayed in the Revelation of John under the image of the Beast and the Lamb. If any one thinks that conflict is being duplicated in our own day, he is not far out of the way.

Whoever declares that the law of Christ is impracticable in actual life, and has to be superseded in business by the laws of capitalism, to that extent dethrones Christ and enthrones Mammon. When we try to keep both enthroned at the same time in different sections of our life we do what Christ says cannot be done, and accept a double life as the normal morality for our nation and for many individuals in it. Ruskin said; "I know no previous instance in history of a nation's establishing a systematic disobedience to the first principles of its professed religion."

The most important advance in the knowledge of God that a modern man can make is to understand that the Father of Jesus Christ does not stand for the permanence of the capitalistic system.

The most searching intensification that a man can experience in his insight into sin and his consciousness of sin is to comprehend the sinfulness of our economic system and to realize his own responsibility for it.

The largest evangelistic and missionary task of the Church and of the individual Christian is to awaken the nation to a conviction of that sinfulness and to a desire for salvation from it.

The bravest act of faith and hope that a Christian can make is to believe and hope that such a salvation is possible and that the law of Jesus Christ will yet prevail in business.

The most comprehensive and intensive act of love in which we could share would be a collective action of the community to change the present organization of the economic life into a new order that would rest on the Christian principles of equal rights, democratic distribution of economic power, the supremacy of the common good, the law of mutual dependence and service, and the uninterrupted flow of good will throughout the human family.

*   *   *

An unChristian economic order tempts men and debases character, sets individuals and classes into unfraternal antagonism to one another, and institutionalizes widespread disloyalty to the common good. A Christian economic order would aid in training sound and strong individuals by its assimilating influence, would place men in righteous relations to one another and to the commonwealth, and so promote the Christian purpose of giving all a chance to live a saved life.

*   *   *

A Christian order must be just. Unjust privilege and unearned incomes debase the upper classes by parasitism, deprive the lower classes of their opportunity to develop their God-given life, and make genuine fraternity impossible between the classes.

A Christian economic order must offer to all members of the community the blessed influence of property rights. If modern industrial conditions no longer permit the workers a chance to own their productive plant and to accumulate enough for security, property must take the new form of a share in social wealth which will guarantee security in sickness and age and give a man an assured position in the workshop of the nation.

Our economic order must work away from one-man power toward the democratizing of industry. It must take the taxing powers of monopoly from an irresponsible aristocracy and put the people in full control of their own livelihood.

458

It must do away with the present unethical inequalities of wealth and approximate a human equality.

A Christian economic order must organize all workers in systematic and friendly cooperation, and so create the material basis for Christian fraternity.

These fundamental demands of the Christian spirit are all simple and almost axiomatic, but they cut deep and are revolutionary enough to prove that they are really the laws of the Kingdom of God on earth.

*　　*　　*

. . . [T]he Kingdom of God includes the economic life; for it means the progressive transformation of all human affairs by the thought and spirit of Christ. And a full salvation also includes the economic life; for it involves the opportunity for every man to realize the full humanity which God has put into him as a promise and a call; it means a clean, rich, just, and brotherly life between him and his fellows; it means a chance to be single-hearted, and not to be coerced into a double life.

But, on the other hand, no outward economic readjustments will answer our needs. It is not this thing or that thing our nation needs, but a new mind and heart, a new conception of the way we all ought to live together, a new conviction about the worth of a human life and the use God wants us to make of our own lives. We want a revolution both inside and outside. We want a moral renovation of public opinion and a revival of religion. Laws and constitutions are mighty and searching, but while the clumsy hand of the law fumbles at the gate below, the human soul sits in its turret amid its cruel plunder and chuckles. A righteous public opinion may bring the proudest sinner low. But the most pervasive scrutiny, a control which follows our actions to their fountainhead where the desires and motives of the soul are born, is exerted only by personal religion.

But here again we are compelled to turn to our economic life. What if the public opinion on which we rely is tainted and purposely poisoned? What if our religion is drugged and sick? The mammonism generated by our economic life is debilitating our religion so that its hand lies nerve-less on our conscience. Jesus told us it would be so. He put the dilemma flatly before us: "Ye cannot serve God and Mammon. If ye love the one, ye will hate the other." Every proof that we love Mammon with all our heart and all our soul raises the presumption that we have lost the love of God and are merely going through the motions when we worship him. We can measure the general apostasy by noting the wonder and love that follow every man who has even in some slight degree really turned his back on money. Men crowd around him like exiles around a man who brings them news from home.

So we must begin at both ends simultaneously. We must change our economic system in order to preserve our conscience and our religious faith; we must renew and strengthen our religion in order to be able to change our economic system. This is a two-handed job; a one-handed man will bungle it.

*　　*　　*

When Archimedes discovered the laws of leverage, he cried Λὸς ποῦ στῶ. He thought he could hoist the bulk of the earth from its grooves if only he had a standing place and a fulcrum for his lever. God wants to turn humanity right side up, but he needs a fulcrum. Every saved soul is a fixed point on which God can rest his lever. A divine world is ever pressing into this imperfect and sinful world, demanding admission and realization for its higher principles, and every inspired man is a channel through which the spirit of God can enter humanity. Every higher era must be built on a higher moral law and a purer experience of religion. Therefore the most immediate and constant need in Christianizing the social order is for more religious individuals.

*　　*　　*

Create a ganglion chain of redeemed personalities in a commonwealth, and all things become possible. "What the soul is in the body, that are Christians in the world." The political events of 1912 have furnished fresh proof that after individuals have preached their faith long enough, the common mind reaches the point of saturation, and moral conviction begins to be precipitated in solid layers. At such times even poor Judas thinks he would like to join the Messianic movement and be an apostle, and the rotten nobility of France follow the peasant girl:

> The White Maid, and the white horse,
> and the flapping banner of God;
> Black hearts riding for money; red hearts
> riding for fame;
> The Maid who rides for France,
> and the king who rides for shame;
> Gentlemen, fools, and a saint riding
> in Christ's high name.

"Force and Right rule the world; Force till Right is ready." The more individuals we have who love the right for its own sake and move toward it of their own will, the less force and compulsion do we need. Here is one of the permanent functions of the Christian church. It must enlist the will and the love of men and women for God, mark them with the Cross of Christ, and send them out to finish up the work which Christ began. Is the church supplying society with the necessary equipment of such personalities? Let us grant that it can never reach all; but is it making Christian revolutionists of those whom it does teach and control? Jesus feared the proselyting efforts of the Jewish church, because it made men worse than they were before. Some people today who carry the stamp of ecclesiastical religion most legibly are the most hopeless cases so far as social spirit and effort are concerned. The spiritual efficiency of the church is therefore one of the most serious practical questions for the Christianizing of the social order. We have shown that the American churches have been to a large extent Christianized in their fundamental organization, and every step in their redemption has facilitated social progress and increased the forces available for righteousness. But the process of Christianizing the church is not yet complete.

To become fully Christian the churches must turn their back on dead issues and face their present tasks. There is probably not a single denomination which is not thrusting on its people questions for which no man would care and of which only antiquarians would know if the churches did not keep these questions alive. Our children sometimes pull the clothes of their grandparents out of old chests in the attic and masquerade in long-tailed coats and crinolines. We religious folks who

air the issues of the sixteenth century go through the same mummery in solemn earnest, while the enemy is at the gate.

*   *   *

To become fully Christian the church must come out of spiritual isolation. In theory and practice the church has long constituted a world by itself. It has been governed by ecclesiastical motives and interests which are often remote from the real interests of humanity, and has almost uniformly set church questions ahead of social questions. It has often built a soundproof habitation in which people could live for years without becoming definitely conscious of the existence of prostitution, child labor, or tenement crowding. It has offered peace and spiritual tranquillity to men and women who needed thunderclaps and lightnings. Like all the rest of us, the church will get salvation by finding the purpose of its existence outside of itself, in the Kingdom of God, the perfect life of the race.

To become fully Christian the church must still further emancipate itself from the dominating forces of the present era. In an age of political despotism our fathers cut the church loose from state control and state support, and therewith released the moral forces of progress. In an age of financial autocracy we must be far more watchful than we have been lest we bargain away the spiritual freedom of the church for opulent support.

We do not want to substitute social activities for religion. If the church comes to lean on social preachings and doings as a crutch because its religion has become paralytic, may the Lord have mercy on us all! We do not want less religion; we want more; but it must be a religion that gets its orientation from the Kingdom of God. To concentrate our efforts on personal salvation, as orthodoxy has done, or on soul culture, as liberalism has done, comes close to refined selfishness. All of us who have been trained in egotistic religion need a conversion to Christian Christianity, even if we are bishops or theological professors. Seek ye first the Kingdom of God and God's righteousness, and the salvation of your souls will be added to you. Our personality is of divine and eternal value, but we see it aright only when we see it as part of mankind. Our religious individuality must get its interpretation from the supreme fact of social solidarity. "What hast thou that thou hast not received?" Then what hast thou that thou dost not owe? Prayer ought to be a keen realization of our fellows, and not a forgetfulness of the world. A religion which realizes in God the bond that binds all men together can create the men who will knit the social order together as an organized brotherhood.

This, then, is one of the most practical means for the Christianizing of the social order, to multiply the number of minds who have turned in conscious repentance from the old maxims, the old admirations, and the old desires, and have accepted for good and all the Christian law with all that it implies for modern conditions. When we have a sufficient body of such, the old order will collapse like the walls of Jericho when the people "shouted with a great shout" and "every man went straight before him" at the wall. No wrong can stand very long after the people have lost their reverence for it and begin to say "Boo" to it.

Mending the social order is not like repairing a clock in which one or two parts are broken. It is rather like restoring diseased or wasted tissues, and when that has to be done, every organ and cell of the body is heavily taxed. During the reconstructive process every one of us must be an especially good cell in whatever organ of the social body we happen to be located. The tissues of society which it will be hardest to replace by sound growth are represented by the class of the poor and the class of the rich. Both are the product of ages of social disease. Christianizing the social order involves a sanitation of the defective and delinquent classes, and of the classes living on unearned incomes. All these need religious salvation.

*   *   *

The sanitation of the wealthy classes is another problem; there we deal, not with the misery and waywardness of the poor, but with excessive material power. Some think it is idle to appeal to the rich to change their own lives; it will have to be changed for them. I do not believe it. As a class they will doubtless go their way, eating and drinking, marrying and giving in marriage till the flood comes. But individuals will respond; more of them, I believe, than in any similar situation in

history before. Large groups of them have of late traveled miles in the direction of the fraternal life.

Even if there are only a few, their coming counts. Something happens when Moses leaves the palace of Pharaoh and joins the fortunes of his people. At a directors' meeting a single steady voice lifted for humanity and six percent and against inhumanity and eight percent, cannot be disregarded forever, and that voice may mean health and decency for hundreds. Socialists justly say that there is no instance in history where one of the possessing classes has voluntarily given up its privileges. But is there any case where a poor and oppressed class has made a permanent and successful advance toward emancipation without help from individuals of the higher classes?

The desire for social esteem is one of the strongest and most subtle forces in social life. The individual always toils for whatever his class regards as the game. He will collect scalps for his belt, Philistine foreskins for a bridal gift to his beloved, silver cups or wreaths of wild olive as athletic trophies, funny titles, shady millions, — it's all the same thing. Now, a few self-confident men can create a new basis of esteem in their class and therewith change the direction of effort. If a few redeemed minds in a given business community begin to yawn at the stale game of piling up and juggling money, and plunge into the more fascinating game of remaking a city, others will follow them. They cannot help it. God and the instinct of imitation will make them.

*   *   *

Every rich man who has taken the Christian doctrine of stewardship seriously has thereby expropriated himself after a fashion and become manager where he used to be owner. If a man in addition realizes that some part of his fortune consists of unearned money, accumulated by one of the forms of injustice which have been legalized by our social order, it becomes his business as a Christian and a gentleman to make restitution in some way. There is no sincere repentance without restitution and confession of wrong. If I discovered that I or my grandfather, had, knowingly or unknowingly, by some manipulation or error of the survey, added to my farm a ten-acre strip which belonged to my neighbor, could I go on harvesting the crops on it and say nothing? It is true that restitution of wealth absorbed from great communities through many years is a complicated matter, and that the giving away of large sums is dangerous business which may do as much harm as good. Yet some way must be found. Since the rich have gained their wealth by appropriating public functions and by using the taxing powers which ought to belong to the community alone, the fittest way of restitution is to undertake public service for which the state in its present impoverished condition has no means, such as the erection and running of public baths, playgrounds, and civic centers. But the moral value of such gifts would be almost incalculably increased if some acknowledgment were made that these funds were drawn from the people and belonged to them. Every time any rich man has indicated that he felt troubled in mind about his right to his wealth, the public heart has warmed toward him with a sense of forgiveness. If some eminent man should have the grace and wisdom to make a confession of wrong on behalf of his whole class, it would have a profound influence on public morality and social peace.

If a rich man has a really redeemed conscience and intellect, the best way to give away his unearned wealth would be to keep it and use it as a tool to make the recurrence of such fortunes as his own forever impossible. The Salvation Army sets a saved girl to save other girls, and that is the best way to keep her saved. By the same token a man whose forefathers made their money in breweries or distilleries ought to use it to fight alcoholism; a man who made his by land speculation should help to solve the housing question or finance the single-tax movement; a man who has charged monopoly prices for the necessaries of life should teach the people to organize cooperative societies; and so forth.

Men and women of the wealthy class who have been converted to the people as well as to God can perform a service of the highest value by weakening the resistance which their classes will inevitably offer to the equalization of property. That resistance has been by far the most important cause why humanity has been so backward in its social and moral development. The resistance of the upper classes has again and again blocked and frustrated hopeful upward movements, kept useful classes of the people in poverty and degrada-

tion, and punished the lovers of humanity with martyrdom of body or soul. The Cross of Christ stands for the permanent historical fact that the men who have embodied the saving power of God have always been ill treated by those who profited by sin.

*   *   *

So far from being dreams these suggestions are hard sense. If I were rich myself, I could state them far more strongly. The call to place unearned wealth at the service of the people's cause is today the daring short cut to great experiences, to the love and confidence of all good men, and almost the only way to fame open to most rich men. It is the "open but unfrequented path to immortality." It is also the path to peace of heart and the joy of life. The sacrifices demanded by a religious conversion always seem sore and insuperable, but every religious man will agree that after the great surrender is made, there is a radiant joy that marks a great culmination of life. All the remaining years are ennobled. God is the great joy. Whenever we have touched the hem of his garment by some righteous action, we get so much satisfaction that we can be well content even if we get no further reward or recognition, or even if we suffer hurt and persecution for it.

82. The Law of Love in Politics and Economics

REINHOLD NIEBUHR

The effort of the modern church to correct the limitations of the orthodox church toward the political order has resulted, on the whole, in the substitution of sentimental illusions for the enervating pessimism of orthodoxy. The orthodox church dismissed the immediate relevancy of the law of love for politics. The modern church declared it to be relevant without qualification and insisted upon the direct application of the principle of the Sermon on the Mount to the problems of politics and economics as the only way of salvation for a sick society. The orthodox church saw the economic order as a realm of demonic forces in which only the most tenuous and tentative order was possible; the modern church approached the injustices and conflicts of this world with a gay and easy confidence. Men had been ignorantly selfish. They would now be taught the law of love. The church had failed to teach the law of love adequately because it had allowed the simplicities of the gospel to be overlaid with a layer of meaningless theological jargon. Once this increment of obscurantist theology had been brushed aside, the church would be free to preach salvation to the world. Its word of salvation would be that all men ought to love one another. It was as simple as that.

Reinhold Niebuhr (1892–1971) was professor of theology at Union Theological Seminary and, arguably, the most important figure in theological ethics in this century. Among his many works are *Moral Man and Immoral Society; Children of Light, Children of Darkness;* and *The Nature and Destiny of Man.*

From Reinhold Niebuhr, *An Interpretation of Christian Ethics* (New York: Harper & Row, 1935).

Thomas Jefferson stated this faith of the liberal Christianity as well as any liberal theologian: "When we shall have done with the incomprehensible jargon of the Trinitarian arithmetic, that the three are one and the one three, when we shall have knocked down the artificial scaffolding, reared to to mask the simple structure of Jesus, when, in short, we shall have unlearned everything which has been taught since his day and got back to the pure and simple doctrines which he inculcated, we shall then be truly and worthily his disciples and my opinion is if nothing had been added to what flowed purely from his lips, the whole world would all this day be Christian."[1] It is fitting that Jefferson, rather than the many theologians of the past two centuries who have repeated such sentiments, should be allowed to state this creed. For Jefferson was a typical child of the Age of Reason; and it is the naive optimism of the Age of Reason, rather than the more paradoxical combination of pessimism and optimism of prophetic religion, which the modern church has preached as "the simple gospel of Jesus." The Age of Reason was right in protesting against theological subtleties which transmuted a religion of love into a support of traditional and historic injustice. It was right in assigning an immediate relevance for politics and economics to the law of love and the ideal of brotherhood. In doing that it recaptured some resources of prophetic religion which historic Christianity had lost.

Yet it was wrong in the optimism which assumed that the law of love needed only to be stated persuasively to overcome the selfishness of the human heart. The unhappy consequence of that optimism was to discourage interest in the necessary mechanisms of social justice at the precise moment in history when the development of a technical civilization required more than ever that social ideals be implemented with economic and political techniques, designed to correct the injustices and brutalities which flow inevitably from an unrestrained and undisciplined exercise of economic power.

The purely moralistic approach of the modern church to politics is really a religio-moral version of *laissez-faire* economics. Jefferson's dictum that

---

1. Quoted by T. C. Hall: *The Religious Background of American Culture,* p. 172.

the least possible government is the best possible government is a secular version of the faith of the modern church that justice must be established purely by appeals to the moral ideal and with as little machinery as possible. It would be as unfair to assume that the anarchistic and libertarian assumptions which underlie this belief represent a conscious conformity of the liberal church to the prejudices of business classes, which have been able to profit from such doctrine, as it would be to accuse Jefferson of devising a political creed for the benefit of his Hamiltonian opponents of the world of finance and industry. It is true, nevertheless, that the plutocracy of America has found the faith of the liberal church in purely moral suasion a conveniently harmless doctrine just as it appropriated Jeffersonian and *laissez-fair* economic theory for its own purposes, though the theory was first elaborated by agrarian and frontier enemies of big business.

The moralistic utopianism of the liberal church has been expressed in various forms. Liberal theologians sometimes go to the length of decrying all forms of politics as contrary to the Christian spirit of love. Sometimes they deprecate only coercive politics without asking themselves the question whether any political order has ever existed without coercion. Sometimes, with greater realism, they merely declare all forms of violent coercion to be incompatible with the Christian ethic.

In justice to the wing of the liberal church which has sought to interpret the "social gospel," it must be admitted that it was usually realistic enough to know that justice in the social order could only be achieved by political means, including the coercion of groups which refuse to accept a common social standard. Nevertheless, some of the less rigorous thinkers of the social gospel school tried to interpret the law of love in terms which would rule out the most obvious forms of pressure for the attainment of justice. In one of the best-known social gospel books of the early part of the century Shailer Mathews wrote: "The impulse to get justice is not evangelical; the impulse to give justice is. The great command which Jesus lays upon his followers is not to have their wrongs righted, but to right the wrongs of others." This note of love perfectionism from the gospel is made applicable to the political order without reservation: "Despite the difficulty of realizing its ideal, the emphasis laid by the gospel upon the giving of justice rather than upon the getting of justice is consonant with life as we know it. Revolutions have seldom, if ever, won more rights than the more thoughtful among the privileged would have been ready to grant."[2] Dr. Mathews partially qualifies this strikingly naïve picture of the political problem by admitting "that to get justice for others by compelling the overprivileged to give it to them may be the quintessence of love, and insofar as the motives of the champions of the underprivileged are of a sort which the gospel declares to be the very quality of God."[3] Unfortunately, this qualification in the interest of political realism fails to find any place in the Kingdom of God for the underprivileged themselves who may be fighting to "get justice." The formula gives moral sanction only to the kindhearted "champions of the underprivileged."

*   *   *

On the question whether coercion should be used to attain justice, the teaching of the liberal church, particularly in America, has been full of confusion. It was impossible for the church to escape the fact of coercion or to deny its necessity, yet it felt that the Christian gospel demanded uncoerced cooperation. It therefore contented itself, as a rule, with the regretful acceptance of the fact and necessity of coercion, but expressed the hope that the Christian gospel would soon permeate the whole of society to such a degree that coercion in the realm of politics and economics would no longer be necessary. Shailer Mathews, in a recent book, which allows the history of the past twenty years to add surprisingly little to his insights of twenty years ago, declares: "There is a general uncertainty as to whether love and cooperation are a practical basis upon which to build economic life. . . . Can men be trusted to cooperate sincerely for their own well-doing or must groups be coerced into doing that which is to their advantage?" The question remains unanswered, but is asked again in the same chapter and answered with a faint hope: "Whether the constructive forces will find capitalist groups sufficiently ready

2. Shailer Mathews, *The Gospel and the Modern Man*, p. 253.

3. Op. cit., p. 255.

to democratize privilege and treat wage-earners as partners in the productive process remains to be seen. Humanity does not seem to be naturally generous and the transformation from acquisitiveness to economic cooperation is difficult. The neglect of the principle of sacrifice which Jesus so clearly saw was involved in that personal cooperation which he called love, continues to prevent the betterment of our economic relations." Upon the basis of the slight hope that men will be more loving than they now are Dr. Mathews then arrives at the conclusion: "The Christian principle of love applied to economic groups stands over against revolutionary coercion. The Christian movement emphasizes a moral process which does not stand committed to an economic philosophy."[4] Christianity, in other words, is interpreted as the preaching of a moral ideal, which men do not follow, but which they ought to. The church must continue to hope for something that has never happened. "The success of (industrial) reorganization depends largely upon the readiness of various groups involved to sacrifice profits in the interest of the general good. The fact that such goodwill is not fully exhibited explains the need of legal coercion. But the emphasis upon cooperation is another testimony to the validity of the principle of love which Christianity, despite the blundering and selfishness of Christians, has embodied and which it is its mission to evoke."[5]

*   *   *

The unvarying refrain of the liberal church in its treatment of politics is that love and cooperation are superior to conflict and coercion, and that therefore they must be and will be established. The statement of the ideal is regarded as a sufficient guarantee of its ultimate realization. . . . Liberal Christian literature abounds in the monotonous reiteration of the pious hope that people might be good and loving, in which case all the nasty business of politics could be dispensed with. In the same vein church congresses have been passing resolutions for the past decades surveying the sorry state of the world's affairs and assuring the world that all this would be changed if only men

lived by the principles of the gospel. Recently the Federal Council of Churches passed resolutions commending the Christian character of Roosevelt's N.R.A. programme, but deprecating the degree of coercion it involved. The implication was that an ideal political programme would depend purely upon voluntary cooperation of the various economic forces of the nation.

The sum total of the liberal church's effort to apply the law of love to politics without qualification is really a curious medley of hopes and regrets. The church declares that men ought to live by the law of love and that nations as well as individuals ought to obey it; that neither individuals nor nations do; that nations do so less than individuals; but that the church must insist upon it; that, unfortunately the church which is to insist upon the law has not kept it itself; but that it has sometimes tried and must try more desperately; that the realization of the law is not in immediate prospect, but the Christian must continue to hope. These appeals to the moral will and this effort to support the moral will by desperate hopes are politically as unrealistic as they are religiously superficial. If the liberal church had had less moral idealism and more religious realism its approach to the political problem would have been less inept and fatuous. Liberal solutions of the social problem never take the permanent difference between man's collective behaviour and the moral ideals of an individual life into consideration. Very few seem to recognize that even in the individual there is a law in his members which wars against the law that is in his mind.

Liberal Christianity has not been totally oblivious to the necessary mechanisms and techniques of social justice in economic and political life. But the total weight of its testimonies has been on the side of sentimental moralism. It has insisted that goodwill can establish justice, whatever the political and economic mechanisms may be. It has insisted on this futile moralism at a moment in history when the whole world faces disaster because the present methods of production and distribution are no longer able to maintain the peace and order of society.

Against this moralism it is necessary to insist that the moral achievement of individual goodwill is not a substitute for the mechanisms of social control. It may perfect and purify, but it cannot

4. Shailer Mathews, *Christianity and Social Progress*, Chap. vi.

5. Op. cit., p. 177.

create basic justice. Basic justice in any society depends upon the right organization of men's common labour, the equalization of their social power, regulation of their common interests, and adequate restraint upon the inevitable conflict of competing interests. The health of a social organism depends upon the adequacy of its social structure as much as does the health of the body upon the biochemical processes. No degree of goodwill alone can cure a deficiency in glandular secretions; and no moral idealism can overcome a basic mechanical defect in the social structure. The social theories of liberal Christianity deny, in effect, the physical basis of the life of the spirit. They seem to look forward to some kind of discarnate spirituality.

The function of a social mechanism is much more important than liberal Christianity realizes and much more positive than that of acting as a "dyke against sin," as in the view of orthodox Christianity. A profound religion will not give itself to the illusion that perfect justice can be achieved in a sinful world. But neither can it afford to dismiss the problem of justice or to transcend it by premature appeals to the goodwill of individuals. Social techniques will not be changed in the interest of justice without the aid of moral incentives. But moral purpose must actually become incorporated in adequate social mechanisms if it is not to be frustrated and corrupted.

Living, as we do, in a society in which the economic mechanisms automatically create disproportions of social power and social privilege so great that they are able to defy and evade even the political forces which seek to equalize and restrain them, it is inevitable that they should corrupt the purely moral forces which are meant to correct them. Christian love in a society of great inequality means philanthropy. Philanthropy always compounds the display of power with the expression of pity. Sometimes it is even used as a conscious effort to evade the requirements of justice, as, for instance, when charity appeals during the Hoover administration were designed to obviate the necessity of higher taxation for the needs of the unemployed. The cynicism of the victims of injustice toward philanthropy is a natural consequence of the inevitable hypocrisy and self-deception which corrupts philanthropy even when its conscious motives are above reproach. There

will never be a social order so perfect as to obviate the necessity of perfecting its rough justice by every achievement of social and moral goodwill which education and religion may be able to generate. But it must be clearly understood that voluntary acts of kindness which exceed the requirements of coercive justice are never substitutes for, but additions to, the coercive system of social relationships through which alone a basic justice can be guaranteed.

In modern society the basic mechanisms of justice are becoming more and more economic rather than political, in the sense that economic power is the most basic power. Political power is derived from it to such a degree that a just political order is not possible without the reconstruction of the economic order. Specifically this means the reconstruction of the property system. Property has always been power, and inequalities in possession have always made for an unjust distribution of the common social fund. But a technical civilization has transmuted the essentially static disproportions of power and privilege of an agrarian economy into dynamic forces. Centralization of power and privilege and the impoverishment of the multitudes develop at such a pace, in spite of slight efforts at equalization through the pressure of political power upon the economic forces, that the whole system of distribution is imperiled. Markets for the ever-increasing flood of goods are not adequate because the buying power of the multitudes is too restricted. Consequently, a periodic glut of goods leads to unemployment crises and general depressions. Efforts to solve this problem, short of the socialization of productive property, lead to a dangerous increase in the power of the state without giving the state final authority over the dominant economic power.

Whatever the defects of Marxism as a philosophy and as a religion, and even as a political strategy, its analyses of the technical aspects of the problem of justice have not been successfully challenged, and every event in contemporary history seems to multiply the proofs of its validity. The political theories of the moralists and religious idealists who try to evade or transcend the technical and mechanical bases of justice are incredibly naïve compared with them. The programme of the Marxian will not create the millennium for which he hopes. It will merely

466

provide the only possible property system compatible with the necessities of a technical age. It is rather tragic that the achievement of a new property system as a prerequisite of basic justice should be complicated by the utopian illusions of Marxism on the one hand and the moralistic evasions of the mechanical problem by liberal Christianity and secular liberalism on the other.

When dealing with the actual human situation realistically and pragmatically it is impossible to fix upon a single moral absolute. Equal justice remains the only possible, though hardly a precise, criterion of value. Since no life has value if all life is not equally sacred, the highest social obligation is to guide the social struggle in such a way that the most stable and balanced equilibrium of social forces will be achieved and all life will thereby be given equal opportunities of development. But so many contingent factors arise in any calculation of the best method of achieving equal justice that absolute standards are useless. How shall a hazardous method of achieving a predictable social end be measured against a safe method of achieving an unpredictable goal? How shall one gauge the security of the moment against an insecure but promising future? Or how shall one test the validity of any social expectation? To what degree is it illusory and in how far does the illusory element invalidate it? Such questions are not answered primarily by nice rational calculations. They are finally answered through exigencies of history in which contingent factors and unpredictable forces may carry more weight than the nicest and most convincing abstract speculation.

Political problems drive pure moralists to despair because in them the freedom of the spirit must come to terms with the contingencies of nature, the moral ideal must find a proper mechanism for its incarnation, and the ideal principle must be sacrificed to guarantee its partial realization. For the Christian the love commandment must be made relevant to the relativities of the social struggle, even to hazardous and dubious relativities. No doubt prophetic religion must place the inevitable opportunism of statesmanship under a religious perspective. But if we are to have prophetic critics of the statesman may they be prophets who know what kind of a world we are living in and learn how to place every type of statesmanship under the divine condemnation. A prophetic criticism of political opportunism, which mistakes moral squeamishness for religious rigour is easily captured and corrupted by the conservative forces in a social struggle. The "decencies" are usually on the conservative side. The more basic moral values are more likely to rest with the standard of the attacking forces, particularly since human burden-bearers usually have more patience than rebellious heroism and are not inclined to attack established institutions and social arrangements until their situation has become literally intolerable.

83. Private Property and the Universal Destination of Material Goods

POPE JOHN PAUL II

. . . The original source of all that is good is the very act of God, who created both the earth and man, and who gave the earth to man so that he might have dominion over it by his work and enjoy its fruits (Gen 1:28). God gave the earth to the whole human race for the sustenance of all its members, without excluding or favouring anyone. This is *the foundation of the universal destination of the earths goods.* The earth, by reason of its fruitfulness and its capacity to satisfy human needs, is God's first gift for the sustenance of human life. But the earth does not yield its fruits without a particular human response to God's gift, that is to say, without work. It is through work that man, using his intelligence and exercising his freedom, succeeds in dominating the earth and making it a fitting home. In this way, he makes part of the earth his own, precisely the part which he has acquired through work; this is *the origin of individual property.* Obviously, he also has the responsibility not to hinder others from having their

---

John Paul II (1920–) (born Karol Wojtyla) is the current bishop of Rome and pope of the Roman Catholic Church. Trained in moral theology, he has written *Sources of Renewal: The Implementation of the Second Vatican Council; Sign of Contradiction; The Redeemer of Man;* and *Christian Meaning of Human Suffering.*

From John Paul II, *Centesimus Annus* (Office for Publishing and Promotion Services U.S. Catholic Conference, 1990).

own part of God's gift; indeed, he must cooperate with others so that together all can dominate the earth.

In history, these two factors — *work* and *the land* — are to be found at the beginning of every human society. However, they do not always stand in the same relationship to each other. At one time *the natural fruitfulness of the earth* appeared to be, and was in fact, the primary factor of wealth, while work was, as it were, the help and support for this fruitfulness. In our time, *the role of human work* is becoming increasingly important as the productive factor both of non-material and of material wealth. Moreover, it is becoming clearer how a person's work is naturally interrelated with the work of others. More than ever, work is *work with others* and *work for others:* it is a matter of doing something for someone else. Work becomes ever more fruitful and productive to the extent that people become more knowledgeable of the productive potentialities of the earth and more profoundly cognizant of the needs of those for whom their work is done.

In our time, in particular, there exists another form of ownership which is becoming no less important than land: *the possession of know-how, technology, and skill.* The wealth of the industrialized nations is based much more on this kind of ownership than on natural resources.

Mention has just been made of the fact that *people work with each other,* sharing in a "community of work" which embraces ever widening circles. A person who produces something other than for his own use generally does so in order that others may use it after they have paid a just price, mutually agreed upon through free bargaining. It is precisely the ability to foresee both the needs of others and the combinations of productive factors most adapted to satisfying those needs that constitutes another important source of wealth in modern society. Besides, many goods cannot be adequately produced through the work of an isolated individual; they require the cooperation of many people in working towards a common goal. Organizing such a productive effort, planning its duration in time, making sure that it corresponds in a positive way to the demands which it must satisfy, and taking the necessary risks — all this too is a source of wealth in today's society. In this way, the *role* of disciplined and creative *human work* and, as an essential part of that work, *initiative and entrepreneurial ability* becomes increasingly evident and decisive.[1]

This process, which throws practical light on a truth about the person which Christianity has constantly affirmed, should be viewed carefully and favourably. Indeed, besides the earth, man's principal resource is *man himself*. His intelligence enables him to discover the earth's productive potential and the many different ways in which human needs can be satisfied. It is his disciplined work in close collaboration with others that makes possible the creation of ever more extensive *working communities* which can be relied upon to transform man's natural and human environments. Important virtues are involved in this process, such as diligence, industriousness, prudence in undertaking reasonable risks, reliability and fidelity in interpersonal relationships, as well as courage in carrying out decisions which are difficult and painful but necessary, both for the overall working of a business and in meeting possible setbacks.

The modern *business economy* has positive aspects. Its basis is human freedom exercised in the economic field, just as it is exercised in many other fields. Economic activity is indeed but one sector in a great variety of human activities, and like every other sector, it includes the right to freedom, as well as the duty of making responsible use of freedom. But it is important to note that there are specific differences between the trends of modern society and those of the past, even the recent past. Whereas at one time the decisive factor of production was *the land*, and later capital — understood as a total complex of the instruments of production — today the decisive factor is increasingly *man himself*, that is, his knowledge, especially his scientific knowledge, his capacity for interrelated and compact organization, as well as his ability to perceive the needs of others and to satisfy them.

However, the risks and problems connected with this kind of process should be pointed out. The fact is that many people, perhaps the majority today, do not have the means which would enable them to take their place in an effective and humanly dignified way within a productive system in which work is truly central. They have no possibility of acquiring the basic knowledge which would enable them to express their creativity and develop their potential. They have no way of entering the network of knowledge and intercommunication which would enable them to see their qualities appreciated and utilized. Thus, if not actually exploited, they are to a great extent marginalized; economic development takes place over their heads, so to speak, when it does not actually reduce the already narrow scope of their old subsistence economies. They are unable to compete against the goods which are produced in ways which are new and which properly respond to needs, needs which they had previously been accustomed to meeting through traditional forms of organization. Allured by the dazzle of an opulence which is beyond their reach, and at the same time driven by necessity, these people crowd the cities of the Third World where they are often without cultural roots, and where they are exposed to situations of violent uncertainty, without the possibility of becoming integrated. Their dignity is not acknowledged in any real way, and sometimes there are even attempts to eliminate them from history through coercive forms of demographic control which are contrary to human dignity.

Many other people, while not completely marginalized, live in situations in which the struggle for a bare minimum is uppermost. These are situations in which the rules of the earliest period of capitalism still flourish in conditions of "ruthlessness" in no way inferior to the darkest moments of the first phase of industrialization. In other cases the land is still the central element in the economic process, but those who cultivate it are excluded from ownership and are reduced to a state of quasi-servitude.[2] In these cases, it is still possible today, as in the days of *Rerum Novarum*, to speak of inhuman exploitation. In spite of the great changes which have taken place in the more advanced societies, the human inadequacies of capitalism and the resulting domination of things over people are far from disappearing. In fact, for the poor, to the lack of material goods has been added a lack of knowledge and training which

1. Cf. Encyclical Letter *Sollicitudo Rei Socialis*, 15: loc. cit., 528-531.

2. Cf. Encyclical Letter *Laborem Exercens*, 21: loc. cit., 632-634.

prevents them from escaping their state of humiliating subjection.

Unfortunately, the great majority of people in the Third World still live in such conditions. It would be a mistake, however, to understand this "world" in purely geographic terms. In some regions and in some social sectors of that world, development programmes have been set up which are centered on the use not so much of the material resources available but of the "human resources."

Even in recent years it was thought that the poorest countries would develop by isolating themselves from the world market and by depending only on their own resources. Recent experience has shown that countries which did this have suffered stagnation and recession, while the countries which experienced development were those which succeeded in taking part in the general interrelated economic activities at the international level. It seems therefore that the chief problem is that of gaining fair access to the international market, based not on the unilateral principle of the exploitation of the natural resources of these countries but on the proper use of human resources.[3]

However, aspects typical of the Third World also appear in developed countries, where the constant transformation of the methods of production and consumption devalues certain acquired skills and professional expertise, and thus requires a continual effort of retraining and updating. Those who fail to keep up with the times can easily be marginalized, as can the elderly, the young people who are incapable of finding their the place in the life of society and, in general, those who are weakest or part of the so-called Fourth World. The situation of women too is far from easy in these conditions.

It would appear that, on the level of individual nations and of international relations, *the free market* is the most efficient instrument for utilizing resources and effectively responding to needs. But this is true only for those needs which are "solvent," insofar as they are endowed with purchasing power, and for those resources which are "marketable," insofar as they are capable of ob-

taining a satisfactory price. But there are many human needs which find no place on the market. It is a strict duty of justice and truth not to allow fundamental human needs to remain unsatisfied, and not to allow those burdened by such needs to perish. It is also necessary to help these needy people to acquire expertise, to enter the circle of exchange, and to develop their skills in order to make the best use of their capacities and resources. Even prior to the logic of a fair exchange of goods and the forms of justice appropriate to it, there exists *something which is due to man because he is man,* by reason of his lofty dignity. Inseparable from that required "something" is the possibility to survive and, at the same time, to make an active contribution to the common good of humanity.

In Third World contexts, certain objectives stated by *Rerum Novarum* remain valid, and, in some cases, still constitute a goal yet to be reached, if man's work and his very being are not to be reduced to the level of a mere commodity. These objectives include a sufficient wage for the support of the family, social insurance for old age and unemployment, and adequate protection for the conditions of employment.

Here we find a wide range of *opportunities for commitment and effort* in the name of justice on the part of trade unions and other workers' organizations. These defend workers' rights and protect their interests as persons, while fulfilling a vital cultural role, so as to enable workers to participate more fully and honourably in the life of their nation and to assist them along the path of development.

In this sense, it is right to speak of a struggle against an economic system, if the latter is understood as a method of upholding the absolute predominance of capital, the possession of the means of production and of the land, in contrast to the free and personal nature of human work.[4] In the struggle against such a system, what is being proposed as an alternative is not the socialist system, which in fact turns out to be State capitalism, but rather *a society of free work, of enterprise, and of participation.* Such a society is not directed against the market, but demands that the market be appropriately controlled by the forces of society and

---

3. Cf. Paul VI, Encyclical Letter *Populorum Progressio,* 33-42: loc. cit., 273-278.

4. Cf. Encyclical Letter *Laborem Exercens,* 7: loc. cit., 592-594.

by the state, so as to guarantee that the basic needs of the whole of society are satisfied.

The Church acknowledges the legitimate *role of profit* as an indication that a business is functioning well. When a firm makes a profit, this means that productive factors have been properly employed and corresponding human needs have been duly satisfied. But profitability is not the only indicator of a firm's condition. It is possible for the financial accounts to be in order, and yet for the people — who make up the firm's most valuable asset — to be humiliated and their dignity offended. Besides being morally inadmissible, this will eventually have negative repercussions on the firm's economic efficiency. In fact, the purpose of a business firm is not simply to make a profit, but is to be found in its very existence as a *community of persons* who in various ways are endeavouring to satisfy their basic needs, and who form a particular group at the service of the whole of society. Profit is a regulator of the life of a business, but it is not the only one; *other human and moral factors* must also be considered which, in the long term, are at least equally important for the life of a business.

We have seen that it is unacceptable to say that the defeat of so-called "Real Socialism" leaves capitalism as the only model of economic organization. It is necessary to break down the barriers and monopolies which leave so many countries on the margins of development, and to provide all individuals and nations with the basic conditions which will enable them to share in development. This goal calls for programmed and responsible efforts on the part of the entire international community. Stronger nations must offer weaker ones opportunies for taking their place in international life, and the latter must learn how to use these opportunities by making the necessary efforts and sacrifices and by ensuring political and economic stability, the certainty of better prospects for the future, the improvement of workers' skills, and the training of competent business leaders who are conscious of their responsibilities.[5]

At present, the positive efforts which have been made along these lines are being affected by the still largely unsolved problem of the foreign debt of the poorer countries. The principle that debts

5. Cf. ibid., 8: loc. cit., 594-598.

must be paid is certainly just. However, it is not right to demand or expect payment when the effect would be the imposition of political choices leading to hunger and despair for entire peoples. It cannot be expected that the debts which have been contracted should be paid at the price of unbearable sacrifices. In such cases it is necessary to find — as in fact is partly happening — ways to lighten, defer, or even cancel the debt, compatible with the fundamental fight of peoples to subsistence and progress.

It would now be helpful to direct our attention to the specific problems and threats emerging within the more advanced economies and which are related to their particular characteristics. In earlier stages of development, man always lived under the weight of necessity. His needs were few and were determined, to a degree, by the objective structures of his physical makeup. Economic activity was directed towards satisfying these needs. It is clear that today the problem is not only one of supplying people with a sufficient quantity of goods, but also of responding to a *demand for quality:* the quality of the goods to be produced and consumed, the quality of the services to be enjoyed, the quality of the environment and of life in general.

To call for an existence which is qualitatively more satisfying is of itself legitimate, but one cannot fail to draw attention to the new responsibilities and dangers connected with this phase of history. The manner in which new needs arise and are defined is always marked by a more or less appropriate concept of man and of his true good. A given culture reveals its overall understanding of life through the choices it makes in production and consumption. It is here that *the phenomenon of consumerism* arises. In singling out new needs and new means to meet them, one must be guided by a comprehensive picture of man which respects all the dimensions of his being and which subordinates his material and instinctive dimensions to his interior and spiritual ones. If, on the contrary, a direct appeal is made to his instincts — while ignoring in various ways the reality of the person as intelligent and free — then *consumer attitudes* and *lifestyles* can be created which are objectively improper and often damaging to his physical and spiritual health. Of itself, an economic system does not possess criteria for correctly distinguishing new and higher forms of satisfying human needs from artificial new needs which hinder the formation of a mature personality. *Thus a great deal of educational and cultural work* is urgently needed, including the education of consumers in the responsible use of their power of choice, the formation of a strong sense of responsibility among producers and among people in the mass media in particular, as well as the necessary intervention by public authorities.

A striking example of artificial consumption contrary to the health and *dignity* of the human person, and certainly not easy to control, is the use of drugs. Widespread drug use is a sign of a serious malfunction in the social system; it also implies a materialistic and, in a certain sense, destructive "reading" of human needs. In this way the innovative capacity of a free economy is brought to a one-sided and inadequate conclusion. Drugs, as well as pornography and other forms of consumerism which exploit the frailty of the weak, tend to fill the resulting spiritual void.

It is not wrong to want to live better; what is wrong is a style of life which is presumed to be better when it is directed towards "having" rather than "being," and which wants to have more, not in order to be more but in order to spend life in enjoyment as an end in itself.[6] It is therefore necessary to create lifestyles in which the quest for truth, beauty, goodness, and communion with others for the sake of common growth are the factors which determine consumer choices, savings and investments. In this regard, it is not a matter of the duty of charity alone, that is, the duty to give from one's "abundance," and sometimes even out of one's needs, in order to provide what is essential for the life of a poor person. I am referring to the fact that even the decision to invest in one place rather than another, in one productive sector rather than another, is always *a moral and cultural choice.* Given the utter necessity of certain economic conditions and of political stability, the decision to invest, that is, to offer people an opportunity to make good use of their own labour, is also determined by an attitude of human

6. Cf. Second Vatican Ecumenical Council, Pastoral Constitution on the Church in the World of Today *Gaudium et Spes*, 35; Paul VI, Encyclical Letter *Populorum Progressio*, 19: loc. cit., 266f.

sympathy and trust in providence, which reveal the human quality of the person making such decisions.

*   *   *

Returning now to the initial question: can it perhaps be said that, after the failure of communism, capitalism is the victorious social system, and that capitalism should be the goal of the countries now making efforts to rebuild their economy and society? Is this the model which ought to be proposed to the countries of the Third World which are searching for the path to true economic and civil progress?

The answer is obviously complex. If by "capitalism" is meant an economic system which recognizes the fundamental and positive role of business, the market, private property and the resulting responsibility for the means of production, as well as free human creativity in the economic sector, then the answer is certainly in the affirmative, even though it would perhaps be more appropriate to speak of a "business economy," "market economy," or simply "free economy." But if by "capitalism" is meant a system in which freedom in the economic sector is not circumscribed within a strong juridical framework which places it at the service of human freedom in its totality, and which sees it as a particular aspect of that freedom, the core of which is ethical and religious, then the reply is certainly negative.

The Marxist solution has failed, but the realities of marginalization and exploitation remain in the world, especially the Third World, as does the reality of human alienation, especially in the more advanced countries. Against these phenomena the Church strongly raises her voice. Vast multitudes are still living in conditions of great material and moral poverty. The collapse of the communist system in so many countries certainly removes an obstacle to facing these problems in an appropriate and realistic way, but it is not enough to bring about their solution. Indeed, there is a risk that a radical capitalistic ideology could spread which refuses even to consider these problems, in the *a priori* belief that any attempt to solve them is doomed to failure, and which blindly entrusts their solution to the free development of market forces.

The Church has no models to present; models

that are real and truly effective can only arise within the framework of different historical situations, through the efforts of all those who responsibly confront concrete problems in all their social, economic, political and cultural aspects, as these interact with one another.[7] For such a task the Church offers her social teaching as an *indispensable and ideal orientation,* a teaching which, as already mentioned, recognizes the positive value of the market and of enterprise, but which at the same time points out that these need to be oriented towards the common good. This teaching also recognizes the legitimacy of workers' efforts to obtain full respect for their dignity and to gain broader areas of participation in the life of industrial enterprises so that, while cooperating with others and under the direction of others, they can in a certain sense "work for themselves"[8] through the exercise of their intelligence and freedom.

The integral development of the human person through work does not impede but rather promotes the greater productivity and efficiency of work itself, even though it may weaken consolidated power structures. A business cannot be considered only as a "society of capital goods"; it is also a "society of persons" in which people participate in different ways and with specific responsibilities, whether they supply the necessary capital for the company's activities or take part in such activities through their labour. To achieve these goals there is still need for a broad associated workers' movement, directed towards the liberation and promotion of the whole person.

In the light of today's "new things," we have re-read *the relationship between individual or private property and the universal destination of material wealth.* Man fulfils himself by using his intelligence and freedom. In so doing he utilizes the things of this world as objects and instruments and makes them his own. The foundation of the right to private initiative and ownership is to be found in this activity. By means of his work man commits himself, not only for his own sake but also *for others* and *with others.* Each person collaborates in the work of others and for their good. Man works in order to provide for the needs of his family, his community, his nation, and ultimately all humanity.[9] Moreover, he collaborates in the work of his fellow employees, as well as in the work of suppliers and in the customers' use of goods, in a progressively expanding chain of solidarity. Ownership of the means of production, whether in industry or agriculture, is just and legitimate if it serves useful work. It becomes illegitimate, however, when it is not utilized or when it serves to impede the work of others, in an effort to gain a profit which is not the result of the overall expansion of work and the wealth of society, but rather is the result of curbing them or of illicit exploitation, speculation or the breaking of solidarity among working people.[10] Ownership of this kind has no justification, and represents an abuse in the sight of God and man.

The obligation to earn one's bread by the sweat of one's brow also presumes the right to do so. A society in which this right is systematically denied, in which economic policies do not allow workers to reach satisfactory levels of employment cannot be justified from an ethical point of view, nor can that society attain social peace.[11] Just as the person fully realizes himself in the free gift of self, so too ownership morally justifies itself in the creation, at the proper time and in the proper way, of opportunities for work and human growth for all.

---

7. Cf. Second Vatican Ecumenical Council, Pastoral Constitution on the Church in the World of Today *Gaudium et Spes,* 36; Paul VI, Apostolic Epistle *Octogesima Adveniens,* 2-5: loc. cit., 402-405.

8. Cf. Encyclical Letter *Laborem Exercens,* 15: loc. cit., 616-618.

9. Cf. ibid., 10: loc. cit., 600-602.
10. Ibid., 14: loc. cit., 612-616.
11. Cf. ibid., 18: loc. cit., 622-625.

84. Key Themes of Liberation Theology

LEONARDO BOFF AND CLODOVIS BOFF

Liberation theology can be understood as the reflection in faith of the church that has taken to heart the "clear and prophetic option expressing preference for, and solidarity with, the poor" (Puebla, §:1134). It is for them, and with them, that the church seeks to act in a liberative manner. Such an option is neither self-interested nor political, as would be the option of the institutional church for an emergent historical power — the popular classes taking an ever more dominant role in the conduct of affairs. No, this option is made for intrinsic reasons, for reasons inherent in the Christian faith itself. Let us look at them one by one.

Leonardo Boff (1938–) was, until his recent resignation from the priesthood, one of the most outspoken proponents of liberation theology among the Catholic clergy in South America. He remains, along with his brother Clodovis Boff (1944–), professor of theology at the Petropolis Institute in Brazil. Leonardo Boff's works include *Jesus Christ: Liberator — A Critical Christology for Our Time; Liberating Grace; Church: Charism and Power;* and *Passion of Christ, Passion of the World.*

From Leonardo Boff and Clodovis Boff, *Introducing Liberation Theology* (Maryknoll, N.Y.: Orbis Books, 1986).

Theological Reasons for the Option for the Poor

Theological Motivation (on God's Part)

The biblical God is fundamentally a living God, the author and sustainer of all life. Whenever persons see their lives threatened, they can count on the presence and power of God who comes to their aid in one form or another. God feels impelled to come to the help of the oppressed poor: "I have seen the miserable state of my people in Egypt. I have heard their appeal to be free of their slave-drivers. Yes, I am well aware of their sufferings. . . . And now the cry of the sons of Israel has come to me, and I have witnessed the way in which the Egyptians oppress them" (Exod. 3:7, 9). The worship that is pleasing to God must be a "search for justice," and a turning to the needy and the oppressed (see Isa. 1:10-17; 58:6-7; Mark 7:6-13). By opting for the poor, the church imitates our Father who is in heaven (Matt. 5:48).

Christological Motivation (on Christ's Part)

Christ undeniably made a personal option for the poor and held them to be the main recipients of his message (see Luke 6:20; 7:21-22). They fulfill his law of love who, like the good Samaritan (Luke 10:25-37), approach those who have fallen by the wayside, who make into neighbors those who are distant from them, and make neighbors into brothers and sisters. The followers of Christ make this option for the poor and needy the first and foremost way of expressing their faith in Christ in the context of widespread poverty in the world of today.

Eschatological Motivation (from the Standpoint of the Last Judgment)

The gospel of Jesus is quite clear on this point: at the supreme moment of history, when our eternal salvation or damnation will be decided, what will count will be our attitude of acceptance or rejection of the poor (Matt. 25:31-46). The Supreme Judge stands by the side of anyone who is oppressed, seen as a sister or brother of Jesus: "I tell you solemnly insofar as you did it to one of these least brothers of mine, you did it to me"

(Matt. 25:40). Only those who commune in his history with the poor and needy, who are Christ's sacraments, will commune definitively with Christ.

Apostolic Motivation
(on the Part of the Apostles)

From its earliest days the church showed concern for the poor. The apostles and their followers held all things in common so that there would be no poor among them (see Acts 2 and 4). In proclaiming the gospel, the one thing they emphasized was that the poor should not be ignored: "The only thing they insisted on was that we should remember to help the poor, as indeed I was anxious to do" (Gal. 2:10). As the greatest of the Greek fathers, St. John Chrysostom, put it, for the sake of the mission of the church, humankind was divided into pagans and Jews, but with reference to the poor there was no division made whatsoever, because they all belonged to the common mission of the church, as much to that of Peter (to the Jews) as to that of Paul (to the pagans).

Ecclesiological Motivation
(on the Part of the Church)

Faced with the marginalization and impoverishment of the great majority of its members, the church of Latin America, moved by the motivations listed above and seized with a humanistic sense of compassion, has made a solemn "preferential option for the poor," defined at the Medellin conference in 1968 and ratified at Puebla in 1979, when the bishops reaffirmed "the need for conversion on the part of the whole church to a preferential option for the poor, an option aimed at their integral liberation" (§1134).

Because of the sufferings and struggles of the poor, the church in its evangelization seeks to urge all Christians to live their faith in such a way that they also make it a factor for transforming society in the direction of greater justice and fellowship. All need to make the option for the poor: the rich with generosity and no regard for reward, the poor for their fellow poor and those who are even poorer than they.

In the Final Analysis, Who Are the Poor?

This question is often posed by those who cannot really be counted among the poor. They come up with so many definitions and subdivisions of poverty that any real meaning in the term is dissipated, and they end up seeing themselves as one sort of poor — usually the "poor in spirit." When those who are actually poor (lacking the means to sustain life) discuss the question, they easily come to an objective assessment of the situation and of specific remedies that would liberate them from their situation of dehumanizing poverty.

In the context of our examination of liberation theology, we can make a distinction between two basic classes of the poor.

The Socioeconomically Poor

These are all those who lack or are deprived of the necessary means of subsistence — food, clothing, shelter, basic health care, elementary education, and work. There is such a thing as innocent poverty, independent of any will or system (infertile land, chronic drought, etc.), but today in most cases, widespread poverty is maintained by the capitalist system that derives cheap labor from it; this prevents a region or people from being developed, excluding them from minimal human advancement.

There is also a socioeconomic poverty that is unjust because it is produced by a process of exploitation of labor, as denounced by John Paul II in his encyclical *Laborem Exercens* (no. 8). Workers are not paid a just wage, the price of raw materials is held down, the interest charged on loans needed by cooperatives is exorbitant. Poverty in such cases means impoverishment and constitutes injustice on a societal and even international scale.

As we have said, there are various forms of poverty brought about by socioeconomic circumstances, which in addition embody specific oppressions and therefore require specific forms of liberation. So there are those who are *discriminated* against by reason of their race (such as blacks), by reason of their culture (such as native tribes), or by reason of their sex (women). The poorest of the poor are often to be found among such groups, for they incur the whole gamut of oppressions and discriminations. In one base community a woman described herself as oppressed and impoverished on six counts: as a woman, as a prostitute, as a single parent, as black, as poor, and because of her tribal origin. Faced with such conditions, what can being a Christian mean except living the faith in a liberating way, trying every possible avenue of escape from such a set of social iniquities? We have to tell poor persons like her that God loves them in a special way, whatever moral or personal situation they find themselves in, because God in Jesus established solidarity with the poor, especially in his passion and death: "For this reason alone, the poor merit preferential attention, whatever may be the moral or personal situation in which they find themselves" (Puebla, §1142). They are preferred by God and by Christ not because they are good, but because they are poor and wronged. God does not will the poverty they suffer.

Their situation of poverty constitutes a challenge to God himself in his innermost nature and to the Messiah in his mission to restore rights taken away, to bring justice to the helpless and comfort to the abandoned.

The Evangelically Poor

They are all those who place themselves and their strength at the service of God and their sisters and brothers; all those who do not put themselves first, who do not see their security and the meaning of their lives and actions in profiting from this world and accumulating possessions, honor, power, and glory, but open themselves to God in gratitude and disinterestedly serve others, even those they hate, building up means of producing a more worthy life for all. Faced with a predatory, consumerist society, the evangelically poor will use the goods of this world with moderation and sharing. They are neither rigid ascetics who disdain God's creation with all the good things God has placed at the disposal of all, nor spendthrifts who intemperately and selfishly take all they can for themselves. The evangelically poor are those who make themselves available to God in the realization of God's project in this world, and thereby make themselves into instruments and signs of the Kingdom of God. The evangelically poor will establish solidarity with the economically poor and even identify with them, just as the historical Jesus did.

Those who, without being socioeconomically poor, make themselves poor — out of love for and solidarity with the poor — in order to struggle against unjust poverty with them and together seek liberation and justice, are evangelically poor to a preeminent degree. They do not seek to idealize either material poverty, which they see as a consequence of the sin of exploitation, or riches, which they see as the expression of oppressive and selfish accumulation of goods; instead they seek the means to social justice for all. In the Third World context, one cannot be evangelically poor without being in solidarity with the lives, causes, and struggles of the poor and oppressed.

Sometimes love for the poor can become so intense that individuals give up their own station in life to share in the sufferings of the poor, even to the point of sharing their premature death. This is perfect liberation, for they have set themselves free from themselves and, in following Jesus, the poor man from Nazareth, they have freed themselves fully for others and for the God dwelling within these others.

Liberation theology would like to see all Christians, including the socioeconomically poor, evangelically poor. It seeks, in the light of the challenges posed by the oppressed poor, to work out and apply the liberating dimension of faith so that the fruits of the Kingdom of God can be enjoyed within history. These fruits are, principally, gratitude to the Father, acceptance of divine adoption, life and justice for all, and universal fellowship.

Let us now see how the classic themes of our faith can be seen in relation to liberation and the kingdom.

Some Key Themes of Liberation Theology

1. *Living and true faith includes the practice of liberation.* Faith is the original standpoint of all theology, including liberation theology. Through the act of faith we place our life, our pilgrimage through this world, and our death in God's hands. By the light of faith we see that divine reality penetrates every level of history and the world. As a way of life, faith enables us to discern the presence or negation of God in various human endeavors. It is living faith that provides a contemplative view of the world.

But faith also has to be true, the faith necessary for salvation. In the biblical tradition it is not enough for faith to be true in the terms in which it is expressed (orthodoxy); it is verified, made true, when it is informed by love, solidarity, hunger and thirst for justice. St. James teaches that "faith without good deeds is useless" and that believing in the one God is not enough, for "the demons have the same belief" (James 2:21, 20). Therefore, orthodoxy has to be accompanied by orthopraxis. Living and true faith enables us to hear the voice of the eschatological Judge in the cry of the oppressed: "I was hungry . . ." (Matt. 25:35). This same faith bids us give heed to that voice, resounding through an act of liberation: "and you gave me to eat." Without this liberating practice that appeases hunger, faith barely plants a seed, let alone produces fruit: not only would we be failing to love our sisters and brothers but we would be failing to love God too: "If a man who was rich enough in this world's goods saw that one of his brothers was in need, but closed his heart to him, how could the love of God be living in him?" (1 John 3:17). Only the faith that leads on to love of God and love of others is the faith that saves, and therefore promotes integral liberation: "Our love is not to be just words and mere talk, but something real and active" (1 John 3:18).

It is the task of liberation theology to recover the practical dimension inherent in biblical faith: in the world of the oppressed this practice can only be liberating.

2. *The living God sides with the oppressed against the pharaohs of this world.* In a world in which death from hunger and repression have become commonplace, it is important to bring out those characteristics of the Christian God that directly address the practice of liberation. God will always be God and as such will constitute the basic mystery of our faith. We cannot struggle with God; we can only cover our faces and, like Moses, adore God (Exod. 3:6). God, who "dwells in inaccessible light" (1 Tim. 6:16), is beyond the scope of our understanding, however enlightened. But beyond the divine transcendence, God is not a terrifying mystery, but full of tenderness. God is especially close to those who are oppressed; God hears their cry and resolves to set them free (Exod. 3:7-8). God is father of all, but most particularly father and defender of those who are oppressed and treated unjustly. Out of love for them, God takes sides, takes *their* side against the repressive measures of all the pharaohs.

This partiality on God's part shows that life and justice should be a universal guarantee to all, starting with those who are at present denied them; no one has the right to offend another human being, the image and likeness of God. God is glorified in the life-sustaining activities of men and women; God is worshiped in the doing of justice. God does not stand by impassively watching the drama of human history, in which, generally speaking, the strong impose their laws and their will on the weak. The biblical authors often present Yahweh as *Go'el*, which means: he who does justice to the weak, father of orphans and comforter of widows (see Ps. 146:9; Isa.1:17; Jer. 7:6, 22:3; Job 29:13, 31:16).

In the experience of slavery in Egypt, which bound the Israelites together as a people, they realized their longing for liberation and witnessed to the intervention of Yahweh as liberator. The liberation from slavery in Egypt was a political event, but one that became the basis for the religious experience of full liberation — that is, liberation also from sin and death. As the bishops of Latin America said at Medellin in 1968:

> Just as formerly the first people, Israel, experienced the saving presence of God when he set them free from slavery in Egypt, so we too, the new people of God, cannot fail to feel his saving deliverance when there is real development — that is, deliverance for each and every one from less human to more human conditions of life. [Introduction to Conclusions, no. 6]

Finally, the Christian God is a trinity of persons, Father, Son, and Holy Spirit. Each distinct from the other, they coexist eternally in a relationship of absolute equality and reciprocity. In the beginning there was not merely the oneness of a divine nature, but the full and perfect communion of three divine persons. This mystery provides the prototype for what society should be according to the plan of the triune God: by affirming and respecting personal individuality, it should enable persons to live in such communion and collaboration with each other as to constitute a unified society of equals and fellow citizens. The society we commonly find today, full of divisions, antagonisms, and discriminations, does not offer an environment in which we can experience the mystery of the Holy Trinity. It has to be transformed if it is to become the image and likeness of the communion of the divine persons.

3. *The Kingdom is God's project in history and eternity.* Jesus Christ, second person of the Blessed Trinity, incarnated in our misery, revealed the divine plan that is to be realized through the course of history and to constitute the definitive future in eternity; the Kingdom of God. The Kingdom is not just in the future, for it is "in our midst" (Luke 17:21); it is not a kingdom "of this world" (John 18:36), but it nevertheless begins to come about in this world. The Kingdom or reign of God means the full and total liberation of all creation, in the end, purified of all that oppresses it, transfigured by the full presence of God.

No other theological or biblical concept is as close to the ideal of integral liberation as this concept of the Kingdom of God. This was well expressed by the bishops at Puebla, in the hearing of John Paul II:

> There are two complementary and inseparable elements. The first is liberation from all the forms of bondage, from personal and social sin, and from everything that tears apart the human individual and society; all this finds its source in egotism, in the mystery of iniquity. The second element is liberation for progressive growth in being through communion with God and other human beings; this reaches its culmination in the perfect communion of heaven, where God is all in all and weeping forever ceases. [§482; cf. *Evangelii nuntiandi,* no. 9]

Because the Kingdom is the absolute, it embraces all things: sacred and profane history, the church and the world, human beings and the cosmos. Under different sacred and profane signs, the Kingdom is always present where persons bring about justice, seek comradeship, forgive each other, and promote life. However, the Kingdom finds a particular expression in the church, which is its perceptible sign, its privileged instrument, its "initial budding forth" and principle (see Puebla, §§227-28) insofar as it lives the gospel and builds itself up from day to day as the body of Christ.

Seeing the Kingdom as God's universal project helps us to understand the link joining creation and redemption, time and eternity. The Kingdom of God is something more than historical liberations, which are always limited and open to further perfectioning, but it is anticipated and incarnated in them in time, in preparation for its full realization with the coming of the new heaven and the new earth.

4. *Jesus, the Son of God, took on oppression in order to set us free.* Jesus is God in our human misery, the Son of God become an individual Jew, at a certain time in history and in a particular social setting. The incarnation of the Word of God implies the assumption of human life as marked by the contradictions left by sin, not in order to consecrate them, but in order to redeem them. In these conditions, Jesus became a "servant" and made himself "obedient even to death on a cross" (Phil. 2:6-11; Mark 10:45). His first public word was to proclaim that the Kingdom of God was "at hand" and already present as "good news" (Mark 1:14). When he publicly set out his program in the synagogue in Nazareth (Luke 4:16-21), he took on the hopes of the oppressed and announced that they were now — "this day" — being fulfilled. So the Messiah is the one who brings about the liberation of all classes of unfortunates. The Kingdom is also liberation from sin (Luke 24:27; Acts 2:38; 5:31; 13:38), but this must not be interpreted in a reductionist sense to the point where the infrastructural dimension in Jesus' preaching stressed by the evangelists is lost sight of.

The Kingdom is not presented simply as something to be hoped for in the future; it is already being made concrete in Jesus' actions. His miracles and healings, besides demonstrating his divinity, are designed to show that his liberating proclamation is already being made history among the oppressed, the special recipients of his teaching and first beneficiaries of his actions. The Kingdom is a gift of God offered gratuitously to all. But the way into it is through the process of conversion. The conversion demanded by Jesus does not mean just a change of convictions (theory) but above all a change of attitude (practice) toward all one's previous personal, social, and religious relationships.

The liberation wrought by Jesus outside the law and customs of the time, and his radical requirements for a change of behavior along the lines of the Beatitudes, led him into serious conflict with all the authorities of his age. He knew defamation and demoralization, persecution and the threat of death. His capture, torture, judicial condemnation, and crucifixion can be understood only as a consequence of his activity and his life. In a world that refused to listen to his message and to take up the way of conversion, the only alternative open to Jesus as a way of staying faithful to the Father and to his own preaching was to accept martyrdom. The Cross is the expression of the human rejection of Jesus, on the one hand, and of his sacrificial acceptance by the Father, on the other.

The resurrection uncovers the absolute meaning of the message of the Kingdom, and of Jesus' life and death. It is the definitive triumph of life and of hope for a reconciled Kingdom in which universal peace is the fruit of divine justice and the integration of all things in God. The resurrection has to be seen as full liberation from all the obstacles standing in the way of the lordship of God and the full realization of all the dynamic forces for life and glory placed by God within human beings and the whole of creation.

The resurrection also, and especially, reveals the meaning of the death of the innocent, of those who are rejected for having proclaimed a greater justice — God's justice — and of all those who, like Jesus, support a good cause and are anonymously liquidated. It was not a Caesar at the height of his power who was raised from the dead, but someone destroyed by crucifixion on Calvary. Those who have been unjustly put to death in a good cause share in his resurrection.

Following Jesus means taking up his cause, being ready to bear the persecution it brings and brave enough to share his fate in the hope of inheriting the full liberation that the resurrection offers us.

5. *The Holy Spirit, "Father of the poor," is present in the struggles of the oppressed.* Like the Son, the Holy Spirit was sent into the world to further and complete the work of integral redemption and liberation. The special field of action for the Spirit is history. Like the wind (the biblical meaning of "spirit"), the Spirit is present in everything that implies movement, transformation, growth. No one and nothing is beyond the reach of the Spirit,

inside and outside the Christian sphere. The Spirit takes hold of persons, fills them with enthusiasm, endows them with special charisms and abilities to change religion and society, break open rigid institutions and make things new. The Spirit presides over the religious experience of peoples, not allowing them to forget the dimension of eternity or succumb to the appeals of the flesh.

The Holy Spirit becomes a participant in the struggles and resistance of the poor in a quite special way. Not without reason is the Spirit called "Father of the poor" in the liturgy: giving them strength, day after day, to face up to the arduous struggle for their own survival and that of their families, finding the strength to put up with a socioeconomic system that oppresses them, one that they have no hope of changing from one day to the next; helping keep alive their hope that some things will get better and that, united, they will eventually set themselves free. Their piety, their sense of God; their solidarity, hospitality, and fortitude; their native wisdom, fed on suffering and experience; their love for their own children and those of others; their capacity for celebration and joy in the midst of the most painful conflicts; the serenity with which they face the harshness of their struggle for life; their perception of what is possible and viable; their moderation in the use of force and their virtually limitless powers of resistance to the persistent, daily aggression of the socioeconomic system with its consequent social marginalization — all these qualities are gifts of the Holy Spirit, forms of the ineffable presence and activity of the Spirit among the oppressed.

But this activity is seen even more clearly when they rise up, decide to take history into their own hands, and organize themselves to bring about the transformation of society in the direction of the dream in which there will be a place for all with dignity and peace. The history of the struggles of the oppressed for their liberation is the history of the call of the Holy Spirit to the heart of a divided world. It is because of the Spirit that the ideals of equality and fellowship, the utopia of a world in which it will be easier to love and recognize in the face of the other the maternal and paternal features of God, will never be allowed to die or be forgotten under the pressure of resignation.

It is also in the light of the action of the Spirit that the emergence of base Christian communities should be understood. More a happening than an institution, they bring into the present the movement Jesus started and commit themselves to the justice of the Kingdom of God. This is where the church can be seen to be the sacrament of the Holy Spirit, endowed with many charisms, ministries, and services for the good of all and the building of the Kingdom in history.

6. *Mary is the prophetic and liberating woman of the people.* The people's devotion to Mary has deep dogmatic roots: she is the Mother of God, the Immaculate Conception, the Virgin of Nazareth, and the one human being taken up into heavenly glory in all her human reality. From the standpoint of liberation, certain characteristics of hers stand out as dear to Christians of the base communities committed in the light of their faith to the transformation of society.

In the first place, all the theological greatness of Mary based on the lowliness of her historical condition. She is Mary from Nazareth, a woman of the people, who observed the popular religious customs of the time (the presentation of Jesus in the temple and the pilgrimage to Jerusalem [Luke 2:21ff. and 41ff.]), who visited her relatives (Luke 1:39ff.), who would not miss a wedding (John 2), who worried about her son (Luke 2:48-51; Mark 3:31-32), and who followed him to the foot of the cross, as any devoted mother would have done (John 19:25). Because of this ordinariness, and not in spite of it, Mary was everything that faith proclaims her to be, for God did "great things" for her (Luke 1:49).

In the second place, Mary is the perfect example of faith and availability for God's purpose (Luke 1:45, 38). She certainly did not understand the full extent of the mystery being brought about through her — the coming of the Holy Spirit upon her and the virginal conception of the eternal Son of the Father in her womb (Luke 1:35; Matt. 1:18), but even so she trusted in God's purpose. She thinks not of herself but of others, of her cousin Elizabeth (Luke 1:39ff.), of her son lost on the pilgrimage (Luke 2:43), of those who have no wine at the marriage feast at Cana (John 2:3). Persons can be liberators only if they free themselves from their own preoccupations and place their lives at the service of others, as did Mary, Jesus, and Joseph.

In the third place, Mary is the prophetess of the Magnificat. Anticipating the liberating proclama-

tion of her son, she shows herself attentive and sensitive to the fate of the humiliated and debased; in a context of praising God, she raises her voice in denunciation and invokes divine revolution in the relationship between oppressors and oppressed. Paul VI gave excellent expression to this whole liberating dimension of Mary in his apostolic exhortation *Marialis Cultus* of 1974:

> Mary of Nazareth, despite her total submission to the will of God, was far from being a passively submissive woman or one given to an alienating religiosity; she was a woman who had no hesitation in affirming that God is the avenger of the humble and oppressed, who pulls down the mighty of this world from their thrones (Luke 1:51-53). We can recognize in Mary, "who stands out among the poor and humble of the Lord" (LG 55), a strong woman, who knew poverty, suffering, flight, and exile (Matt. 2:13-23) — situations that cannot escape the attention of those who with an evangelical spirit seek to channel the liberating energies of man and society. [No. 37]

Finally, Mary is as she appears in the popular religion of Latin America. There is no part of Latin America in which the name of Mary is not given to persons, cities, mountains, and innumerable shrines. Mary loves the poor of Latin America. She took on the dark face of the slaves and the persecuted Amerindians. She is the *Morenita* ("little dark girl") in Guadalupe, Mexico; she is Nossa Senhora da Aparecida, bound like the slaves in Brazil; she is the dark-complexioned Virgin of Charity in Cuba; the list is endless.

The masses of the poor bring their troubles to the centers of Marian pilgrimage; they dry their tears there and are filled with renewed strength and hope to carry on struggling and surviving. In these places Mary becomes "the sacramental presence of the maternal features of God" (Puebla, §291), the "ever-renewed star of evangelization" (*Evangelii nuntiandi*, no. 81), and together with Christ her son, in union with the oppressed, the "protagonist of history" (Puebla, §293).

7. *The church is sign and instrument of liberation.* The church is the inheritor in history of the mystery of Christ and his Spirit, and finds the Kingdom in history as its conscious and institutionalized expression. With this, it is still a mystery

of faith. It is the organized human response made by Christ's followers to God's gift; this makes it, without division or confusion, at once divine and human, sharing in the weakness of all that is human, and in the glory of all that is divine.

From the beginning of its presence in Latin American history, the church has spread its influence throughout the people. It was often an accomplice in the colonization process that entailed the disintegration of Amerindian cultures, but it has also proclaimed freedom and taken part in processes of liberation. In the last few decades, faced with the growing degradation of the lives of the masses, it has made itself conscious that its mission is one of liberating evangelization.

The best way of evangelizing the poor consists in allowing the poor themselves to become the church and help the whole church to become truly a poor church and a church of the poor. In order to accomplish this, thousands of base communities, Bible-study circles, and centers of pastoral work among the people have sprung up in virtually all parts of Latin America. In these communities Christians have been discovering *communion* as the structural and structuring theological value of the church. Rather than church-institution, organized as a "perfect society" and hierarchically structured, the church should be the community of the faithful living in comradely relationships of sharing, love, and service. These communities are better able to embody the meeting between faith and life, between the gospel and the signs of the times, understood in community, and to be a more transparent witness to Christian commitment, than are large parishes, with their more anonymous character. A vast network of base communities has sprung up, in which cardinals, bishops, priests, religious, and various forms of the lay apostolate all come together.

Despite the tensions attendant upon any living body, there is generally a good spirit of convergence between the institutional church and this wide network of base communities. They can recognize in one another the same evangelical spirit and cooperate in proclaiming the good news of Jesus and working for liberation in a divided society.

These Christian communities, united and in communion with their pastors, form the true base from which the church can become, as a matter of fact and not just of rhetoric, the people of God

on pilgrimage, on its way. If they are to be the people of God, Christians have first to become a people — that is, a network of living communities working out their understandings, planning their courses of action, and organizing themselves for action. When this people enters the church through faith, baptism, and evangelical practice, it makes the church the people of God in history, which in Latin America is becoming more and more closely allied with popular culture.

This new route taken by the people of God with its new communities has created the various ministries and services necessary to attend to the religious and human needs that arise; roles and styles of pastoral ministration have been redefined, and the communities as a whole have taken on the task of evangelization.

A church thus born of the faith of the people can truly show itself as the sign of the integral liberation that the Father wills for his children, and as the proper instrument for its implementation in history. In its celebrations, popular dramatizations, ritualization of sacramental life, and its whole variety of religious creativity, it gives symbolical expression to the liberation already experienced by the people — fragile, certainly, but nevertheless true and anticipatory of the full liberation to come in the final Kingdom of the Father.

8. *The rights of the poor are God's rights.* Theological reflection on the primacy of dignity of the poor, as explained in the last chapter, has helped to lead the churches to develop their concern for the defense and promotion of human rights. Pastoral work among the poor has led to the discovery of their historical strength and sacred dignity. Part of integral evangelization consists in fostering a sense of the inviolability of individual human beings and in guaranteeing their basic rights, particularly those in the *social* sphere. The liberal-bourgeois tradition defends individual rights disconnected from society and from basic solidarity with all. Liberation theology has corrected and enriched this tradition by taking account of biblical sources. These speak primarily of the rights of the poor, of outcasts, of orphans and widows. All who are unprotected and downtrodden find their guarantor and advocate in God. God and the Messiah take on the defense of those who have no one to plead for them.

The rights of the poor are the rights of God. The struggle for promotion of human dignity and defense of threatened rights must begin with the rights of the poor. They show us the need for a certain hierarchization of rights; first must come *basic* rights, the rights to life and to the means of sustaining life (food, work, basic health care, housing, literacy); then come the other human rights: freedom of expression, of conscience, of movement, and of religion.

Throughout Latin America there are now hundreds of action groups, Justice and Peace groups, centers for the Defense of Human Rights, for example, in which the poor themselves, together with their allies (lawyers or other "organic intellectuals") make prophetic denunciations of the violations they suffer, discuss their experiences with other movements, organize resistance, and defend those accused in the courts. As the bishops at Puebla said: "The love of God . . . for us today must become first and foremost a labor of justice on behalf of the oppressed, an effort of liberation for those who are most in need of it" (§327; cf. §1145).

9. *Liberated human potential becomes liberative.* Liberation theology, which is essentially practical, has an immediate bearing on human ethics and attitudes. It has produced a new schematization of how to be Christian in the contemporary world, as we shall show at the end of this book. Here, we want only to point out some aspects of the ethical implications.

Christians are faced with the social and structural sin of oppression and injustice under which great numbers of persons are suffering. This is the sin that festers in the institutions and structures of society, inclining individuals and groups to behavior contrary to God's purpose. Let us be clear that "structures" are not just things but forms of relatedness between things and the persons bound up with them. Overcoming social sin requires a will to transformation, to a change of structures, so that they allow for more justice and participation in their functioning. Evangelical conversion requires more than a change of heart; it also requires a liberation of social organization insofar as it produces and reproduces sinful patterns of behavior. This social conversion is brought about through transformative social struggle, with the tactics and strategy suited to bringing about the changes needed. Social sin has to be opposed by social grace, fruit of God's gift and of human endeavor inspired by God.

Charity as a form of being-for-others will always have its validity. But in the social dimension, loving means collaborating in the formation of new structures, supporting those that represent an advance in the campaign for a better quality of life, and political commitment in favor of an option for solidarity with the poor. There is a particular challenge to social love in class struggle, an aspect of the reality of a society marked by class antagonisms. By his example Jesus showed that there can be compatibility between love of others and opposition to their attitudes. We have to love others as such in whatever situation, but we also have to oppose attitudes and systems that do not conform to the ethical criteria of Jesus' message. Social peace and reconciliation are possible only to the extent that the real motives that continually provoke conflict are superseded: unequal and unjust relationships between capital and labor; racial, cultural, and sexual discrimination. So there are specific challenges to the holiness of liberative Christians: to love without hating; to fight for the success of a just cause without being deceived by emotions; and, although respecting different opinions, being objective about one's own position and safeguarding the unity of the community.

Struggle for liberation alongside the oppressed has provoked persecutions and martyrdoms. Living the spirit of the Beatitudes in this context, accepting such consequences as a part of evangelical commitment, forces Christians to be truly free, already members of the Kingdom of God, and therefore effective workers for liberation. Here the spirituality of resurrection takes on its full meaning: rather than celebrate the triumph of life, it demonstrates the victory of a crucified Liberator who, because he freely gave his life for others, inherited the fullness of God's life.

Liberative Christians unite heaven and earth, the building of the human city with the eschatological city of God, the promotion of the minimum of life in the present with the maximum of life in eternity. They reject nothing that is truly human and has therefore been taken up by the Son of God; they do everything they can toward the full liberation that will be realized when the Lord comes, to bring to its fullness all that men and women, and especially the oppressed, have brought about.

Try It Yourself: Can Capitalism Be Saved?

CASE STUDY 7

In this unit you have read several essays which attempt to address the question of what economic system is most compatible with a Christian commitment to the well-being of all persons, especially those who are most frequently neglected. This question gained a new urgency with the fall and dissolution of the greatest communist state, the Soviet Union, in the early 1990s. Listen in on the debate as Max L. Stackhouse and Dennis P. McCann argue for a "reformed capitalism" and Robert Benne and Preston N. Williams challenge their assessment. Can capitalism be saved? What do you think?

85. A Postcommunist Manifesto

MAX L. STACKHOUSE AND DENNIS P. McCANN

The specter that haunted the modern world has vanished. That specter is communism. Nobody who has been paying attention takes it seriously anymore, although a few will echo its slogans for generations. To be more specific: no one thinks anymore that the route to social justice and prosperity necessarily lies in the political control of the marketplace and the means of production. Along with Soviet communism, forms of Marxism, even the gentler forms of European socialism, are under pressure.

We can neither ignore this fact nor deny its implications for Christian social ethics. The Protestant social gospel, early Christian realism, much neoorthodoxy, many forms of Catholic modernism, the modern ecumenical drive for racial and social inclusiveness, and contemporary liberation theories all held that democracy, human rights, and socialism were the marks of the coming Kingdom. For all their prophetic witness in many areas, they were wrong about socialism. The future will not bring what contemporary theology said it would and should. . . .

The failure of the socialist vision, where it does

Max L. Stackhouse (1935–) teaches at Andover Newton Theological School in Newton Centre, Massachusetts. Dennis P. McCann (1945–) teaches at DePaul University in Chicago. They are working on an anthology, *On Moral Business: Theological Perspectives on Business, Ethics, and Economics,* forthcoming from Eerdmans.

From *The Christian Century,* 16 January 1991, pp. 1, 44-47.

not bring a crisis of faith, demands repentance. All too many religious leaders still cling to the belief that capitalism is greedy, individualistic, exploitative, and failing; that socialism is generous, community-affirming, equitable, and coming; and that the transition from the one to the other is what God is doing in the world.

The truth is: no system has a monopoly on greed; modern capitalism engenders greater cooperation; socialism is more exploitative; and no one who has experienced "really existing socialism" now believes that it was God's design. What we now face is more than a delay in the socialist *parousia.* It is the recognition that this presumptive dogma is wrong.

If we can no longer affirm the socialist decision, must we now become enthusiastic neoconservatives? The answer is no, for questions of social justice are a necessary part of modern economics, not an intrusion into it. The economies of the future cannot be based on eighteenth-century theories or a return to nineteenth-century practices. Is it possible that, in face of the new evidence, everyone who holds to a "preferential option for the poor" must now embrace capitalism, since socialism itself impoverishes? In some measure, the answer is Yes. But it must be a reformed capitalism — one that uses law, politics, education, and especially theology and ethics to constrain the temptations to exploitation and greed everywhere.

Whenever capitalism rapes the earth or becomes a pillar of racism, sexism, classism, or nationalism, it must be resisted. But if the age of individualist greed is past, so is the age of collectivist protest against it. Aggregates of possessive egos, each making bottom-line decisions by the utilitarian calculation of cost and benefit, are as false as command economies where political and military leaders control the whole society.

Of course, socialism and Christianity are in theoretical accord on one key point: society is and must be prior to both government and business. But on the issue of what constitutes the core of society the differences appear immediately: more important than class conflict is theology and communities of faith. These transcend political economy both logically and historically and provide the model for the common life.

All politics and all economics must be conducted under the context-transcending principles of truth, justice, and love. Concretely understood, these protect the moral and spiritual rights of persons and groups and disclose purposes for living that are not of this world. Such principles and purposes are, and must be, the formative force in all public life, as well as in personal piety. They must enhance the salvation of both souls and civilizations.

At once more personal and more cosmopolitan than any political ideology or economic interest can be, a genuinely theological vision must constitute the ethics of our postsocialist economic order. Every authority and every policy that is deemed legitimate must recognize the integrity of both material and spiritual matters, of both historical consciousness and the awareness of eternity, of both humanistic interests and metaphysical-moral visions.

Theology is indispensable to the analysis of the human condition and the historical ethos. Interests not guided by theology and channeled by covenanted communities of faith march through the world like armies in the night; but they do not build civilizations and cultures that endure. Communities of intimacy and ultimacy, not class consciousness; institutions of affection and excellence, not revolutionary cadres; organizations of creativity and cooperation, not bureaucratized control mechanisms; and associations dedicated to what is true and just and loving before God, not quasi-scientific dialectics, are what shape social destiny in the long run.

Any account, including a Marxist one, of why things are the way they are that does not speak of theology and ecclesiology errs. It is doomed to fail. But where the political economy honors these, society can become open to a redemptive spirit. Modern theology and ethics have not said this clearly enough.

Yet it is one of the providential aspects of this moment in human history that the failure of communism, and consequently the doubt now thrown on all forms of socialism, cannot justify triumphalism in the West generally or among Christians particularly. The fact that "they" are sick does not prove that "we" are well. The new situation merely means that we can and must examine the relations of theology to political economy with a new openness that does not simply sprinkle holy water on materialist theories, outdated ideologies, and special interests.

The ensemble of problems which we confront is formidable. A full repertoire of solutions is not at hand. Optimism is soured by the nation's growing addiction to debt, a dependence on oil, recurrent hunger in far too many parts of the world, the peril of ecological disaster, the probability of a recession, the high visibility of ethical rot (as in recent junk-bond trading and the savings-and-loan crisis), a lack of commitment to educational excellence, the growing disparity between conspicuous consumption for some and conspicuous poverty for others, and the loss of hope and talent due to discrimination and drugs among far too many.

Even more, many contemporary forms of theology — fideist, fundamentalist, and liberationist — are so alienated from modern science, technology, culture, and especially business that they cannot discern where, in the midst of these sectors of our contemporary life, God is accomplishing something new. And now that the socialist forms of analysis have proven empty, even modern ecumenical thought will have to struggle to provide the framework of meaning, the principles and purposes, necessary to face the new situation.

Any theology able to address the future must reach beyond confessional particularities, exclusive histories, and privileged realms of discourse. In constructing a cosmopolitan social ethics, certain dimensions of theology are more important than others. If theology is only the proclamation of personal sin and redemption, of course, let some continue to preach to their choirs. This message has partial validity, and the old songs replenish the soul. If theology is essentially narrative or metaphor, let others take time to write a novel or a poem. The world needs good ones. If theology is essentially a tradition's confession of faith, still others will want to study their catechisms. People ought to know what their communities believe. And if theology is primarily the reflected experience of some particular gender or race or support group, let them serve the needs of their sectarian enclaves. This, too, is a valid ministry.

But a theology adequate to the cosmopolitan challenges that await us must have another dimension as well: it must develop a social ethic for the emerging world in which democracy, human rights, and a mixed economy are acknowledged as universal necessities. It must address a world linked by technology, trade, and a host of new interdependencies.

This agenda for Christian thought requires a "public theology," a way of speaking about the reality of God and God's will for the world that is intellectually valid in the marketplace of ideas and morally effective in the marketplace of goods and services.

Of course, there are some aspects of Christianity that stand as perennial constraints on every effort of this kind. On the one hand, the Bible knows no economic blueprint. Further, it tells us that to take economic matters too seriously is to miss the point of the lilies of the field, to decline the invitation to the banquet, to turn away sadly, indeed, to worship mammon. This prevents all Christians from identifying any economic system with the Kingdom of God.

On the other hand, the Bible also calls us to be responsible stewards — not only of our talents and personal possessions but of all that is the Lord's until he returns. We are to labor in the vineyards of the world — even when the vineyards reach around the globe in new patterns of corporate capitalism.

We dare not shrink from this task. We cannot say that the new economy now taking shape globally is without theological roots. Nor can we say that it needs no theological help. We must not give the impression that Christianity has nothing to offer it other than condemnation. Islam, and for that matter Hinduism, Buddhism, and the host of secular humanisms and neopagan spiritualities that seek to capture the soul of our times, should not be allowed to shape the future by default. They need a Christian theological perspective to fulfill them and, where necessary, to correct them.

If we refuse the challenge to which providence has called this generation, we betray the gospel. Any pastor who does not preach on these matters, any congregation that does not study them, any seminary that does not teach about them, or any baptized Christian who does not pray about them with a depth that can overcome old ideologies and alter common practices denies that God is Lord over all of creation and history.

What issues, then, are central to this challenge?

1. *The stewardship of capital.* Vast amounts of capital are necessary for the twenty-first century. We must invest in research and development, in new equipment for robotic production, in the development of nonfossil fuels and biotechnology, and in the training of a highly skilled work force. Failure to capitalize means not only economic stagnation but environmental destruction, unemployment, wider hunger, and further homelessness. The undercapitalization that results from policies directed against economic growth inevitably compounds social injustice. The challenge is to capitalize in ways that reflect our responsibilities as faithful stewards. How ought we do it?

Precisely because capitalization by state fiat under socialism has failed to promote economic development and has worsened most of the evils it intended to correct, contemporary Christians must think more deeply about the morality of profits in a world oriented toward markets, corporations and global competition. Creating wealth is the whole point of economic activity, as known to folk wisdom: "If your output is less than your intake, your upkeep is your downfall." What is true of the body's energy level and the family budget is true of every economic effort.

If profits are made by honorable means, we must recognize that working to serve people's needs in the marketplace may be a holy vocation in and for the salvation of the world. We are bound therefore to help businesspeople discover how to exercise this vocation with due respect for employees, customers, and suppliers. Further, public theology must insist upon a regard for the larger social and natural environment. In these ways. the disciplined pursuit of profits within a responsible strategy of capitalization can be a modern form of stewardship — one finding much precedent in the biblical record.

Indeed, a new form of Christian mission today emerges precisely at this point. Convening hearts to God through the grace of Christ is paramount, of course. But outward and material signs of this grace are required. If we care for people's material conditions, the churches should send out to the poorer regions people who can teach others how to develop their own resources — how to form corporations and manage them, how to find markets, how to develop technology, how to work with employees, and how to make profits for the common good.

Enhancing the capacity for capitalization in responsible corporations is as much the new name for mission as development is the new name for peace.

2. *The covenant for corporations.* The corporation has already become the social form distinctive of every cooperative human activity outside the family, the government, and personal friendships. It is historically based on the patterns of association worked out by the church beyond tribe, patriarchy, and nation. The modern business corporation could become a worldly ecclesia no less than hospitals, unions, parties, schools, voluntary organizations, and cultural institutions, virtually all of which are incorporated.

Further, the business corporation has, as much as any other institution, leaped cultural and social boundaries and broken down the walls that divide people. It has found a home in societies far from its roots. Where the opportunities to form corporations are constricted or the skills to sustain them are absent, people remain in an underdeveloped condition. Societies stagnate and people die for want of the ability to form corporations.

Businesses need all the spiritual and moral guidance they can get. The financial environment is in constant flux. Accountability to investors requires a devotion to efficiency that may threaten other principles and goals of covenantal association. Moreover, businesses increasingly operate in a context of global competition. Comparative advantages can make selling out, closing down, or moving to other lands imperative. The failure to move is in some cases a manifestation of a misplaced patriotism, and may fail to aid underdeveloped regions.

Further, such pressures put corporations in a moral bind. On the one hand, the corporations that focus most directly on short-term, bottom-line considerations are those least able to sustain the loyalty of their employees and the trust of the communities they serve. On the other hand, those that spend the most resources on benefits, promote community service, and encourage the personal and social development of their employees are often least equipped to defend themselves against hostile corporate takeovers. For them, liquidation can bring a greater immediate return than quarterly performance. For businesspeople to resign themselves to either alternative, and for the church not to address such questions, is to fail short of the covenantal implications of public theology in corporate life.

If the modern business corporation is to fulfill its calling as a secular form of covenantal community, Christian leaders must assist businesspeople to understand the fateful choice between building an association of interdependent persons seeking to produce goods and services that benefit the commonwealth, and being reduced to an instrument with interchangeable parts, seeking maximum immediate advantage.

If public theology can help us overcome our contempt for corporations as mere money machines, then Christians can begin to articulate what we expect of these institutions. We can even learn to love them as we have learned to love our churches, neighborhoods, nations, schools, and hospitals — although we must not be tempted to seek from them the loves that are proper to other relationships.

We can demand moral responses from them, put a decent measure of loyalty and trust in them, be alert to the strong possibility of sin within them, judge them, forgive them, and convert them when we find them snared in corrigible error. Further, we can encourage churchpeople to work in them and find their callings there, precisely because they may discover valid moral principles already operative there.

While rejecting as both false and unjust the view of the corporation as an inhuman piece of organizational machinery, public theology also must be aware of the limits of this form of covenantal community. Corporations become idols when we become married to firms, when our loyalty is to them only, when we bend all politics to their service, when their distinctive modes of operation get confused with the ideals that must govern health care, education, and culture. Corporations become idols, in short, when we think that they can bring salvation to human life.

The question of limits, however, is not simply one of public ecclesiology. The modern business corporation is not only a voluntary association but an economic institution designed to achieve a degree of control over markets. To the extent that corporations are successful, markets cannot be relied upon exclusively to control corporations. The voice of labor, the demands of government, the rule of law must also be developed.

Furthermore, dramatic increases in corporate mastery of the latest advances in technology enormously enhance any industry's capacity to have a decisive impact on its environment, both culturally and ecologically. While affirming the corporation as a covenantal community, a public theology fully resonant with our emerging world will have to collaborate in developing new systems of public accountability to ensure that corporations respect God's gift of creation.

3. *The vocation of management.* Business managers have not yet become members of a genuine profession in the ways that clergy, teachers, doctors, lawyers, and architects have. There were many reasons for this in the past. They are less valid now, and will become increasingly less so. Managers, no doubt, are already professionals in the way that baseball players, rock stars, and talk-show hosts are: they are experts at what they do, they work at it full time, and they make big bucks. And many do what they do with personal standards of integrity at least as high as those of the clergy. But management itself has not yet developed the rich texture of public responsibility that emerged from the sense of "high" calling historically characteristic of the traditional professions.

In the emerging world of global economic interdependence, management can and should be professionalized. Christians should come to regard it as an honorable and specialized ministry of the laity. If we can no longer dismiss corporations as inhuman machines, we must also confess that it is false and unjust to categorize managers only as bosses. A public theology that is open to the experiences of those who exercise responsibility in modern business corporations will soon discover that managers have more in common with community organizers, pastors, and teachers than they do with impersonal systems of mechanical control. Granted, they must measure performance, both personal and corporate, by standards that aspire to objectivity; but ultimately so must all those who genuinely empower others. There is no longer any reason to deny the holiness of a vocation to business management.

4. *A public theology for a global civilization.* Capitalization and profits, the corporation as a covenanting community and worldly ecclesia, the professionalization of management and tech-

nology? As theological topics? Yes. These are key examples of a public theology that respects the ordering principles of trinitarian thought, with its fundamental commitment to the inclusive community of persons and its dynamic reconception of the biblical message in nonbiblical social and intellectual environments. In a postsocialist world, these are among the decisive areas where the righteous sovereignty of God, the sacrificial presence of Jesus Christ and the dynamic novelty of the Holy Spirit must become concrete.

Such topics are at least as important for the human future as today's theologies of sexuality, literary criticism, and biomedical ethics. The biblical and doctrinal, the ethical and interpretive resources of the ecumenically open traditions have more to offer this new world than we have yet seen. To rediscover these resources is the first requirement for those Protestant and Catholic communities of faith that hope to speak socially and ethically to the momentous changes of our times.

Christians of the world, awake! Now that the specter of communism has vanished, cast off the spell of economic dogmatism! There is nothing to lose but ideology and irrelevance.

86. Responses to "A Postcommunist Manifesto": Ethics, Economics, and the Corporate Life

ROBERT BENNE AND
PRESTON N. WILLIAMS

Less Enthusiasm, Please, I'm Lutheran

I am tempted to endorse wholeheartedly the manifesto presented by Max L. Stackhouse and Dennis McCann. After all, they confirm the argument I made in *The Ethic of Democratic Capitalism — A Moral Reassessment* (1981) that the combination of political democracy and market economic arrangements is not only morally defensible but perhaps the best among possible options. Both men were then open to my argument when others were reluctant to be seen in public with such a benighted fellow.

Further, they had the courage on other issues to swim against the stream of conventional wisdom of the guild of Christian social ethicists. But, more important, they have done two things: (1) they have added their influential voices to the worthy purpose of calling Christian ethicists to turn their constructive attention toward the moral and practical *possibilities* inherent in varieties of

---

Robert Benne (1937–) is Jordan-Trexler Professor of Religion and director of the Center for Church and Society at Roanoke College in Salem, Virginia. Preston N. Williams (1926–) is Houghton Professor of Theology and Contemporary Change at Harvard Divinity School in Cambridge, Massachusetts.

From *The Christian Century*, 23 January 1991.

democratic capitalism rather than diverting their efforts to the unrelenting and exaggerated criticism that has been so characteristic of the past; and (2) they have lent strong support for a renewed *public* relevance of Christian religious and moral claims for the evolving system of democratic capitalism in the face of a world that has marginalized and privatized those claims. These are important contributions.

But, alas, I cannot give three cheers for the particular form of their proposal. In brief, I think they need a dash of Lutheran diffidence to dampen an unseemly enthusiasm. They need a little more exposure to the Norwegian Lutherans of Lake Wobegon. There are two basic fronts on which their enthusiasm needs to be qualified.

First, they confuse the central Christian message of salvation with political and economic practice, in this case capitalist practice. In so doing they make the same mistake that Christian socialists and liberationists often have made, that is, thinking that human efforts at economic and political transformation are in some sense salvatory. The authors claim that if our generation does not respond to the challenge (the constructive engagement with capitalism they commend), we "betray the gospel." Further, that "working to serve people's needs in the marketplace may be a holy vocation in and for the salvation of the world." Or that "enhancing the capacity for capitalization . . . is . . . a new name for mission." The embodied principles of truth, justice and love in public life will "enhance the salvation of both souls and civilizations."

These examples may simply be attributed to the careless exuberance of manifestos. But I think not. They represent a tendency to qualify the radicality and universality of the gospel by conflating a desirable human practice with salvation. On the contrary, the gospel announces God's action in Jesus Christ to save and redeem us. When we are brought by the Holy Spirit to open our repentant hearts to this news, we *receive* it. Salvation is not our work. Even holy vocations do not save. Civilizations as a whole are not saved by the gospel; they have scarcely any capacity to repent, let alone receive the Good News. We do not betray the gospel when our parishes do not foster a constructive engagement with the marketplace. The church's uniquely God-given mission is to communicate the gospel, not encourage capitalization, as worthy as that might be.

The manifesto's tendency to collapse redemption into a particular kind of creative action leads to an inclination to rule others out of the reach of redeeming grace. Earlier it was we proponents of democratic capitalism who were beyond the pale of God's redemption because we supported an unjust system (witness the anathemas of the *The Road to Damascus* document written by "Third World Christians"). Now it is the socialists or other radicals who believe that capitalism is of the devil who are charged with betraying the gospel or denying God's rule in the world.

Both approaches undercut the universality of the gospel. All repentant sinners have the possibility of being grasped by divine grace, not only those with correct political and economic opinions. Those who receive grace may change their political and economic opinions or they may not, but in any case there will continue to be a wide range of opinion among those who call themselves Christian. Not everything goes, but there must be room in the Christian fold for my rock-ribbed Republican father as well as the misguided leftists who wrote *The Road to Damascus*.

The second point at which their enthusiasm needs to be diminished concerns their particular formulation of public theology. It simply claims too much. Theology and communities of faith transcend political economy, they say, and "provide the model for the common life." "Interests not guided by theology and channeled by covenanted communities of faith march through the world like armies in the night." "Any account, including a Marxist one, of why things are the way they are that does not speak of theology and ecclesiology errs." Public theology will construct a "cosmopolitan social ethic" in which "democracy, human rights and a mixed economy are acknowledged as universal necessities."

I too hope for a time when Christian theology and ethics will have more public relevance than they presently have. But Stackhouse and McCann think theology and ecclesiology will be on the front line of the public discussion and sometimes in their enthusiasm seem to claim a dominant role for them that is a bit embarrassing. And presumably it will be theologians and ethicists who will be pressing the project forward. Maybe even pastors and priests.

I would propose a different model of relevance. First, where theologians and ethicists are doing the talking, their publicly significant insights will have to be modulated by a language more universally available than their own professional argot. Their language will be a public philosophy informed by theology and ethics. Reinhold Niebuhr's capacity to speak in the language of such a religiously informed public philosophy made him the last real public theologian we have had in America. Further, as was demonstrated by Niebuhr, that kind of public philosophy will be made up of many notions that are not supplied by theology and ecclesiology. They simply will not provide *the* model.

Moreover, it is my hunch that the most effective public theology will be carried forward by laity who are more expert in their fields than theologians and ethicists will ever be. These laypeople will be informed by theologians but will filter their religious notions through the conceptual apparatus of their own fields. The laity have come of age; they are on the front lines of public theology.

There are exciting signs of this development. Glenn Tinder and Charles Taylor in political philosophy, Robert Bellah in sociology, and a host of topflight Christian philosophers are making a public impact in ways that professional theologians simply can't. This development is also occurring in economics, but we don't yet have a major Christian economist in whose thought Christian claims are clearly evident. If we had, there might have been a different list of priorities for economic action than that proposed by Stackhouse and McCann.

In summary, I strongly affirm the manifesto's basic intentions: to give up the blinding hatred of capitalism enough so that theologians and ethicists can say something useful to the millions of people involved in that dominant economic system; and to summon theology to a rightful and necessary public role. What's more, I agree wholeheartedly with the particulars of its argument. Indeed, the concluding reversal of the *Communist Manifesto's* rousing climax is worth a host of journal articles. But the tendency to draw a straight line between the Christian gospel, and human action in any economic program, as well as the inordinate claims made for its clericalized model of public theology, deserve criticism. This Calvinist and Catholic enthusiasm invites a dash of Lutheran diffidence. If Lutherans can't or won't supply the zest for social transformation exhibited by our Calvinist and Catholic colleagues, then perhaps we can provide a bit of ballast for the balloons they send up.

Robert Benne

Technical Knowledge, Political Will

Stackhouse and McCann conclude their manifesto with the phrase, "Christians of the world awake!" They thus indicate that their public theology is a Christian theology and that its critical and constructive message, while of public importance, is limited by its trinitarian orientation and can claim to be global only in a qualified sense. While the authors announce a desire to reject Christian triumphalism, their statement echoes that orientation. It is the celebration of the victory of one Christian theological perspective over all others. A proper public theology needs to he concerned with more than the squabbles within Christian faith and the revisioning of all societies in terms of specifically Christian theological concepts. As a Christian socialist I would rely more heavily upon a conception of God's common grace and an appeal to all peoples and cultures.

The collapse of communism and socialism among Christians, Muslims, and atheists should concern us because all societies need to find means to produce the goods essential for human living and cultural flourishing. Socialism's failure weakens but does not completely remove it as a competitor to capitalism. The manifesto goes too far when it declares socialism virtually dead and calls all liberals to repent for having made it a mark of the coming Kingdom. Some liberals, like myself, have always preferred a mixed economy to a socialist one because we have seen socialism's inability to deliver either justice or a viable economy in Cuba, Guyana, and Tanzania. The collapse in the Soviet Union, Poland, and Eastern and Central Europe confirms this conclusion but it does not make repentance or a radical change of social vision necessary.

We, as well as the manifesto, need, however, to spell out what is meant by a mixed economy. To speak of reformed or modern capitalism is not enough. What specific "laws, politics, education, and especially theology and ethics" are going to be employed to constrain the temptations to exploitation and greed associated with economic systems? It is not sufficient to urge that "all politics and all economies must be conducted under the context-transcending principles of truth, justice, and love." What is the content of the social ethic that flows from these principles and how do they preserve or enhance the operation of the free market so that it fills the stores with the consumer goods and necessities demanded by the people and provides them with the money to buy these goods?

While the achievements of Reagan-Bush America, Thatcher Britain, and Kohl Germany are better than that of the socialist states, much injustice remains because all capitalism depends to a considerable degree upon individualism and greed and has little concern for the poor. Truth, justice, and love do not arise from capitalism; they are imposed upon it. And while these principles may be grounded in Christianity, they may also be grounded in nontheological conceptions of ultimate reality. One is not quibbling if one suggests that theology and ecclesiology are not essential to all religions and worldviews. Nor is one being unnecessarily annoying if one reminds the authors of the manifesto of their recognition of the Bible and Christianity's unwillingness to identify any economic system with the Kingdom of God.

The three main suggestions that the manifesto makes concerning the theological and ethical guidelines for the mixed economy raise some questions. The Japanese have the most "disciplined pursuit of profits within a responsible strategy of capitalization." Does their success indicate that policies of economic growth and productivity do not need to be propped up by references to holy vocation, world salvation, and Christian mission? Christianity may add something of value to the Japanese pattern and meaning of life, but I wonder whether it is necessary to promote the just creation of wealth.

The concern for the covenant for corporations is puzzling to one who has lived his life in a nation where business success and Christianity are usually joined and are seldom uncoupled by socialist convictions. Certainly business corporations are as necessary as hospitals and schools and need to be viewed as part of God's good creation. They need also to be established in impoverished places where the production of more goods and services are required. But what does it mean to provide them with spiritual and moral guidance? How do we address them in respect to investor profits, competitive success or inclusiveness without seeming to recreate socialism's political control over the market place and the economy? For more than fifty years Roman Catholicism failed in such an enterprise — from *Rerum Novarum* (1891) to *Pacem in Terris* (1963) — and it is difficult to imagine lobbies of theologically correct Christians acting as corporate cheerleaders while guiding policies in ways that would guarantee morally correct decisions in respect to matters such as plant closings, long and short-term performance, and environmental protection. Corporations do need to be seen in a positive light, but that can never mean setting aside the imperatives of efficiency and profit-making, for only when these requirements are met is the corporation able to become "an association of interdependent persons seeking to produce goods and services that benefit the commonwealth." Efficiency and profit-making distinguish the business corporation from the hospital and the school and on occasion break through theological and ethical guidelines to create injustice and inequality.

The spiritual and moral guidance suggested for the covenant for corporations would be better utilized in strengthening the vocation of management. Managers are the decision-making center of the corporation and bear chief responsibility for the creation of a corporate covenantal community and the corporate practice of public service. The character and ethic of managers is most vulnerable to the influence of greed and exploitation. A public theology is, however, only one of their needs. Required also are technological inventiveness and financial astuteness. Indeed, without them theology may be of little worth. The authors' failure to examine the part played by the ignorance of technical skills in the recent collapse of socialism may have resulted in a mislocation of the cause of the failure. Teaching technical skills may then prove to be at least as important as motivating the right spirit toward business institutions.

The manifesto, like Walter Rauschenbusch's *Christianizing the Social Order,* is concerned for a Kingdom of God and a salvation of humanity that includes the economic order. Its task might be more feasible if it were to recognize that socialism's desire to use political forces to control the marketplace still lives in the concern for reformed capitalism. Greater attention needs to be paid therefore to socialism's legacy and its biblical roots if an adequate public theology is to be formulated. Moreover, the manifesto needs to state forthrightly that political forces strong enough to compel action, along with technical knowledge of business and the economy, are as important as any public theology.

Preston N. Williams

Chapter 13

Christian Environmental Ethics

Introduction

Few issues have captured the attention of the Western church as we greet the turn of the century as much as the environmental movement and the concern for the welfare of nonhuman species. Global warming, oil spills and the pollution of the environment, the destruction of the world's rainforests, the accumulation of waste along with the loss of valuable soil and farmlands, and the rapid extinction of plant and animal species are among the most serious environmental problems with which this and future generations must grapple.

The secular world, academic and nonacademic, began seriously examining and occasionally acting upon these issues in the late 1960s. The Christian church, too, has recognized both the gravity and the immediacy of environmental concerns. This is evidenced, among other places, in the decision of the 1983 Assembly of the World Council of Churches to devote study and programmatic emphasis to the theme "Justice, Peace, and the Integrity of Creation." In some of the most provocative and adventuresome writing in Christian theology today, theologians and ethicists are responding to environmental concerns, drawing not only upon Scripture and the tradition of Christian theology but also upon literary, historical, and philosophical analyses, as well as insights from other religions, primarily Native American religions and Buddhism.

Contemporary Christian discussion of environmental issues was sparked by the historian Lynn White, Jr.'s 1967 essay, "The Historical Roots of Our Ecologic Crisis" (*Science,* 10 March 1967). White placed the blame for the ecological crisis squarely upon the shoulders of Western Christianity, identifying the Christian West's reading of Genesis 1 as the source of contemporary ecological ills. It is but a short step, White argues, from the dominion of humankind over creation to the senseless exploitation of nature for the short-term benefit of some, if not all, human beings. The hope for the future lies in a radical rethinking of the relationship between humankind and the nonhuman world. To this end White commends St. Francis as a desperately needed saint for the age of environmentalism.

The readings in this chapter show that, whatever the past history of the Christian church, there are present within the broad Christian tradition the resources for addressing environmental concerns. Our readings begin with a wide range of biblical materials which bear upon Christian concern for the nonhuman world: the creation accounts from Genesis, the psalmist's hymn to God and God's creation, the prophetic recognition of God's judgment upon creation and, following judgment, God's blessing of creation, Jesus' cursing of the fig tree, and Pauline affirmations of the rule of Christ over *all* things.

Following the biblical materials, readers will find selections from the one to whom Lynn White pointed as hope for the future. St. Francis of Assisi's (1182–1226) "Canticle of Brother Sun" (reading 88) reveals not only the tenderness of this Christian saint, but his profound recognition of the unity of all things in Christ. From St. Francis we leap forward some seven hundred years to Karl Barth (1886–1968), the Swiss Calvinist theologian, easily the greatest theologian of the twentieth century. In reading 89 Barth draws heavily upon biblical materials in developing his understanding of how Christians ought to relate to the nonhuman world, forsaking neither the primacy of humankind in the divine economy nor the freedom of the Creator to redeem all that has been wrought by the Creator's hands.

The contemporary theologian Sallie McFague, on the other hand, is skeptical about the adequacy of biblical materials for the present age. In a radical departure from historic Christianity, McFague (reading 90) rejects "triumphalist, monarchial" images of God, and suggests that environmental doom can be averted only if the church begins to think of the world as God's body. In our selection she develops some of the richness of this metaphor for a Christian theology of nature.

Our final two readings address more directly a Christian ethic of the nonhuman world. William F. May (reading 91) draws creatively upon the southern novelist William Faulkner in clarifying covenantal ethics and how a covenantal ethic can inform and guide Christians in addressing the Christian relationship to the nonhuman world. Finally Wendell Berry (reading 92), better known for his poems, novels, and literary essays than for his theological reflection, provides an incisive analysis of the link between economy and ecosystem and observes that the church's fidelity to economic structures has been greater than her faithfulness to Christian Scriptures.

This chapter concludes with a case study asking you to think through a vexing dilemma in which loyalty to the created order seems to be possible only at the expense of benevolence towards other persons.

Suggestions for Further Reading

Granberg-Michaelson, Wesley. *A Worldly Spirituality: The Call to Take Care of the Earth.* San Francisco: Harper & Row, 1984.

Granberg-Michaelson, Wesley, ed. *Tending the Garden: Essays on the Gospel and the Earth.* Grand Rapids, Mich.: Wm. B. Eerdmans, 1987.

Hall, Douglas John. *Imaging God: Dominion as Stewardship.* Grand Rapids, Mich.: Wm. B. Eerdmans, 1986.

Linzey, Andrew. *Christianity and the Rights of Animals.* New York: Crossroad, 1987.

McFague, Sallie. *The Body of God.* Minneapolis: Augsburg Fortress Press, 1993.

Merchant, Carolyn. *The Death of Nature: Women, Ecology, and the Scientific Revolution.* San Francisco: Harper & Row, 1985.

McDaniel, Jay B. *Of God and Pelicans: A Theology of Reverence for Life.* Louisville: Westminster/John Knox Press, 1989.

Rolston, Holmes, III. *Environmental Ethics: Duties and Values in the Natural World.* Philadelphia: Temple University Press, 1988.

Santmire, H. Paul. *Brother Earth: Nature, God, and Ecology in a Time of Crisis.* Camden, N.J.: Thomas Nelson, 1970.

Santmire, H. Paul. *The Travail of Nature: The Ambiguous Ecological Promise of Christian Theology.* Philadelphia: Fortress Press, 1985.

87. Genesis 1:26-31;
Hosea 4:1-3;
Romans 8:18-24a

There is no faithfulness or loyalty,
    and no knowledge of God in the land.
Swearing, lying, and murder,
    and stealing and adultery break out;
    bloodshed follows bloodshed.
Therefore the land mourns,
    and all who live in it languish;
together with the wild animals
    and the birds of the air,
        even the fish of the sea are perishing.

Romans 8:18-24a

I consider that the sufferings of this present time are not worth comparing with the glory about to be revealed to us. For the creation waits with eager longing for the revealing of the children of God; for the creation was subjected to futility, not of its own will but by the will of the one who subjected it, in hope that the creation itself will be set free from its bondage to decay and will obtain the freedom of the glory of the children of God. We know that the whole creation has been groaning in labor pains until now; and not only the creation, but we ourselves, who have the first fruits of the Spirit, groan inwardly while we wait for adoption, the redemption of our bodies. For in hope we were saved.

Genesis 1:26-31

Then God said, "Let us make humankind in our image, according to our likeness; and let them have dominion over the fish of the sea, and over the birds of the air, and over the cattle, and over all the wild animals of the earth, and over every creeping thing that creeps upon the earth."

So God created humankind in his image,
in the image of God he created them;
male and female he created them.

God blessed them, and God said to them, "Be fruitful and multiply, and fill the earth and subdue it; and have dominion over the fish of the sea and over the birds of the air and over every living thing that moves upon the earth." God said, "See, I have given you every plant yielding seed that is upon the face of all the earth, and every tree with seed in its fruit; you shall have them for food. And to every beast of the earth, and to every bird of the air, and to everything that creeps on the earth, everything that has the breath of life, I have given every green plant for food." And it was so. God saw everything that he had made, and indeed, it was very good. And there was evening and there was morning, the sixth day.

Hosea 4:1-3

Hear the word of the LORD, O people of Israel;
    for the LORD has an indictment against
        the inhabitants of the land.

495

88. "The Canticle of Brother Sun" and "How St. Francis Tamed the Very Fierce Wolf of Gubbio"

ST. FRANCIS

The Canticle of Brother Sun

HERE BEGIN THE PRAISES OF THE CREATURES WHICH ST. FRANCIS MADE FOR THE PRAISE AND HONOR OF GOD WHEN HE WAS ILL AT SAN DAMIANO

Most High Almighty Good Lord,
Yours are the praises, the glory, the honor,
    and all blessings!
To you alone, Most High, do they belong,
And no man is worthy to mention you.

Be praised, my Lord, with all your creatures,
Especially Sir Brother Sun,
By whom you give us the light of day!
And he is beautiful and radiant
    with great splendor.
Of you, Most High, he is a symbol!

Be praised, my Lord, for Sister Moon
    and the stars!

In the sky you formed them bright
    and lovely and fair.

Be praised, my Lord, for Brother Wind
And for the air and cloudy and clear
    and all weather,
By which you give sustenance to your creatures!

Be praised, my Lord, for Sister Water,
Who is very useful and humble and lovely
    and chaste!

Be praised, my Lord, for Brother Fire,
By whom you give us light at night,
And he is beautiful and merry and mighty
    and strong!

Be praised, my Lord, for our sister
    Mother Earth,
Who sustains and governs us,
And produces fruits with colorful flowers
    and leaves!

Be praised, my Lord, for those who forgive
    for love of you
And endure infirmities and tribulations.
Blessed are those who shall endure them
    in peace,
For by you, Most High, they will be crowned!

Be praised, my Lord, for our sister
    Bodily Death,
From whom no living man can escape!
Woe to those who shall die in mortal sin!
Blessed are those whom she will find
    in your most holy will,
For the second death will not harm them.

Praise and bless my Lord and thank him
And serve him with great humility!

How St. Francis Tamed the Very Fierce Wolf of Gubbio

At a time when St. Francis was staying in the town of Gubbio, something wonderful and worthy of lasting fame happened.

For there appeared in the territory of that city a fearfully large and fierce wolf which was so rabid

---

St. Francis of Assisi (1182–1226) is among the most popular of Christian saints due to his love of nature and his commitment to simplicity. His words and character are recorded for us in *The Little Flowers of St. Francis.*

From *The Little Flowers of St. Francis,* trans. Beverly Brown (New York: Doubleday, 1958).

with hunger that it devoured not only animals but even human beings. All the people in the town considered it such a great scourge and terror — because it often came near the town — that they took weapons with them when they went into the country, as if they were going to war. But even with their weapons they were not able to escape the sharp teeth and raging hunger of the wolf when they were so unfortunate as to meet it. Consequently everyone in the town was so terrified that hardly anyone dared go outside the city gate.

But God wished to bring the holiness of St. Francis to the attention of those people.

For while the saint was there at that time, he had pity on the people and decided to go out and meet the wolf. But on hearing this the citizens said to him. "Look out, Brother Francis. Don't go outside the gate, because the wolf which has already devoured many people will certainly attack you and kill you!"

But St. Francis placed his hope in the Lord Jesus Christ who is master of all creatures. Protected not by a shield or a helmet, but arming himself with the sign of the Cross, he bravely went out of the town with his companion, putting all his faith in the Lord who makes those who believe in him walk without any injury on an asp and a basilisk and trample not merely on a wolf but even on a lion and a dragon. So with his very great faith St. Francis bravely went out to meet the wolf.

Some peasants accompanied him a little way, but soon they said to him: "We don't want to go any farther because that wolf is very fierce and we might get hurt."

When he heard them say this, St. Francis answered: "Just stay here. But I am going on to where the wolf lives."

Then, in the sight of many people who had come out and climbed onto places to see this wonderful event, the fierce wolf came running with its mouth open toward St. Francis and his companion.

The saint made the sign of the Cross toward it. And the power of God, proceeding as much from himself as from his companion, checked the wolf and made it slow down and close its cruel mouth.

Then, calling to it, St. Francis said: "Come to me, Brother Wolf. In the name of Christ, I order you not to hurt me or anyone."

It is marvelous to relate that as soon as he had made the sign of the Cross, the wolf closed its terrible jaws and stopped running, and as soon as he gave it that order, it lowered its head and lay down at the saint's feet, as though it had become a lamb.

And St. Francis said to it as it lay in front of him: "Brother Wolf, you have done great harm in this region, and you have committed horrible crimes by destroying God's creatures without any mercy. You have been destroying not only irrational animals, but you even have the more detestable brazenness to kill and devour human beings made in the image of God. You therefore deserve to be put to death just like the worst robber and murderer. Consequently everyone is right in crying out against you and complaining, and this whole town is your enemy. But, Brother Wolf, I want to make peace between you and them, so that they will not be harmed by you anymore, and after they have forgiven you all your past crimes, neither men nor dogs will pursue you anymore."

The wolf showed by moving its body and tail and ears and by nodding its head that it willingly accepted what the saint had said and would observe it.

So St. Francis spoke again: "Brother Wolf, since you are willing to make and keep this peace pact, I promise you that I will have the people of this town give you food every day as long as you live, so that you will never again suffer from hunger, for I know that whatever evil you have been doing was done because of the urge of hunger. But, my Brother Wolf, since I am obtaining such a favor for you, I want you to promise me that you will never hurt any animal or man. Will you promise me that?"

The wolf gave a clear sign, by nodding its head, that it promised to do what the saint asked.

And St. Francis said: "Brother Wolf, I want you to give me a pledge so that I can confidently believe what you promise."

And as St. Francis held out his hand to receive the pledge, the wolf also raised its front paw and meekly and gently put it in St. Francis's hand as a sign that it was giving its pledge.

Then St. Francis said: "Brother Wolf, I order you, in the name of the Lord Jesus Christ, to come with me now, without fear, into the town to make this peace pact in the name of the Lord."

And the wolf immediately began to walk along beside St. Francis, just like a very gentle lamb. When the people saw this, they were greatly amazed, and the news spread quickly throughout the whole town, so that all of them, men as well as women, great and small, assembled on the marketplace, because St. Francis was there with the wolf.

So when a very large crowd had gathered, St. Francis gave them a wonderful sermon, saying among other things that such calamities were permitted by God because of their sins, and how the consuming fire of hell by which the damned have to be devoured for all eternity is much more dangerous than the raging of a wolf which can kill nothing but the body, and how much more they should fear to be plunged into hell, since one little animal could keep so great a crowd in such a state of terror and trembling.

"So, dear people," he said, "come back to the Lord, and do fitting penance, and God will free you from the wolf in this world and from the devouring fire of hell in the next world."

And having said that, he added: "Listen, dear people. Brother Wolf, who is standing here before you, has promised me and has given me a pledge that he will make peace with you and will never hurt you if you promise also to feed him every day. And I pledge myself as bondsman for Brother Wolf that he will faithfully keep this peace pact."

Then all the people who were assembled there promised in a loud voice to feed the wolf regularly.

And St. Francis said to the wolf before them all: "And you, Brother Wolf, do you promise to keep this pact, that is, not to hurt any animal or human being?"

The wolf knelt down and bowed its head, and by twisting its body and wagging its tail and ears it clearly showed to everyone that it would keep the pact as it had promised.

And St. Francis said: "Brother Wolf, just as you gave me a pledge of this when we were outside the city gate, I want you to give me a pledge here before all these people that you will keep the pact and will never betray me for having pledged as your bondsman."

Then in the presence of all the people the wolf raised its right paw and put it in St. Francis' hand as a pledge.

And the crowd was so filled with amazement and joy, out of devotion for the saint as well as over the novelty of the miracle and over the peace pact between the wolf and the people, that they all shouted to the sky, praising and blessing the Lord Jesus Christ who had sent St. Francis to them, by whose merits they had been freed from such a fierce wolf and saved from such a terrible scourge and had recovered peace and quiet.

From that day, the wolf and the people kept the pact which St. Francis made. The wolf lived two years more, and it went from door to door for food. It hurt no one, and no one hurt it. The people fed it courteously. And it is a striking fact that not a single dog ever barked at it.

Then the wolf grew old and died. And the people were sorry, because whenever it went through the town, its peaceful kindness and patience reminded them of the virtues and the holiness of St. Francis.

Praised be our Lord Jesus Christ. Amen.

89. Acting Responsibly with Respect to Animals and Plants

KARL BARTH

... The life of beasts as distinct from that of man is merely animally vegetative, and the life of plants as distinct from that of man and beasts is purely vegetative. If only we knew what this really means! If only we knew both forms of life from within, as lived by ourselves! What we first note in animal life (in common with our own) are simply the impulses as such. This is not much. We may well have to reckon on an animal soul, at any rate in the biblical sense of a principle of life. But whether and in what sense we may also ascribe to it a kind of rationality, and how we are to conceive of its relation to the impulses, and above all whether and in what sense it not only derives from God but also moves towards him, remains an enigma. We venture a bold conclusion by analogy if we understand animally vegetative and particularly vegetative life as life in the same sense as human. It can only be said that the analogy forces itself upon us in virtue of the obvious affinity of physical structure at least in the case of animals, and especially of the vital impulses which animals share with man. The close connexion between man and beasts at any rate is a fact, and although our real understanding is so small, and cannot

Karl Barth (1886–1968) was a professor and pastor in Germany and Switzerland. The leading figure in what has come to be known as neoorthodoxy, he is the giant of twentieth-century Protestant theology. His magnum opus is his massive *Church Dogmatics*.

From Karl Barth, *Church Dogmatics*, vol. 3, pt. 4 (Edinburgh: T. & T. Clark, 1961).

derive from a common centre, the relationship is so unmistakable that at the boundary of our present concern for the command of respect for life the question at least arises whether there is a corresponding command in relation to animal life, and at a rather greater distance vegetative life, outside the human sphere. We must refuse to build either ethics as a whole or this particular part of ethics on the view and concept of a life which embraces man, beast and plant. But now that we have spoken of the animal life of man, its right, dignity and sanctification, we cannot refuse to make a temporary halt and to consider the ethical problem of our relation to the life of animals at least, and to some extent of plants as well.

*   *   *

Our starting-point must be that in this matter too, as a living being in coexistence with nonhuman life, man has to think and act responsibly. The responsibility is not the same as he has to his own life and that of his fellow men. Only analogically can we bring it under the concept of respect for life. It can only follow the primary responsibility at a distance. If we try to bring animal and vegetable life too close to human, or even class them together, we can hardly avoid the danger of regarding and treating human life, even when we really want to help, from the aspect of the animal and vegetable, and therefore in a way which is not really apposite. But why should we not be faced here by a responsibility which, if not primary, is a serious secondary responsibility?

The special responsibility in this case rests primarily on this, that the world of animals and plants forms the indispensable living background to the living-space divinely allotted to man and placed under his control. As they live, so can he. He is not set up as lord over the earth, but as lord on the earth which is already furnished with these creatures. Animals and plants do not belong to him; they and the whole earth can belong only to God. But he takes precedence of them. They are provided for his use. They are his "means of life." The meaning of the basis of this distinction consists in the fact that he is the animal creature to whom God reveals, entrusts and binds himself within the rest of creation, with whom he makes common cause in the course of a particular history which is neither that of an animal nor of a plant, and in whose life activity he expects a conscious and deliberate recognition of his honor, mercy, and power. Hence the higher necessity of his life, and his right to that lordship and control. He can exercise it only in the responsibility thus conferred upon him.

But this lordship, and the responsibility which it confers, is in the first instance a differentiated one in respect of the animals and plants. Let us take first the case of plants. We can say unequivocally of these that man may and should exercise his creaturely and relative sovereignty by using them for food. There comes in here what we have stated to be the right of satisfying the animal needs and impulses of man. Man's vegetable nourishment, or the preceding harvest, is not the destruction of vegetation but a sensible use of its superfluity. The only possible limits lie in the nature of man as a rational being and beyond that in his vocation in relation to God and his fellow men.

*   *   *

The question of this human lordship and its corresponding responsibility becomes more difficult when it is a matter of the relation between man and beast. Here, too, lordship can have the primary meaning of requisitioning, disciplining, taming, harnessing, exploiting, and making profitable use of the surplus forces of nature in the animal world. For what is human lordship over the beast if it cannot take this form of "domesticating" animals?

*   *   *

Responsibility within the limits of lordship as understood in this way will consist in what is proposed for our consideration in Proverbs 12:10: "A righteous man regardeth the life of his beast: but the tender mercies of the wicked are cruel." Even within these limits there is still quite enough human stupidity, severity, caprice, and irrationality at work and needing to be curbed. Respect for the fellow creature of man, created with him on the sixth day and so closely related to him, means gratitude to God for the gift of so useful and devoted a comrade, and this gratitude will be translated into a careful, considerate, friendly, and above all understanding treatment of it, in which sympathetic account is taken of its needs and the limits of its possibilities.

*   *   *

So far, so good! But does the lordship of man over the animal consist also in his self-evident freedom to take its life in the service of his own ends? Is he permitted and commanded to kill an animal in the same sense in which he fells a tree, whether for the sake of its meat, for its fur, horns, feathers, or other useful articles, or even to defend himself against the threat of danger or damage which it offers? Those who know respect for life at the point where it arises in the true and primary sense, namely, in the human sphere, will necessarily perceive that there is at least a difference between the two cases. For the killing of animals, in contrast to the harvesting of plants and fruit, is annihilation. This is not a case of participation in the products of a sprouting nexus of life ceaselessly renewed in different forms, but the removing of a single being, a unique creature existing in an individuality which we cannot fathom but also cannot deny. The harvest is not a breach in the peace of creation, nor is the tending and using of animals, but the killing of animals presupposes that the peace of creation is at least threatened and itself constitutes a continuation of this threat. And the nearness of the animal to man irrevocably means that when man kills a beast he does something which is at least very similar to homicide. We must be very clear about this if we maintain that the lordship of man over animals carries with it the freedom to slaughter them. Those who do not hear the prior command to desist have certainly no right to affirm this freedom or cross the frontier disclosed at this point.

*   *   *

If there is a freedom of man to kill animals, this signifies in any case the adoption of a qualified and in some sense enhanced responsibility. If that of his lordship over the living beast is serious enough, it takes on a new gravity when he sees himself compelled to express his lordship by depriving it of its life. He obviously cannot do this except under the pressure of necessity. Far less than all the other things which he dares to do in relation to animals, may this be ventured unthinkingly and as though it were self-evident. He must never treat this need for defensive and offensive action against the animal world as a natural one, nor include it as a normal element in his thinking or conduct. He must always shrink from this possibility even when he makes use of it. It always contains the sharp counterquestion: Who are you, man, to claim that you must venture this to maintain, support, enrich, and beautify your own life? What is there in your life that you feel compelled to take this aggressive step in its favor? We cannot but be reminded of the perversion from which the whole historical existence of the creature suffers and the guilt of which does not really reside in the beast but ultimately in man himself. The slaying of animals is really possible only as an appeal to God's reconciling grace, as its representation and proclamation. It undoubtedly means making use of the offering of an alien and innocent victim and claiming its life for ours. Man must have good reasons for seriously making such a claim. His real and supposed needs certainly do not justify it. He must be authorized to do so by his acknowledgment of the faithfulness and goodness of God, who in spite of and in his guilt keeps him from falling as he saved Noah's generation from the flood and kept it even though it was no better as a result. Man sins if he does it without this authorization. He sins if he presumes to do it on his own authority. He is already on his way to homicide if he sins in the killing of animals, if he murders an animal. He must not murder an animal. He can only kill it, knowing that it does not belong to him but to God, and that in killing it he surrenders it to God in order to receive it back from him as something he needs and desires. The killing of animals in obedience is possible only as a deeply reverential act of repentance, gratitude, and praise on the part of the forgiven sinner in face of the one who is the Creator and Lord of man and beast. The killing of animals, when performed with the permission of God and by his command, is a priestly act of eschatological character. It can be accomplished with a good conscience only as we glance backward to creation and forward to the consummation as the boundaries of the sphere in which alone there can be any question of its necessity. It can be achieved only in recollection of the reconciliation of man by the Man who intercedes for him and for all creation, and in whom God has accomplished the reconciliation of the world with himself.

90. God and the World

SALLIE MCFAGUE

. . . [W]hat if we were to understand the resurrection and ascension not as the bodily translation of some individuals to another world — a mythology no longer credible to us — but as the promise of God to be permanently present, "bodily" present to us, in all places and times of our world?[1] In what ways would we think of the relationship between God and the world were we to experiment with the metaphor of the universe as God's "body," God's palpable presence in all space and time? If what is needed in our ecological, nuclear age is an imaginative vision of the relationship between God and the world that underscores their interdependence and mutuality, empowering a sensibility of care and responsibility toward all life, how would it help to see the world as the body of God?

In making this suggestion, we must always keep in mind its *metaphorical* character: we are not slip-

1. To see the resurrection of Jesus as an expression of God's presence in all space and time cannot in any way restrict that presence to the Christian community. The metaphor of the world as God's body is fundamentally linked not to the resurrection of Jesus but to an understanding of creation. For the Christian community, the resurrection is, however, a powerful and concrete expression of this creational reality. Other religious traditions have other particular expressions of it.

Sallie McFague (1933–) is the E. Rhodes and Leona B. Carpenter Professor of Theology at Vanderbilt Divinity School. Her work includes *Speaking in Parables* and *Models of God*.

From Sallie McFague, *Models of God: Theology for an Ecological, Nuclear Age* (Philadelphia: Fortress Press, 1987).

ping back into the search for unmediated divine presence (which the deconstructionists have criticized so thoroughly). There is no way behind this metaphor or any other construal of the God-world relationship; at most, a metaphor fits with some interpretation of the Christian gospel and is illuminating and fruitful when lived in for a while. Hence, to imagine the world as God's body is to do precisely that: to imagine it that way. It is not to say that the world is God's body or that God is present to us in the world. Those things we do not know; all that resurrection faith can do is imagine the most significant ways to speak of God's presence in one's own time. And the metaphor of the world as God's body presents itself as a promising candidate.

This image, radical as it may seem (in light of the dominant metaphor of a king to his realm) for imagining the relationship between God and the world, is a very old one with roots in Stoicism and elliptically in the Hebrew Scriptures. The notion has tantalized many, including Tertullian and Irenaeus, and though it received little assistance from either Platonism or Aristotelianism because of their denigration of matter and body (and hence did not enter the mainstream of either Augustinian or Thomistic theology), it surfaced powerfully in Hegel as well as in twentieth-century process theologies.[2] The mystical tradition within Christianity has carried the notion implicitly, even though the metaphor of body may not appear: "The world is charged with the grandeur of God" (Gerard Manley Hopkins); "There is communion with God, and a communion with the earth, and a communion with God through earth" (Pierre Teilhard de Chardin).[3]

We are asking whether one way to remythologize the gospel for our time might not be through the metaphor of the world as God's "body" rather than as the king's "realm." If we experiment with this metaphor, it becomes obvious that royalist,

triumphalist images for God — God as king, lord, ruler, patriarch — will be inappropriate. Other metaphors, suggesting mutuality, interdependence, caring, and responsiveness, will be needed. I will suggest God as mother (father), lover, and friend. If the world is imagined as self-expressive of God, if it is a "sacrament" — the outward and visible presence or body — of God, if it is not an alien other over against God but expressive of God's very being, then, how would God respond to it and how should we? Would not the metaphors of parents, lovers, and friends be suggestive, with their implications of creation, nurture, passionate concern, attraction, respect, support, cooperation, mutuality? If the entire universe is expressive of God's very being — *the* "incarnation," if you will — do we not have the beginnings of an imaginative picture of the relationship between God and the world peculiarly appropriate as a context for interpreting the salvific love of God *for our time?*

It is this picture we will be investigating in as much detail as possible in these pages. The issue is how to remythologize the Christian's cry of affirmation "Christ is risen!" — the promise of God's saving presence always — for our space and time. We will first look at the tradition's monarchical mythology for imaging God's relationship to the world. The classical picture, an imaginatively powerful one, employs royalist, triumphalist metaphors, depicting God as king, lord, and patriarch who rules the world and human beings, usually with benevolence. Is this understanding of God's presence in and to the world, and hence, by implication, our presence in and to the world, one that is appropriate and helpful for a holistic, nuclear time? I believe it is not and will suggest below that we consider the world as God's body. In what ways is this metaphor an appropriate context for interpreting the destabilizing, nonhierarchical, inclusive vision of fulfillment for all of creation? How would we feel and act differently in a world that we perceived as the body of God?

Finally, if we accept the imaginative picture of the world as God's body, it is obvious that the triumphalist, imperialistic metaphors of God will no longer be appropriate. I have suggested the metaphors of God as parent, lover, and friend of the earth that is expressive of God's very self. We will in subsequent chapters be investigating these

---

2. For a treatment of some of these theological traditions, see Grace Jantzen, *God's World, God's Body* (Philadelphia: Westminster Press, 1984), chap. 3.

3. Gerard Manley Hopkins, "God's Grandeur," in *Poems and Prose of Gerard Manley Hopkins* (London: Penguin Books, 1953), p. 27; Pierre Teilhard de Chardin, *Writings in Time of War*, trans. René Hague (London: William Collins Sons, 1968), p. 14.

metaphors in detail, but some general issues concerning these images need to be considered first.

For instance, the question arises whether any personal metaphors should be employed for imaging God's presence. Are not more abstract, impersonal, or naturalistic metaphors better for encouraging an ecological sensibility? In the final section of this chapter we will consider the viability of metaphors of personal presence such as mother (and father), lover, and friend. Are these metaphors too intimate, too personal, and indeed, perhaps too individualistic? What defense can be given for imaging God on analogy with human beings and in metaphors expressive of our most important relationships?

As we begin this exercise of the deconstruction and reconstruction of metaphors in which we imagine the saving power of God in our contemporary world, it is necessary to remind ourselves of the nature of our project. We will not be defining or describing the world or universe as God's body nor God's relationship to it as that of mother, lover, or friend. Rather, we will be using descriptions that properly apply elsewhere and letting them try their chance at the difficult task of expressing some significant aspects of the God-world relationship in our time. That they will miss the mark or be nonsense some of the time will come as no surprise. A heuristic theology plays with ideas in order to find out, searches for likely accounts rather than definitions. The object of this kind of theology is to suggest metaphors that create a shock of recognition. Does "the world as God's body" or "God as lover" have both marks of a good metaphor, both the *shock* and the *recognition*? Do these metaphors both disorient and reorient? Do they evoke a response of hearing something new and something interesting? Are they both disclosive and illuminating, both a revelation and in some sense true? I wish at all costs to avoid the "tyranny of the absolutizing imagination," which would insist that our newly suggested metaphors are the only or the permanent ones for expressing God's saving love. No such claims will be made; instead, a case will be presented to show that the metaphors are appropriate, illuminating, and better than some alternatives.

The Monarchical Model

The *monarchical model* of God as King was developed systematically, both in Jewish thought (God as Lord and King of the Universe), in medieval Christian thought (with its emphasis on divine onmipotence), and in the Reformation (especially in Calvin's insistence on God's sovereignty). In the portrayal of God's relation to the world, the dominant western historical model has been that of the absolute monarch ruling over his kingdom.[4]

This imaginative picture is so prevalent in mainstream Christianity that it is often not recognized as a picture. Nor is it immediately perceived as oppressive. More often it is accepted as the natural understanding of the relationship of God and the world — and one we like. Think for a moment of the sense of triumph, joy, and power that surges through us when we join in singing the "Hallelujah Chorus" from Handel's *Messiah*. Probably we do not think about the implications of the images we sing, but we know they make us feel good about our God and about ourselves as his subjects: "King of Kings and Lord of Lords," "for the Lord God omnipotent reigneth." Our God is really God, the almighty Lord and King of the universe whom none can defeat, and by implication we also are undefeatable.

It is a powerful imaginative picture and a very dangerous one. As we have already noted, it has resulted in what Gordon Kaufman calls a pattern of "asymmetrical dualism" between God and the world, in which God and the world are only distantly related and all power, either as domination or benevolence, is on God's side.[5] It supports

4. Ian G. Barbour, *Myths, Models and Paradigms: A Comparative Study in Science and Religion* (New York: Harper & Row, 1974), 156. Edward Farley and Peter C. Hodgson agree: ". . . the Christian movement never abandoned the royal metaphor for God and God's relation to the world. The logic of sovereignty, which presumes that God employs whatever means are necessary to ensure the successful accomplishment of the divine will, eventually pervaded the total criteriology of Christendom" ("Scripture and Tradition," in *Christian Theology: An Introduction to Its Traditions and Tasks*, rev. ed., ed. Peter C. Hodgson and Robert H. King [Philadelphia: Fortress Press, 1985]), 68.

5. See *Models of God* (Philadelphia: Fortress Press, 1987), chap. 1, pp. 16-20, for a discussion of this point.

conceiving of God as a being existing somewhere apart from the world and ruling it externally either directly through divine intervention or indirectly through controlling the wills of his subjects. It creates feelings of awe in the hearts of loyal subjects and thus supports the "godness" of God, but these feelings are balanced by others of abject fear and humiliation: in this picture, God can be God only if we are nothing. The understanding of salvation that accompanies this view is sacrificial, substitutionary atonement, and in Anselm's classic rendition of it the sovereign imagery predominates. Since even a wink of the eye by a vassal against the liege Lord of the universe would be irredeemable sin, we as abject subjects must rely totally on our sovereign God who "became man" in order to undergo a sacrificial death, substituting his great worth for our worthlessness. Again, we feel the power of this picture: because we are totally unable to help ourselves, we will be totally cared for. We not only are forgiven for our sins and reconciled to our King as once again his loyal subjects but we can also look forward to a time when we shall join him in his heavenly Kingdom.

This picture, while simplistic and anachronistic, continues in spite of its limitations, because of its psychological power: it makes us feel good about God and about ourselves. It inspires strong emotions of awe, gratitude, and trust toward God and, in ourselves, engenders a satisfying swing from abject guilt to joyous relief. Its very power is part of its danger, and any picture that seeks to replace it must reckon with its attraction. Many have criticized the monarchical model, and it has been severely rejected by a wide range of contemporary theologians.[6] My criticism of it here focuses on its inability to serve as the imaginative framework for an understanding of the gospel as a destabilizing, inclusive, nonhierarchical vision of fulfillment for all of creation. In that respect, it has three major flaws: in the monarchical model, God is distant from the world, relates only to the human world, and controls that world through domination and benevolence.

The relationship of a king to his subjects is necessarily a distant one: royalty is "untouchable." It is the distance, the difference, the otherness of God that is underscored with this imagery. God as King is in his Kingdom — which is not of this earth — and we remain in another place, far from his dwelling. In this picture God is worldless and the world is Godless: the world is empty of God's presence, for it is too lowly to be the royal abode. Time and space are not filled with God: the eons of human and geological time stretch as a yawning void back into the recesses, empty of the divine presence; the places loved and noted on our earth, as well as the unfathomable space of the universe, are not the house of God. Whatever one does for the world is not finally important in this model, for its ruler does not inhabit it as his primary residence, and his subjects are well advised not to become too involved in it either. The king's power extends over the entire universe, of course, but his being does not: he relates to it externally, he is not part of it but essentially different from it and apart from it.

Although these comments may at first seem to be a caricature rather than a fair description of the classical Western monarchical model they are the direct implications of its imagery. If metaphors matter, then one must take them seriously at the level at which they function, that is, at the level of the imaginative picture of God and the world they project. If one uses triumphalist, royal metaphors for God, certain things follow, and one of the most important is a view of God as distant from and

---

6. Dorothee Soelle claims that authoritarian religion that images God as dominating power lay behind the "obedience" of Nazism and thus behind the Jewish Holocaust (*The Strength of the Weak: Toward a Christian Feminist Identity*, trans. Robert and Rita Kimber [Philadelphia: Westminster Press, 1984]). John B. Cobb, Jr., and David R. Griffin view the classic Western God as "the Cosmic Morality," whose main attribute is power over all creatures rather than responsive love that could lead to the fulfillment of all creatures (*Process Theology: An Introductory Exposition* [Philadelphia: Westminster Press, 1976]). Jürgen Moltmann objects to the "monarchical monotheism" of Christianity which supports hierarchalism and individualism, and insists instead that a social, trinitarian doctrine of God is needed (*The Trinity and the Kingdom of God* [San Francisco: Harper & Row, 1981]). Edward Farley claims that the royal metaphors for God have fueled the notion of "salvation history" and its "logic of triumph" (*Ecclesial Reflection: An Anatomy of Theological Method* [Philadelphia: Fortress Press, 1982]).

basically uninvolved with the world. God's distance from and lack of intrinsic involvement with the world are emphasized when God's real Kingdom is an other-worldly one: Christ is raised from the dead to join the sovereign Father — as we shall be also — in the true Kingdom. The world is not self-expressive of God: God's being, satisfaction, and future are not connected with our world. Not only, then, is the world Godless but God as King and Lord is worldless, in all but an external sense. To be sure, kings want their subjects to be loyal and their realms peaceful, but that does not mean internal, intrinsic involvement. Kings do not have to, and usually do not, love their subjects or realms; at most, one hopes they will be benevolent.

But such benevolence extends only to human subjects; in the monarchical model there is no concern for the cosmos, for the nonhuman world. Here is our second objection to the model. It is simply blank in terms of what lies outside the human sphere. As a political model focused on governing human beings, it leaves out nine-tenths of reality. One could say at this point that, as with all models, it has limitations and needs to be balanced by other models. Such a comment does not address the seriousness of the monarchical model's limitations in regard to nonhuman reality, for as the dominant Western model it has not allowed competing or alternative models to arise. The tendency, rather, has been to draw other models into its orbit, as is evident with the model of God as father. This model could have gone in the direction of parent (and that is clearly its New Testament course), with its associations of nurture, care, guidance, concern, and self-sacrifice, but under the powerful influence of the monarchical model, the parent became the patriarch, and patriarchs act more like kings than like fathers: they rule their children and they demand obedience.

The hegemony of the monarchical model means that its blankness concerning what lies outside the human sphere is a major problem. If we seek a model that will express the inclusive, non-hierarchical vision of the gospel, this is not it. The model's anthropocentrism (the other side of its lack of concern for the natural world) can be seen, for instance, in classical Protestantism's emphasis on the the word of God. The monarchical model and an aural tradition fit together naturally, for kings give orders and subjects obey, but the model

has no place for creatures who cannot hear and obey. An interpretation of Christianity that focuses on hearing the word, on listening to the word as preached and on the Scriptures in which the word is written, is a tradition limited to human beings, for they alone are linguistic. God is present in words and to those who can hear, and if Francis of Assisi preached to the birds, few have followed his example. An aural tradition is anthropocentric: we are the only ones who can "hear the word of the Lord." A visual tradition, however, is more inclusive: if God can be present not only in what one hears but also in what one sees, then potentially anything and everything in the world can be a symbol of the divine. One does not preach to the birds, but a bird can be a metaphor to express God's intimate presence in the world: ". . . the Holy Ghost over the bent world broods with warm breast and with ah! bright wings."[7]

A visual tradition has a place for birds and for much else; if one allows in the other senses of smell, taste, and touch, then, as Augustine puts it in book 10 of the *Confessions,* one loves "light and melody and fragrance and food and embrace" when one loves one's God. In other words, one has let the whole world in: not just words are expressive of God's saving presence but everything can be.[8] The world can be seen as the "body" of God. It is not, then, just a book, the Scriptures, that is special as the medium of divine presence, but the world is also God's dwelling place. If an inclusive vision of the gospel must include the

7. Gerard Manley Hopkins, "God's Grandeur," in *Poems and Prose,* 27.

8. The aural tradition criticized here is obviously only one version of a Logos theology, and one peculiar to Protestantism. I am grateful to Rosemary Radford Ruether for a comment on this point in a letter dated May 16, 1986, in which she writes of "the strong current in neo-Platonism which cultivates a 'cosmos piety' of the visible world as an embodied God, found in Hermetic theology and even in Plotinus and in Plato's *Timaeus.* This tradition flows into a Christian sacramentality which sees the whole cosmos as sacramental, i.e., the bodying forth of the divine Logos. This is a very different understanding of Logos from the 'heard word' that is absent. It is Logos as ground of being bodying forth in not only human being, but all visible things. This older cosmos theology needs to be given more credit for a view very similar to yours."

world, it is evident that the monarchical model, which not only cannot include the world but is totally anthropocentric and excludes alternative models, is sadly lacking.

This anthropocentric model is also dualistic and hierarchical. Not all dualisms are hierarchical; for instance, in the Chinese understanding of yin and yang, a balance is sought and neither is considered superior to the other, for too much of one or the other is undesirable. But a dualism of king and subjects is intrinsically hierarchical and encourages hierarchical, dualistic thinking of the sort that has fueled many kinds of oppression, including (in addition to that of the nonhuman by the human) those arising from the cleavages of male/female, white/colored, rich/poor, Christian/non-Christian, and mind/body. The monarchical model encourages a way of thinking that is pervasive and pernicious, in a time when exactly the opposite is needed as a basic pattern. The hierarchical, dualistic pattern is so widespread in Western thought that it is usually not perceived to be a pattern but is left to be simply the way things are. It appears natural to many that males, whites, the rich, Christians, and the mind are superior, and to suggest that human beings, under the influence of powerful, dominant models such as the monarchical one, have constructed these dualistic hierarchies is to these people not believable. Or to put it with more subtlety, though tolerance is a contemporary civil virtue and not many would say openly that these dualisms are natural, deep down they believe they are.

We come, then, to the third criticism of the monarchical model: in this model God not only is distant from the world and relates only to the human world, but he also controls that world through a combination of domination and benevolence. This is the logical implication of hierarchical dualism: God's action is on the world, not in it, and it is a kind of action that inhibits human growth and responsibility. (Such action represents the kind of power that oppresses — and indeed enslaves — others; but enough has been said already in these pages and by others on that aspect of the model, which is its most obvious fault.) What is of equal importance is the less obvious point that the monarchical model implies the wrong kind of divine activity in relation to the world, a kind that encourages passivity on the part of human beings.

It is simplistic to blame the Judeo-Christian tradition for the ecological crisis, as some have done, on the grounds that Genesis instructs human beings to have "dominion" over nature; nonetheless, the imagery of sovereignty supports attitudes of control and use toward the nonhuman world.[9] Although the might of the natural world when unleashed is fearsome, as is evident in earthquakes, tornadoes, and volcanic eruptions, the power balance has shifted from nature to us, and an essential aspect of the new sensibility is to recognize and accept this. Nature can and does destroy many, but it is not in a position to destroy all as we can. Extinction of species by nature is in a different dimension from extinction by design, which only we can bring about. This chilling thought adds a new importance to the images we use to characterize our relationship to others and to the nonhuman world. If we are capable of extinguishing ourselves and most if not all other life, metaphors that support attitudes of distance from, and domination of, other human beings and nonhuman life must be recognized as dangerous. No matter how ancient a metaphorical tradition may be and regardless of its credentials in Scripture, liturgy, and creedal statements, it still must be discarded if it threatens the continuation of life itself. What possible case can be made for metaphors of the God-world relationship which encourage attitudes on the part of human beings destructive of themselves as well as of the cosmos which supports all life? If the heart of the Christian gospel is the salvific power of God, triumphalist metaphors cannot express that reality *in our time,* whatever their appropriateness may have been in the past.

And this is so even if God's power is seen as benevolence rather than domination. For if God's rule is understood benevolently, it will be assumed that all is well — that the world will be cared for with no help from us. The King as dominating

---

9. See the well-known essay by Lynn White which makes this accusation in its strongest form: "The Historical Roots of Our Ecological Crisis," in *Ecology and Religion in History,* ed. David and Eileen Spring (New York: Harper & Row, 1974). See also a refutation of White's argument in Arthur R. Peacocke, *Creation and the World of Science* (Oxford: At the Clarendon Press, 1979).

sovereign encourages attitudes of militarism and destruction; the King as benevolent patriarch encourages attitudes of passivity and escape from responsibility.[10] In the triumphalist, royal model the victory has already been won on the Cross and in the resurrection of Jesus Christ, and nothing is required of us. We can rest comfortably in the assurance that our mighty Lord will deal with all present end future evil as he has always dealt with evil. Such a view of God's benevolence undercuts human effort of any sort.

The monarchical model is dangerous in our time: it encourages a sense of distance from the world; it attends only to the human dimension of the world; and it supports attitudes of either domination of the world or passivity toward it. As an alternative model, I suggest considering the world as God's body. Questions abound with this piece of "nonsense." It is a shocking idea; is it also an illuminating one? What does it mean from God's side and what from our side? Is it pantheistic? Is God or are we reduced to the world? With this metaphor how would one speak of God knowing and acting in the world as well as loving it? What about evil? About sin? What of *our* freedom, individuality, and behavior in such a world?

The World as God's Body

We are letting the metaphor of the world as God's body try its chance.[11] We are experimenting with

a bit of nonsense to see if it can make a claim to truth. What if, we are asking, the "resurrection of the body" were not seen as the resurrection of particular bodies that ascend, beginning with Jesus of Nazareth, into another world, but as God's promise to be with us always in God's body, our world? What if God's promise of permanent presence to all space and time were imagined as a worldly reality, a palpable, bodily presence? What if, then, we did not have to go somewhere special (church) or somewhere else (another world) to be in the presence of God but could feel ourselves in that presence at all times and in all places? What if we imagined God's presence as in us and in all others, including the last and the least?

As we begin this experiment we must once again recall that a metaphor or model is not a description. We are trying to think in an as-if fashion about the God-world relationship, because we have no other way of thinking about it. No metaphor fits in all ways, and some are more nonsense than sense. The king-realm kind of thinking about the God-world relationship sounds like sense because we are used to it, but reflection shows that in our world it is nonsense. For a metaphor to be acceptable, it need not, cannot, apply in all ways; if it did, it would be a description. One has to realize how not to apply a metaphor (to say God is the Father does not mean that God has a beard!) and also where it fails or treads on shaky ground. The metaphor of the world as God's body has the opposite problem to the metaphor of the world as the king's realm: if the latter puts too great a distance between God and the world, the former verges on too great a proximity. Since both metaphors are inadequate, we have to ask which one is better in our time,

---

10. There is, however, another metaphorical tradition of benevolence that moves in a more positive direction: God as gardener, caretaker, and hence preserver of the world and its life. Here benevolence is not distant good will as in the royal metaphor, but intimate nurture. Gardeners or caretakers "touch" the earth and the life they care for with the goal of creating conditions in which life other than their own can grow and prosper. Such benevolence promotes human responsibility, not escapism and passivity, and hence these metaphors are helpful ones in our time. For further analysis, see Phyllis Trible, *God and the Rhetoric of Sexuality* (Philadelphia: Fortress Press, 1978), 85ff.

11. The metaphor, especially in its form as an analogy — self:body::God:world — is widespread, particularly among process theologians, as a way of overcoming the externality of God's knowledge of and activity in the world. Theologians of nature, who take the

evolutionary reality of the world seriously, also find it attractive as a noninterventionist way of speaking of God's agency in history and nature. See, e.g., Claude Stewart, *Nature in Grace: A Study in the Theology of Nature* (Macon, Ga.: Mercer Univ. Press, 1983). Even among more traditional theologies, the embodiment of God is receiving attention. Grace Jantzen's position, e.g., is that, given the contemporary holistic understanding of personhood, an embodied personal God is more credible than a disembodied one and is commensurate with traditional attributes of God (*God's World, God's Body*).

and to qualify it with other metaphors and models. Is it better to accept an imaginative picture of God as the distant ruler controlling his realm through external and benevolent power or one of God so intimately related to the world that the world can be imagined as God's body? There are, of course, different understandings of "better." Is it better in terms of our and the world's preservation and fulfillment? Is it better in terms of coherence, comprehensibility, and illumination? Is it better in terms of expressing the Christian understanding of the relationship between God and the world? All these criteria are relevant, for a metaphor that is all or mostly nonsense has tried its chance and failed.

Therefore, a heuristic, metaphorical theology, though hospitable initially to nonsense is constrained as well to search for sense. Christians should, given their tradition, be inclined to find sense in "body" language, not only because of the resurrection of the body but also because of the bread and wine of the eucharist as the body and blood of Christ, and the church as the body with Christ as its head. Christians have a surprisingly "bodily" tradition; nonetheless, there is a difference between the traditional uses of "body" and seeing the world as God's body; when the world is viewed as God's body, that body includes more than just Christians and more than just human beings. It is possible to speculate that if Christianity had begun in a culture less dualistic and antiphysical than that of the first-century Mediterranean world, it might have been willing, given the more holistic anthropology and theology of its Hebraic roots, to extend its body metaphor to God.[12] At any rate, in view of the contemporary holistic understanding of personhood, in which embodiment is the *sine qua non*, the thought of an embodied personal deity is not more incredible than that of a disembodied one; in fact, it is less so. In a dualistic culture where mind and body, spirit and flesh, are separable, a disembodied, personal God is more credible, but not in ours. This is only to suggest that the idea of God's embodiment — the idea as such, quite apart from particulars — should not be seen as nonsense; it is less

nonsense than the idea of a disembodied personal God.

A more central issue is whether the metaphor of the world as God's body is pantheistic or, to put it another way, reduces God to the world. The metaphor does come far closer to pantheism than the king-realm model, which verges on deism, but it does not totally identify God with the world any more than we totally identify ourselves with our bodies. Other animals may be said to be bodies that have spirits; we may be said to be spirits that possess bodies.[13] This is not to introduce a new dualism but only to recognize that although our bodies are expressions of us both unconsciously and consciously, we can reflect about them and distance ourselves from them. The very fact that we can speak about our bodies is evidence that we are not totally one with them. On this model, God is not reduced to the world if the world is God's body. Without the use of personal agential metaphors, however, including among others God as mother, lover, and friend, the metaphor of the world as God's body would be pantheistic, for the body would be all there were. Nonetheless, the model is monist and perhaps most precisely designated as panentheistic; that is, it is a view of the God-world relationship in which all things have their origins in God and nothing exists outside God, though this does not mean that God is reduced to these things.[14] There is, as it were, a limit

---

12. See Jantzen's fine study on the dualistic, antimatter context of early Christian theology, in chap. 3 of *God's World, God's Body*.

13. John Cobb makes this point and adds that total identification with our bodies becomes impossible when they are sick, maimed, aging, enslaved, or dying. We are not our bodies at such times. See his "Feminism and Process Thought," in *Feminism and Process Thought*, ed. Sheila Greeve Davaney (New York: Edwin Mellen Press, 1981).

14. Paul Tillich's definition of pantheism is close to Karl Rahner's and Herbert Vorgrimler's definition of panentheism: "Pantheism is the doctrine that God is the substance or essence of all things, not the meaningless assertion that God is the totality of all things" (*Systematic Theology*, vol. 1 [Chicago: Univ. of Chicago Press, 1963], 324); "This form of pantheism does not intend simply to identify the world and God monistically (God = the 'all') but intends, instead, to conceive of the 'all' of the world 'in' God as God's inner modification and appearance, even if God is not exhausted by the 'all'" (*Kleines theologisches Wortenbuchen* [Freiberg: Herder & Herder, 1961], 275).

on our side, not on God's: the world does not exist outside or apart from God. Christian theism, which has always claimed that there is but one reality and it is God's — that there is no competing (evil) reality — is necessarily monist, though the monarchical imaginative picture that has accompanied it is implicitly if not blatantly dualistic. It sets God over against competing, presumably ontological, powers, and over against the world as an alien other to be controlled.

Nevertheless, though God is not reduced to the world, the metaphor of the world as God's body puts God "at risk." If we follow out the implications of the metaphor, we see that God becomes dependent through being bodily, in a way that a totally invisible, distant God would never be. Just as we care about our bodies, are made vulnerable by them, and must attend to their well-being, God will be liable to bodily contingencies. The world as God's body may be poorly cared for, ravaged, and as we are becoming well aware, essentially destroyed, in spite of God's own loving attention to it, because of one creature, ourselves, who can choose or not choose to join with God in conscious care of the world. Presumably, were this body blown up, another could be formed; hence, God need not be seen to be as dependent on us or on any particular body as we are on our own bodies. But in the metaphor of the universe as the self-expression of God — God's incarnation — the notions of vulnerability, shared responsibility, and risk are inevitable. This is a markedly different basic understanding of the God-world relationship than in the monarch-realm metaphor, for it emphasizes God's willingness to suffer for and with the world, even to the point of personal risk. The world as God's body, then, may be seen as a way to remythologize the inclusive, suffering love of the Cross of Jesus of Nazareth. In both instances, God is at risk in human hands: just as once upon a time in a bygone mythology, human beings killed their God in the body of a man, so now we once again have that power, but, in a mythology appropriate to our time, we would kill our God in the body of the world. Could we actually do this? To believe in the resurrection means we could not. God is not in our power to destroy, but the incarnate God is the God at risk: we have been given central responsibility to care for God's body, our world.

If God, though at risk and dependent on others, is not reduced to the world in the metaphor of the world as God's body, what more can we say about the meaning of this model from God's side? How does God know the world, act in it, and love it? How does one speak of evil in this metaphor? In the monarchical model, God knows the world externally, acts on it either by direct intervention or indirectly through human subjects, and loves it benevolently, in a charitable way. God's knowledge, action, and love are markedly different in the metaphor of the world as God's body. God knows the world immediately just as we know our bodies immediately. God could be said to be in touch with all parts of the world through interior understanding. Moreover, this knowledge is empathetic, intimate, sympathetic knowledge, closer to feeling than to rationality.[15] It is knowledge "by acquaintance"; it is not "information about." Just as we are internally related to our bodies, so God is internally related to all that is — the most radically relational Thou. God relates sympathetically to the world, just as we relate sympathetically to our bodies. This implies, of course, an immediacy and concern in God's knowledge of the world impossible in the king-realm model.

Moreover, it implies that the action of God in the world is similarly interior and caring. If the entire universe, all that is and has been, is God's body, then God acts in and through the incredibly complex physical and historical-cultural evolutionary process that began aeons ago.[16] This does

---

15. Most theologians who employ the analogy of self:body::God:world speak in these terms about God's knowledge of the world. Since God is *internally* related to the world, divine knowledge is an immediate, sympathetic awareness. See, e.g., Charles Hartshorne, "Philosophical and Religious Uses of 'God,'" in *Process Theology: Basic Writings*, ed. Ewart H. Cousins (New York: Newman Press, 1977), 109; Schubert Ogden, "The Reality of God," in ibid., 123; and Jantzen, *God's World, God's Body*, 81ff.

16. To understand the action of God as interior to the entire evolutionary process does not mean that some events, aspects, and dimensions cannot be more important than others. See, e.g., the analysis of "act" of God by Gordon Kaufman in *God the Problem* ([Cambridge: Harvard Univ. Press, 1979], 140ff.), in which he distinguishes between "master" act (the entire evolu-

not mean that God is reduced to the evolutionary process, for God remains as the agent, the self, whose intentions are expressed in the universe. Nevertheless, the manner in which these intentions are expressed is internal and, by implication, providential — that is, reflective of a "caring" relationship. God does not, as in the royal model, intervene in the natural or historical process in *deus-ex-machina* fashion nor feel merely charitable toward the world. The suggestion, however, that God cares about the world as one cares about one's body, that is, with a high degree of sympathetic concern, does not imply that all is well or the future is assured, for with the body metaphor, God is at risk. It does suggest, however, that to trust in a God whose body is the world is to trust in a God who cares profoundly for the world.

Furthermore, the model of the world as God's body suggests that God loves bodies: in loving the world, God loves a body. Such a notion is a sharp challenge to the long antibody, antiphysical, antimatter tradition within Christianity. This tradition has repressed healthy sexuality, oppressed women as sexual tempters, and defined Christian redemption in spiritualistic ways, thus denying that basic social and economic needs of embodied beings are relevant to salvation. To say that God loves bodies is to redress the balance toward a more holistic understanding of fulfillment. It is to say that bodies are worth loving, sexually and otherwise, that passionate love as well as attention to the needs of bodily existence is a part of fulfillment. It is to say further that the basic necessities of bodily existence — adequate food and shelter, for example — are central aspects of God's love for all bodily creatures and therefore should be central concerns of us, God's coworkers. In a holistic sensibility there can be no spirit/body split: if neither we nor God is disembodied, the denigration of the body, the physical, and matter should end. Such a split makes no sense in our world: spirit and body or matter are on a continuum, for matter is not inanimate substance but throbs of energy, essentially in continuity with spirit. To love bodies, then, is to love not what is opposed to

tionary process) and "subordinate" acts (such as Jesus' march to the Cross as an essential constituent of the master act).

spirit but what is at one with it — which the model of the world as God's body fully expresses.

* * *

When we turn to our side of this picture of the world its God's body, we have to ask whether we are reduced to being mere parts of the body? What is our freedom? How is sin understood here? How would we behave in this model? The model did not fit God's side in every way, and it does not fit ours in every way either. It seems especially problematic at the point of our individuality and freedom. At least in the king-realm model, human beings appear to have some freedom since they are controlled only externally, not internally. The problem emerges because of the nature of bodies: if we are parts of God's body — if the model is totally organic — are we not then totally immersed, along with all other creatures, in the evolutionary process, with no transcendence or freedom? It appears, however, at least to us, that we are a special part. We think of ourselves as the *imago dei*, as not only possessing bodies but being agents. We view ourselves as embodied spirits in the larger body of the world which influences us and which we influence. That is, we are the part modeled on the model: self:body::God:world. We are agents and God possesses a body: both sides of the model pertain to both God and ourselves. This implies that we are not mere submerged parts of the body of God but relate to God as to another Thou. The presence of God to us in and through God's body is the experience of encounter, not of submersion. For the saving love of God to be present to human beings it would have to be so in a way different from how it is present to other aspects of the body of the world — in a way in keeping with the peculiar kind of creatures we are, namely, creatures with a special kind of freedom, able to participate self-consciously (as well as be influenced unconsciously) in the evolutionary process. This gives us a special status and a special responsibility: we are the ones like God; we are selves that possess bodies, and that is our glory. It is also our responsibility, for we alone can choose to become partners with God in the care of the world; we alone can — like God — mother, love, and befriend the world, the body that God has made available to us as both the divine presence and our home.

Our special status and responsibility, however, are not limited to consciousness of our own personal bodies or even of the human world but extend to all embodied reality, for we are that part of the cosmos where the cosmos itself comes to consciousness. If we become extinct, then the cosmos will lose its human, although presumably not its divine, consciousness. As Jonathan Schell remarks, "In extinction a darkness falls over the world not because the lights have gone out but because the eyes that behold the light have been closed."[17] The tragedy of human annihilation by war, even if some plants and some other animals survived, would be that there were no one to be conscious of embodied reality: the cosmos would have lost its consciousness.

It is obvious, then, what sin is in this metaphor of the world as God's body: it is refusal to be part of the body, the special part we are. as *imago dei.* In contrast to the king-realm model, where sin is against *God,* here it is against the world. To sin is not to refuse loyalty to the liege Lord but to refuse to take responsibility for nurturing, loving, and befriending the body and all its parts. Sin is the refusal to realize one's radical interdependence with all that lives: it is the desire to set oneself apart from all others as not needing them or being needed by them. Sin is the refusal to be the eyes, the consciousness, of the cosmos.

What this experiment with the world as God's body comes to, finally, is an awareness, both chilling and breathtaking, that we as worldly, bodily beings are in God's presence. It is the basis for a revived sacramentalism, that is, a perception of the divine as visible, as present, palpably present in our world. But it is a kind of sacramentalism that is painfully conscious of the world's vulnerability, its preciousness, its uniqueness. The beauty of the world and its ability to sustain the vast multitude of species it supports is not there for the taking. The world is a body that must be carefully tended, that must be nurtured, protected, guided, loved, and befriended both as valuable in itself — for like us, it is an expression of God — and as necessary to the continuation of life. We meet the world as a Thou, as the body of God where God is present to us always in all times and in all places. In the metaphor of the world as the body of God, the resurrection becomes a worldly, present, inclusive reality, for this body is offered to all: "This is my body." As is true of all bodies, however, this body, in its beauty and preciousness, is vulnerable and at risk: it will delight the eye only if we care for it; it will nourish us only if we nurture it. Needless to say, then, were this metaphor to enter our consciousness as thoroughly as the royal, triumphalist one has entered, it would result in a different way of being in the world. There would be no way that we could any longer see God as worldless or the world as Godless. Nor could we expect God to take care of everything, either through domination or through benevolence.

We see through pictures. We do not see directly: the pictures of a king and his realm and of the world as God's body are ways of speaking, ways of imagining the God-world relationship. The one pictures a vast distance between God and the world; the other imagines them as intrinsically related. At the close of day, one asks which distortion (assuming that all pictures are false in some respects) is better, by asking what attitudes each encourages. This is not the first question to ask, but it may well be the last. The monarchical model encourages attitudes of militarism, dualism, and escapism; it condones control through violence and oppression; it has nothing to say about the nonhuman world. The model of the world as God's body encourages holistic attitudes of responsibility for and care of the vulnerable and oppressed; it is nonhierarchical and acts through persuasion and attraction; it has a great deal to say about the body and nature. Both are pictures: which distortion is more true to the world in which we live and to the good news of Christianity?

It may be, of course, that neither picture is appropriate to our time and to Christianity; if so, others should be proposed. Our profound need for a powerful, attractive imaginative picture of the way God is related to our world demands that we not only deconstruct but reconstruct our metaphors, letting the ones that seem promising try their chance.

*   *   *

In particular I would make a case for experimenting in our time with mother, lover, and friend

---

17. Jonathan Schell, *The Fate of the Earth* (New York: Avon Books, 1982), 128. I am indebted to Rosemary Radford Ruether for the import of this paragraph.

as three models that have been strangely neglected in the Judeo-Christian tradition. All three models represent basic human relationships; indeed, one could say that the three, along with the model of father, represent the most basic human relationships.[18] Hence, if one is going to employ a personal model for God it makes sense to consider these three seriously. And they have been considered seriously in most religious traditions, for the simple reason that when people are attempting to express the inexpressible, they use what is nearest and dearest to them: they invoke the most important human relationships. One basic human relationship, that of father, has received massive attention in our tradition; the others have been, at best, neglected and, at worst, repressed. There are traces of them in Scripture and the tradition, but they have never become, or been allowed to become, major models.

Yet I hope that it has become evident that, given the kind of understanding of the gospel appropriate for a holistic, nuclear age, they may well be the most illuminating personal metaphors available. In different ways all three models suggest forms of fundamental intimacy, mutuality, and relatedness that could be a rich resource for expressing how in our time life can be supported and fulfilled rather than destroyed. They are all immanental models, in contrast to the radically transcendent models for God in the Western tradition. As we have seen, part of the difficulty with the dominant model of God is its transcendence, a transcendence undergirded by triumphalist,

sovereign, patriarchal imagery that contributes to a sense of distance between God and the world. The relatedness of all life, and hence the responsibility of human beings for the fate of the earth, is supported by models of God as mother, lover, and friend of the world.

Moreover, these metaphors project a different view of power, of how to bring about change, than the royal model. It is not the power of control through either domination or benevolence but the power of response and responsibility — the power of love in its various forms (agape, eros, and philia) that operates by persuasion, care, attention, passion, and mutuality. The way of being in the world which these metaphors suggest is close to the way of the cross, the way of radical identification with all which the model of servant once expressed. It is a way of being with others totally different from the way of kings and lords.

A final question remains before we close out the case for personal models and especially for the ones chosen. Are they perhaps too intimate and too individualistic? We have already touched on the issue of intimacy: the more intimate, in the sense of the closer to the most basic realities of human existence, the better. An ascetic strain, however, has kept Christianity from acknowledging the physical and often sexual basis of many of its most powerful symbols, and its wariness in dealing with maternal and erotic language for God arises from this same puritanism. Part of the task of a heuristic theology is to consider what has not been considered, especially if the possibilities for illuminating certain aspects of the God-world relationship are great, as I believe they are in the metaphors of mother and lover. (The model of friend is less problematic in this regard, but as we will see, there have been other reasons for its neglect.)

The charge that these metaphors may be individualistic just at a time when radically relational, inclusive metaphors are needed is a serious one. It would be unanswerable if the metaphors had to be interpreted as suggesting a one-to-one relationship between God and individual human beings. Admittedly, in a context where God's saving power is understood as directed to specific individuals (who are also perceived as independent entities), speaking of God as mother, lover, and friend only accentuates the

---

18. To focus on these metaphors is not, of course, to deny the importance of other personal models peculiarly appropriate to our time — such as, e.g., that of God as liberator. That model, however, has received substantial attention, and theologies have been built upon it. The three metaphors I will consider have by comparison been neglected. A basic human relationship with which I do not deal is that of siblings. The "sisterhood" of all women with the Goddess has received some attention, as of course has the relationship of all Christians as brothers and sisters to one another as well as to "Christ as brother." Stress on the sibling model in Christian circles tends to emphasize the dependence of human beings on God as parent, as well as to continue familial imagery as the central model. Much of what I would support as valuable in the models of sister and brother is better dealt with under the model of God as friend.

already particularistic understanding of salvation. But a radically inclusive view of the gospel means that the basic relationship between God and all others cannot be one-to-one; or rather, that it is one-to-one only as it is inclusive of all. The Gospel of John gives the clue: for God so loved the *world*. It is not individuals who are loved by God as mother, lover, and friend but the world. This means that we do not have to interpret these personal metaphors as suggesting a one-to-one relationship between God and individual human beings: we can use the metaphors that have the greatest power and meaning to us in a universal way, and in fact, only as we apply them universally can they also pertain individually. As mother to the world, God mothers each and all: the divine maternal love can be particular only because it is universal. If we understand God's saving presence as directed to the fulfillment of all of creation — with each of us part of that whole — we participate in God's love not as individuals but as members of an organic whole, God's body. Therefore, metaphors that could indeed be individualistic become radically socialized when applied to the world. Moreover, they have the potential for becoming politicized as well, for as the *imago dei,* we are called to mother, love, and befriend the world, both other human beings and the earth. Whether or not we are in our own personal lives mothers or fathers, or have a lover or even a friend, is not important: these most basic of loves lie deeply within us all. The model of God as mother, lover, and friend of the world presents us with an ethic of response and responsibility toward other human beings and other forms of life, in which our deep parental, erotic, and companionable instincts can be socialized and politicized.

In summary, the personal models for the God-world relationship have been defended as the ones we know best, as the richest, and as credible and needed in our time. The particular metaphors of mother, lover, and friend, which come from the deepest level of life and are concerned with its fulfillment, have been suggested as illuminating possibilities for expressing an inclusive, non-hierarchical understanding of the gospel. It has been claimed that the object of this gospel is not individuals but the world, and it has been proposed that the world — the cosmos or universe — be seen as God's body.

We have attempted to imagine the resurrection promise of divine presence — "Lo, I am with you always" — as a worldly reality, as the presence of God in the body of our world. In this, we have imaged God as both caring deeply for that world and calling us to care as well. This imaginative picture is radically different from that of a risen, ascended king in relationship with his realm but remarkably appropriate to an understanding of the story of Jesus of Nazareth as a surprising invitation to the last and the least, expressed in his parables, table fellowship, and Cross. That destabilizing, inclusive, nonhierarchical vision of fulfillment can be perceived as continuing when we conceive of the world as God's body to which God is present as mother, lover, and friend of the last and the least in all of creation.

91. On Slaying the Dragon: The American Nature Myth

WILLIAM F. MAY

Like many other teachers of ethics, I answered the call to make a speech on the first "Earth Day" celebration in the early Seventies. The only memorable part of the assignment was its location — Gary, Indiana.

I raced north from Bloomington (in the rural, Bavarian part of the state) to make my pitch for Mother Earth. No representatives from U.S. Steel, Bethlehem Steel, or (the then) Republic Steel joined me there to tell audiences about company initiatives to sweeten the air, freshen the rivers, and relieve the grass and trees of the industrial grunge that coated them daily.

Rather, it fell to one of the host professors to explain, with a shy trace of local patriotism, that Gary, contrary to popular opinion, was not the most polluted city in the state. That distinction belonged to Terre Haute, whose cement factories produced a fine, air-borne dust that matched the ubiquity of God and settled on everything. Popular opinion notwithstanding, Terre Haute, not Gary, was the Gary of Indiana.

What could anyone say on Earth Day in the industrial underbelly of Chicago — a region that

Carl Sandburg once characterized as "stormy, husky, brawling, City of the Big Shoulders"? I thought back to a conversation with W. H. Auden on a cold winter evening in New England, 1952, in the course of his year as a guest professor at Smith College. In his offhand, epigrammatic way he said, "In Europe, nature is an animal to be trained; in America, a dragon to be slain."

Auden's metaphors anticipated what later came to be called the ecological crisis, a crisis that lies in the background of the Isthmus topic for 1988-89: "The Dynamics of Harmony: Cooperation and Aggression in Nature and Society."

By ecological crisis, I mean four developments chiefly associated with the industrial and agricultural, and increasingly the biological revolutions. First, the pollution of the nonhuman environment on a scale so massive as to affect the life chain to which human beings belong and therefore to threaten banefully human existence itself — if not in this generation then within a biblical three or four. Second, the exhaustion of non-renewable energy sources, chiefly oil, at a pace so rapid as to provoke the nations eventually to turn to energy sources troublesome in their own right, by virtue of their being exhaustible (coal), and/or polluting (coal and nuclear fission), or energy-expensive to produce (fuel from coal shale). Third, the gradual encroachment upon and destruction of the wilderness and various species of nonhuman life. Fourth, the threats to the health and safety of both workers and neighbors of manufacturing plants, as well as to the consumers of their industrial goods and biochemical artifacts, including, in some cases, risks to their progeny. Fifth, threats to the ecology of the human body which result less from an adversarial relation to nature at large than from an antagonistic attitude toward the body itself, an attitude which affects our view of disease and the healing arts.

Auden's phrase — slaying the dragon — invokes a myth. A myth deserves our attention because its importance exceeds that of a merely factually true account of an event. Flannery O'Connor once said, "You know a people by the stories they tell." She had in mind, of course, myths — which people endlessly repeat or relive in their dreams because they order human sensibility and shape human behavior. Myths, like important

William F. May (1927–) is the Cary Maguire Professor of Ethics at Southwestern Methodist University. He has written widely and eloquently in medical ethics including *The Physician's Covenant: Images of the Healer in Medical Ethics* and *The Patient's Ordeal*.

metaphors, have a cognitive and a moral side to them. They offer us a vision of the world and they cue us as to how to behave within it.

The specific myth of slaying the dragon appears, of course, in *Beowulf*. Briefly, it tells the story of a land in the grips of hostile power; and a hero who lifts a curse from the land by killing Grendel, Grendel's dam, and finally an airborne monster. The people prosper through his victory, but in the course of the final battle, Beowulf, abandoned by his fellows, is himself slain.

The myth (except for the Christian ingredients — Beowulf's abandonment and death) includes the following elements. (1) a confrontation with a hostile and destructive power that exceeds the ordinary measure of humankind; (2) the emergence of a hero with special resources for combating the enemy (Beowulf wears a special coat of mail and uses an exceptionally powerful sword. Indeed, giants, that is dragonish figures, who have themselves rebelled against God, have made the sword with which the hard-pressed Beowulf kills Grendel's dam.); (3) the destruction and death of the dragon and the extraction of riches from its slashed belly (or the recovery of stolen goods from its lair); and (4) (by implication) the ugly residue of a vanquished carcass.

I do not want to suggest that the Beowulf myth has "influenced" the American perception of nature through the retelling the story (the biblical stories from Genesis and Deuteronomy figure much more prominently in the ritual life of the American people as they interpreted their settling of a continent). The Beowulf myth, however, roughly corresponds to the lived experience of the American struggle with nature and affects the direction in which Americans took the biblical injunction to subdue the earth.

America was a land of great distances, harsh extremes in climate, and a relatively small population, but a land that also promised extraordinary riches if nature could be conquered. We needed, therefore, heroes: first pioneers, second, scientists/technologists and industrialists, who could subdue the environment. We needed central heating to fight the cold; air-conditioning to fight the humidity and drugs to fight disease; trains, cars, and planes to conquer space; bulldozers to carve up the terrain; shafts and tunnels to mine it; test tubes to manipulate materials into prodigal new

forms; and reactors to unleash their even more prodigal energies.

Once technology subdued the hostile environment, great riches would pour out of the dragon's slashed belly. These riches would create personal fortunes for those who funded the war on nature, and add to the gross product of the nation from which others would more remotely prosper. The battle, to be sure, like human war, would leave a slashed carcass and scorched earth in its path. But the plunder was worth the price and who was to say otherwise? The gain belonged to the getter, the recoverer of what could either be described as unclaimed or stolen goods.

This element of hostility and conflict did not entirely dominate the American account of nature. American poster art, for example, emphasizes nature as pacific — the storied peace and quiet of the country. But the pioneer experienced, in fact, a harsh and inclement environment. Weather on the North American continent is far less temperate than Europe's, moderated as the latter is by the Gulf Stream. Americans so accept today the technologically enforced world-within-a-world which central heating and air-conditioning create, that they are inclined to forget the severity of the climate. But others notice it. Not too long ago, the Russian basketball team made a tour of the United States. Its schedule was rigorous; members of the team were homesick. But when they landed at the airport in Iowa, to play the University of Iowa team, a member of the Russian squad felt the Canadian winds howling and surveyed the banks of snow about him, and suddenly a broad smile crossed his face, as he said, "Siberia."

The heat can be equally extreme. A visitor in Houston asked a wealthy lawyer to what he attributed the rapid growth of the city. Ship channel and cotton port? Oil and petrochemical industry? Space technology and computer industries? "Yes," the lawyer replied. "These developments were all important. But you left off your list the most important factor of all, without which this uninhabitable area would not have become a world class city — central air-conditioning."

Space as well as climate inspired a more hostile attitude toward the natural environment in America because the huge American land mass, largely uninhabited (in most instances the Indians counted for less than the Canaanites), created in Americans the conviction that space had to be conquered.

The Americans, of course, related to space ambivalently. For those weary of social inequality, poverty, and class differences in Great Britain and Europe, the great empty spaces of the North American continent offered sanctuary and opportunity. A latent hostility to humankind lurked in the trek to the West. To have a neighbor was to have an enemy. The romance of the wilderness expressed a yearning for a manless and womanless nature, a desire to recover a pre-political, imperial self, a self without competition and limits.[1] The struggle with nature offered partial relief from the social struggle.

At the same time, however, a harsh climate and huge distances meant loneliness. Limitless space offered relief from the tensions of community but it also deprived pioneers of the solace of community: it severely limited commerce. However, long before America developed a technology with which to conquer space, it needed to devise a political instrument to span distances; the Constitution of the United States solved this problem brilliantly. The document ingeniously exploited both conflict within nature and the vast distances of the continent to solve the political problem which human nature itself presented. Factional self-interest threatened to tear the country to pieces once Americans won the Revolutionary War. But two devices promised to keep the negative effects of factionalism under control. First, the inventors of the Constitution believed that a federal system of checks and balances would pit faction against faction, and thus keep the power of any one faction within limits; second, the device of *representative* government would permit the government to distance itself from the fierce heat of any one local passion. In both cases, the founders of the nation contrived devices that slyly exploited nature itself. The device of pitting "ambition against ambition" through checks and balances mimicked the natural phenomenon of force and counterforce. Second, the device of rep-

resentative government converted continental scale itself into an ally as it permitted leaders to function at some distance from local passion. It would be a mistake, however, to assume that this constitutional system grew organically out of the American's experience of the natural environment. The founders were keenly aware of the political system and its devices as a *conception* and a *contrivance,* a harbinger in politics of the technology to come.

The American experience of an outsize nature derives not only from the huge expanse of the continent but also from its outsized particulars: its coastal plains, mountains, rivers, prairies, skies, deserts, and the great oceans that separate this country from the rest of the world. These boundless particulars do not easily reduce this experience to the image of a tameable animal, drawn up into the orbit of human purposes.

Quite the contrary, nature appears to exceed in grandeur and might and destructive fury the petty calculations of men and women. The best of our novelists had a keen sense for this. Melville devotes a chapter in *Moby Dick* to the size of the white whale but, after attempting to convey its magnitude, concedes that the malevolent beast exceeds all efforts to describe it. In a similar vein, Faulkner tells a story about a convict assigned to rescue a woman trapped on a flooded Mississippi River. The river sweeps them both out into the flood and the man finds himself "in a state in which he was a toy and pawn on a vicious and flammable geography."[2] Not even the original river bed is discernible. He does not know "whether the river had become lost in a drowned world or if the world had become drowned in one limitless river."[3] At one level, the flood appears to be a brief interlude in an otherwise peaceful experience of nature, but, at another level, it ominously recalls the catastrophe from which the country itself derives. "He was now in the channel of a slough, a bayou, in which until today no current had run probably since the old subterranean outrage which had created the country."[4] The jail to which he even-

---

1. See Quentin Anderson's study of Emerson, Thoreau, and Whitman, *The Imperial Self: An Essay in American Literacy and Cultural History* (New York: Knopf, 1971).

tually returns seems like a refuge and sanctuary after his ordeal in the flood.

Still, the harshness of the North American environment, its disheartening weather and size, should not be exaggerated. It challenged, to be sure, the colonists more severely than than the more moderate climates of the "old country" they left, or, for that matter, the West Coast of North America. (What would San Diego weather and avocados have done to soften the Puritan spirit? Can you imagine Jonathan Edwards in a hot tub? Or, sinners in the hands of a laid-back God?) Still, the North American continent hardly presented the colonizers with an environment to match, for example, the harshness of Brazil.

Vianna Moog offers a helpful contrast between the two natural settings in his book on the American pioneers and the Portuguese *bandeirantes* (flagbearers) who explored Brazil.[5] The latter did not have the advantage of excellent coastal plains, the traversable Appalachians, and the broad expanse of the midwestern plains beyond. Brazil's tropical soils were poor, as compared with the great plains of Europe, Asia, and North America; its river system could not match the great hydrographic network of the United States which made this country traversable and colonizable. Brazil's rivers were largely unnavigable; and the Amazon could claim to be the greatest river in the world only in the volume of water it transported. Economically, the Amazon, as opposed to the Mississippi River, proved to be, in Moog's memorable phrase, an "unpatriotic river." It brazenly washes out the soil from Brazil and disgorges it later in the Atlantic where it "is carried along by the Gulf Stream to add new territories to Mexico and the United States, in the alluvial formations of Yucatan and Florida."[6] The river resembles the mythic serpent who steals away treasure not its own.

The word "pioneer," however, should leave no doubt that the Yankees perceived their environment to be strenuous. Like *bandeirantes*, pioneer is a military term (though French in origin): it refers to foot soldiers in advance of a main body of troops, volunteer soldiers at that, because they assume special risks in going beyond the normal

reach of human knowledge and safety. Some of the heroic qualities attached to the pioneer gathered later around the American myth of the freelance entrepreneur and capitalist, who ventured out into the unknown, or, still later, around the scientist, inventor, and technologist who discovered the unknown, invented the wondrous, and applied it with ingenuity. Together, these figures provide the heroic virtues and the magic sword with which to subdue nature and wrest a prodigal life from a new land. They possessed the land by dint of their labors; John Locke taught them that, and Adam Smith reassured them that the people at large would prosper through their own flourishing.

Finally, the Beowulf myth emphasizes the fact that the dragon has stolen its riches from their rightful owner. The hero liberates and restores unclaimed or ill-gotten gain. The pioneers (and later developers) expected the government to back their notion that development is nine-tenths of the law. God may ultimately own the earth, but he has not done much with it during the period of his tenure. The weeds and wilderness take over without vigorous human work. Thus, by rights, he who works the land owns it. The state exists duly to record and back these claims. Thus, American patterns of ownership tended to confer upon the possessor absolute rights of development and disposition. Since development signified moreover *legitimate* ownership, as distinct from God's and the Indian's, the moral basis set for the maximal technological exploitation of everything that the belly of the earth contained.

At least three other myths (I would not want to deny the possibility of more) vie for attention in this Western world for interpreting the natural environment: Franciscan romanticism; European sacramentalism; and American convenantalism. The second part of this paper largely explores the third of these approaches to the nonhuman world.

1. *Franciscan Romanticism.* Lynn White, in his much cited essay on the "Historical Roots of the Ecological Crisis," rejects the dominant Christian tradition, which, he believes, helped produce the current ruthless exploitation of nature; instead, he recommends St. Francis as the patron saint of ecologists. (Pope John Paul II eventually made this designation official.) The Jewish and Christian Scriptures, according to White, gave man domin-

2. William Faulkner, *The Wild Palms* (New York: Random House, 1939), p. 162.

3. Ibid., p. 163.

ion over every creeping thing and commanded him to fill the earth and subdue it. White sees a straight causal line from this scriptural authorization (abstracted from the biblical notion of covenant) through the technologies of the Catholic Middle Ages to the high arrogance of modern times. He prefers the passive religious tradition of nature, "recessive" in the West, that hailed Brother Son and Sister Moon, Brother Wind and Sister Water, Brother Fire and Sister Earth, and Sister Bodily Death, in a kind of holy democracy, or intimate family, of all living things. The wolf of Gubbio marauded the land; St. Francis rescued the land — not by killing the wolf, but by befriending it.

This myth has chiefly shaped that portion of the environmentalist movement that demands the renunciation of technology. Specifically, they have worried more about the destructive powers that an industrial/technological civilization creates than about a dragon to be slain. Worries about air and water pollution, the vanishing of the wilderness and treasured species within it, the depletion of nonrenewable resources, and the potential impacts of powerful new processes and products on workers and consumers are but symptoms of this uneasiness. Technology replaces nature as the mythic monster, plundering riches from their rightful owners. (Giants, after all, forged the sword that Beowulf used to kill Grendel's mother; he owes his equipment to rebellious, dragonish powers.) Thus one looks for ways to call back the dragons unloosed to fight the dragon.

2. *European Sacramentalism.* Biblical scholars have taken White to task for abstracting the Genesis passage from its wider context in Scripture. When one recalls the vegetarianism of Genesis 1 and the Noachic protection of the animals, the command to subdue the earth has a different ring to it than it has for the airport advocates of nuclear energy or the hotel room salesman of plots in Florida.

In addition to noting these exegetical omissions, Catholic theologians have an additional grievance. Lynn White wholly ignores the sacramental traditions of East and West. Sacramentalism provides a second great option in response to nature. It emphasizes the goodness of the nonhuman creation. Far from disdaining natural elements, it takes them up into the orbit of

human purposes — bread, wine, water, and oil — and honors them as the bearer of sacral power. Sacramentalism is far removed from that enmity toward the material realm that characterized dualistic religion in the ancient Near East. Further, sacramentalism associates the reception of these sacred elements with the great turning points in human life — birth, growth, marriage, sickness, and death — and the prosaic bodily actions of washing, eating, and reproducing. Thus sacramentalism presupposes and celebrates the ties of humankind to the great biological rhythms of the nonhuman world. In this respect, sacramentalism is far removed, not only from ancient dualism that viewed the body as evil, but also from modern industrial liberalism that reduces the body to the *incidental.*[7] Sacramentalism knows only too well the intimate dependence of men and women on the prosaic rhythms and needs of the body.

(The liberal illusion of independence from nature had its religious origins in a kind of gnosticism that sought to distance itself — through knowledge — from the body and bodily ties to the world. This aspiration to independence from nature is not entirely, however, an intellectual movement. It has a very prosaic economic base; it depends upon a limitless store of nonrenewable resources, chiefly oil. Thus the eventual exhaustion of oil reserves today, for a moment at least, traumatized the liberal industrial nations. They were forced to rejoin the planet and to attend once again to the rhythms of renewal, care, and tending.)

At the same time, sacramentalism does not indulge in a mystical view of nature that elevates the nonhuman into the divine. It pronounces the nonhuman world good (not absolute good) and draws the natural goods up into the orbit of human purposes. Significantly, the central Christian sacrament takes precisely those elements — bread and wine — that have been compounded with human labor and tending, and makes these elements the bearers of sacred power.

4. Ibid., p. 144.

5. Vianna Moog, *Bandeirantes and Pioneers* (New York: George Braziller, 1964).

6. Ibid., p. 20.

7. D. H. Lawrence understood this point very well. *Lady Chatterly's Lover* has but one "sacrament" —

This sacramentalism is hospitable to the view of nature which W. H. Auden characterized as the European outlook with which we began. Nature is a largely living, creaturely good, not itself directly divine but a fit bearer of the divine. Further, nature is susceptible to, and better for, the respectful interventions of humankind — like an animal to be trained and reared in the household of human purposes.

While the Romantics wished to dismember the beast — dismantle the technology — and repair to a nature, worshipful and adoring, cooler heads like W. H. Auden, E. F. Schumacher, and Rene Dubos were more inclined neither to fear nor to worship nature. They wanted to reduce the experience of nature to a more comfortable, still disciplined domestic scale. They were also disposed to scale down the instruments with which we discipline nature. They look for "intermediate technology," in Schumacher's words, a "technology with a human face." At a practical political level, most look to the regulatory interventions of the federal government as the only agent powerful enough to protect the wilderness, regulate pollution, limit the depletion of nonrenewable resources, and protect producers and users from harmful products.

3. *American Covenantalism.* A third ethic of nature deserves particular attention on the American scene, an ethic associated with the term "covenantal." It differs only in some particulars from the sacramental view in order to provide for special features of the American experience.

An American theology of nature should take seriously two adversarial features of our experience: first, the experience of conflict between humankind and an outsized, powerful nature, not readily tamed; second, the experience of conflict within the human community itself which has often led Americans to flee from their fellows to a harsh environment. A somewhat domesticated view of nature that neglects the adversarial element in our relation to the nonhuman environment provides us with a theology for a continent other than ours; and a theology that prescribes a fidelity to nature but neglects the social covenant only intensifies antagonism in the human community. Environmentalism of the latter sort deteriorates into the political sport of the rich who respect nature but neglect the need of the poor for jobs.

The novelist, William Faulkner, offers, in my judgment, a helpful contemporary restatement of a theological ethic for ecologists on the American scene — a covenantal ethic that embraces one's responsibility to the land and to the community. Significantly he develops that ethic in the context of an essentially adversarial activity — the hunt — an activity for which I have no personal talent or enthusiasm! But that setting and activity offers a fitting contrast to the first half of Auden's epigram, "In Europe, nature is an animal to be trained." The image of the domestic animal suggests that nature can be brought up into the orbit of human purposes.

The image of the hunt, however, suggests a wild animal that can never be fully reconfigured into a world that bears a human face. At the same time, the hunt entails the shedding of blood. Not dragon's blood (the blood of the tyrant oppressor), but the blood of a worthy adversary in the wilderness to whom the hunter in killing becomes bound. ". . . perhaps only a country-bred one could comprehend loving the life he spills."[8]

Faulkner's moral vision offers a covenantal ethic reminiscent of Israel's covenant with Yhwh, begun in the wilderness and sealed in blood. I leave it to others to sort out the various layers of the biblical concept of covenant — the Adamic, Noachian, Mosaic, and Christological notions of covenant. For my limited purposes here, four elements in the biblical covenant deserve attention: (1) An original exchange of gifts, labor, or services, (2) a covenant promise based on this exchange, (3) the shaping of the future life of both partners in the light of the promissory event, and (4) the provision of ritual and other means for the renewal of life between partners in the course of their alienation from one another.

1. *Ritual Return.* The very title of Faulkner's short story, "Delta Autumn," marks the time and place of an annual ritual in which old Isaac McCaslin returns to the decisive moment in his life when, as a boy, he learned to hunt and to kill his first stag in the Delta wilderness. Just as the marked Jew, the errant, harassed, and estranged Jew recovers the covenant of Exodus and Mt. Sinai through ritual renewal, Isaac returns to the Delta every autumn to renew the hunt and to suffer his

sexual love — but Lawrence understood that the greatest modern challenge to that love comes not from own renewal there despite the alienation and pain and compromise and defeat which he has subsequently known across a lifetime. A kind of *anamnesis* occurs in the ritual return, the making-present of the past. In "The Old People," Faulkner describes this representation through the ritual event of storytelling:

> . . . gradually to the boy those old times would cease to be old times and would become a part of the boy's present, not only as if they happened yesterday but as if they were still happening, the men who walked through them actually walking in breath and air and casting an actual shadow on the earth they had not quitted.[9]

In "Delta Autumn," the same boy, now an old man, journeys back to the Delta, makes his camp and, at the end of day, lies down in that state of watchfulness that marks the religiously "observant" man:

> And then, he knew now he would not sleep tonight anyway; he no longer needed to tell himself that perhaps he would. But it was all right now. The day was ended now and night faced him, but alarmless, empty of fret. *Maybe I came for this, he thought: Not to hunt, but for this. I would come anyway, even if only to go back tomorrow.*[10]

That annual trek into the wilderness makes present the event that occurred almost seven decades earlier, what Faulkner calls elsewhere, "the binding instant."

2. *The Promise.* Isaac McCaslin comes of age in the course of the hunt. Sam Fathers, the old Indian of mixed blood, part black and white, his own blood through his mother a battleground, "who had bequeathed to him not only the blood of slaves but even a little of the very blood which had enslaved it"[11] tutors the boy in how to hunt. They track after the deer until the buck looms before them, "looking not like a ghost, but as if all light were condensed in him, and he were the source of it."[12]

And Sam Fathers urges the boy to:

> "Shoot quick and shoot slow": and the gun levelled rapidly without haste and crashed and he walked to the buck lying still intact and still in the shape of that magnificent speed and bled it with Sam's knife and Sam dipped his hands into the hot blood and marked his face forever.[13]

The language recalls the covenant into which the Israelites entered, their foreheads marked forever. McCaslin then binds the whole of his future in the instant.

> *I slew you; my bearing must not shame your quitting life. My conduct forever onward must become your death.*[14]

The episode provides the center for Faulkner's moral vision. His characters take their bearing from a covenantal event. Inevitably, Faulkner wrote about ties — about the ties of marriage and family, and ties to the land. In this respect, Faulkner differs strikingly from his contemporary, Hemingway, who wrote about lovers, but rarely about marriage and the family. Hemingway's typical heroes are war-time fighters or peace-time expatriates, cut off from all permanent ties. Not fidelity to another, but rather the shaping of a code, a portable code that helps one live from moment to moment, constitutes their chief moral task. Hemingway's heroes forget why they fight; the cause fades; and friends and lovers die. The chief moral task comes down to how one fights. Life is a matter of living well, loving well, drinking well, writing well, hunting well, and dying well. The bullfighter thus symbolizes the aesthetic code by which the Hemingway hero lives, and his tragic encounter with the bull in the ring contrasts strikingly with Faulkner's notion of a binding instant:

> . . . the bull charged and Villalta charged and just for a moment they became one. Villalta became one with the bull and then it was over.[15]

---

the "puritan," who viewed the body as evil, but from the liberal who reduced the body to the trivial.

8. William Faulkner, "Old People," in *Go Down Moses* (New York: Viking Books, 1973), p. 181.

9. Faulkner, "Old People," p. 171.

10. Faulkner, "Delta Autumn," in *Go Down Moses*, p. 720.

11. Faulkner, "Old People," p. 168.

12. Ibid., p. 163.

The bull ring encounter resembles sexual intercourse between wartime lovers: they become one, but then it's over. In Faulkner's parallel account of encounter, it's far from over, it's just begun: *"My conduct forever onward must become your death."*

Faulkner writes in the mode of historical rather than natural religion, religion based on election rather than birth, destiny rather than fate, gift rather than possession:

> He seemed to see the two of them — himself and the wilderness — as coevals, his own span as a hunter, a woodsman, not contemporary with his first breath but transmitted to him, assumed by him gladly, humbly, with joy and pride, from that old Major de Spain and that old Sam Fathers who had taught him to hunt. . . .[16]

3. *The Gift.* The foregoing passage gets it just right. A covenantal ethic includes a promise but it does not begin with the promise. It begins before the vow, with what has been received and assumed, gladly and humbly, as a gift; in this case, a gift of the wilderness, its game, and those mentors who have taught the boy how to respect the wilderness and the hunt. In the logic of Scripture — Exodus precedes Mr. Sinai.

A covenantal ethic derives from the transaction of giving and receiving, a transaction that precedes and provides the basis for avowing. The Jews bind themselves to God at Mr. Sinai as those who have already been the recipients of an astonishing gift, the deliverance from Egypt. That is why a covenantal ethic differs from the modern ethics of philanthropy and, equally, the modern ethics of the marketplace.

The modern ethics of philanthropy assumes a one-way street from giver to receiver. It flatters the rich man, the lady bountiful, the self-assured professional, the church, or the powerful nation as the benefactor while others relate to him or her as beneficiaries. But a covenantal ethic always positions the giver in the context of a primordial receiving, a gift not of his deserving, which can only be assumed by him gladly, humbly. Thus Scripture positions the Jewish farmer: when you harvest your crops, do not pick them too clean. Leave some for the sojourner. For you also were sojourners in Egypt. The giver is receiver; the benefactor, beneficiary.

A covenantal ethic differs also from a marketplace ethic that reduces obligations to buying and selling alone. The marketplace offers the illusion that life at its most absorbing and binding level reduces to buying and selling, not giving and receiving. It gives the illusion of ownership rather than bestows the duties of tenancy and stewardship; it thereby misses the human duties to the natural world that resemble those of a guest to host.

> . . . although it had been his grandfather's and then his father's and uncle's and was now his cousin's and someday would be his own land which he and Sam hunted over, their hold upon it actually was as trivial and without reality as the now faded and archaic script in the chancery book in Jefferson which allocated it to them and that it was he, the boy, who was the guest here and Sam Father's voice the mouthpiece of the host.[17]

Faulkner records in fine detail the transmission of the land from buyer to seller, from father to son, from generation to generation but concedes that in an ultimate sense "not even a fragment of it had been his to relinquish or sell."[18] This was true for Isaac himself, his ancestors and the Chickasaw chief from whom it had originally been purchased "for money or rum or whatever."[19]

With a wave of the hand toward that word "whatever," Faulkner puts in its place the libertarian theory of entitlement, the notion that the sacred records of buying and selling have the last word to say on the subject of justice, on the subject of the rightful disposition of people and the land. From an ultimate perspective, before the "Throne Itself" of the primordial host, the courthouse history of buying and selling records no more than "the brown thin ink" of injustice "and a little at least of its amelioration and restitution" but all of it together before the All-knowledgeable fades

13. Faulkner, "Delta Autumn," pp. 350-51.

14. Ibid., p. 351.
15. Ernest Hemingway, "In Our Time," *Hemingway* (Viking Portable).

"back forever into the anonymous communal original dust . . ."[20]

"The Bear" offers the finest account I know of creation as gift that transcends and spans through covenant the marketplace transactions that we know.

> "I cannot repudiate it. It was never mine to repudiate. It was never Father's and Uncle Buddy's to bequeath me to repudiate because it was never Grandfather's to bequeath them to bequeath to me to repudiate because it was never old Ikkematubbe's to sell to Grandfather for bequeathment and repudiation . . . because on the instant when Ikkematubbe discovered, realized, that he could sell it for money, on that instant it ceased ever to have been his forever, father to father to father, and the man who bought it bought nothing!"
>
> "Bought nothing?" and he "Bought nothing. Because he told in the book how he created the earth, made it and looked at it and said it was all right, and then he made man. He made the earth first and peopled it with dumb creatures and then he created man to be his overseer on the earth and to hold suzerainty over the earth and the animals on it in his name, not to hold for himself and his descendants inviolable title forever, generation after generation to the oblongs and squares of the earth, but to hold the earth mutual and intact in the communal anonymity of brotherhood, and all the fee he asked was pity and humility and sufferance and endurance and the sweat of his face for bread."[21]

The passages distinguish sharply and eloquently between the concepts of contract and covenant because, formally considered, they resemble one another. They both include an agreement between parties and an exchange; they look to reciprocal future action. But in spirit, contract and covenant differ sharply.

Contracts involve buying and selling. Covenants include further ingredients of giving and receiving. Contracts are external, while covenants are more internal to the parties involved. Con-

tracts are signed expediently to be discharged; covenants have a gratuitous, growing element which nourishes rather than limits and terminates relationships. Contracts imply a price on everything, goods are extractable, convertible, exchangeable, whereas covenants point to the indefectible. Contracts can be filed away, but a covenant becomes a part of one's history and shapes, in unexpected ways, self-perception and even destiny.

What does this vision of the moral life have to do with the U.S. Steels, the Bethlehem Steels, the Republic Steels or ITV's of the world with which these reflections began? Not that this ethic has no implications for other institutions and movements, e.g., interest group liberalism or ecological pietism, but, for better or for worse, the most powerful group in the country today is its corporate leadership, a leadership which occasionally seasons its ethic with the notion of philanthropy, but which, by and large, has defined corporate responsibility by the contractualist obligation that Milton Friedman summarized as maximizing profits. This paper closes by placing the prevailing marketplace ethic which has driven our development of the natural world in a more spacious covenantal setting.

Friedman argued that management properly discharges its moral responsibilities only by maximally pursuing profits. Otherwise, management exceeds its authority which it derives from stockholders. The entitlements of owners should solely determine whatever decisions management makes about resources, location, wages, technological development, capital improvements, marketing, and sales. Friedman, to be sure, was not an absolute libertarian. He accepted the side constraints of both ethical custom and the law in his essay on maximizing profits. But he holds to a highly individualistic conception of ethical custom — no lying, theft, or murder — and a minimalist understanding of the law. He hardly means by ethics, social ethics, and he hardly wants from the law much more than those protections that permit one to maximize profits.

To this entitlement theory of justice, Friedman adds the further claim that this system yields the best for all. A multiplicity of goods will best be attained through the allocative wizardry of the free market. Far from subordinating self-interest to

16. Faulkner, "Delta Autumn," p. 354.

17. Faulkner, "Old People," p. 171.

18. Faulkner, "The Bear," *Go Down Moses*, p. 255.

some notion of the common good, business institutions in this libertarian view can contribute no more effectively to society than to pursue, without a wandering eye, profit maximization. Otherwise, they exceed their authority (derived from stockholders), their competence (economic decision-making rather than environmental tending or social engineering), and their power (by paternalistically imposing on others their notions of natural and cultural goods).

Friedman's view about the proper goal of the modern corporation gets repeated everyday whenever someone invokes the bottom line. It stands as the single most powerful pressure for extracting riches from the earth and for distributing them unequally as the luck of the market and the wit of the aggressive would have it.

Some of Friedman's critics have sought to expand the notion of corporate responsibility beyond the narrow limits Friedman has set by distinguishing between stockholders and stakeholders. Stockholders are important stakeholders in a company, but by no means the only ones. Workers, customers, neighbors, suppliers, the public, the integrity of the life chain itself, have in varying ways a stake in corporate behavior, sometimes indeed a deeper stake than stockholders, who may dart in and out of their investments more readily than others who cannot withdraw from a company and its impacts and fortunes.

This argument, however, rests on little more than the consonance of the two words — "stock" and "stake" — unless one can show why obligation should extend beyond stockholders in an enterprise. Some help is at hand in the notion of covenant developed in this essay. It expands obligation beyond the limits of commercial contract (the stockholder's purchase) and takes corporate responsibility a notch deeper than token expressions of corporate philanthropy (contributions to the local community chest drive or cosmetic landscaping around the plant). A covenantal ethic concentrates on those obligations that arise in relationships between several parties that are responsive and reciprocal. It acknowledges giving and receiving in extended exchanges between parties, from which permanent agreements arise that give shape to the future. This growing sense of responsibility between parties defines the notion of a stakeholder. Much has happened between us

that gives me a stake in what you do, and you, in what I do. We are covenanted together. *Economic performance at a profit,* rather than the imperial notion of maximizing profits defines the corporate responsibility to stockholders in such a way as to accommodate its indebtedness to other stakeholders in the enterprise.

The ideal of philanthropy also expresses inadequately this indebtedness; it presupposes a one-way street from giver to receiver. The philanthropist pretends to be pure giver alone; others relate to him as receiver. When the philanthropist loses interest, he moves on. Corporate responsibility reduced to philanthropy trivializes corporate ethics; it obscures the depth of the company's obligation. In fact, a corporation does not give as pure benefactor alone. It has already received much from the community and its environment — not only the investments of stockholders, but also the labor of workers, the potential of the terrain and its resources, the ambiance and services of the community in which it is located, the privilege of incorporation by the state, and all the protection bestowed upon persons under the due process clause of the Constitution. Its indebtedness is great.

But not all this indebtedness can be toted up in commercial terms. The corporation, to be sure, pays its workers and its taxes but these transactions build up a life between people and institutions, rather than terminate a connection. The concept of *covenant* surpasses the notion of contract in defining the moral obligations of the corporation. The decision-making of a corporation is massively contractual. But that decision-making rests upon a covenantal base that charters its life, grants it protection, and endows its enterprises with a public significance and responsibility.

Friedman's further argument — that corporations are incompetent to make judgments about matters other than profit-making — exaggerates, and, finally, topples with the collapse of the first argument. In some areas of corporate responsibility (for example, product safety and negative impacts of manufacturing processes on workers, neighbors, and the environment) management usually has more knowledge and competence than most others in the society. In other areas, the corporation may not be competent. But moral responsibility in life can hardly be limited solely to those areas in which persons and institutions have an advance competence. Competent, even virtuoso, lovers may find themselves — willy-nilly — in the somewhat nervous position of being inexperienced, not-yet-competent parents, but, cannot duck morally the obligation to acquire that competence. Economists have had a convenient way of excluding many issues from the manager's responsibility for competence by writing them off as "externalities." But the externalities of water and air pollution, traffic congestion, neighborhood crime, unemployment and the quality of education and culture in a host city have a way of obtruding on the moral and political agenda of citizens and their institutions and require them to develop some measure of wisdom and even expertise.

A covenantal vision of things, with its notion of primordial gift and duties, hardly converts into casuistical principles for resolving dilemmas or into a particular social program or environmental policy. It eliminates neither the world of the marketplace nor the need for governmental regulation. But it places the fallen world of buying and selling, regulating and reforming, within a wider horizon. It lets us see the world for what it is and thus lets it become a little different from what it was. It places the familiar world that we know at the distance of insight and corrective vision.

> . . . he would not sleep tonight but would lie instead wakeful and peaceful on the cot amid the tent-filling snoring and the rain's whisper as he always did on the first night in camp; peaceful, without regret or fretting, telling himself that was all right too, who didn't have so many of them left as to waste one sleeping.[22]

92. God and Country

WENDELL BERRY

The subject of Christianity and ecology is endlessly, perhaps infinitely, fascinating. It is fascinating theologically and artistically because of our never-to-be-satisfied curiosity about the relation between a made thing and its maker. It is fascinating practically because we are unrelentingly required to honor in all things the relation between the world and its Maker, and because that requirement implies another, equally unrelenting, that we ourselves, as makers, should always honor that greater making; we are required, that is, to study the ways of working well, and those ways are endlessly fascinating. The subject of Christianity and ecology also is politically fascinating, to those of us who are devoted both to biblical tradition and to the defense of the earth, because we are always hankering for the support of the churches, which seems to us to belong, properly and logically, to our cause.

This latter fascination, though not the most difficult and fearful, is certainly the most frustrating, for the fact simply is that the churches, which claim to honor God as the "maker of heaven and earth," have lately shown little inclination to honor the earth or to protect it from those who would dishonor it.

Organized Christianity seems, in general, to have made peace with "the economy" by divorcing

---

21. Faulkner, "The Bear," *Go Down Moses*, pp. 256-257.

22. Faulkner, "Delta Autumn," *Go Down Moses*, p. 343.

Wendell Berry (1934–) is a farmer and distinguished professor of English at the University of Kentucky. His works include poetry, short stories, novels and essays. Among these are *The Unsettling of America, A*

19. Faulkner, "The Bear," *Go Down Moses*, p. 255.
20. Faulkner, "The Bear," *Go Down Moses*, p. 261.

itself from economic issues, and this, I think, has proved to be a disaster, both religious and economic. The reason for this, on the side of religion, is suggested by the adjective "organized." It is clearly possible that, in the condition of the world as the world now is, organization can force upon an institution a character that is alien or even antithetical to it. The *organized* church comes immediately under a compulsion to think of itself, and identify itself to the world, not as an institution synonymous with its truth and its membership, but as a hodgepodge of funds, properties, projects, and offices, all urgently requiring economic support. The organized church makes peace with a destructive economy and divorces itself from economic issues because it is economically compelled to do so. Like any other public institution so organized, the organized church is dependent on "the economy"; it cannot survive apart from those economic practices that its truth forbids and that its vocation is to correct. If it comes to a choice between the extermination of the fowls of the air and the lilies of the field and the extermination of a building fund, the organized church will elect — indeed, has already elected — to save the building fund. The irony is compounded and made harder to bear by the fact that the building fund can be preserved by crude applications of money, but the fowls of the air and the lilies of the field can be preserved only by true religion, by the *practice* of a proper love and respect for them as the creatures of God. No wonder so many sermons are devoted exclusively to "spiritual" subjects. If one is living by the tithes of history's most destructive economy, then the disembodiment of the soul becomes the chief of worldly conveniences.

There are many manifestations of this tacit alliance between the organized churches and "the economy," but I need to speak only of two in order to make my point. The first is the phrase "full-time Christian service," which the churches of my experience have used exclusively to refer to the ministry, thereby at once making of the devoted life a religious specialty or career and removing the possibility of devotion from other callings. Thus the $50,000-a-year preacher is a "full-time Christian servant," whereas a $20,000- or a $10,000-a-year farmer, or a farmer going broke, so far as the religious specialists are concerned, must serve "the economy" in his work or in his failure and serve

God in his spare time. The professional class is likewise free to serve itself in its work and to serve God by giving the church its ten percent. The churches in this way excerpt sanctity from the human economy and its work just as Cartesian science has excerpted it from the material creation. And it is easy to see the interdependence of these two desecrations: the desecration of nature would have been impossible without the desecration of work, and vice versa.

The second manifestation I want to speak of is the practice, again common in the churches of my experience, of using the rural ministry as a training ground for young ministers and as a means of subsidizing their education. No church official, apparently, sees any logical, much less any spiritual, problem in sending young people to minister to country churches before they have, according to their institutional superiors, become eligible to be ministers. These student ministers invariably leave the rural congregations that have sponsored or endured their educations as soon as possible once they have their diplomas in hand. The denominational hierarchies, then, evidently regard country places in exactly the same way as "the economy" does: as sources of economic power to be exploited for the advantage of "better" places. The country people will be used to educate ministers for the benefit of city people (in wealthier churches) who, obviously, are thought more deserving of educated ministers. This, I am well aware, is mainly the fault of the church organizations; it is not a charge that can be made to stick to any young minister in particular: not all ministers should be country ministers, just as not all people should be country people. And yet it is a fact that in the more than fifty years that I have known my own rural community, many student ministers have been "called" to serve in its churches, but not one has ever been "called" to stay. The message that country people get from their churches, then, is the same message that they get from "the economy": that, as country people, they do not matter much and do not deserve much consideration. And this inescapably imposes an economic valuation on spiritual things. According to the modern church, as one of my Christian friends said to me, "The soul of the plowboy ain't worth as much as the soul of the delivery boy."

If the churches are mostly indifferent to the work and the people by which the link between economy and ecosystem must be enacted, it is no wonder that they are mostly indifferent to the fate of the ecosystems themselves. One must ask, then: is this state of affairs caused by Christian truth or by the failures and errors of Christian practice? My answer is that it is caused by the failures and errors of Christian practice. The evident ability of most church leaders to be "born again in Christ" without in the least discomforting their faith in the industrial economy's bill of goods, however convenient and understandable it may be, is not scriptural.

Anyone making such a statement must deal immediately with the belief of many non-Christian environmentalists as well as at least some Christians that Genesis 1:28, in which God instructs Adam and Eve to "be fruitful and multiply and replenish the earth, and subdue it," gives unconditional permission to humankind to use the world as it pleases. Such a reading of Genesis 1:28 is contradicted by virtually all the rest of the Bible, as many people by now have pointed out. The ecological teaching of the Bible is simply inescapable: God made the world because he wanted it made. He thinks the world is good, and he loves it. It is his world; he has never relinquished title to it. And he has never revoked the conditions, bearing on his gift to us of the use of it, that oblige us to take excellent care of it. If God loves the world, then how might any person of faith be excused for not loving it or justified in destroying it?

But of course, those who see in Genesis 1:28 the source of all our abuse of the natural world (most of them apparently having read no more of the Bible than that verse) are guilty of an extremely unintelligent misreading of Genesis 1:28 itself. How, for example, would one arrange to "replenish the earth" if "subdue" means, as alleged, "conquer" or "defeat" or "destroy"?

We have in fact in the biblical tradition, rooted in the Bible but amplified in agrarian, literary, and other cultural traditions stemming from the Bible, the idea of stewardship as conditioned by the idea of usufruct. George Perkins Marsh was invoking biblical tradition when he wrote, in 1864, that "man has too long forgotten that the earth was given to him for usufruct alone, not for consump-tion, still less for profligate waste." The Mormon essayist Hugh Nibley invoked it explicitly when he wrote that "man's dominion is a call to service, not a license to exterminate."

That service, stewardship, is the responsible care of property belonging to another. And by this the Bible does not mean an absentee landlord, but one living on the property, profoundly and intimately involved in its being and its health, as Elihu says to Job: "if he gather unto himself his spirit and his breath; All flesh shall perish together." All creatures live by God's spirit, portioned out to them, and breathe his breath. To "lay up . . . treasures in heaven," then, cannot mean to be spiritual at the earth's expense, or to despise or condemn the earth for the sake of heaven. It means exactly the opposite: do not desecrate or depreciate these gifts, which take part with us in the being of God, by turning them into worldly "treasure"; do not reduce life to money or to any other mere quantity.

The idea of usufruct gives this point to the idea of stewardship, and makes it practical and economic. Usufruct, the *Oxford English Dictionary* says, is "the right of temporary possession, use, or enjoyment of the advantages of property belonging to another, so far as may be had without causing damage or prejudice to this." It is hardly a "free-market economy" that the Bible prescribes. Large accumulations of land were, and are, forbidden because the dispossession and privation of some cannot be an acceptable or normal result of the economic activity of others, for that destroys a people as a people; it destroys the community. Usury was, and is, forbidden because the dispossession and privation of some should not be regarded by others as an economic opportunity, for that is contrary to neighborliness; it destroys the community. And the greed that destroys the community also destroys the land. What the Bible proposes is a moral economy, the standard of which is the health of properties belonging to God.

But we have considered so far only those things of the creation that can be included within the human economy — the usable properties, so to speak. What about the things that are outside the human economy? What about the things that from the point of view of human need are useless or only partly usable? What about the places that, as is increasingly evident, we should not use at all?

Obviously we must go further, and the Bible can take us further. Many passages take us beyond a merely economic stewardship, but the one that has come to seem most valuable to me is Revelation 4:11, because I think it proposes an indispensable standard for the stewardship both of things in use and of useless things and things set aside from use: "Thou art worthy, O Lord, to receive glory and honour and power: for thou hast created all things, and for thy pleasure they are and were created."

The implications of this verse are relentlessly practical. The ideas that we are permitted to use things that are pleasing to God, that we have nothing at all to use that is not pleasing to him, and that necessarily implicated in the power to use is the power to misuse and destroy are troubling, and indeed frightening, ideas. But they are consoling, too, precisely insofar as we have the ability to use well and the goodness or the character required to limit use or to forbear to use.

Our responsibility, then, as stewards, the responsibility that inescapably goes with our dominion over the other creatures, according to Revelation 4:11, is to safeguard God's pleasure in his work. And we can do that, I think (I don't know how else we could do it), by safeguarding *our* pleasure in his work, and our pleasure in our own work. Or, if we no longer can trust ourselves to be more than economic machines, then we must do it by safeguarding the pleasure of children in God's work and in ours. It is impossible, admittedly, to give an accurate economic value to the goodness of good work, much less to the goodness of an unspoiled forest or prairie or desert, or to the goodness of pure sunlight or water or air. And yet we are required to make an economy that honors such goods and is conversant with them. An economy that ignores them, as our present one does, "builds a hell in heaven's despite."

As a measure of how far we have "progressed" in our industrial economy, let me quote a part of a sentence from the prayer "For Every Man in His Work" from the 1928 *Book of Common Prayer:* "Deliver us, we beseech thee, in our several callings, from the service of mammon, that we may do the work which thou givest us to do, in truth, in beauty, and in righteousness, with singleness of heart as thy servants, and to the benefit of our fellow men." What is astonishing about that prayer

is that it is a relic. Throughout the history of the industrial revolution, it has become steadily less prayable. The industrial nations are now divided, almost entirely, into a professional or executive class that has not the least intention of working in truth, beauty, and righteousness, as God's servants, or to the benefit of their fellow men, and an underclass that has no choice in the matter. Truth, beauty, and righteousness now have, and can have, nothing to do with the economic life of most people. This alone, I think, is sufficient to account for the orientation of most churches to religious feeling, increasingly feckless, as opposed to religious thought or religious behavior.

I acknowledge that I feel deeply estranged from most of the manifestations of organized religion, partly for reasons that I have mentioned. Yet I am far from thinking that one can somehow become righteous by carrying protestantism to the logical conclusion of a one-person church. We all belong, at least, to the problem. "There is . . . a price to be paid," Philip Sherrard says, "for fabricating around us a society which is as artificial and as mechanized as our own, and this is that we can exist in it only on condition that we adapt ourselves to it. This is our punishment."[1]

We all, obviously, are to some extent guilty of this damnable adaptation. We all are undergoing this punishment. But as Philip Sherrard well knows, it is a punishment that we can set our hearts against, an adaptation that we can try with all our might to undo. We can ally ourselves with those things that are worthy: light, air, water, earth; plants and animals; human families and communities; the traditions of decent life, good work, and responsible thought; the religious traditions; the essential stories and songs.

It is presumptuous, personally and historically, to assume that one is a part of a "saving remnant." One had better doubt that one deserves such a distinction, and had better understand that there may, after all, be nothing left to save. Even so, if one wishes to save anything not protected by the present economy — topsoil, groves of old trees, the possibility of the goodness or health of anything, even the economic relevance of the biblical

Place on Earth, The Remembering, and *What Are People For?*

tradition — one is a part of a remnant, and a dwindling remnant too, though not without hope, and not without the necessary instructions, the most pertinent of which, perhaps, is this, also from Revelation [3:2a]: "Be watchful, and strengthen the things which remain, that are ready to die."

Try It Yourself:
The Spotted Owl

she agrees with the JustWoods action. However, she knows the devastation that an end to the logging would bring to her community, to her church. She writes to you, a regional church committee responsible for providing advice and assistance to pastors for assistance. She requests advice on what specific actions she should take in this latest volley between environmentalists and the logging community and, knowing that she will have to address this issue from the pulpit, she wants theological support for the advice you offer. What advice do you give her?

CASE STUDY 8

The Reverend Mary-Louise Christiansen is pastor of Chapel of the Woods Lutheran Church in Hoquiam, Washington. Her church, like her community, is largely made up of individuals who work or have worked in the lumber industry. Many of these individuals are now out of work as a result of legislation restricting logging in old-growth forests, legislation aimed at protecting the northern spotted owl. It seems to most in her community that with every new season of legislation more restrictions are imposed on the loggers to protect endangered species and the result is higher and higher unemployment in the community, the loss of livelihood and a way of life for many of her parishioners.

As a seminarian, Mary-Louise thought of herself as a "green" theologian and joined numerous environmental activist organizations. She still remains committed to those values and ideals: she is a vegetarian. But now she finds herself in an especially difficult position. The organization Just-Woods (of which she has been a member for ten years) is now making an all-out effort to close down completely the logging of old-growth forests in Washington. Their success will undermine the economy of Hoquiam, will leave a majority of the people of Hoquiam without work and without any prospects of work. Their success will also protect the spotted owl and preserve the natural riches of the state of Washington.

JustWoods would like to have Chapel of the Woods Lutheran Church as their base of operation and would like Mary-Louise to be their major spokesperson in this new protest-offensive against logging. Mary-Louise finds herself torn. In principle

Acknowledgments

The editors and publisher gratefully acknowledge permission granted by the following publishers to reprint these copyrighted works. Works are numbered as they appear in this volume.

2. Verhey, Allen. "Ethics." In *The Oxford Companion to the Bible.* © 1993 Oxford University Press. Used by permission.

3. Gustafson, James M. "The Relationship of Empirical Science to Moral Thought." *The Proceedings of the Catholic Theological Society of America* 26 (1971): 122-137. Used by permission.

4. *Saint Augustine: On Christian Doctrine,* trans. D. W. Robertson, Jr. Copyright © 1958 by Macmillan Publishing Company. Reprinted with the permission of Macmillan Publishing Company.

6. Mouw, Richard J. *The God Who Commands.* © 1990 by the University of Notre Dame Press. Used by permission.

7. Hauerwas, Stanley. *A Community of Character.* © 1981 by the University of Notre Dame Press. Used by permission.

8. Farley, Margaret. "Feminist Consciousness and the Interpretation of Scripture." In *Feminist Interpretation of the Bible,* ed. Letty M. Russell. Copyright © 1985 Letty M. Russell. Used by permission of Westminster/John Knox Press.

9. Cone, James H. "Biblical Revelation and Social Existence." *Interpretation* 28 (October 1974): 422-40. Used by permission.

11. Stout, Jeffrey. "Tradition in Ethics." In *The Westminster Dictionary of Christian Ethics,* ed. James F. Childress and John MacQuarrie. © John Macquarrie 1967; © 1986 The Westminster Press. Used by permission of Westminster/John Knox Press.

12. "The Transmission of Divine Revelation." In Walter M. Abbott, S. J. *The Documents of Vatican II.* Copyright © 1966 by The America Press. Reprinted by permission of The Crossroad Publishing Company.

13. Burtchaell, James T. *The Giving and Taking of Life: Essays Ethical* © 1989 by the University of Notre Dame Press. Reprinted by permission.

14. Ottati, Douglas F. *Jesus Christ and the Christian Vision.* Copyright © 1989 Augsburg Fortress. Used by permission.

15. Ruether, Rosemary Radford. "Feminist Interpretation: A Method of Correlation." In *Feminist Interpretation of the Bible,* ed. Letty M. Russell. Copyright © 1985 Letty M. Russell. Used by permission of Westminster/John Knox Press.

16. Yoder, John Howard. *The Priestly Kingdom: Social Ethics and the Bible.* Copyright © 1985 by the University of Notre Dame Press. Reprinted by permission.

18. Aristotle. *Nicomachean Ethics,* trans. Terence

Irwin, Hackett Publishing Company, Inc., 1985, Indianapolis, IN and Cambridge, MA.

19. Aquinas, Thomas. *Summa Theologica,* trans. Fathers of the English Dominican Province. Benziger Brothers, 1988. Used by permission.

Excerpts from St. Thomas Aquinas, *Summa Contra Gentiles, Book 3,* trans. Vernon J. Bourke. Translation copyright © 1956 by Doubleday, a division of Bantam Doubleday Dell Publishing Group, Inc. Used by permission of Doubleday, a division of Bantam Doubleday Dell Publishing Group, Inc.

21. Mouw, Richard J. *The God Who Commands.* © 1990 by the University of Notre Dame Press. Used by permission.

22. Yannaras, Christos. *The Freedom of Morality.* © 1984 by St. Vladimir's Press. Used by permission.

23. Hauerwas, Stanley. "On Keeping Theological Ethics Theological." In *Revisions: Changing Perspectives in Moral Philosophy,* ed. Stanley Hauerwas and Alasdair MacIntyre. © 1983 by the University of Notre Dame Press. Used by permission.

25. Paul VI. *Humanae Vitae* (Boston: St. Paul Editions, 1968). Used by permission.

26. Wilson, E. O. "Scientific Humanism and Religion." *Free Inquiry* (spring 1991): 20-23, 56.

27. Lewis, C. S. *The Abolition of Man.* London: HarperCollins Publishers Limited, Collins Fount, 1947.

28. Gustafson, James M. "The Relationship of Empirical Science to Moral Thought." *Proceedings of the Catholic Theological Society of America* 26 (1971).

29. Gilligan, Carol. "A Different Voice in Moral Decisions." *Speaking of Faith,* ed. Diana Eck and Devaki Jain. © 1987 by New Society Publishers. Used by permission.

30. Reprinted by permission from *Between the Sexes* by Lisa S. Cahill, copyright © 1985 Fortress Press. Used by permission of Augsburg Fortress.

32. Reprinted from *The American Edition of Luther's Works* by Martin Luther, copyright © 1943 Muhlenberg Press. Used by permission of Augsburg Fortress.

33. Niebuhr, H. Richard. *The Responsible Self.* Copyright © 1963 by Florence Niebuhr. Reprinted by permission of HarperCollins Publishers.

34. Altered from "Three Approaches" from *Situation Ethics: A New Morality* by Joseph Fletcher. Copyright © MCMLXVI W. L. Jenkins. Altered and used by permission of Westminster/John Knox Press.

35. Ramsey, Paul. *War and the Christian Conscience.* © Copyright 1961, Duke University Press, Durham, NC. Reprinted with permission.

36. Gaffney, James. "Values, Victims, and Visions." *Commonweal* © 113 (15 August 1986). Used by permission.

37. *Ethics: Systematic Theology,* vol. 1 by James W. McClendon, Jr. Copyright © 1986 by Abingdon Press. Reprinted by permission of the publisher.

38. Reprinted from Carol Robb, "A Framework for Feminist Ethics," *The Journal of Religious Ethics* 9, no. 1 (Spring 1981): 48-53, 62-68. Reprinted with the permission of Religious Ethics, Incorporated.

40. St. Augustine. *The City of God,* trans. Henry Bettenson. London: Penguin Classics, 1984. Translation copyright © Henry Bettenson, 1972. *Basic Writings of St. Augustine,* ed. Whitney Oates. Copyright 1948 by Random House, Inc. Reprinted by permission of Random House, Inc.

42. Niebuhr, Reinhold. *An Interpretation of Chris-*

tian Ethics. Copyright © 1935 by Harper & Row Publishers, Inc. Reprinted by permission of HarperCollins Publishers.

43. Tillich, Paul J. *Being and Doing,* ed. John J. Carey. © 1987 by Mercer University Press, 1987. Used by permission.

45. Reprinted from *Justice in an Unjust World* by Karen Lebacqz, copyright © 1987 by Augsburg Publishing House. Used by permission of Augsburg Fortress.

46. Graham, Gordon. *The Idea of Christian Charity.* © 1989 by the University of Notre Dame Press. Used by permission.

47. Meilaender, Gilbert. *Friendship.* © 1981 by the University of Notre Dame Press. Used by permission.

48. Callahan, Sidney. *With All Our Heart and Mind: The Spiritual Works of Mercy in a Psychological Age.* Copyright © 1988 by Sidney Callahan. Reprinted by permission of The Crossroad Publishing Company.

50. Colliander, Tito. *Way of the Ascetics: The Ancient Tradition of Discipline and Inner Growth,* pp. 4-6. St. Vladimir's Seminary Press, 575 Scarsdale Road, Crestwood, N.Y. 10707. Used by permission.

51. The Swiss Brethren. "The Schleitheim Confession of Faith." *The Mennonite Quarterly Review* 19, no. 4 (October 1945).

52. Boulton, Wayne G. *Is Legalism a Heresy?* © 1982 by Paulist Press. Used by permission.

53. Murray, John Courtney. *We Hold These Truths.* © 1960 by Sheed & Ward, 1960. Used by permission.

55. Reprinted by permission from *Dietrich Bonhoeffer — His Significance for North Americans* by Larry Rasmussen, copyright © 1990 Augsburg Fortress.

57. From *Incarnate Love: Essays in Orthodox*

Ethics by Vigen Guroian. © 1987 by the University of Notre Dame Press. Reprinted by permission.

58. From *Making the Connections* by Beverly Harrison. Copyright © 1985 by Beverly Harrison. Reprinted by permission of Beacon Press.

59. Excerpts from *Personal Commitments* by Margaret Farley. Copyright © 1987 by Margaret Farley. Reprinted by permission of Harper-Collins Publishers.

61. Nelson, James. *Between Two Gardens.* Reprinted with the permission of The Pilgrim Press.

62. Turner, Philip W. III, ed. *Men and Women: Sexual Ethics in Turbulent Times.* © 1989 by Cowley Publications. Used by permission.

64. Callahan, Daniel. "Religion and the Secularization of Bioethics." *The Hastings Center Report,* July/August 1990. Used by permission.

65. Cahill, Lisa Sowle. "Can Theology Have a Role in 'Public' Bioethical Discourse?" In "Theology, Religious Traditions, and Bioethics," ed. Daniel Callahan and Courtney S. Campbell. Special Supplement, *Hastings Center Report* 20, no. 4 (1990). Copyright © The Hastings Center.

66. From *Suffering Presence: Theological Reflections on Medicine, the Mentally Handicapped, and the Church* by Stanley Hauerwas. © 1985 by the University of Notre Dame Press. Reprinted by permission.

67. Reprinted from *Questions about the Beginning of Life,* edited by Edward D. Schneider, copyright © 1985 Augsburg Publishing House. Used by permission of Augsburg Fortress.

69. Meilaender, Gilbert. "The Distinction between Killing and Allowing to Die." *Theological Studies* 37 (September 1976). Used by permission.

71. Excerpt from *Exodus and Revolution* by Michael Walzer. Copyright © 1985 by Basic Books, Inc.

Reprinted by permission of Basic Books, a division of HarperCollins Publishers Inc.

72. Niebuhr, H. Richard. "The Grace of Doing Nothing." Copyright © 1932 Christian Century Foundation. Reprinted by permission from the March 23, 1932 issue of *The Christian Century.*

73. Niebuhr, Reinhold. "Must We Do Nothing?" Copyright 1932 Christian Century Foundation. Reprinted by permission from the March 30, 1932 issue of *The Christian Century.*

74. Niebuhr, H. Richard. "The Only Way into the Kingdom of God." Copyright 1932 Christian Century Foundation. Reprinted by permission from the April 6, 1932 issue of *The Christian Century.*

75. King, Martin Luther, Jr. *Why We Can't Wait.* Copyright © 1963, 1964 by Martin Luther King, Jr. Reprinted by permission of HarperCollins Publishers and by arrangement with The Heirs to the Estate of Martin Luther King, Jr., c/o Joan Daves Agency as agent for the proprietor.

77. Jordan, Kathleen De Sutter. "An Active Glowing Force: The Nonviolence of Dorothy Day." In *The Universe Bends Toward Justice,* ed. Angie O'Gorman. © 1990 by New Society Publishers. Used by permission.

79. Reprinted by permission of the publishers and the Loeb Classical Library from *Clement of Alexandria,* trans. G. W. Butterworth. Cambridge, Mass.: Harvard University Press, 1919.

80. "On Usury" from *Calvin's Ecclesiastical Advice,* by John Calvin, trans. Mary Beaty and Benjamin Farley. © 1991 Westminster/John Knox Press. Used by permission of Westminster/John Knox Press.

82. Niebuhr, Reinhold. "The Law of Love in Politics and Economics." In *An Interpretation of Christian Ethics.* Copyright 1935 by Harper & Row Publishers, Inc. Reprinted by permission of HarperCollins Publishers.

83. John Paul II. *Centesimus Annus.* Vatican: Libreria Editrice Vaticana. Used by permission.

84. Boff, Leonardo, and Clodovis Boff. *Introducing Liberation Theology.* © 1986 by Orbis Books. Used by permission of Orbis Books, Burns & Oates Ltd., and Editora Vozes.

85. Stackhouse, Max L., and Dennis P. McCann. "A Postcommunist Manifesto." Copyright 1991 Christian Century Foundation. Reprinted by permission from the January 16, 1991 issue of *The Christian Century.*

86. Benne, Robert, and Preston Williams. "Responses to 'A Postcommunist Manifesto': Ethics, Economics, and Corporate Life." Copyright 1991 Christian Century Foundation. Reprinted by permission from the January 23, 1991 issue of *The Christian Century.*

88. From *The Little Flowers of St. Francis* by St. Francis of Assisi. Copyright © 1958 by Beverly Brown. Used by permission of Publishing Group, Inc.

89. Barth, Karl. *Church Dogmatics,* vol. 3. Edinburgh: T & T Clark Ltd. Used by permission.

90. Reprinted from *Models of God* by Sallie McFague, copyright © 1987 Fortress Press. Used by permission of Augsburg Fortress.

92. Berry, Wendell. *What Are People For?* Copyright © 1990 by Wendell Berry. Published by North Point Press and reprinted by permission of Farrar, Straus & Giroux, Inc. and Random House UK Ltd.

Unless otherwise noted, Scripture quotations are from the New Revised Standard Version of the Bible, copyright © 1989 by the Division of Christian Education of the National Council of the Churches of Christ in the U.S.A., and used by permission.

Index